THE
ALL ENGLAND
LAW REPORTS
1996

Volume 4

Editor
CAROLINE VANDRIDGE-AMES LLM

London
BUTTERWORTHS

UNITED KINGDOM	Butterworths a Division of Reed Elsevier (UK) Ltd, Halsbury House, 35 Chancery Lane, **London** WC2A 1EL and 4 Hill Street, **Edinburgh** EH2 3JZ
AUSTRALIA	Butterworths, **Sydney, Melbourne, Brisbane, Adelaide, Perth, Canberra** and **Hobart**
CANADA	Butterworths Canada Ltd, **Toronto** and **Vancouver**
IRELAND	Butterworth (Ireland) Ltd, **Dublin**
MALAYSIA	Malayan Law Journal Sdn Bhd, **Kuala Lumpur**
NEW ZEALAND	Butterworths of New Zealand Ltd, **Wellington** and **Auckland**
SINGAPORE	Reed Elsevier (Singapore) Pte Ltd, **Singapore**
SOUTH AFRICA	Butterworths Publishers (Pty) Ltd, **Durban**
USA	Michie, **Charlottesville**, Virginia

ISBN for the complete set of volumes: 0 406 85159 X
for this volume: 0 406 065047

© Reed Elsevier (UK) Ltd 1996

Printed and bound in Great Britain by William Clowes Ltd, Beccles and London

House of Lords

The Lord High Chancellor of Great Britain: Lord Mackay of Clashfern

Lords of Appeal in Ordinary

Lord Keith of Kinkel
   (retired 30 September 1996)
Lord Goff of Chieveley
Lord Jauncey of Tullichettle
   (retired 30 September 1996)
Lord Browne-Wilkinson
Lord Mustill
Lord Slynn of Hadley
Lord Lloyd of Berwick

Lord Nolan
Lord Nicholls of Birkenhead
Lord Steyn
Lord Hoffmann
Lord Clyde
   (appointed 1 October 1996)
Lord Hope of Craighead
   (appointed 1 October 1996)

Court of Appeal

The Lord High Chancellor of Great Britain

The Lord Chief Justice of England: Lord Bingham of Cornhill
(President of the Criminal Division)

The Master of the Rolls: Lord Woolf
(President of the Civil Division)

The President of the Family Division: Sir Stephen Brown

The Vice-Chancellor: Sir Richard Rashleigh Folliott Scott

Lords Justices of Appeal

Sir Brian Thomas Neill
   (retired 30 September 1996)
Sir Martin Charles Nourse
Sir Thomas Patrick Russell
   (retired 30 September 1996)
Dame Ann Elizabeth Oldfield Butler-Sloss
Sir Murray Stuart-Smith
Sir Christopher Stephen Thomas Jonathan
   Thayer Staughton
Sir Anthony James Denys McCowan
Sir Alexander Roy Asplan Beldam
Sir Andrew Peter Leggatt
Sir Paul Joseph Morrow Kennedy
Sir David Cozens-Hardy Hirst
Sir Simon Denis Brown
Sir Anthony Howell Meurig Evans
Sir Christopher Dudley Roger Rose
Sir John Douglas Waite
Sir John Ormond Roch
Sir Peter Leslie Gibson
Sir John Stewart Hobhouse
Sir Denis Robert Maurice Henry

Sir Mark Oliver Saville
Sir Peter Julian Millett
Sir Swinton Barclay Thomas
Sir Robert Andrew Morritt
Sir Philip Howard Otton
Sir Robin Ernest Auld
   (Senior Presiding Judge for England and
   Wales)
Sir Malcolm Thomas Pill
Sir William Aldous
Sir Alan Hylton Ward
Sir Michael Hutchison
Sir Konrad Hermann Theodor Schiemann
Sir Nicholas Addison Phillips
Sir Mathew Alexander Thorpe
Sir Mark Howard Potter
Sir Henry Brooke
Sir Igor Judge
Sir George Mark Waller
   (appointed 1 October 1996)
Sir John Frank Mummery
   (appointed 1 October 1996)

High Court of Justice

The Lord High Chancellor of Great Britain
The Lord Chief Justice of England
The President of the Family Division
The Vice-Chancellor
The Senior Presiding Judge for England and Wales
The puisne judges of the High Court

Chancery Division

The Lord High Chancellor of Great Britain
The Vice-Chancellor

Sir Jeremiah LeRoy Harman
Sir John Leonard Knox
  (retired 30 September 1996)
Sir Donald Keith Rattee
Sir John Frank Mummery
  (appointed Lord Justice of Appeal
  1 October 1996)
Sir Francis Mursell Ferris
Sir John Murray Chadwick
Sir Jonathan Frederic Parker
  (Vice-Chancellor of the County Palatine
  of Lancaster)
Sir John Edmund Frederic Lindsay

Dame Mary Howarth Arden
Sir Edward Christopher Evans-Lombe
Sir Robin Raphael Hayim Jacob
Sir William Anthony Blackburne
Sir Gavin Anthony Lightman
Sir Robert Walker
Sir Robert John Anderson Carnwath
Sir Colin Percy Farquharson Rimer
Sir Hugh Ian Lang Laddie
Sir Timothy Andrew Wigram Lloyd
  (appointed 1 October 1996)
Sir David Edmund Neuberger
  (appointed 1 October 1996)

Queen's Bench Division

The Lord Chief Justice of England

Sir Christopher James Saunders French
Sir Iain Charles Robert McCullough
Sir Oliver Bury Popplewell
Sir Richard Howard Tucker
Sir Patrick Neville Garland
Sir Michael John Turner
Sir John Downes Alliott
Sir Harry Henry Ognall
Sir John Arthur Dalziel Owen
Sir Francis Humphrey Potts
Sir Richard George Rougier
Sir Ian Alexander Kennedy
Sir Stuart Neill McKinnon
Sir Thomas Scott Gillespie Baker
Sir Edwin Frank Jowitt
Sir Douglas Dunlop Brown
Sir Michael Morland
Sir George Mark Waller
  (appointed Lord Justice of Appeal
  1 October 1996)

Sir Roger John Buckley
Sir Anthony Brian Hidden
Sir John Michael Wright
Sir Charles Barrie Knight Mantell
Sir John Christopher Calthorpe Blofeld
Sir Peter John Cresswell
Sir Anthony Tristram Kenneth May
Sir John Grant McKenzie Laws
Dame Ann Marian Ebsworth
Sir Simon Lane Tuckey
Sir David Nicholas Ramsey Latham
Sir Christopher John Holland
Sir John William Kay
Sir Richard Herbert Curtis
Sir Stephen John Sedley
Dame Janet Hilary Smith
Sir Anthony David Colman
Sir Anthony Peter Clarke
Sir John Anthony Dyson
Sir John Thayne Forbes

[*continued on next page*]

Queen's Bench Division (*continued*)

Sir Michael Alexander Geddes Sachs
Sir Stephen George Mitchell
Sir Rodger Bell
Sir Michael Guy Vicat Harrison
Sir Bernard Anthony Rix
Dame Anne Heather Steel
Sir William Marcus Gage
Sir Jonathan Hugh Mance
Sir Andrew Centlivres Longmore
Sir Thomas Richard Atkin Morison
Sir Richard Joseph Buxton
Sir David Wolfe Keene
Sir Andrew David Collins
Sir Maurice Ralph Kay

Sir Frank Brian Smedley
Sir Anthony Hooper
Sir Alexander Neil Logie Butterfield
Sir George Michael Newman
Sir David Anthony Poole
Sir Martin James Moore-Bick
Sir Julian Hugh Gordon Langley
Sir Roger John Laugharne Thomas
Sir Robert Franklyn Nelson
Sir Roger Grenfell Toulson
Sir Michael John Astill
Sir Alan George Moses
Sir Timothy Edward Walker
    (appointed 1 October 1996)

Family Division
The President of the Family Division

Sir Anthony Barnard Hollis
Sir Edward Stephen Cazalet
Sir Robert Lionel Johnson
Dame Joyanne Winifred Bracewell
Sir Michael Bryan Connell
Sir Jan Peter Singer
Sir Nicholas Allan Roy Wilson
Sir Nicholas Peter Rathbone Wall

Sir Andrew Tristram Hammett Kirkwood
Sir Christopher Stuart-White
Dame Brenda Marjorie Hale
Sir Hugh Peter Derwyn Bennett
Sir Edward James Holman
Dame Mary Claire Hogg
Sir Christopher John Sumner

CITATION

These reports are cited thus:

[1996] 4 All ER

REFERENCES

These reports contain references to the following major works of legal reference described in the manner indicated below.

Halsbury's Laws of England

The reference 26 *Halsbury's Laws* (4th edn) para 577 refers to paragraph 577 on page 296 of volume 26 of the fourth edition of *Halsbury's Laws of England*.

The reference 7(1) *Halsbury's Laws* (4th edn reissue) para 267 refers to paragraph 267 on page 200 of reissue volume 7(1) of the fourth edition of *Halsbury's Laws of England*.

Halsbury's Statutes of England and Wales

The reference 40 *Halsbury's Statutes* (4th edn) 734 refers to page 734 of volume 40 of the fourth edition of *Halsbury's Statutes of England and Wales*.

The reference 19 *Halsbury's Statutes* (4th edn) (1994 reissue) 497 refers to page 497 of the 1994 reissue of volume 19 of the fourth edition of *Halsbury's Statutes of England and Wales*.

The Digest
(formerly The English and Empire Digest)

The reference 37(2) *Digest* (Reissue) 424, *2594* refers to case number 2594 on page 424 of the reissue of green band volume 37(2) of *The Digest*.

The reference 27(1) *Digest* (2nd reissue) 330, *2849* refers to case number 2849 on page 330 of the second reissue of green band volume 27(1) of *The Digest*.

Halsbury's Statutory Instruments

The reference 17 *Halsbury's Statutory Instruments* 305 refers to page 305 of volume 17 of the grey volumes series of *Halsbury's Statutory Instruments*.

The reference 14 *Halsbury's Statutory Instruments* (1994 reissue) 201 refers to page 201 of the 1994 reissue of volume 14 of the grey volumes series of *Halsbury's Statutory Instruments*.

Cases reported in volume 4

Digest of cases reported in volume 4

House of Lords petitions

This list, which covers the period 26 July to 12 December 1996, sets out all cases which have formed the subject of a report in the All England Law Reports in which an Appeal Committee of the House of Lords has, subsequent to the publication of that report, refused leave to appeal. Where the result of a petition for leave to appeal was known prior to the publication of the relevant report a note of that result appears at the end of the report.

F C Jones & Sons (a firm) (trustee of the property of) v Jones [1996] 4 All ER 721, CA. Leave to appeal refused 12 December 1996 (Lord Browne-Wilkinson, Lord Steyn and Lord Hoffmann)

Porter v Secretary of State for Transport [1996] 3 All ER 693, CA. Leave to appeal refused 28 October 1996 (Lord Browne-Wilkinson, Lord Nicholls of Birkenhead and Lord Clyde)

R v Secretary of State for Wales, ex parte Emery

b

QUEEN'S BENCH DIVISION (CROWN OFFICE LIST)

SIR LOUIS BLOM-COOPER QC SITTING AS A DEPUTY JUDGE OF THE HIGH COURT

11, 12 MARCH, 29 APRIL, 4 JUNE 1996

c *Highway – Dedication – Evidence – Definitive map – Public right of way – Riverbank*
footpath – Private landowner refusing access – Application to local authority for order
modifying definitive map of area to show public footpath – Local authority refusing
order – Secretary of State dismissing appeal against refusal of order – Secretary of State
determining appeal on conflicting documentary evidence alone – Whether Secretary of
d *State entitled to do so – Whether Secretary of State acted fairly in doing so – Whether*
Secretary of State should have held public inquiry – Wildlife and Countryside Act 1981,
s 53(5), Sch 14, para 4(2).

Following a private landowner's refusal to allow public access to a riverbank
footpath which crossed his land, the applicant applied to the local authority under
e s 53(5)[a] of the Wildlife and Countryside Act 1981 for an order modifying the
definitive survey map of its area to show the footpath as a public path. The
application included some 23 statements from witnesses together with
photographs and other documentary evidence. After carrying out a statutory
consultation exercise, the local authority rejected the application, relying on an
f undated statement by the former owner of the property, D, whose family had
acquired the property in 1912, which stated that access to the riverbank had been
very strictly controlled and general public access had always been refused. In
particular, the local authority concluded that the evidence was too weak and
conflicting to presume and prove the dedication or existence of the claimed path.
The applicant appealed to the Secretary of State, to whom over 100 statements
g were submitted showing that the path had been used for access to the river for
various activities over a number of years. The Secretary of State held, however,
that the evidence was not conclusive as to dedication as a public footpath and that
D's statement clearly demonstrated no such intention. He accordingly dismissed
the appeal and declined to exercise his powers under para 4(2) of Sch 14 to the
h 1981 Act to direct the local authority to modify the definitive map of its area as
sought. The applicant applied for judicial review of the Secretary of State's
decision, and the question arose whether, in exercising his appellate powers, the
Secretary of State was entitled to rely exclusively on conflicting documentary
evidence or whether he should determine the matter only after a public inquiry.

j **Held** – When considering an appeal from the refusal of an application for a
modification order under the 1981 Act the Secretary of State had a duty to act
fairly and that duty required a public inquiry to be held where the documentary
evidence was conflicting and needed to be tested. In the instant case, moreover,

---

a   Section 53, so far as material, is set out at p 4 *d* to p 5 *c*, post

a legitimate expectation had been created that such a public inquiry would be
held. It followed that by operating the statutory procedure without due regard
to the peculiar facts of the case, strictly in the manner envisaged by Parliament,
the Secretary of State had acted unfairly. The application would accordingly be
allowed (see p 14 c to f, p 15 fg, p 16 c and p 17 e, post).

Notes

For the dedication of public paths and application by individuals for modification
of definitive maps, see 21 *Halsbury's Laws* (4th edn reissue) paras 254, 270.

For the Wildlife and Countryside Act 1981, s 53, Sch 14, see 20 *Halsbury's
Statutes* (4th edn) (1992 reissue) 520, 534.

Cases referred to in judgment

Associated Provincial Picture Houses Ltd v Wednesbury Corp [1947] 1 All ER 498,
[1948] 1 KB 223.

Bryan v UK (1995) 21 EHRR 342, ECt HR.

Doody v Secretary of State for the Home Dept [1993] 3 All ER 92, [1994] 1 AC 531,
[1993] 3 WLR 154, HL.

Fairey v Southampton CC [1956] 2 All ER 843, [1956] 2 QB 439, [1956] 3 WLR 354,
CA.

Jaques v Secretary of State for the Environment [1995] JPL 1031.

Jones v Bates [1938] 2 All ER 237, CA.

Kioa v West (1985) 159 CLR 550, Aust HC.

Lloyd v McMahon [1987] 1 All ER 1118, [1987] AC 625, [1987] 2 WLR 821, CA and
HL.

R v City of London Corp, ex p Matson (1995) 8 Admin LR 49, CA.

R v Ministry of Defence, ex p Smith [1996] 1 All ER 257, [1996] QB 517, [1996] 2 WLR
305, CA.

R v Panel on Take-overs and Mergers, ex p Guinness plc [1989] 1 All ER 509, [1990] 1
QB 146, [1989] 2 WLR 863, CA.

R v Secretary of State for the Environment, ex p Bagshaw (1994) 68 P & CR 402.

R v Secretary of State for the Environment, ex p Cowell [1993] JPL 851, CA.

R v Secretary of State for the Home Dept, ex p Fire Brigades Union [1995] 2 All ER 244,
[1995] 2 AC 513, [1995] 2 WLR 464, HL.

Application for judicial review

Gordon Emery applied, with leave of Latham J granted on 11 October 1995, for,
inter alia, an order of certiorari to quash the decision of the Secretary of State for
Wales by letter dated 16 May 1995 whereby he refused to direct the Clwyd
County Council to make an order modifying its definitive map or alternatively
for an order of mandamus that the Secretary of State hear and determine the
applicant's appeal under para 4(1) of Sch 14 to the Wildlife and Countryside Act
1981. The facts are set out in the judgment.

George Laurence QC and *Edwin Simpson* (instructed by J J Pearlman, Brooke North &
Goodwin, Leeds) for the appellant.

John Hobson (instructed by the *Treasury Solicitor*) for the Secretary of State.

Cur adv vult

a   4 June 1996. The following judgment was delivered.

SIR LOUIS BLOM-COOPER QC. The question in this application for judicial review focuses on the administrative procedures to be deployed when an alleged public right of way (which is deemed reasonably to result from a wealth of evidence from public users) conflicts with evidence from the landowner seeking

b   to establish an intention not to dedicate the way. How, in particular, should the Secretary of State exercise his appellate powers under para 4 of Sch 14 to the Wildlife and Countryside Act 1981, in deciding, on conflicting documentary evidence, whether or not the local surveying authority should be ordered to modify the definitive map of its area? The facts of this case peculiarly raise the issue whether, in so exercising his powers, the Secretary of State should not rely

c   exclusively on the documentary material, but leave the matter to be determined by him only after a public inquiry.

THE STATUTORY FRAMEWORK

(a) *The countryside legislation*

d   Ever since 1949 a county council has been required to carry out a survey of all the lands in its area and prepare a definitive map. Section 27(1) of the National Parks and Access to the Countryside Act 1949 provides that the survey of land—

'over which a right of way to which this Part of this Act applies *is alleged to subsist*, and shall, not later than the expiration of three years after that date ...

e   prepare a draft map ... showing thereon a footpath or a bridleway ... wherever in their opinion such a right of way *subsisted, or is reasonably alleged to have subsisted*, at the relevant date.' (This section survives significantly in s 53 of the 1981 Act.)

Sections 28 to 31 of the 1949 Act provided in detail for definitive maps. Section

f   32 provided for the preparation, publication and effect of definitive maps and statements. Subsection (4), which was the precursor of s 56 of the 1981 Act, provided:

'A definitive map and statement prepared under subsection (1) of this section shall be conclusive as to the particulars contained therein in

g   accordance with the foregoing provisions of this section to the following extent, that is to say—(a) where the map shows a footpath, the map shall be conclusive evidence that there was at the relevant date specified in the statement a footpath as shown on the map; (b) where the map shows a bridleway, or a road used as a public path, the map shall be conclusive

h   evidence that there was at the said date a highway as shown on the map, and that the public had thereover at that date a right of way on foot and a right of way on horseback or leading a horse, so however that this paragraph shall be without prejudice to any question whether the public had at that date any right of way other than the rights aforesaid; and (c) where by virtue of the

j   foregoing paragraphs of this subsection the map is conclusive evidence, as at any date, as to a public path, or road used as a public path, shown thereon, any particulars contained in the statement as to the position or width thereof shall be conclusive evidence as to the position or width thereof at the relevant date, and any particulars so contained as to limitations or conditions affecting the public right of way shall be conclusive evidence that at the said date the said right was subject to those limitations or conditions, but without prejudice to any question whether the right was subject to any other limitations or conditions at that date.'

Section 33 of the 1949 Act provided for periodical revision of maps and statements, sub-s (3) of which provided for the carrying out of the review not later than five years after the relevant date. This timetable for review and potential revision of the maps and statements proved to be wildly ambitious, many reviews not even taking place. By Pt II of Sch 3 to the Countryside Act 1968, the procedure for review was, therefore, changed. Instead, there was put in place a provisional stage of consultation and the review would include the preparation of a revised map. That still did not speed matters up. Hence, the 1981 Act, in Pt III (public rights of way: ascertainment of public rights of way), introduced the incremental review of the definitive map. This was achieved by the method of a modification order.

Section 53 of the 1981 Act (duty to keep definitive map and statement under continuous review) provides:

'(1) In this Part "definitive map and statement", in relation to any area, means, subject to s 57(3),—(a) the latest revised map and statement prepared in definitive form for that area under section 33 of the 1949 Act; or (b) where no such map and statement have been so prepared, the original definitive map and statement prepared for that area under section 32 of that Act; or (c) where no such map and statement have been so prepared, the map and statement prepared for that area under section 55(3).

(2) As regards every definitive map and statement, the surveying authority shall—(a) as soon as reasonably practicable after the commencement date, by order make such modifications to the map and statement as appear to them to be requisite in consequence of the occurrence, before that date, of any of the events specified in subsection (3); and (b) as from that date, keep the map and statement under continuous review and as soon as reasonably practicable after the occurrence, on or after that date, of any of those events, by order make such modifications to the map and statement as appear to them to be requisite in consequence of the occurrence of that event.

(3) The events referred to in subsection (2) are as follows—(a) the coming into operation of any enactment or instrument, or any other event, whereby—(i) a highway shown or required to be shown in the map and statement has been authorised to be stopped up, diverted, widened or extended; (ii) a highway shown or required to be shown in the map and statement as a highway of a particular description has ceased to be a highway of that description; or (iii) a new right of way has been created over land in the area to which the map relates, being a right of way such that the land over which the right subsists is a public path; (b) the expiration, in relation to any way in the area to which the map relates, of any period such that the enjoyment by the public of the way during that period raises a presumption that the way has been dedicated as a public path; (c) the discovery by the authority of evidence which (when considered with all other relevant evidence available to them) shows—(i) that a right of way which is not shown in the map and statement subsists or is reasonably alleged to subsist over land in the area to which the map relates, being a right of way to which this Part applies; (ii) that a highway shown in the map and statement as a highway of a particular description ought to be there shown as a highway of a different description; or (iii) that there is no public right of way over land

shown in the map and statement as a highway of any description, or any other particulars contained in the map and statement require modification …

(5) Any person may apply to the authority for an order under subsection (2) which makes such modifications as appear to the authority to be requisite in consequence of the occurrence of one or more events falling within paragraph (b) or (c) of subsection (3); and the provisions of Schedule 14 shall have effect as to the making and determination of applications under this subsection.

(6) Orders under subsection (2) which make only such modifications as appear to the authority to be requisite in consequence of the occurrence of one or more events falling within paragraph (a) of subsection (3) shall take effect on their being made; and the provisions of Schedule 15 shall have effect as to the making, validity and date of coming into operation of other orders under subsection (2)'.

Section 56 repeated and extended the provision, in effect, that the definitive map and statement was to be conclusive evidence that a footpath shown upon it was subject to a public right of way. Section 66 defines a 'public path' as meaning 'a highway being either a footpath or a bridleway'; and a 'right of way to which this Part applies' means 'a right of way such that the land over which the right subsists is a public path of a byway open to all traffic'.

Schedule 14 to the 1981 Act provides:

'… 2.—(1) Subject to sub-paragraph (2), the applicant shall serve a notice stating that the application has been made on every owner and occupier of any land to which the application relates …

3.—(1) As soon as reasonably practicable after receiving a certificate under paragraph 2(3), the authority shall—(a) investigate the matters stated in the application; and (b) after consulting with every local authority whose area includes the land to which the application relates, decide whether to make or not to make the order to which the application relates.

(2) If the authority have not determined the application within twelve months of their receiving a certificate under paragraph 2(3), then, on the applicant making representations to the Secretary of State, the Secretary of State may, after consulting with the authority, direct the authority to determine the application before the expiration of such period as may be specified in the direction.

(3) As soon as practicable after determining the application, the authority shall give notice of their decision by serving a copy of it on the applicant and any person on whom notice of the application was required to be served under paragraph 2(1).

4.—(1) Where the authority decide not to make an order, the applicant may, at any time within 28 days after service on him of notice of the decision, serve notice of appeal against that decision on the Secretary of State and the authority.

(2) If on considering the appeal the Secretary of State considers that an order should be made, he shall give to the authority such directions as appear to him necessary for the purpose …'

Paragraphs 7(2)(a) and (b) and 10 of Sch 15 provide:

'7 ... (2) Where an order is submitted to the Secretary of State under sub-paragraph (1), the Secretary of State shall either—(a) cause a local inquiry to be held; or (b) afford any person by whom a representation or objection has been duly made and not withdrawn an opportunity of being heard by a person appointed by the Secretary of State for the purpose ...

10.—(1) A decision of the Secretary of State under paragraphs 6, 7 or 8 shall, except in such classes of case as may for the time being be prescribed or as may be specified in directions given by the Secretary of State, be made by a person appointed by the Secretary of State for the purpose instead of by the Secretary of State; and a decision made by a person so appointed shall be treated as a decision of the Secretary of State.

(2) The Secretary of State may, if he thinks fit, direct that a decision which, by virtue of sub-paragraph (1) and apart from this sub-paragraph, falls to be made by a person appointed by the Secretary of State shall instead be made by the Secretary of State; and a direction under this sub-paragraph shall state the reasons for which it is given and shall be served on the person, if any, so appointed, the authority and any person by whom a representation or objection has been duly made and not withdrawn.

(3) Where the Secretary of State has appointed a person to make a decision under paragraph 6, 7 or 8 the Secretary of State may, at any time before the making of the decision, appoint another person to make it instead of the person first appointed to make it.

(4) Where by virtue of sub-paragraph (2) or (3) a particular decision falls to be made by the Secretary of State or any other person instead of the person first appointed to make it, anything done by or in relation to the latter shall be treated as having been done by or in relation to the former.

(5) Regulations under this paragraph may provide for the giving of publicity to any directions given by the Secretary of State under this paragraph.'

(b) *Right of way legislation*

The statutory scheme is completed by the law relating to right of way. Until 1932 the dedication of a footpath as a public right of way was regulated by the common law. The Right of Way Act 1932, while it preserved the common law, for the first time introduced a statutory regime. Section 1(1) of the 1932 Act is strikingly similar to the present statutory provision in s 31 of the Highways Act 1980. The former provides:

'Where a way, not being of such a character that user thereof by the public could not give rise at common law to any presumption of dedication, upon or over any land has been actually enjoyed by the public as of right and without interruption for a full period of twenty years, such way shall be deemed to have been dedicated as a highway unless there is sufficient evidence that there was no intention during that period to dedicate such way ...'

Section 31(1) of the 1980 Act, while preserving the disqualification under the old law, does not replicate the second proviso. The effect of the section is, very broadly, that after 20 years' use a way is deemed to have been dedicated unless there is evidence of a contrary intention: see Riddall and Trevelyan *Rights of Way* (2nd edn, 1992) p 63. Section 31 of the 1980 Act provides, inter alia:

a
'(1) Where a way over any land, other than a way of such character that use of it by the public could not give rise at common law to any presumption of dedication, has been actually enjoyed by the public as of right and without interruption for a full period of 20 years, the way is to be deemed to have been dedicated as a highway unless there is sufficient evidence that there was no intention during that period to dedicate it ...

b
(3) Where the owner of the land over which any such way as aforesaid passes—(a) has erected in such a manner as to be visible to persons using the way a notice inconsistent with the dedication of the way as a highway; and (b) has maintained the notice after 1 January 1934, or any later date on which it was erected, the notice, in the absence of proof of a contrary intention, is sufficient evidence to negative the intention to dedicate the way as a

c
highway ...

(5) Where a notice erected as mentioned in subsection (3) above is subsequently torn down or defaced, a notice given by the owner of the land to the appropriate council that the way is not dedicated as a highway is, in the absence of proof of a contrary intention, sufficient evidence to negative the intention of the owner of the land to dedicate the way as a highway ...

d
(9) Nothing in this section operates to prevent the dedication of a way as a highway being presumed on proof of user for any less period than 20 years, or being presumed or proved in any circumstances in which it might have been presumed or proved immediately before the commencement of this Act.'

e

THE COMMON LAW

The pre-1932 common law position was described by Scott LJ in *Jones* v *Bates* [1938] 2 All ER 237 at 244:

f
'Before [the 1932 Act], the law applicable was the common law. The main alteration is effected by sect. 1, which gives a new statutory effect to mere proof of actual user as of right and without interruption. At the time of the passing of the Act, the main outline of the law affecting proof of a public highway ... had been drawn quite clearly by judicial decisions. Whereas in Scotland proof of 40 years' user as of right, and without interruption in the

g
enjoyment of the right, *ipso facto* established the legal conclusion that the way was public by prescription, in England no such convenient rule of law had been evolved by our courts. Our legal theory had always been ... that the sole origin of a public highway was dedication to the public use by the owners of the land over which it ran, and in consequence that, in case of

h
dispute, the public right could be established only by such evidence as would justify an inference of fact that the way had at some date, known or unknown, been so dedicated. The corollary followed that, on this as on all others issue of fact, the tribunal had to decide, once there was some affirmative evidence before it of user, whether or not on balance it was

j
sufficient to establish dedication ... the task of the tribunal of fact was not limited to deciding the necessary questions of user—Was it of right? Was the exercise of the right interrupted? How long had it continued? These findings would in Scotland have sufficed for the decision of the legal issue. In England, however, the tribunal had to deal with such difficult investigations as the state of the title of the owners and whether there was an owner who could dedicate, and consequently sometimes even the time when the

dedication—usually quite imaginary—had in fact taken place. Above all the
other difficulties, the tribunal had solemnly to infer as an actual fact that
somebody or other had in fact dedicated. It was often a pure legal fiction,
and yet put on the affirmant of the public right an artificial onus which was
often fatal to his success. The practical result of the English rule of law was
that in many cases, although quite a formidable body of evidence was
available to demonstrate what I will call the Scottish premises, the public
claimant failed on the additional English requisites.'

In *Jaques v Secretary of State for the Environment* [1995] JPL 1031 at 1036–1037
Laws J said:

'Taking the passage cited from Scott L.J. in *Jones v. Bates* as a full and
convenient description of the common law, it seemed that the material
change effected by the statute of 1932 (and carried through to the Act of
1980) did not merely consist in a shift of the burden of proof. The common
law required not only that the claimant to the right should show that the
landowner had evinced an intention to dedicate; he had to show *actual*
dedication; and it was precisely because such an event was usually fictitious
or imaginary that the common law was unsatisfactory. But under section 31
the landowner had to prove merely that he had no intention to dedicate;
certainly, he had to prove it by overt acts, directed (as Lord Denning
indicated in *Fairey*) to the public who use the way in question. Lord Denning
contemplated that the traditional means of closing the way for one day in the
year would suffice. The result was, in his view, that under the statute the
landowner had a lesser proposition to disprove than under the common law
the claimant had to prove. That approach vindicated the plain purpose of the
Act of 1932 for the very reason explained by Scott L.J.: it expunged from the
law the Alice in Wonderland requirement of any actual dedication.'
(Laws J's emphasis.)

FACTUAL BACKGROUND

Clwyd County Council was the surveying authority responsible for
maintaining a definitive map and statement of its area, recording rights of way,
and keeping it under continuous review. Its area included a footpath in the
village of Trevor, nr Llangollen, North Wales. The footpath runs from a house,
Llyn Madoc, on Plas-Yn-Pentre Road to, and along the bank of the River Dee at
the Groves, Pontcysyllte, Trevor, Llangollen.

The applicant in these judicial review proceedings is Mr Gordon Emery, a
self-employed publisher from Chester. He challenges the decision of the
Secretary of State for Wales on the grounds that the footpath was presumptively
dedicated, both at common law and under s 31 of the 1980 Act. Stripped of the
detailed statutory provisions for determining public rights of way, the challenge
claims that the only rational decision which the Secretary of State could have
reached was to direct the council to make a modification order which, if objected
to by the landowner, would ensure a public inquiry pursuant to para 7(2) of Sch
15 to the 1981 Act. The initial application to the council had included some 23
statements, from witnesses who filled in a 'Public Rights of Way Evidence Form',
together with photographs and other documentary evidence. Having carried out
a statutory consultation exercise, the council rejected the application. The
council relied heavily upon an undated statement by Mr S J Diggory, whose

a family had owned Llyn Madoc and the riverbank from 1912 until its sale to the
present owner in 1983. The statement reads as follows:

'S J Diggory
56 Pont, Yn Avon
Pen-y-Cae
b Wrexham
Clwyd
To whom it may concern
LLYN MADOC: RIVER BANK BETWEEN HOUSE AND PONTCYSYLLTE BRIDGE The
river bank at Llyn Madoc has been in the control of my family for over the
last century, until it was sold to Mr & Mrs Bromilow in 1983. Due to the
c keen interest of my family in fishing, access to the riverbank was very strictly
controlled, in order to maintain and preserve the standards of fishing. We
were often approached by people enquiring about permission to fish which,
in most cases, we refused. During warm weather, we waged a constant
vendetta on people who considered our river bank and fishing to be a local
swimming pool. Despite abuse we did, whenever possible, refuse
d permission for access to keep people away from the river bank. In later years
from around 1970, we were regularly approached by canoeing clubs and in
particular by the Outdoor Pursuits School at Llanwrst. These bodies fully
acknowledged our complete ownership and control of the river bank when
they applied for permission to use it to practice their white water canoeing.
e My Aunt Ginny, Mrs Martin was born at Llyn Madoc and lived there all of
her life. She died aged 93 years a few years before the property was sold to
the present owners. In all that time, general access to the river was expressly
refused. Indeed Aunty Ginny would often telephone me to come and assist
her when people went onto the river bank, but I was not always available to
do this. Original access to the river bank was from the Llyn Madoc garden.
f Eventually the roadside wall crumbled giving the river bank access from the
road and making it difficult to control. My grandparents grazed a horse on
the river bank and broad steps were built for the horse to get down on the
bank. But these were definitely not for public use. I repeat, the river bank
between Llyn Madoc and the bridge has been in my family's possession for
g well over 100 years and general access to the public has always been refused.
S J DIGGORY.'

The council considered there was insufficient evidence to support the claim;
the evidence was 'too weak and conflicting to presume and prove the dedication
or existence of the claimed path whether under s 31 of the 1980 Act or at common
h law'. Mr Emery took his appeal to the Secretary of State for Wales. By his
decision letter of 16 May 1995 the Secretary of State dismissed the appeal and
declined to exercise his power under para 4(2) of Sch 14 to the 1981 Act. The
decision letter is a fully reasoned decision, and cannot be faulted in any way other
than, potentially, in its approach to the problem whether the conflicting evidence
j on the face of the documentary material should have been tested by oral
examination at a public inquiry.

APPEAL TO THE SECRETARY OF STATE
In considering the appeal, the Secretary of State found that the user evidence
to establish the presumed dedication of the footpath had to be for a full period of
20 years. (Such period is calculated retrospectively from the date when the right

of the public to use the way is first brought into question. There was no
disagreement about the year 1986 having to be regarded as the latest date from   *a*
which the 20-year period had to be retrospectively calculated.) The purchase of
Llyn Madoc in 1983 by a Mr Bromilow, and his subsequent refusal to allow public
access to the riverbank, gave rise to the application to the council. Well over 100
statements had been submitted to the Secretary of State showing use of the path
for walking and for access to the riverbank for swimming, paddling, fishing,   *b*
picnicking and other outdoor activities. The Secretary of State stated that, given
the weight of evidence in the statements, he concluded 'that the path has been
used for purposes claimed for the periods stated'. Turning to the substance of
that evidence, many people were shown to have used the claimed route from
1912 to the time when access was prevented in or around 1986 by Mr Bromilow
taking action to prevent access. The decision letter of 16 May 1995, in   *c*
contradistinction to the conclusion of the council, stated:

> 'The Secretary of State accepts that many of these people may have
> genuinely believed that their unchallenged use of the path had been because
> it had been dedicated as a public right of way.'

d

That finding fell short of establishing that the right of way was 'reasonably alleged
to subsist' within s 53(3)(c)(i) of the 1981 Act. As the decision letter correctly
observed, the appellant's evidence in itself did not provide conclusive evidence of
dedication: 'There has to be examination of the actions of landowners to establish
whether or not they manifested any intention not to dedicate the way' under s 31
of the 1980 Act. The Secretary of State, relying on Mr Diggory's 'clear and   *e*
unequivocal statement' that his family never exhibited any intention to dedicate
the footpath as a public right of way, stated:

> 'While the public has had access to the area in question during the period
> claimed, the actions of the landowners over that period have been such as to
> demonstrate clearly that they had no intention to dedicate it as a public right   *f*
> of way.'

The Secretary of State's conclusion was that the evidence:

> 'Is not such as to indicate that a right of way is reasonably alleged to subsist
> along, or in the immediate vicinity of, the claimed route. Accordingly, the   *g*
> Secretary of State's decision is that the appeal be refused.'

THE LEGAL PROBLEM

It is convenient at this point to observe that the reasonable allegation that the
public right of way subsists may in certain cases not be displaced by the proviso   *h*
to s 31(1) of the 1980 Act, but may merely remain unconsummated as a presumed
dedicated public right of way. The fact that the landowner's intentions not to
dedicate defeat the claim to a right of way cannot, in strict logic, prevent the
subsistence of a reasonable allegation. I respectfully adopt what Laws J said on
this point in *Jaques* [1995] JPL 1031 at 1037–1038:

j

> 'Quite plainly, the second part of section 31(1) imported a further
> requirement. It meant that *even if* use of the required quality was proved, the
> status of right of way would not be established if the landowner
> demonstrated an intention not to dedicate. The logical relationship between
> the two parts of the subsection entailed that proof of an intention not to
> dedicate could be constituted by something less than proof of facts which

a had to have made it clear to the public that they had *no* right to use the way: otherwise, once the interested public had established their case under the first part of the subsection, there would be no room for the operation of the second part. That was not a very satisfactory state of affairs. It was plain that the landowner had to disprove an intention to dedicate by overt acts directed to the members of the public in question, but equally plain that they need not
b actually bring home to the public that there was no right to use the way. He could only conclude that any sufficiently overt act or series of acts indicating an intention to keep the way private would be enough for the landowner's purposes in relation to the second part of the subsection, though they did not in fact bring home to the public his objection to their using his land.' (Laws J's emphasis.)

c In the instant case, there was evidence directly conflicting with that of the users. As Rose LJ said in *R v Secretary of State for the Environment, ex p Cowell* [1993] JPL 851 at 855–856, a case in which horse riders were charged a toll only once a year:

d 'There was nothing in the wording of section 31 to suggest that "sufficient evidence" in subsection (1) was limited either to, or by, the matters identified in subsections (3) to (6). Although proof of matters there identified would provide sufficient evidence in a particular case, what evidence was sufficient in other cases would necessarily vary from case to case ... Whether use was of right and whether there was sufficient evidence of a lack of intention to dedicate were both matters of fact to be determined by the tribunal of fact in
e accordance with the evidence in the particular case. Section 31 contemplated the consideration of evidence directed to both matters.'

Staughton LJ in the same case, while recognising that there was in that case an overlap between the two parts of s 31 of the 1980 Act, said (at 857):

f '... the case concerned two of the requirements of section 31(1) of the Highways Act 1980. First, there was the requirement that the way shall have been actually enjoyed by the public as of right and without interruption for a full period of 20 years. Secondly, there was the proviso where there was sufficient evidence that there was no intention during that period to dedicate it. There might be cases where those two requirements were totally distinct;
g or they might overlap wholly or in part. The first requirement, user as of right, was explained by Farwell J. in *Jones v. Bates* ([1938] 2 All ER 237 at 251). He said it meant that the user had to have been by persons who honestly believed that they had a legal right to do so, as distinguished from user by persons who thought they had the express or tacit licence of the owner, or
h were reckless of the rights of such owner. In the (instant) case the findings of the Inspector showed that some members of the public using this path believed that they had a right to do so. They apparently would not have been using the way on occasions when a toll was demanded. Others, using it on toll days, would have realised that they did not have a right to do so—
j or, at any rate, that the owner of the land challenged their right. It had to surely be a question of fact and degree. One person using the way as of right without knowing that the owner of the land challenged the right to do so, whilst dozens or hundreds of others knew that, might not be sufficient. The Inspector had not been satisfied that there was a sufficient degree of user as of right.'

But in case he was wrong on that, Staughton LJ turned to the second point, that there was sufficient evidence that the owners of the land had no intention to dedicate it (at 857):

> 'There were dicta, in the case of *Fairey* v. *Southampton County Council* ([1956] 2 All ER 843, [1956] 2 QB 439), which said that it was not sufficient for the landowner to have an intention not to dedicate *in pectore*. He had to manifest that intention by some overt act. That was not said in the section itself, but it seemed a sensible rule. Subsections (3), (5) and (6) all dealt with acts which were, to a greater or lesser extent, overt; those were examples of how sufficient intention might be demonstrated. So perhaps it was right to say that evidence of intention had always to be in the form of overt acts. But did it have to be overt to every single user of the way on every single day of the year? There was nothing in the section to say that. Denning L.J. in the *Fairey* case gave as an example the common practice of closing a way for one day in the year. He was not sure that that would always be sufficient for example if the landowners chose to charge a toll on Christmas Day, when nobody would be out riding their horses, or on a day when there was a howling blizzard and when nobody would go out, even on a horse. It might be thought that that was not sufficient evidence of an intention not to dedicate. Again, it was a question of fact.'

George Laurence QC, for the appellant, not unreasonably characterised Mr Diggory's statement as 'about as vague, unclear and unhelpful as one could imagine'. The Secretary of State was, however, the fact finder, and he concluded that Mr Diggory's statement was 'clear and unambiguous', and could, therefore, rely upon it for establishing sufficient evidence of a lack of intention to dedicate. While Mr Laurence did not contend that every time there was conflicting evidence there had to be a public inquiry, if there was, however, a headlong conflict, resoluble only by testing the credibility of witnesses on either side, the Secretary of State should exercise his discretion to ensure a public inquiry. In *Ex p Cowell* the Secretary of State had directed a public inquiry which was held by an inspector. Here, the landowner's statement, Mr Laurence submits, should have been put to the test of oral examination.

The rationale for the decision of Parliament to provide directly for an oral hearing at the Sch 15 stage (ie only as and when an objection is raised to a modification order) and not at the Sch 14 stage, can be discerned on the following footing. Any person (which may of course include a landowner wishing, for example, to downgrade an existing bridleway to a footpath) may apply for a modification order (see s 53(5) of the 1981 Act) and thereby invoke the Sch 14 procedure. In doing so, the applicant is not asserting any private law right or interest but only a right in public law. The decision to be made at that stage is whether to make the order of modification which would require confirmation in accordance with Sch 15. If there is a direction to the local authority to make a modification order, and if objections to it are raised, the public inquiry will be held. This is because the private law rights or interests of the landowner are in jeopardy and require traditional safeguarding. Parliament thereby intended to protect private law rights of landowners, but gave no similar protection to individual citizens who used the footpath or bridleway, simply because such rights as they might have were as members of the public and not as private citizens. It is conceded that, while there is no legal obligation to hold an inquiry other than under the specific provisions of Sch 15, there have been occasions a   when both the Secretary of State for the Environment and the Secretary of State for Wales have directed informal hearings to explore material put before them. No request has been made in the instant case for an oral hearing, but inherent in this application for judicial review is a demand that the imbalance between landowner and the members of the public in their respective rights and interests in private and public law should be redressed if the particular case (such as this

b   one) compels it.

THE APPLICANT'S ARGUMENTS

The main thrust of Mr Laurence's attractive argument is that, having in mind the conflict between the claimants to the footpath as a public right of way and the untested statement of Mr Diggory, the Secretary of State for Wales was acting

c   unreasonably in not directing the council to make a modification order so as to trigger off a public inquiry under the Sch 15 to the 1981 Act, at which there could be a full evaluation of the evidence on both sides.

Mr Laurence relied both on the wording of s 53(3)(c)(i) of the 1981 Act, which refers to evidence that a right of way 'subsists or is reasonably alleged to subsist'

d   and the judgment of Owen J in *R v Secretary of State for the Environment, ex p Bagshaw* (1994) 68 P & CR 402. Owen J said that s 53(3)(c)(i) of the 1981 Act calls for two tests, A and B. Test A relates to the right of way subsisting; test B relates to the reasonable allegation of subsistence. Owen J said (at 408):

'To answer either question must involve some evaluation of the evidence

e   and a judgment upon that evidence. For the first of those possibilities to be answered in the affirmative, it will be necessary to show that on a balance of probabilities the right does exist. For the second possibility to be shown it would be necessary to show that a reasonable person, having considered all the relevant evidence available, could reasonably allege a right of way to subsist'.

f
Owen J went on to say that 'subject to an allegation of *Wednesbury* unreasonableness ... the decision of the Secretary of State had to be final if he had asked himself the right question'. Clearly, the Secretary of State did ask himself the right question, namely whether the right of way as reasonably alleged to subsist was defeated by the proviso to s 31(3) of the 1980 Act, such as not to

g   involve a direction to the local authority to make a modification order. On the basis that the Secretary of State's statutory duty was to decide the issue on the documentary material, it cannot be said that he acted irrationally. Everything depended on the assessment of Mr Diggory's statement. Whatever assessment this court might have made of Mr Diggory's statement, the decision belongs

h   exclusively to the Secretary of State. Even though there was undoubtedly a strong body of evidence in support of the existence of a right of way, together with rebutting evidence in the form of the landowner's declared intention not to dedicate, the Secretary of State was entitled to conclude that it was not reasonable to allege that the right of way subsists, or at least the reasonableness of the

j   allegation could not outweigh the landowner's intention not to dedicate. Even though the Secretary of State said that the right of way could not be 'reasonably alleged to subsist', his acceptance of Mr Diggory's statement such as to satisfy the proviso to s 31(3) of the 1980 Act is conclusive. Mr Laurence seeks to bring the applicant's case within the *Wednesbury* principle of unreasonableness by submitting that Secretary of State, by way of declining to direct a modification order thereby foreclosing on any public inquiry, acted unreasonably (see

Associated Provincial Picture Houses Ltd v Wednesbury Corp [1947] 1 All ER 498, [1948] 1 KB 223). Given the structure of the legislation, I fail to see how the a Secretary of State can be said to have acted irrationally. He was acting entirely within the four corners of the statutory framework. The sole question remains: should the Secretary of State, in performing his duty under para 4 of Sch 14 to the 1981 Act, nevertheless have regard to the fact that the combined effect of that legislative framework and this court's jurisdiction on judicial review may, and in b cases where appeals to the Secretary of State fail, will deprive claimants of public rights of way of the appropriate means of sustaining their claim and testing the landowner's avowed intention not to dedicate?

FAIRNESS

If (as I have found) the Secretary of State was not acting irrationally in c determining the appeal under para 4 of Sch 14 to the 1981 Act, was he acting fairly in declining, in effect, to put the rival claims of the public users of the footpath and of the landowner to the test of oral examination? The law has now developed to the point where, in the making of administrative decisions affecting rights, interests and legitimate expectations, there is a common law duty to act fairly. d That is so, except where manifestly there is a contrary statutory intention. Whereas the court may not interfere with the exercise of an administrative discretion on substantive grounds, save where the decision is so unreasonable that it is beyond the range of responses available to a reasonable decision maker (see Bingham MR in *R v Ministry of Defence, ex p Smith* [1996] 1 All ER 257, [1996] QB 517) it may interfere where the administrative problem focuses on procedural e safeguards. In the course of his judgment in *R v Panel on Take-overs and Mergers, ex p Guinness plc* [1989] 1 All ER 509 at 184, [1990] 1 QB 146 at 531–532, Lloyd LJ indicated that the court is the author and sole judge to set procedural standards, and it may do so to supplement statutory procedures. The courts have not adopted a clear principle about this. There is a general presumption, at least in f cases affecting individuals, that Parliament intends to act fairly and that accordingly the judges can import additional safeguards to those provided by statute, where appropriate.

In *Lloyd v McMahon* [1987] 1 All ER 1118 at 1161, [1987] AC 625 at 702–703 Lord Bridge of Harwich said:
g

'... it is well established that when a statute has conferred on any body the power to make decisions affecting individuals, the court will not only require the procedure prescribed by the statute to be followed, but will readily imply so much and no more to be introduced by way of additional procedural safeguards as will ensure the attainment of fairness.'
h

But the duty does not attach to every decision of an administrative character. Many such decisions do not affect the rights, interests and legitimate expectations of the individual citizen in a direct and immediate way. Thus a decision to impose a tax or a general charge for services rendered to ratepayers, each of j which indirectly affects the rights, interests or legitimate expectations of citizens generally, does not attract the duty to act fairly. This is because the decision affects the person individually only as a member of the public or class of that public. An executive or administrative decision of that kind is truly a policy or political decision, and is not subject to court intervention, except on strict *Wednesbury* grounds. The duty to act fairly depends, therefore, on the a construction of the particular statute. The point is put most helpfully by Mason J in the High Court of Australia in *Kioa v West* (1985) 159 CLR 550 at 585:

> 'The expression "procedural fairness" more aptly conveys the notion of a flexible obligation to adopt fair procedures which are appropriate and adapted to the circumstances of the particular case. The statutory power
>
b> must be exercised fairly, ie in accordance with procedures that are fair to the individual considered in the light of the statutory requirements, the interests of the individual and the interests and purposes, whether public or private, which the statute seeks to advance or protect or permits to be taken into account as legitimate considerations ... When the doctrine of natural justice or the duty to act fairly in its application to administrative decision-making
c> is so understood, the need for a strong manifestation of contrary statutory intention in order for it to be excluded becomes apparent. The critical question in most cases is not whether the principles of natural justice apply. It is: what does the duty to act fairly require in the circumstances of the particular case? It will be convenient to consider at the outset whether the statute displaces the duty when the statute contains a specific provision to
d> that effect, for then it will be pointless to inquire what the duty requires in the circumstances of the case, unless there are circumstances not contemplated by the statutory provision that may give rise to a legitimate expectation. However, in general, it will be a matter of determining *what the duty to act fairly requires in the way of procedural fairness in the circumstances of*
e> *the case.* A resolution of that question calls for an examination of the statutory provisions and the interests which I have already mentioned.' (My emphasis.)

Since the courts have displayed, with whatever degree of judicial restraint might be appropriate, a willingness to supplement the will of Parliament, there
f must exist some room for manoeuvre such as to permit judicial intervention to ensure fairness 'in the circumstances of the particular case'. And where the statute has omitted to supply a procedure that will be fair to all claimants to a public right of way (as well as to landowners who might wish to resist such claims), any implication that such omission is deliberate cannot operate exclusively to all situations. The court's intrusion in a case of judicial review will
g not be to build into the statute a blanket procedure of fairness, but only to inject its notion of fairness, as and when conflicting documentary material in a particular case compels a means of testing the evidence in a public inquiry.

Looking at the procedural structure in Schs 14 and 15 to the 1981 Act, I discern that Parliament has assumed that invariably it is fair for the applicant for a
h modification order to have his or her case determined on documentary material, the decision-maker having regard to all the relevant considerations. Where the public user establishes a public right of way, sufficient to establish a modification order, the landowner's private rights are so engaged as to merit special treatment at that stage. If, however, the basis of the court's power to imply 'additional
j procedural safeguards as will ensure the attainment of fairness' is by way of imposing the common law on the statute (rather than seeking the Parliamentary intention), it seems to me that it is not debarred from intervening; only that it must be careful not to usurp the legislative function. It may supplement, but must not supplant. What the legislature has not written, the court must not write. But if a gap is disclosed, the remedy does not need to await an amending Act; it can be filled instantaneously in appropriate circumstances.

It is not suggested by Mr Laurence that such a safeguard should be available in all cases; only those where (as here) there is a conflict of evidential material between public user and landowner. Although there appears to be no authority for the proposition that the court can supplement a legislative code even only on an ad hominem basis, picking and choosing the cases where the court would demand of the decision maker that he order a public inquiry on the grounds of fairness, I see nothing in the formula for testing the requirement of fairness in Lord Mustill's speech in *Doody v Secretary of State for the Home Dept* [1993] 3 All ER 92 at 106, [1994] 1 AC 531 at 560 that would preclude the court's intrusion, since the question is essentially one of 'intuitive judgment' by the court. My intuition, that the procedural provisions in Schs 14 and 15 produce an imbalance, weighted in favour of private rights at that investigative stage of rival claims, is not displaced by what Parliament has stated so clearly. There is, in my view, room for concluding that the Secretary of State has in this case acted unfairly in operating the statutory procedure, without due regard to the peculiar facts of this case, strictly in the manner envisaged by Parliament. He could have ordered a public inquiry, dehors his statutory powers, as indeed on rare occasions, I am told, has happened. If the decision of 16 May 1995 cannot stand, it will still be a matter for the Secretary of State to decide whether (a) to direct a modification order (leaving the question of a public hearing to be triggered off by the landowner objecting); or (b) to order a public inquiry extra-statutorily; or (c) deem it safe and fair, on a reconsideration of the appeal under para 4(2) of Sch 14 to the 1981 Act, to adhere to his original decision.

LEGITIMATE EXPECTATION

An alternative way of importing fairness into the Secretary of State's consideration of the appeal under para 4(2) of Sch 14 to the 1981 Act, might be to rely on the doctrine of legitimate expectation. The developing case law on legitimate expectation has so far required some express promise, undertaking, representation or published policy statement emanating from the decision maker, upon which the recipient can found an expectation of procedural fairness. But the generality of statutory powers and duties to be exercised as performed by the Executive cannot, in my view, be equated with a 'promise' or 'representation' derived from action of the Executive. As Lord Keith of Kinkel noted in the criminal injuries compensation case, *R v Secretary of State for the Home Dept, ex p Fire Brigades Union* [1995] 2 All ER 244 at 248, [1995] 2 AC 513 at 545:

'... the doctrine of legitimate expectation cannot reasonably be extended to the public at large, as opposed to particular individuals or bodies who are directly affected by certain executive action.'

That proposition might be overcome by acknowledging that, as and when the applicant appealed to the Secretary of State against the adverse decision of the council, any expectation at that point became personalised. But where can any representation be spelt out of the handling of the applicant's appeal to the Secretary of State? How is there an expectation, and whence comes its legitimacy? At no stage did the applicant seek or obtain any express promise or undertaking other than that to which he was entitled by way of fulfilment of the statutory duty of a full consideration of the appeal. In de Smith, Woolf and Jowell *Judicial Review of Administrative Action* (5th edn, 1995) p 426, para 8–058 there is a suggestion—although lacking in direct judicial authority—that lack of knowledge a of a promise or undertaking does not deprive the uninformed of the benefit. The generality of a benefit may thus be conferred on the individual:

b 'Could an applicant claim the benefit of a representation contained in, say, a government circular which he had not seen until after the relevant decision had been made? The fact that the applicant is in the class to which the representation is directed but happens not to be aware of it should not, it is submitted, deprive him of the benefit of the representation. To do so would involve unfair discrimination between those who were and were not aware of the representation and would benefit the well-informed or well-advised. It would also encourage undesirable administrative practice by too readily relieving decision-makers of the normal consequences of their actions.'

c When it was clear from the results of the investigation by the council and the further inquiries made by officials in the Welsh Office that there was a stark conflict between the claimants to a public right of way and the landowner, could it be said that there was an expectation that the particular case, exceptionally, called for a different, fair procedure from the run-of-the-mill appeal under para d 4(2) of Sch 14 to the 1981 Act? To answer that question in the affirmative would be to do no more than to travel down an alternative road to that which permits the court to supplement the statutory code in order to achieve fairness. Whether the court does it by importing fairness into the framework of the statutory code, or compels it because the decision-maker has by implication promised it, matters not. Either way the notion of fairness is implanted. I would be prepared, if it e were necessary, to hold that there was a legitimate expectation in May 1995 that the Secretary of State would act fairly to the applicant in subjecting the case to a public inquiry before he came to make his final decision under para 4(2).

A EUROPEAN DIMENSION

f At a late stage in the course of oral agreement it was mooted whether the procedural safeguards of art 6 of the European Convention for the Protection of Human Rights and Fundamental Freedoms (Rome, 4 November 1950; TS 71, (1953); Cmd 8969), might have some application. Article 6(1) provides, so far as is material, as follows: 'In the determination of his civil rights and obligations ... everyone is entitled to a fair and public hearing ... by an independent and g impartial tribunal established by law.' In his written submissions of 3 May 1996 (after the conclusion of oral hearings) Mr Laurence disavows any argument to that effect. He concedes that the availability of English judicial review saves the Secretary of State's decision from art 6(1) condemnation. And he goes on to concede that, in any event, the threat to the Secretary of State's decision of it h being a nullity is not a matter of concern for the Secretary of State in this case where judicial review is available. This would be so even if the case could be brought within the concepts of 'civil rights' and 'determination' of civil rights. It must be doubtful whether the reliance by the Secretary of State on a decision founded on documented material, rather than hearing the matter to be j determined only after a public inquiry, is encompassed by art 6(1).

Mr Laurence's concession is made upon an analysis of the way in which the European Court of Human Rights has defined the scope of judicial review, in particular in the recent case of *Bryan v UK* (1995) 21 EHRR 342. The facts of that case were as follows. Mr John Bryan was a farmer and contractor, residing in Warrington, Cheshire. In December 1989 an enforcement notice was served on him by a local authority requiring the demolition of two brick buildings on land

bought by Mr Bryan in 1987. The enforcement notice recited an alleged breach
of planning control in that the buildings had been erected without the requisite
planning permission. The notice required demolition within three months. The
authorities acted in accordance with s 172 of the Town and Country Planning Act
1990. Mr Bryan appealed to the Secretary of State for the Environment under
s 174(2) of the 1990 Act. An inspector was appointed to conduct an inquiry and
determine the appeal. The inspector was a Principal Housing and Planning
Inspector, a civil servant and a member of salaried staff of the Department of the
Environment. He had been appointed by the Lord Chancellor. In substance, the
inspector rejected Mr Bryan's appeal. On the application to the High Court for
judicial review Mr Bryan failed, as did his appeal to the Court of Appeal. Before
the European Commission of Human Rights Mr Bryan alleged that art 6(1)
applied to the English proceedings, and that the Secretary of State's inspector did
not satisfy the criteria of independence and impartiality necessary to comply with
the provision, since he was a salaried employee and an individual case could be
removed from him. He also contended that the review by the High Court, which
is limited to points of law, was not able to, and did not in this case, deal with the
central factual inferences which the inspector drew from the primary facts. The
Commission held that the right to property was clearly a 'civil right' within art
6(1) and the enforcement process was concerned directly with the way in which
the applicant was entitled to use his land. The Commission, by 11 votes to 5, in
reviewing the procedure and the inspector's role concluded that there had been
no violation of art 6(1). The court was unanimous in finding that there had been
no violation.

   The ruling of the Commission is notable for a concurring opinion of Nicholas
Bratza QC (the UK member on the Commission). In concluding that the powers
of review of the High Court, when combined with the statutory requirements
under the 1990 Act for appealing against an enforcement notice, satisfied the
requirements of art 6(1), he said (at 354):

   'It appears to me that the requirement that a court or tribunal should have
   "full jurisdiction" cannot be mechanically applied with the result that, in all
   circumstances and whatever the subject matter of the dispute, the court or
   tribunal must have full power to substitute its own findings of fact, and its
   own inferences from those facts, for that of the administrative authority
   concerned. Whether the power of judicial review is sufficiently wide to
   satisfy the requirements of Article 6 must in my view depend on a number
   of considerations, including the subject matter of the dispute, the nature of
   the decision of the administrative authorities which is in question, the
   procedure, if any, which exists for review of the decision by a person or body
   acting independently of the authority concerned and the scope of that power
   of review.'

   Mr Laurence submits that, in the light of the *Bryan* decision, there is adequate
compliance of art 6(1) in the Sch 14 process of this case. He submits that the
statutory review by the High Court, provided for by the legislation in that case,
was available on the same basis as the judicial review application now before the
High Court in the instant case. It is therefore the case that any perceived art 6(1)
inadequacy in the Sch 14 procedure now before the court would be cured by the
availability of the very judicial review application which is now considering the
decision of the Secretary of State under the procedure. The Sch 14 process does

a   not therefore breach art 6(1), because of the availability of judicial review. As was noted in *Bryan* v *UK* (1995) 21 EHRR 342 at 361:

> '... even if the applicant had sought to pursue his appeal under ground (b), the Court notes that, while the High Court could not have substituted its own findings of fact for those of the inspector, it would have had the power to satisfy itself that the inspector's findings of fact or the inferences based on
b   them were neither perverse nor irrational.'

It has to be remembered that Mr Laurence is contending primarily that the defect in the Secretary of State's decision is exposed by its irrationality. Once, however, that ground for alleging a defect is proved to be unsound, the adequacy of judicial review may not be so apparent to the applicant in this case. Given,
c   however, the European Court's approach to English judicial review, it is not for this court to do other than acknowledge the conformity of judicial review with art 6(1) in the eyes of the European Court. Mr Laurence's concessions are rightly made, and preclude any further consideration of the European dimension to this case. I would adopt the words of Neill LJ in *R v City of London Corp, ex p Matson*
d   (1995) 8 Admin LR 49 at 64:

> 'In reaching this conclusion I have not found it necessary to seek the assistance of Article 6 or any of the other Articles in the European Convention on Human Rights, important though those Articles are. I am satisfied that English law provides a fair solution.'

e
CONCLUSION
Had I found myself having to accede to the case for the Secretary of State, I would have recorded my unhappiness at the result. So long as the Secretary of State felt entitled to deal with the matter without a public inquiry, it could not be doubted that the cohort of public users of the footpath in Llangollen would
f   nurture a legitimate grievance that their powerful claim to a public right of way had been kicked into touch by the word of the single landowner, supported by no evidential material other than his untested written statement, unspecific as it clearly is in its content.   The problem arises solely because of the uneven-handedness of the legislative provisions in Schs 14 and 15 to the 1981 Act.
g   The private rights of the landowners are fully protected; the public law rights of the users of the footpath are protected only to the limited extent of a right to apply for a modification order and of appealing to the Secretary of State against the refusal by the county council to make a modification order. The social reality is that individual members of the public are pitting their claims of freedom of
h   movement against the private rights of the landowner and his right to exclusive use of his land. The law rightly lays great, even overriding importance on the latter, but, in sustaining it against claims of a public right of entry, the legal procedures for achieving the right answer to a social issue should be equiparated—in common parlance, the rival claims should be fought out on a level playing field. As Scott LJ said, over 50 years ago, in *Jones v Bates* [1938] 2 All
j   ER 237 at 249:

> 'The rambler—sometimes called the "hiker"—needs the footpath more than ever. The movement represented by the ramblers' societies is of national importance, and to the real lover of the country, who knows that to see it properly he must go on foot, but who is driven off all main roads and a good many others by the din and bustle of motor traffic, the footpath is

everything. In short, it is of real public moment that no genuine public footpath should be lost, without statutory action to close it.'

a

In the course of browsing through the irrelevant parts of the legislation germane to this case, I came across s 302 of the 1980 Act. It empowers the Secretary of State to 'cause such inquiries to be made as he may consider necessary or desirable for the purpose of his functions under this Act ...' Something comparable needs, in my view, to be written into Schs 14 and 15 to the 1981 Act.

b

This application for judicial review is granted. I will hear counsel whether, and if so what relief, if any, is appropriate.

Application granted. Leave to appeal to the Court of Appeal granted.

c

Dilys Tausz   Barrister.

a # Attorney General's Reference (No 1 of 1995)

COURT OF APPEAL, CRIMINAL DIVISION
LORD TAYLOR OF GOSFORTH CJ, BROOKE AND FORBES JJ
23 JANUARY 1996

b
Criminal law – Unlicensed deposit-taking – Director's liability – Directors consenting to acceptance by company of unauthorised deposits – Whether ignorance of law as to requirement for authorisation a defence – Whether mens rea required to show consent – Banking Act 1987, ss 3, 96.

c A company director who knows that acts which can only be performed by the company if it is licensed by the Bank of England are being performed when in fact no licence exists, and who consents to that performance, is guilty of the offence of consenting to the acceptance of a deposit contrary to ss 3[a] and 96[b] of the Banking Act 1987. The fact that he does not know that it is an offence to perform d those acts without a licence is no defence. The mens rea for 'consent' to the acceptance of a deposit contrary to ss 3 and 96 of the 1987 Act requires the defendant to be proved to have known the material facts which constituted the offence by the body corporate and to have agreed to its conduct of its business on the basis of those facts (see p 22 *d e*, p 26 *g* and p 27 *b*, post).

Dicta of Lord Goddard CJ in *Johnson v Youden* [1950] 1 KB 544 at 546 and of
e Viscount Dilhorne in *Churchill v Walton* [1967] 1 All ER 497 at 503 applied.

Secretary of State for Trade and Industry v Hart [1982] 1 All ER 817 distinguished.

Notes
For statutory regulation of banking and restriction on acceptance of deposits, see
f 3(1) *Halsbury's Laws* (4th edn reissue) paras 24–27.

For the Banking Act 1987, ss 3, 96, see 4 *Halsbury's Statutes* (4th edn) (1987 reissue) 532, 625.

Cases referred to in judgment
Churchill v Walton [1967] 1 All ER 497, [1967] 2 AC 224, [1967] 2 WLR 682, HL.
g *Huckerby v Elliott* [1970] 1 All ER 189, DC.
Johnson v Youden [1950] 1 All ER 300, [1950] 1 KB 544, DC.
Secretary of State for Trade and Industry v Hart [1982] 1 All ER 817, [1982] 1 WLR 481, DC.
Westminster City Council v Croyalgrange Ltd [1986] 2 All ER 353, [1986] 1 WLR 674,
h HL.

Reference
The Attorney General referred to the Court of Appeal under s 36 of the Criminal Justice Act 1972 the following questions for consideration: (i) whether, on a
j charge against a company director of consenting to the acceptance of a deposit contrary to ss 3 and 96 of the Banking Act 1987, ignorance of the law as to the requirement of the authorisation of the Bank of England was a defence; and (ii) what mens rea was required to be proved to show 'consent'. The questions arose

---

a   Section 3, so far as material, is set out at p 22 *f*, post
b   Section 96, so far as material, is set out at p 22 *g*, post

after the acquittal, on the trial judge's directions, of the respondents of two counts
charged under s 3(1) of the 1987 Act. The facts are set out in the opinion of the
court.

Michael Worsley QC and *Neville Spencer-Lewis* (instructed by the *Crown Prosecution
Service*) for the Attorney General.
Peter Collier QC and *Jeremy Barnett* (instructed by *Walker Morris*, Leeds) for the
respondents.

LORD TAYLOR OF GOSFORTH CJ. This is a reference by the Attorney
General (No 1 of 1995) under s 36 of the Criminal Justice Act 1972.

On 22 November 1994 the respondents were convicted in the Crown Court at
Teesside of a number of offences under s 35 of the Banking Act 1987. They were
sentenced to a term of imprisonment. The offences involved fraudulent
inducements to make deposits.

They were, however, acquitted on the learned trial judge's directions, of two
counts charged under s 3(1) of the 1987 Act. The judge withdrew those counts
from the jury's consideration following submissions at the conclusion of the case
for the Crown. Her Majesty's Attorney General now seeks the opinion of this
court on points of law, namely: (1) whether on a charge against a company
director of consenting to the acceptance of a deposit contrary to ss 3 and 96 of the
1987 Act, ignorance of the law as to the requirement of the authorisation of the
Bank of England is a defence, and (2) what mens rea is required to be proved to
show 'consent'?

The terms of the two relevant sections of the 1987 Act are as follows, so far as
is relevant. Under s 3(1) of the Act:

'... no person shall ... accept a deposit in the course of carrying on ... a
business which for the purposes of this Act is a deposit-taking business unless
that person is an institution for the time being authorised by the Bank [of
England] under ... this Act.'

Under s 96(1) of the Act:

'Where an offence under this Act committed by a body corporate is proved
to have been committed with the consent or connivance of, or to be
attributable to any neglect on the part of any director, manager, secretary or
other similar officer of the body corporate, or any person who was
purporting to act in any such capacity, he, as well as the body corporate, shall
be guilty of that offence ...'

It is convenient for completeness to refer also to s 96(4) of the Act, which
provides:

'In any proceedings for an offence under this Act it shall be a defence for
the person charged to prove that he took all reasonable precautions and
exercised all due diligence to avoid the commission of such an offence by
himself or any person under his control.'

The facts of the present case can be shortly stated. The respondents were
directors of a company trading in the north of England. It was a small company
dealing in insurance and investment brokerage. The first respondent, F, was the
chairman. He ran the business. He and his wife were the only directors. The
second respondent, B, was his right-hand man and acted as a de facto director.

a There was evidence that from 1987 onwards the company was accepting deposits in the course of carrying on a deposit-taking business and that both men were directly concerned in that activity. Large sums of money were deposited, amounting to some £750,000 in total. In order to induce such deposits the respondents told a number of the depositors that the money would be lent on as bridging loans, for which the company would hold charges as security. In fact the
b money thus raised was being diverted into a night-club venture. When that venture failed in 1989, most of the money was lost. It was in respect of the representations made by the respondents to the depositors that the charges which were proved against the respondents were based.

The company was not authorised by the Bank of England to accept deposits. In February 1992 the respondents were arrested and in October 1992 they were
c charged. Following their arrest, interviews were sought with the two respondents. They declined to answer questions. However, in September 1992 the second respondent, B, volunteered an interview. Towards the end of it, the detective sergeant asked B what explanation he could give for the unlicensed deposit-taking of the company. In the course of questioning, it emerged from the
d respondent, B, that he had no idea that in order to take people's money on deposit, or to take people's money on investment, you have to be licensed by the Bank of England.

The two counts in question were specimen offences. Count 1 related to Mrs B. She had originally invested a total of about £20,000 through the company. She said that at some point after her initial investment the second respondent offered
e her 17% on her money and the respondents had carte blanche from her to invest the money where it would get 17%. The money was then deposited in the company's 'bridging fund'. The deposit was evidenced by a document called a 'property bridging bond', which was signed by the second respondent. It referred to an 'invest', which the prosecution said was truly a deposit, of £19,210 on 25
f November 1988 at a flat rate interest of 17%. The first respondent later acknowledged in a letter dated 27 December 1989 that Mrs B had been offered participation in the bridging fund scheme with fixed interest.

Count 2 concerned Mr and Mrs G, who placed £54,511 in the company's bridging fund via an intermediary. That transaction was evidenced by an agreement with the company signed by the second respondent, which was found
g at the first respondent's house.

At the end of the prosecution case the defence submitted that there was no case to answer on these two counts. It was argued on their behalf that in order to be guilty of consenting to the offence by the company, a defendant director must be aware of the relevant facts. If the director was not aware that the business is as a
h matter of fact deemed to be a deposit-taking business for the purposes of the 1987 Act, he cannot give informed consent and therefore cannot consent to the acceptance of the deposit in contravention of s 3. The issue as to whether the two directors were aware that this was a deposit-taking business was a point raised before the trial judge, but in view of the basis of his decision it was not adjudicated
j upon.

The matter which was determined in the court below was a submission that the directors had to be positively aware of the lack of authorisation by the Bank of England and to have applied their minds to that fact: reference was made to *Secretary of State for Trade and Industry v Hart* [1982] 1 All ER 817, [1982] 1 WLR 481. The trial judge gave an initial ruling, in the course of which he said:

'In my judgment, on the authorities which have been argued before me,
but principally that of *Secretary of State for Trade and Industry v Hart* ([1982] 1   *a*
All ER 817, [1982] 1 WLR 481), and relying upon dicta from both the
judgments of Ormrod LJ and Woolf J, I rule that the Crown would have to
prove not only a deposit-making, not only that it was in the course of a
deposit-taking business, not only that there was no licence, but that these
defendants knew and had applied their mind to the fact that there was no   *b*
licence for them to do this. I think, as against the company, there is what is
in shorthand referred to as strict liability in the criminal jurisdiction. As
against directors it is necessary to prove that they applied their minds to the
lack of a licence. That not being so in this case, and there being no evidence
of it, counts 1 and 2 on this indictment fail and I shall withdraw them from
the jury.'   *c*

The trial judge gave a more extended ruling the next day during the trial, in
which he said:

'I think I can deal shortly with counts 1 and 2, which I indicated yesterday
that I propose to withdraw from the jury, and I will deal with it for the   *d*
purpose of being of assistance, for the sole ground upon which I find there is
no case to answer is that which was centred on the word "consent" in s 96(1)
of the Banking Act 1987, under which counts 1 and 2 are drawn. It does seem
to me that a s 3 offence is indeed a strict liability offence, but that it is made
otherwise where it concerns directors or persons purporting to act as   *e*
directors; that is each of these defendants. In that regard I hold that a
particular awareness must be proved, and at this stage evidence adduced of
a particular awareness of the director or purporting director in question, of
each of the ingredients which go to make up count 3, including a lack of
awareness of authorisation. That lack of awareness of authorisation in my
judgment requires a specific application of the conscious mind to that point   *f*
and not, as [counsel for the prosecution] submitted, that it was a fact that
there was no licence, and had the defendants applied their minds to it they
would have realised [it.] It does seem to me in the way that Parliament has
decided to frame any potential offence as against a director that such a
specific mens rea is needed. I find there is no evidence of that here, rather   *g*
the contrary. The evidence of [B's] awareness was explored by [the]
detective sergeant ... in the course of an interview, and it is apparent that he
expressed his complete ignorance of a need for a licence, and there has been
no evidence to the contrary. The case is no stronger against [F]. For that
reason, and that reason only, I shall withdraw counts 1 and 2 from the jury   *h*
...'

Later, in addressing the jury, the trial judge said:

'... if you think of the evidence of [the] detective sergeant ... in his
interview with [B], [B] was saying: "Well, I don't know anything about a   *j*
licence. Is it necessary?" And if there is not a word of evidence to contradict
his apparent ignorance of the situation—not ignorance of the law, that is
rather different. [Counsel for the prosecution] was quite right when he told
you at the beginning of this trial that ignorance of the law is no excuse—but
ignorance of the fact, the positive fact that the company did not have a
licence to do what it said it was doing; and if there is no evidence to the

a   contrary then there is nothing to support that essential ingredient. However small an ingredient it is, it is still an essential one.'

On behalf of the Attorney General, Mr Worsley QC submits that the judge's rulings and observations to the jury were incorrect. He relies on the well-known principle that ignorance of the law is no excuse. That proposition is not, and indeed could not be, in dispute. The issue on this reference is as to what state of
b   mind has to be established against the accused to make him guilty of 'consenting' under s 96(1).

Mr Worsley submits that if a person mentioned in that subsection knows the facts which constitute the offence under s 3(1) committed by the body corporate and consents to that body's affairs being carried on in accordance with those facts,
c   he is guilty of the offence under s 96(1), subject to any defence he may have under s 96(4). It is no defence to say: 'I had no idea it was an offence to carry on that business without authorisation from the Bank.'

Mr Worsley relies upon dicta in two cases. *Johnson v Youden* [1950] 1 All ER 300, [1950] 1 KB 544 was a case concerned with aiding and abetting. Lord Goddard CJ
d   said:

'If a person knows all the facts and is assisting another person to do certain things, and it turns out that the doing of those things constitutes an offence, the person who is assisting is guilty of aiding and abetting that offence, because to allow him to say, "I knew of all those facts but I did not know that an offence was committed," would be allowing him to set up ignorance of
e   the law as a defence.' (See [1950] 1 KB 544 at 546; cf [1950] 1 All ER 300 at 302.)

That passage was expressly approved in the decision of the House of Lords in *Churchill v Walton* [1967] 1 All ER 497, [1967] 2 AC 224, a conspiracy case.
f   Viscount Dilhorne, with whom all the other members of the Appellate Committee agreed, said:

'The question is "What did they agree to do?" If what they agreed to do was, on the facts known to them, an unlawful act, they are guilty of conspiracy and cannot excuse themselves by saying that, owing to their
g   ignorance of the law, they did not realise that such an act was a crime.' (See [1967] 1 All ER 497 at 503, [1967] 2 AC 224 at 236.)

Mr Collier QC's submission reflected in the judge's rulings was that, unless the accused directors were shown to have addressed their minds specifically to the absence of authorisation or, as it has been called throughout these proceedings, a
h   licence from the Bank of England, they could not be guilty of consenting under s 96(1). He referred to three cases in addition to those cited above. *Huckerby v Elliott* [1970] 1 All ER 189 was a case concerning gaming licences. The company pleaded guilty to operating without a gaming licence. Two directors were charged with offences under s 305 of the Customs and Excise Act 1952, which was
j   in similar terms to s 96(1) of the 1987 Act. A director named L, who was charged with consenting to the offence committed by the company, pleaded guilty. The case concerned another director, H, who was charged with neglect under s 305. She pleaded not guilty. She was convicted and appealed. Her appeal was allowed. The case was, therefore, not directly concerned with the issue before the court at present, which is one of consent. However, in the course of his judgment, Ashworth J (at 194) dealt, en passant, with the question of consent. He

approved the dictum of the stipendiary magistrate from whom the appeal was made, who had said about consent: 'It would seem that where a director consents to the commission of an offence by his company, he is well aware of what is going on and agrees to it.' The rather general nature of that dictum does not throw much light on the issue which has been raised in the present case. Otherwise the point dealt with by Ashworth J was to make it clear that s 305, and by analogy s 96(1) in the present case, does not create an absolute offence involving all directors of the company. With that we entirely agree.

The second case referred to by Mr Collier was *Westminster City Council v Croyalgrange Ltd* [1986] 2 All ER 353, [1986] 1 WLR 674. It dealt with the operation of a sex establishment without a licence. We have considered it with care, but we do not find that it supports Mr Collier's arguments. Indeed, a passage in the speech of Lord Bridge of Harwich is positively unhelpful to Mr Collier's argument (see [1986] 2 All ER 353 at 358, [1986] 1 WLR 674 at 683). It is unnecessary to quote that passage, since the factual background is quite different from that of the present case.

Finally, Mr Collier referred the court to *Secretary of State for Trade and Industry v Hart* [1982] 1 All ER 817, [1982] 1 WLR 481, upon which the learned judge relied. There, a defendant audited the annual accounts of companies of which he was a director, although the Companies Act 1976 disqualified him from doing so. He was charged with an offence under s 13(5) of the 1976 Act, which provided: 'No person shall act as auditor of a company at a time when he knows that he is disqualified for appointment to that office.'

The metropolitan stipendiary magistrate acquitted the defendant, since the prosecution had not, in his judgment, established that the defendant had the requisite knowledge. The decision was challenged on appeal, on the grounds that ignorance of the law is no defence. However, the Divisional Court upheld the decision because of the specific wording of the subsection, which made it an ingredient of the offence that the defendant must know he is disqualified. In our judgment that case was crucially different from the present one. There, knowledge of the unlawfulness of his acting as an auditor was an ingredient of the offence which had to be proved against the defendant.

Here, we are satisfied that the correct approach is that suggested on behalf of the Attorney General. A director who knows that acts which can only be performed by the company if it is licensed by the Bank, are being performed when in fact no licence exists and who consents to that performance is guilty of the offence charged. The fact that he does not know it is an offence to perform them without a licence, ie ignorance of the law, is no defence.

Mr Collier's suggestion that the director must actively have addressed his mind to the question of licences is wholly unreal. If the two directors, who were wholly responsible for the company's business activity, were ignorant of the need for a licence, it can readily be inferred that they knew they did not have one. The concept of a director who is ignorant of the law requiring a licence, focusing his mind on the question of whether he has or has not obtained one is wholly academic. Had anyone approached the defendant directors and asked: 'Have you a licence or authorisation from the Bank of England?' The ready answer would have been No, probably supplemented by 'I did not know I needed one'. There would have been no need for a search, an inquiry or a focusing of the mind. Since the question had not occurred to them, they would know that the company did not have one.

a The ignorance of the law on the point necessarily must, in the context of this case, point to the knowledge that the company is operating unlicensed. That is not to say that s 96(1) creates an absolute offence in respect of directors. There could, for example, in a company with a number of directors responsible for different limbs of the company's business, be a director who believed the licence had been obtained and was not therefore consenting to the offences committed *b* by the company. That was not the situation here. In our view the judge was wrong to withdraw counts 1 and 2 from the jury.

Our answer to the two questions posed is as follows. (1) No. (2) A defendant has to be proved to know the material facts which constitute the offence by the body corporate and to have agreed to its conduct of its business on the basis of those facts.

c

Opinion accordingly.

N P Metcalfe Esq   Barrister.

Re H (a minor) (blood tests: parental rights) *a*

COURT OF APPEAL, CIVIL DIVISION
NEILL AND WARD LJJ
8 FEBRUARY, 5 MARCH 1996

b

Family proceedings – Orders in family proceedings – Parental responsibility order and contact order – Application by putative father – Proof of paternity – Blood test – Child conceived at time when mother having sexual relationship with both her husband and putative father – Husband having had vasectomy – Relationship between mother and putative father ending before child born – Putative father seeking parental *c* *responsibility and contact orders and direction for blood tests – Whether mother's refusal to undergo blood testing determinative of application – Inference to be drawn from refusal – Whether blood tests to determine paternity in child's interests – Family Law Reform Act 1969, ss 20(1), 23.*

d

In December 1994 the mother gave birth to a son, H, and his birth was registered in her husband's name. At the time of H's conception, his mother had been having sexual relations with both her husband, who had had a vasectomy operation in 1990, and the applicant. The mother ended her relationship with the applicant prior to the birth of H, who was then brought up as a child of the family. The applicant, who believed himself to be H's natural father, applied for contact *e* and parental responsibility orders and, if paternity was disputed, for DNA testing to establish paternity. The mother opposed the applications for contact and parental responsibility orders and refused to consent to undergo blood testing to establish paternity. The judge considered that, although there was a good chance that the applicant would succeed in establishing paternity even without the DNA *f* evidence, his chances of obtaining a contact order were remote and that the mother's implacable hostility was a factor that had to be weighed against making a blood test direction. He concluded however that it would be in the interests of H to order blood tests since the applicant would pursue the paternity issue and ordered the applicant, the mother and the child to provide blood samples pursuant to s 20(1)[a] of the Family Law Reform Act 1969 for the purpose of DNA *g* tests to ascertain paternity. The mother appealed.

Held – A mother's refusal to consent to undergo blood testing was not determinative of the question whether the court should exercise its discretion to grant or refuse a putative father's application for a direction under s 20(1) of the *h* 1969 Act, although it was a factor to be taken into account, along with the welfare of the child and the prospects of success in the proceedings in which the paternity issue arose. Moreover, where blood testing could establish the issue of paternity with certainty, the court was entitled to infer that a refusal to provide the blood sample was made to hide the truth, regardless of whether the refusal was made *j* after the court had already made a direction under s 20. Since it was in the child's interests to establish his paternity with certainty, the mother's appeal would be dismissed, but the judge's order would be varied so as to direct the use of blood tests to ascertain paternity, because s 20(1) did not empower the court to order

---

a   Section 20(1), so far as material, is set out at p 36 *e f*, post *a* blood tests, still less to take blood from an unwilling party (see p 36 *j*, p 38 *a b*, p 39 *j* to p 40 *a e*, p 41 *c* to *f*, p 44 *c* to *f* and p 45 *b* to *f*, post).

S v S, W v Official Solicitor [1970] 3 All ER 107 applied.

Re F (a minor) (blood tests: parental rights) [1993] 3 All ER 596 distinguished.

Re CB (a minor) (blood tests) [1994] 2 FLR 762 considered.

b **Notes**

For proof of parentage by blood test sampling, see 5(2) *Halsbury's Laws* (4th edn reissue) paras 714–719, and for cases on the subject, see 27(2) *Digest* (2nd reissue) 101–102, 4494–4501.

For the Family Law Reform Act 1969, ss 20, 23, see 17 *Halsbury's Statutes* (4th edn) (1993 reissue) 192, 195.

c

Cases referred to in judgments

A (a minor) (paternity: refusal of blood test), Re [1994] 2 FLR 463, CA.

CB (a minor) (blood tests), Re [1994] 2 FLR 762.

F (a minor) (blood tests: parental rights), Re [1993] 3 All ER 596, [1993] Fam 314,
d   [1993] 3 WLR 369, CA; *affg* [1993] 1 FLR 225.

G (a minor) (blood test), Re [1994] 1 FLR 495.

G (a minor) (parental responsibility), Re [1994] 2 FCR 1037, CA.

L, Re [1968] 1 All ER 20, [1968] P 119, [1967] 3 WLR 1645, CA.

R v Smith (1985) 81 Cr App R 286, CA.

e *S (a minor) (parental responsibility), Re* [1995] 2 FLR 648, CA.

S v S, W v Official Solicitor [1970] 3 All ER 107, [1972] AC 24, [1970] 3 WLR 366, HL.

W v W (No 4) [1963] 2 All ER 841, [1964] P 67, [1963] 3 WLR 540, CA.

f **Cases also cited or referred to in skeleton arguments**

CG (a minor) (blood tests), Re [1994] 2 FCR 889.

D (a minor) (contact: mother's hostility), Re [1993] 2 FLR 1.

F (a minor: paternity test), Re [1993] 1 FLR 598, CA.

H (minors) (access), Re [1992] 1 FLR 148, CA.

H (minors) (rights of putative fathers), Re (No 2) [1991] FCR 361, CA.

g *J (a minor) (contact), Re* [1994] 2 FCR 741, CA.

O (a minor: access), Re [1985] FLR 716, CA.

R (a minor: contact), Re [1993] 2 FLR 762.

S (a minor) (parental responsibility), Re [1995] 3 FCR 564.

h **Appeal**

By notice dated 1 September 1995 the mother of H (a minor) appealed with leave from the decision of Judge Coningsby QC sitting as a deputy judge of the High Court made on 8 August 1995, whereby he ordered that the applicant (the putative father of H), the mother and H provide blood samples pursuant to *j* s 20(1) of the Family Law Reform Act 1969 for the purpose of DNA testing to establish whether such tests showed that the applicant was or was not thereby excluded from being the father of the child. The facts are set out in the judgment of Ward LJ.

Patricia Scotland QC and *Deborah Archer* (instructed by *Robert Blackford & Co*, Croydon) for the mother.

Bruce Blair QC and *Richard Todd* (instructed by *Ormerod Wilkinson Marshall,* Croydon) for the applicant.   *a*

Cur adv vult

‘ 5 March 1996. The following judgments were delivered.

WARD LJ (giving the first judgment at the invitation of Neill LJ). In this appeal *b* the mother of a young baby seeks to overturn the order of Judge Coningsby QC, sitting as a deputy judge of the High Court, made on 8 August 1995, whereby he ordered that the respondent as the putative father of the child, this appellant, and the child 'do provide blood samples pursuant to section 20(1) of the Family Law Reform Act 1969 for the purpose of DNA testing to ascertain whether such tests *c* · show that the Applicant is or is not thereby excluded from being the father' of the child. I shall say more about the precise form of the order in due time.

The material facts are these. Mrs H married her husband in 1983. They have two children, C, born on 23 January 1981, so he is 15 years old, and J, born on 1 February 1987, who is just 9 years old. Some time in about 1990, Mr H *d* underwent a vasectomy operation. Although he did not return for the second test to check the successfulness of that operation, he and his wife led a full sexual life for some five years without her becoming pregnant again. That led the judge to say:

> 'The impression I have—and I do not make any findings on these matters because this is not the effective hearing of a paternity dispute—is that it was *e* a successful operation ... I have not at this stage, of course, dealt with the law at all but I will just interpose this: that the fact of the vasectomy of the husband is a significant matter which distinguishes this case from other cases which have been decided and which have been reported. There is no reported decision in which that was a factor.'   *f*

By 1993 at the latest the marriage was under strain. The husband was coming home late and was uncommunicative. When challenged by his wife, he admitted seeing another woman but denied adultery. He said that he did not know if he still loved her, his wife. She said in her statement filed in the proceedings:

> '... I began to develop a social life for myself independent of my husband, *g* primarily to annoy him because he likes me to be at home and fulfil the traditional role of wife and mother. I therefore began to make new friends and started going to [a night club] on Friday nights and on occasions [the applicant, Mr B] was invited as well because my friend Linda fancied him.'

h
Notwithstanding, and indeed, as she admits, because of her friend's attraction to him, a kiss on the dance floor led to a developing friendship, which Mrs H enthusiastically embraced because she regarded the attention of this man, 25 years old, 10 years her junior, as 'an ego boost' and also because she desired to hurt her husband.

They began to have sexual intercourse very soon thereafter in November 1993. *j* They did not take contraceptive precautions. They met frequently and she would go to Mr B's home on Friday evenings and occasionally on Saturdays and they regularly had sexual intercourse until about July 1994. The judge rejected her attempts to minimise the extent of this sexual activity. In one of several adverse findings against her, the judge said:

a   '... I am sure that she knows perfectly well that it is not accurate to say that it happened on only six occasions. I believe she has attempted to mislead by giving that evidence.'

She did, however, assert that she was also having some sexual intercourse with her husband throughout this period, including the relevant time of conception, but the judge's view was:

b

'Having regard to other evidence which she gave and some evidence which he gave about the very poor state of their relationship by Christmas of 1993, I am not sure that there was any significant sexual relationship between them at the time. One has to bear in mind that she was a woman who had gone out looking for another sexual relationship and she was the instigator of it. That might indicate something about the state of her sexual life with her husband. Again I do not make any finding because it is not appropriate to do so, but I have to look at the evidence in a provisional way.'

c

In about March 1994 Mrs H became pregnant. The judge found that in the early two or three months of her pregnancy there was a clear understanding between Mrs H and the applicant that they would in due course live together and that he would move into the matrimonial home with her when the husband left, as in fact he did in May 1994. She intended to make a new life for herself with her new man. In preparation for her separating from her husband, she told C, then 13 years old, of her plans for Mr B. Moreover:

d

e

'The other piece of information which is of some importance is that at the time when the mother was thinking of separating permanently from the husband and of having Mr B in the home, she divulged to the elder boy, C, that the child she was expecting—because she was pregnant at that time—was going to be the child of a man other than the husband and C, now aged 14, understood the implications of that and he continues to remember the statement which his mother made to him. When she subsequently decided that she would not go down that road but would remain in the matrimonial home on her own with the children, and also subsequently when she decided to have Mr H back, there has been difficulty with C. He was disturbed by the information which his mother had imparted to him. It may be that this disturbance was, indeed, one of the factors which led her to change her mind about her plans for the children. Mr and Mrs H have had to cope with the problems arising from that statement by the mother and C's difficulties over it, and as a result C has been told not to worry about this but that H is as much part of the family as he is and J is, and that what was said by the mother to him earlier is not significant and he should ignore it or, at any rate, not trouble over it. As far as I am aware, C has accepted this and certainly welcomed his father back into the home, and both the elder boys have welcomed H into the family and there are no immediate problems arising over the distress which was caused to C. Of course, it does mean that there is an ongoing difficulty which could flare up at almost any time. When H becomes old enough to take part in conversations there must be a risk that C will, either intentionally or unintentionally, impart to him something of what his mother told him in 1994 about H's parentage. At the moment H is being brought up to regard Mr H as his father in every sense and the intention of Mr and Mrs H is that they will continue to do that; it is not their intention ever to inform him that his parentage is different—indeed, they do

f

g

h

j

not accept that it is different ... I have no reason to think that C will upset
that arrangement, but on the other hand it is not impossible that information
might come out—I suppose there is a risk it might come out in some other
way—and it is Mr B's case arising from that that it would be much better to
avoid any risk of H discovering that there is an issue about his parentage and
that the best way to do that is for his parentage to be established by these
blood tests; if it emerges that Mr B is the father then he should be told.'

In reciting that passage, I have run ahead a little in the story. When the
applicant learnt from Mrs H that she was pregnant, he became much involved in
her early ante-natal care. He was present on the occasion of her first scan and
indeed has the photographs of its results—odd behaviour, one might think, from
a pregnant lady if she did not then genuinely believe it was the father at her side,
and particularly cynical behaviour if, as she later asserted, she was just using B to
hurt her husband. The judge found:

'... I believe that she did discuss the future with Mr B and until July made
him believe that he would play a part in the life of the child that was to be
born and I do not believe that she regarded or believed at that time that the
baby was her husband's. She was either quite unsure of it or tended to
believe that it was Mr B's child.'

In July Mrs H changed her mind about bringing Mr B into her home. It may
well be that C's reluctance to accept this arrangement was a crucial factor in her
decision. At all events she terminated the affair.

The child H was born on 4 December 1994. His birth was registered in the
husband's name. On 31 January 1995 Mr B made applications for contact to H to
be defined by the court, for a parental responsibility order so that he might be
'involved in the child's upbringing'; and a specific issue order for Mrs H to
disclose the child's full name and date of birth. He also asked that 'if paternity is
disputed there be a DNA test'.

Mr H, who had maintained close contact with the family, returned home in
May 1995 after a year's absence and is reconciled to his wife. In his statement
before the court he said:

'We were still having sexual relations ourselves and therefore, there is a
distinct possibility that I am the father but given that I had a vasectomy 5
years ago, I did think it was unlikely that I would be the father ... I regard
[H] as my own son whether he is biologically my son or not and I am not in
the least bit concerned about his genetic origins as he is part of our family.'

These could not have been easy decisions for him to take and his determined
efforts to hold his marriage and his family together is one of the few laudable
features of this case.

The mother is adamantly opposed to the use of blood testing to establish
paternity. She is totally convinced that blood testing is likely to be detrimental to
H's welfare which she believes depends, for the foreseeable future, on his settled
relationship in a happy family unit, the stability of which may be disturbed by a
blood test and the pursuit of litigation by Mr B which is doomed to fail. She saw
no advantage in establishing the truth by science because, as she said:

'H has a father, it is Mr H ... Even if a blood test or a DNA test were to
show that Mr B is the father, I will never allow contact ... even if Mr H died
I would not let Mr B have any contact with H ... H will never know the

a
truth. My husband's name is on the birth certificate as the father. He is H's father ...'

When asked what would be the position if C were to tell H about the issue of his parentage, her answer was: 'I shall lie to H. I will do that to protect H. In my mind my husband is the father ...' Her attitude was:

b
'She not only regrets the association which she had with Mr B but she wishes in some way to expunge it and treat it almost as if it did not exist ... I have a feeling that they are very aware of the law, in broad terms at least, and are able to express their views and, to some extent mould the facts, with a view to presenting their case as being on that side of the law which would
c
result in directions for blood tests not being given. In particular, I think that they know the importance of categorically stating that they will not in any circumstances give consent to blood tests. It was clear to me that Mr and Mrs H are quite set in their determination never to say anything to J or H and as far as possible to bring C round to a position where he does not continue to regard H as having different parentage. They are totally determined that Mr
d
B should not have anything to do with H at all and in order to achieve that result they are quite prepared to put a gloss on the evidence and interpret the events of 1993/94 in their own way ... The evidence which I heard from the mother does not support any hope that [she would rethink her position and come round to wanting blood tests] so the court has to decide what to do in
e
the circumstances where there is total non co-operation ...'

The learned judge also made other relevant findings:

'... she is as adamantly opposed to Mr B playing any part in the life of this child as any woman could possibly be. There are cases in which expressions
f
like "implacable hostility" are used and that applies with the utmost relevance to this case. She is entirely supported in that by Mr H and there are no influences upon her which would cause her to take a different view. She has, or purports to have, no understanding at all of the kind of problems that can arise when a child grows up and discovers that there are question
g
marks about his paternity and there is a risk that he may have feelings of resentment towards his parents. She sweeps all those problems under the carpet and I do not believe there would be any way of her coming to terms with those sorts of issues—understanding them—even if she were given counselling ...'

h
He took account of the mother's case and her arguments:

'... what is being said here by the mother and by her counsel is that to try to impose either contact or parental responsibility on this situation of implacable hostility would not be in the interests of the child. What is said is
j
that it would lead to great pressure in the home ... All of that would be distressing not only for the adults involved but also the children ... She also says that for the applicant to be pursuing contact would be to de-stabilise her own marriage, which has only recently been put together again ...'

Accordingly, the judge considered it right to take into account the probable outcome of the proceedings. As to the issues of paternity, he held:

'My provisional views about the facts lend considerable support to Mr B. It is difficult to say he has no chance in the paternity proceedings even without the blood tests, having regard to the evidence.'

We were informed by counsel that in the court below the applications for contact and parental responsibility orders were not given any separate consideration. The judge concluded:

'Contact would require her to give over her child contrary to her deeply-held view. In those circumstances I judge that it would be rather unlikely that the court would make an order for contact ... I conclude that the chances of Mr B ever getting contact are remote.'

The judge found this to be 'an acutely difficult case to deal with' and I would agree. He referred to and had well in mind the cases to which our attention has also been drawn, *S v S, W v Official Solicitor* [1970] 3 All ER 107, [1972] AC 24, *Re F (a minor) (blood tests: parental rights)* [1993] 3 All ER 596, [1993] Fam 314, *Re G (a minor) (blood test)* [1994] 1 FLR 495 and *Re CB (a minor) (blood tests)* [1994] 2 FLR 762. He reminded himself that the interests of justice may conflict with the interests of the child. He correctly directed himself that he should follow the fourth principle enunciated by Lord Reid in *S v S, W v Official Solicitor* [1970] 3 All ER 107 at 113, [1972] AC 24 at 45: 'The court ought to permit a blood test of a young child to be taken unless satisfied that would be against the child's interests.' He correctly stated that the court has to weigh the advantage of certainty of parentage against the disadvantage of destabilising the child's family. He confronted the difference of view expressed by Mr Michael Horowitz QC in *Re G (a minor) (blood test)* and Wall J in *Re CB* and considered that an adverse inference could only be drawn against the mother after an order for blood tests had been made and she had refused to take the necessary steps. He declined to follow Wall J and he held that the refusal of the mother with care and control of the child was not determinative of the issue. He held that the mother's implacable hostility was a factor that had to go into the scales against making a blood test direction. At the heart of his decision lay this approach:

'[Mr B] intends to press on. I have already said that he has a substantial case at a paternity hearing. He may succeed in showing that he is the natural father. The court does not have the jurisdiction to stop him pursuing the paternity hearing. If he succeeds in establishing paternity the court cannot stop him applying for contact if he is determined. That means that in spite of my views [of the lack of likely success] I have to anticipate that, whatever order I make, there will be a paternity hearing and if he succeeds there will be a contact hearing after that. Since I know that there will inevitably be a paternity hearing, I have to ask whether the balance changes again, this time in favour of ordering the tests. I have decided that since it is clear that there will be a paternity hearing, it is better to order blood tests than not to do so. There is little to be saved by a refusal. It would only be an advantage to refuse blood tests if by so doing the paternity suit would come to an end. That was the situation in [*Re F (a minor) (blood tests: parental rights)* [1993] 3 All ER 596, [1993] Fam 314] ... I accept that on the basis of Lord Reid's statement of principle I could refuse the tests if satisfied that it would be against the child's interests to order them. The mother's case largely depends upon the disturbance which would be caused. But disturbance will arise from the continuance of the paternity proceedings and those cannot be

a   prevented. If that is a right appreciation then the proviso in the fourth
     principle of Lord Reid's statement ceases to apply. I am unable to say that
     tests are against the child's interests. I am presented with a fait accompli in
     relation to the paternity proceedings which it is not within my power to
     alter. There are some other factors which also go into the scales. The
     present case is highly unusual. Mr H had a vasectomy. The mother did
b   make up her mind to have a future with Mr B and then changed her mind.
     It is also a feature that the case for paternity is strong enough without the
     blood tests ... I do not consider that there is any great prejudice to the child
     in ordering blood tests where the paternity case is already strong.'

     He made his order accordingly.
c   The following issues arise in this appeal: (1) Is refusal to undergo blood testing
     determinative of the application for a direction under s 20(1) of the 1969 Act?
     (2) Can an inference adverse to the refusing party be drawn only if the refusal is
     made after the court has directed the use of blood testing? (3) How does the
     child's welfare influence the decision? (4) How do the prospects of success in the
     proceedings influence the decision? (5) What are this child's best interests?
d

     (1) *Is the refusal determinative?*
         In *Re F (a minor) (blood tests: parental rights)* [1993] 3 All ER 596, [1993] Fam 314
     the Court of Appeal posed the question but may not have given a clear answer.
     In *Re G (a minor) (blood test)* [1994] 1 FLR 495 Mr Michael Horowitz QC sitting as
e   a deputy judge of the High Court answered the question No; but in *Re CB (a
     minor) (blood tests)* [1994] 2 FLR 762 Wall J said Yes. Judge Coningsby declined to
     follow Wall J. Did he misdirect himself? The answer necessitates a somewhat
     semantic review of the authorities.
         The 1969 Act was passed after the Law Commission's report *Blood Tests and the
     Proof of Paternity in Civil Proceedings* (Law Com No 16) (1968). This report had
f   been prompted by the judges of the former Probate, Divorce and Admiralty
     Division of the High Court, possibly as a result of *W v W (No 4)* [1963] 2 All ER
     841, [1964] P 67, where the Court of Appeal refused to allow blood tests to
     determine paternity. Willmer LJ said ([1963] 2 All ER 841 at 843, [1964] P 67 at
     74):

g   'I think that there can be no doubt that, without an order of the court, what
         the court is now being asked to order would prima facie be an unlawful act.'

     Danckwerts LJ said ([1963] 2 All ER 841 at 845, [1964] P 67 at 78):

h   'To compel persons to submit to a blood test without their consent seems
         to me a very serious interference with personal liberty and rights. Very
         convincing reasons would have to be shown before I could conclude that
         such power was within the inherent jurisdiction of the court.'

         In *Re L* [1968] 1 All ER 20 at 26, [1968] P 119 at 159 Lord Denning MR said: 'A
j   blood test which involves the insertion of a needle is an assault, unless consented
     to.'
         In *S v S, W v Official Solicitor* [1970] 3 All ER 107 at 123, [1972] AC 24 at 57 Lord
     Hodson summed it up in the observation: 'No one doubts that so far as adults are
     concerned the law does not permit such an operation to be performed against the
     wishes of the patient.'
         That was and remains established law.

In their report the Law Commission said (at paras 39–40):

'39. A more important question is how the court is to treat the refusal of one of the individuals concerned to submit to blood tests. We do not think that it would be acceptable to public opinion in general or to the medical profession in particular to exert physical compulsion in order to obtain blood samples. We recommend, therefore, that no blood samples should be taken from a person under a direction of the court without that person's consent or, if he is incapable of consenting, without the consent of someone entitled to act on his behalf ... We would recommend that refusal be considered by the court as evidence from which it can draw whatever inferences it thinks warranted in the particular case. For this reason we recommend that the court should be given the power to make a direction for the use of blood tests rather than an order requiring them to be made ...

40. In our Working Paper we suggested that a person refusing to be tested ought to be able to show good cause, on religious or health grounds, why his or her refusal is justified. We still think that it should be open to a person refusing to be tested to satisfy the court that his or her refusal is justified but we do not think that it would be appropriate to provide specific grounds on which refusal can be justified ...'

I venture to think that the distinction made in the last sentence of para 39, which is reflected in the 1969 Act, has not always been fully understood, and the misunderstanding has created confusion.

The scheme of the 1969 Act is as follows:

'20. *Power of court to require use of blood tests.*—(1) In any civil proceedings in which the paternity of any person falls to be determined by the court hearing the proceedings, the court may, on an application by any party to the proceedings, give a direction for the use of blood tests to ascertain whether such tests show that a party to the proceedings is or is not thereby excluded from being the father of that person ...

21. *Consents, etc., required for taking of blood samples.*—(1) Subject to the provisions of subsections (3) and (4) of this section, a blood sample which is required to be taken from any person for the purpose of giving effect to a direction under section 20 of this Act shall not be taken from that person except with his consent ...

(3) A blood sample may be taken from a person under the age of sixteen years ... if the person who has the care and control of him consents ...

23. *Failure to comply with direction for taking blood tests.*—(1) Where a court gives direction under section 20 of this Act and any person fails to take any step required of him for the purpose of giving effect to the direction, the court may draw such inferences, if any, from that fact as appears proper in the circumstances ...'

The Act carried the Law Commission's advice into effect: s 20 does not empower the court to order blood tests, still less to take blood from an unwilling party; all it does is permit a direction for the use of blood tests to ascertain paternity. I drew attention earlier to the actual order made in this case that the applicant, respondent and child 'do provide blood samples'. That order is wrongly drawn. It should be varied to provide that 'it is directed pursuant to s 20 of the Family Law Reform Act 1969 that blood tests be used to ascertain whether the applicant is or is not excluded from being the father of the child'.

a *S v S, W v Official Solicitor* was decided after the Act had been passed, but before it came into operation. Lord Reid said ([1970] 3 All ER 107 at 112, [1972] AC 24 at 44):

b   'I am not at all certain that it is accurate to say that a court orders a blood test ... No case has yet occurred in which a court has *ordered a blood test to be carried out* against the will of the parent who has the care and control of the child, and I am not at all certain that it would be proper to do that or that it will be possible to do that after Part III of the 1969 Act comes into operation.' (My emphasis.)

c I have added the emphasis to draw attention to the order to which Lord Reid was referring. It was the very order the Law Commission recommended against and it is not what the Act permits.

In *Re F (a minor) (blood tests: parental rights)* [1993] 1 FLR 225 at 231 Judge Callman had said: '...this court will not order a blood test by way of DNA profiling or fingerprinting *to be carried out* against the will of a parent ...' Again, I d add the emphasis and I add my agreement with his proposition. Balcombe LJ said ([1993] 3 All ER 596 at 601–602, [1993] Fam 314 at 321):

     'As the judge rightly said, the court will not order a blood test *to be carried out* against the will of a parent who has since birth had sole parental responsibility for the child ... we bear in mind Lord Reid's doubt [in *S v S, W* e   *v Official Solicitor* [1970] 3 All ER 107 at 112, [1972] AC 24 at 44] whether, without the consent of the parent having care and control ... it would be proper for the court *to order a blood test*.' (My emphasis.)

I hope it is not unduly pedantic to point out that the order to which Lord Reid was referring was an order for 'a blood test to be carried out' and so the emphasis f has swung from an obvious assault occasioned by taking blood without consent to a generalised order for a blood test, the looseness of which expression deflects the attention away from the limited terms of the only direction which the court is permitted to make under the Act. If refusal simpliciter were a determinative reason for not giving the direction, then the Act would surely have said so. On g the contrary, the express provisions make it clear that Parliament was content to envisage a direction being made notwithstanding that it might never be carried into effect. The legislature would not have made express provision that a refusal to comply with the direction has a specified consequence, if a refusal to submit to tests would have compelled the court not to make any direction at all.

In *S v S, W v Official Solicitor* [1970] 3 All ER 107 at 113–114, [1972] AC 24 at 46 h Lord MacDermott gave this explanation:

     'I think it must be accepted that, save where Parliament has otherwise ordained, the High Court has no power to direct that a person who is sui juris is to have a blood test taken against his will ... But this lack of power on the j   part of the court to enforce its order physically without consent does not mean that the question under discussion [ie the court's jurisdiction to order a blood test] must be answered in the negative; for much of the jurisdiction of the High Court can only be made effective by indirect means—such as a stay of proceedings, attachment or the treatment of a refusal to comply as evidence against the disobedient party.'

Section 23(1) expressly provides such indirect means, namely the ability to
draw such inference as may be proper from the refusal to take any step required   *a*
of the party for the purpose of giving effect to the court's direction.

I conclude, therefore, that whereas refusal is a factor to take into account (and,
for example, in the case of an haemophiliac it may be a very powerful factor), it
cannot be determinative of the application and I disagree with Wall J's conclusion
in *Re CB (a minor) (blood tests)* [1994] 2 FLR 762 at 773. In my judgment Judge   *b*
Coningsby did not misdirect himself.

*(2) Can an inference be drawn only if the refusal to give blood samples is made
after the court's direction?*

Mr Blair QC supports the judge's conclusion that, 'because of the existence of   *c*
the statutory provision it must be only in the circumstances in which an adverse
inference may be drawn as laid down in the Act that any such inference can be
drawn and this cannot happen outside the Act.' I see the force of that, and was at
first inclined to accept the submission that if there is a statutory scheme, then the
statutory scheme is the only operative scheme. Mr Blair submitted that the Act
permitted an inference to be drawn which, until then, the court had not been able   *d*
to do. I do not agree that this introduced a change to the law of evidence. In *Re L*
[1968] 1 All ER 20 at 26, [1968] P 119 at 159 Lord Denning MR said:

> 'If an adult unreasonably refuses to have a blood test, or to allow a child to
> have one, I think that it is open to the court in any civil proceedings ... to
> treat his refusal as evidence against him, and may draw an inference   *e*
> therefrom adverse to him. This is simply common sense.'

That common sense drove Wall J to a similar conclusion in *Re CB*.

Within the criminal law a refusal without reasonable excuse to supply hair
samples for scientific examination has been held capable of amounting to   *f*
corroboration. In *R v Smith* (1985) 81 Cr App R 286 at 292 the court said:

> '... we have come to the conclusion that the learned judge was entitled to
> leave the appellant's refusal to give the sample, and the circumstances of that
> refusal, as material which was capable of corroborating the evidence of the
> accomplice.'   *g*

The question seems to me to be not so much whether the court is entitled to
draw an adverse inference, but what, if any, inference can be drawn from a
refusal. That is the way the Law Commission approached the question. They
said (at paras 43–45, 47):

h

> '43. So far as adultery is concerned the wife knows, as a fact, whether or
> not she has committed adultery. It is, therefore, proper that the court should
> be able to infer from her refusal to be tested that she is trying to prevent it
> from discovering a fact of which she, herself, has knowledge. On the
> question of the child's paternity however the position is different. Here she   *j*
> does not know which of the two men is the child's father; she is refusing to
> be tested, not in order to hide facts of which she has knowledge, but because
> she does not want to run the risk of her child being shown to be illegitimate.
> Her refusal has no bearing on whether or not the child is illegitimate and the
> court may well decide that it cannot draw any inference on the issue of
> paternity.

44. The problem is not confined to cases where the child's mother refuses to be tested. A husband can also take advantage of the presumption of legitimacy and refuse to be tested if he is anxious to have the child's legitimacy established. Let us take as an example the case where a husband is divorcing his wife on the ground of her adultery. The wife admits her adultery and it is clear that both the husband and the co-respondent had intercourse during the period of conception of the child concerned. The husband and wife are each applying for custody of the child. There is no way, apart from using blood test evidence, by which it can be established which of the men is the child's father. The wife, wanting custody and wanting to prove that the co-respondent, whom she is to marry, is the child's father, asks for blood tests. The husband, also wanting custody, refuses to be blood tested because he wishes the child to be declared his. The court cannot properly draw from his refusal the inference that the child is illegitimate; neither the husband nor anyone else knows who is the child's father. The presumption of legitimacy is therefore applied and the husband is held to be the child's father.

45. How can parties be prevented from refusing to comply with a court order for blood tests, purely as a matter of tactics, so as to prevent the presumption of legitimacy being rebutted? We have already said that we do not think that it would be acceptable to force a person by physical compulsion to submit to an order for blood tests to be taken. We think that it would be equally unacceptable to treat a refusal as contempt of court ...

47. In our view the most effective way of dealing with this problem is to provide that where a direction for blood tests is made and a party to the proceedings is entitled to rely on the presumption of legitimacy in claiming relief, then if that party refuses to be tested the court may either draw inferences against him (if appropriate) or may dismiss his application for relief ...'

It should be remembered that at that time blood testing served only to exclude paternity: it did not establish it. It seems to me that a refusal to comply after the solemnity of the court's decision is more eloquent testimony of an attempt at hiding a truth than intransigent objection made as a forensic tactic. Science has now advanced. The whole truth can now be known. As Waite LJ said in *Re A (a minor) (paternity: refusal of blood test)* [1994] 2 FLR 463 at 473:

'Against that background of law and scientific advance, it seems to me to follow, both in justice and in common sense, that if a mother makes a claim against one of the possible fathers, and he chooses to exercise his right not to submit to be tested, the inference that he is the father of the child should be virtually inescapable. He would certainly have to advance very clear and cogent reasons for this refusal to be tested—reasons which it would be just and fair and reasonable for him to be allowed to maintain.'

Although that was a case of a refusal being made after a direction had been given, I, like Wall J, 'see no intellectual difference between the two situations.' Common sense seems to me to dictate that if the truth can be established with certainty, a refusal to produce the certainty justifies some inference that the refusal is made to hide the truth, even if the inference is not as strong as when the court's direction is flouted.

Although, therefore, Judge Coningsby was wrong, I do not see this to be such a fundamental misdirection as ineluctably to undermine his decision. It is not enough by itself to allow the appeal.

(3) *How do considerations of the child's welfare influence the decision?*
The judge correctly directed himself that he should 'refuse the test if satisfied it would be against the child's interests to order it.' This is wholly in accordance with *S v S, W v Official Solicitor*. There, Lord Reid said ([1970] 3 All ER 107 at 113, [1972] AC 24 at 45):

> 'I would, therefore, hold that the court ought to permit a blood test of a young child to be taken unless satisfied that would be against the child's interest.'

Lord Hodson said ([1970] 3 All ER 107 at 124, [1972] AC 24 at 58):

> 'The court in ordering a blood test in the case of an infant has, of course, a discretion and may make or refuse an order for a test in the exercise of its discretion, but the interests of the other persons than the infant are involved in ordinary litigation. The infant needs protection but that is no justification for making his rights superior to those of others.'

It is clear, therefore, that whereas welfare is the paramount consideration in deciding the applications for parental responsibility and contact orders, welfare does not dominate this decision.

(4) *How do the prospects of success in the proceedings influence the decision?*
In *Re F* [1993] 3 All ER 596 at 600, [1993] Fam 314 at 320 it was held:

> 'If the probable outcome of those proceedings will be the same whoever may be the natural father of E, then there can be no point in exposing E to the possible disadvantages of a blood test.'

The speeches in the House of Lords seem to take a somewhat different view. Lord MacDermott in *S v S, W v Official Solicitor* [1970] 3 All ER 107 at 115, [1972] AC 24 at 48 said:

> ' ... if the court had reason to believe that the application for a blood test was of a fishing nature, designed for some ulterior motive to call in question the legitimacy, otherwise unimpeached, of a child who had enjoyed a legitimate status, it may well be that the court, acting under its protective rather than its ancillary jurisdiction, would be justified in refusing the application. I need not, however, pursue such instances as they do not arise on these appeals.'

He also said ([1970] 3 All ER 107 at 117–118, [1972] AC 24 at 50):

> 'The question raised by a blood test application is quite distinct from the question of custody and the other questions mentioned in s 1 of the Guardianship of Infants Act 1925. It is true that in deciding as to the custody of a child its welfare may depend on the weighing and assessment of various factors, including the rights and wishes of the parents, and that the question of paternity may therefore not only arise but be very relevant. But that is not to make the question of paternity a question of custody. It is only part of the process for determining the facts to be considered in deciding the ultimate

and paramount question, namely, what is best for the welfare of the child. It
would be a backward step to start to whittle down the effect of s 1, but it
would be just as bad to have to apply its final criterion on a finding of fact
which was not reached on the best available evidence, and even worse if that
had to happen because the court, having spied a paternity issue, considered
that it should not be fully explored.'

Lord Morris of Borth-y-Gest said ([1970] 3 All ER 107 at 119, [1972] AC 24 at 53):

'The questions of custody and maintenance do not call for decision in the
legitimacy issue. They will or will not arise for decision according to how
the legitimacy issue is resolved.'

Reading those authorities together, it seems to me that the correct approach
must be as follows. (1) The paternity issue must be judged as a free-standing
application, entitled to consideration on its own. (2) The outcome of the
proceedings in which the paternity issue has been raised, in so far as it bears on
the welfare of child, must be taken into account. (3) Any gain to the child from
preventing any disturbance to his security must be balanced against the loss to
him of the certainty of knowing who he is. (4) The terms of s 10(4) of the
Children Act 1989 are explicit in giving a parent a right to apply for contact
because they provide: 'The following persons *are entitled to apply* to the court for
any section 8 order with respect to a child—(a) any parent ... of the child ...'
There is no statutory justification for transforming the paternity issue into a
disguised application for leave to apply and judging the paternity issue by the
criteria set out in s 10(9). (5) Accordingly, whilst the outcome of the s 8
proceedings and the risk of disruption to the child's life, both by the continuance
of the paternity issue as well as the pursuit of the s 8 order, are obviously factors
which impinge on the child's welfare; they are not, in my judgment,
determinative of the blood testing question.

In this case the judge's conclusion was that 'it would be rather unlikely that the
court would make an order for contact'. That is a conclusion he was plainly
entitled to reach, and one which I would support. He did not, however, expressly
deal with the parental responsibility order. We were told from the Bar that both
counsel treated them as standing or falling together. Whilst that may or may not
be a correct view of this case, parental responsibility orders and contact orders
embrace quite different concepts. The parental responsibility order grants the
status of paternity but it does not deal with the actual exercise of the parental
responsibility thereby conferred on to the father (see *Re S (a minor) (parental
responsibility)* [1995] 2 FLR 648). Features of this case are that at one time the
mother undoubtedly intended to make her future life with the applicant and the
judge found him to have 'quite a strong case for wanting to play a part in the life
of this child'. If that is the true measure of his commitment, if his reasons for
making the application are genuine, and if the child has a right to know who his
father is, the application for parental responsibility may not be as hopeless as his
case for contact.

(5) *What are the child's best interests?*
The mother submits that 'pursuing contact would be to destabilise her own
marriage, which has only recently been put together again, to the disadvantage
of the child'. Miss Scotland QC submits accordingly that the case is
indistinguishable from *Re F*.

I do not agree. The argument is of course similar and what won the day in that case undoubtedly was 'the interests of the child not to be disturbed in [its] present status or ... position as a child of, or residence in, the family of [Mr & Mrs F] in the particular circumstances of this case' (see [1993] 1 FLR 225 at 231 per Judge Callman). It is seldom useful in a case which depends on the exercise of judicial discretion to attempt to draw factual similarities between cases. The reported facts of Re F are sparse and I am totally unpersuaded that there is such a similarity between them as to compel the same conclusion. The material facts of the case under appeal before us include these features which may or may not have applied in Re F.

(1) As the judge found, Mr B has a substantial case for his claim to be this child's father. That can be seen from: (a) the mother's clear belief, at least until she set eyes on her baby, that the child was born of her adulterous relationship. She now closes her mind even to the possibility that might be so; (b) the fact that Mr H has had a vasectomy. He admitted thinking that it was 'unlikely that I would be the father.'

(2) If Mr and Mrs H were reconciled in that state of mind, having their worst fears realised is unlikely of itself to be the cause for the breakdown of a fragile reconciliation. A distinction should be drawn between the effect on their relationship of truth being revealed, as against the effect on the relationship of the strain of litigation, concerned as it is with contesting contact, in which endeavour husband and wife are united, as well as the effect on the relationship in coping with no more than a fear of contact, since actual contact seems to be unlikely.

(3) It may well be correct, as Miss Scotland submits, that denial of the truth is essential to this mother for the restoration of her self esteem and for the expiation of her guilt. That creates a danger in putting her welfare to the forefront, not the child's. The only real chance of setting her mind at rest is that, against all the odds, her husband may indeed be proved to be the father of the child. As Lord Reid observed ([1970] 3 All ER 107 at 110, [1972] AC 24 at 42):

'If one knew or suspected that on the other evidence that the child would be held to be illegitimate then it would be in the child's interest to have a blood test because that would afford some chance that the decision would go the other way.'

With the improvement in scientific techniques, what was then a chance is now a certainty.

(4) This secret cannot be hidden forever. Mr H knows the substantial difficulty of his position. Moreover, and most importantly, 14-year-old C knows, because his mother told him, that his father may not be H's father. It is unrealistic to pretend that the time will not come when H has to face these doubts about his paternity. If his peace of mind is likely to be threatened, and if he has a right to know, the question then becomes one of when it is best he should learn the truth.

(5) In my judgment every child has a right to know the truth unless his welfare clearly justifies the cover up. The right to know is acknowledged in the UN Convention on the Rights of the Child (New York, 20 November 1989; TS 44 (1992); Cm 1976), which has been ratified by the United Kingdom, and in particular art 7, which provides 'that a child has, as far as possible, the right to know and be cared for by his or her parents.' In Re F (a minor) (blood tests: parental rights) the putative father submitted that the child's welfare included her right to know under this article. Balcombe LJ said ([1993] 3 All ER 596 at 601, [1993] Fam 314 at 321):

a

'Whether or not Mr B is included in this definition of a parent within the meaning of this article, it is not in fact possible for E to be cared for by both her parents (if Mr B is such). No family unit exists, or has ever existed, between Mr B and Mrs F, and if Mr B were able to assert his claims to have a share in E's upbringing it would inevitably risk damaging her right to be cared for by her mother, Mrs F.'

b That passage concentrates on the child's right to be cared for by his or her parents. I do not read it as refuting what to me seems the clear intent of the article that there are two separate rights, the one to know, and the other to be cared for by, one's parents. As Balcombe LJ has himself observed in *Re G (a minor) (parental responsibility)* [1994] 2 FCR 1037 at 1042:

c

'... it is well established by authority that, other things being equal, it is always to a child's welfare to know and, wherever possible, to have contact with both its parents, including the parent with whom it is not normally resident, if the parents have separated.'

d (6) This is the whole tenor of the speeches in the House of Lords. Lord Reid (and Lord Guest) said (*S v S, W v Official Solicitor* [1970] 3 All ER 107 at 113, [1972] AC 24 at 45):

'The court must protect the child, but it is not really protecting the child to ban a blood test on some vague and shadowy conjecture that it may turn out to be to its disadvantage; it may equally turn out to be for its advantage or at least do it no harm.'

e

Lord Morris of Borth-y-Gest asked ([1970] 3 All ER 107 at 121–122, [1972] AC 24 at 55):

f

'Will it be in the interests of the child if relatives and friends of those concerned feel that the big doubt which was raised has been unsatisfactorily left by the law so that, though a conclusion has been expressed, the doubt still remains so that it will loom over the whole of the child's future life? Will it be in the interests of the child if, because the court was hampered by not having all the reasonably available evidence, a conclusion is expressed which as the years go on may be demonstrated to have been erroneous and which will command neither confidence nor respect? I would think that in most cases comparable to the present one the interests of a child are best served if the truth is ascertained.'

g

Lord Hodson asked ([1970] 3 All ER 107 at 124, [1972] AC 24 at 59):

h

'Who is to say what is in the interests of the child and whether knowledge of true paternity would or would not favour his or her future prospects in life? How are these interests to be assessed? I find these questions especially difficult to answer in view of the fact that it must surely be in the best interests of the child in most cases that paternity doubts should be resolved on the best evidence, and, as in adoption, the child should be told the truth as soon as possible.'

j

(7) Lord Hodson's reference to adoption produces interesting parallels. The Houghton Committee in 1972 (Report of the Departmental Committee on the Adoption of Children (Cmnd 5107)) called for greater openness in adoption. That call was heeded. Section 51 of the Adoption Act 1976 now enables adopted

persons to obtain access to their birth records. The inter-departmental Review of
Adoption Law in 1992 expressed the opinion that 'it is fundamental to the welfare *a*
of the child that he or she is told (when of sufficient age and understanding) about
his or her adoptive status'. It is a recognition that the child's shock at discovering
the truth about his origins at a later stage in childhood will be increased by the
realisation that his adopted parents have, to date, allowed him to believe in a
falsehood that he was their child.

(8) Section 56 of the Family Law Act 1986 gives H the right to apply for a *b*
declaration: '(a) that a person named in the application is or was his parent; or (b)
that he is the legitimate child of his parents.'

(9) Given the real risk bordering on inevitability that H will at some time
question his paternity, then I do not see how this case is not concluded by the
unassailable wisdom expressed by Lord Hodson ([1970] 3 All ER 107 at 123, [1972] *c*
AC 24 at 57):

> 'The interests of justice in the abstract are best served by the ascertainment
> of the truth and there must be few cases where the interests of children can
> be shown to be best served by the suppression of truth.'
>
d

If, as she should, this mother is to bring up her children to believe in and to act
by the maxim, which it is her duty to teach them at her knee, that honesty is the
best policy, then she should not sabotage that lesson by living a lie.

(10) If the child has the right to know, then the sooner it is told the better. The
issue of biological parentage should be divorced from psychological parentage. *e*
Acknowledging Mr B's parental responsibility should not dent Mr H's social
responsibility for a child whom he is so admirably prepared to care for and love
irrespective of whether or not he is the father. If the cracks in the H marriage are
so wide that they will be rent asunder by the truth, then the piece of paper which
dismisses the application hardly seems adhesive enough to bind them together.

(11) If H grows up knowing the truth, that will not undermine his attachment *f*
to his father figure and he will cope with knowing he has two fathers. Better that
than a time-bomb ticking away.

(6) Conclusions

The judge concluded that it was not within his power to prevent this father *g*
pursuing his application. I agree. Short of striking out the applications for being
frivolous and vexatious or an abuse of the process of the court (and, assuming
there is the power, this is not a striking out case on the findings of the judge) the
proceedings have to be heard. There is strong support for the view taken by the
judge. Lord Morris of Borth-y-Gest said (see *S v S, W v Official Solicitor* [1970] 3 *h*
All ER 107 at 121, [1972] AC 24 at 55):

> 'In a case where a husband repudiates the paternity of a child of his wife
> and where (as in the [*S v S*] case) an issue as to legitimacy has perforce to be
> ordered and, therefore, *must be tried*, it has regrettably become a fact in the
> child's life that its legitimacy is in doubt. It is not as though, when *j*
> considering whether to direct a blood test, a suggestion of illegitimacy is then
> or thereby first being raised. It is not as though the tranquil air is then or
> thereby first being clouded. The events in relation to the child's birth will
> already have been matters of dispute and controversy. The presumption of
> legitimacy cannot be invoked so as to screen and protect the child from being
> involved. The court will have been obliged to order a trial of the issue, and

a   *on the trial of it the court must reach a conclusion.* In the interests of justice the right conclusion ought to be reached ... The most legitimate and most ardent wish to safeguard a child's interests cannot alter the fact that an issue as to paternity has arisen and *must be decided.*' (My emphasis.)

In my judgment Judge Coningsby was not only entitled, but right to conclude:

b   'I have come down in favour of giving a direction for blood tests, since I consider that if I were not to do so it would make it more difficult for the court which will have to deal with the proceedings which follow and I do not consider that there is any great prejudice to the child in ordering blood tests where the paternity case is already strong.'

c   Accordingly, I would dismiss the appeal, but, for the technical reasons I have indicated, the order should be varied and the following direction substituted for paras 1, 2 and 3:

'It is directed pursuant to s 20(1) of the Family Law Reform Act 1969: (a) that blood tests (including DNA tests) be used to ascertain whether such tests
d   show that Mr B is or is not excluded from being the father of H born on 4 December 1994 and; (b) the persons from whom blood samples are required for the purpose of giving effect to this direction are: Mr B, Mrs H and the child H; (c) any blood samples which are required to be taken for the purpose of giving effect to this direction to be taken on or before 1 May 1996; (d) that the person appearing to the court to have care and control of H who is under
e   the age of 16 is Mrs H; and (e) that such tests be carried out by Mr D Ashworth of University Diagnostic Ltd, University College London, Gower Street, London WC1E 6BT.'

f   **NEILL LJ.** I agree that the appeal should be dismissed for the reasons given by Ward LJ. I also agree that the order should be varied in the manner indicated by Ward LJ so as to comply with the terms of s 20(1) of the Family Law Reform Act 1969.

Appeal dismissed. Order varied accordingly.

g
                                        Paul Magrath Esq   Barrister.

Re Cosslett (Contractors) Ltd

CHANCERY DIVISION (COMPANIES COURT)
JONATHAN PARKER J
4, 5, 21 DECEMBER 1995

Charge – Whether fixed or floating – Charge over construction company's plant while on site – Condition in building contract deeming contractor's plant while on site to belong to employer – Whether employer having legal ownership of plant on the site for so long as it remained there – Whether employer's contractual rights constituting equitable proprietary interest in plant – Whether fixed or floating charge – Whether void for want of registration.

The company was contracted by the local authority to undertake engineering works in a land reclamation project, part of which involved the processing of large deposits of coal-bearing shale. In the course of the work two coal-washing plants were established on the site. Under cl 53(2) of the contract all plant, goods and materials owned by the contractor, while on site, were deemed to belong to the local authority as employer. Clause 54 made provision for the transfer of property in goods and materials to the local authority prior to delivery to the site in order to secure payment and cl 63(1) provided that if the contractor went into liquidation or abandoned the contract, the local authority could enter on the site and either use the plant and materials which were deemed to belong to it under cll 53 and 54 to complete the works, or at any time sell such plant and materials and apply the proceeds towards the satisfaction of any sums due from the company under the contract. The company encountered financial difficulties and abandoned the site, leaving the coal-washing plants behind. When the local authority refused to comply with the company's administrator's demand to deliver up the plants or pay for their use, the administrator applied to the court for an order requiring delivery up of the plant, contending that the local authority's contractual rights as employer gave it a property interest in the plant which amounted to an equitable security interest in the nature of a floating charge registrable under s 395[a] of the Companies Act 1985, and that since no floating charge had been registered, the local authority's contractual right to retain the coal-washing plants was void as against the administrator.

Held – On its true construction the contract between the parties did not effect the transfer of the legal ownership in the coal-washing plants to the local authority, but rather created an equitable proprietary interest, since cll 53 and 63 conferred on the local authority contractual rights which were enforceable by means of the remedy of specific performance. Furthermore, the equitable interest so created was not a floating charge for the purposes of s 395 of the 1985 Act but a specific equitable charge, since the plant could not be removed from the site at the will of the company, nor was the company free to use the plant as it pleased, in that the local authority's contractual rights entitled it to sell the plant on the site at the date of forfeiture and to refuse to permit its removal by the company, even where

---

a   Section 395, so far as material, provides: '... a charge created by a company ... is ... void against the liquidator [or administrator] ... unless the prescribed particulars of the charge ... are delivered to ... the registrar ... for registration ...'

a it was not immediately required to complete the works. Accordingly the administrator's application would be dismissed (see p 60 *h*, p 61 *a j* to p 62 *d g h* and p 63 *d* g to p 64 *b*, post).

Re Yorkshire Woolcombers Association Ltd, Houldsworth v Yorkshire Woolcombers Association Ltd [1903] 2 Ch 284 applied.

Bennett & White (Calgary) Ltd v Municipal District of Sugar City No 5 [1951] AC
b 786 distinguished.

Notes

For floating charges or security, see 7(2) *Halsbury's Laws* (4th edn reissue) paras 1260–1266.

For registration of charges at the registrar's office, see ibid para 1299.

c For the Companies Act 1985, s 395, see 8 *Halsbury's Statutes* (4th edn) (1991 reissue) 475.

Cases referred to in judgment

Akron Tyre Co Pty Ltd v Kittson (1951) 82 CLR 477, Aust HC.

d *Atlantic Computer Systems plc, Re (No 1)* [1992] 1 All ER 476, [1992] Ch 505, [1992] 2 WLR 367, CA.

Atlantic Medical Ltd, Re [1993] BCLC 386.

Bennett & White (Calgary) Ltd v Municipal District of Sugar City No 5 [1951] AC 786, PC.

Blake v Izard (1867) 16 WR 108.

e *Bond Worth Ltd, Re* [1979] 3 All ER 919, [1980] Ch 228, [1979] 3 WLR 629.

Brown v Bateman (1867) LR 2 CP 272.

Carreras Rothmans Ltd v Freeman Mathews Treasure Ltd (in liq) [1985] 1 All ER 155, [1985] Ch 207, [1984] 3 WLR 1016.

Hart v Porthgain Harbour Co Ltd [1903] 1 Ch 690.

f *Illingworth v Houldsworth* [1904] AC 355, HL; *affg* sub nom *Re Yorkshire Woolcombers Association Ltd, Houldsworth v Yorkshire Woolcombers Association Ltd* [1903] 2 Ch 284, CA.

Keen & Keen, Re, ex p Collins [1902] 1 KB 555, CA.

Milnes v Huddersfield Corp (1883) 12 QBD 443, CA; *affd* (1886) 11 App Cas 511, [1886–90] All ER Rep 350, HL.

g *R v Norfolk CC* (1891) 60 LJQB 379, DC.

Reeves v Barlow (1884) 12 QBD 436, CA.

Royal Trust Bank v National Westminster Bank plc [1995] BCC 128; *rvsd* [1996] CA Transcript 418.

Stroud Architectural Systems Ltd v John Laing Construction Ltd [1994] 2 BCLC 276.

h *Swiss Bank Corp v Lloyds Bank Ltd* [1980] 2 All ER 419, [1982] AC 584, [1980] 3 WLR 457, CA; *affd* [1981] 2 All ER 449, [1982] AC 584, [1981] 2 WLR 893, HL.

Weibking, Re, ex p Ward [1902] 1 KB 713.

Winter, Re, ex p Bolland (1878) 8 Ch D 225.

j **Cases also cited or referred to in skeleton arguments**

Astor Chemicals Ltd v Synthetic Technology Ltd [1990] BCLC 1.

Beeston v Marriott (1863) 8 LT 690.

Brightlife Ltd, Re [1986] 3 All ER 673, [1987] Ch 200.

Bristol Airport plc v Powdrill [1990] 2 All ER 493, [1990] Ch 744, CA.

Great Eastern Rly Co v Lord's Trustee [1909] AC 109, HL.

Inglefield (George) Ltd, Re [1933] Ch 1, [1932] All ER Rep 244, CA.

Kent and Sussex Sawmills Ltd, Re [1946] 2 All ER 638, [1947] Ch 177.
Metropolitan Water Board v Dick Kerr & Co [1917] 2 KB 1, CA; *affd* [1918] AC 119, HL.
National Provincial and Union Bank of England v Charnley [1924] 1 KB 431, CA.
Newitt, Ex p, re Garrud (1881) 16 Ch D 522, [1881–5] All ER Rep 1039, CA.
Peachdart Ltd, Re [1983] 3 All ER 204, [1984] Ch 131.

Application
Ian Clark, the administrator of Cosslett (Contractors) Ltd (the contractor), applied under s 234 of the Insolvency Act 1986 for an order for delivery up by the respondent local authority, Mid-Glamorgan County Council (the employer), of two coal-washing plants to which the administrator claimed to be entitled pursuant to a contract between the employer and the contractor. The facts are set out in the judgment.

Richard Wilmot-Smith QC and *Alan Maclean* (instructed by *Hammond Suddards*, Manchester) for the administrator.
Simon Mortimore QC and *Antony Zacaroli* (instructed by *Edwards Geldard*, Cardiff) for the employer.

Cur adv vult

21 December 1995. The following judgment was delivered.

JONATHAN PARKER J. This is an application under s 234 of the Insolvency Act 1986 by Mr Ian Clark, the administrator of Cosslett (Contractors) Ltd (the contractor), for delivery up by Mid-Glamorgan County Council, the respondent to the application (the employer), of two coal-washing plants to which the contractor claims title. The employer claims the right to retain the coal-washing plants pursuant to a written contract dated 28 January 1991 and made between the employer and the contractor (the contract). In opposition to the employer's claim, the administrator asserts (a) that the provisions of the contract on which the employer seeks to rely in support of its claim to the right to retain the coal-washing plants constitute or create an equitable charge in favour of the employer, (b) that such charge is in the nature of a floating charge and consequently registrable under s 395 of the Companies Act 1985, and (c) that since the charge was not registered it is void against him by virtue of that section.

Thus, the primary issue before the court on this application is whether the relevant provisions of the contract constitute or create a floating charge over the coal-washing plants in favour of the employer. In the event that the administrator succeeds on this issue, however, the employer nevertheless maintains, as a secondary issue, that its contractual right to retain the coal-washing plants survives non-registration and is not struck down by s 395.

The administrator appears on this application by Mr Richard Wilmot-Smith QC and Mr Alan Maclean of counsel and the employer by Mr Simon Mortimore QC and Mr Antony Zacaroli of counsel.

The factual background can be shortly stated.

The contractor was incorporated in 1962 and carries on the business of engineering, including the carrying out of contracting and demolition works. The employer is responsible, inter alia, for land reclamation schemes in its area. In about 1989 the employer embarked upon a scheme for the reclamation and a redevelopment of some 141 hectares of land in the Upper Garw Valley in Mid-Glamorgan (the site). The greater part of the site was covered with shale tips associated with the former workings of the Garw and International Collieries. Under the scheme, over an estimated period of four years the coal-bearing shale was to be processed through a washing plant, in order to separate the coal from the residue. The residue was to be used for raising the valley floor and providing

b plateaux for possible development. The coal was to be transported off the site and sold. The scheme also involved substantial engineering works, including capping mine shafts, demolition of buildings and construction of new culverts.

In the autumn of 1989 the employer invited the contractor to tender for engineering works comprised in the scheme. The contractor tendered for the works, and in due course its tender was accepted, leading to the signing of the

c contract.

I shall return below to the material provisions of the contract.

Following the signing of the contract, work began on the site. The first of the two coal-washing plants was established on the site by about December 1991 and the second by about September 1992. By mid-1993, however, the contractor had

d encountered financial difficulties in continuing to carry out the works, and in or about August 1993 it abandoned the site. On 31 August 1993 the employer gave notice under the contract expelling the contractor from the site. The coal-washing plants remain on the site.

In September 1993 the administrator demanded delivery up of the coal-washing plants, further or alternatively payment for their use. This demand

e was refused, leading to the present application.

I now turn to the relevant provisions of the contract.

The contract incorporates a set of standard conditions issued by the Institution of Civil Engineers and entitled:

f   'Conditions of Contract and Forms of Tender, Agreement and Bond for use in connection with Works of Civil Engineering Construction, Fifth Edition (June 1973) (Revised January 1979) (Reprinted January 1986).'

I will refer to these conditions as 'the conditions'.

The provisions of the contract on which the employer relies as justifying its

g retention of the coal-washing plants are condition 53 (the standard terms of which were amended by the inclusion of additional words) and condition 64. Also relevant to the issue as to the true construction of these conditions is condition 54. These conditions (with condition 53 in its amended form, the additional words being emphasised) are in the following terms (so far as

h material):

'53.(1) For the purpose of this clause:—(a) the expression "Plant" shall mean any constructional plant *coal-washing plant* temporary works and material for temporary works but shall exclude any vehicles engaged in transporting any labour, plant or material to or from the Site …

j   (2) All plant, goods and materials owned by the Contractor or by any company in which the contractor has a controlling interest shall when on site be deemed to be the property of the Employer. *The washing plant must be owned by the Contractor or by a company in which the Contractor has a controlling interest.*

(3) With a view to securing in the event of a forfeiture under Clause 63 the continued availability for the purpose of executing the works of any hired

Plant the contractor shall not bring on to the site any hired Plant unless there
is an agreement for the hire thereof which contains a provision that the
owner thereof will on request in writing made by the Employer within 7
days after the date on which any forfeiture has become effective and on the
Employer undertaking to pay all hire charges in respect thereof from such
date hire such Plant to the Employer on the same terms in all respects as the
same was hired to the contractor save that the Employer shall be entitled to
permit the use thereof by any other contractor employed by him for the
purpose of completing the Works under the terms of the said clause 63.

(4) In the event of the Employer entering into any agreement for the hire
of Plant pursuant to sub-clause (3) of this Clause all sums properly paid by
the Employer under the provisions of any such agreement and all expenses
incurred by him (including stamp duties) in entering into such agreement
shall be deemed for the purpose of Clause 63 to be part of the cost of
completing the Works.

(5) The contractor shall upon request made by the Engineer at any time in
relation to any item of Plant forthwith notify to the Engineer in writing the
name and address of the owner thereof and shall in the case of hired Plant
certify that the agreement for the hire thereof contains a provision in
accordance with the requirements of sub-clause (3) of this Clause.

(6) No Plant (except hired Plant) goods or materials or any part thereof
shall be removed from the Site without the written consent of the Engineer
which consent shall not be unreasonably withheld where the same are no
longer immediately required for the purposes of the completion of the
Works but the Employer will permit the Contractor the exclusive use of all
such Plant goods and materials in and for the completion of the Works until
the occurrence of any event which gives the Employer the right to exclude
the Contractor from the Site and proceed with the completion of the Works.

(7) Upon the removal of any such Plant goods or materials as have been
deemed to have become the property of the Employer under sub-clause (2)
of this clause with the consent as aforesaid the property therein shall be
deemed to revest in the contractor and upon completion of the Works the
property in the remainder of such Plant goods and materials as aforesaid shall
subject to clause 63 be deemed to revest in the contractor.

(8) If the contractor shall fail to remove any Plant goods or materials as
required pursuant to Clause 33 within such reasonable time after completion
of the Works as may be allowed by the Engineer then the Employer may—
(a) sell any which are the property of the Contractor; and (b) return any not
the property of the Contractor to the owner thereof at the Contractor's
expense and after deducting from any proceeds of sale the costs charges and
expenses of and in connection with such sale and of and in connection with
return as aforesaid shall pay the balance (if any) to the Contractor but to the
extent that the proceeds of sale are insufficient to meet all such costs charges
and expenses the excess shall be a debt due from the Contractor to the
Employer and shall be deductible or recoverable by the Employer from any
monies due or that may become due to the Contractor under the contract or
may be recovered by the Employer from the Contractor at law.

(9) The Employer shall not at any time be liable for the loss of or injury to
any of the Plant goods or materials which have been deemed to become the
property of the Employer under sub-clause (2) of this clause save as
mentioned in Clauses 20 and 65.

(10) The Contractor shall where entering into any sub-contract for the execution of any part of the Works incorporate in such subcontract (by reference or otherwise) the provisions of this Clause in relation to Plant goods or materials brought on to the Site by the sub-contractor.

(11) The operation of this Clause shall not be deemed to imply any approval by the Engineer of the materials at any time by the Engineer.

54.(1) The Contractor may with a view to securing payment ... in respect of goods and materials ... before the same are delivered to the Site transfer the property in the same to the Employer before delivery to the Site provided ...

(2) The intention of the Contractor to transfer the property in any goods or materials to the Employer in accordance with this Clause ...

(3) Upon the Engineer approving in writing the said goods and materials for the purposes of this Clause the same shall vest in and become the absolute property of the Employer and thereafter shall be in the possession of the Contractor for the sole purpose of delivering them to the Employer and incorporating them in the Works and shall not be within the ownership control or disposition of the Contractor ...

(4) Neither the Contractor nor a sub-contractor nor any other person shall have a lien on any goods or materials which have vested in the Employer under sub-clause (3) of this Clause ...

(5) Upon cessation of the employment of the Contractor under this contract before completion of the Works ... the Contractor shall deliver to the Employer any goods or materials the property in which has vested in the Employer by virtue of sub-clause (3) of this Clause ...

63.(1) If the Contractor shall become bankrupt or have a receiving order made against him or shall present his petition in bankruptcy or shall make an arrangement with or assignment in favour of his creditors or shall agree to carry out the Contract under a committee of inspection of his creditors or (being a corporation) shall go into liquidation (other than a voluntary liquidation for the purposes of amalgamation or reconstruction) or if the Contractor shall assign the Contract without the consent in writing of the Employer first obtained or shall have an execution levied on his goods or if the Engineer shall certify in writing to the Employer that in his opinion the Contractor:—(a) has abandoned the Contract ... then the employer may after giving 7 days' notice in writing to the Contractor enter upon the Site and the Works and expel the Contractor therefrom without thereby avoiding the Contract or releasing the Contractor from any of his obligations or liabilities under the Contract or affecting the rights and powers conferred on the Employer or the Engineer by the contract and may himself complete the Works or may employ any other contractor to complete the Works and the Employer or such other contractor may use for such completion so much of the Constructional Plant Temporary Works goods and materials which have been deemed to become the property of the Employer under Clause 53 and 54 as he or they may think proper and the Employer may at any time sell any of the said Constructional Plant Temporary Works and unused goods and materials and apply the proceeds of sale in or towards the satisfaction of any sums due or which may become due to him from the Contractor under the contract ...

(3) The Engineer shall as soon as may be practicable after any such entry and expulsion by the Employer fix and determine *ex parte* or by or after

reference to the parties or after such investigation or enquiries as he may
think fit to make or institute and shall certify what amount (if any) had at the
time of such entry and expulsion been reasonably earned by or would
reasonably accrue to the contractor in respect of work then actually done by
him under the Contract and what was the value of any unused or partially
used goods and materials any Constructional Plant and any Temporary
Works which have been deemed to become the property of the Employer
under Clauses 53 and 54.

(4) If the Employer shall enter and expel the Contractor under this Clause
he shall not be liable to pay to the contractor any money on account of the
contract until the expiration of the Period of Maintenance and thereafter
until the costs of completion and maintenance damages for delay in
completion (if any) and all other expenses incurred by the Employer have
been ascertained and the amount thereof certified by the Engineer. The
Contractor shall then be entitled to receive only such sum or sums (if any) as
the Engineer may certify would have been due to him upon due completion
by him after deducting the said amount. But if such amount shall exceed the
sum which would have been payable to the Contractor on due completion
by him then the Contractor shall upon demand pay to the Employer the
amount of such excess and it shall be deemed a debt due by the Contractor
to the Employer and shall be recoverable accordingly.'

When referring hereafter to condition 53, I refer to that condition as amended.

For the administrator, Mr Wilmot-Smith submits that the combined
contractual effect of conditions 53 and 63 is that plant owned by the contractor is
deemed, for the purposes of the contract, to be the property of the employer whilst
it is on the site, in the sense that while the legal ownership of plant on the site
remains in the contractor, the parties have agreed to proceed *as if* the employer
were the legal owner of such plant. Mr Wilmot-Smith submits that if the parties
had intended legal ownership of the plant to be vested in the employer so long as
it remained on the site they would have used the kind of language to be found in
condition 54.

In support of this submission he cites *R v Norfolk CC* (1891) 60 LJQB 379. In that
case, the court had to consider the meaning of the words in the Highways and
Locomotives (Amendment) Act 1878: 'The following areas shall be deemed to be
highway areas for the purposes of this Act.'

In the course of his judgment, Cave J said (at 380–381):

'Of course that language, it is plain, is slightly loose; because, generally
speaking, when you talk of a thing being deemed to be something, you do
not mean to say that it is that which it is deemed to be. It is rather an
admission that it is not what it is deemed to be, and that, notwithstanding it
is not that particular thing, nevertheless, for the purposes of the Act, it is to
be deemed to be that thing.'

Mr Wilmot-Smith also relies in this connection on *Re Winter, ex p Bolland* (1878)
8 Ch D 225 and *Milnes v Huddersfield Corp* (1883) 12 QBD 443.

In *Re Winter, ex p Bolland*, an engineering contract provided that plant brought
by the contractor onto the site should 'be deemed the property of' the employer,
and that in the event of the contractor's default the employer should have the
right to use the plant in the completion of the works. The contractor defaulted,
leaving items of plant on site. The employer completed the works itself.

a Following completion of the works, the plant was, by agreement, sold. The trustee in bankruptcy of the contractor claimed the proceeds of sale on the footing that the plant was the contractor's property. The employer claimed to be entitled to retain the proceeds of sale on the basis either that the plant was its property, or that it was entitled to set off the value of the plant against the contractor's liability under the contract on the footing that there had been mutual
b dealings between the contractor and the employer for the purposes of the Bankruptcy Act 1869. In the course of his judgment, Bacon CJ said ((1878) 8 Ch D 225 at 228, 229):

c 'The plant was to be deemed, for the purposes of the contract only, to be the property of [the employer] ... [The employer] cannot deduct the £685 which is now ascertained to be the value of this plant from the £2876 [owed to the employer by the contractor], and there is no pretence or reason for saying that this plant, which was the property of [the contractor], and was on these premises, did not become the property of the trustee.'

Accordingly, set-off was not available.
d In *Milnes v Huddersfield Corp* (1883) 12 QBD 443 Lord Coleridge CJ had to consider the meaning and effect of a provision in byelaws enacted under the Huddersfield Waterworks Act 1869 that connecting pipes 'shall be deemed to belong' to the statutory undertaker. Lord Coleridge CJ said (at 449–450):

e 'Now it is important to see what "deemed to belong to them" means, because, except for that expression, there could be no ground whatever, as far as I can see, in the series of clauses which I have been considering, for maintaining that these pipes were anything else than the property of the plaintiff, paid for by him and belonging to him, subject to certain controls, no doubt, but the property of them remaining in him. Now this 6th by-law says they "shall be deemed to belong" to the corporation. For what purpose? For
f all purposes? Certainly I think not. I think only for the purpose for which the corporation were empowered to make the by-law ... It is plain to my mind, therefore, that these by-laws, on the face of them professing to be made under the section of the Act of Parliament which they expressly set out, and under which they expressly say they are acting, must be considered
g to have been made only for the purpose for which they were empowered to be made, namely, "for preventing the waste, misuse, undue consumption, or contamination of the water;" that they do not even attempt to go beyond the line of the powers that are given them by that 66th section [of the Huddersfield Waterworks Act 1869]; and that by the expression "deemed to
h belong to them," it is shewn clearly that they did not mean to claim the property in them, but that they thought it right to claim such control over them as "deeming to belong to them," would give them, namely, access to them at all times, a general power and control, and other powers, which I will not repeat as I have already stated them, for which it is important that they should be in the hands of the corporation.'

j Relying on these authorities, Mr Wilmot-Smith submits that property (ie legal ownership) in plant which is brought by the contractor onto the site remains in the contractor, subject to the employer's contractual rights under condition 63(1) to use the plant to complete the works and to sell it and apply the proceeds of sale in or towards satisfaction of any sums due or which may become due to it from the contractor.

Mr Wilmot-Smith then goes on to submit that these contractual rights of the
employer give the employer a property interest in the plant which, while it is less   *a*
than legal ownership, amounts to what he terms a 'security interest'.

In support of this submission Mr Wilmot-Smith relies on the decision of
Farwell J in *Hart v Porthgain Harbour Co Ltd* [1903] 1 Ch 690 at 692. In that case,
cl 11 of a construction contract provided that plant brought onto the site by the
contractor—   *b*

> 'shall be considered the property of [the employer] until the engineers shall
> have certified completion of the contract, and no plant or materials shall be
> removed or taken away without the consent or order in writing of the
> engineers.'

c

The contractor brought plant onto the site, which was mortgaged to the plaintiff
by a bill of sale. The contractor defaulted and was made bankrupt. The employer
took possession of the plant, which was subsequently sold. The plaintiff claimed
the proceeds of sale of the plant under his bill of sale.

Farwell J said (at 694–695):

d

> 'Now this clause 11 appears to me to be inserted, amongst other things, for
> the purpose of securing to the company the due performance of the contract.
> In my opinion the true construction of the clause, "all such plant and
> material shall be considered the property of the [employer]," is that it vests
> the property in the materials in the company at law subject to a condition   *e*
> that, when the engineer shall have certified the completion of the contract,
> the contractor shall be at liberty to remove them ... the true view is that the
> materials have become the property at law of the [employer] subject to this
> condition; and the condition has not been performed by reason of the default
> of the contractor.'

f

Later in his judgment Farwell J said (at 696):

> 'In my opinion these clauses are put in for the purpose, not merely of
> enabling the contract to be performed, but also as a due security for its
> performance. They are not mere machinery to enable the [employer], either
> themselves or by another contractor, to complete the performance of the   *g*
> contract, but they are also a security for the company that the work shall be
> performed; and the [employer is] entitled to avail [itself] of that security if, by
> the default of the contractor, the work is not performed at all ... The result
> is, although I am sorry that the plaintiff should have lost the money which
> he lent on this security [i e the bill of sale], it is impossible to give effect to his   *h*
> claim, and I must dismiss the action with costs.'

Thus, the ratio of the judgment in *Hart v Porthgain Harbour Co Ltd* was that legal
ownership in the plant vested in the employer, thereby defeating the plaintiff's
claim under his bill of sale. Farwell J's references to the 'security' provided to the
employer by the contractual provision in question must be read in that context.   *j*

Mr Wilmot-Smith also relies in this connection on *Brown v Bateman* (1867) LR
2 CP 272. In that case a building contract provided that—

> 'all materials which shall have been brought upon the premises by [the
> contractor] for the purpose of erecting such buildings, shall be considered as
> immediately attached and belonging to the premises, and that no part

a
thereof shall be removed therefrom without [the employer's] consent.' (See (1867) LR 2 CP 272 at 282.)

The plaintiff in the action had obtained a judgment against the contractor and a writ of fi fa was issued by way of execution. The sheriff seized materials which the contractor had brought onto the site in the performance of the building contract. Subsequently, title to the materials was asserted by the employer, and
b
the sheriff withdrew from possession of such materials and made a return of nulla bona to the writ of fi fa. The plaintiff sued the sheriff for an alleged false return, contending that the materials were the property of the contractor. In the course of his judgment, Bovill CJ said (at 281):

c
'It is not necessary to say whether [the clause in question] creates an express legal interest in the landlord, because in my judgment it confers upon him a clear equitable right to the materials brought upon the premises for the purpose of being used in their construction, without any actual interference on his part; and none of the cases cited shew that such an equitable interest could not be created. That being so, the materials could not be liable to
d
seizure under an execution against the builder. It has been contended that the agreement amounts to no more than a mere licence to [the employer] to take possession. But ... it appears to me that under [the clause in question the employer] took an immediate interest in the materials.'

Bovill CJ accordingly concluded that the agreement did not operate as a mere
e
licence to take possession, but that it created an equitable interest in the employer.

Keating J agreed with Bovill CJ, saying (at 283):

'... if [the clause] gave [the employer] a mere right to seize the materials in question, equity would not give effect to it; but, if it created an interest in [the
f
employer's] favour, a court of equity would (although a court of law would not hold the property to pass) consider it as an equitable charge.'

Montague Smith J also agreed, saying (at 283):

g
'Whatever might be the legal effect of the contract, I think it created such an interest in the goods in equity in [the employer] as was sufficient to prevent the sheriff from selling them under the execution against [the contractor].'

Thus, while all three judges in *Brown v Bateman* concluded that the clause in
h
question gave the employer an equitable interest in the materials, only Keating J described that interest as being in the nature of an equitable charge.

In support of the proposition that the equitable interest created by the operation of conditions 53 and 63 is an equitable interest in the nature of a charge, Mr Wilmot-Smith prays in aid the following passage from the judgment of Slade
j
J in *Re Bond Worth Ltd* [1979] 3 All ER 919 at 939, [1980] Ch 228 at 248:

'In my judgment, any contract which, by way of security for the payment of a debt, confers an interest in property defeasible or destructible on payment of such debt, or appropriates such property for the discharge of the debt, must necessarily be regarded as creating a mortgage or charge, as the case may be.'

Mr Wilmot-Smith submits that an equitable charge may be created to secure
performance not only of an obligation to pay a debt, but of other types of   *a*
obligation as well. In this connection he relies on a passage from the judgment of
Peter Gibson J in *Carreras Rothmans Ltd v Freeman Mathews Treasure Ltd (in liq)*
[1985] 1 All ER 155 at 169, [1985] Ch 207 at 227, where he said:

> 'The type of charge which it is said was created is an equitable charge. Such
> a charge is created by the appropriation of specific property to the discharge   *b*
> of some debt *or other obligation* without there being any change in ownership
> either at law or in equity, and it confers on the chargee rights to apply to the
> court for an order for sale or for the appointment of a receiver, but no right
> to foreclosure (so as to make the property his own) or to take possession ...'
> (My emphasis.)

c

Mr Wilmot-Smith also cited in this connection *Stroud Architectural Systems Ltd
v John Laing Construction Ltd* [1994] 2 BCLC 276, in which Judge John Newey QC
held, following *Re Bond Worth Ltd*, that a retention of title clause in a building
contract created an equitable charge.

Mr Wilmot-Smith's next submission was that the equitable charge created by   *d*
the operation of conditions 53 and 63 is a floating, as opposed to a specific, charge,
and thus registrable under s 395. His citation of authority on this limb of his
argument began with the following well-known passage from the judgment of
Romer LJ in the Court of Appeal in *Re Yorkshire Woolcombers Association Ltd,
Houldsworth v Yorkshire Woolcombers Association Ltd* [1903] 2 Ch 284 at 295:

e

> 'I certainly do not intend to attempt to give an exact definition of the term
> "floating charge," nor am I prepared to say that there will not be a floating
> charge within the meaning of the [Companies Act 1900], which does not
> contain all the three characteristics that I am about to mention, but I
> certainly think that if a charge has the three characteristics that I am about to
> mention it is a floating charge. (1.) If it is a charge on a class of assets of a   *f*
> company present and future; (2.) if that class is one which, in the ordinary
> course of the business of the company, would be changing from time to
> time; and (3.) if you find that by the charge it is contemplated that, until some
> future step is taken by or on behalf of those interested in the charge, the
> company may carry on its business in the ordinary way as far as concerns the   *g*
> particular class of assets I am dealing with.'

In the House of Lords Lord Macnaghten said ([1904] AC 355 at 358):

> 'I should have thought there was not much difficulty in defining what a
> floating charge is in contrast to what is called a specific charge. A specific   *h*
> charge, I think, is one that without more fastens on ascertained and definite
> property or property capable of being ascertained and defined; a floating
> charge, on the other hand, is ambulatory and shifting in its nature, hovering
> over and so to speak floating with the property which it is intended to affect
> until some event occurs or some act is done which causes it to settle and
> fasten on the subject of the charge within its reach and grasp.'   *j*

Mr Wilmot-Smith also referred me to a passage from the judgment of Nicholls
LJ in *Re Atlantic Computer Systems plc (No 1)* [1992] 1 All ER 476, [1992] Ch 505. In
that case the principal issue was whether an assignment by way of charge of the
benefit of certain subleases created a specific or a floating charge over the
subleases. After referring to the passages from the judgments of Romer LJ and

Lord Macnaghten which I have just set out, Nicholls LJ continued ([1992] 1 All
ER 476 at 494, [1992] Ch 505 at 534):

> 'In the light of these observations we cannot accept Mr Heslop's
> submissions [that the charges were floating charges]. The notable feature of
> the present case is that the charges were not ambulatory. The property
> assigned by the company was confined to rights to which the company was
> entitled under specific, existing contracts. The assignments consisted of the
> company's rights "under or by virtue of" subleases each of which was already
> in existence at the time of the assignments and each of which was specifically
> identified in the relevant deeds of assignment. In each case the payments due
> to the company under a specific sublease were charged as security to the
> payments due by the company under the headlease relating to the same
> equipment. The company's right to receive future instalments from
> end-users in due course pursuant to the terms of these subleases was as much
> a present asset of the company, within Romer LJ's reference to "present and
> future" assets of a company, as a right to receive payment of a sum which
> was immediately due. Romer LJ's reference to future assets was a reference
> to assets of which, when the charge was created, the company was not the
> owner. That was the position in that case. That is not the position in this
> case. We have in mind that in practice sums payable by the end-users under
> these subleases were paid to the company and utilised by it in the ordinary
> course of business. In so far as this is relevant, it may well be that this was
> what the parties intended should happen. The company was to be at liberty
> to receive and use the instalments until [the chargee] chose to intervene. We
> are unpersuaded that this results in these charges, on existing and defined
> property, becoming floating charges. A mortgage of land does not become
> a floating charge by reason of the mortgagor being permitted to remain in
> possession and enjoy the fruits of the property charged for the time being.
> This is so even if the land is leasehold and the term is very short, and as such
> the asset is of a wasting character. So here: the mere fact that for the time
> being the company could continue to receive and use the instalments does
> not suffice to negative the fixed character of the charge. This apart, we have
> seen nothing to lend any support to the administrators' contention. In
> particular, we have seen nothing to suggest that after the assignment the
> company was to be at liberty to deal with its rights under the subleases
> without the consent of [the chargee].'

In *Re Atlantic Medical Ltd* [1993] BCLC 386 a similar question arose, and
Vinelott J regarded himself bound by the Court of Appeal decision in *Re Atlantic
Computer Systems plc (No 1)* to conclude that the assignment in question created a
specific charge over the subleases.

Mr Wilmot-Smith submits that the *Atlantic Computer* case is distinguishable on
the facts. In the instant case, he submits, all three of the elements described by
Romer LJ in the *Yorkshire Woolcombers'* case are present. Thus, he submits: (1) the
relevant class of assets consists of plant and other materials brought by the
contractor onto the site, for so long as they remain there; (2) that class of assets is
one which will change from time to time in the ordinary course of the
contractor's business, as the works progress; and (3) the contract contemplates
that until a future step is taken by the employer (ie the giving of notice under
condition 63(1)) the contractor may carry on its business in the ordinary way as
far as concerns that class of assets.

Mr Wilmot-Smith submits that the floating charge crystallised when the
employer served notice under condition 63(1). At that point, he submits, the
employer's security rights became exercisable.

It being common ground that no floating charge was registered pursuant to
s 395, Mr Wilmot-Smith submits that it must follow that the employer's
contractual right to retain the coal-washing plants is void as against the
administrator.

For the employer, Mr Mortimore submits first, that on their true construction
conditions 53 and 63 have the effect of vesting in the employer the absolute legal
ownership in plant which is from time to time on the site for so long as it remains
there, and hence there is no scope for any equitable charge. Second, if that be
wrong, he submits that any equitable charge is a specific, as opposed to a floating,
charge and is accordingly not registrable under s 395.

In support of his primary submission Mr Mortimore relies strongly on *Hart v
Porthgain Harbour Co Ltd* [1903] 1 Ch 690. As I have already noted, that was a case
in which it was held that the legal ownership in building materials from time to
time on site passed to the employer.

As to Mr Wilmot-Smith's submissions as to the meaning of the provision in
condition 53(2) that plant 'shall when on site be deemed to be the property of the
employer', Mr Mortimore submits that it means the same as 'shall be the
property of the employer'. In support of this submission, Mr Mortimore cited
Reeves v Barlow (1884) 12 QBD 436. In that case a building contract provided
that—

'all building and other materials brought by the intended lessee upon the
land shall, whether affixed to the freehold or not, become the property of the
intended lessor.' (See (1884) 12 QBD 436 at 439.)

Bowen LJ, giving the judgment of the court, said (at 442):

'The contract was only to apply to goods when brought upon the
premises, and until this happened there was no right or interest in equity to
any goods at all. Upon the other hand, the moment the goods were brought
upon the premises the property in them passed *in law,* and nothing was left
upon which any equity as distinct from law could attach. No further
performance of the contract was necessary, nor could be enforced. The
builder's agreement accordingly was at no time an equitable assignment of
anything, but a mere legal contract that, upon the happening of a particular
event, the property *in law* should pass in certain chattels which that event
would identify without the necessity of any further act on the part of
anybody, and which could not be identified before.' (My emphasis.)

Mr Mortimore also referred me to *Blake v Izard* (1867) 16 WR 108, where a
provision in a building contract that materials brought onto the land should
become the property of the intended lessors was held, following *Brown v Bateman,*
to take priority over the rights of an execution creditor of the intended lessee.

Mr Mortimore contrasted *Re Keen & Keen, ex p Collins* [1902] 1 KB 555, where a
provision in a building contract that materials brought on site 'shall be considered
to be the property of' the employer was held by Wright J not to confer ownership
of the materials on the employer, with *Re Weibking, ex p Ward* [1902] 1 KB 713,
where a provision that plant and materials brought on site should 'be deemed to
be annexed to the freehold' was held by the same judge to be sufficient to

a   constitute the freeholder the owner for the purposes of the doctrine of reputed ownership.

Mr Mortimore also referred me to the Australian case of *Akron Tyre Co Pty Ltd v Kittson* (1951) 82 CLR 477 as being on all fours with *Reeves v Barlow*. In that case a hire purchase agreement provided that any accessories supplied with or attached to the vehicle 'shall become part of' the vehicle. The High Court of

b   Australia held that that provision was effective to pass the property in replacement tyres which had been fitted to the vehicle.

Finally, in relation to his primary submission, Mr Mortimore referred me to the decision of the Privy Council in *Bennett & White (Calgary) Ltd v Municipal District of Sugar City No 5* [1951] AC 786. In that case a building contract provided

c   that plant provided by the contractor for the works 'shall ... become and until final completion of the said work shall be' the property of the Crown, as employer. The issue was whether the contractors were liable to be assessed to tax as being the 'owners', alternatively in 'legal possession', of such plant for the purposes of a Canadian statute. Lord Reid, giving the judgment of the Privy

d   Council, said (at 813–814):

e   'The first inquiry must ... be, whether the Alberta legislation ... purports to make either the property in question in this case, or the appellants [ie the contractors] in respect of that property, assessable. This involves the further inquiry, whether the appellants were, in 1947—(*a*) "owners", or (*b*) persons "in legal possession" of the chattels in question within [the statutory provision]. Clearly, if they were neither—as, for instance, they would be if the Crown were both—the appellants are exempt. (*a*) Their Lordships are of opinion that the Crown was at all material times the owner of the articles in question ... The English decided cases have dealt not infrequently with

f   clauses of this type: see *Brown v. Bateman* ((1867) LR 2 CP 272); *Blake v. Izard* ((1867) 16 WR 108); *Reeves v. Barlow* ((1884) 12 QBD 436); *In re Keen & Keen* ([1902] 1 KB 555) ... *Hart v. Porthgain Harbour Co. Ld.* ([1903] 1 Ch 690). In some of these cases a distinction has been drawn between clauses which provide that as and when plant or materials are brought to the site they shall be "considered" or "deemed" to become the property of the building owner;

g   and, on the other hand, clauses which provide that they are to "be and become" his property. In the former case it has sometimes been held that the clause was ineffective to achieve its aim and that the property remained in the builder, at the mercy of his creditors and trustee in bankruptcy: see *In re Keen & Keen*. When, as in *Reeves v. Barlow*, a decision of the Court of

h   Appeal and, perhaps, the leading decision in the field, the formula is "be and become" or its equivalent, that case decides that the clause means what it says, operates according to its tenor, and effectively transfers the title. In *Hart v. Porthgain Harbour Co. Ld.* Farwell, J., seems to have thought it immaterial which formula was used; but on any view "be and become" is

j   effective, and the same must hold good of "become and be"—the wording employed in this case. It is true that apart from the case of bargain and sale of goods (and sale of goods is not here in question) either a deed, or a delivery (actual or constructive), is necessary to transfer the title to chattels inter vivos. But in the present case there was delivery on a site owned and occupied by the building owner—the Crown—and on the English cases this has been held sufficient ... If this reasoning is well founded the plant, equipment and materials became the property of the Crown as and when so delivered.'

On the basis of the above authorities, Mr Mortimore submits primarily that on its true construction condition 53 has the effect of vesting in the employer the legal title in plant from time to time on the site for so long as it remains there. It is common ground that if that submission is right, no floating charge is created.

In the event that, contrary to his primary submission, the employer takes an equitable interest only in such plant, Mr Mortimore submits that that equitable interest is not by way of charge. If that is wrong, then it is in the nature of a specific, as opposed to a floating, charge.

Turning to the first of the three characteristics of a floating charge listed by Romer LJ in the *Yorkshire Woolcombers'* case, Mr Mortimore submits that to classify the assets subject to the (assumed) charge by reference to the moment at which they are brought onto the site, is to classify them by reference to the very event which gives rise to the charge. He submits that the instant case is on all fours with *Royal Trust Bank v National Westminster Bank plc* [1995] BCC 128, where I held that a charge over hiring agreements deposited from time to time with the plaintiff created a specific equitable charge over such agreements.

As to the second and third of the characteristics listed by Romer LJ, Mr Mortimore submits that in any event the suggested class of assets (ie plant, goods or materials brought onto the site from time to time) did not change from time to time 'in the ordinary course of the business of [the contractor]'. Mr Mortimore pointed out that under condition 53(6) such plant, goods and materials can only be removed from the site with the written consent of the engineer 'which consent shall not be unreasonably withheld where [the same] are no longer immediately required for the purposes of the completion of the Works'. Mr Mortimore submits that the requirement for the engineer's consent to removal from the site takes this case outside the second and third characteristics listed by Romer LJ.

As his final line of defence, should all his earlier submissions fail, Mr Mortimore submits that even if on their true construction conditions 53 and 63 create a floating charge which is void for non-registration, nevertheless the right conferred on the employer by condition 63(1), having given notice of expulsion to the contractor, to use the plant, goods and materials in completing the works, remains on foot as a contractual right exercisable by the employer.

Conclusions

In expressing my conclusions I use the expression 'relevant plant' to mean plant which the contractor has brought onto the site pursuant to the contract.

I address first the question whether condition 53(2) has the effect of passing the general property in (ie legal ownership in) relevant plant to the employer for so long as it remains on the site, it being common ground that if that question is answered in the affirmative then there is no scope for the existence of any equitable charge.

This is a pure question of construction of condition 53(2), read in the context of the contract as a whole. In addressing that question, I derive some assistance from the authorities which have been cited to me (to which I have already made reference) in which the courts have had to consider contracts to broadly similar effect and expressions more or less similar to the expression 'shall ... be deemed to be the property of' in condition 53(2). In the end, however, the answer must depend on the terms of the particular contract under examination.

a   Reading condition 53(2) in the context of the contract as a whole (and, in particular, condition 54), I conclude that on its true construction it does not have the effect of passing the general property in relevant plant to the employer. The instant case does not, in my judgment, fall within the category of 'be and become' cases identified by the Privy Council in *Bennett & White (Calgary) Ltd v Municipal District of Sugar City No 5*. I accept Mr Wilmot-Smith's submission that on its true

b   construction, the expression 'Shall ... be deemed to be the property of', in condition 53(2) means that legal ownership is not to pass, but that the parties are agreeing to proceed for the purposes of the contract as if it had. The 'deeming' provision in condition 53(2), and the corresponding deemed revesting provision in condition 53(7), are to be contrasted with the clear language employed by the draftsman in condition 54 (the material parts of which I set out earlier). Where

c   the draftsman wished to provide for the transfer of legal ownership, he did so in clear terms.

I conclude, therefore, that on its true construction condition 53(2) does not effect a transfer of the general property in relevant plant for the time being on the site to the employer.

d   It may be that in so far as it embodies an agreement that relevant plant is to be treated as if it belonged in law to the employer for so long as it remains on the site, the contract is effective to transfer special, as opposed to general, property in relevant plant to the employer, so as to constitute the employer a bailee of relevant plant for the time being on the site. But I see no reason in principle why the existence of such a bailor/bailee relationship between contractor and

e   employer (if such a relationship exists) should exclude the possibility that the employer may have some wider equitable rights in relevant plant extending beyond its rights as bailee, so as to give it a floating charge over relevant plant for the time being on the site.

On that footing it is unnecessary to decide whether the contract creates a

f   bailor/bailee relationship in relevant plant. I turn, therefore, to the questions: (a) whether the employer takes an equitable proprietary interest in relevant plant; and (b) if so, what is the nature of that equitable interest.

The answers to these two questions depend, in my judgment, on the intentions of the parties as appearing from the contract, properly construed. The manifestation of a contractual intention to create or assign an equitable

g   proprietary interest may take various forms. In some cases, it may take the form of an express statement of intention to that effect. In others, the existence of the relevant intention may be deduced by inference from the terms of the contract: e g where the contract creates specifically enforceable rights and obligations which, as a matter of law, create an equitable proprietary interest. In cases within

h   the latter category, the parties may not in fact have intended to create an equitable proprietary interest, but they must nevertheless be taken to have intended the legal consequences of the contract which they made.

In the instant case there is no express statement of intention as to whether the employer should take an equitable interest in relevant plant, still less as to the

j   nature of any such equitable interest. It is accordingly necessary to examine the relevant provisions of the contract in order to determine whether such an intention is to be inferred from the rights and obligations which the contract creates in relation to relevant plant. For this purpose, the relevant provisions of the contract are conditions 53 and 63.

I turn first to condition 53. By virtue of condition 53(6) the employer has the following rights in relation to relevant plant: (1) an absolute right to refuse to

permit the contractor to remove from the site relevant plant which is
immediately required for the completion of the works; and (2) a right to refuse to   *a*
permit the contractor to remove from the site relevant plant which is not
immediately required for the completion of the works, provided that the
employer acts reasonably in so refusing. Under condition 53(7) the above rights
come to an end on completion of the works, provided that no forfeiture has
occurred in the meantime.   *b*

For his part, the contractor has the right, under condition 53(6), to exclusive
use of relevant plant in completing the works until the occurrence of a forfeiture
under condition 63.

I turn next to condition 63. Under this condition the employer has the
following rights in relevant plant in the event of a forfeiture: (1) to use relevant
plant on the site at the date of forfeiture to complete the works; and/or (2) to   *c*
allow another contractor to use such relevant plant to complete the works; and/
or (3) at any time thereafter to sell all or any of such relevant plant and to apply
the proceeds of sale in or towards the satisfaction of any sums due or which may
become due to it from the contractor under the contract.

In my judgment, these contractual rights of the employer do have the   *d*
consequence of giving the employer an equitable proprietary interest in relevant
plant, by reason of the fact that equity will aid the enforcement of those rights by
means of the remedy of specific performance.

The next question is whether that equitable interest is in the nature of a charge;
and if so, whether the charge is specific or floating.

In the passage from the judgment of Slade J in *Re Bond Worth Ltd* relied upon   *e*
in this connection by Mr Wilmot-Smith (and quoted above), Slade J refers to
contracts which 'by way of security for a debt' confer property interests defeasible
on payment of the debt. In *Re Bond Worth Ltd* itself, the obligation which was
secured was payment of the purchase price for the goods, but there would appear
to be no reason in principle why the performance of other types of obligation   *f*
may not be secured by an equitable charge (see the reference in *Carreras Rothmans
Ltd v Freeman Mathews Treasure Ltd (in liq)* [1985] 1 All ER 155 at 169, [1985] Ch 207
at 227 per Peter Gibson J to 'some debt or other obligation' and see also *Swiss
Bank Corp v Lloyds Bank Ltd* [1980] 2 All ER 419 at 426, [1982] AC 584 at 595 per
Buckley LJ).

Had condition 63 not contained a right for the employer to sell relevant plant   *g*
on the site at the date of forfeiture and to apply the proceeds in or towards
satisfaction of any sum due from the contractor to the employer under the
contract, it would in my judgment have been impossible to contend that the
equitable proprietary interest of the employer in relevant plant was an interest in
the nature of a charge. But, per contra, the existence of that right does, in my   *h*
judgment, serve to create an equitable charge on relevant plant.

The final question, therefore, is whether that equitable charge is a 'floating
charge' for the purposes of s 395. It is notorious that there is no applicable
statutory definition of that expression, so the question has to be answered by
reference to principle and authority.

As I read the authorities, it is of the essence of a floating charge that unless and   *j*
until the charge crystallises, the chargor should have unfettered freedom to carry
on his business in the ordinary way. This requirement is emphasised by Romer
LJ in each of the second and third characteristics of a floating charge which he
identifies in the *Yorkshire Woolcombers'* case.

Also in that case, Vaughan Williams LJ said ([1903] 2 Ch 284 at 294):

a
'I do not think that for a "specific security" you need have a security of a subject-matter which is then in existence. I mean by "then" at the time of the execution of the security; but what you do require to make a specific security is that the security whenever it has once come into existence, and been identified or appropriated as a security, shall never thereafter *at the will of the mortgagor* cease to be a security. If *at the will of the mortgagor* he can dispose

b
of it and prevent its being any longer a security, although something else may be substituted more or less for it, that is not a "specific security."' (My emphasis.)

See also *Re Bond Worth Ltd* [1979] 3 All ER 919 at 953, [1980] Ch 228 at 266, where Slade J said:

c
'It is in my judgment quite incompatible with the existence of an effective trust by way of specific charge in equity over specific assets that the alleged trustee should be free to use them *as he pleases* for his own benefit in the course of his own business.' (My emphasis.)

d
In the instant case, relevant plant cannot be removed from the site at the will of the contractor; nor is the contractor free to use relevant plant as he pleases. As I pointed out earlier, under condition 53(6) the employer has an absolute right to refuse to permit its removal if it is immediately required to complete the works, and a qualified right so to refuse even if it is not immediately required to complete the works.

e
Mr Wilmot-Smith submitted that the interests of the contractor and the employer coincide in this respect, in that the ordinary course of the contractor's business will inevitably require that relevant plant which is immediately required for the completion of the works will be left on the site for that purpose. In the first place, I am by no means satisfied that that is necessarily so. The ordinary

f
course of the contractor's business (over which the employer will have no control) may well involve deploying its assets to maximum commercial effect over a number of current contracts. It is not to be supposed that the contract is necessarily the only contract which the contractor has on foot. But in the second place, Mr Wilmot-Smith's submission takes no account of the fact that even where relevant plant is not immediately required to complete the works (so that, prima facie, it will be in the contractor's interest to remove it and use it

g
elsewhere), the employer retains the right under condition 53(6) to refuse to permit such removal, provided that it acts reasonably in so refusing. It is not appropriate for me to attempt to define the circumstances in which it may be reasonable for the employer to refuse such permission: it suffices to note that the contract recognises that there may be some circumstances in which it is

h
reasonable for it to do so. That is enough, in my judgment, to lead to the conclusion that the equitable charge created by conditions 53 and 63 is not a floating charge for the purposes of s 395.

In my judgment, on a true analysis, what is created by those conditions is a specific equitable charge on relevant plant for the time being on the site. As and

j
when relevant plant is (with the consent of the employer) removed from the site, it ceases to be subject to the charge. As and when further items of plant are brought onto the site, they become subject to the charge, by way of substitution for the items which have been removed.

For these reasons, I conclude that the employer succeeds in its primary contention that the contract does not create a floating charge over the coal-washing plants. In the light of that conclusion, it is not necessary for me to address the secondary question whether, had a floating charge been created, the contractual rights of the employer would nevertheless have survived the application of s 395.

In the result, therefore, the administrator's contentions fail and the application is accordingly dismissed.

Order accordingly.

Paul Magrath Esq   Barrister.

Kumari v Jalal

a

COURT OF APPEAL, CIVIL DIVISION
NEILL, WARD AND THORPE LJJ
25 JULY 1996

b

Contempt of court – Committal – Breach of court order – Second committal in respect of one breach – Contemnor committed to prison for failure to comply with delivery order within specified time limit – Contemnor's non-compliance continuing – Whether court having power to commit contemnor again for continuing failure to comply with single order.

c

The parties were married in 1989 and then divorced in 1992. Following the dissolution of the marriage the wife applied for ancillary relief, including a request for an order for the delivery to her of certain property. At a hearing on 21 October 1994 to determine the ownership of certain items of property, the district d judge ordered the husband to return certain specified items to the wife within seven days. When the husband failed to comply fully with the order, the wife applied for an order that he be committed to prison for contempt of court. The husband was subsequently found guilty of contempt and sentenced to three months' imprisonment. Following his release, however, he took no further action to return the specified items, with the result that the wife applied to have e him committed again on the ground that he had still failed to comply with the order. The county court judge sentenced the husband to a further six months' imprisonment for contempt and he appealed to the Court of Appeal, on the ground that his failure to comply with the order within the time specified was a single breach which was now spent and that, since a person could not be f sentenced twice for the same offence, he could not be committed again for failure to comply.

Held – A person who had been committed to prison for contempt of court for failure to comply with an order which fixed a specific time for compliance could not be made subject to a further committal order for a continuing failure to g comply with the same court order. In the instant case, the husband's continued failure to comply with the delivery order within the time specified constituted a single breach for which he had already been committed to three months' imprisonment; since his continued failure to comply was not a new breach, it followed that the court had no power to commit him to prison again. The appeal h would accordingly be allowed (see p 69 *d* to p 70 *f* and p 71 *a* to *c*, post).

Danchevsky v Danchevsky (No 2) (1977) 121 SJ 796 and *Lamb v Lamb* [1984] FLR 278 applied.

Notes

j For civil contempt by way of disobedience to an order for delivery of goods, see 9 *Halsbury's Laws* (4th edn) para 67.

Cases referred to in judgments
Danchevsky v Danchevsky (No 2) (1977) 121 SJ 796, [1977] CA Transcript 416.
Lamb v Lamb [1984] FLR 278, CA.
Sondhis v Sondhis (1982) 133 NLJ 420, CA.

Cases also cited or referred to in skeleton arguments

El Capistrano SA v ATO Marketing Ltd [1989] 2 All ER 572, [1989] 1 WLR 471, CA.   *a*
Shoreditch County Court Bailiffs v de Medeiros (1988) Times, 24 February, [1988] CA
   Transcript 141.

Appeal

By notice dated 24 July 1996 Faris Jalal appealed from the order of Judge Harold   *b*
Wilson on 23 July 1996 in the Oxford County Court committing him to prison for
a second term of imprisonment for contempt of court for his continuing failure
to comply with the order of District Judge Campbell made on 21 October 1994
for the delivery up of property to the appellant's former wife, Bimla Kumari,
within seven days, on the ground that he had already been committed to three   *c*
months' imprisonment in respect of the same breach by order of Judge
Wilson-Mellor QC made on 21 February 1995 and could not be sentenced again
in respect of that breach. The facts are set out in the judgment of Neill LJ.

Piers Pressdee (instructed by *Cole & Cole*, Oxford) for Mr Jalal.
Gurnam Gill (instructed by *Haynes Duffell Kentish & Co*, Birmingham) for Mrs   *d*
   Kumari.

NEILL LJ. This is another case which demonstrates the care which has to be
taken before orders for committal for contempt of court are made. There are
technical rules laid down. An order for committal involves the liberty of the   *e*
subject. It is therefore important that, before an order is made, the court should
scrutinise with great care not only the facts but the procedure.

   It is necessary, before I turn to the law and to the arguments that have been
raised on this appeal, to say something about the facts. I think it will avoid
confusion if I refer to the parties as Mr Jalal and Mrs Kumari.   *f*

   The parties were married in 1989. Following a contested hearing, a decree nisi
was granted on 11 May 1992. Subsequently, the decree was made absolute.
Following the dissolution of the marriage, Mrs Kumari made an application for
ancillary relief, including a request for an order for the delivery to her of certain
property. For that purpose she had prepared a list of the property which she said
belonged to her, and Mr Jalal had done the same. But there was a dispute as to   *g*
who owned what. The list which Mrs Kumari had prepared was exhibited to an
affidavit which Mr Jalal swore on 29 October 1993. We have that list in the
documents before us.

   The application relating to the property in dispute came before District Judge
Campbell sitting at the Oxford Combined Court Centre on 10 August 1994. On   *h*
that occasion Mrs Kumari was represented by counsel and Mr Jalal was in person.
A declaration was made in respect of the ownership of certain items of property,
to the effect that they should remain the absolute property of Mr Jalal. But there
was a further order that Mr Jalal should transfer to Mrs Kumari within seven days
all the items listed on pages one to eight of the list which had been exhibited to   *j*
the affidavit of 29 October 1993. The first eight pages of that list contained a
number of household goods, a considerable quantity of clothing and (on the last
page) a number of items of jewellery, some of them quite valuable. It was
ordered further that, in default of delivery, Mr Jalal should pay to Mrs Kumari
two-thirds of the value of the items, such values being stated in a document
attached to the order.

a It seems that no action was taken at that stage to comply with the order, or at any rate no action which satisfied Mrs Kumari. In the result, on 21 October 1994 she went back before the district judge, when she was represented by a solicitor and again Mr Jalal was in person. On this occasion a specific delivery order was made, which did not give Mr Jalal the alternative of paying a sum of money. The order was that within seven days from the date of this order, at his own expense,
b Mr Jalal should deliver to Mrs Kumari all the property which had been ordered to be transferred by the order of 10 August 1994.

What happened following the making of that order is explained in one of the affidavits which we have seen. The precise facts are in dispute, but in broad terms it seems that on 28 October, a week after the order was made, Mr Jalal, his father and several other people went to the community centre at Edgbaston, bringing
c with them a van and a large quantity of belongings. They were contained in a large trunk and suitcases and boxes. It is plain that a considerable number of the items which had been listed on the first eight pages of the list exhibited to Mr Jalal's affidavit of October 1993 were handed over on that occasion. However, it also appears that not everything on the list was handed over. It will be
d remembered that Mr Jalal did not accept the accuracy of the list as representing what in fact belonged to Mrs Kumari.

The next step taken was that in February 1995, about two or three months later, an application was made to the judge in the Oxford County Court, on the basis that Mr Jalal had not complied with the order of 21 October. An affidavit
e dated 2 February 1995 in support of the application was sworn by the solicitor acting on behalf of Mrs Kumari.

The matter came before Judge Wilson-Mellor QC. The judge expressed himself as satisfied that Mr Jalal had been guilty of contempt by failing to deliver the property belonging to Mrs Kumari, in accordance with para 1 of the district judge's order of October 1994, and sentenced Mr Jalal to a term of three months'
f imprisonment. I interpose at this stage only to say this. Although the matter has not been argued before us, it would appear that, where part of an order for the delivery of goods has been complied with but there remain other items still to be delivered, a committal order should specify those items which have not been delivered up. There is a note in the *County Court Practice 1996* p 376 (Ord 29, r (1)
g (drawing attention to the decision of this court in *Sondhis v Sondhis* (1982) 133 NLJ 420) to this effect: '... a committal order is irregular if it does not specify e.g. which of [the] chattels ordered to be delivered up the defendant has failed to return ...' That is an indication of the care that must be taken before a committal order is made at all. But we are not concerned with that matter, and I say no
h more about it.

The next stage in the proceedings was that on 1 March 1995, that is just over a week after he had been committed to prison, Mr Jalal applied by letter to purge his contempt. It was a standard form of letter. He said that he wished to purge his contempt and be released from prison. He promised not to break the order again and he said he understood, if he did break the order again, he might be sent
j back to prison.

That application was due to come before the court on 3 March, but it was adjourned generally by Judge Wilson-Mellor because a letter dated 2 March had been received by the clerk of the court from the medical officer at Her Majesty's Prison at Bullingdon. The letter was to the effect that Mr Jalal was suffering from an acute mental illness such as to make him unfit to attend court. It was said that

he had been seen by a consultant forensic psychiatrist, and the question of what
further assessment or treatment he might need was under consideration.   *a*

On 7 July 1995 Mrs Kumari applied for an order that the application to purge
the contempt should be dismissed and that judgment should be entered for her
in the sum of £5,084. It seems that at that stage she was willing to accept a sum
of money in lieu of the return of the goods. What happened on 7 July is referred
to in an affidavit which Mrs Kumari swore on 20 June 1996, a few weeks ago, in   *b*
support of the application to which I shall come shortly.

In para 7 of that affidavit she said that she had asked for judgment in her favour
for £5,084·96 payable forthwith, that sum being calculated on the basis of
two-thirds of the value of the jewellery and some other items that she said had
not been returned.

The next stage in these proceedings took place a year later. An application was   *c*
made about a month ago, supported by the affidavit of Mrs Kumari sworn on 20
June 1996, seeking an order that Mr Jalal should be committed for contempt
again, on the basis that he had still failed to comply with the order of October
1994. It was that matter which came before Judge Harold Wilson on Tuesday, 23
July 1996, that is two days ago, in the Oxford County Court.   *d*

On that occasion, Mr Pressdee of counsel appeared on behalf of Mr Jalal. He
made a preliminary submission that the application to commit should be
dismissed. That did not succeed and the judge continued with the hearing and
heard evidence. At the end of the hearing he gave a judgment, of which we have
been provided with a transcript which the judge has certified as correct. In the
course of his judgment, the judge recited what had happened in the past. He said: *e*

> 'This is an application to commit the respondent to prison for his failure to
> comply with an order of District Judge Campbell made some time ago,
> requiring him to render up to the applicant certain property within seven
> days. In respect of his failure to comply with that order, the respondent was
> committed to prison for contempt.'   *f*

Later he added:

> 'The orders of the district judge were none of them appealed, and in
> February 1995 the respondent was brought before Judge Wilson-Mellor and
> committed for contempt for a term of three months. This sentence was   *g*
> served and the contempt continues—the former husband has done nothing
> to comply with the orders. He has neither surrendered the balance of goods
> listed in [the list of the goods] nor paid a sum equal to two-thirds of their
> value which was given as an alternative. When asked today what he was
> going to do, he says he can do nothing. The contempt therefore continues   *h*
> and is visited by a further term of six months' imprisonment.'

An order for costs was made against Mr Jalal. There was an application for a stay
of the order for committal but that was refused. It is against that judgment and
that order of Judge Wilson that this appeal is brought today.

In his notice of appeal Mr Pressdee sets out a number of grounds, but I consider   *j*
that it is sufficient for the purpose of this judgment to deal with his first and main
ground. His main ground is that the order made by the district judge was for the
return of these goods by a specific day; that Mr Jalal failed to comply with that
order; and, having failed to comply, that breach was a single breach which is now
spent. He served a term of three months' imprisonment following the order of
Judge Wilson-Mellor in February 1995. But in respect of that breach he cannot

a   be sentenced again. Therefore the learned judge was wrong in making an order on 23 July in effect sentencing him again for the same offence. He has drawn our attention to certain authorities, to one of which I shall have to refer in a moment, and it is right to say that we had the benefit of a fuller argument than did the judge.

b   Where there is a dispute about property, a court can decide the question of title and can make an order for delivery up of the property. Under the Rules of the Supreme Court it is common not to make an order specifying a time for delivery up (see RSC Ord 42, r 2(2)). But, if it is intended that the order is to be enforced by an order for committal, then it is plain from Ord 45, r 5(1), which is substantially the same as CCR Ord 29, r 1(1), that it is necessary that the order for delivery must set out a date for compliance. If no date for compliance is inserted *c*   in the order, then a committal order cannot be made. It is also apparent from Ord 45, r 5(3) that, if an alternative way of complying with the order is given to the person against whom the order is made, then that is not an order which can be enforced by committal. But the order of 21 October 1994 was an order which did give a date and therefore was sufficient to found a committal. However, both as *d*   a matter of principle and on authority, if there is a breach of an order to do a certain act by a certain date, such as the delivery of goods, and that non-compliance is visited with a penalty, the breach cannot be the subject matter of a further committal order. If the failure by the alleged contemnor has continued, then it is necessary to go back to the court and obtain a further order.

e   The position is made very clear by the decision of this court in *Danchevsky v Danchevsky (No 2)* (1977) 121 SJ 796. That case also was between two formerly married people. The order provided that Mr Danchevsky (the respondent) should give up possession of the former matrimonial home to the wife or her solicitors by a specified time on a date in June 1974. He failed to do that and he was committed for contempt of court. He went to prison and, when he came out *f*   of prison, he went back to the same property. He did that not once but twice, and on each of the subsequent occasions his behaviour was punished by a sentence of imprisonment. On the third occasion on which he was sent to prison he applied to be released on the ground that he had already been punished.

It was made clear in that case in the judgments of each member of the court *g*   that where you have an order which has a time fixed for compliance—as you must have if there is to be a committal order at all—and there is non-compliance, then that is a single offence.

Lord Denning MR said:

h   'We had quite a considerable discussion about orders for possession. An order for possession can be made in the first instance without giving a time: but, if it is proposed to commit a man for disobedience of it, you have to have an order specifying the time within which the possession has to be given. [He referred to Ord 42, r 2(2) and Ord 45, r 6(2) and continued] ... In the present case the order of 15 May 1974 did specify the time, namely possession *j*   by 12 June 1974. That was a simple order and non-compliance with it was a single offence, and he cannot be punished twice for it. That is sufficient to decide this case.'

Lawton LJ in his judgment drew attention to the fact that contempt of court was a common law misdemeanour. He said:

'If a man is being dealt with for a common law misdemeanour, it is always relevant to see whether time is a necessary averment in the charge. The inquiry which we have had in this court has established that, if there is going to be an order for committal for breach of an order of the court, that order must have had a time specified in it. There was a time in the relevant order in this case. It follows that the reference to 12 June was a relevant averment. It also follows that, had there been a prosecution for a common law misdemeanour of contempt of court, on all subsequent occasions Mr Danchevsky would have been entitled to plead autrefois convict. It follows therefore that there is no power in the county court to do that which a criminal court could not have done.'

To the same effect was Goff LJ's judgment, where he said:

'... [the] order for breach of which Mr Danchevsky was committed was an order to deliver up possession on a fixed date and was broken once and for all when he failed to deliver up possession on that date. It was not an order requiring a continuance of acts or a continuance of forbearances, so that his returning to possession and remaining in possession was not a new breach or a new offence.'

It seems to me that the principle in that case, which has been recognised in other cases in the Court of Appeal including *Lamb v Lamb* [1984] FLR 278, also applies in this case.

The order of District Judge Campbell on 21 October 1994 which I have already recited was that: 'The Petitioner do within 7 days from the date of this order ... deliver to the Respondent all her belongings.' That order was not complied with, and it was a single breach. It seems to me that it is quite plain that there was no power in the court to commit Mr Jalal again on 23 July.

I would conclude by drawing attention to the fact that Borrie and Lowe *The Law of Contempt* (3rd edn, 1996) p 630, n 15, in a passage dealing with the case of an offender who repeatedly commits contempt, states:

'If [the strategy of seeking increasingly longer sentences] is adopted care should be taken that a fresh order is made on each occasion lest a plea of autrefois convict is raised ...'

Reference is made in the note to the decision in *Danchevsky v Danchevsky (No 2)*, to which I have just referred.

I would add only this. It seems from the quick reading I have been able to make of the affidavits that this is a very unhappy dispute between persons who were formerly married. There is a difference of view as to who owns which pieces of property. Some of it may have been given at the time of the marriage. I understand from what counsel for Mr Jalal has told us, that Mr Jalal would say that he has none of the remaining property in respect of which the order was made. One would therefore hope that, before any further steps are taken to commit this man to prison, every other way of dealing with the matter should be explored. It may be that other methods of execution can be considered.

I have already noted the letter from the medical officer at the prison. We have no information whatever as to Mr Jalal's present state of health, but it does seem to me that, where people belong to the same community, it is unfortunate that this dispute should end up with Mr Jalal being committed to prison for as long a period as six months.

a   For the reasons which I have endeavoured to outline, I would allow this appeal.

WARD LJ. The learned judge did not have the benefit of the guidance in the authorities to which Mr Pressdee today draws our attention. Even deference to as careful and as experienced a judge as Judge Harold Wilson QC does not require

b   my saying more than that I entirely agree with the reasons given by Neill LJ. I too would allow this appeal.

THORPE LJ. I agree with all that Neill and Ward LJJ have said, particularly Neill LJ's postscript as to the future. The reality is that, following the delivery up on 28 October 1994, it is asserted that there are 62 items of property that are still to

c   be delivered in order to achieve complete compliance with the order of 10 August 1994. That order contained a provision for application as to enforcement. The subsequent order of 21 October 1994 resulted from such an application.

     In these circumstances where a respondent is reluctant to comply with an order, for whatever reason, it is so easy to seize upon assertions such as: the

d   property has been lost; the property has been destroyed; I no longer have those items of clothing etc. Those issues arc in practice almost impossible to resolve through the litigation process. It seems to me manifest that it is open to Mrs Kumari to return to the court under the liberty to apply as to enforcement, and to make an application in relation to the delivery up, not of the chattels, but of their money's worth as quantified by the judge on the last occasion. It seems to

e   me that any attempt to continue to enforce through the method of committal is unlikely to produce any practical benefit to either party.

Appeal allowed.

                                                    Paul Magrath Esq   Barrister.

Chief Adjudication Officer and another v Quinn and another

Chief Adjudication Officer and another v Gibbon

HOUSE OF LORDS

LORD KEITH OF KINKEL, LORD MUSTILL, LORD SLYNN OF HADLEY, LORD NICHOLLS OF BIRKENHEAD AND LORD HOPE OF CRAIGHEAD

25, 26, 27 MARCH, 24 JULY 1996

Social security – Income support – Person in need of care and attention – Person in residential accommodation provided by local authority – Accommodation transferred to voluntary organisation – Status of accommodation changed to residential care home – Applicants staying in accommodation but claiming income support – Whether applicants entitled to income support at higher rate applicable to persons in residential care homes – National Assistance Act 1948, ss 21(1), 26 – Income Support (General) Regulations 1987, reg 21, Sch 4, para 6(1).

In two separate appeals the question arose whether a claimant in need of care and attention, who remained in residential accommodation formerly managed by a local authority under Pt III of the National Assistance Act 1948 after the management of that accommodation was transferred to a voluntary organisation, was entitled to income support under the Social Security Act 1986 at the rate payable to claimants in 'residential accommodation' provided by a local authority or at the higher rate payable to claimants in a 'residential care home'. Regulation 19(1) of and para 6(1)[a] of Pt I of Sch 4 to the Income Support (General) Regulations 1987 provided for the payment of income support at a higher rate to eligible aged or infirm persons whose income did not exceed a certain amount and who were accommodated in a 'residential care home', being a home registered under the Registered Homes Act 1984. However, under reg 21[b] of and para 13(1) of Sch 7 to the 1987 regulations eligible aged or infirm persons in need of care and attention who were accommodated in 'residential accommodation' by a local authority pursuant to its duty under s 21(1)[c] of the 1948 Act to provide such accommodation were entitled to income support at a reduced rate. Section 26[d] of the 1948 Act provided that a local authority could fulfil its duty under s 21 by making arrangements for a voluntary organisation to provide residential accommodation for aged or infirm persons in need of care and attention provided that such arrangements made provision for the local authority to make payments to the voluntary organisation in respect of the accommodation provided at such rates as were determined by or under the arrangements. The two applicants lived in residential accommodation provided by their respective local authorities under s 21 of the 1948 Act. In both cases the local authority leased and transferred the management of the homes where the applicants resided to voluntary

---

a Paragraph 6(1), so far as material, is set out at p 75 *j*, post
b Regulation 21, so far as material, is set out at p 76 *b*, post
c Section 21, so far as material, is set out at p 76 *d e*, post
d Section 26, so far as material, is set out at p 76 *j* to p 77 *b*, post

a organisations. In the first case, the local authority transferred the home under a management agreement whereby it provided financial support as a contribution to the voluntary organisation's management and expenses. In the second case, the local authority and the voluntary organisation agreed to co-operate in providing care and attention for elderly persons with the voluntary organisation being responsible for care and management and residents being charged weekly

b sums equal to the residential care allowances paid by the Department of Social Security. In both cases the homes were registered under the 1984 Act. The applicants voluntarily decided to continue staying in their respective homes on the understanding that there would be no change in their conditions. They both applied for income support but in both cases the adjudication officer decided that the applicants were still living in 'residential accommodation' and therefore only

c entitled to income support at the lower rate. Both applicants appealed to the social security appeal tribunal, which allowed one appeal but dismissed the other. On appeal, the social security commissioner found in favour of both applicants, holding, in one case, that the applicant was not in residential accommodation and, in the other case, that the applicant was in a residential care home. The

d Court of Appeal dismissed appeals by the Chief Adjudication Officer and the Secretary of State, who then appealed to the House of Lords.

Held – Since s 26(2) of the 1948 Act provided in unqualified terms that a residential home managed by a local authority under Pt III of the Act could be

e transferred to a voluntary organisation in fulfilment of the local authority's obligations under s 21 of the 1948 Act to provide 'residential accommodation' for aged or infirm persons who were in need of care and attention only if the arrangements made for the transfer provided for the local authority to make payments to the voluntary organisation at rates determined by or under the arrangements, it followed that if the arrangements did not include a provision

f which satisfied s 26(2) then 'residential accommodation' within the meaning of Pt III was not provided and the higher rate of income support was payable. In the applicants' cases there was no evidence of any arrangement between the local authority and the voluntary organisation for payments to be made by the local authority to the voluntary organisation at rates determined by or under the

g arrangement and therefore, on the transfer of their homes to the voluntary organisation, the applicants were no longer in the care of the local authority and fell to be treated like other persons in residential care homes. As such, they were entitled to the higher rate of income support payable to persons in residential care homes. The appeals would therefore be dismissed (see p 74 *j* to p 75 *a*, p 79 *j* to

h p 80 *h*, p 81 *a* to *c* and p 82 *b* to *d*, post).

Notes

For the provision of accommodation by a local authority, see 33 *Halsbury's Laws* (4th edn) paras 919–926.

j For the National Assistance Act 1948, ss 21, 26, see 40 *Halsbury's Statutes* (4th edn) 23, 30.

Case referred to in opinions

Montreal Street Rly Co v Normandin [1917] AC 170, PC.

Appeals

a

Chief Adjudication Officer and anor v Quinn and anor

The appellants, the Chief Adjudication Officer and the Secretary of State for
Social Security, appealed pursuant to leave granted on 17 October 1994 by the
Appeal Committee from the decision of the Court of Appeal (Sir Thomas
Bingham MR, McCowan and Hirst LJJ) ([1994] CA Transcript 439) delivered on   b
15 April 1994 dismissing the appellants' appeal from the decision of the social
security commissioner, Mr J Mitchell, dated 22 December 1992 allowing the
appeal of the claimant, Jane Harris, from the decision of the Bournemouth Social
Security Appeal Tribunal delivered on 6 November 1991 dismissing her appeal
from the decision of the adjudication officer that she was entitled to income
support but only on the basis that she was in residential accommodation at the   c
home run by the Dorset Trust, a voluntary organisation, and transferred to the
trust by the second respondent, Dorset County Council. The first respondent,
Douglas Quinn, was appointed to proceed with the claim on behalf of the
claimant following her death on 5 July 1993. The facts are set out in the opinion
of Lord Slynn of Hadley.

d

Chief Adjudication Officer and anor v Gibbon

The appellants, the Chief Adjudication Officer and the Secretary of State for
Social Security, appealed pursuant to leave granted on 17 October 1994 by the
Appeal Committee from the decision of the Court of Appeal (Sir Thomas   e
Bingham MR, McCowan and Hirst LJJ) ([1994] CA Transcript 439) delivered on
15 April 1994 dismissing the appellants' appeals from the decision of the social
security commissioner, Mr J Mitchell, dated 15 July 1993 dismissing the
adjudication officer's appeal from the decision of the Workington Social Security
Appeal Tribunal delivered on 25 March 1992 allowing the appeal of the
respondent claimant, Freda Gibbon, a resident of Southlands residential home   f
formerly owned and managed by the Cumbria County Council and later leased
to the Westfield Housing Association, a voluntary organisation, from the
decision of the adjudication officer refusing her claim for income support. The
facts are set out in the opinion of Lord Slynn of Hadley.

g

John Howell QC (instructed by the *Solicitor to the Department of Health and Social
    Security*) for the Chief Adjudication Officer and the Secretary of State.
Duncan Ouseley QC and Richard McManus (instructed by *Lawrence Graham*, acting
    also as agents for *David Jenkins*, Dorchester) for the respondents, Mr Quinn and
    Dorset County Council, in the first appeal.   h
Genevra Caws QC and James Richardson (instructed by *Curwen & Co*,
    Cockermouth) for the respondent, Mrs Gibbon, in the second appeal.

Their Lordships took time for consideration.

j

24 July 1996. The following opinions were delivered.

LORD KEITH OF KINKEL. My Lords, for the reasons given in the speech to be
delivered by my noble and learned friend Lord Slynn of Hadley, which I have
read in draft and with which I agree, I would dismiss these appeals.

LORD MUSTILL. My Lords, I have had the advantage of reading in draft the
a speech prepared by my noble and learned friend Lord Slynn of Hadley. For the
reasons he gives I too would dismiss both appeals.

LORD SLYNN OF HADLEY. My Lords, the question which arises on these two
appeals is as to how much 'income support' under the Social Security Act 1986
b each claimant was entitled. Was it during the relevant periods a weekly sum of
£52 or was it £171·40?

Such a difference at first glance suggests that the claimants' standard of living
would have been substantially affected by the answer. In fact it was not; the
essential question, as the social security commissioner found, was whether the
maintenance of the two claimants was to be provided by central or local funds.

c The difficulty of applying the social security legislation, however, is once again
borne out by the fact that in Miss Harris's case the adjudication officer and the
social security appeal tribunal decided against her; the social security
commissioner and the Court of Appeal decided in her favour. In Mrs Gibbon's
case, the adjudication officer decided against her; the tribunal, the commissioner
d and the Court of Appeal decided in her favour. The Chief Adjudication Officer
and the Secretary of State for Social Security now seek to reverse the decision of
the Court of Appeal in each case.

By s 20(3) of the 1986 Act a person in Great Britain was entitled to income
support if, inter alia, he was over the age of 18 and he had no income or his
income did not exceed 'the applicable amount'. If he had no income he received
e the applicable amount; if he had income he got the difference between that
income and the applicable amount, the latter to be prescribed by regulations
(s 22(1) of the 1986 Act).

By s 22 of the National Assistance Act 1948 persons for whom accommodation
was provided under that Part of the Act were required to pay the standard rate
f fixed by the authority managing the premises in which it was provided. If the
person satisfied the local authority that he could not pay the standard rate, a
lower rate was to be fixed.

By the Income Support (General) Regulations 1987, SI 1987/1967, made
pursuant to the 1986 Act, a distinction was drawn between persons in 'a
residential care home' and those in 'residential accommodation'.

g By reg 19(3), as amended by reg 9(b)(i) of the Income Support (General)
Amendment Regulations 1988, SI 1988/663, a 'residential care home' includes,
inter alia, an establishment which is required to be, and is, registered under Pt I
of the Registered Homes Act 1984. By reg 19(1), as amended by reg 9(a) of the
1988 regulations, subject to reductions as prescribed in reg 19(2), for a claimant
h living in such a residential care home the applicable weekly amount (subject to
prescribed exceptions) fell to be calculated in accordance with Pt I of Sch 4 to the
regulations. By para 1 of that Part the applicable amount was to be the weekly
charge for the accommodation, including all meals and services provided for him,
subject to the maximum amount determined in accordance with para 5. That
j paragraph takes one to para 6(1) (as substituted by para 6(1)(a) of Pt I of Sch 5 to
the Social Security Benefits Up-rating Order 1991, SI 1991/503) in the present
case. Subject to special provisions which are not relevant—

> 'where the accommodation provided for the claimant is a residential care
> home for persons in need of personal care by virtue of—(a) old age, the
> appropriate amount shall be [at the relevant time] £160 per week ...'

In addition, by virtue of para 1(b) of Pt I of Sch 4, there is to be added a weekly *a* amount for personal expenses determined in accordance with para 13 of that Part. At the relevant time para 13 prescribed for the claimant a weekly sum of £11·40.

Regulation 21 deals with special cases where the applicable amount is to be reduced. These included by virtue of para 13(1) of Sch 7 'persons in residential accommodation', which is defined in reg 21(3) as meaning—

> 'accommodation for a person whose stay in the accommodation has *b* become other than temporary which is accommodation provided—(a) under sections 21 to 24 and 26 of the National Assistance Act 1948 (provision of accommodation) ...'

For a single claimant in such residential accommodation in addition to *c* amounts which were due under other regulations, the amount of income support was prescribed at the relevant time as being £52 of which £41·60 was in respect of the cost of residential accommodation and £10·40 for personal expenses.

The question is thus whether the two claimants were in accommodation provided under ss 21 to 24 or 26 of the 1948 Act.

By s 21(1) of the 1948 Act, as amended by s 195(6) of and para 2(1) of Sch 23 to *d* the Local Government Act 1972:

> '... a local authority may with the approval of the Secretary of State, and to such extent as he may direct, shall make arrangements for providing—(a) residential accommodation for persons aged eighteen or over who by reason of age, infirmity or any other circumstances are in need of care and attention *e* which is not otherwise available to them ...'

By Department of Health and Social Security circular LAC 13/74 the Secretary of State empowered local authorities to provide accommodation themselves for persons urgently needing it who by reason of age needed care and attention not otherwise available to them. He also authorised the provision of accommodation *f* by such an authority in premises managed by another local authority or pursuant to arrangements in accordance with s 26 of the 1948 Act with a person registered in respect of an old person's home for the provision of accommodation. The Secretary of State also directed local authorities to provide accommodation themselves or in accordance with arrangements for the provision of *g* accommodation in premises managed by another local authority. The local authority empowered to provide residential accommodation is the local authority in whose area the person in question is ordinarily resident and a lower rate may be determined for those unable to pay the standard figure prescribed.

The interpretation of s 26 is the crux of the matter. By that section, as amended *h* by s 44 of the Health Services and Public Health Act 1968 and s 195(6) of and para 2(3) of Sch 23 to the 1972 Act, arrangements under s 21 may include provision by which—

> '(1) ... a local authority—(a) may make, in lieu or in supplementation of the provision, in premises managed by them or another local authority, of *j* accommodation of the kind mentioned in paragraph (a) of subsection (1) of the said section twenty-one, arrangements—(i) with a voluntary organisation managing any premises, for the provision in those premises of accommodation of that kind ... (2) Any arrangements made by virtue of subsection (1) of this section shall provide for the making by the local authority to the other party thereto of payments in respect of the

a
accommodation provided at such rates as may be determined by or under the arrangements. (3) A person for whom accommodation is provided under any such arrangements shall, in lieu of being liable to make payment therefor in accordance with section twenty-two of this Act, refund to the local authority any payments made in respect of him under the last foregoing subsection ...'

b
In 1986 Miss Harris, who was born in 1909, went to live at Heathlands, which was owned by the Dorset County Council, since it was clear that she was in need of care and attention not otherwise available to her. This accommodation was provided pursuant to s 21(4) in Pt III of the 1948 Act. With effect from 28 March 1991 the Dorset County Council granted leases of Heathlands and 17 other of
c their homes providing Pt III accommodation to the Dorset Trust, a voluntary organisation, not under the control of the county council, whose homes are registered under the 1984 Act. A management agreement was made between the county council and the trust which provided for financial support as a contribution to the management and expenses of the trust. Miss Harris and other
d residents of Heathlands were asked whether they would like to stay there under the new arrangement or whether they would like to transfer to one of the homes being retained by the Dorset County Council. Residents were told that their conditions would not change, that they would not have to pay any more and that they could stay as long as they liked at Heathlands if they chose to stay, but that if that they wanted to move to another home so as to remain in the care of the
e Dorset County Council every effort would be made to find a suitable vacancy. Miss Harris through her niece chose, like most other residents, to stay in the home to which she had become accustomed. Her claim for income support, accepted by the adjudication officer on 14 June 1991, was on the basis that under the new arrangements following the transfer of the home she was in 'residential accommodation' and therefore entitled to income support of £32·00 a week.
f That decision was upheld by the social security appeal tribunal on 6 November 1991 on the basis that there were arrangements under s 26 of the 1948 Act which meant that she was in 'residential accommodation'. The social security commissioner held that there were no arrangements under s 26 of the 1948 Act and that she was not in residential accommodation within the meaning of the
g Act.
Mrs Gibbon in 1990 went to live in Southlands, a home providing accommodation under s 21(4) of the 1948 Act, which was owned and managed by the Cumbria County Council, since she was in need of care and attention which was not otherwise available to her.

h
On 11 July 1991 the Cumbria County Council granted a lease of Southlands to the Westfield Housing Association (Westfield), a voluntary organisation, which on the same day became registered as a residential care home under the 1984 Act. An agreement was made between the Cumbria County Council and Westfield under which it was recited that the two parties would co-operate in providing
j care and attention for elderly persons. Westfield undertook to be fully responsible for the care and management of the property and to levy a weekly charge to residents of an amount at least equal to the residential care allowances paid by the Department of Social Security. The council agreed to meet one-quarter of the deficit difference between the amount shown in the budget as collectable for residents and the amount shown in the budget as expendable on the provision of services. The parties are agreed that Westfield also entered into

an agreement with the county council whereby the employees of the authority were to continue to work at Southlands in consideration of a payment by the *a* association to the authority. On 11 July 1991 Mrs Gibbon was told that a transfer would have no direct effect on the services which she would receive, that there would be a weekly charge to residents of £160 and to enable her to pay this she would need to apply for income support. She was told that she could choose between staying at Southlands and moving to another home in the charge of the *b* county council. Mrs Gibbon indicated in a letter of 10 July 1991 that she wished—

> 'to claim income support from Thursday, 11 July because Southlands Home for the Elderly will be owned and run by Westfield from that day. I have chosen to stay here rather than to move to another home run by the county council. The new weekly charge will be £160 and I do not think I *c* have the means to pay all this myself.'

The adjudication officer decided on 31 October 1991 that the applicable amount in her case was £52 a week since she was living in 'residential accommodation', but that given her other resources she was not entitled to income support. The social security appeal tribunal on 25 March 1992 allowed *d* her appeal on the ground that she was in a residential care home and that decision was upheld by the social security commissioner, so that her income support fell to be assessed under reg 19 of and Sch 4 to the 1987 Regulations.

The Court of Appeal agreed with the social security commissioner in both cases.

The appellants stress that the object of the regime established by the 1948 Act *e* is to limit the liability of persons for whom accommodation is provided to an inclusive charge which is itself defined by what they can afford to pay. Thus, for those in accommodation provided by the responsible local authority itself, the standard payment is due subject to a reduction if the person concerned cannot pay that amount. If accommodation is provided under arrangements made with *f* another local authority, the person concerned pays the authority managing it the appropriate charge based on his ability to pay and the managing authority accounts for the sums received to the authority making the arrangements. So it is said in the appellants' case that where accommodation is arranged in premises managed by others the arrangements under s 26 are to—

> 'provide for the making by the local authority to the person managing the *g* premises of payments in respect of the accommodation at such rates as may be determined by or under the arrangements and any individual for whom accommodation is provided under such arrangements is liable to refund to the local authority any payments they have agreed to make to the person *h* providing the accommodation or such part as they are able to pay calculated on the basis of the formula provided for in section 22 of the National Assistance Act 1948: see section 26(2)–(4) of the Act.'

The appellants accept that the relevant question is whether the claimants were in residential accommodation provided pursuant to s 26; the answer to that *j* question, it is said, depends on whether after the transfer of the management of the accommodation the authority had made arrangements for the provision of accommodation of the kind mentioned in s 21(1)(a) of the 1948 Act.

The appellants divide up this question into two parts. First they ask: had in fact arrangements been made pursuant to which the two claimants remained in the homes in which they had been living? It is said that in both cases it is plain that

a   they had. Both claimants were given the option of staying where they were or of
moving to one of the council's remaining homes. Such an option could only have
been offered if the local authority itself had made the arrangements and thereby
given the assurance that the level of care, the security and the charges would
continue as they had been previously. There is nothing to suggest that either
Miss Harris or Mrs Gibbon made any arrangements individually.

b   That, according to the appellants, is enough to establish that s 26 arrangements
had been made. It follows that the claimants were entitled only to the lower rate
of income support and Mrs Gibbon would receive nothing because of her other
income. The fact that there was no provision in such arrangements that the local
authority should make to the housing associations payments in respect of the
accommodation in accordance with sub-s (2) was not fatal to the existence of a
c   valid s 26 arrangement. If it were otherwise it is said in the appellants' case that
local authorities would have—

> 'absolved themselves from their own financial responsibilities to meet that
> part of the cost of accommodation which an individual is unable to meet and
> have transferred them to the national taxpayer by virtue of their own
d   > unlawful arrangements.'

Whether or not a failure to comply with statutory requirements means that what
has been done is devoid of legal effect depends on the intention of Parliament (see
Montreal Street Rly Co v Normandin [1917] AC 170 at 174–175).
      For my part I do not think that the right approach to s 26 is to ask first whether
e   in fact arrangements have been made for persons in need of care to be looked
after by a voluntary organisation and then to ask incidentally whether those
arrangements have provided for payments to be made by the local authority to
the other party, on the basis that if they have not the Secretary of State has the
remedy 'simply to order the authority to make arrangements which comply with
f   the statutory requirements within a reasonable time' (as stated in the appellants'
case). By virtue of s 21(5) the 1948 Act accommodation provided under Pt III of
the Act is to mean 'accommodation provided in accordance with this and the five
next following sections'. That includes s 26. By s 26(1) arrangements under s 21
for the provision of accommodation arrangements clearly include arrangements
between the local authority and a voluntary organisation managing any premises
g   to provide such accommodation, but s 26(2) provides in unqualified terms that—

> 'arrangements made by virtue of subsection (1) of this section shall provide
> for the making by the local authority to the other party thereto of payments
> in respect of the accommodation provided at such rates as may be
h   > determined by or under the arrangements.'

Moreover, the person for whom accommodation is provided under any such
arrangements must refund to the local authority any payments made in respect
of the last foregoing subsection, in lieu of his being liable to make payment for
the accommodation in accordance with s 22 of the Act.
j   This is a separate scheme from that which operates when the local authority
itself provides the accommodation. In my opinion arrangements made in order
to qualify as the provision of Pt III accommodation under s 26 must include a
provision for payments to be made by the local authority to the voluntary
organisation at the rates determined by or under the arrangements. Subsection
(2) makes it plain that this provision is an integral and a necessary part of the
arrangements referred to in sub-s (1). If the arrangements do not include a

provision to satisfy sub-s (2), then residential accommodation within the meaning
of Pt III is not provided and the higher rate of income support is payable.   *a*

This seems to me to result not just from the plain meaning of the words of
sub-s (2) but also from practical necessity. The voluntary organisation needs to
know how much money is to be made available to it pursuant to the
arrangements so that it can be sure that the accommodation can be adequately
provided. The person for whom the accommodation is provided must know   *b*
how much he will receive under the arrangements (which is to be refunded to the
local authority) and whether or not he needs, pursuant to the proviso to s 26(3),
to ask for the amount to be reduced.

It has been suggested that s 26(2) is really no different from s 26(5), which
empowers the local authority to enter and inspect premises where
accommodation is being provided under sub-s (1) in accordance with   *c*
arrangements made by a local authority. This cannot be accepted. The
arrangements under sub-s (1) are intended to be made before the accommodation
is provided; sub-s (5) gives power to enter and inspect the premises after both
sub-s (1) arrangements (including the requirements of sub-s (2)) have been made
and the accommodation has been made available.   *d*

The intention of sub-s (2), in my view, is that rates should be laid down which
are enforceable by either party. The rates are to be agreed between the two
parties to the arrangement. If such a provision is not included in the
arrangements I do not see how it can be imposed either by order of the court or
direction of the minister. The absence otherwise of any power to impose or
enforce the rate to be paid indicates that the plain meaning of the words is the   *e*
right one and that to have valid s 26 arrangements a clause satisfying s 26(2) has
to be included. The arrangement or scheme under which persons are to be
accommodated by the voluntary organisation is intended to be agreed as a
composite whole.

In the case of Miss Harris it is quite impossible to say that there is any evidence   *f*
of any arrangement which complies with s 26(2). She was clearly accommodated
before the transfer of the home to the Dorset Trust in accordance with s 21(4) of
the 1948 Act. Dorset Trust took a lease of the house for 25 years at a full market
rent. It employed its own staff and as a registered home it was independent of the
council. I do not think, as the appellants have contended, that it is an irresistible
inference that financial arrangements had already been made; even if some   *g*
financial arrangements might be inferred, they could only be in general terms
that there was to be some payment. That is not enough to satisfy s 26(2).

Dorset Trust's contention that there is no s 26 arrangement, that Miss Harris
became wholly outside the care of the Dorset County Council and that she fell to
be treated like other persons in a residential care home (as it seems are persons   *h*
admitted subsequently to Southlands after the transfer) is in my view to be
accepted.

In Mrs Gibbon's case there was an agreement between the Cumbria County
Council dated 11 July 1991 which dealt with the framework of the housing
association's future operation and management including some financial and   *j*
monetary provision.

That agreement recites certain powers which the council had to provide or to
assist in the provision of accommodation under a number of statutes including
the 1948 Act, although s 26 of the 1948 Act is not mentioned. The agreement
itself is recited to be one of co-operating and providing care and attention. The
management of the home was, however, to be the full responsibility of the

a association. By cl 5 of the agreement the association was to levy a charge to residents of an amount at least equal to the residential care allowance paid from time to time by the Department of Social Security. The council agreed to pay one quarter of the deficit shown in the budget as collectible from residents and the amount shown in the budget as expendable on the provision of services but subject to an annual limit. The accommodation provided was to be 'available for *b* letting to frailer aged persons of limited means'.

These arrangements seem to me to be inconsistent with the scheme for payment and refund set out in s 26(2) and (3) of the 1948 Act and to lay down provisions which are more akin to an arrangement between a client and a home in the private sector even though in other ways rights and obligations between the parties to the agreement were included in the framework agreement.

c   The claimants have referred to a number of other statutory provisions under which it is said that the local authority could have made the arrangements which it did. Thus by s 45 of the 1968 Act a local authority may, or if directed must, make arrangements for promoting the welfare of old people. By s 65 of the same Act authorities are empowered to give assistance by way of grants or loans for the *d* provision of accommodation similar to that provided by the local authority under Pt III of the 1948 Act. By s 58 of the Housing Associations Act 1985 a local authority may assist a housing association by way of grants or loans. Section 123 of the 1972 Act permits the disposal of surplus land.

Since I, for my part, am quite satisfied that the arrangements made in these two cases did not constitute the provision of residential accommodation within the *e* meaning of Pt III of the 1948 Act, it does not seem to me to be necessary to consider whether any of these other statutory provisions gave the two local authorities power to do what they did. On the basis that these were not s 26 arrangements the vires of what was done has not been put in issue.

On the basis that this was clearly not a s 26 arrangement, it is not strictly *f* necessary to decide the question raised by the commissioner and adverted to by Hirst LJ in the Court of Appeal as to whether once the claimants passed into the care of the housing associations they were no longer in need of the local authority's protection since care and attention acquired by them were 'otherwise available'. However, since the matter has been discussed, I indicate briefly my *g* view on this issue as it arises in the present context. If there had been a s 26 arrangement then, by virtue of s 21(5), residential accommodation would have been provided under statutory arrangements made by the local authority; as there was no such statutory arrangement but Miss Harris and Mrs Gibbon were cared for by the two housing associations, care and attention were otherwise available. If that accommodation no longer became available, or if they became *h* unsuitable for it or it for them, then it might be that they once again were in need of care and attention which was not otherwise available.

There has been some discussion also as to the effect of the Income Support (General) Amendment (No 5) Regulations 1991, SI 1991/1656. This amended para 21 of the 1987 general regulations by providing in reg 2(2) a new paragraph:

j
'(3A) Where on or after 12th August 1991 a person is in, or only temporarily absent from, residential accommodation within the meaning of paragraph (3) and that accommodation subsequently becomes a residential care home within the meaning of regulation 19 (applicable amounts for persons in residential care and nursing homes) that person shall continue to be treated as being in residential accommodation within the meaning of

paragraph (3) if, and for so long as, he remains in the same accommodation and the local authority is under a duty to provide or make arrangements for *a* providing accommodation for that person.'

It is argued on the one hand that this is merely declaratory of the law and, on the other hand, that it changes the law. In any event it does not seem to me that the wording of the amendment is of any assistance in deciding the issue in the present case. On the view to which I have come it did make a change in the law. *b*

It follows that in my opinion the social security commissioner and the Court of Appeal were right to hold that there was no s 26 arrangement in either case and that the higher level of income support fell to be paid. I would dismiss both appeals.

c

LORD NICHOLLS OF BIRKENHEAD. My Lords, I have had the advantage of reading in draft the speech of my noble and learned friend Lord Slynn of Hadley and for the reasons he gives I too would dismiss both appeals.

LORD HOPE OF CRAIGHEAD. My Lords, I have had the advantage of reading in draft the speech of my noble and learned friend Lord Slynn of Hadley. I also *d* would dismiss these appeals for the reasons which he has given.

Appeals dismissed.

Celia Fox   Barrister.   *e*

a # Steane and another v Chief Adjudication Officer and another

HOUSE OF LORDS

b LORD KEITH OF KINKEL, LORD MUSTILL, LORD SLYNN OF HADLEY, LORD NICHOLLS OF BIRKENHEAD AND LORD HOPE OF CRAIGHEAD

26, 27 MARCH, 24 JULY 1996

Social security – Attendance allowance – Entitlement – Person in need of care and attention – Person in residential accommodation provided by local authority –
c *Accommodation transferred to voluntary organisation – Status of accommodation changed to residential care home – Applicant staying in accommodation but claiming attendance allowance – Whether applicant entitled to attendance allowance – Whether cost of applicant's accommodation could be borne out of public or local funds – National Assistance Act 1948, ss 21(1), 26 – National Health Service Act 1977, Sch 8, para 2(1)*
d *– Social Security (Attendance Allowance) Amendment (No 3) Regulations 1983, reg 4(1) – Social Security (Attendance Allowance) Regulations 1991, reg 7(3).*

In 1988 the applicant, who was then aged 79, went to reside in a residential home owned and run by a local authority. The applicant paid for the accommodation from her own resources. Under s 21[a] of the National Assistance Act 1948 a local
e authority was under a duty to provide 'residential accommodation' for aged or infirm persons who were in need of care and attention, but s 26[b] of that Act provided that a local authority could fulfil that duty by making arrangements for a voluntary organisation to provide residential accommodation, provided that such arrangements made provision for the local authority to make payments to
f the voluntary organisation in respect of the accommodation provided at such rates as were determined by or under the arrangements. In 1991 the local authority leased the home to a voluntary organisation set up to manage residential care homes previously run by the local authority and the local health authority. The local authority agreed with the voluntary organisation that it would provide the necessary staff to run the applicant's home and that the
g voluntary organisation would pay the costs. The applicant voluntarily decided to continue staying in the home on the understanding that there would be no change in her conditions. The applicant applied for an attendance allowance under s 35[c] of the Social Security Act 1975. It was accepted that because she was

h   a   Section 21, so far as material, provides: '... a local authority may with the approval of the Secretary of State, and to such extent as he may direct shall, make arrangements for providing ... residential accommodation for persons aged eighteen or over who by reason of age, infirmity or any other circumstances are in need of care and attention which is not otherwise available to them ...'

    b   Section 26, so far as material, provides: '(1) ... arrangements under section 21 ... may include provision whereby a local authority—(a) may make, in lieu or in supplementation of the provision
j   ... of accommodation of the kind mentioned in section 21(1)(a), arrangements—(i) with a voluntary organisation managing any premises, for the provision in those premises of accommodation of that kind ...
        (2) Any arrangements made by virtue of subsection (1) of this section shall provide for the making by the local authority to the other party thereto of payment in respect of the accommodation provided at such rates as may be determined by or under the arrangements.'

    c   Section 35, so far as material, provides: 'A person shall be entitled to an attendance allowance if he ... is so severely disabled physically or mentally that, by day, he requires ... frequent attention in connection with his bodily functions, or ... prolonged or repeated attention during the night ...'

over 65 and so severely disabled that she required frequent attention during the
day or prolonged or repeated attention during the night in connection with her   *a*
bodily functions she fulfilled the physical criteria for entitlement to such an
allowance. However, the adjudication officer decided that the applicant was
disqualified by reg 4(1)^d of the Social Security (Attendance Allowance)
Amendment (No 3) Regulations 1983 from receiving an attendance allowance
because she was living in accommodation provided either by a local authority   *b*
under Pt III of the 1948 Act or in circumstances in which the cost of the
accommodation was or might be borne wholly or partly out of public or local
funds in pursuance of the 1948 Act or para 2^e of Sch 8 to the National Health
Service Act 1977, since the local authority could have provided the
accommodation and paid for it and it was irrelevant that it had chosen not to do
so. The applicant's appeal was allowed by the social security appeal tribunal and   *c*
that decision was subsequently affirmed by the social security commissioner and
the Court of Appeal. The Chief Adjudication Officer and the Secretary of State
appealed to the House of Lords.

Held – The appeal would be dismissed for the following reasons—   *d*
    (1) Since there was no provision in the arrangements made for the transfer of
the applicant's home from the local authority to the voluntary organisation for
the local authority to make payments to the voluntary organisation at rates
determined by or under the arrangements, as the claimant paid the charges for
the accommodation herself, the precondition in s 26 of the 1948 Act for
'residential accommodation' for aged or infirm persons to remain 'residential   *e*
accommodation' under Pt III of the 1948 Act notwithstanding its transfer to
another organisation had not been fulfilled and therefore the accommodation
provided by the voluntary organisation was not provided under Pt III of the 1948
Act (see p 85 *j*, p 87 *d e* and p 92 *b c*, post); *Chief Adjudication Officer v Quinn, Chief
Adjudication Officer v Gibbon* [1996] 4 All ER 72 applied.   *f*
    (2) There was no power for the cost of the applicant's accommodation to be
borne out of public or local funds under para 2 of Sch 8 to the 1977 Act, since that
provision referred to the provision of residential accommodation of persons
suffering from illness and there was no evidence that the applicant was a person
needing accommodation on the ground of illness (see p 85 *j*, p 88 *c*, p 90 *d* to *f* and
p 92 *b c*, post).   *g*
    (3) Nor was there any power under Pt III of the 1948 Act to provide the cost
of the applicant's accommodation out of local authority funds since under
s 21(1)(a) of that Act 'residential accommodation' referred to accommodation for
aged or infirm persons in need of care and attention and the applicant, if and so
long as she remained in the home and was cared for there under the   *h*
arrangements with the voluntary organisation, did not fall within the category of
persons who were in need of care and attention not otherwise available to them
(see p 85 *j*, p 90 *h j* and p 92 *b c*, post).
    Per curiam. The reference to paying 'the whole cost' in reg 7(3)^f of the Social
Security (Attendance Allowance) Regulations 1991 (replacing reg 4 of the 1983   *j*
regulations) is to be read as meaning the payment of the charge fixed for residents
in respect of their individual accommodation. Therefore, if the charge fixed for

---

d   Regulation 4(1) is set out at p 86 *d e*, post
e   Paragraph 2, so far as material, is set out at p 87 *f g*, post
f   Regulation 7, so far as material, is set out at p 91 *a*, post

a residents in respect of their individual accommodation is paid wholly by the resident, reg 7(1)(c) (replacing reg 4(1)(c) of the 1983 regulations) relating to disqualification for attendance allowance where the cost of accommodation may be borne wholly or partly out of public or local funds does not apply. If it is paid wholly or partly by others including payment out of public or local funds, then the resident is required to satisfy the other provisions of reg 7(1)(c) (see p 85 *j* and

b p 91 *j* to p 92 *c*, post).

Notes
For entitlement to attendance allowance, see 33 *Halsbury's Laws* (4th edn) para 448.

For the National Assistance Act 1948, ss 21, 26, see 40 *Halsbury's Statutes* (4th
c edn) 23, 30.

For the National Health Service Act 1977, Sch 8, see 30 *Halsbury's Statutes* (4th edn) (1991 reissue) 914.

Cases referred to in opinions
d *Chief Adjudication Officer v Kenyon* (1995) Times, 14 November, [1995] CA Transcript 1375.

Chief Adjudication Officer v Quinn, Chief Adjudication Officer v Gibbon [1996] 4 All ER 72, [1996] 1 WLR 1184, HL; *affg* [1994] CA Transcript 439.

Jones v Insurance Officer (1984) Times, 20 February, [1984] CA Transcript 60.

e **Appeal**
The Chief Adjudication Officer and the Secretary of State for Social Security appealed from the decision of the Court of Appeal (Hirst, Aldous LJJ and Forbes J) ([1995] Times, 19 December) delivered on 11 December 1995 dismissing the appellants' appeal from the decision of the social security commissioner affirming
f the decision of the social security appeal tribunal allowing the appeal of the first respondent, Vera Mary Steane, from the decision of the adjudication officer refusing her claim for attendance allowance while a resident at Elmdon, a residential care home for the elderly run by the second respondent, Islecare Ltd, a registered charity and company limited by guarantee, following its transfer from the Isle of Wight County Council to the charity. The facts are set out in the
g opinion of Lord Slynn of Hadley.

John Howell QC (instructed by the *Solicitor to the Department of Health and Social Security*) for the Chief Adjudication Officer and the Secretary of State.
Roger McCarthy (instructed by *Sharpe Pritchard*) for Mrs Steane and Islecare Ltd.

h
Their Lordships took time for consideration.

24 July 1996. The following opinions were delivered.

j **LORD KEITH OF KINKEL.** My Lords, for the reasons given in the speech to be delivered by my noble and learned friend Lord Slynn of Hadley, which I have read in draft and with which I agree, I would dismiss this appeal.

LORD MUSTILL. My Lords, I have had the advantage of reading in draft the speech prepared by my noble and learned friend Lord Slynn of Hadley. For the reasons he gives I too would dismiss this appeal.

LORD SLYNN OF HADLEY. My Lords, on 20 May 1991 Mrs Steane claimed an attendance allowance pursuant to s 35 of the Social Security Act 1975. Such an *a* allowance is payable to a person over 65 who is so severely disabled physically or mentally that, inter alia, he requires frequent attention during the day or prolonged or repeated attention during the night in connection with his bodily functions. It is common ground that Mrs Steane satisfied those conditions so as to be eligible, but for the issues raised on this appeal, to an attendance allowance *b* at the higher rate prescribed. The adjudication officer who dealt with her claim rejected it, but the social security appeal tribunal allowed her appeal and its decision in the result was upheld by the social security commissioner and by the Court of Appeal ((1995) Times, 19 December).

Regulation 4(1) of the Social Security (Attendance Allowance) Amendment (No 3) Regulations 1983, SI 1983/1741, made pursuant to s 35(6) of the 1975 Act, *c* provided that except in specified cases, including those specified in reg 4(3), attendance allowance should not be payable in respect of a person who has attained the age of 16 for any period during which that person is living in accommodation—

> '(a) provided for him in pursuance of Part III of the National Assistance Act *d* 1948, paragraph 2 of Schedule 8 to the National Health Service Act 1977, or Part IV of the Social Work (Scotland) Act 1968; or (b) provided for him in circumstances in which the cost of the accommodation is being borne wholly or partly out of public or local funds in pursuance of a Scheduled enactment; or (c) provided for him in circumstances in which the cost of the *e* accommodation may be borne wholly or partly out of public or local funds in pursuance of a Scheduled enactment.'

Regulation 4(3) provided:

> 'Paragraph (1)(c) shall not apply in respect of the following accom- modation—(a) temporary accommodation provided for the homeless; (b) *f* accommodation in such other case or class of case as the Secretary of State may direct.'

The issues raised on this appeal centre on each of the sub-paragraphs of para (1).

The first question is whether accommodation was provided for Mrs Steane in *g* pursuance of Pt III of the National Assistance Act 1948 at the relevant time.

Mrs Steane went to reside on 18 December 1988 (when she was 79 years of age) in a residential home called Elmdon which was then owned and run by the Isle of Wight County Council. She paid the full charge for her accommodation from her own resources.

In 1990 the county council was instrumental in setting up a company called *h* Islecare, limited by guarantee and a registered charity, for the purpose of managing residential care homes, including Elmdon, formerly operated by the council. An agreement was made between the council and Islecare Ltd on 21 January 1991 under which in consideration of the payment referred to therein the *j* council agreed to supply all necessary staff to enable Islecare to operate the properties referred to in the schedule to the agreement as residential care homes and Islecare undertook to pay for the staff so provided.

Before Elmdon was transferred to Islecare Mrs Steane and other residents were asked whether they would prefer to stay at Elmdon under the management of Islecare or to move to other residential accommodation which continued to be

a provided by the council. Mrs Steane was told by letter of 11 April 1991, from the county council to her son, that future charges by Islecare would have to be agreed with the county council but her placement at Elmdon would be secure and that residents who satisfy the appropriate criteria will be entitled to income support from the Department of Social Security in order to assist them in meeting their placement fees, though it was said that Mrs Steane would not satisfy the income
b support criteria by virtue of the level of her capital. She was told, however, that she would receive a personal allowance of £11·40 per week whereas if she had remained in a county council home she would only have been entitled to £10·40 and that it was highly likely that she was entitled to an attendance allowance.

Mrs Steane chose to stay at Elmdon. Whether this accommodation was from then on accommodation provided under Pt III of the 1948 Act depended on the
c proper construction of s 26 of that Act. It was accepted in the Court of Appeal that the decision in this case on that point was covered by the earlier decision of the Court of Appeal in *Chief Adjudication Officer v Quinn, Chief Adjudication Officer v Gibbon* [1994] CA Transcript 439, though the appellants contended that that decision was wrong. For the reasons given in my speech in that case ([1996] 4 All
d ER 72, [1996] 1 WLR 1184) I consider that it is an essential feature of arrangements under s 26 of the 1948 Act that sub-s (2) should be complied with and that the arrangements must 'provide for the making by the local authority to the [other party to the arrangements] of payments in respect of the accommodation provided at such rates as may be determined by or under the arrangements'.

e It is clear that no such provision was included in the arrangements made for Mrs Steane, who was to pay the Elmdon authorities the charges herself. Accordingly no accommodation was provided for her pursuant to Pt III of the 1948 Act.

Paragraph 2 of Sch 8 to the National Health Service Act 1977 is relevant in two
f ways. It is specifically referred to in reg 4(1)(a) of the 1983 regulations and it is a scheduled enactment for the purposes of reg 4(1)(c). Paragraph 2 provides:

'(1) A local social services authority may, with the Secretary of State's approval ... make arrangements for the purpose of the prevention of illness and for the care of persons suffering from illness and for the after-care of
g persons who have been suffering ...'

This provision replaced s 12 of the Health Services and Public Health Act 1968 pursuant to which two circulars had been issued by the Secretary of State. The first, Local Authority circular 19/74 dated 23 April 1974 approved the provision of residential accommodation for the purpose of the prevention of mental
h disorder or in relation to persons who are or who have been suffering from mental disorder. The second is Local Authority circular 28/74 of August 1974, by para 5 of which the Secretary of State approved the making of arrangements under s 12 of the 1968 Act for the provision of social services for the prevention of illness, the care of those suffering from illness and the aftercare of those so
j suffering, namely:

'a. For the purpose of preventing the impairment of physical or mental health, especially of children in families where such impairment is likely; for preventing the break up of such families or for assisting in their rehabilitation; b. To meet the needs of the sick, not provided for under the general approval given in Local Authority Circular 19/1974 (persons who

are under medical care or have been discharged from hospital) and the
provision of night-sitter services; [c. and d. for the provision of meals and of *a*
recuperative holidays].'

These circulars continued to have effect under the 1977 Act by virtue of para
1(1)(b) of Sch 14 to that Act.

No reliance was placed on the 1977 Act by the adjudicating officer or by him
before the social security appeal tribunal. The social security commissioner *b*
found that there was no purported exercise of the power under the 1977 Act
either before or after 10 May 1991. In the Court of Appeal the appellants asked
that the case be referred back to the commissioner for consideration of the
question as to whether the accommodation was provided for Mrs Steane because
she was ill. The Court of Appeal rejected this application. In my opinion they *c*
were plainly right to do so. True Mrs Steane had diabetes and had problems in
moving about but there was no evidence to suggest that she needed accommodation because of illness or that she had been provided with accommodation
because of illness. She had been provided with the accommodation by the
council in 1988 because of her age. She needed care and attention not otherwise
available to her because of her age. *d*

A more difficult question, however, arises under para 4(1)(c) of the 1983
regulations since para 2 of Sch 8 to the 1977 Act and Pt III of the 1948 Act are both
'scheduled enactments'.

Clearly Mrs Steane was living in accommodation provided for her, though on
the opinion which I have expressed it was not provided under either of those *e*
scheduled enactments. Was it provided 'in circumstances in which the cost of the
accommodation may be borne wholly or partly out of public or local funds in
pursuance of a Scheduled enactment'?

Apart from the present case this provision has been considered in two earlier
decisions of the Court of Appeal. In the first case, *Jones v Insurance Officer* (1984)
Times, 20 February, the applicant for an attendance allowance was until *f*
November 1974 in a home for the mentally ill conducted by the local authority.
From that date he resided at a privately owned residential home under
arrangements made by a receiver appointed by the Court of Protection. The cost
of his accommodation was met out of his own resources. He contended that he
would only be disentitled to an attendance allowance if he was in *g*
accommodation physically provided by the local authority; the department
initially contended that 'may be borne' covered the case where there was a real
possibility that there would be a subsidy from local funds although they
apparently abandoned that contention. The commissioner took the view that a
claimant was not entitled to an attendance allowance when under one of the *h*
scheduled enactments the authority had power to subsidise the cost of his
accommodation even if the authority did not in fact do so. Browne-Wilkinson LJ
said:

'Looking at the words of the section, to my mind the prima facie meaning
of them is clear. It seems to me that, on the plain meaning of the words, if *j*
the claimant is being provided by someone with accommodation and the
cost of such provision is being, or could be, met either wholly or in part out
of public funds, then the requirements of the subsection are fulfilled. Plainly
in the case of this claimant the cost of his accommodation, whatever that
may be, could have been met out of local authority funds under Sch 8, para 2,
and indeed was so met in part until November 1980. The crucial question is

a
whether the words "accommodation provided" are to be construed as limited to a case where such accommodation is provided by the local authority or whether the accommodation can be provided by anyone.'

He further held that the accommodation could be provided by anyone not just by the local authority. He concluded:

b
'I therefore reach the conclusion that the commissioner was right in his decision. The claimant is living in accommodation provided for him by a private nursing home in circumstances in which the cost of such accommodation could be, although in fact it is not, met by the local authority.'

c
The other members of the Court of Appeal agreed. The second case is *Chief Adjudication Officer v Kenyon* (1995) Times, 14 November. That was an appeal from a decision of the social security commissioner holding the applicant entitled to an attendance allowance. After some years in hospital the applicant who suffered from a mental disorder moved to live in a hostel owned, administered and funded by the Lancaster Health Authority. The same question arose as to
d
whether this accommodation was provided for her in circumstances in which the cost thereof 'may be borne wholly or partly out of public or local funds' in pursuance of para 2 of Sch 8 to the 1977 Act.

It was common ground in the Court of Appeal (though not earlier) that pursuant to para 2(1) the authority had approval for the making of arrangements
e
for the provision of residential accommodation for the care of persons suffering from the illness from which the claimant suffered and that the local authority could have borne the cost of such accommodation but that his hostel accommodation was not provided under such an arrangement.

The Chief Adjudication Officer's argument was simply that since the local authority could have provided the accommodation and paid for it, it mattered
f
not that it had not done so. The counter-argument was that since the accommodation had not been provided by the local authority it had no power to pay for it.

Simon Brown LJ, with whom other members of the Court of Appeal agreed, said:

g
'Regulation 4(1)(a) is to be regarded as confined to cases of direct public authority provision of residential accommodation, as, of course, is possible under para 2 of Sch 8 ... Regulations 4(1)(b) and 4(1)(c), however, apply where, as is also possible under para 2 of Sch 8, the local authority either pay (reg 4(1)(b)) or have the vires to pay (reg 4(1)(c)) some or all of the cost of
h
accommodation provided by a third party ... The local authority, however, does not have the vires to pay unless and until it makes arrangements for the provision of the accommodation or, once the accommodation has been provided, for its cost. That, of course, is precisely what happened in *Jones v Insurance Officer* so that that case was rightly decided. It has not, however,
j
happened here and the mere existence of para 2 of Sch 8 on the statute book is not of itself sufficient to prohibit the claim.'

The Court of Appeal in the present case distinguished *Jones*'s case from *Kenyon*'s case on the basis that, in the former case, the local authority had made arrangements for the applicant's accommodation since Mr Jones, the receiver, was the Director of Social Services for the local authority. In *Kenyon*'s case no such arrangement had been made so that the question of whether the authority had no vires to pay 'unless and until it makes arrangements for the accommodation or once the accommodation has been provided, for its cost' had to be decided. The Court of Appeal followed the test of vires laid down in *Kenyon's* case and held that in the present case no arrangements had been made by the local authority for Mrs Steane's accommodation so that they had no power to pay for her accommodation.

In my opinion, contrary to that of the Court of Appeal in the present case, there is a distinction in the interpretation adopted in *Jones's* case and in *Kenyon's* case and not simply a difference in the application of the same interpretation to the facts. In *Jones's* case it was clearly held that the power to bear the cost of accommodation out of public or local funds pursuant to a scheduled enactment was sufficient to bring reg 4(1)(c) into play and to exclude the entitlement to an attendance allowance. I agree with the interpretation in *Jones's* case. There is nothing in sub-para (c) which refers to the need for arrangements to have been made under the scheduled enactments before the exclusion applies and I cannot see that there is any necessary inference that this should be implied. The sole question is whether, as a matter of interpretation of the scheduled enactment in question, there is power to bear the cost in whole or in part out of public or local funds of accommodation in which the applicant is living.

I do not consider that in the circumstances there was power here for the residential accommodation at Elmdon to be borne out of public or local funds under para 2 of Sch 8 to the 1977 Act. I agree with the commissioner that Local Authority circular 19/74 had no application since Mrs Steane was in no way mentally disordered or in need of care to prevent mental disorder. Whether the commissioner was right to hold that there was no power to provide residential accommodation pursuant to para 5 of Local Authority circular 28/74, which was limited to meeting very specific needs arising from illness and not to meeting more general needs of residential accommodation, it does not seem to me necessary to decide since I agree with the Court of Appeal that there was no evidence, and it was not contended, that Mrs Steane was in any event a person needing accommodation on the ground of illness. If she was not, there was no power to provide it even if that paragraph is to be given a wider interpretation than that given to it by the commissioner.

The position under Pt III of the 1948 Act is different. There it seems to me that if Mrs Steane was at the relevant time a person who by reason of age was in need of care and attention which was not otherwise available to her then the authority could have made arrangements for her accommodation under s 26(1) of the 1948 Act so long as they provided for the making of payments by them to the voluntary organisation. They clearly had power to arrange the accommodation and to bear part or all of the cost. But since Mrs Steane was living at Elmdon and cared for there under the arrangements with Islecare it seems to me that she was not a person who was in need of care and attention not otherwise available to her so long as she remained there. Accordingly, it seems to me that since she did not fall within the category of persons described in s 21(1)(a) of the 1948 Act as being in need of care and attention the local authority do not have statutory power under Pt III of that Act to provide for her accommodation the cost of which could be borne out of local authority funds.

There is in any event another relevant provision. In the Social Security (Attendance Allowance) Regulations 1991, SI 1991/2740, reg 7, which came into force on 6 April 1992, replaces reg 4 of the 1983 regulations. It provides by a para (3): 'Paragraph (1)(c) shall also not apply ... (b) where the person himself pays the whole cost, and always has paid the whole cost, of the accommodation ...'

Mrs Steane paid £185 per week in 1991 for the accommodation and no doubt more in subsequent years. Before the tribunal, the commissioner and the Court of Appeal it was said that the county council made Islecare a grant of £170 per
b quarter under s 65 of the 1968 Act to assist with management and administration costs. The commissioner and the Court of Appeal both accepted that despite this grant under that Act Mrs Steane was paying and always had paid the whole cost of her accommodation and indeed it is said that before the commissioner, that the issue was not contested. The commissioner said: 'The undisputed evidence, which I accept, is that the claimant currently pays the whole cost of her
c accommodation in Elmdon and has done so continuously since she became resident there.'

The position has changed since it has now been ascertained that a much larger grant was made for the year 1991–92; it was £595,600 and in addition the county council 'rebated' the whole of the rent due to them from Islecare in respect of the
d homes which they took on. For the same year the rent rebated was £234,400 for all the homes. Comparable figures exist for the following years until 1995–96. It is not said how these figures would be apportioned to the particular home, Elmdon.

For my part Mrs Steane objecting to the point being taken at this stage I would not allow the appellants to take advantage of this point before your Lordships but
e since it has been argued I express my view upon it.

It is clear that some matters paid for by public or local funds are to be excluded from the cost of accommodation for the purpose of reg 7 of the 1991 regulations. Thus, by para (5)(c), the cost of improvements made to or furniture or equipment provided for, residential homes in respect of which a grant or payment has been
f made out of public or local funds, except where the grant or payment is of a regular or repeated nature, is not to be included in the cost of the accommodation. Nor is the cost of social and recreational activities provided outside the accommodation in respect of which grants or payments are made out of public or local funds (see also sub-para (d)).

These provisions indicate that other expenses met out of public or local funds
g are to be included in the cost of accommodation and ex-hypothesi the resident does not pay the cost of them. I do not think that the intention of this regulation was to ensure that every item of expenditure was intended to be taken into account in analysing for each resident the whole cost of his or her accommodation. If it were so it seems that a very difficult accountancy exercise
h would be involved. How should there be apportioned to a particular resident payments made for social and recreational activities inside the accommodation provided by individuals or charitable organisations? How should the value of any house or land or equipment given to the voluntary organisation for the benefit of residents be apportioned? I do not accept that if such gifts had been made so as
j to provide for elements of the accommodation the resident is automatically excluded from relying on reg 7(3)(b) of the 1991 regulations unless the cost of such activity or equipment is included in the resident's charge. If it were so a very large number of people would seem to be affected. In my opinion the reference to paying 'the whole cost' is to be read as meaning the payment of the charge fixed for residents in respect of their individual accommodation. If this is paid wholly by the resident, reg 7(1)(c) (formerly reg 4(1)(c) of the 1983 regulations)

does not apply. If it is paid wholly or partly by others including payment out of
public or local funds, then the resident is required to satisfy the other provisions   a
of reg 7(1)(c).

I would accordingly dismiss the appeal and hold that Mrs Steane was entitled
to the attendance allowance which she claims.

LORD NICHOLLS OF BIRKENHEAD. My Lords, I have had the advantage of   b
reading in draft the speech of my noble and learned friend Lord Slynn of Hadley
and for the reasons he gives I too would dismiss this appeal.

LORD HOPE OF CRAIGHEAD. My Lords, I have had the advantage of reading
in draft the speech of my noble and learned friend Lord Slynn of Hadley. I also
would dismiss this appeal for the reasons which he has given.   c

Appeal dismissed.

Celia Fox   Barrister.

a R v Secretary of State for Transport, ex parte Richmond upon Thames London Borough Council and others (No 4)

b QUEEN'S BENCH DIVISION (CROWN OFFICE LIST)

JOWITT J

19, 20, 21 FEBRUARY, 8 MARCH 1996

Air traffic – Noise nuisance – Landing and take-off – Restrictions on landing and taking
c *off to avoid, limit or mitigate noise – Secretary of State proposing new night flying*
restrictions at airports – Restrictions specifying aggregated seasonal limits –
Restrictions for summer period allowing more noise than actually experienced under
1988 restrictions – Whether Secretary of State having to specify limits for each separate
period within aggregate – Whether restrictions having to place further restraints on
d *previous noise levels – Civil Aviation Act 1982, s 78(3)(b).*

In August 1995 the Secretary of State, acting under powers conferred on him by
s 78(3)(b)[a] of the Civil Aviation Act 1982, made an order imposing new night
flight restrictions at Heathrow, Gatwick and Stansted airports for various periods
from October 1995 to 1998. The decision was in line with proposals set out in a
consultation paper issued on 9 June 1995, based on a comparison with noise levels
e in summer 1988, and imposed aggregated seasonal limits on the maximum
number of aircraft movements permitted at each airport. The Secretary of State
indicated that it was not possible to specify the maximum number of movements
in respect of each separate period to which the order applied, since the demand
for night movements varied regularly and not all such variations were
f foreseeable. The restrictions in respect of the summer periods allowed more
noise than had actually been experienced in the summer of 1988, but less noise
than had been permitted under the restrictions in force at that time. The
applicant councils, which were the local authorities for the areas around the three
airports, applied for judicial review of the Secretary of State's decision,
g contending, inter alia, that he had failed to specify the maximum number of
movements in respect of each separate period to which his order applied as
required by s 78(3)(b) and, further or in the alternative, that the power under that
section could only be used to restrict further what had gone before.

h **Held** – The application would be dismissed for the following reasons—
(1) The Secretary of State had power under s 78(3) of the 1982 Act to restrict
the total number of night aircraft movements at designated aerodromes both by
reference to individual specified periods and to the aggregation of specified
periods and the power could be lawfully exercised without specifying the
j maximum number of movements in respect of each separate period. Having
regard to the purpose of s 78(3)(b), the use of the word 'maximum' enlarged
rather than restricted the statutory power to impose limits and indicated that
periods might be aggregated so as to impose a maximum number of permitted
movements in relation to that aggregate. Since the power conferred by s 78(3)

---

a   Section 78(3), so far as material, is set out at p 101 g h, post

was clearly divisible, the Secretary of State's restrictions were within his statutory powers (see p 102 *a b e f*, post).   *a*

(2) The power under s 78(3)(b) of the 1982 Act could only be used for the purpose of avoiding, limiting or mitigating the effect of noise vibration generated by aircraft movements which, but for the exercise of the power, might not be avoided, limited or mitigated; comparisons therefore had to be drawn not between what was proposed and what had been permitted by an earlier order,   *b* but between what was proposed and what the position would have been if there had been no order. In deciding what limits should be imposed, the Secretary of State had to balance a variety of interests which, at different periods, might have to be balanced differently. It followed that the Secretary of State was entitled to relax limits which had been imposed by an earlier order (see p 103 *j* to p 104 *b*, post).   *c*

Notes

For noise and vibration on aerodromes, see 2 *Halsbury's Laws* (4th edn reissue) para 1185.

For the Civil Aviation Act 1982, s 78, see 4 *Halsbury's Statutes* (4th edn) (1987   *d* reissue) 201.

Cases referred to in judgment

Associated Provincial Picture Houses Ltd v Wednesbury Corp [1947] 2 All ER 680, [1948] 1 KB 223, CA.   *e*

Doody v Secretary of State for the Home Dept [1993] 3 All ER 92, [1994] 1 AC 531, [1993] 3 WLR 154, HL.

Liverpool Taxi Owners' Association, Re [1972] 2 All ER 589, sub nom *R v Liverpool Corp, ex p Liverpool Taxi Fleet Operators' Association* [1972] 2 QB 299, [1972] 2 WLR 1262, CA.   *f*

R v Civil Service Appeal Board, ex p Cunningham [1991] 4 All ER 310, CA.

R v Lancashire CC, ex p Huddleston [1986] 2 All ER 941, CA.

R v Secretary of State for Transport, ex p Richmond upon Thames London BC [1994] 1 All ER 577, [1994] 1 WLR 74.

R v Secretary of State for Transport, ex p Richmond upon Thames London BC (No 2)   *g* (1994) Times, 29 December.

R v Secretary of State for Transport, ex p Richmond upon Thames London BC (No 3) (1995) Times, 11 May.

Cases also cited or referred to in skeleton arguments   *h*

Padfield v Minister of Agriculture, Fisheries and Food [1968] 1 All ER 694, [1968] AC 997, HL.

R v Brixton Prison (Governor), ex p Soblen [1962] 3 All ER 641, [1963] 2 QB 243, CA.

R v Governors of Haberdashers' Aske's Hatcham College Trust, ex p Tyrell (1994) Times, 19 October.   *j*

R v Greater Manchester Coroner, ex p Tal [1984] 3 All ER 240, [1985] QB 67, DC.

R v Islington London Borough, ex p Trail [1994] 2 FCR 1261.

R v Lambeth London Borough, ex p Walters [1994] 2 FCR 336.

R v Ministry of Agriculture, Fisheries and Food, ex p Hamble (Offshore) Fisheries Ltd [1995] 2 All ER 714.

Application for judicial review

a Richmond upon Thames London Borough Council, Hillingdon London Borough Council, Hounslow London Borough Council, Surrey County Council, Windsor and Maidenhead Royal Borough Council and Slough Borough Council applied with leave granted by Sedley J on 31 October 1995 for judicial review of the decision of the Secretary of State for Transport announced in a press notice b on 16 August 1995 to introduce new night flying restrictions at Heathrow, Gatwick and Stansted Airports. The relief sought was inter alia (i) an order of certiorari to quash the decision, (ii) a declaration that the decision was unlawful for failing to specify flight numbers in accordance with s 78 of the Civil Aviation Act 1982, (iii) further or alternatively, a declaration that the decision was unlawful for being contrary to statutory purpose and/or the applicants' legitimate c expectations, (iv) further or alternatively, a declaration that the decision was unlawful for allowing noise levels during the night as a whole to increase over 1988 and/or 1993 levels, and (v) orders of mandamus and/or remission requiring the Secretary of State to reconsider his decision according to law. The facts are set out in the judgment.

d
Richard Gordon QC and *Alan MacLean* (instructed by *Richard Buxton*, Cambridge) for the applicants.
Ian Burnett and *Dinah Rose* (instructed by the *Treasury Solicitor*) for the respondent.

Cur adv vult

e
8 March 1996. The following judgment was delivered.

JOWITT J. The Secretary of State for Transport has power under s 78(3) of the Civil Aviation Act 1982 for the purpose of avoiding, limiting or mitigating the effect of noise and vibration connected with the taking-off or landing of aircraft f at aerodromes to make orders imposing restrictions on the number of occasions on which aircraft may take-off or land at an aerodrome during prescribed periods and on the type of aircraft which may take off or land during prescribed periods. It is his exercise of that power in respect of Heathrow, Gatwick and Stansted airports which gives rise to this application for judicial review, for which leave g was given by Sedley J, though the applicants' submissions have been centred on the effect of the Secretary of State's decision on Heathrow airport.

It has been the practice of the Secretary of State to make proposals as to his exercise of this power at five-yearly intervals to cover the following five years and to embark upon a non-statutory consultation in respect of them, inviting responses from interested parties. Although the consultation process occurs at h these intervals and the Secretary of State makes a decision to cover the five-year period, he does not always make a single order to cover that period.

The history of this matter begins with consultation papers published by the Secretary of State in November 1987 for the five-year period 1988–93 in respect of his proposals for future night flight restrictions at Heathrow and Gatwick j airports. Both documents were in similar terms and the Heathrow paper contained the following passage:

'The restrictions as revised in 1981 phased out night flights by the older, noisier aircraft. This, and the airlines' investment in newer and quieter aircraft, has over the years brought about an improvement in the night noise climate around [Heathrow and Gatwick]. That is a significant achievement which we must not throw away. We are therefore determined to ensure *a* that this improvement continues. We believe this can be done without seriously hampering those airlines which need to schedule services at night. *The objectives which underlie the proposals in this paper are therefore:*—to continue to improve the night noise climate so that disturbance of people asleep is further reduced; to allow airlines to produce some scheduled movements during the night periods; to enable the airport to continue to *b* offer a twenty four hour service; to encourage airlines to continue to invest in quieter, modern aircraft.' (Secretary of State's emphasis.)

These proposals were referred to in a subsequent answer to a parliamentary question, as appears from a press notice of 10 February 1988.

c
'In answer to a Parliamentary question [the Secretary of State for Transport] explained that he was determined that night noise around Gatwick should be reduced over the next five years. At Heathrow he will cut back on the number of night flights allowed, first preventing any increase in disturbance. Mr Channon explained that both decisions were in line with the proposals published in last November's consultation papers with one *d* important change: to ensure the improvement of the night noise climate at Gatwick he had undertaken to reconsider the quotas after two years if monitoring showed that the disturbance was getting worse.'

The press notice contained a quotation from the parliamentary answer (12 HC *e* Official Report (6th series) written answers cols 247–248):

'On 6th November last year I published proposals for future night restrictions at the two airports. I set out then my objective—to improve the night noise climate around the airports without imposing unnecessary restrictions on the airline industry ... At Heathrow there is less demand for *f* night flights than at Gatwick. The present quotas are not fully used and I can achieve my objectives in limiting the further growth of night movements by keeping them to their present level, as proposed in the consultation paper ... Take-offs by older, noisier aircraft will not be allowed in the small hours except for a small quota for those planned to take-off earlier which are *g* unavoidably delayed. This should achieve a considerable improvement in the noise climate during this most sensitive period.'

The present application before me concerns the consultations for period 1993–98. A consultation paper was issued in January 1993 outlining the proposals for night flights at all three airports. It pointed out that Heathrow was the world's *h* leading international airport and referred to its importance to the local and national economies. The proposals for 1993–98 were said to be made against this background. Stated objectives of the proposals were as follows. (1) To introduce common arrangements for night restrictions at all three airports. (2) To take account of the effect on UK airports and airlines of competition and *j* of the employment and economic implication of any proposals. The aim was to strike a balance between different interests and the point was made that if the restrictions on night movements are too severe profits will be affected, airfares will increase and business will be lost to continental airports. (3) Striking this balance involved balancing the wish of airlines to operate night services and the desire of local residents to sleep peacefully. (It is obvious that an acceptable

a take-off hour in one part of the world can produce an unwelcome landing time in
another part of the world and vice versa.)
The 1993 consultation paper reads:

b
'34. Since 1988, more of the quieter types of aircraft have been acquired by
airlines, improving the night noise climate. In keeping with the undertaking
given in 1988 [a reference to the answer in Parliament already referred to,
read with the 1987 consultation papers] not to allow a worsening of noise at
night, and ideally to improve it, it is proposed that the quota for the next five
years based on the new quota system should be set at a level so as to keep
overall noise levels below those in 1988. For Heathrow the proposed
summer noise quota is 7,000 and for Gatwick is 9,000. The 1988 summer

c quota for Heathrow would have been about 8,000 if calculated on the new
basis and the summer quota for Gatwick about 11,450.
35. At Stansted where no quotas have been previously set, it is proposed
to introduce a quota linked to the permitted levels of the airports'
development and on a pro rata basis with Gatwick ... On this basis the
Stansted quota will not inhibit development of the airport but it will afford

d local communities protection from night noise on the same basis as people
living around Gatwick and Heathrow. Having the same rules will prevent
Stansted from becoming a dumping ground for noisy aircraft not allowed to
operate at other airports.
36. It is proposed to continue the policy of applying separate quotas to the
winter and summer seasons with the winter season being 5/7ths of the

e summer season one. This will remove the large difference that currently
exists at Gatwick between the seasons to allow for the growth of year-round
scheduled services and more winter charter operations.'

After the consultation process was concluded the Secretary of State announced
f his decision. There were prohibitions on night take-off and landing by aircraft
which generated noise above a certain level (the measurement being known as a
quota count (QC)). No complaint has been made about this aspect of the
decision. A second aspect of control of night take-off and landing was, as
foreshadowed in the consultation paper, through the imposition of a seasonal
noise quota which was not to be exceeded.

g Also, as foreshadowed in the consultation paper, a night quota period was
introduced. This had the effect that, whereas during the period 1988–93 at
Heathrow take-offs and landings in winter between 6 am and 6.30 am on
Mondays to Saturdays and between 6 am and 8.00 am on Sundays had counted
against the movements quota, noise generated during these periods by take-offs

h and landings did not count against the new permitted noise quota. The decontrol
of these periods, save for the ban on take-off and landing of noisy aircraft, has
been the bone of contention before me. In summer during the 1988–93 period
take-offs on Sundays between 6 am and 8.00 am counted against the movements
quota. The decision similarly decontrolled this period, but this aspect of
decontrol has not been the subject of complaint before me. The summer and
j winter periods coincide each year with the operation of British Summer Time
and Greenwich Mean Time.

The decision was announced on 6 July 1993. It stated that the quota levels at
Heathrow (and Gatwick) were designed to keep overall noise levels below those
in summer 1988. In an answer to a parliamentary question the Secretary of State
said (228 HC Official Report (6th series) written answers cols 72–73):

'The central element of our consultation paper was a new system to maintain the protection offered to residents around Heathrow ... Responses to the consultation have clearly demonstrated the importance local people attach to night restrictions. My decisions have sought to maintain the essential balance between the aviation industry and local people. The aviation industry makes an important contribution to the economy and it is essential to preserve employment and business opportunities not only for the 100,000 people who work in it but also for the wider contribution it makes to the local and national economy. The new night noise regime will be tough on industry and is a challenge to them to maintain progress at introducing quieter aircraft. It will help to ensure that local people are able to enjoy a good night's sleep.'

The Secretary of State's decision resulted in a challenge by way of judicial review before Laws J by, among others, a number of the present applicants (see *R v Secretary of State for Transport, ex p Richmond upon Thames London BC* [1994] 1 All ER 577, [1994] 1 WLR 74). A number of challenges were mounted to the Secretary of State's decision, of which only one succeeded. I need not at this stage refer to any of the challenges which failed but it is necessary, as part of the history of this matter, to refer to the one which succeeded. Laws J accepted that while the Secretary of State's intention was, by means of noise quotas, to achieve the statutory purpose set by s 78(3), this was not a means which was open to him under the subsection. The power under the subsection was to place limits on the number of take-offs and landings during specified periods. Laws J granted a declaration that the decision was unlawful and therefore invalid.

The judgment of Laws J was given on 29 September 1993. There was little time left before the winter season began on 24 October. There followed a brief consultation period and a decision on 12 October 1993. This decision, while maintaining overall noise quotas for the winter season, introduced movement limits for take-offs and landings at the three airports.

Then, in November 1993, a further consultation paper was issued containing proposals for the remainder of the 1993–98 period. This referred to a new five-year policy for night restrictions as having been announced in the decision of 6 July 1993. It referred to the need for restrictions to protect local communities from excessive aircraft noise levels at night but without unnecessarily impeding the airline industry. It referred to the objectives of striking a balance which had been referred to in the consultation paper of January 1993. It also referred to other aspects of the demand for night movements not involving passengers.

The paper spoke of the outcome of that consultation exercise. One of the results was that aircraft which had been proposed to have a nil QC were now to be rated at 0·5. This had the effect of reducing the overall noise permitted by any noise quota. Movement quotas were proposed for winters and summers to apply to the periods to which noise quotas had applied in the decision overturned by Laws J but the noise quotas were retained in addition. There was therefore no change proposed to the controlled hours to which restrictions would apply. Comments were also sought on an alternative proposal, though in the event this proposal did not find its way into a decision.

The decision for the summer season of 1994 was announced on 1 February 1994. On 6 May 1994 the Secretary of State announced his decision for the balance of the five-year period. Both these decisions contained a movements quota supplemented by a noise quota and adopted the same controlled periods as a in the July 1993 decision. The Secretary of State said he had given careful consideration to the responses he had received from interested parties during the consultation process and spoke once more of his aim to strike a fair balance between the different interests so as to protect local people from excessive aircraft noise at night without unnecessarily impeding the airline industry.

b These three decisions made subsequently to the hearing before Laws J were in their turn subject to judicial review, this time before Latham J (see *R v Secretary of State for Transport, ex p Richmond upon Thames London BC (No 2)* (1994) Times, 29 December). Of the various challenges two were successful.

He accepted that properly understood the comparison made in the January 1993 consultation paper between what was proposed for the 1993–98 period and 1988 was on the basis of noise levels proposed for the new period and noise levels c extrapolated from the take-off and landing figures which had been permitted for 1988. Mr Gordon QC for the applicants does not dispute this. The learned judge went on, though, to say:

d 'There was, however, one fundamental consequence of this approach which was not referred to in the consultation paper. The summer quota for Heathrow in 1988 was 2,750 movements. That was the basis upon which the consultation paper calculated that the quota count in 1988 would have been 8,000 in comparison with the proposed quota count of 7,000. In fact the actual number of movements for summer 1988 at Heathrow was 1,800: it was accepted on behalf of the respondent that the equivalent noise quota for that number of movements would in all probability be less than 7,000. In e other words, far from there being an improvement over the noise levels experienced in 1988 the new summer quotas if fully utilised would produce an increase over the noise levels experienced in summer 1988, contrary to the apparent and expressed policy of the respondent.'

f Latham J went on to point out that the applicants' representations had been made on the basis that the proposed measure would not have the effect of permitting more noise at Heathrow than had in fact been experienced in 1988 and that there was no clear recognition in the Secretary of State's documents that he appreciated that his department's own data showed his proposed measure would have this effect. The learned judge accepted that the applicants had been misled by the g consultation paper and so had been deprived of the opportunity of making the point that the Secretary of State's proposals would be contrary to his policy, which was to effect an improvement in night-time noise levels. He went on to say:

h 'I do not consider that consultation based upon a document which can mislead in this way can be described as full and fair consultation in the sense that these applicants could legitimately expect. But the issue goes further than the consultation process. I have already said that the documents do not show that the respondent appreciated that the proposals had that effect. The press notice emphasised that noise levels would as a result of the proposals j be below those in summer 1988. That can only sensibly be read as meaning noise levels experienced in summer 1988. I can see nothing to suggest that the respondent, in making the decision in question, took into account the fact that in respect of Heathrow the proposed quotas, if fully utilised, would probably result in an increase in the noise levels experienced in summer 1988 contrary to his expressed policy.'

Latham J held that for these two reasons the decisions attacked were unlawful.
He made a declaration which expressed the unlawfulness in this way: *a*

'... (a) the failure by the [Secretary of State] to provide a full and fair
consultation process; (b) the failure by the [Secretary of State] to take into the
account the fact that the said decisions would permit movements at
Heathrow which would produce greater noise than that which was
experienced at Heathrow in summer 1988 on the basis of his own   *b*
calculations contrary to his expressed policy ...'

Following the judgment of Latham J, a further consultation paper was issued
in March 1995. It was explained that the intention of paras 34 and 35 of the
consultation paper of July 1993 was to explain that the proposal was to set noise
quotas for the new five-year period at a level which would permit less noise than   *c*
had been permitted by the movement quotas for summer 1988. The proposal
was to adhere to the restrictions in the decision of 6 May 1994. Application was
made for leave to challenge this consultation paper by way of judicial review.
The application came before Sedley J on 5 April 1995 (see *R v Secretary of State for
Transport, ex p Richmond upon Thames London BC (No 3)* (1995) Times, 11 May).   *d*

The first ground of challenge was that the Secretary of State had failed in his
consultation paper to recognise and state that he had changed or departed from
his announced policy. Sedley J concluded that despite the way in which the
Secretary of State had expressed and sought to justify his stance (of which he was
highly critical) the consultees knew what was proposed and what they had to deal   *e*
with.

Of the three other challenges it is necessary to mention only one, being a
challenge pursued in the present application. It was said that the Secretary of
State should have placed a nightly limit on aircraft movements rather than simply
a seasonal limit. Sedley J considered that until the Secretary of State had made his
decision it would be premature to canvass this point in judicial review.   *f*

He refused leave. The applicants renewed their application to the Court of
Appeal and were granted leave on the first ground to which I have referred and
on a further ground which has not been pursued before me.

The Secretary of State was anxious to have a decision in place with as little
delay as possible. Accordingly, he issued a further consultation paper and the
applicants agreed to withdraw their application and did so. The new paper was   *g*
issued on 9 June 1995. It contained no proposals to alter the night restrictions
contained in the decision of 6 May 1994. The explanation for para 34 of the
January 1993 consultation paper was repeated and it was explained that the
Secretary of State believed it to be right to compare what was allowed in summer
1988 with what it was proposed to allow for summers under the new system. He   *h*
had used as a reference point the levels of noise which it was considered
reasonable to allow in summer 1988.

The paper acknowledges that the Secretary of State's policies and the proposals
based on them allow more noise than was experienced from aircraft movements
which counted against the quotas in summer 1988 at Heathrow. This was   *j*
acknowledged by the Secretary of State to be contrary to the policy as expressed
in para 34 and went on to say:

'For avoidance of doubt, it remains the case that what is proposed to the
end of summer 1998 would *permit* less noise than was *permitted* at Heathrow
and (Gatwick) for summer 1988.' (Secretary of State's emphasis.)

a   The decision was announced on 16 August 1995 and it is this decision which is
challenged in the present application.   In announcing the decision the
Parliamentary Under-Secretary of State said that the objectives of the review
were, inter alia, to introduce common arrangements for night restrictions at the
three airports, to continue to protect local communities from excessive aircraft
noise levels at night and to ensure that the competitive influences affecting UK
b   airports and airlines and the wider employment and economic implications are
taken into account.   The overall aim was to maintain a fair balance between the
interests of local people and the airline industry, including its customers and that
the decision, when all its elements were taken together, achieved the appropriate
balance.   It represented a sharing of the benefits so far achieved by quieter aircraft
between local people and the airlines and their customers.   In response to the
c   suggestion by some of the consultees that there should be a nightly limit, the
Parliamentary Under-Secretary of State said that the fundamental practical
problem was that demand for night movements at each airport varied from night
to night and from week to week, sometimes substantially.   Not all these
variations were foreseeable. He was not satisfied it would be possible to devise a
d   workable regime of night flying restrictions incorporating a nightly limit.
          The Parliamentary Under-Secretary of State (whose decision this was because
of the proximity to Heathrow of the constituency of the new Secretary of State)
said he had given careful consideration to all the responses received to the
consultation papers of March and June 1995. He said he was unable to refer
specifically to each of them in the space of his announcement and so had arranged
e   for them all (save when the author had requested confidentiality) to be made
available for inspection.

THE CHALLENGES
          The applicants raise four challenges to the decision of 16 August 1995. Having
f   regard to the conclusions I have reached, I propose to consider first the second
and third of them, which both raise points on the construction of s 78(3)(b),
which reads as follows:

          'If the Secretary of State considers it appropriate, for the purpose of
          avoiding, limiting or mitigating the effect of noise and vibration connected
g   with the taking-off or landing of aircraft at a designated aerodrome, to
          prohibit aircraft from taking-off or landing, or limit the number of occasions
          on which they may take-off or land, at the aerodrome during certain periods,
          he may by a notice published in the prescribed manner do all or any of the
          following, that is to say ... (b) specify the maximum number of occasions on
          which aircraft of descriptions so specified may be permitted to take off or
h   land at the aerodrome (otherwise than as aforesaid) during periods so
          specified ...'

The second challenge
j   Mr Gordon, for the applicants, submitted that although the Secretary of State
is entitled, as he has done, to restrict the total of aircraft movements for an
aggregate of periods, he is required also to specify in respect of each separate
period to which his order applies the number of movements which may not be
exceeded in that period.   Having failed to do so, his decision and any order made
giving effect to it is unlawful.   It is necessary, therefore, to consider the ambit of
the power conferred by s 78(3)(b).

Mr Gordon submitted that the 'periods so specified' referred to in para (b) are
the 'certain periods' referred to in the opening words of sub-s (3). I agree. He *a*
argues also that the words 'during periods so specified' should be read as meaning
'during *each* period so specified'. I do not accept the correctness of this suggested
construction. It involves reading in an additional word which is not necessary to
give the words a sensible meaning. Moreover, the inclusion of the word
'maximum' in para (b) has to be born in mind. Subsection (3)(b) has to do with *b*
imposing limits which may not be exceeded. A power to limit by specifying the
permitted number of movements in respect of individual periods has no need of
the word maximum. A reason for including the word is to be found if periods can
be aggregated for the purpose of specifying a maximum number of movements
for the aggregate number of periods. Nor need there be only one aggregate of
periods attracting a maximum. For example, an order could specify different *c*
periods during a 24-hour day or different days of the week and provide different
maxima for the separate aggregate of these different periods. Again, it could
aggregate periods during a shorter time than the summer or winter season, for
example by the week or the month and provide maxima for these.

In my judgment, to read the words 'periods so specified' in the way suggested *d*
by Mr Gordon would make the word 'maximum' surplus and would mean there
was no power to aggregate different periods so as to impose a maximum number
of permitted movements in relation to the aggregate.

Does the reference to maximum mean, then, that the power under sub-s (3)(b)
can only be used in respect of aggregated periods and not in relation to individual
periods? This was not suggested to be the case either by Mr Gordon or by Mr *e*
Burnett for the Secretary of State. Nor do I see any need to give the word this
effect. It would cut down the ambit of the power conferred. In my judgment,
though, having regard to the purpose of the statutory provision, the use of the
word 'maximum' should be regarded as enlarging, rather than restricting, the
statutory power to impose limits on the number of aircraft movements. I *f*
conclude, therefore, that there is power under sub-s (3)(b) to impose limits both
by reference to individual specified periods and to the aggregation of specified
periods.

Mr Gordon argued that since there is a power to impose limits in respect of
individual periods, the power under the subsection cannot lawfully be exercised
unless such limits are imposed. If this is right, then consistency would seem to *g*
require that to be lawful any exercise of the statutory power must impose limits
both by reference to individual periods and to some aggregate of periods. I see
no basis for Mr Gordon's submission and I reject it. The words which precede
paras (a) to (c) in sub-s (3) allow the Secretary of State to do all or any of the things
permitted by those paragraphs. Mr Gordon submitted these words have the *h*
effect that once the Secretary of State decides to exercise a power under one of
the paragraphs, he must exercise every aspect of the power created by that
paragraph; 'any' allows the Secretary of State to chose to act under one or more
of the paragraphs but not to chose to exercise only a part of the powers in a
chosen paragraph, the exercise being indivisible. I see no reason why this phrase *j*
should be read in this restricted way. An example will show how such a reading
could work against the commonsense exercise of the power under para (a),
which allows a ban to be placed on the take-off and landing of noisy aircraft.
Apparently landing creates more of a problem with noisy aircraft than take-off.
One could obviously, therefore, have a time of the day when a landing
movement could be objectionable but not a take-off movement. It would be

a unfortunate and nonsensical if the power under para (a) had to be exercised in respect of both movements or not exercised at all in respect of the particular type of aircraft.

The construction of s 78(3)(b) was argued by Mr Gordon before Latham J and his argument was rejected. Mr Gordon submitted that the learned judge reached the wrong conclusion and, the matter having been re-argued before me, I have
b thought it appropriate to explain my own reasons for reaching the same conclusion as Latham J.

The third challenge

Mr Gordon submitted before me, as he did unsuccessfully before Laws and Latham JJ that the power under s 78(3)(b) can only be exercised so as effectively
c to impose further restraints on noise levels over what has gone before, the so-called ratchet effect. Consequently, since the effect of the decision challenged, though setting a permitted level of noise for the period 1993–98 which is less than the level permitted for the preceding period, is to allow more noise than the actual level for summer 1988, the decision is unlawful. This contention was
d decisively rejected by Laws J. Latham J agreed with him, and not simply for reasons of judicial comity. I also agree and in my turn, not simply for reasons of judicial comity. I propose to confine myself to dealing with one submission which Mr Gordon has made in support of this challenge and to add an example of my own to that given by Laws J in his judgment.

Mr Gordon drew my attention to s 78(5)(a) which imposes a duty on the
e Secretary of State before exercising the power under sub-s (3)(b) to consult any body appearing to him to be representative of operators of aircraft using the aerodrome in relation to which he proposes to exercise his power. Mr Gordon pointed out that the rationale for that duty of consultation is that the aircraft operators may be adversely affected by the exercise of the power and so are given
f the right to be consulted. There is, though, no statutory duty to consult others, for example local residents and the local government bodies representing them, who might be adversely affected by an exercise of the power which allowed a relaxation of the controls which had gone before. Therefore, submitted Mr Gordon, the power under sub-s (3) can only be used to restrict further what has gone before. Were it otherwise a statutory right to be consulted would have
g been provided. This argument is ingenious but quite fails to convince me. I can see a very good reason why Parliament should have singled out bodies representative of aircraft operators as being entitled to be consulted. Aircraft movements cannot sensibly be considered simply in terms of the time of take-off or landing at a particular airport in respect of which it is proposed an order should
h be made. Account has to be taken of where an aircraft is going to or coming from and of the time of landing or take-off at some other airport. Account has to be taken of passenger demand and of the need to have aircraft at the right places and at the right times. An aircraft may touch down at a UK airport en route between two other countries. One type of aircraft may be required for one flight and
j another for another flight. The complexities of all this are such that it is easy to see, on a practical basis, why aircraft operators may have an important contribution to make to the decision-making process, of which the Secretary of State might be largely unaware if there were no consultation.

It is clear that the power under s 78(3) can only be used for the purpose of avoiding, limiting or mitigating the effect of noise and vibration generated by aircraft movements which, but for the exercise of the power, might not be

avoided, limited or mitigated. The comparison drawn by the subsection is not
between what is proposed and what has been permitted by an earlier order, but   *a*
between what is proposed and what the position would be if there were to be no
order. In deciding what limits should be imposed the Secretary of State has to
balance a variety of interests. At different periods the balance may have to be
struck differently. And here I add my own example. Suppose there were to be a
surge in demand for air travel, that is something the Secretary of State would be   *b*
entitled to take into account which might lead him quite properly to conclude
that a new order had to introduce a degree of relaxation of the limits imposed by
an earlier order.

The first and fourth challenges
      The first challenge is divided into two parts, the first relates to policy and the   *c*
second to an alleged failure to give adequate reasons for the decision. The fourth
challenge relates to an allegation that the applicants have been disappointed of
their legitimate expectation to be consulted if there is to be a change of policy. I
propose to consider first the policy point, together with the fourth challenge, and
to come finally to the second part of the first challenge—the reasons challenge.   *d*

First challenge (policy) and the fourth challenge
      Mr Gordon submitted that the 1998 undertaking remains and encapsulates the
Secretary of State's policy, namely to introduce controls which will reduce the
level of night noise at Heathrow below that actually experienced there in the
summer of 1988. It follows he has acted with *Wednesbury* unreasonableness, in   *e*
that while professing to adhere to this policy he has departed from it (see
Associated Provincial Picture Houses Ltd v Wednesbury Corp [1947] 2 All ER 680,
[1948] 1 KB 223). Alternatively, he argues, it is unclear what the Secretary of
State's policy is and (as I understand Mr Gordon) there is no clearly enunciated
policy by which to judge whether his proposals confirm to his policy.   *f*
      Mr Gordon submitted that the Secretary of State has acted consistently so as to
improve the night noise climate at Heathrow and this and the practice of
consultation created a legitimate expectation that he would not depart from this
objective without giving those affected an opportunity to make representations
about it.
      Latham J concluded that the 1988 undertaking covered only the 1988–93   *g*
period and that any undertaking or policy for the subsequent period must be
found in the consultation papers for that period. Mr Gordon does not challenge
this, but he submits that despite the passages in and the quotation from the
consultation paper of 9 June 1995 which I have referred to and set out above, it is
apparent from other material that the Secretary of State still adheres to the 1998   *h*
undertaking as representing his policy. He finds this material first in para 23 of
Miss Duthie's first affirmation filed on behalf of the Secretary of State and second
in an exchange of letters between the applicants' solicitor and the Treasury
Solicitor of 23 and 28 June 1995.
      In para 23 of Miss Duthie's first affirmation she says, referring to para 34 of the   *j*
consultation paper of January 1993:

            'It proposed that the noise levels permitted for summer seasons under the
      new regime should be lower than those permitted under the old regime and
      described this as "in keeping with the undertaking given in 1988 not to allow
      a worsening of noise at night and ideally to improve it".'

a   There, argues Mr Gordon, is the 1988 undertaking still alive and, if not well, still held out as representing ministerial policy. In my judgment this argument is unsustainable. It ignores what is said in the June 1995 consultation paper and lifts a single sentence from Miss Duthie's affirmation from the context in which it should be read.

    The exchange of letters began with an inquiry from the applicants' solicitor. I
b   set out his letter in full.

    'Referring to the recent June 1995 supplement to the April 1995 consultation, I would be grateful if you clarify points regarding the S/S's policy. [The reference should be to March and not April.] It would appear from the new paper that the S/S's policy is not to allow an increase in
c   permitted levels of noise over what was permitted at Heathrow (and Gatwick) for summer 1988. It is not clear however how that relates to the policy "not to allow a worsening of noise at night and ideally to improve it." You will recall that this policy was found by Sedley J to have been repeated in the 1993 and (April) 1995 consultation papers. Please would you clarify whether the S/S has now departed from that policy, ie whether now it is
d   dead and the policy is now to allow an increase of noise; or whether the policy is still extant and the new proposals are merely recognised as a departure from the policy. In any event, the policy (as now appears) only relates to the night quota period (2330–0600). We have no idea what the S/S policy is in relation to the night period (2300–0700) which we understand to be the object of his controls (and presumably the subject of the 1988/93/
e   95 policy/undertaking not to allow worsening of noise at night and ideally to improve it). Does one policy relate to the night quota period and the other policy to the night period? Is that why they are both still extant? What is the policy in relation to the night period and what is the effect of the controls overall on noise during the night period as a whole? I await your
f   clarifications so that informed representations may be made on the S/S's proposals.'

The reply contained the following paragraph:

    'The Secretary of State's position is clearly expressed in Sedley J's summary
g   of the argument put by counsel for the Secretary of State at the leave hearing on 4th April—"Paragraph 7 of the 1995 paper now sets out a new policy, with the consequence that the proposals no longer conflict with it: the new permitted levels will exceed the past actual levels but will be less than the former permitted levels. The policy is now to make a legitimate comparison between one permitted level and another and the Secretary of State's stance
h   is that to do so is in keeping with 1988 undertaking."'

    Again, Mr Gordon argued that the reference to the 1988 undertaking shows it still represents the Secretary of State's professed policy. It seems to me that this amounts to asserting that it is still policy not to permit in the 1993–98 period a
j   night noise climate at Heathrow which is worse than what was actually experienced (as opposed to permitted) in the summer of 1988. This has only to be said and considered in the light of other relevant material to demonstrate that the exchange of letters provides no shred of support for Mr Gordon's submission.

    But he advanced a further possible meaning to be extracted from the reference to the 1988 undertaking. It is this: that the new policy of comparing proposed permission with past permission applies only to the night quota period, but the

ban under sub-s (3)(a) on the take-off and landing of noisy aircraft for the night
period (which is longer than the night quota period) will more than offset the *a*
cumulative adverse effects of the new limits fixed under sub-s 3(b) and of the
winter decontrol of a weekly total of five hours, so achieving by the overall result
compliance with the 1988 undertaking. I find this meaning to be so fanciful and
tortuous as to have no appeal save to a mind seeking a means of avoiding the
obvious. I reject it. The Treasury Solicitor's letter is doing no more than allude *b*
to the spirit of the 1988 undertaking. Moreover, the subject of this application for
judicial review is the Secretary of State's decision and not the letter written by the
Treasury Solicitor containing what might be open to criticism as a loose reference
to a no longer extant undertaking.

I have no hesitation in saying that the 1988 undertaking has gone. It forms no
part of the present policy and cannot be read in substitution for or as a *c*
qualification or addition to the policy stated in the consultation papers issued for
the 1993–98 period as finally explained by the June 1995 paper. Nor, in my
judgment, is there any room for any lingering uncertainty about the present
position. I reject that part of the first challenge relating to policy.

Consultees reading the June 1995 paper and reading in the light of it the earlier *d*
papers, knew what the Secretary of State's policy was for the 1993–98 period.
They knew the 1988 undertaking was not part of that policy. They knew what
the Secretary of State's proposals were and they knew to what they should direct
their representations. It was open to them, if so minded, to make their
representations that the 1988 undertaking should be adhered to and that any
policy contained in it should remain unchanged. There has been no failure to *e*
give effect to the legitimate expectation which is the subject of the fourth
challenge and I reject this challenge.

First challenge (reasons)

Mr Gordon submitted that although there was no statutory duty upon the *f*
Secretary of State to consult the applicants, there was none the less a right to be
consulted and therefore to be given reasons for his decision. He is content to base
that right on the doctrine of legitimate expectation arising out of the Secretary of
State's past practice to consult and to give reasons. Mr Burnett accepted that
there may be a duty based only, he argued, on legitimate expectation but he
asserted that the scope of a duty arising in this way is determined by the extent of *g*
the former practice, in accordance with the principles on which the doctrine of
legitimate expectation is based.

Mr Gordon's arguments do not accept any such limitation. Once there is a
duty to give reasons, however arising, it is a duty to give adequate reasons. He
cited by way of support for this proposition a sentence from de Smith, Woolf and *h*
Jowell *Judicial Review of Administrative Action* (5th edn, 1995) p 468, para 9–053:

> 'Whatever standards are applied by judges to the adequacy of reasons
> under a duty, it seems likely that reasons given voluntarily—where there is
> no duty—will be reviewed in accordance with the same standards as are
> applied to compulsory reasons.' *j*

A fortiori, Mr Gordon submitted, when there is a duty.

He argued that for reasons to be adequate they must satisfy four requirements.
(1) They must explain any change of policy. I understand this to require more of
the Secretary of State than to say simply that he has changed his policy and what
the new policy is. The submission amounts to a requirement that there has to be

a reasoned justification of a change of policy. (2) They must be such as to
demonstrate that all material representations have been properly considered. It
is not enough for the Secretary of State to say that he has taken account of them.
(3) They must deal with all the relevant issues raised by the consultation process
in order to demonstrate what decisions were made on issues about which the
consultation process generated conflict and the reasons for those decisions.
(4) They must set out any further basis for the overall decision not covered by
(3). Mr Gordon accepted, though, that the reasons do not have to be detailed or
elaborate. Relying on *R v Lancashire CC, ex p Huddleston* [1986] 2 All ER 941, he
submitted that once leave to move for judicial review has been granted then even
if no or no adequate reasons have been given a respondent owes to the court a
duty to explain how the decision under review was arrived at so that the court
may know whether it was lawful—as being within the four corners of any
statutory power—and whether or not it is *Wednesbury* unreasonable. *Ex p
Huddleston* was a decision of the Court of Appeal consisting of Donaldson MR,
Parker LJ and Sir George Waller. I take the combined effect of the three
judgments in that case as requiring that once leave has been given the
decision-maker (in so far as this had not already been done) owes to the court a
duty to provide the court with the reasons for its decision which are relevant to
the grounds of challenge.

I have considered the analysis in the decision of the Court of Appeal in *R v Civil
Service Appeal Board, ex p Cunningham* [1991] 4 All ER 310 of the factors which will
often be material in deciding whether or not a requirement to give reasons will
be implied by the common law where there is no statutory duty to give them. I
accept there may be a tendency in recent decisions to add to the cases in which
reasons are required. However, while I appreciate that the analysis may lead to
the identification of cases requiring the giving of reasons not formerly recognised,
I would for myself be hesitant to go beyond what was said in that case and find
new factors calling for reasons. I say this fortified by the recent approval of *Ex p
Cunningham* by the House of Lords in *Doody v Secretary of State for the Home Dept*
[1993] 3 All ER 92, [1994] 1 AC 531. The applicants in the present case were not
parties to any dispute with the respondent or to the resolution by him of any issue
which would determine their rights and I find nothing in *Ex p Cunningham*
(leaving aside legitimate expectation) to lead me to conclude that this is a case in
which the common law should recognise a duty to give reasons.

Mr Gordon submitted, though, that wherever there is a duty to consult, for
whatever reason, there is duty also to give reasons, because if no reasons are
given it cannot be known whether the representations have been considered or
not. He accepts the textbook writers do not suggest that a duty to give reasons
can arise in this way and that no court has decided there is such a duty. But he
submitted that a passage from the speech of Lord Mustill in *Doody* should lead to
this conclusion (see [1993] 3 All ER 92 at 111, [1994] 1 AC 531 at 565). I do not
agree. In my judgment, if the decision-maker says he has considered and taken
into account the representations he has received his assertion must be taken at its
face value unless there is material before the court (and there is none here)
effectively to impugn his assertion. I do not think the receipt of representations
can of itself impose a duty on the decision-maker which would not otherwise
exist to say what conclusions he has reached concerning them and why.
Decision-makers who are neither obliged to consult nor to give reasons not
infrequently do decide to consult and the opportunity to make representations
can be of value to both the decision-maker and the consultees. It seems to me

that to say the fact of consultation automatically imposes a duty to give reasons
could well lead to a reluctance on the part of decision-makers to engage in   *a*
voluntary consultation. In the passage from his speech relied on by Mr Gordon
Lord Mustill was not saying that consultation requires reasons. He was simply
saying why on the facts a conclusion that reasons were required could be reached
by the *Ex p Cunningham* route.

It follows that any duty to give reasons in this case must be based on the   *b*
doctrine of legitimate expectation. What is legitimately expected must depend
on previous practice and utterances by the decision-maker. I do not see that the
doctrine can be applied differently to the giving of reasons so as to require a
breadth or detail of reasons beyond the ambit of previous practice and utterances.
Nor do I think that the paragraph from *de Smith, Woolf and Jowell* can be relied
upon to enlarge the scope of the duty to give reasons. No material has been   *c*
placed before me to suggest that the scope of the reasons given for the decision
which is challenged in these proceedings was narrower than the scope of reasons
given in the past. I would therefore hold that there has been no failure to give
reasons which is open to challenge by way of judicial review. I propose,
however, to review the adequacy of the reasons given by the Secretary of State   *d*
on the further basis that the reasons which will be required in a case of legitimate
expectation do not differ, regardless of previous practice and utterances, from
those required when the duty to give them is imposed in the ordinary way by the
common law.

Mr Gordon accepted that the Secretary of State's policy was to compare   *e*
proposed limits with past limits (inconsistently, it might be thought, with his
submission that the 1988 undertaking still represents his policy) but he complains
the Secretary of State has not said why he considers this to be an appropriate
approach to the exercise of his statutory power. And, Mr Gordon argued, the
failure to explain why renders the change of policy unlawful because the absence
of reasons prevents an examination of the lawfulness of his policy and there is a   *f*
legitimate expectation that an opportunity will be given to examine the question
of lawfulness.

I reject these submissions. There is no unlawfulness in the Secretary of State's
new policy. It falls squarely within the four corners of his statutory powers. Nor
is there the slightest basis for arguing that the new policy is *Wednesbury*   *g*
unreasonable even if it strikes a different balance between competing interests
from the balance in fact experienced in summer 1988. The Secretary of State has
a lawful policy of balancing competing interests. He has to decide how that
balance is struck before he makes any order under s 78(3). That is what he has
done. Having done it he does not have to justify it, because the policy decision
and how within that policy he will exercise his powers are matters for him and   *h*
not for the courts. Consequently, in the absence of anything to indicate
Wednesbury unreasonableness he does not have to justify himself and so does not
have to give reasons on this aspect of the case. Quite simply there is in my
opinion no duty to give reasons on a matter for which the decision-maker is not
accountable to the courts. I consider this view is consistent with a passage from   *j*
the judgment of Lord Donaldson MR in *Ex p Cunningham* [1991] 4 All ER 310 at
315:

'Those of us with experience of judicial review are very much aware that
the scope of the authority of decision-makers can vary very widely and so
long as that authority is not exceeded it is not for the courts to intervene.

a   They and not the courts are the decision-makers in terms of policy. They
         and not the courts are the judges in the case of judicial or quasi-judicial
         decisions which are lawful. The public law jurisdiction of the courts is
         supervisory and not appellate in character.'

         Mr Gordon submitted to Laws J that a policy change must be justified by
b   reference to 'the overriding public interest' (words taken from the judgment of
    Lord Denning MR in Re Liverpool Taxi Owners' Association [1972] 2 All ER 589 at
    594, [1972] 2 QB 299 at 308). Laws J dealt with the submission in these words
    ([1994] 1 All ER 577 at 596–597, [1994] 1 WLR 74 at 94):

         'But this latter condition would imply that the court is to be the judge of
c   the public interest in such cases, and thus the judge of the merits of the
         proposed policy change. Thus understood, Mr Gordon's submission must
         be rejected. The court is not the judge of the merits of the decision-maker's
         policy. In fact Mr Gordon disavowed any such proposition; but if (as must
         be the case) the public authority in question is the judge of the issue whether
         "the overriding public interest" justifies a change in policy, then the
d   submission means no more than that a reasonable public authority, having
         regard only to relevant considerations, will not alter its policy unless it
         concludes that the public will be better served by the change. But this is no
         more than to assert a change in policy, like any discretionary decision by a
         public authority, must not transgress Wednesbury principles. That, however,
e   is elementary and carries Mr Gordon nowhere.'

    Nor indeed could a duty to give reasons on this aspect of the case be imported by
    way of legitimate expectation. In my view there has to be some relevance in
    public law attaching to an expected event before it can become the object of a
    legitimate expectation. So, any legitimate expectation can only be of reasons
f   which will have relevance in public law to the decision.
         Paragraph 55 of the grounds begins at p 31 of form 86A and continues over the
    next five pages. Sub-paragraphs (d) and (e) are no longer relied on. In the rest of
    para 55, complaint is made that issues set out in these pages were not dealt with
    in any reasons contained in the decision. In considering this complaint it is
g   legitimate to look not only at the decision, but at the evidence which has been
    filed in the successive judicial review proceedings and at the consultation papers.
    I do not accept Mr Gordon's proposition that it is impermissible to look at
    consultation papers to see what light they shed on reasons. A passage from a
    consultation paper, when read with a passage from the decision, may throw light
h   on the reasons lying behind it.
         Sub-paragraph (a) raises the question of the night quota period at Heathrow
    in winter and on summer Sundays. This was dealt with in the judgment of
    Latham J:

j   'The applicants point out that standardising the periods of restriction as
         proposed was bound to increase the number of early morning aircraft
         movements in particular. The respondent agrees, but points out that, in
         return, he has effectively prohibited the movement of the noisiest two
         categories of aircraft during the night period. He considered that in the
         overall context of the proposals this achieved a balance which would accord
         with his expressed policy. The applicants had full opportunity to make

representations on this aspect of the proposals. I cannot say that the *a* respondent's conclusions were irrational.'

I respectfully agree. It is said, though, that there was no evidence upon which Latham J could have come to his conclusion and there still is not. I disagree. Miss Duthie's second affirmation contains evidence on the point. To say that because there was no arithmetical calculation in respect of the counter-balancing factor of *b* the ban on noisy aircraft there was no evidence on the point is to confuse a challenge on the merits with a challenge by way of judicial review. In sub-para (b) it is complained that the sleep prevention and health points are not dealt with. In fact a great volume of evidence was placed before Laws J dealing with these matters and he found against the applicants. I should add that research into this subject has continued but is not complete. It cannot be suggested that *c* the Secretary of State has acted with *Wednesbury* unreasonableness because he has failed to take account of a piece of unfinished research.

Sub-paragraph (c) complains that the use of 'Leq' as a measure of noise has not been dealt with. Again, the controversy about this was canvassed before Laws J and the applicants' complaint was rejected.

Sub-paragraph (f) complains that the Secretary of State has not said why he *d* considers his scheme is not detrimental to residents or if it is, why the detriment is irrelevant. It seems to me there are two answers to this complaint. Firstly, this is a matter of policy. Secondly, the Secretary of State has explained why he considers it appropriate to have a standard regime for all three airports and how he has sought to strike a fair balance and considers he has struck a fair balance *e* between the various interests which are in play. It is appropriate at this point to remind myself of Mr Gordon's concession that reasons can be stated quite briefly.

Sub-paragraph (g) complains that the Secretary of State has not explained why he has decided to formulate his scheme for the control of noise during the night period by reference to the shorter night quota period. Again, the answer to this *f* complaint is twofold. The decision is a policy decision. He has also given reasons for it. In reality the complaints in paras (a), (f) and (g) are different facets of a single theme.

Mr Gordon also made a complaint that the Secretary of State has not continued to keep the position under review until a time proximate to the making of his decision. This is perhaps simply another way of saying that he must consider all *g* the material available to him when he makes his decision. However, my attention has not been drawn to any change in circumstances affecting the night noise climate at Heathrow which has occurred since the consultation process in respect of the 1993–98 period was first launched in January 1993. There is nothing in this point. *h*

In my judgment, when the nature of the various issues is considered and the decisions are looked at with the benefit of such light as the consultation papers throw upon them and account is taken of the evidence offered by way of explanation in the various proceedings for judicial review, the complaint that the decision challenged is flawed by inadequacy of reasons is not made out. *j*

Accordingly this application is dismissed.

I return to what I said earlier about the need for reasons to have a relevance in public law to the decision which they accompany. I have read with interest the paragraphs in *de Smith, Woolf and Jowell* pp 457 ff which discuss the right to reasons. It is interesting to note the general use in the discussion of terminology which is apt to refer to decisions which determine people's rights and which *a* probably would be identified, following *Ex p Cunningham*, as needing to be accompanied by reasons. Thus the authors state (p 467, para 9–051):

> 'Some general guidance may be derived from a consideration of the purposes served by a duty to give reasons. Thus, reasons should be sufficiently detailed as to make quite clear to the *parties*—and especially the *losing* party—why the tribunal decided as it did, and to avoid the impression
>
> *b* that the decision was based upon extraneous considerations, rather than the matters raised at the hearing.' (My emphasis.)

Decisions to which this kind of terminology is appropriate are unlike in substance and consequence the decision which has been challenged in these proceedings. Mr Burnett took me to the decision in *Ex parte Cunningham* to demonstrate that *c* this is not a case in which, leaving aside legitimate expectation, the common law would recognise a duty to give reasons. I wonder to what extent, even with the help of legitimate expectation, reasons of the kind which Mr Gordon says were required do in fact have relevance in public law to a decision of the present kind. The point was not argued and I express no view about a point which forms no *d* part of the basis for my decision.

Application dismissed. Leave to appeal refused

Dilys Tausz   Barrister.

Ward v Guinness Mahon & Co Ltd   a
Koppel v Guinness Mahon & Co Ltd
Evans v Guinness Mahon & Co Ltd

b

COURT OF APPEAL, CIVIL DIVISION
SIR THOMAS BINGHAM MR, ROSE AND ROCH LJJ
19 FEBRUARY 1996

Costs – Order for costs – Interlocutory application – Group action – Application by c
plaintiffs in lead actions for anticipatory order – Whether appropriate that plaintiffs'
liability for costs be several and limited to each plaintiff's proportionate share.

The plaintiffs were among a number of investors in three newly formed
companies which had ceased trading. Those investors subsequently brought
actions against the defendant company, which had sponsored the issue of d
prospectuses to raise subscriptions for shares in the companies, offered loan
finance and given advice in respect of the investment. They complained, inter
alia, that the defendant had made material misrepresentations in the
prospectuses, that it was in breach of its duty and that it had made incorrect
statements, and sought damages and rescission of the loan agreements. It was
agreed that the 99 actions concerning one of the companies should be determined e
before those relating to the other two companies, and that six representative lead
actions should be chosen to proceed. The plaintiffs, who were party to three of
the lead actions, applied for an anticipatory costs order to provide that liability for
any costs payable by the plaintiffs to the defendant be several and limited to each
plaintiff's individual share. The judge declined to make the order sought and the f
plaintiffs appealed.

Held – The court had jurisdiction in group actions to make an anticipatory costs
order and would do so in appropriate circumstances, since the purpose of
selecting lead cases would be vitiated if regard were paid not to the issues in
particular actions but to the means and willingness of plaintiffs to accept a high g
degree of risk as to costs. It was therefore fair in the instant case for the costs
liability of the individual plaintiffs to be several and not joint and limited to their
proportionate share of the overall costs, whether incurred by them or payable by
them to the defendant. The appeal would accordingly be allowed and the judge's
order would be set aside (see p117 *fh* to p 118 *c* post).   h
    Davies (Joseph Owen) v Eli Lilly & Co [1987] 3 All ER 94 distinguished.

Notes
For judges' jurisdiction and discretion to award costs in general, see 37 *Halsbury's*
Laws (4th edn) paras 712–725, and for cases on the subject, see 37(3) *Digest* j
(Reissue) 230–286, 4273–4622.

Cases referred to in judgments
A B v John Wyeth & Brother Ltd (1992) 12 BMLR 50, CA.
Davies (Joseph Owen) v Eli Lilly & Co [1987] 3 All ER 94, [1987] 1 WLR 1136, CA;
    affg (8 May 1987, unreported) QBD.

a *Nash v Eli Lilly & Co, Berger v Eli Lilly & Co* [1993] 4 All ER 383, [1993] 1 WLR 782, CA.
Westdock Realisations Ltd, Re [1988] BCLC 354.

Cases also cited or referred to in skeleton arguments
Aiden Shipping Co Ltd v Interbulk Ltd, The Vimeira [1986] 2 All ER 409, [1986] AC
b 965, HL.
Alsop Wilkinson (a firm) v Neary [1995] 1 All ER 431.
Biddencare Ltd, Re [1994] 2 BCLC 160.
Interest Rate Swap Litigation, Re (1991) Times, 19 December.
Wallersteiner v Moir (No 2) [1975] 1 All ER 849, [1975] QB 373, CA.

c
Interlocutory appeal
By notice dated 14 November 1995 the plaintiffs, John Ward, Peter Koppel and
Glynn Evans appealed with leave granted by Waite LJ on 6 October 1995 from
the decision of Alliott J in chambers on 14 June 1995 dismissing their application
for an anticipatory costs order in proceedings brought against the defendant,
d Guinness Mahon & Co Ltd, to provide that, as between them and the defendant,
their liability for any costs ordered to be paid to the defendant should be several
and limited to each plaintiff's proportionate share. The facts are set out in the
judgment of Sir Thomas Bingham MR.

e *James Guthrie QC* (instructed by *Leon Kaye Collin & Gittens*) for the plaintiffs.
Peter Leaver QC (instructed by *Ashurst Morris Crisp*) for Guinness Mahon.

SIR THOMAS BINGHAM MR. This is an appeal by the plaintiffs in certain lead
actions against a decision given by Alliott J in chambers on 14 June 1995. The
f appeal concerns the allocation of costs in a group action, the order being made
well before trial of the action. The point that is raised is one of some general
importance.
  The story, so far as relevant for present purposes, is this. In 1986 to 1988,
prospectuses seeking subscriptions were issued by three companies named,
respectively, Lockton Superstores plc, Lockton Retail Stores plc and Lockton
g Shops plc. Those were newly formed companies formed under the business
expansion scheme, and they were seeking to raise capital by the issue of shares to
the public. The prospectuses were in similar form. The defendant in this action,
Guinness Mahon & Co Ltd (Guinness Mahon), was the sponsor of the
prospectuses and is alleged to have been the promoter of the scheme. In
h connection with the subscription of shares Guinness Mahon offered loan finance,
and it is said that some of the investors took advice from Guinness Mahon.
  The result of the subscription was that a considerable number of investors put
money into the three companies. Unhappily, however, the companies did not
flourish and ceased to trade during the recession of the early 1990s. As a result of
j this misfortune, the investors have complained that material misrepresentations
were made in the prospectuses by Guinness Mahon, that Guinness Mahon was in
breach of its duty, that it made incorrect statements, and other complaints of that
kind. The investors claim damages and rescission of the contracts into which
they entered—that is the loan agreements into which they entered—and
Guinness Mahon counterclaims for sums due and unpaid under the loan
agreements.

A large number of writs were issued relating to investments in each of these
three companies.   Very sensibly, however, it has been agreed that the   *a*
proceedings relating to only one of the companies should in the first instance
proceed, the complaints relating to the other two companies being stayed. It has
therefore been decided that the proceedings relating to Lockton Shops plc should
go ahead, while the other groups of actions should mark time. It has also, very
sensibly, been agreed that among the various writs (and there are 99 of them now   *b*
extant relating to Lockton Shops plc) six lead actions should be identified to
proceed, those actions having been selected with a view to raising the points
which are necessary for decision, so far as can be seen, to resolve all of the 99
actions. It is against that background that the question has arisen concerning the
liability for costs in these six lead actions. This was the subject of the hearing
before Alliott J.   *c*

The argument put forward by Guinness Mahon was, first, that the judge
should simply make no order so that, if Guinness Mahon were successful in the
six lead actions, it would in the ordinary way obtain an order for costs against the
plaintiffs in those actions and Guinness Mahon should be free to enforce its order
against those plaintiffs. What recourse those plaintiffs might have against the   *d*
general body of plaintiffs in the Lockton Shops actions which were not among the
six lead actions was, strictly speaking, nothing to do with Guinness Mahon.
Alternatively, however, it was suggested that, if another order was to be pursued,
then that order should be against all the investors in the Lockton Shops actions
jointly and severally, which would, of course, enable Guinness Mahon to enforce
its order against such plaintiffs as were of sufficient means to pay those costs.   *e*

As against that, the plaintiffs argued that the liability of the plaintiffs in the lead
actions and of all the other investors in the other actions, should be limited by
order of the court to a proportionate share of the total costs. There being 99
plaintiffs in all, it was argued that no plaintiff should be liable for more than one
ninety-ninth, at most, of any costs that were awarded to Guinness Mahon.   *f*
Happily, it appears that a very small number of the total number of plaintiffs is
legally aided, so that the incidence of legal aid is not a major feature of the
argument. A great deal of the debate before Alliott J concerned the true effect and
meaning of an order which Hirst J made when sitting as the allocated judge in the
Opren litigation (see *Davies (Joseph Owen) v Eli Lilly & Co* (8 May 1987,
unreported)). That decision was the subject of an appeal to the Court of Appeal   *g*
([1987] 3 All ER 94, [1987] 1 WLR 1136). There is no doubt, I think, that before
the judge Mr Guthrie QC, who appeared for the plaintiffs then as now, argued
that Hirst J's order was to very much the same effect as the order which he was
seeking. On the other hand, the defendant argued that Hirst J's order related only
to the liability in costs of the plaintiffs among themselves, and did not in any way   *h*
affect the order which would be made in favour of the defendants in that action
if they were ultimately successful. As I say, it appears that the argument before
Alliott J centred very largely on the proper construction of Hirst J's judgment and
the Court of Appeal judgments on it. Mr Guthrie tells us that he, at least, was
under the very clear impression that the argument was whether the court had   *j*
jurisdiction to make the order which he was seeking, and that, accordingly,
attention was being paid to those judgments for the light they threw on whether
the court had such jurisdiction or not.

It is, I think, unnecessary to examine in detail the precise effect either of the
order made by Hirst J or the view taken of that judgment by the Court of Appeal,
since it is now freely accepted by Mr Leaver QC, who appears in this court but

a did not appear below for the defendant, that the court does have jurisdiction to make the orders which the plaintiffs seek, although Mr Leaver vigorously submits that such an order should not be made. The question of the true meaning and effect, both of Hirst J's order and of the Court of Appeal decision, are not therefore fundamental. I would, however, say that, having had occasion to examine both a draft of his judgment and the Court of Appeal's reported

b decision, I am of opinion that the defendant's submissions on this matter are correct, and that his decision was directed to the position of the plaintiffs among themselves, rather than the position of the plaintiffs vis-à-vis the defendants. That is, as I think, how his decision was understood by the Court of Appeal, and also by the Court of Appeal in the later case of *Nash v Eli Lilly & Co, Berger v Eli Lilly & Co* [1993] 4 All ER 383, [1993] 1 WLR 782, and also by Browne-Wilkinson

c V-C in *Re Westdock Realisations Ltd* [1988] BCLC 354. I therefore think that the defendant's argument on this point is correct, and it is right to say that that is the decision which the judge reached. He said:

d '... and at the end of the day, as I have indicated in the course of the argument, I remain unconvinced that the order was other than an order governing the contribution to costs between the plaintiffs themselves.'

As I have mentioned, it is now accepted that the court would have had jurisdiction, had it thought fit to do so, to make the order which Mr Guthrie now seeks. But he submits tentatively, since the judge's judgment in the present case is not entirely clear, that the judge did believe that the court had no jurisdiction

e to make such an order. He draws attention to a discussion following the judgment during which the judge said: 'It is an interesting point as to whether the order can bite on the defendants.' That, Mr Guthrie suggests, points towards the judge's view that there was no jurisdiction.

The judge did, however, deal (albeit briefly) with the situation if Mr Guthrie

f were right. What he said was:

'Finally, Mr Guthrie urged me that even if that were the position I should nevertheless extend the scope of a costs sharing order so that it did bite upon the defendants. That I am disinclined to do, and repeat the invitation that I made to Mr Guthrie to draft a proposed costs sharing order so as to be

g internal only.'

There is, I think, no doubt as to the upshot of the order which the judge did make, since para 7 of the order, as drawn up, is in these terms:

'The application for an Order that as between the investors and [Guinness

h Mahon], the liability for any costs ordered to be paid by the investors to [Guinness Mahon] should be several and limited to that investor's own portion is dismissed.'

The judge refused leave to appeal against that part of the order, but leave has since been given.

j Mr Leaver, at the forefront of his argument, submits that the judge who was allocated to make decisions on this matter has made a decision and that the Court of Appeal should be extremely slow to interfere with that. He draws our attention to some observations of Steyn LJ in *A B v John Wyeth & Brother Ltd* (1992) 12 BMLR 50 at 61, where Steyn LJ emphasises the desirability, in the interests of efficient case management, of the Court of Appeal refraining from interfering with the trial judge's procedural directions.

Furthermore, Mr Leaver emphasises that there is no ground upon which one can challenge the judge's exercise of discretion and, in all the circumstances, he urges that one should leave the order as it stands, which is effectively that the defendant can in the ordinary way obtain—subject, of course, to the order of the trial judge at the end of the trial—an order against the lead plaintiffs, and enforce it. He points out that the plaintiffs all started individual actions before there was any group organisation in existence, that, on the basis of individual actions, each plaintiff was potentially liable for the whole costs of his or her action; and he suggests that the costs of the action will not be very greatly increased by the incidence of the group action. The issues as to what representations were made and as to the effect of them will, he submits, be very much the same as if these 99 actions had been fought out individually. Accordingly, he submits that it would simply be unfair to deprive Guinness Mahon of its right to proceed against each of the lead litigants jointly and severally.

Mr Guthrie strongly opposes that approach. He urges us to take account of the extreme reluctance which any plaintiff would have to be selected as a lead plaintiff if the result of such selection were to leave such a plaintiff at risk of failing to recover a proportionate share of costs against any other plaintiff. It would not seem that legal aid is an important issue in this case, since any order that the judge made at the end of the day could take account of the inability of lead plaintiffs to recover against their brethren who were legally aided. But inevitably, even with that allowance, those who were selected as lead plaintiffs would, under the order as it stands, stand the risk of plaintiffs who were not legally aided either lacking the means to meet, or successfully obstructing enforcement of, the order for costs. Furthermore, Mr Guthrie submits that the selection of lead cases ought, in principle, to take place having regard to the issues in those cases and their suitability to serve as, in effect, test cases, and should not depend on finding a plaintiff sufficiently adventurous to stand what could turn out to be a substantial risk.

To that Mr Leaver counters that the plaintiffs have the organisation of this matter, and that the plaintiffs can, without undue difficulty, organise a fund or a guarantee which would ensure that the lead plaintiffs were adequately protected.

It is, in my judgment, clear that Mr Leaver starts with the advantage—and it is a real advantage—of a decision by the allocated judge in his favour. It does appear that the judge indicated how he would exercise his discretion (if he had one) and one should not lightly interfere with that. On the other hand, it does, I think, appear that the judge probably thought that he had no discretion, having decided that Hirst J's order had the meaning that he held, and having, as I think, understood there to be an argument as to whether the court had discretion to make an order or not.

It is also, I think, open to the plaintiffs to suggest, as they do, that although the judge did indicate how he would exercise his discretion (if he had one) he gave very little in the way of reasons so that one is left in doubt as to what weighed with him in the making of his order. It is also, I think, fair to observe that we are unaware of the view that he took of the points which Mr Guthrie has made as to the fairness or unfairness of the competing orders, and certainly we do not know upon what ground he decided that those considerations were of inadequate weight to justify an order.

Lastly, and this is a matter which is in no sense a criticism of the judge but which it seems right to take into account, there has, since the judge delivered judgment, been consideration of this subject in a long report, *Group Actions Made* a *Easier*, published by the Law Society Civil Litigation Committee in September 1995. In this report there is consideration of the incidence of inter partes costs in group actions. Paragraph 7.4.2 reads as follows:

b 'One point on which there is general agreement is that if defendants win on common issues and costs are ordered against the plaintiffs, the liability of plaintiffs should be several rather than joint. Thus, if a defendant incurs £1m costs defending the common issues of claims brought by 1,000 plaintiffs, the maximum common costs liability of any individual plaintiff will be £1,000 (subject to costs protection for legally-aided claimants). Any other arrangement would make the risk inherent in group actions so great as to limit access to justice solely to those plaintiffs with nothing at all to lose.

c Regardless of the number of plaintiffs sharing costs, no individual plaintiff could hope to satisfy the private client test. Whilst several liability will make it much harder for defendants to recover their costs when they are successful, we see no real alternative to such a rule.'

In the summary, at para 7.4.10, the working party expressed the view that any

d liability of the plaintiffs for common costs should be several and not joint. In a draft rule on group actions, in para 11.1(a), the working party proposed this rule: 'Unless there are exceptional circumstances any liability of the Plaintiffs for common costs shall be several and not joint and several.' Those considerations, taken together, seem to me to justify a reconsideration of this matter, and I consider that the situation is one in which we are not bound by the judge's

e exercise of discretion. It is, I think, plain that whichever decision one makes imposes a risk of non-recovery of costs on someone. If we make the order that Mr Guthrie asks for, then there is a risk that Guinness Mahon (if successful) may fail to enforce all its orders against individual plaintiffs. If, on the other hand, we make the order that Mr Leaver seeks for Guinness Mahon, then there is a risk that

f certain of the lead plaintiffs may fail to be reimbursed by some of the other plaintiffs.

The broad question, as it seems to me, is: What, in this situation, does fairness demand? Mr Leaver suggests that it is premature to make any order at all as to what the outcome at the end of the trial might be. But that submission, I think, runs counter to Donaldson MR's commendation in *Davies (Joseph Owen) v Eli Lilly*

g *& Co* [1987] 3 All ER 94 at 99–100, [1987] 1 WLR 1136 at 1143 of the practice of giving an indication which will enable plaintiffs to know where they stand before they start (subject, always, to the discretion of the trial judge to modify that order at the end of the trial, if it seems appropriate).

Speaking for myself, I am persuaded by Mr Guthrie that it is, in all the

h circumstances, appropriate to make an order that the liability of the individual plaintiffs be limited to the proportionate share of the overall costs, whether incurred by the plaintiffs or payable by the plaintiffs to the defendant, and that such liability should be several and not joint. It appears to me that the defendant is no worse off under such an order than if it had been sued to judgment by 99

j plaintiffs; although it is fair to add, given the sums involved (many of which are quite small) that such an event would appear extremely unlikely. I am, however, persuaded by Mr Guthrie's argument that the role of lead plaintiff would be one which, on the defendant's order no well-advised plaintiff would be wise to accept; and furthermore, that the purpose of selecting lead cases would be vitiated if regard had to be paid not to the issues in particular actions but to the means or willingness of the particular plaintiffs to accept a high degree of risk. It is, in my

judgment, significant that the Law Society working party has come out strongly
in favour of what Mr Guthrie urges as the appropriate rule in this case. I think *a*
that if the judge had had the benefit of that recommendation and had accepted,
as is now not controversial, that the court does have jurisdiction to make such an
order, he would, in all the circumstances, have thought that that was the fair
order to make.

I would therefore, for my part, allow the appeal and make the order for which *b*
Mr Guthrie asks, leaving it to him in the first instance to produce an acceptable
draft.

ROSE LJ. I agree.

ROCH LJ. I also agree.   *c*

Appeal allowed.

                                        L I Zysman Esq   Barrister.

Kpohraror v Woolwich Building Society

COURT OF APPEAL, CIVIL DIVISION
EVANS, WAITE LJJ AND SIR JOHN MAY
25 OCTOBER, 30 NOVEMBER 1995

Contract – Damages for breach – Measure of damages – Foreseeable consequence of breach – Application of rule in Hadley v Baxendale – Building society mistakenly dishonouring cheque drawn on account used by plaintiff for business purposes – Injury to plaintiff's credit – Plaintiff claiming special damages for trading losses sustained by reason of delay – Building society denying knowledge of plaintiff's trading activities – Whether plaintiff who was not established trader entitled to recover damages.

The plaintiff, a Nigerian, converted an existing savings account with the defendant building society to a current account. On the application form he described himself as a self-employed 'exporter/importer' and stated that his annual income was below £5,000. The plaintiff subsequently drew a cheque for £4,550 on his account in favour of P Ltd. When P Ltd presented the cheque for payment with a request for special clearance, the defendants refused payment on the ground that the cheque had been reported lost. Later that same day, the defendants acknowledged that an error had occurred and immediately informed P Ltd that there were sufficient funds in the plaintiff's account to honour the cheque. The following day, P Ltd accepted one of the defendants' own corporate cheques as payment and thereupon released goods which were required by the plaintiff for shipment to Nigeria. The plaintiff subsequently commenced proceedings against the defendants claiming damages for wrongful dishonour of the cheque in breach of his current account contract with the defendants. They admitted liability and the master awarded damages of £5,550 with interest as general damages for the injury to the plaintiff's credit by reason of the dishonour of the cheque and the discreditable reason given by them for so doing. The award included a small allowance for the alleged injury to the plaintiff's credit and reputation in Nigeria. The plaintiff appealed to the Court of Appeal, contending that he was also entitled to recover special damages for trading losses sustained by reason of the delay to the shipment in question and further shipments. The defendants cross-appealed, contending that the damages awarded should be nominal on the ground that they did not know that the account was to be used for trading purposes.

Held – A person who was not a trader could recover substantial rather than nominal damages in contract for loss of credit or business reputation resulting from a cheque being wrongly dishonoured by his bank. It followed that the master's award was consistent with the correct approach to an award of general damages in the circumstances. However, the special damages which the plaintiff sought to recover were too remote, since there was nothing to indicate that a one-day delay in payment would cause the loss of a transaction or a substantial trading loss for the plaintiff, and the defendants could reasonably have expected that they would have been given special notice of the need for immediate clearance so that, if they were willing to do so, a special arrangement could be made. The appeal and cross-appeal would accordingly be dismissed (see p 123 *a*, p 124 *c*, p 125 *b f*, p 127 *b c e f* and p 128 *c*, post).

Hadley v Baxendale [1843–60] All ER Rep 461 applied.

Notes

For the measure of damages in contract, see 12 *Halsbury's Laws* (4th edn) paras *a*
1174–1176 and for a case on the subject, see 17(2) *Digest* (2nd reissue) 248, *1271*.

Cases referred to in judgments

Addis v Gramophone Co Ltd [1909] AC 488, [1908–10] All ER Rep 1, HL.
Bank of New South Wales v Milvain (1884) 10 VLR 3, Vic Full Ct.   *b*
Bliss v South East Thames Regional Health Authority [1987] ICR 700, CA.
Brown v KMR Services Ltd [1995] 4 All ER 598, CA.
Davidson v Barclays Bank Ltd [1940] 1 All ER 316.
Evans v London and Provincial Bank (1917) 3 LDAB 152.
Gibbons v Westminster Bank Ltd [1939] 3 All ER 577, [1939] 2 KB 882.
Hadley v Baxendale (1854) 9 Exch 341, [1843–60] All ER Rep 461, 156 ER 145.   *c*
Heron II, The, Koufos v C Czarnikow Ltd [1967] 3 All ER 686, [1969] 1 AC 350, [1967]
    3 WLR 1491, HL.
Joyce v Sengupta [1993] 1 All ER 897, [1993] 1 WLR 337, CA.
Monarch Steamship Co Ltd v Karlshamns (AB) Oljefabriker [1949] 1 All ER 1, [1949]
    AC 196, HL.   *d*
Parsons (H) (Livestock) Ltd v Uttley Ingham & Co Ltd [1978] 1 All ER 525, [1978] QB
    791, [1977] 3 WLR 990, CA.
President of India v La Pintada Cia Navegacion SA [1984] 2 All ER 773, [1985] AC 104,
    [1984] 3 WLR 10, HL.
Rae v Yorkshire Bank plc [1988] BTLC 35, CA.
Rolin v Steward (1854) 14 CB 595, 139 ER 245.   *e*
Wilson v United Counties Bank Ltd [1920] AC 102, [1918–19] All ER Rep 1035, HL.

Cases also cited or referred to in skeleton arguments

*Hill (Christopher) Ltd   v Ashington Piggeries Ltd, Christopher Hill Ltd v Fur Farm
    Supplies Ltd (Norsildmel, third party)* [1969] 3 All ER 1496 , CA; *rvsd sub nom* *f*
    Ashington Piggeries Ltd v Christopher Hill Ltd, Christopher Hill Ltd v Norsildmel
    [1971] 1 All ER 847, [1972] AC 441 HL.
Marzetti v Williams (1830) 1 B & Ad 415, [1824–34] All ER Rep 150, 109 ER 842.
Prehn v Royal Bank of Liverpool (1870) LR 5 Exch 92.
Seven Seas Properties Ltd v Al-Essa (No 2) [1993] 3 All ER 577, [1993] 1 WLR 1083.
Victoria Laundry (Windsor) Ltd v Newman Industries Ltd (Couldson & Co Ltd, third *g*
    party) [1949] 1 All ER 997, [1949] 2 KB 528, CA.

Appeal and cross-appeal

By notice dated 18 May 1994 the plaintiff, Udele Edirin Kpohraror, appealed from
the decision of Master Tennant in chambers on 16 February 1994 whereby he *h*
awarded the plaintiff damages of £5,500 in respect of an action for breach of
contract for wrongful dishonouring of his cheque against the defendants,
Woolwich Building Society, contending that he was also entitled to recover
special damages for loss of profit on the transaction and on ten further shipments
which would have followed from it. By notice dated 7 June 1994 the defendants
cross-appealed against the award on the ground that the plaintiff was only *j*
entitled to nominal damages. The facts are set out in the judgment of Evans LJ.

Daphne Loebl (instructed by *Anthony Gold Lerman & Muirhead*) for the plaintiff.
Katherine McQuail (instructed by *Morgan Bruce*, Cardiff) for the defendants.

                                                              Cur adv vult

30 November 1995. The following judgments were delivered.

EVANS LJ. On 9 September 1991 the plaintiff drew a cheque for £4,550 on his current bank account with the defendants at their branch at 136 Clapham High Street, London SW4. He is a Nigerian and he had described himself as a self-employed 'exporter/importer' as well as a part-time employee of two south London businesses when he converted his six-month-old savings account to a current account in June 1991. He stated that his income was below £5,000 p a.

The cheque was drawn in favour of Phils (Wholesalers) Ltd in the sum of £4,550. The current balance at the time was about £4,800 including a cheque for £3,000 which was credited to the account on 3 September.

The cheque was presented for payment on 10 September at the payee's bankers with a request for special clearance. Sometime during that day the defendants refused payment on the ground 'Cheque reported lost' and this was reported by the payee to the plaintiff. He went to the defendants' branch where he had his account before 5 p m. The error, for it was an error, was acknowledged and the manageress told the payee by telephone at the plaintiff's request that there were sufficient funds in the account. She persuaded the payee to accept the defendants' own corporate cheque and gave this to the plaintiff at about 5.15 p m. He took it to the payee, Phils (Wholesalers) Ltd, next morning, who accepted it as payment then and agreed to release goods which the plaintiff required for shipment to Nigeria. The goods were cosmetic products which the plaintiff had bought for re-sale there.

The plaintiff claims damages for wrongful dishonour of the cheque in breach of his current account contract with the defendants, and liability is admitted. The assessment of damages came before Master Tennant in chambers on 16 February 1994. He awarded £5,550 with interest as general damages for the injury to the plaintiff's credit by reason of the dishonour of the cheque and the apparently discreditable reason given for it, which was of course unfounded. He rejected the defendants' submission that the damages award should be nominal only, and he likewise rejected the plaintiff's claim for a much greater sum, pleaded as £57,185·68.

The plaintiff and the defendants appeal and cross-appeal respectively. We have had the benefit, as did the master, of detailed and helpful submissions from Miss Loebl for the plaintiff and Miss McQuail for the defendants.

The claim is for general damages for loss of business reputation and credit and for special damages of which particulars are given in the amended statement of claim. These can be set out verbatim:

'PARTICULARS OF SPECIAL DAMAGE

The said cheque was drawn to pay for goods which were due to be collected from the said Phils (Wholesale) on 12th September 1992 for shipment for McTeri Ltd in Nigeria which shipment could not take place by reason whereof the Plaintiff's contract with the said McTeri Ltd was terminated and the said goods had to be sold elsewhere.

(1) Claim from McTeri Ltd in Nigeria for N300,000·00 (Niras) [sic] conversion as at October 18th 1991 Nairas to the pound	15,949·49
(2) Losses due to selling below sale price	4,996·81
(3) Profit loss for December caused by cancellation of Contract	3,294·60

(4) Profit loss for four shipments 1992 caused by cancellation of Contract assessed on the basis of £3,298·49 per shipment	13,178·40	a
(5) Profit loss for four shipments for 1993 based on profits per shipment of £3,298·49	13,178·40	
(6) Profit loss for two shipments/consignments for 1994 assessed on the basis of £3,298·49 per shipment	6,596·98	b
Total	57,185·68'	

(Strangely, a pleaded claim for general damages in para 6 of the original statement of claim was deleted by amendment, but it is not suggested that no such award should be made for this reason.)

The claim is for damages for breach of contract, rather than in tort, although the award of substantial damages for loss of business reputation appears to have an obvious affinity with tortious claims.

In Ellinger and Lomnicka *Modern Banking Law* (2nd edn, 1994) p 387, in their chapter dealing with 'The customer's remedies for wrongful dishonour of his cheques', the authors write: 'A re-examination of the basic principle is timely.' Counsel submit that the present case provides the opportunity for doing so. The basic principle referred to has the authority of the House of Lords in *Wilson v United Counties Bank Ltd* [1920] AC 102, [1918–19] All ER Rep 1035 and of this court (O'Connor and Parker LJJ) as recently as 1987, in *Rae v Yorkshire Bank plc* [1988] BTLC 35. It is open to us, however, to consider what the principle is and what its limits are.

Both parties accept that the claim is governed by the general law, that is to say the plaintiff may recover general damages under the first head of the rule in *Hadley v Baxendale* (1854) 9 Exch 341, [1843–60] All ER Rep 461 and special damages under the second head of the rule when the necessary facts are proved. This is not the only sense in which the terms 'general' and 'special' damages are used nor the only context in which a distinction is made between them. One such distinction is that special damages must be expressly claimed and pleaded, whereas general damages need not (see generally *McGregor on Damages* (15th edn, 1988) para 19).

The claim for general damages rests upon the first part of the rule in *Hadley v Baxendale*, namely, they are claimed as damages 'arising naturally (which means in the normal course of things)' from the defendant's breach (see *Monarch Steamship Co Ltd v Karlshamns (AB) Oljefabriker* [1949] 1 All ER 1 at 12, [1949] AC 196 at 221 per Lord Wright). It is not disputed that a claim does arise for loss of credit or business reputation, but the defendants say that the amount should be nominal unless special facts are proved which were made known to them when the contract was made; in other words, that this should properly be regarded under the second, not the first part of the *Hadley v Baxendale* rule. They rely upon a number of reported cases where nominal damages only were awarded: by a jury in *Evans v London and Provincial Bank* (1917) 3 LDAB 152, by Lawrence J in *Gibbons v Westminster Bank Ltd* [1939] 3 All ER 577, [1939] 2 KB 882 and by this court in *Rae v Yorkshire Bank plc*, where a claim for substantial damages for 'inconvenience and humiliation' was dismissed.

However, the plaintiff relies upon the line of authority which holds that actual damage need not be alleged or proved by 'a trader', which he claims that he was. The defendants say that they were unaware of this, and that the rule does not apply, for that reason alone.

a   As will appear below, the issue in my view is whether a person who is not 'a trader' for the purposes of the common law rule—and it is not at all clear what the limits of that category are—can recover substantial rather than nominal damages for loss of business reputation when his cheque is wrongly dishonoured by the bank. A subsidiary question is how much the measure of damages is affected by the extent of the bank's knowledge of its customer and of the purposes for which he uses his account.

b   I will start with the authorities which establish that a 'trader' is entitled to recover substantial, rather than nominal, damages for loss of business reputation without proof of actual damage. This was recognised and applied, although in a different context, by the House of Lords in *Wilson v United Counties Bank Ltd* [1920] AC 102, [1918–19] All ER Rep 1035. Lord Birkenhead LC said:

c
    'The objection was taken by the defendants that this finding of the jury cannot be supported without proof of special damage. In deciding this point, I do not lay down a rule of general law, but I deal with the exceptional language of an exceptional contract. The defendants undertook for consideration to sustain the credit of the trading customer. On principle the
d   case seems to me to belong to that very special class of cases in which a banker, though his customer's account is in funds, nevertheless dishonours his cheque. The ratio decidendi in such cases is that the refusal to meet the cheque, under such circumstances, is so obviously injurious to the credit of a trader that the latter can recover, without allegation of special damage, reasonable compensation for the injury done to his credit. The leading case
e   upon this point is that of *Rolin* v. *Steward* ((1854) 14 CB 595, 139 ER 245). The direction of Lord Campbell to the jury has been generally accepted and treated as an accurate statement of the law. If it be held that there is an irrebuttable presumption that the dishonour of a trader customer's cheque in the events supposed is injurious to him and may be compensated by other
f   than nominal damages, the conclusion would appear to follow almost a fortiori that such damages may be given where the defendant has expressly contracted to sustain the financial credit of a trading customer and has committed a breach of his agreement.' (See [1920] AC 102 at 112, [1918–19] All ER Rep 1035 at 1037.)

g   (See also [1920] AC 102 at 120, 132–133, [1918–19] All ER Rep 1035 at 1038, 1041 per Viscount Finlay and Lord Atkinson.)
    Two passages should be quoted from *Rolin v Steward* (1854) 14 CB 595, 139 ER 245. Lord Campbell CJ directed the jury to give 'not nominal, nor excessive, but reasonable and temperate damages' (see 14 CB 595 at 605, 139 ER 245 at 249). In
h   the Court of Common Pleas, Williams J said that—

    'when ... the [customer] is a trader ... the jury, in estimating the damages, may take into their consideration the natural and necessary consequences which must result to the [customer] from the [bank's] breach of contract: just as in the case of an action for a slander of a person in the way of his trade, or
j   in the case of an imputation of insolvency on a trader, the action lies without proof of special damage.' (See (1854) 14 CB 595 at 607, 139 ER 245 at 250.)

The rule so stated made it necessary to consider in every case whether or not the plaintiff was a trader. In Australia in 1884 a farmer was not (see *Bank of New South Wales v Milvain* 10 VLR 3). In England, in 1940, a bookmaker was (see *Davidson v Barclays Bank Ltd* [1940] 1 All ER 316), but it is an open question whether professionals such as solicitors and accountants who are 'akin to businessmen' are within the rule (see *Ellinger and Lomnicka* p 387).

It is abundantly clear, in my judgment, that history has changed the social factors which moulded the rule in the nineteenth century. It is not only a tradesman of whom it can be said that the refusal to meet his cheque is 'so obviously injurious to [his] credit' that he should 'recover, without allegation of special damage, reasonable compensation for the injury done to his credit' (see [1920] AC 102 at 112, [1918–19] All ER Rep 1035 at 1037 per Lord Birkenhead LC). The credit rating of individuals is as important as it is for their personal transactions, including mortgages and hire-purchase as well as banking facilities, as it is for those who are engaged in trade, and it is notorious that central registers are now kept. I would have no hesitation in holding that what is in effect a presumption of some damage arises in every case, in so far as this is a presumption of fact.

So the question becomes, whether the authorities compel the conclusion as a matter of law that the presumption cannot extend beyond the category of trader. In my judgment, they do not. The most directly relevant are *Gibbons v Westminster Bank Ltd* [1939] 3 All ER 577, [1939] 2 KB 882 and *Rae v Yorkshire Bank plc* [1988] BTLC 35. In the former case, Lawrence J regarded the presumption in favour of a trader as one of four exceptions to the general rule that the plaintiff in a claim for damages for breach of contract cannot recover substantial damages in the absence of proof that some actual damage has been suffered, and he felt unable to extend the exception to non-traders (see *Addis v Gramophone Co Ltd* [1909] AC 488 at 495, [1908–10] All ER Rep 1 at 5 per Lord Atkinson). He said:

'The authorities which have been cited to me all lay down that a trader is entitled to recover substantial damages without pleading and proving actual damage for the dishonour of his cheque, but it has never been held that that exception to the general rule as to the measure of damages for breach of contract extends to any one who is not a trader.' (See [1939] 3 All ER 577 at 579, [1939] 2 KB 882 at 888.)

In *Rae v Yorkshire Bank plc* the plaintiff's claim was for damages for 'inconvenience and humiliation' (see [1988] BTLC 35 at 37). Parker LJ, with whom O'Connor LJ agreed, cited *Bliss v South East Thames Regional Health Authority* [1987] ICR 700, where Dillon LJ held that the general rule laid down in *Addis v Gramophone Co Ltd* is that—

'where damages fall to be assessed for breach of contract rather than in tort it is not permissible to award general damages for frustration, mental distress, injured feelings or annoyance occasioned by the breach.' (See [1987] ICR 700 at 717–718.)

Dillon LJ also noted a further exception to the general rule which is now permitted 'where the contract which has been broken was itself a contract to provide peace of mind or freedom from distress' (see [1987] ICR 700 at 718). Parker LJ continued ([1988] BTLC 35 at 37): 'That authority, and *Gibbons*, are two of many which in my view make Mr Rae's an appeal which must inevitably fail.' Clearly, the judgment in *Rae v Yorkshire Bank plc* was based primarily in the application of the law as stated by Dillon LJ to the facts of that case, where the claim was for 'inconvenience and humiliation' (only). That is a different kind of damage from loss of reputation or credit, unless 'humiliation' is intended to include such injury in the eyes of third parties, but that point was not taken in a *Rae*'s case because the kinds of damage referred to by Dillon LJ all refer to the injured feelings of the plaintiff himself.

The trial judge in *Rae* had referred to *Gibbons* and said (see [1988] BTLC 35 at 36): 'It is clear that Mr Rae was not a trader and that in those circumstances, damages are purely nominal'. Apart from the passing reference to *Gibbons* in the passage already quoted, the 'trader' rule, or exception, was not considered in the b judgments in the Court of Appeal.

In these circumstances, neither *Rae* nor *Gibbons* itself is binding authority which precludes this court from considering whether a bank's customer who is not a trader is precluded from recovering substantial damages for injury to his reputation or credit, unless special damage is alleged and proved. The trader exception itself recognises, as does the general rule regarding the recovery of c damages for tort, that this is a kind of injury recognised by law. If the trader is an exception to the general rules regarding damages for breach of contract, then the explanation may lie in the tortious analogy with damages for injury to business credit. In *Addis v Gramophone Co Ltd* Lord Atkinson did not refer to any 'trader' rule, but generally to 'actions against a banker for refusing to pay a customer's d cheque when he has in his hands funds of the customer's to meet it' (see [1909] AC 488 at 495, [1908–10] All ER Rep 1 at 5). *McGregor* deals with the rule as applying only to traders but also states generally that 'loss by injury to credit and reputation caused by the defendants' failure to honour the plaintiff's drafts may be presumed' (see paras 1222, 1785). (Damages for loss of reputation simpliciter are excluded, whether in contract or for torts other than defamation (see *Joyce v e Sengupta* [1993] 1 All ER 897, [1993] 1 WLR 337).)

Moreover, if the exception is a presumption of fact then it is open to the court, in my judgment, to hold that changing social circumstances should cause the presumption to be reviewed and if necessary expanded in order to take those changes into account.

f For these reasons, I would reject the defendants' allegation by way of cross-appeal that the master was wrong to award more than a nominal sum by way of general damages. I should, however, also refer to their contention that the master was wrong to do so when the defendants denied that they had knowledge of the fact that he was a trader. In none of the reported cases where a trader has succeeded in recovering substantial damages has the bank's g knowledge been in issue. The master decided this effectively as a preliminary issue. The defendants wished to call as a witness their employee who dealt with the plaintiff when he converted his savings account into a current account in June 1991. She would have denied, as her affidavit evidence indicated, that he told her that the account would be used for trading purposes. So the master gave 'part 1' h of his judgment holding that substantial damages could be awarded even where the bank had no knowledge 'actual or implied of the plaintiff's status as a trader and the use of his account'. If the trader 'exception' is good law then I doubt whether this can be correct, if only because it offends against the basic requirement of both parts of the rule in *Hadley v Baxendale* which is that the test j of remoteness and therefore of the right to recover a particular head of damage depends upon the state of the defendant's knowledge of the likely, or 'not unlikely' (see *The Heron II, Koufos v C Czarnikow Ltd* [1967] 3 All ER 686, [1969] 1 AC 350), consequences of his breach, whether 'in the usual course of things' because of what the defendant is taken to have known or by reason of his actual knowledge of special facts. But it is unnecessary to express a concluded view, because the evidence is that the plaintiff described himself in the application form

as a part-time self-employed 'exporter/importer' although clearly on a modest
scale. This evidence is not and cannot be disputed and it is sufficient in my   *a*
judgment to fix the defendants with knowledge that that was the self-styled
description of the plaintiff for the purposes of the contract between them with
regard to the current account. To this extent, it was a question of 'status' and the
defendants knew what that status was. If it is objected that they should also have
knowledge that the account was to be used for trading purposes, then this is a   *b*
further refinement of the trader exception—the dishonour of a personal cheque
could be no less harmful to the trader's credit than of one drawn on a trading
account, perhaps even more so—and an additional reason why in my judgment,
the exception or rule should not be confined as the defendants say that it should.

Special damages   *c*
    I come therefore to the plaintiff's main ground of appeal. He asserts, in the
'particulars of special damage' already quoted, that he is entitled to recover
damages for his loss of profit on the transaction in question and on ten further
shipments which, he says, would have followed from it if the first shipment had
not been delayed. He claims, moreover, that his losses in respect of the goods   *d*
which were delayed included a very large sum ('Claim from McTeri Ltd in
Nigeria for N300,000 (converted as) £15,949·49') which he was compelled to pay
to his Nigerian customer both by reason of his legal liabilities, as he asserts, owed
to that customer and because considerable pressures, both commercial and
social, were brought to bear upon him and his father and family by that customer
in Nigeria. So, Miss Loebl submits on his behalf, these were all heads of damage   *e*
which could reasonably be contemplated by the defendants when the banking
contract was made, not because they had any knowledge of the circumstances of
the particular transaction or of any intended transaction, but because they knew,
as the plaintiff asserts, that he was an 'exporter/importer' and that he intended to
use the account for his business activities. To these might be added the fact which   *f*
is undisputed that the defendants knew that the plaintiff is Nigerian and so, it
might be submitted, were also aware that exports of goods might be delivered
there.
    The master dealt with this part of the claim on the assumption that the plaintiff
was correct as to the extent of the defendants' knowledge. He held that
nevertheless these damages could not be recovered, either under the first limb of   *g*
Hadley v Baxendale ('this was such an extraordinary outcome it could not possibly
be regarded as a natural consequence of a banker's breach of contract') or under
the second limb, because even on the basis of the defendants' assumed
knowledge 'this claim … raises a narrative of events which though not
unimaginable is certainly not foreseeable in the ordinary course'.   *h*
    Miss Loebl submits that it is not necessary for the plaintiff to prove either that
the precise sequence of events was foreseeable or that the losses might be as
extensive as they were. She relies in particular upon *H Parsons (Livestock) Ltd v
Uttley Ingham & Co Ltd* [1978] 1 All ER 525, [1978] QB 791 and the recent
judgments in *Brown v KMR Services Ltd* [1995] 4 All ER 598. Given the facts which   *j*
were known, or are asserted to have been known by the defendants, they could
reasonably contemplate, it is submitted, that a breach of contract such as
occurred might cause him losses of the kind which he alleges that he has suffered.
    For my part, I cannot regard this as a claim falling within the second limb of
Hadley v Baxendale. It is not a case where the defendant is said to have had
knowledge of 'special circumstances' so that this part of the rule applies. Rather,

a the question is, in my judgment, whether, given the plaintiff's general description of himself and of the purposes for which he intended to use the account, it can be said that damages arising from the loss or late performance of his contract to sell and deliver the goods to Nigeria can reasonably be supposed to have been in the contemplation of both parties when the contract was made, or as the 'not unlikely consequence' of the defendants' breach, if it should occur (*The Heron II*).
b This is the first rather than the second limb of the rule, although as I shall say below I am doubtful whether it assists to make a rigid distinction of this sort.

In my judgment, and in agreement with the master, these damages were too remote to be claimed under this head. Even if the defendants were told that the account was to be used for the plaintiff's business, even trading activities, there was nothing to indicate that a cheque, even one drawn in favour of a goods
c wholesaler, was required for the purposes of international trade and in circumstances where even one day's delay in payment would or might cause the loss of a transaction or a substantial trading loss for the plaintiff. What might perhaps be contemplated was that, if such a situation did arise, then the plaintiff would give the defendants special notice of the need for immediate clearance so
d that, if they were willing to do so, a special arrangement could be made.

There is also the pragmatic reason given by the master, which is that there is no reported case where a bank's customer has recovered damages such as these for the wrongful dishonour of a cheque, where no special circumstances were alleged to exist.

e *Generally*

The above conclusions mean that I would dismiss both the appeal and the cross-appeal, and would uphold the master's award of general damages of £5,550. He said that it was 'somewhat coincidental' that this was £1,000 more than the amount of the cheque, although I think he meant by this that the appropriate sum
f by way of general damages could be calculated in that way in the circumstances of this case. This amount, as he explained, contained some allowance, though not very great, for injury to the plaintiff's credit and reputation in Nigeria such as was alleged to have occurred. This is consistent with a correct approach to the award of general damages in a case where the plaintiff claimed that he was an exporter/importer and therefore the defendants could reasonably contemplate
g that he might suffer some injury to his credit in a country overseas.

The contentions for both parties were presented as if in a straitjacket imposed by the strict application of the rule in *Hadley v Baxendale* so as to require the separate consideration of each of the two limbs. Miss Loebl submitted that there should be an award of general damages for injury to credit and of special damages
h for the trading losses allegedly sustained by reason of the delay to the particular shipment. Miss McQuail for the defendants submitted that general damages should be confined to 'loss flowing naturally being the unavailability to the customer of his money'—a difficult submission, in the light of the House of Lords decision in *President of India v La Pintada Cia Navegacion SA* [1984] 2 All ER 773 esp
j at 778, 789, [1985] AC 104 esp at 115, 129)—and 'other loss depending upon the matters known to the parties at the time of the contract', which might include damages for loss of reputation or credit and for trading losses, in appropriate circumstances. The master held that the bank's knowledge of whether the customer was 'a trader' or whether the account was to be used for trading purposes was irrelevant as a matter of law to the loss of credit claim. I would prefer to hold that the starting point for any application of *Hadley v Baxendale* is

the extent of the shared knowledge of both parties when the contract was made (see generally *Chitty on Contracts* (27th edn, 1994) vol 1, para 26-023, including the *a* possibility that knowledge of the defendant alone is enough). When that is established, it may often be the case that the first and the second parts of the rule overlap, or at least that it is unnecessary to draw a clear line of demarcation between them. This seems to me to be consistent with the commonsense approach suggested by Scarman LJ in *H Parsons (Livestock) Ltd v Uttley Ingham &* *b* *Co Ltd* [1978] 1 All ER 525 at 541, [1978] QB 791 at 813, and to be applicable here.

As stated above, I would dismiss both the appeal and the cross-appeal and uphold the master's award.

WAITE LJ. I agree that the appeal and cross-appeal should both be dismissed for all the reasons given by Evans LJ, with which I am in full agreement.   *c*

SIR JOHN MAY. I also wholly agree with the judgment which Evans LJ has just handed down and that in consequence both the appeal and cross-appeal should be dismissed.

Appeal and cross-appeal dismissed. Leave to appeal to the House of Lords refused.   *d*

Paul Magrath Esq   Barrister.

a # Crédit Suisse v Allerdale Borough Council

COURT OF APPEAL, CIVIL DIVISION

NEILL, PETER GIBSON AND HOBHOUSE LJJ

19–22, 26–28 FEBRUARY, 8 MAY 1996

b

Local authority – Statutory powers – Implied power – Local authority forming company to finance capital project and avoid statutory controls on borrowing – Company borrowing finance to fund leisure pool and time-share development – Local authority guaranteeing loan to company – Company defaulting on loan repayments – Whether c *local authority liable under guarantee – Whether local authority acting ultra vires in forming company and giving guarantee – Whether guarantee enforceable – Local Government Act 1972, s 111 – Local Government (Miscellaneous Provisions) Act 1976, s 19.*

d In 1986 the defendant local authority established a limited liability company, A Ltd, to assist with the financing of a leisure pool complex, with the intention that the company would be able to obtain finance outside the statutory controls imposed on local authority borrowing. In due course the plaintiff bank loaned £6m to A Ltd on terms providing for repayment of the loan by 31 May 1996. The local authority entered into a contract of guarantee which provided for payment e on demand of all moneys owed by A Ltd to the bank in respect of the loan in the event of the winding up of the company. A Ltd purchased a long leasehold of the site and commenced development of the leisure pool complex together with time-share accommodation, with the intention that the proceeds of sale of the time-share units would be used to pay off all bank borrowings. As the development progressed, however, sales of the time-share units were less than f anticipated and the company was unable to meet the repayment instalments. In December 1990 the local authority passed a resolution that A Ltd be put into voluntary liquidation. The bank made demand under the guarantee for payment of the sums owed by the company and thereafter commenced proceedings against the local authority. The judge dismissed the bank's claim on the basis, g inter alia, that the local authority had no statutory power to enter into the guarantee. The bank appealed, contending that the local authority had the requisite statutory powers to enter into the scheme and to give the guarantee under s 19(1)[a] of the Local Government (Miscellaneous Provisions) Act 1976, which empowered local authorities to provide recreational facilities, and s 111[b] h of the Local Government Act 1972, which gave local authorities subsidiary power to do any thing calculated to facilitate the discharge of any of their functions.

Held – A local authority had no express power under s 19 of the 1976 Act to establish a company for the purposes of borrowing the requisite finance to enable it to provide recreational facilities, nor an implied power under s 111 of the 1972 j Act to guarantee a loan made to such a company. The power in s 111 to 'do any thing (whether or not involving the ... borrowing ... of money ...) which is calculated to facilitate, or is conducive or incidental to' the discharge of its

---

a   Section 19, so far as material, is set out at p 142 *d* to p 143 *a*, post
b   Section 111, so far as material, is set out at p 143 *b c*, post

functions had to be construed in the context of the relevant statutory functions and circumstances, including the fact that Sch 13 to the 1972 Act established a *a* comprehensive code which defined and limited the borrowing powers of local authorities, thereby providing the means for a local authority to obtain financial resources to enable it to accomplish its statutory functions. It followed that the only implied power under s 111 could be a power for the local authority itself to borrow and any such power had to be exercised in conformity with other *b* relevant statutory provisions. The use of the company and the giving of the guarantee were therefore ultra vires the local authority's express and implied powers. It followed that the contract of guarantee entered into by the local authority was void and unenforceable. Accordingly the appeal would be dismissed (see p 142 *b c*, p 148 *f j*, p 149 *b d* to *g*, p 152 *c*, p 159 *j*, p 161 *b* to *d f* to *h*, p 162 *e* to *g*, p 163 *d* and p 175 *j*, post); *Hazell v Hammersmith and Fulham London BC* *c* [1991] 1 All ER 545 and *McCarthy & Stone (Developments) Ltd v Richmond upon Thames London BC* [1991] 4 All ER 897 applied.

Notes

For a local authority's power to incur expenditure in general, see 28 *Halsbury's* *d* *Laws* (4th edn) paras 1245–1247, and for cases on the subject, see 33 *Digest* (2nd reissue) 54–57, *135–144*.

For the Local Government Act 1972, s 111, Sch 13, see 25 *Halsbury's Statutes* (4th edn) (1996 reissue) 267, 433. From 1 April 1990, Pt I, Sch 13 to the 1972 Act was repealed by s 194(2) of and Pt I, Sch 12 to the Local Government and Housing Act 1989. *e*

For the Local Government (Miscellaneous Provisions) Act 1976, s 19, see 35 *Halsbury's Statutes* (4th edn) (1993 reissue) 449.

Cases referred to in judgments

A-G v Great Eastern Rly Co (1880) 5 App Cas 473, HL.   *f*
A-G (ex rel Martin) v Finsbury BC [1939] 3 All ER 995, [1939] Ch 892.
Agricultural Horticultural and Forestry Industry Training Board v Aylesbury Mushrooms Ltd [1972] 1 All ER 280, [1972] 1 WLR 190.
Anisminic Ltd v Foreign Compensation Commission [1969] 1 All ER 208, [1969] 2 AC 147, [1964] 2 WLR 163, HL.
Ashbury Rly Carriage and Iron Co Ltd v Riche (1875) LR 7 HL 653, HL; *rvsg* sub nom *g* *Riche v Ashbury Rly Carriage and Iron Co Ltd* (1874) LR 9 Exch 224, Ex Ch.
Associated Provincial Picture Houses Ltd v Wednesbury Corp [1947] 2 All ER 680, [1948] 1 KB 223, CA.
Calvin v Carr [1979] 2 All ER 440, [1980] AC 574, [1979] 2 WLR 755, PC.
Chapleo v Brunswick Permanent Building Society (1881) 6 QBD 696, CA.   *h*
Chief Constable of the North Wales Police v Evans [1982] 3 All ER 141, [1982] 1 WLR 1155, HL.
Colman v Eastern Counties Rly Co (1846) 10 Beav 1, 50 ER 481, MR.
Council of Civil Service Unions v Minister for the Civil Service [1984] 3 All ER 935, [1985] AC 374, [1984] 3 WLR 1174, HL.   *j*
Crane v DPP [1921] 2 AC 299, [1921] All ER Rep 19, HL.
Den Norske Creditbank v Sarawak Economic Development Corp [1989] 2 Lloyd's Rep 35.
Grunwick Processing Laboratories Ltd v Advisory Conciliation and Arbitration Service [1978] 1 All ER 338, [1978] AC 655, [1978] 2 WLR 277, CA and HL.

a   *Hazell v Hammersmith and Fulham London BC* [1991] 1 All ER 545, [1992] 2 AC 1, [1991] 2 WLR 372, HL; *rvsg* [1990] 3 All ER 33, [1990] 2 QB 697, [1990] 2 WLR 17, CA.

Hoffmann-La Roche (F) & Co AG v Secretary of State for Trade and Industry [1974] 2 All ER 1128, [1975] AC 295, [1974] 3 WLR 104, HL.

IRC v National Federation of Self-Employed and Small Businesses Ltd [1981] 2 All ER 93, [1982] AC 617, [1981] 2 WLR 722, HL.

b   *London and Clydeside Estates Ltd v Aberdeen DC* [1979] 3 All ER 876 [1980] 1 WLR 182, HL.

McCarthy & Stone (Developments) Ltd v Richmond upon Thames London BC [1991] 4 All ER 897, [1992] 2 AC 48, [1991] 3 WLR 941, HL.

Norwich Corp v Norfolk Rly Co (1855) 4 E & B 397, 119 ER 143.

c   *NWS 6 v Waltham Forest London BC* (17 November 1992, unreported), QBD.

O'Reilly v Mackman [1982] 3 All ER 1124, [1983] 2 AC 237, [1982] 3 WLR 1096, HL.

Page v Hull University Visitor [1993] 1 All ER 97, [1993] AC 682, [1992] 3 WLR 1112, HL.

Payne (David) & Co Ltd, Re, Young v David Payne & Co Ltd [1904] 2 Ch 608, Ch D

d   and CA.

R v Broadcasting Complaints Commission, ex p Owen [1985] 2 All ER 522, [1985] QB 1153, [1985] 2 WLR 1025.

R v Monopolies and Mergers Commission, ex p Argyll Group plc [1986] 2 All ER 257, [1986] 1 WLR 763, CA.

e   *R v Panel on Take-overs and Mergers, ex p Datafin plc (Norton Opax plc intervening)* [1987] 1 All ER 564, [1987] QB 815, [1987] 2 WLR 699, CA.

R v South Wales Traffic Licensing Authority, ex p Ebbw Vale UDC [1951] 1 All ER 806, [1951] 2 KB 366, CA.

Ridge v Baldwin [1963] 2 All ER 66, [1964] AC 40, [1963] 2 WLR 935, HL.

Rolled Steel Products (Holdings) Ltd v British Steel Corp [1985] 3 All ER 52, [1986] Ch

f   246, [1985] 2 WLR 908, CA.

Salomon v Salomon & Co [1897] AC 22, [1895–9] All ER Rep 33, HL.

Small v Smith (1884) 10 App Cas 119, HL.

Smith v East Elloe RDC [1956] 1 All ER 855, [1956] AC 736, [1956] 2 WLR 888, HL.

Sutton's Hospital Case (1612) 10 Co Rep 1, [1558–1774] All ER Rep 11, 77 ER 937,

g   Ex Ch.

Tamlin v Hannaford [1949] 2 All ER 327, [1950] 1 KB 23, CA.

Tower Hamlets London BC v Chetnik Developments Ltd [1988] 1 All ER 961, [1988] AC 858, [1988] 2 WLR 654, HL.

United City Merchants (Investments) Ltd v Royal Bank of Canada [1982] 2 All ER 720, [1983] 1 AC 168, [1982] 2 WLR 1039, HL.

h   *Wandsworth London BC v Winder* [1984] 3 All ER 976, [1985] AC 461, [1984] 3 WLR 1254, HL.

Wenlock (Baroness) v River Dee Co (1885) 10 App Cas 354, HL.

Wood v Woad (1874) LR 9 Exch 190, [1874–80] All ER Rep 408.

Woolwich Equitable Building Society v IRC [1991] 4 All ER 92, [1990] 1 WLR 1400,

j   HL.

Cases also cited or referred to in skeleton arguments

A-G v Ryan [1980] AC 718, [1980] 2 WLR 143, PC.

A-G v West Ham Corp [1910] 2 Ch 560.

A-G for Ceylon v A D Silva [1953] AC 461, [1953] 2 WLR 1185, PC.

Adams v Cape Industries plc [1991] 1 All ER 929, [1990] Ch 433, Ch D and CA.

An Bord Bainne Co-op Ltd (Irish Dairy Board) v Milk Marketing Board [1984] 2 CMLR 584, CA.

Ashbridge Investments Ltd v Minister of Housing and Local Government [1965] 3 All ER 371, [1965] 1 WLR 1320, CA.

Barned's Banking Co, Re, ex p Contract Corp (1867) LR 3 Ch App 105.

Cocks v Thanet DC [1982] 3 All ER 1135, [1983] 2 AC 286, HL.

DPP v Head [1958] 1 All ER 679, [1959] AC 83, HL.

DPP v Hutchinson [1990] 2 All ER 836, [1990] 2 AC 783, HL.

Dundee Harbour Trustees v D & J Nicol [1915] AC 550, HL.

Dunlop v Woollahra Municipal Council [1981] 1 All ER 1202, [1982] AC 158, PC.

European Society Arbitration Acts, Re, ex p British Nation Life Assurance Association (liquidators) (1878) 8 Ch D 679, CA.

Gale (decd), In the Estate of [1966] 1 All ER 945, [1966] Ch 236, CA.

Galloway v Mayor and Commonalty of London (1866) LR 1 HL 34.

Gardner v London Chatham and Dover Rly Co (1867) LR 2 Ch App 201, LJJ.

General Produce Co v United Bank Ltd [1979] 2 Lloyd's Rep 255.

Goodinson v Goodinson [1954] 2 All ER 255, [1954] 2 QB 118, CA.

Hampshire Land Co, Re [1896] 2 Ch 743.

Hanks v Minister of Housing and Local Government [1963] 1 All ER 47, [1963] 1 QB 999.

Hollier v Eyre (1840) 9 Cl & Fin 1, 8 ER 313, HL.

Holme v Brunskill (1877) 3 QBD 495, CA.

Isaacs v Robertson [1984] 3 All ER 140, [1985] AC 97, PC.

Kent CC v Kingsway Investments (Kent) Ltd, Kent CC v Kenworthy [1970] 1 All ER 70, [1971] AC 72, HL.

Kirklees Metropolitan BC v Wickes Building Supplies Ltd [1992] 3 All ER 717, [1993] AC 227, HL.

Kleinwort Benson Ltd v Glasgow City Council [1996] 2 All ER 257, [1996] 2 WLR 655, CA.

London and Clydesdale Estates Ltd v Aberdeen DC [1979] 3 All ER 876, [1980] 1 WLR 182, HL.

Luby v Newcastle-under-Lyme Corp [1964] 3 All ER 169, [1965] 1 QB 214, CA; affg [1964] 1 All ER 84, [1964] 2 QB 64.

Manchester City Council v Greater Manchester Metropolitan CC (1979) 78 LGR 71, CA.

Marseilles Extension Rly Co, Re, ex p Crédit Foncier and Mobilier of England (1871) LR 7 Ch App 161, LJJ.

Mayhew v Crickett (1818) 2 Swan 185, 36 ER 585, LC.

Meravale Builders Ltd v Secretary of State for the Environment (1978) 36 P & CR 87.

Metropolitan Properties Co (FGC) Ltd v Lannon [1968] 3 All ER 304, [1969] 1 QB 577, CA.

Montreal Street Rly Co v Normandin [1917] AC 170, PC.

National Bank of Greece SA v Pinios Shipping Co No 1 [1990] 1 All ER 78, [1990] 1 AC 637, HL.

Norwegian American Cruises A/S (formerly Norwegian American Lines A/S) v Paul Mundy Ltd, The Vistafjord [1988] 2 Lloyd's Rep 343, CA.

Padfield v Minister of Agriculture Fisheries and Food [1968] 1 All ER 694, [1968] AC 997, HL.

Potato Marketing Board v Merricks [1958] 2 All ER 538, [1958] 2 QB 316.

a *Proctor & Gamble Ltd v Secretary of State for the Environment* (1991) 63 P & CR 317, CA.

Provincial Bank of Ireland v Fisher [1919] 2 IR 249, HL.

R v Greenwich London BC, ex p Lovelace [1991] 3 All ER 511, [1991] 1 WLR 506, CA.

R v Inner London Education Authority, ex p Westminster City Council [1986] 1 All ER 19, [1986] 1 WLR 28.

b *R v Jones (Gwyn)* [1969] 1 All ER 325, [1969] 2 QB 33, CA.

R v Lewisham London BC, ex p Shell UK Ltd [1988] 1 All ER 938, DC.

R v Rochdale Metropolitan BC, ex p Cromer Ring Mill Ltd [1982] 3 All ER 761.

R v Secretary of State for Social Services, ex p Association of Metropolitan Authorities [1986] 1 All ER 164, [1986] 1 WLR 1.

c *R v Secretary of State for Social Services, ex p Cotton* (1985) Times, 5 August, [1985] CA Transcript 840.

R v Secretary of State for Transport, ex p de Rothschild [1989] 1 All ER 933, CA.

R v St Pancras Vestry (1890) 24 QBD 371, CA.

Royal Bank of Canada v IRC [1972] 1 All ER 225, [1972] Ch 665.

d *Simplex (G E) (Holdings) Ltd v Secretary of State for the Environment* (1988) 57 P & CR 306, CA.

Sinclair v Brougham [1914] AC 398, [1914–15] All ER Rep 622, HL.

Smith v Winter (1838) 4 M & W 454, 150 ER 1507.

Smith (A) & Son (Bognor Regis) Ltd v Walker [1952] 2 All ER 1008, [1952] 2 QB 319, CA.

e *Stockton and Darlington Rly Co v Brown* (1860) 9 HL Cas 246, 11 ER 724.

Thames Water Authority v Elmbridge BC [1983] 1 All ER 836, [1983] QB 570, CA.

Thrasyvoulou v Secretary of State for the Environment, Oliver v Secretary of State for the Environment [1990] 1 All ER 65, [1990] 2 AC 273, HL.

Tunstall v Steigmann [1962] 2 All ER 417, [1962] 2 QB 593, CA.

f *Westdeutsche Landesbank Girozentrale v Islington London BC* [1994] 4 All ER 890, [1994] 1 WLR 938, CA; *rvsd* [1996] 2 All ER 961, HL.

Western Fish Products Ltd v Penwith DC [1981] 2 All ER 204, CA.

Woodcock v Oxford and Worcester Rly Co (1853) 1 Drew 521, 61 ER 551.

Woolfson v Strathclyde Regional Council 1978 SLT 159, HL.

g

Appeal

By notice dated 10 August 1994 the plaintiff bank, Crédit Suisse, appealed from the decision of Colman J ([1995] 1 Lloyd's Rep 315) by order dated 29 July 1994 dismissing its claim against the defendant, Allerdale Borough Council, for
h payment under a contract of guarantee dated 23 May 1986 whereby the council had guaranteed repayment of a loan by the bank to Allerdale Development Co Ltd, a company set up by the council, on the grounds that the council had no statutory power to enter into the guarantee. The facts are set out in the judgment of Neill LJ.

j *Christopher Clarke QC* and *Catharine Otton-Goulder* (instructed by *Clyde & Co*) for the bank.

Jules Sher QC and *John Howell QC* (instructed by *Ward Hadaway & Co*, Newcastle) for the council.

Cur adv vult

8 May 1996. The following judgments were delivered.

a

NEILL LJ.

I. INTRODUCTION AND THE FACTS

This is an appeal by Crédit Suisse (the bank) from the order dated 29 July 1994 of Colman J ([1995] 1 Lloyd's Rep 315) dismissing the bank's claim against *b* Allerdale Borough Council (the council) under a contract of guarantee dated 23 May 1986. The appeal raises a number of questions relating to the powers of local authorities, including the subsidiary powers conferred by s 111(1) of the Local Government Act 1972. Before I come to examine these questions, however, it is necessary to set out the relevant facts in some detail.

c

Background to the case

The council was formerly the Allerdale District Council. The council came into existence as a district council on 1 April 1974. The constitution of the council is therefore governed by s 2 of the 1972 Act, which provides (in s 2(2)) that the council is to consist of a chairman and councillors and that the council is to have *d* all such functions as are vested in them by the 1972 Act or otherwise, and (in s 2(3)) that it shall be a body corporate. It is to be noted that by s 101(1) of the 1972 Act a local authority may arrange for the discharge of any of its functions by a committee, a sub-committee or an officer of the authority, though this arrangement is subject to any express provision in the 1972 Act or in any subsequent Act.

e

It is therefore important to remember, as Lord Templeman explained in *Hazell v Hammersmith and Fulham London BC* [1991] 1 All ER 545 at 548, [1992] 2 AC 1 at 22, that a local authority 'although democratically elected and representative of the area, is not a sovereign body and can only do such things as are expressly or impliedly authorised by Parliament'.

It is also important to remember that for many centuries Parliament and *f* central government have exercised a large measure of control over the financial affairs of bodies involved in local administration. Since about the middle of the nineteenth century this control has become increasingly stringent as a larger proportion of local authority expenditure has been funded by moneys contributed by central government. For the purposes of this judgment it is *g* sufficient to refer to two of the principal forms of control: the control of expenditure and the control of borrowing.

At the material time in 1986 and 1987 the capital expenditure of district councils was subject to the provisions set out in Pt VIII of and Sch 12 to the Local Government, Planning and Land Act 1980. Schedule 12 set out the categories of *h* prescribed expenditure which were subject to control. Prescribed expenditure included expenditure on the acquisition of land including buildings as well as the construction of buildings.

At the material time the principal provisions relating to the control of borrowing by district councils were contained in s 172 of the 1972 Act and in Sch *j* 13 to that Act. By para 1 of Sch 13 it was provided (a) that a principal council might borrow money for the purpose of lending money to another authority, and (b) that a local authority might borrow money for any other purpose or class of purpose approved by the Secretary of State and in accordance with any conditions subject to which the approval was given. This power to borrow was expressed to be without prejudice to s 111 of the 1972 Act, but as, by s 111(3), the

a power of the local authority to borrow under s 111(1) could not be exercised except in accordance with the enactments relating to borrowing, a local authority's power to borrow was effectively constrained by the need to obtain the approval of the Secretary of State.

It is further to be noted that in practice the approval of borrowing was effected by means of a block borrowing approval, which in broad terms entitled a district
b council to borrow to meet the cost of its prescribed expenditure. According to the figures which were produced at the trial, the prescribed expenditure limit for the council for 1985/86 was £5,382,000 and for 1986/87 it was £4,685,000. These limits included adjustments and the use of capital receipts. The borrowing limit for the council for 1985/86 was £3,682,000 and for 1986/87 was £2,726,000.

It will be seen therefore that at a time when public spending, including
c spending by local authorities, was under tight restraint, the scope for local authorities to borrow money for capital schemes, however desirable they might seem to be among the local community, was extremely limited. In general terms any borrowing required the approval of the Secretary of State, who would clearly be guided by the economic policy for the time being pursued by central
d government.

It is true that under s 137 of the 1972 Act a local authority was empowered to incur expenditure which in their opinion was in the interests of their area or any part of it or all or some of its inhabitants (including giving financial assistance, such as by giving a guarantee, to persons carrying on commercial or industrial undertakings), but at the relevant time this expenditure was limited to the
e product of a rate of 2p in the pound for the area. For the council the product of a 2p rate was less than £200,000.

It was against this background that the council, following a trend among other local authorities which had already been established for a few years, came to consider the use of a company to borrow the funds which were needed for what
f were thought to be desirable developments in the area.

From the early years of its existence the council, which was then the Allerdale District Council, was urged by the Keswick Town Council, then the lower tier of local government, to consider the provision of a swimming pool. A possible site for the swimming pool was the old railway station and the surrounding land, which had been acquired in 1979 by the Lake District Special Planning Board (the
g LDSPB). The railway station had been closed down some years before.

In his judgment Colman J traced the history of some of the earlier schemes which were considered between 1983 and 1985 which involved the provision of a swimming pool and other recreational facilities. For the purposes of this appeal, however, it is sufficient to restrict my account to a description of the plan which
h began to take shape towards the end of 1985.

On 18 December 1985 Mr A G Perry, the council treasurer, wrote a note for the forthcoming meeting of the council's joint management team. The purpose of the note was to provide an up-to-date report on the plans for the redevelopment of the Keswick station site. By that stage the redevelopment
j envisaged a joint scheme involving both the council and Clifford Barnett Developments Ltd (Clifford Barnett). It was also anticipated that the redevelopment would include a time-share development. In his note Mr Perry recommended that the service company of the Chartered Institute of Public Finance Accountants (CIPFA Services Ltd) should be engaged as financial advisors to the project and should be used in connection with the funding of the scheme.

On 15 January 1986 CIPFA produced a report on the Keswick station site. I
should refer to passages in this report:

'1. The structure chosen to achieve this development is: (a) Allerdale
creates a company limited by shares and underwrites its borrowings. The
reasons for this are that by channelling all the capital expenditure through
the company, the Council completely avoids capital expenditure controls,
whilst at the same time ensuring that the borrowing can be done at the finest
rates. (b) Allerdale appoints 2 or 3 councillors plus the Chief Executive/
Treasurer as Directors of the Board who implement the Council's policy.
(c) The company engages: Aspect Leisure to market the timeshare Cipfa
Services Ltd. to arrange bank finance Clifford Barnett to design and build;
manage the pool; manage the timeshare. (d) Allerdale District Council
purchases the freehold of the 2 sites and grants the company a long lease ...
(f) The proceeds of the timeshare will be used as follows: (i) to pay off all
bank borrowings, fees and rolled-up interest (ii) all marketing expenses (iii)
any other cost attributable to the scheme Only after all costs have been
discharged will there be any distribution between the Company and Clifford
Barnett Developments Ltd ...

3. *Clifford Barnett Developments Ltd.* Three separate agreements are
required: (i) the design and building contract is quite straightforward and
presents no special problems. (ii) the management of the pool has now to be
negotiated in detail. Broad outline of terms are:—25 years at nominal
rental—Company to bear all losses and keep all profits—Council to have
representation on board. Details on opening hours, prices, access of
timesharers etc. still to be finalised. (iii) the management of timeshare.
Many details have still to be worked out but broad outlines are:—the
Company will bear all losses and take all profits of all expenditure other than
marketing expenditure incurred by Aspect Leisure and all income other than
sales or rents of unsold periods ... The major issue to be decided is what ratio
the balance shall be distributed between the parties. Mr. Perry has already
given a lot of thought to this and should for the moment be left for him to
negotiate.

4. *Cipfa Services Ltd.* My Company has been and will continue as financial
advisor and our initial appointment is with the Council although we will
arrange finance for the Company. We will require a Council resolution
guaranteeing the Company's borrowing up to a limit of £6 million and a
Company resolution asking us to proceed ...'

On 17 January 1986 there was a meeting of the council's policy and finance
committee. At this meeting the redevelopment of the Keswick station site was
further considered. Mr Perry reported that it would be advantageous to the
council to create a limited liability company to assist with the financing of the
various capital projects that Allerdale was currently interested in. He advised that
the board of the company should be made up of three members of the council
and one officer and that it would be necessary for the council to provide the
company with a guarantee of £6m in order to be able to borrow the requisite
resources to carry out the capital projects concerned.

This advice was accepted by the committee, though with some dissenters.

The development of a leisure pool at the station site had also been considered
by the recreation and amenities committee on 9 January 1986.

a   A meeting of the full council took place on Wednesday, 29 January 1986. At this meeting the recommendations for the redevelopment made both by the recreation and amenities committee at its meeting on 9 January and of the policy and finance committee at its meeting on 17 January were approved with certain minor amendments. In particular it was resolved to approve the recommendations: (a) that a limited company should be set up to assist with the
b   financing of the council's capital projects and that the board of the company should be composed of three councillors and one officer; (b) that the council should provide the company with a guarantee of £6m; (c) that Allerdale Development Co Ltd should be formed and a guarantee provided accordingly; (d) that the council should purchase the freehold of the station and the adjoining site and grant a long lease of it to the company; and (e) that the proceeds of the
c   time-share unit sales and rental income should be used to pay off all bank borrowings.

On 11 February 1986 there was a meeting attended by Mr Perry, Mr Thwaytes, the council's solicitor, Mr Devas of CIPFA Services Ltd and two representatives of the district auditor. At this meeting the development scheme was explained
d   and it was decided that the opinion of Queen's Counsel should be obtained.

Instructions to advise were sent at once to Mr Gerald Moriarty QC. He was told that the council wished to develop the Keswick Station site as a leisure pool and an adjoining site for time-share accommodation. It was said that it was anticipated that 'the sale of the time-share accommodation will defray the cost of the leisure pool.' Information was given as to the method to be used for carrying
e   out the development which involved the formation of a company to purchase the Keswick Station site and the adjoining land. Reference was made to s 19 of the Local Government (Miscellaneous Provisions) Act 1976 and to s 111 of the 1972 Act. It was also said that on completion of the pool a company to be known as 'Keswick Operating Co' would be formed and franchised to run the pool for 25
f   years at no cost to Allerdale Development Co Ltd. Another company would be established and given a management agreement to promote and manage the time-share development. The instructions concluded: 'The council's real objective is to have a leisure pool built for the inhabitants of the area and tourists at no cost.' Counsel was asked to advise whether the scheme was intra vires the council and whether the concept of recreational facilities could include holiday
g   accommodation managed on a time-share basis, that is, the sale of leases at a premium.

Mr Moriarty advised in consultation and then gave a written opinion dated 12 February 1986. To his opinion he attached some draft resolutions for the council to consider. He drew attention to the wide powers of the council to provide
h   recreational facilities under ss 144 and 145 of the 1972 Act and s 19(1) of the 1976 Act. He also drew attention to the council's powers to acquire land under s 119 of the Town and Country Planning Act 1971 and s 120 of the 1972 Act. In his opinion he continued:

j   'The proposed company will not act as agent for the council but will take a lease granted by the council under s 120 of the [Town and Country Planning Act 1971] and s 123 of the [Local Government Act 1972], on terms that will produce a premium. It is important that any expenditure by the company shall not be prescribed expenditure of the council within Sch 12 to the Local [Government] Planning and Land Act 1980 ... In my view the giving of a guarantee by the council in respect of the company's liabilities is

within s 111 of the Act of 1972, but is not a grant or advance of a capital
nature within para 1(g) of Sch 12 of the Act of 1980. There is no need for any *a*
resolution by the council in respect of the company's management
agreement with the franchised operator of the pool, and it is preferable that
the council should not be directly concerned with that aspect.'

Steps were then taken to put the scheme into operation.

A company was purchased and its name was changed to Allerdale *b*
Development Co Ltd. The memorandum of association of the company was
amended. Clause 3 of the memorandum (as amended) included as objects for
which the company was established:

'(1) To assist, promote, encourage and secure the physical and economic
development of the whole or any part of the District of Allerdale (hereinafter *c*
called "Allerdale"). (2) To assist, promote and encourage existing and new
industry and commerce in Allerdale and to encourage and promote the
creation of employment and training opportunities within Allerdale for the
benefit of that area and its inhabitants. (3) To investigate the needs of
industry and commerce in Allerdale and to advertise and promote the *d*
benefits of Allerdale as a location for the expansion and creation of industry
and commerce ...'

New articles of association were adopted by special resolution on 8 April 1986.

Three members of the council were appointed as directors of the company,
and on 8 April 1986 Mr Perry was appointed as an additional director. Mr *e*
Thwaytes became the company secretary. It may be noted that in 1987,
following the council elections in that year, there were changes in the
membership of the board of directors and a fifth director was appointed.

The share capital of the company was £100 divided into 100 ordinary shares at
£1 each. Two shares were issued, one each to Mr Perry and Mr Thwaytes. By *f*
declarations of trust dated 9 April 1986, Mr Perry and Mr Thwaytes declared that
they held these shares and the rights attaching thereto in trust and as nominees
for the council.

At a meeting of the board of the company on 8 April 1986 it was resolved that
the company would acquire the Keswick Station site from the Lake District
Planning Board and the adjoining archery field from the private owner—   *g*

'for development as a leisure pool complex, car parking, station
refurbishment and housing with a separate time-share development for a
term of 99 years at a nominal ground rent at the respective purchase prices
of not exceeding £300,000 for the station site and at a price to be agreed for *h*
the archery field.'

It was further resolved to borrow sums limited to £6m for the development, with
repayment guaranteed by the council.

Meanwhile, CIPFA Services Ltd had been making inquiries to find a bank who
would be willing to provide a loan to finance the scheme. In the result, by a letter *j*
dated 14 May 1986, the bank made an offer to the company of a facility of £6m,
comprising a maximum of £4·5m by way of principal and £1·5m by way of
interest to be added to the principal as provided in the letter. The amount of
principal and interest outstanding on the third anniversary following the signing
of the letter were together called the 'loan' and it was provided that this loan
would be repayable in full not later than 31 May 1996. The purpose of the loan

a was expressed to be 'Construction of time-share and leisure pool complex'. The letter also contained detailed provisions as to the availability of the loan and as to the rate of interest. Clause 10 of the letter provided for the following security:

'The irrevocable and unconditional guarantee of Allerdale District Council (the "Guarantor"), sealed by the Bank and the Guarantor, in the form of the draft attached.'

b
It seems that the letter dated 14 May was in the same terms as a previous letter from the bank to CIPFA Services Ltd dated 7 May. By a resolution of the board of the company dated 14 May Mr Perry was authorised to accept the facilities offered by the bank as outlined in the letter of 7 May. At a further board meeting on 28 May it was resolved that Mr Perry be authorised to sign the facility letter

c dated 14 May.

Meanwhile, on 23 May 1986 the council entered into the contract of guarantee which is the subject of the present proceedings.

By cl 2 of the guarantee it was provided:

d 'Allerdale District Council hereby irrevocably guarantees to the Bank payment on demand in writing such demand having been made in accordance with the terms of this Guarantee of all moneys whether certain or contingent which are due and owing to the Bank by the Company pursuant to the Loan whether on any current or any other account including all commissions fees and other charges and all expenses incurred by the Bank

e in relation to the Loan or this Guarantee including legal and other costs on a full and unqualified indemnity basis PROVIDED THAT this Guarantee shall only become effective and demand may only be made thereunder by the Bank in the event of an Order being made or an effective resolution being passed for the winding up of the Company.'

f
In the earlier part of the guarantee Allerdale Development Co Ltd was identified as the 'company', and the 'loan' was defined as 'all moneys together with all costs, interest and expenses due thereon or in connection therewith borrowed by the company from the Bank to finance the construction under a loan agreement dated 14 May 1986'. The 'construction' was defined as 'the building by the

g company or its agents of the time-share and leisure pool complex'.

I can trace the ensuing events quite shortly.

On 27 August 1986 the company agreed to purchase the site of the old Keswick Railway Station from the Lake District Planning Board. A 99-year lease at an annual rent of £25 was executed dated 15 September 1986. The freehold

h reversion of the station site was purchased by the council for £250. On 3 September 1986 the company entered into a contract with Clifford Barnett to design and build a leisure pool and to refurbish the station. The date for completion was fixed at 27 July 1987. It was agreed that on completion the company would grant a lease of the leisure pool complex and the station

j buildings to Keswick Operating Co Ltd for a term of 25 years at a nominal rent with an option for a further 25 years at a full market rental.

On 20 August 1986 the company agreed to purchase the archery field by way of the grant of a lease of 99 years at a total rental of £200. The freehold reversion of the archery field was purchased by the council for £100. On 4 September the company entered into a contract with Clifford Barnett to design and build 76 time-share units in phases. The date for completion of the first phase was 27 July

1987.   Keswick Sales Ltd were appointed by the company to market the
time-share units.

The first phase of the time-share development, consisting of 20 units, was
completed on 10 April 1987. The pool was completed on 17 August 1987.

By March 1988 £4,798,696 had been advanced to the company under the loan
agreement. The sale of time-share units, however, had been unsatisfactory. By
5 October 1988 only about £900,000 had been realised from all the sales. The
position was serious because the start of repayments was due to begin in May
1989. Some discussions about rescheduling the debt were begun with the bank.

In December 1988, however, the council were informed by the district auditor
that it was his provisional view that the establishment of the company and the
provision of the guarantee by the council were ultra vires the powers of the
council.

In his judgment Colman J referred to the subsequent attempts to resolve the
position by discussions with the bank and by loans from the council to the
company (see [1995] 1 Lloyd's Rep 315 at 323). In December 1990, however, the
council declined to finance the repayment instalment which had become due in
November 1990 and a resolution was passed that the company should be put into
voluntary liquidation. On 12 December 1990 the bank sent to the company a
formal demand for repayment of £400,000 principal and about £370,000 interest
due in November 1990. The company was unable to pay these sums, however,
and went into liquidation. On 28 December 1990 the bank demanded repayment
of the entire loan. On the same date the bank wrote to the council demanding
immediate repayment of the sums owing to the bank by the company. The total
sum said to be due at the date of the letter including further interest was
£5,233,312·85.

On 25 January 1991 the writ in these proceedings was issued.

II. THE ISSUES AT THE TRIAL

The case came on for hearing before Colman J on 24 June 1993. The hearing
lasted about 25 days over the period between June 1993 and January 1994.
Colman J delivered his judgment on 6 May 1994. I would like to pay tribute to
the quality and in particular the clarity of his judgment.

In the course of his judgment Colman J identified four groups of issues: (A) the
ultra vires issues; (B) the issues relating to the proper construction and scope of
the guarantee; (C) the issues relating to the variation of the principal debt and (D)
the issues relating to quantum (see [1995] 1 Lloyd's Rep 315 at 323–324).

For the purposes of the present judgment, however, I do not propose to
examine the issues relating to quantum or the issues relating to the variation of
the principal debt. I shall concentrate on some of the ultra vires issues and also
on the issue relating to the scope of the guarantee which the judge referred to as
'the severance point'.

The judge formulated the ultra vires issues which had been raised by the
council in these terms (at 323):

'(1) The Council had no statutory power to enter into the guarantee. I
refer to this as the "statutory powers point". (2) If the Council would
otherwise have statutory power to enter into the guarantee it did not have
such power in this case because it was purporting to use the guarantee as part
of a scheme to facilitate the doing by the Company of things which the
Council itself had no power to do, namely (a) to borrow and spend amounts
of money which exceeded its borrowing and spending limits and (b) to carry

a   on a trade in time-share accommodation for profit. I refer to this as the "improper purpose point". (3) The decision of the Council to enter into the guarantee was *Wednesbury* unreasonable because it was entered into when the council had given no or no proper consideration to the likelihood of having to pay under the guarantee and the consequences of any such payment. I refer to this as "the *Wednesbury* point". [See *Associated Provincial*

b   *Picture Houses Ltd v Wednesbury Corp* [1947] 2 All ER 680, [1948] 1 KB 223.] (4) The bank's knowledge of the impropriety of the Council's purpose or of the unreasonableness of its decisions is irrelevant, but, if relevant, the bank did have such knowledge. I refer to this as "the bank's knowledge point".'

I shall turn quite shortly to examine the issue which the judge labelled 'the

c statutory powers point'. Before I do so, however, it will be convenient to refer briefly to 'the *Wednesbury* point' and 'the bank's knowledge point'.

It became clear at an early stage of the trial that in order to support the contention that the decision to give the guarantee was unreasonable in *Wednesbury* terms, the council intended to call over thirty witnesses, most of

d whom were councillors or former councillors. On learning this, the judge directed that no factual witnesses should be called on the *Wednesbury* point until he had reached a conclusion as to the legal effect on the enforceability of the guarantee of a possible finding that the decision to give the guarantee was irrational. Accordingly, the judge made no findings of fact on the rationality of the decision to give a guarantee. Nor did he make any findings of fact as to the

e bank's knowledge of the rational or irrational nature of the decision. Furthermore, though the judge did not refer to any evidence relating to the bank's knowledge of the alleged impropriety of the council's purpose in giving the guarantee, it seems clear that for the same reasons he would have postponed making any findings of fact on this point (see [1995] 1 Lloyd's Rep 315 at 358).

f   I shall have to return later to consider the judge's conclusions of law on the *Wednesbury* point and the bank's knowledge point. At this stage it is sufficient to notice the following.

(a) Before the judge, the bank argued that if the giving of the guarantee was irrational the court was not bound to treat the guarantee as void. Both in private law and in public law the court had a discretion. In this case the court should

g exercise its discretion so as to give effect to the guarantee. It was against public policy to allow the council to avoid a private law claim by reliance on its own abuse of power.

(b) The judge rejected the bank's argument. He declined to recognise the existence of a discretion. He stated his conclusion succinctly (at 356):

h

> 'Once the public body's want of power to act has been established in private law proceedings the Court has no alternative but to recognize the act for what as a matter of substantive law it is—a nullity.'

j   (c) The defences which are raised in this case make it necessary to consider in some detail the legal effect of any finding: (i) that the council had no statutory power to give the guarantee; and (ii) that, even if the council had a statutory power to give the guarantee, the decision to give it was either made for an improper purpose or was irrational.

In this court, counsel for the bank argued that, except in the case of statutory incapacity, the court had a discretion as to how 'invalid' decisions of a local authority were to be treated. His argument in this regard was on a somewhat wider basis than before the judge.

I can now return to the statutory powers point.

III. THE STATUTORY POWERS POINT

It was accepted on behalf of the bank that the council, being a creature of statute, could only act pursuant to and in accordance with powers given to it by statute. It was submitted, however, that the requisite statutory powers existed which entitled the council in 1986 to enter into the scheme and to give the guarantee. It was emphasised that for the purpose of examining the powers of the council one had to look at the scheme at the date of the guarantee, that is 23 May 1986. Any later modifications of the scheme were irrelevant.

For the purpose of developing this argument counsel for the bank drew our attention in particular to s 19 of the 1976 Act and to s 111 of the 1972 Act.

Section 19 of the 1976 Act, which was brought into force on 14 February 1977, is concerned with the provision of recreational facilities. The section, so far as material, is in these terms:

'(1) A local authority may provide, inside or outside its area, such recreational facilities as it thinks fit and, without prejudice to the generality of the powers conferred by the preceding provisions of this subsection, those powers include in particular powers to provide—(a) indoor facilities consisting of sports centres, swimming pools, skating rinks, tennis, squash and badminton courts, bowling centres, dance studios and riding schools; (b) outdoor facilities consisting of pitches for team games, athletics grounds, swimming pools, tennis courts, cycle tracks, golf courses, bowling greens, riding schools, camp sites and facilities for gliding; (c) facilities for boating and water ski-ing on inland and coastal waters and for fishing in such waters; (d) premises for the use of clubs or societies having athletic, social or recreational objects; (e) staff, including instructors, in connection with any such facilities or premises as are mentioned in the preceding paragraphs and in connection with any other recreational facilities provided by the authority; (f) such facilities in connection with any other recreational facilities as the authority considers it appropriate to provide including, without prejudice to the generality of the preceding provisions of this paragraph, facilities by way of parking spaces and places at which food, drink and tobacco may be bought from the authority or another person; and it is hereby declared that the powers conferred by this subsection to provide facilities include powers to provide buildings, equipment, supplies and assistance of any kind.

(2) A local authority may make any facilities provided by it in pursuance of the preceding subsection available for use by such persons as the authority thinks fit either without charge or on payment of such charges as the authority thinks fit.

(3) A local authority may contribute—(a) by way of grant or loan towards the expenses incurred or to be incurred by any voluntary organisation in providing any recreational facilities which the authority has power to provide by virtue of subsection (1) of this section; and (b) by way of grant towards the expenses incurred or to be incurred by any other local authority in providing such facilities; and in this subsection "voluntary organisation"

a

means any person carrying on or proposing to carry on an undertaking otherwise than for profit ...'

The other section on which the bank principally relied was s 111 of the 1972 Act. Section 111 is contained in Pt VII of the 1972 Act, which confers certain miscellaneous powers on local authorities. Section 111 itself, under the rubric b 'Subsidiary powers of local authorities', provides, so far as is material, as follows:

> '(1) Without prejudice to any powers exercisable apart from this section but subject to the provisions of this Act and any other enactment passed before or after this Act, a local authority shall have power to do any thing (whether or not involving the expenditure, borrowing or lending of money c or the acquisition or disposal of any property or rights) which is calculated to facilitate, or is conducive or incidental to, the discharge of any of their functions ...'

Basing himself on these two sections counsel for the bank advanced d submissions on the following lines. (1) The power under s 19(1) of the 1976 Act was a wide power to provide such recreational facilities as the council thought fit. The means to be adopted were for the council to decide, provided the means were lawful. (2) One of the lawful ways of providing recreational facilities was by making use of a company which was under the control of the council. In the present case the directors of the company were nominees of the council and the e only issued shares were held in trust for the council. (3) It was absurd to suggest that a council could not lawfully perform certain of its functions through a company. Independent contractors could be employed for such purposes as the construction of buildings required by the council. There was no reason why a company could not be employed to provided recreational facilities. f (4) Parliament itself had recognised that councils could hold interests in companies. The system of ministerial control relating to companies in which local authorities have interests, introduced by Pt V of the Local Government and Housing Act 1989, was based on an existing state of affairs which had been subjected to scrutiny both in the Widdicombe report of June 1986 (see the Report of the Committee of Inquiry into the conduct of Local Authority Business (1986) g (Cmnd 9797)) and in the subsequent consultation paper published by the Department of the Environment in June 1988 entitled 'Local Authorities' Interests in Companies'. Our attention was drawn to passages in these two documents, including these passages in the consultation paper:

h

> '(4) The survey established that authorities are involved in various ways with companies on a considerably more extensive scale than the Widdicombe Committee were aware of. Companies are used by authorities for a very wide range of activities, and although most of them are small operations their number and the scale of operation is tending to increase. In many cases the companies are engaged in activities that are valuable to local j communities; and operation by means of a company appears to serve a useful purpose in ensuring that the activities are conducted in a business-like way which can involve the private sector where appropriate ...

> (6) It is clear that there are important operational advantages for a local authority in a variety of cases in using a company to conduct an activity in which the authority has an involvement. The Government do not wish to

restrict this flexibility, which has particular usefulness in joint ventures with the private sector ...'

(5) Swimming pools were referred to specifically in s 19(1)(a) and (b) of the 1976 Act. It was true that there was no similar reference to time-share accommodation, but: (a) the facilities listed in s 19(1) were illustrative only and the particular powers to provide these facilities were expressed to be without prejudice to the generality of the powers conferred by the opening words of s 19(1); (b) by s 19(1)(f) the council had power to provide recreational facilities in connection with any other recreational facilities. Time-share accommodation could be enjoyed in conjunction with the swimming pool; (c) in s 19(1)(b) reference was made to 'camp sites'. Time-share accommodation fell into a similar category. In any event, time-share accommodation was a recreational facility which could be used for persons on holiday for the purposes of relaxation. (6) The concluding words of s 19(1) made it clear that the power to provide facilities included the power to provide 'assistance of any kind'. Such assistance could take the form of financial assistance including the provision of a guarantee. The specific power in s 19(3) to contribute to the expenses of a voluntary organisation did not exclude a wider power to provide assistance to companies involved in the provision of recreational facilities. (7) In any event, the council had power to form a company and give a guarantee under its subsidiary powers contained in s 111 of the 1972 Act. Under that section the council had power to do anything (whether or not involving the expenditure, borrowing or lending of money) which was 'calculated to facilitate, or was conducive or incidental to, the discharge of any of [the council's] functions.'

Counsel for the bank also referred, both before the judge and in this court, to a small group of other statutory provisions which, it was submitted, empowered the council to carry out the scheme and to give the guarantee. We were therefore provided with the text of ss 2(1) and 14 of the Local Authorities (Land) Act 1963, the text of ss 120, 123 and 144 of the 1972 Act and the text of ss 112, 119, 123, 124 and 133 of the 1971 Act (which was then in force). As the argument developed in this court, however, counsel confined his submissions based on these subsidiary statutory provisions to those based on ss 2(1) and 14 of the 1963 Act when read in conjunction with s 111 of the 1972 Act. Section 2(1) of the 1963 Act is in these terms:

'Subject to the provisions of this Act, a local authority may, for the benefit or the improvement of their area, erect any building and construct or carry out works on land.'

By s 14, 'erect' is defined to include 'extend, alter and re-erect'.

I propose to deal with these submissions under the following headings: (1) the 'provision' of recreational facilities; (2) time-share accommodation as recreational facilities; (3) the provision of 'assistance of any kind'; and (4) the application of s 111 of the 1972 Act.

(1) The 'provision' of recreational facilities

It is convenient to consider first whether the council, having established the company as the means whereby the swimming pool and time-share facilities were to be made available to the public, could claim that they were 'providing' these facilities within the meaning of s 19(1) of the 1976 Act. For the time being *a* I shall assume that the time-share accommodation constituted recreational facilities within the meaning of s 19.

Our attention was drawn to the decision of the Court of Appeal in *R v South Wales Traffic Licensing Authority, ex p Ebbw Vale UDC* [1951] 1 All ER 806, [1951] 2 KB 366. In that case an omnibus company which had previously been a private enterprise concern had been acquired by the British Transport Commission *b* under the Transport Act 1947. The company became a wholly owned subsidiary of the commission. In due course the company made an application to a licensing authority for public service vehicles to vary the conditions of its road service licences so as to be able to increase the existing scale of fares. Such an application could not be made, however, if the transport services in question were provided by the commission or by any person acting as agent for the commission. The *c* question arose as to whether in the circumstances an application to vary the conditions of the licences could be made. In the course of his judgment Cohen LJ referred to s 3(1) of the 1947 Act, which was in these terms:

d "'It shall be the general duty of the Commission so to exercise their powers under this Act as to provide, or secure or promote the provision of, an efficient ... system of public inland transport ...'" (See [1951] 1 All ER 806 at 809, [1951] 2 KB 366 at 371.)

Later in his judgment Cohen LJ continued ([1951] 1 All ER 806 at 810, [1951] 2 KB 366 at 373):

e 'Where a service is provided through a subsidiary company of the commission, it seems to me that *prima facie*, having regard to the general rule of law, what the commission is doing is securing the provision of road transport facilities, and not providing them ... That the commission can act through an agent is also clear ... but, as I have said, there is no question of agency here ... In the present case I think the commission was securing the *f* provision of an efficient ... system [of public inland transport within the meaning of s 3(1) of the Transport Act 1947] through [the omnibus company], not an independent concern, but a separate legal entity.'

It was argued on behalf of the bank that the *Ebbw Vale* case could be distinguished because of the antithesis in s 3 of the 1947 Act between 'providing' *g* and 'securing or promoting the provision of'. It was also argued, and indeed was pleaded, that in providing the recreational facilities the company was acting as the agent of the council. It was only in obtaining the loan from the bank that the company was acting on its own behalf.

I do not find it necessary to decide whether, in the absence of some statutory *h* power, there may not be cases where a council can lawfully use a wholly-owned subsidiary under its direct control as a means of carrying out certain of its functions. The company might then be the agent of the council. The point does not arise in this case. The purpose of the instant scheme was that the company should operate and incur liabilities independently of the council. This purpose *j* would have been frustrated if the company had been an agent. If, when a sum was drawn down under the loan facility, the company was acting as agent for the council, the borrowing would have been a breach of the statutory control. The borrowing was intended to be outside the statutory control. If, however, the sum was drawn by the company on its own behalf, it is quite plain that the provision of the facilities was by the company and not by the council. I see no escape from this dilemma.

I turn to the next heading.

a

(2) *Time-share accommodation as recreational facilities*
In dealing with this aspect of the case in his judgment the judge referred to dictionary definitions of 'facility' and 'recreation' and continued ([1995] 1 Lloyd's Rep 315 at 340):

> 'Taking the two words in conjunction, therefore, one has opportunities for *b* the easy or easier process of being recreated by some pleasant occupation, pastime or amusement. There seems no reason to suppose that the general words used in the opening to s. 19(1) have any different meaning. It is particularly to be noted that all the specific illustrations contemplate not merely the physical presence in the relevant area of those who enjoy the *c* facilities thus provided, but their participation in what may loosely be described as some form of activity in addition to being merely physically present. The availability of some specific occupation, pastime or amusement for the purpose of which the particular facility is provided is, in my judgment, quite clearly implicit in the words of the sub-section.'

d

Later he added (at 341):

> '... a local authority which provided living accommodation in its area which was available to anyone who wanted to use it and was unrelated to any specific recreational activity or group of activities would not be providing recreational facilities, but would instead be providing living *e* accommodation facilities. It would be nothing to the point that most if not all of those who could be expected to avail themselves of the accommodation would be on holiday at the time or that they might, while using the accommodation, be likely to participate in recreational activities in the area or even in the accommodation itself. I am in particular unable to accept Mr. Clarke's submission that being on holiday away from home is to *f* participate in a recreational activity ... it provides an *opportunity* to participate in such activities. It is not such an activity in itself.' (Colman J's emphasis.)

The judge then considered the specific reference to camp sites in s 19(1)(b), but held that, although this facility came nearer to the time-share unit than any other *g* of the examples listed in the section, it was different in kind from the provision of a time-share unit. He added (at 341):

> 'Those who go on camping holidays pursue the recreational activity of camping ... Camping is not merely living on holiday: it is in itself an *h* occupation, pastime or amusement ... When the local authority provides a camp site it is thus providing space on which the public can enjoy the recreational activity of camping. The occupation of a time-share unit for holiday purposes is not analogous to this because staying in such a unit is not a recognizable recreational activity.'

j

I am content to adopt this careful analysis by Colman J. I also agree with him that reliance could not be placed on s 19(1)(f), which is concerned with the provision of a facility 'in connection with another recreational facility'. It was said that the leisure pool would be used by persons occupying the time-share accommodation and that there was a sufficient connection between the two. As the judge pointed out, however, the only real connection between the pool and *a* the time-share accommodation was the council's intention that the disposal of time-share units would provide a source of funding for the repayment of the bank's loan.

(3) The provision of 'assistance of any kind'

b I come next to the argument based on the concluding words of s 19(1), 'the powers conferred by this subsection to provide facilities include powers to provide ... assistance of any kind'. I can deal with this argument very shortly. The words 'assistance of any kind' have to be construed in their context. The words come at the end of s 19(1) and form part of a sentence or clause:

c '... it is hereby declared that the powers conferred by this subsection to provide facilities include powers to provide buildings, equipment, supplies and assistance of any kind.'

It seems to me quite clear that the powers to provide buildings etc are part of the powers to provide facilities and that the beneficiaries are intended to be those who are to enjoy or make use of the recreational facilities. Thus, for example, *d* 'equipment' is clearly equipment to be used in conjunction with the recreational facilities. In my judgment the words cannot be construed so as to mean that assistance can be given to those who are 'providing' the recreational facilities.

Furthermore, the matter is put beyond doubt by the specific provisions in s 19(3), which empower a local authority to contribute towards the expenses *e* incurred or to be incurred by a voluntary organisation in providing recreational facilities which the authority has power to provide, and to contribute by way of grants to the expenses incurred or to be incurred by another local authority in providing such facilities. These specific powers are inconsistent with the existence of a general power under s 19(1) to give financial assistance to providers *f* of recreational facilities.

(4) The application of s 111 of the 1972 Act

For convenience I should repeat, but with the addition of sub-s (3), the wording of s 111 of the 1972 Act, so far as it is material:

g '(1) Without prejudice to any powers exercisable apart from this section but subject to the provisions of this Act and any other enactment passed before or after this Act, a local authority shall have power to do anything (whether or not involving the expenditure, borrowing or lending of money or the acquisition or disposal of any property or rights) which is calculated to facilitate, or is conducive or incidental to, the discharge of any *h* of their functions ...

(3) A local authority shall not by virtue of this section raise money, whether by means of rates, precepts or borrowing, or lend money except in accordance with the enactments relating to those matters respectively ...'

j The genesis of s 111 is well known. It seems clear that when the doctrine of ultra vires was first being considered in the nineteenth century in relation to the powers of railway companies which had been incorporated by statute, the vires of the company were construed strictly. In the course of time, however, a more liberal approach was adopted. In *A-G v Great Eastern Rly Co* (1880) 5 App Cas 473 at 478 Lord Selborne LC said that the doctrine of ultra vires—

'ought to be reasonably, and not unreasonably, understood and applied, and that whatever may fairly be regarded as incidental to, or consequential *a* upon, those things which the Legislature has authorized, ought not (unless expressly prohibited) to be held, by judicial construction, to be *ultrà vires.*'

Lord Blackburn's speech (at 481) was to the same effect, and both these passages were cited by Lord Templeman in *Hazell v Hammersmith and Fulham London BC* [1991] 1 All ER 545 at 554, [1992] 2 AC 1 at 29. *b*

The effect of s 111 of the 1972 Act has assumed great importance in this case. It was argued on behalf of the bank that the council's powers under s 19 of the 1976 Act and under s 2 of the 1963 Act were extended by s 111 so as to embrace the use of the company and the giving of the guarantee as legitimate means of carrying out the statutory functions under the two sections. *c*

In addition, in the course of the argument we were reminded that, though s 111(1) had to be construed in its context and in conjunction with sub-s (3), it was important to note that 'the making of payments pursuant to an obligation arising under a guarantee' was not included at the material time in the definition of 'prescribed expenditure' in Sch 12 to the 1980 Act. Such payments were added *d* when the schedule was amended by the Local Government Finance Act 1988.

It followed that at the material time there was no express restriction on the making of payments under a guarantee such as that given by the council. It was therefore submitted that one was free to consider the use of the company and the giving of the guarantee to see whether these methods of operation, which were in no way specifically prohibited, were calculated to facilitate or were conducive *e* or incidental to the discharge of any of the council's functions. The answer, it was submitted, was clear. These methods were calculated to assist the discharge by the council of their functions and fell within the statutory wording.

At first sight this submission has some attraction. But in my view it does not survive careful scrutiny. It is clear from the speech of Lord Templeman in *Hazell* *f* and from the speech of Lord Lowry in *McCarthy & Stone (Developments) Ltd v Richmond upon Thames London BC* [1991] 4 All ER 897, [1992] 2 AC 48 that in considering the implied powers of a local authority under s 111 of the 1972 Act it is first necessary to identify the relevant statutory functions. The word 'functions' embraces all the duties and powers of a local authority, that is, the sum total of all the activities Parliament has entrusted to it (see *Hazell* [1991] 1 All ER *g* 545 at 554, [1992] 2 AC 1 at 29 per Lord Templeman). In *Hazell* the question was whether a swap transaction was calculated to facilitate, or was conducive or incidental to, the discharge of the local authority's function of borrowing. In the *Richmond* case the question was whether charging for pre-application planning advice facilitated or was conducive or was incidental to the council's planning *h* functions. In the present case, the statutory functions, as I understand the argument, are those set out in s 19(1) of the 1976 Act and in s 2(1) of the 1963 Act.

It is also necessary, however, in any particular case to examine the context in which the implied powers are to be exercised. The context here includes the following relevant circumstances. (a) It is a basic principle underlying local *j* authority finances that they are to be conducted on an annual basis. Income and expenditure must be attributed to the year in which the income arises or in which the expenditure is incurred. (b) The scheme involved the council in incurring substantial financial obligations. There was no possibility whatever of the council undertaking the scheme out of its ordinary income or without incurring substantial financial obligations. (c) The expenditure of the council is subject to a statutory control. So too is the council's power to borrow. (d) The 1972 Act makes provision for the means whereby the council can accomplish the statutory functions set out in s 19(1) of the 1976 Act and s 2(1) of the 1963 Act. Thus, Parliament clearly intended that the council should discharge these statutory functions by means of its power to borrow. As Lord Templeman explained in *Hazell* [1991] 1 All ER 545 at 558, [1992] 2 AC 1 at 33, Sch 13 to the 1972 Act

b establishes a comprehensive code which defines and limits the powers of a local authority with regard to its borrowing.

In these circumstances, where Parliament has laid down a route whereby a local authority can obtain the financial resources to enable it to carry out its statutory functions, is it possible to say that this scheme facilitates or is conducive or is incidental to the discharge of the relevant functions?

c I agree with the judge where he said that one has to look at the statutory powers of local authorities as a whole (see [1995] 1 Lloyd's Rep 315 at 337–338). I also agree with his conclusion where he said (at 338):

> '... I fail to see how there could be any implication empowering a local authority to acquire the use of borrowed money [to discharge a particular function] by any other means than by borrowing the required funds itself and doing so conformably with Part I of Schedule 13 of the [Local Government Act 1972].'

The only implied power could be a power for the council itself to borrow the money.

e The implied powers in s 111 do not provide an escape route from the statutory controls. In my view that is clear not only as a matter of principle but also on the construction of s 111 itself. Section 111(3) ensures that the powers exercisable under s 111(1) have to be used in conformity with the other statutory provisions.

Accordingly, in my opinion the bank's argument on the statutory powers point

f fails at each stage. The establishment of the company and the giving of the guarantee were part of an ingenious scheme designed to circumvent the no-doubt irksome controls imposed by central government. The council, however, could only do what it was empowered to do by statute. Neither the establishment of a company nor the giving of a guarantee fell within the express or implied powers of the council.

g In the light of the conclusion which I have reached on the statutory powers of the council, it follows that the establishment of the company and the giving of the guarantee were ultra vires acts. In deference to the arguments which were addressed to us, however, I propose to deal shortly with the point which the judge identified as the 'improper purpose point'. At the same time I can deal with

h the issue of severance. Having dealt with these matters I can then turn finally to the question of the effect in private law of the findings I reach on the several ultra vires issues.

IV. THE IMPROPER PURPOSE POINT AND SEVERANCE

The judge identified the improper purpose point as follows ([1995] 1 Lloyd's

j Rep 315 at 323):

> 'If the Council would otherwise have statutory power to enter into the guarantee it did not have such power in this case because it was purporting to use the guarantee as part of a scheme to facilitate the doing by the Company of things which the Council itself had no power to do, namely (a) to borrow and spend amounts of money which exceeded its borrowing and

spending limits and (b) to carry on a trade in time-share accommodation for profit.'

a

In formulating the improper purpose point in this way the judge was summarising the arguments which had been addressed to him on behalf of the council. Similar arguments were addressed to this court.

It was argued on behalf of the bank on the other hand that, on the assumption that the setting up of the company and the giving of the guarantee were prima facie intra vires the council, the fact that the chosen route had the effect of avoiding the statutory financial limits did not render the scheme unlawful. The council had a discretion in the matter. It was further argued that, assuming the council had power to construct the time-share facility, either as a recreational facility or as a form of development, it was under a duty, or at least entitled, to dispose of the units for the best consideration obtainable.

b

c

I feel bound to reject the bank's arguments. The scheme was plainly designed to circumvent statutory controls. Furthermore, the time-share accommodation was erected primarily so that units could be sold in order to provide a fund to finance the construction both of the leisure pool and of the units. The construction of the leisure pool was the primary aim.

d

The statutory powers conferred on local authorities to be exercised for public purposes can only be validly used if they are used in the way which Parliament, when conferring the powers, is presumed to have intended. This is a general principle of public law (see Wade *Administrative Law* (5th edn, 1982) pp 355–356, 357 and *Tower Hamlets London BC v Chetnik Developments Ltd* [1988] 1 All ER 961 at 965, [1988] AC 858 at 872 per Lord Bridge).

e

On analysis the improper purpose point raises questions which are similar to those which I have already considered under s 111. First, it is necessary to identify the function or functions which the council were exercising. Next, it is necessary to see what ancillary powers Parliament has given to enable these functions to be carried out. One then examines whether the route followed by the council in purporting to exercise those functions involved taking into account irrelevant or improper considerations.

f

In the present case the decision to adopt the scheme involved: (a) an attempt to circumvent the statutory borrowing machinery and the statutory financial controls incorporated in that machinery; (b) an attempt to use the anticipated surplus receipts from the disposal of one form of development (the time-share units) to finance the creation of another form of development (the leisure pool); (c) the exposure of the council to a substantially greater financial risk than if the borrowing had been limited to the sums needed to construct the time-share units alone. If the sale of the units failed to generate sufficient surplus funds the council would be left with a substantial financial burden.

g

h

I am quite unable to treat the decision to adopt such a scheme as a decision made for a proper purpose and within the discretionary powers of the council. The nature of the scheme has only to be stated to expose its divergence from what Parliament must be assumed to have intended.

The judge expressed his conclusion on this point as follows ([1995] 1 Lloyd's Rep 315 at 349):

j

'... the Council's decision to give the guarantee was, on both the grounds of its purpose of evading the borrowing and spending controls on local authorities and of its creating a revenue producing development to fund the provision of the leisure pool, a decision tainted by irrelevant considerations a   the effect of which was to make it an invalid exercise of the Council's powers.'

I agree with the judge's conclusion. I would, however, prefer to base my decision on the general principle to which I have already referred. Statutory powers are conferred on local authorities upon trust. These powers can only be

b   used in the way which Parliament is presumed to have intended. Parliament has created an elaborate structure to provide for and regulate the manner in which a local authority can obtain funds to carry out its statutory functions. Parliament has already made changes in this structure since 1986 and more changes may lie in the future. We are concerned, however, with the structure as it existed in 1986.

The purposes of the scheme were to circumvent the restrictions on borrowing

c   and spending to which at the time the council were subject and to produce profits from the development of the time-share units for the financing of the scheme. These were not proper purposes for the council to pursue. Even if, contrary to my earlier conclusion, the council had power under s 111 to set up the company and to give a guarantee, this power could not be exercised in the way and for the

d   purposes in which it was exercised in this case.

I turn therefore to the question of severance.

It was argued on behalf of the bank that if the scheme was permissible in part the guarantee was enforceable pro tanto. As I am of the opinion that the scheme was beyond the capacity of the council and was adopted for improper reasons, this argument is in one sense academic. Nevertheless, I think it is right to explain

e   why I consider that this argument too must be rejected.

Counsel for the bank developed his argument on the following lines. If the council had no power to provide time-share accommodation but the scheme was otherwise a permissible discharge by the council of its statutory functions to provide recreational facilities, the guarantee was enforceable against the council

f   in relation to that part of the borrowing which was applied exclusively in relation to the provision of the leisure pool. Counsel drew our attention to a number of authorities including *Baroness Wenlock v River Dee Co* (1885) 10 App Cas 355 and *United City Merchants (Investments) Ltd v Royal Bank of Canada* [1982] 2 All ER 720, [1983] 1 AC 168. It was said that these authorities supported the proposition that where it was possible to isolate the lawful part of a contract that part could be

g   upheld.

How then is the possibility of severance to be approached? The answer is to be found by considering whether, if one isolated that part of the company's indebtedness which related to the leisure pool, a fundamentally different contract would result. I should refer to a passage in the speech of Lord Oliver in *Woolwich*

h   *Equitable Building Society v IRC* [1991] 4 All ER 92 at 104, [1990] 1 WLR 1400 at 1413:

'One has to ask ... the question whether the deletion of that which is in excess of the power so alters the substance of what is left that the provision

j   in question is in reality a substantially different provision from that which it was before deletion.'

This passage occurs in a case in which the House of Lords was considering the validity of certain provisions in the Income Tax (Building Societies) Regulations 1986, SI 1986/482. But the approach which Lord Oliver explained is, in my view, of general application.

In the present case the provision of the time-share units was an integral part of
the scheme. Indeed the scheme would not and could not have gone ahead   *a*
without the time-share development. In these circumstances it seems to me that
the contract without the time-share development would have been a quite
different contract. The leisure pool development was inextricably linked with the
development which, it was hoped, would provide the finance. The guarantee
was part of one composite scheme. On the facts of the present case, I am quite   *b*
satisfied that if a question of severance were a relevant consideration, it would
not be possible to enforce the guarantee pro tanto.

V. THE EFFECT OF THE INVALIDITY OF THE SCHEME AND THE GUARANTEE

In his closing submissions counsel for the bank accepted that if the council had
no statutory capacity to implement the scheme by the creation of the company   *c*
and the giving of the guarantee, the guarantee was void and unenforceable. If,
however, the court concluded that the scheme was ultra vires because (a) it had
been adopted for improper purposes, either in order to avoid the financial
controls imposed on the council or because it involved the trading in the
time-share units for a profit, or (b) because it involved some improper delegation   *d*
or, (c) because it was unreasonable in a *Wednesbury* sense, then, it was submitted,
the court had a discretion. The doctrine of ultra vires did not have to be applied
in a uniform manner in all circumstances. Thus, in proceedings for judicial
review the court had always had a discretion whether or not to give relief to
someone who complained that a decision of a public authority was ultra vires.
Furthermore, even before the recent statutory changes in the law relating to the   *e*
doctrine of ultra vires in relation to limited companies, the courts had recognised
a distinction between acts which were ultra vires the company and acts which
were ultra vires the directors.

In the light of the conclusion which I have reached on the issue of the statutory
power of the council, these submissions are no longer of direct relevance to the   *f*
outcome of this appeal. Nevertheless, I have decided that I should express some
opinion on the questions which were raised. I propose to consider these
questions as shortly as possible under four headings. (1) The development of the
doctrine of ultra vires. (2) The doctrine of ultra vires in relation to limited
companies. (3) The doctrine of ultra vires in public law. (4) The present case.

          g

(1) *The development of the doctrine of ultra vires*

Since the abolition of the Court of Star Chamber, the Court of King's Bench
and subsequently the High Court have played a supervisory role in relation to
decisions made by local administrative bodies. It is not necessary, however, in
this judgment to consider the nature or the extent of this control in so far as it   *h*
affected municipal corporations or other bodies established otherwise than by
statute. Blackburn J may or may not have been right when in his judgment in the
Exchequer Chamber in *Riche v Ashbury Railway Carriage and Iron Co Ltd* (1874) LR
9 Exch 224 at 263, after referring to *Sutton's Hospital Case* (1612) 10 Co Rep 1,
[1558–1774] All ER Rep 11, he said: *j*

'This seems to me an express authority that at common law it is an incident
to a corporation to use its common seal for the purpose of binding itself to
anything to which a natural person could bind himself, and to deal with its
property as a natural person might deal with his own. And further, that an
attempt to forbid this on the part of the King, even by express negative

a   words, does not bind at law. Nor am I aware of any authority in conflict with
         this case.'

The incorporation of some municipalities by statute dates from the Municipal
Corporations Act 1835. In this case we are concerned with a local authority
which is a body corporate within the meaning of s 2(3) of the 1972 Act.

b   It seems, however, that the origins of the modern doctrine of ultra vires are to
         be found not so much in the cases where the courts sought to exercise control
         over local administrative bodies allegedly acting in excess of jurisdiction by, for
         example, passing impermissible byelaws, but in cases where consideration was
         given to the powers of trading companies, and in particular of railway companies,
         incorporated by statute towards the end of the first half of the nineteenth century.
c   The courts found themselves in unfamiliar territory. In *Colman v Eastern Counties
         Rly Co* (1846) 10 Beav 1 at 13, 50 ER 481 at 486 Lord Langdale MR referred to some
         of the recently established railway companies and said:

> 'I think it right to observe, that companies of this kind, possessing most
> extensive powers, have so recently been introduced into this country, that
d   > neither the Legislature nor Courts of Justice have been yet able to
> understand all the different lights in which their transactions ought properly
> to be viewed. We must, however, adhere to ancient general and settled
> principles, so far as they can be applied to great combinations and companies
> of this kind.'

e   A little later he expressed the view that a railway company had to be scrutinised
         more closely than a partnership. He added (10 Beav 1 at 14, 50 ER 481 at 486):

> '... I am clearly of opinion that the powers which are given by an Act of
> Parliament, like that now in question, extend no farther than is expressly
> stated in the Act, or is necessarily and properly required for carrying into
f   > effect the undertaking and works which the Act has expressly sanctioned.'

Thereafter the courts progressed cautiously until the position was clarified by
the important decisions in the House of Lords in *Ashbury Rly Carriage and Iron Co
Ltd v Riche* (1875) LR 7 HL 653, *A-G v Great Eastern Rly Co* (1880) 5 App Cas 473
and *Small v Smith* (1884) 10 App Cas 119.

g   In the last hundred years, and particularly in the last fifty, the doctrine of ultra
         vires has become a potent force in many areas of the law. In public law it has been
         used as the foundation for the intervention by the courts in judicial review
         proceedings. In private law it has been used as a method of confining the lawful
         activities of limited companies to those which are authorised by the
         memorandum of association.
h   But despite the great importance which the doctrine of ultra vires has assumed
         in the field of public law and, until recently, in relation to the activities of limited
         companies, the doctrine still gives rise to conceptual and practical difficulties. It
         is easy to state that if a body with limited powers makes a decision which it has
         no power to make, the decision is void and of no legal effect. But such a
j   statement may not accord with the reality of the situation.

The problem is illustrated by the well-known dictum of Lord Radcliffe in *Smith
v East Elloe RDC* [1956] 1 All ER 855 at 871, [1956] AC 736 at 769, where he said:

> 'An order, even if not made in good faith, is still an act capable of legal
> consequences. It bears no brand of invalidity upon its forehead. Unless the
> necessary proceedings are taken at law to establish the cause of invalidity and

to get it quashed or otherwise upset, it will remain as effective for its
ostensible purposes as the most impeccable of orders.'

Moreover, even an order which is manifestly bad can be effective until its
invalidity has been exposed in court. The counterfeit is as good as the genuine
article until it has been weighed.

It is no doubt because it has been difficult to find an appropriate epithet to
describe the quality of an ultra vires decision in the period before it has been
pronounced ineffective ab initio that judges have deprecated the use of the word
'void'. By way of example one can take a passage in the speech of Lord Diplock
in *F Hoffmann-La Roche & Co AG v Secretary of State for Trade and Industry* [1974] 2
All ER 1128 at 1154, [1975] AC 295 at 366, where he said:

'I think it leads to confusion to use such terms as "voidable", "voidable ab
initio", "void" or "a nullity" as descriptive of the legal status of subordinate
legislation alleged to be ultra vires for patent or for latent defects, before its
validity has been pronounced on by a court of competent jurisdiction.'

The problem, however, is not merely one of terminology. Even after an order or
decision has been declared to be void or a nullity or has been quashed, it may
return as a ghost to show that it was once very much alive. The law has not yet
found a way to deal satisfactorily with the simulacrum of a decision.

I turn next to the application of the doctrine in relation to limited companies.

(2) The doctrine of ultra vires in relation to limited companies

I referred earlier to the fact that the courts have drawn a distinction between
the effect of acts which are ultra vires a company and of acts which are beyond
the powers of the directors. This matter was discussed, together with the various
uses of the words 'ultra vires', by Browne-Wilkinson LJ in his important
judgment in *Rolled Steel Products (Holdings) Ltd v British Steel Corp* [1985] 3 All ER
52 at 91–92, [1986] Ch 246 at 302 where he said, in a case decided before the
Companies Act 1985:

'In my judgment, much of the confusion that has crept into the law flows
from the use of the phrase "ultra vires" in different senses in different
contexts. The reconciliation of the authorities can only be achieved if one
first defines the sense in which one is using the words "ultra vires". Because
the literal translation of the words is "beyond the powers", there are many
cases in which the words have been applied to transactions which, although
within the capacity of the company, are carried out otherwise than through
the correct exercise of the powers of the company by its officers; indeed, that
is the sense in which the judge seems to have used the words in this case. For
reasons which will appear, in my judgment, the use of the phrase "ultra
vires" should be restricted to those cases where the transaction is beyond the
capacity of the company and therefore wholly void. A company, being an
artificial person, has no capacity to do anything outside the objects specified
in its memorandum of association. If the transaction is outside the objects,
in law it is wholly void. But the objects of a company and the powers
conferred on the company to carry out those objects are two different things
... If the concept that a company cannot do anything which is not authorised
by law had been pursued with ruthless logic, the result might have been
reached that a company could not (ie had no capacity) to do anything
otherwise than in *due* exercise of its powers. But such ruthless logic has not

a
been pursued and it is clear that a transaction falling within the objects of the company is capable of conferring rights on third parties even though the transaction was an abuse of the powers of the company: see eg *Re David Payne & Co Ltd, Young v David Payne & Co Ltd* [1904] 2 Ch 608. It is therefore established that a company has capacity to carry out a transaction which falls within its objects even though carried out by the wrongful exercise of its

b
powers ... If the transaction is beyond the capacity of the company it is in any event a nullity and wholly void; whether or not the third party had notice of the invalidity, property transferred or money paid under such a transaction will be recoverable from the third party. If, on the other hand, the transaction (although in excess or abuse of powers) is within the capacity of the company, the position of the third party depends on whether or not

c
he had notice that the transaction was in excess or abuse of the powers of the company.' (Browne-Wilkinson LJ's emphasis.)

It may be noted that this distinction between the capacity of a company and the powers of directors in relation to the rights of a third party must have been in the

d
mind of Lord Campbell CJ in *Norwich Corp v Norfolk Rly Co* (1856) 4 E & B 397 at 443, 119 ER 143 at 160 when he suggested that the purchase of a large quantity of iron rails by the directors of a railway company for the purposes of a private speculation would be treated differently from a similar purchase of a thousand gross of green spectacles.

e
In the last two decades, however, the doctrine of ultra vires in its application to ordinary limited companies has been fundamentally changed by legislation.

Section 35 of the 1985 Act was enacted as part of a number of measures introduced in order to bring UK law into conformity with EU law, as contained in Council Directive (EEC) 68/151 (as amended), the First Company Law Directive. By s 108(1) of the Companies Act 1989, however, a new s 35 was

f
substituted. The substitution was brought into force on 4 February 1991. The 1989 Act also introduced provisions relating to charitable companies. For the purposes of this judgment it is sufficient to refer to part only of s 35 (as substituted):

g
'*A company's capacity not limited by its memorandum.*—(1) The validity of an act done by a company shall not be called into question on the ground of lack of capacity by reason of anything in the company's memorandum ...

(3) It remains the duty of the directors to observe any limitations on their powers flowing from the company's memorandum; and action by the

h
directors which but for subsection (1) would be beyond the company's capacity may only be ratified by the company by special resolution. A resolution ratifying such action shall not affect any liability incurred by the directors or any other person; relief from any such liability must be agreed to separately by special resolution ...'

j
No comparable changes have been introduced by legislation in relation to local authorities. Nevertheless, it is for consideration whether in a private law claim by a third party a distinction can be drawn, similar to that drawn in *Rolled Steel*, between decisions and acts which are beyond the capacity of a public authority and decisions and acts which involve a misuse of power by those controlling the authority.

(3) *The doctrine of ultra vires in public law*

At one time a distinction was drawn between cases where the public authority
lacked capacity and the impugned decision was said to be void or a nullity, and
cases of wrong decisions 'within jurisdiction', in which the decisions were said to
be voidable. But in the recent authorities the term 'void' has been generally
adopted, though, as I have already observed, some concern has been expressed as
to the confusion to which the use of the term may lead.

A useful starting point is the speech of Lord Reid in *Anisminic Ltd v Foreign
Compensation Commission* [1969] 1 All ER 208, [1969] 2 AC 147, where in a
landmark decision the House of Lords held that an error by the commission
within jurisdiction rendered their determination a nullity. Lord Reid said ([1969]
1 All ER 208 at 213–214, [1969] 2 AC 147 at 171):

> 'It has sometimes been said that it is only where a tribunal acts without
> jurisdiction that its decision is a nullity. But in such cases the word
> "jurisdiction" has been used in a very wide sense, and I have come to the
> conclusion that it is better not to use the term except in the narrow and
> original sense of the tribunal being entitled to enter on the enquiry in
> question. But there are many cases where, although the tribunal had
> jurisdiction to enter on the enquiry, it has done or failed to do something in
> the course of the enquiry which is of such a nature that its decision is a
> nullity. It may have given its decision in bad faith. It may have made a
> decision which it had no power to make. It may have failed in the course of
> the enquiry to comply with the requirements of natural justice. It may in
> perfect good faith have misconstrued the provisions giving it power to act so
> that it failed to deal with the question remitted to it and decided some
> question which was not remitted to it. It may have refused to take into
> account something which it was required to take into account. Or it may
> have based its decision on some matter which, under the provisions setting
> it up, it had no right to take into account. I do not intend this list to be
> exhaustive.'

It follows therefore that where in judicial review proceedings an order or
decision is declared to be ultra vires on any of the grounds which are now
available, the order or decision is as a matter of law void and a nullity. In legal
theory this result is comprehensible and indeed the all-embracing doctrine of
ultra vires accords with the jurisdictional basis on which the court acts. The court
can only intervene where the body which made the original decision made an
error which undermined its capacity to act. As Lord Reid explained, in the
absence of such error, the body to whom the question was remitted was as much
entitled to decide the question wrongly as to decide it rightly (see [1969] 1 All ER
208 at 214, [1969] 2 AC 147 at 171.)

The public law cases, however, demonstrate some of the conceptual and
practical problems to which, as I mentioned earlier, the doctrine of ultra vires
gives rise.

In the first place, an ultra vires decision will in the ordinary way take effect
unless and until it is challenged, and challenged promptly, by someone who has
the right to do so. Applications for judicial review, which include applications to
quash ultra vires decisions of public authorities, are subject to the provisions of
s 31 of the Supreme Court Act 1981 and of RSC Ord 53. Section 31, so far as is
material, is in these terms:

a
'... (3) No application for judicial review shall be made unless the leave of the High Court has been obtained in accordance with rules of court; and the court shall not grant leave to make such an application unless it considers that the applicant has a sufficient interest in the matter to which the application relates ...

b
(6) Where the High Court considers that there has been undue delay in making an application for judicial review, the court may refuse to grant—(a) leave for the making of the application; or (b) any relief sought on the application, if it considers that the granting of the relief sought would be likely to cause substantial hardship to, or substantially prejudice the rights of, any person or would be detrimental to good administration.'

c
It will be seen, therefore, that in the context of judicial review a decision of a public authority, which as a matter of law is ultra vires, may survive and remain effective if the applicant for a remedy is adjudged to have no sufficient interest or there has been undue delay and the case falls within the concluding words of s 31(6) of the 1981 Act.

d
An illustration of the continuing existence of a void decision is provided by the fact that an appeal can be brought against such a decision. In *Calvin v Carr* [1979] 2 All ER 440, [1980] AC 574 the plaintiff, who was the part-owner of a horse, was disqualified for a year by the stewards of the Australian Jockey Club. The plaintiff appealed from the decision of the stewards to the committee of the Jockey Club but his appeal was dismissed. In subsequent proceedings he claimed, inter alia,

e
that because the proceedings before the stewards had been in breach of the rules of natural justice they were void, so that the committee of the Jockey Club had no jurisdiction to hear or determine an appeal. The Privy Council rejected this argument. Lord Wilberforce said ([1979] 2 All ER 440 at 446, [1980] AC 574 at 590):

f
'The decision of the stewards resulted in disqualification, an effect with immediate and serious consequences for the appellant ... These consequences remained in effect unless and until the stewards decision was challenged and, if so, had sufficient existence in law to justify an appeal.'

g
Lord Wilberforce drew attention to the analogy provided by appeals in criminal proceedings where irregularities at the trial may have rendered the trial a nullity (see *Crane v DPP* [1921] 2 AC 299, [1921] All ER Rep 19.)

I have already referred to the fact that in a case where the court considers that there has been undue delay in making an application for judicial review, it has a

h
discretion under s 31(6) of the 1981 Act to refuse to grant relief if, for example, it considers that the granting of relief would be, for example, 'detrimental to good administration'. But it seems clear that in public law cases the court, as a court of review, has some general as opposed to a merely statutory discretion as to the relief which it will grant. It is true that in *Grunwick Processing Laboratories Ltd v Advisory Conciliation and Arbitration Service* [1978] 1 All ER 338 at 364, [1978] AC

j
655 at 695 Lord Diplock said that—

'where a statutory authority had acted ultra vires any person who would be affected by its act if it were valid is normally entitled ex debito justiciae to have it set aside, if he has proceeded by way of certiorari, or to have it declared void ...'

More recently, however, in *Chief Constable of the North Wales Police v Evans* [1982] 3 All ER 141, [1982] 1 WLR 1155 the House of Lords, though it held that the chief *a* constable had failed in the performance of his duty to act fairly in dealing with a probationary constable, granted only a limited declaration. Lord Brightman said ([1982] 3 All ER 141 at 156, [1982] 1 WLR 1155 at 1176):

'I feel that the choice of remedy is a difficult one. It is a matter of discretion. From the point of view of the respondent who has been wronged in a matter *b* so vital to his life, an order of mandamus is the only satisfactory remedy ... But it is unusual, in a case such as the present, for the court to make an order of mandamus, and I think that in practice it might border on usurpation of the powers of the chief constable, which is to be avoided. With some reluctance and hesitation, I feel that the respondent will have to content *c* himself with the less satisfactory declaration that I have outlined [affirming that, by reason of such unlawfully induced resignation, the respondent thereby became entitled to the same rights and remedies, not including re-instatement, as he would have had if the appellant had unlawfully dispensed with his services under reg 16(1) of the Police Regulations 1971].'

d
The existence of this general discretion was also affirmed by Donaldson MR in *R v Panel on Take-overs and Mergers, ex p Datafin plc (Norton Opax plc intervening)* [1987] 1 All ER 564 at 578, [1987] QB 815 at 840, where he said:

'I think that it is important that all who are concerned with take-over bids should have well in mind a very special feature of public law decisions, such *e* as those of the panel, namely that however wrong they may be, however lacking in jurisdiction they may be, they subsist and remain fully effective unless and until they are set aside by a court of competent jurisdiction. Furthermore, the court has an ultimate discretion whether to set them aside and may refuse to do so in the public interest, notwithstanding that it holds and declares the decision to have been made ultra vires (see e g *R v Monopolies* *f* *and Mergers Commission, ex p Argyll Group plc* [1986] 2 All ER 257, [1986] 1 WLR 763). That case ... further illustrates an awareness that such decisions affect a very wide public which will not be parties to the dispute and that their interests have to be taken into account as much as those of the immediate disputants.'
g
I come now to the present case.

(4) *The present case*
It is important to remember the nature of the present claim. It is not a claim against a limited company. Nor is it a claim in public law where the court is being *h* asked to exercise a supervisory jurisdiction. It is a private law claim, albeit against a public authority.

I have made some reference to proceedings for judicial review where the court, in the exercise of its supervisory jurisdiction, can grant remedies which, to an extent which I need not further examine, are discretionary. Part of this *j* discretion is conferred by statute. Part of the discretion seems to arise from the nature of the jurisdiction itself.

It was argued on behalf of the bank that in private law proceedings against a public authority the court should exercise a similar discretion where the decision was ultra vires not for lack of statutory capacity, but because of some procedural impropriety. In private law too, it was said, there were gradations of ultra vires.

a It was also submitted that it is profoundly unsatisfactory if a decision which is procedurally ultra vires can survive a challenge in judicial review proceedings but can nevertheless be treated as a nullity in a claim in private law.

I feel bound to reject these submissions. I know of no authority for the proposition that the ultra vires decisions of local authorities can be classified into categories of invalidity. I do not think that it is open to this court to introduce b such a classification. Where a public authority acts outside its jurisdiction in any of the ways indicated by Lord Reid in *Anisminic*, the decision is void. In the case of a decision to enter into a contract of guarantee, the consequences in private law are those which flow where one of the parties to a contract lacks capacity. I see no escape from this conclusion.

Furthermore, this conclusion seems to me to accord with the decision of the c House of Lords in *Wandsworth London BC v Winder* [1984] 3 All ER 976, [1985] AC 461. In that case the defendant, who occupied a flat let by the council on a secure weekly tenancy, sought to contest his liability to pay arrears of rent by claiming that the notices of increase of rent were ultra vires and void as being in breach of s 111 of the Housing Act 1957. The council applied to strike out the defence as d an abuse of the process of the court and contended that it was contrary to public policy to challenge the conduct of a public authority otherwise than by way of an application for judicial review. The House of Lords upheld the defendant's right to challenge the increase. Lord Fraser said ([1984] 3 All ER 976 at 981, [1985] AC 461 at 509):

e '[The respondent] puts forward his defence as a matter of right, whereas in an application for judicial review, success would require an exercise of the court's discretion in his favour. Apart from the provisions of [RSC] Ord 53 and s 31 of the Supreme Court Act 1981, he would certainly be entitled to defend that action on the ground that the plaintiff's claim arises from a resolution which (on his view) is invalid ... I find it impossible to accept that f the right to challenge the decision of a local authority in course of defending an action for payment can have been swept away by Ord 53, which was directed to introducing a procedural reform. As Lord Scarman said in *IRC v National Federation of Self-Employed and Small Businesses Ltd* [1981] 2 All ER 93 at 109, [1982] AC 617 at 647: "The new RSC Ord 53 is a procedural reform of g great importance in the field of public law, but it does not, indeed cannot, either extend or diminish the substantive law ..."'

I do not consider the present law to be satisfactory. I say nothing about the merits of this case which have not been investigated. But there may be cases where it is beyond argument that a third party has entered into a contract with a h public body in ignorance of any procedural defect which may later entitle the public body to claim that the contract was made ultra vires and so reject liability under it. But if, as I believe there to be, there is only one category of ultra vires decisions where a local authority is concerned, I see no room for a judicial discretion. Furthermore, in view of the fact that by s 2(2) of the 1972 Act it is j provided that the council is to consist of a chairman and councillors, there is no scope for an argument that a distinction can be drawn between the powers of the council and the powers of the councillors.

VI. CONCLUSION

Accordingly, for the various reasons which I have outlined, I would dismiss this appeal.

PETER GIBSON LJ. It is an unattractive feature of the case of the Allerdale
Borough Council (the council) that it is seeking to assert the illegality of its own   *a*
action in entering into the contract of guarantee in order to resist the claim of
Crédit Suisse (the bank) to enforce the guarantee. As was pointed out by Peter
Cane in his perceptive article on Colman J's judgment ([1995] 1 Lloyd's Rep 315),
'Do banks dare lend to local authorities?' (1994) 110 LQR 514 at 517, where a
governmental body wishes to escape an ultra vires contract with a citizen, two of   *b*
the main aims of the doctrine of ultra vires might appear to be in conflict, viz the
aim to protect citizens against illegal actions by government and the aim to
protect the public and the public purse from the effects of illegal conduct by
government. As a matter of policy, there is much to be said for the view that a
citizen who contracts in good faith with a governmental body should not have to
bear the risk that the contract may be beyond the legal powers of that body.   *c*

But in the present case Mr Clarke QC for the bank, whilst drawing attention
with justification to the fact that the council is seeking to rely on its own breach
of the duties which it owes to the public in order to renege on its private law
obligations, accepts that the position of a local authority acting beyond its
capacity by purporting to do what it could never do, may be different from that   *d*
of a local authority which asserts the invalidity of its actions on the ground that it
took into account irrelevant considerations or otherwise acted with *Wednesbury*
unreasonableness (see *Associated Provincial Picture Houses Ltd v Wednesbury Corp*
[1947] 2 All ER 680, [1948] 1 KB 223). In the former case, he appeared to accept,
the council could ask the court to hold that its action was invalid. Further, the
bank was well aware of the essential nature of the scheme, viz that it was lending   *e*
£6m to a company with a nominal capital of £2 on the security of a guarantee
from the council to assist the council to avoid its capital expenditure and
borrowing limits, and that it was not lending to the council. Accordingly, the
bank knew, or ought to have known, that it could not bring itself within the
protection of para 20 of Sch 13 to the Local Government Act 1972. It follows that,   *f*
as with any person dealing with a local authority and not coming within para 20,
the bank took the risk that the local authority did not have the power to do what
it contracted to do. It is of course elementary that a local authority, being the
creature of statute, can only do what it is required or authorised by statute to do.

Did the council have the capacity to enter into the guarantee? The judge first
considered whether the use of a company and the guarantee of its borrowings as   *g*
a means of procuring the provision of recreational facilities automatically
involved the council exceeding its statutory powers. In addressing that issue, the
judge was perhaps attributing to the council an extreme position which the
council, as I understand it, was not adopting. Mr Sher QC, for the council,
accepted that a local authority can in two particular circumstances use a company   *h*
to discharge a statutory function. One is where statute has expressly empowered
a local authority to do so, in circumstances not relevant here. The other is where
a company is set up to be the agent or nominee of the local authority. But that
was not the position in law in this case. True it is that Allerdale Development Co
Ltd was wholly owned by the council. But just as a wholly-owned subsidiary is a   *j*
separate entity in law from its holding company, so the company was a separate
entity from the council, and there was never any arrangement between the
council and the company under which the company was to act as the council's
agent or which required the company to do only the things which the council had
previously directed or authorised the company to do. It was always crucial to the
scheme entered into by the council that the company, and not the council, was

a the borrower and the expender of the moneys borrowed. Notwithstanding the fact that the council appointed the directors of the company, the directors' duties were owed to the company. It is not difficult to conceive of circumstances in which the company's interests and the council's interests might conflict. For example, if the company fell into financial difficulty, its interests, which the directors would be obliged to further, might dictate the disposal of the swimming

b pool to the purchaser who offered the best price and who might want to develop the site, whereas the council's interests would lie in the continued availability of the pool as such. In my judgment, on the facts of this case, the judge was wrong to consider that the use of the company was not necessarily an impermissible means of discharging the council's function of providing recreational facilities, or indeed any other statutory function.

c   Mr Clarke contended that the scheme involved the council providing recreational facilities in the form of the swimming pool and the time-share accommodation. For the reasons given by Neill LJ, the provision of the time-share accommodation did not fall within the provision of recreational facilities referred to in s 19 of the Local Government (Miscellaneous Provisions)

d Act 1976, nor did the scheme involve the council itself providing any recreational facilities. The provider under the scheme was the company. Thereby there was no discharge of the council's functions in a manner authorised by s 101 of the 1972 Act. The judge took the view that s 101 was only concerned with the decision-taking (as distinct from the ministerial) part of the local authority's statutory functions, but for my part I cannot see any justification for so limiting

e s 101. In that section, as in s 111, the references to functions must have their ordinary meaning as the duties and powers of a local authority. It is of course possible for a council (meaning the chairman and councillors: see s 2(1)) in the discharge of its functions to act through its own staff (s 112). It can also employ outside contractors. That, in my judgment, is permitted by s 111. But when such

f a contractor is used, whether to build a swimming pool or to run it, the arrangements must be such as to leave the local authority itself discharging its statutory function. On the facts of the present case, the use of the company meant that the council was not discharging any function under s 19 of the 1976 Act. To my mind it is apparent from the structure of s 19 itself that a local authority, if it is not itself to provide the recreational facilities under sub-s (1), can

g only provide assistance to another person providing such facilities if (a) that person is another local authority or a voluntary organisation within the meaning of sub-s (3), and (b) the assistance is in the limited form indicated in sub-s (3).

   Mr Clarke also argued that the council did come within the concluding words of s 19(1), as providing 'assistance of any kind'. But for the reasons given by Neill

h LJ I would reject that argument. That conclusion is supported by the decision of Mr Michael Barnes QC, sitting as a deputy judge of the High Court in the Queen's Bench Division, in NWS 6 v Waltham Forest London BC (17 November 1992, unreported), who rejected a similar argument that those words conferred a general power to provide financial assistance to others providing recreational

j facilities.

   Mr Clarke placed chief reliance on the wide language of s 111. He submitted that the giving of a guarantee was prima facie within s 111, and sought to derive support from the decision of this court in Den Norske Creditbank v Sarawak Economic Development Corp [1989] 2 Lloyd's Rep 35. In that case legislation containing general words somewhat similar to s 111 was construed by this court as extending to the giving of a guarantee, notwithstanding an express reference to a more limited power to give a guarantee elsewhere in the same section. But that was a case which turned on particular wording in a particular context not the same as that of s 111, and for my part I do not derive any assistance from that decision.

Section 111(1) commences with words that make clear that the provisions of the section are not to conflict with other statutory provisions. It sets out what previously had been implicit and merely authorises the local authority to do what is calculated to assist the discharge by the local authority of its functions. Where the relevant function is that in s 19, to provide recreational facilities, s 111 cannot, in my judgment, be utilised by a local authority to procure another person to discharge the local authority's function in contravention of s 101.

Further, even if that is wrong, in my opinion s 111 is not a power that can be utilised in a manner inconsistent with the statutory controls on borrowing and expenditure by local authorities. Mr Clarke relied on *A-G (ex rel Martin) v Finsbury BC* [1939] 3 All ER 995, [1939] Ch 892 as exemplifying the ability of a local authority to use a route available to it to achieve an end which by another route could not be achieved. In that case the defendant council devised a scheme to get around restrictions to build an air-raid shelter. The scheme was attacked as a sham, but Simonds J held that what that council did was valid and within its powers. No doubt today a different attack would have been made on the lawfulness of what was patently a device to evade a statutory restriction. In the light of more modern authorities such as *Tower Hamlets London BC v Chetnik Developments Ltd* [1988] 1 All ER 961, [1988] AC 858, it may be doubted whether the statutory power used in that case was properly so used. For my part, I cannot see that it can be within the scope of s 111 for a local authority, wishing one of its functions to be performed but unable, without contravening statutory controls on borrowing and expenditure, to borrow or expend the funds necessary for the performance of that function, to set up a company to perform that function and to guarantee the debts of that company, regardless of the statutory borrowing and expenditure limits.

For these and the other reasons given by Neill LJ, I would hold that the council had no power to enter into the guarantee. I am also in agreement with what he has said in his judgment on the severance point.

Mr Clarke accepted that if the council lacked the capacity to give the guarantee, it could not be enforced. Accordingly, it follows that this appeal must be dismissed.

In the light of that conclusion, it is unnecessary and I prefer not to express any obiter views on the difficult question of the effect of the invalidity on other grounds of the guarantee, particularly when it is the council which seeks to rely on its own improper conduct.

HOBHOUSE LJ.

Introduction

The claim of the plaintiffs in this action, Crédit Suisse, the well-known bank, which carries on business in a number of countries and in the City of London, is made under a contract of guarantee dated 23 May 1986 executed by the parties under seal. It is a straightforward contractual document. It guarantees the indebtedness of a company incorporated under the Companies Acts called Allerdale Development Co Ltd (the company) to the bank in respect of a loan facility of up to £6m granted by the bank to the company. The company failed to *a* repay the full amount of the advances which had been made to it and in December 1990 the company went into liquidation owing the bank a sum of the order of some £5·5m. In this action the bank seeks to recover the deficiency from the guarantor.

The other party to the guarantee was Allerdale District Council, the predecessor of the defendants. It was a relatively small district council in the *b* county of Cumbria whose area includes the town of Keswick. At the material time its annual spending limit was about £5m. The district council has denied liability to the bank under the guarantee. It says that although the affixing of the council's seal to the contract of guarantee was authorised by the council, the purported contract is not binding on the council as the making of such a contract was beyond the powers of the council or was not a lawful exercise of its powers. *c* It has also raised defences based on the allegation that the liability of the company had been varied by the bank without the consent of the council, and points on the quantum of the bank's claim.

Colman J in a detailed and careful judgment considered all the defences raised by the council (see [1995] 1 Lloyd's Rep 315). He decided against the bank *d* substantially on the ground that the council had exercised its powers unlawfully and for an improper purpose. For reasons that will become apparent, I agree with Colman J and Neill LJ that the claim must fail, having regard to the defences which have been raised in relation to the powers of the council. I do not follow in all respects the same analysis and consequently the reasons for my conclusion to some extent differ.

e This appeal has raised questions of the inter-relationship of public and private law concepts and has touched upon certain fundamental difficulties in the terminology which is used in connection with administrative law and judicial review.

f *Local authorities*

The bank's counterparty was a local authority. Local authorities are statutory corporations. They carry out governmental and administrative functions and have powers of taxation. They are governed by a complex scheme of legislation which regulates to a greater or lesser degree every aspect of their activities and finances. This legislative scheme is subject to continuing revision with additions *g* and amendments to the legislation. It is therefore necessary to have in mind that the present case has to be decided by reference to the legislation in force in May 1986. Later Acts, for example the Local Government and Housing Act 1989, would certainly have been relevant if they had been in force at the time that this guarantee was given.

h Unlike natural persons of full age and (effectively) companies incorporated under the Companies Act 1985, local authorities are corporations of limited capacity and competence. Any third party dealing with a local authority should be aware of that fact and of the potential legal risk. Where a bank lends to a local authority it has the protection of para 20 of Sch 13 to the Local Government Act *j* 1972:

'A person lending money to a local authority shall not be bound to inquire whether the borrowing of the money is legal or regular or whether the money raised was properly applied and shall not be prejudiced by an illegality or irregularity, or by the misapplication or non-application of any of that money.'

There is thus an acceptable framework within which private sector finance can
be made available to local authorities without legal risk to the private sector *a*
lender. More recently, further means of making private sector finance available
to local authorities have, with appropriate safeguards, been authorised by statute.
In the present case, however, the bank was not lending to a local authority; it was
lending to a company and taking a guarantee of the company's liability from a
local authority. This transaction, as the bank was aware, was a transaction of a *b*
different character, where they did not enjoy the protection of para 20. They
took a legal risk and it is that risk which has resulted in the present litigation.

It has long been established in English law that statutory corporations have
limited capacity. In *Chapleo v Brunswick Permanent Building Society* (1881) 6 QBD
696 at 712–713 Baggallay LJ said:

c

'... persons who deal with corporations and societies that owe their
constitution to or have their powers defined or limited by Acts of Parliament,
or are regulated by deeds of settlement or rules, deriving their effect more or
less from Acts of Parliament, are bound to know or to ascertain for
themselves the nature of the constitution, and the extent of the powers of the
corporation or society with which they deal. The plaintiffs and everyone else *d*
who have dealings with a building society are bound to know that such a
society has no power of borrowing, except such as is conferred upon it by its
rules, and if in dealing with such a society they neglect or fail to ascertain
whether it has the power of borrowing, or whether any limited power it may
have has been exceeded, they must take the consequences of their *e*
carelessness. It may be that the plaintiffs in the present case have been
misled, by the misrepresentations or conduct of others, into the belief that
the company had full authority to accept the loan from them; that is a
question which I shall have to consider when dealing with the other appeal;
such representations or conduct may doubtless give rise to a claim against
the parties making such misrepresentations or so conducting themselves, *f*
but in my opinion they can in no way give rise to or support a claim against
the society.'

The effect of exceeding the statutory authority was clearly stated by the House
of Lords in *Ashbury Railway Carriage and Iron Co Ltd v Riche* (1875) LR 7 HL 653.
The company had in good faith entered into a contract which in the opinion of *g*
their Lordships was not authorised by the memorandum of the company and the
Companies Act 1862. Lord Cairns LC (at 673) adopted the words of Blackburn J
((1874) LR 9 Exch 224 at 262):

'If so, every court, whether of law or equity, is bound to treat that contract *h*
entered into contrary to the enactment, I will not say as illegal, but as *extra*
vires, and wholly null and void, and hold also that a contract wholly void
cannot be ratified.'

Other members of the House stressed that such a contract was not voidable but
'absolutely void' and '*ultra vires* of the corporation itself' (see (1875) LR 7 HL 653 *j*
at 679, 694).

In the present century the same principles have been reaffirmed. In the interest
rate swaps case, *Hazell v Hammersmith and Fulham London BC* [1991] 1 All ER 545
at 548, [1992] 2 AC 1 at 22, Lord Templeman reaffirmed the limited powers of a
local authority:

'A local authority, although democratically elected and representative of the area, is not a sovereign body and can only do such things as are expressly or impliedly authorised by Parliament ... The expenditure incurred by a local authority in the discharge of its functions is funded partly by grants from Parliament, derived from the taxpayer, partly by rates and community charges derived from local residents and partly by income lawfully generated by the council in the due performance of some of its functions, for example rents from council houses. Authorised expenditure by a local authority may be short term or long term ... Parliament has conferred on a local authority controlled power to borrow short term and long term. The borrowing powers of a local authority are defined and controlled by the provisions of Pt I of Sch 13 to the [Local Government Act 1972] ... Those provisions limit the purpose and method of borrowing by a local authority and dictate internal accounting for repayment.'

Later he continued ([1991] 1 All ER 545 at 556, [1992] 2 AC 1 at 30):

'Individual trading corporations and others may speculate as much as they please or consider prudent. But a local authority is not a trading or currency or commercial operator with no limit on the method or extent of its borrowing or with powers to speculate. The local authority is a public authority dealing with public moneys, exercising powers limited by Sch 13 [of the Local Government Act 1972].'

Finally, he said ([1991] 1 All ER 545 at 560, [1992] 2 AC 1 at 36): 'The object of the doctrine of ultra vires is the protection of the public.'

The relationship of public, private and administrative law

Where a statutory corporation purports to enter into a contract which it is not empowered by the relevant statute to enter into, the corporation lacks the capacity to make the supposed contract. This lack of capacity means that the document and the agreement it contains does not have effect as a legal contract. It exists in fact but not in law. It is legal nullity. The purported contract which is in truth not a contract does not confer any legal rights on either party. Neither party can sue upon it. This conclusion gives rise to no conflict between public law and private law principles. The role of public law is to answer the question: what is the capacity of the local authority to contract? The role of private law is to answer the question: when one of the parties to a supposed contract lacks contractual capacity, does the supposed contract give rise to legal obligations? When a plaintiff is asserting a private law right—a private law cause of action, typically a claim for damages for breach of contract or tort—the plaintiff must establish his cause of action. Any defence raised by the defendant must be one which is recognised by private law. Lack of capacity to contract is a defence recognised by private law.

When one gets beyond situations which can be described as lack of capacity, the private law position becomes more complicated, as was recognised in *Rolled Steel Products (Holdings) Ltd v British Steel Corp* [1985] 3 All ER 52, [1986] Ch 246. That case concerned the law relating to companies incorporated under the Companies Act 1948. Slade LJ said ([1985] 3 All ER 52 at 79, [1986] Ch 246 at 286):

'For many years the phrase "ultra vires" has from time to time been used by company lawyers in two senses. Primarily it is used to describe acts which are beyond the *capacity* of a company. As is pointed out by the editors of

Gore-Browne on Companies (43rd edn, 1977) para 3–1, the phrase is also
sometimes used to describe acts which are not beyond the capacity of the *a*
company but simply beyond the *authority* of either the board of directors or
a majority of the shareholders.' (Slade LJ's emphasis.)

Browne-Wilkinson LJ said ([1985] 3 All ER 52 at 91–92, [1986] Ch 246 at 302–304):

'In my judgment, much of the confusion that has crept into the law flows *b*
from the use of the phrase "ultra vires" in different senses in different
contexts. The reconciliation of the authorities can only be achieved if one
first defines the sense in which one is using the words "ultra vires". Because
the literal translation of the words is "beyond the powers", there are many
cases in which the words have been applied to transactions which, although
within the capacity of the company, are carried out otherwise than through *c*
the correct exercise of the powers of the company by its officers; indeed, that
is the sense in which the judge seems to have used the words in this case. For
reasons which will appear, in my judgment, the use of the phrase "ultra
vires" should be restricted to those cases where the transaction is beyond the
capacity of the company and therefore wholly void ... The critical *d*
distinction is, therefore, between acts done in excess of the capacity of the
company on the one hand and acts done in excess or abuse of the powers of
the company on the other. If the transaction is beyond the capacity of the
company it is in any event a nullity and wholly void; whether or not the third
party had notice of the invalidity, property transferred or money paid under
such transaction will be recoverable from the third party. If, on the other *e*
hand, the transaction (although in excess or abuse of powers) is within the
capacity of the company, the position of the third party depends on whether
or not he had notice that the transaction was in excess or abuse of the powers
of the company ... The two badges of a transaction which is ultra vires in
that sense are (1) that the transaction is wholly void and (consequentially) (2) *f*
that it is irrelevant whether or not the third party had notice.'

The decision of the Court of Appeal was that if the relevant transaction was not
ultra vires in the sense in which Slade and Browne-Wilkinson LJJ were using it,
the defence has to be based on the principles applicable to agents and fiduciaries.
   Thus, the question of capacity and ultra vires properly so-called does not *g*
involve any consideration of questions of fault or notice. On the other hand
questions of abuse of power may involve such considerations.
Browne-Wilkinson LJ summarised his conclusions ([1985] 3 All ER 52 at 93–94,
[1986] Ch 246 at 306–307):

'(1) To be ultra vires, a transaction has to be outside the capacity of the *h*
company, not merely in excess or abuse of the powers of the company.
(2) The question whether a transaction is outside the capacity of the
company depends solely on whether, on the true construction of its
memorandum of association, the transaction is capable of falling within the
objects of the company as opposed to being a proper exercise of the powers *j*
of the company ... (4) If a transaction falls within the objects, (and therefore
the capacity) of the company, it is not ultra vires the company and
accordingly it is not absolutely void. (5) If a company enters into a
transaction which is intra vires (as being within its capacity) but in excess or
abuse of its powers, such transaction will be set aside at the instance of the
shareholders. (6) A third party, who has notice (actual or constructive) that

a a transaction, although intra vires the company, was entered into in excess
or abuse of the powers of the company, cannot enforce such transaction
against the company ...'

If local authorities were companies incorporated under the Companies Acts,
the *Rolled Steel* case would provide the necessary guidance on the treatment of
lack of capacity and excess or abuse of power. But local authorities are public law
b bodies and fall within the purview of administrative law. This means that their
decisions are amenable to judicial review and the remedies which that procedure
provides. The essence of the modern law of judicial review is that decisions
which involve illegality, irrationality or procedural impropriety are treated as
ultra vires (see *Council of Civil Service Unions v Minister for the Civil Service* [1984] 3
c All ER 935 at 951, [1985] AC 374 at 410 per Lord Diplock). That ultra vires was
the basis of the jurisdiction of the courts in judicial review proceedings was
emphatically reaffirmed by Lord Browne-Wilkinson, with the agreement of the
other members of the House, in *Page v Hull University Visitor* [1993] 1 All ER 97 at
107, [1993] AC 682 at 701, where he adopted what Lord Diplock had said in
O'Reilly v Mackman [1982] 3 All ER 1124 at 1129, [1983] 2 AC 237 at 278 (again with
d the agreement of the other members of the House):

'[*Anisminic Ltd v Foreign Compensation Commission* [1969] 1 All ER 208,
[1969] 2 AC 147] "has liberated English public law from the fetters that the
courts had theretofore imposed upon themselves so far as determinations of
inferior courts and statutory tribunals were concerned, by drawing esoteric
e distinctions between errors of law committed by such tribunals that went to
their jurisdiction, and errors of law committed by them within their
jurisdiction. The breakthrough that *Anisminic* made was the recognition by
the majority of this House that if a tribunal whose jurisdiction was limited by
statute or subordinate legislation mistook the law applicable to the facts as it
had found them, it must have asked itself the wrong question, ie one into
f which it was not empowered to inquire and so had no jurisdiction to
determine. Its purported 'determination', not being 'a determination' within
the meaning of the empowering legislation, was accordingly a nullity."'

It is an inescapable conclusion that the same words and phrases have a breadth
g of meaning which differs in administrative law and other parts of the law. In
some contexts the terms are clearly used in an equivalent sense. If a tribunal of
limited jurisdiction acts in excess of its jurisdiction, its purported decision is a
nullity (though such nullity will not prevent an appellate court from deciding that
there has been an excess of jurisdiction). A minister who purports to exercise a
delegated power to legislate must act within that power and, if he does not, the
h purported delegated legislation is void and of no legal effect. But in other areas,
such as procedural impropriety, difficulties arise. For example, breach of the
rules of natural justice has long been held to render invalid and void a decision so
reached. In *Ridge v Baldwin* [1963] 2 All ER 66 at 81, [1964] AC 40 at 80 Lord Reid
(representing the view of the majority of their Lordships) said:

j 'Then there was considerable argument whether in the result the watch
committee's decision is void or merely voidable. Time and again in the cases
I have cited it has been stated that a decision given without regard to the
principles of natural justice is void and that was expressly decided in *Wood* v.
Woad ((1874) LR 9 Exch 190, [1874–80] All ER Rep 408). I see no reason to
doubt these authorities. The body with the power to decide cannot lawfully

proceed to make a decision until it has afforded to the person affected a
proper opportunity to state his case.'

Lord Devlin expressed a different view, agreeing with Lord Evershed on this
point: 'the miscarriage rendered the watch committee's decision voidable and
not null and void ab initio' (see [1963] 2 All ER 66 at 120, [1964] AC 40 at 142).

Lord Hailsham addressed these problems in *London and Clydeside Estates Ltd v
Aberdeen DC* [1979] 3 All ER 876 at 883, [1980] 1 WLR 182 at 189–190:

> 'In this appeal we are in the field of the rapidly developing jurisprudence of
> administrative law, and we are considering the effect of non compliance by
> a statutory authority with the statutory requirements affecting the discharge
> of one of its functions. In the reported decisions there is much language
> presupposing the existence of stark categories such as "mandatory" and
> "directory", "void" and "voidable", a "nullity", and "purely regulatory".
> Such language is useful; indeed, in the course of this opinion I have used
> some of it myself. But I wish to say that I am not at all clear that the language
> itself may not be misleading in so far as it may be supposed to present a court
> with the necessity of fitting a particular case into one or other of mutually
> exclusive and starkly contrasted compartments, compartments which in
> some cases (eg "void" and "voidable") are borrowed from the language of
> contract or status, and are not easily fitted to the requirements of
> administrative law. When Parliament lays down a statutory requirement for
> the exercise of legal authority it expects its authority to be obeyed down to
> the minutest detail. But what the courts have to decide in a particular case is
> the legal consequence of non compliance on the rights of the subject viewed
> in the light of a concrete state of facts and a continuing chain of events. It
> may be that what the courts are faced with is not so much a stark choice of
> alternatives but a spectrum of possibilities in which one compartment or
> description fades gradually into another. At one end of this spectrum there
> may be cases in which a fundamental obligation may have been so
> outrageously and flagrantly ignored or defied that the subject may safely
> ignore what has been done and treat it as having no legal consequences on
> himself. In such a case if the defaulting authority seeks to rely on its action
> it may be that the subject is entitled to use the defect in procedures, simply
> as a shield or defence without having taken any positive action of his own.
> At the other end of the spectrum the defect in procedure may be so nugatory
> or trivial that the authority can safely proceed without remedial action,
> confident that, if the subject is so misguided as to rely on the fault, the courts
> will decline to listen to his complaint. But in a very great number of cases, it
> may be in a majority of them, it may be necessary for a subject, in order to
> safeguard himself, to go to the court for declaration of his rights, the grant of
> which may well be discretionary, and by the like token it may be wise for an
> authority (as it certainly would have been here) to do everything in its power
> to remedy the fault in its procedures so as not to deprive the subject of his
> due or themselves of their power to act. In such cases, though language like
> "mandatory", "directory", "void", "voidable", "nullity" and so forth may be
> helpful in argument, it may be misleading in effect if relied on to show that
> the courts, in deciding the consequences of a defect in the exercise of power,
> are necessarily bound to fit the facts of a particular case and a developing
> chains of events into rigid legal categories or to stretch or cramp them on a
> bed of Procrustes invented by lawyers for the purposes of convenient

exposition. As I have said, the case does not really arise here, since we are in the presence of a total non compliance with a requirement which I have held to be mandatory. Nevertheless, I do not wish to be understood in the field of administrative law and in the domain where the courts apply a supervisory jurisdiction over the acts of subordinate authority purporting to exercise statutory powers, to encourage the use of rigid legal classifications. The jurisdiction is inherently discretionary and the court is frequently in the presence of differences of degree which merge almost imperceptibly into differences of kind.'

In *F Hoffmann-La Roche & Co AG v Secretary of State for Trade and Industry* [1974] 2 All ER 1128 at 1154, [1975] AC 295 at 366 Lord Diplock said:

'I think it leads to confusion to use such terms as "voidable", "voidable ab initio", "void" or "a nullity" as descriptive of the legal status of subordinate legislation alleged to be ultra vires for patent or latent defects, before its validity has been pronounced on by a court of competent jurisdiction.'

In the same vein, it can be added that the use of the term 'illegal' or 'unlawful' in administrative law is to be contrasted with the use of the term 'illegal' in private law.

Chief Constable of the North Wales Police v Evans [1982] 3 All ER 141, [1982] 1 WLR 1155 illustrates such considerations. Like *Ridge v Baldwin*, it was a case of wrongful dismissal (Evans having been constructively dismissed) and the House of Lords discussed what remedies were appropriate. The fact that the decision of the relevant authority had been arrived at unlawfully and was therefore to be treated for the purposes of administrative law as ultra vires did not carry with it the conclusion that the decision and subsequent actions should be treated as if they never had occurred.

The use of terminology for the purposes of administrative law in a different way to that which would be recognised in private law can be found in very many authorities, as can examples of the use by the court of the discretion to grant or withhold remedies of proceedings for judicial review. One further example will suffice to illustrate the point. In *R v Broadcasting Complaints Commission, ex p Owen* [1985] 2 All ER 522, [1985] QB 1153 the Divisional Court held that the commission had acted unlawfully in refusing to consider a certain complaint. But the court refused to grant further relief notwithstanding the invalidity of the decision. May LJ said ([1985] 2 All ER 522 at 533, [1985] QB 1153 at 1177):

'... the grant of what may be the appropriate remedies in an application for judicial review is a matter for the discretion of this court. Where one is satisfied that although a reason relied on by a statutory body may not properly be described as insubstantial, nevertheless without it the statutory body would have been bound to come to precisely the same conclusion on valid grounds, then it would be wrong for this court to exercise its discretion to strike down, in one way or another, that body's conclusion.'

The discretion of the court in deciding whether to grant any remedy is a wide one. It can take into account many considerations, including the needs of good administration, delay, the effect on third parties, the utility of granting the relevant remedy. The discretion can be exercised so as partially to uphold and partially quash the relevant administrative decision or act (see e g *Agricultural*

Horticultural and Forestry Industry Training Board v Aylesbury Mushrooms Ltd [1972]
1 All ER 280, [1972] 1 WLR 190).

These factors have in their turn given rise to fundamental difficulties for the
theoretical basis of administrative law as discussed by a number of authors—
Wade *Administrative Law* (7th edn, 1994), Lord Woolf's *Hamlyn Lecture* (41st
series, 1990), Sir John Laws 'Illegality: The Problem of Jurisdiction' in
Supperstone and Goudie, *Judicial Review* (1992) and de Smith Woolf and Jowell
Judicial Review of Administrative Action (5th edn 1995). What is the status of an
ultra vires decision which the courts have declined to quash on proceedings for
judicial review? In principle any such decision is to be regarded as 'void' and a
'nullity'. Yet the effect of the exercise of the court's discretion is to allow it to
stand. Similar questions of theory and terminology exist in relation to the status
of an unlawful decision or administrative act before it has been challenged and
held to be 'ultra vires' (see *Smith v East Elloe RDC* [1956] 1 All ER 855, [1956] AC
736 and *Hoffmann-La Roche*).

In my judgment, the answer lies in what has been said by Lord Hailsham and
Lord Diplock in the passages which I have quoted and the recognition that terms
are used differently in administrative law and other branches of the law. Before
using the phrase 'ultra vires' or the words 'void' and 'nullity', it is necessary to
pause and consider the breadth of the meaning which one is giving them. It is not
correct to take terminology from administrative law and apply it without the
necessary adjustment and refinement of meaning to private law. Where private
law rights are concerned, as in the present case, the terminology must be used in
the sense which is appropriate to private law.

There is a further dimension which is also fundamental. In judicial review all
that an applicant need show in order to have a locus standi is 'a sufficient interest
in the matter to which the application relates' (see RSC Ord 53, r 3(7)). This need
not be any recognisable legal interest and need not involve any assertion of any
infringement of the rights of the applicant. On the other hand, in civil
proceedings the rights and liabilities of the parties before the court are of the
essence of the subject matter of the proceedings. Therefore, whereas in judicial
review proceedings it may be appropriate for a court to consider whether an
abuse of power should be publicly exposed, in civil proceedings the court is only
concerned with whether that abuse of power has affected the private law rights
of the parties.

Thus, in *Wandsworth London BC v Winder* [1984] 3 All ER 976, [1985] AC 461 the
local authority was seeking to evict and obtain a possession order against one of
its tenants. It was asserting a private law right. The ground upon which it relied
was the tenant's refusal to pay an increased rent. The tenant said that the
resolutions of the council and the notices of the increases in rent were ultra vires
and void in that they did not comply with s 111 of the Housing Act 1957.
Accordingly, although the tenant was raising an issue which could have been the
subject of judicial review proceedings (had he brought them in time), he was
actually raising a narrower point: whether or not he was civilly liable to pay the
increased rent. The Court of Appeal by a majority and the House of Lords held
that it was not an abuse of process for him to raise this defence in the possession
proceedings. The existence of private law rights has to be determined as a private
law issue.

In resolving a private law issue it is always necessary to have regard to who are
the actual parties to the issue. This may affect the analysis of the issue and the
answer which private law gives to it. Some improper conduct of the

a decision-making body may be material within the broader spectrum of administrative law, but it will not necessarily be material as between the parties to a private law dispute. A want of natural justice is specifically material to the respective private law rights of the aggrieved party and the decision-maker or a person who asserts rights based upon the decision. The private law rights of a third party who himself has not been a victim of any want of natural justice will
b not be affected.

Similarly, if the abuse of power by one party can properly be categorised as a 'fault' of that party, it cannot on private law principles be used as a basis for conferring rights which would not otherwise exist upon the party at fault against another party, who would otherwise have rights against the party at fault or
c would not be liable to the party at fault. Again, similarly, considerations of the knowledge of, or degree of notice to, a party who is asserting a private law right may be relevant to the question whether the right is enforceable against another where there has been some irregularity in the transaction which is alleged to have given rise to the right.

d Private law issues must be decided in accordance with the rules of private law. The broader and less rigorous rules of administrative law should not without adjustment be applied to the resolution of private law disputes in civil proceedings. Public law, that is to say, the law governing public law entities and their activities, is a primary source of the principles applied in administrative law
e proceedings. The decisions of such entities are the normal subject matter of applications for judicial review. When the activities of a public law body (or individual) are relevant to a private law dispute in civil proceedings, public law may in a similar way provide answers which are relevant to the resolution of the private law issue. But after taking into account the applicable public law, the civil proceedings have to be decided as a matter of private law. The issue does not
f become an administrative law issue; administrative law remedies are irrelevant.

In the present case, counsel have advanced arguments which have called into question the relationship between private law and administrative law. Mr Sher QC, for the council, has argued that an element of irrationality ('*Wednesbury* unreasonableness*'*: see *Associated Provincial Picture Houses Ltd v Wednesbury Corp*
g [1947] 2 All ER 680, [1948] 1 KB 223) or improper motive would provide the council with a defence to the bank's claim. Mr Clarke QC, for the bank, has argued that any defence should be regarded as discretionary and should be approached in the same way as the decision whether to grant a remedy in judicial review proceedings. These arguments were considered by Colman J in his
h judgment (see [1995] 1 Lloyd's Rep 315 at 342–358). In my judgment, both these arguments make the error which I have identified of using administrative law language and concepts without making the necessary adjustments. It remains necessary to ask what amounts to a defence to a private law cause of action. Want of capacity is a defence to a contractual claim; breach of duty, fiduciary or
j otherwise, may be a defence depending upon the circumstances. To say that administrative law categorises all grounds for judicial review as ultra vires does not assist. In civil proceedings the question is whether, after taking into account the relevant public law, there is on the facts a private law defence. By a parity of reasoning, how a divisional court would have decided an application for judicial review and what remedy (if any) it would have granted in the exercise of its discretion is not material.

The transaction

The document upon which the bank sues is a guarantee given by the council in respect of the liabilities of a company. This is not, as such, the exercise of a legitimate power of a local authority. If it is to be within the capacity of the council this must be demonstrated from considering its role in some larger transaction.

As their solicitors put it, the council's 'real objective' was to have a leisure pool built for the inhabitants of their area and tourists at no cost to the council. The council could not, without an unacceptable reduction in its existing programme, have built the pool within its then current borrowing and spending limits. It could not itself build the leisure pool. Therefore it formed a limited liability company with the intention that the company should do so. In Keswick there were two parcels of land belonging to third parties which were available for purchase. If the company could purchase the land or take it on long lease and could raise the necessary finance, the company would then be able to build the pool. As part of this scheme, therefore, it was intended that the company should build time-share accommodation on one of the parcels of land and sell time-share entitlements producing a sufficient profit to defray the cost of building the leisure pool and possibly provide an additional sum of money as well. The time-share part of the scheme was essentially a trading activity designed to yield a trading profit sufficient to finance the leisure pool part of the scheme.

The relationship of the council to the company was solely that of shareholder. There was no contractual relationship between the council and the company . The council did not employ the company to do anything. The company was under no obligation to the council to do anything. It was an essential and overt part of the scheme that the company was not to be the agent of the council. The memorandum of the company, as adopted on 8 April 1986, contains objects which are broadly drafted and include the carrying on of trading activities. There are references in the objects clause to the district of Allerdale but not to the council. There is nothing beyond its shareholding which entitles the district council to exercise any control over the company. Paragraphs in the memorandum preclude the distribution of profits, or surpluses on liquidation, to the members of the company. The articles of association are in general terms and give rise to no special consideration. There were four directors of the company, three councillors and Mr Perry (the chief executive of the council).

The company needed finance to cover the construction costs of the leisure pool and time-share development for the period before which the time-share entitlements had been sold. One of the institutions approached was the bank. The bank appreciated that—

> 'the borrowing company has been specifically formed as a vehicle to develop the complex under the guarantee of the council to avoid the initial cost being set against prescribed capital expenditure.'

At the trial, the head of corporate marketing at the bank gave evidence that he appreciated that the reason for the involvement of the company was that the council's borrowing and spending limits did not enable the council to finance the scheme itself and that the finance had to be taken 'off balance sheet'. It was thus appreciated that it was essentially an artificially structured scheme designed to avoid the statutory controls upon local authorities and that the company was involved specifically because it was not the council or its agent and therefore not subject to those controls.

a By a letter dated 14 May 1986 the bank offered the company a facility. The purpose was stated to be: 'Construction of time-share and leisure pool complex.' The security was to be an irrevocable unconditional guarantee provided by the council. The bank considered that the interest rate which it was obtaining was advantageous. If the guarantee had not been forthcoming, other security would have to had to be found and the interest rates would no doubt have been
b different. The scheme might well have ceased to make sufficient business sense to be commercially acceptable. However, on 23 May 1986 the council's seal was affixed to the guarantee and the scheme went ahead. The facility was drawn down by the company. The relevant land was acquired by the company and the buildings erected by its contractors. The time-share entitlements were marketed, but without the anticipated success. The scheme was a commercial failure and
c the company was unable to repay the sums which had been advanced to it by the bank.

The capacity of the district council to give the guarantee
I will not set out again the relevant statutory provisions. This has already been
d done by Neill LJ.
The provision relied upon by the bank is s 111(1) of the 1972 Act. The power, therefore, has to be a power to grant a guarantee which is calculated to facilitate or conducive or incidental to the discharge of some function of the council. The word 'functions' as used in this section has been given a wide interpretation as 'the sum total of the activities Parliament has entrusted to' the local authority:
e 'Those activities are its functions' (see *Hazell v Hammersmith and Fulham London BC* [1991] 1 All ER 545 at 554, [1992] 2 AC 1 at 29; [1990] 3 All ER 33 at 83, [1990] 2 QB 697 at 785). There is no ambiguity in s 111; it embodies well-established principles authorising incidental powers. Similarly, I do not consider that for present purposes relevant assistance is to be found in sub-s (3); the subsection has
f been given a restricted interpretation in *McCarthy & Stone (Developments) Ltd v Richmond upon Thames London BC* [1991] 4 All ER 897, [1992] 2 AC 48.
It is implicit in s 111(1) that it refers to the discharge by the council of its functions. In my judgment, this necessary implication was not sufficiently recognised by Colman J and the argument of the bank. It interrelates with points considered by the judge and by Neill LJ in his judgment but is more radical. The
g activity must be one which can, as a matter of fact, be properly categorised as an activity of the council. The primary statutory provision relevant to this is s 101(1) in Pt VI of the 1972 Act, headed 'Discharge of functions'. It authorises a local authority to arrange for the discharge of any of its functions by a committee, sub-committee or an officer of the authority or by any other authority. Save for
h immaterial exceptions, this delimits how a local authority may discharge its functions. Any delegation beyond those prescribed limits is unlawful. Thus, a local authority may not delegate the discharge of this functions to members of the council. Still less may it delegate them to the directors of a company.
However, without any such delegation, a local authority may employ
j contractors or agents; this is what is permitted by s 111(1). It is still the local authority that is discharging its functions. The employment of a contractor or the use of an agent facilitates that discharge. But that was not what happened under the present scheme. The company was not the agent of the council. It was not employed by the council; it had no contract with the council. The company was a free-standing entity trading on its own account without obligation to the council. It acquired the interests in the land on its own account and employed

contractors similarly on its own account. The loans made by the bank were made to the company and for the account of the company. Were this not so, the guarantee would have strictly been unnecessary—and the borrowing would have been improper borrowing by the council and the expenditure likewise improper.

It is elementary law that shareholders are not to be identified with the corporate entity even if there is only one shareholder (see *Salomon v Salomon & Co* [1897] AC 22, [1895–9] All ER Rep 33). Similarly, the existence of a shareholding does not suffice to make the company the agent of the shareholders; separate and distinct evidence of an agency relationship is required. Even where there are wider powers of control over a company, such identification is not to be made. In *Tamlin v Hannaford* [1949] 2 All ER 327, [1950] 1 KB 23 the question was whether or not the British Transport Commission was a servant or agent of the Crown so as to be able to claim the immunities and privileges of the Crown. The Minister of Transport had extensive powers of control over the commission ([1949] 2 All ER 327 at 328–330, [1950] 1 KB 23 at 24, 25):

'He is given powers over this corporation which are as great as those possessed by a man who holds all the shares in a private company, subject, however, as such a man is not, to a duty to account to Parliament for his stewardship. It is the Minister who appoints the directors—the members of the commission—and fixes their remuneration. They must give him any information he wants, and, lest they should not prove amenable to his suggestions as to the policy they should adopt, he is given power to give them directions of a general nature in matters which appear to him to affect the national interest, as to which he is the sole judge, and they are then bound to obey. These are great powers, but still we cannot regard the corporation as being his agent, any more than a company is the agent of the shareholders or even of a sole shareholder. In the eye of the law the corporation is its own master and is answerable as fully as any other person or corporation … In the absence of any [express provision that a corporation should act on behalf of the Crown] the proper inference, in the case, at any rate, of commercial corporation, is that it acts on its own behalf, even though it is controlled by a government department.'

Whatever was being done in acquiring interests in the land, erecting buildings, providing recreational facilities to the users of the swimming pool, giving rights to occupy accommodation to purchasers of time-share entitlements, all this was being done by the company alone. It was not in fact or in law a local authority doing anything. It was not the council discharging any function.

It is possible for a function of a local authority to be secondary—to encourage or assist others to do something or arrange for others to do something. If so, it can be a discharge of the authority's function to provide such encouragement or assistance or to make such arrangements. This distinction, which is obvious and requires no citation, was acknowledged in *R v South Wales Traffic Licensing Authority, ex p Ebbw Vale UDC* [1951] 1 All ER 806 at 808–809, [1951] 2 KB 366 at 370–371 (per Cohen J). There the Court of Appeal held that when the relevant service was provided by an independent company not acting as the agent of the council, the service was not provided by the council:

'Under the ordinary rules of law a parent company and a subsidiary company, even a hundred per cent. subsidiary company, are distinct single entities, and in the absence of a contract of agency between the two a companies one cannot be said to be the agent of the other ... I would emphasise the distinction that is plainly drawn [in the Transport Act 1947] between providing, on the one hand, and securing or promoting, the provision of an efficient system of transport, on the other. It seems to me that that clearly visualises that the commission may either provide the system themselves or may secure or promote the provision thereof by b others.'

Similar distinctions of wording exist in the statutory provisions upon which the bank has sought to rely in the present case. The primary provision was s 19 of the Local Government (Miscellaneous Provisions) Act 1976. Section 19(1) includes the function: to provide recreational facilities including swimming pools. But it c also, by the concluding phrase in the subsection, says that the power to provide facilities includes the power to provide 'assistance of any kind'. It is possible to provide assistance without yourself providing the facility. Similarly, in s 144 of the 1972 Act, a local authority was empowered (among other things) to 'provide or encourage any other person or body to provide, facilities for' various purposes (see also s 145). The scheme of the relevant Acts clearly recognises the distinction d between the local authority providing something and its assisting or encouraging someone else to do so. Therefore, in so far as the bank relies upon functions which involve the council doing something or providing something, the bank's case must fail. This conclusion covers all the primary ways in which the bank presented its case and the bank's reliance upon s 2(1) of the Local Authorities e (Land) Act 1963. As regards the other secondary ways in which the bank put its case, I agree with what Neill LJ has said about the construction of the various statutory provisions relied upon and their inapplicability to the facts of this case.

Had the bank got over this difficulty, there would have come next the question: what was giving the guarantee incidental to? In my judgment it was clearly incidental to the use of an independent company to provide the relevant f service. On this approach, the bank has to argue that (contrary to my view) the use of the company was something which was authorised by s 111(1) of the 1972 Act. It is not suggested that at the material time there was any other power which permitted setting up the company. Assuming that the setting up of the company was a proper exercise of an incidental power under s 111(1), the giving of the guarantee was, in my judgment, incidental to that incidental activity. The g function of the guarantee was to assist the company to borrow at favourable rates and without providing other security. It flowed from the needs of the company. It was not incidental to the discharge of the function. The principle recognised in cases such as *McCarthy & Stone* is applicable.

Similarly, I agree with Neill LJ that the time-share scheme was an integral and h essential part of the transaction at the time it was entered into. The facility was expressly for the 'Construction of time-share and leisure pool complex' and the guarantee was an all-indebtedness guarantee. The business of constructing and marketing time-share flats was clearly not an activity which was covered by s 19(1) of the 1976 Act: the suggested analogy with camp sites was unreal.
j The appeal should be dismissed.

Appeal dismissed.

Paul Magrath Esq   Barrister.

Crédit Suisse and another v Waltham Forest London Borough Council

a

COURT OF APPEAL, CIVIL DIVISION

NEILL, PETER GIBSON AND HOBHOUSE LJJ

19–22, 26–28 FEBRUARY, 8 MAY 1996

b

Local authority – Statutory powers – Implied power – Local authority forming and partly owning company to fund property acquisitions – Local authority guaranteeing company's obligations to bank and indemnifying company against losses – Company entering into speculative property transactions – Company incurring losses following c *collapse of property market – Whether local authority liable under indemnity and guarantee – Whether local authority having implied power to form company and give indemnity and guarantee – Local Government Act 1972, s 111 – Housing Act 1985, ss 65, 69.*

d

In October 1988 the defendant local authority established a company, N Ltd, in which it retained a 50% interest, for the purpose of purchasing properties which would be leased to the local authority on short three-year leases. The arrangement was intended to enable the local authority to discharge its statutory function under s 65 of the Housing Act 1985[a] of providing housing for homeless persons. The local authority planned to apply the profits made from the e arrangement with N Ltd to the acquisition of further housing stock. In order to facilitate the scheme, N Ltd borrowed £11m from the plaintiff bank to purchase approximately 100 properties and simultaneously the local authority guaranteed the loan and agreed to indemnify N Ltd from and against all losses arising out of the scheme. The local authority intended that the properties would be sold at the f end of the lease period and that the loan would be repaid in September 1993. However, following a collapse in the property market in 1990, there was a shortfall in the proceeds of sale with the result that N Ltd failed to repay the loan. Thereafter the bank and N Ltd (which was then in administrative receivership) issued a writ against the local authority claiming recovery under the guarantee and the indemnity respectively. The judge gave summary judgment for the g plaintiffs on the basis that s 111[b] of the Local Government Act 1972 gave the local authority implied power to guarantee the loan and to indemnify N Ltd. The local authority appealed.

Held – A local authority had no implied power under s 111 of the 1972 Act to h discharge its housing functions by means of a partly-owned company or to give such a company assistance in the form of a guarantee or indemnity. Where Parliament had made detailed provisions as to how certain statutory functions were to be carried out, there was no scope for implying the existence of additional powers which lay wholly outside the statutory code, and since the only means by which the local authority could discharge its housing function under s 65 of the *j*

---

a   Section 65, so far as material, provides: 'Where [the local authority] are satisfied that [the applicant] had a priority need and are not satisfied that he became homeless intentionally … they shall … secure that accommodation becomes available for his occupation.'

b   Section 111, so far as material, is set out at p 183 *c d*, post

a 1985 Act were set out in s 69^c of that Act, the guarantee and indemnity could not properly be characterised as calculated to facilitate, or as conducive or incidental to, the discharge of any function of the local authority within the meaning of s 111 of the 1972 Act. The scheme thereafter involved an impermissible delegation of the local authority's powers in relation to the acquisition of properties, and, as such, the guarantee and indemnity were unlawful. It followed

b that the purported transactions were not contracts which the local authority had the capacity to enter into and gave rise to no legal obligations enforceable against the local authority. The appeal would accordingly be allowed (see p 184 *d* to *g*, p 185 *d* to *g*, p 188 *e* to *j* and p 189 *e*, post).

Crédit Suisse v Allerdale BC [1996] 4 All ER 129 considered.

c **Notes**

For a local authority's power to incur expenditure in general, see 28 *Halsbury's Laws* (4th edn) paras 1245–1247, and for cases on the subject, see 33 *Digest* (2nd reissue) 54–57, *135–144*.

For the Local Government Act 1972, s 111, see 25 *Halsbury's Statutes* (4th edn)
d (1996 reissue) 267.

For the Housing Act 1985, ss 65, 69, see 21 *Halsbury's Statutes* (4th edn) (1990 reissue) 104, 108.

Cases referred to in judgments

e *Crédit Suisse v Allerdale BC* [1996] 4 All ER 129, CA; *affg* [1995] 1 Lloyd's Rep 315.
Hazell v Hammersmith and Fulham London BC [1991] 1 All ER 545, [1992] 2 AC 1, [1991] 2 WLR 372, HL.

Cases also cited or referred to in skeleton arguments

Puhlhofer v Hillingdon London BC [1986] 1 All ER 467, [1986] AC 484, HL.
f *McCarthy & Stone (Developments) Ltd v Richmond upon Thames London BC* [1991] 4 All ER 897, [1992] 2 AC 48, HL.

Appeal

By notice dated 2 December 1994 the defendant, Waltham Forest London
g Borough Council, appealed with leave from the decision of Gatehouse J on 2 November 1994 whereby he granted an application by the plaintiffs, Crédit Suisse and North East London Property Co Ltd (in administrative receivership) (NELP), for summary judgment and/or disposal on a point of law under RSC Ord 14 and 14A of their claim for payment from the council under a contract of guarantee
h dated 28 October 1988 pursuant to which the council had guaranteed repayment of a loan by the bank to the company. The facts are set out in the judgment of Neill LJ.

Andrew Arden QC and *Richard Sheldon* (instructed by *Gerard Curran*, Waltham
  Forrest) for the council.
j *Christopher Clarke QC* and *Catharine Otton-Goulder* (instructed by *Lawrence Graham*) for the bank and NELP.

Cur adv vult

---

c   Section 69, so far as material, is set out at p 178 *d e*, post

8 May 1996. The following judgments were delivered.

a

NEILL LJ. Part III of the Housing Act 1985 imposes certain duties on local authorities with regard to housing homeless persons. If a person applies to a local authority for accommodation or for assistance in obtaining accommodation and the authority have reason to believe that he may be homeless or threatened with homelessness then, in accordance with s 62(1) of the 1985 Act, they are required *b* to make such inquiries as are necessary to satisfy themselves as to whether he is homeless or threatened with homelessness. Section 65 of the 1985 Act sets out the duties which are owed to an applicant where the local authority are satisfied that he is homeless. Under s 65(2) and (3) duties are imposed on a local housing authority to secure that accommodation becomes available for the applicant's occupation.   *c*

Section 69 of the 1985 Act contains provisions supplementary to s 65 (and to other sections in Pt III). So far as is material, s 69(1) (as substituted by s 14(3) of the Housing and Planning Act 1986) is in these terms:

> 'A local housing authority may perform any duty under section 65 ... *d*
> (duties to persons found to be homeless) to secure that accommodation becomes available for the occupation of a person—(a) by making available suitable accommodation held by them under Part II (provision of housing) or any enactment, or (b) by securing that he obtains suitable accommodation from some other person, or (c) by giving him such advice and assistance as will secure that he obtains suitable accommodation from some other person, *e*
> and in determining whether accommodation is suitable they shall have regard to Part IX (slum clearance), X (overcrowding) and XI (houses in multiple occupation) of this Act.'

In 1988 Waltham Forest London Borough Council, which was a local housing authority, became concerned that owing to the stringent financial controls *f* imposed by central government they would not be able adequately to perform their duties under Pt III of the 1985 Act. Furthermore, they were reluctant to make use of bed and breakfast accommodation because such accommodation was usually very expensive and often provided unsatisfactory facilities. In these circumstances the director of housing considered what steps could be taken to *g* improve the stock of accommodation available. The director therefore invited the National Leasing and Finance Co (NLF) and a firm of solicitors to advise and to prepare a report.

In due course a report was prepared which set out the structure of a proposed scheme for the provision of additional housing. In para 3 of the report the *h* principal ingredients of the scheme were stated as follows:

> '(a) An appropriate Housing Association or a specially created Company would acquire or develop suitable property (within a price band determined by the Council). (b) The property would be leased to [the council] for a period of three years (less one day). The lease payments would be set at the *j* level determined by the Council ... (c) At the end of the three year period the properties would be sold and the sale proceeds used to discharge the debt raised.'

On 5 July 1988 a report based on the NLF report was submitted to the council's housing committee. The report was entitled 'Provision of Housing for the

Homeless—Leasing'. I should refer to passages in this report. I can turn at once
a to para 2:

'Shortfall in Housing Provision.

2.1 The report on Housing for Homeless submitted to the last Housing
Committee identified a potential shortfall of 200 properties for homeless
families over the next 12 months. The effects of the [Local Government
b (Prescribed Expenditure) (Amendment) Regulations 1988, SI 1988/434]
announced (and coming into effect) on 9 and 10 March this year effectively
prevented leasing of properties for longer than 3 years and the leasing of any
property for any period where the Council had had a prior interest in the land
or involvement through development.

c 2.2 These new regulations have had a major impact on the Council's
strategy to provide new housing for the homeless. At best there will be a
delay in new developments whilst alternative funding is identified, at worst
it may prove impossible to develop some of the sites for long term rented
housing ...

d 2.4 It is essential, given the projected shortfall for housing for the
homeless and the likely increased demand for leasing within Waltham
Forest, that this Council takes all steps necessary to secure accommodation
to prevent the use of bed and breakfast. To date provision has been made for
100 properties to be leased from the private sector, of which 27 have so far
been leased and 20 are in the pipeline. Given the market conditions that are
e likely to prevail, it is unlikely that the Council will be able to lease more than
an extra 100 properties over the next 12 months and authority is sought to
increase provision of leased accommodation to maximise this potential.'

The report drew attention to the fact that house prices in Waltham Forest had
f risen by 28% in the previous 12 months. It was suggested that this increase in
prices provided a potential profit for anyone who purchased a house and then
leased it to the council at a price which covered the cost of borrowing. The report
then referred to a possible way in which this potential capital gain might be
harnessed for the benefit of the public sector rather than private speculators. The
report continued in para 4.4:

g '... A proposal has been put forward by [NLF] ... which by establishing a
company which was 50% owned by [NLF] and 50% owned by the Council
would enable the capital gain to be channelled through a charitable trust for
the provision of additional rented housing.'

h In para 5 of the report details of the proposal were set out:

'5.1 A deadlock company (one where neither party has a majority), will be
established with the principal objectives of purchasing housing properties,
leasing them to the Council for the 3 year period then re-selling once the
j lease has expired.
5.2 [NLF] have indicated that a borrowing facility would be available for
such a venture with a drawdown to match an appropriate purchase profile.
In order to gain the best interest rates it is suggested that the borrowing be
guaranteed by the Council. The number of properties to be purchased over
the next 12 months would be about 100 to match the homelessness need and
the likely availability as indicated above ...

5.4 The Council would lease properties in exactly the same way that it is currently leasing from the private sector at the moment. This would mean *a* that the Council would be determining property types and standards required. The company would be authorised to purchase properties as directed by the council and this is likely to take the form of monthly or quarterly instructions.

5.5 The purchase of each property would need the authorisation of both *b* share-holders so that effectively the Council, through the deadlock arrangement would be able to control property purchases. In the same way, the Council would have control over subsequent sales and the current price achieved in that sale.

5.6 The company would pass all capital gains achieved from the sale of *c* property to a charitable trust which would be established to provide rented housing for those in need in the borough.

5.7 As with properties currently being leased from the private sector, all properties would be managed and maintained by the Council.

5.8 The Council's directors to the company would be appointed by the *d* Chief Executive.'

In para 6 of the report the financial implications of the proposal were set out. Reference was made to the fact that the new regulations, which were effective from 10 March 1988 (Local Government (Prescribed Expenditure) (Amendment) Regulations 1988, SI 1988/434), required that the full value of properties leased *e* for more than three years counted against the council's prescribed expenditure. In para 6.3 it was suggested that the council should provide a guarantee for the £10m loan facility which the company required for the purchase of the properties. At that stage it was envisaged that about 100 properties would be bought at an average cost of about £100,000 each. Attention was drawn to the fact that if *f* payments had to be made under the guarantee, they would count as prescribed expenditure under the new provisions to be introduced in pending legislation. This was a reference to an addition to the categories of prescribed expenditure in Sch 12 to the Local Government, Planning and Land Act 1980, which was subsequently introduced by the Local Government Finance Act 1988.

Having considered the proposals set out in the report, the housing committee *g* recommended that the scheme should go forward and that the council should take a 50% interest in a private leasing company to be established as described in the report. The recommendation was later approved and adopted by the council at their meeting on 28 July 1988.

In the meantime the matter had also been considered and approved by the *h* council's resources strategy committee. In addition, a favourable opinion had been obtained from a distinguished leading counsel. It will be seen that the potential benefits to the council included the following. (1) Provided the leases from the company did not exceed three years, the restrictions on expenditure imposed by the new regulations which came into force on 10 March 1988 would *j* be avoided. In fact, when the scheme was put into effect the term of the leases was three years less one day. (2) The cost of the acquisition of the houses would be borne by the new company. (3) As the houses would not be acquired by the council, the restrictions on disposal contained in s 32 of the 1985 Act would not apply. (4) Provided all went well and the value of real property continued to rise, the council would not have to meet any obligations under the guarantee. Indeed

it was hoped that capital gains would accrue to the charitable trust which in due
a course could be applied for the provision of further housing.

The company used for the purpose of the scheme was Briarhurst Ltd. A
general meeting of the company took place on 5 October 1988. The name of the
company was then changed to North East London Property Co Ltd (NELP). At
the same time four directors of the company were appointed, including two
b directors nominated by the council. It was agreed that NLF would provide
secretarial services for the first year and that NLF would be paid a fee for this
function and the accounting function.

NELP had an authorised share capital of £100. The share capital was split into
50 class A ordinary shares, which were issued to the council, and 50 class B
ordinary shares, which were issued to NLF Investments Ltd.
c At the meeting on 5 October certain amendments were made to the objects
clause in the memorandum of association. It is not necessary to refer to the
whole of the objects clause. It is sufficient to notice that the objects in the clause
included:

d '(A) 1. To carry on business as property managers undertaking the
management of property, real or personal, or of any interest therein as
owners, trustees, agents, receivers or otherwise ... 2. To carry on business
as caterers, proprietors of hotels, motels, clubs, theatres, restaurants ...
(B) To carry on any other trade or business which can, in the opinion of
the Board of Directors, be advantageously carried on by the Company in
e connection with or as ancillary to any of the above businesses or the general
business of the Company, or further any of its objects.
(C) To purchase, take on lease or in exchange, hire or otherwise acquire
and hold for any estate or interest any lands, buildings, easements ...'

It is not necessary to make any detailed reference to the articles of association. It
f is to be noted, however, that there were provisions in articles 6.2 and 6.4 to
ensure that to be effective, any resolutions had to be passed by the unanimous
resolution of all the members entitled to attend and vote.

In the next few weeks a number of documents putting the scheme into
operation came into existence. On 28 October 1988 a loan agreement was made
between Crédit Suisse (the bank) as lenders and NELP. Under the loan
g agreement the bank agreed to make available a loan of up to £11m to be used for
the acquisition by NELP of properties to be leased to the council for a period not
exceeding three years for the purpose of providing accommodation for homeless
persons in the borough. It was provided that the loan should be repaid on 28
September 1993.

h By a guarantee in writing of the same date the council guaranteed the punctual
payment of all sums payable by NELP to the bank under the loan agreement and
undertook that if NELP failed to pay any sum on its due date they would
immediately on demand pay that sum to the bank.

By a further agreement between the council and NELP dated 28 October 1988
j the council granted to NELP the right for NELP to require the council to take a
lease of any property on the terms and in the manner set out in the agreement.
It was provided, however, that the value of the total number of properties to be
demised to the council should not exceed £11m or such higher figure as the
parties should agree.

Finally, by a further agreement dated 28 October 1988 between the council and
NELP, NELP agreed to apply any final surplus from the sale of the properties to

a registered charity to provide housing for people in necessitous circumstances in the borough. The council agreed that, if called upon to do so between certain specified dates, it would pay to NELP such sum as was certified to represent the shortfall between the amount required to repay the moneys due under the loan agreement and the sale proceeds of the properties leased to the council (after deduction of expenses). In addition, by cl 3(3), the council agreed to indemnify NELP 'from and against all losses arising out of the Scheme'.

The scheme was then put into operation. Unfortunately, however, in about 1990 the property market collapsed. NELP was unable to repay the loan. NELP is now in administrative receivership, receivers having been appointed on 13 December 1993.

In due course both the bank and NELP issued a writ against the council. The claim by the bank was under the guarantee. The claim by NELP was under cl 3(3) of the final agreement dated 28 October 1988 whereby the council agreed to indemnify NELP 'from and against all losses arising out of the Scheme'. On 28 July 1994 the bank and NELP issued a summons for judgment under RSC Ord 14, alternatively under Ord 14A.

The summons came on for hearing before Gatehouse J in chambers. As his decision was of interest to other local authorities and lenders, he delivered his judgment in open court on 2 November 1994.

The judge summarised the argument put forward on behalf of the council in these terms:

'The council's argument amounted to this: that Pt II of the [Housing Act 1985], as added to by ss 58 and 60 of the Housing Associations Act 1985 and s 24 of the Local Government Act 1988, comprised a corpus of law relating to the housing functions of a local authority; that where Parliament intended an authority to have power to enter into a guarantee it made express provision, and there was no room for the implication of any further, implied powers.'

The judge rejected this argument. He said that the case seemed to be a proper one for the application of s 111 of the Local Government Act 1972. He took the view that the facts were quite different from those considered by the House of Lords in *Hazell v Hammersmith and Fulham London BC* [1991] 1 All ER 545, [1992] 2 AC 1. He continued:

'Here, the giving of the guarantee to the bank was a sine qua non of the scheme designed to fulfil the council's duty under s 65, and in my judgment, was "calculated to facilitate, or was conducive to, or incidental to" the discharge of that function.'

He therefore held that s 111 gave the council implied power to guarantee the payments by NELP under the loan agreement and to indemnify NELP. He gave judgment in favour of the bank.

The judge granted leave to appeal.

In this court we have had the advantage of more detailed arguments than those which were addressed to Gatehouse J. In addition we have had the opportunity of considering the scope of s 111 of the 1972 Act in determining the appeal in the proceedings between the bank and Allerdale Borough Council (see *Crédit Suisse v Allerdale BC* [1996] 4 All ER 129).

By s 2(3) of the 1972 Act it was provided that the council should be a body corporate. Their only powers are those given by statute. It is clear that they had a no express statutory power either to guarantee the obligations of NELP under the loan agreement with the bank or to indemnify NELP against losses suffered as a result of the scheme. Though it is true that local authorities are entitled under s 58 of the Housing Associations Act 1985 to guarantee the payment of money borrowed by a housing association, this power is restricted, so that assistance can only be given to a registered housing association. NELP, however, b is neither a registered housing association nor indeed a housing association of any kind.

The bank and NELP rely, however, on s 111 of the 1972 Act. Section 111, so far as material, is in these terms:

c '(1) Without prejudice to any powers exercisable apart from this section but subject to the provisions of this Act and any other enactment passed before or after this Act, a local authority shall have power to do any thing (whether or not involving the expenditure, borrowing or lending of money or the acquisition or disposal of any property or rights) which is calculated to facilitate, or is conducive or incidental to, the discharge of any of their functions …

d (3) A local authority shall not by virtue of this section raise money, whether by means of rates, precepts or borrowing, or lend money except in accordance with the enactments relating to those matters respectively.'

The argument on behalf of the bank and NELP was developed on the following lines. (1) The council had a duty under s 65 of the 1985 Act to secure e that accommodation became available for occupation by homeless people. (2) Under s 69(1) of the 1985 Act (which I have already set out) the council had power to perform that duty by making available suitable accommodation held by it under Pt II of the Act. (3) Part II of the 1985 Act was concerned with the provision of housing accommodation. Section 9(1) in Pt II provided:

f 'A local housing authority may provide housing accommodation—(a) by erecting houses, or converting buildings into houses, on land acquired by them for the purposes of this Part, or (b) by acquiring houses.'

(4) The council duly acquired houses, in accordance with the powers conferred by s 9(1)(b) of the 1985 Act, by leasing them from NELP. (5) The scheme g whereby the council, in conjunction with NLF, established NELP as a means of purchasing and leasing the houses so that accommodation could be made available to homeless people was calculated to facilitate, or be conducive or incidental, to the discharge of the council's functions. (6) The provision of the guarantee to the bank and the grant of an indemnity to NELP also were h calculated to facilitate, or to be conducive or incidental, to the discharge of the council's functions. (7) The relevant functions were those contained in ss 65, 69 and 9 of the 1985 Act. (8) In these circumstances, the provision of the guarantee and the indemnity were within the council's powers under s 111 of the 1972 Act.

This is a powerful argument. Furthermore, one must take account of the fact j that the purpose of this scheme was to alleviate hardship and to make the best provision possible for the accommodation of homeless persons. With regret, however, I have come to the conclusion that the council had no power to give the guarantee or to grant the indemnity.

It was argued on behalf of the council that the housing legislation, which included the Housing Act 1985 and the Housing Associations Act 1985, provided a comprehensive code regulating the powers of local housing authorities in the provision of housing. The rights to acquire property including houses, the rights to dispose of property and the rights to provide financial assistance were set out *a* in the legislation. In addition, Parliament had made provision for the sources of finance which could be used to carry out these functions, and had placed a limit on the sums which could be so expended.

The scheme for the leasing of the additional houses had a number of features which included the following. (a) The houses were to be acquired not by the *b* council but by NELP. NELP was not the agent of the council. Though two of the four directors of the company were appointed by the council and resolutions had to be approved by *all* the directors, there was a possibility of a conflict of interest between the duties of the two council directors as directors and their duties as employees of the council. (b) Under the option agreement the council were obliged, subject to the cap, to lease properties offered to them by NELP. *c* (c) The success of the scheme depended on continuing inflation in house prices. The council would no doubt have been able to cope with an isolated loss resulting from the unsuccessful sale of an individual property, but the potential exposure of the council was very large.

In my judgment in *Crédit Suisse v Allerdale BC* [1996] 4 All ER 129 at 148, I *d* pointed out that it is necessary, when considering the implied powers of a local authority under s 111 of the 1972 Act, to identify the relevant statutory functions. It is also necessary to examine the context in which the implied powers are to be exercised.

Section 101 of the 1972 Act contains provisions relating to what arrangements can be made for the discharge of functions by local authorities. These powers are *e* very limited. They do not entitle a local housing authority to discharge any of their functions by means of a partly-owned company. Can this power, or the power to give such a company assistance in the form of a guarantee or an indemnity, be implied by reason of s 111?

I am afraid that I have come to the conclusion, as I did in the *Allerdale* case, that *f* where Parliament has made detailed provisions as to how certain statutory functions are to be carried out, there is no scope for implying the existence of additional powers which lie wholly outside the statutory code. Section 111(3) makes it clear that the power to enter into financial obligations is subject to any statutory controls which may be imposed.

The scheme had no doubt a very laudable object. It may be that later similar *g* schemes have or will become within the powers of local authorities. But we have to look at the position in October 1988.

In these circumstances I feel bound to allow the appeal.

PETER GIBSON LJ. As in *Crédit Suisse v Allerdale BC* [1996] 4 All ER 129, the *h* council in this case seeks to escape from liability under its contractual obligations to the bank by asserting the invalidity of its own conduct. Again, in this case it is not disputed by the bank that if the council lacked the power to enter into the guarantee and indemnity which it gave the bank, then the council cannot be held to its promises.

The judge said, no doubt correctly, that the council's guarantee was an *j* indispensable condition of the loan to North East London Property Co Ltd (NELP) and that, without it, the scheme would not have got off the ground. In accepting the bank's argument that the power conferred on the council by s 111 of the Local Government Act 1972 extended to the giving of the guarantee (as calculated to facilitate or as conducive or incidental to the discharge of the

a council's function under s 65 of the Housing Act 1985 to secure that accommodation was available for the homeless for whom it was responsible), the judge followed that part of the judgment in *Allerdale* in which Colman J had said:

b 'In my judgment, the guarantee by a local authority of the obligation of a company set up by the local authority to enable it to provide recreational facilities under s.19 is not necessarily impermissible any more than is the setting up of the company itself. Moreover, in as much as the giving of a guarantee involves incurring an obligation to the party guaranteed I see no reason why, if that is calculated to facilitate the provision by the local authority of recreational facilities, that should not fall within the ancillary powers given to the local authority by s. 111 of the [Local Government Act c 1972].' (See [1995] 1 Lloyd's Rep 315 at 328–329.)

For the reasons given in my judgment in *Allerdale* [1996] 4 All ER 129 at 160–162, I disagree with the views of Colman J on those points.

I cannot accept that the council had the power to set up the company, which was not its agent or nominee, to carry out any statutory function of the council. d The directors of the company who were appointed by the council owed duties to the company. Section 101 of the 1972 Act could not authorise the council to arrange for the company to discharge any of the council's functions. For the reasons given by Hobhouse LJ, the scheme involved an impermissible delegation of the function of providing housing accommodation under s 9 of the 1985 Act. Nor, in my judgment, were the actions of the council authorised under s 111 of e the 1972 Act. The only means by which the council could discharge its function under s 65 of the 1985 Act were set out in s 69 of that Act. The guarantee and indemnity cannot properly be characterised as calculated to facilitate, or as conducive or incidental to, the discharge of any function of the council, being too remote therefrom. Further, I agree with Neill LJ that, having regard to the f detailed statutory scheme governing the housing functions of a local authority and in particular the express provisions relating to raising money to provide housing and to giving financial assistance to others to acquire housing, there is no scope for treating s 111 as authorising a local authority to give a guarantee and indemnity such as were given in the present case. It is simply inconsistent with the statutory scheme that a local authority should have the power to set up a g company and give a guarantee of the company's liabilities and an indemnity. I too would allow this appeal.

HOBHOUSE LJ. In this case, like *Crédit Suisse v Allerdale BC* [1996] 4 All ER 129, the claims are made under documents bearing the seal of a local authority, h Waltham Forest London Borough Council. They are contractual claims. The first plaintiffs, Crédit Suisse, claim under a letter of guarantee probably dated 28 October 1988. The letter guaranteed the repayment to the bank by second plaintiff, North East London Property Co Ltd, of the sums up to £11m plus interest advanced to the company by the bank under a facility granted by the j bank to the company. The facility document is lengthy. Its purpose is said to be:

'This Agreement sets out the terms and conditions upon and subject to which the Bank agrees to make available to the Borrower a term loan of up to £11,000,000 to be used for the acquisition by the Borrower of properties to be leased to the Council for a period not exceeding three years [for] the purpose of providing accommodation to homeless persons in the Borough.'

The facility called for the provision of various 'security documents'. One was the guarantee already referred to. Others were a floating charge on the assets of the company and mortgages of the properties purchased. Also stipulated for were various contractual documents to be executed as between the company and the council. Thus, there was to be an option agreement (also executed on 28 October 1988) whereby the council, in consideration of the sum of £1m, granted to the company an option to require the council to take three-year leases (less one day) at a rack rent of any properties containing one or more units of accommodation in areas (or such larger area as might be agreed) which the council considered suitable for the provision of accommodation for homeless persons; the obligations of the council under this option were limited to an aggregated freehold value of property of £11m. The option was to remain enforceable for three years. The leases were also to be treated as security documents and certified copies were to be delivered to the agent of the bank. Clause 9 of the facility agreement included undertakings by the company fully to enforce its rights against the council under and in relation to the leases and comply with any directions of the bank in that connection.

The final security document was the 'Agreement as to Surpluses and Indemnity'. This is the document upon which the company (the second plaintiff), in the interests of the bank, also sues the council. It recites:

'1. (1) The council has certain statutory duties under Part II of the Housing Act 1985 to provide accommodation for homeless persons.

(2) With that object in mind the Council approached [the company] with an offer of financial support for a scheme proposed by [the company] to provide various properties in the Borough and in other locations considered suitable by the Council for rent using private finance ("the Scheme").

(3) Having duly considered the Scheme the Council has agreed to support it by (among other things) entering into the Guarantees hereinafter mentioned and further indemnifying [the company] against all losses arising out of the Scheme in accordance with the provisions of this Agreement...'

It is a detailed document. It refers, inter alia, to the facility being granted by the bank, the guarantee being given by the council and the option agreement and provides that the council will 'indemnify [the company] from and against all losses arising out of the Scheme referred to in recital 1(3) hereof'. It also includes an entitlement to require the council after the expiry of three years to pay to the company, by way of grant under any statutory power so enabling the council, such sum of money as the company certifies it believes will represent a shortfall arising on sale of the properties leased to the council under the terms of the option agreement. For its part, the company agrees to apply the rents to meeting its obligations to the bank and defraying its own costs; to sell each property on the expiry of the relevant lease and apply the net proceeds of sale towards the repayment of the loan; and, finally, to apply any surplus remaining upon the expiry of the agreement, so far as prudent to do so, to the charitable objective of providing housing for people in necessitous circumstances in the borough, after consultation with the council.

This scheme, like that in the *Allerdale* case, arose from the wish of the council to avoid the statutory restrictions upon its borrowing and spending powers. The salient features of the scheme are summarised in the minutes of the council's resources strategy committee for 18 July 1988:

a 'The noting that Housing Committee approved proposals for the Council to take a 50% interest in a new private company to be established in conjunction with an existing private sector finance and leasing company. The principal objective of the new company is to acquire housing properties on the open market, lease them to the Council for a period of three years, and then re-sell them once the lease has expired. All capital gains achieved

b from the sale of properties will be passed by the company to a charitable trust which will be established to provide rented housing for those in need in the borough. To meet the cost of the purchase of the properties and to cover the value of any deferred interest not covered by lease rentals, a borrowing facility will be available to the company with a drawdown matching an appropriate purchase profile. In order that the most competitive interest

c rates for this facility can be achieved in the financial markets, we have agreed that the company be given a Council guarantee for a borrowing facility up to £11M.'

d The decision of Gatehouse J in the present action was given on an application by the plaintiffs for summary judgment under RSC Ord 14 or 14A. He held that the giving of the guarantee to the bank and the indemnity to the company were within the statutory powers of the council under Pt III of the 1985 Act and s 111(1) of the 1972 Act.

In my judgment it is necessary at the outset to take a view about the same aspects of the scheme as those which I considered important in the *Allerdale* case.

e However, the present case is different from the *Allerdale* case in a number of respects. First, the relationship between the company and the local authority is different and the company was differently structured. Secondly, the statutory functions of the authority, being housing functions, were differently defined. There was a third point of distinction which was, indeed, the point which was put

f in the forefront of his argument by Mr Arden QC, who appeared for the council. This was that the housing functions and powers of local authorities were (and still are) contained in a scheme of provisions which effectively form an exhaustive code and which therefore, having regard to the words 'but subject to the provisions of this Act and any other enactment passed before or after this Act' in s 111(1), mean that there was no scope for the lawful exercise of any further

g incidental powers in relation to housing matters.

The company was what is commonly called a deadlock company. The shareholding was split 50/50 between the council and a finance company, called the National Leasing and Finance Co, which apparently made a business of advising upon, setting up and running such schemes. Any decisions of a general

h meeting of the company or of the board had to be unanimous and the quorum for a meeting of the board was all four of its directors, being two directors nominated by the council and two nominated by the finance company. The objects of the company were those of a trading company primarily concerned with property, but without any restriction.

j The company was thus a separate entity from the council. The powers of the company were exercised through its board of directors, which included two councillors. But under s 101 of the 1972 Act, the activities of the company could not and did not amount to a discharge of the functions of the council. Further, the company was not an entity to which the council was entitled to delegate any of its functions or powers under s 101 nor did it come within the provisions of Pts I and II of the Housing Associations Act 1985 or s 73 of the Housing Act 1985.

Under s 65 of the Housing Act 1985 the council was under a duty to house the
homeless, and it is accepted that this was one of its functions. However, s 69(1)   *a*
provided (as amended by the Housing and Planning Act 1986):

'A local housing authority may perform any duty under section 65 or 68
(duties to persons found to be homeless) to secure that accommodation
becomes available for the occupation of a person—(a) by making available   *b*
suitable accommodation held by them under Pt II (provision of housing) or
any enactment, or (b) by securing that he obtains suitable accommodation
from some other person, or (c) by giving him such advice and assistance as
will secure that he obtains suitable accommodation from some other person
...'

c

Section 69, as a matter of language, defines three alternative ways in which a local
authority may perform its function under s 65. Section 69 is, as a matter of
language, exhaustive and there is no reason for giving the words used any
meaning other than their natural meaning. The plaintiffs accept that the relevant
alternative is that in sub-para (a). The council was discharging its function of   *d*
housing the homeless by letting out to them the properties which had been let to
the council for three years less one day by the company.

The council's renting of the properties from the company was the discharge of
another function of the council—the function of providing housing
accommodation 'by acquiring houses' under s 9(1)(b) of the 1985 Act.

Focusing on these functions—(1) the housing of the homeless by making   *e*
available suitable accommodation and (2) the acquisition of properties for the
purposes of providing housing accommodation—it is necessary to consider the
application of s 111 of the 1972 Act. Section 111 empowers the local authority to
do anything which is calculated to facilitate or is incidental to the discharge by the
authority of its functions. Here, the only thing which was incidental to the actual   *f*
letting out of housing to the homeless was the renting by the council of the
properties from the company. The critical function is therefore the second, the
acquisition of properties. It is submitted on behalf of the council that the scheme
involved an impermissible delegation of the council's powers in relation to the
acquisition of properties.

I consider that this submission is well founded. The council, properly so   *g*
understood and in accordance with s 101, did not have control as a council of the
activities of the company. Directors of companies are not permissible delegates
of a local authority. Once appointed they have the character of individuals with
the duties of directors of a company incorporated under the Companies Acts.
The effect of the scheme and the option which the council purported to grant to   *h*
the company was unlawfully to delegate to the company the discharge of the
council's function of acquiring properties for the purposes of providing housing
accommodation under s 9: the option transferred to the company the selection
and purchase of properties and the company was then entitled (and could be
compelled by the bank) to require the council to take leases of the properties. It   *j*
follows from this conclusion that any purported exercise of powers incidental to
such a purported discharge of function cannot be lawful or valid. The option was
a remarkable document. For a nominal consideration it transferred to the
company the complete control over the relevant additions to the council's
housing stock. It is no answer to say that it was a deadlock company and that two
of the directors were elected by the council.

a   But, in my judgment, there is a further difficulty in the way of the plaintiffs.
The primary exercise of any power that existed under s 111 was in setting up, and
taking a shareholding in, the company. This was, on the plaintiffs' case, an
exercise of the incidental power. The further transactions upon which the
plaintiffs have to rely in this action were remote from the exercise of any function
by the council and not incidental to it. The grant of the guarantee and the
b   indemnity were to facilitate the borrowing by the company at advantageous
rates. That is how it is put in the minute of the resources strategy committee
from which I have quoted. The giving of the indemnity to the company had a
similar character. Both documents were essentially aspects of an exercise in
property speculation. It was hoped that this scheme would be profitable and that
the capital values of the properties purchased by the company would increase.
c   The documents executed by the council would only become relevant if property
values fell and the venture became loss-making, not profitable. These
transactions were remote from the actual function of housing the homeless or the
acquisition of housing for the purpose of providing accommodation. They
related to an exercise in property speculation on borrowed money and the needs
d   of a trading company, not to the needs of the council and the discharge of its
functions. (The parallel with what was said by Lord Templeman in *Hazell v
Hammersmith and Fulham London BC* [1991] 1 All ER 545 at 556, 558, [1992] 2 AC 1
at 31, 34 is striking.)

    Accordingly, without needing to examine the more elaborate argument of Mr
Arden based upon a review of the corpus of the statutory provisions regarding
e   local authority housing, I consider that the claims of both plaintiffs must fail. The
purported transactions were not transactions which the council had the capacity
to enter into. It follows that they were not contracts and gave rise to no legal
obligations enforceable against the council.

    The council's appeal must be allowed against both plaintiffs.
f

Appeal allowed.

                                            Paul Magrath Esq   Barrister.

Logan v R

a

PRIVY COUNCIL

LORD KEITH OF KINKEL, LORD BROWNE-WILKINSON, LORD MUSTILL, LORD STEYN AND
SIR BRIAN HUTTON

22, 23, 24 JANUARY, 21 FEBRUARY 1996

b

*Privy Council – Leave to appeal – Special leave – Jurisdiction – Belize – Whether Privy
Council having jurisdiction to hear petition for special leave after expiry of time limits
laid down in proclamation providing for postponement of death sentence pending
appeal – Whether Privy Council having jurisdiction to hear petition for special leave*   c
*after petition for mercy has been refused – Judicial Committee (General Appellate
Jurisdiction) Rules Order 1982, r 5.*

*Belize – Criminal law – Murder – Provocation – Whether words alone can amount to
provocation under law of Belize – Belize Criminal Code, ss 116–119.*

d

The appellant was charged in Belize with the murder of his ex-girlfriend. It was
alleged that he met the victim and stabbed her with a knife. At his trial the Crown
relied on a statement made by the appellant in which he admitted to the police
that he had intentionally and unlawfully killed the victim. The appellant relied
on the defence of provocation and claimed in an unsworn statement that the   e
victim had goaded him to such extent that he had lost his self-control. The judge
left the issue of provocation to the jury after stating that provocation referred to
all the things said and done and did not specifically refer to provocation by words
alone. Under s 116[a] of the Belize Criminal Code extreme provocation was a
defence which reduced murder to manslaughter. Section 117[b] defined four
specific forms of physical provocation, s 118[c] provided that provocation 'whether   f
by things done or by things said or by both together' was to be left to the jury to
determine whether the provocation was extreme enough to make a reasonable
man do as the defendant did, while s 119[d] provided that provocation would not
reduce murder to manslaughter if the defendant had not lost his self-control as
the result of the provocation, or if there was a prior or independent intent to kill,   g
or if the defendant had sufficient time to recover his self-control before killing the
victim, or if his retaliation was disproportionate to the provocation received. The
appellant was convicted of murder and sentenced to death. His appeal to the
Court of Appeal of Belize was dismissed. He then petitioned the Governor to
exercise the prerogative of mercy but the Governor dismissed that petition on the   h
advice of the Belize Advisory Council. The appellant then applied to the Privy
Council for special leave to appeal even though he had not complied with the
time limits laid down in a proclamation made in 1978 by the Governor for
applying to the Privy Council for special leave. The 1978 proclamation, which
was issued before Belize became independent in 1981, stated that the execution
of a person sentenced to death was to be postponed if an application for special   j
leave was notified to the authorities within 10 days of the refusal of a pardon or

---

a   Section 116, so far as material, is set out at p 200 c, post
b   Section 117 is set out at p 200 d to f, post
c   Section 118 is set out at p 200 g h, post
d   Section 119, so far as material, is set out at p 200 j to p 201 a, post

a 14 days of the dismissal of an appeal by the Court of Appeal and if the application
was lodged with the Privy Council within 21 days. On the hearing of the petition
for special leave before the Privy Council the questions arose (i) whether the
Privy Council had jurisdiction to hear the petition after the expiry of the time
limits laid down in the 1978 proclamation or after a petition for mercy had been
refused, and (ii) whether the judge had misdirected the jury on provocation.

b
Held – (1) At the time the 1978 proclamation was issued the procedure and time
limits for making applications for special leave to the Privy Council from Belize
were regulated by the Judicial Committee Acts 1833 and 1844 enacted by the
United Kingdom Parliament and under the royal prerogative. The only temporal
requirement for lodging a petition for special leave to appeal was that contained
c in r 5^e of the Judicial Committee (General Appellate Jurisdiction) Rules Order
1982 (made under the 1833 and 1844 Acts), which simply required that the
petition be lodged with the least possible delay after the date of the judgment
from which special leave to appeal was sought. Since the proclamation could not
have any greater legal effect than when it was first made in 1978 and since, at that
d date, the procedure and the time limits for making applications for special leave
were regulated by the 1833 and 1844 Acts, the Governor had no power to curtail
any right of the citizens of Belize to petition for special leave or in any other way
to affect the jurisdiction of the Privy Council and nor did the proclamation
purport to do so. The proclamation merely provided for the postponement of
the death sentence provided that the petitioner complied with the specified
e timetable and did not provide time limits within which the right to petition the
Privy Council was to be exercised (see p 198 *a* to *f*, post).
       (2) The refusal of a petition for mercy did not prevent a convicted person
appealing to the Privy Council, since there was no inconsistency between a
refusal to grant a pardon and a subsequent appeal. The function of the Advisory
Council was to decide whether the prerogative of mercy should be exercised in
f relation to a person lawfully convicted, whereas the function of the Privy Council
was to rule on the legality of the conviction and if it did so after the refusal of a
petition for mercy it was not thereby arrogating to itself the power of final
prerogative of mercy. If, for good reason, no appeal against conviction had been
brought before the refusal to exercise the prerogative of mercy and it was shown
g that there might have been a wrongful conviction, the Privy Council, as the
ultimate legal court of appeal under the Constitution of Belize, had power to set
such conviction aside on legal grounds, whether or not the prerogative of mercy
had been or would be exercised. It followed that the grant of special leave to
appeal was within the jurisdiction of the Privy Council (see p 199 *a* to *g*, post).
h   (3) On the substantive issue relating to provocation, the category of
provocation 'by things done or by things said or by both together' referred to in
s 118 was to be read as supplemental to the four categories of provocation by acts
referred to in s 117, and since s 118 clearly referred to provocation by things said
it followed that words alone could amount to provocation under the law of
j Belize. Furthermore, the situations referred to in s 119 in which provocation
could not reduce murder to manslaughter were not rules of law entitling the trial
judge to withdraw the issue of provocation from the jury, but merely
circumstances relevant to the merits of the defence of provocation which were to
be left to the jury to consider in determining whether there was evidence that the

e   Rule 5 is set out at p 198 *c*, post

defendant had lost his self-control as a result of provocation. On the facts, the failure of the judge to provide a clear and correct direction to the jury that words *a* alone could amount to provocation was a material misdirection. The appeal would therefore be allowed, the conviction of murder and sentence of death quashed and a verdict of manslaughter substituted (see p 201 *f j* to p 202 *a d*, p 203 *e* to *g* and p 204 *b c h*, post).

b

Notes

For provocation as a defence to murder, see 11 *Halsbury's Laws* (4th edn reissue) 438.

For the Judicial Committee (General Appellate Jurisdiction) Rules Order 1982, SI 1982/1676, r 5, see 5 *Halsbury's Statutory Instruments* (1994 reissue) 404. *c*

Cases referred to in opinion

DPP v Camplin [1978] 2 All ER 168, [1978] AC 705, [1978] 2 WLR 679, HL.

DPP v Walker [1974] 1 WLR 1090, PC.

d

Lauriano v A-G of Belize (17 October 1995, unreported), Bel CA; *affg* (20 September 1995, unreported), Bel SC.

Mancini v DPP [1941] 3 All ER 272, [1942] AC 1, HL.

Parker v R [1964] 2 All ER 641, [1964] AC 1369, [1964] 3 WLR 70, PC.

R v Duffy [1949] 1 All ER 932, CCA.

e

Vasquez v R, O'Neill v R [1994] 3 All ER 674, [1994] 1 WLR 1304, PC.

Appeal

Linsberth Logan appealed with special leave granted by the Judicial Committee *f* from the decision of the Court of Appeal of Belize delivered on 7 September 1993 dismissing his appeal against his conviction in the Supreme Court of Belize on 10 February 1993 for murder for which he was sentenced to death. A preliminary point of law arose on the hearing of the appeal, namely whether the Judicial Committee had jurisdiction to hear the petition for special leave after the expiry of the time limits laid down in the proclamation of the Governor of Belize *g* contained in Statutory Instrument No 62 of 1978 or after a plea for mercy had been rejected by the Belize Advisory Committee. The Attorney General of Belize and counsel for Alfred Codrington, Nicholas Antonio Guevara, and Ellis Taibo, all of whom had appealed separately to the Privy Council, were heard on the preliminary point of law. The facts are set out in the judgment of the Board. *h*

James Dingemans (instructed by *Edwin Coe*) for the Attorney General on the jurisdiction issue and as amicus curiae on the appeal.

James Guthrie QC and *Simeon Sampson SC* (of the Belize Bar) (instructed by *Ingledew Brown Bennison & Garrett*) for Guevara on the jurisdiction issue. *j*

Edward Fitzgerald QC, Simeon Sampson SC (of the Belize Bar) and *Paul Taylor* (instructed by *Ingledew Brown Bennison & Garrett*) for the appellant and for Codrington on the jurisdiction issue.

Michael Grieve, Anthony Metzer and *Julian Knowles* (instructed by *Simons Muirhead & Burton*) for Taibo on the jurisdiction issue.

a   The Board took time for consideration.

21 February 1996. The following judgment of the Board was delivered.

LORD STEYN. This is an appeal by Linsberth Logan from the judgment of the Court of Appeal of Belize given on 7 September 1993, which dismissed his appeal
b   against his conviction for murder in the Supreme Court of Belize on 10 February 1993. Important questions of law arose. The first was whether the Privy Council had been deprived of jurisdiction, as the Chief Justice of Belize has held in an unrelated recent case, by virtue of the effluxion of time limits on the prosecution of criminal appeals imposed in Belize or by reason of the dismissal of the appellant's plea for mercy. After hearing submissions on behalf of the
c   prosecution and the defence the Board ruled that it had jurisdiction to entertain this appeal. This judgment gives the reasons for that decision.

Jurisdiction having been established, their Lordships heard submissions on the merits of the appeal. The appellant accepted at the trial that he intentionally and unlawfully killed Linda Vasquez. He relied on the defence of provocation. By
d   their unanimous verdict the jury rejected that defence. The appellant appealed as of right to the Court of Appeal. The Court of Appeal dismissed the appeal. On the appeal to the Privy Council the principal argument for the appellant was that the trial judge misconstrued relevant sections of the Criminal Code of Belize and accordingly misdirected the jury on the law of provocation. In particular this argument raised issues regarding the interaction of ss 116 to 119 of the Criminal
e   Code. Those issues are of great importance for the criminal justice system in Belize and will have to be considered in some detail. In the light of the resolution of those issues it will then be necessary to consider the directions of the trial judge.

It will be convenient now to provide a narrative relevant to the issues which
f   arise on this appeal both in regard to the jurisdiction of the Privy Council and the merits of the appeal.

THE NARRATIVE

The trial: February 1993
The trial took place in February 1993. The appellant had previously lived
g   together with Linda Vasquez. She was then aged 17 years. By July 1992 they had separated but they still continued to see one another. On 2 July 1992 the appellant and Linda Vasquez met in Belize City. At the end of that meeting the appellant produced a knife and cut the throat of Linda Vasquez. She died almost immediately.

h   At the trial the only issue was provocation. The focus was therefore on why the appellant acted as he did. The prosecution put their case on the basis that it was a premeditated and unprovoked killing. The prosecution case can be summarised quite briefly. The mother of the deceased testified that the appellant had, in the past, beaten her daughter and threatened to kill her if she left him.
j   Wilfred Martinez gave evidence about the earlier part of the meeting between the appellant and the deceased on 2 July 1992. He said that he saw the appellant come up to the deceased and walk back with her in the direction of the Chateau Caribbean Hotel. He said the deceased was not resisting. Ronald Fraser testified to a later part of the incident. He said that at 2 pm on 2 July 1992, and at the alley behind the Chateau Caribbean, he saw a man harassing a woman by trying to kiss her. He said that the man pushed the woman in the alley. He went to report the

matter. When he returned he found the woman lying in the alley with her throat
cut. Dennis and Linsford Reneau testified that they approached the alley and saw
the appellant bending over a woman. The appellant appeared to pick up a knife.
When the appellant saw the two witnesses he ran away.

It further emerged during the prosecution case that, after the killing, the
appellant went straight to the nearest police station. He handed in the knife and
admitted cutting the throat of the deceased. The police questioned him. He said:
'I mean to do it. I love the girl and she abstract me.' Their Lordships were
informed that 'abstract' is a colloquial expression which means goad. The
appellant made a statement under caution, which was produced as part of the
prosecution case. In that statement he said that she refused to take him back. He
said he threatened her with a knife. There was a struggle. She fell to the ground.
He said that he got on top of her and cut her throat. Their Lordships observe that
on the face of this statement read in isolation there was no evidence of
provocation for the jury to consider.

The prosecution relied on two other facts as controverting the defence of
provocation. First, a few hours before the killing the appellant had bought the
knife and had it sharpened. Secondly, there were several knife wounds including
a fatal one to the deceased's neck.

The defendant did not testify. Instead he made an unsworn statement. The
appellant said that in May 1992 he left the house where he lived with the
deceased. He continued to support the deceased and they continued a sexual
relationship. About three weeks before the killing he saw the deceased meeting
another man. She told him she was pregnant. He gave her money to go to a
doctor. On 2 July 1992 he bought a knife but without any intention of doing any
harm. He described their meeting on that day. He said they kissed. He then
pressed her for answers about the future of their relationship. He continued:

'At this moment she told me that she was not pregnant for me as to only
keep me from going to the United States where I normally go to buy my stuff
that I bring and sell. She also told me that she had another boyfriend and if
I want we could still have something on the side without her Mum knowing
of this. At this moment I lost total control of myself, I then take out the knife
and cut her.'

No other evidence was adduced by the defence.

After closing speeches on behalf of the prosecution and the defence the judge
summed up the case to the jury. The judge left the issue of provocation for the
jury to consider and directed the jury that the verdict had to be either murder or
manslaughter by reason of provocation. The jury retired to consider their verdict
for almost three hours. The jury then returned to render a unanimous verdict of
guilty of murder. The judge then passed the death sentence.

The proceedings in the Court of Appeal: September 1993

Their Lordships were informed that the appellant appealed as of right to the
Court of Appeal. The grounds of appeal were primarily directed at the trial
judge's directions on provocation. The Court of Appeal dismissed the appeal.
Their Lordships were informed that no reasons were given for the decision of the
Court of Appeal.

Subsequent events

a   On 17 January 1994 the prison authorities informed the appellant that his mercy petition had been dismissed by the Governor General. In early December 1994 the appellant was notified that he was due to be executed on 9 December 1994. On 6 December the appellant applied to the Privy Council for a conservatory order prohibiting his execution pending the lodging of a petition for
b   special leave to appeal. On the same day the Privy Council granted such a conservatory order. On 11 January 1995 the Privy Council granted special leave to appeal to the appellant.

The judgment of the Chief Justice in Lauriano's case

c   On 20 September 1995 the Chief Justice of Belize gave a judgment in *Lauriano v A-G of Belize* (unreported). The Chief Justice acknowledged that he was not addressing any issue between the parties. Nobody had applied for any order. The Chief Justice granted a two-fold declaration, viz: (a) that the Privy Council has no jurisdiction to grant special leave to appeal after the expiry of the periods of time stipulated in the proclamation of the Governor of Belize contained in Statutory
d   Instrument No 62 of 1978 (the proclamation); (b) that, in any event, the Privy Council had no jurisdiction after a plea for mercy by a man sentenced to death had been rejected by the Advisory Committee.

The Chief Justice said that if the Privy Council acted contrary to his declaration it would be seeking to 'arrogate' a power it did not have, and that it would amount to 'rule by decree by Her Majesty in Council'.
e   Subsequently, the Court of Appeal of Belize had to consider the merits of the appeal of *Lauriano* (17 October 1995, unreported). His appeal was dismissed. Given that the declaration of the Chief Justice, which related to the jurisdiction of the Privy Council, was not an issue on the appeal before it, the Court of Appeal did not examine its validity. At the same time the Court of Appeal made clear
f   that it was not endorsing the declaration of the Chief Justice.

It is the judgment, therefore, of the Chief Justice which was the basis of the argument that the Privy Council had no jurisdiction to entertain the appeal of the appellant.

g   JURISDICTION
    In making the two-fold declaration in *Lauriano*'s case the Chief Justice founded himself on the proclamation made by the Governor of Belize before Belize became fully independent in 1981. It was expressed to be made by the Governor 'in exercise of my authority to respite sentences of death' and was headed 'Rules for the prosecution by persons under sentence of death of petitions for special
h   leave to appeal to the Judicial Committee of the Privy Council'. So far as relevant the proclamation provided as follows:

'1.(1) If he intends to apply for Special Leave, the applicant should as soon as possible and in any case within the period prescribed in paragraph (2) of
j   this Rule notify his intention to the Governor through his legal representative or if personally, through the officer in charge of the prison where he is confined.

(2) The period prescribed for notification under paragraph (1) of this Rule is ten clear days after notification that the Governor has not granted a pardon or respite, or, in the event of an appeal to the Court of Appeal, fourteen days after the dismissal of the appeal, if the latter should be longer.

2. On receipt of a notification under Rule 1, the applicant will be informed
that the execution will be postponed for twenty-one days, during which   a
period the applicant must furnish the Governor with proof that the necessary
instructions, papers and funds have been sent to a solicitor practising in
London, the instructions and funds by air mail and the papers by registered
ordinary mail; and also where the application is to be made in *forma pauperis*
that the procedure relating to such applications as set out in Rule 3(c) has   b
been complied with.'

Rules 3 to 7 contain certain administrative particulars not directly relevant to this
case. The rules then proceeded:

'8. If the proof required by the provisions of Rule 2 is not furnished to the
Governor before the expiration of the period of twenty-one days referred to   c
in that Rule, the execution will not be further postponed unless the
Governor considers that there are special reasons that would justify
exceptionally an extension of the date for furnishing such proof. The
applicant or his advisers will be informed by the Governor of the new date
by which the required proof must be furnished.   d
9. If the proof required by the provisions of Rule 2 is furnished within the
period of twenty-one days referred to in that Rule or on or before such date
as the Governor may have fixed under the provisions of Rule 8, execution
will be postponed ...
11. If the Governor is informed by the Foreign and Commonwealth   e
Office—(a) that the application for special leave has not been lodged by the
date fixed; (b) that the application has been dismissed by the Judicial
Committee; (c) that the appeal has been dismissed by the Judicial
Committee; the execution will not be further postponed, subject, however,
to the power of the Governor to exercise the Prerogative of Mercy.'

In effect, therefore, the proclamation provided for a stay of execution of the   f
death penalty pending an application to the Judicial Committee for special leave
to appeal provided that a strict timetable was adhered to by the applicant in
prosecuting his application for leave.

In reaching his conclusion, the Chief Justice first referred to s 104 of the Belize
Constitution, which, after providing in sub-ss (1) and (2) for appeals to the Privy   g
Council as of right and with leave of the Court of Appeal, by sub-s (3) provides
that an appeal shall lie to Her Majesty in Council with the special leave of Her
Majesty from any decision of the Court of Appeal in any civil, criminal or other
matter. Then, after referring to the proclamation, he stated that it regulates 'the
time within which application may be made for special leave' and that, despite   h
the coming into force of the Constitution, the proclamation was preserved in
force by s 28(3) of the Interpretation Act, which provides:

'Where any Act authorising the making of any statutory instrument
repeals a previous Act under which any statutory instrument was lawfully
made and was in force at the commencement of the repealing Act, the   j
statutory instrument made under the repealed Act shall ... remain in
operation so far as it is not inconsistent with the provisions of the repealing
Act or of any statutory instrument made thereunder.'

He therefore held that, after the coming into force of the Constitution in 1981,
the provisions in the proclamation laying down time limits for applications for

a special leave to appeal from decisions of the Court of Appeal were still in force. However, he held that the provisions providing for application for special leave after the refusal of a respite or pardon by the Belize Advisory Council were inconsistent with the Constitution and had to be severed. He therefore held that any right of appeal to the Privy Council after the Advisory Council had reached a decision whether or not to grant mercy was impossible and 'would make *b* mockery' of the Advisory Council's decision. He said:

'I say this on the basis that it is a fundamental principle of law in an Independence Constitution like that of Belize that the prerogative of mercy is at the end of judicial process only where there is certainty as to time and opportunity for the exhaustion of such redress so that the Belize Advisory *c* Council can act after all legal process has been exhausted.'

The Chief Justice accordingly held that the time limits in the proclamation continued to apply to applications for special leave to appeal from the Court of Appeal but that there could be no application to the Privy Council for special leave after the Advisory Council have decided whether or not to exercise the *d* prerogative of mercy. He concluded:

'Based upon my findings and observations I declare that the Belize government is, therefore, not bound to abide by the terms of any special leave granted out of conformity with this declaration. This case, and any other similar case, were therefore unlawfully before Her Majesty in Council *e* having been all there after the Belize Advisory Council had acted and the grounds were never as to any unconstitutional proceedings of the Belize Advisory Council. The petitions were [in] relation to the Court of Appeal's decision. The Belize Advisory Council had already subsequently met in committee, after a reasonable time had elapsed, before any of the applications had been made to Her Majesty in Council. To hold otherwise *f* would be sanctioning the ouster of our constitutional provisions and the rule of law that goes with them and supporting what amounts to no more than rule by decree by Her Majesty in Council.'

There is one factor that must be mentioned before turning to the substance of the Chief Justice's reasoning. As was common ground before their Lordships, the *g* Chief Justice was in error in relying on s 28(3) of the Interpretation Act to preserve the proclamation in force. In the Interpretation Act, the word 'Act' is defined as 'an Act of Parliament' (see s 3(1)). Therefore the Interpretation Act has no impact on proclamations made under the prerogative such as No 62 of 1978. This factor, however, does not affect the reasoning of the Chief Justice since it *h* was also common ground that s 134 of the Belize Constitution does operate so as to perpetuate the legal effect, whatever it may be, of the proclamation. In that section 'existing law' is defined by sub-s (6) as including, inter alia, any 'rule, regulation, order or other instrument having effect as part of the law', a definition which must include the proclamation. Section 134 provides that, notwith- *j* standing the revocation of the Letters Patent and the Constitution Ordinance, the 'existing laws' are to continue in force and effect as if they had been made in pursuance of this Constitution 'but they shall be construed with such modifications, adaptations, qualifications and exceptions as may be necessary to bring them into conformity with this Constitution'. Therefore the proclamation remains in force, but must be so construed as to make it conform with the Constitution.

Turning then to the substance of the Chief Justice's reasons, there is no
provision which can give the proclamation any greater legal effect than it had   a
when it was first made in 1978, ie before independence. The first question,
therefore, is what was the original effect of the proclamation. In 1978 appeals to
the Privy Council were regulated by two Acts of the United Kingdom Parliament,
the Judicial Committee Act 1833 and the Judicial Committee Act 1844, and under
the royal prerogative. Section 3 of the 1833 Act established the Judicial   b
Committee to hear appeals and s 24 provided for the making of rules by the Privy
Council 'regulating the mode, form and time of appeal' (see also s 1 of the 1844
Act). At all material times the only rule made under the statutory power which
regulated the time for lodging a petition for special leave to appeal is that now
contained in r 5 of the Judicial Committee (General Appellate Jurisdiction) Rules
Order 1982, SI 1982/1676:   c

'A petition for special leave to appeal shall be lodged with the least possible
delay after the date of the judgment from which special leave to appeal is
sought.'

Since the procedure and the time limits for making applications for special   d
leave were regulated by those Acts, in 1978 the Governor of Belize, acting under
his Letters Patent, had no power to curtail any right of the citizens of Belize to
petition for special leave or in any other way to affect the jurisdiction of the
Judicial Committee. Nor indeed did the proclamation purport to do so.

The document sets out the way in which the Governor will exercise the   e
prerogative to grant 'a respite ... from the execution of any punishment' which
was conferred on him by art 26(1)(b) of the Letters Patent of 1964. The
proclamation does not provide time limits within which the right to petition the
Privy Council is to be exercised: all it does is to provide that, so long as the
petitioner complies with the timetable stated in the proclamation, the Governor
will not cause the death sentence to be carried out.   f

Accordingly, the proclamation as it operated before the introduction of the
Constitution of 1981 did not, and could not, limit the jurisdiction of the Judicial
Committee in relation to the grant of special leave to appeal. There is nothing in
the Constitution which can operate to give the proclamation any greater effect
after independence. Section 104(3) of the Constitution, by expressly conferring a g
right of appeal to the Judicial Committee with special leave, introduces into the
law of Belize the existing procedures and rules of the Judicial Committee. It
follows that the proclamation can have no effect on the jurisdiction of the Judicial
Committee to grant special leave to appeal where such right is conferred by the
Constitution of any country.

Turning then to the right of appeal to the Privy Council at any time after the   h
Advisory Council of Belize has determined whether or not to grant mercy, the
Chief Justice did not base himself on the proclamation: on the contrary in his view
he had to strike out of the proclamation those parts which expressly provided for
an appeal after the Advisory Committee had come to its decision. On
applications for special leave after such decision the reasoning of the Chief Justice j
is based on the proposition that, in an independent state, the decision as to the
exercise of the prerogative of mercy is necessarily the last stage in the process and
a subsequent appeal is therefore constitutionally irregular. The Chief Justice
gives no examples of jurisdictions where his proposition holds sway nor were
their Lordships referred by counsel for the Attorney General to any such

a jurisdiction. Although their Lordships were not referred to any specific case, it appears that in the United States of America such appeals are often brought.

There is no inconsistency between a refusal to grant a pardon and a subsequent appeal. All appellate courts are familiar with cases where the circumstances of the crime are so heinous that no authority would be inclined to exercise the prerogative of mercy. But if the trial leading to the conviction is legally
b unsatisfactory, the conviction cannot stand, however great the suspicion of guilt of the crime. It is for the court to rule on the legality of the conviction, and for the Advisory Council to decide whether to exercise the prerogative of mercy in relation to a person lawfully convicted. There are two separate functions. If, for good reason, no appeal against conviction has been brought before the refusal to
c exercise the prerogative of mercy and it is shown that there may have been a wrongful conviction, it must be possible to set such conviction aside on legal grounds, whether or not the prerogative of mercy has been or will be exercised.

This confusion between the respective roles of the Advisory Council and of the Judicial Committee seems to lie at the root of the Chief Justice's decision. He
d speaks of the Privy Council arrogating to itself the power of final prerogative of mercy and, in the final paragraph quoted above, of the 'ouster of our Constitutional provisions and the rule of law that goes with them and supporting what amounts to no more than rule by decree by Her Majesty in Council'. The Judicial Committee has no function in relation to the prerogative of mercy. What it does have under the Constitution of Belize is the function of being the ultimate
e legal court of appeal. That function can be abolished or modified by the people of Belize by amending the Constitution. But so long as the Constitution remains unamended, no law of Belize (whether pre-dating or post-dating the Constitution) can validly curtail the constitutional right of the citizens of Belize to apply to the Judicial Committee, in compliance with the rules made under the
f 1833 and 1844 Acts, for special leave to appeal or the right of the Judicial Committee to grant such an application in a proper case.

For these reasons their Lordships conclude that the Chief Justice was in error in making the declaration in his judgment in the *Lauriano* case and that the special leave to appeal granted in this and other cases was within the jurisdiction of the
g Judicial Committee.

THE MERITS

A case for the jury to consider

h There was a strong prosecution case, notably because the appellant bought the knife a few hours before he used it in cutting the deceased's throat. On the other hand, a combination of the appellant's statement at the police station that the deceased had goaded him, being part of a 'mixed' statement, and his explanation in his unsworn statement at the trial, amounted to evidence of provocation fit for the jury to consider. An unsworn statement, untested by cross-examination, is in
j principle evidence markedly inferior in quality to sworn evidence. And a trial judge is entitled to explain this fact to the jury in accordance with the guidance given by the Board in *DPP v Walker* [1974] 1 WLR 1090 at 1096. Nevertheless, it is for the jury to consider what weight they should attach to such an unsworn statement. In these circumstances the judge rightly left the issue of provocation for the jury to consider.

The law of provocation in Belize

It will be convenient first to consider the law of provocation in Belize before   *a*
examining the judge's directions to the jury on provocation. On 20 September
1981 Belize became independent. On 1 October 1981 a new Criminal Code came
into effect. It is necessary to refer in extenso to the provisions of the Criminal
Code so far as it is relevant to provocation. Section 114 provides that every
person who intentionally and unlawfully causes the death of another is guilty of   *b*
murder unless his crime is reduced to manslaughter by reason of 'such extreme
provocation ... as in the next following sections mentioned'. Section 115 then
makes provision for a partial defence of diminished responsibility. Section 116
provides that intentional and unlawful homicide is reduced to manslaughter if it
is proved on the defendant's behalf that he was deprived of the power of
self-control 'by such extreme provocation given by the other person as is   *c*
mentioned in section 117'. The next three sections then provide as follows:

'**117.** *Provocation defined.* The following matters may amount to extreme
provocation to one person to cause the death of another person, namely—
(a) an unlawful assault or battery committed upon the accused person by the   *d*
other person, either in an unlawful fight or otherwise, which is of such a kind
either in respect of its violence or by reason of words, gestures or other
circumstances of insult or aggravation, as to be likely to deprive a person,
being of ordinary character, and being in the circumstances in which the
accused person was, of the power of self-control; (b) the assumption by the
other person, at the commencement of an unlawful fight of an attitude   *e*
manifesting an intention of instantly attacking the accused person with
deadly or dangerous means or in a deadly manner; (c) an act of adultery
committed in the view of the accused person with or by his or her wife or
husband, or the crime of unnatural carnal knowledge committed in his or
her view upon his or her wife or child; (d) a violent assault and battery   *f*
committed in the view or presence of the accused person upon his or her
wife, husband, child or parent, or upon any other person being in the
presence and in the care or charge of the accused person.

118. *Provocation to be left to jury.* Where on a charge of murder there is
evidence on which the jury can find that the person charged was provoked
(whether by things done or by things said or by both together) to lose his   *g*
self-control, the question whether the provocation was extreme enough to
make a reasonable man do as he did shall be left to be determined by the jury;
and in determining that question the jury shall take into account everything
both done and said according to the effect which, in their opinion, it would
have on a reasonable man.   *h*

119. *When provocation shall not be admitted.* (1) Notwithstanding proof on
behalf of the accused person of such matter of extreme provocation as
mentioned in section 117, his crime shall not be deemed to be thereby
reduced to manslaughter if it appear, either from the evidence given on his
behalf, or from evidence given on the part of the prosecution—(a) that he   *j*
was not in fact deprived of the power of self-control by the provocation; or
(b) that he acted wholly or partly from a previous purpose to cause death or
harm, or to engage in an unlawful fight whether or not he would have acted
on that purpose at the time or in the manner in which he did act but for the
provocation; or (c) that after the provocation was given, and before he did
the act which caused the harm, such a time elapsed or such circumstances

a occurred that a person of ordinary character might have recovered his self-control; or (d) that his act was, in respect either of the instrument or means used, or of the cruel or other manner in which it was used, greatly in excess of the measure in which a person of [ordinary] character would have been likely under the circumstances to be deprived of his self-control by the provocation ...'

b It is necessary to describe the contextual scene of those provisions. First, ss 116, 117 and 119 are based on the common law of provocation in Victorian times and have formed part of the statute law of British Honduras and then Belize since 1888. But s 118 only became part of the law of Belize in 1981. Secondly, subject to one qualification s 118 reproduces verbatim the provisions of s 3 of the c Homicide Act passed in England in 1957. The qualification is that in s 118 the word 'extreme' was inserted in the Belize text in the phrase 'the provocation was extreme enough'. The word 'extreme' does not appear in the English text. Thirdly, it is of some significance that what has been described as the old law (ss 116, 117 and 119) and the new law (s 118) were in 1981 respectively re-enacted and enacted at the same time to form part of the same legislative code. Fourthly, d in 1994 the Privy Council held that ss 116(a) and 119(1) of the code, by placing the burden of proof upon the defendant, are in conflict with s 6(3)(a) of the Constitution of Belize and should be modified to make clear that the burden of disproving provocation is on the prosecution (see *Vasquez v R, O'Neill v R* [1994] 3 All ER 674, [1994] 1 WLR 1304).

e

The relationship between ss 116, 117 and 118

Counsel for the appellant submitted that s 118 of the Criminal Code of Belize was a reforming measure intended to mitigate the harshness of earlier law. In particular he submitted that the words 'by things done *or* by things said *or* by both f together' in s 118 were intended to reverse the old rule which prescribed that words alone could never amount to provocation. Their Lordships accept this submission. No other interpretation of the plain words 'by things done *or by things said* or by both together' is possible.

Counsel for the appellant then submitted that s 118 implicitly abrogated ss 116 and 117 in all material respects. He relied by analogy on the principle that where g a later enactment is inconsistent with an earlier enactment the later enactment by implication amends the earlier enactment so far as it is necessary to remove the inconsistency. The difficulty is, however, that ss 116, 117 and 118 were respectively re-enacted and enacted at the same time and by means of the same legislative text. In these circumstances invocation of the principle of implied h abrogation must be a measure of last resort.

Their Lordships consider it of paramount importance first to consider whether the language of ss 116 and 117, on the one hand, can be reconciled with the language of s 118, on the other hand. The wording of these provisions sit together uncomfortably. Given the unambiguous provision that words alone may amount to provocation, which cannot be ignored, their Lordships consider j that these sections can be reconciled. That course is possible since s 116 provides that provocation 'as is mentioned in section 117' is a defence and s 117 lists four specific cases which *may* amount to provocation. It is not expressly made an exhaustive list. It is therefore possible to read the words 'by things done or things said or by both together' as supplemental to the four specific categories in s 117. In other words, those words can be treated as if they constitute a category (e)

immediately following paras (a), (b), (c) and (d) of s 117. That is the basis on
which their Lordships conclude that words alone may under the law of Belize   a
amount to provocation.

The interaction between ss 118 and 119

Counsel for the appellant next invited their Lordships' attention to what he
described as the inconsistency between ss 118 and 119. He said that s 118 was   b
intended to make clear that, in a case where there was evidence fit to go to the
jury that the defendant had been provoked so as to lose his self-control, the judge
was always obliged to leave the defence for the jury to consider. He said that
s 119(b), (c) and (d) was inconsistent with s 118 because it allowed the judge to
withdraw the case from the jury in circumstances falling in those categories. He
argued that s 118 impliedly abrogated s 119(1)(b), (c) and (d). Given that ss 118 c
and 119 were respectively enacted and re-enacted at the same time and in the
same code, their Lordships feel compelled to reject this argument.

That left a choice between two feasible solutions. One is to say that the
categories listed in s 119(b), (c) and (d) are exceptions to the general provision in
the second part of s 118. The second possible solution is that, by reason of the   d
introduction of s 118, as a matter of interpretation the two sections should be
reconciled on the basis that the matters mentioned in s 119(b), (c) and (d) are not
rules of law but important circumstances relevant to the merits of the defence of
provocation.

Their Lordships have found this a difficult question. The literal language of
s 119 (even as modified in *Vasquez v R*) argues in favour of treating s 119(b), (c)   e
and (d) as exceptions to the general rule spelt out in s 118. And their Lordships
observe that in the process of statutory interpretation ultimate loyalty to the
legislative text is of paramount importance. On the other hand, there are
important factors pointing the other way.

Only if there is some evidence that the defendant lost his self-control by reason f
of provocation must the judge leave the defence to be determined by the jury. If
there is no such evidence, the judge ought to refuse to leave the case to the jury.
That has always been law, and there has never been anything controversial about
it. On the other hand, and particularly after the adoption of the reasonable man
test in the second half of the last century, judges withdrew cases where the
defendant wished to rely on provocation on the basis of rules or supposed rules   g
of law which were judicially developed. By converting commonsense criteria
into fixed rules of law judges empowered themselves to invoke those rules to
withdraw cases from the jury. One such rule has already been mentioned: the
judges held that words alone could not amount to provocation. That rule
prevailed until it was reversed by statute in England and Belize. For present   h
purposes three other rules, which in practice enabled judges to withdraw cases
from the jury, must be considered. First, the rule was developed that the defence
of provocation cannot apply if the act was 'done pursuant to an "intent" to take
life which was either formed previously to, or was formed independently of, the
provocation' (see *Parker v R* [1964] 2 All ER 641 at 652, [1964] AC 1369 at 1391). j
This common law rule formed the basis of the statutory rule in s 119(1)(b).
Secondly, the rule was established that if a defendant who was provoked had a
sufficient time to cool down the defence of provocation was not available to him
(see *Mancini v DPP* [1941] 3 All ER 272, [1942] AC 1 and *R v Duffy* [1949] 1 All ER
932). This common law rule is mirrored by the rule in s 119(1)(c). Thirdly, the
rule was laid down that disproportionate retaliation may bar the defence, or, as it

a was later put, that the retaliation must bear a reasonable relationship to the provocation received (see *Mancini v DPP* and *R v Duffy*). That common law rule is reflected in s 119(1)(d). Plainly all three rules reflect common sense criteria which are highly relevant to the defence of provocation. And it has never been doubted that these matters, where relevant, ought to be placed before the jury.

The perceived mischief was that judges withdrew cases from the jury on the ground of fixed rules of law such as have been set out. In addressing this matter
b the English legislature in s 3 of the Homicide Act 1957 provided that if there is some evidence of loss of self-control by reason of provocation 'the question whether the provocation was enough to make a reasonable man do as he did shall be left to be determined by the jury'. In *DPP v Camplin* [1978] 2 All ER 168 at 173, [1978] AC 705 at 716 (per Lord Diplock) the House of Lords held that s 3
c abolished all previous rules as to what can or cannot amount to provocation.

The question is now whether s 118 in the Criminal Code of Belize is to be given a different effect. There are two differences. First, as already observed, the legislature in Belize inserted the word 'extreme' before 'provocation' in s 118. That does not, however, touch on the point presently under consideration.
d Secondly, and more importantly, there is the fact that the legislature when it enacted s 118 simultaneously re-enacted s 119(1)(b), (c) and (d). This factor cannot be brushed aside. On the other hand, if one adopts the view that s 118 has no impact whatever on the specific rules of law enshrined in s 119, it follows that s 118 is fundamentally emasculated in a major purpose which appears on the face of s 118. That would fail to do justice to the words and manifest purpose of s 118.
e
Given the real difficulties of interpretation created by the introduction of s 118 while leaving s 119 intact, their Lordships conclude that the two sections can be reconciled by construing the three matters mentioned in s 119(1)(b), (c) and (d) as relevant circumstances for the jury to consider if there is evidence that the defendant lost his self-control as a result of provocation. This is the solution that
f makes the best sense. And their Lordships would observe that this conclusion ought to simplify the task of trial judges. It eliminates the need for directions of law under s 119 while leaving the judge free to place before the jury the common sense criteria enshrined in s 119(1). For these reasons their Lordships rule that properly construed s 119(b), (c) and (d) do not contain exceptions to rules contained in s 118.
g

The summing up on provocation

It is important to bear in mind that the appellant's case, as explained in his unsworn statement, was that the deceased taunted him. He relied on
h provocation by words alone. Relying on ss 116 and 117 the counsel for the prosecution argued in her closing speech that words alone cannot in law amount to provocation. Counsel for the appellant made a contrary submission. When he came to sum up the judge read ss 117 and 118 to the jury. He left provocation as an issue to be considered by the jury. Logically, the jury ought to have realised that the legal submission of the prosecution was wrong. But the judge never said
j to the jury that the prosecution was wrong. And the judge never said that words alone can amount to provocation. He referred somewhat loosely to 'all the things said *and* all the things done'. Indeed the judge read to the jury a definition of provocation formulated by Devlin J in *R v Duffy* and quoted by Lord Goddard CJ in the Court of Criminal Appeal which no longer represented the law. The definition read as follows ([1949] 1 All ER 932):

'Provocation is *some act, or series of acts*, done by the dead man to the
accused which would cause in any reasonable person, and actually causes in   *a*
the accused, a sudden and temporary loss of self-control, rendering the
accused so subject to passion as to make him or her for the moment not
master of his mind.' (Our emphasis.)

The judge quoted Lord Goddard CJ as saying that the direction of Devlin J was
'as good a definition of provocation as it has ever been my lot to read'. At the end   *b*
of his summing up the judge therefore left the jury with a definition of
provocation which excluded provocation by words alone. At the very least the
relevant passages in the judge's summing up could have left the jury in
uncertainty as to whether words alone could or could not amount to
provocation. The failure of the judge to provide a clear and correct direction to   *c*
the jury on this central issue was a material misdirection.

Counsel for the appellant also argued that the judge misdirected the jury by
reading s 119 to the jury and by presenting it as containing fixed rules of law.
Read in context their Lordships are satisfied that the judge was simply drawing
attention to s 119(1)(b), (c) and (d) as spelling out matters of common sense
relevant to the defence of provocation. This argument is rejected.   *d*

Additional arguments

Counsel for the appellant advanced certain other grounds of appeal of a less
substantial nature. Their Lordships do not propose to discuss these additional
grounds.   *e*

THE CORRECT DISPOSAL OF THE APPEAL

Given that the judge misdirected the jury on the central issue in the case, the
possibility that the jury might have returned a verdict of manslaughter if they had
been correctly directed cannot be excluded. It is sufficient to say that a
miscarriage of justice may have taken place.   *f*

Their Lordships have carefully considered whether the right disposal might be
to remit the matter to the Court of Appeal in Belize to decide whether there
should be a retrial. The prosecution case was strong. The delay since the killing
and the trial is not unusually long. Moreover, the judge had dealt with the case
in a very fair manner, and he had been confronted with a very difficult problem   *g*
regarding the relevant sections of the Criminal Code of Belize. These factors
afford a substantial basis for ordering a remission to the Court of Appeal in Belize
to consider whether there should be a retrial. Ultimately, their Lordships have
concluded that, in the light of the fact that the appellant has been under sentence
of death for some three years, and very close to execution before the
conservatory order was granted, such an order would be unjust. In the result   *h*
their Lordships will humbly advise Her Majesty that the conviction of murder
and sentence of death should be quashed; that a verdict of manslaughter should
be substituted and that the matter should be remitted to the Court of Appeal of
Belize to pass sentence.

j

Appeal allowed.

Celia Fox   Barrister.

a Begg-MacBrearty (Inspector of Taxes) v Stilwell (trustee of the G E Coke Settlement)

CHANCERY DIVISION

KNOX J

b 5, 6 MARCH 1996

Capital gains tax – Settlement – Beneficiary becoming absolutely entitled to settled property – Date that beneficiary becoming absolutely entitled – Trustees under settlement exercising special power of appointment in favour of settlor's grandchildren
c *and thereafter holding in trust for them contingently on attaining age of 21 – Whether grandchildren entitled to an interest in possession on attaining age of 18 – Whether grandchildren's interest arising under the settlement or under the appointment – Trustee Act 1925, s 31.*

The settlor made a discretionary settlement dated 16 February 1959 in favour of
d his children and grandchildren. The terms of the settlement conferred on the trustees a special power of appointment which they exercised by deed of appointment dated 11 September 1975, thereafter holding the capital fund on trusts for the settlor's three grandchildren in equal shares contingently upon their attaining the age of 21. The trusts incorporated the provisions of s 31[a] of the Trustee Act 1925 relating to maintenance and accumulation and the right of a
e beneficiary to the income from trust property at the age of 21. With effect from 1 January 1970 the age of majority under s 31 was reduced by s 1[b] of the Family Law Reform Act 1969 from 21 to 18, but by para 5(1)[c] of Sch 3 to the 1969 Act, s 1 was disapplied in relation to 'any interest under an instrument made before' 1 January 1970. On 27 July 1990 M, the eldest grandchild, attained the age of 21
f and became absolutely entitled as against the trustees to a one third share in the fund. For the purposes of capital gains tax, that entitlement was deemed to be a disposal giving rise to a chargeable gain, which the trustees and M elected to hold over. The inspector refused the claim for hold-over relief on the ground that M's interest existed under the 1975 appointment and that, pursuant to s 1 of the 1969
g Act, M had become entitled to an interest in possession on attaining the age of 18 three years previously. The special commissioner allowed an appeal by one of the trustees against the consequent assessment to capital gains tax for the year 1990–91 on the basis that M's interest was an interest under the 1959 settlement and therefore para 5(1) applied, so that M had only become absolutely entitled to her share in the settled property on attaining the age of 21. The Crown appealed
h by way of case stated on the question whether s 1 of the 1969 Act applied to reduce the age of majority in relation to an interest created under an instrument made after the commencement of the 1969 Act by the exercise of a special power of appointment contained in a settlement made before the coming into force of that Act.

j
Held – On its true construction, para 5(1) of Sch 3 to the 1969 Act clearly connoted that the reduction in the age of majority contained in s 1 of the Act

---

a Section 31, so far as material, is set out at p 209 *d* to p 210 *d*, post

b Section 1, so far as material, is set out at p 211 *b* to *d*, post

c Paragraph 5(1), so far as material, is set out at p 211 *h*, post

would affect s 31 of the 1925 Act in its application to any interest under an
instrument made after the commencement of the 1969 Act. It followed that   *a*
where a settlement made before the coming into force of the 1969 Act created a
special power of appointment which was exercised after the Act came into force,
and the trusts under the appointment incorporated the provisions of s 31 of the
1925 Act, the appointment was the relevant instrument under which the
beneficiary's interest existed, since before the appointment the beneficiary had no   *b*
relevant interest to which s 31 of the 1925 Act could attach. In the instant case the
trusts under the appointment were therefore affected by the statutory reduction
of the age of majority, with the result that M had obtained a vested interest in
income on the attainment of her majority at 18. The election to hold over the
gain which arose on the deemed disposal when M attained the age of 21 was
therefore ineffective and the appeal would accordingly be allowed (see p 207 *j* to   *c*
p 208 *a*, p 212 *b c f g j* and p 223 *a*, post).

    Re Dickinson's Settlements, Bickersteth v Dickinson [1939] Ch 27 and *Re de la Bere
Marriage Settlement Trusts, de la Bere v Public Trustee* [1941] 2 All ER 533 considered.

Notes
    d
For the disposal which is deemed to occur on a beneficiary becoming absolutely
entitled to settled property as against the trustee, see 5(1) *Halsbury's Laws* (4th edn
reissue) para 143.

    For the Trustee Act 1925, s 31, see 48 *Halsbury's Statutes* (4th edn) (1995 reissue)
289.

    e

Cases referred to in judgment
Batty (decd), Re, Public Trustee v Bell [1952] 1 All ER 425, [1952] Ch 280.
Beyfus v Lawley [1903] AC 411, [1900–3] All ER Rep 796, HL.
Brinkley's Will Trusts, Re, Westminster Bank Ltd v Brinkley [1967] 3 All ER 805,
    [1968] Ch 407, [1968] 2 WLR 217.   *f*
de la Bere Marriage Settlement Trusts, Re, de la Bere v Public Trustee [1941] 2 All ER
    533, [1941] Ch 443.
Delamere's Settlement Trusts, Re, Kenny v Cunningham-Reid [1984] 1 All ER 584,
    [1984] 1 WLR 813, CA.
Dickinson's Settlements, Re, Bickersteth v Dickinson [1939] Ch 27.
Dowie's Will Trusts, Re, Barlas v Pennefather [1949] 1 All ER 968, [1949] Ch 547.   *g*
Fane, Re, Fane v Fane [1913] 1 Ch 404, CA.
Hoff, Re, Carnley v Hoff [1942] 1 All ER 547, [1942] Ch 298.
IRC v Jamieson [1963] 2 All ER 1030, [1964] AC 1445, [1963] 3 WLR 156, HL.
Marlborough (Duke of) v Lord Godolphin (1750) 2 Ves Sen 61, [1558–1774] All ER
    Rep 264, 28 ER 41, LC.   *h*
Muir or Williams v Muir [1943] AC 468, HL.
Northumberland (Duke of) v IRC [1911] 2 KB 343.
Rush, Re, Warre v Rush [1922] 1 Ch 302.

Case stated
    j
By case stated by a Special Commissioner dated 16 February 1995 the Crown
appealed from the Special Commissioner's decision dated 27 October 1994
whereby he allowed the appeal of the taxpayer, James Reginald Skey Stilwell, one
of the trustees of a settlement dated 16 February 1959 in favour of the children
and grandchildren of G E Coke, against a capital gains tax assessment for the
period 1990–91. The question for the High Court was whether, as a consequence

a of s 31 of the Trustee Act 1925 as amended by s 1 of the Family Law Reform Act 1969, one of the settlor's grandchildren, Miranda Mary Wilson (the beneficiary), obtained an interest in possession on 27 July 1987 in a one third share of the property in trusts created in 1975 under a special appointment incorporating the provisions of s 31 in circumstances where the settlement creating the power of appointment was made before the coming into force of the 1969 Act, and in

b particular whether a vested interest in income from the trust was conferred on the beneficiary on the attainment of majority at 18, or at 21, for the purposes of assessment of capital gains tax. The facts are set out in the judgment.

Michael Furness (instructed by the *Solicitor of Inland Revenue*) for the Crown. The taxpayer did not appear.

c

KNOX J. This is an appeal under s 56 of the Taxes Management Act 1970 by way of case stated by a Special Commissioner dated 16 February 1995. In his written decision dated 27 October 1994 he allowed the appeal of Mr James Reginald Skey Stilwell (the taxpayer) against a capital gains tax assessment dated 16 October

d 1991. The taxpayer was a trustee of a settlement (the settlement) dated 16 February 1959 made by Mr Gerald Edward Coke as settlor. It was a fairly common form discretionary settlement in favour, so far as relevant, of his children and grandchildren and their spouses.

The only problem which arises is one of statutory construction in connection with the trusts of an appointment (the appointment) dated 11 September 1975

e made by the trustees of the settlement in exercise of a special power of appointment created by the settlement.

The statute in question is the Family Law Reform Act 1969, which came into force on 1 January 1970. Amongst other things, it reduced the age of majority from 21 to 18 years.

f The short, but not entirely straightforward, question is whether in a case such as the present, where a settlement made before the coming into force of the 1969 Act creates a special power of appointment which is exercised after the Act comes into force, and the trusts under the appointment incorporate the provisions of s 31 of the Trustee Act 1925, the latter trusts under s 31 are affected by the change of law reducing the age of majority so as to confer a vested interest in income on

g the attainment of majority at 18, or whether, as the taxpayer successfully contended before the Special Commissioner, the original trusts under s 31 of the Trustee Act 1925, as enacted in 1925—under which majority is attained only at the age of 21 years—are incorporated into the appointment so that no interest in possession exists before the age of 21 is attained.

h There appeared before me Mr Furness for the Crown. No one appeared for the taxpayer. However, fortunately before the Special Commissioner counsel appeared on behalf of the taxpayer. Mr Furness, in accordance with the Bar's traditions, took me through not only the skeleton argument used by taxpayer's counsel before the Special Commissioner, but also indicated what he understood

j the taxpayer's arguments would be as the case progressed.

The facts are not in dispute, nor indeed are the fiscal consequences of the two constructions contended for. It was common ground before the Special Commissioner that if the Revenue were right and the reduction in the age of majority operated in connection with the appointment, the beneficiary in question, Miranda Mary Wilson (the beneficiary), a grandchild of the settlor born on 27 July 1969, attained an interest in possession on 27 July 1987 in income only

and an absolute interest in both capital and income three years later on attaining
21 on 27 July 1990. Therefore, there was a deemed disposal for capital gains tax *a*
purposes under s 54(1) of the Capital Gains Tax Act 1979 on the latter occasion
when she became absolutely entitled as against the trustees. On that basis the
election made on 3 December 1990 under s 147A(2)(d) of the 1979 Act to hold
over the consequent chargeable gain was ineffective.

Conversely, if the taxpayer is right the beneficiary became entitled to an *b*
interest in possession only on attaining the age of 21 years and the election to hold
over the trustees' chargeable gain was effective. There is no issue before me on
the figures involved, although they are not yet agreed. The gain in the
assessment was one of £93,340.

I turn to the trust documents. The settlement recited a desire to make
provision for the settlor's wife and issue. The settlor had four children: Lavinia *c*
Mary Coke who was born on 21 September 1944 and three others whose names
I need not recite. There are various definitions in the settlement. The only ones
that I need refer to are three in number. First, 'the beneficiaries' was defined as
including the settlor's wife and 'the said children of the settlor'—that is, all four
of them—'and any other child or children of the settlor hereafter born, the *d*
children of any child of the settlor and the wives or husbands of any children or
grandchild of the settlor'. There were provisos enabling in particular the settlor's
wife to be excluded, as indeed she subsequently was.

Secondly, 'vesting day' is defined as meaning the day on which the period of 60
years expires, or a royal life period, from the date of settlement. The vesting day *e*
foreseeably would be almost certain to occur in 2019.

Thirdly, 'the accumulation period' is defined as 'the period from the date
hereof until either the expiration of five years or the death of the Settlor
whichever shall first happen'. That cannot have extended beyond the period of
five years after the date of the settlement.

Clause 2 of the settlement, so far as material, reads as follows: *f*

> 'THE Trustees shall stand possessed of the Trust Fund and the income
> thereof upon such trusts ... for the respective benefits of the Beneficiaries or
> any one or more of them exclusive of the others or other and for such
> interests whether absolute or for life or for any other period or periods and *g*
> with such provisions for their respective advancement maintenance or
> education at the discretion of the Trustees or of any other persons or person
> other than the Settlor as the Trustees being not less than two in number may
> at any time or times and from time to time at their absolute and uncontrolled
> discretion by any deed or deeds revocable or irrevocable executed before the
> Vesting Day appoint ...' *h*

There are two provisos that I need not read.

There is a discretionary trust of income in default, which I need not read in
detail. In cl 4 there is a power of accumulation, which reads as follows:

j

> 'Notwithstanding the trusts of Clause 3 hereof the following powers are
> conferred on the Trustees (but without imposing any trust or legal
> obligation as to the exercise or non-exercise of any such powers) namely:—
> (a) DURING the Accumulation Period the Trustees may in their absolute and
> unfettered discretion accumulate the whole or any part or parts of the
> income of the Trust Fund by investing the same and the resulting income

a
thereof in any manner hereby authorised as an accretion to the capital of the
Trust Fund and so as to form one fund therewith for all purposes ...'

There were trusts in default of appointment which, save for a substitutional
provision, operate in favour of the children of the settlor, not in favour of the
beneficiary, who was a grandchild of the settlor. I need not read the rest of the
settlement.

b
The appointment was made on 11 September 1975 by the three persons who
were then the trustees of the settlement. It contains lengthy recitals of earlier
deeds, partly of appointment of new trusts but mostly of revocable appointments
which in some measure had been revoked. The first two operative clauses
contain revocations of such of the revocable appointments as have previously

c
been made but have not yet been revoked. The operative clause with which this
decision is concerned is cl 3:

'The Present Trustees in exercise of the power conferred upon them by
Clause 2 of the Settlement and of every or any other power then enabling
HEREBY APPOINT that from the date hereof the Capital Fund shall be held UPON

d
the following Trusts that is to say:—(a) the Present Trustees shall stand
possessed of the investments set out in the Schedule hereto (being part of the
Capital Fund) UPON TRUST for such of the children of Lavinia Mary Wilson
(daughter of the Settlor) as shall attain the age of twenty-one years and if
more than one in equal shares absolutely ...'

e
Of course, Lavinia Mary Wilson was the same person as Lavinia Mary Coke who
was the first-named child in the recital at the outset of the settlement.

Most of the rest of the appointment was concerned with another part of the
fund with which this decision is not concerned. The only other clause in the
appointment that I need read is cl 8:

f
'THE provisions of Section 31 (relating to maintenance and accumulation)
and of Section 32 (relating to advancement) of the Trustee Act 1925 shall
apply hereto with the following variations:—(a) Section 31 shall have effect
as if the words "the Trustees think fit" were substituted in paragraph (i) of
sub-section (1) for the words "may in all the circumstances be reasonable"
and as if the provision at the end of subsection (1) were omitted ...'

g
A more usual or traditional form of that clause is to refer to the proviso at the end
of sub-s (1), but I do not think that anything turns on that small misprint. There
are modifications of the statutory power of advancement, which is incorporated
by reference to s 32, but I need not read them.

h
I turn now to the relevant statutory provisions. I begin with the Trustee Act
1925. So far as material, s 31(1) reads as follows:

'Where any property is held by trustees in trust for any person for any
interest whatsoever, whether vested or contingent, then, subject to any prior
interests or charges affecting that property—(i) during the infancy of any

j
such person, if his interest so long continues, the trustees may, at their sole
discretion, pay to his parent or guardian, if any, or otherwise apply for or
towards his maintenance, education, or benefit, the whole or such part, if
any, of the income of that property as may, in all the circumstances, be
reasonable, whether or not there is—(a) any other fund applicable to the
same purpose; or (b) any person bound by law to provide for his
maintenance or education; and (ii) if such person on attaining the age of

twenty-one years has not a vested interest in such income, the trustees shall
thenceforth pay the income of that property and of any accretion thereto
under subsection (2) of this section to him, until he either attains a vested
interest therein or dies, or until failure of his interest ...'

There follows a proviso which is excluded by the terms of the appointment.
Subsection (2), so far as material, reads as follows:

'During the infancy of any such person, if his interest so long continues, the
trustees shall accumulate all the residue of that income in the way of
compound interest by investing the same and the resulting income thereof
from time to time in authorised investments ...'

It goes on to give directions as to how those accumulations are to be dealt with,
with which matter I am not directly concerned.

The only other subsection I need read is sub-s (5):

'This section does not apply where the instrument, if any, under which the
interest arises came into operation before the commencement of this Act [on
1 January 1926].'

Somewhat similar but different provisions obtained under the Conveyancing Act
1881 in regard to earlier instruments.

Section 32 contains the statutory power of advancement. The only part which
I need read is sub-s (3), which defines the cases where the power is applicable:
'This section does not apply to trusts constituted or created before the
commencement of this Act.'

Section 164 of the Law of Property Act 1925 regulates the extent to which
accumulations are permitted. Subsection (1), so far as material, reads as follows:

'No person may by any instrument or otherwise settle or dispose of any
property in such manner that the income thereof shall, save as hereinafter
mentioned, be wholly or partially accumulated for any longer period than
one of the following, namely:—(a) the life of the grantor or settlor; or (b) a
term of twenty-one years from the death of the grantor, settlor or testator;
or (c) the duration of the minority or respective minorities of any person or
persons living or en ventre sa mere at the death of the grantor, settlor or
testator; or (d) the duration of the minority or respective minorities only of
any person or persons who under the limitations of the instrument directing
the accumulations would, for the time being, if of full age, be entitled to the
income directed to be accumulated.'

There were two further permitted periods added by s 13 of the Perpetuities
and Accumulations Act 1964: the term of 21 years from the date of making the
disposition and the duration of the minority, or respective minorities, of any
person or persons in being at that date. That is qualified by s 165 of the Law of
Property Act 1925, which reads as follows:

'Where accumulations of surplus income are made during a minority
under any statutory power or under the general law, the period for which
such accumulations are made is not (whether the trust was created or the
accumulations were made before or after the commencement of this Act) to
be taken into account in determining the periods for which accumulations
are permitted to be made by the last preceding section, and accordingly an
express trust for accumulation for any other permitted period shall not be

a deemed to have been invalidated or become invalid, by reason of accumulations also having been made as aforesaid during such minority.'

I turn to the Family Law Reform Act 1969. The relevant provisions are as follows:

b '**1.**—(1) As from the date on which this section comes into force a person shall attain full age on attaining the age of eighteen instead of on attaining the age of twenty-one; and a person shall attain full age on that date if he has then already attained the age of eighteen but not the age of twenty-one.

(2) The foregoing subsection applies for the purposes of any rule of law, and, in the absence of a definition or of any indication of a contrary intention, for the construction of "full age", "infant", "infancy", "minor", "minority" c and similar expressions in—(a) any statutory provision, whether passed or made before, on or after the date on which this section comes into force; and (b) any deed, will or other instrument of whatever nature (not being a statutory provision) made on or after that date.

(3) In the statutory provisions specified in Schedule 1 to this Act for any d reference to the age of twenty-one years there shall be substituted a reference to the age of eighteen years ...'

Schedule 1 contains a long list of statutory provisions which are amended by substituting 18 for 21 years, and in that list is s 31(1)(ii) and (2)(i)(a) and (b) of the Trustee Act 1925.

e Subsection (4), so far as material, provides that the transitional provisions and savings contained in Sch 3 to the 1969 Act shall have effect in relation to s 1.

Subsection (7) provides:

'Notwithstanding any rule of law, a will or codicil executed before the date on which this section comes into force shall not be treated for the purposes f of this section as made on or after that date by reason only that the will or codicil is confirmed by a codicil executed on or after that date.'

Schedule 3 contains the following provisions:

g '**1.**—(1) In this Schedule "the principal section" means section 1 of this Act and "the commencement date" means the date on which that section comes into force [1 January 1970].

(2) Subsection (7) of the principal section shall apply for the purposes of this Schedule as it applies for the purposes of that section.'

h I come to the critical provision in para 5:

'(1) The principal section shall not affect section 31 of the Trustee Act 1925—(a) in its application to any interest under an instrument made before the commencement date ...'

j I need not deal with (b) which deals with statutory trusts under the Administration of Estates Act 1925 upon an intestacy.

It will be seen at once that the crucial words are 'any interest under an instrument made before the commencement date'. The question in this appeal can be put as follows: Is the beneficiary's interest in one-third of the appointed fund contingently upon attaining the age of 21 an interest under the settlement or the appointment, or is it perhaps both?

I can dispose of the suggestion that para 5(1)(a) of Sch 3 applies to interests under instruments made both before and after the commencement date and therefore operates to preserve the pre-1970 version of the Trustee Act 1925. That was an argument advanced on behalf of the taxpayer before the Special Commissioner. In my view, para 5(1) was clearly intended to provide a dividing line between those interests in respect of which s 31 of the Trustee Act 1925 applied still unaltered and those in respect of which it applied in its post-1969 altered form.

The following points can be made on para 5(1)(a) of Sch 3. First, the paragraph clearly connotes that the principal section shall affect s 31 of the 1925 Act in its application to any interest under an instrument made after the commencement date. One has to choose as regards any particular interest whether it is one under an instrument made before the commencement date or not.

Secondly, the paragraph is elliptical in that there is no verb connecting 'interest' and 'under an instrument', although one has to be supplied to obtain the full sense of the provision. The most likely verb that can grammatically be supplied is 'arising' or possibly 'existing'. 'Created' or 'constituted' does not fit very happily.

Thirdly, the scheme of this part of the Family Law Reform Act 1969, in particular s 1(2), seems to me to be consistent with an approach to resolving questions of construction by treating documents which are not statutory, and which are effectively written after 1969, in the new climate of majority supervening at 18 or as including that concept. A dictionary is provided in which those who speak post-1969 are presumed to use Family Law Reform Act language, but those who spoke before that time have their words respected in their necessarily pre-1970 form. Section 1(7) in its treatment of wills seems to me to emphasise that approach in requiring the rather technical doctrine of republication of wills by confirmation to be ignored in deciding whether or not a will is to be treated as written before or after the commencement date of the 1969 Act.

Fourthly, if for the reasons given above one has to decide, as I believe one does, under which of the two instruments—the settlement and appointment—the beneficiary's interest exists, and one is not allowed to say that it exists under both, the commonsense approach points to the appointment as the relevant instrument. Before the appointment the beneficiary had no relevant interest to which s 31 of the 1925 Act could attach. It is true that immediately before the appointment she was entitled to a revocable interest, but it was revoked. She was an object of the power of appointment, but s 31 could never attach to that, even if it is properly describable as an interest. The immediate cause of the existence of a relevant interest is the appointment. Under the settlement alone she had no relevant interest. She was not incidentally entitled in default of appointment. Under the appointment she had the relevant interest. True it is that without the settlement the appointment would not have been made, and to that extent her interest is one under the settlement. But of the two instruments it seems clear to me that the appointment is the one under which the beneficiary's interest arises and to which it directly owes its existence.

Fifthly, since the appointment itself undoubtedly falls to be construed under s 1(2) in the post-1969 sense that majority is attained at 18, it seems a priori more probable that the trust incorporated by reference to s 31 of the 1925 Act should be similarly construed.

Sixth and last, para 9 of Sch 3 of the 1969 Act reads as follows:

a
'The principal section shall not affect the construction of any statutory provision where it is incorporated in and has effect as part of any deed, will or other instrument the construction of which is not affected by that section.'

In my view, that paragraph lends support to the view that s 31 of the 1925 Act as incorporated in the appointment, is affected by the change in the age of majority.

b
The construction of the appointment is affected by the principal section, in the sense that it is clearly within the ambit of s 1(2). If it had used the words 'full age' or 'infancy' they would have been used as referring to the attainment of the age of 18 as the age of majority. The appointment does not use any of those words, but that does not detract from the fact that the provision for preserving unaltered statutory provisions which are incorporated by reference is limited to those

c
which are incorporated by documents unaffected by the principal section. In my view, this must be a reference to documents falling within the ambit of s 1(2), that is to say 'any deed, will or other instrument of whatever nature made on or after 1 January 1970', rather than whether or not by accident the words 'full age', 'minority', etc figure in the document in question. Those are my views on the Act unaided by any authority.

d
The only authority in which the question before me has been considered, even marginally, is the decision of the Court of Appeal in *Re Delamere's Settlement Trust, Kenny v Cunningham-Reid* [1984] 1 All ER 584, [1984] 1 WLR 813. In that case the plaintiffs were trustees of a settlement dated 8 March 1963. They had made a revocable appointment under a power created by the settlement on 19 February

e
1971 in favour of six dependants. Those dependants were at that stage all under the age of 18, the eldest being 14. The plaintiff trustees revoked that revocable appointment on 1 October 1980. By that time two of the appointees had attained not only the age of 18 but the age of 21 years. None of the other four had yet attained the age of 18. The eldest was very nearly 18, but the revocation supervened—perhaps not accidentally—just before her eighteenth birthday.

f
Questions arose with regard to the destination of the income that had been retained. The revocable appointment, which was subsequently revoked, had been in favour of the six infant beneficiaries 'in equal shares absolutely'. The decision was concerned with the effect of the use of the word 'absolutely' in relation to the ultimate destination of the accumulations. That is not a subject

g
which is of any relevance to anything that I have to decide here. But it will be seen that it was a case where there was a pre-Family Law Reform Act settlement dated 8 March 1963 and a post-Family Law Reform Act appointment dated 19 February 1971. Factually, it was on all fours with the present case. In the judgment of Slade LJ one finds the following ([1984] 1 All ER 584 at 588, [1984] 1

h
WLR 813 at 818):

'Before setting out the relevant provisions of s 31, I should mention two further points. First, the section was amended by the Family Law Reform Act 1969, which substituted references to 18 years for references to 21 years, but not so as to affect its application to any interest under an instrument

j
made before 1 January 1970. I shall hereafter refer to s 31 as so amended. Second, it is common ground that the interests of the appointees under the 1971 appointment must be treated as arising under the 1971 appointment, made after 1 January 1970, rather than under the settlement itself, which was made before that date, so that 18 years is the relevant age for all present purposes.'

It was common ground before the Special Commissioner in this case that the
construction for which the Crown contended was adopted by the parties in *Re*   a
Delamere and not questioned, as far as one can tell, by the Court of Appeal. It is
noticeable that Slade LJ inserted the word 'arising' in describing the interests
under the appointment. This lends some support to the view I expressed earlier
that that is the natural verb to supply in para 5 of Sch 3. However, the point
which has been argued before me obviously was not argued before the Court of   b
Appeal but went by concession. I think that that leads to the conclusion that what
was said on the subject by Slade LJ is not binding upon me.

Before the Special Commissioner the taxpayer relied primarily on what was
said obiter by Lord Romer in *Muir or Williams v Muir* [1943] AC 468. That was a
decision on appeal from the Second Division of the Court of Session on the
proper application of s 9 of the Trusts (Scotland) Act 1921. Lord Thankerton and   c
Lord Macmillan held that it was purely a matter of Scots law, not affected or
illuminated by English decisions. But Lord Romer, with whom Lord Wright and
Lord Clauson agreed, made observations on English law which, although plainly
obiter, have often been cited since and obviously command great respect. Lord
Romer said (at 481):
                                                                              d

'My Lords, if the question arising on the present appeal had to be decided
in accordance with English law it is plain that the validity and effect of the
liferents appointed by Matthew William Muir to his daughter, Mrs.
Williams, and his son, Ian Kay Muir, would fall to be determined as though
they had been given by the trust disposition and settlement of the testator,   e
Sir John Muir. In other words, the appeal would have to be allowed, for it is
a well-settled principle of English law in its relation to special, as
distinguished from general, powers of appointment that "when the power is
exercised the limitations created under it are to be written into the
instrument which created the power": see per Buckley L.J. in *In Re Fane. Fane
v. Fane* ([1913] 1 Ch 404 at 413). It necessarily follows from this principle that   f
the donee of such a power cannot create any estate or interest that the donor
of the power could not himself have created. "It is well-established," said an
eminent author, "that under a particular power, as a power to appoint to
children, no estate can be created which would not have been valid if limited
in the deed creating the power. The test of the validity of the estates raised   g
is to place them in the deed creating the power in lieu of the power itself.":
Sugden on Powers ((8th edn, 1861) p 396). Whether this principle also forms
part of the law of Scotland seems to me to be the question to be determined
upon this appeal.'

Later in his judgment, having considered Scots and English authorities and the   h
decision of Lord Hardwicke LC in *Duke of Marlborough v Lord Godolphin* (1750) 2
Ves Sen 61, [1558–1774] All ER Rep 264, Lord Romer says (at 485):

'No statement of the principle that I have ever seen has suggested that the
appointees under an appointment in their favour take any interest in the
subject-matter of the power until the appointment takes effect. It is, on the   j
contrary, quite plain that they do not, and that is all that [Lord Hardwicke
LC] decided in the case in question.'

He goes on to recite the facts of *Duke of Marlborough v Lord Godolphin*. It was a
straightforward case of an appointment in favour of persons who were at the date
of the appointment already dead. Lord Hardwicke LC decided that such an

a appointment could not be effected in their favour, although they were alive when the power was created and indeed, when living, were objects of the power itself. Lord Romer went on to say (at 485–486):

> 'My Lords, that the interests appointed in pursuance of a special power only arise in point of time when the appointment takes effect was also one of the questions decided by Russell J., as he then was, in [*Re Rush, Warre v Rush*
>
> *b* [1922] 1 Ch 302]. The particular question was this. Under the Treaty of Peace Order, 1919, all property, rights and interests within His Majesty's dominions belonging to German nationals at the date when it came into force were subjected to the charge mentioned in the treaty. Now at that date certain German nationals were entitled to reversionary interests in a settled
>
> *c* fund and these interests were unquestionably subject to the charge. The interests were, however, liable to be defeated by the exercise of a special power of appointment of which the German nationals were among the objects. After the said date the donee of the power exercised it in favour of the German nationals in question. It was held that the interests that had been so appointed to them were not interests to which they were entitled at the
>
> *d* date when the Treaty came into force. But no one could have successfully contended that the interests appointed to them were not created by the instrument from which the power was derived or that they did not take such interests by virtue of that instrument.'

e I think that the last few words are the high point in the tide of authority in favour of the taxpayer. I accept that they are authority for the proposition that it is a proper use of language to refer to an interest under the exercise of a power of appointment as created by the instrument from which the power is derived. But, since Lord Romer also said that the appointees took no interest until the appointment took effect, it is clear that the appointment was also an essential element in the creation of the appointed interest. It is also the fact that in the

f passage from the judgment of Buckley LJ in *Re Fane* [1913] 1 Ch 404 at 413, which Lord Romer read with approval, there is reference to the interests under a power of appointment being created under the exercise of the power: 'When the power is exercised the limitations created under it are to be written into the instrument which created the power ...' So, even within Lord Romer's speech one has an

g acceptance that the creation of the interests which arise under the exercise of a special power of appointment can be attributed, per Buckley LJ in *Re Fane*, to the exercise of the power and, per Lord Romer, to the instrument from which the power is derived.

It is also to be observed that the decision in *Muir or Williams v Muir* was

h concerned with s 9 of the Trusts (Scotland) Act 1921, which, as far as relevant, reads:

> 'It shall be competent to constitute or reserve by means of a trust or otherwise a liferent interest in moveable and personal estate in Scotland in favour only of a person in life at the date of the deed constituting or reserving
>
> *j* such liferent ...'

The decision was concerned with the question whether, where there was in succession a power created and an exercise of the power, the deed constituting or reserving a liferent which had been appointed by the exercise of the power was the original deed which created the power or the deed which exercised it. I have used English law terms which doubtless would be rejected by a Scots lawyer, but

that was essentially the point of the case. It was concerned with what an English
lawyer would call remoteness of vesting. It did not deal in any way with   *a*
questions of construction, but the bounds of what was permissible in what an
English lawyer would describe as perpetuity terms.

The second authority relied upon by the taxpayer was *Re Brinkley's Will Trusts,
Westminster Bank Ltd v Brinkley* [1967] 3 All ER 805, [1968] Ch 407. The case was
concerned with the effect of the Adoption Act 1950. Confusingly, there were   *b*
three successive generations in a family all called Thomas. Buckley J referred to
them respectively as Thomas I, Thomas II and Thomas III. Thomas I was the
testator who created a power which was exercisable by his son, Thomas II.
Thomas II exercised that power in favour of Thomas III, the testator's grandchild.
Thomas III adopted two children in 1950, just before Thomas II made a will
exercising the power of appointment in favour of his grandchildren who should   *c*
be living 21 years after his death, that is to say Thomas II's grandchildren. There
was also a natural child of Thomas III. The question was whether the two
adopted children of Thomas III were capable of taking. That question hinged on
s 13(2) of the Adoption Act 1950, which reads:

> 'In any disposition of real or personal property made, whether by   *d*
> instrument inter vivos or by will (including codicil), after the date of an
> adoption order ... (c) any reference (whether express or implied) to a person
> related to the adopted person in any degree shall, unless the contrary
> intention appears, be construed as a reference to the person who would be
> related to him in that degree if he were the child of the adopter born in lawful   *e*
> wedlock and were not the child of any other person.'

It will be seen, therefore, that the question turned entirely on identifying the
disposition in question. Was it the will of the testator (the grandfather, Thomas I)
or the exercise by the intervening generation (Thomas II) of the power of
appointment? Buckley J held that the dispositive instrument was the original will   *f*
which created the power. He referred to the earlier case of *Re Hoff, Carnley v Hoff*
[1942] 1 All ER 547, [1942] Ch 298, which raised a similar question under the
Legitimacy Act 1926. The taxpayer placed reliance on the following passage in
the judgment of Buckley J ([1967] 3 All ER 805 at 809, [1968] Ch 407 at 412–413):

> 'FARWELL, J., [in *Re Hoff* [1942] 1 All ER 547 at 550, [1942] Ch 298 at 303], if   *g*
> I may say so with respect, put the position very clearly and accurately in the
> passage which I have read. Anyone who can take any interest under the
> appointment made by Thomas II takes it as a result of the disposition made
> of his property by Thomas I in his will. The exercise of the power of
> appointment amounts to a selection among permitted objects of the   *h*
> particular persons to take; such selection will exclude, it may be, other
> persons who would otherwise take under the gift in default of appointment,
> but nevertheless it remains true that the dispositive document—the source
> of the disposition—is in the present case the will of Thomas I.'

He deals with arguments that are advanced as to the curious results which are   *j*
achieved in certain circumstances. Having rejected those, Buckley J says ([1967]
3 All ER 805 at 810, [1968] Ch 407 at 413):

> '... for anyone who takes under the appointment takes as the result of the
> disposition made by the grantor of the power, and the appointment must be
> read back into the document that creates the special power, and is really only

a part of the machinery of carrying that initial disposition into its final operation.'

In my judgment, that is of marginal relevance to this particular case. The subject matter of the decision was the identification of the dispositive instrument in those circumstances. That is not quite the same as the question of construction of the latter of the two documents in issue.

b Re Dowie's Will Trusts, Barlas v Pennefather [1949] 1 All ER 968, [1949] Ch 547 was also relied upon. That case concerned a pure question of construction on the expression 'expectant interests' in an after-acquired property clause. It was held by Roxburgh J that in the circumstances of that particular case the words 'expectant interest' were apt to include a future interest under an appointment that had yet to be made. That is purely a question of the interpretation of the

c individual words concerned and is of no assistance to me. But reliance was placed on an observation of Roxburgh J in the course of his judgment, following a long quotation from the speech of Lord Romer in Muir or Williams v Muir, which I have already cited. Referring to the concluding part of that passage—'But no one could have successfully contended that the interests appointed to them were not

d created by the instrument from which the power was derived or that they did not take such interests by virtue of that instrument'—Roxburgh J said ([1949] 1 All ER 968 at 971, [1949] Ch 547 at 553–554):

e 'In my judgment, that last sentence, in which LORD CLAUSON concurred, shows clearly that, though the interest created by the appointment did not arise until the appointment was executed, when it did arise the beneficiary took his interest by virtue of the instrument creating the power, or, in other words, the will. That, however, is by no means the end of the case, for it is settled and clear also from LORD ROMER'S speech that the interest which arises under the appointment is a different interest from that which the

f beneficiary had in default of appointment, and, accordingly, it is clear at the date of the marriage settlement the expectancy which the beneficiary had was not a present interest.'

He goes on to deal with the question of construction, with which I need not concern myself. I do not find that to be anything more than a lucid explanation

g of what Lord Romer said in Muir or Williams v Muir.

Reliance was also placed on the decision of Vaisey J in Re Batty decd, Public Trustee v Bell [1952] 1 All ER 425, [1952] Ch 280. That case concerned the applicability of the statutory power of advancement. I have read the critical provision of the Trustee Act 1925, s 32(3): 'This section does not apply to trusts constituted or created before the commencement of this Act.' The circumstances

h were parallel to those obtaining here, that is to say, before the 1925 Act came into force the power was created but it was exercised after the Act came into force. The question was whether the statutory power of advancement, which was introduced in 1925 (unlike the statutory power of maintenance), applied to the trusts contained in the appointment. Vaisey J held that it did not. He said ([1952]

j 1 All ER 425 at 426, [1952] Ch 280 at 283):

'In [Re Dickinson's Settlements, Bickersteth v Dickinson [1939] Ch 27], a decision of CROSSMAN, J., the headnote is: "Where a power of appointment is exercised, the document exercising the power and not the document creating the power is for the purposes of [s 31 of the 1925 Act] the instrument under which the appointed interest arises, as a new interest is created by the appointment." In a sense in the present case the origin of the trusts by virtue of which the power of advancement is said to arise is the deed of *a* appointment, and not the testamentary disposition which conferred the power of appointment, but I think that a distinction has to be drawn between the expressions "trusts constituted" and "trusts created" in s. 32(3). In my judgment, in the present case the trusts were constituted by the testator's will; i.e., they originated by reason of the constitution of the original trusts *b* as contained in the codicil of August 1925. No doubt they were created in one sense when the power of appointment was exercised, but it must be noted that the language of s. 32(3) differs very materially from that of s. 31(5). Section 32(3) refers to trusts "constituted or created before the commencement of [the] Act", and not to "the instrument ... under which the interest arises."' *c*

He goes on to deal with some authorities, including *Muir or Williams v Muir*, and says ([1952] 1 All ER 425 at 427, [1952] Ch 280 at 285):

'I think it must be noticed that s. 32(1) is a revolutionary provision in that *d* it has a confiscatory effect since it enables half of the property held contingently on an infant attaining the age of twenty-one to be applied for his advancement, i.e., it gives half of the capital to a beneficiary who, under the terms of the instrument creating the trust, is only entitled to that capital contingently. In my judgment, it may well be that the difference between the language of s. 31(5) and s. 33(2), on the one hand, and that of s. 32(3), on *e* the other hand, may be referable to a distinction between the three sub-sections. It seems to me that, if the legislature intended the section to apply to interests which arise under the constitution of a testamentary instrument which came into operation, by reason of the testator's death, before the commencement of the Trustee Act, 1925, words of a much *f* stronger character would have been employed.'

It is plain that that decision was concerned with the different words 'trusts constituted or created'.

The other authorities relied upon in the skeleton argument of the taxpayer can be dealt with a good deal more briefly. In my judgment, *Re Hoff* does not add *g* anything to what was said by Buckley J in *Re Brinkley*. It was concerned with the effect of the 1926 Act and the meaning of the word 'disposition' used in that legislation.

IRC v Jamieson [1963] 2 All ER 1030, [1964] AC 1445 was concerned with the meaning of the words 'determination of the settlement' in the Income Tax Act *h* 1952 and is of no assistance as far as I can see.

Beyfus v Lawley [1903] AC 411, [1900–3] All ER Rep 796 was cited in support of the proposition that an appointee derived title to appointed property from the instrument creating the power. That seems to me to be an unexceptional proposition. Indeed, it is parallel with the analysis in the 1926 Act case of *Re Hoff* *j* and the 1950 Act case of *Re Brinkley* as to where the dispositive instrument is to be found. All of those authorities cited by the taxpayer adopt the approach, for the purposes of testing the validity of appointments, of reading back the appointment into the instrument creating the power or identifying as the dispositive source of the appointee's interest the creation rather than the exercise of the power, because the power does not dispose.

a   The other approach is that favoured by the Crown in this case. It seeks to identify the instrument under which the appointed interests arise. Re Dickinson's Settlements, Bickersteth v Dickinson [1939] Ch 27, to which reference was made by Vaisey J in the decision in Re Batty, was concerned with s 31(5), which reads: 'This section does not apply where the instrument, if any, under which the interest arises came into operation before the commencement of this Act.' Crossman J

b   held that in the same circumstances as here of a power being created before the Act came into force, but exercised after it came into force by creating the trusts, those trusts were ones to which s 31 of the 1925 Act applied, because the appointed interests arose as a result of the appointment. He said (at 30–31):

c   'It has been argued that estates created under powers are to be regarded as created by the instrument under which the powers arose. In support of that principle, Farwell on Powers ((3rd edn, 1916) p 576), has been cited. The same learned author at pp. 310, 311, states that an appointment creates a new estate, using the words "the exercise of a power of appointment divests ... the estates limited in default of appointment and creates new estates, and that, too, whether the property be real or personal." The last mentioned

d   statement from Farwell on Powers was adopted as correct by Hamilton J. in Duke of Northumberland v. Commissioners of Inland Revenue ([1911] 2 KB 343, 354). The principle finds support in the case of In re Rush. Warre v. Rush ([1922] 1 Ch 302), a case arising out of the Treaty of Peace Order, 1919. In my judgment the interests of the three grandchildren of George Dickinson

e   arose for the purpose of s. 31, sub-s. 5, of the Trustee Act, 1925, under the appointment made in 1932. I hold, therefore, that s. 31 applies to the contingent interests of those three grandchildren ...'

    It is true that emphasis is made by Crossman J on the use of the word 'arises' in the subsection in question, but if it is right, as I think it is, that that is the verb

f   which needs to be supplied in para 5 of Sch 3 to the 1969 Act that is very helpful authority. I also observe that, although it was cited to the House of Lords in Muir or Williams v Muir, it was not criticised, far less overruled, by their Lordships in that case.

    Re Rush, Warre v Rush [1922] 1 Ch 302 was dealt with and described by Lord

g   Romer in the passage that I have cited from Muir or Williams v Muir. He, also, did not suggest that it had been wrongly decided. That is in line with the approach that the court concentrates on the instrument under which the interests in question are created or arise.

    Finally, in the cycle of authorities the Crown relied on Re de la Bere's Marriage

h   Settlement Trusts, de la Bere v Public Trustee [1941] 2 All ER 533, [1941] Ch 443. That was an after-acquired property clause case. The headnote reads as follows:

    'A marriage settlement, executed in 1919, on the marriage of R.B. and M.H., contained a covenant by the wife, M.H., to settle any after-acquired property, excepting (inter alia) any property regarding which an intention was expressed in the instrument under which the property was acquired that

j   it should be exempt from the covenant. In 1938 a settlor made a settlement of property by which, after declaring certain trusts in favour of the wife, M.B., and her two sisters for a term of years, the trustees were empowered to appoint the funds to or for the benefit of M.B. and her issue and other beneficiaries in such shares and to such beneficiaries as they should in their absolute discretion determine. In 1941 the trustees of this settlement by deed

poll appointed that on the expiry of the trusts declared by the settlement of
1938 the funds should go to M.B. and her sisters in equal shares, and declared *a*
their intention that each share should be exempt from the covenant to settle
after-acquired property contained in the marriage settlements of each of
them ...' (See [1941] Ch 443.)

The instrument which created the power did not express an intention that any *b*
appointed interest would be outside the after-acquired property clause, but the
instrument which exercised the power did so. The question was whether the
property thus appointed was property which was expressed in the instrument
under which the property was acquired to be exempt from the covenant. That
involved identifying what the instrument was.

Simonds J had *Re Dickinson* cited to him. He said of it ([1941] 2 All ER 533 at *c*
535, [1941] Ch 443 at 447):

> 'I think that it is reasonably clear that the instrument under which the
> daughter acquired her share of the trust fund was the deed poll of
> appointment under which the power was exercised. In coming to that *d*
> conclusion, I am following the close analogy of the recent decision of
> CROSSMAN, J., in *Re Dickinson's Settlements, Bickersteth* v. *Dickinson* ([1939] Ch
> 27). There the judge had to consider the effect of the Trustee Act, 1925,
> s. 31.'

He describes what Crossman J decided, which I need not repeat. He refers to *e*
Re Rush and the *Duke of Northumberland*'s case. He continues ([1941] 2 All ER 533
at 535–536, [1941] Ch 443 at 448):

> 'In fact, both those cases are examples of a principle which seems to be
> perfectly clear—namely, that, where one has an instrument creating a power
> and an instrument exercising that power, the interest created by the exercise *f*
> of the power arises under the latter instrument, for in fact there never was
> such an interest until the power was exercised so as to create it. Accordingly,
> I come to the conclusion upon the first point here that the instrument under
> which the daughter acquired her interest was the instrument which
> contained the expression of opinion that it should be exempt from the *g*
> covenant for the settlement of her after-acquired property.'

Taken as a whole, the authorities do not detract from the view I formed earlier
from the terms of the 1969 Act itself. On the contrary, the nearest case seems to
me to be in *Re Dickinson* and possibly *Re de La Bere's Marriage Settlement*, more
especially if I am right in thinking that 'arising' is the appropriate verb to be *h*
supplied in para 5 of Sch 3 to the 1969 Act.

The taxpayer's skeleton argument also relied on the exactly contemporaneous
Scottish Act, the Age of Majority (Scotland) Act 1969, which is quite explicit on
the question that I have to decide. That Act received Royal Assent on exactly the
same day as the Family Law Reform Act 1969. Section 1(2)(b) of the Scottish Act *j*
refers to—

> 'any deed executed on or after that date other than a deed made in the
> exercise of a special power of appointment where the deed creating the
> power was executed before that date.'

a That passage is incorporated with the parallel provision to s 1(2) of the Family Law Reform Act 1969, and indeed is in almost, but not quite, the same terms. The first part of the subsection reads:

'The foregoing subsection [altering the age of majority] applies for the purposes of any rule of law, and, in the absence of a definition or of any indication of a contrary intention, for the construction of "full age", "infant",
b "infancy", "minor", "minority" and similar expressions ...'

There is an express exclusion of this particular case, which is that of a deed made in exercise of a special power of appointment where the deed creating the power is executed before that date. It seems to me that the arguments go either way in relation to that enactment. The taxpayer submits that the courts should
c seek to construe the English Act so as to make English and Scots law the same. My imperfect knowledge of Scots law does not extend beyond the belief that there are many cases where English and Scots law on the law of trusts is not identical. The Crown says that the fact that the explicit provisions in the Scots Act have not been incorporated in the English Family Law Reform Act is an
d indication that a different result was intended. I do not find any conclusive guide from those conflicting arguments as to that parallel but radically different provision.

Arguments were also put forward based on what was said to be the intention of the 1969 Act. In particular, reliance was sought to be placed on the provisions of s 1(7) which deals with wills. In my judgment, what the 1969 Act does in that
e context is preserve the meaning of instruments written before the Act came into force, notwithstanding the technical republication argument. I do not find any guide in s 1(7) as to what was intended regarding the construction of instruments written after the 1969 Act came into force.

Equally, it was argued that there could be anomalous results. As has frequently
f been observed particularly in taxation cases, the ingenuity of counsel nearly always is capable of producing a variety of startling results and circumstances in support of particular constructions of legislative enactments. I do not find the fact that some curious results can be constructed as conclusive, as compared with the general considerations as to the wording and policy of the Act, which seem to me to be of much more import.

g It is accepted that in some cases, where, as here, there has been an election as to which of the permitted periods should be used for accumulation, there is a slight restriction involved in the Revenue's construction of the extent of the powers of the trustees to direct accumulation and maintenance trusts, whether they are declared expressly or by reference to the s 31 of the Trustee Act 1925. It
h will be recalled that under s 164 of the Law of Property Act 1925 only one period can be selected for accumulations to be directed. Equally, there is a statutory accumulation period which is exempt from that restrictive rule. The exemption is in s 165, which I have read and need not repeat.

In my view, the reduction of the age of majority to 18 prevents accumulations
j being directed at the age of 21 if a period other than the minority of beneficiaries, who would be entitled at full age, has been selected and that period has expired. That is the case here. It will be recalled that the period chosen was the lifetime of the settlor or five years, whichever was the first. Whichever was the first, it had long expired before the beneficiary attained the age of 18. Between the ages of 18 and 21 there was no minority or statutory power available. In those circumstances, there would be no permissible accumulation period. That seems

to me to be more the natural consequence of the reduction in the age of
majority—after all, it was the intention of the legislature to bring it into
immediate effect on 1 January 1970—rather than an indication that the legislature
intended a post-1969 instrument to have a pre-1970 meaning.

On the principal point, such textbook authority as I have been able to find
supports the view that I have expressed. In Underhill and Hayton *Laws Relating
to Trusts and Trustees* (15th edn, 1995) p 689 one finds the following:

> 'The statutory powers of maintenance and accumulation contained in
> Trustee Act 1925, section 31, and set out below have been affected by the
> Family Law Reform Act 1969. They relate to a beneficiary's infancy or
> minority which ends at the age of twenty-one for inter vivos or testamentary
> trusts under instruments made before 1 January 1970 and at the age of
> eighteen for beneficiaries under settlements or appointments made after
> 1969.'

There follows a reference to the rule regarding wills. It goes on (p 690):

> 'Thus, in the case of, what might be termed in short, pre-1970 trusts
> trustees continue to have power to pay income to the parent or guardian of
> a person aged between eighteen and twenty-one though they may pay
> income directly to such person if they wish. However, such person has no
> right to income till he is twenty-one years of age unlike a beneficiary under
> a post-1969 settlement or appointment who has a right to income as from the
> age of eighteen.'

No reason is given in support of the proposition, but the proposition is
undoubtedly there stated.

Similarly, in *Snell's Equity* (29th edn, 1990) p 276 under the heading 'Statutory
power of maintenance', one sees a description of the power in s 31(1), which I
need not read. The author goes on to say:

> 'If on attaining full age, namely, 18, or 21 if the interest arises under an
> instrument made before 1970, the beneficiary still has no vested interest in
> the income, the trustees "shall thenceforth" pay the whole of the income to
> him until he either attains a vested interest in it or dies, or until failure of his
> interest.'

That, too, while not containing any reasoning on the subject, seems to express
the conclusion which I have myself reached.

The taxpayer's argument before the Special Commissioner included a
submission that, even if the Crown's construction of the 1969 Act was correct, as
I have held it is, there was, on the true construction of the appointment, a
sufficient indication that what was intended to be imported by cl 8 was the
Trustee Act 1925 in its unamended form. In my judgment, there is no positive
indication in that regard in the several references to s 31, which I have read and
need not repeat. They are all neutral and just as comprehensible in relation to the
amended as in relation to the unamended form of s 31. But there is also a
significant argument to the contrary in that, for the reasons I gave a few moments
ago, there is no available accumulation period between the attainment of the ages
of 18 and 21 by the several appointees. The reference to the unamended s 31, if
there was one, would no longer be to the statutory power, because ex hypothesi
the statute had been amended. It would be an express exercise by incorporation
of the unamended s 31 as an identified document. As such, it would not have the

a protection of s 165 and would be void so far as the accumulation provision was concerned. That consideration makes it an unlikely intention to impute to the authors of the appointment.

For all those reasons, I am of the opinion that the appeal must be allowed.

Order accordingly.

b
                                                    Susan J Murphy   Barrister.

Practice Direction

a

QUEEN'S BENCH DIVISION

Practice – Trial – Setting down action – Setting down action for new trial – Queen's Bench Division – Setting down after time ordered has expired – Leave of court required b *– RSC Ord 3, r 6, Ord 25, r 8, Ord 34, r 2(1)(2).*

1. A plaintiff must obtain the leave of the court before setting an action down for trial after the expiry of the period fixed by an order made under RSC Ord 34, r 2(1) or in the case of the action to which Ord 25, r 8 relates.

2. The application should be made ex parte to the practice master, who may c require an inter partes summons to be issued or refer the application to the assigned master.

3. This direction does not relieve a plaintiff from complying, in appropriate cases, with Ord 3, r 6 (requirement of service of notice of intention to proceed after a year's delay).   d

4. Where the plaintiff has failed to set an action down for trial within the time fixed by the order of the court or by rule, the failure may entail the dismissal of the action for want of prosecution under Ord 34, r 2(2).

5. The practice direction dated 16 July 1979 ([1979] 3 All ER 193, [1979] 1 WLR 1040) is hereby revoked.   e

R L TURNER
2 July 1996   Senior Master of the Queen's Bench Division.

a # Re N (a minor) (sexual abuse: video evidence)

COURT OF APPEAL, CIVIL DIVISION
NEILL AND WARD LJJ
12, 13 FEBRUARY, 14 MARCH 1996

b
Family Proceedings – Orders in family proceedings – Contact order – Allegation of sexual abuse – Evidence – Reliability – Video recorded interview with child – Weight and credibility of video taped interview – Whether child to be believed – Expert's evidence of his belief in truth of what child was saying – Admissibility – Functions of judge.

c
The parents of a young girl were divorced in April 1993; the mother had custody of the child and the father had contact on Sundays. In July 1993, the mother refused to allow further contact between the father and the child and alleged that after the child had visited her father the previous Sunday, she had made remarks
d which suggested that she had been sexually abused by the father. The father denied the allegation and applied for a contact order. The local authority's child protection team arranged a videotaped interview of the child by a police officer and social worker with the mother present. At that interview the child did not respond to open questions and both the police officer and social worker resorted to leading questions; there were also signs that the child was being put under
e pressure. The child was subsequently interviewed by the court welfare officer, an expert on the subject of child sexual abuse, but whose qualifications were limited to her experience as a social worker, and by the guardian ad litem, a witness of considerable experience in child welfare, but with limited expertise in child psychology. At the hearing of the father's application, the judge held that
f the recorded interview was insufficient of itself to establish that sexual abuse had occurred and was sceptical of the mother's evidence. However, he was persuaded by the opinions of (a) the court welfare officer, who reported that she accepted the opinions of the officers who had conducted the recorded interview that the child had been sexually abused by her father, and (b) the guardian ad litem, who indorsed the conduct of the interview and stated that although the
g child had made no voluntary statements incriminating the father, her account was genitally focused and appeared to relate to an unpleasant experience in her life connected with her father. The judge therefore dismissed the application and the father appealed.

h **Held** – (1) Where a videotaped interview with a child was put before a court considering the refusal of contact with the father on the grounds of alleged sexual abuse, the judge had to decide the weight and credibility of the video recording and whether the child was to be believed. An expert's evidence of his belief in the truth of what the child was saying was ordinarily inadmissible because it
j trespassed on the judge's domain and usurped his function; the question whether or not the child was telling the truth was ultimately one for the judge, not the expert (see p 231 h j, p 232 d and p 233 b f, post); dicta of Glidewell LJ and Stocker LJJ in *Re S and B (minors) (child abuse: evidence)* [1990] 2 FLR 489 at 498–499 and Morritt LJ in *Re F S (minors)* [1996] 1 FLR 666 at 676–677 applied.
    (2) The evidence obtained from the videotaped interview was so tainted by pressure and leading questions as to be unreliable and consequently the judge had

been correct in his conclusion that there was insufficient for him to be satisfied to
the requisite standard of proof that sexual abuse had occurred. However, he a
erred by accepting as admissible evidence which was inadmissible in particular,
that of the guardian ad litem that he had no doubt that the child was giving a
truthful account of sexual abuse of herself by her father. The judge had therefore
been wrong to find that the father had sexually abused his daughter and since that
finding informed his decision on contact, his decision to dismiss the father's b
application was fatally flawed. The appeal would accordingly be allowed and the
case remitted for a rehearing of the application (see p 234 *g j*, p 236 *h*, 237 *h j* and
p 238 *g h*, post).

Notes

For the admissibility of expert opinion, see 11(2) *Halsbury's Laws* (4th edn reissue) c
para 1137, and for cases on the subject, see 15(2) *Digest* (2nd reissue) 105, *19055–
19057*

For evidence of children, see 11(2) *Halsbury's Laws* (4th edn reissue) paras 1178–
1179 and for a case on a video recording of a child in a case concerning sexual
abuse, see *Digest Quarterly Survey* (December 1995) 57–58, 60. d

Cases referred to in judgments

A and B (minors) (investigation of alleged abuse), Re (No 1) [1995] 3 FCR 389.
B v B (child abuse: contact) [1994] 2 FLR 713.
F S (minors), Re, [1996] 1 FCR 666, CA.
S and B (minors) (child abuse: evidence), Re [1990] 2 FLR 489, CA. e
W (minors) (wardship: evidence), Re [1990] 1 FLR 203, CA.

Cases also cited or referred to in skeleton arguments

A and B (minors), Re (No 2) [1995] 1 FLR 351.
B (minors) (evidence: alleged sexual abuse), Re [1995] 3 FCR 572, CA. f
D (child abuse: investigation procedure), Re [1995] 3 FCR 581.
E (a minor) (child abuse: evidence), Re [1991] 1 FLR 420.
G v G [1985] 2 All ER 225, [1985] 1 WLR 647, HL.
*H v H and C (Kent CC intervening) (child abuse: evidence), K v K (Haringey London BC
    intervening) (child abuse: evidence)* [1989] 3 All ER 740, [1990] Fam 86, CA. g
M (a minor) (application for care order), Re [1995] 3 FCR 611.
M (child abuse: video evidence), Re [1995] 2 FLR 571.
R (child abuse: video evidence), Re [1995] 1 FLR 451.

Appeal h

The father appealed against the order of Judge Cotterill made in the Taunton
County Court on 14 March 1995 dismissing his application for contact with his
child M. The facts are set out in the judgment of Ward LJ.

Judith Parker QC, Christopher Naish (instructed by *Ford Simey Daw Roberts,* j
    Exmouth) for the father.
Patricia Scotland QC, Ralph Dixon (instructed by *Gilbert Stephens,* Exeter) for the
    mother.
Bruce Coleman (instructed by *Kay Firth-Butterfield,* Taunton) for the guardian ad
    litem.

Cur adv vult

a   14 March 1996. The following judgments were delivered.

WARD LJ (giving the first judgment at the invitation of Neill LJ). This is an appeal by the father of a young girl, M, who was born on 20 July 1989, from an order made by Judge Cotterill dismissing his application for contact with the child.

b   The appellant married the respondent in May 1987. The marriage became seriously unhappy and in July 1992 the father vacated the former matrimonial home and a decree absolute of divorce was pronounced in April 1993. The circumstances of that breakdown were not explored in any great detail. The mother's general complaint was that her husband was a particularly jealous man who continued to keep watch on her activities even after they had separated. He *c* admitted to his challenging her about an affair with another man who worked at the same bus depot as he did. He expressed concern, for M's sake, about her 'somewhat rumbustious life'. Words were harshly exchanged on Sunday, 11 July 1993 when he collected M for contact and chose to comment on the state of the house following the previous night's party. Until that time he had enjoyed *d* contact every Sunday for four or five hours and at other times when he was off work, including a period of six weeks when he was recovering from a broken shoulder. The judge found: 'That contact seems to have been entirely satisfactory until May of 1993 when ill-defined problems began to arise.'

The mother said that M returned from that contact very quiet and pale, clinging to her without saying goodbye to her father, leading her to believe that *e* M might be ill. In her statement the mother asserted that on the Tuesday, two days later, whilst at the maternal grandmother's home:

'M had now apparently got over what was troubling her when she returned home from her contact with the Applicant. I began to talk things *f* over with her to see if I could find out what was wrong, and she quite suddenly came out with the words "Daddy played with my tuppence" (by which I understood M to mean her vagina). I was absolutely horrified and managed to keep myself in control while I hugged M ...'

This remark was apparently repeated to a neighbour but there was no *g* evidence from the neighbour. The following day the mother consulted her solicitors. She had apparently also recollected an earlier remark made by the little girl that 'Daddy's got a hairy willy', which led the child to question whether she would in time develop breasts and grow pubic hair. The solicitors reported the matter to the local authority. The social worker confirmed the mother's account, *h* which now included not only the allegation that Daddy played with her tuppy but also that he made her sore. The child had an inflamed vulva but this was not unique, for she had suffered similarly in the past and had been prescribed the appropriate ointment to cure this soreness. The child protection team arranged an interview with the child to be video recorded. I shall deal with that in detail later. They interviewed the father, who denied the allegations levelled at him. *j* No criminal proceedings followed. After the mother had indicated through her solicitors, on 22 July 1993, that no further contact was to be allowed, the father made his application on 13 August 1993. The court welfare officer reported in November. Although these were not 'specified' proceedings for the purposes of the Children Act 1989, a guardian ad litem from the panel was appointed in April 1994 and he filed his report in September. Having heard the parties, the court welfare officer and the guardian ad litem, the judge made his findings on the issue

of 'whether there was indeed sexual abuse of this child and, if so, by whom'. He
held: a

'To assist me in coming to that conclusion I have had, as I have already
made clear, the assistance of the video recording of the interview. More
particularly, I have had the evidence of the mother and the independent
evidence of the court welfare officer and the guardian ad litem. I say "more
importantly" not in disparagement of [the mother], but since it is the view of   b
[the father] that she is hostile to him and is in fact the perpetrator of the
complaints by having tutored the child, it is right that I approach her
evidence with a good deal of caution, if not scepticism. Having said that, I
found her a not unimpressive witness, although there were certain
revelations which she said had been made by the child which seemed to have   c
seen the light of day at a very late stage in this history. For example, the
references to the child having seen her father's "hairy willy".'

The judge was right to approach this evidence with caution, not only because
of the father's challenge to the mother's bona fides, but also because, generally,
per Butler-Sloss LJ in *Re W (minors) (wardship: evidence)* [1990] 1 FLR 203 at 214:   d

'Such [grave] allegations [of sexual abuse made in a statement by a child
naming a perpetrator] would, unsupported, rarely be sufficiently cogent and
reliable for a court to be satisfied, on the balance of probabilities, that the
person named was indeed the perpetrator.'

The judge then considered the video recording and concluded: e

'If matters ended there, that would be insufficient for me to be satisfied to
the requisite standard of proof that sexual abuse had occurred.'

That finding may be sufficient for the appellant's purpose, but it would not do
justice to his case not to refer to some unsatisfactory features of the mother's   f
evidence. According to her statement she recalled M's speaking of Daddy's 'hairy
willy' as part of the early 'disclosure', rather than 'at a very late stage in the
history' as the judge wrongly stated. When this remark is considered in the
context of her going on to ask about her own development, the conversation
with the father is consistent with a wholly innocent discussion from which it
would be impossible to draw any inference of sexual abuse.   g
The respect in which I suspect the learned judge found the mother to be
unimpressive was her evidence of the 'revelations' which did see 'the light of day
at a very late stage in this history'. That was her relating to the guardian ad litem,
according to him, as part of the first 'disclosures', that M had also said, 'Daddy's
penis goes hard.' She told the guardian ad litem that since those disclosures and   h
the contact stopping on 22 July 1993, no further disclosures were made. In her
statement she said that the remark was made 'after M spoke to the police'. Under
cross-examination she said that the remark was made in the 'autumn time'. She
could not adequately explain the contrast between that assertion and what she
had told the guardian ad litem. There was nothing in the court welfare officer's   j
evidence to suggest that this remark had been conveyed to her. It was not part
of the complaint as recorded by the investigating social worker. Given the
importance of the allegation and the admittedly surprising reference to 'penis' as
opposed to 'willy', the mother's evidence is altogether unconvincing.
The judge then turned to the video. Contrary to good practice, and most
unfortunately, there was no transcript of the recording, which was only seen for

a the first time by the parties and the guardian ad litem on the day of the hearing. The judge said:

> 'The interpretation of the video evidence I have not found easy. What took place is conveniently summarised, in part, [in] the bundle of documents before me.'

b I believe that summary is the one contained in the social services records and it reads as follows:

> '[M] uncomfortable in video suite—did not respond to "open" questions. [Police officer] asked her if anything had hurt her "tuppy"—[M] said that Daddy had touched her tuppence "like a toy" and said he has put a stick in *c* her vagina. She demonstrated by opening her pants and her genitals. She said the stick tickled and had prickles on it. [M] said she had her pants on and Daddy had "lots of pants on" when he touched her.'

The judge described the video as follows:

> 'Essentially what appeared in that film, which was of some significant *d* length, was a child of four years of age, either ill-disciplined or very much ill at ease, who did not spontaneously recount any incident between herself and her father until prompted by the direct questioning by the interviewing officers, who quite clearly were unable to bring her to the sticking point without taking such a course. [Counsel] on behalf of the father, says that *e* their taking such an approach invalidates the responses of the child, but the guardian ad litem differs from that view. [The guardian] is a man of vast experience in social work and, I should say at this stage, a man who greatly impressed me in the presentation of his evidence. It seemed to me that he was cautious and measured in his approach and interpretation. As will *f* appear in due course, I attach a great deal of significance to what he had to say. What he had to say in relation to the video interview was that it is commonly the case that children will shy away from talking about a disagreeable experience spontaneously. It is only when they are, as it were, forced to confront the disagreeable that they will, in fact, speak about the disagreeable. His view was that the approach adopted by the police officers *g* was perfectly proper and understandable, and was necessary. In his view it reinforced his conclusion that there had in fact been a very disagreeable experience in that child's life a short time before that interview took place. He instanced the way in which on three occasions, no fewer, the child sought refuge in her mother's bosom, when the subject of relations between child and father were broached by the interviewing officer, however tenderly that *h* had been done. The child's account, in the course of that video interview, was, as [father's counsel] said at times difficult to follow, at times inconsistent and at times fanciful. But it did seem to me that it was genitally focused, that it is her history of the experience, and the experience was related to the father, to whom she had developed an antipathy over a relatively short *j* period. Having regard to those matters, there seemed to me to be a substantial foundation, if no more, for the belief that some sexual impropriety had taken place between the father and the daughter.'

We now have a transcript of the relevant passages of the video. The video was made available to us and I have seen it. The salient features might be limited to these.

1. The mother was present and participating. I agree with Wall J in *Re A and B (minors) (investigation of alleged abuse) (No 1)* [1995] 3 FCR 389 at 409:

'From a forensic viewpoint, para. 12.35 of the *Cleveland Report* [*Report of the Inquiry into Child Abuse in Cleveland 1987* (Cm 412)—the unsuitability of having a parent present at an interview] remains a correct statement of the proper practice, particularly in a case where the only evidence of abuse up to the date of the first interview was what the mother has said the child has said to her. Quite apart from any pressure which the mother's presence may place on the child, the golden rule is that each interview is to be approached with an open mind: such a rule is in my view immediately broken if the mother is present at the interview.'

2. There were many (counsel has counted 15) leading questions seeking to elicit that the child had been hurt. This is one flagrant example from the social worker:

'I think Mummy's been worried about you. Have you been telling Mummy a secret? Have you been telling her a bad secret, because you said you had a sore place? Can you tell us where that was M?'

The child who had been sitting on her mother's lap giving her mother a hug as her mother had just requested, responded by moving off to play with her dominoes.

3. Showing obvious concern that no progress was being made in the interview the sergeant then asked the child, once again sitting with her mother:

'You said something about your tuppence earlier? Do you want to tell us about your tuppence? M. Daddy played about with my tuppence like a toy.'

This is a blatantly leading question offending the clear rule of practice set out in para 12.34 of the *Report of the Inquiry into Child Abuse in Cleveland 1987* that 'the style of the interview should be open-ended questions to support and encourage the child in free recall' and that 'the interview should go at the pace of the child and not of the adult'.

4. Shortly afterwards the sergeant said: 'M, can you listen to me, can you listen to me. What did he play with your tuppence for?' The child's response was to moan. This is a child being put under pressure.

5. Then this exchange followed:

'*Social worker.* M, did it hurt when Daddy played with your tuppence? M. No. (moaning)

Social worker. Can you tell Mummy? M. No.

Mother. Did it hurt? M. Yes.

Mother. Did Daddy use anything? How did Daddy touch your tuppence? M. He hurt myself, hurt me.

Mother. How did Daddy touch you? M. I don't know.

Sergeant. With his fingers?

Mother. Did he use his hands to touch your tuppence? Eh? M. He went whack he did.

Sergeant. He smacked you on the tuppence? M. He went whack on my tuppence. He went whack with a stick and he put it all the way *up to* my tuppence.

a   *Social worker.* What did he put *in* your tuppence? *M.* A big stick, a long stick (laughing).

    Sergeant. A long stick? *M.* Yes, a big heavy stick.

    Social worker. Did it hurt? *M.* No, it went bong bong.

    Social worker. Bong bong? Did it go inside your tuppence? *M.* No.

b   *Social worker.* Can you show us where the stick was? *M.* In the middle of there (point between her legs).

    Social worker. In the middle of there? *M.* Then he went ding dong when he pressed the bell on it ...

    Mother. What did the stick look like M? *M.* It had a slug which came inside and came out again, it climbed up on my leg.

    Social worker. A slug? *M.* Yes.

c   *Social worker.* Went inside and came out again? *M.* Yes.

    Social worker. Where was the slug? *M.* He climbed up my leg and went that way—just in the middle bit. Ding dong.

    Sergeant. Do you know what a willy is? *M.* I didn't play with Daddy's willy.

    Sergeant. You didn't play with Daddy's willy? Have you seen Daddy's

d   willy? *M.* When he shuts the door when he goes to toilet and he doesn't show me.

    Sergeant. He doesn't show you? So you haven't seen Daddy's willy, M? *M.* No reply.

    Sergeant. So you haven't seen Daddy's willy? *M.* No.

    Social worker. Can you tell Mummy if you have seen Daddy's willy?

e   *Mother.* Have you seen Daddy's willy? *M.* No.

    Mother. You haven't? *M.* No ...

    Social worker. Did the stick have anything on it, M?

    Sergeant. Can I just ask ...? *M.* No, it just had prickles.

    Social worker. Just had prickles. Where were the prickles? *M.* On top of

f   the flower.

    Social worker. On top of the flower? *M.* Yes.

    Social worker. Right, where was the flower? *M.* Bing bong, bing bong.

    Social worker. It went bing bong, bing bong? Did the stick make a noise?

    Mother. Did the stick make a noise, M?

g   *Sergeant.* I was just wondering how the stick made your tuppence hurt? Can you remember how the stick made your tuppence hurt? You don't want to tell me do you? What's Daddy's name, could you tell me? *M.* Michael.' (My emphasis.)

A judge approaching a recording like that should remind himself of the following.

h   1. The recording is admitted as a form of hearsay evidence. It is for the judge to decide its weight and credibility. He will accordingly have regard to the fact that the evidence from the child is elicited in response to leading questions, under some pressure. He will judge the internal consistency and inconsistency of the story. He will look for any inherent improbabilities in the truth of what the child

j   relates and will decide what part, if any, he can believe and whether stripped of embellishments of fancy or exaggeration, there remains, none the less, a hard core of truth.

   2. The judge will also receive expert evidence to explain and interpret the video. This expert evidence will cover such things as the nuances of emotion and behaviour, the gestures and the body movements, the use or non-use of language and its imagery, the vocal inflections and intonations, the pace and pressure of the

interview, the child's intellectual and verbal abilities, or lack of them, and any signs or the absence of signs of fantasising.

3. There are particular problems in the reception of expert evidence in separating out that which is admissible from that which is inadmissible. To make the point, take a simple but sadly regular occurrence—an incident of domestic violence. The wife goes to the general practitioner, he takes her history, and he makes his examination. This is not a case where any real diagnosis is required. The proper and relevant evidence from the doctor is that he saw bruises and that the bruising was consistent with an assault. If he gives evidence of the history, that is hearsay and, assuming that it is admissible as such, its weight is a matter for the court's judgment and if the wife does not herself give evidence of those facts then considerable caution must be exercised by the court before relying on the hearsay. What the doctor is not permitted to say is that he believed the wife when she gave him the history, he is not permitted to say that because of the nature of the injuries he saw, he believed or was fortified in his belief of her having been assaulted, and he is certainly not entitled to say he believed that the husband was the one who had committed such an assault.

It is the judge's duty to decide and only the judge's duty to decide whether or not the child should be believed. In *Re S and B (minors) (child abuse: evidence)* [1990] 2 FLR 489 at 498 Glidewell LJ drew this distinction:

'In that role [as an expert witness] her opinions about A's psychiatric state and her propensity to fantasise or invent were properly admissible. To the extent that she was supporting these opinions by an expression of view that A's account of her previous history was apparently credible, this was also admissible. What, however, was not admissible was any direct expression of opinion that A was telling the truth, and not telling malicious lies. The boundary between the two expressions of view is fine, but it does seem to me that Miss Tranter's evidence crossed that line, so that her expression of "little doubt that the accounts given to me by A are accurate" was a matter for the judge and not for her.'

Stocker LJ said (at 499):

'... in giving as her opinion that A was telling the truth and not telling lies to the court she crossed the boundary—a fine one—between what was admissible and what was not.'

In *Re F S (minors)* [1996] 1 FCR 666 at 676–677 Morritt LJ said of the proper role of expert evidence:

'The use of child psychiatrists is obviously of the greatest assistance to the court in many cases. In some instances that will extend to pointing out features of the child's evidence which tend either to support or undermine its credibility. But it is usurping the function of the Judge to give an opinion directly on whether the man did that of which he is accused. In this case three of the experts stated their respective beliefs that the father had sexually abused N in the way of which she complained, not because of the results of medical examination, but because they believed what she said in the video interview. Not only was such evidence inadmissible, it was capable of being highly prejudicial ... Though Judges are often required to put out of their mind inadmissible and prejudicial matters they are entitled to expect the parties and their representatives to use care to see that they are not faced

a   with it in the first place. Moreover, not only may the wrongful admission of
    such evidence cause problems for the Judge, it is also susceptible to giving to
    the accused person the impression that he is being tried by the experts and
    not the Judge.'

    By way of summary, the position appears to me to be this: (i) The expert's
    evidence of his or her belief in the truth of what the child is saying is ordinarily
b   inadmissible because it trespasses upon the judge's domain and usurps his
    function. (ii) Proper evidence from an expert will be couched in terms that fact
    (a) or (b) is consistent with or inconsistent with sexual abuse, that it renders the
    child's evidence capable or incapable of being accepted by the judge as true.
    I must now introduce another subtle distinction. Medical witnesses are
c   frequently called upon to give evidence of their diagnoses. To take another sad
    but regular example; a very young baby is brought to the hospital with head
    injuries. The paediatrician will give evidence of his diagnosis that the child is
    suffering from a sub-dural haematoma. He will give evidence of the clinical
    features leading to that conclusion and (assuming his expertise) the results of the
    x-rays and CT scans. He will express his opinion that the injuries are consistent
d   with the child having been severely shaken. A diagnosis of sexual abuse is
    sometimes a proper medical question in the case of obvious physical injury to the
    genital area. In other cases the diagnosis is heavily dependent upon what the
    child says. It is difficult for that diagnosis to be made without having formed a
    view as to the veracity of the child and the court has to be sympathetic with the
e   clinician in such a case if in the course of his evidence he says that he believed the
    child. The strict law of evidence is contained in the three citations above. One
    cannot, however, expect the subtleties of the law of evidence to be understood
    by the child psychiatrist and the child psychologist. Experience shows that the
    subtleties are not always understood by the legal practitioners. I agree with
    Morritt LJ that more care must be taken but, in the imperfect world in which
f   these difficult cases are conducted, the ultimate safeguard is the judge. It is for
    the judges always to ensure that the decision at the end of the day is theirs.
    Whether or not the child is telling the truth is ultimately one for them not for the
    expert.
    4. Evidence of a diagnosis of sexual abuse of the kind I have been discussing
g   calls for a very high level of expertise, about which the court must always be
    satisfied. As Wall J said in B v B (child abuse: contact) [1994] 2 FLR 713 at 731:

        '... the analysis of interviews with children is a highly specialised skill
        which should only be undertaken by an expert in the field. The dangers of
        misinterpretation are manifest ...'

h   Whilst the courts have accepted that Miss Tranter, a psychiatric social worker
    with vast experience of working with Dr Bentovim, is an expert in this field, that
    accreditation should not ordinarily be given to social workers generally,
    notwithstanding their experience in a child abuse team. For the court to rely on
    opinion evidence—even to admit it—the qualifications of the witness must
j   extend beyond experience gained as a social worker and require clinical
    experience as or akin to a child psychologist or child psychiatrist.
    5. A guardian ad litem on the guardian's panel usually brings his experiences
    as social worker to bear in the discharge of his duties as guardian ad litem. I
    indorse the passage in the Manual of Practice Guidance for Guardians ad Litem and
    Reporting Officers (1992), which recommends:

'The Guardian should not attempt to appear in Court as an expert witness in matters on which he is not competent and credible in the Court's eyes as this can only undermine the child's case. The Guardian is expected to be an expert in general child care matters, not an expert in specialist areas.'

6. There is a further danger to the guardian ad litem giving evidence as an expert. His duties—certainly in specified proceedings, and I see no reason why that should not apply when, exceptionally, he acts in private law matters as well—are to safeguard the interests of the child in the manner described by the rules (see s 41(2)(b) of the 1989 Act). By the Family Proceedings Rules 1991, SI 1991/1247, his duty is to 'advise the court' on a number of matters including what orders should be made in determining the applications (r 4.11(4)). It is impossible for him to advise without having come to his own conclusion about the harm the child is alleged to have suffered. He has to decide in the exercise of his own duty to safeguard the child's interests whether or not he believes the child. Judges cannot complain if he states that belief as the reason for coming to the conclusion and giving the advice he advances. It may be better if his report and his evidence expressly acknowledge that he realises and accepts that this is the court's decision, and even if it is not expressly acknowledged, the judge must make it clear to the guardian and particularly to the parties that the ultimate decision would be his and his alone.

As one reads the rules, it is not without significance to note that under r 4.11(9) the guardian is able to obtain such professional assistance which he thinks appropriate, which is an indication by itself of the limitations of his own expertise.

7. It is a function of the judicial art and skill to apply these observations with discretion and with circumspection as the facts of the particular case demand. The point is well made in this case that there was neither the time nor the money nor the availability of expertise which would have enabled this particular guardian ad litem to have achieved the counsel of perfection which is implicit in the foregoing. Where opinions are proffered on subjects beyond the competence of the witness, then the judges must sift the admissible from the inadmissible and give weight to what they admit as may be appropriate. The business of the court must be conducted with some eye to the practicalities as well as the technicalities.

Applying those observations to the present case I conclude that: (a) the evidence obtained from this video taped interview was so tainted by pressure and leading questions as to be unreliable. (b) As a consequence, future 'disclosures' may also be tainted. (c) This guardian ad litem's experience in a child abuse team was not sufficient to establish his ability to express an opinion on the emotional responses of the child to the matters being pressed upon her. In so far as he expressed the view that the approach adopted by the police officer (and social worker) was 'perfectly proper and understandable and necessary', he was plainly wrong, for the interview was in flagrant breach of established practice. This error undermines the validity of the evidence of his observations of the child during his interview with her. (d) The judge was correct in his conclusion that there was insufficient for him to be satisfied to the requisite standard of proof that sexual abuse had occurred.

Having made that correct finding, the judge continued:

'However, the evidence did not stop there. The child was subsequently interviewed by the court welfare officer. The court welfare officer had been alerted to the allegation. She was herself independently able to form a view about the child's attitude towards her. Her interpretation of the child's a response to her in November 1993 (some four months after the alleged incident) was that this was a child who had been the victim of a painful experience and had no wish to renew her acquaintance with her father, who was perceived to be the cause, or the perpetrator, of that distress.'

The welfare officer had spoken to the sergeant who conducted the video interview and recorded that 'he stated categorically that he believed that M had been abused by (her father)'. She also spoke to the social worker, who said 'that the child had made a very clear disclosure and that there was no doubt in her mind that (father) had abused her.' In the light of the criticisms I have heaped upon that interview, their belief was unfounded. The communication of their firm, but forensically mistaken belief, creates the prejudice which Morritt LJ deprecated. The prejudicial consequence in this case was that it induced the court welfare officer to write:

'I must accept their opinions and be aware of the concern which would be caused should unsupervised contact between [the father] and [M] take place. In my own contact with [M], she made it clear to me that she does not want to see her father (because he hurt her). In view of the background and the opinions of other professionals, I cannot disregard what [M] has said … Because of concerns from [the child protection team] any contact between [M] and [the father] would, in my opinion, need to be supervised. However, in view of the fact that [M] has said she does not want to see her father, I do not believe that contact between her and [the father] would be in her best interests at this time.'

In her evidence she said that the child had said to her, 'I don't want to see Daddy. He hurt me.' She said that at the time she believed the child had suffered a certain amount of trauma, that she was frightened and that she did not wish to see her father.

Her perceptions have clearly been influenced by the prejudicial opinions of her fellow professionals. She did not keep an open mind. Assuming the truth of the child's assertion that father had hurt her and that the child was in fear, these matters do not justify the judge's findings that the painful experience of which the child was the victim was one of sexual abuse, as opposed to some other painful experience. The information is equivocal.

The judge then referred to the guardian ad litem, who saw the child approximately 12 months after the incident. He said:

'He … was apparently entirely uncontaminated, for want of a better way of putting it—certainly uninfluenced—by the views of others at this time. Certainly he had not seen the video evidence which has been seen before the court today. He said that the story he was given by the child on that occasion was, in his view, an entirely credible story and consistent with sexual abuse of that child by her father. It was suggested to him that the account she gave him … emanated not from the child's recollection of any such incident, but from the "tutoring", as it was put, of the child by her mother. [He] would not have that. He gave what seemed to me to be very cogent reasons for his not accepting such a proposition; namely, that in his experience, where a child has been tutored, the child is eager to press upon the willing listener the story which he or she has been trying to tell. The account is superficial and painless to the child. His impression , when interviewing M, was that this was not the situation; that her account of the events which she related was

not only consistent with the story she had previously given, but was clearly
a painful experience for her. He had no doubt in his mind that she was giving   *a*
him a truthful account of sexual abuse of herself by her father. The fact
remains that contact between child and father had been on any view good
until May 1993. Something significant happened to bring that harmony
between child and father to an abrupt end—the harmony that has not been
in any degree restored by the passage of time. The guardian ad litem has   *b*
been unable to discern, through any of his inquiries or observations of the
child, any evidence of emotional disturbance in that child sufficient to have
caused her to fantasise about what might have taken place, or in any way to
have dissimulated in relation to her experience. In any event, he said, in his
view it is impossible, or at least very difficult for a child to maintain such
fantasies or dissimulation over the sort of time which the court is concerned,   *c*
namely the period between July 1993 and the summer of 1994 when he first
saw her. This was not merely a cooling down in relationships between child
and father, but a hostility between child and father on the child's part.'

This guardian is very experienced and he was undoubtedly an impressive
witness. I do not suggest, or even begin to suggest, that he did not wish to   *d*
discharge his responsibilities in accordance with his duty to do what was best for
this little girl. Nevertheless, his opinions ranged over areas of child psychology
of which he may have considerable experience but limited expertise. The child
told him, from the comfort of her mother's lap, speaking only with mother's
permission, that 'Daddy had 'touched her tuppence' and had used a stick in a   *e*
field. One hour later, and of course, after much more conversation and play she
repeated, 'Daddy hurt me, on my tuppence'. He believed that to be and
persuaded the judge that it was 'an entirely credible story and consistent with
sexual abuse'. When regard is had to how the child described in the video
interview what use was made of a stick, then I regret that I cannot share the
conclusion that this was an entirely credible story. Nor am I convinced by the   *f*
guardian's trespass into the field of child psychology, when he said in an answer
in cross-examination:

> 'It is also perfectly possible to interpret a little girl's reaction to being
> physically abused between her legs as feeling as if she had been whacked.
> That could be her only way of actually saying, "It hit me like a thunderbolt."   *g*
> Here was this massive reaction. That's what it felt like. I don't put forward
> that myself, but it is a perfectly reasonable interpretation of what she has
> said.'

When the guardian ad litem said in evidence that the 'child, in my opinion,   *h*
very strongly and very clearly believes she has been sexually abused' and when
the judge accepted that the guardian ad litem 'had no doubt in his mind that she
was giving a truthful account of sexual abuse of herself by her father', then the
learned judge fell into the error of accepting as admissible evidence that which
Glidewell, Stocker and Morritt LJJ have each said was inadmissible.

The possibility of the child's evidence having been contaminated by a very   *j*
pressured, driven interview by the child protection team, the lapse of time, the
absence of repeated complaint, the mother's presence, all this should have given
rise to anxiety about the reliance to be placed on what M was saying. There was
no 'constellation' of factors pointing to sexual abuse, only unsatisfactory hearsay
evidence and unsatisfactory 'expert' opinion. I repeat the warning in *Re W*
(minors) (wardship: evidence) [1990] 1 FLR 203 at 228, this time citing Neill LJ:

a
'... the court will be very slow indeed to make a finding of fact adverse to a parent if the only material before it has been untested by cross-examination.'

That was not enough to prove on the balance of probabilities that this serious allegation was true. Yet the judge found:

b
'I am satisfied beyond the mere balance of probabilities that the child has indeed been the victim of sexual abuse, and that that abuse was at the hands of [the father]. Precisely what form that abuse took, I am in no position to conclude, although I am inclined to believe that it involved digital or manual interference with the child's genitalia. Whether it was the sole cause of

c
soreness in the child must be a matter for speculation in the light of some history of vulval soreness in the past when the parties were on good terms. I interpose the observation that I do not interpret that earlier soreness as being evidence of sexual malpractice by the [father] on a previous occasion. The child, as I have made clear, is hostile to her father and remains hostile to him at this date. A measure of her hostility is, in my view, evidenced by her

d
attitude to the use of his name by herself. She, I am told, has chosen to be known by the name adopted by [the mother], who has reverted to her maiden name. [The mother] has said that the decision ... by M was her own and was spontaneous. I have little doubt that the child was not discouraged from this approach and may, indeed, have been encouraged by the [mother].

e
But the fact that the child is eager to put her father from her life supports my conclusion that she has indeed been the victim of a very disagreeable experience of the kind I have already outlined'.

That last conclusion demonstrated the fallibility of this judgment. Eagerness 'to put her father from her life' does not justify any inference that she had been the

f
victim of the very disagreeable experience of sexual abuse. The facts in relation to the change of name, properly looked at, put her hostility to her father in an entirely different context. The mother's evidence relating to the change of name was that M came to her decision a month after mother had changed her name and that was within months of her separating from her husband. This was long

g
before any sexual abuse is alleged to have taken place. That the mother 'saw no reason to have to carry [the father's] name' speaks eloquently of her antipathy, and the risk of communication of such hostility to her daughter was a matter to which little attention seemed to have been paid.

I have come to the clear conclusion that the learned judge was wrong to find

h
that this father had sexually abused his daughter. Since that finding informed his decision on contact, his decision to dismiss the father's application is fatally flawed. The appeal must, therefore, be allowed. There is no alternative but to send the matter back for the rehearing of the father's application to be considered in the light of events as they now stand and upon the basis that any hostility evidenced by this child to her father has not been occasioned by his having

j
sexually abused her.

NEILL LJ. The judge had an opportunity to see the witnesses, and in particular the mother, giving evidence. One must therefore treat his conclusions with great care and respect. Nevertheless, I am satisfied that for the reasons explained by Ward LJ the judge was not justified in making a finding that the father had sexually abused his daughter.

The judge identified the evidence which he had to consider on the issue of
sexual abuse as being: (1) the video recording of the interview; (2) the evidence of *a*
the mother; (3) the evidence of the court welfare officer; and (4) the evidence of
the guardian ad litem.

The evidence provided by the recording of the interview with M was very
unsatisfactory. Ward LJ has drawn attention to the faults in the procedure which
was followed and to the leading nature of some of the questions. Among many *b*
criticisms which can be made of the procedure, it is to be noticed that after the
interview had continued for some time the sergeant said to M: 'You said
something about your tuppence earlier.' I have not been able to find any
reference in the transcript to any earlier statement by M about her 'tuppence'.

The judge was clearly right to treat the mother's testimony with 'a good deal
of caution, if not scepticism', but it is unfortunate that he did not make specific *c*
findings as to the passages in her evidence which he either accepted or rejected.
In my view, however, the judge should have been even more careful about
accepting the mother's evidence. Her evidence that M had told her that the
father's 'penis goes hard' was particularly unconvincing.

In agreement with Ward LJ, I am also troubled by the fact that the welfare *d*
officer's approach to the case had been influenced by the opinions expressed both
by the police sergeant and by the social worker. It is essential that in these very
difficult cases of alleged sexual abuse the interviewer should approach an initial
interview with an open mind.

The guardian ad litem was in a different position because he was able to *e*
interview M without being influenced by seeing the video or by any discussions
with the other professionals. But he did not see M until 12 months after the
alleged incident and in the course of his evidence he ventured opinions which fell
outside the range of his expertise. I have no doubt that the guardian is a man of
ability and is very experienced in the art of interviewing children, but in my view
the judge was in error in attaching importance to the guardian's comments about *f*
the video interview. Indeed I find it disturbing that the guardian regarded the
approach adopted by the police officers at the recorded interview as being
'perfectly proper'.

I have had an opportunity of reading Ward LJ's judgment in draft. In his
judgment he analyses the evidence on which the judge relied. I agree with his *g*
analysis. A finding of sexual abuse is a grave matter. I am quite satisfied that the
quality of the evidence which was before the judge in this case was insufficient to
support such a finding.

I too would allow the appeal and send the case back for a rehearing of the
father's application.

h

Appeal allowed.

Paul Magrath Esq   Barrister.

a # Re M and R (minors) (sexual abuse: expert evidence)

COURT OF APPEAL, CIVIL DIVISION

BUTLER-SLOSS, HENRY AND SAVILLE LJJ

b 22 APRIL, 21 MAY 1996

Family proceedings – Orders in family proceedings – Care order – Conditions to be satisfied before making care order – Threshold conditions – Allegation of sexual abuse – Whether child likely to suffer significant harm if order not made – Whether real
c *possibility of significant harm sufficient – Whether care order can be made if no proof but merely suspicion of abuse – Children Act 1989, ss 1(3), 31.*

Family proceedings – Evidence – Expert evidence – Whether relevant expert evidence inadmissible as going to ultimate issue – Civil Evidence Act 1972, s 3.

d In 1994 R, one of six children, alleged that he and several of the other children had been sexually abused by their mother and two men. The four younger children were placed with foster parents pending the local authority's application for full care orders. At the hearing of the application, the judge considered medical evidence, video recorded interviews with the children and the expert evidence of
e two child psychiatrists. He concluded that, although the balance of the psychiatric evidence was unanimously to the effect that sexual abuse had probably occurred, he was not satisfied on the balance of probabilities that the allegations of sexual abuse were proved. He was, however, satisfied that the threshold criteria in s 31[a] of the Children Act 1989 were met in respect of emotional abuse and made interim care orders after having regard to the welfare principle in s 1[b] of the 1989 Act, on
f the basis that the children had suffered such abuse and were likely to suffer significant harm in the future. The local authority, supported by the guardian ad litem, appealed, contending principally that the judge, having found that there was a real possibility that sexual abuse had occurred, had erred in law in not taking into account the allegations of sexual abuse in his assessment of the welfare of the
g children.

Held – When assessing under s 1(3)(e) of the 1989 Act whether a child was at risk of suffering harm, the court could have regard only to any harm that the child had suffered or was at risk of suffering if it was satisfied on the balance of probabilities
h that such harm or risk of harm (ie a real possibility of future harm) in fact existed. If, as in the instant case, the court concluded that the evidence was insufficient to prove sexual abuse in the past, and if such abuse was the only basis for asserting a risk of sexual abuse in the future, it followed that there was no basis, other than suspicion or mere doubt, for finding a risk of future sexual abuse. The appeal would accordingly be dismissed (see p 246 j, p 247 b, 248 j and p 255 g, post).
j *Re H and ors (minors) (sexual abuse: standard of proof)* [1996] 1 All ER 1 applied.

---

a   Section 31, so far as material, provides: '... A court may only make a care order or a supervision
    order if it is satisfied—(a) that the child concerned is suffering, or it is likely to suffer, significant
    harm ...'
b   Section 1(3)(e), so far as material, provides: '... a court shall have regard in particular to ... any
    harm which [a child] has suffered or is at risk of suffering ...'

Per curiam. The practice of family law judges to receive expert opinion
evidence as to the accuracy or truthfulness of child complainants is consistent with   *a*
s 3ᶜ of the Civil Evidence Act 1972, which makes it clear that such evidence cannot
be held to be inadmissible solely on the ground that it goes to the ultimate
question to be determined by the court. The passing of the Act should not operate
to force the court to listen to superfluous and cumbersome testimony, provided
the judge never loses sight of the central truths, namely that the ultimate decision   *b*
is for him, as are all questions of weight and relevance. If the expert's opinion is
clearly irrelevant the judge will say so; if this opinion is arguably relevant, but in
the judge's view ultimately unhelpful, he can generally prevent its reception by
indicating that the expert's answer would carry little weight with him. The
modern view is to regulate such matters by way of weight, rather than
admissibility (see p 251 *j*, p 252 *j* and p 253 *j* to p 254 *a*, post).   *c*

Re S and B (minors) (child abuse: evidence) [1990] 2 FLR 489 and Re N (a minor)
(sexual abuse: video evidence) [1996] 4 All ER 225 considered.

Notes

For the application of the welfare principle in making a care order, see 5(2)   *d*
Halsbury's Laws (4th edn reissue) para 787, and for cases on the subject, see 28(3)
Digest (2nd reissue) 418–424, 3549–3575.

For the Children Act 1989, ss 1, 31, see 6 Halsbury's Statutes (4th edn) (1992
reissue) 392, 431.

For the Civil Evidence Act 1972 , s 3, see 17 Halsbury's Statutes (4th edn) (1993
reissue) 201.   *e*

Cases referred to in judgment

B (child sexual abuse: standard of proof), Re [1995] 1 FLR 904.
DPP v A & BC Chewing Gum Ltd [1967] 2 All ER 504, [1968] 1 QB 159, [1967] 3 WLR
493, DC.   *f*
F S (minors), Re [1996] 1 FCR 666, CA.
G v G [1985] 2 All ER 225, [1985] 1 WLR 647, HL.
H and ors (minors) (sexual abuse: standard of proof), Re [1996] 1 All ER 1, [1996] AC
563, [1996] 2 WLR 8, HL.
K (minors) (alleged sexual abuse: evidence), Re [1996] 2 FCR 425.
Liddell v Middleton (1995) Times, 17 July, [1995] CA Transcript 875.   *g*
Lowery v R [1973] 3 All ER 662, [1974] AC 85, [1973] 3 WLR 235, PC.
N (residence: hopeless appeals), Re [1995] 2 FLR 230, CA.
N (a minor) (sexual abuse: video evidence), Re [1996] 4 All ER 225, CA.
R v Silcott, R v Braithwaite, R v Raghip (1991) Times, 9 December, CA.
R v Stockwell (1993) 97 Cr App R 260, CA.   *h*
S and B (minors) (child abuse: evidence), Re [1990] 2 FLR 489, CA.

Appeal

By notice dated 14 March 1996 Surrey County Council appealed with leave from
the decision of Connell J on 7 March 1996 whereby he refused to make full care   *j*
orders in respect of four children but made interim care orders on the basis of
emotional abuse and neglect, finding that allegations that the children had been
sexually abused by the respondents, the mother of the children and her partner,
were not proved. The facts are set out in the judgment of the court.

c   Section 3 is set out at p 250 *g* to *j*, post.

a   *Clive Newton* (instructed by *J H Jessup*, Kingston upon Thames) for the local authority.
Alison Ball QC and *David Turner* (instructed by *Ratip Partnership*, Southall and Darlington & Parkinson, Ealing) for the respondents.
Andrew McFarlane (instructed by *Sheridan & Co*, Kingston upon Thames) for the guardian ad litem.

b   *Cur adv vult*

21 May 1996. The following judgment of the court was delivered.

BUTLER-SLOSS LJ. This appeal by the Surrey County Council, the local
c   authority, supported by the guardian ad litem, is from the refusal of Connell J on
7 March 1996 after a 15-day hearing to make full care orders in respect of four
children. The judge made interim care orders based upon emotional abuse and
neglect but found that allegations of sexual abuse were not proved. He adjourned
the case for three months to consider whether to return the four children to their
mother and her partner, Mr R, who are respondents to the appeal.
d

HISTORY
The children are P (born 16 February 1986, now ten), D (born 7 February 1987),
both apparently the children of Mr M, although there is some doubt as to P's
paternity, E (born 3 July 1993, aged two) and A (born 21 July 1994, aged one), the
children of Mr R. The mother of all four children is A. The father of P and D has
e   played no part in these proceedings.
The mother has two elder children, E (born on 27 April 1982, just 14) and R
(born on 21 August 1983, who is 12). The father of E and R is Mr S, who met the
mother in 1980 when she was 18. They lived together until August 1984 when Mr
S was sentenced to a short term of imprisonment for burglary and perverting the
f   course of justice. On his release from prison he was unable to find the mother and
his children, who had moved to council accommodation in Woolwich. In 1985
the mother met Mr M and they lived together until November 1991, when they
separated. The mother began a relationship with Mr R, which is still continuing.
The M and S children lived with them.
Education welfare officers investigated a number of justified complaints about
g   the physical care of the children. In 1992 E and R started to stay at weekends with
their father, who was living with T. In March 1993 they ran away from home to
their father and have since lived principally with him. He and T experienced
considerable difficulties in caring for them and sought the help of social workers.
In November 1993 E returned to her mother but in January 1994 there was a fire
h   in the mother's flat. The mother has alleged that E's father was responsible for the
fire. Mr M continued to have problems in the care of R, who has displayed very
disturbed behaviour, and he has been placed in a children's home from time to
time where he remains at present.

ALLEGATIONS OF SEXUAL ABUSE
j   The proceedings the subject of these appeals were started by a complaint by R
to T that he had been sexually abused by his mother. His father was told and
informed the police. There were then a series of video recorded interviews of both
children. On 15 February 1994 R was interviewed by a woman police officer in the
presence of a social worker. He alleged abuse by his mother and a Mr W. He
alleged that his mother touched him and that Mr W touched him, E and D. He
also described the conditions in which he lived with his mother as 'terrible', being

dirty and smelly and that he was the victim of excessive punishment by Mr R. He
said of his mother that: 'I'm still upset with her, I've got a lot of anger with her.'   a
  On 22 February 1994 E was similarly interviewed. She complained about the
state of her mother's house but made no complaints of abuse. She then returned
to live with her father. The mother was arrested on 23 February and released on
bail, but the police did not pursue their investigations.
  In April 1995 E and then R spoke to T about further abuse. Both children were   b
again interviewed by the police. In her interview E, for the first time, made
allegations of indecent touching by her mother of herself, D, P and R. In his
interview, R described abuse by his mother and anal penetration by Mr R and Mr
W of himself, E, P and D. The mother, Mr R and Mr W were arrested and held in
custody. They denied all the allegations. The mother was charged with two
offences of indecent assault and Mr R and Mr W each with two offences of   c
buggery, but all the proceedings were subsequently discontinued. The four
younger children were placed with two sets of foster parents with whom they
remain.

MEDICAL EVIDENCE
  All six children have been examined for any relevant physical signs which might   d
be consistent with the allegations of serious sexual abuse. The examinations of E,
R, E and A showed no physical signs. On 23 May 1995 P was examined jointly by
Dr Lauder and Dr Holden, who observed a wedge-shaped healed tear at the 9
o'clock position in the external anal sphincter. The fissure was not recent and had
occurred between three months and eighteen months previously. D was   e
examined by the same two doctors on the same day and was found to have three
healed fissures in the external anal sphincter. Upon general examination she was
seen to be constipated or, more accurately, faecally loaded. Neither child had any
other signs of bruising or recent injury. Dr Lauder and Dr Hamner gave evidence
at the hearing.
                                                                                         f
INTERVIEWS
  R has had four video recorded interviews, E three, P four, D three, and P and D
a joint interview. In contrast to the detailed allegations of R and E implicating the
mother, Mr R and Mr W, neither P nor D has made any allegation of sexual abuse
against any of the adults. In addition to women police officers and social workers,   g
two consultant child psychiatrists have taken part in some of the interviews. Dr
Baker interviewed both P and D with Dr Heller watching the interviews. Dr
Heller interviewed R in January 1996. In addition, two further consultant child
psychiatrists have been involved, Dr Briscoe, who read the papers and saw the
video recordings, and Dr Hodes, who at one time had both R and briefly E as his
patients. Dr Baker, Dr Heller and Dr Hodes gave evidence at the hearing and Dr   h
Briscoe's report was before the judge.

JUDGMENT
  The judge gave a lengthy and careful judgment. He set out the salient features
of the interviews with the four children and the allegations made, which was, as   j
he pointed out, the foundation of the local authority's case. He considered how
they came to make the allegations to T. He found:

    'R is known to be untruthful and to be capable of carrying out extended
    deceptions. For example, he managed to continue his life under an assumed
    identity for at least a month in August 1995. He is also a very disturbed child.
    Further, as his statements in interview make clear, he is very angry towards

a the adults and in particular towards his mother. He believes that she failed properly to look after him and he is jealous of what he sees as her preference for Mr R. Rather less is known about E, although she too alleges ill treatment—sexual abuse apart—at the hands of her mother and Mr R. This might give her a motive for invention. In short, it is a matter of great concern that these two children should have made such specific and serious allegations b of sexual abuse at the hands of these adults but, if the case depended upon their evidence alone, which is hearsay evidence as previously indicated, it would not in my judgment be sufficient to prove these serious allegations against these adults to the requisite standard.'

He then turned to consider the other evidence in the case. He concluded that the c medical evidence was—

'consistent either with sexual use of these children or, alternatively, with constipation. The findings in respect of D are noteworthy but they do not eliminate the possibility of constipation.'

d He looked at the circumstantial evidence about R and E, the manifestations of unhappiness at home and the treatment of them by the mother and Mr R. He set out in some detail the psychiatric evidence about the interviews, the concerns of the psychiatrists, the significance attached by them to answers given by each of the children and their expert opinion that these children have been the subjects of sexual abuse at the hands of their mother, Mr R and Mr W. He saw all the video e recordings. He set out the explanations from the mother and Mr R, both of whose evidence he found in many ways to be unsatisfactory.

In coming to his final conclusion about the allegations of sexual abuse, he carefully reminded himself that the balance of the psychiatric evidence was unanimously to the effect that sexual abuse had probably occurred and he said: f 'Given the expertise of those expressing this view, in my judgment this is an important aspect of the evidence.' He then considered pointers to the contrary and concluded:

'In all the circumstances, therefore, I am not satisfied on the balance of probabilities that these serious allegations of sexual abuse are proved against g these adults, contrary to the submission made by Mr Newton on behalf of the local authority, that there is no sensible explanation existing for the children making up these serious allegations. I conclude that there is a reasonable alternative on the evidence that I have heard which is just as likely to be correct as the possibility of sexual abuse.'

h He set out his alternative proposition and added:

'It is implicit in what I have said that I likewise conclude that there is a real possibility that such abuse did occur, but in the light of the majority decision of the House of Lords in *Re H and ors (minors) (sexual abuse: standard of proof)* j [1996] 1 All ER 1, [1996] AC 563, such a possibility cannot justify a conclusion that the threshold criteria are satisfied.'

The judge then made findings that R, E, D and P had suffered emotional abuse at the hands of the mother and Mr R and that D, P, E and A were likely to suffer significant harm in the future and he found the threshold criteria in s 31 of the Children Act 1989 were met. There is no appeal by the mother and Mr R against the findings of emotional abuse.

ISSUES ON APPEAL

On the appeal Mr Newton for the local authority, supported by Mr McFarlane *a* for the guardian ad litem, has raised two main issues: (1) that the judge was plainly wrong not to find the allegations of serious sexual abuse proved on the balance of probabilities; and (2) that the judge, having found that there was a real possibility that such abuse had occurred, erred in law in not taking into account the allegations of sexual abuse in his assessment of the welfare of the children at the *b* discretionary stage.

Mr Newton also raised in his skeleton argument, but did not pursue in oral argument, the question whether the judge correctly directed himself on his approach to the expert psychiatric evidence.

(1) *Evidence of sexual abuse*   *c*

Both the skeleton arguments of Mr Newton and Mr McFarlane set out in great detail an analysis of the judgment and the judge's approach to the volume of evidence over the fifteen-day hearing. Mr Newton asked us to find that the judge had failed properly to examine all the pieces of evidence or to put them together to form an overall picture which clearly portrayed abuse. He submitted that if a *d* proper approach had been adopted, a finding of serious sexual abuse perpetrated by the mother and Mr R would have been inevitable. He further submitted that the Court of Appeal should set aside the judge's findings in respect of the allegations and make our own findings of sexual abuse. On the basis of such findings we should ourselves make full care orders in respect of the four younger children. *e*

The main evidence to which our attention was directed was the paediatric and psychiatric evidence. There was one element only in the medical evidence, the presence of three healed fissures found in D's external anal sphincter. The paediatric experts considered that the fissures were noteworthy and raised concern but were not diagnostic of abuse. Mr Newton criticised the judge for failing to give sufficient weight to the expert opinion as to the reasons for these *f* injuries and the absence of evidence of constipation as an alternative possibility for the injuries.

Mr Newton has criticised the judge for his failure to give proper weight to or take sufficient account of a number of factors that the three child psychiatrists considered pointed to the truth of the allegations of sexual abuse. He dissected the *g* judgment to show, as an example, that the judge may have in one place slightly underestimated the degree of concern expressed by Dr Heller. We have also been asked to find that the alternative explanations of the facts suggested by the judge are implausible and far-fetched and that the judge ought not to have relied upon them. *h*

Mr Newton has sought to demonstrate a sufficient number of errors of detail so as to attempt to cast doubt upon the conclusions of the judge. Whatever might be the success of this approach in other cases, and in our view it would only be in the rarest case that it would succeed, Mr Newton has singularly failed to do so in this case.

The judgment, which was reserved only for twenty four hours, is a model of *j* clarity and cohesion. The facts were set out clearly; the judge correctly directed himself as to his approach to the factual disputes, which he carefully explored. He looked at alternative explanations; he most carefully took into account the expert evidence; he made clear findings of fact and gave reasons for the conclusions which he reached. He was not satisfied upon the evidence that the sexual abuse was proved. He was, to the surprise of the local authority, satisfied that there had a been a much more serious degree of emotional abuse than the local authority perceived, sufficient to meet the threshold criteria for a care order. It was an extremely worrying and anxious case, which left the judge, as it must leave any court which has studied the evidence, with feelings of suspicion and concern for these children. That residual suspicion should not, and did not in this case, obscure the duty of the judge, and the judge alone, to make up his mind on the facts and come to a decision.

b Once the judge has made a decision in a child case, it is not for the Court of Appeal to second-guess the judge, to trawl through the evidence on paper, to consider whether the judge has given sufficient weight to one matter or too great weight to another matter, nor to allow minor discrepancies to provide the opportunity for a rehearing of the facts and a fresh exercise of discretion. That is c properly the function of the trial judge, who has been immersed in the case and has that unique opportunity, denied to the appellate court, of seeing and hearing the witnesses and gaining the feel of the case. It is the function of the appellate court to make sure that the judge has correctly directed himself to and applied the relevant law, has properly approached his task in deciding disputed facts and has not erred in principle. The appellate court then has to stand back and consider d whether his decision is plainly wrong. If he is not, it is not for the appellate court to intervene.

Lord Fraser of Tullybelton, in G v G [1985] 2 All ER 225 at 228, [1985] 1 WLR 647 at 652 said:

e   '... in cases dealing with the custody of children, the desirability of putting an end to litigation ... is particularly strong because the longer legal proceedings last, the more are the children, whose welfare is at stake, likely to be disturbed by the uncertainty.'

In the present case there is further litigation over these children, but it is equally f appropriate to bring to an end an arid area of dispute which may distract those engaged in important assessments of the future of these children from concentrating on the relevant issues.

Subject to the second part of the appeal, which raises an issue of law and in respect of which leave was rightly granted, the issues raised on the first part of this appeal are unappealable and without any prospect of success. On several g occasions in the last year or so, such as in Re N (residence: hopeless appeals) [1995] 2 FLR 230, this court has expressed a view about the bringing of hopeless appeals in an effort to discourage continuation of litigation over children which has no prospect of success. The new requirement for leave acts as an useful filter, but we strongly urge those advising litigants, whether individuals or local authorities, to h hesitate before seeking to set aside the trial judge's assessment of these serious issues raised in child applications.

(2) Future risk
We now turn to consider the question of law that has arisen on this appeal.

Where a court is faced with an application for a care order under s 31 of the 1989 j Act it must first consider whether the requirements of that section are met. If they are, then the court is given a discretion as to what to do, but in exercising that discretion the court must act in accordance with s 1 of the Act. These two stages have conveniently been described as, respectively, the threshold stage and the welfare stage.

The decision of the House of Lords in Re H and ors (minors) (sexual abuse: standard of proof) [1996] 1 All ER 1, [1996] AC 563 provides clear guidance on the

threshold stage. The appeal was concerned with the need (under s 31(2)(a)) for the
court to be satisfied that the child is suffering significant harm or is likely to do so.   *a*
The House of Lords held that in either case the standard of proof required was the
ordinary civil standard of the preponderance of probability, and that the word
'likely' meant a real possibility. The question then arose as to what was required
to establish such a real possibility. The primary case made by the local authority
was that a Mr R had sexually abused one child and that it therefore was likely that   *b*
he would abuse the other children unless they were taken into care.

The judge held that the allegation of sexual abuse by Mr R had not been made
out, though he expressed himself as more than a little suspicious that Mr R had
abused the child and would have been prepared to hold that there was a real
possibility that such abuse had occurred. The local authority submitted that
although it had not established that Mr R had abused the one child, the real   *c*
possibility that he had done so was sufficient to satisfy the court that the other
children were likely to suffer significant harm through sexual abuse by Mr R

By a majority the House of Lords rejected this submission on the grounds that
the court must base its conclusion on facts, not on judicial or other suspicions or
doubts. There was only a risk to the children if Mr R had in fact abused the other   *d*
child. In the absence of proof of that fact on the preponderance of probabilities,
there was nothing to suggest that the other children were at risk of harm. As Lord
Nicholls said ([1996] 1 All ER 1 at 22, [1996] AC 563 at 592):

> 'To decide that the others are at risk because there is a *possibility* that D1 was
> abused would be to base the decision, not on fact, but on suspicion: the   *e*
> suspicion that D1 *may* have been abused.' (Lord Nicholls' emphasis.)

In the case before us Mr Newton submitted that the House of Lords were
concerned only with the threshold stage and that the majority view had no
relevance to the welfare stage. So far as the latter stage was concerned, he
submitted that since the judge in the present case was also clearly of the view that   *f*
there was a real possibility that the children had been sexually abused, this was
sufficient to establish that the children were at risk of suffering like harm in the
future. Since a risk of harm is included in the welfare checklist set out in s 1(3) of
the 1989 Act, the judge was wrong to exclude it from consideration. Mr Newton
submitted that the justification for approaching s 1 in a way rejected by the House   *g*
of Lords for s 31 was that under s 1 the welfare of the child was the paramount
consideration, which justified and indeed required the court to act on possibilities
rather than proof on the preponderance of probability. These submissions were
supported by Mr McFarlane.

In our judgment these submissions cannot be supported. They amount to the   *h*
assertion that under s 1 the welfare of the child dictates that the court should act
on suspicion or doubts, rather than facts. To our minds the welfare of the child
dictates the exact opposite.

Section 1(3) requires a court, when considering whether, among other things,
to make an order under s 31, to have regard in particular to a number of matters.   *j*
The subsection then sets out those matters in the welfare checklist. Item (e) of this
list is: 'any harm which [the child] has suffered or is at risk of suffering'. If there is
a dispute as to whether the child has suffered or is at risk of suffering harm, the task
of the judge, when considering whether to make any order, whether it be a care
or supervision order under s 31 or a s 8 order (residence, contact and other orders
with respect to children), must be to resolve that dispute. Unless this is done, it
will remain in doubt whether or not the child has suffered harm or is at risk of

a suffering harm and thus it will remain in doubt whether or not there exist factors which Parliament expressly considered to be of particular importance to be taken into account. The question is how such a dispute is to be resolved.

To our minds there can be only one answer to this question, namely the same answer as that given by the majority in *Re H.* The court must reach a conclusion based on facts, not on suspicion or mere doubts. If, as in the present case, the court

b concludes that the evidence is insufficient to prove sexual abuse in the past, and if the fact of sexual abuse in the past is the only basis for asserting a risk of sexual abuse in the future, then it follows that there is nothing (except suspicion or mere doubts) to show a risk of future sexual abuse.

Mr Newton submitted that this is not so. His point was that if there is a real possibility of harm in the past, then it must follow (if nothing is done) that there is

c a risk of harm in the future. To our minds, however, this proposition contains a non sequitur. The fact that there might have been harm in the past does not establish the risk of harm in the future. The very highest it can be put is that what might possibly have happened in the past means that there may possibly be a risk of the same thing happening in the future. Section 1(3)(e), however, does not deal

d with what *might* possibly have happened or what future risk there *may* possibly be. It speaks in terms of what *has* happened or what *is* at risk of happening. Thus, what the court must do (when the matter is in issue) is to decide whether the evidence establishes harm or the risk of harm.

We cannot see any justification for the suggestion that the standard of proof in performing this task should be less than the preponderance of probabilities. Were

e such a suggestion to be adopted, it would mean in effect that instead of acting on what was established as probably the case, the court would have to act on what was only possibly the case, or even on the basis of what was probably not the case. This, as Lord Nicholls pointed out in *Re H,* is the same as saying that the court should act on the basis of suspicion rather than on the basis of fact.

f Such a proposition has, to our minds, only to be stated to be rejected. The same applies to the suggestion that the paramountcy of the welfare of the child requires such a method of proceeding, for this equally entails the proposition that the future of the child should be decided on the basis of suspicion rather than fact. We can find nothing in the 1989 Act which begins to suggest that Parliament intended that all-important decisions as to the future of a child should be made on such a

g basis, which to our minds would be a recipe for making decisions which were not in the best interests of the child.

Mr Newton suggested that it is inappropriate in the context of s 1 and the welfare principle to apply the ordinary rule in civil proceedings that something which is established on the preponderance of probabilities should be treated as

h certain, while something which is not so established should be treated as not having happened at all. We disagree, for this really amounts to no more than saying that the court may get it wrong in deciding whether or not a fact exists. Courts do indeed on occasion get it wrong, but this is because of the fallibility of human institutions. Such fallibility cannot be cured by adopting the test Mr Newton propounds, for the scope for going wrong would be broadened, not

j narrowed, were the court to proceed not on the basis of proven facts, but on the basis of suspicion.

Mr Newton sought to draw support for his submission from a number of cases in wardship proceedings before the 1989 Act came into effect, where he submitted that the courts had accepted the validity of his approach. We are not convinced by these submissions. In the cases cited there is to our minds no detailed analysis of the question. More importantly, the cases were not concerned with s 1 of the

1989 Act, which is part of a new code for children and which (as Lord Nicholls observed at the end of his speech in Re H [1996] 1 All ER 1 at 22–23, [1996] AC 563 *a* at 592–593) is to be approached and interpreted accordingly.

Finally, we find support for our analysis of the position from the odd results which would follow were Mr Newton's submissions to be accepted.

Firstly, it would be extraordinary if Parliament intended that evidence which is insufficient to establish that a child is likely to suffer significant harm for the *b* purposes of s 31, should nevertheless be treated as sufficient to establish that a child is at risk of suffering harm for the purposes of s 1. Were this so, then as Miss Ball QC (on behalf the mother and Mr R) submitted, the result would be that where a case was proved, sufficient to surmount the threshold stage and remove the child, but the concerns were capable of resolution and the children returned home, the court could make a care order permanently removing the child from its *c* home on the basis of allegations which were not proven for the purposes of s 31; whereas in the absence of the other concerns, the court could not make any order at all. We agree with Miss Ball that this would produce a random result which could not have been intended by Parliament.

Secondly, it is clear from the speech of Lord Nicholls in Re H [1996] 1 All ER 1 *d* at 22, [1996] AC 563 at 592 that s 31 provides, among other things, protection for parents. He said:

'They are not to be at risk of having their child taken from them and removed into the care of the local authority on the basis only of suspicions, whether of the judge or of the local authority or anyone else.' *e*

That protection would be entirely removed in circumstances similar to those of the present case, if, on reaching the second stage for reasons which might well not justify permanently removing the children, the court could act on the basis of such suspicions to make an order for permanent removal which would not be justified *f* on the matters that had been properly proved.

Thirdly, the submission, if adopted, would be to create a fundamental difference between public and private law cases; for whereas the local authority would have to surmount the threshold stage by proving matters on a preponderance of probabilities, one parent seeking, for example, permanently to exclude the other parent from any relationship, such as contact, with the child, *g* would only have to establish possibilities rather than probabilities. Again, we can find nothing in the Act which suggests that Parliament intended that this was to be the position nor any good reason why it should have done so.

In conclusion, we should emphasise, just as Lord Nicholls did in Re H, that what the evidence is required to establish depends upon the issue the court has to *h* decide. Thus, where (under Pt V of the 1989 Act) a local authority are under a duty to investigate where they have 'reasonable cause to suspect' that a child is suffering or likely to suffer harm, the court has to be satisfied that the applicant does have such reasonable cause, not that the child is actually suffering or likely to suffer harm.

In the present case, however, the question is the latter, not the former, and for *j* the reasons we have given, the court can only have regard to any harm that the child has suffered or is at risk of suffering if satisfied on the balance of probabilities that such harm or risk of harm in fact exists. In our view risk of harm means the real possibility of future harm. Lord Nicholls said ([1996] 1 All ER 1 at 21–22, [1996] AC 563 at 592–593):

a
'It is, of course, open to a court to conclude there is a real possibility that the child will suffer harm in the future although harm in the past has not been established. There will be cases where, although the alleged maltreatment itself is not proved, the evidence does establish a combination of profoundly worrying features affecting the care of the child within the family. In such cases it would be open to a court in appropriate circumstances to find that,

b
although not satisfied that the child is yet suffering significant harm, *on the basis of such facts as are proved* there is a likelihood that he will do so in the future.' (Lord Nicholls' emphasis.)

That passage sets out, in our view, the correct approach to the question how to assess any harm the child is at risk of suffering in s 1(3)(e) of the welfare test.

c
(3) *Expert evidence*
Many, if not all, family law cases involving children feature expert opinion evidence. Recently the proper limits of such evidence have been the subject of a number of decisions. A conflict exists between obiter dicta of this court in *Re S and B (minors) (child abuse: evidence)* [1990] 2 FLR 489 (since followed—also obiter—by

d
two other Court of Appeal decisions) and the Civil Evidence Act 1972, which was not cited to the court in any of those three decisions. This conflict has been and is the source of much unnecessary forensic activity, and should be resolved. The point in question was taken in this appeal, though not persisted in. We think it right to express our views on this point in an attempt to resolve the conflict.

e
In cases involving children, expert medical and psychiatric evidence from paediatricians and allied disciplines is often quite indispensable to the court. As Lord Parker CJ said in *DPP v A & BC Chewing Gum Ltd* [1967] 2 All ER 504 at 506, [1968] 1 QB 159 at 165, when dealing with children, the court needs 'all the help [it] can get'. But that dependence in no way compromises the fact that the final decision in the case is the judge's and his alone.

f
In cases involving suspected child abuse, the expert evidence may relate to the presence and interpretation of physical signs. But it may also relate to the more problematic area of the presence and interpretation of mental, behavioural and emotional signs. That evidence often necessarily includes, if not a conclusion, at least strong pointers as to the witness's view of the likely veracity of the child (ie credibility): indeed, his diagnosis and the action taken by the local authority may

g
depend on the conclusion reached. The evidence also frequently includes a conclusion as to whether or not the child has been abused. At one time it was thought that an expert witness could not give evidence of his opinion on an issue in the case, especially not when it was the ultimate issue, determinative of the case. To give such evidence was said to 'usurp the function of the jury', a reason

h
Wigmore was particularly scornful of, condemning it as 'empty rhetoric' (see *Wigmore on Evidence*, (3rd edn, 1940) vol 7, para 1921). First, the witness is not attempting to 'usurp' the judge or jury's function—at worst he is simply offering as evidence that which is not, and second he could not usurp it if he would, because no power could compel the judge or jury to accept it, and they know the

j
decision is theirs.
Wigmore was equally dismissive of the dicta that opinion evidence on the ultimate issue was inadmissible:

'The fallacy of this doctrine is, of course, that it is both too narrow and too broad, measured by the principle. It is too broad because, even when the very point in issue is to be spoken of, the jury should have help if it is needed. It is too narrow, because opinion may be inadmissible even when it deals with

something other than the point in issue. Furthermore, the rule if carried out
strictly and invariably would exclude the most necessary testimony. When all   a
is said, it remains simply one of those impracticable and misconceived
utterances which lack any justification in principle.'

The Law Reform Committee was asked to consider this question. A strong
committee was set up. Its members included those who were or subsequently   b
achieved the following offices: two Lords of Appeal, five members of the Court of
Appeal, a Vice-Chancellor and Professors Guest and Heuston. That Committee
made the following recommendations (see Law Reform Committee Report No 17
(1970) Cmnd 4489):

'63. Although expert witnesses have for long been allowed to express their   c
opinions on matters in issue (e g as to value, cause of death, etc) the rule which
we discussed in paragraph 4 prohibiting a witness from expressing his opinion
on the ultimate issue for decision in the case applies to expert witnesses as well
as witnesses of fact. Where the issue is whether a person holding himself out
as possessing reasonable skill and competence in some specialised field did act
with reasonable skill and competence, the opinion of an expert in that field as   d
to whether that person did so or not is a useful aid to the judge who has to
decide the issue. We think that the rule has even less justification in the case
of expert witnesses than in the case of witnesses of fact and we see no reason
why an expert witness should not be asked the direct question as to his
opinion on an issue in the action which lies within the field of his expertise.   e
The rule which excludes this evidence is frequently ignored in practice even
in criminal proceedings. [The Committee quotes a passage from Lord Parker
CJ in *DPP v A & BC Chewing Gum Ltd* [1967] 2 All ER 504 at 505, [1968] 1 QB
159 at 164.] We accordingly recommend that a statement by an expert
witness, whether given orally in the witness-box or in writing in a report, shall
not be inadmissible upon the ground *only* that it expresses his opinion on the   f
issue in the proceedings, and that a question put to him to elicit his opinion
on such issue, if it lies within the field of his expertise, should be permissible.'
(Our emphasis.)

That recommendation led directly to the Civil Evidence Act 1972. Relevant for
our purposes is s 3:   g

'3. *Admissibility of expert opinion and certain expressions of non-expert
opinion.*—(1) Subject to any rules of court made in pursuance of Part I of the
Civil Evidence Act 1968 or this Act, where a person is called as a witness in any
civil proceedings, his opinion on any relevant matter on which he is qualified   h
to give expert evidence shall be admissible in evidence.

(2) It is hereby declared that where a person is called as a witness in any civil
proceedings, a statement of opinion by him on any relevant matter on which
he is not qualified to give expert evidence, if made as a way of conveying
relevant facts personally perceived by him, is admissible as evidence of what
he perceived.   j

(3) In this section "relevant matter" includes an issue in the proceedings in
question.'

So it is right to say (as the textbooks do) that the ultimate issue rule has been
abandoned (unmourned by the ghost of Wigmore and the editor of *Cross and
Tapper on Evidence* (8th edn, 1995) p 552).

a   The Criminal Law Revision Committee [eleventh report (1972) Cmnd 4991] also recommended abrogating the rule. While this has not happened, evidence that would technically offend it is frequently admitted in criminal courts.

Lord Taylor CJ said in *R v Stockwell* (1993) 97 Cr App R 260 at 265:

b
'The rationale behind the supposed prohibition [on the ultimate issue question] is that the expert should not usurp the functions of the jury. But since counsel can bring the witness so close to opining on the ultimate issue that the inference as to his view is obvious, the rule can only be ... a matter of form rather than substance.'

That is why we find the suggestion (to be found in the authorities) that it is prejudicial for a judge to hear such evidence difficult to justify.

c   And even in criminal cases, where the evidence is relevant, expert opinion evidence on the ultimate issue has for a long time been received even before juries. Thus, Lord Parker CJ said in *DPP v A & BC Chewing Gum Ltd* [1967] 2 All ER 504 at 506, [1968] 1 QB 159 at 164:

d
'I myself would go a little further, in that I cannot help feeling that, with the advance of science, more and more inroads have been made into the old common law principles. Those who practise in the criminal courts see every day cases of experts being called on the question of diminished responsibility, and, although technically the final question "Do you think he was suffering from diminished responsibility?" is strictly inadmissible, it is allowed time and

e
time again without objection. No doubt when dealing with the effect of certain things on the mind science may still be less exact than evidence as to what effect some particular thing will have on the body, but that, as it seems to me, is purely a question of weight.'

f   And the criminal law also recognises that such opinion evidence may be relevant, even in questions of credibility, an example of such 'scientific inroads'. This is shown not only by the exceptional case of *Lowery v R* [1973] 3 All ER 662, [1974] AC 85, but by a line of cases dealing with the expert evidence of psychologists on the reliability of confessions made by those on or below the borderline of mental handicap (see *R v Silcott, R v Braithwaite, R v Raghip* (1991) Times, 9 December).

g   This is now an accepted area for expertise. Ten years before such evidence would have been rejected. But now—

'it is possible to discern a more indulgent attitude [to the reception of expert evidence as to the defendant's mental state] in the Court of Appeal (and in the practice of judges in the Crown Court) in recent years'. (See *Archbold*

h   *Criminal Pleading Evidence and Practice* (1995) vol 1, para 4–339 and see the cases there cited.)

Against that background it is not surprising that family law judges have received (without, it would seem, objection, demur, embarrassment, or prejudice) expert opinion evidence, including evidence as to the accuracy or truthfulness of child

j   complainants. Johnson J in *Re B (child sexual abuse: standard of proof)* [1995] 1 FLR 904, lists a few out of many possible examples where experienced family judges have admitted such evidence without question. While loyally following *Re S and B (minors) (child abuse: evidence)* [1990] 2 FLR 489, he wryly quotes Professor Spencer as commenting that the judgment of the court in that case had been given 'in a slightly conservative mood' (see [1995] 1 FLR 904 at 911–912). It would be curious if a non-adversarial trial before a judge to which the 1972 Act applied were

more restrictive as to the reception of expert evidence than a criminal trial before
a jury to which the Act did not apply.   a

But this practice was challenged by obiter dicta of this court in *Re S and B*.
There, wardship proceedings relating to child abuse were criticised as a result of
the complaints of A, who had been abused, who admitted abusing her own
children, and who had had psychiatric problems. The court accepted as an expert
the psychiatric social worker, Miss Tranter (experienced in dealing with, and   b
hearing accounts of abuse given by women who had themselves been abused and
had abused their own children) to whom these allegations had initially been made.
She believed that A was telling the truth, and said so in her report, which was
received without objection. But on appeal it was argued that her evidence that A
was telling the truth was inadmissible. But it seems that the court was never
referred to the 1972 Act.   c

The majority of the court (Glidewell and Stocker LJJ) found that Miss Tranter,
as an expert, could express her opinion on A's psychiatric state and her propensity
to fantasise, and could support those opinions by her opinion that A's account was
apparently credible, but—

> 'what ... was not admissible was any direct expression of opinion that A was   d
> telling the truth, and not telling malicious lies. The boundary between the
> two expressions of views is fine, but it does seem to me that Miss Tranter's
> evidence crossed that line ...' (See [1990] 2 FLR 489 at 498.)

But as the trial judge recognised that ultimately the question of credibility was for
him, it was clear that he did not rely on her expression of opinion, and so the   e
appeal failed.

In the analysis of the third member of the court, Sir Roualeyn Cumming-Bruce,
the distinction was even finer. His view was that A was Miss Tranter's patient. As
such, she had to form a view as to her veracity in deciding whether to act on or
reject her allegations. He said (at 502–503):   f

> 'I accept the submissions of Mr Cole as to the admissibility of their opinions
> as to A's veracity for the purposes of their assessments of A's veracity when
> they were forming a view of A as a patient and had to decide whether she was
> so unbalanced that her account of her experiences as victim of her mother,
> her stepfather, and her brother Mr B, ought to be rejected as the illusions of g
> an unbalanced mind. As this was a prominent part of the defendants' attack
> on her credibility their opinions as to A's veracity were relevant and the judge
> was right to admit those opinions. The opinions of Miss Tranter and Dr Little
> were thus relevant in the context of their testimony, but irrelevant and
> inadmissible on the issue of whether A's evidence should be rejected on the
> alternative ground propounded by the defendants to the effect that her   h
> accusations were not the illusions of a disordered mind but deliberate
> fabrications concocted out of malice and spite, motivated by an attempt to
> destroy the family relationships of other members of her extended family as a
> compensation for her sense of the loss of her own children.'

The only legal reason given by the court for finding Miss Tranter's opinions on A's j
veracity inadmissible for some (but not for all) purposes are that this was
ultimately a question for the court. But that objection would seem to be
insufficient after the passing of the 1972 Act, which makes clear (see p 12, para 63
of the Law Reform Committee Report) that the evidence cannot be held
inadmissible *only* on that ground. It seems to us that the obiter remarks were
made per incuriam.

Two further decisions of the Court of Appeal have followed that authority, *Re*
a *F S (minors)* [1996] 1 FCR 666 (with dicta as to 'usurping the function of the judge'),
and *Re N (a minor) (sexual abuse: video evidence)* [1996] 4 All ER 225. Unfortunately,
in neither of these cases was the court referred to the 1972 Act, and we do not
believe that those courts would have expressed themselves in the terms they did
had they been aware of that Act. Accordingly, we regard those obiter remarks also
b as having been made per incuriam.

Wall J in *Re K (minors) (alleged sexual abuse: evidence)* [1996] 2 FCR 425 rejected
the per incuriam submission that we have accepted above.

The submission rejected by him (made by Mr Cryan for the Official Solicitor)
was that the 'issue' in s 3(3) of the 1972 Act *can* be the ultimate issue, and *can*
include an issue of credibility.   As a matter of construction, both of those
c submissions seem to us to be plainly right. But that is not the end of the story. The
legal limitation imposed by the section is that the expert's opinion must be on a
matter on which he is qualified to give expert evidence. Thus a witness's evidence
as to the right answer on the ultimate issue will often be inadmissible because he
has no expertise on the final question, for example whether adult A's evidence
d should be preferred to adult B's. It would not (because of the Act) be inadmissible
because it went to the ultimate issue or usurped the judge's function. But it would
be inadmissible as not being relevant.   As we shall seek to demonstrate, the
practical limitations on the Act lie not in its wording, but first, in the over-arching
requirement of relevance, and second (more questionably) on the court's
discretion under s 5(3).

e   Wall J did not reach his decision by construing the 1972 Act himself. He relied
primarily on the Court of Appeal case of *Liddell v Middleton* (1995) Times, 17 July
and in particular Stuart-Smith LJ's statement that '[s 3 of the 1972 Act] in no way
extends the principle upon which expert evidence is admissible.' When that
sentence is read in context, it is clear that it does not bear the construction Wall J
f seeks to impose on it. The court was there dealing with a claim for personal
injuries arising from a traffic accident. In some traffic accidents there is scope for
expert evidence to assist the court. But this was not one of those cases: expert
evidence was 'entirely irrelevant and inadmissible'. The reason for that lay in the
fact that the primary evidence did not involve technical matters (such as length of
skid marks) that required expert interpretation, but simply the evaluation of
g eye-witness accounts, on which the so-called expert had nothing to contribute that
was outside the competence and experience of a layman. His evidence was
inadmissible because it was not relevant. Had the evidence been relevant (ie going
to a matter on which a layman would require instruction on the essentials of the
necessary field of expertise to make a properly informed decision), then s 3 makes
h clear that such evidence is admissible, whether or not it goes to an issue (or even
in appropriate circumstances the ultimate issue) in the litigation.

But while Wall J was wrong in his construction of s 3, we have no reason to
believe that he was wrong in holding the doctor's evidence on the credibility of
two women giving evidence of abuse of them when they were children dealt with
an issue that did not require his expertise. The evidence was inadmissible because
j irrelevant, and not because it went to the ultimate issue in the case. Thus the
requirement of relevance will usually lead to the same result as the old ultimate
issue rule, which as Wigmore suggested, is at once 'too narrow and too broad'.

So the passing of the Act should not operate to force the court to, in Wigmore's
words 'waste its time in listening to superfluous and cumbersome testimony',
provided that the judge never loses sight of the central truths: namely that the
ultimate decision is for him, and that all questions of relevance and weight are for

him. If the expert's opinion is clearly irrelevant, he will say so. But, if arguably relevant but in his view ultimately unhelpful, he can generally prevent its reception by indicating that the expert's answer to the question would carry little weight with him. The modern view is to regulate such matters by way of weight, rather than admissibility.

But when the judge is of the opinion that the witness's expertise is still required to assist him to answer the ultimate questions (including, where appropriate, credibility) then the judge can safely and gratefully rely on such evidence, while never losing sight of the fact that the final decision is for him.

In summary, there were four problems arising from the court's decision in Re S and B. (1) The fact that the 1972 Act was clearly relevant but not referred to. (2) The question under the ultimate issue rule was both too wide and too narrow, for the reasons given by Wigmore. (3) That the test there put forward led to impossibly fine distinctions. Ward LJ in Re N (a minor) (sexual abuse: video evidence) [1996] 4 All ER 225 at 233 recognised that:

'One cannot ... expect the subtleties of the law of evidence to be understood by the child psychiatrist and the child psychologist. Experience shows that the subtleties are not always understood by the legal practitioners.'

The law of evidence should not be subtle and difficult to understand. And fine distinctions should be only tolerated if both unavoidable and user-friendly—ie easy to make. (4) The state of the authorities meant that the finding that the expert's opinion on an issue that was ultimately for the court was inadmissible provided a fertile ground for appeal, on the basis that the evidence was in law admissible under the 1972 Act and consequently that in not admitting it the court had not given it any weight while it deserved some.

The result of those four problems is that what should be a simple matter of assessment of the weight of evidence for the trial judge has become a legal minefield. By way of illustration from this case, Connell J received evidence from three experts that in their opinion sexual abuse of the children had occurred. He disagreed with their conclusion, as he was entitled to do once he had taken their evidence into account (as he had). He said:

'In my judgment however it is a proper function of the expert to draw attention to the particular passages in the course of interviews which they believe are significant and relevant to the issues which fall for decision by the court.'

To that he need only have added that, having taken account of those matters, he derived little or no additional assistance from the experts' expressed conclusion that abuse probably had occurred, for the reasons he gave. But instead he was faced with a complicated task. First, he had to draw the fine line distinguishing this case from Re S and B. Second, he had to acknowledge the 1972 Act, saying that in the light of that he paid 'careful attention to those passages to which they referred'. But he was still appealed on the basis that (and we quote from the guardian's skeleton argument)—

'the learned judge erred in failing to regard as admissible evidence the conclusions of the expert witnesses which it is submitted were admissible by virtue of the Civil Evidence Act 1972, s 3(1) and (3). Whilst it must be accepted that the ultimate decision on the issue remained a matter for the learned judge, if he had regarded the expert's conclusions as admissible, given the even balance of evidence found by the judge on the other aspects of the *a* case, the learned judge must have inevitably found that the sexual abuse allegations were proved.' (Counsel's emphasis).

While that ground of appeal was not pressed before us, we regard the current state of the authorities as unsatisfactory, distracting, wasteful of court time at first instance, and unnecessarily productive of appeals. For those reasons, and as it seems that there was no authority from this court dealing with the 1972 Act in this

b context, we felt that it required our attention despite the fact that it was not argued before us.

Lastly, we consider s 5(3) of the 1972 Act:

> 'Nothing in this Act shall prejudice—(a) any power of a court, in any civil proceedings, to exclude evidence (whether by preventing questions from
>
> *c* being put or otherwise) at its discretion ...'

We take that subsection to assume that the court has a discretionary power to exclude admissible (ie relevant) evidence. But the statute does not define what that power is. *Phipson on Evidence* (14th edn, 1990) p 705 states that 'The courts

d have on occasions disclaimed any general discretion in civil cases to exclude evidence'. The editors then go on to deal with two limited exceptions not relevant to this appeal. While this is not the occasion to find that the court has such a power, still less to define it, in our judgment there plainly should be some such power in the court, particularly in the modern era of the interventionist judge, and a fortiori in non-adversarial proceedings such as these.

e We would draw attention to rr 102 and 403 of the American Federal Rules of Evidence. Rule 102 requires the trial judge, while securing fairness '... to eliminate unjustifiable expense and delay ... to the end that the truth may be ascertained and the proceedings justly determined.' Rule 403 provides:

> *f* 'Although relevant, evidence may be excluded if its probative value is substantially outweighed by the danger of unfair prejudice, confusion of the issue, or misleading the jury, or by considerations of undue delay, waste of time, or needless presentation of cumulative evidence.'

The introduction of such a rule into criminal law was recommended by the Royal Commission on Criminal Justice (Cmnd 2263 (1993), chairman Lord Runciman).

g We are clearly of opinion that the judge in proceedings such as these should have such a power. We express no opinion on whether he presently has it or not.

We dismiss the appeal.

Appeal dismissed.

h

Carolyn Toulmin   Barrister.

Tan Te Lam and others v Superintendent of Tai A Chau Detention Centre and another

PRIVY COUNCIL

LORD KEITH OF KINKEL, LORD BROWNE-WILKINSON, LORD MUSTILL, LORD STEYN AND SIR BRIAN HUTTON

30, 31 JANUARY, 1 FEBRUARY, 27 MARCH 1996

Immigration – Detention – Illegal entrant – Detention pending deportation – Unauthorised migrants from Vietnam detained in Hong Kong pending removal – Repatriation to Vietnam constituting sole means of removal – Vietnamese authorities not accepting repatriation of non-nationals – Whether statutory power of detention limited – Whether court having jurisdiction to determine reasonableness of duration of detention – Whether non-Vietnamese nationals being detained 'pending removal' – Immigration Ordinance (Hong Kong), s 13D.

The applicants, who were of Chinese ethnic origin, arrived in Hong Kong by boat as unauthorised migrants from Vietnam, and were detained by the Director of Immigration in detention centres under the powers contained in s 13D[a] of the Immigration Ordinance to detain migrants pending a decision whether to grant or refuse permission to remain in Hong Kong or, after a decision to refuse permission, 'pending ... removal'. In due course the applicants were refused permission to remain and were further detained for extended periods pending their removal from Hong Kong and repatriation to Vietnam. The applicants sought their release and applied for writs of habeas corpus against the superintendents of the detention centres where they were being detained. The judge ordered the release of the first three applicants, holding that while their periods of detention were reasonable, they were not lawfully detained pending removal, since the Vietnamese authorities operated a policy of refusing to accept the repatriation of those whom they regarded as non-nationals, which applied to the first three applicants, who could not therefore be removed to Vietnam. The judge, however, refused any relief to the fourth applicant, finding that he would be accepted as a Vietnamese national and removed from Hong Kong in the near future. On appeal, the Court of Appeal of Hong Kong held that the legality of the detentions fell to be determined solely by reference to the statutory power, that it was for the director and not the court to determine whether the duration of the detentions was reasonable or whether repatriation was possible, and that evidence from the director that attempts were on foot to effect repatriation was conclusive proof that the applicants were lawfully detained pending removal. The court accordingly allowed the appeals against the release of the first three applicants and dismissed the fourth applicant's appeal. The applicants appealed to the Privy Council.

Held – (1) Where a statute conferred power to detain an individual pending his removal from the country, in the absence of contrary indications in the statute, it was to be implied that that power could only be exercised during the period necessary, in all the circumstances of the particular case, to effect that removal,

---

a   Section 13D, so far as material, is set out at p 261 *b* to *f*, post

a that the person seeking to exercise the power of detention had to take all
reasonable steps within his power to ensure the removal within a reasonable time
and that, if it became clear that removal was not going to be possible within a
reasonable time, further detention was not authorised. The courts would
construe strictly any statutory provision purporting to allow the deprivation of
individual liberty by administrative detention and would be slow to hold that
b statutory provisions authorised administrative detention for unreasonable
periods or in unreasonable circumstances (see p 265 h j and p 266 a, post); *R v
Governor of Durham Prison, ex p Singh* [1984] 1 All ER 983 approved.

(2) The question whether the applicants could be repatriated to Vietnam and
were therefore being detained pending removal was prima facie a jurisdictional
question; if removal was not pending within s 13D of the Immigration
c Ordinance, the director had no power to detain at all. Accordingly, that question
was for the court to determine and it was for the director to prove to the court,
on the balance of probabilities, the facts necessary to justify the conclusion that
the applicants were being detained pending removal. Since no sufficient reason
had been shown for overturning the judge's finding that it was the policy of the
d Vietnamese government not to accept repatriation of non-Vietnamese nationals,
it followed that the first three applicants were not being detained pending their
removal and that the judge's decision to order their release was therefore correct.
However, the judge's finding that the fourth applicant would be removed from
Hong Kong in the near future had in the event been proved to be wrong and,
since it appeared that the Vietnamese government's policy of refusal was still
e being applied to him, it was right to order his release. The appeals would
accordingly be allowed (see p 266 j to p 267 a h, p 268 g and p 270 c e to h, post);
Khawaja v Secretary of State for the Home Dept [1983] 1 All ER 765 and *Bugdaycay v
Secretary of State for the Home Dept* [1987] 1 All ER 940 considered.

f **Notes**
For habeas corpus proceedings, see 37 *Halsbury's Laws* (4th edn) paras 584–590.
    For protection of fundamental rights and freedoms in United Kingdom
dependencies, see 6 *Halsbury's Laws* (4th edn reissue) paras 984–986.
    For legislative powers of United Kingdom dependencies, see ibid paras 1026–
1037.
g

Cases referred to in judgment
Associated Provincial Picture Houses Ltd v Wednesbury Corp [1947] 2 All ER 680,
    [1948] 1 KB 223, CA.
Bugdaycay v Secretary of State for the Home Dept [1987] 1 All ER 940, [1987] AC 514,
h   [1987] 2 WLR 606, HL.
Khawaja v Secretary of State for the Home Dept [1983] 1 All ER 765, [1984] AC 74,
    [1983] 2 WLR 321, HL.
Liew Kar-seng v Governor-in-Council [1989] 1 HKLR 607, Hong Kong HC.
Pham Van Ngo, Re [1991] 1 HKLR 499, Hong Kong HC.
j *R v Governor of Durham Prison, ex p Singh* [1984] 1 All ER 983, [1984] 1 WLR 704.

Appeals
The applicants, (1) Tan Te Lam, (2) Phung Hoan, (3) Ly Hue My and (4) Luu Tai
Phong appealed with leave from the decision of the Court of Appeal of Hong
Kong (Power, Litton V-PP and Mortimer JA) ([1995] 3 HKC 339) on 12 April 1995
(i) allowing the appeal of the first respondent, the Superintendent of Tai A Chau

Detention Centre, from the decision of Keith J (sub nom *Re Chung Tu Quan* [1995] 1 HKC 566) on 24 January 1995 whereby he granted orders of habeas corpus in *a* respect of the first three applicants and ordered their release from detention, and (ii) dismissing the appeal of the fourth applicant from the same judgment of Keith J on 24 January 1995 whereby he discharged a writ of habeas corpus directed to the second respondent, the Superintendent of High Island Detention Centre, in respect of the fourth applicant. The facts are set out in the judgment of the Board. *b*

Michael Beloff QC and *G J X McCoy* (of the English and Hong Kong Bars) (instructed by *Haldanes*) for the applicants.
David Pannick QC, William Marshall QC (of the English and Hong Kong Bars), *Roxana Cheng* (of the Hong Kong Bar) and *Java Herberg* (instructed by *Macfarlanes*) for the detention centre superintendents. *c*

The Board took time for consideration.

27 March 1996. The following judgment of the Board was delivered.

d

LORD BROWNE-WILKINSON. Since 1985 some 80,000 migrants from Vietnam have arrived by boat in Hong Kong (the Vietnamese boat people). This enormous influx has placed great strains, economic, human and legal, on the colony. It has had to seek a balance between the claims of the immigrants to humane treatment and the practicalities of handling such a multitude of *e* uninvited visitors. This appeal concerns four applicants, each of whom has been detained for years under statutory powers authorising such detention 'pending his removal from Hong Kong'. The Hong Kong government is, of course, anxious to remove the boat people from Hong Kong as soon as possible. But, in practice, the only country to which they can be removed is Vietnam and the delay in these applicants' removal is substantially due to the attitude adopted by the *f* Vietnamese authorities over whom the government of Hong Kong has no direct control. In particular, these applicants allege that the Vietnamese authorities have a policy of refusing to accept repatriation of those whom they regard as being non-Vietnamese nationals, including these four applicants. In these habeas corpus proceedings the applicants allege that, given the very long periods of *g* detention and the policy of Vietnam, their further detention is not authorised by the statutory powers and their detention is unlawful.

BACKGROUND
Before turning to the matters directly in issue, it is necessary to set out some of the background. The exceptionally comprehensive and lucid judgment of the *h* trial judge, Keith J (sub nom *Re Chung Tu Quan* [1995] 1 HKC 566), sets out the facts in full from which their Lordships derive the following comparatively short summary. The Vietnamese boat people started to arrive in Hong Kong after the fall of Saigon in 1975. The Hong Kong government originally adopted the policy of granting to the boat people first asylum in Hong Kong. But this was only done *j* on the basis that those granted asylum in Hong Kong would in due course be resettled elsewhere by the rest of the international community. Between 1975 and 1982 the boat people arriving in Hong Kong were not placed in detention pending their resettlement elsewhere in the world. This policy changed in 1982 when the Hong Kong government, whilst adhering to the policy of granting the migrants first asylum in Hong Kong, took, and exercised, power to detain all

a those arriving from Vietnam in closed centres pending resettlement elsewhere in the world.

By 1988 it had become clear that that policy was not working. Between 1984 and 1987 some 8,800 migrants arrived. In 1988 there were 18,328 arrivals; in 1989, 34,114. Due to what the judge called 'compassion fatigue' the rest of the world was not accepting the Vietnamese migrants for resettlement elsewhere at b anything like the rate that they were being granted first asylum in Hong Kong. In consequence, the policy of first asylum was abandoned. In consultation with the United Nations High Commission for Refugees (the UNHCR) a new policy was adopted which involved two stages. First, on arrival the migrant would be 'screened' to see if he qualified for refugee status in Hong Kong. Second, if he did not so qualify, he would be repatriated to Vietnam. The migrant was to be held c in a detention centre pending, first, the determination of whether he was entitled to refugee status in Hong Kong and, second, if not granted refugee status, for a further period pending his removal to Vietnam. Alongside this change of policy by the Hong Kong government, the UNHCR entered into an understanding with the government of Vietnam under which a voluntary repatriation scheme to be d run by the UNHCR was established. The government of Vietnam agreed to accept the repatriation of Vietnamese citizens who volunteered to be repatriated.

In November 1991 the government of Hong Kong established a scheme, the Orderly Repatriation Programme, for the compulsory repatriation to Vietnam of those migrants who had not qualified for refugee status in Hong Kong, but refused to volunteer for repatriation under the UNHCR voluntary scheme.

e The result of the implementation of these two schemes of repatriation, one voluntary, the other compulsory, was that the number of boat people detained in Hong Kong decreased from a peak of 65,000 in 1991, to approximately 23,000 in 1994. Their Lordships were told that today there are something over 20,000 migrants remaining in Hong Kong awaiting repatriation to Vietnam, the f overwhelming majority of whom have, according to the government, declined to apply for voluntary repatriation.

THE REPATRIATION SCHEMES

(1) *The voluntary scheme*

g In June 1989 the International Conference on Indo-Chinese Refugees, after noting that since 1975 over 2,000,000 people had left their countries of origin in the Indo-China area, adopted a comprehensive plan of action under which, amongst other things, migrants who volunteered were to be returned to and accepted by their countries of origin under a scheme to be administered by the UNHCR. The UNHCR and the government of Vietnam signed a memorandum h of understanding under which the general policy was to be implemented in relation to migrants from Vietnam. Under that scheme, a migrant wishing to volunteer for repatriation obtains from the UNHCR a form which includes a box in which he is required to state his nationality. This form, when completed, is forwarded by the UNHCR to the Vietnamese authorities for processing. If the j Vietnamese are prepared to accept the applicant for repatriation, they issue the necessary travel documents. The understanding provided that the processing by the Vietnamese authorities should be completed, and the UNHCR informed of their decision, within three months of the application being submitted. But the judge found that this timetable had not been adhered to by the Vietnamese authorities. If the Vietnamese authorities notify the UNHCR that the application is acceptable, the UNHCR is required to arrange for the repatriation to take place

within one month after such notification. By the end of 1995, some 45,228
migrants had been repatriated from Hong Kong to Vietnam under this voluntary   *a*
scheme.

Two points are to be stressed. First, the application form discloses the
nationality of the applicant. Second, the scheme is not run by the Hong Kong
government but by the UNHCR: the Hong Kong government has no direct
control over how it is run.   *b*

(2) *The compulsory scheme*

This scheme is organised by the Vietnamese Refugees Branch of the Hong
Kong government in conjunction with the Vietnamese authorities.   The
Vietnamese Refugees Branch periodically submits the particulars of proposed
returnees to the Vietnamese authorities for them to process.   The Vietnamese   *c*
Refugees Branch cannot submit the particulars of too many returnees at any one
time, for fear that the Vietnamese authorities (who have administrative
problems) will be swamped. The submission of particulars is therefore staggered.
None of the particulars submitted in 1994 had been processed by the Vietnamese
authorities by 14 December 1994.   The branch aimed to have submitted the   *d*
particulars of all proposed returnees by the end of 1995, which would have been
well ahead of the current capacity for the Vietnamese authorities to process. At
the time of the trial before the judge, particulars of about 12,000 proposed
returnees under the compulsory scheme had been submitted to the Vietnamese
authorities.   Of that number, about 5,500 had been processed and identified by   *e*
the Vietnamese authorities.

The particulars of proposed returnees under the compulsory scheme are
submitted to the Vietnamese authorities in a form agreed with the government
of Vietnam.   There is no specific box for recording a returnee's nationality.
However, the judge found that if a returnee is not a Vietnamese national, that is
likely to be picked up by the Vietnamese authorities in the processing exercise. *f*
That is because the form gives sufficient details to enable the Vietnamese
authorities to check his particulars against his local household registration or his
residential file, from which they are likely to glean the fact that he is a foreign
national or has a foreign resident's permit if that be the case.

Although the compulsory scheme has been in force since November 1991, by
the end of 1994 only about 1,175 migrants had been repatriated to Vietnam under   *g*
it. Their Lordships were told that in 1995 a further 864 were repatriated under
the compulsory scheme.

Three things are to be noted about the compulsory scheme.   First, the
documents forwarded to the Vietnamese authorities do not specify the
nationality of the migrant, but the checks made by the Vietnamese authorities are   *h*
likely to disclose his nationality as recorded in the files in Vietnam. Second, the
delay in compulsory repatriation is largely due to the inability of the Vietnamese
authorities to process the large numbers involved. Third, the number repatriated
under the compulsory scheme is very small when compared with those
repatriated under the voluntary scheme.   *j*

THE LEGISLATION

Since 1981 the immigration status of the Vietnamese boat people has been
regulated by a special legislative regime contained in Pt IIIA of the Immigration
Ordinance of Hong Kong. Although it is unnecessary in the present case to
determine whether the Vietnamese boat people are technically 'illegal

a immigrants', it is clear that at all times since the ending of the first asylum policy in 1988, a migrant arriving in Hong Kong has had no right to enter or stay there save to the extent that such right is recognised by Pt IIIA of the Ordinance.

The power to detain Vietnamese migrants is contained in s 13D of the Ordinance, the terms of which have been amended from time to time as the policies for the time being in force have changed. It is not necessary for the b purpose of this appeal to trace the development of s 13D, which was finally amended to its present form in 1991. It provides as follows:

'(1) As from 2 July 1982 any resident or former resident of Vietnam who—
(a) arrives in Hong Kong not holding a travel document which bears an unexpired visa issued by or on behalf of the Director; and (b) has not been c granted an exemption under section 61(2), may, whether or not he has requested permission to remain in Hong Kong, be detained under the authority of the Director in such detention centre as an immigration officer may specify pending a decision to grant or refuse him permission to remain in Hong Kong or, after a decision to refuse him such permission, pending his removal from Hong Kong ...

d (1A) The detention of a person under this section shall not be unlawful by reason of the period of the detention if that period is reasonable having regard to all the circumstances affecting that person's detention, including— (a) in the case of a person being detained pending a decision under section 13A(1) to grant or refuse him permission to remain in Hong Kong as a e refugee—(i) the number of persons being detained pending decisions under section 13A(1) whether to grant or refuse them such permission; and (ii) the manpower and financial resources allocated to carry out the work involved in making all such decisions; (b) in the case of a person being detained pending his removal from Hong Kong—(i) the extent to which it is possible to make arrangements to effect his removal; and (ii) whether or not the f person has declined arrangements made or proposed for his removal.'

It will be seen that the legislation contains two separate powers of detention: the first relates to the period during which the Vietnamese migrant is being 'screened' to determine whether he is to be given refugee status in Hong Kong; the second relates to the period between the refusal of refugee status and g repatriation to Vietnam. Each of the applicants in this case have been detained during both periods, but the present appeal turns on the legality of their continued detention only during the second period, i e 'pending his removal from Hong Kong'.

h THE APPLICANTS

Applicants A9, A10 and A11
These three applicants, Tan Te Lam, Phung Hoan and Ly Hue My, are all of Chinese ethnic origin. A9 and A10 were born in China and subsequently went to Vietnam. A11 was born in Vietnam but claims to be Taiwanese because her j father was Taiwanese. The judge found that, whatever their true nationality, all three were treated by the Vietnamese authorities as non-nationals because each, whilst resident in Vietnam, was issued with a foreign resident's permit which described him or her as having Taiwanese nationality and which had to be renewed periodically.

All three of these applicants have been refused refugee status by Hong Kong. All three have refused to apply for repatriation under the voluntary scheme and do not wish to return to Vietnam. A9's detention started on 6 April 1991: he was detained for 25 months pending determination of his refugee status and 20 *a* months pending removal from Hong Kong. A10's detention started on 18 August 1989: he was detained for 10 months pending determination of his refugee status and 25 months thereafter. A11 was first detained on 18 May 1989: she was detained for 24 months pending determination of her refugee status and 44 months thereafter.   *b*

Since these three applicants have not volunteered for repatriation, they can only be removed from Hong Kong by repatriation to Vietnam under the compulsory scheme. The government of Hong Kong did not set in motion the machinery for their compulsory repatriation by submitting their particulars to the Vietnamese authorities until 8 December 1994, ie six days after the start of these proceedings. The Vietnamese authorities did not respond in any way to *c* their proposed compulsory repatriation and, so their Lordships were told, that remains the position today. Were it not for these proceedings they would still be detained today.

Applicant A8   *d*

A8, Luu Tai Phong, is also Chinese by ethnic origin, but was born in Vietnam. All his family (including his wife and children) are still in Vietnam. After being refused refugee status in Hong Kong, he applied for voluntary repatriation in August 1993 but stated, incorrectly, on his application form that his nationality was Taiwanese. The reason for making this misstatement was that, whilst in Vietnam, his father had produced a forged Taiwanese document showing A8 to *e* be a Taiwanese national in order to enable him to escape conscription in Vietnam. As a result, A8 was issued by the Vietnamese authorities with a foreign resident's permit. A8 claimed that, when interviewed by a Vietnamese official in September 1993, he was told that his application for voluntary repatriation would not be accepted because he was a Taiwanese national. The judge found that the *f* Hong Kong officials were not aware of this rejection of his application. They were informed by the UNHCR (who had the sole conduct of the voluntary repatriation) that A8 had withdrawn his application. On being so informed, on 25 February 1994 the Hong Kong authorities forwarded the particulars of A8 to the Vietnamese authorities with a view to compulsory repatriation. No response had been received from the Vietnamese authorities at the date of trial and, so *g* their Lordships were informed, until the present day.

A8 was in detention for 22 months pending determination of his refugee status. He is still in detention 'pending removal', such latter detention having lasted, so far, for 40 months.
                                                                                             h
THE PROCEEDINGS

These proceedings were started by 11 Vietnamese boat people seeking writs of habeas corpus against the superintendents of the detention centres where they were being detained. Applicants 1 to 7 were released from detention at various stages between the commencement of proceedings on 2 December 1994 and the *j* delivery of judgment by Keith J on 24 January 1995. The judge did not in his judgment deal with their applications.

The remaining applicants, A8 to A11, put their case before the judge in four ways. First, they submitted that their original detention (as opposed to its later continuance) was unlawful. Second, they submitted that in the absence of any order for their removal, their detention was unlawful. The judge held against the a applicants on both these submissions which were not persisted in before their Lordships. The third submission (the length of detention issue) was that, given the very long periods during which the applicants had already been detained, their further detention for an indefinite period would be unreasonable and therefore unlawful. Finally, they submitted (the nationality issue) that the Vietnamese authorities had a policy under which Vietnam would not accept the

b repatriation of those they treated as non-Vietnamese nationals; therefore, there was no possibility of their removal from Hong Kong under the compulsory scheme; accordingly, their detention could not be 'pending removal'.

As to the length of detention issue, the judge directed himself by reference to the principles laid down by Woolf J in *R v Governor of Durham Prison, ex p Singh* [1984] 1 All ER 983, [1984] 1 WLR 704. That case was concerned with an Indian

c national who had been a lawful immigrant into the United Kingdom. Following the commission by him of two criminal offences, a deportation order had been made by the Secretary of State, who ordered his detention pending his removal. He had been detained for nearly five months at the time he applied for habeas corpus. Woolf J said ([1984] 1 All ER 983 at 985, [1984] 1 WLR 704 at 706):

d   'Although the power which is given to the Secretary of State ... to detain individuals is not subject to any express limitation of time, I am quite satisfied that it is subject to limitations. First of all, it can only authorise detention if the individual is being detained ... pending his removal. It cannot be used for any other purpose. Second, as the power is given in order to enable the machinery of deportation to be carried out, I regard the power of detention

e   as being impliedly limited to a period which is reasonably necessary for that purpose. The period which is reasonable will depend on the circumstances of the particular case. What is more, if there is a situation where it is apparent to the Secretary of State that he is not going to be able to operate the machinery provided in the Act for removing persons who are intended

f   to be deported within a reasonable period, it seems to me that it would be wrong for the Secretary of State to seek to exercise his power of detention. In addition, I would regard it as implicit that the Secretary of State should exercise all reasonable expedition to ensure that the steps are taken which will be necessary to ensure the removal of the individual within a reasonable time.'

g

Keith J accepted these principles as being applicable to the present case. As to the first and third propositions stated by Woolf J, the judge held that it was for the court (not the director) to determine whether in all the circumstances the length of detention was reasonably necessary to achieve removal and whether the

h director had taken all reasonable steps. As to the second of the propositions of Woolf J, the judge held that Woolf J was not merely giving guidance but stating a proposition of law and that, accordingly, it was for the court, not the director, to determine whether deportation could be effected within a reasonable time. The judge further held that, in determining whether removal can be effected within a reasonable time, the court has to take into account whether the delay

j was caused by factors outside the control of the detainer.

Applying those principles to the present case, the judge held that the periods of detention pending determination of their application for refugee status were, despite their length, reasonable. In dealing with the second period of detention, ie the period pending their removal from Hong Kong, he said ([1995] 1 HKC 566 at 596):

'When coupled with the length of their detention pending screening, the time which these applicants have been in detention is truly shocking. They are, at first blush, an affront of the standards of the civilized society which Hong Kong aspires to be.'

Their Lordships agree. But the judge held that, even so, the detention was not unreasonable and therefore unlawful when viewed in context. He pointed out that A9, A10 and A11 had never applied for voluntary repatriation and that the authorities were entitled to believe that A8 had withdrawn his application. As a result, compulsory repatriation was the only possible mode of removal from Hong Kong and the speed of such compulsory repatriation was controlled, not by the Hong Kong authorities, but by the response of the Vietnamese authorities. He held that in all the circumstances the delay, though very great, had not been unreasonable.

The judge then considered the nationality issue. After reviewing the evidence (which their Lordships will have to consider later) he expressed himself as being 'quite satisfied that Vietnam is not prepared to accept the repatriation of detainees whom it regards as non-Vietnamese nationals'. He held accordingly that Vietnam would refuse to accept A9, A10 and A11 for repatriation. He accordingly ordered their immediate release. As to A8, however, he reached a different conclusion. He referred to the fact that the governments of Hong Kong and Vietnam had recently agreed a procedure for dealing with cases where the giving of false information by Vietnamese migrants impeded the repatriation programme. He expressed himself as being 'quite sure' that when the true facts relating to A8 had been made clear to the Vietnamese authorities, they would accept A8 for repatriation and that there was therefore 'every prospect of him being removed from Hong Kong in the near future' (see [1995] 1 HKC 566 at 600). The judge therefore refused any relief to A8.

The government appealed to the Court of Appeal of Hong Kong against the judge's order to release A9, A10 and A11. A8 appealed against the judge's decision refusing him relief. The Court of Appeal (Power, Litton V-PP and Mortimer JA) ([1995] 3 HKC 339) held that the judge's approach to the cases had been wrong in law. They held that the principles enunciated in *Singh* had no application in determining the legality of the detentions of Vietnamese boat people, which fell to be determined solely by reference to the terms of Pt IIIA of the Ordinance and in particular s 13D. They further held that, in relation to the Vietnamese refugees, the court's jurisdiction was supervisory only. It was not for the court to determine whether the duration of the detention was reasonable or whether repatriation was possible: those were matters for the director to determine. The court could only intervene on the usual grounds for judicial review of executive decision ie if the decision of the director was *Wednesbury* unreasonable (see *Associated Provincial Picture Houses Ltd v Wednesbury Corp* [1947] 2 All ER 680, [1948] 1 KB 223). They held that the director had discharged any burden of showing that the detentions were lawful by showing that the applicants were detained for the purpose of repatriation and that that purpose was not spent. There was no burden on the director to prove to the court that it was more likely than not that Vietnam would accept these applicants for repatriation. It was enough for the director to show that attempts were on foot to effect repatriation: this was 'conclusive proof of the legality of the detention' (see [1995] 3 HKC 339 at 353). On those grounds, the Court of Appeal allowed the appeals relating to A9, A10 and A11 and dismissed the appeal of A8. However, the Court a of Appeal also indicated that they doubted whether, even if the judge had been right to enter into the question whether Vietnam would in fact accept repatriation, the judge had made the correct findings of fact on the nationality issue.

All four applicants appealed to the Board against the decision of the Court of Appeal. Following that decision, steps were taken to redetain A9, A10 and A11 b but, after the issue of judicial review proceedings, the director gave an undertaking not to seek their redetention pending the decision of this appeal by their Lordships. A8 has remained in detention throughout.

THE ISSUES

On the appeal before their Lordships Mr Beloff QC, for the applicants, c submitted that the Court of Appeal was in error (a) in holding that the *Singh* principle has no application to the present case and (b) that it was for the director, not the court, to determine whether or not there was sufficient prospect of the applicants being repatriated to Vietnam to justify their continued detention. Mr Beloff submitted that, on both issues, the approach of Keith J was correct. Mr d Beloff then submitted that the judge had erred in applying that correct approach to the length of detention issue, but had reached the correct conclusion on the facts in deciding the nationality issue in favour of A9, A10 and A11. As to A8, Mr Beloff submitted that the judge's finding was wrong and had been proved to be wrong by subsequent events.

Mr Pannick QC, for the respondents, took issue on all these points. He e submitted that the Court of Appeal were right in their approach in law. Alternatively, if the judge's approach were right in law, the judge reached the right conclusion on the length of detention issue and on the nationality issue so far as A8 was concerned. As to A9, A10 and A11 the judge's conclusions of fact were erroneous.

f Their Lordships will deal with these issues in turn.

THE CORRECT APPROACH IN LAW

The Singh principles

Section 13D(1) confers a power to detain a Vietnamese migrant 'pending his removal from Hong Kong'. Their Lordships have no doubt that in conferring g such a power to interfere with individual liberty, the legislature intended that such power could only be exercised reasonably and that accordingly it was implicitly so limited. The principles enunciated by Woolf J in *Singh* are statements of the limitations on a statutory power of detention pending removal. In the absence of contrary indications in the statute which confers the power to h detain 'pending removal', their Lordships agree with the principles stated by Woolf J. First, the power can only be exercised during the period necessary, in all the circumstances of the particular case, to effect removal. Second, if it becomes clear that removal is not going to be possible within a reasonable time, further detention is not authorised. Third, the person seeking to exercise the power of j detention must take all reasonable steps within his power to ensure the removal within a reasonable time.

Although these restrictions are to be implied where a statute confers simply a power to detain 'pending removal' without more, it is plainly possible for the legislature by express provision in the statute to exclude such implied restrictions. Subject to any constitutional challenge (which does not arise in this case) the legislature can vary or possibly exclude the *Singh* principles. But in their

Lordships' view the courts should construe strictly any statutory provision
purporting to allow the deprivation of individual liberty by administrative *a*
detention and should be slow to hold that statutory provisions authorise
administrative detention for unreasonable periods or in unreasonable
circumstances.

Their Lordships are unable to agree with the Court of Appeal that there is any
conflict between the *Singh* principles and the provisions of s 13D. Section *b*
13D(1A), which was inserted in 1991, expressly envisages that the exercise of the
power of detention conferred by s 13D(1) will be unlawful if the period of
detention is unreasonable. It expressly provides that 'the detention ... shall not
be unlawful by the reason of the period of detention *if that period is reasonable*
having regard to ...' What s 13D(1A) does is to provide expressly that, in deciding
whether or not the period is reasonable, regard shall be had to all the *c*
circumstances including (in the case of a person detained pending his removal
from Hong Kong) 'the extent to which it is possible to make arrangements to
effect his removal' and 'whether or not the person has declined arrangements
made or proposed for his removal'. Therefore the subsection is expressly based
on the requirement that detention must be reasonable in all the circumstances *d*
(the *Singh* principles), but imposes specific requirements that in judging such
reasonableness those two factors are to be taken into account.

The two additional factors specifically mentioned in s 13D(1A) reflect the
delays in arranging with the Vietnamese authorities to accept repatriation and the
fact that detainees in refusing to be repatriated under the voluntary scheme are
declining to take advantage of a scheme which could effect their repatriation, and *e*
therefore their release, much more speedily. The requirement that these factors
should be taken into account was directly attributable to earlier decisions in the
Hong Kong courts suggesting that these factors were not relevant in determining
whether the period of detention was reasonable (see *Re Pham Van Ngo* [1991] 1
HKLR 499, where Sears J indicated that, whatever the difficulties, detention for *f*
18 months was unreasonable, and *Liew Kar-seng v Governor-in-Council* [1989] 1
HKLR 607 at 609).

For these reasons, their Lordships consider that Keith J was entirely correct in
applying the *Singh* principles as amplified by the provisions of s 13D(1A) to the
facts of this case.

g

Is it for the court or the director to determine the facts?

The Court of Appeal held that the return to each of the writs of habeas corpus,
stating simply that the applicant was detained under s 13D(1) pending removal
from Hong Kong, was an adequate return and the judge should have made no
further inquiry into facts beyond finding 'that attempts were still being made for *h*
the repatriation of the applicant' (see [1995] 3 HKC 339 at 353). In their view, the
application could only succeed if the applicant could demonstrate (and the
burden was on him) that the director was *Wednesbury* unreasonable in reaching
his conclusion that removal from Hong Kong would at some time prove
practicable. They held that the court's jurisdiction, even in a case of habeas *j*
corpus, is purely supervisory: it was not for the court to reach findings as to the
underlying facts, viz whether or not the period of detention was reasonable or
whether Vietnam would accept repatriation of non-Vietnamese nationals. The
Court of Appeal considered that those facts were not precedent or jurisdictional
facts which are for the court to decide (see *Khawaja v Secretary of State for the Home
Dept* [1983] 1 All ER 765, [1984] AC 74), but matters incidental to the exercise of

a the discretionary powers conferred on the director by s 13D and accordingly for the director to decide (see *Bugdaycay v Secretary of State for the Home Dept* [1987] 1 All ER 940, [1987] AC 514).

In *Khawaja* the House of Lords had to consider the legality of an order for the detention of the applicant as an illegal immigrant pending his removal from the United Kingdom. The order for detention was made under paras 9 and 16 of b Sch 2 to the Immigration Act 1971, which conferred on the executive the power to order the removal of an 'illegal immigrant' and his detention pending removal. The applicant had obtained leave to enter. But it was alleged that he had obtained such leave by fraud as a result of which he was an 'illegal immigrant'. There was a dispute of fact as to whether the leave to enter had been obtained by fraud. The House of Lords held that, since the very existence of the power to detain c depended on the question whether the applicant was an illegal immigrant, the burden lay on the executive to prove to the court on the balance of probabilities that he was an illegal immigrant, ie that he had obtained leave to enter by fraud. That was a precedent or jurisdictional fact which, in the case of deprivation of liberty, had to be proved to exist before any power to detain was exercisable at all.

d In *Bugdaycay* the applicants, having obtained leave to enter by admitted fraud, then sought to claim asylum in the United Kingdom as refugees. The relevant legislation provided that, in the event of a claim for asylum, the matter was to be 'referred to the Home Office for decision'. It further provided that leave to enter would not be refused if removal would be contrary to provisions of the Convention and Protocol relating to the Status of Refugees (Geneva, 28 July e 1951; TS 39 (1954); Cmd 9171; New York, 31 January 1967; TS 15 (1969); Cmnd 3906). The applicants were refused leave to enter and an order made for their removal. The applicants claimed, in reliance on *Khawaja*, that the question whether or not they were entitled to asylum (because a refusal of their application would conflict with the convention) was a question of jurisdictional f or precedent fact which was for the court, not the executive, to determine. Their Lordships rejected this submission, saying that the question whether or not the applicants were refugees was but one of a large number of factual issues which had been committed by Parliament to the executive to determine in the course of exercising their discretion whether or not to give leave to enter. The facts were not, as in *Khawaja*, a condition precedent to the existence of any discretionary g power, but matters for determination in the course of exercising such power.

The issue therefore in the present case is whether the determination of the facts relevant to the question whether the applicants were being detained 'pending removal' goes to the jurisdiction of the director to detain or to the exercise of the discretion to detain. In their Lordships' view the facts are prima h facie jurisdictional. If removal is not pending, within the meaning of s 13D, the director has no power at all. The case is analogous to one where a continuing discretion to detain is conferred on A if a notice has been served on B and no counternotice has been served by B. If there were a dispute as to whether a notice or counternotice had been served, it must prima facie be for the court to j determine the question: if no notice has been served, A's power has never arisen; if a counternotice has been served, A's power has come to an end. In the absence of express words to the contrary, it is for the court to determine whether the power exists and for that purpose the court has to be satisfied as to the existence of the underlying facts.

Their Lordships do not exclude the possibility that, by clear words, the legislature can confer power on the executive to determine its own jurisdiction.

Say, for example, the power to detain was expressly made exercisable during such
period as in the opinion of the director removal from Hong Kong was pending. *a*
In such a case the court's only power would be to review the director's decision
on *Wednesbury* principles. Where human liberty is at stake, very clear words
would be required to produce this result. As was emphasised by all their
Lordships in *Khawaja*, in cases where the executive is given power to restrict
human liberty, the courts should always 'regard with extreme jealousy any claim *b*
by the executive to imprison a citizen without trial and allow it only if it is clearly
justified by the statutory language relied on' (see [1983] 1 All ER 765 at 790, [1984]
AC 74 at 122 per Lord Bridge of Harwich). Such an approach is equally applicable
to everyone within the jurisdiction of the court, whether or not he is a citizen of
the country (see [1983] 1 All ER 765 at 782, [1984] AC 74 at 111–112 per Lord
Scarman). *c*

In the present case their Lordships can find no indication that the legislature
intended the director to have the power to determine jurisdictional fact. First,
such a provision would be very surprising, given the basic constitutional
importance of habeas corpus. If a jailer could justify the detention of his prisoner
by saying 'in my view, the facts necessary to justify the detention exist' the *d*
fundamental protection afforded by a habeas corpus would be severely limited.
The court should be astute to ensure that the protection afforded to human
liberty by habeas corpus should not be eroded save by the clearest words.
Second, there is nothing in the language of the Ordinance to suggest that this was
intended. Third, there is some indication to the contrary. Before 1991, the courts
of Hong Kong had on a number of occasions reached the conclusion that the *e*
detention was not authorised by s 13D because repatriation was not pending and
in so doing had reached their own conclusions of fact on the evidence adduced.
In 1991 the legislature substantially amended s 13D, in particular by the
introduction of sub-s (1A). Yet the legislature introduced no provision limiting
the court's power to determine jurisdictional issues of fact. *f*

For these reasons their Lordships are unable to agree with the Court of Appeal.
Keith J directed himself rightly in law in holding that the burden lay on the
executive to prove to the court on the balance of probabilities the facts necessary
to justify the conclusion that the applicants were being detained 'pending
removal'.

g

The length of detention issue

For the reasons already given, their Lordships consider that Keith J approached
this issue on the correct basis in law. The applicants contend that he reached the
wrong conclusion, but their Lordships find it unnecessary to reach any decision
on this issue since, as will appear, the appeal succeeds on the nationality issue. *h*

However, since there are a large number of Vietnamese boat people still in
Hong Kong who may only be able to bring proceedings on the basis that the
inordinate length of their detention renders it unreasonable, it is desirable to
emphasise one point. The large majority of those in detention do not wish to
return to Vietnam and have declined to apply for voluntary repatriation. The *j*
evidence shows that, if they did so apply, most of them would be repatriated in a
comparatively short time, thereby regaining their freedom. It follows that, in
such cases, the Vietnamese migrant is only detained because of his own refusal to
leave Hong Kong voluntarily, such refusal being based on a desire to obtain entry
to Hong Kong to which he has no right. In assessing the reasonableness of the
continuing detention of such migrants, s 13D(1A)(b)(ii) requires the court to have

a regard to 'whether or not the person has declined arrangements made or proposed for his removal'. In their Lordships' view the fact that the detention is self-induced by reason of the failure to apply for voluntary repatriation is a factor of fundamental importance in considering whether, in all the circumstances, the detention is reasonable.

b *The nationality issue: A9, A10 and A11*

Keith J expressed himself as being 'quite satisfied that Vietnam is not prepared to accept the repatriation of detainees whom it regards as non-Vietnamese nationals' (see [1995] 1 HKC 566 at 599). In reaching this conclusion, he referred specifically to three elements in the evidence. First, the evidence of A8 and three other detainees that they had been told by the Vietnamese officials who

c interviewed them that their applications could not be accepted because they were Taiwanese nationals. Second, evidence indicating that UNHCR officials had been told by Vietnamese officials that they would not accept non-Vietnamese nationals: since this evidence was in the form of double hearsay, the judge attached no weight to it. Third, evidence from a witness that the Vietnamese

d vice-consul in Hong Kong had twice said that non-Vietnamese nationals would not be accepted. The judge further attached weight to the fact that the Hong Kong government had not led any evidence that, in its talks with the Vietnamese authorities, the latter had disowned any such policy or stated that there might be any exception to such policy.

e On the other side, the Hong Kong government produced evidence that in a random check of 50 files of ethnic Chinese detainees who had been accepted for repatriation by Vietnam, four had had foreign resident's permits describing them as being of Taiwanese nationality and one of those four also had a Taiwanese passport. The judge discounted this evidence on the grounds that three out of the four cases related to applications for compulsory repatriation, the forms for

f which do not disclose the nationality of the applicant. Moreover, he pointed out that it could not be demonstrated whether the box relating to nationality on the application for voluntary repatriation had been honestly completed or whether the applicant had followed the advice given by the UNHCR that applicants should conceal non-Vietnamese nationality.

g The Court of Appeal criticised the judge's findings of fact on grounds which were supported in argument before their Lordships. As to the first ground relied on by the judge, the Court of Appeal considered that the account given by the four detainees as to their interviews with the Vietnamese officials amounted only to opinion evidence. In their Lordships' view, this is not correct. The detainees were stating as a fact that the ground stated for the rejection of their applications

h by the Vietnamese officials was that they were non-Vietnamese nationals. As to the statements made by the Vietnamese vice-consul, the Court of Appeal dismissed these on the grounds that the vice-consul was not responsible for national policy and therefore he was only expressing an opinion. Their Lordships are again unable to accept this analysis: the vice-consul is a representative of the

j Vietnamese government in Hong Kong concerned with repatriation; prima facie his statement as to Vietnamese policy on repatriation is likely to be correct.

There is more substance in the criticism of the way in which the judge dealt with the random check evidence led by the government. The evidence in fact showed that out of the four cases relied upon, three were applicants for voluntary repatriation (who were required to disclose nationality) and one for compulsory repatriation (who was not so required) whereas the judge reversed the position.

But in their Lordships' view this error by the judge is not sufficient to upset his
decision on the facts: as he pointed out, the applicants for voluntary repatriation
may well have suppressed their true nationality in completing their application
forms as the UNHCR were suggesting.

Finally, although more than a year has elapsed since the judge made his
decision, there is still no reaction from the Vietnamese authorities to the
applications for repatriation relating to A9, A10 and A11. This is retrospective
support for the judge's finding. In all the circumstances their Lordships can see
no sufficient reason to overturn the finding of the judge that it is the policy of the
Vietnamese government not to accept repatriation of non-Vietnamese nationals.
In these circumstances, it is not contended that these applicants are being
detained 'pending removal'. Accordingly, the decision of Keith J to order their
release was correct.

The nationality issue: A8

It will be remembered that A8 is in fact a Vietnamese national but, due to the
dishonest production to the Vietnamese authorities of papers indicating that he
was Taiwanese, the Vietnamese authorities regard him as a non-national and
refused him voluntary repatriation on that ground. However, the judge refused
to order his release because, immediately before the hearing, the governments of
Hong Kong and Vietnam had agreed a procedure which was to apply in cases
where false information given by the detainee prevents the Vietnamese
authorities from determining whether to allow him to be repatriated. The judge
was 'quite sure' that when this new procedure was operated in relation to A8 the
Vietnamese authorities would accept him for repatriation as a result of which he
would be removed from Hong Kong 'in the near future'.

Their Lordships are far from saying that, on the evidence before him, the judge
reached a wrong conclusion. But time has shown his forecast to be wrong. Far
from A8 having been removed from Hong Kong 'in the near future', nothing
further has been heard from the Vietnamese authorities about his case and a year
later he remains in detention. It therefore appears that the policy of not accepting
those whom they regard as non-Vietnamese nationals is still being applied by the
Vietnamese authorities to A8. In these circumstances, strictly A8 should be
required to make a fresh application for habeas corpus. But in view of the fact
that he has already been in detention for over six years, their Lordships think it
right to reverse the judge's decision and order his immediate release, given that
no progress towards his repatriation has taken place.

Their Lordships will therefore humbly advise Her Majesty that all four appeals
should be allowed, that the order of Keith J in relation to A9, A10 and A11 should
be restored and the order of Keith J as to A8 should be set aside and an order made
for the immediate release of A8. The respondents must pay the appellants' costs
in the courts below and before their Lordships' Board.

Appeals allowed.

Celia Fox   Barrister.

Parkes v Legal Aid Board

a

COURT OF APPEAL, CIVIL DIVISION
BUTLER-SLOSS, WAITE AND HOBHOUSE LJJ
14, 16 FEBRUARY 1996

b

Legal aid – Charge on property recovered for deficiency of costs – Property recovered or preserved in proceedings – Property recovered or preserved – Home of unmarried couple held in joint names on trust for sale – Respondent issuing proceedings for immediate sale with vacant possession – Appellant obtaining legal aid and defending proceedings – Consent order permitting appellant to remain in occupation – Whether charge for benefit of legal aid fund extending to appellant's continued enjoyment of right of possession – Whether shares of beneficial interests in issue – Law of Property Act 1925, s 30 – Legal Aid Act 1988, s 16.

c

The appellant purchased a house jointly with her partner, B, the title to which *d* was transferred into their joint names on trust for sale. On the breakdown of the relationship, B left the property and brought proceedings for an order for its immediate sale with vacant possession and for distribution of the proceeds, under s 30[a] of the Law of Property Act 1925. The appellant obtained legal aid to defend the claim. The parties agreed a compromise, and the outcome of the proceedings was embodied in a consent order postponing sale and allowing the appellant to *e* remain in possession until one of a number of events occurred, in which case the house would be sold and the proceeds would be divided equally between the co-owners. Following the conclusion of the litigation, the Legal Aid Board claimed a charge on the appellant's beneficial interest in the property, as property 'recovered or preserved in proceedings' within the meaning of s 16[b] of the Legal *f* Aid Act 1988, so as to secure repayment to the board of costs incurred on her behalf. The appellant issued proceedings against the board for a declaration that the charge did not apply, contending that (i) the beneficial interests in the house had not been in issue in the original proceedings, and (ii) the right of possession she had obtained under the compromise was insufficient to bring the property within the definition of property 'recovered or preserved in proceedings' to *g* which the statutory charge attached. The judge held that there had been no contest between the co-owners as to the extent of their beneficial interests, but that the rights of occupation that the appellant had acquired or retained under the compromise had brought the property within the statutory charge. The appellant appealed.

h

Held – In the case of unmarried co-owners the parties' rights were regulated solely by their legal status as beneficiaries under the trust for sale imposed by the 1925 Act, and the effect of an order postponing sale was to enlarge that beneficial interest by transforming the transient right to remain in possession for so long as *j* the parties agreed to postpone sale, into a right to enjoy possession for a substantial period and to have the occupation protected by an enforced postponement of sale. Thus, from the date of the consent order, the appellant's rights under the trust for sale of the house were preserved to the extent that she

---

a   Section 30, so far as material, is set out at p 276 *j* to p 277 *a*, post
b   Section 16, so far as material is set out at p 273 *g* to *j*, post

continued to enjoy a right of possession; and were the subject of recovery to the
extent that where her possession had been formerly shared it was now exclusive, *a*
and that where postponement of sale had formerly been consensual it was now
imperative. It followed that the appellant's beneficial interest in the house, which
was not in issue by the time the parties agreed the terms of the consent order, fell
within s 16 of the 1988 Act, and the statutory charge attached accordingly. The
appeal would therefore be dismissed (see p 273 *c e f*, p 276 *h*, p 280 *f g* and p 281 *a* *b*
to *c*, post).

Hanlon *v* Law Society [1980] 2 All ER 199 and *Curling v* Law Society [1985] 1 All
ER 705 applied.

Notes
For the statutory charge for the benefit of the legal aid fund on property *c*
recovered or preserved, see 27(2) *Halsbury's Laws* (4th edn reissue) paras 1972–
1974, and for cases on the subject, see 27(3) *Digest* (2nd reissue) 97–99, 9669–9673.

For the Law of Property Act 1925, s 30, see 37 *Halsbury's Statutes* (4th edn) 108.

For the Legal Aid Act 1998, s 16, see 24 *Halsbury's Statutes* (4th edn) (1989
reissue) 28. *d*

Cases referred to in judgments
Curling v Law Society [1985] 1 All ER 705, [1985] 1 WLR 470, CA.
Hanlon *v* Hanlon [1978] 2 All ER 889, [1978] 1 WLR 592, CA.
Hanlon *v* Law Society [1980] 2 All ER 199, [1981] AC 124, [1980] 2 WLR 756, HL. *e*

Cases also cited or referred to in skeleton arguments
Goodman v Gallant [1986] 1 All ER 311, [1986] Fam 106, CA.
Van Hoorn v Law Society [1984] 3 All ER 136, [1985] QB 106.
Williams v Williams [1977] 1 All ER 28, [1976] Ch 278, CA.

f

Appeal and cross-appeal
By notice dated 3 June 1994 Anita Parkes appealed from the order of Thorpe J in
the Family Division of the High Court on 13 May 1994 ([1994] 2 FLR 850)
whereby he dismissed the appellant's summons for declarations (i) that she did
not recover or preserve any property within the meaning of s 16 of the Legal Aid
Act 1988, as a result of an order granting her a continued right to remain in *g*
possession of a house held in trust for sale, in proceedings under s 30 of the Law
of Property Act 1925 for an order for immediate sale of the house, and (ii) that the
respondent, the Legal Aid Board, was not entitled to a charge pursuant to s 16 of
the 1988 Act over the property in respect of the costs incurred on behalf of the
appellant in those proceedings. By respondent's notice dated 12 April 1995 the *h*
respondent cross-appealed on the question whether the beneficial interests in the
property had been at issue in the proceedings. The facts are set out in the
judgment of Waite LJ.

John Robson (instructed by *Churchers*, Lee-on-Solent) for the appellant. *j*
Charles Utley (instructed by *Colin Stutt*) for the board.

WAITE LJ (giving the first judgment at the invitation of Butler-Sloss LJ). The
appellant is the co-owner, jointly with the man who was formerly her partner in
an unmarried relationship, of a property which was transferred into their joint
names and in which they lived together until he left the house when their

a relationship ended shortly after the birth of their child. After his departure he sought a sale of the former joint home with vacant possession, but she objected and wished to remain in occupation. When he brought proceedings against her for an order for sale of the property and distribution of the net proceeds, she obtained legal aid to defend them. The proceedings were compromised at the door of the court, on terms that upon her undertaking full responsibility for the

b mortgage payments she would be allowed to remain in occupation with the child until the child's seventeenth birthday, or her own death, or that of the child, or her marriage or cohabitation with another partner, whichever of those events should first happen. Upon the occurrence of the relevant event, the house would be sold and the net proceeds would be divided equally between the co-owners. The consent order embodying those terms stated that there should be no order

c as to costs.

Following the conclusion of that litigation, the Legal Aid Board claimed a charge on the appellant's beneficial interest in the property to secure repayment to the board of the costs that had been incurred on her behalf. In this current action she claims a declaration against the board that the charge did not apply.

d That declaration was refused by Thorpe J on 13 May 1994 ([1994] 2 FLR 850). There had been two issues before him. The first was whether (as the Legal Aid Board contended) the beneficial interests had been in contest in the original proceedings or (as the appellant contended) were undisputed; the second was whether the right she had obtained under the compromise to force a postponement of sale and to remain in occupation was sufficient (as the board

e contended) or insufficient (as she contended) to bring the property within the definition in the relevant provisions of the Legal Aid Act 1988, of property recovered or preserved in the proceedings. The judge held, in the appellant's favour on the first question, that there had been no contest between the co-owners as to the extent of their beneficial interests; but on the second question

f he held, favourably to the board, that the rights of exclusive possession she had acquired or retained under the compromise brought the property within the charge. In this court she now appeals against the latter holding, and the board (by a respondent's notice) cross-appeals against the former.

THE LAW

g Section 16 of the 1988 Act provides, so far as relevant:

'... (6) Except so far as regulations otherwise provide—(a) any sums remaining unpaid on account of a person's contribution in respect of the sums payable by the Board in respect of any proceedings, and (b) a sum equal to any deficiency by reason of his total contribution being less than the net

h liability of the Board on his account, shall be a first charge for the benefit of the Board on any property which is recovered or preserved for him in the proceedings.

(7) For the purposes of subsection (6) above it is immaterial what the nature of the property is and where it is situated and the property within the

j charge includes the rights of a person under any compromise or settlement arrived at to avoid the proceedings or bring them to an end ...'

In *Hanlon v Law Society* [1980] 2 All ER 199, [1981] AC 124 the House of Lords was concerned with a case where the legal title to a matrimonial home was vested in the husband alone. The wife asserted, and the husband disputed, that she had a beneficial interest in the property. Without prejudice to that issue, each side

claimed a transfer of property order in respect of the other's interest under the
Matrimonial Causes Act 1973. The upshot of the proceedings was an order (on   a
appeal) that the husband should transfer the property to the wife (see *Hanlon v
Hanlon* [1978] 2 All ER 889, [1978] 1 WLR 592). An issue later arose under the
equivalent of s 16 of the 1988 Act when the legal aid authorities claimed a charge
on the property for the wife's costs. That claim was upheld in the House of Lords
on the ground that the charge attaches to any property that has been in issue   b
between the parties; that the whole beneficial interest had been in contest—
either as a matter of established right on ordinary equitable principles, or as the
subject matter of a property transfer claim—and that accordingly the true view
of the case was that the house became property recovered by the wife to the
extent of any interest in it of the husband, and property preserved, to the extent
of any interest of her own. That reasoning was expressed thus by Lord Simon   c
([1980] 2 All ER 199 at 209, [1981] AC 124 at 180–181):

> '... property has been recovered or preserved if it has been in issue in the
> proceedings: recovered by the claimant if it has been the subject of a
> successful claim, preserved to the respondent if the claim fails. In either case   d
> it is a question of fact, not of theoretical "risk". In property adjustment
> proceedings, in my view, it is only property the ownership or transfer of
> which has been in issue which has been "recovered or preserved" so as to be
> the subject of a legal aid charge. What has been in issue is to be collected as
> a matter of fact from pleadings, evidence, judgment and/or order. I can see   e
> no reason for extending the words to items of property the ownership or
> possession of which has never been questioned. I think this interpretation
> also accords with the structure of the legal aid scheme. Items of property the
> ownership of which is not questioned and which are not the subject of
> dispute, fall (subject to disregards) to be taken into account for the initial
> contribution from the legally-aided litigant. It would seem to be contrary to   f
> the general scheme to take them into account again for the purpose of the
> legal aid charge. Although no doubt the subject matter in part determined
> the change of wording of reg 18(10)(c) in 1976 [see the Legal Aid (General)
> Regulations 1971, SI 1971/62, as amended by SI 1976/628], that change also
> marginally supports the construction which I venture to favour. The 1971
> regulation referred to "any property affected by an order". These are the   g
> very words used by counsel for the respondent as one of the tests for
> "property recovered or preserved". But in the 1976 amendment these words
> disappear. If therefore it had been conceded that the appellant had a
> beneficial half share of the house, I would presume to agree with Arnold P
> that it was only the husband's beneficial half share which was "recovered";   h
> and I would hold consonantly that only if it was disputed that the appellant
> had or should retain a beneficial half share in the house would she have
> "preserved" her beneficial half share. But though I therefore respectfully
> agree with Arnold P's general approach, I venture to differ on its application
> to the facts of the instant case. What is crucial, to my mind, is that at the very   j
> outset, in the original pleadings, each spouse was claiming the transfer of the
> other's interest in the house. I cannot find that the husband's claim was ever
> withdrawn. On scrutiny of the evidence it is apparent that there never was
> any real agreement that the appellant had a beneficial half or any share in the
> house: it was at most a hypothesis on which various contingent financial
> courses could be canvassed. This conclusion involves that the house was

a   property which was recovered by the appellant (the husband's interest) or
    preserved to her (her own interest).'

    The section was considered, again in the context of a matrimonial home, by
    this court in *Curling v Law Society* [1985] 1 All ER 705, [1985] 1 WLR 470. In that
    case the house was in the joint names of husband and wife. The husband wanted
    to remain in occupation and resist a sale, and also to exclude the wife from the
b   house. The wife wanted the house sold, so that she could buy a new home out
    of the proceeds. The proceedings were settled by a consent order by which the
    husband bought out the wife's interest in the matrimonial home for £15,000—
    representing the approximate value of her (admitted) half share in the beneficial
    interest. In subsequent proceedings the wife challenged a claim by the legal aid
c   authorities to a charge on her £15,000 payment, on the ground that, since it
    represented no more than payment for her admitted half interest, it constituted
    property neither recovered nor preserved, but only the price of an asset whose
    ownership had never been in dispute. It was held that even though the beneficial
    title to the property had not been in issue, the wife had 'recovered' property
    within the terms of the section, because she achieved an immediate or
d   accelerated right to her share of the proceeds of sale under the trust for sale to
    which the house was subject. Neill J, who was a member of the court, said ([1985]
    1 All ER 705 at 710–711, [1985] 1 WLR 470 at 477–488):

       'What then was in issue in the divorce proceedings apart from the question
       of the custody of the children? It was submitted on behalf of the Law Society
e   that the husband put in issue the wife's entitlement to a share in the
       matrimonial home merely by including in his petition a claim for a property
       adjustment order in respect of the house. That claim, however, has to be
       looked at in the light of the other evidence and in particular of the husband's
       concession that *as a matter of prior entitlement* the wife should have a half share
f   in the net proceeds of the sale of the house. I would therefore accept the
       submission of counsel for the wife that at no material time was there an issue
       in the divorce proceedings as to the *ownership* of the matrimonial home. But
       in my judgment the ownership of the house cannot be looked at in isolation
       in considering whether the wife has recovered any property in the
       proceedings. I have already made reference to the correspondence and to
g   the affidavits which throw light on the dispute between the parties about the
       matrimonial home in the period between September 1981 and January 1982.
       The husband wished to remain in the house and to postpone the sale, at any
       rate for the time being. In addition he wished to exclude the wife from the
       house. The wife for her part wanted the house to be sold so that she could
h   receive her share of the proceeds and use it towards the purchase of a new
       house. The wife achieved her aim by the compromise which was reached
       on 26 January 1982 and by the consent order which was made on the same
       day. It is true that the sum of £15,000 merely represented her agreed share
       of the proceeds of sale (or indeed perhaps rather less than her full share), but
j   the fact that a party to legal proceedings recovers in the proceedings that to
       which he or she is in law already entitled cannot by itself prevent the
       attachment of the statutory charge. The question is whether the party's right
       to recover the property has been in issue in the proceedings and for this
       purpose I can see no reason to limit the relevant issue to that of ownership
       alone. The judge took the view that the wife recovered the £15,000 in the
       proceedings because she achieved an immediate or at any rate an accelerated

right to her share of the proceeds of sale. He referred to the mention made
by Lord Simon in Hanlon's case [[1980] 2 All ER 199, [1981] AC 124] of both   *a*
ownership and possession. I agree with the judge. In my opinion the
recovery of possession of property may constitute the recovery of property
within s 9(6) [of the Legal Aid Act 1974], just as the defeat of a claim by
another party to a possessory interest in property may constitute the
preservation of property ...' (Neill J's emphasis.)   *b*

Oliver LJ said ([1985] 1 All ER 705 at 715, [1985] 1 WLR 470 at 483):

> 'Where, even though the *title* to property may not be in issue, the
> proceedings are necessary in order to reduce it into or restore it to the
> possession of its owner, it seems to me that, quite literally, the property has
> been "recovered". For instance, a landlord seeking to forfeit a lease or a   *c*
> landowner seeking to evict a squatter who claims no title but merely refuses
> to move is pursuing property the title to which is not in issue. But I find it
> unarguable that the property reduced to possession by the judgment has not
> been "recovered" by the proceedings. Equally, if a trustee for sale wrongly
> refuses to concur in selling so that proceedings are necessary under s 30 of   *d*
> the Law of Property Act 1925 to compel a sale and the distribution of
> proceeds, I would have thought it quite clear that, as a result of the
> proceedings, the beneficiary had "recovered" his share. It seems to me
> entirely inappropriate and irrelevant in such a case to seek to assess the
> increment to the plaintiff of the value of his interest. He has, quite literally,
> recovered (ie got into his hands) property which he would not have in his   *e*
> hands had it not been for the proceedings. That, as it seems to me, equally
> applies in the instant case. The wife's interest, though undisputed, was
> effectively locked away from her by the husband's insistence on remaining
> in possession and his seeking, by the threatened ouster, to convert his
> possession into sole possession, unless and until she either obtained an order   *f*
> in the proceedings for the property to be sold and its proceeds distributed or
> prevailed on the husband to pay her the monetary equivalent of her interest.'
> (Oliver LJ's emphasis.)

The present case is the first, so far as counsels' researches have been able to
discover, in which a charge has been asserted by the Legal Aid Board against   *g*
property in relation to which the assisted party is an unmarried co-owner who
has obtained (whether by agreement or after trial) an order postponing sale and
permitting her to remain in exclusive occupation. There are obvious parallels
between the joint property rights of married and unmarried cohabitants, but
there is a material distinction in that there are no statutory powers to vary the   *h*
beneficial interests, and the parties' rights are regulated solely by their legal status
as beneficiaries under the trust for sale imposed upon the house by ss 35 and 36
of the Law of Property Act 1925. Those rights include the entitlement of each
party to the net rents and profits pending sale (s 35) and a power to postpone
execution of the trust for sale (s 25(1)). Section 30 of the 1925 Act is designed to
deal with cases where agreement to a sale cannot be obtained from the trustees   *j*
(or all of them) and reads:

> '(1) If the trustees for sale refuse to sell or to exercise any of the powers
> conferred by either of the last two sections, or any requisite consent cannot
> be obtained, any person interested may apply to the court for a vesting or
> other order for giving effect to the proposed transaction or for an order

a directing the trustees for sale to give effect thereto, and the court may make such order as it thinks fit ...'

The effect of those provisions is now well established, and is described in Megarry and Wade The Law of Real Property (5th edn, 1984) p 441. To express it shortly, the appellant's status in law immediately before the compromise order was that of a beneficiary under a trust for sale of which she was herself a trustee; she had a right
b to possession pending sale, but not an exclusive right as against her co-tenant in common; she had no right to force a postponement of the sale of the house, but that disability was subject to the discretion of the court under s 30 to give directions designed to give effect to the equity of the case. Such directions could potentially include not only an order postponing sale, but also the granting to her
c of a right of exclusive possession pending sale—subject to whatever terms the court might regard as fair and reasonable between the parties.

THE FACTS

On 30 July 1986 the appellant and her partner, Mr Bradford, took a transfer into their joint names of a property, 9 Freshfields Gardens, Waterlooville, Hampshire,
d for which they paid £38,000. That sum was raised as to £3,800 by a cash deposit put up by Mr Bradford, and as to the balance by a mortgage. The appellant put up a sum of £1,000 to buy furniture. The parties remained in occupation, sharing the outgoings, including mortgage instalments, until August 1988 when the relationship broke down and Mr Bradford left the house. A child, R, had been born of the association on 5 May 1988.
e In June 1989 Mr Bradford issued an originating application in the Portsmouth County Court entitled: 'In the matter of [section 30 of] the Law of Property Act 1925' and 'In the matter of [the house]'. The relief prayed for was an order for sale of the house and a declaration that the first £3,800 of the proceeds of sale belonged to him, and the balance to the appellant and himself in equal shares.
f The grounds of application did not refer to the basis of the claim to the first £3,800, but concentrated on the need for a sale order because the house had been bought for joint occupation and that purpose was now over. The appellant was granted legal aid in September 1989 to defend what were described on the face of the certificate as proceedings under s 30 of the 1925 Act. There was at that stage a discussion of terms of settlement which came to nothing. The appellant swore
g an affidavit in the proceedings on 9 November 1989, in which she agreed that the initial deposit of £3,800 had been paid by Mr Bradford and referred to her furniture contribution of £1,000. She submitted that the purposes of the original purchase were still continuing, because of the need for accommodation of R and herself. She concluded her affidavit by submitting:
h
'In the circumstances I respectfully ask the Court to consider that the purpose for which the property was acquired has not come to an end and accordingly to order that the sale of the property be postponed until [R] attains his majority. As regards the distribution of the proceeds of sale, I respectfully ask the Court to find that the Applicant and I have equal
j beneficial interests in the property and to order that when a sale does take place the proceeds should be divided equally between us.'

In January 1990 the value of the house was agreed at £65,000.

The proceedings were listed for hearing on 30 March 1990. On that day the parties agreed to a consent order under which, upon the appellant undertaking to discharge all future mortgage instalments and to inform Mr Bradford of structural alterations to the house and of any future marriage or cohabitation, it was ordered that sale be postponed until the first to happen of the events already mentioned, that the cost of future structural repairs should be born by the parties equally, and that there be no order as to costs. Nothing was said on the face of the order as to the nature or extent of the rights of possession which would be enjoyed by the appellant during the period of postponement of sale. It was assumed before the judge in the present action that, by necessary inference, the consent order was intended to provide that she would enjoy an exclusive right of possession, but (as will shortly appear) that assumption has been challenged on appeal by the counsel now representing her.

In due course the appellant's costs were taxed under the 1988 Act at a figure of £1,968.

THE PRESENT PROCEEDINGS

There arose, as a result, the claim by the board to a charge on the appellant's beneficial interest in the house. It was claimed on two bases. The first was that the appellant had established as a result of the proceedings a one half beneficial interest in the proceeds of sale—whereas until the consent order (so it was contended) there had been a dispute as to the extent of her interest—at least in relation to the first £3,800 of the equity which was claimed on the face of the originating application by Mr Bradford. The second was that she had recovered or preserved a substantially enhanced beneficial interest, in that the consent order gave her exclusive possession of the house in place of the shared possession rights she had hitherto enjoyed, and moreover secured that possession by postponing for a substantial period the sale upon which Mr Bradford would otherwise have been entitled (subject to the court's discretion under s 30 of the 1925 Act) to insist.

The judge dealt with the first claim by finding that whatever appearances to the contrary might be inferred from the formal relief claimed by Mr Bradford and the remarks I have quoted in the affidavit sworn in the original proceedings by the appellant, there was in fact no real issue between the parties as to beneficial entitlement. He accepted the statement by the appellant, sworn in an affidavit filed in these current proceedings, that there had never been a dispute as to the parties' respective shares in the house, on which she was not cross-examined.

On the second claim, the judge, founding himself on the passages already quoted from the speeches of Lord Simon and Lord Scarman in *Hanlon* and on the judgments of Oliver LJ and Neill J in *Curling*, held that the appellant had received 'an interest in property, namely the right to exclusive use and enjoyment over an extensive period of years, recovered within the language of s 16(6) of the [Legal Aid Act 1988].' (See [1994] 2 FLR 850 at 855–856.)

This was a conclusion which the judge reached with understandable reluctance, because the appellant, as a single parent mother on a low income already committed to discharging mortgage instalments, had no realistic prospect of being able to pay off the legal aid costs of nearly £2,000 in one lump, and under the Civil Legal Aid (General) Regulations 1989, SI 1989/339, then in force, the board had no power to postpone the charge. That situation has fortunately improved, in that under regulations which have since become operative (the Civil Legal Aid (General) (Amendment) (No 2) Regulations 1994, SI 1994/1822) the board is empowered to postpone enforcement and has told the court that, if successful in this appeal, it intends to do so.

THE ARGUMENTS

a   Before turning to the main submissions of the parties, it will be convenient to deal with a point that was not taken before the judge, but has been raised by Mr Robson, who appears for the appellant in this court, but did not appear below. He draws attention to the fact (to which I have already referred) that the consent order made in the original proceedings does not on its face contain any provision which either entitles the appellant to exclusive occupation of the property or

b   excludes the right of joint occupation to which Mr Bradford is entitled in law as an incident of his continuing status as a beneficial part-owner. He acknowledges that it is highly unlikely that anyone contemplated, during the discussions which preceded the making of the consent order, that Mr Bradford would seek to exercise rights of joint occupation after the order had taken effect—the more so

c   as he was on the point of emigrating to Australia. Nevertheless, he submits that a technical view is justifiable on the part of those resisting a statutory charge for costs on their property, and he relies on this lacuna in the order to support a submission that the judge was wrong to have regarded it as having placed the appellant in the position of a party entitled to exclusive possession. I would, for my part, reject that submission. It is indeed a pity that those with responsibility

d   for drafting the consent order overlooked the necessity to provide expressly that the appellant was thenceforth to have a right of exclusive possession until the property came to be sold, but the intention that she should be so entitled is so obvious an inference from all the circumstances in which the order came to be made, that I have not the slightest doubt that in the unlikely event of Mr Bradford

e   returning and seeking to exercise rights of joint occupation, she would have no difficulty in restraining him from doing so in proceedings for a declaration that the order must be construed as excluding his possessory rights by implication. The case is so clear that it might even provide occasion for an amendment of the order under the slip rule.

f   The parties' submissions on the two main issues are as follows.

(1) *The judge's finding that there was no contest as to the proportion of the beneficial interests*

Mr Utley, for the board, acknowledges that: 'what has been in issue is to be collected as a matter of fact from pleadings, evidence, judgment and/or order.'

g   (See *Hanlon* [1980] 2 All ER 199 at 209, [1981] AC 124 at 180 per Lord Simon.)

He accepts, also, that (as is made clear in *Curling* [1985] 1 All ER 705 at 713–714, [1985] 1 WLR 470 at 481) the question of what assets or interests of the parties have been in dispute requires a full survey of the course of dealing between the parties, and is not to be resolved merely by recourse to their original pleading. He

h   accepts, further, that on that basis there was room for the judge's finding of no contest as to the beneficial interests above £3,800. But in relation to the first £3,800 of the proceeds of a future sale, he submits that the judge's finding of no dispute was not open to him on the evidence. That was an issue on which, he submits, Mr Bradford, by his assertion of entitlement to the full amount on the face of his originating application, threw down a gauntlet which was promptly

j   taken up by the appellant in the passage already quoted from her initial evidence, and on which neither side thereafter gave any overt sign of surrender or agreement. Mr Robson replies that a mere assertion of the claim on the face of a summons which failed to state any grounds in support of it, provides too uncertain a note to constitute a call to arms, and that the statements in the appellant's evidence are routine and generalised and do not necessarily denote

any understanding on her part that there was a serious issue as to whether the
ownership of the home was to be treated otherwise than fifty-fifty.

*(2) Did the appellant recover or preserve property under the consent order to which
the statutory charge attaches?*

Mr Robson distinguishes *Hanlon* and *Curling* upon their facts—pointing out
that in the one case the wife obtained the whole interest in the home and in the
other a sum of money representing the value of her interest in it, and that in both
cases the court was concerned with a discretionary jurisdiction incorporating
power to re-write all interests in the matrimonial assets. It is much easier in such
circumstances, he says, to infer that what has been ordered for one spouse has
been recovered or preserved from the other. In the present case, by contrast,
there has been no disposition of property by order of the court, or (he would add)
at all. The appellant is simply to be regarded as someone whose only interest in
the property was as beneficial owner of a half share in the proceeds of a trust for
sale. That was not changed by the consent order: she recovered nothing and
preserved nothing. Any enlargement of her property rights obtained as a result
of having the sale of the property postponed is illusory. The power of sale was in
practice, he submits, already postponed, because of the terms of s 25(1) of the
1925 Act, which (in the absence of contrary intention—which is not here alleged)
imports into every trust for sale a power of postponement. That power, he says,
is one which is bound to be exercised so long as the parties agree and (in the event
of disagreement) will become subject to the terms of s 30. The result is that when
the machinery of the trust for sale set up by the 1925 Act is regarded as a whole,
the consequence, for all practical purposes, is that it incorporates not just a power
to postpone sale, but (subject to s 30) a binding direction to postpone. The order
therefore changed nothing.

Mr Utley accepts that, to the mere extent that she was a beneficial co-tenant in
equity under a trust for sale both before and after the consent order, the appellant
neither recovered nor preserved anything. But he submits that the effect of the
order was to enlarge her beneficial interest substantially by transforming the
transient right which the law allowed her (to remain in possession for so long as
the parties agreed to postpone sale) into a right—whether her co-owner agreed
or not—to enjoy possession for a substantial period and to have her occupation
protected by an enforced postponement of sale.

CONCLUSION

On the first issue I prefer the submission of Mr Robson. There was ample
material for the judge, viewing the evidence in the round and taking note of the
absence—after the first exchanges—of any serious indications of controversy
over the proportions of ownership, to reach the conclusion that the beneficial
interests were not in issue, and that by the time they came to agree the terms of
the consent order, both parties regarded themselves as entitled in equal shares.

On the second issue I find the argument of Mr Utley wholly persuasive. Mr
Robson's suggested interpretation of s 25(1) of the 1925 Act is ingenious, but is
not, in my view, maintainable. The power to postpone is a power properly
so-called and cannot be elevated into a direction. On the more general aspects of
the case, it is obviously desirable that wherever possible the law should avoid
distinction between the rights of the married and the unmarried, and Mr Utley's
approach (which was clearly also in the mind of the judge) has the advantage of
applying to the case of unmarried co-owners the underlying principles of *Hanlon*

a and *Curling*, without invading the distinctions which still exist in law when property is recovered or preserved through an exercise of the court's discretion under s 25 of the 1973 Act, on the one hand, and s 30 of the 1925 Act, on the other. The correct view of this case, in my judgment, is that from the date of the consent order the appellant's rights under the trust for sale of the home were preserved to the extent that she continued to enjoy a right of possession; and were the b subject of recovery to the extent that where her possession had been formerly shared, it was now exclusive, and where postponement of sale had formerly been consensual, it was now imperative. The decision of the judge was entirely correct.

I would dismiss the appeal.

c **HOBHOUSE LJ.** I agree.

BUTLER-SLOSS LJ. I also agree.

Appeal dismissed. No order on the respondent's notice.

d
Paul Magrath Esq   Barrister.

Garston and others v Scottish Widows' Fund   a
and Life Assurance Society

CHANCERY DIVISION

RATTEE J
                                                                    b
20, 21 MARCH 1996

Landlord and tenant – Business premises – Application for new tenancy – Request by
tenant for new tenancy – Lease of office premises for term of years with option to
determine – Lessee serving invalid notice to determine on landlord together with request
for new tenancy – New tenancy commencing before expiry of existing tenancy but after c
date of option to determine – Whether request effective to determine existing tenancy –
Whether request valid – Landlord and Tenant Act 1954, s 26(1)(2)(5).

In 1988 the plaintiffs took an assignment of a lease dated 10 July 1985 for a term
of 20 years from 24 June 1985. Clause 7 of the lease contained an option for d
determination by the plaintiffs by the service of 'six months' previous notice in
writing ... on expiration of the tenth year of the term'. In 1994 the plaintiffs
purported to give notice by letter to determine the lease on 9 July 1995. The letter
enclosed a request for a new tenancy under s 26[a] of the Landlord and Tenant Act
1954 for a term of nine years from 10 July 1995. However, the plaintiffs had
mistakenly given notice to determine on the tenth anniversary of the date of the e
lease and not, as cl 7 required, on the tenth anniversary of the commencement of
the term of the lease (ie 24 June). They accepted that the notice was therefore
ineffective, but contended that their request for a new tenancy was effective to
bring the lease to an end under s 26(5) of the 1954 Act. The defendant landlord
rejected that contention on the ground that the commencement date of the new f
tenancy was earlier than the date on which the existing tenancy would come to
an end by the effluxion of time and that therefore the request infringed the
proviso to s 26(2) of the 1954 Act and was accordingly invalid. The plaintiffs
thereafter applied for a declaration that, since the commencement date of the
new tenancy was not earlier than the date on which, as at the date of request, the
existing tenancy could be brought to an end by notice to quit, the request did not g
infringe the proviso, and the lease had effectively been determined.

Held – On its natural construction, the proviso to s 26(2) of the 1954 Act
contemplated only one relevant date in respect of a given tenancy, and the two
alternative definitions of that date were to take account of the fact that the h
relevant tenancy might be either (a) one granted simply for a term of years, in
which case the relevant date under the proviso would be the date on which it
would come to an end by effluxion of time, or (b) one granted for a term of years
certain and thereafter from year to year, which would never come to an end by
effluxion of time, and in which case the only possible relevant date specified in the j
proviso was the date on which, as at the date of request under s 26(1), the existing
tenancy could be brought to an end by notice to quit given by the tenant. In the
instant case, the tenancy had been granted for a term of years and, since the date
specified by the plaintiffs for the commencement of the new tenancy was earlier

---

a   Section 26, so far as material, is set out at p 285 *e* to *j*, post

a than the date on which the existing tenancy would otherwise come to an end, the request was invalid. It followed that the request was not effective to terminate the tenancy and the application would accordingly be dismissed (see p 287 *e f* and p 288 *c* to *e*, post).

Notes

b For option to determine lease and notice to exercise option, see 27(1) *Halsbury's Laws* (4th edn reissue) paras 116–118, and for cases on the subject, see 31(1) *Digest* (2nd reissue) 274–275, 2289–2300.

For the Landlord and Tenant Act 1954, s 26, see 23 *Halsbury's Statutes* (4th edn) (1989 reissue) 151.

c **Cases referred to in judgment**
Hankey v Clavering [1942] 2 All ER 311, [1942] 2 KB 326, CA.
Mannai Investment Co Ltd v Eagle Star Life Assurance Co Ltd [1996] 1 All ER 55, [1995] 1 WLR 1508, CA.

d **Case also cited or referred to in skeleton arguments**
Scholl Mfg Co Ltd v Clifton (Slim-Line) Ltd [1966] 3 All ER 16, [1967] Ch 41, CA.

Originating summons
By an originating summons dated 29 June 1995 the plaintiff lessees, Eric Michael Garston, Alan Kilsha Toulson, Paul Denzil Nicholas and Charles Edward
e Cameron Gardner, applied for a declaration against the defendant landlord, Scottish Widows' Fund and Life Assurance Society, that the contractual term of a commercial lease dated 10 July 1985 of office premises in Holborn, London had been validly determined by the plaintiffs' request for a new tenancy made under s 26 of the Landlord and Tenant Act 1954. The facts are set out in the judgment.

f *David Hodge* (instructed by *Reynolds Porter Chamberlain*) for the plaintiffs.
Kim Lewison QC (instructed by *Freshfields*) for the defendant.

RATTEE J. The plaintiffs in this originating summons are former partners or partners in the well-known firm of solicitors, Messrs Reynolds Porter
g Chamberlain. As such they took an assignment of a lease from a predecessor of the defendant, being a lease of office premises in Holborn, at a rent which has come to be in excess of the current market rent. The proceedings raise the question whether the plaintiffs have succeeded in extricating themselves from that lease. Neither they nor their successors wish to occupy the premises any
h longer.
The lease was dated 10 July 1985 and made between Merchant Navy Officers Pension Fund Trustees Ltd as lessor and Manufacturers Hanover Finance Ltd as lessee. The plaintiffs took an assignment of the lease on 29 September 1988. The reversion has become vested in the defendant. The term of the lease is 20 years from 24 June 1985, subject to earlier termination as therein provided. The rent
j was £47,000 pa subject to rent review. The only provision of the lease which I need read is cl 7, which is in the following terms:

'IF the Tenant shall desire to determine the term hereby granted at the expiration of the tenth year of the term and shall give to the Landlord at least six months' previous notice in writing of such his desire then immediately on the expiration of the tenth year of the term hereby granted the demise and

everything herein contained shall cease and determine but without prejudice
to the rights and remedies of either party against the other in respect of any   *a*
antecedent claim or breach of covenant.'

According to unchallenged affidavit evidence, the plaintiffs decided to exercise
their power to determine the lease at the expiration of the tenth year of the term
in accordance with cl 7 thereof.

On 4 October 1994 Reynolds Porter Chamberlain, on behalf of the plaintiffs,   *b*
wrote to the defendant a letter which referred to the lease and said:

> 'Pursuant to clause 7 of the Lease the lessee hereby serves notice on the
> Lessor to determine the Lease and this notice shall expire on the 9 July 1995.'

The letter enclosed a request for a new tenancy under s 26 of the Landlord and   *c*
Tenant Act 1954, the new tenancy requested being one at a rent of £5 per square
foot, compared with a rent of some £34 per square foot then currently payable
under the lease, for a term of nine years from 10 July 1995 with three-yearly rent
reviews.

In fact, on 14 September 1994 Reynolds Porter Chamberlain had served an   *d*
identical notice and request on the defendant, saying that they did so on behalf of
their firm, rather than on behalf of the plaintiffs. In order to cure any doubt that
there might have been as to the effectiveness of that earlier letter and request as
given on behalf of the plaintiffs, the actual tenants, the later letter and request
were served, as I have said, on 4 October 1994. I shall refer in the remainder of
this judgment only to the later documents. Nothing turns on the fact that others   *e*
had been served on 14 September 1994.

The draftsman of the letter and request for a new tenancy made the mistake of
thinking that the relevant date for breaking the lease under cl 7 was the tenth
anniversary of the date of the lease, rather than the tenth anniversary of the
commencement of the term granted by the lease. The letter should have given   *f*
notice to terminate the lease on 24 June 1995 and not on 9 July 1995. This was a
plain slip. A layman, or even a lawyer unversed in the finer details of landlord and
tenant law, might be forgiven for thinking that the court should find it possible to
rectify this error without much difficulty. Unfortunately such a course is not
open to me. The Court of Appeal, most recently in *Mannai Investment Co Ltd v
Eagle Star Life Assurance Co Ltd* [1996] 1 All ER 55, [1995] 1 WLR 1508, following   *g*
an earlier decision of the Court of Appeal in *Hankey v Clavering* [1942] 2 All ER 311,
[1942] 2 KB 326, has held that such a mistake in a notice purportedly given
pursuant to a break clause in a lease is fatal to its effectiveness.

Mr Hodge, counsel for the plaintiffs in the present case, accepts that, by virtue
of that decision, I am bound to hold that the notice given in the present case was   *h*
not an effective notice to terminate the lease under cl 7 thereof. Mr Hodge made
plain that he wished to keep open the possibility of arguing in a higher court that
the Court of Appeal decision to which I have referred should not be followed,
particularly since there is apparently an appeal pending in the *Mannai Investment
Co Ltd* case to the House of Lords.   *j*

However, Mr Hodge argued (if I may say so, most persuasively) that the
request for a new tenancy served with the purported cl 7 notice was effective to
bring the lease to an end by virtue of the provisions of Pt II of the 1954 Act. To
explain the argument, I must first refer to some of the provisions of that Act. As
is apparent to the long title to the 1954 Act, the purpose of Pt II is: '... to enable
tenants occupying property for business, professional or certain other purposes

a   to obtain new tenancies in certain cases …' Section 23(1) of the 1954 Act provides that, in general, Pt II applies to—

'any tenancy where the property comprised in the tenancy is or includes premises which are occupied by the tenant and are so occupied for the purposes of a business carried on by him or for those and other purposes.'

b   Section 23(2) provides that the expression 'business' includes a trade, profession or employment. It is not disputed that the premises subject to the lease in the present case were so occupied at all material times.

Section 24(1) of the 1954 Act provides that a tenancy to which Pt II applies shall not come to an end unless terminated in accordance with the provisions of Part II of the Act. That subsection gives a right to the tenant under such a tenancy, c   subject to the provisions of s 29, which are not material for present purposes, to apply to the court for a new tenancy (a) if the landlord has given notice under s 25 of the Act to terminate the tenancy, or (b) if the tenant has made a request for a new tenancy in accordance with s 26 of the Act. Section 24(2) provides that s 24(1) shall not prevent the coming to an end of a tenancy by, inter alia, notice d   to quit given by the tenant, except in certain immaterial circumstances. By virtue of s 69(1) of the Act a notice to quit for this purpose means a notice to terminate a tenancy given in accordance with the provisions of the tenancy.

Section 26 of the 1954 Act is the section particularly relevant to the argument in this case, and I should read such of its provisions as are material for present purposes. Section 26 reads as follows:

e
'(1) A tenant's request for a new tenancy may be made where the tenancy under which he holds for the time being (hereinafter referred to as "the current tenancy") is a tenancy granted for a term of years certain exceeding one year, whether or not continued by section twenty-four of this Act, or granted for a term of years certain and thereafter from year to year.

f
(2) A tenant's request for a new tenancy shall be for a tenancy beginning with such date, not more than twelve nor less than six months after the making of the request, as may be specified therein: Provided that the said date shall not be earlier than the date on which apart from this Act the current tenancy would come to an end by effluxion of time or could be g   brought to an end by notice to quit given by the tenant …

(4) A tenant's request for a new tenancy shall not be made if the landlord has already given notice under the last foregoing section to terminate the current tenancy, or if the tenant has already given notice to quit or notice under the next following section; and no such notice shall be given by the h   landlord or the tenant after the making by the tenant of a request for a new tenancy.

(5) Where the tenant makes a request for a new tenancy in accordance with the foregoing provisions of this section, the current tenancy shall, subject to the provisions of subsection (2) of section thirty-six of this Act and the provisions of Part IV of this Act as to the interim continuation of j   tenancies, terminate immediately before the date specified in the request for the beginning of the new tenancy …'

Section 36(2) of the 1954 Act is not relevant, and the only relevant provision of Pt IV is s 64, to which I shall refer.

Succeeding sections of the 1954 Act contain provisions as to the grounds on which a landlord may oppose the grant of a new tenancy and the terms to be included in any new tenancy granted, which are not relevant for present purposes.

The only other section of the Act to which I should refer is s 64, which provides for: 'Interim continuation of tenancies pending determination by court.' So far as material, s 64(1) provides that, where a request for a new tenancy has been made under Pt II of the 1954 Act and an application for such a new tenancy has been made to the court, then if, apart from s 64, the effect of the request would be to terminate the tenancy before the expiration of the period of three months beginning on the date on which the application to the court is finally disposed of, the effect of the request shall be to terminate the tenancy at the expiration of such a period of three months and not at any other time.

Section 64(2) provides that if the application to the court is withdrawn, the reference in s 64(1) to the date on which the application is finally disposed of shall be construed as a reference to the date of its withdrawal.

Having made their request for a new tenancy on 4 October 1994, the plaintiffs applied to the county court for the grant of such a tenancy on 23 January 1995. The defendant, by its solicitors, indicated that it did not accept that the plaintiffs were entitled to a new tenancy. On 24 May 1995 the plaintiffs gave notice of discontinuance of their application to the county court.

Mr Hodge's argument on behalf of the plaintiffs is as follows.

(1) It is not disputed that the tenancy created by the lease, being a tenancy granted for a term of years exceeding one year, was at the material time a tenancy within s 26(1) of the 1954 Act and, therefore, one in respect of which the plaintiffs were entitled, subject to the other provisions of s 26, to make a request for a new tenancy under s 26.

(2) By virtue of s 26(2) the request had to be for a new tenancy beginning not more than 12 nor less than 6 months after the making of the request. This condition was satisfied by the request made by the plaintiffs on 4 October 1994, being for a tenancy commencing on 10 July 1995.

(3) The request did not infringe the proviso to s 26(2), in that the commencement date of the new tenancy requested was not earlier than the date on which, as at the date of the request, the existing tenancy could be brought to an end by notice to quit, ie notice under cl 7 of the lease given by the plaintiffs as tenants.

(4) The plaintiffs were not disabled from making a request for a new tenancy by s 26(4), because the tenants had not given notice to quit before making their request. The purported cl 7 notice was given at the same time as the request for a new tenancy, and anyway was, it must be assumed for the purposes of the present argument, not a valid notice to quit because of the mistake as to the date.

(5) Therefore, by virtue of s 26(5), subject to s 64, the tenancy under the lease [would have] terminated immediately before 10 July 1995, the date specified in the plaintiffs' request as the beginning of the new tenancy.

(6) In fact the old tenancy was prolonged by s 64 until 24 August 1995, being three months after the date of the discontinuance of the plaintiffs' application to the county court.

(7) Thus, irrespective of any invalidity of the purported notice under cl 7 of the lease, the lease terminated on 24 August 1995.

The defendant's argument, put very clearly and concisely by Mr Lewison QC, is much shorter. It is that the plaintiffs' purported request for a new tenancy under s 26 of the 1954 Act was invalid, because it infringed the proviso to s 26(2). For ease of reference I repeat the proviso:

a 'Provided that the said date [ie the date of commencement of the new tenancy requested] shall not be earlier than the date on which apart from this Act the current tenancy would come to an end by effluxion of time or could be brought to an end by notice to quit given by the tenant.'

b Mr Lewison's argument was that in the present case, the relevant tenancy being of the first of the two types to which s 26 applies, namely a tenancy granted for a term of years exceeding one year, the date relevant for the purposes of the proviso to s 26(2) is the date on which, apart from the Act, that tenancy would have come to an end by effluxion of time, namely 23 June 2005. The date of the commencement of the new tenancy specified in the plaintiffs' request was earlier than this date; therefore the request infringed the proviso to s 26(2).

c Despite the persuasiveness of Mr Hodge's submissions, I prefer the argument of Mr Lewison. Mr Hodge's argument requires the proviso to s 26(2) to be read as though it said:

d 'Provided that the said date shall not be earlier than (1) the date on which apart from this Act the current tenancy would come to an end by effluxion of time or (2) if earlier, the date on which it could be brought to an end by notice to quit given by the tenant.'

This is not what in fact the proviso says. In my judgment, the actual words of the proviso on their natural construction contemplate one relevant date only in respect of a given tenancy, and the two alternative definitions of that date are to e take account of the fact that the relevant tenancy may be (a) one granted simply for a term of years, in which case the relevant date under the proviso will be the date on which it would come to an end by effluxion of time, or (b) one granted for a term of years certain and thereafter from year to year, in which case, as Mr Lewison pointed out, the tenancy will never come to an end by effluxion of time, f and the only possible relevant date specified in the proviso to s 26(2) is the date on which, as at the date of the request under s 26(1), the existing tenancy could be brought to an end by notice to quit given by the tenant. Thus, in the case of a tenancy granted for a term of years exceeding one year, the date for the commencement of a new tenancy cannot be earlier than the date on which the current tenancy would, apart from the 1954 Act, come to an end by effluxion of g time.

This seems to me to be the natural construction of the words of the proviso in the context of s 26 as a whole, bearing in mind that the proviso has to be applicable to either of the two particular types of tenancy specified in s 26(1). Such a construction seems to me to produce a perfectly rational result in the h context of Pt II of the 1954 Act. I do not find it surprising that the Act does not, as would Mr Hodge's construction of it, mean that the inclusion in a lease for a term of years of a power for the tenant to break the lease has the effect that the tenant can not only terminate his enjoyment of the benefit and suffering of the burdens of the lease on the terms agreed on its grant, but can at the same time j obtain the benefit of a new tenancy on, in times of recession, terms much more favourable to him than those of the lease into which he entered or which he took by way of assignment.

Mr Hodge sought to derive some support for his argument on the construction of the proviso to s 26(2) of the 1954 Act, from the fact that s 25 of the Act enables a landlord to give notice terminating a tenancy to which Pt II of the Act applies on the earliest date on which he could, apart from the Act, have brought the tenancy to an end by notice to quit. Mr Hodge submitted that, to be consistent, s 26 should be construed so as to give a tenant power to request a new tenancy on the earliest date on which the tenant is entitled, apart from the Act, to bring the existing tenancy to an end by notice to quit.

I do not accept this argument. Nothing in the Act prevents a tenant bringing his original tenancy to an end at any date on which he could do so apart from the Act (see s 24(2)). The question is whether s 26 empowers him to request a new tenancy on new terms at the same time as exercising his power under a break clause to bring the old tenancy to an end. In my judgment, it does not. I see nothing in this conclusion inconsistent with the preservation by s 25 of the landlord's contractual right to give notice to quit, but subject to the tenant's right to apply for a new tenancy if the landlord does give such notice.

Accordingly, in my judgment, the purported request by the plaintiffs for a new tenancy under s 26 of the 1954 Act was invalid, because the date specified in it for the commencement of the new tenancy was earlier than the date on which the existing tenancy would come to an end by effluxion of time. It follows that the request was not effective to terminate the tenancy created by the lease and, since the error in the date specified in the notice purportedly given under cl 7 of the lease made that notice ineffective, the lease continues in force. I will hear counsel as to what order I should make.

Application dismissed. Certificate granted under s 12(3) of the Administration of Justice Act 1969 to appeal direct to the House of Lords.

3 July 1996. The Appeal Committee of the House of Lords (Lord Browne-Wilkinson, Lord Slynn of Hadley, Lord Nicholls of Birkenhead, Lord Steyn and Lord Hoffmann) refused leave to appeal.

Celia Fox   Barrister.

Secretary of State for Trade and Industry v Davies and others

COURT OF APPEAL, CIVIL DIVISION

NEILL, HOBHOUSE AND MILLETT LJJ

2, 3 APRIL, 24 MAY 1996

Company – Director – Disqualification – Director unfit to be concerned in management of a company – Application for leave to commence proceedings out of time – Principles applicable to exercise of court's discretion – Weight to be given to inadequacy of reasons for delay – Company Directors Disqualification Act 1986, ss 6, 7(2).

On 1 July 1992 the Secretary of State for Trade and Industry commenced disqualification proceedings against five company directors pursuant to s 6[a] of the Company Directors Disqualification Act 1986. The originating summons was issued just within the statutory time limit of two years from the date on which the companies became insolvent, so that the leave of the court under s 7(2)[b] of the Act was not required. However, the Secretary of State was unable to file evidence in support as required by the relevant rules. The summons was therefore accompanied by an application for an extension of time to file the evidence and an affidavit which sought to explain the delay in commencing the proceedings and disclosed the grounds on which the disqualification orders were sought. The evidence in support was subsequently served before the hearing of the application for extension of time, but more than five months after the two-year period had expired. Following various procedural steps, the registrar granted the application for an extension in January 1994 and his decision was upheld on appeal. The judge considered that while the reasons given for the delay were far from satisfactory, that consideration was outweighed by others, such as the gravity of the charges and the absence of any prejudice to the respondents, which pointed towards the granting of leave. One of the directors appealed on the question whether the inadequacy of reasons for a delay was merely one of the considerations to be taken into account on an application for leave to commence disqualification proceedings out of time, or whether the absence of a satisfactory explanation required the court to dismiss the application without regard to countervailing considerations.

Held – The 1986 Act imposed no limitation on the exercise of a judge's discretion on an application for leave under s 7(2) for an extension of time within which to file evidence in support of disqualification proceedings against a company director. The sole requirement was that he should exercise his discretion judicially, taking into account all the circumstances of the particular case, and having regard to the statutory purpose for which the discretion had been given to him and to the public interest. It followed that the inadequacy of reasons for a delay in bringing disqualification proceedings was only one of the considerations which the judge would take into account when deciding whether to grant leave for the proceedings to be commenced out of time. In the instant case, the judge

---

a   Section 6, so far as material, is set out at p 301 *f*, post
b   Section 7(2), so far as material, is set out at p 291 *g*, post

had applied the correct test, and although the Secretary of State had not given a
satisfactory explanation for the delay, leave should nevertheless be granted, since *a*
the charges against D were particularly serious, there was an obvious public
interest in having them determined and the delay had occasioned no prejudice to
the directors. The appeal would accordingly be dismissed (see p 296 *f* to p 297 *a*,
p 299 *j* to p 300 *a f* to *j*, p 301 *a b*, p 302 *c* to *g*, p 303 *e f* and p 304 *a* to *e*, post).

Dictum of Scott LJ in *Re Probe Data Systems Ltd (No 3), Secretary of State for Trade* *b*
and Industry v Desai [1992] BCLC 405 at 416 and of Hoffmann LJ in *Secretary of*
State for Trade and Industry v McTighe, Re Copecrest Ltd [1994] 2 BCLC 284 at 287
considered.

Notes
For powers and duty of the court to make disqualification orders, see 7(2) *c*
Halsbury's Laws (4th edn 1996 reissue) paras 1417–1427.

For the Company Directors Disqualification Act 1986, ss 6, 7, see 8 *Halsbury's*
Statutes (4th edn) (1991 reissue) 786, 787.

Cases referred to in judgments   *d*
Cedar Developments Ltd, Re [1994] 2 BCLC 714.
Costellow v Somerset CC [1993] 1 All ER 952, [1993] 1 WLR 256, CA.
Erskine Communications Ltd v Worthington (1991) Times, 8 July, [1991] CA
  Transcript 725.
Kleinwort Benson Ltd v Barbrak Ltd, The Myrto (No 3) [1987] 2 All ER 289, [1987] AC
  597, [1987] 2 WLR 1053, HL.   *e*
Lo-Line Electric Motors Ltd, Re [1988] 2 All ER 692, [1988] Ch 477, [1988] 3 WLR 26.
Manlon Trading Ltd, Re [1995] 4 All ER 14, [1996] Ch 136, [1995] 3 WLR 839, CA.
Noble Trees Ltd, Re [1993] BCLC 1185.
Polly Peck International plc, Re (No 2), Secretary of State for Trade and Industry v Ellis
  [1994] 1 BCLC 574.   *f*
Probe Data Systems Ltd, Re (No 3), Secretary of State for Trade and Industry v Desai
  [1992] BCLC 405, CA.
Ratnam v Cumarasamy [1964] 3 All ER 933, [1965] 1 WLR 8, PC.
Revici v Prentice Hall Inc [1969] 1 All ER 772, [1969] 1 WLR 157, CA.
Savill v Southend Health Authority [1995] 1 WLR 1254, CA.
Secretary of State for Trade and Industry v Langridge [1991] 3 All ER 591, [1991] Ch *g*
  402, [1991] 2 WLR 1343, CA; *rvsg sub nom Re Cedac Ltd* [1990] BCC 555.
Secretary of State for Trade and Industry v McTighe, Re Copecrest Ltd [1994] 2 BCLC
  284, CA.
Van Stillevoldt (CM) BV v El Carriers Inc [1983] 1 All ER 699, [1983] 1 WLR 207, CA.
                                                                      h
Cases also cited or referred to in skeleton arguments
Crestjoy Products Ltd, Re [1990] BCLC 677.
Rastin v British Steel plc [1994] 2 All ER 641, [1994] 1 WLR 732, CA.
Regalbourne Ltd v East Lindsey DC [1994] RA 1, CA.
Sevenoaks Stationers (Retail) Ltd, Re [1991] 3 All ER 578, [1991] Ch 164, CA.   *j*

Interlocutory appeal
By amended notice dated 13 February 1995 the first respondent, Vernon John
Everleigh Davies, appealed with leave of the Court of Appeal (Millett and Otton
LJJ) granted on 7 November 1995 from the decision of Carnwath J made on 2 May
1995 whereby he dismissed his appeal from an order of the registrar dated 27

a January and granted the Secretary of State for Trade and Industry an extension of time for the service of evidence in support of his originating summons dated 1 July 1992 seeking the disqualification of the first respondent and the second to fifth respondents, Nicholas Andrew Thomas, William Cummings Thompson, Alexander Douglas Andrew, and Nigel Anthony Eastaway, as company directors pursuant to s 6 of the Company Directors Disqualification Act 1986. The facts are

b set out in the judgment of Millett LJ.

Michael Briggs QC and *Paul Girolami* (instructed by *Peters & Peters*) for the first respondent.
A W H Charles and *Richard Gillis* (instructed by the *Treasury Solicitor*) for the Secretary of State.

c
Cur adv vult

24 May 1996. The following judgments were delivered.

d **MILLETT LJ** (giving the first judgment at the invitation of Neill LJ). This is an appeal by the first respondent, Mr Vernon Davies, from an order of Carnwath J dated 2 May 1995 dismissing his appeal from an order of the registrar dated 27 January 1994 and granting the Secretary of State for Trade and Industry an extension of time for the service of evidence in support of his originating summons dated 1 July 1992 and issued under s 6 of the Company Directors

e Disqualification Act 1986.

Section 6 of the Act requires the court to make a disqualification order against any person where, on an application made under the section, it is satisfied that he is or has been a director of a company which has become insolvent and that his conduct as a director of that company makes him unfit to be concerned in the

f management of a company. The minimum period of disqualification under the section is two years and the maximum period is 15 years. Section 7 of the Act authorises the Secretary of State to make an application for a disqualification order under s 6 if it appears to him to be expedient in the public interest that such an order should be made.

Section 7(2) of the Act provides:

g
'Except with the leave of the court, an application for the making under [s 6] of a disqualification order against any person shall not be made after the end of the period of 2 years beginning with the day on which the company of which that person is or has been a director became insolvent.'

h Section 6 is not the only provision which confers power on the court to make a disqualification order against a director, though it is the only one which makes such an order mandatory where the necessary conditions are satisfied. The court may, for example, also make a disqualification order under s 2 of the Act against a person who has been convicted of an indictable offence in connection with the

j promotion, formation or management of a company, and the maximum period of disqualification under this section is also 15 years. No time limit is laid down for the making of an application for an order under s 2.

Applications by the Secretary of State under s 7 are governed by the Insolvent Companies (Disqualification of Unfit Directors) Proceedings Rules 1987, SI 1987/2023. Rule 3(1) provides:

'There shall, at the time when the summons is issued, be filed in court
evidence in support of the application for a disqualification order; and copies   a
of the evidence shall be served with the summons on the respondent.'

In the present case, the originating summons was issued within the relevant
period of two years, so that the leave of the court under s 7(2) of the Act was not
required. But the Secretary of State was unable to file detailed evidence in
support of the application with the summons, as required by the 1987 rules.   b
Accordingly, at the same time as issuing the originating summons he made an
application to the registrar for an extension of time for the service of evidence
until a date long after the two-year period was due to expire. In the event, the
Secretary of State completed and served the evidence in support of the
originating summons before the hearing of his application for an extension of   c
time, which became the subject of successive adjournments by the registrar, but
more than five months after the two-year period had expired. The registrar
granted the application and his decision was upheld by the judge.

In dismissing the appeal of the first respondent and thereby granting the
extension of time sought by the Secretary of State for the filing of evidence, the
judge was exercising a judicial discretion. He considered that the reasons given   d
by the Secretary of State for the delay were far from satisfactory, but that this
consideration was outweighed by others which pointed towards the granting of
leave. It was common ground that in exercising his discretion to enable the
Secretary of State to file evidence out of time, without which the originating
summons must necessarily have been dismissed, the judge should treat the   e
application as if it had been an application for leave to issue the originating
summons on the date on which the Secretary of State was first in a position to
serve his supporting evidence.

This court gave leave to appeal against the judge's decision in order to enable
the first respondent to raise an issue of principle. The question is whether (as the
Secretary of State submits) the inadequacy of the reasons for delay is merely one   f
of the considerations which must be taken into account when deciding whether
to give leave for disqualification proceedings to be commenced out of time; or
whether (as the first respondent submits) it is always necessary for a satisfactory
explanation to be given for the delay, so that, if no such explanation is
forthcoming, the respondent is entitled to have the Secretary of State's   g
application dismissed and countervailing considerations, such as the absence of
prejudice to the respondent, do not fall to be taken into account.

THE HISTORY OF THE PROCEEDINGS

The proposed disqualification proceedings concern the conduct of five persons
who were directors of four companies in a group of companies known as the   h
Blackspur Group. The companies were engaged in the business of computer
leasing. Administrative receivers were appointed in respect of each of the
companies in July 1990. Nearly 14 months later, at the end of August 1991, Mr
Brierley, a partner in Messrs Arthur Andersen & Co and one of the joint
administrative receivers, reported to the Secretary of State on the conduct of the   j
directors of the companies. According to Mr Brierley, the transactions entered
into by the companies were extremely complicated, and it took time to unravel
them and to consider the true extent of the liabilities of the companies to third
parties and the liabilities of third parties to the companies. It was his opinion that
the profits of the companies were overstated, and it became necessary to consider
the accounting policies which had been adopted by the companies since the

a inception of trading. Together with his staff, Mr Brierley carried out a detailed examination of the accounting policies adopted by the companies and the effect which they had on the reported profits of the companies. Because of the poor condition of the companies' books and records and the complicated nature of the transactions into which they had entered, this task took a long time to complete and delayed his report to the Secretary of State.

b On 30 September 1991, as a result of Mr Brierley's report, the Secretary of State made a formal decision to bring disqualification proceedings. In his report, Mr Brierley had recommended close liaison with the Serious Fraud Office (the SFO), which since August 1990 had been carrying out its own investigation into the conduct of the directors of the companies in the Blackspur Group, following complaints from creditors, and which had taken charge of the books and papers

c of one of the companies (though without denying the administrative receivers access to them).

Accordingly, on 1 October the Department of Trade and Industry contacted the SFO and requested its assistance. It received no substantive reply until 6 December. On that date it was informed that the SFO would make no final

d decision on whether to prosecute until after the receipt of the report of the inspectors who had been appointed by the Secretary of State to investigate the affairs of Atlantic Computers plc, a company with which some of the directors of companies in the Blackspur Group had been associated. The Atlantic report was expected to be received by the end of January 1992, and it was thought that the SFO would make a decision during February. The department decided that

e 'there was no alternative but to wait for the decision of the SFO'.

By the beginning of March 1992, the Atlantic report had still not been received. On 4 March the department contacted the SFO again, only to be informed that the SFO was still not in a position to make a final decision. Shortly afterwards, the SFO informed the department that it was not at that stage willing to disclose

f any of the information in its possession to the Secretary of State.

Once this was known, the department decided to begin the preparation of the evidence needed to support its own proceedings. Discussions were held with Mr Brierley's assistant, from which it became clear that the principal grounds on which the applications would be made would be based upon information in the possession of the SFO, in respect of which Mr Brierley's knowledge was

g incomplete. Preliminary steps were taken to prepare an affidavit by Mr Brierley.

On 13 May the Treasury Solicitor was instructed in the matter on behalf of the Secretary of State. On 21 May a meeting took place between the Treasury Solicitor's office, the department and the SFO, at which the SFO reversed its previous decision and agreed to make available to the Secretary of State whatever

h information it properly could in order to enable him to bring proceedings. By now, it was obviously too late to prepare the detailed evidence in support of the application by the two-year deadline, which was due to expire in early July.

The department served the 'ten-day letters' required by s 16(1) of the 1986 Act in June. The letter to the first respondent was sent to him on 9 June. Unusually,

j it set out the main allegations upon which the proposed proceedings would be based. Shortly afterwards, all five respondents were arrested and interviewed under caution. On 1 July the second to fifth respondents were charged and brought before the Dartford Magistrates' Court. The first respondent was not and never has been charged with any offence.

On the same day, the present proceedings were commenced by the issue of an originating summons. This was one day before the expiry of the two-year period

in relation to three of the companies and nine days before the expiry of the period
in relation to the fourth. The originating summons was accompanied by an   *a*
application for an extension of time until 12 October 1992 to file evidence. This
was supported by an affidavit, which sought to explain the delay and which
disclosed the grounds on which the disqualification orders were sought. These
included allegations of false accounting as a result of which the companies were
shown to be profitable and solvent when in fact they were unprofitable and   *b*
insolvent; and allegations that the companies had traded while insolvent,
obtained credit by misrepresentation, paid grossly excessive remuneration to the
directors, and engaged in uncommercial transactions.

The proceedings were served on 13 July. Meanwhile, the solicitors acting for
the first and fourth respondents had written to the Treasury Solicitor referring to
the fact that the fourth respondent had been charged and had asked that if   *c*
disqualification proceedings were to be pursued at all they should be stayed until
after the conclusion of the criminal proceedings. Surprisingly, in view of his own
position, the Treasury Solicitor refused this request and expressed the hope that
all interlocutory matters including the filing of evidence would be completed
before the conclusion of the criminal trial.   *d*

The Secretary of State's application for an extension of time to file evidence
was the subject of successive adjournments. The evidence in support of the
originating summons was completed and filed on 14 December 1992. This
included a second affidavit of Mr Brierley of 77 pages accompanied by 800 pages
of exhibits and an affidavit of 94 pages from a Mr Bellamy accompanied by more   *e*
than 1,000 pages of exhibits. Mr Bellamy was a partner in Price Waterhouse on
secondment to the SFO. He had led a team of accountants investigating the
affairs of the Blackspur Group. He had begun these investigations in October
1990.

Meanwhile, the respondents had applied to strike out the proceedings for
failure to comply with r 3(1) of the 1987 rules. In May 1993 they applied to stay   *f*
all proceedings until after the verdict in the criminal proceedings. On 27 January
1994 the registrar granted the Secretary of State an extension of time to file
evidence and dismissed the respondents' application to strike out the
proceedings. In view of the imminence of the criminal trial, the respondents'
solicitors invited the Treasury Solicitor to agree that the time for appealing the   *g*
registrar's order should be extended until 28 days after the conclusion of the trial.
The Treasury Solicitor refused this request, and the respondents duly gave notice
of appeal. The criminal trial began on 7 March 1994, and shortly afterwards it was
agreed between the Secretary of State and the respondents that all
disqualification proceedings, including the appeal, should be stayed until after the   *h*
verdict.

The Atlantic report was eventually signed by the inspectors in April 1994 and
published in July. In June the fourth and fifth respondents were acquitted and the
second and third respondents were convicted; their convictions were later
quashed on appeal in February 1995. The appeal of the respondents from the   *j*
registrar's orders came before Carnwath J on 1 May 1995 and was dismissed by
him on 2 May. Only the first respondent appeals to this court.

THE REASONS FOR THE DELAY

No criticism is made by the first respondent in respect of the period prior to 1
October 1991. But serious criticism is made of the delay between then and 13

a May 1992, when the Treasury Solicitor was instructed and progress at last began in earnest to assemble the evidence for disqualification.

Once the formal decision to bring disqualification proceedings was taken, it was decided that the first step should be to approach the SFO to establish the current position of its inquiry. This was clearly not unreasonable. It was in accordance with Mr Brierley's own recommendation. Moreover, the SFO had undertaken a far more comprehensive investigation of the matters which would be relevant to the fitness of the individual directors, and the main allegations on which disqualification proceedings would be based were matters which were being fully investigated by the SFO but not by the joint administrative receivers, since the investigation of these matters was not necessary for the purposes of the receivership.

It was not to be expected that the SFO would take two months to reply, or that its response would be so unhelpful. The delay to 6 December 1991 is, therefore, understandable, though it suggests a want of any sense of urgency (or even of the passage of time) on the part of the department. The same cannot be said of the period between 6 December 1991 and April 1992. Nothing at all was done during this period. This was due to the department's decision that it 'had no alternative' but to wait for the decision of the SFO whether to bring criminal proceedings.

I do not for my own part find this decision easy to understand. The Secretary of State had already decided that it was expedient in the public interest to seek mandatory disqualification orders, and as subsequent events demonstrate, this was not conditional on the absence of criminal proceedings. Even if such proceedings were brought, they might not be brought against all the directors considered to be unfit; they might be unsuccessful against all or some of the accused; and the making of disqualification orders against those who were convicted would be discretionary. What the department needed from the SFO was not a decision on whether it intended to prosecute, but its assistance in the preparation of the evidence needed for the bringing of successful disqualification proceedings. It is possible, of course, that the two were thought to be connected, but if so this is not spelled out in the evidence.

While the Secretary of State did not act unreasonably in trying to secure the assistance of the SFO, I do not think that he can escape criticism for the failure to instruct the Treasury Solicitor in December 1991 or to approach Mr Bellamy at that time to see if he was willing to provide the necessary evidence for the disqualification proceedings. At the very least, inquiries should have been made of Mr Brierley (and possibly Mr Bellamy) to enable the department to estimate how long would be needed to assemble the evidence so that the work could be put in hand in time. Where such an estimate is made and the work is later found to take longer than expected, the court is likely to be sympathetic to an application for leave to extend time.

The judge appears to have accepted the first respondent's submission that with proper diligence the evidence could have been prepared in time. He recognised that it was sensible to avoid unnecessary duplication of work, and that it was reasonable to try to obtain Mr Bellamy's assistance. The trouble was that there was no evidence that the department made a considered judgment to that effect in December 1991. Indeed, it did not appear that any of the officials concerned had addressed their minds to the statutory time limit and the problem of assembling the evidence by July 1992. On any view, the case was going to take some months to prepare even with the full co-operation of the SFO, and the July deadline was not far off. No one tried to establish a realistic programme. It was

not until the meeting with the SFO in May 1992 following the involvement of the
Treasury Solicitor that the work was put in hand in earnest, and by then there was   *a*
no hope of meeting the deadline. Accordingly, the judge said, he 'saw some force
in the criticisms made by [the respondents], if the reasons for the delay are looked
at on their own'.

I agree with the judge's assessment. Indeed, I would put it more strongly. I
see considerable force in these criticisms, and would hold that the reasons which   *b*
the Secretary of State has put forward for his failure to assemble the necessary
evidence before the expiry of the two-year period, while not contumelious or
wholly unacceptable, are nevertheless far from satisfactory.

The question is whether they must be looked at 'on their own'.

THE PRINCIPLES ON WHICH THE DISCRETION IS TO BE EXERCISED   *c*

The principles which govern the exercise of the discretion were most recently
stated by this court in *Secretary of State for Trade and Industry v McTighe, Re
Copecrest Ltd* [1994] 2 BCLC 284 at 287, where Hoffmann LJ said:

'The judge asked himself whether the Secretary of State had shown a good
reason for an extension. This seems to me a correct way of putting the   *d*
question. The matter was elaborated by Scott LJ in *Re Probe Data Systems Ltd
(No 3), Secretary of State for Trade and Industry v Desai* [1992] BCLC 405 at 416
where he said: "In considering an application under s 7(2) for leave to
commence disqualification proceedings out of time the court should, in my
opinion, take into account the following matters: (1) the length of the delay,   *e*
(2) the reasons for the delay, (3) the strength of the case against the director
and (4) the degree of prejudice caused to the director by the delay."'

It is common ground that the statutory language places the onus on the
Secretary of State to satisfy the court that an extension should be granted. He
must, in the words of Hoffmann LJ, always show a good reason for the extension.   *f*
The reference to 'good reason' is derived from the speech of Lord Brandon in
Kleinwort Benson Ltd v Barbrak Ltd, The Myrto (No 3) [1987] 2 All ER 289 at 297,
[1987] AC 597 at 622. That case was concerned with an extension of time for
service of a writ. Lord Brandon made it clear that it was always necessary to show
good reason for the extension, while observing that it was not possible to define
or circumscribe the scope of that expression.   *g*

The four factors which Scott LJ described derive from a number of cases,
including *C M Van Stillevoldt BV v El Carriers Inc* [1983] 1 All ER 699, [1983] 1 WLR
207, a case concerned with the extension of time for leave to appeal to this court.
There, Griffiths LJ approved the approach taken by the registrar, who had said:

h

'In my judgment, all the relevant factors must be taken into account in
deciding how to exercise the discretion to extend time. Those factors include
the length of the delay, the reasons for the delay, whether there is an
arguable case on the appeal, and the degree of prejudice to the defendant if
time is extended.' (See [1983] 1 All ER 699 at 704, [1983] 1 WLR 207 at 212.)   *j*

I do not read the passage in the judgment of Scott LJ in *Re Probe Data Systems
Ltd (No 3), Secretary of State for Trade and Industry v Desai* [1992] BCLC 405 as
intended to be exhaustive. Plainly all relevant circumstances must be taken into
account, including but not limited to the four particular factors to which Scott LJ
drew attention. One factor which is always present but always relevant is the
nature of the proceedings. The Secretary of State is not seeking to vindicate a

a private right, but to protect the public from the actions of a person alleged to be unfit to be a director of a company. Scott LJ's reference to 'the strength of the case against the director' must be read in this light. It is not, in my opinion, a reference to the strength or credibility of the evidence which he seeks leave to file, but to the gravity of the charges which he makes.

b THE JUDGE'S DECISION
    The judge accepted the parties' invitation to exercise his discretion anew. He referred to and applied the test propounded by Hoffmann LJ in *Re Copecrest Ltd*. He rejected the respondents' submissions that he should treat the adequacy of the explanation given by the Secretary of State for the delay as a preliminary or free-standing issue, and that the failure to give a satisfactory explanation was the
c same as giving no explanation at all. He saw force in the criticisms of the department's failure to act much earlier than it did, and appears to have accepted that it could have assembled the evidence in time if it had acted more diligently. But he thought that this was outweighed by other countervailing considerations; in particular the gravity of the charges, the absence of any prejudice to the
d respondents, and the fact that the timetable for the hearing of the disqualification proceedings had not been delayed at all. It was always clear that the hearing of those proceedings would have to await the outcome of the criminal trial, and the five-month delay in assembling the evidence in support of the proceedings had not caused any overall delay. The judge concluded by saying:

e   'If, as must be accepted, there is a serious case against the [respondents] which the Secretary of State considers it right in the public interest to pursue, it does not seem to me that should be defeated merely because of some delay in getting his tackle in order, where that delay has not in itself added to the overall time scale nor materially affected the [respondents'] ability to defend themselves.'

f This passage has been strongly criticised by the first respondent. It has been suggested that the judge was laying down a rule of law of general application. If so, he was in error, for there is no such rule, and the error vitiated his decision. But I do not think that he was intending to enunciate any general rule, but rather to summarise the way in which he considered the balance came out on the
g particular facts of the case before him.

THE RIVAL CONTENTIONS
The first respondent
    The first respondent's submissions may be summarised as follows. Section
h 7(2) of the 1986 Act is, in effect, a limitation provision. Failure to comply with its provisions has the automatic consequence that no proceedings may be brought. The requirement to proceed timeously against delinquent directors of insolvent companies is imposed partly for their protection, so that they may be able to organise their affairs once the two-year period has passed free of the risk of future
j disqualification; and partly in the public interest, for it is obviously wrong that a person whom the Secretary of State considers to be unfit to act as a director should be left free to do so any longer than is necessary (see *Re Noble Trees Ltd* [1993] BCLC 1185 at 1190 per Vinelott J and *Re Polly Peck International plc (No 2)*, *Secretary of State for Trade and Industry v Ellis* [1994] 1 BCLC 574 at 590 per Lindsay J). Accordingly, it is submitted, while the existence of a discretionary power to extend the time for the taking of a step in litigation occurs in a wide range of

different circumstances, the jurisdiction to extend the time within which
Parliament has decided that proceedings must be brought should be exercised
sparingly and with great caution. If the extension is granted, its effect is to deprive
the respondent of an accrued statutory immunity from suit.

It is always necessary for an applicant for an extension of time to explain the
reasons for the delay; in the absence of some explanation there is no material
upon which the court can exercise its discretion (see *Ratnam v Cumarasamy* [1964]
3 All ER 933 at 935, [1965] 1 WLR 8 at 12 per Lord Guest, *Revici v Prentice Hall Inc*
[1969] 1 All ER 772 at 774, [1969] 1 WLR 157 at 160 per Edmund Davies LJ, and
Savill v Southend Health Authority [1995] 1 WLR 1254 at 1259 per Balcombe LJ). In
the last-mentioned case, the delay was minimal; the court recognised that it
might be satisfied with an explanation for a minimal delay, even possibly
forgetfulness, which it would not accept for a substantial period of delay, but it
upheld the judge's refusal to extend time where no explanation was given at all.

In this context, the first respondent submits, an unsatisfactory reason for the
delay is no better than no reason at all; what is needed is an acceptable reason on
which the court can properly act. Reliance for this proposition, which the judge
rejected, is placed on *Ratnam v Cumarasamy*, where the appellant gave an
explanation for the delay, albeit an unacceptable one (he had not instructed his
solicitors in time to issue proceedings within the time limit because he had hoped
to effect a compromise); yet (it is submitted) the judicial committee treated the
case as one in which no explanation was given of the delay.

It is, therefore, always necessary for the Secretary of State to show a
satisfactory reason for or explanation of the delay which is sufficient to justify the
extension sought. Mr Cherryman QC was right in *Re Cedar Developments Ltd*
[1994] 2 BCLC 714 at 719 when he suggested that there can hardly be a good
reason for leave without a good reason for having missed the time limit. If the
Secretary of State cannot meet the threshold test by giving an adequate
explanation of the delay, leave should not be given. It cannot be a sufficient
ground for granting leave that the delay has been slight or that no prejudice has
been caused to the respondent. This would reverse the onus and justify
extensions being granted virtually as a matter of course unless the putative
respondent could show prejudice. This cannot have been the intention of
Parliament.

The Secretary of State

The Secretary of State accepts that he must satisfy the court that the extension
should be granted, and that as part of that process he must explain why he did not
serve the process (or in this case the supporting evidence) in time. But, he
submits, that explanation is merely one of the factors which must be taken into
account in the exercise of the discretion. There is no justification for treating the
adequacy of the explanation of the delay as a free-standing or threshold test which
must be satisfied before other considerations can be taken into account. The
judge was right to reject the equation of an unsatisfactory reason for delay with
the giving of no reason at all. The court is always entitled to an explanation for
the delay, but once an explanation is given, then it becomes a matter to be
considered in the light of all the relevant circumstances.

CONCLUSION

I do not find it helpful to describe s 7(2) of the 1986 Act as a limitation
provision, or to regard the grant of leave as depriving the respondent of an

a accrued immunity from suit. The grant of leave is built into the two-year period. Parliament clearly recognised that the two-year period might not be sufficient in every case. Even before the period expires, proceedings cannot be brought unless the Secretary of State has first determined that it is expedient in the public interest that they should be brought; after it has expired, the further requirement is imposed that the leave of the court should be obtained. There are then two

b preconditions instead of one, but that is all. Once the two-year period has expired, delinquent directors are not immune from disqualification proceedings; they are immune from such proceedings brought without the leave of the court, but that is a very different thing.

Further, while it is true that the requirement that disqualification proceedings must be brought within the statutory period unless the leave of the court is

c obtained is imposed in part at least in the public interest, in that the sooner directors who are unfit to take part in the management of a company are disqualified from doing so the better, I fail to see how this consideration assists the first respondent, when the only result of refusing leave is that the proceedings may not be brought at all. If correct, the first respondent's argument on this point

d would suggest that the more serious the charges made against a director, the more difficult it should be for the Secretary of State to obtain leave. I do not think that either Scott LJ or Hoffmann LJ intended to be so understood.

Nor, even though it was common ground, do I accept the proposition that in considering an application by the Secretary of State for an extension of time in which to file evidence without which proceedings started in time must

e necessarily be dismissed, the court should treat the application as if it were an application for leave to bring the proceedings out of time. I agree that the court should adopt a similar approach, and that it should take the same factors into account. But it must be more difficult to justify a failure even to issue the originating process within the time limit than to justify the failure to serve

f adequate supporting evidence at the same time; and the fact that the process has been issued within time must be a relevant factor to be taken into account, particularly if it is accompanied, as it was in the present case, with a statement of the grounds upon which the Secretary of State alleges that the respondent is unfit to be a director of a company. One of the purposes which Parliament had in mind in enacting the two-year time limit must have been to allow directors of

g companies which have become insolvent a reasonable degree of security from disqualification with the passage of time. If they have been notified within the time limit, not only of the Secretary of State's decision to bring disqualification proceedings against them but also of the nature of the allegations upon which they are to be based, the statutory purpose has to this extent been fulfilled.

h Moreover, once the proceedings have been started, the time for the filing of evidence is under the control of the court. Any application for an extension of time will be heard inter partes, and any attempt by the Secretary of State to delay matters unreasonably after the commencement of proceedings can be resisted by the respondent and ought to be frustrated by the court.

j In all other respects, I reject the submissions of the first respondent. An applicant for an extension of time must always explain why his application is necessary; this necessarily involves his giving an explanation of the delay. The Secretary of State is, therefore, obliged to explain why he failed to issue the proceedings or serve the supporting evidence (as the case may be) in time. But once an explanation is given it becomes a matter to be considered together with all the other relevant circumstances. There is, in my opinion, no justification for treating the adequacy of the explanation as a free-standing or threshold test which must be satisfied before other considerations can be taken into account. There is no support for such an approach in the authorities, and it is incorrect in principle as well as unworkable in practice. In the absence of a deliberate decision to disregard the rules, or to overreach, or take an unfair advantage of the other side, there is no such thing as a reason for delay which is 'good' or 'bad' in itself, regardless of the circumstances, or which is inherently acceptable or unacceptable in all circumstances. There is only a reason for delay which may reasonably be accepted as sufficient to justify an extension of time in all the circumstances of the particular case. Balcombe LJ recognised as much in *Savill v Southend Health Authority* [1995] 1 WLR 1254 at 1259, when he pointed out that the court might be satisfied with an explanation such as forgetfulness for a minimal delay which it would not accept for a longer period of delay. What he was saying, in my view, was that even forgetfulness, while not in itself a satisfactory reason for delay, might be accepted as sufficient to justify an extension of time where it was supported by other considerations, and that the minimal length of the delay might be such a consideration.

The first respondent's reliance on *Ratnam v Cumarasamy* [1964] 3 All ER 933, [1965] 1 WLR 8 in this connection was in my opinion misplaced. The case is not authority for the proposition that a 'bad' reason for delay is the same as no reason. Lord Guest described the explanation of the delay which had been put forward below, and after restating the principles upon which a court acts when reviewing the discretion exercised by a lower court and confirming that on questions of procedure the board was slow to interfere with the discretion of the local court, stated that the court below were entitled to take the view that the explanation 'did not constitute material on which they could exercise their discretion in favour of the appellant.' It does not, of course, follow that the board would have been entitled to interfere if the court below had decided differently.

There is no suggestion in the formulation of the appropriate test made by Scott LJ and approved by Hoffmann LJ that any of the factors which they enumerated is to be taken by itself as constituting a free-standing or threshold test which must be satisfied before any extension of time can be granted. The Secretary of State must show a good reason for being granted the extension of time which he seeks; but this is not the same as having to show a good reason for the delay, as is clear from the speech of Lord Brandon in *Kleinwort Benson Ltd v Barbrak Ltd, The Myrto (No 3)* [1987] 2 All ER 289, [1987] AC 597. The Secretary of State must explain the delay; the better the explanation, the easier it will be for him to obtain leave.

In the present case he gave an explanation. It was not a good one. The judge thought that, despite this, leave should be given. In my opinion, he applied the correct test, and the view which he took was one to which he was entitled to come. If, contrary to my opinion, his decision was vitiated by the error of law to which I have already referred, it would make no difference, for this would entitle us to substitute our own decision, and I would come to the same conclusion as the judge did. The case is brought in the public interest to disqualify directors alleged to be unfit. The charges (particularly of false accounting and trading while insolvent) are particularly serious and there is an obvious public interest in having them determined. The delay was not minimal and the explanation for it is unsatisfactory, but it has not affected the timing of the hearing and has caused no prejudice to the first respondent. The proceedings were initiated in time, and the first respondent was made aware of the nature of the allegations intended to be made against him before the statutory period had expired. Thereafter, the a respondents' main concern was to delay the proceedings until after the conclusion of the criminal trial, not to hurry them on. In those circumstances, I, for my part, would also have granted the extension sought had the discretion been mine to exercise. In saying this, I would emphasise that I would have exercised it in the light of all the circumstances and not merely because there was no prejudice to the first respondent.

b   I would dismiss the appeal.

HOBHOUSE LJ. The purpose of the Company Directors Disqualification Act 1986 is to give effect to the public interest that persons who are unfit to be directors of companies should be disqualified from so acting. It exists for the proper regulation of the economic life of this country. It imposes administrative c duties upon government and the persons responsible for this regulation. It charges the courts with the judicial duty to make appropriate orders of disqualification in the public interest. The powers which the 1986 Act gives affect the rights of individuals who may be the subject of proceedings for disqualification and who, unless disqualified, would be free to continue to act as d directors of companies. The Act therefore has to impose appropriate duties upon those responsible for protecting the public interest and at the same time have proper regard to the rights and interests of individual citizens who may be affected by proceedings or orders made under the Act.

          The Act covers a number of situations which give rise to the need to consider the fitness of an individual to be a director and whether a disqualification order e should be made. Section 6 deals with the duty of the court to disqualify unfit directors of insolvent companies. Section 6(1) is mandatory:

> 'The court shall make a disqualification order against a person in any case where, on an application under this section, it is satisfied—(a) that he is or has been a director of a company which has at any time become insolvent f (whether while he was a director or subsequently), and (b) that his conduct as a director of that company (either taken alone or taken together with his conduct as a director of any other company or companies) makes him unfit to be concerned in the management of a company.'

g The duty of the court to disqualify under this subsection only arises where an application has been made. Section 7(1) provides that the application shall be made by the Secretary of State or, when he so directs, by the Official Receiver. Section 7(3) defines classes of 'office-holders' who are required to report apparent unfitness to the Secretary of State.

          As was pointed out by Hoffmann LJ in his judgment in *Secretary of State for* h *Trade and Industry v McTighe, Re Copecrest Ltd* [1994] 2 BCLC 284 at 285, the Insolvent Companies (Reports on Conduct of Directors) No 2 Rules 1986, SI 1986/2134, lay down a timetable which must be followed by office-holders in reporting to the Secretary of State. These rules impose a duty upon the office-holder to make his report within six months of the commencement of the j winding up or administration. It is a criminal offence for the office-holder 'without reasonable excuse' to exceed this time limit. If the office-holder has performed his duty within the six-month period, there should ordinarily be no reason why the Secretary of State, or the Official Receiver, should not be able to make up his mind within the succeeding 18 months whether or not to apply under s 6 of the 1986 Act and assemble the evidence necessary to support the application.

This is clearly the assumption which underlies s 7(2) of the 1986 Act:

'Except with the leave of the court, an application for the making under that section of a disqualification order against any person shall not be made after the end of the period of 2 years ...'

Good administration requires that appropriate timetables be followed and that any investigations be carried out with appropriate diligence and despatch, and that disqualification orders be applied for and obtained with reasonable promptitude. Indeed, the worse the case of unfitness, the greater the need that a disqualification order be applied for and made at the earliest practicable date; but, equally, the lapse of two years does not make it any the less necessary that such persons should be disqualified.

An important part, therefore, of the purpose of s 7(2) is to aid good administration: it reflects the public interest in good administration. But it clearly has a further purpose as well—the protection of the legitimate interests of persons who have been directors of insolvent companies. Although to be a director of a company is a privilege, it is not one of which a person should be unjustly deprived. It represents, or may represent, his means of livelihood and his ability to carry on his business activities. He has a legitimate expectation that if he is going to have to defend disqualification proceedings he should know about it within a reasonable time following the insolvency and not be left in a state of uncertainty. This policy is also reflected by s 16 of the 1986 Act, which requires ten days prior notice to be given to the person affected of the intention to make an application for a disqualification order.

However, further than this s 7(2) does not go. It simply requires that the applicant shall apply to the court for leave. The discretion of the court is unfettered. There is no statutory threshold for the exercise of the discretion or the grant of leave. It is not a limitation period or time bar such as is found in the Limitation Acts. The expiry of the two-year period creates no vested right in the former director. It gives rise to no question of competing private law rights.

But it does give the former director the procedural right and opportunity to oppose the giving of leave. He is entitled to object that he should not be subjected to a stale or oppressive or unmeritorious application. The imposition of the requirement for the leave of the court gives him, after the two years have elapsed, an additional procedural protection. Thereafter, the Secretary of State does not have the unqualified power to make an application under s 6 against him. The application may only proceed if the court, in the exercise of its discretion, considers that it should.

I consider that there is a close analogy with the situation considered in *Re Manlon Trading Ltd* [1995] 4 All ER 14, [1996] Ch 136. In that case the application under s 6 had been made within two years. But there had then been inordinate and inexcusable delay in the prosecution of the application. The respondent applied to have the proceedings dismissed for want of prosecution. The Court of Appeal based its decision upon an assessment of the public interest in allowing the proceedings to continue. They upheld the judge's order dismissing the proceedings. Peter Gibson LJ ([1995] 4 All ER 14 at 21–22, [1996] Ch 136 at 161) affirmed that—

'the proceedings are not brought to enforce private rights but are brought in the public interest in order to protect the public ... It is of course true that a disqualification order has serious consequences for the disqualified person a and that the contravention of an order carries criminal penalties (s 13 of the 1986 Act). But the primary purpose of disqualification proceedings is the protection of the public and not the punishment of the director (see *Re Lo-Line Electric Motors Ltd* [1988] 2 All ER 692 at 696, [1988] Ch 477 at 486).'

b In *Secretary of State for Trade and Industry v Langridge* [1991] 3 All ER 591, [1991] Ch 402 the Court of Appeal had to consider the consequences of a failure to serve the ten-day notice required by s 16(1). The leading judgment was given by Balcombe LJ, with whom Leggatt LJ agreed. Balcombe LJ stressed that 'the purpose of the 1986 Act is to protect the public' and said ([1991] 3 All ER 591 at 599, [1991] Ch 402 at 415):

c 'The general object of the 1986 Act is the protection of the public: the object of the ten-day notice is the protection of the person against whom an application for a disqualification is to be made; the relationship between these two objects clearly involves a balancing exercise.'

d In that case, Mummery J had given leave to commence the proceedings outside the two-year period. One of the factors which he took into account was that 'Refusal of leave would mean that the truth or otherwise of grave allegations against the respondent would never be determined by the court' (see *Re Cedac Ltd* [1990] BCC 555 at 565). His exercise of his discretion was upheld by the Court of Appeal, notwithstanding that there had been significant and unexplained delay on the part of the Secretary of State.

e The statute imposes no restriction upon the exercise of the judge's discretion. Therefore the sole requirement is that he exercise his discretion judicially, taking into account all the circumstances of the particular case and having regard to the purpose for which the discretion has been given to him. This purpose is shown by the statutory context. It is not for the courts to impose fetters upon a f discretion which has been given in unqualified terms. (See *Costellow v Somerset CC* [1993] 1 All ER 952 at 957–958, [1993] 1 WLR 256 at 262 per Bingham MR, applying *Erskine Communications Ltd v Worthington* (1991) Times, 8 July.)

With the addition of a reference to the need to have regard to the public interest, there should, in my judgment, be no greater elaboration of the guidance to be given by this court to those whose task it is to exercise the discretion than g is contained in the judgment of Scott LJ in *Re Probe Data Systems Ltd (No 3), Secretary of State for Trade and Industry v Desai* [1992] BCLC 405 at 416. The four factors which he says should be taken into account, whilst not exhaustive, conveniently summarise the considerations which should ordinarily enable the judge to balance the public interest and the legitimate interests of the director. h This passage in the judgment of Scott LJ has been followed and applied on many occasions, including by this court.

It is significant that Scott LJ expressly bases himself upon *C M Van Stillevoldt BV v El Carriers Inc* [1983] 1 All ER 699, [1983] 1 WLR 207. That was a case in which Griffiths LJ had to consider the exercise of a discretion to extend time for setting j down in the Court of Appeal. It was an example of an unfettered procedural discretion.

The argument of Mr Briggs QC on behalf of the director on this appeal was that different and additional criteria were to be applied. He cited authorities which dealt with cases where either there was some qualification of the discretion given or the exercise of the discretion would interfere with a vested right of the affected party; *Kleinwort Benson Ltd v Barbrak Ltd, The Myrto (No 3)* [1987] 2 All ER

289, [1987] AC 597 was one such case. This citation was in my judgment
misplaced and wrong. If a 'good reason' has to be looked for, it is not a reason for   *a*
the delay but a reason for giving leave. But that reason will normally be found in
the public interest that unfit directors be disqualified unless the proposed
application under s 6 lacks substance or there is some sufficient countervailing
factor. I agree that Carnwath J was right to reject the argument based upon such
citation. He said: *b*

> 'If, as must be accepted, there is a serious case against the [respondents]
> which the Secretary of State considers it right in the public interest to pursue,
> it does not seem to me that should be defeated merely because of some delay
> in getting his tackle in order, where that delay has not in itself added to the
> overall timescale nor materially affected the [respondents'] ability to defend   *c*
> themselves.'

The judge weighed up the relevant factors following the guidance given by Scott
LJ. There is no basis for this court to interfere with the judge's exercise of his
discretion. Indeed, on the evidence I would have unhesitatingly exercised my
discretion in the same way as he did.   *d*
   I agree that this appeal should be dismissed.

NEILL LJ. I agree that the appeal should be dismissed for the reasons given in
the judgments of Hobhouse and Millett LJJ, which I have had the advantage of
reading in draft.
          e
Appeal dismissed.

                              Carolyn Toulmin   Barrister.

a
Union Bank of Finland Ltd v Lelakis

QUEEN'S BENCH DIVISION (COMMERCIAL COURT)

THOMAS J

25 JANUARY, 15 FEBRUARY 1996

b

COURT OF APPEAL, CIVIL DIVISION

HENRY AND SAVILLE LJJ

29 APRIL, 13 MAY 1996

c *Practice – Service out of the jurisdiction – Order for examination as to assets – Action against guarantor resident in Greece – Guarantee conferring exclusive jurisdiction on High Court – Writ claiming amount owing under guarantee served on guarantor's agent in England – Judgment entered in default of acknowledgement of service for amount claimed – Order made for defendant to attend before court to be examined as to*
d *assets – Order served on defendant outside jurisdiction – Whether order could be served on defendant outside jurisdiction without leave – Civil Jurisdiction and Judgments Act 1982, Sch 1, art 17 – RSC Ord 11, r 9(4), Ord 48, r 1.*

The defendant, a Greek national resident in Greece, entered into two personal guarantees of loans amounting to $US10m made by the plaintiff bank to a
e company of which the defendant was the principal shareholder for the purpose of funding the construction of a new ship. The guarantees provided that they were governed by English law and that in the event of any dispute the defendant would 'irrevocably and unconditionally' submit to the jurisdiction of the High Court in England and appoint a London agent for service. The bank
f subsequently served notices of default and demands for payment under the guarantees on the defendant and later issued a writ for recovery of the sums due. The writ was served on the defendant's agent in London. The bank then obtained judgment in default of acknowledgement of service for a sum in excess of $US8m and applied for an order under RSC Ord 48, r 1[a] that the defendant attend before the court in London to be examined as to his assets. The master
g granted the order, which was served personally on the defendant in Greece for one appointment and New York for another. The defendant applied to set aside the order on the ground that it could not be served out of the jurisdiction. His application was refused and he appealed to the judge, contending that his submission to the court under the guarantee was only for the purpose of adjudicating on the dispute and that the court had no power under Ord 48 to
h order the examination of a judgment debtor who was resident outside the jurisdiction. The judge dismissed the appeal, holding that the defendant's submission to the court extended to its enforcement jurisdiction as well its jurisdiction to adjudicate on the dispute, and that there was jurisdiction to make an order under Ord 48 which could be served on him in Greece. The defendant
j

---

a   Rule 1, so far as material, provides: '(1) Where a person has obtained a judgment or order for the payment by some other person (... "the judgment debtor") of money, the Court may, on an application made *ex parte* by the person entitled to enforce the judgment or order, order the judgment debtor ... to attend before such ... officer as the Court may appoint and be orally examined on the questions ... (b) whether the judgment debtor has any and, if so, what ... property or means of satisfying the judgment or order ...'

appealed on the issue of jurisdiction to serve the order out of the jurisdiction, contending that the procedure for such service was exclusively covered by Ord 11, that an order made under Ord 48 for a judgment debtor to attend for examination was an 'order ... made in any proceedings' which, under Ord 11, r 9(4)[b], required leave unless the writ had been served out of the jurisdiction, and that leave had not been obtained and the writ had not been served out of the jurisdiction.

Held – Service out of the jurisdiction of orders ancillary to execution after judgment, such as an order under RSC Ord 48, r 1 to attend before the court to be examined as to assets, was valid if the proceedings were appropriate for service of the writ out of the jurisdiction without leave, in that they complied with Ord 11, r 9(4). Order 11, r 9(4) was concerned with substance (ie the nature of the process) rather than mere form. It followed that if the proceedings were appropriate for service of the writ out of the jurisdiction without leave, it did not matter whether service was in fact made within or out of the jurisdiction in determining whether service of subsequent orders, such as orders made under Ord 48, could be made out of the jurisdiction; nor did it matter if a writ which was legitimately used for service within the jurisdiction was not in the requisite form for service out. Since under art 17[c] of Sch 1 to the Civil Jurisdiction and Judgments Act 1982 the writ against the defendant could have been served out of the jurisdiction without leave because the guarantee was an agreement conferring jurisdiction to which art 17 applied and the defendant was domiciled in a Convention country, the order made under Ord 48 for the defendant to attend for examination could also be served out of the jurisdiction without leave and it was irrelevant that the writ had not in fact been served out of the jurisdiction. The appeal would therefore be dismissed (see p 316 j and p 317 b to g, post).

Re Tucker (a bankrupt), ex p Tucker [1988] 1 All ER 603 distinguished.

Per curiam. A submission to the exclusive jurisdiction of the court contained in a guarantee is a submission to both the adjudicative and enforcement jurisdiction of the court (see p 315 h j, post).

Notes

For service out of the jurisdiction generally, see 37 *Halsbury's Laws* (4th edn) para 171.

For the Civil Jurisdiction and Judgments Act 1982, Sch 1, art 17, see 11 *Halsbury's Statutes* (4th edn) (1991 reissue) 1145. A new text of art 17 was substituted by the Civil Jurisdiction and Judgments Act 1982 (Amendment) Order 1990, SI 1990/2591, with effect from 1 December 1991.

Cases referred to in judgments

Alcom Ltd v Republic of Colombia (Barclays Bank plc and ors, garnishees) [1984] 2 All ER 6, [1984] AC 580, [1984] 2 WLR 750, HL.

Anglo African Steamship Co, Re (1886) 32 Ch D 348, CA.

Arab Banking Corp v International Tin Council (1986) 77 Int LR 1, QBD.

Busfield, Re, Whaley v Busfield (1886) 32 Ch D 123, CA.

---

b   Rule 9(4), so far as material, is set out at p 311 c, post
c   Article 17, so far as material, is set out at p 315 e, post

a *Clark (Inspector of Taxes) v Oceanic Contractors Inc* [1983] 1 All ER 133, [1983] 2 AC
   130, [1983] 2 WLR 94, HL.
   Interpool Ltd v Galani [1987] 2 All ER 981, [1988] QB 738, [1987] 3 WLR 1042, CA.
   MacKinnon v Donaldson Lufkin & Jenrette Securities Corp [1986] 1 All ER 653, [1986]
   Ch 482, [1986] 2 WLR 453.
   Maclaine Watson & Co Ltd v Dept of Trade and Industry, Re International Tin Council,
b *Maclaine Watson & Co Ltd v International Tin Council, Maclaine Watson & Co Ltd
   v International Tin Council (No 2)* [1988] 3 All ER 257, [1989] Ch 286, [1988] 3
   WLR 1190, CA.
   Tucker (a bankrupt), Re, ex p Tucker [1988] 1 All ER 603, [1990] Ch 148, [1988] 2
   WLR 748, CA.

c **Cases also cited or referred to in skeleton arguments**
   Allen v Taylor [1992] 1 PIQR P255, CA.
   Banque Russe et Francaise v Clark [1894] WN 203, CA.
   Barclays Bank plc v Khaira [1992] 1 WLR 623.
   Barclays Bank plc v O'Brien [1993] 4 All ER 417, [1994] 1 AC 180, HL.
d *Chetwynd-Talbot v Midland Bank Ltd* (21 June 1982, unreported), QBD.
   Cornish v Midland Bank plc (Humes, third party) [1985] 3 All ER 513, CA.
   Galoo Ltd (in liq) v Bright Grahame Murray (a firm) [1995] 1 All ER 16, [1994] 1 WLR
   1360, CA.

Appeal

e The defendant guarantor, Antonios Lelakis, appealed from the decision of Master
Miller on 5 December 1995 refusing to set aside his order made ex parte on 25
November 1994 that the defendant be orally examined as a judgment debtor
under RSC Ord 48, r 1 in relation to a claim by the plaintiff, Union Bank of
Finland Ltd, for the payment of sums due under a loan, on the ground that the
court had no power to make such an order since he was resident in Greece out of
f the jurisdiction of the court. The appeal was heard and judgment was given in
chambers. The case is reported by permission of Thomas J. The facts are set out
in the judgment.

Simon Gault (instructed by *Holman Fenwick & Willan*) for the defendant.
g *Andrew Hochhauser* (instructed by *Watson Farley & Williams*) for the plaintiff.

Cur adv vult

15 February 1996. The following judgment was delivered.

h **THOMAS J.** This appeal is brought by the defendant, an experienced Greek
shipowner, against the refusal of Master Miller to set aside an order that he be
orally examined as a judgment debtor under RSC Ord 48. The principal issue in
the appeal is whether the court has power to make such an order in
circumstances where the judgment debtor is resident out of the jurisdiction of the
j court.
  The circumstances giving rise to the order made under Ord 48 are briefly as
follows. In May and August 1992 the defendant entered into two personal
guarantees of loans of some $US6m and $US4m made by the plaintiff bank to a
company of which the defendant was the sole shareholder; the loans were in
connection with the building of a new ship. In August 1994 the plaintiff bank
served notices of default and demands for repayment on the borrower and

notices of default and demands for payment under the guarantees on the
defendant. On 14 September 1994 a writ was issued by the plaintiff bank; they
contended that it was properly served upon the defendant pursuant to the
jurisdiction clause of the guarantees. On 28 September 1994 the plaintiff bank
entered judgment in default of acknowledgment for an amount of over $US8m.

The defendant applied to the Commercial Court to set aside the judgment on
the grounds that the writ had not been properly served; this application was
heard by Clarke J on 3 November 1994. It failed and a stay of execution was
refused. Leave to appeal to the Court of Appeal was sought by the defendant
from Saville LJ, but refused on 27 March 1995. The application was renewed
before Aldous and Hutchison LJJ on 16 May 1995 and the application for leave to
appeal was granted; by further order of the Court of Appeal made on 31 July 1995
a stay of execution was refused save in respect of a sum deposited by way of cash
collateral.

In the meantime the plaintiff bank had on 25 November 1994 obtained an
order ex parte from Master Miller that the defendant be examined under Ord 48
before an officer of the court; the purpose of this order was to examine the
defendant as to his assets. A copy of the order was sent to the defendant's London
solicitors and the order itself was served on the defendant personally in Greece.
Whilst there was an issue over whether the order had been served personally on
the defendant, an order was made on 6 February 1995 for substituted service of
the order under Ord 48 on the defendant's solicitors in London.

On 6 February and 13 March 1995 the defendant applied to set aside the order
for his examination under Ord 48 and the order for substituted service. Master
Miller held on 5 December 1995 that personal service had been effected on the
defendant in Greece and he set aside the order for substituted service. There is
no appeal from that part of Master Miller's decision. However, the more
important point before Master Miller and the main point in this appeal was the
defendant's contention that there was no power under the jurisdiction clause in
the guarantees or under Ord 48 to make an order for examination of the
defendant as a judgment debtor as he was outside of the jurisdiction of the court.
Master Miller held in a carefully reasoned judgment that there was such
jurisdiction and with that judgment I entirely agree.

Clause 13.02 of the two guarantees provided for the jurisdiction of the English
High Court:

> 'In relation to any dispute arising out of or in connection with this
> Guarantee, and for the exclusive benefit of the Lender, the Guarantor hereby
> irrevocably and unconditionally: (a) submits to the jurisdiction of the High
> Court of Justice in England and waives any objection to proceedings with
> respect to this Agreement in such Court on the grounds of venue or
> inconvenient forum; and (b) appoints [Internav (Chartering) Ltd] of ...
> London ... as his agent for service of process in respect of proceedings before
> such Court and undertakes that, throughout the term of this Guarantee, he
> will maintain an agent in England for such purpose.'

The plaintiff bank contended that the submission to the jurisdiction of the
English High Court in this clause was a submission to all the Rules of the
Supreme Court including those relating to the enforcement of judgments of the
court; under the rules of court and in particular Ord 48, there was power to order
service out of the jurisdiction on the defendant in Greece.

a   It was the defendant's case, attractively presented by Mr Gault, that the
defendant's submission to the jurisdiction of the English High Court under
cl 13.02 only extended to the jurisdiction of the English High Court to adjudicate
upon the dispute. There was no submission to the jurisdiction of the court for
the purposes of enforcement; once judgment had been given, there was no
longer a submission to the jurisdiction and it was for the plaintiff bank to enforce
b   the judgment at the place of the defendant's residence, or in any other jurisdiction
where assets could be found and the judgment enforced in accordance with the
procedure of that jurisdiction. Mr Gault further contended that, even if the
submission to the English jurisdiction contained in cl 13.02 extended beyond
adjudication upon the dispute, the court did not have power under the Rules of
the Supreme Court, in particular Ord 48, to order the examination of a judgment
c   debtor resident outside of the jurisdiction; hence, it was contended that the terms
of the clause could not, even on a wide construction, cover the examination of
the defendant as the court had no power to order it. It is easiest first to consider
the issue on cl 13.02.

d   *The construction of cl 13.02*
Mr Gault contended that if regard were had to the language of cl 13.02 and in
particular to the opening words: 'In relation to any dispute arising out of or in
connection with this Guarantee', and the words in sub-cl (a): 'proceedings with
respect to this Agreement', it was clear that the submission was limited to an
adjudication on the dispute relating to the agreement and did not extend to
e   jurisdiction in respect of a judgment emanating from an adjudication on that
dispute.
The plaintiff bank, in support of the argument that the words in cl 13.02 should
bear a wide construction, relied upon a passage in the judgment of Hoffmann J in
MacKinnon v Donaldson Lufkin & Jenrette Securities Corp [1986] 1 All ER 653, [1986]
f   Ch 482; the case concerned an unsuccessful attempt to obtain under the Bankers'
Books Evidence Act 1879 information from a bank in New York which was not a
party to the action. Hoffmann J said ([1986] 1 All ER 653 at 659, [1986] Ch 482 at
494):

'... I am not concerned with the discovery required by RSC Ord 24 from
g   ordinary parties to English litigation who happen to be foreigners. If you join
the game you must play according to the local rules. This applies not only
to plaintiffs but also to defendants who give notice of intention to defend.'

Mr Gault, whilst accepting that a party to litigation who had submitted to the
adjudicative jurisdiction of the High Court was clearly bound by the Rules of the
h   Supreme Court relevant to the adjudication of the dispute, contended that this
passage did not provide much assistance, as Hoffmann J was not concerned with
the distinction that he sought to draw between submission to the adjudicative
and enforcement jurisdiction of the court. I agree.
Some assistance can, however, be derived in relation to this issue of
j   construction and the more general issue in relation to the Rules of the Supreme
Court from the distinction that is made in sovereign immunity cases between
submission to the court for the purpose of adjudication, and submission for
enforcement. It was fairly well established at common law that a submission to
the jurisdiction by a diplomat or foreign sovereign extended to the court's
adjudicative powers and not to the powers of execution, for which a separate
submission was required (see *Dicey and Morris on the Conflict of Laws* (9th edn,

1973) p 155, footnote 26, but now see the State Immunity Act 1978). In *Arab Banking Corp v International Tin Council* (1986) 77 Int LR 1 Steyn J held that a submission by the International Tin Council in a banking facility to 'the non-exclusive jurisdiction of the English Courts' did not, in the context of sovereign immunity, involve a submission to the enforcement jurisdiction of the English courts; there was therefore no power to grant a Mareva injunction against it, as that was relief ancillary to execution. After referring to the judgment of Lord Diplock in *Alcom Ltd v Republic of Colombia (Barclays Bank plc and ors, garnishees)* [1984] 2 All ER 6 at 10, [1984] AC 580 at 600, where Lord Diplock drew the distinction between the adjudicative jurisdiction and enforcement jurisdiction of the English court, Steyn J said (77 Int LR 1 at 5):

> '... it was stressed that the word "jurisdiction" was used by Lord Diplock in the only speech in the case, as covering both the adjudicative and enforcement powers of the court. Undoubtedly the word "jurisdiction" is capable of more than one meaning and, in particular, is capable of comprehending both the adjudicative and enforcement powers of the court. However, illuminating as Lord Diplock's speech is in relation to the dispute in *Alcom* ([1984] 2 All ER 6, [1984] AC 580), it casts, in my judgment, no light on the meaning of the word "jurisdiction" in the context of the facility letter. Words and phrases in a contract such as the facility letter do not always have one fixed and immutable meaning. Often there is more than one possible meaning. The applicable meaning can not be found simply by turning to a dictionary. In selecting the appropriate meaning, the contextual scene will usually be the paramount consideration. It will dictate the applicable meaning or nuance. That is how the question of construction in this particular case ought to be approached.'

Although it is useful to refer to the analogy with state immunity as an example of where a distinction can be drawn between the adjudicative and enforcement jurisdiction of the court, it is the context, as Steyn J observed, that will usually be the paramount consideration in determining the scope of a submission to the jurisdiction. Thus, the considerations in the sovereign immunity cases that led to the distinction between the adjudicative and enforcement jurisdiction of the English court are not applicable to a commercial agreement of the type entered into between the defendant and the plaintiff bank.

It is therefore necessary to consider the phrases used in cl 13.02 in the context of a commercial agreement. In my view, reading the whole of cl 13.02 together, it is clear that there was a submission to both the adjudicative and enforcement jurisdiction of the court. There is no limitation on or qualification to the word 'jurisdiction' as used in the clause; it would be artificial to construe the use of the term 'proceedings' with respect to this guarantee as importing only those proceedings that cover adjudication and not the enforcement consequent upon that. Furthermore, having regard to the terms of cl 13.02(b), the appointment of the agent in London was in respect of 'proceedings before such Court' without any expressed limitation. The contract in question is a guarantee of a commercial transaction and it would be unlikely that the parties intended the submission to the court to have been limited to its adjudicative and not to its enforcement jurisdiction.

I therefore consider that the plaintiff bank are correct on the issue of construction and that there was a submission to the whole of the jurisdiction of *a* the High Court, including its enforcement jurisdiction. It is therefore necessary to consider whether the court has power under Ord 48 to make an order against this defendant which could properly have been served in Greece.

The scope of Ord 48

b Mr Gault contended that the court had no power under Ord 48 to order the examination of the defendant as a judgment debtor; as personal service of an order under Ord 48 was generally required, there was no power to order such service of an order for examination of a defendant outside of the jurisdiction contained in Ord 48 or elsewhere in the Rules of the Supreme Court.

It is correct that Ord 48 contains no specific provision permitting service out of the jurisdiction of an order made under that rule, but the general provisions for *c* service out are contained in Ord 11. Order 11, r 9(4), so far as relevant, provides:

'... service out of the jurisdiction of any summons, notice or order issued, given or made in any proceedings is permissible with the leave of the Court but leave shall not be required for such service in any proceedings in which the writ, originating summons, motion or petition may by these rules or *d* under any Act be served out of the jurisdiction without leave.'

The plaintiff bank served the order under Ord 48 in Greece without leave, as they contended that the claim in respect of which the writ had been issued fell within art 17 of the Convention on Jurisdiction and the Enforcement of Judgments in Civil and Commercial Matters 1968, as set out in Sch 1 to the Civil *e* Jurisdiction and Judgments Act 1982.

Mr Gault contended that service of the order requiring the defendant's examination under Ord 48 could not have been made under Ord 11, r 9(4), with or without leave, because the word 'proceedings' was restricted to that part of the procedure until final judgment was given (after any appeal) and was inapplicable *f* to any procedure after final judgment had been given. It was accepted by him that if this argument were good in respect of Ord 48, it would also apply to any attempt to enforce other orders of the court made after final judgment. One example put in argument will suffice; an employee of a multinational company working overseas sought to work for a competitor of his employer in breach of a restrictive covenant in a contract governed by English law; Mr Gault, whilst *g* accepting that an interlocutory injunction restraining breach of the restrictive covenant could be served on the employee out of the jurisdiction and be enforced against the employee up to the time of final judgment, contended that any permanent injunction made on a final judgment could not effectively be enforced because the court would have no power to serve the employee personally out of *h* jurisdiction with any process that could lead to proceedings for the sequestration of any assets within the jurisdiction.

Mr Gault also accepted that the same must apply to a Mareva injunction after judgment, as no personal service of any process against the defendant could be effected overseas; it is, however, difficult to see why, on Mr Gault's argument, *j* this should not also apply to a Mareva injunction prior to final judgment being given in the action. Order 48 provides an ancillary mechanism for the enforcement jurisdiction of the court, as it enables a judgment debtor to be examined as to the assets which are available to satisfy the judgment. A Mareva injunction is also, as was pointed out by Steyn J in *Arab Banking Corp v International Tin Council* 77 Int LR 1 at 4, relief ancillary to execution:

'If this were not the position and a *Mareva* injunction were to be regarded
as part of the adjudicative process of the court as opposed to the process of   *a*
enforcement, then it must be borne in mind that the power of committal
would undoubtedly be part of the enforcement process. If it is unavailable
in respect of a breach of a *Mareva* injunction, a court would not be inclined
to grant a *Mareva* injunction, which would then be a *brutum fulmen.*'

Thus if Mr Gault's argument is correct, the power of the court to enforce   *b*
orders ancillary to execution or other similar orders against a person resident
outside of the jurisdiction has significant limitations; this is of importance in cases
like the present where the defendant is amenable to a sanction because of the
presence of assets or other pending proceedings in the jurisdiction.

Mr Gault rightly contends that it is necessary to approach the construction of   *c*
the Rules of the Supreme Court in the light of the principles summarised in *Clark*
(*Inspector of Taxes*) v *Oceanic Contractors Inc* [1983] 1 All ER 133 esp at 139, 144,
[1983] 2 AC 130 esp at 145, 152 in the speeches of Lord Scarman and of Lord
Wilberforce; in essence the principle is that, unless the contrary is expressly
enacted or so plainly implied that the courts must give effect to it, United
Kingdom legislation is applicable only to British subjects or to foreigners who by   *d*
coming to the United Kingdom, whether for a short or a long time, make
themselves subject to English jurisdiction. That principle was applied to the
Bankruptcy Act 1914 and the Bankruptcy Rules 1952, SI 1952/2113, in *Re Tucker*
(*a bankrupt*), *ex p Tucker* [1988] 1 All ER 603, [1990] Ch 148 by the Court of Appeal
when deciding that there was no power under r 86 of the 1952 rules (as amended)   *e*
to compel a person resident outside of the jurisdiction to attend for examination.
That decision has been heavily relied upon by the defendant before me, in
particular because in *The Supreme Court Practice 1995* para 48/1–3/6 the editors
state:

'Although the Court has express powers in specified circumstances to give   *f*
leave for service of process out of the jurisdiction (see, *e.g.* O.11 rr. 1 and 9),
it has no general power to do so, and accordingly, the Court will not make
an order under r.1 for the examination of a person who is outside the
jurisdiction (see *Re Tucker* ([1988] 1 All ER 603, [1990] Ch 148)).'

Master Miller held that *Re Tucker* neither supported the paragraph in *The Supreme*   *g*
Court Practice 1995 to which I have referred, nor the defendant's argument. I
entirely agree with that conclusion. It seems to me that there are only two points
that can be derived from *Re Tucker* which are relevant to the construction of the
Rules of the Supreme Court, in particular Ord 48 and Ord 11: (1) the principles of
restrictive construction to which I have already referred, and (2) the principle that
the court must, when deciding whether a rule permits the exercise of   *h*
extra-territorial jurisdiction, take into account the fact that there are generally
procedures available within the jurisdiction of the overseas courts for
enforcement of judgments of the English courts.

Although there is no evidence before me of the position in Greece or
elsewhere, I am prepared to assume that the courts of Greece (as indeed the   *j*
courts of most countries) would have procedures for the examination of a
judgment debtor to ascertain the whereabouts of his assets for the purposes of
enforcing an English judgment.

Applying therefore the restrictive principle of construction and assuming also
in the defendant's favour that there are procedures available in Greece to
examine him as to his assets, I turn to consider whether the word 'proceedings'

a in Ord 11 should bear the construction advanced that it is applicable only to adjudicative and not enforcement proceedings and that therefore an order made under Ord 48 is not an order in 'proceedings'. I see no justification for construing 'proceedings' as restricted to the adjudicative proceedings of the court; there is nothing in the language of Ord 11 or any other passage to which I have been referred that would support such a construction. The word 'proceedings'
b naturally means the whole of the proceedings from adjudication up to and including enforcement. Moreover, such a construction would have the limiting and anomalous effects on orders of the court to which I have already referred.

The fact that Ord 48 itself contains no provision for service out is not in my view significant, as the general provisions for service out of the jurisdiction are contained in Ord 11. There is nothing in the language of Ord 48 from which it is
c possible to imply that such orders are only to be served on persons within the jurisdiction. On the contrary, a purposive construction would favour Ord 48 being given a broad construction. In *Maclaine Watson & Co Ltd v Dept of Trade and Industry, Re International Tin Council, Maclaine Watson & Co Ltd v International Tin Council, Maclaine Watson & Co Ltd v International Tin Council (No 2)* [1988] 3 All ER
d 257, [1989] Ch 286, where an attempt was made to examine an officer of the International Tin Council (which was a judgment debtor) both under Ord 48 and under the inherent jurisdiction of the court, Kerr LJ said of Ord 48:

> '[The plaintiff's] objective to compel the International Tin Council to comply with the judgment which has been entered against it is in accordance
> *e* with the policy of the law to assist judgment creditors.' (See [1988] 3 All ER 257 at 378, [1989] Ch 253 at 300.)

It was also pointed out by the plaintiff bank that the decision of the Court of Appeal in *Interpool Ltd v Galani* [1987] 2 All ER 981, [1988] QB 738 that a judgment debtor was bound to answer questions about assets both within and without the
f jurisdiction was consistent with such a purposive construction.

I therefore hold that there was jurisdiction to make an order for the examination of the defendant under Ord 48 which could be served on him in Greece.

g *The discretion*
The defendant finally contended that it was premature to make the order before the merits of the appeal had been heard, as the order was draconian and imposed a substantial burden on the defendant; the plaintiff bank, it was said, would suffer no prejudice if the examination were delayed until after the hearing of the appeal.
h There is no merit in either of these points. The Court of Appeal has itself refused a stay of execution and there is therefore no reason to delay procedures ancillary to execution. Furthermore, it is quite clear that the plaintiff bank may well suffer prejudice if the examination is delayed. Delay in this procedure will delay execution in the event the appeal is dismissed and, in the meantime, a
j delayed examination will frustrate the plaintiff bank in taking any steps it might be entitled to take to secure its position.
I therefore dismiss the appeal.

Appeal dismissed.

K Mydeen Esq   Barrister.

Appeal

The defendant appealed on the issue of jurisdiction to serve the Ord 48 order out *a* of the jurisdiction. The facts are set out in the judgment of Henry LJ.

Stephen Gee QC and *Vasanti Selvaratnam* (instructed by *Holman Fenwick & Willan*) for the defendant.

Andrew Hochhauser (instructed by *Watson Farley & Williams*) for the plaintiff.　　*b*

Cur adv vult

13 May 1996. The following judgments were delivered.

HENRY LJ. Captain Lelakis is, in the words of Thomas J 'an experienced Greek *c* shipowner'. He is the defendant in this action, and the appellant before us. In 1992 he wished to build a new ship. A company, of which he was the principal shareholder and sole beneficial owner, borrowed a total of $US10m from the plaintiff bank. He entered into two personal guarantees in relation to that loan. In August 1994 the plaintiffs served notices of default and demands for payment under the guarantees on the defendant. On 14 September 1994 they issued a writ *d* for recovery of the sums due. That writ was purportedly served in the United Kingdom under submission to jurisdiction clauses contained in the guarantees. Judgment in default of acknowledgment of service was obtained on the first available day, for a sum in excess of US$8m. The defendant applied to set aside that judgment, first on the ground that he had not been properly served, and *e* second on the merits. That application was heard by Clarke J and failed. A stay was refused. The single judge (Saville LJ) refused leave on paper, but the full court (Aldous and Hutchison LJJ) granted leave to appeal. However, by order made on 31 July 1995 they refused a stay of execution save in respect of a sum deposited by way of cash collateral.

That is all by way of background. This appeal stems from the purported *f* service out of the jurisdiction of an order made under Ord 48, r 1 that the defendant attend before a court examiner in London to be questioned as to his assets. By summons dated 6 February 1995 the defendant sought to set aside this order on the basis that it could not lawfully be served out of the jurisdiction. Master Miller refused that application in a full and carefully reasoned judgment. *g* Various points were taken before him—but the only one which survives is the broad proposition that there was no jurisdiction in the court to approve such service. That in its turn was appealed, the appeal coming before Thomas J. He dismissed the appeal by judgment delivered on 15 February. This appeal is launched against that dismissal. We heard the appeal on 29 April, the appointed *h* day for the examination of the judgment debtor as to his assets being 1 May. The proximity of those two dates is caused by what seemed to Thomas J as attempts by the defendant to achieve delay by 'playing the system'. However, as the points before us are pure points of law, we do not find it necessary to say any more on this score.

The starting point for consideration of this problem lies in the contractual *j* submission to the jurisdiction to be found in cl 13 of the agreements of guarantee, which reads:

'13 LAW AND JURISDICTION
13.01 This Guarantee shall be governed by, and construed in accordance with, English law.

a   13.02 In relation to any dispute arising out of or in connection with this
Guarantee, and for the exclusive benefit of the Lender, the Guarantor hereby
irrevocably and unconditionally: (a) submits to the jurisdiction of the High
Court of Justice in England and waives any objection to proceedings with
respect to this Agreement in such Court on the grounds of venue or
inconvenient forum; and (b) appoints [Internav (Chartering) Ltd] of Suite 2,

b   Telford Yard, 6–8 The Highway, London E1 OBQ as his agent for service of
process in respect of proceedings before such Court and undertakes that,
throughout the term of this Guarantee, he will maintain an agent in England
for such purpose. Nothing in this Clause shall affect the right of the Lender
to serve process in any manner permitted by law or limit the right of the
Lender to take proceedings with respect to this Guarantee against the

c   Guarantor in any jurisdiction nor shall the taking of proceedings with respect
to this Guarantee in any jurisdiction preclude the Lender from taking
proceedings with respect to this Guarantee in any other jurisdiction,
whether concurrently or not.'

Captain Lelakis is domiciled in Greece.

d   The significance of that provision is that it brings into operation art 17 of the
Convention on Jurisdiction and the Enforcement of Judgments in Civil and
Commercial Matters 1968, as set out in Sch 1 to the Civil Jurisdiction and
Judgments Act 1982:

e   'If the parties, one or more of whom is domiciled in a Contracting State,
have agreed that ... the courts of a Contracting State are to have jurisdiction
to settle any disputes which have arisen or which may arise in connection
with a particular legal relationship ... those courts shall have exclusive
jurisdiction ...'

f   The preamble to the convention indicates that it operates within the European
Community 'to secure the simplification of formalities governing the reciprocal
recognition and enforcement of judgments', it being necessary—

'to determine the international jurisdiction of their courts, to facilitate
recognition and to introduce an expeditious procedure for securing the
g   enforcement of judgments ...'

In purported performance of cl 13.02(b) the writ was served at Internav's office in
London.
Before the judge the first point raised on behalf of the plaintiff was that cl 13.02
only gave jurisdiction to the English courts to adjudicate upon the dispute, but
h   was not a submission to the jurisdiction of the court for the purposes of
enforcement. This distinction has been drawn in cases relating to the sovereign
immunity of states, but the judge was right to find that the considerations that led
to that distinction in those cases were not applicable to a commercial agreement
between lender and borrower. He was satisfied that cl 13.02 was a submission
j   both to the adjudicative and enforcement jurisdiction of the court. In this he was
clearly right, and Mr Stephen Gee QC realistically no longer relies on this ground
of appeal.
The question therefore is whether the enforcement jurisdiction of the court
was effectively invoked by the purported personal service of the Ord 48, r 1 order
on Capt Lelakis, in Greece for one appointment, and in New York for another. It
is not necessary for us to consider whether service of the order might not have

been validly achieved under cl 13.02, because that was not done. The actual
service was either authorised by the rules, or it was not good service.   *a*

I have no problem in uncritically accepting Mr Gee's initial propositions: first,
that Ord 11 contains the entire code authorising service out of the jurisdiction,
and second, that any gaps in that code cannot be filled by the court's inherent
powers, but require statutory authority (ie express provision under Ord 11) to
permit such service (see *Re Busfield, Whaley v Busfield* (1886) 32 Ch D 123 at 132   *b*
and 133 and *Re Anglo African Steamship Co* (1886) 32 Ch D 348 at 350).

The scheme of Ord 11 is that r 1 applies to the service of writs out of the
jurisdiction and r 9(1) extends Ord 11 beyond writs to the service out of other
sorts of originating process 'originating summons, notice of motion or petition as
it applies to service of a writ'. Those rules do not cover the service of this order.

Order 11, r 9(4) deals with the service out of certain formal documents   *c*
ancillary to the process 'any summons, notice or order issued, given or made in
any proceedings'. The order made under Ord 48 for the judgment debtor to
attend for examination is clearly such an 'order ... made in any proceedings', as
Mr Gee accepts. Nor does he contend (as counsel for Capt Lelakis did before the
judge) that the 'proceedings' in question finished with the signing of judgment.   *d*
The word covers both the adjudicative proceedings leading to judgment and the
enforcement proceedings consequent upon that adjudication.

The rule then goes on to provide the two circumstances in which such
ancillary orders may be served out of the jurisdiction. First, with the leave of the
court. That was neither sought nor obtained in this case. Second, the second
limb of the rule provides: *e*

'... leave shall not be required for [service out of the jurisdiction of, e g Ord
48, r 1 orders] in any proceeding in which the writ ... may by these rules or
under any Act be served out of the jurisdiction without leave.'

The competing arguments may be shortly stated. The plaintiff's first   *f*
contention is that the writ here could have been served out of the jurisdiction
without leave under Ord 11, r 1(2):

'Service of a writ out of the jurisdiction is permissible without the leave of
the Court provided that each claim made by the writ is either:—(a) a claim
which by virtue of the Civil Jurisdiction and Judgments Act 1982 the Court   *g*
has power to hear and determine, made in proceedings to which the
following conditions apply—(i) no proceedings between the parties
concerning the same cause of action are pending in the courts of any other
part of the United Kingdom or of any other Convention territory, and (ii)
either—the defendant is domiciled in any part of the United Kingdom or in   *h*
any other Convention territory, or the proceedings begun by the writ are
proceedings to which Article 16 of Schedule 1, 3C or 4 refers, or the
defendant is a party to an agreement conferring jurisdiction to which Article
17 of Schedule 1, 3C or 4 to that Act applies ...'

That submission is right in so far as it goes. The 1982 Act applies, Capt Lelakis   *j*
is domiciled in a convention territory, and there is an agreement conferring
jurisdiction to which art 17 of Sch 1 to the 1982 Act applies. That much is clear.

But Mr Gee argues that, while the writ in this case might have been served out
of the jurisdiction without leave, in fact it was not. It was served within the
jurisdiction and the writ actually used was not suitable for service out in that: (1)
the time for acknowledgment of service was 14 days (the normal time in relation

a to service within the jurisdiction) and not 21 days (as required by Ord 11, r 1(3)), and (2) the writ actually served did not carry the indorsement required by Ord 6, r 7(1)b. Therefore, it is submitted that Ord 11, r 9(4) is not complied with.

The point of construction at issue then is whether this limb of Ord 11, r 9(4) comes into play where the nature of the process complies with the rule, or only where the writ on its face complies with the rule, i e was a writ in proper form for b service out of the jurisdiction (even though it was to be served within the jurisdiction)?

I am in no doubt as to the answer. The rule is concerned with the substance (the nature of the process) and not with mere form. The use of the word 'may' recognises that the writ might not be served out of the jurisdiction, and will not be in art 17 cases. If the proceedings are appropriate proceedings (i e compliant c with Ord 11, r 9(4)) which permit the writ to be served out of the jurisdiction without leave, then when it comes to the service of subsequent orders (such as Ord 48, r 1 orders) it matters not whether the service of the writ was in fact made within the jurisdiction, under e g art 17, or without. Nor does it matter that the writ, legitimately used for service in, was not in the requisite form for service out. d Not only does it not matter, but there is no reason why it should matter.

Our attention was drawn to *The Supreme Court Practice 1995* para 48/1/1–3/6, which reads:

> 'Although the Court has express powers in specified circumstances to give leave for service of process out of the jurisdiction (see, *e.g.* O. 11, rr. 1 and 9), it has no general power to do so, and accordingly, the Court will not make e an order under r. 1 for the examination of a person who is outside the jurisdiction (see *Re Tucker* ([1988] 1 All ER 603, [1990] Ch 148)).'

I have no quarrel with that passage down to and including the words 'no general power to do so'. What follows seems to me to be plainly wrong: the court can f give leave for service out under the first limb of Ord 11, r 9(4), and no such leave is required under the second limb. And nor is *Re Tucker* relevant to the construction of Ord 11, r 9. That case turned on the construction of and jurisdictional limitations contained in s 25 of the Bankruptcy Act 1914, and did not touch on the question we had to consider.

Accordingly, I would dismiss this appeal.

g
SAVILLE LJ. I agree.

Appeal dismissed. Leave to appeal to the House of Lords refused.

Carolyn Toulmin   Barrister.

John Munroe (Acrylics) Ltd v London Fire and Civil Defence Authority and others

QUEEN'S BENCH DIVISION

ROUGIER J

26, 27, 28 MARCH, 15 APRIL 1996

Negligence – Duty to take care – Fire brigade – Negligence in attendance at fire – Duty of fire brigade in relation to fire – Persons to whom duty owed – Plaintiffs' premises damaged by fire caused by explosion on adjoining land – Fire brigade investigating site of explosion but failing to notice smouldering debris and combustible materials on plaintiffs' premises – Whether fire brigade owing duty of care to plaintiffs – Whether special relationship existing between fire brigade and plaintiffs giving rise to duty of care – Whether fire brigade assuming responsibility by responding to calls.

Following an explosion on a piece of adjoining land, the plaintiffs' industrial premises were showered with flaming debris. Emergency services were called and when the fire brigade arrived at the scene of the explosion they satisfied themselves that the fires there had been extinguished; they did not, however, inspect the plaintiffs' premises. If they had done so, they would have seen smouldering debris and combustible materials which later resulted in the premises being seriously damaged by fire. Thereafter, the plaintiffs brought an action against the defendant fire authority, seeking damages for the negligent actions of the fire brigade. In the course of the proceedings an application was made for the determination of a preliminary issue of law, namely whether, in the circumstances, the defendant owed any duty of care to the plaintiffs in relation to the fire. The plaintiffs contended (i) that within the relevant statutory framework there was an implied common law duty on the fire brigade to respond to calls made to it and therefore a duty of care in making the response, and (ii) that if there was no such duty at common law, nevertheless, by electing to respond to an emergency call, the fire brigade assumed responsibility and thereby owed a duty of care to the owners of premises in foreseeable danger from the fire.

Held – No sufficient proximity nor special relationship existed between the fire brigade and the owner of any property which might be on fire such as to impose on the fire brigade a personal duty at common law to respond to any call for assistance; indeed, many public policy considerations militated against the imposition of such a common law duty. Further, in the absence of a general duty to respond to a call, a fire brigade did not, merely by responding to a call, assume a particular responsibility towards those in foreseeable danger sufficient to trigger an automatic common law duty of care. Before the necessary proximity could be established, something more had to be shown to demonstrate that, besides the mere performance of its public duty, the fire brigade had undertaken a personal responsibility to some individual during the course of its activity. It followed that, in the circumstances, the fire brigade did not owe a duty of care to the plaintiffs in relation to the fire (see p 329 f, p 331 j, p 333 e, p 334 c and p 335 j, post).

Hill v Chief Constable of West Yorkshire [1988] 2 All ER 238 and *Alexandrou v Oxford* [1993] 4 All ER 328 applied.

Notes

a For the nature of negligence and the duty to take care generally, see 34 *Halsbury's Laws* (4th edn) paras 1–5, and for cases on the subject, see 36(1) *Digest* (2nd reissue) 7–64, 1–325.

Cases referred to in judgment

Alexandrou v Oxford [1993] 4 All ER 328, CA.
b *Ancell v McDermott* [1993] 4 All ER 355, CA.
Anns v Merton London Borough [1977] 2 All ER 492, [1978] AC 728, [1977] 2 WLR 1024, HL.
Barnett v Chelsea and Kensington Hospital Management Committee [1968] 1 All ER 1068, [1969] 1 QB 428, [1968] 2 WLR 422.
c *Barrett v Ministry of Defence* [1995] 3 All ER 87, [1995] 1 WLR 1217, CA.
Caparo Industries plc v Dickman [1990] 1 All ER 568, [1990] 2 AC 605, [1990] 2 WLR 358, HL.
Crown River Cruises Ltd v Kimbolton Fireworks Ltd (1996) Times, 6 March.
Donoghue v Stevenson [1932] AC 562, [1932] All ER Rep 1, HL.
Duff v Highland and Islands Fire Board (1995) Times, 3 November, Ct of Sess.
d *East Suffolk Rivers Catchment Board v Kent* [1940] 4 All ER 527, [1941] AC 74, HL.
Fellowes v Rother DC [1983] 1 All ER 513.
Hill v Chief Constable of West Yorkshire [1988] 2 All ER 238, [1989] AC 53, [1988] 2 WLR 1049, HL.
Home Office v Dorset Yacht Co Ltd [1970] 2 All ER 294, [1970] AC 1004, [1970] 2 WLR
e 1140, HL.
Kirkham v Chief Constable of the Greater Manchester Police [1990] 3 All ER 246, [1990] 2 QB 283, [1990] 2 WLR 987, CA.
Knightley v Johns [1982] 1 All ER 851, [1982] 1 WLR 349, CA.
M (a minor) v Newham London BC, X and ors (minors) v Bedfordshire CC [1994] 4 All ER 602, [1995] 2 AC 633, [1994] 2 WLR 554, CA; *affd* [1995] 3 All ER 353, [1995] 2
f AC 633, [1995] 3 WLR 152, HL.
Murphy v Brentwood DC [1990] 2 All ER 908, [1991] 1 AC 398, [1990] 3 WLR 414, HL.
Osman v Ferguson [1993] 4 All ER 344, CA.
R v Metropolitan Police Comr, ex p Blackburn [1968] 1 All ER 763, [1968] 2 QB 118, [1968] 2 WLR 893, CA.
g *Rich (Marc) & Co AG v Bishop Rock Marine Co Ltd, The Nicholas H* [1995] 3 All ER 307, [1996] 1 AC 211, [1995] 3 WLR 227, HL.
Rigby v Chief Constable of Northamptonshire [1985] 2 All ER 985, [1985] 1 WLR 1242.
Skinner v Secretary of State for Transport (1995) Times, 3 January.
Stovin v Wise (Norfolk CC, third party) [1994] 3 All ER 467, [1994] 1 WLR 1124, CA; *rvsd* [1996] 3 All ER 801, [1996] 3 WLR 388, HL.
h *Sutherland Shire Council v Heyman* (1985) 60 ALR 1, Aust HC.
Swinney v Chief Constable of the Northumbria Police [1996] 3 All ER 449, CA.

Cases also cited or referred to in skeleton arguments

Alcock v Chief Constable of the South Yorkshire Police [1991] 4 All ER 907, [1992] 1 AC
j 310, HL.
Curran v Northern Ireland Co-ownership Housing Association (Stewart, third party) [1987] 2 All ER 13, [1987] AC 718, HL.
Elguzouli-Daf v Comr of Police of the Metropolis, McBrearty v Ministry of Defence [1995] 1 All ER 833, [1995] QB 335, CA.
Galoo Ltd (in liq) v Bright Grahame Murray (a firm) [1995] 1 All ER 16, [1994] 1 WLR 1360, CA.

Harris v Marter (1874) 2 Pug 165.
Joyce v Metropolitan Board of Works (1881) 44 LT 811.　　　　　　　*a*
Kilboy v South Eastern Fire Area Joint Committee 1952 SC 280, Ct of Sess.
Lavis v Kent CC (1992) 90 LGR 416, CA.
Rondell v Worsley [1967] 3 All ER 993, [1969] 1 AC 191, HL.
Sands v DPP (1990) Times, 23 March, DC.
Sheppard v Glossop Corp [1921] 3 KB 132, [1921] All ER Rep 61, CA.　　　*b*
Smith v Littlewoods Organisation Ltd (*Chief Constable, Fife Constabulary, third party*)
　　[1987] 1 All ER, [1987] AC 241, HL.
Ultramares Corp v Touche (1931) 255 NY 170, NY Ct of Apps.
Yuen Kun-yeu v A-G of Hong Kong [1987] 2 All ER 705, [1988] AC 175, PC.

Preliminary issue　　　　　　　　　　　　　　　　　　　　　　*c*
The plaintiffs, John Munroe (Acrylics) Ltd, brought an action for damages against
the defendants, London Fire and Civil Defence Authority, Any Effects Ltd (in liq)
and Thomas Charles Harris (trading as Any Effects Ltd (in liq)), for negligence in
respect of the fire which severely damaged the plaintiffs' premises. In the course
of the proceedings an application was made for determination of a preliminary
issue, namely whether the first defendants owed a duty of care to the plaintiffs in　*d*
relation to the fire. The second and third defendants took no part in the trial of the
preliminary issue. The facts are set out in the judgment.

Ronald Walker QC and *Toby Hooper* (instructed by *Hextall Erskine & Co*) for the
　plaintiffs.　　　　　　　　　　　　　　　　　　　　　　　　*e*
Michael de Navarro QC, Graham Eklund and *Jennifer Gray* (instructed by *S J F Starling*)
　for the first defendants.

Cur adv vult

15 April 1996. The following judgment was delivered.　　　　　　　*f*

ROUGIER J. During the evening of 27 March 1991, the plaintiffs' industrial
premises at Unit 69, Weir Road, Wimbledon were severely damaged by fire. They
seek to recover damages against the first defendants, who are the local fire
authority for the area and would be vicariously liable for negligence on the part of
their servants, in particular the fire brigade.　　　　　　　　　　*g*
　The matter comes before me as a preliminary issue of law, namely whether in
the circumstances the first defendants owed any duty of care to the plaintiffs in
relation to the fire. As a matter of history, the plaintiffs have also sued the second
and third defendants who, in the course of their operations, had created an
explosion on wasteland not far from the plaintiffs' premises and which, for the　*h*
purposes of this hearing, must be assumed to have been the ultimate origin of the
fire which subsequently occurred on the plaintiffs' premises. Since the second and
third defendants are not involved in the present inquiry, I propose to refer to the
first defendants purely as 'the defendants'.
　The relevant facts I take from a joint statement of facts which has been agreed
solely for the purposes of the hearing of this issue. The explosion was deliberate　*j*
and took place just before 6.30 in the evening. A shower of flaming debris was
scattered over a fairly wide area, and relatively small fires were seen to have
started, separated by quite a substantial distance. Debris was seen to fall onto the
plaintiffs' premises and smoke to come from a corner of the yard of those premises.
　Members of the public dialled the emergency services and within a short time
no fewer than four fire engines, complete with their crews and a leading

a fire-fighter, arrived on the scene. In the meantime the staff of the second
defendants had extinguished the burning debris and the fires on the wasteland, and
there was no visible evidence of any continuing conflagration to be seen.

On arrival the defendants' officers took steps to satisfy themselves that all fires
had been extinguished and there was no residual danger. They made inquiries of
the staff of the second defendant and learnt what had happened. The response of
b the second defendant's staff to the question 'Where had the explosion taken place?'
was decidedly imprecise. Having looked around, the defendants' crews took the
view that the fires were out and the danger had passed, and they left the scene at
about 6.50 pm. They did not inspect Unit 69, which abutted one side of the
wasteland. Had they done so, there was combustible material to be seen. It is also
likely that there would have been smouldering debris. There is no record of any
c conversation passing between the defendants' crews and any member of the
plaintiffs' staff. Indeed, there is no suggestion that any member of the plaintiffs'
staff was present at the scene, either at the time of the explosion or subsequently,
until the fire was well underway.

It is agreed by both sides that in determining the question before me I should
d adopt what is referred to as the 'incremental approach' developed into the law of
negligence by a succession of cases over the last 20 years, culminating in the
decision of the House of Lords in *Caparo Industries plc v Dickman* [1990] 1 All ER 568,
[1990] 2 AC 605. Such an approach involves the triple consideration of (1)
foreseeability of damage, whether economic or physical; (2) whether sufficient
proximity in the legal sense exists between plaintiff and defendant to cast upon the
e latter a duty to take care; (3) whether, even if the first two conditions are satisfied,
there are considerations of public policy whereby it would not be just, fair or
reasonable to saddle the defendant with such a duty.

With the assistance and industry of counsel for both sides, for which I am
profoundly grateful, I have been referred to a well nigh exhaustive list of
f authorities where the possible liability of public bodies or organisations performing
public functions has been considered.

The first step must be to consider the statutory framework under, or by reason
of which, the fire brigade was operating. It is not contended that the defendants
were under any personal duty to the plaintiffs. Any liability which may attach to
them would be vicarious only for the negligence, if any, of the fire brigade. The
g relevant statute is the Fire Services Act 1947. Section 1(1) provides as follows:

'It shall be the duty of every fire authority in Great Britain to make provision
for fire-fighting purposes, and in particular every fire authority shall secure—
(a) the services for their area of such a fire brigade and such equipment as may
be necessary to meet efficiently all normal requirements; (b) the efficient
h training of the members of the fire brigade; (c) efficient arrangements for
dealing with calls for the assistance of the fire brigade in case of fire and for
summoning members of the fire brigade … (f) efficient arrangements for the
giving, when requested, of advice in respect of buildings and other property in
the area of the fire authority as to fire prevention …'

j It is common ground that s 30 of the Act (which I need not recite) gives a fire
brigade power to fight fires and, if necessary, enter premises without the owner's
permission. By sub-s (3) the senior fire brigade officer present is stated to 'have the
sole charge and control of all operations for the extinction of the fire'.

Two further matters are not in issue. First, from the foregoing wording of the
statute it is clear that there is no statutory duty on the fire brigade, or for that
matter the defendants, to fight fires. If the duty exists it can only exist at common

law. Second, the first limb of the *Caparo* trio is satisfied. There was the   *a*
foreseeability of damage to the plaintiffs' premises.

The rival contentions, in essence, are these. For the plaintiffs it is argued that
within the statutory framework of a duty to make arrangements to respond to calls
there should be implied a common law duty on the part of the fire brigade to
respond to those calls. Mr Walker QC went so far as to contend that the necessary
proximity was established whenever a call on the fire brigade was made and the   *b*
endangered premises or persons identified. If such a duty exists, it is argued, there
must be a companion duty to act with due care in making the response. The
relevance of the statute is in providing the background to the position contended
for, so as to distinguish the fire brigade from an ordinary member of the public who
is under no duty and can watch the premises burn. It is also claimed to be relevant
to the issue of the third limb of *Caparo*.   *c*

As a secondary position, the plaintiffs submit that even if there is no duty at
common law to respond, but nevertheless the fire brigade elect to make a
response, then they are in the position of those who have assumed responsibility
and have effectively put themselves in the same position as if there were a duty to
respond. By their actions in responding and visiting the premises where the fire is   *d*
burning, it is said that they put themselves within the range of legal proximity to
the owner of the premises and to the owners of neighbouring premises in the area
of foreseeable danger from the fire.

In so far as considerations of public policy are concerned, it is contended that
there are no, or at any rate no sufficient, factors to make it either unfair, unjust or   *e*
unreasonable to make the fire brigade and, through them, the defendants,
answerable for any negligence in the course of carrying out their response. In this
context it is claimed that the police, who on more than one occasion have had the
benefit of the public policy consideration, are a special case and that the fire brigade
is, if one is to look at the matter on the incremental basis, in a position much more
closely akin to that of a hospital or medical services.   *f*

The defendants' submissions are, first, that the emergency services should be
regarded as being in a somewhat special category, principally for two reasons;
namely, first, the often desperate and dangerous situations in which they are
operating, of which the recent tragic death of a young fire officer gives a poignant
reminder. Second, that they are almost always operating reactively to a peril or to   *g*
damage which they did not themselves create. The defendants' primary position
is that, like the police, the duty they owe is a public duty to the public at large and
that neither the statute nor the circumstances in which they operate suggest that
any duty is owed to private individuals to respond to emergency calls.

The secondary position is that if a response is made there are very limited   *h*
situations when a duty may arise, but those situations are entirely coextensive with
circumstances when a duty would be likewise cast upon an ordinary member of
the public. These situations are (1) specific assumption of responsibility to an
individual; (2) damage over and above that created by the original event; (3) fresh
damage. The distinction between (2) and (3) above is nice, but for present purposes
I think they can be regarded as one and the same.   *j*

As an alternative, reliance is placed on the older case of *East Suffolk Rivers
Catchment Board v Kent* [1940] 4 All ER 527, [1941] AC 74. This, it is submitted, is
authority for the proposition that if a public body is exercising a statutory power
only and not fulfilling a statutory duty, their duty in exercising that power is limited
to not making matters worse, and that the fact that they may purport to exercise
their power but do so in a careless or inadequate fashion cannot found the basis of

a a claim against them. In a sentence, it is contended that for all relevant purposes the position of the fire brigade, and indeed of other emergency services, should be equated to that of the police.

I do not propose to recite the many details into which the basic arguments developed. I have little doubt that this court is not the final resting place of the issue, and the arguments will have to be paraded again. The principles of
b proximity and those of justice, fairness and reasonableness, which I propose to label *Caparo* 2 and *Caparo* 3, must be considered in relation to two separate questions. (1) Is there a duty owed to private individuals to respond at all? This is the primary question. (2) If No, is the position different if the fire brigade nevertheless do respond? This is the secondary question. I should say in passing that if the answer to (1) is Yes, I think it axiomatic that a duty to respond would take
c with it a satellite duty to use all due care and skill in the response.

The primary question

The only case concerning the fire services that the researches of counsel have been able to find is *Duff v Highland and Islands Fire Board* (1995) Times, 3 November.
d It is a decision of Lord Macfadyen in the Outer House of the Court of Session. The learned judge, without going fully into the competing arguments, held that the fire services were under a duty to respond. In this country, in *Crown River Cruises Ltd v Kimbolton Fireworks Ltd* (1996) Times, 6 March, heard before Potter J, the duty appears to have been conceded so that the learned judge was not asked to give it his consideration.

e I first consider proximity: *Caparo* 2. It is clear that this is a relevant factor whether the damage is physical damage or merely economic loss (see *Marc Rich & Co AG v Bishop Rock Marine Co Ltd, The Nicholas H* [1995] 3 All ER 307 at 326, [1996] 1 AC 211 at 235). In *Caparo* itself, Lord Bridge summarised the development to which the modern law had reached. He said ([1990] 1 All ER 568 at 573–574, [1990]
f 2 AC 605 at 617):

> 'But since [*Anns v Merton London Borough* [1977] 2 All ER 492, [1978] AC 728]
> a series of decisions of the Privy Council and of your Lordships' House,
> notably in judgments and speeches delivered by Lord Keith, have emphasised
> the inability of any single general principle to provide a practical test which can
g be applied to every situation to determine whether a duty of care is owed and,
> if so, what is its scope … What emerges is that, in addition to the foreseeability
> of damage, necessary ingredients in any situation giving rise to a duty of care
> are that there should exist between the party owing the duty and the party to
> whom it is owed a relationship characterised by the law as one of "proximity"
h or "neighbourhood" and that the situation should be one in which the court
> considers it fair, just and reasonable that the law should impose a duty of a
> given scope on the one party for the benefit of the other … Whilst
> recognising, of course, the importance of the underlying general principles
> common to the whole field of negligence, I think the law has now moved in
> the direction of attaching greater significance to the more traditional
j categorisation of distinct and recognisable situations as guides to the existence,
> the scope and the limits of the varied duties of care which the law imposes.
> We must now, I think, recognise the wisdom of the word of Brennan J in the
> High Court of Australia in *Sutherland Shire Council v Heyman* (1985) 60 ALR 1
> at 43–44, where he said: "It is preferable, in my view, that the law should
> develop novel categories of negligence incrementally and by analogy with
> established categories, rather than by a massive extension of a prima facie duty

of care restrained only by indefinable 'considerations which ought to negative, or to reduce or limit the scope of the duty or the class of person to whom it is owed'.""

Following, I hope, this line of approach, it seems to me necessary to consider what are the services or organisations and their operations which are sufficiently comparable in kind, so that the incremental approach referred to can enable one to say that a duty of common law should or should not be implied to the fire brigade. In doing so, I regard as an essential feature of true comparability that the duty postulated should be a duty to protect or assist the plaintiff from the harm done or threatened by third parties, or from some peril not brought about by any act or omission of the fire brigade itself.

This leads me straight to the principal case on the subject, namely the decision of the House of Lords in *Hill v Chief Constable of West Yorkshire* [1988] 2 All ER 238, [1989] AC 53, where the mother of one of the victims of the so-called Yorkshire Ripper attempted to sue the police for their alleged negligence in failing to identify and apprehend the killer in good and sufficient time. The House held that there was no general duty of care owed by police officers, either to identify or apprehend an unknown criminal; nor did they owe a duty of care to individual members of the public who might suffer injury through the criminal's activities, except in situations where their failure to apprehend him had created an exceptional added risk beyond that to which all, or at any rate, a large section of the public were subject. Their Lordships further held that the fact that the plaintiff's daughter had been young and female, in line with the killer's other victims, did not of itself place her at special risk, and that there were no other additional characteristics capable of establishing sufficient proximity to cast upon the police a common law duty of care.

Therein, Lord Keith, delivering the leading opinion of the House, expressed the principle in these terms ([1988] 2 All ER 238 at 240–241, [1989] AC 53 at 59):

'By common law police officers owe to the general public a duty to enforce the criminal law: see *R v Metropolitan Police Comr, ex p Blackburn* [1968] 1 All ER 763, [1968] 2 QB 118. That duty may be enforced by mandamus, at the instance of one having title to sue. But as that case shows, a chief officer of police has a wide discretion as to the manner in which the duty is discharged. It is for him to decide how available resources should be deployed, whether particular lines of inquiry should or should not be followed and even whether or not certain crimes should be prosecuted. It is only if his decision on such matters is such as no reasonable chief officer of police would arrive at that someone with an interest to do so may be in a position to have recourse to judicial review. So the common law, while laying on chief officers of police an obligation to enforce the law, makes no specific requirements as to the manner in which the obligation is to be discharged. That is not a situation where there can readily be inferred an intention of the common law to create a duty towards individual members of the public.'

His Lordship further considered *Home Office v Dorset Yacht Co Ltd* [1970] 2 All ER 294, [1970] AC 1004, on which Mrs Hill and the present plaintiffs placed reliance, and illustrated the essential distinction between that case and *Hill's* case as follows ([1988] 2 All ER 238 at 241–242, [1989] AC 53 at 60):

'The *Dorset Yacht* case dealt with a situation where some borstal boys, who having records of previous escapes, were encamped on Brownsea Island

under the supervision of prison officers and escaped in the night while their
guardians slept, boarded a yacht moored nearby in order to make their way to
the mainland and manoeuvred it so as to damage the plaintiffs' yacht. One of
the features of the case was that the damage sustained by the plaintiffs was the
direct consequence of a tortious act done with conscious volition by a third
party responsible for his own acts, which was interposed between the
allegedly negligent conduct of the prison officers and the damage suffered.
The actual decision, which was on a preliminary point of law, was that a
special relationship existed on the one hand between the prison officers and
the Borstal boys who were in their custody, and on the other hand between
the prison officers and the owners of yachts moored near the encampment.
That the boys might seek to make use of a yacht in order to get away to the
mainland and might damage it in the process was the very thing which the
prison officers ought reasonably to have foreseen. The prison officers had
brought the boys, of whose propensity to attempt escape they were aware,
into the locality where the yachts were moored and so had created a potential
situation of danger for the owners of those yachts. Accordingly liability was
capable of being established on the facts.'

In other words, the *Dorset Yacht* case is explicable on the basis that, by their actions
in bringing the youths, known to be criminal, into close physical proximity with
the yachts moored nearby, and leaving them unsupervised, the prison officers had
effectively created an additional risk and brought themselves into legal proximity
with the owners of the boats.

Finally, comparing the situation in the *Dorset Yacht* case with that of the police,
Lord Keith ended his opinion with these words ([1988] 2 All ER 238 at 242–243,
[1989] AC 53 at 62):

'The *Dorset Yacht* case was concerned with the special characteristics or
ingredients beyond reasonable foreseeability of likely harm which may result
in civil liability for failure to control another man to prevent his doing harm to
a third. The present case falls broadly into the same category. It is plain that
vital characteristics which were present in the *Dorset Yacht* case and which led
to the imposition of liability are here lacking. Sutcliffe was never in the
custody of the police force. Miss Hill was one of a vast number of the female
general public who might be at risk from his activities but was at no special
distinctive risk in relation to them, unlike the owners of yachts moored off
Brownsea Island in relation to the foreseeable conduct of the borstal boys. It
appears from the passage quoted from the speech of Lord Diplock in the *Dorset
Yacht* case that in his view no liability would rest on a prison authority, which
carelessly allowed the escape of an habitual criminal, for damage which he
subsequently caused, not in the course of attempting to make good his
getaway to persons at special risk, but in further pursuance of his general
criminal career to the person or property of members of the general public.
The same rule must apply as regards failure to recapture the criminal before
he had time to resume his career. In the case of an escaped criminal his
identity and description are known. In the instant case the identity of the
wanted criminal was at the material time unknown and it is not averred that
any full or clear description of him was ever available. The alleged negligence
of the police consists in a failure to discover his identity. But, if there is no
general duty of care owed to individual members of the public by the
responsible authorities to prevent the escape of a known criminal or to
recapture him, there cannot reasonably be imposed upon any police force a

duty of care similarly owed to identify and apprehend an unknown one. Miss Hill cannot for this purpose be regarded as a person at special risk simply *a* because she was young and female. Where the class of potential victims of a particular habitual criminal is a large one the precise size of it cannot in principle affect the issue. All householders are potential victims of an habitual burglar, and all females those of an habitual rapist. The conclusion must be that although there existed reasonable foreseeability of likely harm to such as *b* Miss Hill if Sutcliffe were not identified and apprehended, there is absent from the case any such ingredient or characteristic as led to the liability of the Home Office in the *Dorset Yacht* case. Nor is there present any additional characteristic such as might make up the deficiency.'

A further case, which in my opinion is of great significance, is the decision of the *c* Court of Appeal in *Alexandrou v Oxford* [1993] 4 All ER 328. This was the case of the shop owner whose burglar alarm recorded a telephone message to the local police station saying it had been activated. Officers attended the scene but failed to inspect the back of the shop properly, where the burglars had already forced entry. The bell on the premises would be activated and would continue to ring until either it was turned off or the control panel or the system sustained damage. The *d* investigating police officer's assertion that he gave the shop passing attention while on his beat after finding everything apparently secure at his initial visit was not accepted by the trial judge. The court, having reviewed the authorities—notably the *Dorset Yacht* case and *Hill's* case—held that there was no such special relationship as would cast a common law duty of care between the plaintiff and the *e* police, because the communication to the police was by way of an emergency call which in no way differed from a call which might have been made by an ordinary member of the public. If a duty of care owed to the plaintiff was to be imposed on the police, it was held that that same duty would be owed to all members of the public who informed the police of a crime being committed or about to be committed against them or against their property. The court also held that it *f* would be against public policy to impose such a duty, but for the moment I merely draw attention to the fact that, despite the fact that the police had a public duty to prevent crime and to apprehend criminals, in the circumstances recited it was held that they were not in sufficient proximity to the very owner of the shop that was the burglars' target and whose message had alerted the police. *g*

Besides relying upon the primary finding in that case, Mr de Navarro QC placed great reliance on one passage from the judgment of Glidewell LJ wherein, having posed the question, 'Did the police owe the plaintiff a duty of care?' he said (at 334):

'The difficulty in answering this question arises from the fact that the *h* plaintiff's loss was not caused directly by any act or failure on the part of the police, but by the activities of the burglars. The police, on the judge's findings of fact, were indirectly responsible for the plaintiff's loss, because of Pc Smith's failure properly to inspect the rear of the shop when he realised at 9.26 pm that the alarm bell had stopped ringing, and his consequent failure to prevent or intercept the theft.' *j*

For the defendants it is contended that this is authority for the proposition that the necessary proximity is harder to establish in cases of indirect loss. Mr de Navarro claims further support for that proposition in the opinion of Lord Steyn in *Marc Rich & Co AG v Bishop Rock Marine Co Ltd, The Nicholas H* [1995] 3 All ER 307 at 328, [1996] 1 AC 211 at 237, where he said:

'Counsel for the cargo owners argued that the present case involved the infliction of *direct* physical loss. At first glance the issue of directness may seem a matter of terminology rather than substance. In truth it is a material factor. The law more readily attaches the consequences of actionable negligence to directly inflicted physical loss than to indirectly inflicted physical loss. For example, if the NKK surveyor had carelessly dropped a lighted cigarette into a cargo hold known to contain a combustible cargo, thereby causing an explosion and the loss of the vessel and cargo, the assertion that the classification society was in breach of a duty of care might have been a strong one.' (Lord Steyn's emphasis.)

For my part, I find some difficulty in appreciating how the nature of the ultimate damage, whether direct or indirect, can affect the question of proximity, for it seems to me that this is arguing backwards, since proximity, which surely implies a relationship, is either there before the damage is sustained or it is not. Nor do I think that Glidewell LJ intended to convey the meaning which Mr de Navarro suggests. As I read the passage it seems to me that he was merely saying that proximity was harder to establish in cases where the main or direct cause of the damage was the act of someone else, and I note that Lord Steyn's remarks were in the context of public policy (*Caparo 3*) rather than in relation to proximity. Nevertheless, *Alexandrou*'s case, as Mr Walker frankly conceded, presents considerable difficulties for him.

I have been referred to a series of other cases concerning the possible liability of the police. But with the exception of the most recent I do not propose to discuss them at any length because I have not found them particularly helpful in deciding the primary question. In *Knightley v Johns* [1982] 1 All ER 851, [1982] 1 WLR 349 and *Rigby v Chief Constable of Northamptonshire* [1985] 2 All ER 985, [1985] 1 WLR 1242 it is clear to my mind that the liability of the police stemmed from the fact that they had created the additional danger themselves, additional that is to the original accident or crime that had occurred. In *Osman v Ferguson* [1993] 4 All ER 344 the Court of Appeal, whilst dismissing the plaintiff's action on the ground of public policy did however, albeit obiter, take the view that there was an arguable case that there was a very close degree of proximity amounting to a special relationship between the plaintiff's family and the investigating police officers. However, a glance at the extremely unusual facts of that case suggests to me that it is merely an example of what Lord Keith in *Hill*'s case was referring to as an exceptional added risk. In *Ancell v McDermott* [1993] 4 All ER 355 it was held that the police were under no duty of care to protect road users from, or to warn them of, hazards discovered by the police whilst going about their duties on the highways, so that there was no special relationship giving rise to an additional duty to prevent harm from dangers created by another. The decision was basically on grounds of public policy, but in so far as proximity is concerned the fact that duties in relation to the highway lay primarily upon the highway authority must, to my mind, have been a telling factor.

The most recent case is that of *Swinney v Chief Constable of the Northumbria Police* [1996] 3 All ER 449. In that case the first plaintiff had information which could have helped to identify the driver of a hit and run vehicle. Being public spirited, she passed on that information to one of the defendant's officers in strict confidence and it found its way onto a document which included her name, address and telephone number, and which also stated several times that the information was given in total confidence and was not to be leaked for fear of reprisals from the person named in the document who was known to be of a violent disposition. The

document was stolen whilst in the custody of the police. Giving the judgment of
the court, Hirst LJ took the view that the case fell into the *Dorset Yacht* category *a*
rather than the *Hill* category in respect of proximity, principally because of the
repeated references to confidentiality and the fact that the plaintiffs were at
particular risk. This case is another interesting example of what one might term
the exceptions to the *Hill* principle.

Prison officers feature in the *Dorset Yacht* case, but since I have already dealt with *b*
that and the way in which it was distinguished in *Hill*, I propose to say no more
about it. There has been one interesting case concerning the coastguard service,
namely *Skinner v Secretary of State for Transport* (1995) Times, 3 January, a decision
of Judge Gareth Edwards. This was the case arising out of the sinking of the fishing
vessel Inspire near Fishguard by an enormous wave. The lone survivor sued the
coastguard service for failure to respond to some form of Mayday call. I should like *c*
to say at once that I found the judgment and reasoning of the learned judge
extremely careful, well expressed and most persuasive. He reviewed the
authorities current at the time, including all those to which I have referred with the
exception of the most recent case of *Swinney*, and in particular he distinguished
such cases as *Knightley*, *Rigby* and the *Dorset Yacht*. He came to the conclusion that *d*
none of the cases were any authority for the proposition that the police are under
a legal duty of care to a member of the public making an emergency call and, by
analogy, applied the same reasoning to the coastguard service. He summarised his
conclusions in these words:

e

> 'Accordingly, it seems to me that the incremental approach yields a definite
> and negative answer to the question whether the coastguard owes a duty of
> care to mariners in respect of its watching, search and rescue functions. There
> is no way to arrive at a duty of care by analogy with the position of other
> emergency services or by analogy with the position of public bodies exercising
> statutory functions. In fact, the relevant precedents to which I have referred *f*
> appear to give a negative answer whether or not the incremental approach is
> adopted.'

Not unnaturally, the plaintiffs rely on the analogy with local authorities in
relation to their duties of inspection of buildings, expressed in a series of cases, of *g*
which perhaps the most important and far reaching was *Anns v Merton London
Borough* [1977] 2 All ER 492, [1978] AC 728. In passing, it is a remarkable
coincidence that this fire also took place in the London Borough of Merton. In
Anns's case it was held that the borough would be liable to the house owner for
breach of a duty if it were proved that their inspector, having assumed the duty of *h*
inspecting the foundations of the house and acting otherwise than in the bona fide
exercise of any discretion under the statute, did not exercise reasonable care to
ensure that the byelaws applicable to the foundations were complied with.

I do not derive assistance from this case for two reasons. First, I do not think it
can validly be said that the local authority are reacting to peril created by someone
else and are not in the same position as the emergency services. Second, one *j*
cannot but be conscious of a distinct retreat from the somewhat extreme position
which the *Anns* case reached. The House of Lords has already departed from it in
relation to economic loss (see *Murphy v Brentwood DC* [1990] 2 All ER 908, [1991] 1
AC 398). I am informed that they are in the process of deciding whether to do so
altogether as a result of *Stovin v Wise* (*Norfolk CC, third party*) [1994] 3 All ER 467,
[1994] 1 WLR 1124, so that it must be doubted whether, quite apart from the first

a factor that I have mentioned, *Anns* can any longer be relied on as an authority for the principle contended for by the plaintiffs.

It is the contention of Mr Walker that the true analogy is with the hospitals and allied medical services who are under a public duty to provide medical care and who, in a succession of cases—for example, *Barnett v Chelsea and Kensington Hospital Management Committee* [1968] 3 All ER 1068, [1969] 1 QB 428—have been held to be
b under a personal duty to those who come to them for such care. But the statutory framework under which hospitals and allied medical services act is very different from that governing the fire brigade. The relevant statute is the National Health Service Act 1977, which begins by reciting a series of duties on the part of the Secretary of State to make arrangements for the promotion of a comprehensive health service designed to secure improvement of the physical and mental health
c of persons in England and Wales, and in the prevention, diagnosis and treatment of illness.

Section 29(2) of that Act provides:

d 'Regulations may provide for the definition of the personal medical services to be provided and for securing that the arrangements will be such that all persons availing themselves of those services will receive adequate personal care and attendance ...'

I consider that against the background of the highly personal element involved in 'adequate medical care', proximity has effectively been imposed upon hospital authorities by the statute. In obedience to that statute they hold themselves out as
e being prepared to assume responsibility for the sick and injured. Patients are invited in, whether to the ward or the casualty department, and are entitled to rely upon the hospital assuming responsibility for them. Firemen, on the other hand, are not dealing personally with the sick and injured, save in so far as they may be injured during the course of the fire. Their duty is to fight fires—a duty owed to
f the general public. In summary, therefore, I have come to the firm opinion that as regards the fire brigade there exists no sufficient proximity nor special relationship between them and the owner of any property that may be ablaze to cast upon them a personal duty at common law to respond to any call for assistance. Where public policy is concerned, one naturally returns to *Hill*'s case, where Lord Keith
g listed the various reasons whereby it was not in the public interest to saddle police officers with personal common law duties towards individuals who were affected by crimes which the officers were supposed to prevent ([1988] 2 All ER 238 at 243–244, [1989] AC 53 at 63):

h 'Application of that second stage is, however, capable of constituting a separate and independent ground for holding that the existence of liability in negligence should not be entertained. Potential existence of such liability may in many instances be in the general public interest, as tending towards the observance of a higher standard of care in the carrying on of various different types of activity. I do not, however, consider that this can be said of police
j activities. The general sense of public duty which motivates police forces is unlikely to be appreciably reinforced by the imposition of such liability so far as concerns their function in the investigation and suppression of crime. From time to time they make mistakes in the exercise of that function, but it is not to be doubted that they apply their best endeavours to the performance of it. In some instances the imposition of liability may lead to the exercise of a function being carried on in a detrimentally defensive frame of mind. The possibility of this happening in relation to the investigative operations of the

police cannot be excluded. Further, it would be reasonable to expect that if
potential liability were to be imposed it would be not uncommon for actions a
to be raised against police forces on the ground that they had failed to catch
some criminal as soon as they might have done, with the result that he went
on to commit further crimes. While some such actions might involve
allegations of a simple and straightforward type of failure, for example that a
police officer negligently tripped and fell while pursuing a burglar, others b
would be likely to enter deeply into the general nature of a police
investigation, as indeed the present action would seek to do. The manner of
conduct of such an investigation must necessarily involve a variety of
decisions to be made on matters of policy and discretion, for example as to
which particular line of inquiry is most advantageously to be pursued and
what is the most advantageous way to deploy the available resources. Many c
such decisions would not be regarded by the courts as appropriate to be called
in question, yet elaborate investigation of the facts might be necessary to
ascertain whether or not this was so. A great deal of police time, trouble and
expense might be expected to have to be put into the preparation of the
defence to the action and the attendance of witnesses at the trial. The result d
would be a significant diversion of police manpower and attention from their
most important function, that of the suppression of crime. Closed
investigations would require to be reopened and retraversed, not with the
object of bringing any criminal to justice but to ascertain whether or not they
had been competently conducted.'

Lord Templeman added some further reflections ([1988] 2 All ER 238 at 244–245, e
[1989] AC 53 at 64):

'The question for determination in this appeal is whether an action for
damages is an appropriate vehicle for investigating the efficiency of a police
force. The present action will be confined to narrow albeit perplexing f
questions, for example whether, discounting hindsight, it should have been
obvious to a senior police officer that Sutcliffe was a prime suspect, whether a
senior police officer should not have been deceived by an evil hoaxer, whether
an officer interviewing Sutcliffe should have been better briefed and whether
a report on Sutcliffe should have been given greater attention. The court
would have to consider the conduct of each police officer, to decide whether g
the policeman failed to attain the standard of care of a hypothetical average
policeman. The court would have to decide whether an inspector is to be
condemned for failing to display the acumen of Sherlock Holmes and whether
a constable is to be condemned for being as obtuse as Dr Watson. The plaintiff
will presumably seek evidence, for what it is worth, from retired police h
inspectors, who would be asked whether they would have been misled by the
hoaxer and whether they would have identified Sutcliffe at an earlier stage. At
the end of the day the court might or might not find that there had been
negligence by one or more members of the police force. But that finding
would not help anybody or punish anybody ... Moreover, if this action lies,
every citizen will be able to require the court to investigate the performance j
of every policeman. If the policeman concentrates on one crime, he may be
accused of neglecting others. If the policeman does not arrest on suspicion a
suspect with previous convictions, the police force may be held liable for
subsequent crimes. The threat of litigation against a police force would not
make a policeman more efficient. The necessity for defending proceedings,
successfully or unsuccessfully, would distract the policeman from his duties.

a   This action is in my opinion misconceived and will do more harm than good. A policeman is a servant of the public and is liable to be dismissed for incompetence. A police force serves the public and the elected representatives of the public must ensure that the public get the police force they deserve. It may be that the West Yorkshire police force was in 1980 in some respects better and in some respects worse than the public deserve. An action for

b   damages for alleged acts of negligence by individual police officers in 1980 could not determine whether and in what respects the West Yorkshire police force can be improved in 1988.'

For a list of considerations which have influenced the courts in deciding what is fair, just and reasonable within the terms of public policy, I can do no better than
c   quote from *Clerk and Lindsell on Torts* (17th edn, 1995) para 7/15. The authors refer to justice and reasonableness:

'At its narrowest, it focuses on the relationship between the parties and, in particular the proportionality, *i.e.* the weight of the burden of liability in relation to the nature of the conduct. Assessing the burden may involve
d   considering the relative exposure to risk of the class of plaintiff and defendant concerned and the availability of protection through insurance or contractual arrangements. Thus, in *Donoghue v. Stevenson* [1932] AC 562, [1932] All ER Rep 1 the fact that, but for negligence liability, the consumer who was not also the purchaser would be left with no remedy at all, was a key factor in justifying the duty. Beyond the particular relationship of the parties, the criterion may
e   involve consideration of the so-called floodgates argument, *i.e.* that if a duty is to be imposed on the facts of the particular case, it will have to be imposed in a wide range of similar situations with the result that the burden of liability on the class of defendant may be considered to be disproportionate to the conduct involved. The overall framework of the legal system may also be
f   relevant on the ground that it would not be just and reasonable to impose negligence liability if the rights and duties of the parties have been clearly defined by equity, statute or other tort actions. The wider interests of the legal system may include concerns about the evidentiary difficulties and length of litigation following imposition of a duty, for example in relation to nervous shock. At the broadest level, "perceptions of community attitudes and goals"
g   may also be relevant. The existence of statutory regulation may be taken as evidence of community values and "may encourage the court to hold that certain interests warrant protection" but in other situations it may be taken as evidence that the plaintiff is so adequately protected that a further common law remedy would not be just and reasonable. The general "public good" may
h   also be invoked: thus a duty has been denied on the grounds that it would lead to defensive policing, defensive social services, defensive regulatory activity or inhibit the work of advocates. The counter-argument is that the deterrent effect of negligence liability in such situations makes a desirable contribution to the maintenance of standards. On occasion, broader consequential
j   arguments are invoked but judges are rightly hesitant to pursue such arguments when they have neither the full information nor the basis on which to evaluate the information that is presented.'

I think that as regards the fire brigade, many of these considerations are applicable and militate on grounds of public policy against the imposition of any common law duty. In particular, I would single out the following. (1) I do not think that any extra standard of care would be achieved. (2) Rather the reverse; if a common law duty of care can lead to defensive policing, by the same token it can lead to defensive fire-fighting. Fearful of being accused of leaving the scene too early, the officer in charge might well commit his resources when they would have been better employed elsewhere. He would be open to criticism every time there was a balance to be struck or that sort of operational choice to be made. (3) If the efficiency of the emergency services is to be tested, it should be done not in private litigation but by an inquiry instituted by national or local authorities who are responsible to the electorate. This follows the reasoning of Lord Templeman in *Hill's* case. (4) The case of *Marc Rich & Co AG v Bishop Rock Marine Co Ltd, The Nicholas H* [1995] 3 All ER 307, [1996] 1 AC 211 suggests that the fact that a defendant in the position of the fire brigade acts for the collective welfare is one that should be taken into account. (5) Last, and to my mind by far the most important consideration, is what is sometimes referred to as the 'floodgates' argument.

I have read the statement of Martin Coffey, agreed for the purposes of this issue, which gives some indication of the enormously wide scope and frequency of the fire brigade's activities, which are by no means merely confined to fighting fires. I am told that the fire services are the prime rescue service in the land. It is a truism to say that we live in the age of compensation. There seems to be a growing belief that every misfortune must, in pecuniary terms at any rate, be laid at someone else's door, and after every mishap, every tragedy, the cupped palms are outstretched for the solace of monetary compensation. Claims which would have been unheard of 30 years ago are now being seriously entertained, and public money provided for pursuing them. When performing their primary function, namely fighting fires, the fire brigade are very often reacting to a situation created either by the hand of God or that of a lunatic or of a criminal. Pecuniary compensation is notoriously difficult to obtain from such persons, particularly the first named. The consequence of this is that the party suffering damage will be eager to fix his cannon against a defendant who may be in a position to meet the claim. Just as with the police, as part of any action brought against the fire brigade it may be necessary to institute an elaborate investigation into the facts so that one can decide whether or not any decision or exercise of discretion was one which the courts would allow to be called in question. This is in relation to decisions which are almost always made in dangerous and rapidly developing situations. One can envisage protracted arguments between various experts in this field. In relation to such claims as may succeed, the money to meet those claims will, whether by straight award or increased premium, ultimately, have to be subscribed by the general public.

In this context I respectfully adopt the reasoning of Staughton LJ in *M (a minor) v Newham London BC, X and ors v Bedfordshire CC* [1994] 4 All ER 602 at 630, [1995] 2 AC 633 at 674:

'The question whether it will be just and reasonable to extend an established category to some new situation can give rise to a number of familiar arguments, to which there are a number of familiar answers. For example, it is often said that a new development will open the floodgates to litigation: to that the answer is either a denial, or the assertion that if there is so much negligence there ought to be so much litigation, and the courts must cope with it. It may be said that the legal aid authorities will fund unjustified claims, resulting in hardship to defendants; in answer, that is a fault of the legal aid system, and should not be met by denying a cause of action to all. Similarly it is said that child plaintiffs will be able to delay bringing claims against local

a
authorities until many years later when they reach the age of 21; the answer is that the fault lies in the law of limitation of actions, and not in an incremental duty of care. Again it may be said that professional people with difficult tasks to perform should only be held liable if they really are negligent, but in practice will be blamed for mere errors of judgment—or at any rate some payment will have to be made to settle such cases; that again will be attributed

b
to error in the operation of the law rather than error in its substance. To all those points the answer given is sound in logic. But I fear that the time has come to recognise that it is unsound in practice. If a new duty of local authorities is established in these appeals, I do not doubt that many claims will be brought, placing further strain on an already stretched system (which will be provided with no more resources). I do not doubt that many claims with

c
little or no prospect of success will be financed by the legal aid fund. Nor that many will be delayed for years, perhaps until the plaintiff is 21. Nor that many claims will be settled, or even decided in favour of a plaintiff whose misfortunes attract sympathy, although there has been no more than an error of judgment.'

d
Having listened carefully to the submissions of both counsel, I can discern no countervailing arguments for the imposition of a duty on the grounds of public policy which have anything like the weight of the arguments against so doing.

I turn now to the subsidiary question: can it be said that despite the absence of a common law duty to respond at all, once the fire brigade have, as they invariably

e
do, elected to respond, they thereby put themselves into sufficient proximity to the building owner; and second, are the considerations of public policy any different in such a situation?

Again I start with Caparo 2. Mr Walker has referred me to a number of cases where, despite what for convenience I would call the general immunity, police and

f
other public bodies have been held to have been in sufficient proximity to a particular plaintiff during the course of discharging their public duty. This, in the case of a fire brigade, would be analogous to answering an emergency call. Those where the police themselves have created the added danger I have dealt with under the primary question, but my attention has been drawn to Kirkham v Chief Constable

g
of the Greater Manchester Police [1990] 3 All ER 246, [1990] 2 QB 283. In that case the police took into custody a man known to be a suicide risk, but did not communicate that information to the prison authorities, with the result that he was not sufficiently supervised and did indeed commit suicide. It was held that the police, by the fact of arresting the man, assumed responsibility towards him and brought themselves under a duty to pass on information which might affect his

h
wellbeing when being transferred to the custody of the prison authorities.

In Barrett v Ministry of Defence [1995] 3 All ER 87, [1995] 1 WLR 1217—the case of the drunken sailor—it was held that the mere existence of public duty did not create a special relationship between the defendants and naval personnel so as to impose a duty in private law so that they were entitled to leave a responsible adult

j
to assume responsibility for his own actions as to how much alcohol he chose to consume. However, after the deceased had collapsed through drink the petty officer on duty organised a stretcher party and the deceased was taken to his cabin insensible, where he was placed in his bunk in the recovery position although he was tossing and turning. He was monitored only in the most cursory fashion and died through inhaling his own vomit. The Court of Appeal held that once the defendants, by their officers, had decided to assume what was in effect total control

of the deceased's movement, they thereby assumed personal responsibility for him.

     These cases, in my judgment, are examples of situations where, by words or conduct, the defendants have ventured beyond a mere discharge of public duty and have assumed a particular responsibility. It was pointed out that the fact that persons affected would be expected to rely on the public body discharging the responsibility that they had assumed was sufficient to create the necessary proximity to give rise to a duty at common law. The present plaintiffs argued, by parity of reasoning, that when, to use the words of Hilaire Belloc, 'Members of the gallant band come pouring in from every hand', and pursuant to the powers given by s 30(3) of the 1947 Act the chief fire officer starts giving orders to all and sundry, they are assuming responsibility to those likely to be affected by the fire. But the flaw in that argument, so it seems to me, is that it postulates that whenever one of the emergency services is merely discharging its public duty, for instance fighting fires, chasing burglars or manning the lifeboats, by the very same token, and no more, it is assuming responsibility towards the householder or to those in peril on the sea. In other words, the mere discharge of public duty would trigger an automatic common law duty, which is exactly what the authorities have declared does not happen. Before the necessary proximity can be established something more—it has been termed a special ingredient—must be shown to demonstrate that besides the mere performance of their public duty the fire brigade, or for that matter other emergency services, undertook a personal responsibility to some individual during the course of their activity. If the police arrest a man they drastically curtail his freedom and, to a large extent, determine his movement. If superior officers pick up a drunken and insensible rating in order to dispose of him in accordance with Admiral Smith's system, they have taken charge of a man who cannot take charge of himself and must deal carefully with him.

     Probably the greatest support for the defendant's contention on this issue is to be found in *Alexandrou*'s case. Therein, as the facts show, not only did the police respond to the fact that there had been a '999' call and the burglar alarm had been activated but, like the fire brigade in the present case, they went as far as inspecting the premises and keeping a periodic eye on them during the course of their duties. This, however, was not enough to bring them within the range of legal proximity. Glidewell LJ said ([1993] 4 All ER 328 at 338):

     'It is possible to envisage an agreement between an occupier of a property protected by a burglar alarm and the police which would impose a contractual liability on the police. That is not, however, the situation in this case. The communication with the police in this case was by a 999 telephone call, followed by a recorded message. If as a result of that communication the police came under a duty of care to the plaintiff, it must follow that they would be under a similar duty to any person who informs them, whether by 999 call or in some other way, that a burglary, or indeed any crime, against himself or his property is being committed or is about to be committed. So in my view if there is a duty of care it is owed to a wider group than those to whom the judge referred. It is owed to all members of the public who give information of a suspected crime against themselves or their property. It follows, therefore, that on the facts of this case it is my opinion that there was no such special relationship between the plaintiff and the police as was present in the *Dorset Yacht* case.'

a Mr Walker points out that in the passage quoted Glidewell LJ only seems to be considering the matter at the moment when the 999 call was made, but I cannot for one moment believe that in the face of the facts, which he was careful to recite, Glidewell LJ was unmindful of the fact that the police had, in effect, responded in the matter described. Slade LJ clearly had both situations in mind when he disclaimed any duty owed by the police on or after the 999 call (see [1993] 4 All ER

b 328 at 344).

Since I regard the position of the police force as properly comparable for present purposes with that of the fire brigade, this decision is effectively binding upon me, irrespective of the fact that in accordance with the authorities I should have reached the same conclusion independently.

c Those conclusions are sufficient to determine the preliminary issue. Consequently, I do not propose to deal at length with the public policy argument within the framework of what I have described as the secondary question. *Swinney's* case illustrates that considerations of public policy do not form a blanket immunity to the police in all situations. Other considerations of public policy, notably the encouragement and protection of informants, might override the

d more general principle. However, in the facts of the present case I can discern no special overriding considerations which would have that effect. Once it is appreciated that the public policy immunity can be overridden by particular considerations and that immunity does not necessarily prevail when the fire brigade either creates the risk itself or makes an assumption of responsibility upon which others are likely to rely, then I do not think that there is any justifiable reason

e for holding that the public policy considerations relevant to the primary question do not apply with equal force once the fire brigade have responded to a call out.

Mr de Navarro also urged upon me the principle in *East Suffolk Rivers Catchment Board v Kent* [1940] 4 All ER 527, [1941] AC 74 to the effect that where a statutory authority has a mere power rather than a duty, it cannot be made liable for any

f damage sustained by an individual by reason of a failure to exercise the power or a failure to exercise it properly. However, in *Anns*, Lord Wilberforce (without expressly departing from the *East Suffolk* case) gave as his opinion that the rule was by no means absolute and that, following the decision of *Donoghue v Stevenson* [1932] AC 562, [1932] All ER Rep 1, it had to be realised that common law duties might co-exist with those of public law. In *Fellowes v Rother DC* [1983] 1 All ER 513

g Goff J (as he then was) stated that the principle had to be read in the light of the later decision in *Anns*.

Some doubt has been expressed whether the *East Suffolk* case has withstood the onslaught of later developments and expansion of the principle of proximity as creating a common law duty. Again, I am informed that the House of Lords may

h well make some definitive pronouncement on the subject as a result of the appeal in *Stovin's* case. Since I have decided this issue on other grounds, it is unnecessary and would be positively impertinent for me to try and resolve the problem.

In conclusion therefore, reverting to the terms of the preliminary question, my answer is No.

j

Order accordingly.

K Mydeen Esq   Barrister.

Capital and Counties plc v Hampshire County Council and others

Digital Equipment Co Ltd v Hampshire County Council and others

QUEEN'S BENCH DIVISION (OFFICIAL REFEREES' BUSINESS)

JUDGE RICHARD HAVERY QC

3–5, 9–12, 16–18, 26 OCTOBER, 2, 6–9, 13–16, 20–23, 27–30 NOVEMBER, 4–7, 11–12, 18–21 DECEMBER 1995, 28 MARCH 1996, 4, 7 JUNE 1996

Negligence – Duty to take care – Fire brigade – Negligence in attendance at fire – Duty of fire brigade in relation to fire – Plaintiffs' property destroyed by fire – Fire brigade switching off sprinkler system – Whether fire brigade owing duty of care to plaintiffs – Whether fire brigade immune from liability at common law on ground of public policy – Whether fire brigade having statutory immunity – Fire Services Act 1947, s 30(1).

The two plaintiffs were the head lessee and sublessee respectively of a commercial building. A fire broke out in the roof void of the building, and the fire brigade were called. Although the building was fitted with a sprinkler system which included sprinklers in the roof void, the fire officer initially in charge of fire-fighting at the scene mistakenly believed that there were no sprinklers in the roof and that the sprinkler system was not therefore assisting in fighting the fire, but merely hampering the fire-fighters. Accordingly, he ordered the whole sprinkler system to be turned off. Thereafter, the fire spread rapidly across the roof, with the result that the whole building was eventually destroyed. Several actions were brought in respect of the loss and destruction of the building, but by the time of trial, following the settlement of various proceedings, the claims remaining before the court were the claims by the two plaintiffs against the defendant fire authority for damages for negligence in switching off the sprinkler system. The questions arose in particular: (i) whether the fire service was liable at common law for negligence in turning off the sprinkler system or immune from liability on the grounds of public policy, and (ii) whether the fire service was immune from liability by reason of s 30(1)[a] of the Fire Services Act 1947.

Held – (1) In carrying out its professional activities the fire service owed a duty of care not to commit positive acts of negligence, and there was no reason why the service should be immune on grounds of public policy from liability in relation to such acts. Accordingly, since it was reasonably foreseeable that if the sprinklers were turned off there would be a significantly increased risk of the fire spreading, and the owners and occupiers of the building were foreseeably likely to suffer physical damage as a direct result of the negligent shutting down of the sprinkler system, it followed that the fire service was liable for negligence at common law (see p 340 *g j* to p 341 *a* and p 344 *e f*, post); *Alexandrou v Oxford* [1993] 4 All ER 328, *Church of Jesus Christ of Latter Day Saints v West Yorkshire Fire and Civil Defence Authority* (1996) Times, 9 May and *John Munroe (Acrylics) Ltd v London Fire and Civil Defence Authority* [1996] 4 All ER 318 distinguished.

---

a   Section 30(1) is set out at p 344 *h j*, post

a (2) Section 30(1) of the 1947 Act conferred immunity on the fire service only to the extent necessary to give effect to the powers conferred by the section on the service. Thus, a fire-fighter was immune from liability in carrying out activities such as applying water to a plaintiff's building, setting into a hydrant on a plaintiff's land, or in turning a sprinkler system on or off, only provided that he was acting within the statutory power. The section did not, however, grant
b immunity from liability for causing damage by negligence. Accordingly, since the decision to turn off the sprinkler system had been found to be negligent, the statutory immunity did not apply. Damages would therefore be awarded for the plaintiff (see p 344 *g* and p 345 *e f*, post); dictum of Lord Blackburn in *Geddis v Proprietors of Bann Reservoir* (1878) 3 App Cas 430 at 455–456 and of Lord Jauncey in *X and ors (minors) v Bedfordshire CC, M (a minor) v Newham London BC, E (a minor)*
c *v Dorset BC* [1995] 3 All ER 353 at 362 applied.

Notes

For the nature of negligence and the duty to take care generally, see 34 *Halsbury's Laws* (4th edn) paras 1–5, and for cases on the subject, see 36(1) *Digest* (2nd
d reissue) 7–64, *1–325*.

For the Fire Services Act 1947, s 30, see 18 *Halsbury's Statutes* (4th edn) (1991 reissue) 31.

Cases referred to in judgment

Alexandrou v Oxford [1993] 4 All ER 328, CA.
e *Associated Provincial Picture Houses Ltd v Wednesbury Corp* [1947] 2 All ER 680, [1948] 1 KB 223, CA.
Barrett v Ministry of Defence [1995] 3 All ER 87, [1995] 1 WLR 1217, CA.
Caparo Industries plc v Dickman [1990] 1 All ER 568, [1990] 2 AC 605, [1990] 2 WLR 358, HL.
f *Church of Jesus Christ of Latter Day Saints v West Yorkshire Fire and Civil Defence Authority* (1996) Times, 9 May.
East Suffolk Rivers Catchment Board v Kent [1940] 4 All ER 527, [1941] AC 74, HL.
Geddis v Proprietors of Bann Reservoir (1878) 3 App Cas 430, HL.
Hill v Chief Constable of West Yorkshire [1988] 2 All ER 238, [1989] AC 53, [1988] 2
g WLR 1049, HL.
Holgate-Mohammed v Duke [1984] 1 All ER 1054, [1984] AC 437, [1984] 2 WLR 660, HL.
Home Office v Dorset Yacht Co Ltd [1970] 2 All ER 294, [1970] AC 1004, [1970] 2 WLR 1140, HL.
h *Kilboy v South Eastern Fire Area Joint Committee* 1952 SC 280, Ct of Sess.
Munroe (John) (Acrylics) Ltd v London Fire and Civil Defence Authority [1996] 4 All ER 318.
Rigby v Chief Constable of Northamptonshire [1985] 2 All ER 985, [1985] 1 WLR 1242.
Skinner v Secretary of State for Transport (1995) Times, 3 January.
Swinney v Chief Constable of the Northumbria Police [1996] 3 All ER 449, CA.
j *X and ors (minors) v Bedfordshire CC, M (a minor) v Newham London BC, E (a minor) v Dorset BC* [1995] 3 All ER 353, [1995] 2 AC 633, [1995] 3 WLR 152, HL.

Cases also cited or referred to in skeleton arguments

Alexander v Cambridge Credit Corp Ltd (1987) 9 NSWLR 310, NSW CA.
Ancell v McDermott [1993] 4 All ER 355, CA.
Anns v Merton London Borough [1977] 2 All ER 492, [1978] AC 728, HL.

Banque Bruxelles Lambert SA v Eagle Star Insurance Co Ltd [1995] 2 All ER 769, [1995]
QB 375, CA; *rvsd sub nom South Australia Management Corp v York Montague,*
United Bank of Kuwait plc v Prudential Property Services Ltd, Nykredit Mortgage
Bank plc v Edward Erdman Group Ltd [1996] 3 All ER 365, [1996] 3 WLR 87, HL.
Brind v Secretary of State for the Home Dept [1991] 1 All ER 720, [1991] 1 AC 696, HL.
Calvely v Chief Constable of the Merseyside Police [1989] 1 All ER 1025, [1989] QB 136,
HL.
Cooper v Nevill (1961) Times, 10 March.
Cutler v Wandsworth Stadium Ltd (in liq) [1949] 1 All ER 544, [1949] AC 398, HL.
Dawson & Co v Bingley Urban DC [1911] 2 KB 149, [1911–13] All ER Rep 596.
Donoghue v Stevenson [1932] AC 562, [1932] All ER Rep 1, HL.
Duff v Highland & Islands Fire Board (1995) Times, 3 November, Ct of Sess.
Elguzouli-Daf v Comr of Police of the Metropolis, McBrearty v Ministry of Defence [1995]
1 All ER 833, [1995] QB 335, CA.
Fellowes v Rother DC [1983] 1 All ER 513.
Galoo Ltd (in liq) v Bright Grahame Murray (a firm) [1995] 1 All ER 16, [1994] 1 WLR
1360, CA.
Horsley v McLaren, The Ogopogo [1971] 2 Lloyd's Rep 410.
Hughes v National Union of Mineworkers [1991] 4 All ER 278.
Kirkham v Chief Constable of the Greater Manchester Police [1990] 3 All ER 246, [1990]
2 QB 283, CA.
Knightley v Johns [1982] 1 All ER 851, [1982] 1 WLR 349, CA.
Mahon v Osborne [1939] 1 All ER 535, [1939] 2 KB 14, CA.
March v E & M H Stramare Pty Ltd (1991) 171 CLR 506, Aust HC.
Marshall v Osmond [1983] 2 All ER 225, [1983] QB 1034, CA.
Maynard v West Midlands Regional Health Authority [1985] 1 All ER 635, [1984] 1
WLR 634, HL.
Minories Finance Ltd v Arthur Young [1989] 2 All ER 105.
Murphy v Brentwood DC [1990] 2 All ER 908, [1991] 1 AC 398, HL.
National Justice Cia Naviera SA v Prudential Assurance Co Ltd, The Ikarian Reefer
[1995] 1 Lloyd's Rep 455, CA.
Osman v Ferguson [1993] 4 All ER 344, CA.
Pasmore v Oswaldtwistle UDC [1898] AC 387, [1895–99] All ER Rep 191, HL.
Philcox v Civil Aviation Authority (1995) Times, 8 June, [1995] CA Transcript 821.
Quinn v Burch Bros (Builders) Ltd [1966] 2 All ER 283, [1966] 2 QB 370, CA.
R v Deputy Governor of Parkhurst Prison, ex p Hague [1991] 3 All ER 733, [1992] 1 AC
58, HL.
R v Inner London Education Authority, ex p Ali (1990) 2 Admin LR 822, DC.
Rich (Marc) & Co AG v Bishop Rock Marine Co Ltd, The Nicholas H, [1995] 3 All ER
307, [1996] 1 AC 211, HL.
Rondell v Worsley [1967] 3 All ER 993, [1969] 1 AC 191, HL.
Saif Ali v Sydney Mitchell & Co [1978] 3 All ER 1033, [1980] AC 198, HL.
Tojo Maru, The [1971] 1 All ER 1110, [1972] AC 242, HL.
Ward v London CC [1938] 2 All ER 341.
Yorkshire Dale Steamship Co Ltd v Minister of War Transport, The Coxwold [1942] 2
All ER 6, [1942] AC 691, HL.

Actions

By reereamended writs dated respectively 22 June 1995 and 5 July 1995 the
plaintiffs, Capital and Counties plc and Digital Equipment Co Ltd, brought
actions against, inter alia, Hampshire County Council (the fire authority),

a   claiming damages for the destruction of their commercial office property known as 'The Crescent', Jays Close, Basingstoke arising from the fire authority's breach of duty of care and/or negligence in switching off the building's sprinkler system during a fire. The facts are set out in the judgment.

b   *John Slater QC, Simon Brown QC* and *Alexander Antelme* (instructed by *Cameron Markby Hewitt*) for Capital and Counties plc.

John Slater QC and *Nigel Tozzi* (instructed by *Barlow Lyde & Gilbert*) for Digital Equipment Co Ltd.

James Munby QC and *Robert Beecroft* (instructed by *Peter C B Robertson*, Winchester) for Hampshire County Council.

c
Cur adv vult

28 March 1996. The following judgment was delivered.

d   **JUDGE HAVERY QC.** These actions arise out of a fire which occurred at Basingstoke on 6 March 1990. The fire destroyed a commercial building; there was no personal injury. The building was known as 'The Crescent' and it was situated in Jays Close, a modern commercial estate. The two plaintiffs are the head lessee of the building, Capital and Counties plc (Capco) and the lessee of Capco, Digital Equipment Co Ltd (Digital). The Crescent was practically
e   completed in September 1988 and Digital, its first occupant, went into occupation in 1989. Digital occupied the building, which contained much computer equipment, as the headquarters of its computer business in the United Kingdom. Where appropriate, I shall refer to the two plaintiffs indiscriminately as 'the plaintiffs'. There were numerous defendants; but by the time of the opening of
f   the trial, only five defendants and one third party were left in the action. At an early stage of the hearing, the claims involving all those parties except Hampshire County Council were settled, and they took no further part in the proceedings. Hampshire County Council are the fire authority for the relevant area, Hampshire, and are sued by the plaintiffs for breaches of duty alleged to have been committed by the Hampshire fire brigade (the fire brigade) (now known as
g   the Hampshire Fire and Rescue Service) in relation to the fire. In this judgment, I shall for convenience sometimes refer to the fire brigade as though they were the defendants. [The judge proceeded to describe the facts of the case, namely that the building was a two-storey building consisting of three inter-connected blocks, A, B and C. The accommodation was at ground and first floor level, with
h   pitched perimeter roofing above. Neither the roof voids over the three blocks nor the link block had any fire barriers. The whole building was protected by a sprinkler system divided into zones: A1, A2, B1, B2 and C. Station Officer Mitchell decided to switch off the building's sprinkler system at an early stage in proceedings under the mistaken belief that there were no sprinklers in the roof
j   void (where the fire originated) and that the sprinkler system was not assisting in fighting the fire, but merely hampering the fire-fighters. The judge concluded that in the circumstances Station Officer Mitchell's decision was so unreasonable that it could not be described as other than negligent, and that the defendant could not avoid liability for damages by claiming that it was not under a duty to fight the fire and that the building would have burnt down completely even if the fire brigade had done nothing at all, and continued:]

Liability at common law and immunity on the ground of public policy

I now consider the question of liability at common law for negligence in a turning off the sprinkler system, regardless of any duty to fight the fire.

Both parties have cited to me the criteria laid down in *Caparo Industries plc v Dickman* [1990] 1 All ER 568 at 573–574, [1990] 2 AC 605 at 617–618, by reference to which the existence or otherwise of a duty of care is to be decided. The first two of those criteria are: (i) was the damage to the plaintiff reasonably b foreseeable? (ii) Did there exist between the plaintiff and the defendant a relationship characterised by the law as one of 'proximity' or 'neighbourhood'? In my judgment, it is manifest that those two criteria are satisfied in the instant case in relation to turning off the sprinklers. However, I have heard argument on both points and I must deal with it.

Mr Munby QC argued that Station Officer Mitchell was entitled to assume that c there would be one-hour fire separation between blocks A and B and, accordingly, to believe that the A/B link would make a suitable fire break at which, with the resources he had to hand, he would be able to fight and extinguish the fire whether or not the sprinklers were on. It was accordingly not reasonably foreseeable that turning off the sprinklers would imperil either block d B or block C.

Mr Munby's argument is, on its face, insufficient to establish fulfilment of criterion (i). Mr Munby did not argue that the risk of further damage to block A was not reasonably foreseeable. Damage to blocks B and C, though representing damage greater in extent than, does not represent damage differing in kind from, that to block A. But I reject his argument even in relation to blocks B and C. e Assuming that Station Officer Mitchell had reason to expect the existence of the one-hour fire separation between blocks A and B, there might be circumstances (though I find there not to have been in this case) where, in weighing the reasonably perceived smallness of the risk of spread of fire into block B, against countervailing advantages in turning off the sprinkler system, it would have been f reasonable to turn off the system. That would negative negligence, but would not prevent the risk from being reasonably foreseeable. Even given Station Officer Mitchell's actual knowledge of the building, I do not accept that a reasonable assumption for the purposes of fighting the fire renders the falsity of the assumption not reasonably foreseeable. Station Officer Mitchell knew that it was necessary to fight the fire in order to prevent its spreading into block B, and g I am satisfied, even on the stated assumption, that it was reasonably foreseeable that if the sprinklers were switched off there was a significantly increased risk of the fire spreading to block B.

In relation to criterion (ii), the proximity or neighbourhood criterion, Mr Munby argued that the mere existence of regulatory or other public duties does h not of itself create a special relationship imposing a duty in private law. There will not be a special relationship, or assumption of responsibility, and thus there cannot be any liability in tort, unless the authority acts in such a way as would give rise to a special relationship or assumption of responsibility, and thus to liability, if a non-statutory undertaker acted in the same way. That argument was j addressing the general field of negligence in this case: at this point, I am concerned only with negligence in turning off the sprinkler system. The position of Station Officer Mitchell as respects proximity was in my judgment the same as that of any other visitor lawfully on the premises who negligently switched off the sprinkler system. The owners and occupiers of the property were clearly his neighbours, in that they were persons foreseeably likely to suffer physical damage a as a direct result of the negligent act. The damage was physical damage: the damage to buildings and other property greater in extent than that which would otherwise have been sustained. If such a visitor, not a member of the fire brigade, had negligently caused the sprinklers to be turned off, it is obvious that he would be liable for the ensuing damage. Criterion (ii) would be satisfied.

b Mr Munby relied on *Alexandrou v Oxford* [1993] 4 All ER 328, a case about the police responding to a burglar alarm. The police had responded to a shopkeeper's intruder alarm, which was connected to the police station, by detailing a constable to give passing attention to the shop during the course of his patrols. The trial judge found that the constable had failed in his duty to visit the back of the premises when, some two hours after the alarm call had been received by the police, the alarm ceased ringing. As a result, he failed to prevent a burglary. It

c was not argued that the police owed a particular duty to the owner of the shop because the constable was present when the alarm stopped ringing and could readily have caught the burglars red-handed. Nor was it argued that there was an assumption of responsibility on the part of the police by responding to the call in the way that they did. The argument was that the class of persons to whom the

d police owed a duty was owners of intruder alarms connected to the police station. The Court of Appeal (Glidewell, Parker and Slade LJJ) decided that if, as a result of the communication to the police station, the police came under a duty of care to the plaintiff, it must follow that they would be under a similar duty to any person who informed them, whether by 999 call or in some other way, that any crime against himself or his property was being committed or was about to be

e committed. The court held that there was no special relationship between the plaintiff and the police and hence no duty of care. In my judgment, it was of crucial importance in that case that what was complained of was an omission. The Court of Appeal held that there was no duty to act. If some positive act had been complained of, the result might have been different, in that the positive act

f might have created a situation of proximity.

Mr Slater QC relied on *Rigby v Chief Constable of Northamptonshire* [1985] 2 All ER 985, [1985] 1 WLR 1242, a case where the police were held liable for accidentally burning a shop by firing into it a CS gas canister in order to immobilise a psychopathic intruder. It was necessary to fire the canister, but the defendants were held liable in negligence for failing to arrange for the presence of

g fire-fighting equipment. Mr Slater submitted that when Station Officer Mitchell gave the order to turn off the sprinklers, his knowledge of the plaintiffs and their position was akin to that of the police in *Rigby's* case. In each case there was a positive act which was foreseeably likely to cause, or give rise to a risk of, damage to a specific property owner.

h Mr Munby accepted that if the police or fire brigade so acted as to create the danger, then they might be liable; and equally, they might be liable if, as in the driving cases, there was a citizen-to-citizen duty of care. I do not think that the test of proximity is whether the defendant acted so as to create the danger. It is sufficient to establish proximity that the defendant acted so as foreseeably to

j increase the risk of direct physical damage to the plaintiff or his property.

Criterion (iii), as applicable here, is whether it is fair, just and reasonable that the law should impose upon the defendants, for the benefit of the plaintiffs, a duty not negligently to turn off the sprinklers. Mr Munby submitted that it was not fair, just or reasonable to impose a common law duty of care on the emergency services in relation to their professional activities even when they are responding to an emergency call from the specific individual at risk. He relied again on

Alexandrou v Oxford. A second reason for the decision of the Court of Appeal in
that case was that it was not fair or reasonable that the police should be under any
common law duty. In arriving at that conclusion, the Court of Appeal ([1993] 4
All ER 328 at 339–340) drew from the speeches of Lord Keith of Kinkel and Lord
Templeman in *Hill v Chief Constable of West Yorkshire* [1988] 2 All ER 238 at 243–
244, [1989] AC 53 at 63–65. Lord Keith of Kinkel said:

b

'Potential existence of [liability in negligence] may in many instances be in
the general public interest, as tending towards the observance of a higher
standard of care in the carrying on of various different types of activity. I do
not, however, consider that this can be said of police activities. The general
sense of public duty which motivates police forces is unlikely to be
appreciably reinforced by the imposition of such liability so far as concerns   c
their function in the investigation and suppression of crime … In some
instances the imposition of liability may lead to the exercise of a function
being carried on in a detrimentally defensive frame of mind. The possibility
of this happening in relation to the investigative operations of the police
cannot be excluded. Further, it would be reasonable to expect that if   d
potential liability were to be imposed it would be not uncommon for actions
to be raised against police forces on the ground that they had failed to catch
some criminal as soon as they might have done, with the result that he went
on to commit further crimes. While some such actions might involve
allegations of a simple and straightforward type of failure, for example that a
police officer negligently tripped and fell while pursuing a burglar, others   e
would be likely to enter deeply into the general nature of a police
investigation, as indeed the present action would seek to do. The manner of
conduct of such an investigation must necessarily involve a variety of
decisions to be made on matters of policy and discretion, for example as to
which particular line of inquiry is most advantageously to be pursued and   f
what is the most advantageous way to deploy the available resources. Many
such decisions would not be regarded by the courts as appropriate to be
called in question, yet elaborate investigation of the facts might be necessary
to ascertain whether or not this was so. A great deal of police time, trouble
and expense might be expected to have to be put into the preparation of the
defence to the action and the attendance of witnesses at the trial. The result   g
would be a significant diversion of police manpower and attention from their
most important function, that of the suppression of crime. Closed
investigations would require to be reopened and retraversed, not with the
object of bringing any criminal to justice but to ascertain whether or not they
had been competently conducted.'

h

Although those observations were of a general nature, I do not read them as
casting doubt on cases such as *Rigby*. In any event, they are not expressed to be
applicable to a fire brigade. I see no reason why it should not be fair, just and
reasonable to hold the defendants liable for Station Officer Mitchell's act in   j
ordering the sprinklers to be turned off.

Finally in this connection, Mr Munby submitted that the firemen were in any
event immune from action on the grounds of public policy. The reasons given
by the Court of Appeal in *Alexandrou v Oxford* for holding that it was not fair or
reasonable that the police should be under any common law duty were expressed
to be a matter of general policy, and Lord Keith of Kinkel had said that the

a considerations in the passage quoted above were those of public policy (see [1993] 4 All ER 328 at 338).

As to the considerations specifically referable to the investigation and suppression of crime, similar considerations do not in my judgment apply to the fire-fighting activities of the fire brigade with anything like the same force. Potential liability is not likely to lead to fire-fighting being carried on in a frame b of mind which is defensive in any relevant respect, though firemen are of course concerned with the defence of persons and property. The decisions made on site in fighting a fire may be said to include tactical or strategic decisions, but they are entirely operational; they do not include the decision of questions of priority in the allocation of resources between one fire and another. I am not here concerned with any decision made off site whether to respond to a call for c appliances, or for more appliances. As to the consideration mentioned towards the end of the passage I have quoted, if the police were potentially liable for failure to catch a criminal as soon as they might have done, they might be subjected to a large number of unmeritorious actions, thereby diverting substantial resources from their intended use. I doubt that fire brigades would be d likely to be subjected to large numbers of unmeritorious actions in relation to fighting fires.

Mr Munby submitted that the courts have consistently barred claims against the emergency services in relation to their professional activities (eg preventing and detecting crime, undertaking rescues at sea) on grounds of public policy, and invited me to conclude, by parity of reasoning with the police cases and a e coastguard case, that fire authorities and firemen are likewise immune on grounds of public policy in relation to their fire-prevention and fire-fighting activities, save where they themselves create the danger and then negligently let it loose. As to the coastguard, Mr Munby relied on the decision of Judge Gareth Edwards QC, sitting as a judge of the High Court, in *Skinner v Secretary of State for f Transport* (1995) Times, 3 January. The complaint in that case was that the coastguard had negligently failed to respond to an emergency call. Judge Edwards applied the questions of public policy considered in *Hill* to the situation of the coastguard, and reached the conclusion that public policy considerations conferred immunity from action. In my judgment, the situation of the coastguard is dissimilar to that of the fire brigade. I do not think that parity of g reasoning necessarily leads to the same conclusion in relation to the fire-fighting activities of the fire brigade. In any case, Judge Edwards did say:

> 'Naturally the coastguard will be under a duty of care if they undertake any activity which involves creating danger, such as the putting of one of their own vessels to sea, but in their ordinary function of watching, listening and h co-ordinating search and rescue the coastguard owes no legally enforceable duty of care to any member of the seagoing public, even in an emergency.'

Mr Slater relied, both in relation to the question of proximity and in relation to the question of public policy, on the fact that, by virtue of s 30 of the Fire Services j Act 1947, the fire brigade have exclusive control of all operations for the extinction of a fire and no one is allowed to interfere. The way he put it was that the defendants were saying:

> 'You can safely leave fighting this fire to us. If you seek to interfere you will be committing a criminal offence. By the way, if we act negligently, having assumed exclusive control, you will have no remedy.'

Whilst I do not accept that the fire brigade in any way warrant the success of their fire-fighting operations, I accept that the provision as to their exclusive *a* control of those operations while they are carrying them out, which may prevent anyone else from fighting the fire at the same time, is a consideration against immunity on the ground of public policy. It is also a consideration supporting the fairness, justice and reasonableness of the existence of a duty of care.

In *Kilboy v South Eastern Fire Area Joint Committee* 1952 SC 280 at 288 Lord Keith *b* (later Lord Keith of Avonholm) said, obiter:

'I would add that, where the duty of providing fire fighting services has been committed by the Legislature to a fire authority, I should doubt whether there is any method by which the authority could free itself from liability for the negligence of persons expressly or impliedly authorised by *c* the authority to deal with fires in the manner in which they carry out that task. But it is unnecessary here to consider that aspect of the matter.'

Finally, in *X and ors (minors) v Bedfordshire CC, M (a minor) v Newham London BC, E (a minor) v Dorset BC* [1995] 3 All ER 353 at 380, [1995] 2 AC 633 at 749 Lord Browne-Wilkinson, with whom Lord Jauncey of Tullichettle, Lord Lane, Lord *d* Ackner and Lord Nolan agreed, expressed his agreement with the view of Bingham MR that the public policy consideration which has first claim on the loyalty of the law is that wrongs should be remedied, and that very potent counter-considerations are required to override that policy.

The foregoing considerations seem to me to afford weighty reasons why, *e* where the fire brigade are fighting a fire, they should be under a duty to exercise reasonable care in doing so. However, it is unnecessary for me to decide that general proposition, and I do not do so. What I do decide is that it is fair, just and reasonable that the defendants should have owed a duty of care, and that they did owe a duty of care, to the plaintiffs in relation to the shutting down of the sprinkler system, and that there is no immunity on grounds of public policy from *f* liability in relation to the decision to shut it down. Here there was a positive act: shutting down the sprinkler. If the sprinklers had not been automatic, but operated manually, and the complaint had been of negligent failure to turn them on, the position might be different.

Statutory immunity

g

Mr Munby submitted that the defendants were immune from liability for negligence on the day of the fire (and specifically for the positive act of turning off the sprinklers) by reason of the language of s 30 of the 1947 Act. Section 30(1) provides as follows:

h

'Any member of a fire brigade maintained in pursuance of this Act who is on duty, any member of any other fire brigade who is acting in pursuance of any arrangements made under this Act, or any constable, may enter and if necessary break into any premises or place in which a fire has or is reasonably believed to have broken out, or any premises or place which it is necessary to enter for the purposes of extinguishing a fire or of protecting the premises *j* or place from acts done for fire-fighting purposes, without the consent of the owner or occupier thereof, and may do all such things as he may deem necessary for extinguishing the fire or for protecting from fire, or from acts done as aforesaid, any such premises or place or for rescuing any person or property therein.'

a Mr Munby drew attention to the distinction between the presence of the requirement of reasonable belief in relation to the power to enter premises, and the absence of such a requirement in relation to the things a fire-fighter was empowered to do. Station Officer Mitchell had complete discretion (subject to the requirement to act honestly, which was not in issue) to do whatever he deemed necessary for extinguishing the fire. In the latter case, there was no *b* criterion of reasonableness. That was borne out by the provisions of sub-s (3), which gave the senior officer present (who was Station Officer Mitchell when he gave the order to turn off the sprinklers), the sole charge and control of all operations for the extinction of the fire. The language was so wide that, as a matter of statutory construction and having regard to the demand of public policy, a fireman should not be regarded as having gone outside the ambit of his *c* statutory discretion unless he was acting dishonestly. Not even the test of *Wednesbury* unreasonableness applied (see *Associated Provincial Picture Houses Ltd v Wednesbury Corp* [1947] 2 All ER 680, [1948] 1 KB 223). As to public policy, Mr Munby referred to sub-s (2), which makes it a criminal offence for anybody wilfully to obstruct or interfere with any member of a fire brigade who is engaged *d* in the operation of fire-fighting. The reason for that was that it was imperative in the public interest that the fire brigade should be able to act instantly as they professionally thought proper to control fire. The public policy was further shown by the absence of any provision in the statute for compensation.

Considerations of public policy go beyond statutory construction. To the extent that they do, I have considered them above. So far as statutory *e* construction is concerned, I reject Mr Munby's argument. The statute confers powers on the fire-fighter. The fire-fighter cannot lawfully be prevented from fighting the fire however he may think fit. It is a criminal offence to obstruct him. The statute confers immunities on the fire-fighter only to the extent necessary to give effect to those powers. Thus, the fire-fighter is immune from liability for *f* trespass in setting foot on the plaintiff's land, in applying water to the plaintiff's building, in setting into a hydrant on the plaintiff's land, in turning off a sprinkler system, in turning on a sprinkler system, and so on, always provided that he acts within the power. Whether the test of acting within the power is that of honesty or that of reasonableness is not relevant for present purposes. The Act does not grant immunity from liability for causing damage by negligence.

g That the above conclusion represents the law is, in my judgment, clear from a well-known passage from the speech of Lord Blackburn in *Geddis v Proprietors of Bann Reservoir* (1878) 3 App Cas 430 at 455–456 (quoted by Lord Romer in *East Suffolk Rivers Catchment Board v Kent* [1940] 4 All ER 527 at 541, [1941] AC 74 at 99):

h   '... no action will lie for doing that which the legislature has authorized, if it be done without negligence, although it does occasion damage to anyone; but an action does lie for doing that which the legislature has authorized, if it be done negligently. And I think that if by a reasonable exercise of the powers, either given by statute to the promoters, or which they have at *j* common law, the damage could be prevented it is, within this rule, "negligence" not to make such reasonable exercise of their powers.'

It is also clear from *X and ors (minors) v Bedfordshire CC, M (a minor) v Newham London BC, E (a minor) v Dorset BC.* In that case Lord Jauncey of Tullichettle said, with reference to an act authorised by statute to be done:

'If … the authorised act is performed carelessly whereby unnecessary
damage is caused a common law action will lie. This is because the act
would, but for the statute, be actionable at common law and the defence
which the statute provides extends only to the careful performance of the
act. The statute only authorises invasion of private rights to the extent that
the statutory powers are exercised with reasonable and proper regard for the
holders of such rights. Thus careless performance of an authorised act rather
than amounting to breach of a new duty simply ceases to be a defence to a
common law right of action.' (See [1995] 3 All ER 353 at 362, [1995] 2 AC 633
at 728–729.)

Lord Jauncey continued by quoting with approval from the speech of Lord
Reid in *Home Office v Dorset Yacht Co Ltd* [1970] 2 All ER 294 at 300–301, [1970] AC
1004 at 1030:

'Parliament deems it to be in the public interest that things *otherwise
unjustifiable* should be done, and that those who do such things with due care
should be immune from liability to persons who may suffer thereby. But
Parliament cannot reasonably be supposed to have licensed those who do
such things to act negligently in disregard of the interests of others so as to
cause them *needless* damage.' (Lord Jauncey's emphasis.)

And Lord Browne-Wilkinson drew a distinction between, on the one hand,
claims based solely on the careless performance of a statutory duty in the absence
of any other common law right of action, claims which, with the unanimous
support of Lord Jauncey, Lord Lane, Lord Ackner and Lord Nolan, he held not to
found any cause of action; and, on the other hand, actions based on a common
law duty of care arising either from the imposition of the statutory duty or from
the performance of it (see [1995] 3 All ER 353 at 362, [1995] 2 AC 633 at 732).

Mr Munby had a further argument which is not dependent upon the language
of s 30 of the 1947 Act. He described Station Officer Mitchell's order to turn off
the sprinkler system as the exercise of an executive discretion under powers given
by s 30 of that Act. He submitted that in *Holgate-Mohammed v Duke* [1984] 1 All
ER 1054 at 1057, [1984] AC 437 at 443 Lord Diplock had made it clear that the
lawfulness of the exercise of an executive discretion conferred by statute cannot
be questioned in any court save upon *Wednesbury* principles. In the passage relied
on, Lord Diplock said:

'So the condition precedent to Det Con Offin's power to take the appellant
into custody and the power of the other constables at Southsea Police Station
to detain her in custody was fulfilled; and, since the wording of the
subsection under which he acted is "*may* arrest without warrant", this left
him with an executive discretion whether to arrest her or not. Since this is
an executive discretion expressly conferred by statute upon a public officer,
the constable making the arrest, the lawfulness of the way in which he has
exercised it in a particular case cannot be questioned in any court of law
except upon those principles laid down by Lord Greene MR in *Associated
Provincial Picture Houses Ltd v Wednesbury Corp* [1947] 2 All ER 680, [1948] 1
KB 223, that have become too familiar to call for repetitious citation. The
Wednesbury principles, as they are usually referred to, are applicable to
determining the lawfulness of the exercise of the statutory discretion of a
constable under s 2(4) of the [Criminal Law Act 1967], not only in
proceedings for judicial review but also for the purpose of founding a cause

a of action at common law for damages for that species of trespass to the person known as false imprisonment, for which the action in the instant case is brought.'

In my judgment, that passage does not support the proposition for which Mr Munby contended. Provided that the constable is acting within his powers in arresting a person, the deprivation of liberty which that person suffers, and which
b would otherwise constitute the tort of wrongful imprisonment, is lawful. It follows that the constable is immune from an action for wrongful imprisonment arising out of the arrest. Lord Diplock did not suggest that the power of a constable under s 2 of the Criminal Law Act 1967 to arrest a person whom he reasonably suspected to be guilty of an offence, afforded the constable immunity
c from other claims, e g a claim for negligently injuring the detained person. [The judgment concluded with a consideration of damages; the events before the fire; the need for two appliances; contributory negligence; and the history of discovery in the proceedings.]

d 7 June 1996. The following supplementary judgment was delivered.

JUDGE HAVERY QC. I appointed a hearing on 4 June 1996 to hear submissions on quantum, an application on the part of the plaintiffs for indemnity costs, an application on the part of the defendants for leave to appeal, and submissions on whether I should refer questions raised in my judgment to the Director of Public
e Prosecutions and to the Law Society. At that hearing I have also heard an application on the part of the defendants for a stay of execution. In addition, Mr James Munby QC for the defendants asked me to reconsider my judgment on liability in the light of two decisions relating to the liability of the fire services, which, coincidentally, were delivered within five weeks of my own.

f My judgment on liability is not reflected in the form of a perfected order and, accordingly, it is open to me to reconsider it. In my judgment, it would not be satisfactory to the parties to have a judgment which does not take those decisions into account. Accordingly, I have acceded to Mr Munby's submission that I ought to reconsider the matter. In those circumstances the applications for costs, leave to appeal and a stay of execution were heard de bene esse. It was, of course,
g necessary for me to determine quantum in any event, since this case is likely to go further.

The two recent decisions in question were *Church of Jesus Christ of Latter Day Saints v West Yorkshire Fire and Civil Defence Authority* (1996) Times, 9 May, a decision of Judge Crawford QC sitting as a judge of the High Court, and *John*
h *Munroe (Acrylics) Ltd v London Fire and Civil Defence Authority* [1996] 4 All ER 318, a decision of Rougier J.

I say at once that those two decisions have not caused me to change my mind. They are distinguishable from the instant case on their facts, but there is no doubt that the blanket immunity from liability held in both of those cases to exist would
j also negative liability in this case.

Both decisions were made on applications to strike out claims. In the first case the complaint was that the fire brigade had negligently, and in breach of its statutory duty, failed properly to maintain fire hydrants or to secure an adequate supply of water. The statutory duties in question were to be found in ss 1 and 13 of the Fire Services Act 1947. It was held that no action lay in private law for breach of the statutory duty.

I have not found it necessary in this case to decide whether the defendants are
liable to the plaintiffs for breach of statutory duty. It is thus unnecessary for me   a
to consider the point further.

In both of the other cases the matters complained of were entirely or
substantially negative in character: in the one case failure properly to maintain
the hydrants; in the other failure to discover on site that a fire was still
smouldering. The existence of liability in those cases must depend on the   b
existence of a duty, whether absolute or a duty of care, to maintain the hydrants
or to fight the fire. My decision in the instant case does not depend on the
existence of such a duty. I have found that the fire brigade have committed a
positive act of negligence for which anyone else would be liable; and that neither
on grounds of fairness, justice and reasonableness nor on considerations of public
policy (which overlap with those grounds) should the fire brigade not be liable.   c

The reasoning which appears in both judgments in relation to those
overlapping matters appears to me to apply with far greater force to the exercise
of administrative discretion than it does to operational matters. Of course, there
can be an overlap between the two. For example, there is the possibility that a
fire brigade on the site of a fire might have other urgent calls on its hands   d
justifying its removal from the site before fully investigating whether the fire was
still smouldering. I derive that example from what Rougier J said in the context
of defensive fire-fighting. But it seems to me a strong thing to say that, because
of possibilities of that kind, the brigade should have a blanket immunity so that
no remedy would be available to an injured plaintiff even in the case of the most
glaring negligence.   e

The floodgates argument has been persuasive. It does not persuade me. The
courts are not astute to find professional persons who make a mistake guilty of
negligence. I have considered the law on this aspect of the matter in my earlier
judgment. In the case of the fire brigade there are often, as there were here, the
added elements of danger and urgency. Unmeritorious actions against fire   f
brigades will not be successful. I do not think it likely that there would be a flood
of such actions in the absence of blanket immunity. Certainly, I do not consider
that the possible risk of that is a reason for denying an otherwise just claim.

Further, it is said that the fire brigade should not be insurers; plaintiffs should
take out their own insurance. I do not consider that considerations of insurance
are relevant. It is not claimed in the instant case that the defendants were   g
insurers; moreover, the plaintiffs were insured.

Mr Munby submitted that the fire brigade, like the police, were immune from
suit unless either (a) there were an assumption of responsibility on the part of the
defendant, or (b) the fire brigade had caused the danger, ie had caused the fire.

As to (a); the expression 'assumption of responsibility' seems to me to beg the   h
question. The question is whether the law imposes responsibility on the
defendant in the given circumstances. Mr Munby cited the example of *Barrett v
Ministry of Defence* [1995] 3 All ER 87, [1995] 1 WLR 1217, the case of the drunken
sailor who was placed in his bunk by the officers of the defendants and died
following neglect. In the Court of Appeal in *Barrett's* case the trial judge's finding   j
that the defendant was in breach of duty to take care of the deceased once he had
collapsed and it had assumed responsibility for him, was not challenged (see
[1995] 3 All ER 87 at 93, [1995] 1 WLR 1217 at 1223). The Court of Appeal did not
have to decide that point, as can be seen from the brevity of the reference to it
([1995] 3 All ER 87 at 96, [1995] 1 WLR 1217 at 1225). Moreover, here, the fire
brigade had assumed total control of the fire-fighting; just as in *Barrett's* case the

a defendants had assumed control of the deceased. So Mr Munby's argument may not help him.

As to (b), I have already rejected the argument that causation of the danger is the test of proximity. I also reject any argument that the fire brigade are immune from liability unless they caused the danger. In my judgment, my rejection is borne out by the recent decision of the Court of Appeal (Hirst, Peter Gibson and *b* Ward LJJ) in *Swinney v Chief Constable of the Northumbria Police* [1996] 3 All ER 449, another striking out case. It was there alleged that the officers of the defendant had negligently released information about an informant who had named an alleged criminal and, in consequence, the plaintiffs, who included the informant, had suffered psychological damage from the alleged criminal. There was no question of the defendant's having created the danger. The Court of Appeal *c* nevertheless held: (a) that it was arguable that a sufficient relationship of proximity such as to give rise to a duty of care, existed between the defendants' officers and the plaintiffs, rendering the plaintiffs distinguishable from the general public as being particularly at risk, and (b) that the police did not have a blanket immunity and it was arguable that they were not immune in that case. [The *d* judge concluded with a consideration of other issues arising from the case.]

Judgment for the plaintiff for damages to be assessed if not agreed.

K Mydeen Esq   Barrister.

R v Governor of Brixton Prison and another, ex parte Levin

a

QUEEN'S BENCH DIVISION

BELDAM LJ AND MORISON J

b

19, 20, 21 FEBRUARY, 1 MARCH 1996

Extradition – Committal – Evidence – Evidence sufficient to justify committal – Computer misuse and unauthorised transfers of money – Whether computer print-outs admissible in extradition proceedings – Whether extradition proceedings 'criminal *c* *proceedings' – Police and Criminal Evidence Act 1984, ss 69, 72.*

The applicant, a Russian national located in St Petersburg, used his skill as a computer programmer to gain unauthorised access to the computer of a bank located in the United States and divert funds from the bank's customer accounts to accounts controlled by his accomplice at another US bank. The scheme was *d* however discovered and the relevant accounts were frozen. At the request of the US government, the applicant was detained in England in execution of a warrant under s 1(3) of the Extradition Act 1989. At the committal hearing the magistrate found that the US government had made out a prima facie case on 66 criminal charges, including theft, forgery, false accounting, unauthorised access to a *e* computer and unauthorised modification of computer material and ordered that the applicant be committed in custody to await extradition. The applicant applied for a writ of habeas corpus challenging the legality of his detention, contending principally that records of the instructions and transfers contained in the computer print-outs were hearsay and not admissible under s 69[a] of the *f* Police and Criminal Evidence Act 1984 before the magistrate in extradition proceedings, because that section applied only to criminal proceedings by virtue of s 72[b] of that Act.

Held – Since the extradition proceedings before the magistrate had their origin in acts or conduct punishable under the criminal law they were properly classed as *g* criminal and were therefore criminal proceedings for the purposes of s 72 of the 1984 Act. Further, unauthorised use of the computer was not of itself a ground for believing that the statements recorded by it were inaccurate and it would be absurd to hold that a computer print-out could not be given in evidence to prove that an accused had obtained unauthorised access to the computer for the *h* purposes of crime. It followed that the computer print-outs of the bank's records were admissible under s 69 and, since the evidence produced by the US government was sufficient according to English law to justify the applicant's committal for trial if his acts or omissions had been committed in England, the magistrate had been right to commit the applicant to custody and his application *j*

---

a   Section 69, so far as material, provides: 'In any proceedings, a statement in a document produced by a computer shall not be admissible as evidence of any fact stated therein unless it is shown—(a) that there are no reasonable grounds for believing that the statement is inaccurate because of improper use of the computer ...'

b   Section 72, so far as material, provides: 'In this Part of this Act ... "proceedings" means criminal proceedings ...'

a for a writ of habeas corpus would be dismissed accordingly (see p 358 *f*, p 359 *c f*, p 362 *b* and p 365 *a e*, post).

Ex p Woodhall (1888) 20 QBD 832 and *Amand v Secretary of State for Home Affairs* [1942] 2 All ER 381 followed.

R v Governor of Belmarsh Prison, ex p Francis [1995] 3 All ER 634 doubted.

b **Notes**

For evidence in committal proceedings for extradition, see 18 *Halsbury's Laws* (4th edn) paras 224–228, and for cases on the subject, see 25 *Digest* (2nd reissue) 47–50, *229–263*.

For the Police and Criminal Evidence Act 1984, ss 69, 72, see 17 *Halsbury's Statutes* (4th edn) (1993 reissue) 222, 223.

c For the Extradition Act 1989, s 1, see 17 *Halsbury's Statutes* (4th edn) (1993 reissue) 560.

Cases referred to in judgment

Amand v Secretary of State for Home Affairs [1942] 2 All ER 381, [1943] AC 147, HL.

d *Chan Man-sin v A-G of Hong Kong* [1988] 1 All ER 1, [1988] 1 WLR 196, PC.

R v Atakpu [1993] 4 All ER 215, [1994] QB 69, [1993] 3 WLR 812, CA.

R v Gold [1988] 2 All ER 186, [1988] AC 1063, [1988] 2 WLR 984, HL.

R v Governor of Belmarsh Prison, ex p Francis [1995] 3 All ER 634, [1995] 1 WLR 1121, DC.

e *R v Governor of Brixton Prison, ex p Savarkar* [1910] 2 KB 1056, [1908–10] All ER Rep 603, CA.

R v Governor of Pentonville Prison, ex p Lee, R v Bow Street Metropolitan Stipendiary Magistrate, ex p Lee [1993] 3 All ER 504, [1993] 1 WLR 1294, DC.

R v Governor of Pentonville Prison, ex p Osman [1989] 3 All ER 701, [1990] 1 WLR 277, DC.

f *R v Hale* [1974] 1 All ER 1107, [1974] QB 819, [1974] 3 WLR 249.

R v King's Lynn Magistrates' Court, ex p Holland [1993] 2 All ER 377, [1983] 1 WLR 324, DC.

R v Oxford City Justices, ex p Berry [1987] 1 All ER 1244, [1988] QB 507, [1987] 3 WLR 643, DC.

R v Shepherd [1993] 1 All ER 225, [1993] AC 380, [1993] 2 WLR 102, HL.

g *Woodhall, Ex p* (1888) 20 QBD 832, CA.

Cases also cited or referred to in skeleton arguments

A-G's Reference (No 1 of 1990) [1992] 3 All ER 169, [1992] QB 630, CA.

Air-India v Wiggins [1980] 2 All ER 593, [1980] 1 WLR 815, HL.

h *Armah v Government of Ghana* [1966] 3 All ER 177, [1968] AC 192, HL.

Associated Provincial Picture Houses Ltd v Wednesbury Corp [1947] 2 All ER 680, [1948] 1 KB 223, CA.

Churchill v Walton [1967] 1 All ER 497, [1967] 2 AC 224, HL.

Farinha, Re [1992] Imm AR 174, DC.

j *Lawrence v Comr of Police for the Metropolis* [1971] 2 All ER 1253, [1972] AC 626, HL.

Liangsiriprasert v US Government [1990] 2 All ER 866, [1991] 1 AC 225, PC.

R v Anderson [1985] 2 All ER 961, [1986] AC 27, HL.

R v Bow Street Magistrates' Court, ex p Van der Holst (1985) 83 Cr App R 114, DC.

R v Brixton Prison Governor, ex p Schtraks [1962] 3 All ER 529, [1964] AC 556, HL.

R v Coventry Justices, ex p Bullard (1992) 95 Cr App R 175, DC.

R v El-Hakkaoui [1975] 2 All ER 146, [1975] 1 WLR 396, CA.

R v Gomez [1993] 1 All ER 1, [1993] AC 442, HL.
R v Governor of Pentonville Prison, ex p Naghdi [1990] 1 All ER 257, [1990] 1 WLR   *a*
  317, DC.
R v Hornett [1975] RTR 256, CA.
R v Kohn (1979) 69 Cr App R 395, CA.
R v More [1987] 3 All ER 825, [1987] 1 WLR 1578, HL.
R v Navvabi [1986] 3 All ER 102, [1986] 1 WLR 1311, CA.   *b*
R v Siracusa (1989) 90 Cr App R 340, CA.
R v Thompson [1984] 3 All ER 565, [1984] 1 WLR 962, CA.
R v Tobierre [1986] 1 All ER 346, [1986] 1 WLR 125, CA.
R v Tomsett [1985] Crim LR 369, CA.
R v Wille (1987) 86 Cr App R 296, CA.   *c*
Shaw v DPP [1993] 1 All ER 918, DC.
Treacy v DPP [1971] 1 All ER 110, [1971] AC 537, HL.

Application for habeas corpus
By notice dated 3 October 1995 Vladimir Leonidovich Levin applied for a writ of
habeas corpus ad subjiciendum directed to the governor of HM Prison Brixton   *d*
whereto he had been committed to custody pursuant to an order made on 20
September 1995 under the Extradition Act 1989 by Mr R D Bartle, the
metropolitan stipendiary magistrate sitting at Bow Street Magistrates' Court, to
await the direction of the Secretary of State for his extradition to the United States
of America. The facts are set out in the judgment of the court.   *e*

Alun Jones QC and *James Lewis* (instructed by *Reynolds Dawson*) for the applicant.
Paul Garlick (instructed by the *Crown Prosecution Service Headquarters*) for the
  respondents.

                                                        Cur adv vult *f*

1 March 1996. The following judgment of the court was delivered.

BELDAM LJ. Vladimir Levin, a Russian citizen, moves for a writ of habeas
corpus challenging the legality of his detention pursuant to the order of Mr R D
Bartle, the metropolitan stipendiary magistrate, who on 20 September 1995   *g*
ordered his committal in custody on 66 criminal charges to await the direction of
the Secretary of State under para 7 of Sch 1 to the Extradition Act 1989. The
applicant is from St Petersburg. He is an expert computer programmer. He was
detained at Stansted Airport on 3 March 1995 in execution of a warrant under
s 1(3) of the 1989 Act at the request of the United States government. The   *h*
applicant was accused of having committed in the United States offences of wire
fraud and bank fraud and of conspiring to commit such offences. A warrant was
issued for his arrest in the US District Court for the Southern District of New York
on 24 February 1995. No single criminal offence under the law of England and
Wales equates to the offence of wire fraud or bank fraud, which are respectively *j*
violations of 18 United States Code §§ 1343 and 1344. Conspiracy to commit
these offences is a violation of 18 United States Code § 371.
     In summary, wire fraud consists of devising a plan or trick to defraud or to
obtain money or property by fraud and executing such plan or trick by
transmitting writings or signals by wire, radio or television communication in
interstate or foreign commerce.

a Similarly, bank fraud consists of knowingly executing or attempting to execute such a scheme to defraud or to obtain the money or property of a financial institution under its custody or control by false or fraudulent pretences.

The fact that acts or conduct committed in England and Wales and in the United States could give rise to the commission of different criminal offences is recognised by art 3 of the extradition treaty made in 1972 between the United
b Kingdom and the United States of America (set out in Sch 1 to the United States of America (Extradition) Order 1976, SI 1976/2144) so that extradition is to be granted for an act or omission the facts of which disclose an offence within any of the descriptions listed in the schedule to the treaty, or any other offence if the offence is punishable under the laws of both countries by imprisonment for more than one year and the offence consists of a felony under the law of the United
c States. Further, under the rule of 'specialty', a person extradited and returned to the United States cannot be proceeded against for any offence other than an extraditable offence established by the facts in respect of which his extradition has been granted.

In proof of the charges laid against the applicant in the US District Court, the
d prosecuting authority gave details of acts and conduct which translated into a schedule of 66 offences under the criminal law of England and Wales, they were offences of theft, forgery, false accounting, unauthorised access to a computer with intent to commit or facilitate further offences, conspiracy to commit offences under the Computer Misuse Act 1990 and unauthorised modification of computer material.

e Schedule 1 of the 1989 Act lays down the procedure to be followed after the request for extradition and for the hearing of the case. Paragraph 6(1) requires the magistrate to hear the case in the same manner and exercising the same jurisdiction and powers as near as may be as if the prisoner were brought before him charged with an indictable offence committed in England or Wales. That is
f to say, he is to inquire into the circumstances as near as may be as on committal for trial for an indictable offence. By para 7(1), if such evidence is produced as would according to the law of England and Wales justify the committal for trial of the prisoner if the crime of which he is accused had been committed in England or Wales, the magistrate shall 'commit him to prison, but otherwise shall order him to be discharged.'

g The case against the applicant was that he and others, including an accomplice called Korolkov, had put into execution a scheme to obtain money, credits and assets under the custody of Citibank by entering unauthorised instructions into Citibank's computer at Parsipenny in New Jersey, thereby securing substantial credits to be made to accounts maintained by Korolkov or companies controlled
h by him with the Bank of America in San Francisco. The applicant, using his skill as a computer programmer to gain unauthorised access to the Citibank computer, was able to monitor transactions on the accounts of substantial customers and to insert unauthorised instructions to make payment from those accounts to the accounts of Korolkov or his companies.

j Had the scheme been successful, sums in excess of $US10m would have been obtained. However, although some amounts were withdrawn successfully, when Korolkov's wife tried to withdraw moneys from the accounts in San Francisco in August 1994 she was arrested, and thereafter Korolkov agreed to assist the investigating authorities. His evidence formed the backbone of the case presented to the magistrate. Korolkov said that in October 1992 he had opened accounts with the Bank of America in San Francisco in favour of himself and his

wife, and of a company called Shore & Co. Later in 1993 he opened a further
account in the name of Primorye (USA) Corp. In July 1994 the applicant   *a*
approached him privately and told him he had succeeded in transferring a large
amount of money through the Citibank computer system to an account at a
Finnish bank (KOP) and that an acquaintance of theirs (Lamin) had obtained
$US120,000 from that account. The applicant then proposed that he and
Korolkov should use the bank accounts at Bank of America in San Francisco for   *b*
a similar fraud. The applicant would transfer large amounts of money to the
accounts of Shore & Co and Primorye at the Bank of America; Korolkov would
withdraw the money and return with it to St Petersburg and they would divide
the proceeds equally.   The applicant explained that he could monitor by
computer the accounts of companies using the money transfer system and that
he would transfer money only from accounts of companies that were engaging   *c*
in large transactions so that the unauthorised transfers would not be immediately
noticed. He mentioned the account of a company in Jakarta which had been
transferring millions of dollars on an almost daily basis and which he thought
would be less likely to detect the fraud quickly. At the end of July Korolkov went
to San Francisco and on Friday, 5 August 1994, the applicant telephoned him and   *d*
told him that the transfers had been made. After confirming that $US304,000 had
been transferred into the account of Shore & Co and $US218,000 into the
Primorye (USA) Corp account, on the following Monday, 8 August, Korolkov
went to the Bank of America with a cheque for $US8,000 and another for
$US40,000 drawn on the Primorye account. He drew $US8,000 in cash and wired
the proceeds to his wife in St Petersburg. The $US40,000 cheque he paid into the   *e*
joint account of himself and his wife at the Bank of America. He then drew
further cheques, but by 9 August the transfers to the Primorye account had been
questioned and that account and his personal account had been frozen.
Thereupon he returned to Russia.

Korolkov then began planning with the applicant a series of additional transfers   *f*
by which sums were intended to be transferred to accounts in the Netherlands,
Finland, Germany, the United States and Israel. In pursuance of this plan,
Korolkov's wife flew to San Francisco and opened six different accounts, the
numbers of which she telephoned to Korolkov, who gave them to the applicant.
The fraudulent transfers were made by the applicant at night, to correspond with
the operational hours of banking in New York. Thus, near midnight on the   *g*
evening of 23 August 1994, Korolkov, the applicant and another man known as
'Sascha' met to carry out further transfers. Using two computers, the applicant
and Sascha were seen by Korolkov to execute transfers to an account at the ABN
Amro Bank in Middleberg, Netherlands, an account at a bank in Finland, an
account at the Deutsche Bank in Germany and to a further account held in a bank   *h*
in Finland. On the following night Korolkov saw the applicant and Sascha make
ten additional fraudulent wire transfers: five transfers totalling just under
$US200,000 were made to the accounts opened in San Francisco by Korolkov's
wife, and additional transfers totalling just under $US1m were transferred to five
accounts opened by a man called Alex in Israel.   *j*

About a month later the applicant used a laser printer to print out information
concerning one of the transfers, but then tore the printed details into pieces and
discarded them. Korolkov, however, retrieved the pieces of paper which related
to the transfer of $US983,770 to the account of Autorig Import/Export at AMB
Amro Bank in the Netherlands, which was one of the transfers he had witnessed
on the night of 23 August 1994.

a   Further evidence was given by Mr Yancy, an executive director of Citibank Global Cash Management Services, whose responsibilities included the management of a service called the Financial Institutions Citibank Cash Manager (FICCM). He explained that the service enabled Citibank's financial institution customers to transfer funds from accounts at Citibank to accounts at other financial institutions throughout the world, that to gain access to the system the

b   customer's employee had to identify himself with a code and a password which were unique to him and request the transfer. The transaction had to be separately reviewed and approved by a second employee using a different code and password before it went ahead. Mr Yancy produced records of the transactions recorded in the electronic banking system in the form of computer print-outs maintained by Citibank in the ordinary course of their business. In all

c   there were some 40 transfers totalling more than $US10·7m in which, after investigation, Citibank either cancelled the transfer or recredited the customer's account with the full amount, accepting that the transfers had been made without the customer's instructions. Evidence of the operation of the Citicorp FICCM system was given by Mr Shearan.

d
He described how transactions would be entered into the system and explained how the entries on the computer print-outs corresponded with the electronic instructions received by the computer in New Jersey. Entries onto the magnetic storage medium in that computer in the form of customer instructions created a payment request which was then stored in the funds transfer system in

e   New York. That system created a payment instruction which was copied back to the customer service system known as AIRS. This system is also within the computer complex in New Jersey and contains historical records of payment transactions. Thus, the print-out is a representation of data stored in the magnetic disc of the computer system in New Jersey. He explained how all the

f   data is stored in the computer in New Jersey and that it was not possible to create a record outside that system. However, by using a personal computer which contains an additional program designed to copy the actions taking place within the computer in New Jersey, it is possible to print out the records contained in the New Jersey computer. He confirmed that all those who use the FICCM system

g   are customers of Citibank, New York. That is to say their current records are contained in the Citibank computer in New Jersey.

On the basis of this evidence, the magistrate considered that the US government had made out a prima facie case on all 66 charges and committed the applicant in custody to await extradition. It is now contended that the evidence

h   before the magistrate did not establish that the offences charged would have been committed if the conduct of the applicant had been carried out in England.

The first ground on which Mr Alun Jones QC for the applicant challenges the lawfulness of his committal, is that the records of the instructions and transfers contained in the computer print-outs were hearsay and not admissible. They

j   could not be admitted under s 69 of the Police and Criminal Evidence Act 1984, since that section did not apply to extradition proceedings. Even if it did, the proceedings were not 'criminal proceedings' within s 72 of that Act. Further, he contends that even if the proceedings were criminal proceedings and the computer records were prima facie admissible, the requirements of s 69 were not complied with.

Does s 69 apply to the proceedings before the magistrate?

As previously stated, the magistrate hearing extradition proceedings is hearing
evidence to decide whether it discloses proof to the standard necessary to 'justify
the committal for trial of the prisoner if the crime of which he is accused had been
committed in England or Wales'(para 7(1) of Sch 1 to the 1989 Act). When sitting
in the ordinary way as examining magistrate on a committal for trial, the
proceedings are criminal proceedings to which the 1984 Act applies (see *R v King's
Lynn Magistrates' Court, ex p Holland* [1993] 2 All ER 377, [1983] 1 WLR 324 and *R
v Oxford City Justices, ex p Berry* [1987] 1 All ER 1244, [1988] QB 507).

If, on the evidence, the magistrate decides to commit the fugitive criminal to
prison, he must inform him that he will not be surrendered for 15 days, during
which he has the right to apply for a writ of habeas corpus.

That is the foundation for the application now made to this court. The writ of
habeas corpus is available to any subject who claims he is being unlawfully
detained. His detention may arise from criminal proceedings or from an
infringement of his civil rights. Depending on the origin of the detention, the
subject has different rights of appeal. If the origin is infringement of civil rights,
he may appeal to the Court of Appeal; if it is criminal proceedings, he has no right
of appeal to that court, but may appeal to the House of Lords (see ss 1, 14 and 15
of the Administration of Justice Act 1960). In *Amand v Secretary of State for Home
Affairs* [1942] 2 All ER 381, [1943] AC 147 the question for the House of Lords was
whether a soldier of the Netherlands army, absent without leave, who was
detained under an order made under the Allied Forces Act 1940 for return to the
Netherlands military police, and whose application for habeas corpus had been
refused, could appeal to the Court of Appeal. The Court of Appeal had held he
could not, as the proceedings were criminal proceedings and s 31 of the Supreme
Court of Judicature (Consolidation) Act 1925 precluded an appeal in a criminal
cause or matter. The House of Lords held that no such appeal lay, as the
judgment appealed from was in a criminal cause or matter within s 31(1)(a) of the
1925 Act. Viscount Simon LC, after reviewing the authorities and the provisions
of the Habeas Corpus Act 1679 and the Habeas Corpus Act 1816, concluded:

> 'It will be observed that these decisions, which I accept as correct, involve
> the view that the matter in respect of which the accused is in custody may be
> "criminal" although he is not charged with a breach of our own criminal law;
> and (in the case of the Fugitive Offenders Act, 1881) although the offence
> would not necessarily be a crime at all if committed here. It is the nature and
> character of the proceeding in which *habeas corpus* is sought which provide
> the test. If the matter is one the direct outcome of which may be trial of the
> applicant and his possible punishment for an alleged offence by a court
> claiming jurisdiction to do so, the matter is criminal.' (See [1942] 2 All ER
> 381 at 385, [1943] AC 147 at 156.)

Lord Wright said ([1942] 2 All ER 381 at 387, 388, [1943] AC 147 at 159, 162):

> 'The words "cause or matter" are, in my opinion, apt to include any form
> of proceeding. The word "matter" does not refer to the subject-matter of the
> proceeding, but to the proceeding itself ... The principle which I deduce
> from the authorities I have cited and the other relevant authorities which I
> have considered is that, if the cause or matter is one which, if carried to its
> conclusion, may result in the conviction of the person charged and in a
> sentence of some punishment, such as imprisonment or fine, it is a criminal

a   cause or matter. The person charged is thus put in jeopardy. Every order
made in such a cause or matter by an English court, is an order in a criminal
cause or matter, even though the order, taken by itself, is neutral in character
and might equally have been made [in] a cause or matter which is not
criminal. The order may not involve punishment by the law of this country,
but, if the effect of the order is to subject by means of the operation of
b   English law the persons charged to the criminal jurisdiction of a foreign
country, the order is, in the eyes of English law for the purposes being
considered, an order in a criminal cause or matter, as is shown by Ex p.
Woodhall ((1888) 20 QBD 832) and R. v. Brixton Prison (Governor), Ex p.
Savarkar ([1910] 2 KB 1056, [1908–10] All ER Rep 603).'

c   Lord Porter also pointed out that if the underlying proceeding was a criminal
cause or matter, the application for the writ of habeas corpus was also a criminal
cause or matter (see [1942] 2 All ER 381 at 389, [1943] AC 147 at 164).

        Notwithstanding these opinions, Mr Jones contended that this court was
bound by and should follow its own decision in R v Governor of Belmarsh Prison, ex
d   p Francis [1995] 3 All ER 634, [1995] 1 WLR 1121, which he contended established
that extradition proceedings were not criminal proceedings to which the 1984 Act
applied. In that case the question was whether the magistrate could in such
proceedings apply the provisions of s 78 of the 1984 Act. An application had been
made to him to exclude the evidence of an accomplice under that section. He
considered that s 78 did apply to the proceedings, but exercised his discretion not
e   to exclude the evidence. In the Divisional Court the respondent argued that s 78
did not apply to extradition committal proceedings, because they were not
criminal proceedings; they were extradition proceedings concerning a criminal
cause or matter and were to be regarded as 'sui generis'.

        In accepting the respondent's submissions, the court found support for the
f   suggestion that extradition proceedings are sui generis, not criminal proceedings
and that the magistrate could not exercise the power under s 78 to exclude
evidence in such proceedings in the earlier case of R v Governor of Pentonville
Prison, ex p Lee, R v Bow Street Metropolitan Stipendiary Magistrate, ex p Lee [1993] 3
All ER 504 at 509–510, [1993] 1 WLR 1294 at 1299–1300. The passage cited,
however, does no more than suggest that certain aspects of domestic criminal
g   procedure, such as the duty to make available relevant unused material, cannot
be imported into the committal proceedings before the magistrate in extradition
proceedings. McCowan LJ, giving the judgment in Ex p Francis [1995] 3 All ER
634 at 639, [1995] 1 WLR 1121 at 1125 said: 'For all those reasons I conclude that
s 78 has no application to extradition proceedings.'

h   One of the reasons which had been advanced was that in such proceedings the
magistrate is not concerned to decide the effect that the evidence may have; only
whether it would justify committal for trial and on this basis the decision is
obviously right. But it is now argued that McCowan LJ must be taken to have
accepted the submission of counsel that the proceedings before the committing
j   magistrate were not criminal proceedings. This, it is said, is supported by the
unequivocal assertion in the headnote of the report ([1995] 1 WLR 1121) that
extradition proceedings are not criminal proceedings. If indeed the decision in Ex
p Francis is to be taken to have decided that the proceedings before the magistrate
are not criminal proceedings, in our view it is wrong and should not be followed.
It is inconsistent with the opinions in Amand v Secretary of State for Home Affairs
[1942] 2 All ER 381, [1943] AC 147, which approved the decision of the Court of

Appeal in *Ex p Woodhall* (1888) 20 QBD 832, which binds this court. In that case
Bowen LJ put the matter with characteristic clarity. He said (at 838):

'Whether we have jurisdiction or not depends upon whether the decision
of the Queen's Bench Division was a judgment in a criminal cause of matter
within s. 47. That decision was given in an application to obtain the
discharge from custody of a person committed under s. 10 of the Extradition
Act, 1870. It is necessary to look at that section in order to see how she came
to be committed. The section in terms is to apply "in the case of a fugitive
criminal accused of an extradition crime." It must therefore be the case of a
person who has fled from foreign justice; and the crime of which he is
accused must be one of those specified in the schedule which would be a
crime according to the law of this country. The magistrate is charged with
the duty of considering, upon the evidence before him, whether that
evidence is sufficient according to English law to justify the committal for
trial of the accused person. *How can the matter be other than criminal from first
to last?* It is a matter to be dealt with from first to last by persons conversant
with criminal law, and competent to decide what is sufficient evidence to
justify a committal. The questions upon which the application for a writ of
habeas corpus depend, are whether or not there was evidence before the
magistrate of a crime, which would be a crime according to English law,
having been committed in a foreign country, and whether or not that
evidence was sufficient to justify him in committing the accused for trial if
the crime had been committed in England. These must be questions arising
in a criminal matter; and it follows that the judgment given upon the
application for a writ of habeas corpus is a judgment in a criminal matter.'
(Our emphasis.)

It is further to be noted that in Sch 1 to the 1989 Act reference is repeatedly made
to 'a fugitive criminal' and to 'such criminal'. In our view the proceedings before
the committing magistrate are properly classed as criminal, having their birth or
origin in acts or conduct punishable under the criminal law. They are not in a
separate class of their own.

Further, in so far as it was suggested that Pt VII of the 1984 Act did not apply
to committal proceedings, we adhere to the view expressed in *R v King's Lynn
Magistrates' Court, ex p Holland* [1993] 2 All ER 377, [1983] 1 WLR 324 that the
words 'criminal proceedings' where used in ss 72 and 82 include committal
proceedings for the reasons given in that case. The magistrate is to apply the
provisions of the Act exercising his powers 'as near as may be' as if he were
hearing ordinary committal proceedings (see para 6(1) of Sch 1 to the 1989 Act).

It was next submitted that the magistrate should not have admitted the
computer print-outs of the FICCM records because the requirements of s 69 were
not properly complied with. Mr Yancy and Mr Shearan explained how the
records were produced and what they showed. They were records made in the
course of Citibank's business between 30 June 1994 and 3 October 1994. Under
the heading 'Certification' Mr Yancy testified in his affidavit that there were no
grounds for believing that the information and material in those records was
inaccurate because of improper use of the computer and that at all material times
the computer was operating properly or, if not, that any respect in which it was
not operating properly or was out of operation was not such as to affect the
production of the information or material or the accuracy of its content. It was
objected that this was merely paying lip-service to the requirements of s 69.

a Further, it was argued that the charges against the applicant were based on his improper use of the computer and accordingly the requirements of s 69 could not be satisfied. For the US government Mr Garlick argued that, save for the four theft charges, he did not rely on the records for any purpose but to show that there had been unauthorised access, and the records represented the electronic instructions contained upon the recording medium in the computer. To that *b* extent they were admissible as real evidence. They were not being relied upon for the purpose of proving a fact stated in the document, for example the actual state of the account of Citibank's customers.

They were, however, being relied on to show that instructions had been entered which caused customers' accounts to be debited and other accounts to be credited and those were facts shown in the documents. Merely because there has *c* been unauthorised use of the computer, this is not of itself a ground for believing that the statements recorded by it were inaccurate in the sense that the instruction had not been given. It would be absurd to hold that a computer print-out could not be given in evidence to prove that an accused had obtained unauthorised access to the computer for the purposes of crime. In our judgment *d* the requirements of s 69(1) were complied with.

A further argument was that there had been no compliance with the requirements of para 8 of Sch 3. Paragraph 8 is permissive, not mandatory, and clearly does not exclude the calling of a witness to give evidence of the matters which could be proved by a certificate. This it seems to us is clear from para 9, and was the interpretation put upon s 69 and the schedule in *R v Shepherd* [1993] *e* 1 All ER 225, [1993] AC 380.

Between them Mr Shearan and Mr Yancy fully covered all the requirements necessary to render the information printed out from Citibank's computer admissible in evidence. We therefore reject the submission that the records were not admissible before the magistrate.

f The next question for the court is whether the evidence produced by the US government was sufficient according to English law to justify the applicant's committal for trial if the acts or omissions constituting the crime with which he was accused had been committed in England.

Although the US government had to prove that there was evidence to support *g* all 66 of the charges which went to make up the acts or omissions contained in the charges of wire fraud, bank fraud and conspiracy charged in New York, the question for this court is whether the acts done by and the conduct of the applicant and his accomplices amounted to the commission of the equivalent offences under English law with which he was charged.

h It is convenient first to consider the charges of offences under s 2 of the 1990 Act. The applicant's first act said to amount to the commission of a crime was of causing the Citibank computer in New Jersey to perform a function to give him unauthorised access to data held in that computer. He intended to secure unauthorised access and knew that his access was unauthorised. Accordingly, *j* had the computer he caused to perform that function been in England, he would have committed an offence under s 1 of the 1990 Act, and s 4 would give the English courts jurisdiction.

The applicant next inserted into the data in the Citibank computer as if it was authorised, an instruction which would cause the computer to create a debit entry on the account chosen; for example, in charge 13, the account of the bank Artha Graha in Jakarta.

Being guilty of an offence under s 1 in gaining unauthorised access, he is charged that he did so with intent to commit offences of forgery and false *a* accounting. Such offences are offences within s 2 of the 1990 Act and it is clear that on the evidence he had the intent to commit or facilitate the commission of those offences. It is argued on the applicant's behalf that the charges thus framed are bad for uncertainty because they do not specify the particular offence of each kind he intended to commit, and for duplicity because they encompass more than *b* one offence in the same charge. In our view it is not necessary to do more than specify the type of offence which the accused had in mind so as to bring it within the requirements of s 2(2). The offence charged is the commission of an offence under s 1 of the Act with the required intent. A person commits the offence whether he intends to commit one or more than one such subsequent offence. The charges laid are not bad for either reason. *c*

The second category of offences alleged under the 1990 Act was under s 3, by which it is an offence to do any act which causes an unauthorised modification of the contents of a computer intending to impair the reliability of the data held in the computer. The evidence before the magistrate established clearly that the data in the computer was relied upon not only by Citibank but by their *d* customers; the introduction of an unauthorised instruction to transfer money from the accounts into other accounts would undoubtedly impair the ability of Citibank and its clients to rely upon data held in the computer and to our mind the applicant by his actions committed offences under s 3 of the Act.

The offences in relation to the bank Artha Graha particularised in charges 13 and 14 were committed on 5 August 1994. On the same date similar offences *e* were committed in respect of the accounts held by Citibank for Banco Del Sud as set out in charges 17 and 18.

Further charges were laid in respect of these activities. It was contended that the conduct of the applicant resulted in the commission of offences of forgery and false accounting. Charge 15 accused the applicant on that day of making an *f* instruction to Citibank to transfer $US218,000 from the account of Bank Artha Graha, Jakarta, to the account of Primorye at Bank of America in San Francisco, but the instruction was false because it purported to be made in the form in which it was made on the authority of a person who did not in fact authorise its making and with the intention that he or another should use it to induce Citibank to accept it as genuine and by so accepting it to act to his or another person's *g* prejudice. For the applicant it was argued that the offence could not be committed by entering a computer password and other information because it did not create an instrument within the meaning of s 8(1)(d) of the Forgery and Counterfeiting Act 1981. Section 8(1) of that Act provides:

'... "instrument" means ... (d) any disc, tape, soundtrack or other device on *h* or in which information is recorded or stored by mechanical, electronic or other means.'

According to Mr Shearan's evidence, the records contained in the computer are stored in magnetic disc media. That disc is in our view within the definition *j* of 'instrument'. Did the applicant make a false disc? We consider the disc embraces the information stored as well as the medium on which it is stored, just as a document consists both of the paper and the printing upon it. Thus, by entering false instructions onto the disc it was, in our opinion, falsified. But Mr Jones argued that the decision of the House of Lords in *R v Gold* [1988] 2 All ER 186, [1988] AC 1063 precludes the court from holding that the applicant made an a instrument. In that case the House decided that a process by which a number and password were held momentarily in a control segment of the computer for verification before being irretrievably expunged was not a process to which the words 'recorded or stored' in s 8(1)(d) of the 1981 Act could reasonably have been intended to apply.

b In his opinion, with which the other Lords concurred, Lord Brandon drew attention to para 22 of the Law Commission's Report on Forgery and Counterfeit Currency (Law Com No 55) (1973) and that in the ordinary case of forgery a document contains two messages of distinct kinds: firstly about the nature of the document and secondly a message to be found in the words used in the document that it is to be accepted and acted upon (see [1988] 2 All ER 186 at 191, [1988] AC 1063 at 1071). Thus, for a document to require protection by the law of forgery

c it must contain both types of message. Construing s 8(1)(d), Lord Brandon said ([1988] 2 All ER 186 at 192, [1988] AC 1063 at 1072):

> 'The words "recorded" and "stored" are words in common use which should be given their ordinary and natural meaning. In my opinion both words in their ordinary and natural meaning connote the preservation of the
> d thing which is a subject matter of them for an appreciable time with the object of subsequent retrieval and recovery. Further, in relation to information recorded or stored on or in a disc, tape or sound track, that is the meaning of the two expressions which appears to me to be clearly intended.'

e The instructions inserted into the recording medium of the Citibank computer in New Jersey clearly come within that definition. They were not merely held momentarily, but were inserted onto the disc with the purpose that they should be recorded, stored and acted upon. The instructions purported to be authorised instructions given by Bank Artha Graha to Citibank. They were not authorised and, in our view, the disc with the instructions recorded and stored on it

f amounted to a false instrument.

It was also argued that there was no evidence of any intention that the applicant or another should use the false instrument to induce somebody to accept it as genuine and by reason of so accepting it to do an act. We consider the only inference to be drawn from the evidence of Mr Korolkov and the actions of the applicant is that the instructions were inserted with the intention that they

g should be acted upon by Citibank by causing a transfer to be made from the account of Bank Artha Graha and subsequently a transfer to the account of Primorye with the Bank of America in San Francisco.

But it was said that even if the instrument amounted to a forgery, it had been made in Russia and not, had the computer been situated in England, in England.

h The applicant, as he operated his keyboard in St Petersburg, made an instrument there. We would reject this submission. The applicant's keyboard was connected electronically with the Citibank computer in Parsipenny; as he pressed the keys his actions, as he intended, recorded or stored information for all practical purposes, simultaneously on the magnetic disc in the computer. That is

j where the instrument was created and where the act constituting the offence was done.

The US government argued that the actions of creating unauthorised instructions on the Citibank computer amounted to offences under s 17(1)(a) of the Theft Act 1968 of dishonestly, and with a view to gain for himself or another or with intent to cause loss to another, falsifying a record made or required for an accounting purpose; but the applicant argued that the magistrate was wrong to

commit him on the false accounting charges because an instruction to a bank by
computer cannot amount to a record within the meaning of s 17(1)(a). Did the *a*
applicant falsify a record made or required for an accounting purpose?

By s 17(2) a person who makes in an account an entry which is or may be
misleading, false or deceptive in a material particular is to be treated as falsifying
the account. The applicant made an entry into a continuous record stored on the
computer's disc which was unquestionably false or misleading, and in our view *b*
the applicant must be treated as having falsified the account.

We therefore conclude that the evidence before the magistrate of the acts and
omissions of the applicant would have been sufficient to justify the magistrate
committing him for trial on the charges of computer misuse, forgery and
falsification of accounts.
c
We now come to the four offences of theft based upon the drawing of cheques
by Korolkov on the accounts of himself and his wife, of Shore & Co, and of
Primorye with the Bank of America in San Francisco. There was clearly evidence
before the magistrate from which he could conclude that the applicant was an
accomplice to the acts of Korolkov, but it was contended that he could not be
guilty of theft assuming that Korolkov's actions had been carried out in England. *d*
The first ground rested on the assertion that the applicant in inserting the
instructions on the Citibank computer had performed an act of appropriation in
St Petersburg as he sat before his computer and typed in the instructions. He
thereby assumed the rights of the Bank Artha Graha and of the Banco Del Sud.
That action having occurred in St Petersburg, the courts of England would have *e*
no jurisdiction. Mr Jones relied on the authority of *R v Governor of Pentonville
Prison, ex p Osman* [1989] 3 All ER 701, [1990] 1 WLR 277, in which it was held that
a person who sent a telex instruction to the bank to debit an account had assumed
the account holder's right to have his instructions met and that the sending of the
telex amounted to an appropriation, and that on the facts of that case the
appropriation had taken place where the telex was sent in Hong Kong. *f*

In *Ex p Osman* the court quoted from Lord Oliver's opinion in giving the advice
of the Privy Council in *Chan Man-sin v A-G of Hong Kong* [1988] 1 All ER 1 at 4,
[1988] 1 WLR 196 at 199, where he said:

> 'Ownership, of course, consists of a bundle of rights and it may well be that *g*
> there are other rights which an owner could exert over the chose in action in
> question which are not trespassed on by the particular dealing which the
> thief chooses to assume.'

The court in *Ex p Osman* was concerned with the assumption of the right of the
account-holder to give instructions and to have them met. Those instructions *h*
could be given by telex without more ado. Osman was simply sending an
instruction to the correspondent bank in the United States. But in the present
case no instructions could be given without first gaining entry into the Citibank
computer in Parsipenny. No doubt there was an appropriation of the right of the
client to gain access to the computer, but that is a different right of property, *j*
which on Korolkov's evidence had been appropriated by the applicant many
times before he actually set about entering the computer for the purpose of
giving any instructions. We see no reason why the appropriation of the client's
right to give instructions should not be regarded as having taken place in the
computer. Lloyd LJ in *Ex p Osman* did not rule out the possibility of the place
where the telex was received also being regarded as the place where the

a appropriation occurred if the courts ever adopted the view that a crime could have a dual location.

For the reasons we have already indicated, the operation of the keyboard by a computer operator produces a virtually instantaneous result on the magnetic disc of the computer, even though it may be 10,000 miles away. It seems to us artificial to regard the act as having been done in one rather than the other place. b But in the position of having to choose on the facts of this case whether, after entering the computer in Parsipenny, the act of appropriation by inserting instructions on the disc occurred there or in St Petersburg, we would opt for Parsipenny. The fact that the applicant was physically in St Petersburg is of far less significance than the fact that he was looking at and operating on magnetic discs located in Parsipenny. The essence of what he was doing was done there. c Until the instruction is recorded on the disc, there is in fact no appropriation of the rights of Bank Artha Graha. It has been held that theft in the course of a robbery in which it was necessary to prove that force was used 'at the time of the stealing' was not merely a momentary event (see *R v Hale* [1974] 1 All ER 1107, [1974] QB 819). A further difficulty is pointed up by Professor Griew, *The Theft* d *Acts* (7th edn, 1995) para 2–153, where he says:

> 'The conclusion that theft of P's bank credit is complete when D assumes any right of an owner in it, as by delivering to a payee a cheque drawn upon it or sending to the bank an instruction relating to it, may exceptionally give rise to a serious practical problem. It could require an investigation of the
> e state of the account at the moment when D delivered the cheque or sent the instruction. For if the account was then overdrawn (beyond any agreed limit); there will have been no relevant property belonging to P for D to steal. Yet it may be difficult or impossible to show at what time D's relevant act (e.g. the issue of a post-dated cheque) took place. This problem would not arise if the time of the theft were the time of the debiting of the account;
> f for there need be no doubt about the state of the account at that time. A possible solution, not excluded by the cases, is to treat D's act as continuing (as an appropriation or potential appropriation) until the account is debited ...'

g In the case of a virtually instantaneous instruction intended to take effect where the computer is situated, it seems to us artificial to regard the insertion of an instruction onto the disc as having been done only at the remote place where the keyboard is situated. Be that as it may, it does not resolve the next objection raised by Mr Jones.

Basing his argument on the decision in *R v Atakpu* [1993] 4 All ER 215, [1994] h QB 69, Mr Jones argues that the applicant could not steal the same property more than once and accordingly, having appropriated the chose in action represented by Bank Artha Graha's credit balance by inserting the instruction in the computer to debit the account, the applicant could not subsequently be guilty of stealing the same property. So the question remains, even if the applicant was guilty of an j appropriation in England, whether the actions of Korolkov, if also carried out in England, amounted to a further assumption of the rights of the owner of the same property.

The result of the applicant's activities on the computer was to cause Citibank to debit the account of Bank Artha Graha and via the Bank of America to create a credit in the accounts of Korolkov, Shore & Co and Primorye. This Citibank did in the mistaken belief that it was authorised by its customer to carry out these transactions. Korolkov and the applicant at all times knew that, in so far as Shore & Co, Primorye or Korolkov were shown in the accounts maintained by Bank of America as entitled to a credit balance, they had no right of action in respect of such balances. On 8 August 1994 Korolkov, by cheques drawn on the Primorye account, drew $US8,000 in cash and paid a cheque for $US40,000 into his joint account at the same bank. On 9 August Korolkov drew two cheques on the Shore & Co account payable to cash for $US12,113 and $US9,000 respectively. It was these four transactions which formed the basis of the four charges of theft. In the first two charges it is alleged that the sums of $US8,000 and $US40,000 belonged to Bank Artha Graha and in the third and fourth charges that the sums belonged to Banco Del Sud. In each case the property the subject matter of the charge was different from the property appropriated by the applicant when he inserted the instructions into the computer. It was no longer the chose in action represented by the client banks' credit balances. In so far as the property was dollar bills, the sums were the property of the Bank of America. In so far as the cheque for $US40,000 caused Bank of America to create a credit balance of $US40,000 in Korolkov's joint account, Bank of America had a right to recover such balance. Undoubtedly in all four cases Korolkov and the applicant appropriated property belonging to another. But Mr Jones objected that in each case the charge alleged that the property was either the property of the Bank Artha Graha or of the Banco Del Sud.

However, in the law of theft when several persons have enforceable rights or interests in property which is stolen, the property may be regarded as belonging to any of them whose right or interest is appropriated. So under s 5(1) of the 1968 Act, property is to be regarded as belonging to any person who has any proprietary right or interest, legal or equitable, in the property, saving only an equitable interest arising out of an agreement to transfer or grant an interest. In our view both the Bank Artha Graha and Banco Del Sud, until their credit balances had been restored, retained an interest in the funds which represented the balances extracted from them. Even if it were argued that they could not trace the proceeds after they became mixed with Bank of America's funds, nevertheless the applicant and Korolkov knew when Korolkov obtained cash or gave instructions for the transfer of credit to the joint account and then drew cash that the proceeds represented part of the balances extracted from Bank Artha Graha's and Banco Del Sud's accounts. Thus, when Korolkov received the property he did so from or on account of those two banks and the applicant and Korolkov were under an obligation to retain it and deal with the property or its proceeds for the benefit of the banks. Therefore, under s 5(3) of the 1968 Act the property or the proceeds was to be regarded as belonging to the banks. Further, the applicant and Korolkov had induced Citibank and Bank of America to debit the two banks' accounts in the mistaken belief that they had the banks' instructions to do so. Korolkov and the applicant got the property as a result of the mistake they had induced and were under an obligation to restore the property or its proceeds or the value, and accordingly, under s 5(4), the property or its proceeds was to be regarded as belonging to the banks who were entitled to restoration. By appropriating the property Korolkov and the applicant committed the offences of theft. But even if that is incorrect, we do not think a misstatement of the name of the owner of the property stolen vitiates the magistrate's decision to commit the applicant on the charges of theft. Generally speaking, in English law the name of the owner of the property is not regarded as material unless the mistake is shown to have prejudiced the accused (see rr 5 and a   6(b) of the Indictment Rules 1971, SI 1971/1253). In our view, even if there was a doubt whether the ownership of the property stolen had been properly attributed, the magistrate would have been justified in the circumstances of this case in committing for trial (see s 6(1) of the Magistrates' Court Act 1980).

For these reasons, we would hold that the magistrate was right to commit on the theft charges.

b   Finally, it is said that the two charges of conspiracy were bad for duplicity. The conspiracy alleged was that between 1 June and 31 October the applicant conspired with Korolkov and others to contravene s 2(1) of the 1990 Act by gaining unauthorised access to a computer with intent to commit the offences of forgery and false accounting. The second conspiracy alleged is that between the same dates the applicant and others conspired to contravene the provisions of

c   s 3(1) of the Act. It is objected to these charges that they are bad for uncertainty and duplicity. They are uncertain because a particular offence or offences of forgery and false accounting which was intended to be committed or facilitated is not specified and duplicitous because the charge could refer to an unlawful agreement to commit more than one offence.

d   This, however, is often the case in a conspiracy and it is to be remembered that the offence consists in the agreement with another person or persons to pursue a course of conduct which, if that agreement is carried out in accordance with the parties' intentions, will necessarily amount to or involve the commission of any offence or offences by one or more of the parties to the agreement. In our view only one agreement is alleged and the fact that the course of conduct involved the

e   carrying out of more than one offence does not make the charge duplicitous or uncertain.

For these reasons we consider that the magistrate, on the evidence produced, was right to commit the applicant in custody to await extradition and we would refuse the application for habeas corpus.

f   *Application dismissed.*

Dilys Tausz   Barrister.

Co-operative Bank plc v Tipper   a

CHANCERY DIVISION AT MANCHESTER
JUDGE ROGER COOKE SITTING AS A JUDGE OF THE HIGH COURT
7 NOVEMBER 1995

b

*Guarantee – Alteration – Alteration made in pencil – Company directors personally
guaranteeing the provision of banking facilities to company – Guarantee erroneously
describing directors as both debtor and guarantor – Plaintiff bank making alterations
in pencil to correct misdescription – Whether alterations rendering guarantee void –
Whether plaintiff able to maintain rectification.*

c

The defendants were the directors of a limited company which successfully
applied for facilities from the plaintiff bank. The facilities were secured by a
personal guarantee from the defendants and a third party charge on their house.
The guarantee was a printed standard form document; however, it erroneously
described the defendants personally as both 'the customer' (ie the principal d
debtor) and the guarantors. After the execution of the guarantee, the description
of the defendants which defined them as the customer was altered by an
employee of the bank in pencil. The defendants' details were crossed out and the
name and address of the company were inserted. The company subsequently
went into liquidation and the plaintiff, in order to enforce the guarantee, applied
for rectification of the error. The defendants, however, contended that the e
guarantee had been altered in a material particular and was therefore
unenforceable, with or without rectification. The plaintiff thereafter issued a
summons under RSC Ord 14A to determine the question whether,
notwithstanding the alterations on the face of the deed, it was entitled to
rectification. The judge answered the question posed in the negative. The f
plaintiff appealed.

Held – Where a document consisted of print, type and ink writing, the most
natural inference to draw from an amendment in pencil was that it was not, and
was not intended to be, an operative and final alteration and as such it would not
stop a plaintiff's claim in relation to the document in limine. In the instant case, g
it was clear that the alteration to the guarantee was in the form of a note or a
drafting amendment; it was not final and did not alter the substance of the
document. It followed that the plaintiff was not precluded from setting up
rectification by reason of the pencil addition. The appeal would accordingly be
allowed (see p 372 *d e g* to *g* and p 373 *f*, post). h

Master v Miller (1791) 4 Term Rep 320 considered.

Notes
For alteration of deeds after execution by party entitled, see 12 *Halsbury's Laws*
(4th edn) para 1378.

j

Cases referred to in judgment
Adams' Goods, Re (1872) LR 2 P & D 367.
*Amalgamated Investment and Property Co Ltd (in liq) v Texas Commerce International
    Bank Ltd* [1981] 3 All ER 577, [1982] QB 84, [1981] 3 WLR 565, CA.
Bishop v Chambre (1827) 3 C & P 55, 172 ER 320; *rvsd* (1828) Dan & Ll 83.

a *Hall's Goods, Re* (1871) LR 2 P & D 256.

Hawkes v Hawkes (1828) 1 Hag Ecc 321, 162 ER 599.

Master v Miller (1791) 4 Term Rep 320, 100 ER 1042; *affd* (1793) Hy Bl 141, 126 ER 474, Ex Ch.

Parkin v Bainbridge (1820) 3 Phillim 321, 161 ER 1338.

Pigot's Case (1614) 11 Co Rep 26b, [1558–1774] All ER Rep 50, 77 ER 1177.

b *Suffell v Bank of England* (1882) 9 QBD 555, CA.

Appeal

The plaintiff, Co-operative Bank plc (the bank), appealed from the decision of District Judge Beattie whereby he answered the question in the bank's summons *c* under RSC Ord 14A, in an action to enforce a guarantee against the defendants, Mr and Mrs Tipper, against the bank by deciding that pencil alterations to the guarantee precluded it from maintaining rectification or enforcing the guarantee. The case was heard and judgment was given in chambers in Manchester. The case is reported by permission of Judge Roger Cooke. The facts are set out in the *d* judgment.

Ian Leeming QC and *Nigel Bird* (instructed by *Brian Lord & Co*, Manchester) for the bank.

Jeffrey Terry (instructed by *Stunt & Son*, Chelmsford) for Mr and Mrs Tipper.

e **JUDGE ROGER COOKE.** I have before me an appeal from the district judge, who came to the firm conclusion, in answer to the plaintiff's summons under RSC Ord 14A, that the plaintiff was unable to maintain rectification or, indeed, enforce a deed of guarantee which was dated, or purports to be dated 27 March 1987 and made between the plaintiff, Co-operative Bank plc (the bank), and the *f* defendants, Mr and Mrs Gilbert Tipper.

The guarantee appears to have come into being in a familiar way. Not all the surrounding facts are fully before me, but in short summary it worked like this: the defendants were the directors of a limited company called G Tipper & Co Ltd (a short version of a rather longer title), which sought facilities from the bank. The bank (as is common with small companies in private ownership) was *g* prepared to give facilities on the basis that it got security. The security that it sought was a personal guarantee from Mr and Mrs Tipper and a third party charge on their house.

The guarantee itself is a wholly unremarkable document; it is a printed document in the bank's standard form. As executed, it has certain oddities *h* because the person whose task it was to type in the parties to the document, including the name and particulars of the principal debtor, failed—for reasons that nobody has been able to explain—to carry out that simple task efficiently. Instead of typing out—as everybody, I think, accepts as common ground—what should have been the name of the company and its place of business or registered *j* office, they typed out instead the names of Mr and Mrs Tipper with their address, describing them as 'The Customer', which they were not, and then proceeding to type out their name and address all over again as guarantors. It was a crass mistake; the culprit has not been identified, but it is the clearest possible error. So drawn, such a document was virtually worthless; no man can effectively guarantee his own indebtedness for more than he could pay anyway. It is of no value to the bank whatsoever because Mr and Mrs Tipper's indebtedness might or might not have extended to various other accounts but certainly was not the company's indebtedness.

There is, however, a further oddity. When the document came to be executed by Mr and Mrs Tipper it was witnessed by their then solicitor, Mr Wetton. It may very well be that the reason for this was that the bank had in mind all the well-known authorities about undue influence and that it may have been a good idea for them to have their separate legal adviser dealing with them at the point of execution—I know not. At all events, that is what he did.

The date appears at least likely—I put this neutrally at this stage—to be in the same hand, or at least the same pen, as Mr Wetton's signature and particulars as attesting witness and is clearly over a previous date that has been 'Tipp-Exed' out. The date that appears on the deed is 27 March 1987; an examination reveals the possibility, at least, that the original date may have been April. I make no finding about that, although I do observe that references to April are made in other documents in this case. So there are these two rather strange features.

The document appears to have been kept, as one would expect, in the custody of the bank. At some stage when it was in the custody of the bank, some person— whom the bank's principal witness accepts on affidavit must have been an employee of the bank—took a pencil and struck through with five fairly light pencil lines, going diagonally across the page, the description of Mr and Mrs Tipper and their address above the line defining them wrongly as 'The Customer' and inserted, with a certain amount of brevity, the name and address of the company which should have been there to begin with. All of that is in pencil and, of course, it is clear to see what was there before (so far as that matters).

It would appear, though I have not been taken to this part of the evidence in any detail—and I need not be I think—that fairly early on a dispute arose between the bank and Mr and Mrs Tipper as to what the bank guarantee ought to contain and it was never resolved, and in the event the company is now in liquidation and the bank, not unnaturally, wish to enforce their guarantee.

It is also clear from the evidence—and, I think, is accepted by everybody as common ground before me—that it was the common intention of everyone that 'The Customer' whose indebtedness was sought to be guaranteed was indeed the company, and this particular company, and that had proceedings for rectification been taken before anybody started making markings on the face of this guarantee they would have been incapable of defence, subject to other issues which are not before me today.

What is sought by the bank is to say that notwithstanding these curiosities on the face of the deed they are entitled to rectification and the deed remains good. I pause to say that there are issues not before me on this appeal and were not before the district judge under the summons under Ord 14A, because there is a laches argument which has not been deployed and that will, if the appeal goes in favour of the bank, be a shot still in Mr and Mrs Tipper's locker which they can take to trial and have determined there. There are other possible issues as well that will have to be determined, not before me today.

Putting it shortly, the argument raised by the guarantors is this. This document has been altered—whether it is a deed or instrument not under seal does not matter for this purpose, a fortiori perhaps because it is a deed—and that accordingly, it having been altered in a material particular, the document is totally unenforceable for all time, rectified or unrectified. That argument found favour with the district judge and it is from that decision that the appeal is made to me.

a I pause to say that different considerations apply to the alteration of the date and the alteration to the principal debtor and I will deal briefly first, in order to dispose of it, with the alteration of the date. The district judge was (I think one can say) incensed by the alteration to the date; it is clear that his judgment is quite strongly expressed. That undoubtedly weighed heavily with him. But there is before me, and was not before him, evidence from Mr Wetton. That evidence is b not accepted by the defendants and, accordingly, so far as that raises material issues, there would have to be a trial about it. What Mr Wetton says is that the alteration was made by him—and I pause to say he was, of course, the guarantor's solicitor and nothing whatever to do with the bank—and it was made by him before execution. The guarantors do not accept the latter; they make, I think, at this stage, no affirmative case about the former but they would obviously, if c nothing else, put Mr Wetton to proof and if they got the opportunity would cross-examine him.

If Mr Wetton was wrong about that, then it may very well be that what the district judge said is quite right on that issue. If Mr Wetton is right about that, then of course it would very probably follow—though I make no actual finding d about it—that (a) the alteration was made in, effectively, the custody of the guarantors or their solicitor and (b) was not an alteration made after execution, and it may also be (c) that the date is not actually a material alteration anyway. But those are matters which will have to be considered, if it goes that far, at a trial of that issue and are not matters upon which I can express any view now.

I am now simply concerned with what is the effect of the pencil alterations to e the identity of the principal debtor ('The Customer'), and whether the learned district judge was right that that stops the plaintiff's case in limine. To that I now turn.

The doctrine upon which the defendants rely is an ancient one. It goes back at least to *Pigot's Case* (1614) 11 Co Rep 26b, [1554–1774] All ER Rep 50. It may very f well not even originate there, in the year 1614; it has indeed overall echoes of the medieval world. But it is this, and very simply this, that Coke CJ said (11 Co Rep 26b at 27a, [1554–1774] All ER Rep 50 at 51):

'... when any deed is altered in a point material, by the plaintiff himself, or by any stranger, without the privity of the obligee, be it by interlineation, g addition, rasing, or by drawing of a pen through a line, or through the midst of any material word, that the deed thereby becomes void ...'

It is a harsh and ancient common law doctrine with which, interestingly, the Courts of Equity never sought to interfere. It is good law today.

h The reason for the harshness is this. It acts as a firm deterrent—particularly so in the days when *Pigot's Case* was decided, when deeds were all-important—to any person seeking to alter (all too easily then) writing upon which important rights turned and which might very well be of importance between people who were not the parties. To make it plain, the penalty for alteration was severe and absolute.

j It is apparent from later authority that what also may lie behind it is that the forgery of deeds appears to have been a misdemeanour rather than a felony and, therefore, in order to make the punishment the greater it was thought that a deed should be void as it would appear the forger was not liable to be hanged.

The doctrine has, in later authorities—some of themselves of some antiquity—been further elaborated upon. Thus (and it seems to me a particularly important

authority) in *Master v Miller* (1791) 4 Term Rep 320 at 329, 100 ER 1042 at 1047
Lord Kenyon CJ said:

> '... why, in point of policy, would it [ie the doctrine] have had that effect
> in a deed? Because no man shall be permitted to take the chance of
> committing a fraud, without running any risk of losing by the event, when it
> is detected.'

It was he, indeed, who referred to the fact that it had originally been a
misdemeanour and not a felony. He said:

> 'Therefore those decisions, which were indeed confined to deeds, applied
> to the then state of affairs: but they establish this principle, that all written
> instruments which were altered or erased, should be thereby avoided.' (See
> (1791) 4 Term Rep 320 at 330, 100 ER 1042 at 1047.)

He was concerned in that particular case with the extension of that doctrine to
bills of exchange.

In a later authority, *Suffell v Bank of England* (1882) 9 QBD 555 at 560, Jessel MR
repeated what was said in *Master v Miller* in what was a comprehensive and
historical review of this doctrine. Jessel MR was sitting then in the Court of
Appeal, therefore having, whatever the earlier authorities may have had, clear
Court of Appeal status.

It may well be, as it may well be in this case, that how any alteration came
about and whether the alteration was indeed intended to be an alteration or
capable of being an alteration may simply not be known, or may be known by
one party and not another. Therefore, it is important to consider where the
burden of proof lies. As early as 1827 in *Bishop v Chambre* 3 C & P 55, 172 ER 320
it said (and I think I can simply quote the headnote, which really encapsulates the
charge to go to the jury):

> 'In an action on a note, if it appear on the inspection of the note, that it has
> been altered, it lies on the plaintiff to shew that the alteration took place
> under such circumstances as will entitle him to recover.'

I pause to say the evidence here accepts that the alteration might have been while
it was in the custody of the bank and, therefore, it follows from other extensions
to the document (which I perhaps need not spell out) that it is treated, initially at
least, as if it had been made by the bank and therefore, all other things apart, the
bank would fail. But try as they will, the bank's officials have not been able to
discover who did it or why. There are all sorts of guesses that one can make but
none of them, I think, is very satisfactory.

It does, however, seem to me that although the burden of proof inevitably
shifts to the person setting up the apparently altered document, it may be possible
to discharge their burden of proof by necessary inference as opposed to direct
evidence. I would not, if necessary, shrink from that.

It is material next to consider whether there is any law that assists me as to the
effect of an alteration made not in ink but, as here indeed, in pencil. In *Norton on
Deeds* (2nd edn, 1928) ch 2, p 34 (which is the last edition and which I think may
now safely be taken as a work of authority so far as it goes) as to pencilled
alterations, the editors say, first of all quoting from *Williams on Executors* (11th
edn, 1921) vol 2, Pt 1:

a
'It has been held that the general presumption and probability are, that where alterations (in a will) in pencil only are made, they are deliberative; where in ink they are final and absolute ...'

Norton continues:

b
'There does not appear to be any authority as to the effect of pencil alterations in deeds, but they would probably be disregarded, whether made before or after execution.'

He cites no authority and, indeed, says (as I have quoted) that there is none. Of course, distinguished conveyancing textbooks have an authoritative status of their own so far as they go, but that is, of course, a statement really of first
c impression. There are four will cases, two of them before and two after the Wills Act 1837. I can refer to them, I think, reasonably briefly, and they are in turn these. The two before the 1837 Act are *Parkin v Bainbridge* (1820) 3 Phillim 321, 161 ER 1338 and *Hawkes v Hawkes* (1828) 1 Hag Ecc 321, 162 ER 599, both decisions in the Prerogative Court of Canterbury by Sir John Nichol, who was the
d Dean of Arches at that date.

In the earlier case, *Parkin v Bainbridge*, Sir John Nichol, having deliberated a little on whether pencil was to be disregarded, said in the end he would reserve his opinion until he got an appropriate case in which to decide it. Coming back to the matter in *Hawkes v Hawkes*, on the particular case before him, but without any further authority being put to him, he said that he was of the opinion that the
e pencil marks were not finally revocatory but only deliberative and depending on future acts, but I think it has to be said that this really took in the context of the particular will. I do not think those two cases are of themselves of enormous assistance.

In the later cases, which were decided after the 1837 Act, rather different
f considerations came about. Both were decided by Lord Penzance. One is *Re Hall's Goods* (1871) LR 2 P & D 256 and the other is *Re Adams' Goods* (1872) LR 2 P & D 367. They both really turned, I think, on the particular circumstances, though perhaps some assistance can be got in *Re Hall's Goods* LR 2 P & D 256 at 258, where Lord Penzance said:

g
'If, under all the circumstances, the Court considered that such words, although found in a testamentary paper, had not been written as a fixed testamentary disposition, but merely deliberatively, in order that the testator on further consideration, should determine whether or not they should be ultimately carried out, it rejected the words as part of the will.'

h That seems to me to turn really not on whether they are in pencil but on evidence at large. He continues: 'In this case the alterations in pencil, lines are scored through certain paragraphs, and opposite others the word "query" is placed.' He placed a deal of emphasis on the word 'query'. I think it may be fair to say that the fact that the words in that case were words in pencil was a factor, though not
j necessarily the decisive one. I do not for my part think that those authorities are necessarily authority for what *Norton* says. *Norton* says they would probably be disregarded, and I think the reality of what *Norton* is saying is that this is not so much a question of legal principle but a question of evidence.

It is really to the evidential effect of words of this kind being in pencil that I now turn. I think it is very important to remember that the court must live in the real world and some judicial notice must be taken of the way in which, in modern times, particular writing media are used. The pencil is quite an old writing instrument, as writing instruments go; it certainly seems to have been around in the 1820s (or earlier from the authorities) and I suspect a good deal earlier than that. No doubt in its early days its great advantage was it was a writing instrument you could carry with you anywhere and use at any time without the need to cart round all the paraphernalia of ink pots and sanders and the like. With the arrival of the fountain pen and later, half a century or so ago, of the original ball-point pen, it probably became of less significance simply as a portable writing instrument.

In modern times individuals, of course, may use it for writing and note taking in preference to the ink pen or the ball-point pen, but one cannot help noticing in legal documents it commonly appears as a form of annotation, or perhaps most commonly of all as the medium in which the initials of the persons to execute a deed and the words 'Do not date' across the gap for the date appear. Also, as I indicated to counsel, there has almost entered into the language the expression 'We will pencil this date in our diary'.

I would, for my part, consider that where a document consists otherwise of print, type and ink writing that the most natural inference to draw of an amendment to that in pencil is that it is not, and is not intended to be, an operative and final alteration. 'Deliberative' is perhaps a rather old-fashioned expression to come from the authorities, but it has, perhaps, some merit as a convenient word of description. But the inference is, perhaps, more, that it is something that *may* be done, something that is there for consideration; above all, something that may well very simply be rubbed out—because the one thing, of course, that distinguishes pencil from anything else is the ability to rub it out completely so that (except to a forensic scientist) it was never there at all.

So that is an inference that can be drawn, I think, from the use of pencil. It is not, I emphasise, a question of law at all. It is a question of looking at the individual document, the individual circumstances and seeing what inference you can draw. For instance, if the document was entirely in pencil between persons who liked doing everything in pencil, pencilled alterations would have much greater force than in a document produced on a word processor.

Here, if one looks at this document, it is apparent that the pencilling out of the names of 'The Customer' is very light; there is no attempt to obliterate. It merely shows that it ought to be taken out. Underneath it is pencilled in what undoubtedly ought to have been there in the first place. There is no attempt at any less ephemeral alteration than that. I think here what seems to me critical is this. If one looks back at what the old authorities say, and in particular if one looks at *Master v Miller*—'no man should be permitted to take the chance of committing a fraud without running any risk of losing by the event when it is detected'—what, in truth and in commercial reality, is the chance of committing a fraud here, with a pencilled alteration to an instrument of this kind? It seems to me that the proper evidential inference to draw is that this was in the nature of a note, a drafting amendment, a proposal, but not something final and that could ever deceive. For my part, I cannot think that if an attempt was made at court to enforce this document with this pencilled alteration it could succeed. That may be in the end, perhaps, the test.

For all those reasons, therefore, I would think that the reality is that this is not in truth an alteration of the document at all. It may be an annotation, it may be a suggestion, but it does not actually alter the substance of the document and I would not infer it was ever intended to. Had it been an alteration, I for my part *a* would have regarded it as a highly material one because of the nature of the principal debtor whose debt you are prepared to guarantee is critical to the obligation which you undertake. I would not doubt that.

Mr Leeming QC raised a very interesting argument before me, really partly, I think, in support of his principal submissions and partly standing on its own, that this was a case to which there might very well apply the doctrine of estoppel by *b* convention based on the well-known judgment of the Court of Appeal in *Amalgamated Investment and Property Co Ltd (in liq) v Texas Commerce International Bank* [1981] 3 All ER 577, [1982] QB 84, on the basis that the parties had throughout treated this instrument as in fact guaranteeing the indebtedness of the company and not the indebtedness of Mr and Mrs Tipper and that therefore they would be estopped from saying that the doctrine applied and that the *c* instrument should not be rectified. That is a most interesting argument and, so far as it is not a free-standing argument, it is there to support this assertion that this was not a material alteration. As I have held it is not an alteration, I do not have to decide in the event whether it is material—nor, does it seem to me, is it desirable I should.

d The issue of estoppel, if it has to arise at all in view of what I have said is, I think, something that must depend on evidence. I see how it is put—for all I know Mr Leeming is right—but it is, I note, contentious as to what stage it was that the parties ceased to be of one mind as to how far the estoppel extended. If that issue is to be pursued at all it seems to me (1) it must be very clearly and fully pleaded (and it has not actually been pleaded at all), and (2) that it must be a matter of *e* evidence, because there is obvious cross-examination of the bank's witnesses which would have to take place.

In the event, I have come to the conclusion, on the narrow issue before me—and it is, of course, only one of the issues in this case—that the district judge was wrong and that rectification would, all other issues being in favour of the plaintiff, *f* be open to the plaintiff. It therefore follows, I think, that I simply declare in those terms that the plaintiff is not, by reason of the pencil addition to the document, precluded from setting up rectification.

Appeal allowed.

Celia Fox   Barrister.

Ketchum International plc v Group Public Relations Holdings Ltd and others

a

COURT OF APPEAL, CIVIL DIVISION

STUART-SMITH, PETER GIBSON AND WARD LJJ

b

9, 24 MAY 1996

Court of Appeal – Jurisdiction – Injunction – Unsuccessful plaintiff seeking injunction pending appeal to restrain defendants' disposal of assets – Relief denied at first instance – Plaintiff issuing summons in Court of Appeal seeking same relief – Whether Court of Appeal having concurrent original jurisdiction to grant injunction – Whether appeal more appropriate – RSC Ord 59, r 10(9).

c

The plaintiff company entered into an agreement to purchase from the defendant company 40% of the shares in a third company. The agreement made provision for a put option under which the defendant had the right at the end of a three-year period to require the plaintiff to purchase the remaining 60% of the shares and for the payment of dividends. In litigation arising out of the purported exercise of the put option, the judge ordered specific performance of the agreement and dismissed the plaintiff's claims for damages in relation to two dividend payments. The plaintiff complied with the order, but exercised its right to appeal in the first dividend action and sought the damages which it had originally claimed; it subsequently sought an injunction restraining the defendant from dealing with the proceeds of sale pending the appeal. The judge dismissed the application for an injunction and refused leave to appeal. Thereafter the plaintiff applied to the Court of Appeal for the same injunctive relief or, alternatively, for leave to appeal and, if granted, orders setting aside the judge's decision and granting the injunction sought. The question arose whether the Court of Appeal had an original jurisdiction to grant injunctive relief in such circumstances.

d

e

f

Held – The Court of Appeal had an original jurisdiction pursuant to RSC Ord 59, r 10(9)[a] to grant injunctive relief to restrain a defendant from disposing of assets pending the unsuccessful plaintiff's substantive appeal. That jurisdiction was similar to the jurisdiction exercised where an unsuccessful defendant sought a stay of execution pending an appeal and it was based on the principle that justice required that the court should be able to take steps to ensure that its judgments were not rendered valueless by an unjustifiable disposal of assets. Further, there was no reason in principle why the considerations applicable to the grant of a Mareva injunction should not be applied in favour of such a plaintiff; the test would be whether he had a good arguable appeal, and where leave was not required to appeal from the substantive judgment (as in the instant case) injunctive relief of the type sought should not be granted unless leave to appeal would have been granted, had it been required. Since the plaintiff did not have a sufficiently good arguable appeal to warrant the relief sought, his application

g

h

j

---

a   Rule 10(9), so far as material, provides: 'In any proceedings incidental to any cause or matter pending before the Court of Appeal, the powers conferred by this rule on the Court ... shall be exercisable ... in relation to (a) the grant, variation, discharge or enforcement of an injunction ... and (b) the grant or lifting of a stay of execution or proceedings.'

a would accordingly be dismissed (see p 378 *j* to p 379 *b*, p 381 *c* to *f j* to p 382 *b*, p 383 *b c* and p 384 *c d*, post).

Wilson v Church (No 2) (1879) 12 Ch D 454, Polini v Gray, Sturla v Freccia (1879) 12 Ch D 438 and Orion Property Trust Ltd v Du Cane Court Ltd, General London and Urban Properties Ltd v Du Cane Court Ltd [1962] 3 All ER 466 considered.

b **Notes**

For original jurisdiction of the Court of Appeal, see 10 *Halsbury's Laws* (4th edn) para 899, and for cases on the subject, see 16 *Digest* (2nd reissue) 362–363, *2575–2576*.

c **Cases referred to in judgments**

British Bakeries (Midlands) Ltd v Michael Testler & Co Ltd [1986] 1 EGLR 64.

Bromley Park Garden Estates Ltd v Moss [1982] 2 All ER 890, [1982] 1 WLR 1019, CA.

Derby & Co Ltd v Weldon (No 2) [1989] 1 All ER 1002, [1990] Ch 65, [1989] 2 WLR 412, CA.

d *Erinford Properties Ltd v Cheshire CC* [1974] 2 All ER 448, [1974] Ch 261, [1974] 2 WLR 749.

Ninemia Maritime Corp v Trave Schiffahrtsgesellschaft mbH & Co KG, The Niedersachsen [1984] 1 All ER 398, [1983] 1 WLR 1412, QBD and CA.

Orion Property Trust Ltd v Du Cane Court Ltd, General London and Urban Properties Ltd
e *v Du Cane Court Ltd* [1962] 3 All ER 466, [1962] 1 WLR 1085.

Polini v Gray, Sturla v Freccia (1879) 12 Ch D 438, CA; *affd* (1880) 5 App Cas 623, [1874–80] All ER 657, HL.

R v Secretary of State for the Home Dept, ex p Muboyayi [1991] 4 All ER 72, [1992] QB 244, [1991] 3 WLR 442, CA.

f *Wilson v Church* (1879) 11 Ch D 576, CA.

Wilson v Church (No 2) (1879) 12 Ch D 454, CA.

Application

g By summons dated 23 April 1996 the plaintiff, Ketchum International plc (Ketchum), applied to the Court of Appeal for (i) an injunction restraining the first defendant, Group Public Relations Holdings Ltd (Holdings), from removing from the jurisdiction or disposing of the proceeds of sale of a 60% holding in another company, EPR (Jersey) Ltd, together with interest, pending the outcome of Ketchum's appeal in a related action, or alternatively (ii) leave to appeal from
h the decision of Blackburne J on 3 April 1996, whereby he dismissed Ketchum's notice of motion dated 28 March 1996 seeking the same injunctive relief against Holdings, refused leave to appeal and granted an injunction in terms of the motion for a limited period pending an application to the Court of Appeal. The second and third defendants, Christopher O'Donoghue and Pamela Ann Poe,
j took no part in the proceedings. The facts are set out in the judgment of Stuart-Smith LJ.

George Leggatt (instructed by *Clifford Chance*) for Ketchum.
Romie Tager QC and *James Ayliffe* (instructed by *Lewis Silkin*) for Holdings.

Cur adv vult

24 May 1996. The following judgments were delivered.

a

STUART-SMITH LJ. A Jersey company, EPR (Jersey) Ltd (EPRJ), is the owner of all the shares in an English public relations company which, until January 1993, was called Group Public Relations plc. Prior to 14 January 1991 all the shares in EPRJ were owned by the first defendant, Group Public Relations Holdings Ltd (Holdings). The second defendant, Christopher O'Donoghue, and the third *b* defendant, Pamela Ann Poe, own Holdings in equal shares. On 14 January 1991 by a share purchase agreement the plaintiff, Ketchum International Inc (Ketchum), a Delaware corporation, agreed to purchase from Holdings 40% of the shares in EPRJ. That agreement provided that the purchase price was payable in tranches over a three-year period and was geared to the profits of EPRJ and its subsidiaries after tax during that period. It also provided for both put and call *c* options. By a put option, Holdings had the right after the end of that period to require Ketchum to purchase the remaining 60% holding in EPRJ at a price also geared to those profits in that period. It also provided (by cl 8(1)) that EPRJ should not make any distribution by way of dividend without the prior written approval of Ketchum, such consent not to be unreasonably withheld or delayed. *d*

In August 1993 EPRJ paid a dividend of just over £800,000 and in October 1993 a dividend of just under £200,000, on each occasion without the approval of Ketchum, although Ketchum received and retained its 40% share of those dividends. In March 1994 Holdings purported to exercise the put option, requiring Ketchum to purchase the 60% holding in EPRJ for some £2·6m. Those events in 1993 and 1994 led to the commencement of three actions. By the action *e* with which this appeal is directly concerned, (the first dividend action), Ketchum claimed against Holdings, Mr O'Donoghue and Miss Poe that the payment of the first dividend without its consent was a breach of the agreement and it claimed damages therefore. The loss was particularised as being that Holdings, by that dividend payment, 'rendered less valuable [Ketchum's] option, and/or [had] *f* rendered more onerous [Ketchum's] liability pursuant to [Holdings'] option, by the amount of the dividend', that loss being quantified as £483,477. That is 60% of the dividend payment. By another action (the second dividend action), Ketchum made a similar claim, mutatis mutandis, in respect of the second dividend, the claimed loss being quantified as £119,673. The third action (the put *g* action) was brought by Holdings against Ketchum and its parent corporation and related to the exercise by Holdings of its put option. The principal issues were the validity of the exercise of that option, and, if it was validly exercised, the price payable by Ketchum.

The three actions came before Blackburne J at the same time, the claims by Ketchum in the first and second dividend actions being treated as counterclaims *h* to Holdings' claim in the put action. In the course of the hearing Ketchum discontinued the counterclaim against Mr O'Donoghue and Miss Poe. In his closing address to the judge, leading counsel then appearing for Ketchum conceded the validity of the exercise of the put option. The judge on 21 February 1996 in the put action determined the price to be paid as a little over £2·4m and *j* ordered specific performance of the agreement, directing that completion of the purchase should take place on 3 April 1996. He ordered that Ketchum should pay 80% of the costs until day three of the trial and 75% of the costs thereafter. He refused to order Ketchum to pay interest prior to 28 February 1996. In the first dividend action the judge dismissed with costs Ketchum's claim, holding that it had unreasonably withheld its consent to the first dividend. In the second a dividend action, he awarded Ketchum damages as claimed and nearly £24,000 interest, but ordered Holdings to pay only 50% of Ketchum's costs. Ketchum is not appealing against the orders made against it in the put action, but Holdings is appealing on the question of interest. In the first dividend action Ketchum has exercised its right to appeal and it is seeking the damages which it originally claimed. Holdings is appealing in the second dividend action.

b   The purchase price ordered to be paid in the put action, less the damages and interest which were awarded to Ketchum in the second dividend action, a net sum of about £2m, has been duly paid by Ketchum to Holdings' solicitors. But by a notice of motion dated 28 March 1996 Ketchum applied for an injunction restraining Holdings from removing from the jurisdiction or disposing of or dealing with the proceeds of the sale of the 60% holding in EPRJ up to the value
c of £585,736, together with interest thereon, pending the outcome of Ketchum's appeal in the first dividend action. That maximum sum is made up of the £483,477 damages claimed plus interest. That motion was heard, but dismissed, by the judge on 3 April 1996 and he refused leave to appeal. However, he granted an injunction in the terms of the notice of motion for a limited period, pending
d an application to this court.

The application before us is a summons by which Ketchum seeks precisely the same relief as that which it unsuccessfully sought before the judge. In other words Ketchum is thereby asking this court, not for leave to appeal from the decision of the judge and, if leave is granted, the reversal of that decision and the
e grant of an injunction, but to exercise an original jurisdiction to grant an injunction. If that is wrong and this court holds that an appellate route should have been followed, Mr Leggatt for Ketchum asks this court to give leave to appeal, to set aside the order of the judge and to grant the injunction sought.

At this point it is convenient to summarise the arguments presented to the judge and his conclusions.
f
(1) Mr Leggatt for Ketchum submitted that a trilogy of cases in 1879—*Wilson v Church (No 1)* (1879) 11 Ch D 576, *Wilson v Church (No 2)* (1879) 12 Ch D 454 and *Polini v Gray, Sturla v Freccia* (1879) 12 Ch D 438—established the principle that when a party is bringing a bona fide appeal as of right, the Court of Appeal ought to ensure that the appeal, if successful, is not nugatory by restraining the hitherto
g successful party from disposing of its assets. This principle could and should be applied at first instance (see *Erinford Properties Ltd v Cheshire CC* [1974] 2 All ER 448, [1974] Ch 261 and *Orion Property Trust Ltd v Du Cane Court Ltd, General London and Urban Properties Ltd v Du Cane Court Ltd* [1962] 3 All ER 466, [1962] 1 WLR 1085). Blackburne J distinguished the 1879 cases on the grounds that, on their
h facts, they involved competing claims to a fund and did not apply to an action for damages. He said that the *Erinford* case, which concerned the question whether the court had jurisdiction to grant a limited injunction preserving the status quo pending an appeal against the court's refusal to grant an interlocutory injunction pending trial, was not relevant.

j (2) Mr Leggatt submitted in the alternative that the principles which apply when the court grants Mareva relief should be applicable pending an appeal to the Court of Appeal by an unsuccessful plaintiff, provided the relevant conditions are satisfied. The judge rejected his submission. He said there was no authority for such a proposition and the plaintiff was faced with the formidable difficulty of showing that he had a good arguable case, when the judge had just held that he did not.

(3) On the assumption that jurisdiction based on Mareva principles exists, the
judge acknowledged that Ketchum might have good arguable grounds for   *a*
appealing the decision in the first dividend action. But he said:

'I have seen nothing in the evidence to show that Holdings is about to or
may take action designed to ensure that any subsequent order of the Court
of Appeal will be rendered less effective than would otherwise be the case.
Not only is there nothing in evidence that Holdings would seek to render   *b*
itself judgment-proof, I have seen nothing to indicate that, if Ketchum's
appeal were to succeed, those who control Holdings, namely Miss Poe and
Mr O'Donoghue, would not seek to ensure that Holdings would honour the
court's order.'

Basing himself on a dictum of Lord Donaldson MR in *Derby & Co Ltd v Weldon*   *c*
(No 2) [1989] 1 All ER 1002 at 1006–1007, [1990] Ch 65 at 76, Blackburne J said:

'The fundamental principle underlying this jurisdiction is that, within the
limits of its powers, no court should permit a defendant to take action
designed to ensure that subsequent orders of the court are rendered less
effective than would otherwise be the case.'   *d*

Before us Mr Leggatt submitted as follows. (1) This court has an original
jurisdiction to grant the injunction sought. The application is by way of a
renewed application and is similar to the renewed application for a stay of
execution after refusal by the trial judge. (2) Alternatively, if the matter is to be
brought before this court by way of appeal, leave to appeal should be granted.   *e*
(3) The jurisdiction arose when there was a bona fide appeal as of right or
alternatively when there was a good arguable appeal and, in the absence of
injunctive relief, the appeal was likely to be rendered nugatory. (4)(a) There was
a good arguable appeal and the judge accepted this. (b) The judge posed too
high a test in requiring an intention on the part of the defendant to make itself   *f*
judgment-proof; it is sufficient if the defendant's actions have the consequence
that the judgment will not be met. (c) On the facts, this likelihood was
established and the judge in reaching a contrary conclusion took into account
irrelevant matters.

Mr Tager QC, on the other hand, submits as follows. (1) The judge was right   *g*
to distinguish the *Wilson v Church* line of cases on the grounds that he did.
(2) Mareva relief is not appropriate where the plaintiff has failed at first instance
and therefore ex hypothesi does not have a good arguable case. (3) In any event,
the court has no original jurisdiction to entertain this application; it must be
brought by way of appeal and leave should not be granted. (4) If the question is
whether Ketchum has a good arguable appeal, he submits it does not. (5) The   *h*
judge was right to hold that there was no risk of dissipation of assets; this was a
finding of fact based in part upon the judge's assessment of the witnesses and this
court should not interfere.

Does this court have an original jurisdiction to grant an injunction in the terms
sought? If so, in what circumstances should it be exercised? Mr Leggatt submits   *j*
that in principle courts should be able to take steps to ensure that their judgments
are not rendered valueless by an unjustifiable disposition of assets. The High
Court has power to grant injunctions under s 37 of the Supreme Court Act 1981
in any case in which it appears just and convenient to do so. This jurisdiction is
exercisable by the Court of Appeal by reason of s 15 of that Act, and RSC Ord 59,
r 10(1), and this court has power to grant injunctions in any proceedings

a instituted in any cause or matter pending before the Court of Appeal (Ord 59, r 10(9)). There is no reason in principle why this jurisdiction should not be exercised in favour of a plaintiff who has lost in the court below if there is a real risk that as a successful appellant his right of appeal is rendered nugatory. He submits that there is no difference in principle between granting an injunction in such circumstances and granting a stay of execution to an unsuccessful defendant

b who wishes to appeal. In each case justice requires that a successful party be prevented from reaping the fruits of his success until the Court of Appeal has been able to decide if there is a real likelihood that the appeal might otherwise be rendered nugatory.

In *Wilson v Church (No 2)* (1879) 12 Ch D 454 the plaintiff brought an action on behalf of himself and all other holders of Bolivian bonds issued in connection with

c the construction of a railway against the trustees for the bond holders, seeking a declaration that a trust fund of a large amount in the hands of the trustees should be returned to the bond holders and not applied to the payment of the work on the railway. The plaintiff failed before Fry J, but succeeded on appeal. Based on prior authority it was said that Fry J, having dismissed the action, had no

d jurisdiction to restrain the trustees from paying the money out until the determination of the appeal. On this assumption, the Court of Appeal granted the injunction sought, pending determination of the appeal to it. When the trustees lost in the Court of Appeal they sought a similar injunction to restrain disposal from the trust to the bond holders pending appeal to the House of Lords, which at that time they enjoyed without leave. The court again granted the

e injunction.

Cotton LJ said (at 458):

'But then there comes the question whether or no that part of the order which directs payment to the bondholders should be stayed. I will state my opinion that when a party is appealing, exercising his undoubted right of

f appeal, this Court ought to see that the appeal, if successful, is not nugatory; and, acting on that principle, when there was an appeal to this Court from the judgment of Mr. Justice *Fry* dismissing the Plaintiff's action altogether, and it was urged therefore that this Court had no jurisdiction to stay the execution of the order, we were of opinion that we ought to stay the

g execution of a judgment in another action made by Mr. Justice *Fry*, ordering the fund to be dealt with—that is to say, by granting an injunction against the trustees to restrain them from parting with any portion of the fund in their hands till the appeal was disposed of (*Wilson v Church* (1879) 11 Ch D 576). That possibly was rather novel, but it was right, in my opinion, to make that order to prevent the appeal, if successful, from being nugatory. Acting on

h the same principle, I am of opinion that we ought to take care that if the House of Lords should reverse our decision (and we must recognise that it may be reversed), the appeal ought not to be rendered nugatory.'

Brett LJ said (at 459):

j 'This is an application to the discretion of the Court, but I think that Mr. *Benjamin* has laid down the proper rule of conduct for the exercise of the judicial discretion, that where the right of appeal exists, and the question is whether the fund shall be paid out of Court, the Court as a general rule ought to exercise its best discretion in a way so as not to prevent the appeal, if successful, from being nugatory.'

James LJ dissented on the facts, but not I think on the principle.

In so far as dicta in that case suggests that it is enough that the appeal is bona fide and not brought for some improper purpose such as delay or exerting pressure on the other party, that in my opinion is inconsistent with what is said in *Polini v Gray, Sturla v Freccia* (1879) 12 Ch D 438. In that case, S claimed that she was next of kin of a testator and was entitled under his will. She failed at first instance and in the Court of Appeal, but intended to appeal. The Court of Appeal granted an injunction staying disposal of the fund pending appeal to the House of Lords.

I think it may well be right that Jessel MR based his judgment on the rule of court that gave the court jurisdiction to make 'any order for the detention, preservation ... of any property being the subject of such action' (see (1879) 12 Ch D 438 at 443). But Cotton LJ (1879) 12 Ch D 438 at 446 seems to have put it on a broader basis. He said:

> 'I see no difference in principle between staying the distribution of a fund to which the Court has held the Plaintiff not to be entitled, and staying the execution of an order by which the Court has decided that a Plaintiff is entitled to a fund. In that case, as in this case, the Court, pending an appeal to the House of Lords, suspends what it has declared to be the right of one of the litigant parties. On what principle does it do so? It does so on this ground, that when there is an appeal about to be prosecuted the litigation is to be considered as not at an end, and that being so, if there is a reasonable ground of appeal, and if not making the order to stay the execution of the decree or the distribution of the fund would make the appeal nugatory, that is to say, would deprive the Appellant, if successful, of the results of the appeal, then it is the duty of the Court to interfere and suspend the right of the party who, so far as the litigation has gone, has established his rights. That applies, in my opinion, just as much to the case where the action has been dismissed, as to the case where a decree has been made establishing the Plaintiff's title.'

In *Orion Property Trust Ltd v Du Cane Court Ltd, General London and Urban Properties Ltd v Du Cane Court Ltd* [1962] 3 All ER 466, [1962] 1 WLR 1085 Pennycuick J followed the judgment of Cotton LJ which I have cited and held that the court of first instance had jurisdiction to make an order restraining the issue of shares pending an appeal, even though the action seeking such relief had failed. And in *Erinford Properties Ltd v Cheshire CC* [1974] 2 All ER 448 at 454, [1974] Ch 261 at 268 Megarry J applied the same principle to an interlocutory injunction which he had refused, but granted it for a limited time so that application could be made to the Court of Appeal to extend it. He said:

> 'There may, of course, be many cases where it would be wrong to grant an injunction pending appeal, as where any appeal would be frivolous, or to grant the injunction would inflict greater hardship than it would avoid, and so on. But subject to that, the principle is to be found in the leading judgment of Cotton LJ in *Wilson v Church (No 2)* ((1879)12 Ch D 454 at 458), where, speaking of an appeal from the Court of Appeal to the House of Lords, he said, "when a party is appealing, exercising his undoubted right of appeal, this Court ought to see that the appeal, if successful, is not nugatory". That was the principle which Pennycuick J applied in the *Orion* case ([1962] 3 All ER 466, [1962] 1 WLR 1085); and although the cases had not then been

a   cited to me, it was on that principle, and not because I felt any real doubts about my judgment on the motion, that I granted counsel for the plaintiffs the limited injunction pending appeal that he sought. This is not a case in which damages seem to me to be a suitable alternative ... Although the type of injunction that I have granted is not a stay of execution, it achieves for the application or action which fails the same sort of result as a stay of execution

b   achieves for the application or action which succeeds. In each case the successful party is prevented from reaping the fruits of his success until the Court of Appeal has been able to decide the appeal.'

In my judgment, this jurisdiction is not limited, as the judge thought, to cases concerned with the preservation of a fund or property the subject of the action,

c   but is based on the wider principle enunciated by Cotton LJ that justice requires that the court should be able to take steps to ensure that their judgments are not rendered valueless by an unjustifiable disposal of assets. Moreover, I cannot see any reason in principle why the considerations which are applicable when the court is considering the grant of a Mareva injunction should not be applied in favour of a plaintiff, even if he has lost in the court below, though the question

d   will not be 'does he have a good arguable case?' but 'does he have a good arguable appeal?' This is likely to be a more difficult test to satisfy, and, if the case turns upon questions of fact which the judge has resolved against the plaintiff, may well be insuperable. This threshold must be at least as high as that which has to be satisfied when the court considers whether or not to grant leave to appeal, where

e   that is required.

The analogy with a stay of execution is appropriate. Where an unsuccessful defendant has to obtain leave to appeal and seeks a stay of execution, for example in a possession action, this court will normally grant a stay if it grants leave to appeal, since otherwise a successful appeal will be of no effect. Where leave is not

f   required to appeal the substantive judgment, as in this case, injunctive relief of the type sought should not be granted unless leave to appeal would be granted, had it been required. In my opinion, the judge was in error in thinking that he did not have jurisdiction to make the order sought.

But this still leaves the question whether Ketchum is able to renew its application before this court or is required to appeal, for which it needs leave to

g   appeal. Mr Tager points out that it is unfair that an unsuccessful plaintiff, having failed to obtain an injunction before the trial judge, should have a second bite at the cherry without the hurdle of leave, where this court is being asked to exercise its discretion afresh, without the well-known fetter on interfering with the trial judge's exercise of discretion. Leave to appeal is now required from the grant or

h   refusal of an interlocutory injunction. And as Mr Tager points out, a trial judge who has heard the action and dismissed it may be in a much better position to determine whether such relief should be granted. I see the force of Mr Tager's submission. On the other hand, Ord 59, r 10(9) expressly seems to contemplate an original jurisdiction and this undoubtedly exists in the case of applications for

j   a stay of execution. Order 59, r 14(4) requires that where an application can be made either to the court below or the Court of Appeal, it must in the first instance be made to the court below save in special circumstances. Not without considerable hesitation, I have come to the conclusion that the court has concurrent original jurisdiction in such a case as this, similar to that exercised where a stay of execution is sought, and that the matter does not have to be raised by way of appeal. If I am wrong, in the circumstances of this case I would grant

leave to appeal. I do not envisage that this court will be inundated with renewed
applications; it is only in exceptional cases that the facts will justify an application   a
to the judge, and I think an appellant who has a right of appeal may well be
reluctant to risk being told by this court that in its opinion there is no good
arguable appeal on the substantive appeal. Furthermore, this court will not
interfere with relevant findings of fact which the trial judge has made based in
part on his assessment of the witnesses, and in so far as the grant of injunctive   b
relief is a matter of discretion, is unlikely to differ from the trial judge, save on
well-established principles. The only matter on which this court may, as a rule,
be in a better position to decide than the trial judge, is whether the plaintiff has a
good arguable appeal.

I turn then to consider the question whether Ketchum has shown that it has a
good arguable appeal. Mr Leggatt initially took his stand on which he claimed   c
was the judge's view of this. The judge said:

'... I am modest enough to acknowledge that my decision in the first
dividend action may be upset on appeal and that Ketchum may be able to
demonstrate that there are good arguable reasons for indicating why that
should happen ...'   d

In my judgment, the judge is doing no more than assuming that there may be
such grounds, because he then went on to refuse relief on the ground that he did
not think that Holdings intended to make itself judgment-proof. He never really
analysed the strength of the grounds of appeal. Mr Tager submits that if the
grounds of appeal are considered, the prospects for Ketchum are poor and would   e
not justify granting leave to appeal, if that was required.

Ground 1 raises a point of law which, in the field of landlord and tenant relating
to the question of unreasonable withholding of consent, is very similar to cl 8(1)
of the share purchase agreement in this case, and has been determined against
Ketchum by the Court of Appeal in *Bromley Park Gardens Estates Ltd v Moss* [1982]   f
2 All ER 890, [1982] 1 WLR 1019 and *British Bakeries (Midlands) Ltd v Michael
Testler & Co Ltd* [1986] 1 EGLR 64. I agree with Mr Tager that it is most unlikely
that leave to appeal to the House of Lords would be granted or the effect of those
decisions, which have not been criticised, overruled.

The second ground of appeal is: (i) that the judge failed to have regard to the
correct test, namely whether no reasonable shareholder in Ketchum's position   g
would have withheld its consent to the dividend; and (ii) the judge failed to hold
or take account of the fact that, in deciding whether to give its consent to the first
dividend, Ketchum was entitled to have regard to its own interests unless the
detriment caused to Holdings by withholding consent was wholly
disproportionate to the advantage gained by Ketchum. Again, I agree with Mr   h
Tager that there is little prospect in this ground. It seems to me the judge had
regard to the correct test and did take into account the point made in ground 2(ii).

Mr Leggatt's principal criticism of the judge's decision was that Ketchum was
not objecting to any dividend being paid, but only to one of £800,000 proposed;
that it was entitled to take the view that it was unfair that the price it had to pay   j
for the shares was inflated by interest that was earned on accumulated and
undistributed profits during the earn-out period, and it did not acquire a
corresponding asset when it acquired the shares. Mr Leggatt said that the judge
should have but failed to, hold that this was a reasonable ground for withholding
consent to the first dividend. But to my mind Mr Tager has a formidable answer
to these points. First, he says that it is clear from the correspondence, and the

a judge so held, that Ketchum was objecting to any dividend, however modest. Secondly, he says that the judge did have regard to the alleged unfairness, and indeed this was the reason why he held in Ketchum's favour on the second dividend. The judge carefully analysed this point and decided that the dividing point came at the £800,000 dividend. We cannot, of course, in this hearing decide whether this submission is correct. But since Ketchum eventually appears to

b have accepted that some dividend was payable, the question was one of quantum and the judge assessed this having regard to the evidence and submissions made to him, both in relation to the unfairness point and the cash requirements of the company. I have come to the conclusion that Ketchum's prospects of appeal are not sufficiently good to justify grant of the relief sought.

All the other grounds appear to me to be challenges to the judge's findings of
c fact which were based in part at least on his assessment of the witnesses who gave evidence before him. While it is not an insuperable task to persuade this court to interfere with such findings, it is obviously a difficult one.

That is sufficient to dispose of the application in Holdings' favour. But since we have heard considerable argument upon the point of whether there was a
d serious risk that Holdings would dispose of its assets before the hearing of Ketchum's appeal, and since I have come to the conclusion that the judge was in error on this point, I shall state my reasons as briefly as possible.

In my judgment, the judge misdirected himself by relying on the passage already quoted from *Derby & Co Ltd v Weldon (No 2)* [1989] 1 All ER 1002, [1990] Ch 65 for the proposition that the plaintiff must show that the defendant intends
e to deal with his assets for the purpose of ensuring that a judgment will not be met. It is sufficient if there is a real risk that the judgment in favour of the plaintiff will remain unsatisfied if injunctive relief is refused (see *Ninemia Maritime Corp v Trave Schiffahrtsgesellschaft mbH & Co KG, The Niedersachsen* [1984] 1 All ER 398 at 419, [1983] 1 WLR 1412 at 1422 and *R v Secretary of State for the Home Dept, ex p*
f *Muboyayi* [1991] 4 All ER 72 at 81, [1992] QB 244 at 257, where Lord Donaldson MR clarified what he had said in *Derby & Co Ltd v Weldon* by explaining that in this context 'designed to' does not mean 'intended' but 'having the consequence that').

The judge's finding was that he had 'seen nothing to indicate that, if Ketchum's appeal were to succeed, those who control Holdings, namely Miss Poe and Mr
g O'Donoghue, would not seek to ensure that Holdings would honour the court's order'. I find this difficult to reconcile with the expressed opposition to the grant of injunctive relief on the basis that it will frustrate long laid plans by Mr O'Donoghue and Miss Poe as to use by them of the money, which implicitly if not expressly indicates that they will seek to effect a distribution of the money to
h themselves.

The judge appears to have given three or possibly four grounds for reaching his conclusion; first, the favourable view which he had formed of Miss Poe and Mr O'Donoghue from seeing them in the witness box. But for my part, I cannot see how this has any bearing on their intentions of keeping the proceeds of the
j sale of the shares within the jurisdiction, a question which was not in issue at the trial, and to which they have given no undertaking or evidence contrary to that to which I have referred. In the absence of injunctive relief the money will clearly go out of the jurisdiction to Jersey and I am not persuaded that there is any legal restraint on its distribution to the shareholders. Secondly, the judge referred to the fact that throughout Holdings had been represented by well-known and extremely competent solicitors and counsel. I doubt whether the judge really

intended to advance this as a reason; but if he did, it is plainly irrelevant. Thirdly, the judge pointed to the fact that Mr O'Donoghue is now living in this country. Again I cannot see that this is relevant. There is nothing to prevent Holdings taking the money out of the jurisdiction to Jersey where it is registered and judgment against Holdings would not be enforceable against the shareholders. Finally, the judge observed that it 'merely happens' that Holdings has sold the retained shares and received the proceeds of sale in this country. But I do not think this is anything to the point. Prior to trial, Holdings' only assets were the shares; it could not dispose of these since it was seeking to enforce the put option; there was therefore no question of Ketchum seeking Mareva relief before trial. But if the sole questions in the action had been those which arose in the dividend actions, and Holdings had cash assets within the jurisdiction and there was a real risk that these cash assets would be removed, it might well have been a classic case for Mareva relief. That, in effect, is the situation which now exists. Had I been satisfied that Ketchum has a sufficiently good arguable appeal, I would have granted the relief sought. As it is, in my judgment, the application should be dismissed.

PETER GIBSON LJ. I agree.

WARD LJ. I also agree.

Application dismissed.

Carolyn Toulmin   Barrister.

a
R v Secretary of State for Social Security, ex parte Joint Council for the Welfare of Immigrants

b
R v Secretary of State for Social Security, ex parte B

COURT OF APPEAL, CIVIL DIVISION

NEILL, SIMON BROWN AND WAITE LJJ

c   13, 14 MAY, 21 JUNE 1996

Social security – Income support – Urgent cases payments – Asylum seekers – Entitlement of asylum seekers to urgent cases payments – Secretary of State making regulations removing entitlement to urgent cases payments from those seeking asylum
d *otherwise than immediately on arrival in United Kingdom and from all claimants pending appeal from an adverse determination by Home Secretary – Whether regulations ultra vires – Social Security Contributions and Benefits Act 1992, ss 135(1)(2), 137(2)(a), 175(3)(a) – Social Security (Persons From Abroad) Miscellaneous Amendments Regulations 1996, reg 8.*

e   In order to discourage asylum claims by economic migrants the Secretary of State, acting under powers conferred on him by ss 135(1)(2), 137(2)(a) and 175(3)(a) of the Social Security Contributions and Benefits Act 1992, made the Social Security (Persons From Abroad) Regulations 1996. Regulation 8 amended the Income Support (General) Regulations 1987, which by reg 70 had enabled
f   persons seeking asylum in the United Kingdom who were not eligible for income support to claim urgent cases payments amounting to 90% of the normal income support level, so as to exclude from such entitlement those who sought asylum otherwise than immediately on arrival in the United Kingdom and those whose claims had been rejected by the Home Secretary and were awaiting appeal. The applicants applied for judicial review of the 1996 regulations, contending that
g   they were not within the powers conferred by the 1992 Act because they conflicted with the regime under the Asylum and Immigration Appeals Act 1993 and interfered with the rights of asylum seekers under that Act to immunity from removal pending determination of their applications and/or fundamental human rights. The Divisional Court dismissed the applications and the applicants
h   appealed.

Held (Neill LJ dissenting) – In order to be valid, subordinate legislation had to be not only within the powers of the enabling statute, but also so drawn as not to conflict with statutory rights already enacted by other primary legislation. While
j   the Secretary of State was entitled to discourage economic migrants by restricting their entitlement to benefits and while there was no conflict between the 1996 regulations and the 1993 Act merely because those regulations were designed to reduce the numbers of those invoking rights of application and appeal under the 1993 Act, the effect of the 1996 regulations was to render the rights of asylum seekers under the 1993 Act nugatory, since they would either be deterred by penury from pursuing their claims or be forced to live a life of destitution until

their claims were finally determined. That effect was so draconian that the 1996
regulations had to be held to be ultra vires. The appeals would accordingly be
allowed (see p 398 *f g*, p 399 *a*, p 400 *j* to p 401 *a d e* and p 402 *c d h j*, post).

R v Secretary of State for the Home Dept, ex p Leech [1993] 4 All ER 539 applied.
Hammersmith and Fulham London BC v Secretary of State for the Environment [1990]
3 All ER 589 distinguished.

Notes

For income support and urgent cases payments, see 33 *Halsbury's Laws* (4th edn)
para 856A.

For the Social Security Contributions and Benefits Act 1992, ss 135, 137, 175,
see 40 *Halsbury's Statutes* (4th edn) 673, 675, 715.

For the Asylum and Immigration Appeals Act 1993, see 31 *Halsbury's Statutes*
(4th edn) (1994 reissue) 215.

Cases referred to in judgments

Associated Provincial Picture Houses Ltd v Wednesbury Corp [1947] 2 All ER 680,
    [1948] 1 KB 223, CA.
Hammersmith and Fulham London BC v Secretary of State for the Environment [1990] 3
    All ER 589, [1991] 1 AC 521, [1990] 3 WLR 898, QBD, CA and HL.
R v Eastbourne (Inhabitants) (1803) 4 East 103, 102 ER 769.
R v Secretary of State for the Home Dept, ex p Anderson [1984] 1 All ER 920, [1984] QB
    778, [1984] 2 WLR 725, DC.
R v Secretary of State for the Home Dept, ex p Leech [1993] 4 All ER 539, [1994] QB 198,
    [1993] 3 WLR 1125, CA.
Raymond v Honey [1982] 1 All ER 756, [1983] 1 AC 1, [1982] 2 WLR 465, HL; affg
    [1981] 2 All ER 1084, [1981] QB 874, [1981] 3 WLR 218, DC.
Sandralingham v Secretary of State for the Home Dept, Rajendrakumar v Immigration
    Appeal Tribunal [1996] Imm AR 97, CA.
Solosky v R (1979) 105 DLR (3d) 745, Can SC.

Cases also cited or referred to in skeleton arguments

Airey v Ireland (1979) 2 EHRR 305, ECt HR.
Garland v British Rail Engineering Ltd [1982] 2 All ER 402, [1983] 2 AC 751, ECJ and
    HL.
Khaboka v Secretary of State for the Home Dept [1993] Imm AR 484, CA.
Padfield v Minister of Agriculture Fisheries and Food [1968] 1 All ER 694, [1968] AC
    997, CA and HL.
R v Hillingdon BC, ex p Streeting [1980] 3 All ER 413, [1980] 1 WLR 1425, DC and
    CA.

Appeals

By notices dated 29 March and 9 April 1996 respectively the applicants, the Joint
Council for the Welfare of Immigrants and B, an asylum seeker, appealed from
the decision of the Queen's Bench Divisional Court (Beldam LJ and Buxton J) on
26 March 1996 dismissing their applications for judicial review by way of a
declaration that the Social Security (Persons From Abroad) Miscellaneous
Amendments Regulations 1996, SI 1996/30, were invalid. The facts are set out in
the judgment of Neill LJ.

a   *Nicholas Blake QC* and *Frances Webber* (instructed by *Christian Fisher & Co*) for the applicants.
Stephen Richards and *Steven Kovats* (instructed by the *Solicitor to the Department of Social Security*) for the Secretary of State.

Cur adv vult

b   21 June 1996. The following judgments were delivered.

NEILL LJ.   After anxious consideration and despite the powerful reasons advanced by Simon Brown LJ, I find myself unable to agree with the conclusions which he has reached in his judgment.

c   The appellants seek to challenge the validity of the Social Security (Persons From Abroad) Miscellaneous Amendments Regulations 1996, SI 1996/30. The 1996 regulations came into force on 5 February 1996. I propose to direct my attention to the effect of these regulations on the eligibility of asylum seekers to receive income support under the urgent cases provisions.

d   Income support was introduced by the Social Security Act 1986. The principal Act now dealing with the criteria for eligibility for income support is the Social Security Contributions and Benefits Act 1992. Provisions relating to income-related benefits are contained in Pt VII of the 1992 Act. Section 124 in Pt VII of the 1992 Act provides, so far as is material, as follows:

e   '(1) A person in Great Britain is entitled to income support if—(a) he is of or over the age of 18 or, in prescribed circumstances and for a prescribed period, of or over the age of 16 ... (b) he has no income or his income does not exceed the applicable amount; (c) he is not engaged in remunerative work and, if he is a member of a married or unmarried couple, the other member is not so engaged; and (d) except in such circumstances as may be f   prescribed—(i) he is available for, and actively seeking, employment; (ii) he is not receiving relevant education ...'

Certain categories of persons, however, are ineligible for income support. These categories are set out in reg 21(3) of and Sch 7 to the Income Support (General) Regulations 1987, SI 1987/1967. The 1987 regulations have been amended from g   time to time, most recently by the 1996 regulations. The 1987 regulations were made under the Social Security Act 1986 and certain other enabling provisions; they now have effect as if made under, inter alia, the 1992 Act (see s 2(2)).

Regulation 21 of the 1987 regulations is concerned with special cases. Regulation 21 has to be read in conjunction with Sch 7, which sets out the h   categories of special cases and prescribes the amount if any (ie the applicable amount) which may be recovered by a person in one of these categories. A 'person from abroad' is one of these categories. Regulation 21(3) contains a definition of the term 'person from abroad' for the purposes of Sch 7. It is, however, unnecessary for the purposes of this judgment to examine the j   definition of 'person from abroad' in detail. It is sufficient to say that at all material times the definition has covered persons coming to this country seeking asylum.

Part VI of the 1987 regulations, however, contains provisions relating to claimants who fall into one of a number of categories of 'urgent cases'. One of these categories consists of certain persons from abroad as defined in reg 70(3) of the 1987 regulations. In the past and until 1993, persons seeking asylum, though

not within a defined group in reg 70(3), were in practice treated as 'urgent cases'
pending the final determination of their applications for asylum. Urgent cases   a
payments are paid at 90% of the normal income support level.

Until the enactment of the Asylum and Immigration Appeals Act 1993, persons
seeking asylum from abroad had no special status in UK immigration law. The
1993 Act was passed to make provision for persons who claimed asylum and to
introduce certain specified rights of appeal under the Immigration Act 1971. In   b
addition, it was provided in s 2 of the 1993 Act that nothing in the immigration
rules should lay down any practice which would be contrary to the Convention
relating to the Status of Refugees (Geneva, 28 July 1951; TS 39 (1954); Cmd 9171)
and the Protocol to that convention (New York, 31 January 1967; TS 15 (1969);
Cmd 3906). I shall refer to this convention as 'the 1951 convention'.

Following the coming into force of the 1993 Act, certain amendments were   c
made to the 1987 regulations. Regulation 70 of the 1987 regulations was
amended (by reg 2(2)(3) of the Income Support (General) Amendment No 3
Regulations 1993, SI 1993/1679) so as to include as a special category of 'person
from abroad', who might be treated as an urgent case, 'an asylum seeker' who
was such for the purposes of the newly introduced para (3A) of reg 70. The new   d
para (3A) was in these terms:

'For the purposes of this paragraph, a person—(a) becomes an asylum
seeker when he has submitted a claim for asylum to the Secretary of State
that it would be contrary to the United Kingdom's obligations under the
Convention for him to be removed from, or required to leave, the United   e
Kingdom and that claim is recorded by the Secretary of State as having been
made; and (b) ceases to be an asylum seeker when his claim is recorded by
the Secretary of State as having been finally determined or abandoned.'

In 1994 the 1987 regulations were further amended so that in reg 21(3), after the
definition of 'person from abroad', there was inserted the following definition: f

'"person from abroad" also means a claimant who is not habitually resident
in the United Kingdom, the Republic of Ireland, the Channel Islands or the
Isle of Man, but for this purpose, no claimant shall be treated as not
habitually resident in the United Kingdom who is ... (b) a refugee within the
definition in Article 1 of the [1951] Convention ... or (c) a person who has   g
been granted exceptional leave to remain in the United Kingdom by the
Secretary of State.'

This amendment was introduced by reg 4 of the Income-related Benefits
Schemes (Miscellaneous Amendments) (No 3) Regulations 1994, SI 1994/1807.

In broad terms the position at the end of 1995 was as follows. (1) Persons from   h
abroad, which included asylum seekers, were treated as special cases under the
1987 regulations. (2) Subject to exceptions, persons from abroad were not
entitled to income support. (3) Asylum seekers, however, as specified in para
(3A) of reg 70 of the 1987 regulations, were treated as 'urgent cases'. In the period
during which an asylum seeker was treated as an urgent case, he was entitled to   j
receive 90% of the normal income support benefit, until his claim for asylum had
been finally determined. (4) If an asylum seeker was successful or was granted
exceptional leave to remain, he would then become entitled to income support
in the usual way. He would no longer be treated as a person from abroad. (5) If,
however, his claim was finally rejected or abandoned he was no longer treated as
an urgent case and any right to any benefit as an urgent case came to an end.

a It was against this legislative background that the 1996 regulations were introduced. I turn next to the factual background.

It will be convenient to refer first to the statement made by the Secretary of State for Social Security to the Social Security Advisory Committee in accordance with s 174(2) of the Social Security Administration Act 1992, in which the purpose of the 1996 regulations was explained as follows:

b
'... 3. The purpose of these regulations—together with measures in the Asylum and Immigration Bill announced by the Home Secretary since the Regulations were referred to the Committee—is: to ensure that the UK remains a haven for those genuinely fleeing from persecution, whilst discouraging unfounded applications from those who are actually economic *c* migrants. The growing number of these unfounded applications prevents speedy processing of applications from those who genuinely merit asylum and imposes an unjustifiable cost on the British taxpayer.

4. The Government recognises that genuine refugees do not come to the UK to obtain social security benefits but to escape persecution. Their rights *d* to asylum will not be curtailed in any way by these regulations or the Bill. And those who make their true intentions clear when they arrive in this country, and seek asylum at the port of entry, will continue to have access to benefits while their claims are considered by the Home Office. However, well over 90 per cent of those claiming asylum are eventually found not to be genuine refugees. Most of these applicants are economic migrants. The *e* number of such applicants coming here is influenced by the ready availability of benefits. British benefits compare favourably with average wages in many countries from which asylum seekers come. And other European countries offer more limited benefits, less opportunity to work, and have tightened up the procedures applying to asylum seekers. As a result the number of asylum *f* claims in Western Europe as a whole has fallen by over a third since 1993 while in the same period the number of claims in Britain has doubled. So the proportion of all those claiming asylum in Europe who came to Britain has risen from 4 per cent to 13 per cent over ten years. Consequently, the total cost of social security benefits for asylum seekers already exceeds £200 million a year ...

g
6. The proposed regulations mean that people claiming asylum at the port of entry will continue to be eligible for benefits while their claim is processed by the Home Office. In addition benefits will be available to those who claim asylum after arrival in the UK as a result of a significant upheaval in their home country since their arrival here.

h
7. However, 70 per cent of all asylum claims are made by people who entered this country as tourists, students, business people or illegally and subsequently make a claim. The Government will continue to consider such asylum claims. But benefits will no longer be available to those who enter the country on one basis and subsequently make an asylum claim (except *j* following a significant upheaval in their home country).

8. Any British citizen whose claim for social security benefit is refused is not entitled to receive that benefit while appealing against refusal. Yet under the existing rules any asylum seeker whose claim for asylum is rejected by the Home Office can continue to claim benefits while appealing against refusal. As a result a high proportion of asylum seekers whose asylum claim is rejected appeal against the decision, even though only 4 per cent of such

appeals are upheld. The regulations submitted to the Committee would put
asylum seekers on a similar basis to British benefit claimants. They will *a*
continue to be entitled to appeal, but will not be entitled to receive benefits
while doing so ...'

The 1996 regulations came into force on 5 February 1996. The effect of the
1996 regulations in relation to income support was to exclude from the definition *b*
of asylum seekers those who sought asylum otherwise than on arrival in the
United Kingdom and those whose claims for asylum had been determined by the
Secretary of State or abandoned. An exception was made in cases where the
Secretary of State made a declaration that the country of which the asylum seeker
was a national was subject to a fundamental change in circumstances, such that a
person would not normally be asked to return to that country.   *c*

It was accepted on behalf of the appellants that, if looked at in isolation, the
enabling powers in the primary legislation empowered the Secretary of State to
make regulations specifying the persons who were or were not entitled to receive
income support and other income-related benefits. But, it was argued,
Parliament did not intend these enabling powers to be used in such a way that *d*
persons might be deprived of their common law or statutory rights, or in such a
way as to interfere with fundamental human rights. As the argument developed,
however, counsel for the appellants concentrated his attention on the suggested
conflict and inconsistency between the 1996 regulations and the rights conferred
and the regime established by the 1993 Act.

Counsel for the appellants drew our particular attention to s 6 of the 1993 Act. *e*
This section provides:

'During the period beginning when a person makes a claim for asylum and
ending when the Secretary of State gives him notice of the decision on the
claim, he may not be removed from, or required to leave, the United *f*
Kingdom.'

He also drew attention to the provisions in Sch 2 to the 1993 Act, which set out
the rights of appeal given to an asylum seeker who has received an adverse
decision from the Secretary of State. The schedule confers on a person making
use of the appeals procedure a similar immunity from being removed from the *g*
United Kingdom until his appeal has been finally determined.

The argument for the appellants was developed on the following lines.

(a) Post-entry claims were no more likely to be unfounded than claims on
entry into the United Kingdom. The statistics showed that post-entry claims and
on-entry claims had broadly similar prospects of success. There were many *h*
reasons why some genuine refugees were unable to or were inhibited from
claiming asylum at the port of entry.

(b) The statistics also showed that the claims of many asylum seekers were
successfully established only after an appeal brought in accordance with the 1993
Act. In addition, many asylum seekers were granted exceptional leave to remain *j*
at the conclusion of the appeal process.

(c) The effect of the 1996 regulations was to prevent many asylum seekers
from establishing a valid claim to refugee status or from obtaining the grant of
exceptional leave to remain.

(d) A further effect of the 1996 regulations was to render nugatory, in many
cases, the right to appeal conferred by the 1993 Act.

a (e) The categories of asylum seekers excluded from income support by the 1996 regulations were in effect rendered destitute. They were fugitives from their own country and were almost certain to have no financial resources of their own. The conditions imposed on them on entry made it impossible for them to seek employment.

(f) In summary, the 1996 regulations ran counter to the expressed will of
b Parliament that persons seeking asylum should not be required to leave the United Kingdom until their claims had been finally decided. The 1996 regulations were also in conflict with the obligations of the United Kingdom under the 1951 convention.

These are powerful arguments.

c In determining whether secondary legislation is ultra vires the enabling statute, however, it is necessary to consider both the primary purpose and the main effect of the legislation. It is also necessary to remember that a court faces particular difficulties when it is examining a decision which involves the allocation of public funds.

It is clear that, as the appellants contend, the inability to claim income support
d would have an adverse effect on a significant number of genuine asylum seekers. Some may be obliged to return to conditions of danger. Others may be obliged to live in penury or to abandon their claims to asylum. Yet others will be unable to exercise their rights to appeal or may forfeit the chance of being granted exceptional leave to remain. On the other hand, it is equally clear that the
e legislation is not aimed at the genuine asylum seeker.

The Secretary of State is given by Parliament the responsibility of deciding the categories of persons who are entitled to income support and other similar benefits. The choice of these categories and the allocation of resources between different groups is prima facie a matter for the Secretary of State, though it is accepted on his behalf that he could not exercise his powers in such a way as to
f act in direct contravention of an Act of Parliament.

It is not suggested that in framing the 1996 regulations, the Secretary of State acted irrationally or for an improper purpose. The appellant's arguments are founded on the alleged illegality of the 1996 regulations. But the Secretary of State has to try to strike a balance. The statistics demonstrate that a majority of
g asylum seekers are not found to be genuine refugees, though it is true that many may be granted exceptional leave to remain. In the view of the Secretary of State, the claims of the unsuccessful asylum seekers have placed an increasing and unsustainable burden on the resources, both in money and in manpower, which he has available.

h It must be a matter of great regret that some of those who are genuinely seeking asylum in this country will be turned away because they have no one to whom they can look for assistance and no money with which to obtain food or shelter. But Parliament has not imposed on the Secretary of State any express obligation to provide funds to enable persons claiming asylum to exercise all the
j rights conferred on them by the 1993 Act.

I regard the decision of this court in *R v Secretary of State for the Home Dept, ex p Leech* [1993] 4 All ER 539, [1994] QB 198 as plainly distinguishable. In that case, the prison rules had a direct effect on prisoners' rights to communicate with their legal representatives. Furthermore, it was recognised in *Ex p Leech* [1993] 4 All ER 539 at 555, [1994] QB 198 at 217 that s 47(1) of the Prison Act 1952 authorised some screening of correspondence passing between a prisoner and a solicitor.

As I have already said, in determining whether secondary legislation is ultra
vires, it is necessary to consider both the primary purpose and the main effect of *a*
the legislation. If secondary legislation brought into force under one statute has
an impact on rights conferred by another statute, or rights established by the
common law, the court has to consider the extent of that impact and, provided
the secondary legislation is prima facie within the enabling powers, to examine
the objects which the secondary legislation seeks to achieve. In my judgment, a *b*
court is only entitled to intervene where the interference with the other rights is
disproportionate to the objects to be achieved.

In the present case, the 1996 regulations were aimed primarily at those who are
not genuine asylum seekers and the principal impact of the 1996 regulations will
be on them. I accept that the 1996 regulations will also have a very serious effect
on a considerable number of genuine asylum seekers and those who might be *c*
hoping to obtain exceptional leave to remain, but I am not satisfied that the
Secretary of State has exceeded his powers. Parliament has entrusted the
Secretary of State with the administration of the system of benefits which
includes the allocation of the resources made available to him. He has to strike a
balance. The changes will interfere with existing rights and expectations. But the *d*
extent of that interference is important. Looking at the objects to be achieved by
the legislation and its results, I do not consider that the threshold of illegality has
been crossed.

I have found this to be a very anxious case, but, in my judgment, the court is
not entitled to declare the 1996 regulations to be illegal. I would dismiss the *e*
appeal.

SIMON BROWN LJ.

INTRODUCTION

In recent years the number of persons seeking asylum in the United Kingdom *f*
has risen significantly, both in absolute terms and in relation to the rest of
Western Europe. Of those applying, only some 25% are ultimately found to be
genuine refugees: 4 to 5% as strictly defined by the Convention relating to the
Status of Refugees (Geneva, 28 July 1951; TS 39 (1954); Cmd 9171) (as amended
by the 1967 Protocol (New York, 31 January 1967; TS 15 (1969); Cmd 3906); some
20% being granted exceptional leave to remain as, for example, fugitives from *g*
civil war or torture for a non-1951 convention reason, the borderline between the
two categories being often a very fine one. The 75% whose claims fail are
regarded as economic migrants. With the numbers now applying, the time taken
to resolve their claims is inevitably too long and the cost of all this to the taxpayer
is enormous. *h*

To speed up the process of decision-making and to reduce the expenditure on
benefits, the respondent Secretary of State for Social Security made the Social
Security (Persons From Abroad) Miscellaneous Amendments Regulations 1996,
SI 1996/30, which came into force on 5 February 1996. What in essence the 1996
regulations do is to remove all entitlement to income-related benefit from two *j*
particular categories of asylum seeker—those who submit their claims for asylum
otherwise than immediately upon arrival in the United Kingdom (subject to a
limited exception where the Home Secretary makes what is called an 'upheaval
declaration'), and those whose claims have been rejected by the Home Secretary
but who then appeal to the independent appellate authorities. The Secretary of
State's intention is to discourage economic migrants from making and pursuing

asylum claims. This, in turn, will speed up the system to the advantage of genuine refugees. All this is expected to save the taxpayer some £200m p a.

No one could dispute the desirability of these aims. There is, however, a problem. A significant number of genuine asylum seekers now find themselves faced with a bleak choice: whether to remain here destitute and homeless until their claims are finally determined, or whether instead to abandon their claims and return to face the very persecution they have fled.

The appellants' case, in essence, is that the 1996 regulations are in the result ultra vires. The enabling power, widely drawn though it is, cannot, they submit, have been intended to permit this degree of interference with statutory rights under the Asylum and Immigration Appeals Act 1993 and/or with fundamental human rights. The argument failed before the Divisional Court on 26 March 1996. It is now renewed before us.

THE ASYLUM REGIME

Until the 1993 Act, there was no primary immigration legislation dealing with asylum seekers. Rather, our 1951 convention obligations were acknowledged in the various immigration rules made under the Immigration Act 1971. These prohibited action not in accordance with the 1951 convention and provided the skeleton of a determination procedure in accordance with guidance contained in the UNHCR Handbook. The 1993 Act put into statutory form our recognition of the primacy of the 1951 convention (s 2) and our obligation of non-refoulement under art 33 of the 1951 convention. As to this, s 6 provides:

'During the period beginning when a person makes a claim for asylum and ending when the Secretary of State gives him notice of the decision on the claim, he may not be removed from, or required to leave, the United Kingdom.'

Section 8 and paras 7, 8 and 9 of Sch 2 to the 1993 Act give parallel protection until the end of the appeal process. In short, the 1993 Act provides determination procedures, protection from refoulement, and appeal rights to all categories of asylum seekers, the appeal procedures being part of the overall asylum determination process: see *Sandralingham v Secretary of State for the Home Dept, Rajendrakumar v Immigration Appeal Tribunal* [1996] Imm AR 97 at 112:

'... in asylum cases the appellate structure as applied by the 1993 Act is to be regarded rather as an extension of the decision-making process.'

It is further relevant to note that all asylum seekers are treated alike, subject only to this exception: there is provision in the 1993 Act (see para 5 of Sch 2) whereby the Home Secretary can certify that a claim is without foundation either as not raising any 1951 convention issue or as being otherwise frivolous or vexatious. This procedure, conveniently called the 'without foundation procedure', is typically used for what are known as 'safe third country cases'. When used, there are expedited time limits at all stages of the procedure and, if the special adjudicator agrees with the Secretary of State's certificate, there is no further appeal to the Immigration Appeal Tribunal.

THE POSITION OF ASYLUM SEEKERS BEFORE THE 1996 REGULATIONS

Although we were treated to the very fullest exposition of the legislative history of the benefits system, both generally and more particularly as it applied

to various categories of immigrants and asylum seekers down the years, it seems
to me that in fact only the broadest appreciation is required.   *a*

The principal (consolidating) Act now dealing with the criteria for eligibility for
state benefits is the Social Security Contributions and Benefits Act 1992. Part VII
(ss 123 to 137) deal with income-related benefits—income support, housing
benefit, family credit and council tax benefit—which together are designed to
ensure a basic minimum provision for those not entitled to contributory benefits   *b*
(such as unemployment or sickness benefit).

The Income Support (General) Regulations 1987, SI 1987/1967 (as amended by
SI 1993/1679 to deal specifically with asylum seekers, who for the first time
entered the statutory language by way of the 1993 Act) have effect as if made
under, inter alia, the 1992 Act. This is the principal statutory instrument
governing entitlement to income support. Regulation 21(3) of and Sch 7 to the   *c*
1987 regulations set out categories of persons who are generally ineligible for
income support. 'Persons from abroad', who include asylum seekers, are
amongst them. Their requirements are deemed to be nil. By reg 70 of the 1987
regulations, however, certain persons from abroad, including asylum seekers, are
eligible for 'urgent cases payments'. These are paid at 90% of the normal income   *d*
support level. These payments are sometimes called the 'safety net within the
safety net'. They act, moreover, as the gateway to other safety net benefits such
as housing benefit, and to other benefits in kind such as free school meals, free
prescriptions and free dental treatment.

Prior, therefore, to the coming into force of the 1996 regulations now
impugned, all asylum seekers were entitled to urgent cases payments amounting   *e*
to 90% of normal income support benefit and, in addition, to housing benefit and
the other benefits 'passported' through income support. When homeless, they
were in the same position under Pt III of the Housing Act 1985 as other homeless
people, save only that they had to be content with 'any accommodation,
however temporary', and any need they established was to be regarded as   *f*
'temporary only' (see s 4 of the 1993 Act).

THE 1996 REGULATIONS

The regulations impugned were made in the exercise of powers conferred in
particular by the following provisions in the 1992 Act:

g

'**135.**—(1) The applicable amount, in relation to any income-related
benefit, shall be such amount or the aggregate of such amounts as may be
prescribed in relation to that benefit.

(2) The power to prescribe applicable amounts conferred by subsection
(1) above includes power to prescribe nil as an applicable amount ...

137 ... (2) Regulations may make provision for the purposes of this Part of   *h*
this Act—(a) as to circumstances in which a person is to be treated as being
or not being in Great Britain ...

175 ... (3) ... any power under this Act to make regulations ... may be
exercised—(a) either in relation to all cases to which the power extends, or
in relation to those cases subject to specified exceptions, or in relation to any   *j*
specified cases or classes of case ...'

Regulation 8 of the 1996 regulations amends regs 21 and 70 of the 1987
regulations so as to remove entitlement to urgent cases payments from all asylum
seekers, save those who submit a claim for asylum on arrival in the United
Kingdom and, even then, entitlement ceases on the date when the Home

a Secretary records the claim to have been determined by him or abandoned. The only exception to this is when the Home Secretary makes an 'upheaval declaration'—when, that is, an in-country claim is made within three months of the Home Secretary making a declaration that the country of which the claimant is a national is subject to such a fundamental change in circumstances that he would not normally order the return of a person to that country. The rest of this

b judgment will take this 'upheaval declaration' exception as read.

Regulation 7 of the 1996 regulations amends the regulations governing entitlement to housing benefit (the Housing Benefit (General) Regulations 1987, SI 1987/1971, as amended) in such a way as to remove that particular entitlement in precisely corresponding circumstances.

It is, I think, unnecessary to recite the actual language of any of the regulations

c by which these various results are achieved: the route is somewhat tortuous.

THE EFFECT OF THE 1996 REGULATIONS ON ASYLUM SEEKERS

It follows that from 5 February 1996 two main categories of asylum seeker are wholly excluded from benefit: (1) in-country (as opposed to on-arrival) claimants;

d and (2) all claimants pending appeal from an adverse determination of the Home Secretary. These I shall call 'the deprived asylum seekers'.

In the event of homelessness, the deprived asylum seekers are peculiarly disadvantaged. Not, of course, if they have a priority need for accommodation (as do roughly a third who have dependent children): then the housing authority is obliged to house them, even though they can pay no housing benefit. (The

e Secretary of State has now reached agreement with local authorities to pay them a substantial part of the costs involved and thereby bought off judicial review challenges to the 1996 regulations, which the authorities themselves had instituted.) But local authorities have refused to accept that asylum seekers deprived of all benefits have a priority need on the grounds of being 'vulnerable'

f for 'other special reason' within the meaning of s 59(1)(c) of the 1985 Act—this being a separate issue raised before us on an immediately following appeal.

If the local authorities are correct in that view, it follows that those of the deprived asylum seekers not otherwise in priority need face the following situation.

g (1) They have no access whatever either to funds or to benefits in kind.

(2) They have no accommodation and, being ineligible for housing benefit, no prospect of securing any.

(3) By the express terms of their leave to stay, they are invariably forbidden from seeking employment for six months and, even assuming that thereafter they

h apply for and obtain permission to work, their prospects of obtaining it are likely to be poor, particularly if they speak no English.

(4) They are likely to be without family, friends or contacts and thus in a position of peculiar isolation with no network of community support.

(5) Their claims take on average some 18 months to determine, on occasions

j as long as four years. An individual has no control over this and no means of hastening a final decision. If eventually the claim succeeds there is no provision for back payment.

(6) Quite apart from the need to keep body and soul together pending the final determination of a claim, expense is likely to be incurred in pursuing it. Applicants must attend for interviews with the Home Office and with any advisers they may have. They must have an address where they can be contacted

with notices of appointments or decisions. To miss an appointment or the time *a* for appeal is to forgo their claim.

Others, it is true, face the same total loss of benefits under the various regulations: prisoners, those in holy orders and virtually all other immigrants. But prisoners and the clergy each have their own obvious support systems, respectively the state and their religious communities. And non-asylum-seeking immigrants have, since 1980, invariably been admitted subject to the condition of *b* 'no recourse to public funds' and, more importantly, unlike asylum seekers, can in any event return to their country of origin. Truly, deprived asylum seekers are in a unique position and one which threatens total destitution. No doubt, as Mr Richards submits, voluntary organisations do what they can to help. The need, however, far exceeds their capacity. As Mr Blake puts it, charity cannot bridge the gap between the 1996 regulations and the 1993 Act. *c*

Before leaving this section of the judgment, I should just add this. Whatever may be the correct decision on the homelessness appeal, its effect, we are told, is likely to be comparatively short-lived. The Secretary of State proposes to bring into force this summer further legislation to relieve local authorities of any duty to house deprived asylum seekers, whether in priority need or not. The position *d* will, in short, worsen.

Mr Richards submits, and I would accept, that the 1996 regulations must be judged as at the date they were brought into force and not by reference to later legislation. By the same token, however, the Secretary of State must have known that local housing authorities would deny any liability to house most of the deprived asylum seekers. And whatever effect the 1996 regulations may have in *e* terms of accelerating the decision-making process for those who remain, that effect, too, could only be for the future.

THE APPELLANTS' ARGUMENTS

The 1996 regulations are said to be ultra vires because of implied restrictions in *f* the enabling power. Two central arguments are advanced. The first and wider one is that the 1996 regulations are inconsistent with the 1993 Act in the sense that they create various sub-categories of asylum seekers in a way that the 1993 Act itself does not. It is not, submits Mr Blake, for the Secretary of State in regulations to redefine how asylum seekers should be treated, even with regard to benefit payments. *g*

Secondly, and more narrowly, Mr Blake submits that the 1996 regulations materially interfere with the exercise of rights by asylum seekers under the 1993 Act. This I shall call 'the conflict argument'. Let me consider each in turn.

(1) *Inconsistency* *h*

The 1993 Act makes no distinction between on-arrival and post-arrival (sometimes called 'in-country') claimants nor, indeed, in terms of entitlement to remain, between those awaiting the Home Secretary's decision and those awaiting decision on appeal. There is, therefore, in this sense a clear lack of consistency between the 1996 regulations and the 1993 Act.

Similarly, the mechanism available in the 1993 Act by way of the 'without *j* foundation procedure' for speedily weeding out obviously bogus claims finds no reflection in the 1996 regulations.

Moreover, submits Mr Blake, the Secretary of State has no good reason to distinguish, as he does, between the different categories of asylum seeker with a view to discouraging unmeritorious claims. The available statistics, as well as the facts of B's case, make the point. B, it may be noted, despite having claimed a asylum on the day she reached the United Kingdom, forfeited her 'on-arrival' status by waiting to do so until she arrived, via Waterloo, at Lunar House, the Home Office's immigration centre at Croydon, rather than applying on the Eurostar train into Waterloo itself. As for the statistics, these appear to show no significant difference in the rate of recognition as refugees between those applying on arrival (about one third) and those who apply after entry. Similarly,

b no significant difference exists between the rates recognised respectively by the Home Secretary and, following his initial refusal, on appeal (sometimes by way of exceptional leave granted thereafter upon the appellate authorities' recommendation). Accordingly, submits Mr Blake, the mechanism of deterrence falls on the just and unjust alike. In general terms, perhaps, the later an asylum application is made, the more likely it is to be bogus. But, as the Social Security

c Advisory Committee (the SSAC) stated in para 38 of their report (to which I shall shortly refer):

> 'There are many valid reasons why people do not make their asylum claim immediately on arrival. Lack of knowledge of the procedures, arriving in a confused and frightened state, language difficulties or fear of officialdom
d > may all be insuperable barriers to making any kind of approach to the authorities at port of entry. Many intending applicants will quite reasonably want to get help and advice before making their claim. We are told by refugee organisations that there is a common fear that making an asylum application while still in port is more likely to result in immediate deportation, or being held in detention. For these and other reasons, it is
e > easy to see why for the majority of asylum seekers it appears much safer to make their claim from inside the UK.'

No doubt, submits Mr Blake, the asylum scheme itself could properly dictate that in-country applications not made within say four or six weeks of arrival should be
f treated as prima facie frivolous and vexatious and dealt with under the 'without foundation procedure' but, the argument runs, the benefit system, so long as it is contained in regulations rather than in primary legislation, must remain in harmony with the statutory asylum regime.

For my part, I would reject this argument. The responsibility for the benefit budget lies with the Secretary of State and not with the Home Secretary. Subject
g always to the conflict argument, the Secretary of State is perfectly entitled to reach his own decision as to how asylum seekers should be treated and as to whether all should be treated in the same way. The enabling power is amply wide for these purposes—see particularly s 175(3)(a) of the 1992 Act. He is under no obligation to align the benefit scheme to the approach adopted in the 1993 Act.

h As to the distinction made by the Secretary of State between the different categories of asylum seeker, there may or may not be good reason for this. With regard to these matters, however, the Secretary of State is answerable to Parliament rather than to the courts, not least given the absence of any irrationality challenge. As Mr Richards points out, moreover, a detailed scheme exists for parliamentary oversight and control of the benefit system. Part XIII of
j the Social Security Administration Act 1992 (ss 170 to 176) provides for the Secretary of State to seek advice from specialist bodies, here the SSAC. True, that committee advised that the proposed 1996 regulations should be abandoned, but the Secretary of State was not bound to follow it. His duty, rather, was to present to Parliament a reasoned response to their report. This he did. The regulations were made subject to negative resolution on 11 January 1996 and debated that day in both Houses of Parliament. They then became the subject of a further

report by the all-party Social Security Committee of the House of Commons. Following a further House of Commons debate on 23 January 1996, they came *a* into force on 5 February. One can argue, as Parliament did, about the justice and logic of the approach followed by the 1996 regulations in contrast to that adopted in the 1993 Act. That, however, as Mr Richards rightly submits, cannot found a vires challenge. I repeat, the Secretary of State was not obliged to follow the same indiscriminate approach to asylum seekers as the 1993 Act adopts. *b*

(2) *The conflict argument—interference with rights*
    The right of access to refugee determination procedures, including appeals, is, submits Mr Blake, fundamental to the protection granted by the 1951 convention to which the 1993 Act gives effect. To deprive large categories of asylum seeker of the most basic subsistence benefits constitutes a serious impediment to such *c* access, significantly reducing their ability to make and process asylum claims (including attending interviews and hearings, collecting supporting evidence, keeping in touch with legal advisers, and above all, staying alive and healthy). In the result, he submits, a number of asylum seekers will either be forced by the 1996 regulations to forgo their claims (or appeals) and leave the country, or else *d* be so seriously handicapped in bringing them to a successful conclusion that refugee status may, on occasions, be wrongly refused them.
    Furthermore, submits Mr Blake, not only are the 1996 regulations bound to cause many asylum seekers to forgo their claims, they are positively intended to do so: as the Secretary of State accepts, their very object is to discourage numbers of asylum seekers from coming to this country or, at any rate, from pursuing their *e* claims here. So be it, responds Mr Richards, but the intention is to discourage bogus asylum seekers rather than genuine ones and, by the nature of things, it is the bogus ones—economic migrants out to exploit the benefit system—who are most likely to be deterred. These, after all, are by definition (a) here for benefit rather than protection, (b) able without risk to return whence they came, and (c) *f* less expectant of obtaining long-term leave at the end of the determination process, and thus presumably less prepared to await the outcome in penury.
    This part of Mr Richards' argument, I would accept. To my mind, there is no conflict between the 1996 regulations and the 1993 Act merely because the 1996 regulations are designed to reduce the numbers of those invoking rights of application and appeal under the 1993 Act. That said, however, it can hardly be *g* doubted that some genuine asylum seekers, as well as bogus ones, are likely to be deterred by penury from pursuing their claims and thus be forced to return to the very persecution which they have sought to escape. As the UNHCR stated in their evidence to the SSAC:

h
    'UNHCR is concerned that asylum seekers may be forced into unlawful exploitative conditions to support themselves whilst exercising their appeal rights. It is difficult to speculate on the range of illegal activities that increasingly desperate persons may resort to, but these are likely to include unlawful employment, dishonesty offences and perhaps more serious *j* criminality involving drugs, prostitution or violent crimes. Such activity could bring them into conflict with the law and undermine the delicate balance of reciprocity that exists between the State offering asylum and the asylum seeker. Confronted with these choices even genuine but desperate refugees might be compelled to return to face persecution in the country of origin, rather than remain in an impossible position in the United Kingdom. In our opinion, this could amount to *"constructive refoulement"* and may place

a   the United Kingdom in violation of its obligations under the Refugee Convention.'

Specific statutory rights are not to be cut down by subordinate legislation passed under the vires of a different Act. So much is clear. These asylum seekers' rights, submits Mr Blake, are being gravely interfered with by the 1996 regulations.

b   They should, therefore, be struck down, just as this court struck down a prison rule giving an unrestricted power to read, and in certain circumstances stop, correspondence between a prisoner and his solicitor: see *R v Secretary of State for the Home Dept, ex p Leech* [1993] 4 All ER 539, [1994] QB 198. The prisoner's basic rights in question were identified as those of legal professional privilege, together with unimpeded access both to the court and to legal advice. It was with these

c   rights that the rule conflicted. The Court of Appeal said ([1993] 4 All ER 539 at 554, [1994] QB 198 at 216–217):

'The question is whether r 33(3) [of the Prison Rules 1964] creates an impediment to these basic rights. Frequently, it may not be possible for a solicitor to visit a prisoner as soon or as often as may be required. Moreover,

d   correspondence will often be the most effective medium, e g in giving advice. A prisoner may wish to obtain legal advice about the conduct of those in authority over him. He may want to know whether he has a remedy against the police, individual prison officers, the governor of the prison or the Home Office. In *Solosky v R* (1979) 105 DLR (3d) 745 at 760 Dickson J described the impact of a right to read a prisoner's correspondence as follows: "Nothing is

e   more likely to have a 'chilling' effect upon the frank and free exchange and disclosure of confidences, which should characterise the relationship between inmate and counsel, than knowledge that what has been written will be read by some third person, and perhaps used against the inmate at a later date." We respectfully agree. An unrestricted right to read

f   correspondence passing between a solicitor and a prisoner must create a considerable disincentive to a prisoner exercising his basic rights as expounded in *Honey v Raymond* [1982] 1 All ER 756, [1983] 1 AC 1 and *R v Secretary of State for the Home Dept, ex p Anderson* [1984] 1 All ER 920, [1984] QB 778. In our view it creates a substantial impediment to the exercise of those basic rights. And the right to stop letters on the grounds of

g   objectionability or prolixity means that access to a solicitor by the medium of correspondence can be denied altogether. In our view r 33(3) is ultra vires so far as it purports to apply to correspondence between prisoners and their legal advisers.'

This case, submits Mr Blake, is a fortiori to *Ex p Leech*, the 1996 regulations here

h   involving an even more direct effect upon an even greater human right.

THE RESPONDENT'S REPLY TO THE CONFLICT ARGUMENT

Mr Richards' arguments in response are essentially these. First that the court should be reluctant to read into the broad power conferred by the 1992 Act any

j   further restriction than that regulations made under it should not actually contravene other primary legislation. The question of benefit control is one for the political judgment of the Secretary of State, subject only to the approval of Parliament. A parallel exists with the situation under consideration by the House of Lords in *Hammersmith and Fulham London BC v Secretary of State for the Environment* [1990] 3 All ER 589, [1991] 1 AC 521. In both cases, the Secretary of State was acting within a carefully defined system of parliamentary scrutiny and control in an important area of the national economy and with the legitimate aim of removing an unwarranted burden on public funds. Accordingly, here as there, the court should be yet more reluctant than usual to interfere with governmental *a* action: the super-*Wednesbury* test should apply (see *Associated Provincial Picture Houses Ltd v Wednesbury Corp* [1947] 2 All ER 680, [1948] 1 KB 233).

Second, Mr Richards submits that the appellants' argument, although couched in terms of an implied limitation on powers conferred by the 1992 Act, in effect contends for a positive duty upon the Secretary of State under that Act, a duty at *b* least to make urgent needs payments to those claiming asylum under the 1993 Act. If it was unlawful for the 1996 regulations to deprive certain categories of asylum seeker of such benefit, it would, he suggests, have been unlawful not to grant it in the first place. There is, however, submits Mr Richards, no such duty on the Secretary of State, either under the 1951 convention or in domestic law. True, such a duty arises under art 24 of the 1951 convention if and when a *c* claimant's refugee status is recognised; before that, however, there is none. It would, he submits, be extraordinary if, albeit not in breach of the 1951 convention, a state should be found guilty of constructive refoulement merely by failing to provide economic assistance to claimants.

Third, Mr Richards submits that only direct interference with established *d* rights constitutes a sufficient basis for holding regulations ultra vires on the ground of repugnancy. Here, he contends, the effect of the 1996 regulations is at most indirect and speculative.

THE DIVISIONAL COURT'S JUDGMENT

The appellants' challenge below failed on the ground that the exercise of the *e* regulation-making power is 'only to be taken to be ultra vires ... when it involves a plain and direct interference with other provisions'. A little earlier the court had said:

> 'Withdrawal of benefit cannot in our view be characterised as deportation, expulsion or refoulement. The UN Convention, the UNHCR Handbook *f* and the 1993 Act cannot be read as requiring or creating an expectation of any particular form of positive support to be extended to refugees or asylum seekers. What is prohibited is state action to enforce removal. Although we accept that conditions might be imposed so hostile to the continued presence of asylum seekers that a decision to leave in order to escape those conditions *g* amounted to constructive deportation, we do not think that the withdrawal of benefit can properly be regarded as positive action on the part of the state amounting to returning the asylum seeker to the country of origin.'

CONCLUSIONS   *h*

I do not pretend to have found this by any means an easy case. Powerful arguments are advanced on both sides. The *Leech* principle is undoubtedly of assistance to the appellants and yet the analogy with *Leech* is not, as it seems to me, exact. As stated, I, for my part, have no difficulty in accepting the Secretary of State's right to discourage economic migrants by restricting their benefits. That of itself indicates that the 1996 regulations are not invalid merely because of *j* their 'chilling effect' (Dickson J's phrase in *Solosky v R*) upon the exercise of the deprived asylum seekers' rights under the 1993 Act.

It is, moreover, as I recognise, one thing, as in *Ex p Leech,* to condemn direct interference with the unquestioned basic rights there identified; another to assert that the Secretary of State, here, is bound to maintain some benefit provision to asylum seekers so as to ensure that those with genuine claims will not be driven a by penury to forfeit them, whether by leaving the country before their determination or through an inability to prosecute them effectively.

The present challenge, I therefore acknowledge, involves carrying the *Ex p Leech* principle a step further and this, moreover, in a field where Parliament has been closely involved in the making of the impugned 1996 regulations.

I have nevertheless concluded that it is a step the court should take.
b Parliamentary sovereignty is not here in question: the 1996 regulations are subordinate legislation only. The *Hammersmith* approach cannot, in my judgment, avail the respondent: it applies only once the court has determined that the 1996 regulations do not contravene the express or implied requirements of a statute—the very question here at issue. Parliament, for its part, has clearly demonstrated by the 1993 Act a full commitment to the United Kingdom's 1951
c convention obligations. When the regulation-making power now contained in the 1992 Act was first conferred, there was no question of asylum seekers being deprived of all benefit and thereby rendered unable to pursue their claims. Although I reject Mr Blake's argument that the legislative history of this power (including, in particular, an indication to Parliament in 1986 that the government was then intending to exercise it in continuing support of asylum seekers) itself
d serves to limit its present scope, the fact that asylum seekers have hitherto enjoyed benefit payments appears to me not entirely irrelevant. After all, the 1993 Act confers on asylum seekers fuller rights than they had ever previously enjoyed, the right of appeal in particular. And yet these regulations for some genuine asylum seekers at least, must now be regarded as rendering these rights
e nugatory. Either that, or the 1996 regulations necessarily contemplate for some a life so destitute that, to my mind, no civilised nation can tolerate it. So basic are the human rights here at issue, that it cannot be necessary to resort to the Convention for the Protection of Human Rights and Fundamental Freedoms (Rome, 4 November 1950; TS 71 (1953); Cmd 8969) to take note of their violation.
f Nearly 200 years ago Lord Ellenborough CJ in *R v Eastbourne (Inhabitants)* (1803) 4 East 103 at 107, 102 ER 769 at 770 said:

> 'As to there being no obligation for maintaining poor foreigners before the statutes ascertaining the different methods of acquiring settlements, the law of humanity, which is anterior to all positive laws, obliges us to afford them relief, to save them from starving ...'

g
True, no obligation arises under art 24 of the 1951 convention until asylum seekers are recognised as refugees. But that is not to say that up to that point their fundamental needs can properly be ignored. I do not accept they can. Rather, I would hold it unlawful to alter the benefit regime so drastically as must inevitably
h not merely prejudice, but on occasion defeat, the statutory right of asylum seekers to claim refugee status.

If and when that status is recognised, refugees become entitled under art 24 to benefit rights equivalent to nationals. Not for one moment would I suggest that prior to that time their rights are remotely the same; only that some basic provision should be made, sufficient for genuine claimants to survive and pursue
j their claims.

It is not for this court to indicate how best to achieve this consistently with the Secretary of State's legitimate aim of deterring unmeritorious claims. I content myself merely with noting that many European countries, so we are told, provide benefits in kind by way of refugee hostels and meal vouchers; that urgent needs payments could be made at a significantly lower rate than the 90% rate hitherto paid; and that certain categories of claim (perhaps, as suggested, in-country

claims brought more than four or six weeks post-arrival) could be processed
under the 'without foundation procedure'. All that will doubtless be for   *a*
consideration. For the purposes of this appeal, however, it suffices to say that I,
for my part, regard the 1996 regulations now in force as so uncompromisingly
draconian in effect that they must indeed be held ultra vires. I would found my
decision not on the narrow ground of constructive refoulement envisaged by the
UNHCR and rejected by the Divisional Court, but rather on the wider ground   *b*
that rights necessarily implicit in the 1993 Act are now inevitably being
overborne. Parliament cannot have intended a significant number of genuine
asylum seekers to be impaled on the horns of so intolerable a dilemma: the need
either to abandon their claims to refugee status or alternatively to maintain them
as best they can but in a state of utter destitution. Primary legislation alone could
in my judgment achieve that sorry state of affairs.   *c*
    I would allow this appeal.

WAITE LJ. The principle is undisputed. Subsidiary legislation must not only be
within the vires of the enabling statute, but must also be so drawn as not to
conflict with statutory rights already enacted by other primary legislation. Once   *d*
that is accepted, the question in the present case becomes one of degree and
extent. Do the impugned regulations contained in the Social Security (Persons
From Abroad) Miscellaneous Amendments Regulations 1996, SI 1996/30,
deprive a significant number of asylum seekers of the rights conferred by the
Asylum and Immigration Appeals Act 1993 to remain in the United Kingdom
while their claims are considered and any appeal is disposed of? The public as a   *e*
whole, and those asylum seekers with genuine claims to press in particular, have
an interest in discouraging spurious or ill-founded applications. The question is
not to be answered, however, by appeal to such considerations of policy,
persuasive though they may be. Nor, in my judgment, is the answer to be found
through an inquiry as to whether the effect of the 1996 regulations on the rights   *f*
conferred by the 1993 Act is direct or indirect. It involves looking with an
objective eye at the practical result for most of those affected by the 1996
regulations. The class of asylum seeker comprehended by the regulations is a
wide one—embracing all those who have made their application after arrival or
who are awaiting the determination of an appeal against refusal of an application.
They are not permitted to work for reward. Among their number there may be   *g*
a few—but it can only be a very few—who are able to benefit from the efforts of
the charities who work devotedly, but with severely limited resources, to house
and help asylum seekers. But the effect of the 1996 regulations upon the vast
majority will be to leave them without even the most basic means of subsistence.
The stark question that has, therefore, to be answered is whether regulations   *h*
which deprive a very large number of asylum seekers of the basic means of
sustaining life itself have the effect of rendering their ostensible statutory right to
a proper consideration of their claims in this country valueless in practice by
making it not merely difficult, but totally impossible for them to remain here to
pursue those claims. For all the reasons stated by Simon Brown LJ, with which I   *j*
agree entirely, the answer to the question, when it is so expressed, can only, in
my view, be Yes. I would allow the appeal.

Appeal allowed.

                                        Paul Magrath Esq   Barrister.

a # Wallace Smith Trust Co Ltd (in liq) v Deloitte Haskins & Sells (a firm) and another

COURT OF APPEAL, CIVIL DIVISION

b NEILL, SIMON BROWN AND WAITE LJJ

15, 16 MAY, 10 JULY 1996

Discovery – Production of documents – Order for production for inspection – Transcripts and tapes of interviews – Interviews of partner and employee of defendants conducted by Serious Fraud Office under statutory powers – Plaintiff seeking
c *production of transcripts and tapes – Whether production necessary for fair disposal of action – Whether court should inspect documents when considering application for order for production – RSC Ord 24, r 13.*

Discovery – Production contrary to public interest – Documents containing information
d *obtained under statutory powers – Transcripts and tapes of interviews of partner and employee of defendants conducted by Serious Fraud Office – Whether public interest immunity attaching to transcripts and tapes – Whether defendants entitled to withhold production of transcripts and tapes – Criminal Justice Act 1987, s 2.*

e The plaintiff company carried on business as a bank authorised and regulated by the Bank of England and its auditors were the first defendant, which subsequently merged with the second defendant. In April 1991 joint liquidators were appointed in respect of the company, which shortly afterwards ceased business. The Serious Fraud Office thereupon investigated the affairs of the company and served notices pursuant to s 2 of the Criminal Justice Act 1987 on D and G, a
f partner and employee respectively of the defendants. D and G were interviewed by the Serious Fraud Office in February 1992 and the interviews were recorded on tape and transcripts were produced. In July the liquidators commenced proceedings against the defendants, alleging that they were in breach of their duties both in contract and in tort in failing to detect that the company's business was being fraudulently conducted. The liquidators sought discovery of the tapes
g and transcripts of interviews with D and G and applied for an order for their production for inspection pursuant to RSC Ord 24, r 13. The defendants claimed that those documents were privileged from production as being subject to public interest immunity on the grounds that they contained information disclosed to a public body under compulsion of law and that it had not been shown that their
h production was necessary for fairly disposing of the action, as required by Ord 24, r 13. The judge, who did not inspect the documents, held that the documents did not attract public interest immunity, but he dismissed the liquidators' application on the ground that he was not satisfied that production of the tapes and transcripts was necessary for the fair disposal of the action. The liquidators
j appealed.

Held – (1) Where an application was made to the court for an order for the production of documents pursuant to RSC Ord 24, r 13 and the applicant showed that such production might be necessary for the fair disposal of the action, the court should inspect the documents and should only refuse an order if, after considering them in the light of the material already in the applicant's possession, it concluded that they were not in fact necessary for such disposal. In considering the application, the court should examine the facts of the case and in particular *a* should consider the central issues of the action, the nature of the documents and the information they were likely to contain; it could also take into account whether the documents were confidential and, if so, whether the information sought could be obtained by some other means. Since the tapes and transcripts were undoubtedly likely to contain material necessary for the fair disposal of the *b* action as the witnesses would have been well informed at the time of their interviews owing to an internal inquiry by the defendants, and the tapes were likely to provide an insight into the state of knowledge of the defendants in the period leading up to the collapse of the company, it followed that the judge had misdirected himself in failing to inspect the documents. The appeal would therefore be allowed and the matter referred back to the judge so that he could *c* do so (see p 412 *e* to *j*, p 413 *e* to *g j* to p 414 *b*, p 416 *g*, p 417 *a*, p 418 *c*, p 419 *d* and p 420 *c j*, post); *Science Research Council v Nassé, BL Cars Ltd (formerly Leyland Cars) v Vyas* [1979] 3 All ER 673 and *Kaufmann v Credit Lyonnais Bank* (1995) Times, 1 February applied.

(2) Although the tapes and transcripts came into existence by reason of the *d* special powers conferred on the Serious Fraud Office by the 1987 Act, which contained detailed provisions setting out the use which the Serious Fraud Office might make of the information which was provided to it and the persons to whom that information might be disclosed, there was no basis on which the defendants could claim public interest immunity for the copies of those documents in their hands. It followed that that claim was without foundation *e* (see p 416 *c f*, p 417 *a* and p 420 *d e j*, post).

Notes

For production of documents by order of the court, see 13 *Halsbury's Laws* (4th edn) para 64, and for withholding documents on the ground of public interest *f* immunity, see ibid paras 86–91, and for cases on those subjects, see 18 *Digest* (2nd reissue) 203–219, *1822–1879*.

For the Criminal Justice Act 1987, s 2, see 12 *Halsbury's Statutes* (4th edn) (1994 reissue) 1103.

Cases referred to in judgments *g*

Air Canada v Secretary of State for Trade (No 2) [1983] 1 All ER 910, [1983] 2 AC 394, [1983] 2 WLR 494, HL.

Arbuthnott v Fagan (1994) Independent, 11 July, [1994] CA Transcript 841.

Arrows Ltd, Re (No 4), Hamilton v Naviede [1994] 3 All ER 814, [1995] 2 AC 75, [1994] *h* 3 WLR 656, HL.

Bellenden (formerly Satterthwaite) v Satterthwaite [1948] 1 All ER 343, CA.

Cie Financière et Commerciale du Pacifique v Peruvian Guano Co (1882) 11 QBD 55, CA.

Dolling-Baker v Merrett [1991] 2 All ER 890, [1990] 1 WLR 1205, CA. *j*

Kaufmann v Credit Lyonnais Bank (1995) Times, 1 February.

Lonrho plc v Fayed (No 4) [1994] 1 All ER 870, [1994] QB 775, [1994] 2 WLR 209, QBD and CA.

Macmillan Inc v Bishopsgate Investment Trust Ltd [1993] 4 All ER 998, [1993] 1 WLR 1372, Ch D and CA.

a R v *Chief Constable of the West Midlands Police, ex p Wiley, R v Chief Constable of the Nottinghamshire Constabulary, ex p Sunderland* [1994] 3 All ER 420, [1995] 1 AC 274, [1994] 3 WLR 433, HL.

R v *Reading Justices, ex p Berkshire CC* [1996] 1 Cr App R 239, DC.

Science Research Council v Nassé, BL Cars Ltd (formerly Leyland Cars) v Vyas [1979] 3 All ER 673, [1980] AC 1028, [1979] 3 WLR 762, HL.

b *Smith v Director of Serious Fraud Office* [1992] 3 All ER 456, [1993] AC 1, [1992] 3 WLR 66, HL.

Taylor v Anderton (Police Complaints Authority intervening) [1995] 2 All ER 420, [1995] 1 WLR 447, CA.

Ventouris v Mountain [1991] 3 All ER 472, [1991] 1 WLR 607, CA.

c
Cases also cited or referred to in skeleton arguments

Barlow Clowes Gilt Managers Ltd, Re [1991] 4 All ER 385, [1992] Ch 208.

Burmah Oil Co Ltd v Bank of England [1979] 2 All ER 461, [1979] 1 WLR 473, CA; affd on other grounds [1979] 3 All ER 700, [1980] AC 1090, HL.

d *Conway v Rimmer* [1968] 1 All ER 874, [1968] AC 910, HL.

Crompton (Alfred) Amusement Machines Ltd v Customs and Excise Comrs [1973] 2 All ER 1169, [1974] AC 405, HL.

G v G [1985] 2 All ER 225, [1985] 1 WLR 647, HL.

Hargreaves (Joseph) Ltd, Re [1900] 1 Ch 347, CA.

McDonald v Horn (20 February 1995, unreported), Ch D.

e *Makanjuola v Comr of Police of the Metropolis* [1992] 3 All ER 617, CA.

Marcel v Comr of Police of the Metropolis [1992] 1 All ER 72, [1992] Ch 225, CA.

Morris v Director of the Serious Fraud Office [1993] 1 All ER 788, [1993] Ch 372.

Palermo, The (1883) 9 PD 6, CA.

Svenska Handelsbanken v Sun Alliance and London Insurance plc [1995] 2 Lloyd's Rep
f 84.

Westminster Airways Ltd v Kuwait Oil Co Ltd [1950] 2 All ER 596, [1951] 1 KB 134, CA.

Interlocutory appeal

g By notice dated 10 April 1995 Christopher Hayward and Philip Wallace, the liquidators of Wallace Smith Trust Co Ltd, appealed from the decision of Carnwath J on 21 December 1994 refusing their application for an order for the production of tapes and transcripts of the interviews of Gareth Davies and Wolfie Ginsberg, a former partner and manager respectively of the defendants, Deloitte
h Haskins & Sells and Coopers & Lybrand Deloitte, conducted by the Serious Fraud Office in February 1992 pursuant to notices served under s 2 of the Criminal Justice Act 1987. By a respondent's notice dated 26 April 1995 the defendants challenged Carnwath J's rejection of their alternative objection to production of the tapes and transcripts on public interest immunity grounds. The facts are set out in the judgment of Neill LJ.
j

Mark Hapgood QC and *Philip Sales* (instructed by *Allen & Overy*) for the plaintiffs.
Ian Croxford QC and *Andrew Onslow* (instructed by *Barlow Lyde & Gilbert*) for the defendants.

Cur adv vult

10 July 1996. The following judgments were delivered.

a

NEILL LJ.

Introduction

This appeal relates to an application by the liquidators of a company in liquidation for the production for inspection of certain tapes and transcripts of interviews which took place in February 1992 when the affairs of the company *b* were being investigated by the Serious Fraud Office (the SFO).

The application, which was brought pursuant to RSC Ord 24, r 13, was dismissed by Carnwath J on 21 December 1994 on the ground that he was not satisfied that the production of the documents was necessary for the 'fair disposal of the cause'. In the course of his judgment, however, he rejected an alternative *c* argument advanced on behalf of the defendants to the effect that the documents were protected from production by the rules of public interest immunity. The respondents to the appeal seek, if necessary, to challenge the judge's ruling on public interest immunity.

I propose to deal first with the issue arising under RSC Ord 24, r 13, as I am satisfied that it is right to consider this issue before the issue relating to public *d* interest immunity: see *R v Chief Constable of the West Midlands Police, ex p Wiley, R v Chief Constable of the Nottinghamshire Constabulary, ex p Sunderland* [1994] 3 All ER 420 at 423, [1995] 1 AC 274 at 280 per Lord Templeman. I must start, however, by giving some account of the facts.

e

The facts

Until about 30 April 1991 Wallace Smith Trust Co Ltd (WSTC) carried on business as a bank authorised and regulated by the Bank of England under the Banking Acts 1979 and 1987. WSTC's banking business consisted of, inter alia, the taking of and making of deposits from and to other banks and trading in *f* financial instruments, namely certificates of deposit, bills of exchange and bankers' acceptances.

At all material times the chairman and managing director of WSTC was Mr Wallace Duncan Smith (Mr Smith).

From about 1976 until about April 1990 Deloitte Haskins & Sells (Deloitte), a firm of chartered accountants, acted as auditors of the accounts produced each *g* year by WSTC. In particular they acted as auditors of the accounts for the financial years 1984–85 to 1988–89. In about April 1990 Deloitte merged with another firm of chartered accountants. The merged firm subsequently in 1992 changed its name to Coopers & Lybrand (Coopers). After the merger, Coopers acted as auditors of the accounts produced by WSTC for the financial year 1989– *h* 90. In each of the financial years between 1984–85 and 1989–90, the end of WSTC's financial year was 30 April.

On 28 April 1991 Mr Smith informed the Bank of England that WSTC had a deficiency of about £70m. On 30 April 1991 Mr Christopher Hayward and Mr William Radford were appointed by the Companies Court as joint provisional *j* liquidators of WSTC. On 12 June 1991 it was ordered by the court that WSTC should be wound up and Mr Hayward and Mr Radford were appointed as joint liquidators. On 23 February 1993 Mr Radford retired and was replaced as a joint liquidator by Mr Philip Wallace.

After WSTC ceased business on 30 April 1991 its affairs were investigated by the SFO. At about the end of April 1991 Mr Smith was arrested.

a On 14 May 1991 a notice was served on Mr Gareth Davies pursuant to s 2 of the Criminal Justice Act 1987. Mr Davies was a former partner in Deloitte and also a partner in the merged firm. He had been engaged in the audit of the accounts of WSTC in the relevant financial years.

The notice, which was from the SFO, was, as far as is material, in the following terms:

b
'NOTICE REQUIRING ATTENDANCE TO ANSWER QUESTIONS FURNISH INFORMATION AND PRODUCE DOCUMENTS

PERSONS UNDER INVESTIGATION: Wallace Duncan Smith and Wallace Smith Trust Co. Limited

1. The Director of the Serious Fraud Office has decided to investigate *c* suspected offences which appear to her to involve serious or complex fraud. 2. Pursuant to s 2(11) of the Criminal Justice Act 1987 (the Act) I have been authorised by the director of the Serious Fraud Office to exercise on her behalf all the powers conferred by s 2 of the Act for the purpose of investigating the affairs of the persons under investigation. 3. There appears to me, for the purposes of the investigation referred to at 1 above, to be good *d* reason to exercise the powers conferred by s 2(2) and (3) of the Act for the purpose of investigating the affairs of the persons under investigation. I have reason to believe that you have relevant information about the affairs of the persons under investigation, and I therefore require you to answer questions or otherwise furnish information to me with respect to matters relevant to *e* the investigation forthwith. I also require you to produce to me forthwith the following documents which appear to me to relate to the matters relevant to the investigation: All files, documents and papers relating to the persons under investigation and connected companies as per the attached list.'

f Enclosed with the notice was a list of 17 identified documents and also a list of ten companies connected with WSTC.

On 20 June 1991 a further notice under s 2 of the 1987 Act was sent to Mr Davies. The notice was in substantially the same terms as the notice dated 14 May 1991 but in the June notice the persons under investigation were identified as being Mr Smith and WSTC and also a number of other companies additional *g* to those set out in the list enclosed with the earlier notice. The names of the persons under investigation concluded with the words '... and related companies and persons'.

The final paragraph of the notice dated 20 June was in these terms: 'All files, documents and papers relating to the persons under investigation.' On 5 *h* February 1992 a third notice under s 2 of the 1987 Act was sent to Mr Davies. This notice was in similar terms to the earlier notice save that (a) the persons under investigation were stated to be 'Wallace Duncan Smith, Wallace Smith Trust Company Limited and related companies and persons'; and (b) the last paragraph of the letter was in these terms—

j
'I have reason to believe that you have relevant information about the affairs of the persons under investigation, and I therefore require you to answer questions or otherwise furnish information to me with respect to matters relevant to the investigation at Elm House ... on Thursday 13 February 1992 at [as amended on 13 February] 2.30 p.m. I also require you to produce to me at the same place on the same date at the same time the

following documents which appear to me to relate to matters relevant to the
investigation: All audit working papers and any additional documents and *a*
records in the possession of Coopers Lybrand Deloitte which support the
audit opinions on the financial statements of Wallace Smith Trust Company
Limited for the year ended 30 April 1987 and for the year ended 30 April
1990.'

In addition, on 5 February 1992 a notice under s 2 of the 1987 Act was served on *b*
Mr W Ginsberg, who had been a manager employed by Deloitte and who
subsequently became a manager in the audit department of Coopers. The notice
served on Mr Ginsberg was in the same terms as the notice served on Mr Davies
on 5 February 1992 save that he was asked to attend at Elm House at 10.30 am on
13 February.   *c*

On 13 February 1992 Mr Davies and Mr Ginsberg duly attended for interviews
at Elm House, the offices of the SFO. The interviews were recorded and tapes of
the interviews together with transcripts were subsequently prepared. In both
cases the tapes of the interviews extended over three tapes.

I shall have to refer later to the correspondence which took place before these *d*
interviews were arranged.

The proceedings and the application for production of documents
The first writ in these proceedings was issued in July 1992 and further writs
were issued in 1993. A consolidated statement of claim was served on 22 July
1994.   *e*

It was alleged in the statement of claim that both Deloitte and Coopers had
held themselves out as being firms which had particular experience and
knowledge of the banking industry. It was further alleged that both firms were
in breach of implied terms of their respective contracts of engagement and were
also in breach of the duties owed by them to WSTC in tort. The allegations of *f*
breach and of negligence included allegations that in planning and conducting the
audits of WSTC and in making their reports to the board and to the shareholders
the two firms: (a) had failed to review the business and internal controls of WSTC
properly or at all; and (b) had failed to acquire evidence of the assets held by
WSTC and in particular had failed to count or arrange for the counting of
financial instruments which were recorded as being in WSTC's custody or *g*
control.

In summary, it was alleged that the two firms as auditors were in breach of
their duties both in contract and in tort in failing to detect that the business of
WSTC was being conducted fraudulently. In para 48(1) of the statement of claim
it was stated that the net deficiency of shareholders' funds as at 22 July 1994 was *h*
estimated as being about £98,413,076.

In July and August 1994 correspondence took place between the solicitors
acting for the liquidators and the solicitors acting for the two firms (the
defendants). The solicitors for the liquidators were seeking discovery and
production of a number of documents including the documents which form the *j*
subject matter of the present appeal. By a letter dated 18 August 1994 the
defendants' solicitors set out the documents for which public interest immunity
was claimed.

On 13 September 1994 a summons was issued on behalf of the liquidators
seeking the production for inspection of the documents for which public interest
immunity was claimed by the defendants. The only documents with which we

a are presently concerned are those to which I have already referred, namely: (a) the three tapes of the interview with Mr Davies on 13 February 1992; (b) the transcript of that interview; (c) the three tapes of the interview with Mr Ginsberg on 13 February 1992; (d) the transcript of that interview.

The summons for production for inspection of the tapes and transcripts was heard with certain other interlocutory applications by Carnwath J. On 21
b December 1994 Carnwath J dismissed the liquidators' application.

The judgment of Carnwath J

Before turning to the arguments before the judge and the judge's judgment I should refer briefly to the rules relating to the discovery and inspection of documents. Under RSC Ord 24, r 2(1) a party to proceedings must make
c discovery by providing a list to the other party of all documents which are or have been in his possession, custody or power relating to any matter in question between them in the action. By Ord 24, r 9 a party is prima facie required to allow the other party to inspect the documents referred to in his list. But objections to production can be made and the issue will then have to be decided by the court.
d Order 24, r 11(2) provides:

'... subject to rule 13(1) the Court may, on the application of any party to a cause or matter, order any other party to permit the party applying to inspect the documents in the possession, custody or power of that other party relating to any matter in question in the cause or matter.'

e Order 24, r 13 provides:

'(1) No order for the production of any documents for inspection or to the Court, or for the supply of a copy of any document, shall be made under any of the foregoing rules unless the Court is of opinion that the order is necessary either for disposing fairly of the cause or matter or for saving costs.
f (2) Where on an application under this Order for production of any document for inspection or to the Court, or for the supply of a copy of any document, privilege from such production or supply is claimed or objection is made to such production or supply on any other ground, the Court may inspect the document for the purpose of deciding whether the claim or
g objection is valid.'

Before the judge the defendant firms raised a number of objections to the production of the tapes and the transcripts. The two main objections, which were also the objections which were pursued in this court, were that the documents were protected by the principle of public interest immunity and that
h in any event it had not been shown that their production was necessary within the terms of r 13.

The judge dealt first with the claim to public interest immunity. Earlier in his judgment he had outlined the circumstances in which copies of the tapes and the transcripts had come into the possession of the defendants. I shall have to refer
j to the relevant correspondence later. The judge noted that there had been no absolute assurance by the SFO of confidentiality in respect of the interviews and that the SFO had not objected to disclosure of the documents. He referred to some recent authorities, including the decision of the House of Lords in *Ex p Wiley* [1994] 3 All ER 420, [1995] 1 AC 274, and he rejected the claim of public interest immunity. He also rejected a variant of this claim which had been referred to before him as a form of 'quasi-privilege'.

The judge next turned to consider whether production should be ordered in the light of the test of 'necessary' in Ord 24, r 13. He expressed his conclusion as follows:

'In the present context, in my view, it is relevant that the documents in this case came into existence under statutory compulsion. It is also relevant that they are not themselves part of the story, but are subsequent reconstructions by potential witnesses. Fair disposal under current procedures normally requires that the parties should have the opportunity to hear and question relevant witnesses in person, and that they should have advance notice of what they will say in the form of witness statements. It does not require that they should be assisted by prior interviews by public authorities carried out under statutory powers. Of course, there may be cases where the results of an earlier investigation will be of special value, particularly where the trial is significantly delayed. However I do not see this as an overriding factor in this case. We are dealing with professional witnesses who will be relying to a large extent on their own contemporary notes and other documents. The events in question extended back over seven years prior to the interview. It is unlikely that their recollections will be materially affected by the lapse of the further time to trial. This leaves only the possibility that there may be matters in the interviews which would provide fuel for cross-examination. However, this is pure speculation at least at the present stage ... on the present evidence I am not persuaded that the production of these documents is necessary for fair disposal of the cause ...'

Arguments on the appeal on Ord 24, r 13

The argument on behalf of the liquidators was advanced on the following lines.

(1) The general principle underlying discovery was that set out by Brett LJ in *Cie Financière et Commerciale du Pacifique v Peruvian Guano Co* (1882) 11 QBD 55 at 63, where he said:

'It seems to me that every document relates to the matters in question in the action, which not only would be evidence upon any issue, but also which, it is reasonable to suppose, contains information which *may*—not which *must*—either directly or indirectly enable the party requiring the affidavit either to advance his own case or to damage the case of his adversary ... a document can properly be said to contain information which may enable the party requiring the affidavit either to advance his own case or to damage the case of his adversary, if it is a document which may fairly lead him to a train of inquiry, which may have either of these two consequences ...' (Brett LJ's emphasis.)

(2) In the present case it was true that the liquidators had been supplied with the witness statements of Mr Davies and Mr Ginsberg but these had been much abridged. The tapes and the transcripts contained accounts given in February 1992 by Mr Davies and Mr Ginsberg of their roles in the audits of the plaintiff. The trial of the action had been fixed for June 1997. Mr Davies and Mr Ginsberg might not give evidence until late 1997, which would be nearly six years after the interview.

(3) The interviews would contain answers to questions posed by experienced investigators who had by then acquired a detailed knowledge of the case.

a   Moreover, as the answers were intended to provide material for evidence at a criminal trial they were likely to be considered and frank. The witness statements on the other hand would have been subjected to some editing.

(4) At the trial of Mr Smith, which concluded in February 1994, the evidence was directed to the events in 1990 and 1991. The interviews, however, would have covered the whole period of the relevant audits.

b   (5) The tapes and the interviews would have contained expressions of opinion which would have been removed for the purpose of the preparation of the witness statements.

(6) The tapes and transcripts would be a useful source of material for cross-examination and might contain admissions. One of the crucial issues at the trial was whether the auditors had any suspicions about the activities of Mr

c   Smith.

(7) The tapes and transcripts were also likely to disclose some information as to what Mr Smith had said to the SFO.

(8) The tapes and transcripts were clearly necessary for the fair disposal of the action. Without them the liquidators would be left with a sense of unfairness. At

d   this stage the liquidators could not be sure what the tapes and transcripts contained, but they were clearly of direct relevance to the issues in this case and the accounts given by Mr Davies and Mr Ginsberg at the beginning of 1992 were recorded at a time when their recollection of the relevant events was still quite fresh.

(9) In any event the judge could not properly have ruled against the

e   liquidators without inspecting the documents himself. In this context we were referred to passages in the speeches in *Science Research Council v Nassé, BL Cars Ltd (formerly Leyland Cars) v Vyas* [1979] 3 All ER 673, [1980] AC 1028, and in particular to the speech of Lord Salmon, where he said:

f   'In my view, it would be impossible for a tribunal to decide whether the disclosure of confidential documents was necessary for fairly disposing of the proceedings without examining the documents.' (See [1979] 3 All ER 673 at 685, [1980] AC 1028 at 1072.)

On behalf of the defendants, on the other hand, it was submitted that the liquidators' application was based on a fundamental misconception that the tests

g   for discovery on the one hand and for production for inspection on the other hand were the same. As Parker LJ explained in *Ventouris v Mountain* [1991] 3 All ER 472 at 486, [1991] 1 WLR 607 at 622, in a case involving r 13 'the burden is on the applying party to satisfy the court that production *is necessary* for the purposes specified' (Parker LJ's emphasis). Moreover the court will not inspect the

h   documents itself unless a prima facie case has been made out that the documents are necessary for the fair disposal of the action or for saving costs.

In the present case, it was said, the liquidators had already been provided with copies of the witness statements and knew the evidence which had been given by Mr Davies and Mr Ginsberg at the trial of Mr Smith. The judge's conclusion that

j   the tapes and the transcripts were not necessary was correct, and, moreover, was made by the judge in the exercise of his discretion. The Court of Appeal could not interfere with that discretion unless the judge had acted on some wrong principle or had been clearly wrong. It was relevant, as the judge accepted, that the documents came into existence under statutory compulsion and were merely a subsequent reconstruction of the relevant events. It was a pure speculation to assume that the interviews might provide material for cross-examination. Our attention was drawn to a passage in the judgment of Bingham MR in *Taylor v Anderton (Police Complaints Authority intervening)* [1995] 2 All ER 420 at 434, [1995] 1 WLR 447 at 462, where he said:

> 'The crucial consideration is, in my judgment, the meaning of the expression "disposing fairly of the cause or matter". Those words direct attention to the question whether inspection is necessary for the fair determination of the matter, whether by trial or otherwise. The purpose of the rule is to ensure that one party does not enjoy an unfair advantage or suffer an unfair disadvantage in the litigation as the result of a document not being produced for inspection. It is, I think, of no importance that a party is curious about the contents of a document or would like to know the contents of it if he suffers no litigious disadvantage by not seeing it and would gain no litigious advantage by seeing it. That, in my judgment, is the test.'

Accordingly, it was submitted on behalf of the defendants, the judge's decision should not be disturbed. The liquidators might be curious about the contents of the tapes but that was not enough.

The application under Ord 24, r 13: conclusions

I shall consider later the impact of the principles of public interest immunity. At this stage I am concerned with the question whether, subject to any immunity from production, the test laid down in Ord 24, r 13 has been satisfied.

I can start by setting out what I consider to be the correct approach.

(1) The general principles underlying discovery remain those contained in the judgment of the Court of Appeal in the *Peruvian Guano* case. I anticipate, however, that these principles and the present practice may have to be re-examined in the near future. The scope of discovery in a complex action imposes obligations with regard to the examination and identification of documents which are often extremely expensive properly to fulfil.

(2) In a case, however, where the court is asked to make an *order* for the production of documents for inspection it is clear that an order is not to be made unless the court 'is of opinion that the order is necessary either for disposing fairly of the cause or matter or for saving costs'.

(3) It is for the party making the application for production to satisfy the court that the test of necessity is satisfied (see *Ventouris v Mountain* [1991] 3 All ER 472 at 486, [1991] 1 WLR 607 at 622 per Parker LJ).

(4) In considering the application the court should bear in mind the words of Bingham MR in *Taylor v Anderton* [1995] 2 All ER 420 at 434, [1995] 1 WLR 447 at 462 that the 'purpose of the rule is to ensure that one party does not enjoy an unfair advantage or suffer an unfair disadvantage in the litigation as the result of a document not being produced for inspection'.

(5) In addition the court is entitled to take into account whether the documents are confidential and, if so, whether the necessary information could be obtained by some other means. In *Science Research Council v Nassé* discovery was sought, in the context of a complaint of discrimination, of the records of other persons interviewed for the post for which the complainant had applied. In giving guidance on the matter, Lord Wilberforce said ([1979] 3 All ER 673 at 679–680, [1980] AC 1028 at 1065–1066):

> 'There is no principle in English law by which documents are protected from discovery by reason of confidentiality alone. But there is no reason

a   why, in the exercise of its discretion to order discovery, the tribunal should
     not have regard to the fact that documents are confidential, and that to order
     disclosure would involve a breach of confidence ... The ultimate test in
     discrimination (as in other) proceedings is whether discovery is necessary for
     disposing fairly of the proceedings. If it is, then discovery must be ordered
     notwithstanding confidentiality. But where the court is impressed with the
b   need to preserve confidentiality in a particular case, it will consider carefully
     whether the necessary information has been or can be obtained by other
     means, not involving a breach of confidence ... In order to reach a
     conclusion whether discovery is necessary notwithstanding confidentiality
     the tribunal should inspect the documents. It will naturally consider
     whether justice can be done by special measures such as "covering up",
c   substituting anonymous references for specific names, or, in rare cases,
     hearing in camera.'

We were also referred to a passage to the same effect in the judgment of Parker
LJ in *Dolling-Baker v Merrett* [1991] 2 All ER 890 at 895, [1990] 1 WLR 1205 at 1211.
As Bingham LJ explained in *Ventouris v Mountain* [1991] 3 All ER 472 at 485, [1991]
d   1 WLR 607 at 622:

     'While the court's ultimate concern must always be to ensure the fair
     disposal of the cause or matter, it need not be unmindful of other legitimate
     concerns nor is it powerless to control the terms on which production and
     inspection may be ordered.'
e

     (6) The court should examine the facts of the individual case and in particular
should consider: (a) the central issues in the action; (b) the nature of the
documents; and (c) the information which the documents are likely to contain.
     This was the approach which was adopted by Arden J in *Kaufmann v Credit*
f   *Lyonnais Bank* (1995) Times, 1 February, where she set out the material which she
thought that the applicants for production would hope to find in the documents
sought.
     (7) The judge has a discretion whether or not to inspect the documents. But
if the party seeking discovery shows that the production of the documents *may*
be necessary for the fair disposal of the action an order should normally only be
g   refused after the court has examined the documents and considered them in the
light of the material already in the applicant's possession. Indeed, as is apparent
from the speech of Lord Wilberforce in *Science Research Council v Nassé* [1979] 3
All ER 673 at 680, [1979] 3 WLR 762 at 769–770 the court will need to inspect the
documents where relevance is admitted but it is asserted that the documents are
h   confidential. Similarly, inspection is likely to be the only safe course where it
seems probable that the documents contain a version of events given soon after
their occurrence and at a time when the recollection of the witness would have
been fresh.
     I turn then to apply these propositions to the facts of the present case.
j   I have well in mind the passage in the judgment of Asquith LJ in *Bellenden*
     (formerly Satterthwaite) v Satterthwaite [1948] 1 All ER 343 at 345 as to the limited
circumstances in which an appellate court can interfere with a judicial discretion.
It seems to me, however, with the greatest respect to the judge, that, unless
protected by some immunity, these tapes and transcripts are *undoubtedly* likely to
contain material necessary for the fair disposal of this action. In the months
preceding the interviews, as is apparent from the documents to which I shall

shortly refer, an internal inquiry was carried out by Coopers into the events
leading up to the liquidation of WSTC. In February 1992 therefore Mr Davies *a*
and Mr Ginsberg must have had the matters which will be relevant to the issues
in these proceedings at their fingertips. The tapes are likely to include not only
matters of fact but expressions of opinion. Moreover, they are likely to provide
an insight into the state of knowledge of the auditors in the period leading up to
the collapse of WSTC. I would therefore allow the appeal. *b*

In my judgment the judge misdirected himself in failing to inspect the
documents. I consider that this court is therefore entitled to exercise its own
discretion.

I must turn next therefore to the matters raised by the respondent's notice.

c
Public interest immunity: the argument
It was argued on behalf of the defendant firms that the tapes and the transcripts
were protected from production by the principles of public interest immunity.
Before I consider this argument in detail it is necessary to refer to the legislative
background against which the tapes and the transcripts came into existence and
to some of the correspondence which took place in 1992 and 1994. *d*

The SFO was established by the 1987 Act. Section 1(3) of the 1987 Act
provides: 'The Director may investigate any suspected offence which appears to
him on reasonable grounds to involve serious or complex fraud.' Section 2 of the
1987 Act sets out the 'investigation powers' of the director. Section 2(2) (as
amended) is in these terms: *e*

'The Director may by notice in writing require the person whose affairs are
to be investigated ("the person under investigation") or any other person
whom he has reason to believe has relevant information to answer questions
or otherwise furnish information with respect to any matter relevant to the
investigation at a specified place and either at a specified time or forthwith.' *f*

Section 3 is concerned with the disclosure of information obtained by the SFO.
Section 3(4) provides:

'Without prejudice to his power to enter into agreements apart from this
subsection, the Director may enter into a written agreement for the supply *g*
of information to or by him subject, in either case, to an obligation not to
disclose the information concerned otherwise than for a specified purpose.'

By s 3(5), information can be disclosed to 'any competent authority'. By s 3(6)
competent authorities include the Official Receiver but do not include other
liquidators. *h*

I turn next to the correspondence.

In 1991 Coopers carried out a review of the work that had been done earlier on
the auditing of the accounts of WSTC. This review was referred to in a letter
from the defendants' solicitors to the SFO dated 10 January 1992 when it was said
that all the files in their possession had been collected 'partly to assist them in *j*
undertaking internal reviews of their own work and partly to facilitate inspection
by members of the SFO in due course'. Later in the letter the solicitors wrote:

'We should be grateful if you would confirm that the liquidators of [the
bank] have not been shown or provided with copies of any of the documents
which the SFO have received from our clients pursuant to the Section 2

a Notice. Could you please also confirm that the SFO will not give such access or provide any such copies in the future.'

The SFO replied on 17 January 1992. The writer said: 'I can confirm that documents obtained under section 2 of the Criminal Justice Act 1987 are treated as confidential.'

b The defendants' solicitors returned to the question of confidentiality shortly before the interviews took place. On 11 February 1992 they wrote:

'We note that documents obtained under Section 2 of the Criminal Justice Act 1987 are treated by your office as confidential. Nonetheless, we should still be grateful to receive the specific confirmations requested in the last paragraph of our letter.'

c
As far as I have seen there was no reply by the SFO to that request for 'specific confirmations'.

The interviews took place on 13 February 1992. Three weeks later, on 6 March 1992, the SFO wrote to the defendants' solicitors to inform them that draft witness statements had been prepared following the interviews. The letter
d continued:

'As you will see, I have attempted to keep both statements as short as possible and, to the maximum extent possible, have restricted the contents to matters of fact, as opposed to matters of opinion ... As agreed at the interviews on 13 February, I also enclose copies of the tapes of the interviews
e and unchecked copies of the transcript of these interviews.'

Finally, I should refer to the correspondence which took place in October 1994 between the solicitors acting for the liquidators and the SFO. In a letter dated 4 October 1994 the liquidators' solicitors referred to the fact that a claim to immunity had been made. The letter to the SFO continued:
f
'In advance of receiving details of the claim, it would be most helpful if you could confirm the following points to me: (1) Were the documents that have been disclosed to [the plaintiffs] (as on the attached schedule) disclosed to the defence? (2) Does the Crown believe that public interest immunity exists to cover these classes of documents?; and (3) Has any claim for public
g interest immunity been made by the Crown in respect of these particular documents?'

On 7 October 1994 the SFO replied:

h '1. All matters referred to in your schedule were disclosed to the defendant as part of the prosecution's duty in the criminal trial. 2. The documents referred to in the schedule as between prosecution and defence: I do not believe that PII could be claimed in respect of these documents. 3. I am not aware of any claim to public interest immunity having been made by the prosecution at any stage in these proceedings in respect of the documents
j referred to in your schedule.'

I come now to the arguments advanced on behalf of the defendants.
It was submitted that the principles which preclude the disclosure of documents on the grounds of the public interest apply broadly to three categories of documents. (a) Documents which contain state secrets or which are concerned with such matters as national security or the workings of central government.

(b) Documents which contain information disclosed to public bodies on a confidential basis, where knowledge of the possibility of wider disclosure might inhibit the free flow of information or discourage candour. (c) Documents containing information disclosed to public bodies under compulsion of law.

It was submitted that the transcripts and tapes fell into category (c).

Counsel drew our attention to passages in the speech of Lord Mustill in *Smith v Director of Serious Fraud Office* [1992] 3 All ER 456 at 463–464, [1993] AC 1 at 30 where he referred to the several immunities which are commonly grouped under the title of 'a right to silence'. These immunities are of great importance and they are all concerned with the protection of citizens against the abuse of powers by those investigating crimes.

In the present case, it was emphasised, the tapes and transcripts came into existence by reason of the special powers conferred on the SFO by the 1987 Act. The 1987 Act contained detailed provisions setting out the use which the SFO might make of the information which was provided to it and the persons to whom that information might be disclosed.

The fact that copies of the tapes and transcripts were in the hands of the defendants did not remove the public interest immunity. If the immunity ceased to exist when documents reached the hands of witnesses, it would be likely that in future witnesses would be careful to decline to accept such documents.

I have not been persuaded by these submissions.

Lord Mustill's analysis of the right of silence was concerned with the protection of an individual from self-incrimination. The tapes and transcripts came into existence for the purpose of the trial of Mr Smith and perhaps some of the companies which were being investigated. Mr Davies and Mr Ginsberg were witnesses for the prosecution. As Lord Woolf underlined in *Ex p Wiley* [1994] 3 All ER 420 at 446, [1995] 1 AC 274 at 305: 'The recognition of a new class-based public interest immunity requires clear and compelling evidence that it is necessary.' The trial of Mr Smith has been concluded. It is unnecessary to decide whether the records of these interviews have any public interest immunity in the hands of the SFO, though it is to be noted that the SFO do not claim such an immunity. But I can see no basis on which the auditors can claim such an immunity for the copies of the tapes and transcripts in their hands.

I am satisfied that the claim to public interest immunity is without foundation. I would therefore allow the appeal and reject the matters raised in the respondent's notice.

In these circumstances I would direct that the matter should be referred back to the judge so that he can inspect the documents himself.

SIMON BROWN LJ. On 13 February 1992 the defendants' audit partner, Mr Davies, and manager, Mr Ginsberg, were interviewed by the Serious Fraud Office (the SFO) with regard to the collapse of the plaintiff bank. Copies of the tapes and transcripts of those interviews (the documents) were, as earlier requested, sent to them on 6 March 1992. The liquidators, unsurprisingly, wish to see them. This interlocutory appeal concerns whether or not they may.

The relevancy of the documents to the issues raised in the action is not in dispute. The defendants, however, object to their production for inspection. The central question arising is whether or not that objection is soundly based. Carnwath J held that it was, on the ground that production is not necessary for disposing fairly of the action. Against that ruling the plaintiff appeals. The defendants for their part by respondent's notice challenge the judge's rejection of their alternative objection on public interest immunity grounds.

a   Although I agree with all that Neill LJ has said and gratefully adopt his detailed exposition of the facts, the arguments, and the main provisions of the Criminal Justice Act 1987 in play, I would nevertheless wish to add a short judgment of my own.

The appeal: is production necessary here?

b   The directly relevant words in RSC Ord 24 are these:

'... **11.**—(1) If a party ... (b) objects to produce any document for inspection ... then, subject to rule 13(1), the Court may, on the application of the party entitled to inspection, make an order for production of the documents in question for inspection ...

c   **13.**—(1) No order for the production of any documents for inspection ... shall be made under any of the foregoing rules unless the Court is of opinion that the order is necessary either for disposing fairly of the cause or matter or for saving costs.

d   (2) Where on an application under this Order for production of any document for inspection ... objection is made to such production ... the Court may inspect the document for the purpose of deciding whether the ... objection is valid.'

I take the basic principles governing the proper application of these rules to be as follows.

e   (1) The burden lies upon the party holding the documents to show that they are not discoverable, ie not relevant. (There is, I repeat, no present issue as to that.)

(2) The burden lies on the party seeking inspection to show that that is necessary for the fair disposal of the action. (I need not refer further to the question of 'saving costs', the other limb of r 13(1), that not being relevant here.)

f   (3) If no element of confidentiality (or, of course, public interest immunity— but that only becomes relevant on the cross-appeal) is asserted in the documents, routinely they will be produced for inspection without the need for a r 13 hearing on the issue of necessity. As Lord Scarman said in *Air Canada v Secretary of State for Trade (No 2)* [1983] 1 All ER 910 at 924, [1983] 2 AC 394 at 444:

g   'It may well be that, where there is no claim of confidentiality or public interest immunity or any objection on the ground of privilege, the courts follow a relaxed practice, allowing production on the basis of relevance. This is sensible, bearing in mind the extended meaning given to relevance in *Compagnie Financière et Commerciale du Pacifique v Peruvian Guano Co* (1882) 11 QBD 55.'

h

(4) If, however, confidentiality is asserted or any other ground of objection arises, r 13 assumes relevance and it becomes necessary to decide whether inspection is necessary for the fair disposal of the action. As Lord Scarman had earlier said in *Science Research Council v Nassé, BL Cars Ltd (formerly Leyland Cars) v Vyas* [1979] 3 All ER 673 at 699, [1980] AC 1028 at 1089:

j

'The only complicating factor is the confidential nature of relevant documents in the possession of the party from whom redress is sought. The production of some of these may be necessary for doing justice to the applicant's case. If production is necessary, they must be produced. The factor of confidence however militates against general orders for discovery and does impose upon the tribunal the duty of satisfying itself, by inspection if need be, that justice requires disclosure.'

(5) Disclosure will be necessary if: (a) it will give 'litigious advantage' to the party seeking inspection (see *Taylor v Anderton (Police Complaints Authority intervening)* [1995] 2 All ER 420 at 434, [1995] 1 WLR 447 at 462 per Bingham MR); (b) the information sought is not otherwise available to that party by, for example, admissions, or some other form of proceeding (eg interrogatories) or from some other source (see eg *Dolling-Baker v Merrett* [1991] 2 All ER 890 at 899, [1990] 1 WLR 1205 at 1214); and (c) such order for disclosure would not be oppressive, perhaps because of the sheer volume of the documents (see eg *Nassé* [1979] 3 All ER 673 at 688, [1980] AC 1028 at 1076 per Lord Edmund-Davies).

(6) If a prima facie case is made out for disclosure, then as several of the speeches in *Nassé* make plain, the court will first inspect the documents: (a) to ensure that inspection is indeed necessary (that very safeguard of itself making the court generally readier to accept that the threshold test for disclosure is satisfied) and (b) assuming it is, to see if the loss of confidentiality involved can be mitigated by: (i) blanking out parts of the documents, and/or (ii) limiting disclosure to legal advisers only.

Those basic principles I have sought to distil from all the many authorities which were placed before us. Several passages in the various judgments are relevant; it would however be wearisome and, I think, ultimately unproductive to cite them.

Turning to the present appeal, the first question to ask must be this: were these principles properly recognised and applied by the judge below? If they were, the evaluation of the relevant factual considerations was essentially a matter for him and this court would inevitably be most reluctant to interfere.

Mr Hapgood QC for the appellant criticises the judge's approach in two particular respects. First and foremost for acceding to Mr Croxford QC's argument, repeated before us, derived essentially from this court's decision in *Dolling-Baker v Merrett*, to the effect that the court's task under r 13 is to strike a balance between the likely utility of the documents at trial and, in this particular instance, the defendants' legitimate concern as to their intrinsic confidentiality. Second, he criticises the judge for relying, at least in part, on *Macmillan Inc v Bishopsgate Investment Trust Ltd* [1993] 4 All ER 998, [1993] 1 WLR 1372, a decision of this court which he says is of no help but rather, in the present circumstances, calculated to mislead the court. Let me take each in turn.

(1) *Dolling-Baker v Merrett*

The relevant passage in Carnwath J's judgment below is as follows:

'In the normal case, therefore, where documents are shown to be relevant, particularly if they are contemporary with the matters in dispute, the court will require little persuasion that their production is necessary in the interests of fair disposal. However, as *Dolling-Baker* shows, in special cases the court can and should take into account the genesis of the document, and may balance its likely utility in the trial against other factors: in that case the "implied obligation" of privacy. In the present context, in my view, it is relevant that the documents in this case came into existence under statutory compulsion.'

The first point that Mr Hapgood takes in this regard is that no question of confidentiality arises in the present case at all. The fact that these documents

a came into existence under statutory compulsion is, he submits, nothing to the point: these are the defendants' documents, containing their own account of matters within their own knowledge, in their possession at their own request. The whole process of discovery is by definition an invasion of confidentiality and day after day it requires parties routinely to disclose their private documents. Only when third party confidentiality of one sort or another is involved—for
b example through an implied undertaking to other parties to arbitration proceedings as in *Dolling-Baker v Merrett* itself, or an employer's duty to employees as in *Nassé*—does there arise the element of special confidentiality relevant for r 13 purposes. This submission I would reject. Whatever may be the impact of statutory compulsion upon the public interest immunity claim here, in my judgment it suffices at least to found a proper assertion of confidentiality in
c the documents.

It by no means follows, however, that such confidentiality then falls to be weighed against the likely utility of these documents to the plaintiff in the manner adopted by the judge. On this point rather I could accept Mr Hapgood's submissions to the contrary. As stated, once it is recognised that inspection of the
d documents may give 'litigious advantage' to the party seeking it, then, assuming, as is here plain, that the information they contain is not otherwise going to be available to that party, and that disclosure would not be oppressive, the threshold test for inspection is made out and the court can only properly refuse disclosure if, having itself first inspected the documents, it concludes that they will not after all assist him. Confidentiality at this point is frankly immaterial (save as to
e possible partial blanking out or limiting inspection to legal advisers), unless only 'the probative value of [the] documents [is] ... clearly ... so slight as to render unjustifiable an order for their inspection' (see *Nassé* [1979] 3 All ER 673 at 688, [1980] AC 1028 at 1076 per Lord Edmund-Davies). 'Probative value' in this context, having regard to the *Peruvian Guano* principle, must refer to the
f documents' overall use in the proceedings. Nothing short of such a finding—one which in effect destroys the contended for 'litigious advantage'—would justify a refusal to order inspection.

What above all needs to be emphasised is that there is no balancing exercise to be performed under r 13. The weighing of loss of confidentiality on the one hand against litigious disadvantage on the other is, obviously, difficult enough at the
g best of times: these are wholly disparate interests not readily matched against one another. Such a task is, of course, necessary if and when a prima facie claim to public interest immunity is made out. It is not, however, desirable to introduce this difficulty in some diluted form into the present type of r 13 proceedings; that rather is wholly unnecessary and inappropriate (see *Nassé* [1979] 3 All ER 673 at
h 681, [1980] AC 1028 at 1066 per Lord Wilberforce).

(2) *Macmillan v Bishopsgate Investment Trust*

Macmillan was a case where a plaintiff unsuccessfully sought to subpoena a witness to produce documents whilst that witness was giving evidence for the
j defendant, the plaintiff hoping that such documents might provide fuel for cross-examination.

As Mr Hapgood points out, very different considerations arise in Ord 38 proceedings of that nature, not least because there is no *Peruvian Guano* dimension to such a case. The position there is, perhaps, more akin to that regarding the disclosure of documents by third parties in criminal proceedings: see *R v Reading Justices, ex p Berkshire CC* [1996] 1 Cr App R 239.

In referring (twice) to *Macmillan*, in terms suggesting that he found it a useful
analogy, Carnwath J, it is said, allowed himself to become deflected from the true   *a*
question, the question whether the documents here in question might assist the
preparation of the plaintiffs' case in any material way whatever? I acknowledge
that possibility, but, were this criticism to stand alone, would not myself find it a
sufficient basis for concluding that the judge so misdirected himself in law as to
entitle, indeed require, this court to exercise a fresh discretion in the matter.   *b*
Having regard, however, to the judge's error, as I see it, on the *Dolling-Baker v
Merrett* question, I conclude that that is indeed now the position.

As to how our discretion ought now to be exercised in the matter, I agree
entirely with all that Neill LJ has said. Two authorities in particular are closely in
point: *Arbuthnott v Fagan* (1994) Independent, 11 July, [1994] CA Transcript 841
and *Kaufmann v Credit Lyonnais Bank* (1995) Times, 1 February. An ample prima   *c*
facie case is here made out on the facts for the matter to be remitted to the judge
below so that he may inspect the documents in line with the sixth and last of the
basic principles I earlier sought to identify.

The respondent's notice—are these documents protected by public interest   *d*
immunity?

There is little I wish to say on this part of the case.

Clearly it is necessary first to disentangle two questions.   (i) Do these
documents attract public interest immunity in the hands of the SFO? (ii) Do they
attract public interest immunity in the defendants' own hands?

Assuming, without deciding, that despite the House of Lords decision in *Re*   *e*
Arrows Ltd (No 4), Hamilton v Naviede [1994] 3 All ER 814, [1995] 2 AC 75, question
(i) falls to be answered Yes—as this court's decision in *Lonrho plc v Fayed (No 4)*
[1994] 1 All ER 870, [1994] QB 775 strongly suggests—it is nevertheless in my
judgment plain that the answer to question (ii) is No. On this second question,
indeed, I regard *Lonrho* as decisive. Mr Croxford submits that only a Secretary of   *f*
State—and not, therefore, the SFO—can disclose documents prima facie within
a recognised public interest immunity class, a submission founded upon a passage
in Lord Woolf's speech in *R v Chief Constable of West Midlands Police, ex p Wiley, R
v Chief Constable of the Nottinghamshire Constabulary, ex p Sunderland* [1994] 3 All ER
420 at 438, [1995] 1 AC 274 at 296. Let me assume that is so. I nevertheless fail to
see how it assists the defendants here. Rather it begs the very question which falls   *g*
for determination: the question whether, given that the documents are already in
the defendants' hands—and given too, as is clearly the case, that the nature of
these particular documents is not such (as, for example, in fields like national
security or international relations) that public interest immunity must inevitably
cover the documents in whosesoever hands they may be—public interest   *h*
immunity attaches to the documents in the first place. In my judgment it does
not.

In the result, therefore, I too would allow the appeal and dismiss the
respondent's notice.

WAITE LJ. I agree with both judgments.   *j*

Appeal allowed. Respondent's notice dismissed.

Paul Magrath Esq   Barrister.

a
R v Gloucestershire County Council and another, ex parte Barry

R v Lancashire County Council and another, ex parte Royal Association for Disability and Rehabilitation and another

b

COURT OF APPEAL, CIVIL DIVISION

HIRST, SWINTON THOMAS LJJ AND SIR JOHN BALCOMBE

c 7, 8, 9 MAY, 27 JUNE 1996

Social security – Services for sick and disabled persons – Assessment of needs of sick and disabled persons – Duty of local authority to assess needs of sick and disabled persons and to provide services to meet such needs – Whether local authority entitled to take account of its resources in assessing and reassessing needs – Chronically Sick and Disabled Persons Act 1970, s 2(1).

d

In two separate appeals the issue arose whether a local authority, when making an assessment under s 2(1)[a] of the Chronically Sick and Disabled Persons Act 1970 of a disabled person's needs and the arrangements required to meet them, was entitled to take into account the resources available to it in both human and financial terms.

e   In the first case, the applicant, B, was 79 years of age and gravely disabled. The local authority assessed him under s 2(1) of the Act as needing home care assistance, including the provision of cleaning and laundry services, which it then provided until September 1994, when some of the services were withdrawn

f owing to a shortage of financial resources. B's application for judicial review was granted, but the court declined to make a declaration that, in assessing the needs of a disabled person and the arrangements required to meet them, a local authority was not permitted to take account of the resources available to it. B appealed.

g   In the second case, the applicant, Mrs I, who was 88 years of age at the material time, was chronically ill. In May 1994 the local authority assessed her needs under s 2 and instituted 24-hour care in her home from a housekeeper. The local authority later decided to reassess Mrs I's needs and determined that they were best met by residential care in a nursing home. Financial considerations were among the factors taken into account in both decisions. Mrs I's application for

h judicial review was dismissed and, following her death, her daughter and the Royal Association for Disability and Rehabilitation appealed, seeking the same declaration as that sought by B.

j **Held** (Hirst LJ dissenting) – A local authority was not entitled to take into account the availability of resources when deciding under s 2 of the 1970 Act whether to make provision to meet the needs of a disabled person. Once the local authority had determined that it was necessary to make such provision, it owed an absolute duty to that person to make appropriate arrangements; at that stage the

___

a   Section 2(1), so far as material, is set out at p 425 *h* to p 426 *d*, post

availability of resources might well be relevant to the manner in which provision
would be made to meet the needs of the disabled person concerned. Since B's *a*
cleaning and laundry services had been withdrawn solely on financial grounds,
the local authority had acted unlawfully. B's appeal would accordingly be
allowed, and a declaration would be granted in the terms sought. In Mrs I's case
the local authority had decided that her needs could be better met by residential
placement in a nursing home, and while the availability of resources had played *b*
a part in that decision, the local authority had not acted improperly or unlawfully.
That appeal would therefore be dismissed (see p 437 *h*, 438 *d*, p 439 *a d g j*, p 440 *a*
b e f and p 442 *h j*, post).

Notes

For welfare services, see 33 *Halsbury's Laws* (4th edn) paras 927–932.   *c*

For the Chronically Sick and Disabled Persons Act 1970, s 2, see 40 *Halsbury's
Statutes* (4th edn) 70.

Case referred to in judgments

Associated Provincial Picture Houses Ltd v Wednesbury Corp [1947] 2 All ER 680, *d*
[1948] 1 KB 223, CA.

Cases also cited or referred to in skeleton arguments

Ainsbury v Millington [1987] 1 All ER 929, [1987] 1 WLR 379, HL.
IRC v National Federation of Self-Employed and Small Businesses Ltd [1981] 2 All ER *e*
93, [1982] AC 617, HL.
London CC v Central Land Board [1958] 3 All ER 676, [1959] Ch 386, CA.
R v Brent London BC, ex p Connery [1990] 2 All ER 353.
R v Canons Park Mental Health Review Tribunal, ex p A [1994] 2 All ER 659, [1995] *f*
QB 60, CA.
R v Central Birmingham Health Authority, ex p Walker, R v Secretary of State for Social
Services, ex p Walker (1987) 3 BMLR 32.   •
R v Dartmoor Prison Board of Visitors, ex p Smith [1986] 2 All ER 651, [1987] QB 106,
CA.   *g*
R v Inner London Education Authority, ex p Ali (1990) 2 Admin LR 822, DC.
R v Inspectorate of Pollution, ex p Greenpeace Ltd (No 2) [1994] 4 All ER 329.
R v Islington London BC, ex p Rixon (1996) Times, 17 April.
R v Secretary of State for Foreign Affairs, ex p World Development Movement Ltd [1995]
1 All ER 611, [1995] 1 WLR 386, DC.   *h*
R v Secretary of State for Social Services, ex p Hincks (1980) 1 BMLR 93, CA.
R v Secretary of State for the Environment, ex p Friends of the Earth (1995) Times, 8
June, [1995] CA Transcript 348.
R v Secretary of State for the Environment, ex p Rose Theatre Trust Co [1990] 1 All ER
754, [1990] 1 QB 504.   *j*
R v Wandsworth London BC, ex p Beckwith [1996] 1 All ER 129, [1996] 1 WLR 60,
HL.
Smith v Williams [1922] 1 KB 158.
Wynne v Secretary of State for the Home Dept [1993] 1 All ER 574, [1993] 1 WLR 115,
HL.

a **Appeals**

R v Gloucestershire CC and anor, ex p Barry

By notice dated 14 December 1995 Michael Barry appealed with leave of the Court of Appeal granted on 12 December 1995 from the decision of the Queen's Bench Divisional Court (McCowan LJ and Waller J) on 16 June 1995 ((1995) 30 BMLR 20) granting judicial review of decisions by Gloucestershire County
b Council to withdraw services under s 2(1) of the Chronically Sick and Disabled Persons Act 1970, but refusing his application for a declaration that in assessing or reassessing the needs of a disabled person under that Act a local authority was not entitled to take into account the resources available to it. The Secretary of State for Health was heard with leave of the court. The facts are set out in the
c judgment of Hirst LJ.

R v Lancashire CC and anor, ex p Royal Association for Disability and
Rehabilitation and anor

By notice dated 26 July 1995 the Royal Association for Disability and Rehabilitation and Beryl Gilpin appealed from the decision of Hidden J on 5 July
d 1995 whereby he dismissed an application by Mrs Gilpin's mother, Mrs Annie Ingham, for judicial review of decisions made by the Lancashire County Council on 5 October 1994 and 9 December 1994 under s 2(1) of the Chronically Sick and Disabled Persons Act 1970 reviewing Mrs Ingham's care arrangements and determining that her needs would be most appropriately met by placement in
e residential care. By leave of the Court of Appeal granted on 12 December 1995 the appellants were added and substituted following the death of Mrs Ingham, and leave was given for the Secretary of State for Health to be heard. On appeal the appellants sought a declaration that in assessing or reassessing the needs of a disabled person under the 1970 Act a local authority was not entitled to take into account the resources available to it. The facts are set out in the judgment of
f Hirst LJ.

Richard Gordon QC and *Alan MacLean* (instructed by *Stephen Cragg*, Public Law
   Project, London) for Mr Barry.
Cherie Booth QC and *Helen Mountfield* (instructed by *Stephen Cragg*, Public Law
g   Project, London) for the Royal Association for Disability and Rehabilitation
   and Mrs Gilpin.
Partick Eccles QC and *Christopher Fraser* (instructed by *R I M Wotherspoon*,
   Gloucester) for Gloucestershire County Council.
Genevra Caws QC and *Clive Lewis* (instructed by *Gordon Johnson*, Preston) for
h   Lancashire County Council.
Nigel Pleming QC and *Stephen Kovats* (instructed by the *Solicitor to the Department of*
   Health) for the Secretary of State for Health.

Cur adv vult

j 27 June 1996. The following judgments were delivered.

HIRST LJ. These two appeals raise important questions concerning the scope of the duty owed by a local authority to a disabled person as contained in s 2 of the Chronically Sick and Disabled Persons Act 1970, and its place within the framework of the community care legislation as a whole. The particular point at issue is whether such authorities are entitled, when making an assessment of a disabled person's needs and of the arrangements required to meet them, to take *a* into account the resources available to them in both human and financial terms.

In the first case Michael Barry appeals against part of the decision of the Divisional Court (McCowan LJ and Waller J) ((1995) 30 BMLR 20) dated 16 June 1995 whereby they allowed his motion for judicial review of decisions by the Gloucestershire County Council withdrawing services under s 2 of the 1970 Act on a ground no longer in dispute, but refused his application for further additional *b* declaratory relief that, inter alia, in assessing or reassessing the needs of a disabled person and the arrangements required to meet them, a local authority is not entitled to take account of the resources available to such local authority.

In the second case, in substitution for the original applicant Mrs Annie Ingham deceased, pursuant to an order of the Court of Appeal dated 12 December 1995, *c* the Royal Association for Disability and Rehabilitation (Radar), and Beryl Gilpin (Mrs Ingham's daughter), appeal against the decision of Hidden J dated 5 July 1995 whereby he dismissed Mrs Ingham's application for judicial review to quash the decision of the Lancashire County Council dated 5 October 1994 to review Mrs Ingham's care arrangements, and the decision of the Social Services Special Cases Sub-Committee dated 9 December 1994 that Mrs Ingham's needs for *d* 24-hour care could most appropriately be met by the provision of residential care. The appellants in this case now seek a declaration similar to Mr Barry's.

The facts of Mr Barry's case are very simple. He is 79 years old, and is gravely disabled. Prior to 29 September 1994 he was in receipt of home care services providing him with cleaning, laundry, shopping and community meals pursuant *e* to s 2 of the 1970 Act. By letter dated 29 September 1994 the Gloucestershire County Council withdrew his cleaning services and reduced his laundry provision, on the ground that it had been necessary to reassess the service hitherto provided due to shortage of financial resources.

Mrs Ingham, who was aged 88 at the material time, was chronically ill, *f* suffering from poor mobility, incontinence and confusion, and in need of 24-hour care. After a spell in hospital in late 1993 she was discharged to a nursing home. On 23 May 1994 her needs were assessed at the request of her daughter, and an agreed care plan was instituted to move her from the nursing home for 24-hour care in her home from a housekeeper. Her needs were reassessed on 5 October *g* 1994 and, at this juncture, it was decided that her needs could best be met by a residential placement back in a nursing home. Mrs Ingham's daughter then sought a review panel hearing, which took place, with the result that the sub-committee on 9 December 1994 upheld the decision of 5 October. In both decisions financial considerations were one of a number of factors taken into account. *h*

During the course of the hearing, these two decisions in Mrs Ingham's case were attacked by Miss Cherie Booth QC on the ground that they were *Wednesbury* unreasonable (see *Associated Provincial Picture Houses Ltd v Wednesbury Corp* [1947] 2 All ER 680, [1948] 1 KB 223) whatever the outcome of the appeal on the main point of principle, but in view of Mrs Ingham's death, the question is *j* now academic, and I propose to say no more than that, having considered the documents, I am not satisfied that Miss Booth has made good her contention that there was any such impropriety in either of these decisions.

It follows that both appeals stand or fall on the same point of principle, which itself turns on the proper construction of the relevant legislation.

a Section 29 of the National Assistance Act 1948 is the legislative starting point, and is within Pt III of the 1948 Act, headed 'Local authority services'. It presently provides, so far as relevant as follows, under the sub-heading 'Welfare services':

b 'Welfare arrangements for blind, deaf, dumb and crippled persons, etc.—(1) A local authority [may, with the approval of the Secretary of State, and to such extent as he may direct in relation to persons ordinarily resident in the area of the local authority shall] make arrangements for promoting the welfare of persons to whom this section applies, that is to say persons [aged eighteen or over] who are blind, deaf or dumb [or who suffer from mental disorder of any description], and other persons [aged eighteen or over] who are substantially and permanently handicapped by illness, injury, or congenital *c* deformity or such other disabilities as may be prescribed by the Minister ...

(4) Without prejudice to the generality of the provisions of subsection (1) of this section, arrangements may be made thereunder—(a) for informing persons to whom arrangements under that subsection relate of the services available for them thereunder; (b) for giving such persons instruction in their own homes or elsewhere in methods of overcoming the effects of their *d* disabilities; (c) for providing workshops where such persons may be engaged (whether under a contract of service or otherwise) in suitable work, and hostels where persons engaged in the workshops, and other persons to whom arrangements under subsection (1) of this section relate and for whom work or training is being provided in pursuance of the Disabled *e* Persons (Employment) Act 1944 [or the Employment and Training Act 1973] may live; (d) for providing persons to whom arrangements under subsection (1) of this section relate with suitable work (whether under a contract of service or otherwise) in their own homes or elsewhere; (e) for helping such persons in disposing of the produce of their work; (f) for providing such persons with recreational facilities in their own homes or elsewhere; (g) for *f* compiling and maintaining classified registers of the persons to whom arrangements under subsection (1) of this section relate ...'

The words in square brackets have been inserted by subsequent legislation, and in its original form, and as it stood in 1970, it was, subject to minor grammatical changes, in the form it presently appears without the square brackets. *g* The description in sub-s (1) has stood ever since as the definition of disabled persons.

Section 2 of the 1970 Act is the bedrock of the appellant's case, and is in the following terms:

h 'Provision of welfare services.—(1) Where a local authority having functions under section 29 of the National Assistance Act 1948 are satisfied in the case of any person to whom that section applies who is ordinarily resident in their area that it is necessary in order to meet the needs of that person for that authority to make arrangements for all or any of the following matters, *j* namely—(a) the provision of practical assistance for that person in his home; (b) the provision for that person of, or assistance to that person in obtaining, wireless, television, library or similar recreational facilities; (c) the provision for that person of lectures, games, outings or other recreational facilities outside his home or assistance to that person in taking advantage of educational facilities available to him; (d) the provision for that person of facilities for, or assistance in, travelling to and from his home for the purpose

of participating in any services provided under arrangements made by the
authority under the said section 29 or, with the approval of the authority, in
any services provided otherwise than as aforesaid which are similar to
services which could be provided under such arrangements; (e) the provision
of assistance for that person in arranging for the carrying out of any works of
adaptation in his home or the provision of any additional facilities designed
to secure his greater safety, comfort or convenience; (f) facilitating the taking
of holidays by that person, whether at holiday homes or otherwise and
whether provided under arrangements made by the authority or otherwise;
(g) the provision of meals for that person whether in his home or elsewhere;
(h) the provision for that person of, or assistance to that person in obtaining,
a telephone and any special equipment necessary to enable him to use a
telephone, then ... subject ... [... to the provisions of section 7(1) of the Local
Authority Social Services Act 1970 (which requires local authorities in the
exercise of certain functions, including functions under the said section 29, to
act under the general guidance of the Secretary of State)] [and to the
provisions of section 7A of that Act (which requires local authorities to
exercise their social services functions in accordance with directions given by
the Secretary of State)], it shall be the duty of that authority to make those
arrangements in exercise of their functions under the said section 29 ...'

I shall in future refer to paras (a) to (h) inclusive as 'the service list'.

Section 4 of the Disabled Persons (Services, Consultation and Representation
Act) 1986 provides as follows:

> 'Services under s 2 of the 1970 Act: duty to consider needs of disabled persons.—
> When requested to do so by—(a) a disabled person, (b) his authorised
> representative, or (c) any person who provides care for him in the
> circumstances mentioned in section 8, a local authority shall decide whether
> the needs of the disabled person call for the provision by the authority of any
> services in accordance with section 2(1) of the 1970 Act (provision of welfare
> services).'

Section 47 of the National Health Service and Community Care Act 1990
provides, so far as relevant, as follows:

> 'Assessment of needs for community care services.—(1) Subject to subsections
> (5) and (6) below, where it appears to a local authority that any person for
> whom they may provide or arrange for the provision of community care
> services may be in need of any such services, the authority—(a) shall carry
> out an assessment of his needs for those services; and (b) having regard to the
> results of that assessment, shall then decide whether his needs call for the
> provision by them of any such services.
>
> (2) If at any time during the assessment of the needs of any person under
> subsection (1)(a) above it appears to a local authority that he is a disabled
> person, the authority—(a) shall proceed to make such a decision as to the
> services he requires as is mentioned in section 4 of the Disabled Persons
> (Services, Consultation and Representation) Act 1986 without his requesting
> them to do so under that section; and (b) shall inform him that they will be
> doing so and of his rights under that Act.
>
> (3) If at any time during the assessment of the needs of any person under
> subsection (1)(a) above, it appears to a local authority—(a) that there may be
> a need for the provision to that person by such District Health Authority as

a   may be determined in accordance with regulations of any services under the
     National Health Service Act 1977, or (b) that there may be a need for the
     provision to him of any services which fall within the functions of a local
     housing authority (within the meaning of the Housing Act 1985) which is not
     the local authority carrying out the assessment, the local authority shall
     notify that District Health Authority or local housing authority and invite
b   them to assist, to such extent as is reasonable in the circumstances, in the
     making of the assessment; and, in making their decision as to the provision
     of the services needed for the person in question, the local authority shall
     take into account any services which are likely to be made available for him
     by that District Health Authority or local housing authority.

c   (4) The Secretary of State may give directions as to the manner in which
     an assessment under this section is to be carried out or the form it is to take
     but, subject to any such directions and to subsection (7) below, it shall be
     carried out in such manner and take such form as the local authority consider
     appropriate ...'

     In future I shall refer to these four key statutory provisions as s 29, s 2, s 4, and s 47
d   respectively.
          During the course of the argument considerable reference was made on all
     sides to official guidance and advice, starting with the 1989 White Paper entitled
     'Caring for people; Community Care in the Next Decade and Beyond' (1989) (Cm
     849), which was the progenitor of the 1990 Act.
e   Before citing the relevant material, it is important to note the extent to which
     it is appropriate to refer to it, and the weight which it should bear.
          It falls into two categories, namely on the one hand official guidance issued by
     the Secretary of State and, on the other hand, official statements in, for example,
     ministerial circulars.
          So far as the former is concerned, local authorities are obliged by s 7(1) of the
f   Local Authority Social Services Act 1970 (LASSA 1970) to act under the general
     guidance of the Secretary of State in the exercise of their social services functions,
     including s 2, which specifically refers to LASSA 1970.
          The latter, which do not come strictly within the scope of s 7 of LASSA 1970,
     are, as stated in 44(1) *Halsbury's Laws* (4th edn reissue) para 1427 on the authority
g   of the cases there cited, persuasive authority on the proper construction of the
     legislation.
          I propose to go through this material in chronological order, starting with the
     White Paper.
          The White Paper, which of course preceded the 1990 Act, describes in
h   para 1.11 one of the government's six key objectives to be '*to promote the
     development of domiciliary, day and respite services to enable people to live in their own
     homes wherever feasible and sensible*'.
          Paragraph 3.3.1 provides:

          'Once an individual assessment has been completed, and a decision has
j   been taken that publicly funded care can and should be arranged, it will be
          the responsibility of the social services authority to design care arrangements
          in line with individual needs ...'

     Department of Health circular 12/70, issued on 17 August 1970 and headed
     'The Chronically Sick and Disabled Persons Act 1970', provides under the
     heading 'General' in para 3:

'PURPOSE OF THE ACT ... Its underlying purposes are to draw attention to the problems, varying with age and incapacity, of people who are handicapped by chronic sickness and disablement; to express concern that these problems should be more widely known and studied and to urge that when priorities are settled, full weight is given to finding solutions. While recognising the effect of constraints on resources, the Government are confident that local authorities will have these purposes in mind in the administration of Sections with which they are concerned.'

In relation to s 2 specifically, the circular states in para 7:

'The duty requires the authority to assess the requirements of individuals determined by them to be substantially and permanently handicapped as to their needs in these matters. If they are satisfied that an individual is in need in any (or all) of these matters, they are to make arrangements that are appropriate to his or her case. The task of assessment should be undertaken as a normal part of the authority's social work service, *i.e.* it should be an occasion for considering all relevant needs and not merely those to which the Section refers; and a judgment whether those needs are of prior importance should be drawn from a complete and not a partial picture of the situation. Criteria of need are matters for the authorities to determine in the light of resources.'

Policy Guidance 'Community Care in the Next Decade and Beyond', issued following the 1990 Act, states that the White Paper and the 1990 Act itself set out the government's policy framework for community care in the next decade and beyond. This document of course falls into the former category. Paragraph 1.9 provides:

'The objective must be to provide a service in which the boundaries between primary health care, secondary health care and social care do not form barriers seen from the perspective of the service user. How this is done will reflect the way local and health authorities work together and organise their resources. Care must be focused on meeting the needs of individuals and their carers appropriately and sensitively.'

Paragraph 1.15 provides: 'A major objective of Government policy is that over a period of time services should increasingly respond to the needs of individuals.' Paragraph 3.7 provides:

'Care management is based on a needs-led approach which has two key aspects: a progressive separation of the tasks of assessment from those of service provision in order to focus on needs, where possible having the tasks carried out by different staff; a shift of influence from those providing to those purchasing services.'

Paragraph 3.9 provides:

'For the purpose of this guidance, care management in its most comprehensive form covers three distinct processes: assessment of the user's circumstances in the round, including support required by carers; design of a "care package" in agreement with users, carers and relevant agencies, to meet the identified needs within the care resources available, including help from willing and able carers. Any preferred solutions which prove *a*   unavailable either because of resource constraints or because the services have not been developed will be fed back into the planning process ...'

Paragraph 3.15 provides:

b   'Although assessment is a service in its own right it can be distinguished from the services which are arranged as a consequence. The needs-led approach pre-supposes a progressive separation of assessment from service provision. Assessment does not take place in a vacuum: account needs to be taken of the local authority's criteria for determining when services should be provided, the types of service they have decided to make available and the overall range of services provided by other agencies, including health authorities.'

c   Paragraph 3.24 provides:

'Once needs have been assessed, the services to be provided or arranged and the objectives of any intervention should be agreed in the form of a care plan.'

d   Paragraph 3.25 provides:

'The aim should be to secure that the most cost-effective package of services that meets the user's care needs, taking account of the user's and carers' own preferences. Where supporting the user in a home of their own would provide a better quality of life, this is to be preferred to admission to

e   residential or nursing home care. However, local authorities also have a responsibility to meet needs within the resources available and this will sometimes involve difficult decisions where it will be necessary to strike a balance between meeting the needs identified within available resources and meeting the care preferences of the individual.'

f   Paragraph 3.30 provides:

'In accordance with the Section 47(2) of the Act, if at any time during their assessment, an individual is found to be a person to whom Section 29 of the National Assistance Act 1948 applies, the authority must so inform them, advise them of their rights and make a decision as to their need for services,

g   as required by Section 4 of the Disabled Persons' (Services, Consultation and Representation) Act 1986. Once an individual's need for welfare services, specified in Section 2 of the Chronically Sick and Disabled Persons Act 1970 has been established, the authority must make necessary arrangements to meet it.'

h   The Care and Management Assessment: Practitioners' Guide (1991) provides in paras 3, 11–13, under the heading 'Summary of practice guidance', as follows:

'3. Care management and assessment constitute one integrated process for identifying and addressing the needs of individuals within available

j   resources, recognising that those needs are unique to the individuals concerned ... 11. Need is a complex concept which has been analysed in a variety of different ways. In this guidance, the term is used as a shorthand for the requirements of individuals to enable them to achieve, maintain or restore an acceptable level of social independence or quality of life, as defined by the particular care agency or authority. 12. Need is a dynamic concept, the definition of which will vary over time in accordance with: changes in

national legislation; changes in local policy; the availability of resources; the
patterns of local demand. 13. Need is thus a relative concept. In the context   *a*
of community care, need has to be defined at the local level. That definition
sets limits to the discretion of practitioners in accessing resources.'

Finally, the letter from Mr Herbert Laming CBE, the Chief Inspector, Social
Services Inspectorate, dated 14 December 1992 (the Laming letter), which falls
into the former category, states in the attached guidance as follows: *b*

'3. The assessment process should be structured so that the needs of the
individual ie their capacities and incapacities and their circumstances are
identified before consideration is given to any requirements for service
provision. Such consideration will need to take into account for example
whether other organisations could more appropriately meet the needs   *c*
identified. It will also have to take into account the resources available to the
authority ... 13. An authority may take into account the resources available
when deciding how to respond to an individual's assessment. However,
once the authority has indicated that a service should be provided to meet an
individual's needs and the authority is under a legal obligation to provide it   *d*
or arrange for its provision then the service must be provided. It will not be
possible for an authority to use budgeting difficulties as a basis for refusing to
provide the service ... 28. Authorities will need regularly to review their
criteria of eligibility for resources and services to take account of: the new
policy objectives; more efficient targeting of resources; newly available
resources; changing volumes and types of assessed needs and user   *e*
preferences; available resources ... 31. The care plans of all users should be
subject to regular review. For frail people in the community, frequent
reviews and adjustments of their care plans are likely to be needed. Before
any changes in services are made for existing users, they should be
re-assessed. In those cases, where assessments have been undertaken,   *f*
particularly under Section 2(1) of the [Chronically Sick and Disabled Persons
Act 1970] authorities must satisfy themselves, before any reduction in service
provision takes place that the user does not have a continuing need for it. So
long as there is a continuing need, a service must be provided although,
following review, it is possible that an assessed need might be met in a
different way ...'   *g*

In the Gloucestershire case, McCowan LJ giving the leading judgment, with
which Waller J agreed, having stated that at first sight the arguments on behalf of
Mr Barry appeared to have much force, proceeded as follows ((1990) 30 BMLR 20
at 30–31):   *h*

'A person's need is none the less a need because there is a shortage of
resources to meet it and competing needs of other persons; and once a need
has been established it cannot be reduced or eliminated by virtue of a
reduction in the resources available to meet it. On further reflection,
however, I have been driven to the view that such an interpretation would   *j*
be impractical and unrealistic and hence one to be avoided if at all possible.
In assessing need, those doing so will inevitably compare the extent of the
disabilities of the persons concerned in order to arrive at a view as to who
needs help more. That comparative exercise is obviously related to
resources. Indeed, it seems to me that a local authority faces an impossible
task unless they can have regard to the size of the cake so that in turn they

a know how fairest and best to cut it. I am strengthened in that view by the following factors: (1) The broad nature of the factors under (a) to (h) [of s 2 of the Chronically Sick and Disabled Persons Act 1970] seems to demonstrate the very broad spectrum covered by the word "needs". (2) The expression "necessary in order to meet the needs" again suggests to my mind that resources are a relevant factor. (3) The demand for resources and the resources themselves are bound to fluctuate. Hence inevitably resources

b will be a relevant factor. (4) Under s 2(1) the local authority is to make the arrangements in exercise of their functions under s 29 of the [National Assistance Act 1948]. Those functions are to make welfare arrangements for persons who are substantially and permanently handicapped by among other things disabilities. This points, in my view, in the direction of having

c to take account of other needs of other disabled persons when looking at the needs of a particular disabled person. For these reasons I for my part have concluded that a local authority is right to take account of resources both when assessing needs and when deciding whether it is necessary to make arrangements to meet those needs. I should stress, however, that there will,

d in my judgment, be situations where a reasonable authority could only conclude that some arrangements were necessary to meet the needs of a particular disabled person and in which it could not reasonably conclude that a lack of resources provided an answer. Certain persons would be at severe physical risk if they were unable to have some practical assistance in their homes. In those situations, I cannot conceive that an authority would be

e held to have acted reasonably if it used shortage of resources as a reason for not being satisfied that some arrangement should be made to meet those persons' needs. On any view s 2(1) is needs-led by reference to the particular needs of a particular disabled person. A balancing exercise must be carried out assessing the particular needs of that person in the context of the needs of others and the resources available, but if no reasonable authority could

f conclude other than that *some* practical help was necessary, that would have to be its decision. Furthermore, once they have decided that it is necessary to make the arrangements, they are under an absolute duty to make them. It is a duty owed to a specific individual and not a target duty. No term is to be implied that the local authority is obliged to comply with the duty only if

g it has the revenue to do so. In fact, once under that duty, resources do not come into it.' (McCowan LJ's emphasis.)

In the Lancashire case Hidden J, having resolved the *Wednesbury* issue in the council's favour, also upheld their submissions based on the Gloucestershire case,

h which had been decided some three weeks previously, and concluded that the council were entitled to have regard to their available resources both at the first stage of assessing needs and also at the second stage of deciding whether it was necessary to make arrangements to meet those needs.

In his argument on behalf of Mr Barry in the Gloucestershire case, Mr Richard

j Gordon QC crystallised his submissions in ten propositions. (1) Section 47(1) establishes a two-stage framework for local authorities considering a community care provision for an individual person, viz the assessment stage and the provision stage. (2) The framework applicable to disabled persons under s 2 is materially different from that otherwise applicable in the community care field. (3) In the case of a disabled person requiring or possibly requiring s 2 services, the local authority is obliged to go through an analytical process involving a judgment and not a discretion, ie to decide whether it is necessary to provide one or more of the services described in s 2 for that individual; and then as a matter of *a* strict obligation, to implement that decision, if it is favourable to the disabled person. (4) A s 2 decision pre-supposes a judgment by the local authority of the needs of each individual disabled person. (5) The determination of the needs of any individual disabled person under s 2 cannot depend on the resources available to the local authority, nor on the number of or needs of other disabled *b* persons in their area. (6) Having formed the judgment as to need, and the necessity of meeting it, the duty to make provision is automatically activated. (7) Section 2(1) is to be contrasted with every other community care service, as laying a unique specific individual duty at the local authority's door. (8) Just as resources are irrelevant to judgments under s 2, so are they irrelevant to the provision of the requisite arrangements. (9) It is unlawful to withdraw or reduce *c* s 2 services, once implemented, on the ground of inadequate resources. (10) If money is tight, proper priority must be given to fulfilling this statutory duty, and if necessary, money must be found elsewhere by pruning other (discretionary) services.

Mr Gordon submitted that the essence of s 2 is that it constitutes a minimum *d* basic provision or safety net, in order to achieve a key objective of community care for the disabled, in contrast to other provisions in this field, which lay down target powers or duties with a discretionary element.

This, he submitted, is manifest from the language of s 2 itself, with its use of the plain words 'needs' and 'necessity to meet', which left no room for any discretion or value judgment. *e*

This approach, he submitted, was strongly borne out by s 47, and in particular by the contrast he painted between sub-ss (1) and (2). The former required first an assessment under para (a) and secondly a provision under para (b), the latter being subject to an element of discretion in view of the opening words 'having regard to'. *f*

Sub-section (2), on the other hand, was an entirely discrete and free-standing provision introducing a separate assessment process for the disabled, and requiring the local authority to proceed to a mandatory decision under ss 4 and 2.

Mr Gordon also relied on a number of passages in the guidance and advisory material, in particular paras 1.11 and 3.3.1 of the White Paper, paras 1.9, 1.15, 3.7 and especially para 3.30 of the policy guidance and para 31 of the Laming letter. *g*

In the Lancashire case, Miss Booth adopted Mr Gordon's submissions on the general framework of the legislation, and in particular on s 2, which she submitted lays down specific duties, enacted to give a disabled person rights to essential services to meet that person's minimum need. The s 2 exercise, she submitted, required a personal inquiry scrutinising, and focusing exclusively *h* upon, the needs of the individual disabled person, and without any regard to available resources; only if an identified need could equally well be met by a less expensive arrangement (eg a nursing home rather than home care) was it legitimate to take into account such resources. It was incumbent on the court, she submitted, to give effect to the difference between, on the one hand, s 2 *j* arrangements which are individual rights and needs-based entitlements regardless of the local authority's resources and, on the other hand, the services provided under a range of other statutory discretions, which provide similar arrangements, but contingent upon competing demands for resources.

Persuasively though the appellants' arguments were addressed, I am unable to accept them, substantially for the reasons advanced by Mr Patrick Eccles QC on a behalf of Gloucestershire County Council, Miss Genevra Caws QC on behalf of Lancashire County Council, and Mr Nigel Pleming QC on behalf of the Secretary of State for Health.

On Mr Gordon's and Miss Booth's arguments, the opening words of s 2 provide a complete and conclusive answer in the light of their construction of the critical phrase 'necessary in order to meet the needs of that person', which they
b say demonstrates that the underlying purpose is to provide a safety net or minimum standard of care for the disabled. This latter concept was central to their argument, and they both recognised that, if it is unsound, it goes some considerable way to undermine their case.

It is common ground that, once the test laid down in the critical phrase is satisfied, an absolute duty rests on the authority to make the identified
c arrangement or arrangements, so the case turns entirely on the correct interpretation of the critical phrase.

None of the words in the critical phrase are defined in the 1970 Act, and I for my part do not find that, taken by itself, it bears a sufficient degree of clarity to rule out the wider interpretation adopted in both courts below and supported by
d the respondents, encompassing a value judgment which would allow resources to be taken into account.

The heading 'Provision of welfare services' does not suggest that s 2 is referring to a minimum standard of care. Nor do I consider that the safety net concept fits several of the individual items in the service list, in particular items (b) to (f) conclusive, which hardly rate as basic requirements, and whose selection would
e seem to involve choices in which cost would be an inevitable consideration. Despite Mr Gordon's plea to the contrary, I do not think it proper to ignore the service list when construing the opening words of the section, which in any event does not specifically categorise the service list as minimum standards.

The opening words of s 2 ('Where a local authority having functions under
f section 29 of the National Assistance Act 1948 ...') demonstrate clearly that the provision of welfare services under s 2 is to be treated as one of the s 29 functions. These functions, as is common ground, are ones which the local authority is empowered but not obliged to carry out, and where financial considerations are legitimate. While I accept that this does not rule out the appellant's construction of s 2, it does seem to me to tell against it, in order to fit s 2 into the general s 29
g discretionary framework.

Moreover, s 2 cannot be construed in a vacuum, and I consider there is great force in the respondents' argument that it would be surprising to say the least if Parliament intended s 2 to impose a strict duty on a local authority, completely regardless of that authority's resources to carry it out. Parliament in 1970 must
h of course have been well aware of the financial constraints under which local authorities have always laboured, even though the present capping regime was far away in the future.

Consequently, if in s 2 Parliament did intend to create what Mr Gordon and Miss Booth portray as a unique category, I would have expected to find that
j intention spelt out in the section in clear and unequivocal words, which it is not.

I now turn to the provisions in the subsequent legislation, which cannot alter the meaning of s 2 if it bears the plain meaning for which the appellants contend, but which are, in my judgment, pertinent as showing how Parliament itself interpreted s 2 subsequently.

Section 4 imposes a duty on the local authority on request to 'decide whether the needs of the disabled person call for the provision by the authority of any

services in accordance with section 2 ...' In my view the words 'call for' in their
natural meaning import an element of discretion or value judgment, and this is
borne out by the use of the same words in s 47(1)(b) to which I am about to refer.

Section 47 is part of a major piece of legislation following upon the White
Paper. Section 47(1)(a) lays a duty on the local authority to carry out an
assessment of the needs of any person in their area for the provision of
community care services, which are defined in s 46(3) as including not only those
specified in Pt III of the 1948 Act (ie including s 2) but also provisions in several
other statutes including s 117 of the Mental Health Act 1983. Thus, s 47(1)(a) has
a very wide conspectus, embracing a very wide variety of community care
services, including, but not restricted to, those for the disabled.

Section 47(1)(b) requires the local authority to decide whether that person's
needs call for provision by them of any such services having regard to the results
of that assessment. The appellants concede that this gives the local authority a
discretion in which resources can be taken into account, but they say that this
flexibility is to be derived simply and solely from the opening words 'having
regard to the results of that assessment'. I prefer to read s 47(1)(b) as a whole, and
am satisfied that the discretionary aspect is to be derived from the combination
of the words 'having regard to' and 'called for'.

Section 47(2) is central to the appellant's argument, and is portrayed by them
as a discrete free-standing provision which, in Mr Gordon's words, 'by-passes'
s 47(1)(b) and is 'entirely distinct from' the s 47(1) exercise.

I reject this contention, which neither fits into the pattern of s 47 as a whole,
nor accords with the wording of sub-s (2) itself. The pattern is exemplified by the
opening words of sub-s (2), which establish a direct link with the s 47(1) exercise.
The wording itself shows that once the person in question is identified as a
disabled person, the local authority is directed to 'proceed to make such a
decision as to the services he requires as is mentioned in section 4', ie to decide
whether his needs call for the provision of s 2 services, without his requesting
them to do so under s 4. This, mutatis mutandis, is identical to the s 47(1)(b)
exercise.

Finally, s 47(4), which clearly applies to both sub-ss (1) and (2), stipulates that,
subject to any directions from the Secretary of State, the assessment shall be
carried out in such manner and take such form as the local authority consider
appropriate, which seems to me to demonstrate that the local authority have a
considerable degree of flexibility fully consistent with the respondents'
construction of s 2.

I turn finally to the guidance and other official statements issued by the
Secretary of State, which in my judgment support the construction I favour.

I fully accept the appellants' submissions that this material emphasises over
and over again the basic principle that community care is based upon an
assessment of individual needs and upon the tailoring of service provisions to
meet them, and that a special place in the assessment of such care needs is
accorded to s 2 by para 3.30 of the policy guidance.

However, it is manifest from the other passages which I have quoted from the
policy guidance and from the Laming letter that there is a repeated recognition
and assertion that resources can properly be taken into account, and also that it is
appropriate for local authorities to draw up eligibility criteria and schemes of
priority. Nothing in para 3.30 or in the Laming letter in any way suggests that s 2
is immune from these considerations. Added to that is the persuasive authority

a of the other material, in particular circular 12/70 and the paragraphs which I quoted from the practitioners' guide, which are quite categorical.

Taking all these manifold aspects into account, I for my part am satisfied that both the Divisional Court and Hidden J were correct in holding that under s 2 the local authority is entitled to take into account resources in assessing a disabled person's needs and the arrangements necessary to meet those needs.

b I stress that this is no more than one factor in an overall assessment, where no doubt the objective needs of the individual disabled person will always be the paramount consideration, but not to the total exclusion of resources as one element in the overall value judgment, nor in disregard of any eligibility criteria or priorities established by the local authority.

The same considerations must logically apply to any reassessment, and I reject c the appellants' submission that once a s 2 arrangement has been made, it is sacrosanct and can only be changed if the disabled person's circumstances have changed.

I would therefore dismiss both appeals.

d **SWINTON THOMAS LJ.** I have had the advantage of reading the judgment to be delivered by Hirst LJ, and I gratefully adopt his statement of the facts relating to these appeals and the legislative framework.

Although the very ably argued and valuable submissions in these two appeals lasted three days before us, all parties were agreed that the point in issue was one of pure construction of s 2 of the Chronically Sick and Disabled Persons Act 1970. e Section 2(1) provides:

> 'Where a local authority having functions under section 29 of the National Assistance Act 1948, are satisfied in the case of any person to whom that section applies who is ordinarily resident in their area that it is necessary in order to meet the needs of that person for that authority to make f arrangements for all or any of the following matters, namely ...'

and the matters are then set out at (a) to (h).

The appellants submit that on a proper construction of those words, the resources available to the local authority are not a relevant consideration to a g decision made under s 2. The respondents submit that on a proper construction of the section, 'need' imports a consideration of the resources available to the authority.

It is common ground between the parties that neither earlier nor later legislation provides direct assistance on the construction of s 2. However, the h respondents submit that both earlier and later legislation are of assistance in ascertaining the intention of Parliament when the 1970 Act was enacted, and it is, therefore, necessary to look at that legislation.

The National Assistance Act 1948 gave power to local authorities to provide welfare services for the disabled. Section 29(1) provides:

j > 'A local authority [may, with the approval of the Secretary of State, and to such extent as he may direct in relation to persons ordinarily resident in the area of the local authority shall] make arrangements for promoting the welfare of persons to whom this section applies, that it is to say persons [aged eighteen or over] who are blind, deaf or dumb [or who suffer from mental disorder of any description], and other persons [aged eighteen or over] who are substantially and permanently handicapped by illness, injury, or

congenital deformity or such other disabilities as may be prescribed by the
Minister.'   *a*

It is clear that this section is an empowering section, and that there is no duty to
exercise the powers unless and until the minister so directs. I accept that s 29 does
not impose a duty on the local authority to provide services and that, accordingly,
it is entitled to take into account resources when making a decision whether or   *b*
not to provide such services.

The 1970 Act resulted from a Private Member's Bill (the Act becoming known
as the 'The Alf Morris Act'). Section 2 provided that local authorities who have
functions under s 29 of the 1948 Act should be under a duty to exercise those
functions as provided in the section. Thus, the power in s 29 became a duty
under s 2.   *c*

Section 4 of the Disabled Persons (Services, Consultation and Representation)
Act 1986 provides:

> 'When requested to do so by—(a) a disabled person, (b) his authorised
> representative, or (c) any person who provides care for him in the
> circumstances mentioned in section 8, a local authority shall decide whether   *d*
> the needs of the disabled person call for the provision by the authority of any
> services in accordance with section 2(1) of the [Chronically Sick and Disabled
> Persons Act 1970] (provision of welfare services).'

This section was enacted because local authorities were not required by s 2 of   *e*
the 1970 Act to make any decision under it, and in some instances they were
failing to do so. Hence a duty was laid on them to make such a decision. That
was the only effect of s 4 and it was not submitted on behalf of the respondents
or the Secretary of State that the section has any relevance to the resolution of the
question as to whether in carrying out their duties under s 2 a local authority can
or can not take into account available resources. However, the words used in s 4,   *f*
'shall decide whether the needs of the disabled person call for the provision by the
authority of any services' have some materiality, as does the concession made by
the respondents and the Secretary of State, because one finds those words picked
up again in s 47(1) of the National Health Service and Community Care Act 1990.
Further, a decision as to whether the needs of a disabled person call for the   *g*
provision of services must be very close if not identical to a decision that it is
necessary to meet the needs of a disabled person to make arrangements for that
provision.

Section 46(3) of the 1990 Act provides:

> '... "community care services" means services which a local authority may   *h*
> provide or arrange to be provided under any of the following provisions—
> (a) Part III of the National Assistance Act 1948; (b) section 45 of the Health
> Services and Public Health Act 1968; (c) section 21 of and Schedule 8 to the
> National Health Service Act 1977; and (d) section 117 of the Mental Health
> Act 1983 ...'   *j*

Section 47(1) and (2) provides:

> '(1) Subject to subsections (5) and (6) below, where it appears to a local
> authority that any person for whom they may provide or arrange for the
> provision of community care services may be in need of any such services,
> the authority—(a) shall carry out an assessment of his needs for those

a services; and (b) having regard to the results of that assessment, shall then decide whether his needs call for the provision by them of any such services.

(2) If at any time during the assessment of the needs of any person under subsection (1)(a) above it appears to a local authority that he is a disabled person, the authority—(a) shall proceed to make such a decision as to the services he requires as is mentioned in section 4 of the Disabled Persons

b (Services, Consultation and Representation) Act 1986 without his requesting them to do so under that section; and (b) shall inform him that they will be doing so and of his rights under that Act.'

Section 47(1)(a) provides for the provision of community care services generally, the need for such services, and the carrying out of an assessment and

c s 47(1)(b) gives the local authority a discretion as to whether to provide those services. The discretion in making the decision under s 47(1)(a) arises by reason of the use of the words 'having regard to the results of that assessment'. In making that decision they will be entitled to take into account available resources.

Then s 47(2) turns to consider the position of the disabled. It is absolutely clear

d that if, when an assessment is being carried out under s 47(1), it appears that the person who is being assessed is disabled, then he or she falls into a distinct category. That in turn triggers the duty laid down in s 4 of the 1986 Act to make a decision which, in turn, triggers the duty to decide whether the needs of the disabled person call for the provision of any services in accordance with s 2(1) of

e the 1970 Act. Accordingly s 47(2) of the 1990 Act takes one back to the provisions of s 2 of the 1970 Act.

I can find nothing in the provisions of the legislation enacted by Parliament either before or after the passing of the 1970 Act which in any way indicates that it was the intention of Parliament when passing the 1970 Act that resources should be a relevant consideration when a local authority is required to carry out

f its statutory duty to a disabled person under s 2(1). If Parliament had intended to incorporate the duties laid down by s 2 of the 1970 Act into the Community Care regime of the 1990 Act it could readily have passed amending or repealing legislation within the provisions of the 1990 Act. That Parliament chose not to do so supports the contentions argued for by the appellants in these appeals.

g Our attention was drawn to a number of passages in ministerial policy guidance, departmental circulars and guides. Hirst LJ has referred to a number of the passages and, unsurprisingly, both sides found passages which assisted their respective cases. From time to time resources are mentioned. As I will indicate a little later, resources are clearly a relevant consideration which a local authority is entitled to take into account when, having concluded that it is necessary to

h make provision to meet the needs of the disabled person concerned under s 2, they decide the nature of the provision to be made to meet those needs. There was nothing in the guidance or the circulars which would lead me to the view that it was the considered departmental opinion that resources were relevant to the former consideration rather than the latter. If that was the view, then, in my

j opinion, it was wrong. Furthermore, the following passage may be relevant.

Policy Guidance 'Community Care in the Next Decade and Beyond' para 3.30 provides:

'In accordance with Section 47(2) of the Act, if at any time during their assessment, an individual is found to be a person to whom Section 29 of the National Assistance Act 1948 applies, the authority must so inform them, advise them of their rights and make a decision as to their needs for services

as required by Section 4 of the Disabled Persons (Services, Consultation and
Representation) Act 1986. Once an individual's need for welfare services,
specified in Section 2 of the Chronically Sick and Disabled Persons Act 1970,
has been established, the authority must make necessary arrangements to
meet it.'

Paragraph 31 of the letter from Mr Herbert Laming CBE, the Chief Inspector,
Social Services Inspectorate, dated 14 December 1992 includes:

'... where assessments have been undertaken, particularly under Section
2(1) of the [Chronically Sick and Disabled Persons Act 1970] authorities must
satisfy themselves, before any reduction in service provision takes place that
the user does not have a continuing need for it. So long as there is a
continuing need, a service must be provided although, following review, it
is possible that an assessed need might be met in a different way.'

One must, then, in my judgment, construe the words in s 2 of the 1970 Act in
accordance with their natural meaning. It is conceded by Mr Patrick Eccles QC
for Gloucestershire that, once the duty under s 2 has arisen it is an absolute duty
owed to a specific individual. The duty in the section is aimed at 'any person to
whom that section applies' and to meet the needs of 'that person', ie the disabled
person. Accordingly, the duty is plainly individually orientated. It was said on
behalf of the respondents and the Secretary of State that the word 'need' is not
defined in s 2 or in any of the other sections in the legislation to which we were
referred. That is true but hardly surprising. 'Need' is an ordinary English word
and in my judgment, in this context, it means a basic or essential requirement.
The *Oxford English Dictionary* equates need with requirement. It was the central
plank of the respondents' submissions that an assessment of need involves a
discretion. In my view, that is the fundamental flaw in the argument. A need is
a question of assessment and judgment, not discretion. Whether or not a
disabled person has a need must be assessed in precisely the same way as an
assessment as to whether he is disabled.

A clear distinction must be drawn in the case of a disabled person between a
need and what it may be desirable for the disabled person to have. There is a duty
to meet the need under s 2 of the 1970 Act. There is a power to provide that
which is desirable under s 29 of the 1948 Act and s 47(1) of the 1990 Act. Thus,
for example, in the case of Mr Barry, his need is for laundry and cleaning services.
The need for cleaning services may be met by a person cleaning his house once a
week, even though it may be desirable that his house be cleaned every day. In
the case of some disabled persons the assessment might be that it is desirable that
they are provided with assistance in the house but they do not have that need. In
such a case, no duty under s 2 arises. It was submitted by the respondents that it
would be difficult and unwieldy to operate a system whereby needs would be
met under s 2 of the 1970 Act and services provided by the local authority to a
disabled person over and above those necessary to meet their needs would be
provided under s 47 of the 1990 Act. I do not myself see that this creates any great
difficulty, bearing in mind that s 47 gives the local authority very broad powers
to provide community care services, whereas s 2 only imposes a duty to make
provision to meet an identified need. In any event, it is by no means unusual in
social security legislation to find basic provision provided for in one statute and
further potential provision provided for in another.

In my judgment an individual's need is something which can be assessed or in
respect of which a judgment can be formed. It is difficult indeed to see how a

a third party's resources or the needs of others can be relevant to making such an assessment or making such a judgment in relation to a disabled person. Once the need is identified, then, following the language of s 2, it becomes a duty to make the provision that is necessary to meet that need.

Resources cannot, in my judgment, be relevant to a judgment that provision is necessary to meet the needs of the disabled person. If it were otherwise, then it b seems to me to be inescapable that if a local authority has no money in the relevant budget, then it would be open to the local authority to make an assessment or judgment that a disabled person has a need which it is necessary to meet applying objective criteria, but they are not required to meet it because of shortage of funds, resulting in an unmet need. The concept of an unmet need seems to me to fly in the face of the plain language of s 2 of the 1970 Act. Indeed c Mr Nigel Pleming QC on behalf of the Secretary of State concedes that if a local authority have satisfied themselves that in order to meet the needs of a person to whom the section applies it is necessary to make particular arrangements for any of the matters listed in s 2(1), it would not be permissible for a local authority to decline to make those arrangements because of an absence of funds.

d Once the assessment has been made then resources may well be relevant to the manner in which provision is made to meet the need. Take the facts of these appeals. Mrs Ingham's needs were identified as being '24 hour care'. Lancashire County Council's duty was to meet that need. They could do so either by making arrangements for her to go into a residential home or by providing 24-hour care in her own home. In making that decision they were entitled to take into account e the alternative costs. In Mr Barry's case his need was identified as, amongst other things, 'cleaning and laundry service'. Once the need was identified, there was a duty laid on Gloucestershire County Council to meet it. However, the manner in which the need was met, for example by someone doing his laundry at home in a washing machine or by it being taken away, was within the discretion of the f authority and costs would be a relevant consideration. If the need is the provision of meals (s 2(1)(g) of the 1970 Act) then the need can be met by someone going to the home of the disabled person to cook, or by the provision of meals on wheels, and costs will again be a relevant factor for the local authority to take into account. If the need is the provision of a television set (s 2(1)(b)) the needs can be met by the provision of a new or a second-hand set.

g On the issue of principle that arises in these appeals, I conclude that the local authority is not entitled to take into account the availability or otherwise of resources when carrying out the duty under s 2(1) of the 1970 Act of making a decision as to whether they are satisfied in the case of a disabled person that it is necessary in order to meet the needs of that person to make arrangements for all h or any of the matters set out in the section. I agree with Hirst LJ that if a person had been assessed under the provisions of s 2 of the 1970 Act and arrangements had been made to provide services for that person, he or she can be reassessed. However, that assessment cannot be based solely on an absence of resources to meet the person's need.

j I turn to deal very briefly with the relief sought on the facts of the two cases.
Mrs Ingham's needs were assessed on 23 May 1994, as needing 24-hour care. On 5 October 1994 the respondents decided that care could be provided more cheaply by returning the applicant to a nursing home. On 9 December 1994 the relevant sub-committee concurred with the reassessment of 5 October 1994, that Mrs Ingham's needs could best be met by a nursing home placement.

Mrs Karimullah of the Lancashire County Council Social Services Department, in an affidavit sworn on 27 April 1994, which was not challenged, made reference to Mrs Ingham's needs in para 16 and said: 'I concluded that the needs of Mrs Ingham could be better met in a residential placement in a nursing home.'

Then, later, she referred to a report from the district nurse which stated that Mrs Ingham 'needs a placement provided in a suitable nursing home which caters for confused patients'. It is true that resources played a part in the decision that was made as to placement, but I am not persuaded that the Lancashire County Council behaved in any way improperly or unlawfully in carrying out the duties laid on them by s 2 of the 1970 Act. Consequently I would refuse the relief sought in her case.

Mr Barry was assessed as needing home care assistance, including the provision of cleaning and laundry services. On 29 September 1994 Gloucestershire County Council wrote to him as follows:

'As you may have heard on local radio, or read in the newspapers, the demand for Community Care in Gloucestershire is far greater than the Government estimated it would be. The money the Government allocated to Gloucestershire, and which they suddenly reduced by a further £2·5 million earlier this year, is nowhere near enough to meet demand. In order to try to continue to offer some help to people at greatest risk, we are therefore having to reduce, or stop altogether, the services we have been providing to some people. I very much regret that the service we have been providing to you is affected. Until further notice we will no longer be able to provide you with cleaning and laundry.'

A letter in identical terms was sent to a number of residents in Gloucestershire.

Mr Barry's needs had been assessed as requiring the provision of cleaning and laundry services. It was not suggested that it was not longer necessary to provide those services in order to meet his needs. The services were withdrawn solely on financial grounds. For the reasons set out above, that, in my judgment, was unlawful. I would allow the appeal in the Gloucestershire case and grant the declaration sought on behalf of Mr Barry. I would dismiss the appeal in the Lancashire case solely on the facts.

SIR JOHN BALCOMBE. The issues in these appeals turn upon the construction of the following words in s 2(1) of the Chronically Sick and Disabled Persons Act 1970:

'Where a local authority ... are satisfied in the case of any [disabled] person ... that it is necessary in order to meet the needs of that person for that authority to make arrangements for all or any of the following matters ... then ... it shall be the duty of that authority to make those arrangements ...'

The respondents to the appeals, supported by the Secretary of State for Health, submit that in considering a disabled person's needs, and the arrangements necessary in order to meet those needs, it is open to a local authority to take into account the resources available to it. That submission found favour in both the courts below.

'Need' as a noun is a common English word. The *Shorter Oxford English Dictionary* (3rd edn, 1944) gives as definition six of 'need': 'A condition marked by the lack or want of some necessary thing, or requiring some extraneous aid or addition.' Simply as a matter of the ordinary use of language, I do not see how the resources available to a local authority can be relevant to the determination of the needs of a particular disabled person. If it were otherwise, then the logical a consequence would be that if the local authority had no resources, then no disabled person resident in its area could have any needs. When this was put to the respondents during the course of argument, they submitted that there could come a point when it would be unreasonable for the local authority to rely on a lack of resources in its determination of the needs of a disabled person. But that submission begs the question whether the resources of some outside provider

b are, or can ever be, relevant to the assessment of an individual's needs. Those needs can, in my judgment, be determined only by reference to the circumstances of the individual concerned. That is not to say that the needs of a disabled person are susceptible to a wholly objective assessment. Clearly need is a relative concept, and the needs of an individual will vary according to outside circumstances; thus, the needs of a disabled person may be assessed differently

c now than they would have been in years gone by, because standards rise and expectations change. But the point of reference in assessing those needs can only be the requirements of the individual concerned: it cannot extend to a consideration of the resources available to the local authority.

Once the needs of the disabled person have been assessed, then the question

d arises: is it necessary for the local authority to make arrangements to meet those needs? Again the dictionary meaning of 'necessary' is enlightening: 'Indispensable, requisite, needful; that cannot be done without.' Any arrangements beyond what is essential to meet the needs of the disabled person will not be necessary, although they may well be desirable and may be within the power of the local authority to provide under other parts of the relevant

e legislation.

If the local authority were not under a duty to make arrangements to meet the needs of a disabled person, but had a power to do so, then clearly its resources would be a factor relevant to the exercise of its discretion in deciding whether and to what extent to exercise the power. Even if the local authority is under a duty

f to make arrangements, because they are necessary in order to meet the needs of a disabled person, the local authority is entitled to take resources into account in its decisions as to the manner in which it makes those arrangements. If there are two ways in which the needs of a disabled person can be met, the local authority does not have to choose the more expensive way merely because of the preference of the individual concerned.

g So far I have considered the matter simply by reference to the language used in s 2(1) of the 1970 Act. I turn to consider the arguments which persuaded the courts below to depart from what I believe to be the clear meaning of the words used in the section.

(1) The wide nature of the matters set out in paras (a) to (h) of s 2(1): what

h Hirst LJ has conveniently defined as the service list. I accept that, on first impression, some of those matters seem to call into question the validity of the appellants' primary submission: that the essence of s 2 is that it provides for a basic minimum or safety net. Thus, the provision of recreational facilities, or facilitating the taking of holidays, may appear to go beyond what is essential and to extend to what is merely desirable. But it must be realised that the section

j originally extended to children as well as to adults, and that a disabled person's needs may be psychological as well as physical. With this realisation it becomes apparent that what in many cases may well be only desirable may in some cases be essential to meet the disabled person's needs.

(2) The argument that Parliament cannot have intended to impose duties on local authorities without regard to the resources available to them. I am unimpressed by this argument. Legislation imposing specific duties on local

authorities which they are required to perform without regard to the resources available to them is not unknown; an example in a different field is that of the duty of the local education authority towards children with special educational needs. Parliament knows very well how to confer a power, which will enable resources to be taken into account; if it uses language apt to impose a duty it presumably means what it says. If the fulfilment of that duty now imposes upon local authorities financial demands inconsistent with current government financial policies, that does not mean that local authorities are relieved from their obligations under the 1970 Act.

(3) Section 29 of the National Assistance Act 1948 already gave to local authorities power to make welfare arrangements for disabled persons. The obvious purpose of s 2 of the 1970 Act was to impose a duty on local authorities to make such arrangements, and it would not have been a significant alteration to their existing position if local authorities had been intended to be able to escape from fulfilling the obligations imposed upon them by the 1970 Act by pleading a lack of financial resources.

(4) The subsequent legislative history is entirely consistent with this interpretation of s 2 of the 1970 Act. In particular, the distinction drawn between a local authority's general powers under s 47(1) of the National Health Service and Community Care Act 1990 and its specific duties under s 47(2), highlights the special position of s 2 of the 1970 Act.

(5) The emphasis on the availability of resources in the official guidance and circulars is explained by the fact that these documents are primarily concerned with the general powers of local authorities in this field. It is noteworthy that in most cases where there is an express reference to a local authority's duties under s 2 of the 1970 Act, as in para 3.30 of the Policy Guidance 'Community Care in the Next Decade and Beyond' and in para 31 of the letter from Mr Herbert Laming CBE, the Chief Inspector, Social Services Inspectorate, dated 14 December 1992, there is an absence of reference to resources being relevant to the determination of needs. Paragraph 7 of Department of Health circular 12/70, issued on 17 August 1970 and headed 'The Chronically Sick and Disabled Persons Act 1970', is an exception to this general rule, but a government circular attempting to explain the effect of a statute resulting from a private member's bill is unlikely to be of much assistance when that statute falls to be construed by the courts.

For these reasons, as well as those given by Swinton Thomas LJ, with which I agree, in my judgment a local authority is not entitled to take into account the availability of resources when carrying out its duties under s 2 of the 1970 Act, save only to the extent that it may make the necessary arrangements in the most economical way open to it.

On the application of the law to the facts of the two appeals, I would allow the appeal in Mr Barry's case. I am not satisfied on the evidence in Mrs Ingham's case that there was any breach by the Lancashire County Council of its duties towards her under s 2 of the 1970 Act, and in that case I would dismiss the appeal.

Appeal in Barry allowed; appeal in Royal Association for Disability and Rehabilitation dismissed. Leave to appeal to the House of Lords granted.

Paul Magrath Esq   Barrister.

R v Acott

a

COURT OF APPEAL, CRIMINAL DIVISION

HIRST LJ, ROUGIER AND MITCHELL JJ

1, 8 MARCH 1996

b

Criminal law – Murder – Provocation – Direction to jury – Defendant charged with mother's murder – Prosecution suggesting defendant provoked into losing self-control – No evidence of active provocation – What evidence required before judge obliged to leave issue of provocation to jury – Homicide Act 1957, s 3.

c

A's mother was found dead in the bungalow where she and A had lived. Examination revealed that she had sustained multiple injuries and that she had also consumed a substantial quantity of alcohol. Expert evidence disagreed as to whether the injuries were explicable in terms of accident or had been deliberately inflicted as a result of a sustained attack. During A's trial for his mother's murder, *d* the prosecution suggested in cross-examination that he had assaulted his mother after a sudden explosion of temper, inferring that his mother's uncharacteristic consumption of alcohol, and the fact that she had treated him as if he were a child, had suddenly caused his self-control to snap. The recorder left to the jury the issue of what inference could be drawn from those suggestions. A was convicted *e* and appealed against his conviction on the ground, inter alia, that the prosecution had put to the jury a possible reason for the killing as a factor probative of guilt, and that the jury should therefore have been invited to consider the partial defence of provocation which the same reason might indicate. In particular, the question arose what evidence was required to trigger the judge's duty to leave the issue of provocation to the jury.

f

Held – Before a judge was required by s 3[a] of the Homicide Act 1957 to leave the issue of provocation to the jury, there had to be some evidence of provocation in its active sense, ie of what was done or said to provoke the homicidal reaction. Such evidence could be either direct or inferential, but could not merely indicate *g* that the defendant had lost his temper, possibly as a result of some unidentified words or actions; otherwise the jury would have no material on which they could make the objective judgment demanded by the statute. It followed, in the instant case, that since there was no evidence to enable the jury to come to any determination of fact as to what provocation if any was offered to A, it was not *h* incumbent on the recorder to put the issue before them, and he had been right not to do so. The appeal would accordingly be dismissed (see p 453 *b* to *h*, post).

R v Stewart [1995] 4 All ER 999 explained.

Notes

j For provocation as a defence to a charge of murder, see 11(1) *Halsbury's Laws* (4th edn reissue) paras 438–439, and for cases on the subject, see 14(2) *Digest* (2nd reissue) 33–48, *5260–5409*.

For the Homicide Act 1957, s 3, see 12 *Halsbury's Statutes* (4th edn) (1994 reissue) 280.

---

a   Section 3 is set out at p 450 *f*, post

Cases referred to in judgment

Bullard v R [1961] 3 All ER 470n, [1957] AC 635, [1957] 3 WLR 656, PC.

Lee Chun-Chuen v R [1963] 1 All ER 73, [1963] AC 220, [1962] 3 WLR 1461, PC.

R v Cambridge [1994] 2 All ER 760, [1994] 1 WLR 971, CA.

R v Duffy [1949] 1 All ER 932, CCA.

R v Gilbert (1977) 66 Cr App R 237, CA.

R v Rossiter [1994] 2 All ER 752, CA.

R v Stewart [1995] 4 All ER 999, CA.

Cases also cited or referred to in skeleton arguments

R v Cox [1995] 2 Cr App R 513, CA.

R v Newell (1980) 71 Cr App R 331, CA.

R v Sawyer (1980) 71 Cr App R 283, CA.

Appeal against conviction

Brian Gordon Acott appealed with leave against his conviction in the Central Criminal Court on 19 June 1995 before the Recorder of London and a jury of murder for which he was sentenced to life imprisonment. The facts are set out in the judgment of the court.

Michael Gale QC and *Louis French* (assigned by the *Registrar of Criminal Appeals*) for the appellant.

Heather Hallett QC and *Simon Russell-Flint* (instructed by the *Crown Prosecution Service*, Maidstone) for the Crown.

At the conclusion of the argument the court announced that the appeal would be dismissed for reasons to be given later.

8 March 1996. The following judgment of the court was delivered.

ROUGIER J. On 19 June 1995 at the Central Criminal Court before the Recorder of London, the appellant, on retrial, was convicted by a majority of ten to two of the murder of his mother. He appeals against that conviction by leave.

At the time of his mother's death, the appellant was 48 years old, and of good character. His disposition was mild, even self-effacing, according to those that knew him. He had been in continuous work until early in 1991 when he gave up his job and returned, in order to live with his mother, to Rainham, where he stayed until her death. It is clear that he wished to resume gainful employment if he could find a suitable job and made many applications which had not, so far, been successful. This had had an inevitable effect on his finances and, after living for a year on his savings, thereafter he became financially almost totally dependent on his mother, who paid his bills and gave him pocket money. This was a situation which he found somewhat irksome, but there was ample and uncontradicted evidence to show that he was extremely fond of her and, until her death at any rate, appeared to submit with good grace to the fact that she treated him in many ways as if he were a child. According to his mother's most recent will, made approximately a year before her death, and found in the appellant's briefcase, he was the sole beneficiary.

Mrs Acott was 78 years old at the time of her death; her physical and mental condition were such as were to be expected in a woman of her age with the possible exception that, according to the pathologists, she suffered from quite *a* marked osteoporosis which would have had the effect of making her bones unusually brittle.

At 9.15 pm on 17 February 1993 the appellant, apparently in a state of great agitation, telephoned the emergency services requesting an ambulance and saying that his mother was injured as a result of a fall. Mrs Acott was found lying dead on the floor of the hallway of her bungalow and examination both on the *b* spot and later in the mortuary revealed that she had sustained multiple injuries, both internally and externally, the latter being mostly in the area of the head, face and neck. Additionally, to the surprise of all who knew her, she was found to have recently drunk a fair quantity of alcohol, and, as confirmation, a bottle of brandy was found in her bedroom.

c When questioned by the police, the appellant's account of the matter was that his mother had put her head around his bedroom door to say 'good night' and then almost immediately after he had heard her fall. He came to the door and saw that she was lying on the floor of the hallway, and as he went to her she rolled over and began to sit up; he took hold of her, but as he did so she lurched forward and her head hit the wall, sliding down to the floor near the radiator and hitting *d* the wainscot. Blood was everywhere; he tried to pick her up again but his hands slipped and she fell down again hard, apparently senseless. He had tried to get her up; he had also thumped her chest and slapped her face in an effort to bring her round.

The first autopsy was performed by Dr Paula Lannas who came to the firm *e* conclusion that the totality of the injuries could not be reconciled with the appellant's account, and were not explicable in terms of accident, but had been deliberately inflicted as a result of a sustained attack. The appellant was accordingly arrested and charged. On his behalf, another pathologist, Dr Gibson was instructed and performed a second autopsy as the result of which, contrary to the views of Dr Lannas, he came to the equally firm conclusion that the injuries *f* *were* explicable on the basis of the appellant's account, and he gave his opinion that the appellant had no case to answer. This also was the view of the metropolitan stipendiary magistrate who heard committal proceedings on 23 November 1993.

The prosecution thereupon instructed yet a third pathologist, Professor *g* Michael Green. Professor Green did not perform an autopsy, but gave his opinion purely on the documentary evidence before him. It will be necessary later to analyse the professor's opinion in greater detail, but in summary, he was strongly of the opinion that Dr Lannas' view was correct. The prosecution accordingly applied for a voluntary bill and the appellant duly stood trial at *h* Maidstone in July 1994, at the end of which the jury failed to agree. Such a protracted progress of the case is most unfortunate, particularly for the appellant but, so far as this court is concerned, can only operate as illustrative of the difficulties which were encountered. We are solely concerned with the conduct of the second trial, and the verdict of the jury in relation to the evidence and *j* summing up which they heard.

The first ground of appeal is that these difficulties and the divergence of views amongst expert witnesses should by themselves have created sufficient doubt to render the verdict unsafe; it is contended that Professor Green's stated position was that he could not reject the opinion of Dr Gibson; and it is further contended that there was no other cogent evidence to assist the jury in arriving at their verdict.

We are unable to agree. In the first place, to say that Professor Green's stated view was that he could not reject Dr Gibson's opinion is to oversimplify and thereby distort the effect of his evidence. In the passage most heavily relied upon he was asked: 'But you are not saying Dr Gibson is wrong?' And he answered:

'No, but I think that in this particular case looking at the injuries overall and the view that I have formed I cannot see Dr Gibson and I coming more than very slightly closer together.'

But it is necessary to consider other answers both before and after those quoted which make Professor Green's view abundantly plain. Earlier the professor makes the point that in the job of the pathologist everything is a question of probabilities and he said: 'It is a well-known aphorism in forensic pathology that one should never say never.' He added:

'Looking at the whole events and the account given repeatedly by the defendant this is where he and I and Dr Gibson part company and, you know, not just by a narrow margin but by a wide one.'

Finally, he summed up his position in these telling words: 'I think that the range of disagreement between us is about as wide as I have ever experienced with a colleague in the course of my career.' Once the entire context of Professor Green's evidence on the subject is read, we think the one answer so eagerly seized upon was no more than an expression of Hippocratic caution from an expert whose training and experience had conditioned him never wholly to discount any possibility, however unlikely. His strong preference for Dr Lannas' view was manifest. Reliance was also placed on a passage of which the recorder reminded the jury of the summing up, saying: 'Professor Green accepts that both theories [he was referring to theories of the two other pathologists] are reasonable.'

However, a reading of the context of Professor Green's remarks, and indeed of the summing up, demonstrates that the theories referred to were nothing to do with the overall conclusion but merely related to one detail concerning one specific injury, referred to as number one, which was a severe bruise and laceration on the forehead caused, it was agreed, when Mrs Acott's head came in contact with the radiator. The direction from which such contact had occurred was a point of little concern to the prosecution on their reconstruction of events, but was extremely important for the defence who wished to demonstrate that Mrs Acott had fallen in a particular direction because she had tripped on a tear in the carpet.

Nor can we agree that there was a lack of other cogent evidence. In the first place, the appellant's account of what had occurred is not, in our judgment, one which would command instant credence. And any reservations that the jury might have felt about it were bound to have been heightened by a description of the injuries which were found on the deceased. These are helpfully set out at the back of the skeleton argument of the respondent. Without going into great detail, Mrs Acott had sustained 40 external bruises, not counting what were described as two areas of multiple bruising, together with lacerations and petechial haemorrhages which were present in the facial skin. Internally, there was also extensive bruising, again principally to the face and neck. Her neck was broken at the 6/7 cervical level; there were fractures of the nasal bones, the right zygoma, the lower end of the thyroid bone; the right superior horn of the hyoid, and virtually every rib in this woman's body was broken, some of them in two places. These injuries, at any rate the external ones, are dramatically illustrated

a
in photographs which are with our papers. Making every allowance for the frailties of age, one glance at those photographs might well have made any jury extremely reluctant to believe that they could possibly have been caused in the way described by the appellant.

Finally, the recorder did no more than state the law correctly when he told the jury:

b
> 'In trials by jury it is not unusual to find that experts disagree. It does not follow that in those circumstances it is impossible for the jury to reach a decision. The evidence of experts is evidence which you can, and should, evaluate in exactly the same way as you do other evidence in this case ...
> Proof does not depend upon the number of witnesses who say the same
c
> thing but on the quality of the evidence and that is something which you decide.'

The second ground concerns the way in which the recorder dealt with the expert evidence and in particular certain comments he made or did not make concerning it. It is submitted that he created an unfair imbalance by making
d
certain remarks to suggest that Dr Gibson had shifted his ground and was therefore not impartial, without providing or commenting on certain features, where the same criticism might have been levelled at Dr Lannas. The recorder's comments concerning Dr Gibson of which complaint is made are three in number; the first deals with the view of Dr Lannas that injury number one had been caused by the radiator valve, where the recorder said:

e
> 'Dr Gibson accepts that this is correct so you may be entirely satisfied as to at least some of the immediate causation in this instance, but Dr Gibson may not agree that it was this contact which first broke the skin and caused the laceration and so started the bleeding in that area. Certainly at one stage he thought that there was an earlier contact with the wall and he never wholly
f
> abandoned that stance.'

We are quite unable to see that the passage quoted contains the slightest suggestion that Dr Gibson may not have been impartial; indeed, it is difficult to see that it is in any way critical of him.

The second passage referred to is as follows:
g
> 'The doctor [he is referring to Dr Gibson] says it is an account which is not only intrinsically probable but it contains details which the defendant as a layman could not have invented. Even he as a doctor would not have been able to invent such a story at such short notice. The story does not appear to account for the bloodstain which was superimposed on the other such
h
> stain on the wall outside the bedroom but otherwise Dr Gibson is convinced that it explains everything which he has seen and heard and he maintains his opinion that in the circumstances no criminal offence is made out.'

We would make the same comment as that in relation to the first passage.
j
Mr Gale QC does, however, demonstrate a potentially adverse comment on Dr Gibson's evidence in the final passage relied upon. It is necessary first to examine the context in which it was made, and the technical issue to which it referred. It will be remembered that, according to the appellant's account, the second fall sustained by his mother occurred when she half rose in an attempt to get to her feet but fell back again. Not unnaturally, the prosecution were quick to make the point that this would have hardly been possible for a woman with a

broken neck, to which Dr Gibson had replied by saying that, provided the spinal
cord was not injured, Mrs Acott would not have been paralysed. It appears that *a*
at some early stage during the pathological investigation a Dr Doshey, who was
not called as a witness, had examined part of the affected area of the spinal cord
but had found no bleeding or softening indicative of damage. Dr Lannas, who,
on the other hand, had examined the entire area, did find evidence of bleeding.
Dealing with that issue the recorder had this to say: *b*

'Dr Gibson asserts that the cord itself is not shown to have been damaged
and that accordingly movement of limbs is not precluded. He emphasises
that Dr Doshey found no bleeding or softening of the area which she was
asked to examine, which was only a portion of the whole. He accepts that
Dr Lannas found evidence of bleeding around the cord but states that he *c*
prefers the account of Dr Doshey who found none. It may be questioned to
what extent that attitude demonstrates the impartiality of the expert or the
partisanship of the advocate.'

A judge is by no means precluded from commenting on any part of the
evidence, if he thinks it desirable, always provided that the comment is not unfair. *d*
In our opinion, so far from being unfair, when one bears in mind that Dr Gibson
not only lacked the advantage of having heard what Dr Doshey had to say, but
also was well aware that she had only examined a portion of the potentially
affected area whereas Dr Lannas had examined the whole, the comment was
perfectly justified. It was certainly perfectly proper to ask the jury to consider *e*
whether Dr Gibson's acceptance of Dr Doshey's findings in preference to those
of Dr Lannas owed more to the fact that they fitted in with his own theory than
to any objective analysis.

Mr Gale's main contention, however, was that, if one accepts that such a
comment was permissible, there were instances of similar shifting of ground or
lack of objectivity on the part of Dr Lannas which the recorder should also have *f*
commented on in order to keep the scales evenly balanced. Mr Gale listed and
helpfully sought to analyse five such instances, as follows.

First, in relation to the percentage of injuries that Dr Lannas accepted might be
accounted for by the appellant's version of events. It is claimed that this figure
dwindled significantly as the case progressed.   *g*

Second, the strength or otherwise of Dr Lannas' view that the rib fractures
were the result of an attack rather than of clumsily attempted resuscitation is said
to have hardened considerably.

Third, the significance of a particular stippling mark seen on Mrs Acott's face.
It was suggested that, from a stance whereon she was merely of the opinion that *h*
the closest match of this mark from materials present at the scene was a plaster
which the appellant had on his foot, Dr Lannas progressed to a position whereby
she positively asserted cause and effect.

Fourth, Dr Lannas had stated in her evidence in chief that what she described
as most of the classical signs of strangulation were present. In cross-examination, *j*
Mr Gale was able to put to her a list of other such signs which were absent.

Lastly, her view as to the cause of what was referred to as injury number five,
being described as a 'tram line injury'; in line with their reconstruction, the
defence were suggesting that this injury had been caused when, on falling, Mrs
Acott's face came into contact with the skirting board. According to the notes
taken at the committal, Dr Lannas had replied to a question that this injury might

a have been caused by a fall against the skirting board, whereas, when it came to the second trial, she gave it as her view that this was not a feasible explanation.

In pursuit of these five criticisms, we have considered carefully the evidence relating to what Dr Lannas has stated at various stages. It is not necessary to go into precise detail, for it suffices to say that we remain entirely unpersuaded that the criticisms levelled at Dr Lannas are justified, or that her recorded utterances
b on the subjects in question betray any lack of objectivity, rather the reverse. In particular, we would point out that in relation to the first two matters, the only record of what Dr Lannas actually said consists of some rather terse notes made by the police officer who was present at the autopsy listening to comments being made almost as asides while Dr Lannas was at work. Further, in relation to the last criticism, if it be right to say that Dr Lannas' opinion that the skirting board
c was not the cause of the tram line injury became firmer, that was because, after the suggestion had been put to her at committal, she conducted her own personal experiment and was quite unable to reproduce the contact suggested. Throughout the whole of her evidence it is clear that she has always been firmly of the view that the injuries, when considered in their totality, could not have
d been due to anything other than a sustained attack, although in accordance with what we might call the 'never say never' principle, she was prepared to make certain concessions in relation to individual injuries and other possible reasons for them.

For these reasons, we do not think that this second ground of appeal succeeds.

e The third ground relates to the fact that the recorder, in the exercise of his discretion, allowed the prosecution to admit evidence concerning an earlier will of the deceased woman which had been found in her bedroom after her death. In view of the evidence concerning the amiable relationship between mother and son, the prosecution were clearly in some difficulty in advancing a possible motive and they wished to introduce this earlier will to provide one. Since
f motive is clearly a highly relevant factor in any case of murder we do not think the recorder can be criticised for allowing the prosecution to explore this possibility, even though it is somewhat difficult to see how an earlier will, which presumably had been superseded by the will found in the appellant's briefcase, could have provided any understandable motive. In any event, the prosecution
g appear to have abandoned this line by the end of the case, since in the summing up the recorder told the jury that the possibility of the inheritance was not seriously advanced as a motive. In the light of these factors, plus the fact that the second will was more favourable to the appellant than the first, we cannot think that the jury attached any significance to this evidence.

h The final ground of appeal is to the effect that the recorder should have left the issue of provocation to the jury and should have directed them upon it. It is this ground which has caused this court some anxiety. If the appellant had indeed attacked his mother then, against the background of the case, it was difficult to account for such a brutal and sustained assault other than by reason of a sudden explosion of temper. This was suggested to the appellant in terms by Miss Hallett
j QC during the course of her cross-examination, wherein she put to him that he had for some time been in a state of smouldering resentment occasioned by his financial dependency on his mother and her taking advantage of it so as to treat him like a child, and that finally his self-control had snapped. This suggestion emerges most clearly in the cross-examination where such questions were asked as:

'Even calm, quiet men sometimes snap Mr Acott? ... Was she becoming
increasingly difficult with what was according to you her secret drinking? ... *a*
You were treated like a 13-year-old ... like a small boy, were you not?'

The matter was later put in its starkest form: 'Mr Acott I have to suggest that
something went wrong that night and the two of you had a row and you attacked
your mother.' And later: 'Because you had lost your temper totally, everything
had built up and snapped.' When it came to summing up the recorder echoed *b*
this suggestion in the following passages:

'Was there some underlying resentment which suddenly boiled over on 17
February? That is what the prosecution suggests ... The suggestion that
there had been some underlying resentment which boiled over was put to
the defendant in cross-examination.'   *c*

And perhaps most pointedly of all:

'Could alcohol have caused her to be unsteady on her feet, or could it have
caused her to behave in a way which made the defendant lose his
self-control? The consumption is an established fact. What inference, if any, *d*
should be drawn from it is a matter for you.'

It is undeniable that these are words commonly used when a jury is being
directed on the issue of provocation. The complaint that is made is that the
prosecution were putting to the jury a possible reason for the killing as a factor
probative of guilt, without at the same time their being invited to consider the *e*
partial defence which the same reason might indicate.

We start with the oft-quoted words of s 3 of the Homicide Act 1957, which
have received consideration on very many occasions by this court:

'Where on a charge of murder there is evidence on which the jury can find
that the person charged was provoked (whether by things done or by things *f*
said or by both together) to lose his self-control, the question whether the
provocation was enough to make a reasonable man do as he did shall be left
to be determined by the jury; and in determining that question the jury shall
take into account everything both done and said according to the effect
which, in their opinion, it would have on a reasonable man.'   *g*

As a matter of legal history, it is perhaps not without significance that this Act
was passed in order to resolve the question of whether or not mere words alone
could be sufficient to amount to provocation. But, as a result of the manner in
which the section is worded, it is now well established that if the requisite
evidence exists so as to trigger the operation of the section, then it is the duty of *h*
the trial judge to place the matter before the jury for them to make the two
decisions enjoined by the statute, namely: (1) *did* the accused lose his self-control
as a result of the provocation? and (2) (the objective test) would a reasonable man
in his position have behaved as he did? This is so even though the defence may
not have raised the issue (see *Bullard v R* [1961] 3 All ER 470n, [1957] AC 635), or *j*
when the judge considers that any favourable verdict on that issue would be
perverse (see *R v Gilbert* (1977) 66 Cr App R 237).

The vital question in this case is what sort of evidence must exist before the
judge's duty to leave the issue of provocation to the jury is triggered? And by
evidence we include inferences which may be drawn from evidence. On the facts
of this case we accept that it was certainly possible for the jury to draw the

a inference that, if this was an attack and not an accident, the appellant must have been gripped by overmastering passion. It is difficult otherwise to account for such sustained savagery. We would also accept that there was a possible, but by no means unavoidable, inference that his mother must have either done or, more probably, said something to produce such passion in the defendant. But what? No evidence whatever, either direct or indirect, exists to afford any answer to that *b* question.

On the foregoing basis the crucial question can be simply stated: before a judge is obliged to leave the issue of provocation to the jury, must there be *some* evidence, either direct or inferential, as to what was either done or said to provoke the accused?

In our view it is essential to bear in mind that the word 'provocation' is used in *c* an active and not a passive sense. Provocation is that which provokes; it is not the state of being provoked, ie being in a temper as a result of provocation. The classic illustration of this is to be found in the direction of Devlin J in *R v Duffy* [1949] 1 All ER 932: 'Provocation is some act, or series of acts [we must now include words], done by the dead man to the accused ...' In *Lee Chun-Chuen v R* *d* [1963] 1 All ER 73 at 79, [1963] AC 220 at 231 the same judge, delivering the judgment of the Privy Council, said: 'Provocation in law consists mainly of three elements—the act of provocation, the loss of self-control ... and the retaliation proportionate to the provocation.' More recently in *R v Rossiter* [1994] 2 All ER 752 at 758 Russell LJ, after quoting the section, said:

e   'We take the law to be that wherever there is material which is capable of amounting to provocation, however tenuous it may be, the jury must be given the privilege of ruling upon it.'

Russell LJ was clearly using the word 'provocation' in its active sense, as was confirmed by Lord Taylor CJ in *R v Cambridge* [1994] 2 All ER 760, [1994] 1 WLR *f* 971, where, dealing with the submission that different considerations applied when the defence was one of alibi, Lord Taylor CJ, having cited the words of Russell LJ in *R v Rossiter* above, said:

       'We cannot agree. The authorities cited above draw no such distinction. Moreover, by way of example, a defendant may rely on an alibi whilst the *g* prosecution witnesses identifying him as the killer may describe provocative acts or words followed by an apparent loss of self-control on the defendant's part ... But what sort of evidence gives rise to the duty? Clearly, it is not for the judge to conjure up a speculative possibility of a defence which is not relied on and is unrealistic.' (See [1994] 2 All ER 760 at 764–765, [1994] 1 *h*   WLR 971 at 975.)

Before leaving the authorities, however, it is necessary to consider the recent case of *R v Stewart* [1995] 4 All ER 999, upon which Mr Gale places great reliance. The facts were very nearly identical to those in the present case. The appellant's wife, who suffered from bulimia, was found dead with a depressed skull fracture *j* consistent with repeated impact on or by a blunt object. Charged with murder, the appellant raised a defence of accident which was as improbable as that of the present appellant. He denied losing self-control or being provoked. Evidence was given by the wife's former doctor that, as a result of her illness, the deceased woman was prone to irritability, anger and impulsive actions, this evidence being led in order to lend credence to the appellant's account that he thought she was going to commit suicide, rather than to any likelihood of her acting in a

provocative way. Despite the defence, after consultation with counsel, the judge
left the issue of provocation to the jury. However, having done so, he failed to *a*
give them any further guidance as to what evidence might support the conclusion
that the accused had lost his self-control, and this omission was held to be a
non-direction. The court, however, dismissed the appeal, holding that even if the
jury's attention had been directed to evidence concerning the possibility that the
appellant did lose his self-control, they could not properly have concluded that a *b*
reasonable man would have lost his self-control as a result of those matters, since
it was only from the appellant's own evidence as to what the deceased said or did
that the provocative acts or words could be gleaned, and he had given no such
evidence. Despite the non-direction, therefore, the court applied the proviso.

The passage upon which Mr Gale relies occurs where Stuart-Smith LJ deals
with whether or not the issue of provocation should have been left to the jury *c*
([1995] 4 All ER 999 at 1006):

> 'We were at one stage minded to take the view that there was nothing in
> the evidence of the appellant which could raise a case of provocation. But
> we have been persuaded by Mr Calvert-Smith's analysis that this is not so and
> that the circumstances of the killing itself, rather than the appellant's own *d*
> evidence as to what happened, do amount to sufficient evidence that it was
> incumbent on the judge to leave the issue to the jury. Mr Calvert-Smith
> pointed out that the pathologist's evidence showed that there might have
> been as many as five blows, three to the back of the scalp and two to the face.
> It occurred in the middle of the night and was perpetrated by a man who had *e*
> not shown any tendency to violence hitherto. It was an unusually messy
> way to carry out a premeditated murder and suggested loss of self-control
> causing a frenzied attack. But while there is evidence that the appellant in
> fact may have lost his self-control, the jury can look only at what the
> appellant said the deceased did or said as provoking such loss of control, since
> there is no other testimony which bears on this vital time before the killing. *f*
> In other words, it is not open to the jury to speculate that the deceased may
> have done or said something else, simply because she had a predisposition to
> anger or provocative behaviour as a result of her disease.'

With great respect we find some difficulty in reconciling the reasoning
underlying the first two sentences of the above passage with that which *g*
prompted the last two. At first Stuart-Smith LJ appears to accept that the mere
fact of a brutal murder committed by a man not prone to violence, thereby
indicating loss of self-control, is enough to trigger the section. In the later extract,
however, he draws attention to the fact that the jury had no material on which to
work other than that provided by the defendant himself, which expressly denied *h*
provocation, and that it was not open to them to speculate so as to fill the blank
on the screen. It could be said that this last passage is tantamount to saying that
there was no evidence of provocation in its active sense, so that the court might
have resolved the problem more correctly by adhering to their initial view, rather
than by operation of the proviso which might come perilously close to usurping *j*
the jury's function.

We think that the difficulty to which this case gives rise is explained by the fact
that whether or not provocation should have been left to the jury was not the
central issue with which their Lordships were concerned, for the simple reason
that the jury *had* been invited to consider it. Given that invitation, what the court
was concerned with was the absence of any further guidance on the subject in

a relation to the evidence. If and in so far as the passage quoted contains any dichotomy, we consider that it is the concluding part which correctly states the position.

b In our judgment, having considered the authorities, before a judge is required by the statute to leave the issue of provocation to the jury, there must be some evidence of provocation in its active sense, in other words some evidence of *what* was done or *what* was said to provoke the homicidal reaction. Such evidence will, in the vast majority of cases, be direct. It is possible that it could arise by inference—for instance if, shortly before his death, the deceased was heard to say that he proposed to go and taunt the defendant upon a matter whereon the latter was known to be particularly sensitive. But it is not enough that the evidence should merely indicate that the defendant had lost his temper, *possibly* as a result

c of some unidentified words or actions, for people occasionally work themselves into a fury and erupt with no external provocation at all. If it were otherwise, the jury would have no material upon which they could make the objective judgment demanded by the statute. To direct them to determine whether the provocation in question was enough to make a reasonable man do as the

d defendant did, without the slightest inkling of what the provocation was, would be to ask the impossible. The fallacy of the appellant's argument lies in reading the first clause of the section but omitting the words in brackets.

It has been suggested that, in the above circumstances, namely where there is an inference of loss of self-control plus the possibility of some provocation as the cause, but an entire absence of evidence identifying that provocation, a jury

e would be left in doubt, a doubt which would have to be resolved in the defendant's favour. This we reject; if a defendant elects to advance a defence, be it alibi, accident or other, which is false, and thereby conceals from the jury what really happened and precludes them from considering the truth, to hold that he has, through falsity, created a second line of defence for himself we consider

f repugnant both to common sense and justice.

From the foregoing it follows that since there was no evidence to enable the jury to come to any determination of fact as to what provocation, if any, was offered to the appellant, we do not consider that it was incumbent on the recorder to put the issue before them, and he was right not to do so. That being so, in repeating the suggestions made by Miss Hallett as to the reason for the

g killing, the recorder was not in any danger of misdirecting the jury. It might, perhaps, have been better had he not used language which lawyers tend to associate with provocation, but from the jury's point of view those matters were merely put before them as material for their consideration as possibly probative of murder so that no confusion would have arisen.

h For the above reasons this final ground of appeal also fails and the appeal must be dismissed.

Appeal dismissed.

Carolyn Toulmin Barrister.

Harris (formerly Manahan) v Manahan

COURT OF APPEAL, CIVIL DIVISION
SIR THOMAS BINGHAM MR, EVANS AND WARD LJJ
25 APRIL, 24 MAY 1996

Divorce – Financial provision – Consent order – Setting aside order – Jurisdiction – Consent order incorporating agreement of spouses following dissolution of marriage to division of proceeds of sale of matrimonial home and dismissal of wife's claim for periodical payments – Wife applying to set aside consent order on basis that she had received bad legal advice at the time – Whether consent order should be set aside – Whether bad legal advice a ground for setting aside consent order.

Following the dissolution of their marriage in 1993 the parties agreed a 'clean break' settlement which was approved by the district judge and embodied in a consent order. Under that order, the former matrimonial home was to be sold and the net proceeds of sale divided between the husband and wife, and their respective claims for ancillary relief (including the wife's claim for periodical payments) were to be dismissed together with any future claims under s 2 of the Inheritance (Provision for Family and Dependants) Act 1975. Prior to the consent order, the wife had received an offer to purchase the matrimonial home for £195,000, which would have left her with a net sum of £29,000, and the husband with between £10,000 and £15,000; however, the wife's then solicitors advised her not to proceed with the sale until the ancillary proceedings had been concluded. As a result, the prospective purchasers withdrew and she was unable thereafter to find any other purchaser due to the slump in the property market. The mortgage was in arrears and in due course the building society foreclosed and an order for possession was made. A sale subsequently would produce a deficit because of mortgage charges and other debts so that there would be no lump sum for either party. The effect of the consent order was therefore that the wife (who was then 51) would have nowhere to live and would be dependent on income support. The wife brought an action for damages against her former solicitors for negligently advising her to agree to the dismissal of her claim for periodical payments and not to proceed with the sale of the matrimonial home, and in April 1995 she applied to the court to set aside the consent order on the ground it was vitiated by their bad legal advice. The judge dismissed her application and she appealed.

Held – When considering whether to approve financial arrangements agreed between the parties in ancillary relief proceedings, the court was required by s 25[a] of the Matrimonial Causes Act 1973 to have regard to all the circumstances and accordingly should take account of 'bad legal advice' whether as a good justification or as a weak excuse for a party not being held to his or her bargain. Once a consent order had been made, bad legal advice was not one of the considerations which could justify the setting aside of the order in view of the fact that the policy of the law was to encourage a clean break and the public interest

---

a   Section 25, so far as material, provides: '(1) It shall be the duty of the court in deciding whether to exercise its powers under section 23, 24 or 24A above and, if so, in what manner, to have regard to all the circumstances of the case ...'

a demanded that there should be some end to litigation. Since the judge had made the consent order after hearing submissions from the parties' representatives and the husband had not misled the wife or the court, it would be unfair on the husband, in view of the lapse of time, to set the order aside merely because of the inadequacy of the legal advice given to the wife. The appeal would therefore be dismissed (see p 494 *j* to p 470 *a d* to *j*, p 471 *g h*, p 472 *d e* and p 473 *c d*, post).

b   Per curiam. It is arguable that an appeal still lies as of right and without leave against a consent order made by a district judge and therefore if the appeal is entered in time the judge is bound to approach the matter de novo by virtue of r 8.1(3)[b] of the Family Proceedings Rules 1991 and is not bound to approve an agreement which, owing to 'bad legal advice', produces a manifestly unjust result (see p 464 *c*, p 472 *j* and p 473 *c d*, post).

c

Notes
For consent orders embodying spouses' agreement on financial provisions, see 13 *Halsbury's Laws* (4th edn) para 1158.

    For the Matrimonial Causes Act 1973, s 25, see 27 *Halsbury's Statutes* (4th edn)
d (1992 reissue) 763.

    For the Inheritance (Provision for Family and Dependants) Act 1975, s 2, see 17 *Halsbury's Statutes* (4th edn) (1993 reissue) 391.

    For the Family Proceedings Rules 1991, r 8, see 12 *Halsbury's Statutory Instruments* (1995 reissue) 116.

e **Cases referred to in judgments**
Ampthill Peerage Case [1976] 2 All ER 411, [1977] AC 547, [1976] 2 WLR 777, HL.
B v B (consent order: variation) [1995] 1 FLR 9.
Barder v Barder (Caluori intervening) [1987] 2 All ER 440, [1988] AC 20, [1987] 2 WLR 1350, HL.
f *Birkett v James* [1977] 2 All ER 801, [1978] AC 279, [1977] 3 WLR 38, HL.
B-T v B-T (divorce: procedure) [1990] 2 FLR 1.
C (financial provision: leave to appeal), Re [1993] 2 FLR 799.
Camm v Camm (1982) 4 FLR 577, CA.
D v D [1963] 1 All ER 602, [1963] 1 WLR 194, DC.
g *de Lasala v de Lasala* [1979] 2 All ER 1146, [1980] AC 546, [1979] 3 WLR 390, PC.
Dinch v Dinch [1987] 1 All ER 818, [1987] 1 WLR 252, HL.
Doyle v Olby (Ironmongers) Ltd [1969] 2 All ER 119, [1969] 2 QB 158, [1969] 2 WLR 673, CA.
Edgar v Edgar [1980] 3 All ER 887, [1980] 1 WLR 1410, CA.
h *Jakeman v Jakeman and Turner* [1963] 3 All ER 889, [1964] P 420, [1964] 2 WLR 90, DC.
Livesey (formerly Jenkins) v Jenkins [1985] 1 All ER 106, [1985] AC 424, HL.
Marsh v Marsh [1993] 2 All ER 794, [1993] 1 WLR 744, CA.
Martin v Martin [1977] 3 All ER 762, [1978] Fam 12, [1977] 3 WLR 101, CA.
   Minton v Minton [1979] 1 All ER 79, [1979] AC 593, [1979] 2 WLR 31, HL.
j *Morris-Thomas v Petticoat Lane Rentals* (1986) 53 P & CR 238, CA.
O'Connor v Din (1993) Times, 15 February, [1993] CA Transcript 150.
Peek v Peek [1947] 2 All ER 578, [1948] P 46, DC; *affd* [1948] 2 All ER 297, CA.
Pounds v Pounds [1994] 4 All ER 777, [1994] 1 WLR 1535, CA.

---

b   Rule 8.1, so far as material, is set out at p 462 *g* to *j*, post

Purcell v F C Trigell Ltd (t/a Southern Window and General Cleaning Co) [1970] 3 All
ER 671, [1971] 1 QB 358, [1970] 3 WLR 884, CA.
Thwaite v Thwaite [1981] 2 All ER 789, [1982] Fam 1, [1983] 3 WLR 96, CA.
Tommey v Tommey [1982] 3 All ER 385, [1983] Fam 15, [1982] 3 WLR 909.

Cases also cited or referred to in skeleton arguments
Cornick v Cornick [1994] 2 FLR 530.
Rondel v Worsley [1967] 3 All ER 993, [1969] 1 AC 191, HL.
Saif Ali v Sydney Mitchell & Co (a firm) (P, third party) [1978] 3 All ER 1033, [1980]
AC 198, HL.
Somasundaram v M Julius Melchior & Co (a firm) [1989] 1 All ER 129, [1988] 1 WLR
1394, CA.

Appeal
By notice dated 14 December 1995 Mrs Harris (the wife) appealed with leave
from the order of Connell J made on 17 November 1995 dismissing her
application (which had been transferred to him) to set aside a consent order dated
17 November 1993 made by District Judge Hall in ancillary relief proceedings
following the dissolution of her marriage to the respondent, Mr Harris (the
husband), on the ground that it was vitiated by the bad legal advice given to her
by her then legal advisers. The facts are set out in the judgment of Ward LJ.

Nicholas Carden (instructed by *Wynne Baxter & Godfree*, Brighton) for the wife.
The husband appeared in person.

Cur adv vult

24 May 1996. The following judgments were delivered.

WARD LJ (giving the first judgment at the invitation of Sir Thomas Bingham
MR). This is an appeal with the leave of Connell J from his order dismissing the
appellant's application which was to set aside an order dated 17 November 1993
'on the ground that it is vitiated by the bad legal advice given to her by her then
legal advisers'.
    That November 1993 order was a consent order made in the ancillary relief
proceedings following the dissolution of the marriage of the appellant and her
husband, the respondent. They had married in 1962 and separated 30 years later
in September 1992. They have five adult children. Decree nisi of divorce was
pronounced in February 1993 on the wife's petition and she pursued her claim for
ancillary relief. Affidavits of means were exchanged. The court appointed 17
November 1993 as a date for a pre-trial review, the main purpose of which was,
we were told, to give the parties an opportunity to explore the possibility of
settling the dispute. Both parties attended, the wife being represented by her
solicitor and the husband by solicitor and counsel. Negotiations took place
leading to an agreement which was approved by the district judge who then
made the order by consent, the material elements of which were: (1) the former
matrimonial home was to be sold forthwith and—

> 'The net proceeds of sale (defined as gross sale price less the outstanding
> charges to Woolwich Building Society and Barclays Bank Plc and the
> reasonable costs of estate agents and solicitors incurred in the sale) be divided
> as follows:—(a). In the event that said matrimonial home be sold for more

a than £185,000 the respondent to receive £25,000 with the balance to the petitioner; or (b). In the event that the said matrimonial home is sold for £185,000 or less, the respondent to receive a sum calculated as 12·82% of the gross sale price, and the petitioner to receive the balance'; and

b (2) the division of the proceeds of sale was to effect a clean break between the parties and there were, accordingly, further provisions in the order for the dismissal of their respective claims for ancillary relief, which included the wife's claim for periodical payments, and further provision for the dismissal of their claims under the Inheritance (Provision for Family and Dependants) Act 1975, with no order for costs.

c The background to the making of that order is very shortly this. At the time of the separation in September 1992, the matrimonial home was thought to be worth £240,000 and was subject to a first charge in favour of the building society, approximately £87,000 being outstanding on the mortgage at that time. Following the separation, the respondent husband ceased to make any further mortgage repayments notwithstanding his employment on the Channel Tunnel *d* earning £500 per week. The parties owed about £7,000 to Barclays Bank and in June 1993 voluntarily charged the property to secure that joint loan. She owed Lloyds Bank about £10,000, and he owed them nearly £8,000. In November 1993 the bank obtained charging orders against the property in respect of those debts.

As Connell J observed: 'From late 1992 onwards the story becomes somewhat familiar.' It was not possible to sell the property for £240,000. By April 1993 the *e* wife had reduced the asking price to £200,000, which substantially reduced the net capital which would have become available on any sale. In June 1993 an offer was in fact received to purchase the property for £195,000, completion being sought by October 1993. The husband did not object to that sale. The wife's solicitors were, however, advising that contracts could not be exchanged until *f* there was agreement between husband and wife resolving the claims for ancillary relief. The offerors became impatient and set a deadline of 8 November 1993 but, notwithstanding this ultimatum, the wife's solicitors continued to advise her that she should not sell until the ancillary relief proceedings had been concluded. The prospective purchasers withdrew. A week or so later the consent order was made.

g Had it been possible to sell for £195,000, then the husband would have received his £25,000 leaving, it is said, some £36,500 available to the wife, about £3,000 of which would have been needed to discharge miscellaneous debts. Taking her costs of £4,500 into account, she would have been left with a net sum of about £29,000. After payment of his bank borrowing, his debts and costs, the husband *h* would have had between £10,000 and £15,000 net. But he had his income and although a man presumably in his 50s, he still had a good earning capacity. She was 51 and had no earnings of any significance nor any prospect of any. It would not appear to me ever to have been an appropriate case for a clean break and it is no surprise at all that she has commenced proceedings against her former *j* solicitors seeking damages for their negligently advising her to agree to the dismissal of her claim for periodical payments when she had no obvious sources of income or means of support and was receiving no significant capital sum to compensate her for the dismissal of her maintenance claims. She also alleges that negligent advice cost her the chance of concluding a sale at £195,000. In the events that have occurred, the loss of that sale was significant. Despite all her best endeavours the wife was unable to secure any other purchaser. Meanwhile the

mortgage arrears which had been mounting for over a year continued to rise and
the building society foreclosed in April 1994 and a possession order was made on a
3 August 1994. The mortgagees remained sympathetic and agreed a stay on the
order for possession until February 1995. They granted a further indulgence
because there was some prospect in the spring of 1995 that the property might
sell for £170,000. It was not to be. We were informed by counsel that the
building society have now taken possession. They have marketed the property b
for £150,000 but a sale at that price has fallen through. Even if that price is
achieved today there would be a deficit because there would fall to be deducted
legal and estate agents' costs, say £5,000, the mortgage redemption figure of
about £117,000, the Barclays Bank charge of about £11,000 and the Lloyds Bank
loans of about £21,000. There will be no lump sum for either party. The effect
of the order would be that the wife would have nowhere to live and would be c
dependent on income support. Her claim for damages for negligence is being
met with the not very attractive defence that the solicitor was entitled to an
advocate's immunity from suit in respect of any incompetence he displayed in the
conduct of the proceedings at court. It is an altogether sorry tale indeed.

One approaches this appeal, therefore, with considerable sympathy for the d
wife but sympathy may not be enough.

It was not until 4 April 1995 that the wife instituted these proceedings by a
notice of application issued in the county court of her intention to apply to the
district judge for orders that the consent order be set aside on the ground I have
set out and also for an order that the application be transferred to the High Court
to be heard by a judge thereof. That was duly ordered by the district judge who e
transferred the application to the Divorce Registry for listing before a High Court
judge 'for argument on the preliminary point as to whether the ground pleaded
in the application is within the classes entitling a party to seek to re-open a
consent order of this nature'. In that way it came before Connell J.

Bearing in mind the pending negligence action, Connell J held: f

> 'Naturally, it would not be appropriate for me to venture an opinion as to
> whether or not the advice given was negligent, because I have not heard any
> submissions on behalf of the solicitors in that respect and I do not know what
> their defence to the charge may be. However, I can say, to put it at its lowest,
> that the advice given to the wife, on the basis of the facts as described herein, g
> was plainly bad advice.'

I agree. The learned judge found, and again I entirely agree:

> 'The compromise of a claim to periodical payments after a 30-year h
> marriage is a compromise which should only be agreed to by a wife who is
> confident that she will be left with sufficient resources to house and maintain
> herself in the future. Likewise, advice to reject an offer of £195,000, i e close
> to the then asking price, in a volatile market, has, in the result, been shown
> to be bad advice.'

j

The volatile market conditions prevailing at that time created risks which have
now become realities that: (a) the slump in the property market would further
depress property prices thereby reducing the amount upon which the wife was to
be dependent for establishing her home and/or for her support; (b) mortgage
arrears would continue to accrue through the husband's continuing default but,
since the husband took his share either as the fixed price of £25,000 or as a

a percentage of the gross selling price, the mounting debts would be borne by the wife alone.

It was, therefore, on any view, an improvident and ill-advised bargain for the wife to have struck.

The question in the appeal is whether bad legal advice justifies the setting aside of a consent order. It is an important question. An affirmative answer could

b dramatically affect the workload of the family courts because, in a field of jurisprudence where the solution is found by 'trial and error and imagination' (see Martin v Martin [1977] 3 All ER 762 at 768, [1978] Fam 12 at 20 per Ormrod LJ), and where the unhappiness of the breakdown of a marriage easily transfers to disenchantment with the ancillary arrangements made consequent

c upon it, the disgruntled have wide scope for blaming bad legal advice for their dissatisfaction. The question raises difficult issues of precedent, procedure and policy. It is, therefore, necessary to examine the nature and effect of consent orders, the function of the court in approving agreed terms and the procedures for challenging the order before turning directly to the question posed in the appeal.

d

(1) THE EFFECT OF AN ORDER BEING MADE BY CONSENT

In giving the advice of the Judicial Committee in de Lasala v de Lasala [1979] 2 All ER 1146 at 1155, [1980] AC 546 at 560, Lord Diplock said:

e   'Financial arrangements that are agreed on between the parties for the purpose of receiving approval and being made the subject of a consent order by the court, once they have been made the subject of the court order no longer depend on the agreement of the parties as the source from which their legal effect is derived. Their legal effect is derived from the court order ...'

f That was considered by this court in Thwaite v Thwaite [1981] 2 All ER 789 at 794, [1982] Fam 1 at 8, where Ormrod LJ (with Dunn LJ and Wood J) gave the judgment of the court in these terms:

         'This statement of principle is effectively binding on this court because the relevant provisions of the Hong Kong Ordinance are identical to the
g   corresponding provisions of the Matrimonial Causes Act 1973. We respectfully adopt it and believe that it removes much of the confusion about consent orders which has prevailed in this jurisdiction. It does, however, represent a significant departure from the general principle frequently stated in cases arising in other divisions of the High Court, that the force and effect
h   of consent orders derives from the contract between the parties leading to, or evidenced by, or incorporated in the consent order ... A distinction, therefore, has to made between consent orders made in this and other types of litigation ... The effect of eliminating the contractual basis of these consent orders should simplify the problem. If their legal effect is derived
j   from the court order it must follow, we think, that they must be treated as orders of the court and dealt with, so far as possible, in the same way as non-consensual orders ... As orders of the court, they must be subject to the provisions which apply to appeals from orders made at first instance, though with one important exception. Where the court of first instance has not adjudicated on the evidence, its decision cannot be challenged on the ground that the court has reached a wrong conclusion on the evidence before it.

Final orders of all kinds, however, can be challenged on appeal and may be set aside on other grounds.'

Any doubt about this was removed by Lord Brandon of Oakbrook's emphasising as his fourth basic principle in *Livesey (formerly Jenkins) v Jenkins* [1985] 1 All ER 106 at 112, [1985] AC 424 at 435:

'... when parties agree the provisions of a consent order, and the court subsequently gives effect to such agreement by approving the provisions concerned and embodying them in an order of the court, the legal effect of those provisions is derived from the court order itself, and does not depend any longer on the agreement between the parties ...'

(2) THE FUNCTION OF THE JUDGE

The first three principles Lord Brandon wished to emphasise in *Livesey (formerly Jenkins) v Jenkins* were:

'The first matter is that the powers of a judge of the Family Division of the High Court or of a judge of a divorce county court to make orders for financial provision and property adjustment following a divorce are conferred on them, and conferred of them solely, by statute ... The second matter is that there no difference in this respect between a judge's powers to make such orders after a disputed hearing involving evidence on both sides and his powers to make such orders by the consent of the parties without having heard any evidence at all. The third matter is that the powers of registrars to make such orders, when delegated to them by rules of court, are exactly the same as those of judges, whether the proceedings concerned are in the principal registry of the Family Division, or in the registry of a divorce county court.'

The Matrimonial Causes Act 1973, as amended, makes clear what those powers are. Under s 25 it shall be the duty of the court in deciding whether to exercise its powers, and if so, in what manner, to have regard to the listed matters. Under s 25A:

'Where ... the court decides to exercise its powers ... it shall be the duty of the court to consider whether it would be appropriate so to exercise those powers that the financial obligations of each party towards the other will be terminated as soon after the grant of the decree as the court considers just and reasonable.'

Under s 15(1) of the Inheritance (Provision for Family and Dependants) Act 1975 the court may order that the parties shall not be entitled to apply for orders under s 2 of the Act 'if it considers it just to do so'.

Implicit in the order are, therefore, decisions made by the district judge that it was appropriate to order a clean break and that the court considered that the order was just and reasonable and that it was also just to disentitle future claims under the 1975 Act.

The question, however, is how assiduous the judge must be before approving the compromise. In *Tommey v Tommey* [1982] 3 All ER 385 at 390, [1983] Fam 15 at 21 Balcombe J said:

'A judge who is asked to make a consent order cannot be compelled to do so: he is no mere rubber stamp. If he thinks that there are matters about a   which he needs to be more fully informed before he makes the order, he is entitled to make such inquiries, and require such evidence to be put before him, as he considers necessary. But, per contra, he is under no obligation to make inquiries or require evidence. He is entitled to assume that parties of full age and capacity know what is in their best interests, more especially when they are represented before him by counsel or solicitors. The fact that

b   he was not told facts which, had he known them, might have affected his decision to make a consent order, cannot of itself be a ground for impeaching the order.'

Lord Brandon in *Livesey (formerly Jenkins) v Jenkins* [1985] 1 All ER 106 at 116, [1985] AC 424 at 441 said that 'there is a great deal of practical common sense' in

c   that passage, even though he rejected the implication that there was no duty to give full and frank disclosure.

Section 7 of the Matrimonial and Family Proceedings Act 1984 introduced into the 1973 Act a new s 33A, which provided:

d   '(1) Notwithstanding anything in the preceding provisions of this Part of this Act, on an application for a consent order for financial relief the court may, unless it has reason to think that there other circumstances into which it ought to inquire, make an order in the terms agreed on the basis only of the prescribed information furnished with the application ...'

e   In this case the parties had attended in person having filed their affidavits and the need to file the necessary r 2.61 summary of relevant information must have been dispensed with.

In *Pounds v Pounds* [1994] 4 All ER 777 at 781–782, [1994] 1 WLR 1535 at 1539–1540 Waite LJ said:

f   'When the House of Lords ruled in *Livesey (formerly Jenkins) Jenkins* [1985] 1 All ER 106, [1985] AC 424 that the duty of disclosure of assets was owed by spouses not only to each other but to the court, it did so upon the basis that it was the function of the court in every case, whether it was proceeding by consent of the parties or after a contested hearing, to be satisfied that the provision made by the order fulfilled the criteria laid down by s 25 of the 1973

g   Act. It is clear, however, that this was intended to be an assertion of general principle only, and not to impose on the court the need to scrutinise in detail the financial affairs of parties who came to it for approval of an independently negotiated bargain. It could not be otherwise, for earlier that year Parliament had specifically enacted a more cursory regime for the

h   scrutiny of consent orders ... The effect of s 33A and the rules and directions made under it is thus to confine the paternal function of the court when approving financial consent orders to a broad appraisal of the parties' financial circumstances as disclosed to it in summary form, without descent into the valley of detail. It is only if that survey puts the court on inquiry as

j   to whether there are other circumstances into which it ought to probe more deeply that any further investigation is required of the judge before approving the bargain that the spouses have made for themselves.'

Waite LJ thus eloquently states the principle which I had brashly reduced to the observation that whilst the court is no rubber stamp, nor is it some kind of forensic ferret.

It is important to stress the practical common sense of Balcombe J's approach. The realities of life in the principal registry and the divorce county courts are that the district judges are under inevitable pressure and the system only works because the judges rely on the practitioners' help. I would, therefore, be very slow to condemn any judge for a failure to see that bad legal advice is being tendered to a party. The statutory duty on the court cannot be ducked, but the court is entitled to assume that parties who are sui juris and who are represented by solicitors know what they want. Officious inquiry may uncover an injustice but it is more likely to disturb a delicate negotiation and produce the very costly litigation and the recrimination which conciliation is designed to avoid.

In this case the petitioner frankly states in her affidavit that District Judge Hall—

'asked me if I was happy with the Order that was to be made. Having been told by Mr Fagg [her solicitor] that the terms were "pretty fair" I naturally replied in the affirmative. Mr Fagg had explained to me, before we entered the Judge's chambers, that the terms of the Order prevented me from ever claiming maintenance from the Respondent. Again, I accepted that because I was told that the deal was fair.'

In those circumstances there can be no possible criticism of the district judge and Mr Carden made it quite clear that he was not suggesting there was.

(3) THE PROCEDURE

How can an order like this be challenged? There seem to be four possibilities. I covered three of them in *B-T v B-T (divorce: procedure)* [1990] 2 FLR 1 and Thorpe J suggested a fourth in *Re C (financial provision: leave to appeal)* [1993] 2 FLR 799.

(i) *Appeal*

The Matrimonial Causes Rules 1977, SI 1977/344, permitted an appeal even against a consent order (see r 124). That was the position when I gave judgment in *B-T v B-T*. It is now submitted by Mr Carden that the rule has changed and that a consent order cannot be appealed. Rule 8.1 of the Family Proceedings Rules 1991, SI 1991/1247, reads:

'*Appeals from district judges.*—(1) Except where paragraph (2) applies, any party may appeal from an order or decision made or given by the district judge in family proceedings in a county court to a judge on notice; and in such a case—(a) CCR Order 13, rule 1(10) (which enables the judge to vary or rescind an order made by the district judge in the course of proceedings), and (b) CCR Order 37, rule 6 (which gives a right of appeal to the judge from a judgment or final decision of the district judge), shall not apply to the order or decision.

(2) Any order or decision granting or varying an order (or refusing to do so)—(a) on an application for ancillary relief ... shall be treated as a final order for the purposes of CCR Order 37, rule 6.

(3) On hearing an appeal to which paragraph (2) above applies, the judge may exercise his own discretion in substitution for that of the district judge ...'

CCR Ord 37, r 6 reads:

'Appeal from district judge.—(1) Any party affected by a judgment or final order of the district judge may, except where he has consented to the terms thereof, appeal from the judgment or order to the judge, who may, upon such terms as he thinks fit—(a) set aside or vary the judgment or order or any part thereof ...'

I do not find the construction of these rules easy. There is a clear attempt to separate interlocutory orders under r 8.1(1) from final orders under r 8.1(2). I had pointed out in *B-T v B-T* [1990] 2 FLR 1 at 13–15 the uncertainties about the extent to which ancillary relief orders ranging from variable periodical payments orders to non-variable lump sum and property adjustment orders could or should be treated as interlocutory or final orders. The practical effect of the difference in the practice of the county court is that on appeal the judge has the ability to deal with the former as hearings de novo whereas with the latter the appeal is akin to an appeal from the judge to the Court of Appeal. The value of that distinction was eroded by *Marsh v Marsh* [1993] 2 All ER 794, [1993] 1 WLR 744, which decided that the provisions of r 8.1(3) give the judge the power to exercise his own discretion so that the strict appellate approach was not intended to apply in ancillary relief appeals. It would seem, therefore, to be a distinction without a difference.

Mr Carden submits that r 8(2) of the 1991 rules must be more widely construed than that. He submits that ancillary relief orders must not only be treated as final orders for the purposes of Ord 37, r 6, but that appeals against ancillary relief orders must be entirely governed by that rule. Since that rule excludes an appeal where a party has consented to the terms thereof, no appeal lies against a consent order for ancillary relief. Counsel who then represented the respondent in the court below apparently agreed and the case proceeded upon that basis. I am far from convinced that Mr Carden is correct. My reservations are these.

(a) Rule 8.1 does not seem to apply to orders made in the High Court where the rules would seem to permit an appeal against a consent order. RSC Ord 58, r 1 provides: '(1) ... an appeal shall lie to a Judge in Chambers from any judgment, order or decision of ... a Registrar of the Family Division ...' Rule 3 provides a similar appeal from the district registrar. Whether or not leave to appeal is required may be a matter of debate. The decision of this court in *Purcell v F C Trigell Ltd (t/a Southern Window and General Cleaning Co)* [1970] 3 All ER 671, [1971] 1 QB 358 was that because 'court or judge' in s 31(1)(h) of the Supreme Court of Judicature (Consolidation) Act 1925 included the district registrar, leave was necessary, but *The Supreme Court Practice 1995* vol 2, para 4606 seems to suggest that with the repeal of the successor section, s 18(1)(f) of the Supreme Court Act 1981, there is no longer any need for leave. It is not necessary to enter that debate.

(b) If the purpose of the rule were as Mr Carden contends, then the rule-making committee could very simply have said: 'Ord 37, r 6 shall apply to appeals against ancillary relief orders.'

(c) *Marsh v Marsh* demonstrates that Ord 37, r 6 does not fully apply to ancillary relief appeals.

(d) If the established learning of the Privy Council, Court of Appeal and House of Lords in *de Lasala v de Lasala* [1979] 2 All ER 1146, [1980] AC 546, *Thwaite v Thwaite* [1981] 2 All ER 789, [1982] Fam 1 and *Barder v Barder (Caluori intervening)* [1987] 2 All ER 440, [1988] AC 20 was being swept overboard by a change in the rules then: (i) one would have expected the rules to say so clearly, for example:

'No appeal shall lie against a consent order for ancillary relief'; (ii) one would have expected to have been able to identify quite easily what mischief this change *a* was curing. It may be that the Rules Committee had in mind that a right of appeal was unnecessary because there was a right of rehearing under Ord 37, r 1. I do not see why the two remedies cannot live side by side. In matters heard by a judge there is a right of rehearing as well as a right of appeal to the Court of Appeal and although this court in *O'Connor v Din* (1993) Times, 15 February *b* suggested that the remedy of rehearing should be exhausted before going on appeal, there was no reservation about these two routes being available.

In my judgment, it is at least arguable that an appeal against a consent order will still lie as of right and without leave. If it does, and if the right to appeal is exercised in time, then the appeal proceeds by virtue of the provisions of r 8.1(3) as one where the judge exercises his own discretion in substitution for that of the *c* district judge. The judge is accordingly under a duty to have regard to the provisions of s 25 of the 1973 Act and, as I shall set out in a moment, he is not bound to approve an agreement which, due to 'bad legal advice', produces a manifestly unjust result.

d

(ii) *Rehearing*

Some justification for excluding appeals against consent orders may be the acknowledgment that if the judge gives his imprimatur of approval to the compromise placed before him, then it can hardly be asserted that he was in error. Accordingly, Ord 37, r 1 applies. That reads:

e

'*Rehearing.*—(1) In any proceedings tried without a jury the judge shall have power on application to order a rehearing when no error of the court at the hearing is alleged.

(2) Unless the court otherwise orders, any application under paragraph (1) shall be made to the judge by whom the proceedings were tried ... *f*

(4) Where the proceedings were tried by the district judge, the powers conferred on the judge by paragraphs (1) ... shall be exercisable by the district judge and paragraph (2) shall not apply ...'

Once again the practice in the county court and the High Court differ in that there is no comparable provision in the Rules of the Supreme Court, even though *g* the power so to provide is given by s 17(2) of the 1981 Act.

Given that the function of the judge is as I have set it out above, then, as Lord Merriman P said in *Peek v Peek* [1947] 2 All ER 578 at 584, [1948] P 46 at 58: '... it is impossible to say that the court was in error merely because the judge did not conduct some more exhaustive enquiries.' That would cover this case. It is *h* possible to imagine that such a manifestly unjust order is in fact made when no reasonable judge would ever have made it, then it would be hard to say there was no error of the court. That would be a reason for having a fall-back right of appeal.

As to whether or not 'bad legal advice' would justify a rehearing, I observe that *j* the solicitor's negligence was treated as a sufficient justification for a rehearing under the comparable provisions for rehearing divorce causes (see *D v D* [1963] 1 All ER 602, [1963] 1 WLR 194 and *Jakeman v Jakeman and Turner* [1963] 3 All ER 889, [1964] P 420). It should not, however, be thought that a rehearing would follow inevitably. As Ralph Gibson LJ pointed out in *Morris-Thomas v Petticoat Lane Rentals* (1986) 53 P & CR 238 at 254:

a
'Justice normally requires that when an action has been fought and duly lost upon the ground apparently chosen by the plaintiff, with the advice of solicitors and counsel, such a plaintiff should not, save in most exceptional circumstances, be permitted to start again in order to fight the claim on different grounds, and the claim that solicitor or counsel made a mistake would rarely if ever justify a departure from that principle. The court will

b
not permit the litigant to suffer for the mistake of his lawyer if the mistake can be corrected without injustice on the other side: see *Doyle* v. *Olby Ltd.* ([1969] 2 All ER 119, [1969] 2 QB 158); but when the mistake is of the nature that can only be corrected by letting the plaintiff start again with a fresh trial it will rarely be possible to assist such a plaintiff.'

c
If, however, the application is made in time, and if it is granted, then on the rehearing a fresh discretion must be exercised on the facts then before the court.

It is not quite clear from the terms of the notice of application issued in this case whether the wife had Ord 37, r 1 in mind. It is possible so to construe the application. Although the rehearing should be by the district judge who made the original order, I can see no objection to the difficult case being transferred by him

d
into the High Court to be resolved by the High Court judge as was done here. The application was, however, way out of time. There was no application to extend time and no consideration appears to have been given to that matter at all.

(iii) *Fresh action*

e
In *de Lasala v de Lasala* [1979] 2 All ER 1146 at 1155–1156, [1980] AC 546 at 561 Lord Diplock said:

'Since their Lordships have already held that Huggins J, in the exercise of the divorce jurisdiction ... had no power to vary the consent order ... the only means now open to the wife to set it aside on grounds of fraud or

f
mistake would be by bringing a fresh action for this purpose.'

Where the vitiating factor is said to be bad advice, then I can imagine circumstances where the bad advice gives rise to a mistaken belief which, if shared by the other side, may enable the underlying agreement to be attacked on the ground of mistake. I find it very difficult to envisage a cause of action in which

g
the negligence of one's own solicitor justifies the setting aside of an agreement made with a third party. I do not find this route at all attractive.

(iv) *Application in the suit*

In *Re C (financial provision: leave to appeal)* [1993] 2 FLR 799 at 801 Thorpe J took

h
a pragmatic approach to problems of this kind and suggested:

'... if an order made by a judge of the Division has been secured by some vitiating factor, then the aggrieved party can reopen the proceedings by the issue of a judge's summons for which no leave is required.'

j
I suspect this was the course followed by this appellant. The parties before Thorpe J took the appeal route when they could perhaps have applied for a rehearing by the district judge who would not appear to have been in error. That they had to go through the hoop of seeking an extension of time does not appear to me to be a serious obstacle because it gives the court a chance to filter out the hopeless case before the expense of a full blown contest is incurred. Whilst I am ordinarily totally sympathetic to practicality overcoming technicality, nevertheless, where the rules sufficiently provide the remedy, as they do, I see no

justification for importing ad hoc procedures. Thorpe J has far greater experience of these matters than I do and his judgment commands respect, but I venture to think that the extension he proposed goes further than is necessary.

There was no dispute before Connell J about the correctness of the procedure that was followed in this case. He proceeded to determine the matter upon its merits as I will soon turn to do. It is a pity that we have not been able to have full argument on these procedural matters which remain far from clear. The Family Proceedings Rules Committee could usefully look again at r 8.1. I tentatively make the following suggestions.

(a) There ought to be the same rule for county court proceedings as for those transferred into the High Court both as to appeals and as to rehearings.

(b) The right to seek a rehearing under Ord 37, r 1 should enable consent orders to be reconsidered in most cases because it is most unlikely that an error of the court can then be established.

(c) Because the ratio of *de Lasala v de Lasala*, *Thwaite v Thwaite* and *Livesey (formerly Jenkins) v Jenkins* demands that consent orders be treated no differently from non-consensual orders, consent orders ought, in my opinion, to be capable of being appealed in exactly the same way as contested orders. Judicious application of *O'Connor v Din* (1993) Times, 15 February should ensure that the appeal route is discouraged where rehearing is more appropriate.

(d) The time limit of 14 days provided both for rehearings as for appeals is a valuable filter which ought not to be overlooked. It should be rigorously enforced whether the case is one of fraud, mistake, non-disclosure, fresh evidence, or supervening events as in *Barder v Barder*. It is, in my judgment, all the more important if the reason advanced for the rehearing or appeal is 'bad legal advice'. The guidelines set by Lord Brandon of Oakbrook in *Barder v Barder* [1987] 2 All ER 440 at 453, [1988] AC 20 at 43 apply with equal force whenever leave is required or, I suggest, whenever any extension of time is sought. He suggested that leave should only be given if certain conditions are satisfied:

> 'The first condition is that new events have occurred since the making of the order which invalidate the basis, or fundamental assumption, on which the order was made, so that, if leave to appeal out of time were to be given, the appeal would be certain, or very likely, to succeed. The second condition is that the new events should have occurred within a relatively short time of the order having been made. While the length of time cannot be laid down precisely, I should regard it as extremely unlikely that it could be as much as a year, and that in most cases it would be no more than a few months. The third condition is that the application for leave to appeal out of time should be made reasonably promptly in the circumstances of the case. To these three conditions, which can be seen from the authorities as requiring to be satisfied, I would add a fourth, which it does not appear has needed to be considered so far, but which it may be necessary to consider in future cases. That fourth condition is that the grant of leave to appeal out of time should not prejudice third parties who have acquired, in good faith and for valuable consideration, interests in property which is the subject matter of the relevant order.'

If leave had to be sought in this case, I would be likely to refuse it because, as I shall show, success was unlikely, there was a long delay before protesting about the negligence and the proceedings were not brought promptly.

a In the light of the way in which this litigation was conducted, I propose to assume that the wife has overcome all procedural hurdles so that the question of her appeal should be dealt with on its merits. I turn now to the nub of that appeal.

(4) BAD LEGAL ADVICE AS A FACTOR AFFECTING THE MAKING OF THE ORDER

The first reference to bad legal advice to which we have been referred, was made in *Edgar v Edgar* [1980] 3 All ER 887, [1980] 1 WLR 1410. There the wife had
b entered into a separation deed and had agreed to terms that on the husband's buying her a house for £100,000 and maintaining her at the rate of £16,000 per annum she would not claim any lump sum or property adjustment orders. This was against the advice of Mr Robert Johnson QC leading Mr Nicholas Wilson. She in time presented a petition for divorce and her prayer for ancillary relief
c included the claims she had agreed to forgo. Eastham J none the less awarded her a further £670,000, but in the course of allowing the appeal Ormrod LJ said ([1980] 3 All ER 887 at 893, [1980] 1 WLR 1410 at 1417):

> 'To decide what weight should be given, in order to reach a just result, to
> a prior agreement not to claim a lump sum, regard must be had to the
d > conduct of both parties leading up to the prior agreement, and to their
> subsequent conduct in consequence of it. It is not necessary in this
> connection to think in formal legal terms, such as misrepresentation or
> estoppel; *all* the circumstances as they affect each of two human beings must
> be considered in the complex relationship of marriage. So the circumstances
> surrounding the making of the agreement are relevant. Undue pressure by
e > one side, exploitation of a dominant position to secure an unreasonable
> advantage, inadequate knowledge, *possibly* bad legal advice, an important
> change of circumstances, unforeseen or overlooked at the time of making
> the agreement, are all relevant to the question of justice between the parties.
> Important too is the general proposition that, formal agreements, properly
f > and fairly arrived at with competent legal advice, should not be displaced
> unless there are good and substantial grounds for concluding that an
> injustice will be done by holding the parties to the terms of their agreement.
> There may well be other considerations which affect the justice of this case;
> the above list is not intended to be an exclusive catalogue.' (My emphasis.)

g The point arose in *Camm v Camm* (1982) 4 FLR 577 at 580, where Sir Roger Ormrod, having referred to his judgment in *Edgar v Edgar*, said:

> '... I made it clear [in *Edgar v Edgar*] that that was not, of course, an
> exclusive list. I still think it was right to refer to bad legal advice, although in
> that passage I was not thinking in terms of negligence by the solicitor. The
h > unfortunate fact in this case was that the hearing below was occupied to a
> considerable extent in questioning the wife's solicitor, who is himself the
> defendant in a pending action for negligence which may or may not be
> proceeded with. In that passage I was certainly not thinking in terms of
> negligence: I was thinking in terms of exactly what I had said, "bad legal
j > advice", and we are all familiar with cases in which parties are badly advised.
> That is to say, it is not necessarily negligent advice to take a course or permit
> a client to take a course which a more experienced, or a stronger minded
> legal adviser would have discouraged ... I think the quality of legal advice is
> relevant on the issue of justice, but not in terms of negligence actions.'

Eveleigh LJ neatly encapsulated the court's approach (at 588):

'One has to ask in relation to the wife, how far did she know what she was
doing, and what her choices were and in what circumstances did she make   *a*
the agreement? Then one has to ask whether it is just to allow her to ignore
the agreement, to go behind it, and one might say in a given case that the
agreement was made in such circumstances that it should be binding unless
a radical change of circumstances could be shown. On the other hand, one
might in another case say that the circumstances in which the agreement was   *b*
made were such that it would be wrong to hold the party (in this case the
wife) to it or for it to affect the case at all. One should also consider whether
the husband has altered his position for the worse on the strength of the
agreement.'

Hoffmann LJ understandably enough did not find the law to be in a satisfactory   *c*
state. To one schooled in the Chancery Division, the familiar approach of the
Family Division to paint with the broad brush seemed only to be slapdash. He
pointed out in *Pounds v Pounds* [1994] 4 All ER 777 at 792–793, [1994] 1 WLR 1535
at 1550:

'... it does seem to me that the law is in an unsatisfactory state ... The   *d*
result of the decision of this court in *Edgar v Edgar* [1980] 3 All ER 887, [1980]
1 WLR 1410 and the cases which have followed it is that we have, it seems
to me, the worst of both worlds. The agreement may be held to be binding,
but whether it will be can be determined only after litigation and may
involve, as in this case, examining the quality of the advice which was given
to the party who wishes to resile. It is then understandably a matter for   *e*
surprise and resentment on the part of the other party that one should be
able to repudiate an agreement on account of the inadequacy of one's own
legal advisers, over whom the other party had no control and of whose
advice he has no knowledge.'

Waite LJ had said, with the agreement of Neill and Hoffmann LJJ ([1994] 4 All ER   *f*
777 at 779, [1994] 1 WLR 1535 at 1537):

'So long as that bargain remained an out-of-court agreement, it would be
impossible to claim for it the finality which both sides hoped to achieve. The
common law will not enforce, and statute law renders void, any provision in   *g*
an agreement purporting to restrict rights to apply to a court for an order
giving financial relief. Far from being clean, the break would become liable
to a painful rejoining if either side, whether because of second thoughts or
because of change in circumstances, became dissatisfied with the bargain.
The only safe way of making their agreement watertight would be to   *h*
incorporate it in an order of the court.'

In this case the clean break agreement was approved and initialled by the district
judge before decree nisi was pronounced. The wife changed her mind—and her
solicitors, and her new eagle-eyed advisers spotted the timing of the order and
successfully argued before Singer J that the order was a nullity having been made   *j*
before decree nisi. That finding was reversed on appeal. It therefore became
unnecessary for the court to express any view about the effect of bad legal advice
and the above observations are obiter, but they are not lacking persuasive force,
and Connell J rightly placed considerable reliance on their views.

This case was not referred to Thorpe J in *B v B (consent order: variation)* [1995] 1
FLR 9. There, a consent order had been made providing a lump sum and a term

a of periodical payments on the expiry of which the wife's claim would be
   dismissed, but the order did not contain the direction under s 28(1A) of the 1973
   Act which would have provided that the wife was not entitled to apply for a
   variation of the order by extending that term. She in time duly applied for just
   such an extension and for increased periodical payments from her wealthy
   husband whose earnings had increased and who had substantial pension
b entitlements. Thorpe J found (at 21):

> 'What these two non-specialist solicitors intended is, to me, manifestly
> plain. I am in no doubt at all that Mr G, Mr W, the husband, and the wife,
> must all have understood in their differing ways that there was to be a
> deferred dismissal of the periodical payments claim at the expiration of 7
c > years.'

He accepted the wife's submission that the fact of bad legal advice should be
taken into consideration on the application to vary and he held (at 22–23):

> 'So, what should be done at this stage? The responsibility for the creation
> of this quite unnecessary further litigation seems to lie with Mr G and
d > possibly with Mr W, although I must bear in mind that I have not heard from
> either in defence of what they did during the course of their respective
> professional relationships. Each of the parties has issued a protective writ
> within the limitation period and it would therefore arguably be enough for
> this court to say that the matrimonial causes settlement has been achieved
e > by a consent order, and if that order is unfair to either then each has their
> remedy in negligence. For many reasons I do not think that it is the
> appropriate response. The decisions of the Court of Appeal in relation to
> applications that invoke ss 23–25 in the face of contracts that prevent such
> application is none the less to grant relief in exceptional circumstances. I
> reject the submission that different principles apply where the contract has
f > been made the subject of order by consent and the application is under s 31
> in breach of a provision in the consent order that expressly or by implication
> debars it. The general considerations expressed by Ormrod LJ in *Edgar* and
> in *Camm* in my judgment apply. The rationalisation contained in the
> judgment of Eveleigh LJ in *Camm* ((1982) 4 FLR 577 at 588) is, in my
g > judgment, of equal application to variation and extension applications.
> Fundamentally, where the parties come before the court with a proposed
> order to satisfy a wife's rights to financial provision the court at that stage has
> a statutory duty to have regard to a number of factors and considerations.
> That function was seemingly performed by the district judge who
> considered the draft and the r 76(A) statement. That function was distorted
h > by the incomplete and slanted presentation of the essential circumstances as
> by the failure of the negotiators, and in consequence of the court, to face the
> important question—was the right to apply for extension alive or dead? So if
> the statutory exercise that should have accompanied the making of the
> consent order was not properly performed, it seems to me that it is my
j > function to perform it now.'

As Connell J correctly observed, Thorpe J was dealing with an application to vary,
not an application to set aside a consent order.
   The effect of these authorities seem to me to amount to this: because the court
is under a duty imposed by s 25 of the 1973 Act to have regard to *all* the
circumstances, and then under the duty itself to decide whether it will exercise

any of its powers and if so how they are to be exercised, 'bad legal advice' must
be taken into account whether as a good justification or as a weak excuse for a   *a*
party not being held to his or her bargain. The quality of advice clearly has a part
to play.

(5) BAD LEGAL ADVICE AS A GROUND FOR SETTING AN ORDER ASIDE

In *de Lasala v de Lasala* [1979] 2 All ER 1146, [1980] AC 546 Lord Diplock had,   *b*
as I have set out, referred to challenges being made to the validity of the order
there on the ground of fraud or mistake. In *Thwaite v Thwaite* [1981] 2 All ER 789,
[1982] Fam 1 Ormrod LJ observed that there were other grounds, mentioning
fresh evidence properly admitted by an appellate court and material
non-disclosure, this latter ground being confirmed by *Livesey (formerly Jenkins) v
Jenkins* [1985] 1 All ER 106, [1985] AC 424. *Barder v Barder (Caluori intervening)*   *c*
[1987] 2 All ER 440, [1988] AC 20 established another category where new events
occurring since the making of the order invalidate the basis upon which it had
been made. In *de Lasala v de Lasala* the wife was asserting that she had been
induced to agree to the consent order (a) by misrepresentations by the husband
as to his financial position at the time, and (b) by the bad advice she had received   *d*
from her then legal advisers as to what her tax position would be. It was not
necessary for the Privy Council to rule upon that latter submission.

So, as Connell J held, the question posed sharply as it is here, has not yet
directly arisen for decision. Connell J held:

> 'In the present case I observe that the court has given its imprimatur to the   *e*
> agreement reached between the parties by making the order after hearing
> submissions from the parties' representatives, and by expressing the view
> that it was just to disentitle either party from applying for an order under s 2
> of the Inheritance (Provision for Family and Dependants) Act 1975. The role
> of the court was not therefore entirely passive, and the step between
> agreement and order was important ... Further, it is not said here that the   *f*
> husband misled the wife or the court, or behaved in any way improperly. No
> doubt, since 17 November 1993, he has believed that the agreement reached
> on that day, which was embodied in the order of the court, was final and
> binding and he was fully entitled so to believe. When considering the justice
> of the case it would, in my judgment, be unfair to this husband to set the   *g*
> order of the court aside. That is not by any means conclusive of the issue
> because the wife's situation must also be borne in mind. She has issued
> proceedings against her solicitors, although these may not be without
> problems ... So far as her application before me is concerned, bearing in
> mind in particular the dicta, albeit an obiter dicta of Waite and Hoffmann LJJ   *h*
> in *Pounds v Pounds* [1994] 4 All ER 777, [1994] 1 WLR 1535, I conclude that
> there is a line to be drawn between the court's approach to agreements, on
> the one hand, and consent orders, on the other hand, and that it would not
> be right to add bad legal advice to the list of considerations which can justify
> the setting aside of consent orders of the court.'

j

In broad terms, I agree with his conclusion and with his sentiments.

In reaching my own decision, I derived help from the approach of Balcombe J
in *Tommey v Tommey* [1982] 3 All ER 385, [1983] Fam 15, even though his actual
conclusion was doubted by Lord Brandon in *Livesey (formerly Jenkins) v Jenkins*.
There, it was agreed that the wife would receive a sum in full and final settlement
of all her financial claims and the court, approving that agreement, accordingly

a dismissed those claims. She then applied to set aside that part of the order on the ground that the husband had exerted undue influence in obtaining her consent to the agreement. Balcombe J held ([1982] 3 All ER 385 at 392, [1983] Fam 15 at 24):

b '... whether that development [of the existing law by holding that undue influence is an additional ground upon which a matrimonial order can be set aside] should take place involves considerations of policy. In my judgment, this involves holding a balance between two important principles which are often expressed by the Latin phrases: ubi jus ibi remedium and interest reipublicae ut sit finis litium.'

c Mr Carden mounts a powerful argument that the law should provide a remedy for the wrong suffered by this appellant. It cannot be gainsaid that she has been wronged and that she has suffered an injustice. As between husband and wife an unfair order was made. It may, but perhaps it may not, be fully redressed by her claim against her former solicitors. This alternative remedy should, however, be as irrelevant as it is in applications to strike out an action for want of prosecution (see *Birkett v James* [1977] 2 All ER 801, [1978] AC 279). This aspect of justice

d demands that she have a remedy against her husband.

There are, however, other public policy considerations. Procedural delays and escalating costs are common scars on the face of justice. Consequently every impetus is given to encourage and to enhance early settlements of disputed claims. A conciliatory approach to find accord is the essence of good practice extolled by the Family Law Bar Association and the Solicitors' Family Law

e Association.

Lord Scarman said in *Minton v Minton* [1979] 1 All ER 79 at 87–88, [1979] AC 593 at 608 that two principles inform the modern legislation:

f 'One is the public interest that spouses, to the extent that their means permit, should provide for themselves and their children. But the other, of equal importance, is the principle of "the clean break". The law now encourages spouses to avoid bitterness after family breakdown and to settle their money and property problems. An object of the modern law is to encourage the parties to put the past behind them and to begin a new life which is not overshadowed by the relationship which has broken down.'

g To allow a bargain struck to be set aside is inevitably to fuel recrimination. Bitterness and anger are inevitable concomitants of the conflict which arises from contested claims. Parties suffer. So do their children. It is inevitable that the focus of recrimination will swing from the incompetent solicitor and will be heaped upon the other party even though his conduct in the negotiations may

h not fairly be capable of being impeached. If the policy of the law is to encourage the clean break, then the law should also ensure that break with the past is final and that there is no turning back.

This is in the public interest that there be some end to litigation. The point is made by Lord Wilberforce in *Ampthill Peerage Case* [1976] 2 All ER 411 at 417–418,

j [1977] AC 547 at 569:

'English law, and safe it is to say, all comparable legal systems, place high in the category of essential principles that which requires that limits be placed upon the rights of citizens to open or reopen disputes ... Any determination of disputable fact may, the law recognises, be imperfect: the law aims at providing the best and safest solution compatible with human fallibility and having reached that solution closes the book ... For a policy of closure to be compatible with justice, it must be attended with safeguards: so the law allows appeals; so the law, exceptionally, allows appeals out of time; so the law still more exceptionally allows judgments to be attacked on the ground of fraud ... But these are exceptions to a general rule of high public importance, and as all the cases show, they are reserved for rare and limited cases, where the facts justifying them can be strictly proved.'

That last observation bears examination. What is bad legal advice? Must it be manifestly bad legal advice? Must it be confined to legal advice opposed to the advice of other professionals? How is it to be established? Privilege will have been waived, but is it invidious that a party's solicitor and counsel be called by the other side? Mr Carden submits that in practice these are not real problems and that a case of bad legal advice is as instantly recognisable as the elephant. Yet when pressed to propose the principle which supports his submission, he is driven to assert it in terms of fairness and justice. I think it inevitable that the test be framed in those terms. It is a wide test. Justice is a multi-faceted jewel and it is precious even if it has a minor flaw. To deny justice to the wife is hard—and to that extent justice is imperfect; but justice must also be done to the husband; to do justice to children is paramount; to do justice to the system into which these disputes are fed is also essential. Like Connell J, I conclude, not without sympathy for the wife and not without regret that a wronged individual is again to be sacrificed on the high altar of policy, that justice demands that there be finality to this litigation and that bad legal advice should not be a ground for interfering. I draw consolation from the speech of Lord Oliver of Aylmerton in *Dinch v Dinch* [1987] 1 All ER 818 at 820–821, [1987] 1 WLR 252 at 255:

'The hardship and injustice that such failure [of the solicitors] inevitably causes, particularly in cases where one or both parties are legally aided and the only substantial family asset consists of the matrimonial home, are so glaring in the instant case that I feel impelled once again to stress in the most emphatic terms that it is in all cases the imperative professional duty of those invested with the task of advising the parties to these unfortunate disputes to consider with due care the impact which any terms that they agree on behalf of their clients have and are intended to have ... It is, of course, also the duty of any court called on to make such a consent order to consider for itself, before the order is drawn up and entered, the jurisdiction which it is being called on to exercise and to make clear what claims for ancillary relief are being finally disposed of. I would, however, like to emphasise that the primary duty in this regard must lie on those concerned with the negotiation and drafting of the terms of the order and that any failure to fulfil such duty occurring hereafter cannot be excused simply by reference to some inadvertent lack of vigilance on the part of the court or its officers in passing the order in the form which the parties have approved.'

CONCLUSIONS

(1) If, as I believe, there may be or ought to be, a right of appeal, then if the appeal is entered in time, the judge is bound to approach the matter de novo and the materiality of 'bad legal advice' will be governed by the considerations of *Edgar v Edgar* [1980] 3 All ER 887, [1980] 1 WLR 1410 and *Camm v Camm* (1982) 4 FLR 577.

a   (2) If there is a right of rehearing, and I believe there is, and if that application is made in time, then the court will not necessarily permit the rehearing for bad legal advice but, on the assumption that the error is discovered (and perhaps acknowledged) within such a short time, then the respondent's claim to be adversely affected by rehearing is not likely to weigh substantially.

   (3) If the leave of the court is necessary, then the strict control suggested by
b   *Barder v Barder (Caluori intervening)* [1987] 2 All ER 440, [1988] AC 20 should be rigorously enforced.

   (4) The requirement that the appeal or rehearing would be 'certain or very likely to succeed' assumes special significance. Only in the most exceptional case of the cruellest injustice will the public interest in the finality of litigation be put aside.

c   (5) This is not such a case.

Accordingly, I would dismiss the appeal.

EVANS LJ. I agree.

d   **SIR THOMAS BINGHAM MR.** I also agree.

Appeal dismissed. Leave to appeal to House of Lords refused.

Mary Rose Plummer   Barrister.

Dobson and another v North Tyneside Health Authority and another

a

COURT OF APPEAL, CIVIL DIVISION

b

BUTLER-SLOSS, PETER GIBSON AND THORPE LJJ

4, 26 JUNE 1996

Human tissue – Property – Right of possession – Next of kin – Brain preserved in *c*
paraffin following post mortem and body buried – Brain later disposed of by hospital –
Health authority joined in negligence claim – Whether next of kin having cause of
action against health authority – Whether next of kin having right of possession to or
property in brain of deceased.

The deceased collapsed at work and later died from brain tumours at a hospital *d*
run by the second defendant health authority.   During a post-mortem
examination, the deceased's brain was removed, preserved in paraffin by the
doctor who conducted the autopsy, and delivered to the hospital for storage. The
rest of the body was returned to the family and was buried. Some two years later,
the deceased's next of kin contacted the hospital asking for the histology relating *e*
to the brain tumours; they were informed that the brain had been disposed of.
The next of kin subsequently commenced proceedings against the first defendant
health authority for medical negligence in failing to diagnose the tumours at a
time when early diagnosis might have saved the deceased's life or ameliorated
her pain with radiotherapy.   They also joined the second defendant to the *f*
proceedings, seeking damages for its failure to preserve the deceased's brain,
which had thereby deprived them of evidence which might have assisted them in
their claims against the first defendant.   The second defendant applied for and
obtained an order striking out the claim against it; the district judge held that the
plaintiffs had no cause of action against the second defendant, since there was no
property in a dead body and no duty of a hospital to preserve parts of a body *g*
indefinitely after a post mortem and inquest had been concluded.   The judge
dismissed the plaintiff's appeal from the district judge's order.   The plaintiffs
appealed.

Held – Although there was no property in a corpse, unless it had undergone a *h*
process or other application of human skill, such as stuffing or embalming, the
executors or administrators or other persons charged by law with the duty of
interring the body had a right to its custody and possession until it was buried.
Since, in the instant case, there were no such persons until long after the body had
been buried and no such duty lay on next of kin as such, and there was nothing *j*
in the pleadings or the evidence to suggest that the actual preservation of the
brain after post mortem was on a par with stuffing or embalming a corpse, it
followed that the plaintiffs had no right to possession of or property in the
deceased's brain and therefore no cause of action against the second defendant.
The appeal would accordingly be dismissed (see p 478 *c* to *h*, p 479 *g* and p 480 *g*,
post).

Notes

a For the duty to dispose of and property in a dead body, see 10 *Halsbury's Laws* (4th edn) paras 1015–1019.

   For the striking out of pleadings showing no reasonable cause of action, see 36 *Halsbury's Laws* (4th edn) para 73, and for cases on the subject, see 37(1) *Digest* (Reissue) 273–286, *1783–1837*.

b

Cases referred to in judgments

Armory v Delamirie (1772) 5 Stra 505, [1558–1774] All ER Rep 121, 93 ER 664.

Clark v London General Omnibus Co Ltd [1906] 2 KB 648, CA.

Doodeward v Spence (1908) 6 CLR 406, Aust HC.

c *Norwich Pharmacal Co v Customs and Excise Comrs* [1973] 2 All ER 943, [1974] AC 133, [1973] 3 WLR 164, HL.

Williams v Williams (1882) 20 Ch D 659.

Cases also cited or referred to in skeleton arguments

Coldman v Hill [1919] 1 KB 443, CA.

d *Dyson v A-G* [1911] 1 KB 410, CA.

E (a minor) v Dorset CC [1994] 4 All ER 640, [1995] 2 AC 633, CA; *rvsd in part* [1995] 3 All ER 353, [1995] 2 AC 633, HL.

Hubbuck & Sons Ltd v Wilkinson Heywood & Clark Ltd [1899] 1 QB 86, [1885–9] All ER Rep 244, CA.

e *Moore v Regents of the University of California* (1988) 215 Cal App 3d 709, Calif CA.

Parker v British Airways Board [1982] 1 All ER 834, [1982] QB 1004, CA.

Appeal

By notice dated 4 September 1995 the plaintiffs, Brenda Dobson suing as administratrix of the estate of Deborah Dobson, deceased, and as next friend of

f the deceased's infant son, Andrew Steven Dobson, appealed with leave from the decision of Judge Harkins in the North Shields County Court on 7 August 1995, whereby he dismissed the plaintiffs' appeal from the order of District Judge Marley on 22 May 1995 striking out their claim against the second defendant, Newcastle Health Authority, for damages for failure to preserve the deceased's

g brain. The first defendant, North Tyneside Health Authority, took no part in the proceedings. The facts are set out in the judgment of Peter Gibson LJ.

Richard Hone (instructed by *Hindle Campbell*, North Shields) for the plaintiffs.

Michael Curwen (instructed by *Samuel Phillips & Co*, Newcastle upon Tyne) for the second defendant.

h

Cur adv vult

26 June 1996. The following judgments were delivered.

j **PETER GIBSON LJ** (giving the first judgment at the invitation of Butler-Sloss LJ). This is an appeal by the plaintiffs, Brenda Dobson (the grandmother) suing as the administratrix of the estate of the late Deborah Dobson (the deceased), and Andrew Steven Dobson (the son), the deceased's infant son suing by his grandmother and next friend, the grandmother. They appeal from the order of Judge Harkins on 7 August 1995 in the North Shields County Court. The judge dismissed the plaintiffs' appeal from the order of District Judge Marley, who had acceded to the application of the second defendant, the Newcastle Health Authority, to strike out the claim against it. The judge gave leave to appeal.

The facts of this case are unusual. I take them not only from the plaintiffs' pleadings but also from the affidavit of the second defendant's solicitor, Miss Searl, filed in support of the application to strike out. Although that affidavit is strictly inadmissible under the rules, because the sole ground for the application was that the particulars of claim disclosed no reasonable cause of action, Mr Hone, for the plaintiffs, relies on part of the affidavit and takes no objection to the admission of the facts to which Miss Searl deposed. And he has given us further factual information to which Mr Curwen, for the second defendant, has not objected.

The deceased was born on 28 January 1969. She does not appear to have married but gave birth to the son on 18 December 1988. She collapsed at work on 5 October 1991 and was taken to North Tyneside General Hospital and was then transferred to Preston Hospital, both being hospitals of the first defendant. Electroencephalograms were taken and the report made on her suggested a liability to primary generalised epilepsy. No CT scan was taken and she was discharged on 10 October 1991. Her condition deteriorated and on 12 December 1991 she became very ill and was taken to the Royal Victoria Infirmary in Newcastle for a CT scan. This showed two brain tumours. She was taken to the Newcastle General Hospital, a hospital of the second defendant, where an operation was to have been performed on her on 15 December 1991 at 10 am but she died four hours before.

The coroner required a post-mortem examination to be carried out to determine the cause of death. Dr Robert Perry, a consultant neuropathologist at Newcastle General Hospital, was asked by the coroner to carry out the autopsy. It is not in dispute that Dr Perry was employed for a fee as an independent consultant. The autopsy was performed on 16 December 1991 in the course of which Dr Perry removed the brain and fixed (or preserved) it in paraffin. In his report to the coroner he summarised the cause of death thus: 'Death was due to: (1a) Brain-stem herniation due to; (1b) a multi-focal brain tumour (probable terminal haemorrhage into the tumour cavity—natural causes).' Following that report the deceased's body (minus the brain) was returned to the deceased's family for burial and was buried.

Dr Perry was not required by the coroner to carry out a histological examination of the tumours. However it was Dr Perry's normal practice to undertake histological tests and he intended to do so in due course. That practice was not followed and that intention was not carried out in the present case. The brain was delivered to the Newcastle General Hospital by Dr Perry for storage. But when, by letter dated 29 September 1993, the plaintiffs' solicitors asked the Department of Neuropathology at the hospital for the histology relating to the tumours, they were told by Dr Perry, by letter dated 12 November 1993, that no report additional to the post-mortem report was requested by the coroner within 12 months of the autopsy and that they had almost certainly disposed of any material which they had. The solicitors wrote again on 25 February 1994 asking if paraffin blocks were available, but on 9 March 1994 Dr Perry confirmed that the department did not have paraffin blocks from the autopsy. Miss Searl, exhibiting the correspondence to her affidavit, commented that the requests of the plaintiffs' solicitors could not be complied with since there had not in fact been any histological examination of the tumours nor was the brain by that time extant.

On 5 October 1994 the plaintiffs commenced these proceedings. Immediately
a before that letters of administration to the deceased's estate had been take out by
the grandmother. The plaintiffs sued the first defendant in negligence. Their case
is that if the tumours had been detected in October or November 1991 by a
routine CT scan, the deceased would have survived if the tumours were benign;
if they were malignant, she would probably have died, but the pain which she
b suffered could have been ameliorated with radiotherapy. It was therefore
important for the plaintiffs to discover whether the tumours were benign or
malignant. Mr Hone told us that the second defendant was originally joined
because it was assumed that histological specimens would have been taken, and
it was sought to obtain discovery and production of the specimens from the
second defendant. That is surprising in the light of the correspondence to which
c I have referred and which preceded the commencement of proceedings.

I find it difficult to discern from the existing particulars of claim what cause of
action was being asserted against the second defendant. But that is unimportant
as it is well established that if a pleading can be saved from striking out by an
amendment which shows that the plaintiff has a proper cause of action, the court
d will allow the pleading to be so amended. The plaintiffs, when faced with the
application to strike out, applied for leave to amend the particulars of claim.
They wish to make the following allegations against the second defendant:

'2 ... The Plaintiffs' case against the Second Defendants is that they failed
... to keep and preserve the brain of the Deceased pending further
e investigation or to take a section of the brain tumours (which seems almost
unimaginable). It is now asserted that the brain of the Deceased is no longer
extant. That deprives the Plaintiffs of definitive proof that the brain tumours
concerned were benign rather than malignant. The Plaintiffs accordingly
rely upon the maxim omnia praesumuntur contra spoliatorem to the effect
that the evidential burden is shifted to the Second Defendants to prove that
f the tumours were malignant ...

10. Further or alternatively, the Second Defendants either failed to keep
and preserve the brain of the Deceased pending further investigation or to
take sections of the brain tumours for histology (which is almost
unimaginable).

g 10A. The Plaintiffs claim as the next of kin of the Deceased and assert that
the Second Defendants were gratuitous bailees and were not entitled to
destroy, lose, convert or otherwise wrongfully interfere with the brain of the
Deceased. In either event, the Second Defendants have deprived the
Plaintiffs of being able to prove definitively that the brain tumours found in
the Deceased were benign and that the Deceased's life could have been saved
h by early surgery. The Plaintiffs will rely on the maxim omnia praesumuntur
contra spoliatorem to shift the evidential burden of proof onto the
Defendant to prove that the two brain tumours identified in the brain of the
Deceased were malignant rather than benign.'

j The pleading ends with a general claim for damages exceeding £5,000 and
interest, and Mr Hone told us that claim applied to the second defendant as well
as the first defendant.

On 17 January 1995 the second defendant applied to strike out the plaintiffs'
claim against it. The first defendant took no part in the hearing before the district
judge or in the subsequent appeals. The district judge took the view that there is
no property in a dead body and no duty on a hospital to preserve parts of a body

indefinitely after a post mortem and inquest had been concluded. She therefore
struck out the claim and refused leave to amend. On appeal by the plaintiffs the *a*
judge agreed with the district judge.

Before us, Mr Hone has rightly reminded us that it is only in plain and obvious
cases, where the legal basis of the claim is unarguable or almost incontestably
bad, that the court will strike out the claim. He submitted that the present case
raises an important question of law, the plaintiffs' case on which cannot be *b*
described as unarguable or almost incontestably bad. He described that question
as whether it remains established law that there is no property in a dead body or
part of a dead body so that personal representatives of a deceased cannot
maintain a cause of action in respect of human tissue. That was modified before
us, as he accepted that the deceased's brain was almost certainly destroyed before
the grandmother became the administratrix, and on the primary way in which he *c*
put his case, viz in conversion, it is trite law that a person has title to sue if and
only if he has at the time of conversion either actual possession or the immediate
right to possession. He acknowledged that the plaintiffs were claiming as the
deceased's next of kin and that is of course how the case is pleaded in para 10A.

As the question of law as framed by Mr Hone indicates, in the present state of *d*
the English authorities there is no property in a corpse (see *Williams v Williams*
(1882) 20 Ch D 659 at 662–663 and *Clerk and Lindsell on Torts* (17th edn, 1995)
p 653, para 13-50). However, that bare statement needs some qualification.

First, as is stated in *Clerk and Lindsell*, 'the executors or administrators or other
persons charged by the law with the duty of interring the body have a right to the
custody and possession of it until it is properly buried'. In the present case there *e*
were no executors and there was no administratrix until October 1994, long after
the body of the deceased was buried. The other persons who are charged by the
law with the duty of interring the body include, for example, the parent of an
infant child who dies where the parent has the means to do so (see *Clark v London
General Omnibus Co Ltd* [1906] 2 KB 648 at 659 and 10 *Halsbury's Laws* (4th edn) *f*
para 1017); but I am not aware that there is any authority that there is such a duty
on the next of kin as such. If there is no duty, there is no legal right to possession
of the corpse. However, even if that is wrong and the next of kin do have some
right to possession of the body, there is no authority stating that right is otherwise
than for the interment or other proper disposition of the body.

The second qualification is also to be found in *Clerk and Lindsell* p 653, para *g*
13-50, where it is said:

> 'Once a body has undergone a process or other application of human skill,
> such as stuffing or embalming, it seems it can be the subject of property in
> the ordinary way; hence it is submitted that conversion will lie for a skeleton *h*
> or cadaver used for research or exhibition, and the same goes for parts of and
> substances produced by, a living person.'

Mr Hone relies on the tentatively expressed proposition in the first part of that
statement, the authority for which is said to be *Doodeward v Spence* (1908) 6 CLR
406. That case involved the preserved foetus of a two-headed child, still-born 40 *j*
years previously, which the appellant had purchased. He sought to recover it
from the police so that he could exhibit it for gain. He succeeded in an action in
detinue. In the High Court of Australia Griffith CJ pointed out that it was not
unlawful to possess a mummy or a prepared skeleton or a skull or other parts of
the human body, and he referred to the many collections of anatomical and
pathological specimens formed and maintained by scientific bodies (see 6 CLR

a 406 at 413). He stated (at 414): '... so far as it constitutes property, a human body, or a portion of a human body, is capable by law of becoming the subject of property.' He expressed the view that—

b
> 'when a person has by the lawful exercise of work or skill so dealt with a human body or part of a human body in his lawful possession that it has acquired some attributes differentiating it from a mere corpse awaiting burial, he acquires a right to retain possession of it, at least as against any person not entitled to have it delivered to him for the purpose of burial ...'

He said that some work and skill had been bestowed on the foetus and that it had acquired an actual pecuniary value, and so an action in detinue would lie. Barton J was prepared to agree that the action did lie only in relation to a still-born *c* foetus, and did not wish to cast the slightest doubt on the general rule that an unburied corpse was not the subject of property. Higgins J dissented, being of the view that no one could have property in another human being, live or dead. *Doodeward v Spence* is therefore not a decision establishing the proposition in *Clerk and Lindsell on Torts*. However, I am prepared to accept that proposition is *d* properly arguable, particularly in the light of the academic writings to which Mr Hone referred us: Paul Matthews 'Whose Body? People as Property' [1983] CLP 193, *Palmer on Bailment* (2nd edn, 1991) p 9ff and Roger Magnusson 'Proprietary Rights in Human Tissue', in *Interests in Goods* edited by Palmer and McKendrick (1993) p 237ff.

Does this mean that it is arguable that when Dr Perry fixed the brain in *e* paraffin, he thereby transformed it into an item the right to possession of which or the property in which belonged to the plaintiffs? For my part, I do not think so. The removal of the brain was lawfully performed in the course of the post mortem which at the coroner's request Dr Perry had undertaken to determine the cause of the deceased's death. Dr Perry was under an obligation imposed by *f* r 9 of the Coroners Rules 1984, SI 1984/552, to make provision for the preservation of material which in his opinion bore upon the cause of death, but only for such period as the coroner thought fit. It is not alleged that Dr Perry was in breach of that obligation, and once the cause of death had been determined by the coroner with Dr Perry's help and the time for challenge to that determination had passed, there could be no continuing obligation under the rule to preserve *g* that material. There is nothing in the pleading or evidence before us to suggest that the actual preservation of the brain after the post mortem was on a par with stuffing or embalming a corpse or preserving an anatomical or pathological specimen for a scientific collection or with preserving a human freak such as a double-headed foetus that had some value for exhibition purposes. There was no *h* practical possibility of, nor any sensible purpose in, the brain being reunited with the body for burial purposes. Mr Hone accepted that organs would not usually be preserved by the pathologist who carries out a post mortem and that if Dr Perry had disposed of the brain without fixing it in paraffin, the plaintiffs would have no cause for complaint. I do not see how the fact that the brain was so fixed *j* rendered it an item to possession of which the plaintiffs ever became entitled for the purpose of interment or any other purpose, still less that the plaintiffs ever acquired the property in it.

Mr Hone told us that the plaintiffs wished to discover the answers to a number of questions, including why the brain was delivered to the hospital laboratory for storage and what were the relevant protocols or procedures of the hospital laboratory as to the period for which human tissue was to be stored. But the fact

that a plaintiff would like more information from a defendant than the plaintiff
has does not justify the bringing of an action against that defendant unless it is a
case (which is not suggested here) to which the principle of *Norwich Pharmacal Co
v Customs and Excise Comrs* [1973] 2 All ER 943, [1974] AC 133 applies. Further,
even if the hospital laboratory protocols were not followed (and there is
absolutely nothing to suggest there was such a contravention), I cannot see how
that breach of internal rules could help the plaintiffs.

I return to the specific way in which the plaintiffs' case is sought to be pleaded.
The primary claim is in conversion, but as next of kin they have not shown and
cannot show that they had actual possession or the immediate right to possession
at the time the brain was disposed of. They claim in bailment, but they
acknowledge that the only bailment of the brain was not by them but by Dr Perry
to the second defendant. They claim a wrongful interference with the brain, but
they have not shown and cannot show as next of kin the possession or right to
possession or ownership of the brain or that anything done by the second
defendant was wrongful. They claim in negligence, but I cannot see how the
second defendant in storing the brain at Dr Perry's behest can be said to owe a
duty of care to the plaintiffs. I would add that I am far from persuaded that it
would be right to impose a duty on hospitals to retain tissue removed in a post
mortem against the possibility that it might be material evidence in civil litigation
commenced at some future time.

Finally, I should briefly refer to the maxim omnia praesumuntur contra
spoliatorem, appearing as it does more than once in the plaintiffs' pleading. Mr
Hone said that the maxim meant that all things are presumed against the interests
of a party who destroys goods. That is a mistranslation. A spoliator is a
wrongdoer. Thus in *Armory v Delamirie* (1772) 5 Stra 505, [1558–1774] All ER Rep
121, the servant of the defendant goldsmith to whom the plaintiff had handed a
piece of jewellery wrongfully took out the jewels and refused to hand them back
to the plaintiff. The defendant was held liable to the plaintiff for the greatest
value which the jewels might have. But the maxim is of no assistance to the
plaintiffs unless and until they can establish that the second defendant is a
wrongdoer. This the plaintiffs have not done and cannot do.

For these reasons I would dismiss this appeal.

THORPE LJ. I agree.

BUTLER-SLOSS LJ. I also agree.

Appeal dismissed.

                              Paul Magrath Esq   Barrister.

a
St Albans City and District Council v International Computers Ltd

COURT OF APPEAL, CIVIL DIVISION

NOURSE, HIRST LJJ AND SIR IAIN GLIDEWELL

b

4–7, 10–12 JUNE, 26 JULY 1996

Contract – Damages for breach – Measure of damages – Defendant supplying computer system to plaintiff local authority for use in administering collection of community charge – Software erroneously overstating population and plaintiff accordingly
c *undersetting charge – Plaintiff suffering loss of charge receipts and additionally having to make increased precept payments to county council – Plaintiff recouping lost revenue from chargepayers the following year – Whether plaintiff entitled to recover damages from defendant for breach of contract in respect of total loss caused.*

d *Sale of goods – Implied terms as to quality and fitness for purpose – Goods – Computer disk – Whether computer disk 'goods' – Sale of Goods Act 1979, ss 14, 61 – Supply of Goods and Services Act 1982, ss 9, 18.*

The plaintiff local authority entered into a contract with the defendant company for the supply of a computer system to be used in administering its collection of
e community charge. In December 1989 the plaintiff used the system to extract the population figures for its area, but due to an error in the software the figure was overstated by 2,966. The plaintiff set its community charge in accordance with that figure, with the result that its charge receipts in 1990–91 were £484,000 less than they ought to have been. In addition it had to pay a net sum of £685,000 by way of
f increased precept payments to the county council. The plaintiff recouped its lost revenue from its chargepayers by setting a higher community charge in 1991–92. Thereafter it commenced proceedings against the defendant for damages for breach of contract, contending that it was entitled to recover the total loss caused by the faulty software. The defendant contended, inter alia, (i) that the plaintiff did not itself suffer loss as a result of any breach of contract, and (ii) that the plaintiff's
g lost revenue was not recoverable, since it had been recouped the following year by setting a higher community charge. The judge held that the loss caused by the defendant's breach was recoverable by the plaintiff and awarded it damages, drawing no distinction between the £685,000 and £484,000. The defendant appealed.

h

Held – Although not strictly a trustee, the plaintiff local authority had no less capacity than a trustee to recover damages from the defendant for breach of contract for the benefit of the inhabitants, since it had to administer its funds for their benefit and owed them a duty to collect all sums which were owed to it.
j However, in determining the amount recoverable by the plaintiff it was necessary to distinguish between the two amounts of loss which formed the basis of its claim. The plaintiff could recover damages in respect of the increased precept payments, because otherwise it would have to recover that loss from its chargepayers who would then be out of pocket; but it could not recover damages in respect of the community charge receipts, since the additional cost thereby caused to the chargepayers in 1991–92 was intrinsically the same as the sum which, but for the defendant's breach, they would have had to have paid in 1990–91. It followed that

the plaintiff could not recover the £484,000 or the interest lost thereon during
1991–92 and the judge's order would accordingly be reduced by that amount. The *a*
appeal would therefore be allowed in part (see p 489 *c* to *j*, p 490 *a* to *c* and p 492 *c*
to *f*, post).

Parry *v Cleaver* [1969] 1 All ER 555 and *Palatine Graphic Arts Co Ltd v Liverpool City
Council* [1986] 1 All ER 366 applied.

Per Sir Iain Glidewell. A computer disk is within the definition of 'goods' *b*
contained in s 61 of the Sale of Goods Act 1979 and s 18 of the Supply of Goods and
Services Act 1982. A computer program, however, is not. Nevertheless, if a disk
onto which a program designed and intended to instruct or enable a computer to
achieve particular functions has been encoded is sold or hired but the program is
defective, so that it will not instruct or enable the computer to achieve the intended
purpose, the seller or hirer of the disk will be in breach of the terms as to quality *c*
and fitness for purpose implied by s 14 of the 1979 Act and s 9 of the 1982 Act (see
p 493 *a* to *c f* to *h*, post).

Notes
For legal proceedings by and against local authorities, see 28 *Halsbury's Laws* (4th *d*
edn) para 1339.

For the Sale of Goods Act 1979, ss 14, 61, see 39 *Halsbury's Statutes* (4th edn) (1995
reissue) 80, 119.

For the Supply of Goods and Services Act 1982, ss 9, 18, see ibid 141, 147.

Cases referred to in judgments   *e*
Advent Systems Ltd v Unisys Corp (1991) 925 F 2d 670, US Ct of Apps (3rd Cir).
Design 5 v Keniston Housing Association Ltd (1986) 10 Con LR 123.
Linden Gardens Trust Ltd v Lenesta Sludge Disposals Ltd [1993] 3 All ER 417, [1994] 1
   AC 85, [1993] 3 WLR 408, HL.
Mitchell (George) (Chesterhall) Ltd v Finney Lock Seeds Ltd [1983] 2 All ER 737, [1983] 2 *f*
   AC 803, [1983] 3 WLR 163, HL
Palatine Graphic Arts Co Ltd v Liverpool City Council [1986] 1 All ER 366, [1986] QB
   335, [1986] 2 WLR 285, CA.
Parry v Cleaver [1969] 1 All ER 555, [1970] AC 1, [1969] 2 WLR 821, HL.
Salvage Association v CAP Financial Services Ltd [1995] FSR 654.
Saphena Computing Ltd v Allied Collection Agencies Ltd [1995] FSR 616, CA.   *g*
Toby Constructions Products Pty Ltd v Computa Bar (Sales) Pty Ltd [1983] 2 NSWLR 48,
   NSW SC.
Trollope & Colls Ltd v North West Metropolitan Regional Hospital Board [1973] 2 All ER
   260, [1973] 1 WLR 601, HL.

          h
Cases also cited or referred to in skeleton arguments
*A/S Det Dansk-Franske Dampskibsselskab v Cie Financiere d'Investissements SA
   (Compafina), The Himmerland* [1965] 2 Lloyd's Rep 353.
Adamson (TH) & Sons v Liverpool and London and Globe Insurance Co Ltd [1953] 2
   Lloyd's Rep 355.
Ailsa Craig Fishing Co Ltd v Malvern Fishing Co Ltd [1983] 1 All ER 101, [1983] 1 WLR *j*
   964, HL.
Aswan Engineering Establishment Co v Lupdine Ltd (Thurgar Bolle Ltd, third party)
   [1987] 1 All ER 135, [1987] 1 WLR 1, CA.
Baily v de Crespigny (1869) LR 4 QB 180, [1861–73] All ER Rep 332.
Barclays Bank plc v Fairclough Building Ltd [1995] 1 All ER 289, [1995] QB 214, CA.
Berwick upon Tweed Corp v Oswald (1854) 3 E & B 653, 118 ER 1286.

a *Cassel v Lancashire and Yorkshire Accident Insurance Co Ltd* (1885) 1 TLR 495.
EE & Brian Smith (1928) Ltd v Wheatsheaf Mills Ltd [1939] 2 All ER 251, [1939] 2 KB 302.
Fillite (Runcorn) Ltd v APV Pasilac Ltd [1995] CA Transcript 62.
Flamar Interocean Ltd v Denmac Ltd (formerly Denholm Maclay Co Ltd), The Flamar Pride [1990] 1 Lloyd's Rep 434

b *Forsikringsaktieselskapet Vesta v Butcher (No 1)* [1989] 1 All ER 402, [1989] AC 852, HL.
Gamble v Accident Insurance Co (1869) IR 4 Cl 204.
Heron II, The, Koufos v C Czarnikow Ltd [1967] 3 All ER 686, [1969] 1 AC 350, HL.
Motor and General Insurance Co Ltd v Pavy [1994] 1 WLR 462, PC.
Motor Oil Hellas (Corinth) Refineries SA v Shipping Corp of India, The Kanchenjunga [1990] 1 Lloyds's Rep 391, HL.

c *Murray (Edmund) Ltd v BSP International Foundations Ltd* (1992) 33 Con LR 1, CA.
Patton v Employers' Liability Assurance Corp Ltd (1887) 20 LR Ir 93.
Phillips Products Ltd v Hyland [1987] 2 All ER 620n, [1987] 1 WLR 659n, CA.
Photo Production Ltd v Securicor Transport Ltd [1980] 1 All ER 556, [1980] AC 827, HL.
R & B Customs Brokers Co Ltd v United Dominions Trust Ltd (Saunders v Abbott (1980)

d *Ltd, third party)* [1988] 1 All ER 847, [1988] 1 WLR 321, CA.
Shine v General Guarantee Corp Ltd (Reeds Motor Co (a firm), third party) [1988] 1 All ER 911, CA.
Smith v Eric S Bush (a firm), Harris v Wyre Forest DC [1989] 2 All ER 514, [1990] 1 AC 831, HL.

e *Stag Line Ltd v Tyne Shiprepair Group Ltd, The Zinnia* [1984] 2 Lloyd's Rep 211.
Treml v Ernest W Gibson & Partners (1984) 272 EG 70.

Appeal

f By amended notice dated 1 May 1995 the defendant, International Computers Ltd, appealed from the decision of Scott Baker J ([1995] FSR 686) on 3 October 1994 whereby he awarded the plaintiffs, St Albans City and District Council, damages of £1,314,846 in respect of the defendant's breach of contract to supply the plaintiffs with a computer system to be used in their collection of community charge, on the grounds (i) that the plaintiffs themselves had suffered no loss, and (ii) that any loss suffered by the plaintiffs was not recoverable since it had been recouped from their

g chargepayers. The facts are set out in the judgment of Nourse LJ.

Conrad Dehn QC, Timothy Lamb QC and *Adam Tolley* (instructed by *Masons*) for the defendant.
Richard Mawrey QC (instructed by *Michael Lovelady*, St Albans) for the plaintiffs.

h   *Cur adv vult*

26 July 1996. The following judgments were delivered.

NOURSE LJ. On 3 October 1994, in a judgment reserved after a ten-day trial in
j July of that year, Scott Baker J ([1995] FSR 686) awarded the plaintiffs, St Albans City and District Council, damages of £1,314,846 against the defendant, International Computers Ltd, and judgment was entered accordingly. The basis of the award was that the defendant had breached its contract to supply the plaintiffs with a computer system to be used in their collection of community charge by providing faulty software which significantly overstated the relevant population of their area and thus caused them to suffer a loss of revenue. The defendant now appeals to this court.

The material facts and many of the judge's findings are set out in his judgment (see [1995] FSR 686 at 688–696). It is unnecessary to restate them at length, although reference will necessarily be made to them in the course of dealing with the arguments advanced in this court.

The essence of the problem was that the faulty software caused the total figure for the relevant population of the plaintiffs' area extracted from the computer on 4 December 1989 to be stated at 97,384·7, whereas it ought to have been 94,418·7. Thus there was an overstatement of 2,966. That meant that when, at the end of February 1990, the plaintiffs came to calculate the amount needed to defray their budgeted expenditure, they proceeded on the footing that they had a larger number of chargepayers to call on than they in fact had. So they set the charge at a lower figure than they would have done had they known the true number. In the result, their community charge receipts for the year 1990–91 were £484,000 less than they ought to have been.

That was not the plaintiffs' only loss. They suffered a small reduction (£14,000) in revenue support grant. Their real and substantial additional loss was in having to pay an extra £1,795,000 by way of precept to the Hertfordshire County Council, which was only partially offset by a reduced contribution to the 'safety net' (£259,000) and an increase in the receipt from the national non-domestic rate pool (£865,000).

The figures for the plaintiffs' loss, as agreed before the judge, were as follows:

Increased precept to county council	£1,795,000
Reduced revenue support grant	£14,000
Reduced contribution to 'safety net'	(£259,000)
Increased receipt from national non-domestic rate pool	(£865,000)
Reduced community charge receipts	£484,000
Total net income loss	£1,169,000
Interest loss 1990–91	£73,509
Interest loss 1991–92	£72,377
Total	£1,314,846

The losses thus fell into two different categories. There was the £484,000 which the plaintiffs did not receive for community charge in 1990–91. There was also the extra £685,000 net which they had to pay out, ie £1,795,000 plus £14,000 less £259,000 and £865,000. The distinction between the two categories is of importance on the question of damages.

The issues argued before and decided by Scott Baker J are summarised in the holdings which appear in the headnote to the report (see [1995] FSR 686 at 687–688). In this court the defendant's appeal has been argued by Mr Dehn QC, who did not appear below. In an opening which lasted for nearly three and a half days he raised several new arguments, including one which went to the heart of the contract between the parties. Some of his arguments overlapped, particularly in relation to construction and breach on the one hand and causation, failure to mitigate and remoteness on the other. The convenient course is to take the various issues still in dispute, so far as practicable in the same order as the judge, and to deal with Mr Dehn's arguments as they affect each issue.

The first step is to identify the material terms of the contract into which the parties entered on 24 December 1988. This process is not as simple as might have been expected since the contract was expressed to consist not only of the plaintiffs' invitation to tender dated June 1988 and the defendant's tender dated 18 July 1988, a but of seven other documents as well. I propose to refer only to those provisions which are directly material to the arguments advanced in this court.

The invitation to tender

Under the heading 'Applications software—general requirements', the plaintiffs' invitation to tender stated that they required the development and replacement of a large number of systems. Reference was made to the various
b systems in order of priority, financial information and community charge being the two which were listed as priority one (see cl 3.2E). Under the sub-heading 'Tried and Tested Software', it was stated that software should as far as possible be based on a package tried and tested in a local authority environment and that tailoring of software to meet requirements should be completed before
c installation and payment. The most important provision of the invitation to tender, indeed the contractual provision to which the arguments in this court were mainly directed, was contained in cl 1.1 of the 'Community charge and non-domestic rates, statement of user requirements' under the sub-heading 'Introduction and Objectives':

d   'The Council invites tenders from a pre-selected list of suppliers for the provision of a computerised system for Community Charge and Non-Domestic rates. This is necessary to cope with the requirements of the Local Government Finance Bill currently proceeding through Parliament. As the Bill has not yet received the Royal Assent, and a large number of Statutory Instruments/Regulations have still to be laid before Parliament, prospective
e   suppliers will be expected to give a firm commitment to provide a system to cope with all the Statutory Requirements for registration, billing, collection and recovery and financial management of the Community Charge and Non-Domestic Rates; including Community Charge Rebates.'

f Clause 5 of that statement, under the sub-heading 'Register Content', noted that the legislative requirements were not yet complete, but stated that the 16 data items thereunder listed might be included in the requirements for the content of the register 'subject to addition/amendment as a result of the continuing Parliamentary process'. Clause 15 under the sub-heading 'Collection Fund' stated that payments out of that fund would include precepts issued to the charging
g authority, and non-domestic rating contributions.

The defendant's tender

Chapter 1 of the defendant's tender was entitled 'Management summary'. Under the sub-heading 'The ICL solution' the products which were said to meet
h the plaintiffs' requirements were listed, including: 'COMCIS, a comprehensive solution for Community Charge being developed in conjunction with English Authorities ...' In response to cl 3.6E of the invitation to tender (tried and tested software) it was stated that all applications software proposed had been tried and tested within local government environments—'with the exception of Community Charge (under development)'. In the introduction to ch 5 of the
j defendant's tender entitled 'Community charge and [non-domestic] rates', it was stated that part of the defendant's very clear strategy in its development to community charge was: 'To develop a system using a 70 strong development team, which meets fully the legislative requirements, and which is easy to use and operate.' Later it was said that in summary the plaintiffs had the opportunity not only to implement the best system for community charge, but also—'to input into the development process in order to be sure that this product meets your specific

requirements'. In response to cl 5 of the plaintiffs' statement of user requirements (register content), the defendant's tender stated:

> 'The register will contain the data items necessary to meet at the very least the legal requirements plus any other fields the User Design Group deem advantageous. The system is planned to handle all debits. All other requirements will be met.'

Clause 9.5.7E stated that the defendant was unable to provide performance guarantees. Clause 10.6.2E stated:

> 'Implementation plans, due to changing legislation, are relatively fluid. However ICL is committed to provide a full system by April 1990 with the canvass register on stream in the last quarter of 1988. Individual plans are being produced as customers commit to the ICL solution.'

The tender contained a statement headed 'ICL Statement' which stated that the defendant warranted that the equipment and programmes supplied would conform with their relevant product descriptions and would be of merchantable quality, but that—

> 'none of the statements contained in this document constitutes representations for which ICL can accept liability and St Albans must satisfy themselves that the equipment and programs are fit for the purpose to which they will be put.'

The defendant's general conditions

The judge found that the contract incorporated the defendant's general conditions of contract for the supply of equipment, programmes and services (February 1985 edn). Clause 2 of those conditions provided that all equipment, programmes and services were supplied by description. Clause 3 granted the plaintiffs a licence under the defendant's patents, copyrights and other intellectual property rights to use the equipment, programmes and any items related to the provision of services, in the form and for the purpose for which they were supplied. Clause 9, headed 'ICL's Liabilities', provided, by sub-cl (a), that the defendant's liability for negligently causing injury to or the death of any person would be unlimited; and, by sub-cl (b), for negligently or otherwise being responsible for damage to or loss of any physical property would be limited to £250,000. Sub-clause (c) provided:

> 'In all other cases ICL's liability will not exceed the price or charge payable for the item of Equipment, Program or Service in respect of which the liability arises or £100,000 (whichever is the lesser). Provided that in no event will ICL be liable for: (i) loss resulting from any defect or deficiency which ICL shall have physically remedied at its own expense within a reasonable time; or (ii) any indirect or consequential loss or loss of business or profits sustained by the Customer; or (iii) loss which could have been avoided by the Customer following ICL's reasonable advice and instructions.'

Accepting the submissions which had been advanced on behalf of the plaintiffs by Mr Mawrey QC, the judge held that the defendant was under an obligation to provide software that would maintain a reliable database of the names entered onto the community charge register, accurately count the names and accurately retrieve and display the figures resulting from the count (see [1995] FSR 686 at 697).

a   The basic submission of Mr Dehn as to the construction of the contract, advanced for the first time in this court, was that the defendant agreed to supply a system which was to be fully operative by the end of February 1990, when the amount of the community charge would have to be set. It was a system, as the contractual provisions recognised, which until then would still be in course of development. Thus, except where the defendant had acted negligently, the plaintiffs had impliedly agreed to accept the software supplied, bugs and all. Mr

b   Dehn relied on observations of Staughton LJ in *Saphena Computing Ltd v Allied Collection Agencies Ltd* [1995] FSR 616 at 652. Specifically, he submitted that the defendant was not contractually bound to provide software which would enable the correct figure to be extracted from the computer on 4 December 1989.

   These submissions must be rejected. Parties who respectively agree to supply

c   and acquire a system recognising that it is still in the course of development cannot be taken, merely by virtue of that recognition, to intend that the supplier shall be at liberty to supply software which cannot perform the function expected of it at the stage of the development at which it is supplied. Moreover, and this is really an anterior point, the argument is concluded against the defendant by cl 1.1 of the

d   plaintiffs' statement of user requirements which, having referred to the Bill that later became the Local Government Finance Act 1988, stated:

> 'As the Bill has not yet received the Royal Assent, and a large number of Statutory Instruments/Regulations have still to be laid before Parliament, prospective suppliers will be expected to give a firm commitment to provide a system to cope with *all* the Statutory Requirements for registration, billing,
>
> *e*   collection and recovery and financial management of the Community Charge and Non-Domestic Rates ...' (My emphasis.)

   Mr Dehn sought to avoid the clear impact of that provision and others to the like effect by arguing that the statutory requirements there referred to were only those

f   derived from the 1988 Act and any statutory instruments or regulations made under it. He pointed to the fact that the Secretary of State's requirement that all charging authorities should make returns of their relevant populations on Form CCR1 not later than 8 December 1989 derived from amendments to the 1988 Act made by the Local Government and Housing Act 1989. In my view that is to put an altogether too narrow construction on the provision. What it clearly

g   contemplated was that the system must meet the statutory requirements, many of them still unknown, whatever they might prove to be. On a commonsense interpretation of cl 1.1, it would be immaterial whether those requirements arose under the 1988 Act in its original form or as amended by the 1989 Act.

   I therefore agree with the judge that the defendant was under an express

h   contractual obligation in the terms stated by him. Accordingly, once the defendant knew, soon after 2 November 1989, that the Secretary of State had notified all charging authorities of his intention to require them to make a return of relevant population on Form CCR1 not later than 8 December 1989, it became under an express contractual obligation to supply the plaintiffs with software which would enable them accurately to complete the return by that date. On that footing, it

j   becomes strictly unnecessary to consider whether the contract was subject to an implied term to the same effect. However, having had the advantage of reading in draft the judgment to be delivered by Sir Iain Glidewell, I would, like him and for the reasons he gives, have answered that question in the affirmative.

   Having established the nature of the defendant's contractual obligation, I turn to the question of breach. The judge held that there was a plain breach of contract on the defendant's part because the COMCIS software produced erroneous figures for

the population return to the department (see [1995] FSR 686 at 697). On the basis
of his findings of fact, he held that the fault was that of the defendant and not the   a
plaintiffs. His material findings were, first, that release 2036 was prepared for the
statistics to be provided to the department; secondly, that for some reason
unknown 2036 was not delivered to the plaintiffs; thirdly, that 2037 was installed
on 4 December 1989, after the figures had been extracted (see [1995] FSR 686 at 690,
692).   b

Mr Dehn's submissions on this question covered much the same ground as his
submissions on the construction of the contract. He added, however, that after
2037 had been installed on 4 December 1989 there was still time for a rerun of the
figures which would have enabled the plaintiffs to get in a correct return by 8
December. I disagree. The judge's finding that the operation had in practice to be
carried out over the weekend of 2/3 December is unassailable. Moreover, the   c
mere installation of 2037 on 4 December could not have put the plaintiffs on notice
that the figures already extracted might be wrong. The judge was clearly right to
hold that the contract had been breached in the manner stated by him.

The views already expressed also make it unnecessary to consider the plaintiffs'
alternative case based on Mr Turton's negligent misrepresentation. The facts   d
material to this matter are stated by the judge ([1995] FSR 686 at 691–692; his
holding that there was a negligent misrepresentation appears at 697). Mr Dehn
attacked the judge's decision both on the facts and in law. I remain unpersuaded
that the decision was incorrect on either score.

At this point it is convenient to deal with two further, closely-linked,   e
arguments of Mr Dehn's which were not advanced in the court below. First, he
submitted that the plaintiffs had been at fault in not doing a rerun of the figures
after release 2040 had been installed, as the judge found, on 11 December 1989.
Secondly, he submitted that the plaintiffs ought in any event to have realised
from a printout made on 9 February 1990 that the December figure was or might
be wrong and ought not to have continued to act on it.   f

As to the first of these arguments, Mr Dehn was unable to satisfy me of any good
reason for the plaintiffs' doing a rerun between 11 December and 9 February.
There was nothing at that stage, any more than there had been on 4 December, to
put them on notice that the figures on which they were working might be wrong.
The second argument was effectively countered by the unchallenged evidence of   g
Mr Emery, a principal registration assistant (finance department) with the
plaintiffs. He said that his section carried out an account scan on 9 February 1990
which produced a total figure of 94,757. Suspecting that something was wrong, he
spoke to Mr Thake of the defendant on the telephone, who indicated that he
considered the figures to be incorrect. However, at a meeting in St Albans on 15   h
February, Mr Thake said there would be a further release of software which would
correct the error shown on 9 February, and that that would be produced in due
course. In my view, the plaintiffs were entitled to act on that assurance. I would
therefore reject both these new arguments of Mr Dehn's.

Mr Dehn further submitted that when the printout made on 26 February 1990
produced a figure at variance with that returned on Form CCR1 in December, the   j
plaintiffs ought then, if not before, to have realised that the December figure was
or might be wrong and ought not to have continued to act on it. This matter was
considered by the judge and he concluded that, by acting as they did, the plaintiffs
took the only practical course open to them ([1995] FSR 686 at 693). Mr Dehn
submitted that that finding was against the weight of the evidence. Again I disagree
and would reject the submission accordingly.

a   I turn to the question of damages, which was dealt with by the judge (see [1995] FSR 686 at 699–704). He explained the system which required the plaintiffs to maintain collection and general funds, the main payments required to be made into and out of the collection fund and the difference between the losses of £484,000 and £685,000. He had to deal with two arguments advanced on behalf of the defendant: first, that the plaintiffs did not themselves suffer loss as a consequence of any breach

b   of contract or negligence on the part of the defendant; secondly, that any loss that the plaintiffs suffered was recouped from the 1991–92 chargepayers and therefore, in law, amounted to an irrecoverable loss.

The first of those arguments was rejected by the judge, in my view correctly. Assuming that it is right to say that the plaintiffs did not themselves suffer loss, I nevertheless regard it as clear that that is no bar to their recovery of damages.

c   Although it would be incorrect, except in a broad sense, to describe a local authority as a trustee for the inhabitants of its area, it can only act in their interests. It must administer its funds for their benefit. Equally, it owes them a duty to get in, if necessary by action, all sums which are owed to it. Otherwise the inhabitants themselves, who are the ultimate source of its funds, will be out

d   of pocket. So, although not strictly a trustee, a local authority has no less a capacity than a trustee to recover damages in circumstances such as these, broadly for the benefit of the inhabitants.

The judge also rejected the second argument. In doing so he made no distinction between the £685,000 and £484,000. I think that that must have been because the distinction between the two amounts was not urged on him as

e   forcefully as it has been urged on us. In my view, the distinction must be made. Once it is made, it is seen that the £685,000 is recoverable and the £484,000 is not. This is the most important and difficult question in the case. In the end I have come to a clear opinion in regard to each of the two amounts.

Authority apart, I would approach the matter in this way. If the software had

f   not been faulty, the plaintiffs would not have had to pay out the £685,000. Having paid it out, they were unable to recover it from the county council or any other third party. They could only recover it, they were bound to recover it, from their chargepayers. Viewing the plaintiffs as having, for this purpose, the like capacity as a trustee for the chargepayers, I am in no doubt that they can recover the £685,000 from the defendant. Otherwise the chargepayers would be out of pocket.

g   The £484,000 stands on a different footing. Although Mr Mawrey argued to the contrary, I think that we can only work on the inference that if the software had not been faulty, the plaintiffs would have collected the £484,000 by way of an additional charge in 1990–91. Having not collected it, they were unable to recover it from any third party. They could only recover it, they were bound to recover it,

h   from their chargepayers in 1991–92. In this instance, however, the chargepayers were under an obligation to pay in 1991–92 precisely what they ought to have paid, but did not pay in 1990–91. Viewing the plaintiffs in the like capacity as before, I am in no doubt that they cannot recover the £484,000 from the defendant. The effect of the recovery would be to relieve the chargepayers of an obligation to which they were always subject or, if you prefer, to give them a bonus to which

j   they were not entitled. They have not been out of pocket. The plaintiffs, on the other hand, are entitled to recover interest on the £484,000 for the year 1990–91.

The judge referred to authority on this question, in particular to *Design 5 v Keniston Housing Association Ltd* (1986) 10 Con LR 123 and *Linden Gardens Trust Ltd v Lenesta Sludge Disposals Ltd* [1993] 3 All ER 417, [1994] 1 AC 85. He did not refer to *Parry v Cleaver* [1969] 1 All ER 555, [1970] AC 1 or to *Palatine Graphic Arts Co Ltd v Liverpool City Council* [1986] 1 All ER 366, [1986] QB 335, no doubt because, as I

understand it, those decisions were not cited to him. Had he been asked to
consider them, it is well possible that he would have distinguished between the
£685,000 and the £484,000.

I believe that the key observation in the authorities is to be found in the speech
of Lord Reid in *Parry v Cleaver* [1969] 1 All ER 555 at 559, [1970] AC 1 at 15:

> 'Surely the distinction between receipts which must be brought into account
> and those which must not must depend not on their source but on their
> intrinsic nature.'

That observation was quoted by Glidewell LJ in *Palatine Graphic Arts Co Ltd v
Liverpool City Council* [1986] 1 All ER 366 at 371, [1986] QB 335 at 344 and applied by
this court in that case. Here, since the 1990–91 shortfall was an unintended
subtraction from the 1990–91 charge which had to be made good by an equivalent
addition to the 1991–92 charge, the two are intrinsically the same. As Mr Dehn well
put it, the addition to the 1991–92 charge was not the result of benevolence or an
accidental circumstance, but the very sum which, but for the defendant's breach of
contract, would have been received from the chargepayers in 1990–91 and which
the plaintiffs were required to obtain from them in 1991–92. Accordingly, the test
propounded by the authorities leads to the same conclusion as that to which I
would have come without them.

I come finally to the Unfair Contract Terms Act 1977. As I have said, the judge
found that the contract incorporated the defendant's general conditions of contract
for the supply of equipment, programmes and services. It has not been suggested
that those conditions were not written standard terms of business for the purposes
of the 1977 Act. The material provision was contained in cl 9(c) whose effect, if it
stands, would be to limit the damages recoverable by the plaintiffs to £100,000.

So far as material, s 3 of the 1977 Act provides:

> '(1) This section applies as between contracting parties where one of them
> deals as consumer or on the other's written standard terms of business.
> (2) As against that party, the other cannot by reference to any contract
> term—(a) when himself in breach of contract, exclude or restrict any liability
> of his in respect of the breach ... except in so far as (in any of the cases
> mentioned above in this subsection) the contract term satisfies the
> requirement of reasonableness.'

So far as material, s 12 provides:

> '(1) A party to a contract "deals as consumer" in relation to another party
> if—(a) he neither makes the contract in the course of a business nor holds
> himself out as doing so ...'

By s 14 'business' is defined to include a profession and the activities of any
government department or local or public authority. The requirement of
reasonableness is dealt with in s 11.

The first question is whether, as between the plaintiffs and the defendant, the
plaintiffs dealt as consumer or on the defendant's written standard terms of
business within s 3(1). In the light of s 12(1)(a) and the definition of 'business' in
s 14, it is accepted on behalf of the plaintiffs that they did not deal as consumer. So
the question is reduced to this. Did the plaintiffs 'deal' on the defendant's written
standard terms of business?

Mr Dehn submitted that the question must be answered in the negative, on the
ground that you cannot be said to deal on another's standard terms of business if,

a as was here the case, you negotiate with him over those terms before you enter into the contract. In my view that is an impossible construction for two reasons: first, because as a matter of plain English 'deals' means 'makes a deal', irrespective of any negotiations that may have preceded it; secondly, because s 12(1)(a) equates the expression 'deals as consumer' with 'makes the contract'. Thus it is clear that in order that one of the contracting parties may deal on the other's written standard *b* terms of business within s 3(1) it is only necessary for him to enter into the contract on those terms.

Mr Dehn sought to derive support for his submission from observations of Judge Thayne Forbes QC in *Salvage Association v CAP Financial Services Ltd* [1995] FSR 654 at 671–672. In my view, those observations do not assist the defendant. In that case the judge had to consider, in relation to two contracts, whether certain terms *c* satisfied the description 'written standard terms of business' and also whether there had been a 'dealing' on those terms. In relation to the first contract he said (at 671):

'I am satisfied that the terms in question were ones which had been written and produced in advance by CAP as a suitable set of contract terms for use in many of its future contracts of which the first contract with [the Salvage *d* Association] happened to be one. It is true that Mr Jones felt free to and did negotiate and agree certain important matters and details relating to the first contract at the meeting of February 27, 1987. However, although he had read and briefly considered CAP's conditions of business, he did not attempt any negotiation with regard to those conditions, nor did he or Mr Ellis consider *e* that it was appropriate or necessary to do so. The CAP standard conditions were terms that he and Mr Ellis willingly accepted as incorporated into the first contract in their predetermined form. In those circumstances, it seems to me that those terms still satisfy the description "written standard terms of business" and, so far as concerns the first contract, the actions of Mr Jones and Mr Ellis constituted "dealing" on the part of [the Salvage Association] with *f* CAP on its written standard terms of business within the meaning of section 3 of the [Unfair Contract Terms Act 1977].'

It is true that the judge found that the Salvage Association did not negotiate with CAP over the latter's standard terms and that he held that, in entering into the contract, the Salvage Association dealt with CAP on those terms within s 3. I do *g* not, however, read his observations as indicating a view that the 'dealing' depended on the absence of negotiations. I think that even if there had been negotiations over the standard conditions his view would have been the same.

Scott Baker J dealt with this question as one of fact, finding that the defendant's general conditions remained effectively untouched in the negotiations and that the *h* plaintiffs accordingly dealt on the defendant's written standard terms for the purposes of s 3(1) (see [1995] FSR 686 at 706). I respectfully agree with him. The consequence of that finding is that the defendant cannot rely on cl 9(c) except in so far as it satisfies the requirement of reasonableness. The judge carefully considered that question and held that clause 9(c) did not pass that test (see [1995] FSR 686 at *j* 707–711).

In *George Mitchell (Chesterhall) Ltd v Finney Lock Seeds Ltd* [1983] 2 All ER 737 at 743, [1983] 2 AC 803 at 816 Lord Bridge of Harwich, with whose speech the others of their Lordships agreed, said of the answer given by a judge of first instance to the question whether the requirement of reasonableness has been satisfied or not:

'There will sometimes be room for a legitimate difference of judicial opinion as to what the answer should be, where it will be impossible to say that one view is demonstrably wrong and the other demonstrably right. It must follow, in my view, that, when asked to review such a decision on appeal, the appellate court should treat the original decision with the utmost respect and refrain from interference with it unless satisfied that it proceeded on some erroneous principle or was plainly and obviously wrong.'

Adopting that approach to the answer given by Scott Baker J in this case, and despite Mr Dehn's well-sustained argument to the contrary, I am certainly not satisfied that his decision proceeded upon some erroneous principle or was plainly and obviously wrong. Indeed, I believe that I would have given the same answer myself.

I therefore differ from the judge only on the single, but important, question of the recoverability of the £484,000. I would vary his order by reducing the award by that amount and the amount of the interest loss thereon during the year 1991–92, the plaintiffs being entitled to the amount of the interest loss for 1990–91. To that extent I would allow the appeal.

HIRST LJ. I agree.

SIR IAIN GLIDEWELL. I have read in draft the judgment prepared by Nourse LJ and, like Hirst LJ, I agree with him that Scott Baker J was right in concluding that International Computers Ltd (ICL) were in breach of an express term of their contract with St Albans City and District Council (St Albans), that in the alternative the contract was subject to an implied term as to the fitness for purpose of the COMCIS program of which ICL were also in breach, and that they are not saved from the consequences of such breach by any terms of exclusion or limitation of liability in the contract. It follows that I agree with Nourse and Hirst LJJ that ICL are, as the judge held, liable in damages to St Albans. I too would therefore dismiss this part of the appeal.

However, before I turn to the subject of damages there is one aspect of the case on liability on which I wish to express my own opinion. This is the second issue to which I have already referred, namely, was the contract between the parties subject to any implied term as to quality or fitness for purpose, and if so, what was the nature of that term? Consideration of this question during argument led to discussion of a more general question, namely: 'Is software goods?' To seek to answer this question, it is necessary first to be clear about the meaning of some of the words used in argument.

In his judgment, Scott Baker J ([1995] FSR 686 at 698) adopted a description of a computer system which contains the following passage which I have found helpful:

'By itself hardware can do nothing. The really important part of the system is the software. Programs are the instructions or commands that tell the hardware what to do. The program itself is an algorithm or formula. It is of necessity contained in a physical medium. A program in machine readable form must be contained on a machine readable medium, such as paper cards, magnetic cards, magnetic tapes, discs, drums or magnetic bubbles.'

In relation to COMCIS the property in the program, ie the intangible 'instructions or commands', remained with ICL. Under the contract, St Albans were licensed to use the program. This is a common feature of contracts of this kind. However, in order that the program should be encoded into the computer itself, it was necessarily first recorded on a disk, from which it could be transferred to the computer. During the course of the hearing, the word 'software' was used to include both the (tangible) disk onto which the COMCIS program had been

a encoded and the (intangible) program itself. In order to answer the question, however, it is necessary to distinguish between the program and the disk carrying the program.

In both the Sale of Goods Act 1979, s 61, and the Supply of Goods and Services Act 1982, s 18, the definition of goods includes 'all personal chattels other than things in action and money'. Clearly, a disk is within this definition. Equally

b clearly, a program, of itself, is not.

If a disk carrying a program is transferred, by way of sale or hire, and the program is in some way defective, so that it will not instruct or enable the computer to achieve the intended purpose, is this a defect in the disk? Put more precisely, would the seller or hirer of the disk be in breach of the terms as to quality and fitness for purpose implied by s 14 of the 1979 Act and s 9 of the 1982 Act? Mr

c Dehn QC, for ICL, argues that they would not. He submits that the defective program in my example would be distinct from the tangible disk, and thus that the 'goods'—the disk—would not be defective.

There is no English authority on this question, and indeed we have been referred to none from any common law jurisdiction. The only reference I have found is an

d article published in 1994 by Dr Jane Stapleton. This is to a decision in *Advent Systems Ltd v Unisys Corp* (1991) 925 F 2d 670 that software is a 'good'; Dr Stapleton notes the decision as being reached 'on the basis of policy arguments'. We were referred, as was Scott Baker J, to a decision of Rogers J in the Supreme Court of New South Wales, *Toby Constructions Products Pty Ltd v Computa Bar (Sales) Pty Ltd* [1983] 2 NSWLR 48. The decision in that case was that the sale of a whole

e computer system, including both hardware and software, was a sale of 'goods' within the New South Wales legislation, which defines goods in similar terms to those in the English statute. That decision was in my respectful view clearly correct, but it does not answer the present question. Indeed, Rogers J specifically did not answer it. In expressing an opinion I am therefore venturing where others have, no doubt wisely, not trodden.

f Suppose I buy an instruction manual on the maintenance and repair of a particular make of car. The instructions are wrong in an important respect. Anybody who follows them is likely to cause serious damage to the engine of his car. In my view, the instructions are an integral part of the manual. The manual including the instructions, whether in a book or a video cassette, would in my

g opinion be 'goods' within the meaning of the 1979 Act, and the defective instructions would result in a breach of the implied terms in s 14.

If this is correct, I can see no logical reason why it should not also be correct in relation to a computer disk onto which a program designed and intended to instruct or enable a computer to achieve particular functions has been encoded. If

h the disk is sold or hired by the computer manufacturer, but the program is defective, in my opinion there would prima facie be a breach of the terms as to quality and fitness for purpose implied by the 1979 Act or the 1982 Act.

However, in the present case, it is clear that the defective program 2020 was not sold, and it seems probable that it was not hired. The evidence is that, in relation to many of the program releases, an employee of ICL went to St Albans' premises

j where the computer was installed taking with him a disk on which the new program was encoded, and himself performed the exercise of transferring the program into the computer.

As I have already said, the program itself is not 'goods' within the statutory definition. Thus a transfer of the program in the way I have described does not, in my view, constitute a transfer of goods. It follows that in such circumstances there is no statutory implication of terms as to quality or fitness for purpose.

Would the contract then contain no such implied term? The answer must be
sought in the common law. The terms implied by the 1979 Act and the 1982 Act   *a*
were originally evolved by the courts of common law and have since by analogy
been implied by the courts into other types of contract. Should such a term be
implied in a contract of the kind I am now considering, for the transfer of a
computer program into the computer without any transfer of a disk or any other
tangible thing on which the program is encoded?   *b*

The basis upon which a court is justified in implying a term into a contract in
which it has not been expressed is strict. Lord Pearson summarised it in his speech
in *Trollope & Colls Ltd v North West Metropolitan Regional Hospital Board* [1973] 2 All
ER 260 at 268, [1973] 1 WLR 601 at 609:

> 'An unexpressed term can be implied if and only if the court finds that the   *c*
> parties must have intended that term to form part of their contract: it is not
> enough for the court to find that such a term would have been adopted by the
> parties as reasonable men if it had been suggested to them: it must have been
> a term that went without saying, a term which, although tacit, formed part of
> the contract which the parties made for themselves.'

d
In my judgment, a contract for the transfer into a computer of a program intended
by both parties to instruct or enable the computer to achieve specified functions is
one to which Lord Pearson's words apply. In the absence of any express term as to
quality or fitness for purpose, or of any term to the contrary, such a contract is
subject to an implied term that the program will be reasonably fit for, i e reasonably
capable of achieving the intended purpose.   *e*

In the present case if, contrary to my view, the matter were not covered by
express terms of the contract, I would hold that the contract was subject to an
implied term that COMCIS was reasonably fit for, that is, reasonably capable of
achieving the purpose specified in the 'Statement of User Requirements' in ch 5 of
St Alban's invitation to tender, and that as a result of the defect in release 2020 ICL   *f*
were in breach of that implied term.

I turn now to the issue of damages. When the judge was considering whether
the plaintiffs' loss was irrecoverable as damages because it had already been
recouped in 1991–92, he drew no distinction between the £685,000 and the
£484,000. Moreover, it seems that he was not referred directly to the decision of
this court in *Palatine Graphic Arts Co Ltd v Liverpool City Council* [1986] 1 All ER 366,   *g*
[1986] QB 355, nor to the passages from the speech of Lord Reid in *Parry v Cleaver*
[1969] 1 All ER 555 esp at 559, [1970] AC 1 esp at 15 quoted in the judgments in that
case, which Nourse LJ has set out in his judgment.

Applying the principles derived from those authorities, I entirely agree with
Nourse LJ that St Albans suffered a loss of £685,000 which, with interest, must form   *h*
part of the damages. As to the £484,000, however, St Albans recouped their loss of
this sum from their chargepayers in 1991–92. For the reasons given by Nourse LJ
they are not entitled to recover the £484,000 as damages, but only the interest on
that sum for one year.

To this limited extent I would allow the appeal.
j

Appeal allowed in part.

L I Zysman Esq   Barrister.

National Westminster Bank plc v Kitch

a

COURT OF APPEAL, CIVIL DIVISION
SIMON BROWN, PETER GIBSON AND SCHIEMANN LJJ
19 APRIL, 3 MAY 1996

b

Jurisdiction – High Court of Justice – Divisions of High Court – Action triable in two separate divisions – Action commenced by bank in Queen's Bench Division for recovery of loan secured by mortgage – Mortgage not relied on in proceedings – Whether action properly commenced in Queen's Bench Division – Whether action a 'mortgage action' – RSC Ord 88, r 1.

c

An action by a bank against a customer for the recovery of an overdraft which is secured by a mortgage or charge is not a 'mortgage action' within the meaning of RSC Ord 88, r 1[a] where the bank does not rely on the mortgage in making its claim. It follows that the provisions of Ord 88 do not apply and, as a result, such *d* an action can properly be commenced in the Queen's Bench Division of the High Court (see p 496 *g h*, p 499 *j* and p 502 *c*, post).

Dictum of Donaldson J in *Midland Bank Ltd v Stamps* [1978] 3 All ER 1 at 3 disapproved.

Notes

e For commencement of mortgage actions in the High Court, see 32 *Halsbury's Laws* (4th edn) paras 804–808.

Cases referred to in judgments

Barclays Bank Ltd v Beck [1952] 1 All ER 549, [1952] 2 QB 47, CA.
f *Midland Bank Ltd v Stamps* [1978] 3 All ER 1, [1978] 1 WLR 635.
Newnham v Brown [1966] 2 All ER 229, [1966] 1 WLR 875, CA; *rvsg* [1966] 1 All ER 281, [1966] 1 WLR 875.
Redditch Benefit Building Society v Roberts [1940] 1 All ER 342, [1940] Ch 415, CA.
Samuel v Jarrah Timber and Wood Paving Corp Ltd [1904] AC 323, HL.
Temperance Permanent Building Society v Nevitt [1940] 3 All ER 237, CA.
g

Cases also cited or referred to in skeleton arguments

Al-Tobaishi v Aung (1994) Times, 10 March, [1994] CA Transcript 233.
Anlaby v Praetorius (1888) 20 QBD 764, CA.
Bank of America National Trust and Savings Association v Chrismas [1994] 1 All ER
h   401.
Bernstein v Jackson [1982] 2 All ER 806, [1982] 1 WLR 1082, CA.
Birmingham Citizens Permanent Building Society v Caunt [1962] 1 All ER 163, [1962] Ch 883.
Charlesworth v Focusmulti Ltd [1993] CA Transcript 228.
j *Dawson (Bradford) Ltd v Dove* [1971] 1 All ER 554, [1971] 1 QB 330.
Dubai Bank Ltd v Galadari (No 4) (1990) Times, 23 February.
Four-Maids Ltd v Dudley Marshall (Properties) Ltd [1957] 2 All ER 35, [1957] Ch 317.
Hamp-Adams v Hall [1911] 2 KB 942, CA.

---

a   Rule 1, so far as material, provides: 'This Order applies to any action ... by a mortgagee ... in which
     there is a claim for ... payment of moneys secured by the mortgage ...'

Harkness v Bell's Asbestos and Engineering Ltd [1966] 3 All ER 843, [1967] 2 QB 729, CA.

Hinckley and South Leicestershire Permanent Building Society v Freeman [1940] 4 All ER 212, [1941] Ch 32.

Isaacs v Robertson [1984] 3 All ER 140, [1985] AC 97, PC.

Leal v Dunlop Bio-Processes International Ltd [1984] 2 All ER 207, [1984] 1 WLR 874, CA.

MacFoy v United Africa Co Ltd [1961] 3 All ER 1169, [1962] AC 152, PC.

Marsh v Marsh [1945] AC 271, PC.

Peachey Property Corp v Robinson [1966] 2 All ER 981, [1967] 2 QB 543, CA.

Singh v Atombrook Ltd [1989] 1 All ER 385, [1989] 1 WLR 810, CA.

White v Weston [1968] 2 All ER 842, [1968] 2 QB 647, CA.

Willowgreen Ltd v Smithers [1994] 2 All ER 533, [1994] 1 WLR 832, CA.

Appeal

The defendant, John Stephen Kitch, appealed with leave granted by the Court of Appeal (Glidewell and Waite LJJ) on 5 April 1995 from the decision of Curtis J on 10 October 1994, dismissing his application to set aside a judgment entered in default of defence by the plaintiff, National Westminster Bank plc, on the basis that it had been irregularly obtained. The facts are set out in the judgment of Schiemann LJ.

Robert Deacon (instructed by *Lucas & Co*, Cowbridge) for the defendant.

Michael Lerego QC and *Paul Gott* (instructed by *Osborne Clarke*, Bristol) for the plaintiff.

Cur adv vult

3 May 1996. The following judgments were delivered.

SCHIEMANN LJ (giving the first judgment at the invitation of Simon Brown LJ). This case raises a question of some general importance in relation to actions by banks against their customers for repayment of overdrafts given by the banks. Many such loans are secured by a mortgage or charge. Often the bank starts proceedings for repayment of the overdraft, which proceedings make no mention of the fact that the bank has the mortgage as security. The question which faced Curtis J, from whom this is an appeal, was this: is such an action a 'mortgage action' to which the provisions of RSC Ord 88 are applicable? Curtis J held that it was not. In so holding, he departed from a dictum of Donaldson J upon which various notes to the order in *The Supreme Court Practice* are based. In my judgment, Curtis J was right.

The factual background need not detain us long for we are not asked to concern ourselves with the merits. The bank issued a writ out of the Bristol district registry of the Queen's Bench Division claiming sums allegedly due on two accounts which the customer had with the bank. The writ, which was indorsed with a statement of claim, makes no mention of any mortgage. The defence legal team deliberately decided to file no defence taking the view that this was a mortgage action which had been improperly commenced in the Queen's Bench Division. The bank then, without first seeking the leave of the court, entered judgment in default of defence under Ord 13, r 1 whereupon the *a*   customer applied to set the judgment aside on the basis that it had been irregularly obtained.

The customer's submissions

Mr Deacon, who appeared for the customer, relied on Ord 88, r 6 and on a note to that rule.

b   In order to do so he had to persuade the court that this action was a mortgage action as defined in Ord 88, r 1(1). His argument was simple. He pointed out three undisputed facts: (1) the action was begun by a mortgagee; (2) the action was one in which there was a claim for payment of moneys; and (3) the payment of those moneys was secured by the mortgage. So he submitted that the action fell neatly within the definition in Ord 88, r 1(1)(a). Moreover, he pointed to

c   *Midland Bank Ltd v Stamps* [1978] 3 All ER 1 at 3, [1978] 1 WLR 635 at 638, where the foregoing three facts were equally present, where the statement of claim made no mention of any mortgage and where Donaldson J said:

'The bank is without doubt claiming payment of moneys secured by a mortgage of real property and the action is thus a mortgage action to which
d   Ord 88 applies.'

The bank's submissions

Mr Lerego QC submitted as follows.

e   (1) In cases where Ord 88, r 1(1)(b) to (g) has no application, r 1(1)(a) only applies *if the claim is described in the document originating the action* as a claim for payment of moneys secured by a mortgage (as defined in r 2). In my judgment, that is a possible construction of the order, although the construction contended for by the defendant is equally possible.

(2) No purpose is served by requiring a plaintiff who does not found his claim
f   upon a mortgage to include in the originating process a statement as to the whereabouts of the mortgaged property (r 3(3)) or to exhibit a copy of the mortgage as part of his evidence and to produce the original (rr 6(4) and 5(2)). Moreover, the particulars which are required by r 5(6) and (3) are inappropriate to claims made on a current bank account. It would be highly unusual for the rules to require the production of irrelevant material.

g   (3) He drew attention to the legislative history and context of Ord 88. Throughout the rules there are two variables in play—whether the case is heard by the Queen's Bench Division or by the Chancery Division, and whether the case is started by writ or by originating summons. Two cases in the Court of Appeal in 1940 indicate the history of Ord 88: *Redditch Benefit Building Society v*
h   *Roberts* [1940] 1 All ER 342, [1940] Ch 415 and *Temperance Permanent Building Society v Nevitt* [1940] 3 All ER 237. Those cases were decided shortly after the introduction into the Rules of the Supreme Court of Ord 55, r 5A, which is the predecessor of the present Ord 88, r 1. The background and purpose of the changes introduced into the rules in 1936 as explained by the Court of Appeal
j   were in summary: (i) to cure an anomaly in that judgment for possession could automatically be obtained in the King's Bench Division in default of appearance to a writ, whereas proceedings for possession in the Chancery Division were commenced by originating summons and judgment could only be obtained after a hearing before the master; (ii) the form of order for payment and possession in the King's Bench Division failed to indicate to the defendant mortgagor that upon payment he was, or might be, entitled to relief against the order for possession—

this was a defect which it was wished to cure; (iii) even if the defendant was aware of this right, he had to take separate proceedings in the Chancery Division to establish or enforce that right, thereby producing the multiplicity of proceedings which it was the object of the Judicature Acts to avoid; (iv) to enable judgment to be given for a monetary sum in mortgage proceedings by originating summons in the Chancery Division; and (v) to achieve uniformity in the treatment of mortgage actions whether begun by writ or originating summons.

(4) He drew attention to the fact that Ord 13 of the present rules also distinguishes between possession and money claims; under r 4(1) a plaintiff seeking a default judgment for possession must certify that he is not claiming relief specified in Ord 88, r 1, but a plaintiff seeking a money judgment under rr 1 and 2 does not have to do so.

(5) Prior to the changes, all money claims had to be made by writ. But following the changes, a mortgagee could make a claim for payment of money by originating summons, but, by the terms of Ord 55, r 5A, the summons had to *specify* that the plaintiff was claiming money secured by the mortgage. Unless it did so it was not a proper method of commencing proceedings to recover money and would not have been issued by the court.

(6) Although at first blush it seemed strange for the rules to distinguish between simple money claims based on a mortgage and simple money claims not based on a mortgage and to prescribe the Chancery Division for the former, even when there was no concurrent claim for possession, there was good reason for so doing. The law relating to mortgages is notoriously complex and there was much to be said for allocating claims for money under mortgage documentation to masters and judges familiar with this branch of the law. He drew our attention to Lord Macnaghten's statement in *Samuel v Jarrah Timber and Wood Paving Corp Ltd* [1904] AC 323 at 326 that—'no one ... by the light of nature ever understood an English mortgage of real estate.' These considerations are of no relevance to a case such as the present.

(7) The construction contended for by the bank achieves consistency with the corresponding provision of the County Court Rules (CCR Ord 6, r 5(1)).

None of this was disputed by Mr Deacon.

One is of course always hesitant before differing from Donaldson J. However, the issue which he had to decide in *Midland Bank Ltd v Stamps* was whether he had jurisdiction, notwithstanding the provisions of Ord 88 to retain the action in the Commercial Court. He held that he had. He based his decision on a direction made by the Lord Chancellor under s 57 of the Supreme Court of Judicature (Consolidation) Act 1925 and upon the exercise of his discretion under s 58 of that Act. I accept that whereas, if the decision of Curtis J is right, Donaldson J could have based his decision on a finding that he was not concerned with a mortgage action at all, he in fact said ([1978] 3 All ER 1 at 3, [1978] 1 WLR 635 at 638):

'The bank is without doubt claiming payment of moneys secured by a mortgage of real property and the action is thus a mortgage action to which Ord 88 applies.'

I consider the phraseology of Ord 88, r 1 is capable of the construction contended for both by the appellant and by the respondent. While in no way criticising the result achieved by Donaldson J in *Midland Bank Ltd v Stamps*, I disagree with the single sentence in that decision relied upon by the appellant and the editors of *The Supreme Court Practice*. That sentence was not necessary to the judge's decision and it seems clear that Donaldson J was not treated to the careful analysis of the

a history of this rule and the previous decisions concerning it which have been placed before the court by the respondent. I accept the points made by Mr Lerego, and Mr Deacon has not put before us any cogent policy reasons for construing the rule in the manner for which he contends.

I confess I reached this conclusion with satisfaction. There seems to be no reason in principle why, if a bank chooses not to rely on a mortgage in an action,
b that action should be classified as a mortgage action. Most cases based upon or concerning the operation of ordinary bank accounts have been and are brought in the Queen's Bench Division. In complex cases, they will be heard in the Commercial Court of that division. The most appropriate place for the trial of ordinary bank claims is often the trial centre closest to the customer and bank branch, and during the last few years a series of Mercantile Court lists have been
c established outside London under practice directions which presuppose that ordinary banking disputes will form part of the Queen's Bench lists.

In cases such as the present the legal mortgages are charges to the bank created to secure running accounts. The distinction between such charges and, for instance, a mortgage deed to a building society is referred to in *Barclays Ltd Bank*
d *v Beck* [1952] 1 All ER 549 at 552–553, [1952] 2 QB 47 at 54 by Denning LJ who points out the distinction between specialty debts and simple contract debts:

> 'If they are created under and by virtue of a deed, they are specialty debts from their commencement, but if they are created by a simple contract outside a deed, they remain simple contract debts even though there is a
e deed in existence which gives collateral security for them. The distinction is clearly shown by considering the difference between a mortgage debt to a building society and a charge to a bank to secure a running account. The mortgage debt to a building society is created under and by virtue of a deed and is a specialty debt from its commencement, but a future debt on a running account is a debt created by parol and it remains a simple contract
f debt even though the customer has previously given a charge to secure it which includes a covenant under seal. The future debt on running account is not created under the deed. It may be that it would never have been created but for the deed, but that is a different thing. It only means that the deed is collateral security for its repayment.'

g As Donaldson J himself said in *Midland Bank Ltd v Stamps* [1978] 3 All ER 1 at 2, [1978] 1 WLR 635 at 637: '… the fact that the moneys claimed by the bank are secured by a mortgage is wholly irrelevant in the context of the bank's claim.' I see no policy reason why we should construe an ambiguous rule in the way contended for by the appellant. So far as the money claim is concerned, he
h deserves no more protection than any other debtor. There may well be cases where there is a real doubt as to whether the bank is secured or not. In such cases I can see no disadvantage in the bank being allowed to sidestep any problems which this might raise. So far as the possibility of being turned out of his house is concerned, he still has all the protection which the law gives to a mortgagor
j who is at risk of action by the mortgagee.

I would dismiss this appeal and invite the editors of *The Supreme Court Practice* to reconsider their notes to Ord 88, rr 2 and 6.

PETER GIBSON LJ. The first and in the event determinative question raised on this appeal is whether an action brought by a creditor claiming a sum owed by the debtor on two current accounts is a mortgage action within RSC Ord 88, r 1

when the sum is secured by a mortgage, but the creditor does not rely on the
mortgage in making his claim.   *a*

There are two possible constructions of the definition of a mortgage action in
Ord 88, r 1.   The wider construction, which has the weighty support of
Donaldson J in *Midland Bank Ltd v Stamps* [1978] 3 All ER 1 at 3, [1978] 1 WLR 635
at 638, is that it embraces any action by a person who is in fact a mortgagee and
claims in the action payment of moneys which in fact are secured by a mortgage,   *b*
whether or not the mortgage is relied on. The narrower construction, which was
favoured by the judge, is that it is an action brought by the plaintiff as mortgagee
in which action there is a claim for payment of moneys secured by a mortgage in
the sense that it must be claimed that the moneys are so secured.

In arguing in favour of the wider construction Mr Deacon, for the appellant,   *c*
found himself in the curious position of saying that Donaldson J in the *Midland*
Bank case was wrong to decide, as he did, that he could disregard the assignment
by Ord 88, r 2 to the Chancery Division of 'any action in which there is a claim
for ... payment of moneys secured by a mortgage of any real or leasehold
property' by reason of the discretion given to him by proviso (2) to s 58 of the
Supreme Court of Judicature (Consolidation) Act 1925, but that he was right to   *d*
assert, as that judge did, that:

> 'The [plaintiff] bank is without doubt claiming payment of moneys secured
> by a mortgage of real property and the action is thus a mortgage action to
> which Ord 88 applies.' (See [1978] 3 All ER 1 at 3, [1978] 1 WLR 635 at 638.)
>   *e*

Donaldson J pointed out that the fact that the moneys claimed by the plaintiff
bank were secured by a mortgage was wholly irrelevant in the context of the
bank's claim and that neither the bank nor the defendant needed to refer to the
mortgage (see [1978] 3 All ER 1 at 2, [1978] 1 WLR 635 at 637). In exercising his
discretion not to transfer the action from the Commercial Court, he took into   *f*
account the fact that the case was primarily a banking dispute and not a mortgage
dispute.   Donaldson J may not have had the benefit of as extensive an argument
as we have had.   He referred to no authorities and does not appear to have
considered the origins of Ord 88.

Mr Deacon suggested that the purpose of a requirement that an action in   *g*
which there is a claim for moneys which happen to be secured by a mortgage, but
in which no reliance is placed on the mortgage, was to enable the court to check
the interest calculation to ensure that the state of the account between the
mortgagor and mortgagee was correct, not just from the mortgagor's viewpoint
but also for the benefit of any second mortgagee. He referred us to Ord 88, r 5,
prescribing what evidence is required to support a mortgage action. By r 5(6)   *h*
where the plaintiff claims payment of moneys secured by the mortgage, the
affidavit must prove that the money is due and payable and give the particulars
mentioned in para (3), viz (a) the amount of the advance, (b) the amount of the
periodic payments required to be made, (c) the amount of any interest or
instalments in arrears at the date of the issue of proceedings and at the date of the   *j*
affidavit, and (d) the amount remaining under the mortgage.   These particulars
do not appear appropriate to a simple case of a running account which is
overdrawn and the overdraft is secured by a mortgage. Nor does Ord 88 give any
support to the suggestion that the draftsman had in mind a second mortgagee (if
indeed there is one).   Why should there be concern on behalf of a second
mortgagee? He is not likely to be a party to the proceedings between the creditor

a and the debtor and so would not be bound in any judgment obtained against the debtor.

In my judgment, the narrower construction is to be preferred for the following reasons.

First, as already indicated, Ord 88, r 5(3) and (6) do not appear to have been drafted with the case of an action for payment of moneys due on an overdraft on
b a running account in mind, common enough though that was and is. It is not in dispute that a debt on a running account remains a simple contract debt even if it is secured by a charge (see *Barclays Bank Ltd v Beck* [1952] 1 All ER 549 at 553, [1952] 2 QB 47 at 54).

Second, Ord 88, r 5(2) requires the supporting affidavit to exhibit a copy of the mortgage, and also requires the production of the original mortgage or, in the
c case of a registered charge, the charge certificate at the hearing of the mortgage action. That, to my mind, clearly indicates that Ord 88 was drafted on the basis that the mortgage would be a relevant document in the action and that is wholly inconsistent with an action in which the existence of the mortgage is irrelevant to any issue in the proceedings.

d Third, the history of Ord 88 does not suggest that it was ever intended to apply to a case in which there was no reliance on the mortgage. It was introduced in 1936 (as Ord 55, r 5A), accompanied by practice directions described as 'relating to proceedings under a mortgage or charge' (see [1936] WN 326). Mr Lerego QC, for the bank, showed us the explanations given in this court for the introduction of the new rule, and Schiemann LJ in his judgment has set them out in para (3) of
e his summary of Mr Lerego's submissions. Cross J accurately summarised the new provisions in *Newnham v Brown* [1966] 1 All ER 281 at 283, [1966] 1 WLR 875 at 877–878:

'In 1936, however, the rules were changed so as to provide—speaking generally—(a) that all actions claiming payment or possession under
f mortgages of land should be brought in the Chancery Division; (b) that orders for payment or possession under mortgages could be obtained on originating summons as well as by writ, and (c) that, if the claim was made by writ, judgment in default should not be entered without the leave of the court obtained in the same way as it would have to be obtained if the claim was being made by originating summons.'
g

In this court Lord Denning MR expressed a similar view ([1966] 2 All ER 229 at 230, [1966] 1 WLR 875 at 881):

'The object of R.S.C., Ord. 55, r. 5A, was to ensure that all claims on a mortgage or charge, where the defendant was in possession, should be
h brought in the Chancery Division and be subject to the control of the judges of that division.'

Fourth, while it is easy to see the sense of assigning to the Chancery Division proceedings in which the specific expertise of that division in dealing with the
j notoriously difficult subject of mortgages was to be utilised, no satisfactory reason can be given for assigning to that division cases where no reliance is placed on the mortgage. Moreover, in some cases there may be real doubt as to whether in fact the moneys claimed are secured by a mortgage. The definition of a mortgage in Ord 88, r 2 includes an equitable mortgage or charge. This, prior to s 2 of the Law of Property (Miscellaneous Provisions) Act 1989, would include informal equitable mortgages created by the mere deposit of title deeds with the

requisite intention of creating a mortgage. Why should it matter whether or not
such a mortgage was created when the plaintiff does not rely on his security?   *a*

Fifth, in Ord 13 a distinction is drawn between a claim for possession of land
(r 4) and a claim for a liquidated demand (r 1). Only in the former must the
plaintiff, wishing to enter a default judgment, state that he is not claiming any
relief in the action of the nature specified in Ord 88, r 1.

Sixth, the narrower construction is consistent with the corresponding   *b*
provisions of the County Court Rules. Ord 6, r 5(1) only applies where the
plaintiff claims 'as mortgagee' payment of moneys secured by a mortgage of real
or leasehold property or possession of such property.

For these reasons, for which I am largely indebted to the excellent arguments
of Mr Lerego, I would agree with the judge's conclusion that the action is not a
mortgage action. Accordingly I would dismiss this appeal.   *c*

SIMON BROWN LJ. I agree with both judgments.

Appeal dismissed. Leave to appeal to the House of Lords refused.

Paul Magrath Esq   Barrister.   *d*

a   # Racoon Ltd v Turnbull and another

PRIVY COUNCIL

LORD GOFF OF CHIEVELEY, LORD GRIFFITHS, LORD JAUNCEY OF TULLICHETTLE, LORD
STEYN AND LORD HOFFMANN

b   27 MARCH, 22 MAY 1996

*Land registration – Rectification of register – Entry obtained by mistake – Landowner
granting lease of strip of road – Registrar erroneously recording against lessor's title
general right of way over landowner's land for duration of lease – Plaintiff purchasing
land after expiry of lease but claiming right of way in reliance on register – Whether
c   right of way enforceable – Whether plaintiff having knowledge of error – Whether
defendant entitled to rectification – Registered Land Ordinance 1970 (British Virgin
Islands), ss 38, 140.*

G Ltd was granted a lease for a term of five years from 21 December 1971 of a
d   strip of road which connected its estate to a public road. In 1972 part of the estate
was sold and the new owners applied to register the title. The registrar
erroneously recorded as an appurtenance a general right of way over the lessor's
land. The lessor's title was subsequently registered and this entry also
misconstrued the lease as a grant of a right of way, but accurately reflected the
limited duration of the right thereby conferred. In 1979 the plaintiff company
e   purchased the estate, but did not search the register entry relating to the lessor's
land, since by s 38(1)[a] of the Registered Land Ordinance 1970 a subsequent
purchaser was not required to ascertain the circumstances in which the title had
been registered. The lease was not renewed and in 1982 access to the road was
blocked. The plaintiff thereafter applied for a declaration against the defendant
f   executor of the lessor's estate that, as the registered proprietor of the estate, it was
entitled to a right of way over the road, and for an injunction against interference
with the exercise of that right. The judge held that the plaintiff had established
20 years' continuous use of the road and was therefore entitled to the right of way
and injunction sought. The Court of Appeal of the British Virgin Islands allowed
the defendant's appeal, set aside the order and ordered that the entry in the
g   register recording a general right of way be cancelled on the ground that the
plaintiff had established neither 20 years' user nor acquiescence by the lessor for
a lesser period and was presumed to have had knowledge of the error since he
should have searched the title. The plaintiff appealed to the Privy Council,
contending (i) that it was a purchaser for value without notice of the error for the
h   purposes of s 140(2)[b] of the 1970 Ordinance and could therefore avoid
rectification, and (ii) that the proper remedy was to rectify the lessor's title under
s 140(1), which would enable the defendant to claim compensation.

Held – The appeal would be dismissed for the following reasons—

j   (1) The power to rectify an entry in the register under s 140(1) of the 1970
Ordinance could be exercised only where registration was obtained, made or
omitted by fraud or mistake. In the instant case the only mistake was the
description of the right conferred by the lease as right of way rather than a right

---

a   Section 38, so far as material, is set out at p 506 *j*, post
b   Section 140, so far as material, is set out at p 508 *b c*, post

of occupancy; the reference to the lease and the duration of the right were
accurate. It followed that there was no relevant mistake which could be rectified *a*
under s 140(1) (see p 508 *j* to p 509 *a*, post).

(2) Where an entry in the register indicated a purported appurtenant right or
burden over another parcel of land, s 38 of the 1970 Ordinance did not absolve
the purchaser of the dominant tenement from the need to examine the entry in
the register relating to the servient tenement. In those circumstances, it was *b*
entirely reasonable and consistent with the scheme of registration that the
purchaser should satisfy himself as to the validity of his right by examining the
other registered entry; he was not required to go behind the register, but merely
to examine two entries instead of one. It followed that a prudent purchaser of the
estate would and should have examined the registered entry of the lessor's land
and that the plaintiff was deemed to have had knowledge of the mistake in the *c*
register. Accordingly, the plaintiff's title fell to be rectified under s 140(2) to
remove the right of way over the defendant's land (see p 509 *c d h* and p 510 *b*,
post).

### Notes											*d*
For the basis of systems of land registration generally, see 26 *Halsbury's Laws* (4th
edn) paras 913–917.

Cases referred to in judgment
Breskvar v Wall (1971) 126 CLR 376, Aust HC.
Frazer v Walker [1967] 1 All ER 649, [1967] 1 AC 569, [1967] 2 WLR 411, PC.				*e*

Appeal
Racoon Ltd appealed with final leave granted by the Court of Appeal of the
British Virgin Islands from the decision of that court (Sir Vincent Floissac CJ,
Byron and Liverpool JJA) given on 10 January 1994 allowing the appeal of the *f*
respondent, Harris Turnbull (as executor of James Turnbull, deceased, and in his
own right) from the judgment of Bertrand J in the High Court of the British
Virgin Islands on 30 May 1991, whereby she declared that the appellant was
entitled to a right of way over land which had been registered in the name of the
deceased and granted injunctive relief. The facts are set out in the judgment of *g*
the Board.

Fenton Ramsahoye QC and *Gerard Farara* (both of the British Virgin Islands Bar)
	(instructed by *Simons Muirhead & Burton*) for the appellant.
Michael Douglas and *Peter Foster* (of the British Virgin Islands Bar) (instructed by *h*
	Winckworth & Pemberton) for the respondents.

The Board took time for consideration.

22 May 1996. The following judgment of the Board was delivered.							*j*

LORD JAUNCEY OF TULLICHETTLE. This appeal arises out of a disputed
right of way over land in Tortola in the British Virgin Islands and involves
consideration of certain sections of the Land Adjudication Ordinance 1970 and
the Registered Land Ordinance 1970 which changed the system of land
registration from one of deeds to one of title.

a The background to the action may conveniently be summarised chronologically.

28 August 1965. Samuel Penrose acquired 100·68 acres of land known as Greenbank Estate which was bounded on the south, inter alia, by lands belonging to James Turnbull.

8 September 1967. Penrose conveyed to Greenbank Estate Co Ltd (GECL) *b* 49·87 acres of the above land including that part bounded by the land of Turnbull.

21 June 1968. GECL agreed to sell to Simrose Ltd a part of the above 49·87 acres which included the part bounded by the land of Turnbull. Penrose was a director of both GECL and Simrose.

11 February 1972. Turnbull granted to GECL a lease for five years from 21 December 1971 of 'a strip of graded road approximately 20 feet wide and *c* approximately 100 feet long connecting land of the lessee known as Greenbank Estate to the public road' which bounded Turnbull's land. There was an estate road over Greenbank Estate which terminated at the above strip of graded road. Although at the date of the lease the land abutting that of Turnbull was owned by Simrose, it appears that GECL retained responsibility for the estate road and *d* that the buyers of parcels of ground from Simrose were obliged to pay to GECL an annual maintenance charge in respect of the road.

5 December 1972. Simrose conveyed 1·22 acres to Mr and Mrs Schaum. This area did not abut on the land of Turnbull and the Schaums were required to contribute towards the upkeep of the Greenbank Estate road.

12 June 1979. The Schaums conveyed the above 1·22 acres to Racoon Ltd, the *e* appellant.

The lease of the road was not renewed and in 1982 Turnbull blocked the road as a result of which the appellant raised the present action.

The Land Adjudication Ordinance 1970 requires the preparation of an adjudication record consisting of a form relating to each parcel of land which is *f* to form the basis of the land register prepared under the Registered Land Ordinance 1970. Section 9 of the latter Ordinance provides that the land register shall comprise a register in respect of every parcel of land adjudicated upon and shall be divided into three sections namely the property section, the proprietorship section, and the incumbrances section 'containing a note of every incumbrance and every right adversely affecting the land or lease'. Section 10 is *g* in the following terms:

> 'Whenever an adjudication record has become final under section 23 of the Land Adjudication Ordinance and the adjudication officer has delivered the adjudication record to the registrar, the registrar shall prepare a register for each parcel shown in the adjudication record and for any lease required to be *h* registered, and shall register therein any of the particulars in the adjudication record which requires registration.'

The Schaums submitted an adjudication claim form dated 4 April 1973 which made no reference to any right of way over Turnbull's land, but the adjudication *j* record prepared in response thereto contained the following entry: '3A. APPURTENANCES. 1. EASEMENT: 20ft Right of Way over 2638B 27 from Public Road to Greenbank Estate Road (see lease No. 195 of 1972).' This was a reference to the lease by Turnbull to GECL and suggests that the adjudication officer misconstrued the lease of the strip of land as a grant of a right of way. However, when the Schaums' title came to be registered on 28 June 1974 bearing parcel number 16 there was recorded as an appurtenance: '20ft Right of Way over

2638B 27 from Public Road to Greenbank Estate Road.' In omitting the reference
to the lease the registrar completely altered the character of the appurtenance
which appeared in the adjudication record. This was an alteration which he was
not empowered by s 10 to make and which was clearly erroneous.

Turnbull's title was registered bearing parcel number 27 on 25 September 1974
and the incumbrances section contained the following entry: '20ft Right of Way
to Greenbank Estate created for five years from 21.12.71 by lease No. 195 of 1972
(filed with this parcel).' This entry also misconstrued the lease as a grant of a right
of way but accurately reflected the limited duration of the right which was
conferred thereby. The result of these two entries was to produce a discrepancy
in that the title to parcel 16 was shown as having a general right of way over
parcel 27 whereas that of the latter merely showed a right in favour of parcel 16
limited in duration to five years.

On 20 October 1982 after the blocking of the road the appellant raised the
present action against Turnbull's executor seeking a declaration that as registered
proprietor of parcel 16 it was entitled to a right of way 20 ft wide for pedestrians,
horses and vehicles over parcel 27 and for an injunction against interference with
the exercise of the right. A hearing took place in the High Court of the British
Virgin Islands before Bertrand J on seven days in June and July 1988, and on 30
May 1991 she gave judgment in which she held that the appellant had established
more than 20 years continuous use of the road and was therefore entitled to the
declaration and injunction sought.

The Court of Appeal of the British Virgin Islands set aside the order of Bertrand
J holding that the appellant had established neither appropriate user for 20 years
nor acquiescence on the part of Turnbull for a lesser period and that accordingly
the entry in the register recording as an appurtenance to parcel 16 a general right
of way should be cancelled.

Before this Board Dr Ramsahoye QC, for the appellant, argued that as a
subsequent purchaser for value and without notice of parcel 16 he was entitled to
rely on the entry in the register, and that the proper remedy for the respondents
was to have the entry relating to parcel 27 rectified and to claim compensation as
provided for in the Ordinance. Mr Douglas, for the respondents, submitted that
registration of a right of way in the title of the dominant tenement was
insufficient without a corresponding entry in that of the servient tenement to
create a right enforceable against the latter. He further argued that the title to
parcel 27 could not be rectified under the Ordinance.

The philosophy underlying a system of registration of title is that it confers
indefeasibility of title to the specified parcel of land upon the registered proprietor
and dispenses with any need on the part of persons dealing with him to
investigate further his right thereto. Thus it is provided in s 38(1) of the
Registered Land Ordinance 1970:

'No person dealing or proposing to deal for valuable consideration with a
proprietor shall be required or in any way concerned—(a) to inquire or
ascertain the circumstances in or the consideration for which such proprietor
or any previous proprietor was registered; or ... (c) to search any register
kept under the Registration and Records Ordinance.'

The register referred to in para (c) is a register of deeds prepared in accordance
with the previous system of land registration. The Ordinance also makes
provision for rectification of the register and for indemnification out of public
funds of persons suffering damage as a result of rectification or impossibility

a thereof. Their Lordships were informed that the registration system in the British Virgin Islands was modelled on similar systems in Australia and New Zealand and were referred to observations of this Board in *Frazer v Walker* [1967] 1 All ER 649, [1967] AC 569. In that case a forged memorandum of mortgage granted by one of two joint proprietors was registered and subsequently enforced by the mortgagees on default by the mortgagor. A purchaser in good faith at

b auction whose title was thereafter registered was held entitled to found on his registered title in proceedings for possession against the other joint proprietor. Lord Wilberforce, delivering the judgment of the Board, referred to the phrase 'indefeasibility of title' and continued ([1967] 1 All ER 649 at 652, [1967] 1 AC 569 at 580–581):

c   'The expression, not used in the [Land Transfer Act 1952] itself, is a convenient description of the immunity from attack by adverse claim to the land or interest in respect of which he is registered, which a registered proprietor enjoys. This conception is central in the system of registration. It does not involve that the registered proprietor is protected against any claim whatsoever; as will be seen later, there are provisions by which the entry on

d   which he relies may be cancelled or corrected, or he may be exposed to claims in personam. These are matters not to be overlooked when a total description of his rights is required; but as registered proprietor, and while he remains such, no adverse claim (except as specifically admitted) may be brought against him.'

e Their Lordships were also referred to *Breskvar v Wall* (1971) 126 CLR 376 in which the High Court of Australia held that the fact that an instrument of transfer of land was void or voidable did not prevent the transferee from acquiring an indefeasible interest in accordance with the instrument when it was registered.

f   Section 23 of the Registered Land Ordinance provides that—

       'the registration of any person as the proprietor with absolute title of a parcel shall vest in that person the absolute ownership of that parcel, together with all rights and privileges belonging or appurtenant thereto, free from all other interests and claims whatsoever, but subject—(a) to the leases, charges and other incumbrances and to the conditions and restrictions, if

g   any, shown in the register; and (b) unless the contrary is expressed in the register, to such liabilities, rights and interests as affect the same and are declared by section 28 of this Ordinance not to require noting on the register.'

h Section 28 provides that in the absence of a contrary intention all registered land shall be subject to such of certain specified overriding interests, including rights of way, as may for the time being subsist and affect the land without their being noted in the register. It might appear from s 23 that the effect of registration was to render unchallengeable any right recorded as an appurtenance. But Dr

j Ramsahoye conceded, correctly in their Lordships' view, that the registrar had no power under that section on first registration to create a right of way or other easement which did not exist at the time of registration. How then has parcel 16 acquired a right of way over parcel 27? Dr Ramsahoye argued that the appellant was a purchaser for value without notice and that therefore the registered entry for parcel 16 could no longer be rectified. It followed that the right of way referred to in the register had become indefeasible.

The two principal rectification provisions are s 139, which empowers the
registrar to rectify what may broadly be described as minor errors and omissions,   *a*
and s 140, which empowers the court to order rectification and is in the following
terms:

'(1) Subject to the provisions of subsection (2) of this section, the court
may order rectification of the register by directing that any registration be
cancelled or amended where it is satisfied that any registration including a   *b*
first registration has been obtained, made or omitted by fraud or mistake.
(2) The register shall not be rectified so as to affect the title of a proprietor
who is in possession or is in receipt of the rents or profits and acquired the
land, lease or charge for valuable consideration, unless such proprietor had
knowledge of the omission, fraud or mistake in consequence of which the   *c*
rectification is sought, or caused such omission, fraud or mistake or
substantially contributed to it by his act, neglect or default.'

The Ordinance also makes provision for indemnification in s 141(1):

'Subject to the provisions of this Ordinance and of any written law relating   *d*
to the limitation of actions, any person suffering damage by reason of—(a)
any rectification of the register under this Ordinance; or (b) any mistake or
omission in the register which cannot be rectified under this Ordinance,
other than a mistake or omission in a first registration; or ... shall be entitled
to be indemnified by the Government out of moneys provided by the
Legislative Council.'   *e*

Had the Schaums sought to enforce a right of way over parcel 27 in reliance on
the entry on their title, Turnbull could have applied to the court under s 140(1)
for rectification of that title to conform to the true state of affairs. However, the
position of the appellant, Dr Ramsahoye argued, is different in as much as it
purchased for value without knowledge of the error in the Schaums' title and   *f*
therefore could rely on s 140(2) to avoid rectification. The Court of Appeal were
accordingly in error in ordering such rectification. The proper course now was
to rectify the title to parcel 27 under s 140(1) which would enable the respondents
to claim compensation under s 141. Mr Douglas argued that the Court of Appeal
were correct to hold that any purchaser of a dominant tenement who did not
search the title of the servient tenement was presumed to have knowledge. He   *g*
further argued that the provisions of s 93 demonstrated that the system presumed
that an easement was only effective where it was registered in the titles of both
dominant and servient tenements. This section, so far as relevant to the
argument, is in the following terms:

h
'(1) The proprietor of land or a lease may, by an instrument in the
prescribed form, grant an easement over his land or the land comprised in his
lease, to the proprietor or lessee of other land for the benefit of that other
land ...
(4) The grant or reservation of the easement shall be completed by its
registration as an incumbrance in the register of the land burdened and in the   *j*
property section of the land which benefits, and by filing the instrument.'

In their Lordships' view rectification of the respondent's title cannot take place
under s 140(1). That subsection refers to the registration having been 'obtained,
made or omitted by fraud or mistake'. When Turnbull's title was registered on
25 September 1974 the only mistake therein was to describe the right conferred

a by the lease as a right of way rather than a right of occupancy. The reference to the lease and the duration of the right were entirely accurate. There was accordingly no relevant mistake which could be rectified under s 140(1). The existence of the error in the registered entry of parcel 16 could not ipso facto convert the subsequent substantially accurate entry of parcel 27 into a mistaken one. If Dr Ramsahoye is correct that the entry of parcel 16 cannot be rectified, it

b must follow that two inaccurate entries will remain on the register. Furthermore, it would also appear to follow that Turnbull, due to the registrar's error, has had imposed upon his land and without his knowledge a burden in respect of which he can obtain compensation neither from public funds nor from anyone else. This would be an unhappy situation and one which it seems unlikely that the Ordinance was intended to produce. Sections 140 and 141

c provide broadly that a person adversely and unknowingly affected by an error in the register should be entitled either to rectification or compensation.

Dr Ramsahoye argued that s 38 absolved a purchaser from looking at anything other than the entry of the parcel in the register. The section is undoubtedly concerned primarily with obviating the need for an individual to go behind the

d register in order to discover whether the seller, mortgagor or lessor derives his title from valid deeds. It does not, however, follow that where there is noted in the register a right or burden related to another parcel of land the individual can rely on s 38 to ignore the registered entry in relation to that parcel. Section 93 provides that where an easement is granted by instrument it is completed when registered in relation to both parcels of land. It would be surprising if an

e erroneous entry by the registrar could become effective against the servient tenement without the knowledge of the proprietor thereof when an express grant by him is only completed by registration in relation to both properties. The fact that an examination of the title of the servient tenement might reveal nothing because an overriding interest was not noted in the register is nothing to the

f point. The person dealing with the proprietor of the dominant tenement would be put on his guard.

It is one thing to protect a proprietor with a registered title in relation to his rights over his own land. This was the position in *Frazer v Walker* [1967] 1 All ER 649, [1967] 1 AC 569 and *Breskvar v Wall* (1971) 126 CLR 376, where only one parcel of land was involved and where the issue was whether an adverse claim to

g land or an interest therein could succeed against the registered proprietor. It is, however, another thing to protect a proprietor in relation to his rights over another registered parcel of land in circumstances where the other proprietor has no knowledge of the asserted right and consequential burden. In a situation where the rights of A extend over B's land, it is entirely reasonable and consistent

h with the scheme of registration that someone dealing with A should satisfy himself as to the validity of his right by examining the registered entry of B. This does not require him to go behind the register but merely to examine two entries instead of one.

The system cannot have been designed solely to protect benefits conferred ex

j facie on proprietors without regard to the consequential burdens imposed on other proprietors. Where the registered entry of proprietor A erroneously detracts from his rights or fails to give him full advantage, he has the opportunity of having the matter corrected. Where on the other hand the error in A's title benefits him at the expense of proprietor B, the latter has no opportunity of taking any corrective steps. In short, a burden is imposed on his land without his knowledge and in circumstances in which he may be powerless to take any action and unable to claim compensation from anyone. He would thus be subjected to a form of compulsory acquisition without compensation. This cannot have been intended and shows that the general philosophy of indefeasibility of title cannot be applied without qualification to a situation in which the register shows that the titles of two or more proprietors are involved.

In these circumstances their Lordships consider that s 38 was not intended to apply to a situation such as the present and that the Court of Appeal were correct to conclude that a prudent purchaser of parcel 16 would and should also have examined the registered entry of parcel 27. It therefore follows that the appellant must be deemed to have had knowledge of the mistake in the registered entry of parcel 16 and that, subject to any further considerations, that entry falls to be rectified under s 140(2).

As a secondary submission Dr Ramsahoye submitted briefly that Bertrand J was entitled on the facts to find that there was acquiescence on the part of Turnbull. This contention was rejected by Liverpool JA in a carefully reasoned judgment in which the other members of the court agreed and which found no evidence to support acquiescence of Turnbull between the expiry of the lease in 1976 and the blocking of the road in 1982. Their Lordships see no reason to differ from this conclusion.

Their Lordships will accordingly humbly advise Her Majesty that the appeal should be dismissed. The appellant must pay the respondents' costs before their Lordships' Board.

Appeal dismissed.

Celia Fox   Barrister.

a   # C v Mirror Group Newspapers and others

COURT OF APPEAL, CIVIL DIVISION

NEILL, MORRITT AND PILL LJJ

4, 5, 21 JUNE 1996

b

Libel and slander – Limitation of action – 'Facts relevant' – Knowledge of fact relevant to cause of action – Newspapers publishing allegations made by a party to proceedings – Plaintiff receiving information outside limitation period that allegations not privileged – Whether information constituting fact relevant to cause of action – Whether grounds for extension of time limit – Limitation Act 1980, s 32A.

c

In 1986 C, who was given custody of her two children on her divorce, took them on holiday abroad with the approval of the court, but did not return to England. The father subsequently received information that the children were in Australia and made an application relating to them. At the conclusion of the hearing the

d   judge decided to adjourn the matter from chambers to open court and to lift reporting restrictions to enlist the help of the media in locating the children. The father spoke to the press and made serious and untrue defamatory allegations about C, in particular that she was connected with a drugs gang, which were published by the respondent newspapers in March 1988. C received a copy of the article in Australia and telephoned the newspaper in England to complain about

e   it; she was told that the newspaper had merely reported what had been said in court. In August 1993, following her return to England, C received a letter from the judge who had presided over the hearing, stating that the allegations complained of had not been made in court. In March 1994 C issued proceedings against the newspapers, claiming damages for libel and malicious falsehood. The

f   respondents applied to strike out both claims, and their application was granted by the judge on the grounds that the libel claim, which had been brought well outside the three-year limitation period, was statute-barred and that C did not have an arguable case on damages in respect of her claim of malicious falsehood. C appealed, and sought to rely on s 32A[a] of the Limitation Act 1980, which provided that an action for libel or slander could be brought with leave at any

g   time within one year from the earliest date on which the applicant knew all the facts relevant to that cause of action, to defeat the limitation defence to her libel claim.

Held – (1) For the purposes of s 32A of the 1980 Act the reference to the 'facts

h   relevant' to a cause of action for libel or slander related only to facts establishing the existence of a cause of action (ie those which ought to be pleaded in the statement of claim) and did not extend to facts tending to rebut any possible defences to the libel action. It followed that the fact on which C sought to rely, namely that it was only on receipt of the judge's letter in August 1993 that she

j   realised that her involvement in drug smuggling had not been mentioned in court and therefore that the newspaper reports had not been privileged as accounts of court proceedings, was not a relevant fact within the meaning of s 32A. C's libel claim was therefore statute-barred and her appeal against that part of the judge's decision would accordingly be dismissed (see p 516 *b e* to *g*, p 518 *b e* to *g* and

---

a   Section 32A is set out at p 515 *g h*, post

p 522 *b*, post); *Johnson v Chief Constable of Surrey* (1992) Times, 23 November
applied.   *a*

(2) However, the claim of malicious falsehood was not time-barred and, since
proof of publication and falsity had been admitted, C only had to prove malice or
assumed damage in order to establish her claim. In view of the seriousness of the
allegation in fact made and the statutory relaxation of the burden of proof in
actions for malicious falsehood under s 3(1)[b] of the Defamation Act 1952, it   *b*
would not be appropriate to strike out the action for lack of an arguable case on
damages. It followed that C's appeal would be allowed in respect of that part of
the judge's decision striking out her claim of malicious falsehood (see p 519 *a* and
p 521 *j* to p 522 *a e*, post).

Notes   *c*
For extension or postponement of limitation periods in general, see 28 *Halsbury's
Laws* (4th edn) para 864.

For the Defamation Act 1952, s 3, see 24 *Halsbury's Statutes* (4th edn) (1989
reissue) 109.

For the Limitation Act 1980, s 32A, see ibid 685.   *d*

Cases referred to in judgments
Frisby v Theodore Goddard & Co (1984) Times, 3 March, [1984] CA Transcript 84.
Horrocks v Lowe [1974] 1 All ER 662, [1975] AC 135, [1974] 2 WLR 282, HL.
John v MGN Ltd [1996] 2 All ER 35, [1996] 3 WLR 593, CA.
Johnson v Chief Constable of Surrey (1992) Times, 23 November, [1992] CA   *e*
    Transcript 961.
Law v Llewellyn [1906] 1 KB 487, [1904–7] All ER Rep 536, CA.

Cases also cited or referred to in skeleton arguments
Blackshaw v Lord [1983] 2 All ER 311, [1984] QB 1, CA.   *f*
Burr v Smith [1909] 2 KB 306, [1908–10] All ER Rep 443, CA.
Central Electricity Board v Halifax Corp [1962] 3 All ER 915, [1963] AC 785, HL.
Collins v Jones [1955] 2 All ER 145, [1955] 1 QB 564, CA.
Fothergill v Monarch Airlines Ltd [1980] 2 All ER 696, [1981] AC 251, HL.
Kemsley v Foot [1952] 1 All ER 510, [1952] AC 345, HL.
Kitchen v Royal Air Force Association [1958] 2 All ER 241, [1958] 1 WLR 563, CA.   *g*
Nash v Eli Lilly & Co [1993] 4 All ER 383, [1993] 1 WLR 782, CA.
Oyston v Blaker [1996] 2 All ER 106, CA.
Phillips-Higgins v Harper [1954] 2 All ER 51n, [1954] 1 QB 411n, CA; *affg* [1954] 1
    All ER 116, [1954] 1 QB 411.
Sheldon v RHM Outhwaite (Underwriting Agencies) Ltd [1995] 2 All ER 558, [1996]   *h*
    AC 102, HL; *rvsg* [1994] 4 All ER 481, [1996] AC 102, CA.
Spring v Guardian Assurance plc [1993] 2 All ER 273, [1993] ICR 412, CA; *rvsd* [1994]
    3 All ER 129, [1995] 2 AC 296, HL.

Appeal   *j*
By notice dated 21 April 1995 C appealed from the decision of Sir Michael Davies,
sitting as a judge of the High Court, on 20 March 1995 affirming the decision of
Master Eyre on 30 November 1994 whereby he struck out the appellant's claims
in libel and malicious falsehood against the respondents, Mirror Group

---

b   Section 3(1), so far as material, is set out at p 519 *d*, post

a Newspapers, South-West Wales Newspapers, Swansea Press and the Western Mail & Echo Ltd on the grounds that the libel claim was statute-barred and that she did not have an arguable case on damages in respect of the claim of malicious falsehood. The facts are set out in the judgment of Neill LJ.

The appellant appeared in person.

b *Patrick Moloney* (instructed by *Davenport Lyons*) for the first respondent.

Thomas Shields QC and *Jane Phillips* (instructed by *Oswald Hickson Collier & Co* and *Sharpe Pritchard* as agents for *Loosemores*, Cardiff and *Sharpe Pritchard* as agents for *Foot & Bowden*, Plymouth) for the second, third and fourth respondents.

Andrew Caldecott QC (instructed by the *Treasury Solicitor*) as amicus curiae.

c   *Cur adv vult*

21 June 1996. The following judgments were delivered.

NEILL LJ. I shall refer to the former husband of the appellant as 'the father'. The
d father and the appellant were married on 16 January 1975. The first child, D, was born on 17 February 1977. He is now 19. The younger child, J, was born on 7 February 1980. He is now 16.

The parties separated in 1980. Divorce proceedings followed. The decree absolute was dated 24 October 1984. In the divorce proceedings the appellant was given the custody of the two children.

e In June 1986, with the approval of the court, the appellant took the two children to Tenerife for a holiday. However, she did not return to this country. On 3 October 1986, on the application of the father, an order was made that the two children become wards of court. On 7 November 1986 Hollis J ordered that the children should return. On 16 December Waterhouse J made an order giving
f interim care and control to the father.

In March 1987 the father went to Tenerife to try to find the appellant and the children. He later reported that they had been 'spirited away'. It is now clear that in or about March 1987 the appellant and the two children had left Tenerife and travelled to Australia.

g At about the end of February 1988 the father received information to the effect that the children might be in Australia. He made an application to the High Court in Swansea relating to the children. The application was supported by an affidavit sworn on 5 November 1987

The matter came before Judge Michael Evans QC sitting as a judge of the High Court in the Family Division in Swansea. The father appeared in person. At the
h conclusion of the hearing, which took place in chambers, the judge decided to adjourn into open court and reporting restrictions were lifted. After the adjournment into open court the judge made the following statement:

j '1. [D] and [J] are the children of [the father] and [the mother] who married on the 16th day January 1975 at Aldershot in Hampshire. The marriage unhappily ended in divorce and there has been a long history of dispute over the children.

2. On 3rd of October 1986 by an Application filed at the Swansea District Registry the children were made Wards of Court. By an order dated the 7th November 1986 Mr Justice Hollis made an order that the wards be returned to the jurisdiction of this Court within 14 days and that the Mother ... should

disclose her whereabouts to the Plaintiff's Solicitors. This was because it was believed that the wards had left the United Kingdom.

3. In spite of attempts to find out the whereabouts of the wards from those who would have such knowledge, the children were not found or returned. On the 16th December 1986 Mr Justice Waterhouse ordered that the interim care and control be committed to ... the father, and that the children should be handed over to him and not removed from him without the leave of the Court.

4. In March 1987 [the father] eventually traced the children to Tenerife and went there to secure the transfer of care and control to him under the order of the Court, having taken all proper steps to enlist the help of the local Courts. To use his words "the children were spirited away from the island" and have not been seen since.

5. Great concern is now felt about the welfare of these children because we have no knowledge of how they are cared for or, for example, what education they are receiving if any. About three weeks ago, [the father] received information that the children might be in Australia. This is the only country, so far as he is aware, who has issued a visa for them to enter.

6. I have adjourned this matter to Open Court in order that I may enlist the help not only of the National Media, but through them all other agencies who may be able to help. I call upon anyone who has any information as to the whereabouts of these children to inform [the solicitors]. A photograph which is $2\frac{1}{2}$ years old is available but the children are obviously older and their looks may well have changed.

7. In the unusual events which have happened, I want to make it plain that the usual restriction on publication of the details of these events does not apply. I have informed [the father] that he is free to discuss with the media or anyone else any details which will enable the court to find where the children are, to ensure their safe return to the jurisdiction, and to a final resolution of this troublesome matter.'

Following the hearing in court, the father spoke to representatives of the press. It also seems clear that he gave an interview on television. In the course of speaking to the press the father made serious and defamatory allegations against the appellant including, in particular, an allegation to the effect that she was in some way connected with a drugs gang. It is right to emphasise at the outset that this allegation was completely untrue. It was later withdrawn by the father.

Unfortunately, however, the father's allegations against the appellant were published in a number of newspapers. One of the newspaper reports was in the issue of the Daily Mirror dated 22 March 1988. It is not necessary to refer to this report or to the other newspaper reports in detail. It is, however, necessary to mention that the report in the Daily Mirror did not make clear that the words attributed to the father were spoken outside court rather than in the course of the court proceedings. The reports in the other newspapers, and in particular the report in the Western Mail dated 22 March, made it clear that the father had spoken to the press after the hearing in the court in Swansea.

In March 1988 the appellant was working in Australia. When she had arrived in Australia a year before she had been admitted on the basis that she did not take employment.

In March 1988 the appellant received a copy of the Daily Mirror article in Australia. She rang the newspaper in England to complain about it and was *a* referred to a man she believed to be the editor. The appellant did not want the call to be traced as she had 'gone to great lengths to avoid [her] ex-husband and harassment'. The appellant says that the editor told her that there was nothing he could do 'as they were just repeating what my ex-husband has said in court'. The appellant plainly had no intention at that time of commencing proceedings.

b The appellant attempted to stay in Australia, but fell foul of the immigration authorities there. She was deported to the United Kingdom in December 1990, her children accompanying her. In early 1991 she consulted solicitors who told her that they did not specialise in this area of law but advised her, sensibly it appears to me, that she would need a copy of the transcript of the hearing of 21 March 1988. When she inquired of the court, she was told that no transcript was available.

c On 4 July 1991, at the library at Aberystwyth, the appellant examined the relevant articles in the newspapers owned by the second, third and fourth respondents (the Welsh newspapers).

There was a further court hearing with respect to the children before Rattee J in Swansea on 12 November 1991. The wardship of the children was continued, *d* with care and control to the appellant and reasonable access to the father. It was at court on that day that the father signed a retraction of his allegation that the appellant had been involved in drug smuggling.

There was then an interval of 18 months before the appellant wrote letters before action, in June 1993, to each of the respondents. By his clerk, Judge Michael Evans wrote to the appellant on 25 August 1993 stating that to the best *e* of his recollection the father had on 21 March 1988 'said nothing in court about drug smuggling nor that [the appellant] was a drug smuggler'.

The appellant issued writs on 21 March 1994. That is, of course, well outside the ordinary three-year limitation period in defamation, but just within the six-year limitation period for malicious falsehood.

f
Libel

The court has heard submissions from the appellant in person and from Mr Caldecott QC as amicus curiae. To defeat a claim of limitation in defamation, the appellant seeks to rely on s 32A of the Limitation Act 1980, inserted into the Act by the Administration of Justice Act 1985. Section 32A provides:

g
'Where a person to whom a cause of action for libel or slander has accrued has not brought such an action within the period of three years mentioned in section 4A of this Act (or, where applicable, the period allowed by section 28(1) as modified by section 28(4A)) because all or any of the facts relevant to that cause of action did not become known to him until after the expiration *h* of that period, such an action—(a) may be brought by him at any time before the expiration of one year from the earliest date on which he knew all the facts relevant to that cause of action; but (b) shall not be so brought without the leave of the High Court.'

j The appellant's submission is that only upon receipt of Judge Michael Evans' letter of 25 August 1993 did she realise that her alleged involvement in drug smuggling had not been mentioned in court on 21 March 1988. Until then, she believed that the newspaper reports were privileged as accounts of court proceedings. Her writ was issued within one year of the receipt of the judge's letter. It was issued without the leave of the High Court, but no point was taken before Sir Michael Davies as to the absence of leave. The point has not seriously been taken against her in this court and, for the purposes of this appeal only, I would be prepared to treat the writ on the basis that leave had been obtained.	*a*

The appellant relies upon her alleged lack of knowledge of facts relevant to the cause of action, within the meaning of that expression in s 32A, until 25 August 1993. Counsel for the respondents, Mr Shields QC and Mr Moloney, submit that the expression in the section covers only facts establishing the existence of a cause of action, that is those which ought to be pleaded in the statement of claim, and	*b* does not extend to facts tending to rebut an anticipated defence such as privilege. Even if the broader construction is correct, they submit, the appellant knew all the relevant facts by 1991. The appellant admits having been told in Australia that her ex-husband had said on television and the radio that she was in a drug smuggling gang. By July 1991, the appellant had read the offending articles, from three of which it was clear that the words attributed to the father were spoken	*c* outside court rather than in the course of court proceedings. Further, at the latest in November 1991, when the case came before Rattee J, the appellant had a copy of Judge Michael Evans' order and was aware that it contained no reference to drugs or drug smuggling. At the same time, the father withdrew his allegation of drug smuggling. The respondents also rely on the fact that detailed and	*d* appropriate letters before action were written two months before the judge's letter. The appellant told the respondents that she was ready to serve writs. She believed she had a cause of action prior to her receipt of the judge's letter.

In *Johnson v Chief Constable of Surrey* (1992) Times, 23 November the plaintiff sought to bring an action for damages for false imprisonment after the expiry of six years from the accrual of the cause of action. He relied on s 32(1)(b) of the	*e* 1980 Act, which provides for the postponement of the limitation period where 'any fact relevant to the plaintiff's right of action has been deliberately concealed from him by the defendant'. The plaintiff contended that the police had concealed material from him which demonstrated that they did not have reasonable grounds to suspect the relevant offence at the time of the arrest.	*f*

The court had to construe the expression 'fact relevant to the plaintiff's right of action' which in material respects is the same as the expression now under consideration. It is common ground that the difference between 'right of action' and 'cause of action' is irrelevant for present purposes, the former being used merely to embrace equitable rights.

The court construed the expression narrowly. Rose LJ stated:	*g*

> 'For my part, I accept [the] submission that, in construing the section, there is no middle ground between facts and evidence ... Facts which improve prospects of success are not, as it seems to me, facts relevant to his right of action ... I accept that the construction proposed ... is a narrow one, but	*h* unless it is correct it is difficult to see what purpose is served by the special provisions with regard to personal injury actions which are contained in s 33 of the Act.'

It is clear that Rose LJ accepted what in this court has been described as the statement of claim test, that is knowledge of the facts which should be pleaded in	*j* the statement of claim.

Russell LJ stated:

> 'In order to give relief to the plaintiff any new fact must be relevant to the plaintiff's "right of action" and is to be contrasted with the facts relevant, for example, to "the plaintiff's action" or "his case" or "his right to damages".

a   The right of action in this case was complete at the moment of arrest. No other ingredient was necessary to complete the right of action. Accordingly, whilst I acknowledge that new facts might make the plaintiff's case stronger or his right to damages more readily capable of proof they do not in my view bite upon the "right of action" itself. They do not affect the "right of action", which was already complete, and consequently in my judgment are not
b   relevant to it.'

Neill LJ referred to the plaintiff's submission that the tort of false imprisonment has two elements, first the detention and second the absence of any reasonable cause by the police officers to suspect guilt. Neill LJ stated:

c   'In one sense it is true to say that the tort of false imprisonment has two ingredients; the fact of imprisonment and the absence of lawful authority to justify it ... But as I understand the law, the gist of the action of false imprisonment is the mere imprisonment. The plaintiff need not prove that the imprisonment was unlawful or malicious; he establishes a prima facie case if he proves he was imprisoned by the defendant. The onus is then
d   shifted to the defendant to prove some justification for it. If that be right, one looks at the words in s 32(1)(b), "any fact relevant to the plaintiff's right of action". It seems to me that those words must mean any fact which the plaintiff has to prove to establish a prima facie case.'

    Mr Caldecott submits that the primary purpose of the cause of action in
e   defamation, unlike that in other actions including malicious falsehood, is to obtain vindication, and the court should consider a broader construction of s 32A. Had Parliament intended the narrow meaning, the word 'necessary' would have been used instead of 'relevant'. Serious injustice may in some cases result if the 'facts relevant' do not include, for example, facts tending to prove malice, in cases
f   where there was no cogent evidence of malice previously and where in consequence a defence of fair comment or qualified privilege would have succeeded, or facts tending to establish that the occasion of publication was not protected by privilege where previously it had appeared that the occasion was privileged. Mr Caldecott gave the example of a musician who discovered, years after an adverse review of his performance, facts which went to prove malice in
g   the reviewer. Mr Caldecott accepts, rightly in my view, that ignorance of the facts must have been the cause of the plaintiff's decision not to commence proceedings and that the facts must be facts of a decisive character in the proposed action.

    Mr Caldecott has sought to distinguish Johnson on the basis that s 32A, unlike
h   s 32(1)(b), is specific to defamation, where a distinction between facts necessary to make out a prima facie case and facts bearing on the existence or otherwise of a good defence is difficult to justify as a matter of policy. The narrowness of s 32(1)(b) encourages a broad construction of s 32A. Leave is required under s 32A and the court has a discretion, which will protect a defendant in appropriate
j   cases, absent in the other section. The comparison with s 33, thought relevant by Rose LJ in Johnson, has no relevance in the context of an action in defamation.

    Mr Caldecott accepts that a court will not usually construe the same words in the same statute in different ways. He also accepts the importance of the principles of finality and certainty in questions of limitation.

    The respondents rely upon the decision of this court in Johnson. They also rely upon the statement of Donaldson MR when considering the relevance of an alleged concealment of the right of action under s 26 of the Limitation Act 1939 in *Frisby v Theodore Goddard & Co* (1984) Times, 3 March. Donaldson MR stated that it was to be remembered that a right of action arose out of a basic set of essential facts. That right could be concealed by the hiding of one or more of those facts, but concealment of evidence was wholly different and related to the proving of the case rather than the existence of the right of action.

The respondents submit that relevant facts are those which must be proved to establish a cause or right of action in the absence of a defence. The facts on which the appellant seeks to rely are relevant not to the cause of action, but to the possible existence of a defence under the Law of Libel Amendment Act 1988, which confers a privilege upon fair and accurate newspaper reports of proceedings publicly heard before any court.

Counsel submit that, unlike the broad construction, the narrow construction provides a clear, certain and workable test. On the broad test there would be considerable complication and uncertainties, for example, if facts relevant to a possible defence of justification were to come within the scope of the section or facts claimed to throw light on earlier facts relevant to a possible defence of fair comment. The present case gives a further example of the complexity which would arise upon a broad construction. Given the appellant's knowledge in 1991, would the judge's 1993 letter permit the issue of a writ?

In my judgment, the decision in *Johnson*, which is of course binding upon this court, must be applied to the relevant expression in s 32A as it applies to the expression in s 32(1)(b). The relevant facts are those which the appellant has to prove to establish a prima facie case. That being so, the fact alleged to have come known to the appellant only in August 1993, that drug smuggling had not been mentioned in court, is not a relevant fact within the meaning of s 32A.

As well as being bound by it, I respectfully agree with the decision in *Johnson*. In s 32A Parliament has for actions for libel or slander breached the protection which a period of limitation ordinarily gives to a defendant. I do not consider that Parliament has intended, in the words used in s 32A, to create a breach so wide as to enable facts relevant to possible defences to the action to be a relevant consideration. Given the public interest in finality and the importance of certainty in the law of limitation, I would have expected Parliament to use words different and more general had the broad construction, with the uncertainties it involves, been intended. The facts relevant to the cause of action are confined to the limited class of facts contemplated in *Johnson*.

I would make one reservation and it relates to whether there is a cause of action when it is clear on the face of the statement of claim that the occasion was absolutely privileged, such as proceedings in Parliament and in courts. Mr Caldecott referred to *Law v Llewellyn* [1906] 1 KB 487, [1904–7] All ER Rep 536 where an action against a magistrate for a statement made in the course of his judicial duties was struck out as not actionable. Counsel agreed that the court itself should take the point in such an action and strike it out. I would leave this question open.

The point has not been seriously pursued, but I would not hold that the alleged representation on the telephone to Australia by an editor of the Daily Mirror that there was nothing he could do 'as they were just repeating what my ex-husband had said in court' was a deliberate concealment within the meaning of that term in s 32(1)(b) of the 1980 Act. On the basis of *Johnson*, the facts given were not in any event facts relevant to the plaintiff's right of action within the meaning of that paragraph.

Malicious falsehood

a
The claim for damages for malicious falsehood is not defeated by limitation. It requires proof of publication and falsity, which are admitted, and malice and damage or assumed damage, which are not.

The statement of claim alleges in relation to each defendant:

b
> 'The Plaintiff avers that the above article was published maliciously, the First Defendant knowing that the matters complained of were untrue or alternatively acting recklessly, not caring whether they were true or false. If it be necessary the Plaintiff avers that the malice can be inferred from the grossness and falsity of the assertions and the cavalier way in which they were published. Further the Plaintiff relies on Section 3(1)(a) of the
c
> Defamation Act 1952.'

Section 3(1) of the 1952 Act provides:

> 'In an action for ... malicious falsehood, it shall not be necessary to allege or prove special damage—(a) if the words upon which the action is founded are calculated to cause pecuniary damage to the plaintiff and are published in
d
> writing or other permanent form ...'

The appellant does also plead financial loss in Australia, alleging that as a result of the Daily Mirror article she felt the need to leave her employment and also that she was dismissed from subsequent employment when her employers became aware of the article. The appellant does not suggest that the Welsh newspapers
e
circulate in Australia.

The appellant submits that there is an arguable case that the respondents acted maliciously. They should have checked the story before printing. The judge had not given the press a licence to print anything. The respondents had never been prepared to apologise, a sure sign of malice, it is submitted. In relation to the
f
third respondent, the appellant draws attention to the fact that a major drugs trial was being conducted in Swansea in March 1988 and, in the editions of their newspaper, on either side of the prominent report about her appear prominent reports of that drugs trial.

As amicus curiae, Mr Caldecott has analysed the content of Judge Michael Evans' statement in the context of the allegation that the respondents acted
g
maliciously. It contains no reference to drugs. There is no reference to the police, which might have been expected if criminal conduct was suspected by the judge. Far from expressing suspicion of the children being subjected to drug smuggling, it is stated that the court has 'no knowledge of how they are cared for'. Mr Caldecott also submits that if the father did not tell the judge of his fears
h
about drugs, that is an indication that he had no such fears. In the circumstances, the respondents should have made further inquiries about the allegations made by the father out of court before publishing them.

For the respondents, it is submitted that there is no arguable case that they acted maliciously. The wording of the court statement and in particular para 7,
j
gave credence to the word of the father. It cloaked him with authority to speak outside court. The judge did not distance himself from the father and at para 4 quoted what the father had said. The press had been requested by the judge to help in tracing children who were with a mother who had flouted an order of the court. A judge who took the exceptional course the judge took can be assumed by the press to have had very serious concerns about the way the children were being treated. It is, as Mr Shields put it, a majestic leap from a finding of

publication to a finding that words were published without an honest belief in
their truth.   *a*

In *John v MGN Ltd* [1996] 2 All ER 35 at 57 Bingham MR, giving the judgment
of the court, stated:

> 'Where actual knowledge or unlawfulness is not in issue, a jury direction
> based on reference to "reckless, not caring whether the publication be true   *b*
> or false" is sanctioned by long usage and is not incorrect. The crucial
> ingredient of this state of mind is, however, a lack of honest or genuine belief
> in the truth of what is published. That is what makes the publisher's conduct
> so reprehensible (or "wicked") as to be deserving of punishment.
> Carelessness alone, however extreme, is not enough unless it properly
> justifies an inference that the publisher had no honest belief in the truth of *c*
> what he published.'

Mr Caldecott also referred to Lord Diplock's analysis of honest belief in *Horrocks
v Lowe* [1974] 1 All ER 662 at 669, [1975] AC 135 at 150:

> 'If he publishes untrue defamatory matter recklessly, without considering   *d*
> or caring whether it be true or not, he is in this, as in other branches of the
> law, treated as if he knew it to be false. But indifference to the truth of what
> he publishes is not to be equated with carelessness, impulsiveness or
> irrationality in arriving at a positive belief that it is true.'

The finding of the judge on this point was: *e*

> 'In the special circumstances arising out of the judge's request and his very
> unusual open licence to [the father] to talk to the press, the assistance in
> tracing the children being given by the press—in all the circumstances, I do
> not find that the plaintiff has any possibility on the facts and on her pleadings
> of establishing the necessary ingredient of malice in malicious falsehood.   *f*
> The defendants may or may not, any of them, have been negligent but that
> is something which would be insufficient and with which I do not deal.'

The respondents also submit that, on the pleaded case, there are no prospects
of proving special damage and that words published are not 'calculated to cause *g*
pecuniary damage to the plaintiff'.

The jurisdiction to strike out should be exercised, as the judge recognised, only
if plainly and obviously the action cannot succeed.

The essence of the appellant's case on malice is that the respondents were
reckless. It is not suggested that any of the newspapers acted out of spite towards *h*
the appellant or that they actually *knew* that what they published was false. The
appellant pleads that 'malice can be inferred from the grossness and falsity of the
assertions and the cavalier way in which they were published'.

It is to be remembered, however, that malice connotes an actual or presumed
state of mind, and that the presence or absence of malice is a matter of inference.
Furthermore, though earlier or subsequent events may throw light on a *j*
defendant's state of mind the court is concerned with the question of whether the
publication was actuated by malice. It is therefore necessary to examine the
circumstances surrounding the moment of publication with great care.

The facts in this case were most unusual. I should set out again the last three
paragraphs of the statement which Judge Michael Evans made in open court:

a

'5. Great concern is now felt about the welfare of these children because we have no knowledge of how they are cared for or for example what education they are receiving, if any. About three weeks ago, [the father] received information that the children might be in Australia. This is the only country, so far as he is aware, who has issued a visa for them to enter.

b

6. I have adjourned this matter to Open Court in order that I may enlist the help, not only of the National Media, but through them all other agencies who may be able to help. I call upon anyone who has any information as to the whereabouts of these children to inform [the solicitors]. A photograph which is 2½ years old is available but the children are obviously older and their looks may well have changed.

c

7. In the unusual events which have happened, I want to make it plain that the usual restriction on publication of the details of these events does not apply. I have informed [the father] that he is free to discuss with the media or anyone else details which will enable the court to find where the children are, to ensure their safe return to the jurisdiction, and to a final resolution of this troublesome matter.'

d

On the one hand, account must be taken of a number of points about this statement, including the following: (a) the judge said that he had no knowledge of how the children were cared for; (b) in the statement the judge made no reference to drugs; and (c) though it was apparent that the judge had informed the father that he was free to discuss the case with the media, the judge's permission to the father could not be construed as a licence to him to say what he liked.

e

It can therefore be said that a journalist should have noticed and been warned by the contrast between the judge's apparent lack of knowledge of how the children were being cared for and the very serious allegations made by the father. Further inquiries, it could be said, were clearly called for.

f

On the other hand, in considering whether the respondents acted recklessly and published the allegations about the appellant without any genuine belief in their truth, it is important to recognise that the judge had enlisted the help of the press to find the children and that he had given express permission to the father 'to discuss with the media or anyone else any details which will enable the court to find where the children are to ensure their safe return to the jurisdiction'.

g

The fact that the father was allowed to speak to the press might well have led the press to conclude that the judge regarded the father as a reliable informant.

I see great force in the submissions made on behalf of the respondents on the issue of malice. Moreover, it is a striking feature of the case that the court had invited the assistance of the media in order to trace the children. If, however, we accede to these submissions the appellant will be denied the opportunity of putting her case on malicious falsehood before a court and of seeking to prove after discovery and cross examination her assertion that the respondents were in fact reckless in a relevant sense.

h

j

Bearing in mind the seriousness of the allegation in fact made and the effect of s 3(1)(a) of the 1952 Act, I would not have struck out the action for lack of an arguable case on damages.

I have found this to be an anxious case. In the end, however, I do not think it would be right to strike out the appellant's claim in malicious falsehood at this stage. The court's power to strike out a claim is one to be exercised with the greatest care. I consider that on this aspect of the case the appellant's appeal should be allowed.

a

MORRITT LJ. I agree.

PILL LJ. On the issues in libel I agree and do not wish to add anything. On the issue of malice in the malicious falsehood claim, I too see great force in the *b* submissions made on behalf of the respondents and the conclusion reached by Sir Michael Davies. The fact that Judge Michael Evans QC took the unusual step of issuing the statement at all would encourage the press reasonably to assume (though wrongly as it turned out) that the appellant, who was in breach of a court order with respect to the children, and had removed them from Tenerife, was acting so as to put their safety in peril. While I accept that, by his statement, the *c* judge did not licence the father to say anything outside court he chose to say, the statement did in effect confer a credibility upon the father and a freedom in him to speak to the media. When conferring that freedom, the judge said in terms that he was enlisting the help of the media and other agencies and that can reasonably be construed as an encouragement to publish material arising from *d* any interview with the father. Nothing has so far emerged to indicate anything which I would construe as ill-will or improper purpose on the part of the respondents towards the appellant at the time of publication.

However, having regard to the apparent lack of further inquiry by the respondents before they published the serious allegation made by the father, and to the nature of striking out proceedings, I do not find a need to dissent from the *e* course proposed by Neill and Morritt LJJ.

Appeal allowed in part.

Paul Magrath Esq   Barrister.

a
Percy and another v Hall and others

COURT OF APPEAL, CIVIL DIVISION
SIMON BROWN, PETER GIBSON AND SCHIEMANN LJJ
17, 18, 19 APRIL, 10 MAY 1996

b
*Byelaws – Validity – Challenge to validity – Offences of entering protected military area
in breach of byelaws – Whether byelaws invalid for uncertainty – Military Lands Act
1892, s 17(1) – HMS Forest Moor and Menwith Hill Station Byelaws 1986.*

c
*False imprisonment – Arrest without warrant – Power to arrest without warrant –
Statutory power to remove and take into custody persons committing an offence against
byelaws – Defendant constables arresting plaintiffs for breach of byelaws regulating use
of military lands – Whether defendants entitled to plead defence of lawful justification
if byelaws invalid.*

d
Between April 1990 and October 1991 the plaintiffs were, between them, arrested
without warrant on over 150 occasions and removed from the vicinity of
Menwith Hill Station, a military communications installation, for alleged
breaches of the HMS Forest Moor and Menwith Hill Station Byelaws 1986. The
plaintiffs were acquitted of criminal charges and sought judicial review of their
arrests, contending that the byelaws were void for uncertainty and could never
e
have founded any lawful arrest. On an appeal by the Director of Public
Prosecutions against their acquittals, the Divisional Court held that the byelaws
were insufficiently certain under s 17(1)[a] of the Military Lands Act 1892 due to an
inability to accurately ascertain the boundaries of the protected areas which were
the subject of the byelaws. The plaintiffs thereafter commenced civil proceedings
f
against the arresting Ministry of Defence police constables, seeking damages for
false imprisonment and wrongful arrest; the Attorney General was also sued in
place of the Secretary of State for Defence for breach of statutory duty for making
allegedly defective byelaws. The constables pleaded lawful justification on the
basis of a reasonable belief that the plaintiffs had been committing an offence at
the time of their arrests. On a trial of preliminary issues, the judge held that the
g
byelaws were invalid, but that that finding of invalidity did not preclude the
constables from pleading lawful justification. The defendants appealed.

Held – (1) A byelaw would be treated as valid unless it was so uncertain in its
language as to have no ascertainable meaning, or so unclear in its effect as to be
h
incapable of certain application in any case. So long as in certain circumstances
an offence would undoubtedly be committed, byelaws should (subject to any
issue of severance) be upheld and to that extent enforced; if that test was not met
they should be struck down for uncertainty. The byelaws in the instant case fell
to be upheld, even though the plan annexed to the byelaws could have been
j
clearer, and the boundaries of the protected areas could have been better
described; there would always be a borderline of uncertainty, but that should not
invalidate the byelaws and make them void and unenforceable even against those
who deliberately and flagrantly trespassed within the very centre of the protected
areas. The defendants' appeal would accordingly be allowed (see p 532 j to

---

a   Section 17(1), so far as material, is set out at p 527 *f g*, post p 533 *b*, p 535 *h j*, p 537 *c e*, p 543 *f j* to p 544 *d* and p 545 *h*, post); *Fawcett Properties Ltd v Buckingham CC* [1960] 3 All ER 503 applied; *Bugg v DPP, Percy v DPP* [1993] 2 *a* All ER 815 considered; *Kruse v Johnson* [1895–9] All ER Rep 105 not followed.

(2) Even if the byelaws were void for uncertainty, that would not deprive the constables of the defence of lawful justification to allegations of wrongful arrest and false imprisonment, provided they could show that they had acted in the reasonable belief that the plaintiffs were committing a byelaw offence. For, while *b* a subsequent declaration that the byelaws were invalid would operate retrospectively to entitle a person convicted of their breach to have that conviction set aside, it could not convert conduct which, at the time, had been regarded as the lawful discharge of the constables' duty into actionably tortious conduct (see p 541 *h j*, p 542 *c* and p 544 *c d*, post); *F Hoffmann-La Roche & Co AG v Secretary of State for Trade and Industry* [1974] 2 All ER 1128 and *Wills v Bowley* *c* [1982] 2 All ER 654 applied.

Notes

For validity of byelaws generally, see 28 *Halsbury's Laws* (4th edn) paras 1326–1330, and for cases on the subject, see 13 *Digest* (Reissue) 259–267, 2314–2404. *d*

For byelaws regulating the use of military lands, see 41 *Halsbury's Laws* (4th edn) para 116.

For the Military Lands Act 1892, s 17, see 3 *Halsbury's Statutes* (4th edn) 1142.

Cases referred to in judgments

A-G v Denby [1925] 1 Ch 596. *e*
Alderson v Secretary of State for the Environment (1984) 49 P & CR 307, CA.
Bentley v Brudzinski (1982) 75 Cr App R 217, DC.
Bernstein (Lord) of Leigh v Skyviews and General Ltd [1977] 2 All ER 902, [1978] QB 479, [1977] 3 WLR 136.
Bugg v DPP, Percy v DPP [1993] 2 All ER 815, [1993] QB 473, [1993] 2 WLR 628, DC. *f*
Collins v Wilcock [1984] 3 All ER 374, [1984] 1 WLR 1172, DC.
DPP v Hutchinson [1990] 2 All ER 836, [1990] 2 AC 783, [1990] 3 WLR 196, HL.
Fawcett Properties Ltd v Buckingham CC [1960] 3 All ER 503, [1961] AC 636, [1960] 3 WLR 831, HL.
Graham v Philcox [1984] 2 All ER 643, [1984] QB 747, [1984] 3 WLR 150, CA.
Hall & Co Ltd v Shoreham-by-Sea UDC [1964] 1 All ER 1, [1964] 1 WLR 240, CA. *g*
Hoffmann-La Roche (F) & Co AG v Secretary of State for Trade and Industry [1974] 2 All ER 1128, [1975] AC 295, [1974] 3 WLR 104, HL.
Kruse v Johnson [1898] 2 QB 91, [1895–9] All ER Rep 105, DC.
Leyton UDC v Chew [1907] 2 KB 283.
London and North Eastern Rly Co v Berriman [1946] 1 All ER 255, [1946] AC 278, HL. *h*
Miller-Mead v Minister of Housing and Local Government [1963] 1 All ER 459, [1963] 2 QB 196, [1963] 2 WLR 225, CA.
Mixnam's Properties Ltd v Chertsey UDC [1964] 2 All ER 627, [1965] AC 735, [1964] 2 WLR 1210, HL; *affg* [1963] 2 All ER 787, [1964] 1 QB 214, [1963] 3 WLR 38, CA.
Nash v Findlay (1901) 18 TLR 92, DC. *j*
R v Central Criminal Court, ex p A J D Holdings Ltd [1992] Crim LR 669.
R v Reading Justices, ex p South West Meat Ltd [1992] Crim LR 672.
R v Secretary of State for Trade and Industry, ex p Ford (1984) 4 Tr L 150.
R v Wicks (1995) 93 LGR 377, CA.
Scott v Martin [1987] 2 All ER 813, [1987] 1 WLR 841, CA.

a	Scott v Pilliner [1904] 2 KB 855, DC.
	Smith v East Elloe RDC [1956] 1 All ER 855, [1956] AC 736, [1956] 2 WLR 888, HL.
	Staden v Tarjanyi (1980) 78 LGR 614, DC.
	Todd v DPP [1996] Crim LR 344.
	United Bill Posting Co Ltd v Somerset CC (1926) 42 TLR 537.
	Wigginton & Milner Ltd v Winster Engineering Ltd [1978] 3 All ER 436, [1978] 1 WLR
b		1462, CA.
	Wills v Bowley [1982] 2 All ER 654, [1983] 1 AC 57, [1982] 3 WLR 10, DC and HL.

Cases also cited or referred to in skeleton arguments
	An Bord Bainne Co-op Ltd (Irish Dairy Board) v Milk Marketing Board [1984] 2 CMLR
		584, CA.
c	Avon CC v Buscott [1988] 1 All ER 841, [1988] QB 656, CA.
	Basely v Clarkson (1682) 3 Lev 37, 83 ER 565.
	Calvin v Carr [1979] 2 All ER 440, [1980] AC 574, PC.
	Cinnamond v British Airports Authority [1980] 2 All ER 368, [1980] 1 WLR 582, CA.
	Cooper v Wandsworth Board of Works (1863) 14 CBNS 180, 143 ER 414.
d	Firman v Ellis [1978] 2 All ER 851, [1978] QB 886, CA.
	Forbes v New South Wales Trotting Club Ltd (1979) 143 CLR 242, Aust HC.
	Hazell v Hammersmith and Fulham London BC [1990] 3 All ER 33, [1990] 2 QB 697,
		CA.
	Liversidge v Anderson [1941] 3 All ER 338, [1942] AC 206, HL.
	London and Clydeside Estates Ltd v Aberdeen DC [1979] 3 All ER 876, [1980] 1 WLR
e		182, HL.
	Lovelock v Minister of Transport (1980) 40 PC & R 336.
	Martin v Ryan [1990] 2 NZLR 209, NZ HC.
	McEldowney v Forde [1969] 2 All ER 1039, [1971] AC 632, HL.
	Mercury Ltd v Director General of Telecommunications [1996] 1 All ER 575, [1996] 1
f		WLR 48, HL.
	Plymouth City Council v Quietlynn Ltd [1987] 2 All ER 1040, [1988] QB 114, DC.
	R v Hendon Justices, ex p DPP [1993] 1 All ER 411, [1994] QB 167, DC.
	R v Panel on Take-overs and Mergers, ex p Datafin plc (Norton Opax plc intervening)
		[1987] 1 All ER 564, [1987] 1 QB 815, CA.
	R v Secretary of State for Defence, ex p Greaves (26 November 1991, unreported), DC.
g	Ridge v Baldwin [1963] 2 All ER 66, [1964] AC 40, HL.
	Roy v Kensington and Chelsea and Westminster Family Practitioner Committee [1992] 1
		All ER 705, [1992] 1 AC 624, HL.
	Shearer v Shields [1914] AC 808.
	Wandsworth London BC v Winder [1984] 3 All ER 976, [1985] AC 461, HL.
h	Waverley BC v Hilden [1988] 1 All ER 807, [1988] 1 WLR 246.

Appeal
	By notice dated 4 May 1995 the defendants, 66 Ministry of Defence police
	constables, and the Attorney General, who was sued by the plaintiffs in place of
j	the Secretary of State for Defence for making allegedly defective byelaws,
	appealed from the decision of Sir Peter Webster, sitting as a deputy judge of the
	High Court on 4 April 1995, hearing preliminary issues in an action brought by
	the plaintiffs, Lindis Elizabeth Percy and Rachel Diane Greaves, against the
	defendants claiming damages for wrongful arrest and false imprisonment,
	whereby he held (i) that the HMS Forest Moor and Menwith Hill Station Byelaws
	1986, SI 1986/481, made by the Secretary of State under s 14(1) of the Military

Lands Act 1892 in relation to certain military installations, were invalid as
insufficiently certain, and (ii) that their invalidity did not prevent the police   *a*
constables from raising a defence of lawful justification. The plaintiffs challenged
the second part of the judge's decision. The Chief Constable of North Yorkshire
Police, who was sued in respect of the plaintiffs' various detentions by civilian
police officers into whose custody the military police had passed them, took no
part in the appeal. The facts are set out in the judgment of Simon Brown LJ.   *b*

John Howell QC and *Robin Tam* (instructed by the *Treasury Solicitor*) for the
    defendants.
Nigel Pleming QC, Heather Williams and *Keir Starmer* (instructed by *Stephens
    Innocent*) for the plaintiffs.
    c

Cur adv vult

10 May 1996. The following judgments were delivered.

SIMON BROWN LJ. During the 18-month period from April 1990 to October   *d*
1991 the plaintiffs, Lindis Elizabeth Percy and Rachel Diana Greaves, between
them were arrested over 150 times and removed from the vicinity of the
Menwith Hill Station, a military communications installation in North Yorkshire
used jointly by the United States National Security Agency and by GCHQ
personnel. The plaintiffs' activities, they say, are designed to stop abuses of
power by the Ministry of Defence (the MOD).   *e*

Trespass is not, of course, an arrestable offence—not, indeed, a criminal
offence at all. The plaintiffs were arrested rather for alleged breaches of the HMS
Forest Moor and Menwith Hill Station Byelaws 1986, SI 1986/481 (the byelaws).
It is the validity, and effect of any invalidity, of these which are the issues at the
heart of this appeal. In a sentence, the plaintiffs contend that the byelaws were   *f*
void for uncertainty and can never, therefore, have founded any lawful arrest.

The defendants are 66 constables of the MOD Police who carried out the
arrests, together with the Chief Constable of North Yorkshire Police and the
Attorney General. The individual constables are each sued for wrongful arrest
and false imprisonment. The chief constable is sued pursuant to s 48 of the Police
Act 1964 in respect of the plaintiffs' various detentions by civilian police officers   *g*
into whose custody the military police had passed them—further occasions of
alleged false imprisonment. The Attorney General is sued in place of the
Secretary of State for Defence pursuant to s 17 of the Crown Proceedings Act
1947, his liability being said to arise by way of breach of statutory duty for making
allegedly defective byelaws.   *h*

On 21 July 1994 Master Miller ordered the trial of two preliminary issues: first,
as to the validity or otherwise of the byelaws; second, as to whether, if the
byelaws were invalid, the plaintiffs' claims against the constables must necessarily
succeed; whether, in short, such a finding of invalidity would deny the constables
any defence of lawful justification. Those issues were substantially reformulated   *j*
by Sir Peter Webster (sitting as a deputy judge of the High Court) at the trial. For
present purposes, however, the precise formulations do not matter: it is sufficient
to indicate merely that the judge found essentially for the plaintiffs on the first
issue and for the defendants on the second. Neither side, however, is entirely
happy with the judge's actual rulings on either issue and both now are either
appealing or at least seeking variations of them.

a   With that brief introduction let me at once turn to the relevant parts of the byelaws and the empowering legislation. The byelaws were made by the Secretary of State for Defence under Pt II of the Military Lands Act 1892. Section 14(1) of the Act provides:

b
> 'Power of Secretary of State to make byelaws as to use of land held for military purposes and securing safety of public.—(1) Where any land belonging to a Secretary of State or to a volunteer corps is for the time being appropriated by or with the consent of a Secretary of State for any military purpose, a Secretary of State may make byelaws for regulating the use of the land for the purposes to which it is appropriated, and for securing the public against danger arising from that use, with power to prohibit all intrusion on the land
c
> and all obstruction of the use thereof. Provided that no byelaws promulgated under this section shall authorise the Secretary of State to take away or prejudicially affect any right of common.'

(That proviso, it may be noted, although immaterial to the present appeal, proved fatal to the Greenham Common byelaws: see *DPP v Hutchinson* [1990] 2
d All ER 836, [1990] 2 AC 783.)

To understand the full territorial scope of s 14(1) the following additional two provisions are relevant. Subsection (3) provides:

> 'For the purposes of this section, "land belonging to a Secretary of State" means land under the management of a Secretary of State, whether vested
e
> in Her Majesty or in the Secretary of State, or in a person as trustee for Her Majesty or the Secretary of State; and "land belonging to a volunteer corps" means any land vested in that corps or in any person as trustee for that corps.'

Section 23 provides: '... the expression "land" includes any easement in or over lands ...' Section 17 provides:

f
> 'Notice and enforcement of byelaws.—(1) A Secretary of State, before making any byelaws under this Act, shall cause the proposed byelaws to be made known in the locality, and give an opportunity for objections being made to the same, and shall receive and consider all objections made; and when any such byelaws are made, shall cause the boundaries of the area to which the
g
> byelaws apply to be marked, and the byelaws to be published, in such a manner as appears to him necessary to make them known to all persons in the locality; and shall provide for copies of the byelaws being sold at the price of [5p] for each copy to any person who desires to obtain the same ...'

Section 17(2) (more directly relevant to the second issue than the first) provides:
h
> 'If any person commits an offence against any byelaw under this Act, he shall be liable, on conviction before a court of summary jurisdiction, to a fine not exceeding [level 2 on the standard scale], and may be removed by any constable or officer authorised in manner provided by the byelaw from the area, whether land or water, to which the byelaw applies, and taken into
j
> custody without warrant, and brought before a court of summary jurisdiction to be dealt with according to law, and any vehicle, animal, vessel, or thing found in the area in contravention of any byelaw, may be removed by any constable or such officer as aforesaid, and on due proof of such contravention, be declared by a court of summary jurisdiction to be forfeited to Her Majesty.'

As will appear, s 2(5) of the Military Lands Act 1900 (an Act to be construed as part of the 1892 Act—see s 6) is also relevant upon the issue of certainty:

> 'Where an area to which byelaws under this section apply consist of any sea or tidal water, or the shore thereof, and the boundaries of the area cannot, in the opinion of the authority making the byelaws, be conveniently marked by permanent marks, those boundaries shall be described in the byelaws, and shall be deemed to be sufficiently marked within the meaning of section seventeen of the Military Lands Act, 1892, if, while the area is in use for military of naval purposes, sufficient means are taken to warn the public from entering the area.'

Now to the byelaws themselves. They were made on 10 March 1986 to come into operation on 26 March 1986. Byelaw 1, under the heading 'Application of Byelaws', provides:

> 'The areas to which these byelaws apply consist of lands belonging to the Secretary of State in the parishes of Menwith with Darley and Birstwith and Felliscliffe and Norwood and Fewston in the County of North Yorkshire, which lands are for convenience of identification shown by a thick black line on the plan annexed to these byelaws and identified as "Plan of HMS FOREST MOOR and Menwith Hill Station" all of which is hereinafter referred to as "the protected Areas".'

The plan annexed is clearly small-scale (it is put by the plaintiffs at about 1:25,000). It depicts two large areas (respectively Forest Moor and Menwith Hill) defined by thick black lines separated at one point by what appears to be a road. In places the areas depicted are crossed by what a legend shows to be public footpaths. A third very small square area appears just north of Menwith Hill, perhaps connected to it by a footpath.

Byelaw 2 specifies the prohibited activities which include entering the protected areas except by way of an authorised entrance, and remaining in them after being directed to leave. Byelaw 3 provides that anyone contravening or attempting to contravene byelaw 2 shall be guilty of an offence. Byelaw 4 defines the persons 'authorised to remove from the Protected Areas and to take into custody without warrant any person committing an offence against byelaw 2' (and to remove too any objects found inside).

An explanatory note at the end contains information as to where copies of the byelaws and plan may be inspected and obtained.

Let me next indicate something more of the history of this dispute. Having been prosecuted for a number of breaches of the byelaws, Miss Percy (and a man named John Bugg, now deceased, earlier a third plaintiff in the action) were in May 1991 acquitted of all charges by the stipendiary magistrate at Ripon. It is not necessary to relate the precise course of those proceedings; suffice it to say that the enforceability of the byelaws was in question.

The following month Miss Greaves was twice arrested, whereupon, acting in person, she sought judicial review of her arrests. She attacked the validity of the byelaws on a number of different grounds. Her renewed application for leave was refused by the Divisional Court (Woolf LJ and Pill J) on 26 November 1991. One short passage of the judgment (given by Pill J) is relevant to the present appeal:

a 'I do not consider it an arguable ground for declaring the byelaws invalid that ... the map is inadequate ... The map was not required to be a definitive marking and it is sufficient to comply with the law. The first paragraph of the byelaws does set out sufficiently the area to be covered.'

(The writ in the present action, one may note, had been issued the previous month.)

b Finally, and most importantly in the history, in July 1992 there came before the Divisional Court two conjoined appeals by way of case stated: one by John Bugg and Miss Greaves against the Director of Public Prosecutions (the DPP) in respect of their convictions under byelaws promulgated for RAF Alconbury; the other by the DPP against the dismissal (above referred to) of the charges against Miss c Percy and John Bugg under the Forest Moor and Menwith Hill byelaws. The first appeal was allowed, the second dismissed (see Bugg v DPP, Percy v DPP [1993] 2 All ER 815, [1993] QB 473; again Woolf LJ and Pill J).

The court's judgment on that occasion was given by Woolf LJ. The argument had extended over five days and the great bulk of it, together with most of the d judgment, was concerned with the important question, raised by both appeals, as to the circumstances in which the validity of subordinate legislation can be challenged in the course of criminal proceedings. Of altogether greater relevance to the present appeal, however, are the Divisional Court's conclusions on the selfsame issue as now arises with regard to the validity of these particular byelaws. The court there found them to be insufficiently certain and in the result e 'defective on their face in this regard'. The most critical passages in the judgment are these ([1993] 2 All ER 815 at 829–830, [1993] QB 473 at 503):

'Are the byelaws sufficiently certain? Byelaws such as are here under consideration which create offences must clearly state what action is required in order to commit an offence. A person who is subjected to the f byelaws is, therefore, entitled to be given the necessary details to enable him to avoid contravening the byelaws ...

In the case of the Forest Moor byelaws, there is no description contained in the byelaws as to the boundary of the protected area. The only reference is to the lands belonging to the Secretary of State. Mr Bishop [appearing as g amicus curiae, the Ministry of Defence having declined an invitation to present argument to the court] says that this does not matter because of the obligation under s 17(1) of the 1892 Act of the Secretary of State to mark the boundary on the ground. However, if this submission is right, it would mean that the area subject to the byelaws would be dependent upon action being taken by the Secretary of State which he may or may not take and h which would enable him to fix the boundary at will as long as he defined that boundary within his own lands. We do not accept that this can be the situation. In our judgment, before the Secretary of State is entitled to rely on what is marked on the ground, or for that matter on some other document, there must be some reference to the marking on the ground or the other j document in the byelaws themselves. This does not occur in the case of Forest Moor.'

The court had earlier noted that it was common ground that the black line surrounding the protected areas on the plan would represent approximately 60 feet on the ground. Mr Howell QC for the defendants, I should perhaps note, makes no such concession here.

Mr Pleming QC for the plaintiffs not surprisingly places considerable reliance
on the decision in *Bugg*. Plainly, as he recognises, this court is not bound by *Bugg*,   *a*
and, of course, the MOD not having been a party to those proceedings, no
question of issue estoppel arises. Having regard to the constitution of that court,
however, its decision clearly commands the greatest respect.

That, understandably, was a major consideration in Sir Peter Webster's
approach to the case. Put shortly, he thought it right to follow *Bugg*, although he   *b*
then went on to indicate that but for *Bugg* he would have decided—

    'that the boundaries of the protected area are sufficiently defined by the
black lines shown on the plan and by the permanent marks along the
boundaries marked by the black line, sufficient to identify those boundaries
to a person approaching them, if at all material times there were such marks,   *c*
and provided that those marks are consistent with the black lines but not
otherwise.'

Mr Howell, however, does not invite us to decide the case that way. On the
contrary, he recognises that the validity of the byelaws must be determined as at
the date they are made and cannot depend upon the proper fulfilment of a duty   *d*
which only arises thereafter—the s 17(1) duty to mark the boundaries on the
ground. He accepts, therefore, that the court in *Bugg* was right to reject Mr
Bishop's argument—the argument that the byelaws' failure to describe the
boundary of the protected areas did not matter because of the s 17(1) duty. Mr
Howell's argument is rather that there was never in the first place any obligation   *e*
to describe the boundaries in the byelaws themselves. This, he points out, is an
obligation expressly imposed by Parliament under s 2(5) of the 1900 Act with
regard to particular (watery) areas, and for obvious good reason: it would not in
those circumstances be right for the court to impose a similar requirement in all
cases. Rather, it is the area to which the byelaws apply which has to be described,
not the boundaries as such. That, of course, requires that the boundaries are   *f*
capable of ascertainment but, submits Mr Howell, this was sufficiently achieved
here by the identification of the areas themselves in byelaw 1. He so submits,
indeed, even had no plan been annexed. Here, however, for good measure one
was, and although it was provided 'for convenience of identification', it could
none the less still properly be used to identify the limits of the protected areas (see
Wigginton & Milner Ltd v Winster Engineering Ltd [1978] 3 All ER 436, [1978] 1 WLR   *g*
1462, *Graham v Philcox* [1984] 2 All ER 643, [1984] QB 747 and *Scott v Martin* [1987]
2 All ER 813, [1987] 1 WLR 841).

Mr Pleming accepts that the boundaries themselves do not have to be
described as such and further accepts that the plan is properly available to assist
in identifying the protected areas. He disputes, however, the sufficiency of the   *h*
description in byelaw 1, with or without the plan. The limits of the protected
areas must, he argues, be clear and certain and they must be readily ascertainable
not merely by the Secretary of State but by any interested citizen. The
boundaries, he concedes, need not necessarily be ascertainable within the four
corners of the byelaws themselves; if not, however, they must be ascertainable by   *j*
reference to some available Ordnance Survey plan or central register or the like,
to be notified by the byelaws. At the very least, he argues, there should be more
precise identification of the protected areas than was afforded by the 1986
byelaws—as perhaps by the RAF Menwith Hill Byelaws 1996, which revoked the
earlier byelaws and which identify the new applicable area by reference to all the
land shown on a different (and undoubtedly clearer) map 'which lies within the

a   outermost edges of the red lines on that map'—although even this is not conceded by Mr Pleming to be sufficiently certain.

One of Mr Pleming's points is that byelaw 1 does not state even that it applies to *all* the lands belonging to the Secretary of State in the specified parishes. That clearly was not a point which troubled the court in *Bugg*—the judgment there referring simply to 'the' lands belonging to the Secretary of State. Nor does it

b   trouble me. Whatever else was achieved by the map, it at least served to depict the essential areas covered. Whether or not these were indeed *all* 'the lands belonging to the Secretary of State' falling within the extended statutory definition of these terms—which Mr Howell contends to be the natural meaning of byelaw 1—really matters not.

c   Mr Pleming further argues that, because of the extended statutory definitions, there exist no means outside the byelaws of checking just what lands do belong to the Secretary of State so as to be capable of being properly brought within the byelaws. That certainly is true. The Secretary of State himself will of course know, but anyone else will have to ask him (and if necessary litigate) for the relevant information. That is equally true, however, with regard to the question

d   whether the land has been properly appropriated for military use. I cannot see why the citizen's inability to discover either of these matters for himself unaided should be thought to create any particular uncertainty as to the limits of the areas designated as protected.

As to the plaintiffs' central complaint about uncertainty, upheld as this was in

e   *Bugg*, namely that the precise boundaries of the protected areas are unclear either from their description or from the map, Mr Howell points out that all maps, however good, ultimately leave an element of uncertainty: the lines on the map always have to be translated into lines on the ground. In reality, the thickness of the line on the map and the scale of the map are likely to be of less importance than the lie of the land itself. In all cases it will be necessary to go to the land to

f   find out what is represented by the map. Sometimes this will be obvious; other times, however apparently precise the map, less so.

If, submits Mr Howell, there is indeed any uncertainty on the ground as to whether or not the byelaws apply at a particular point, then the benefit of that doubt ought clearly be given to the citizen and he or she ought not to be

g   convicted of a byelaw offence. That, however, is no reason to strike down the byelaws in their entirety.

As to the obligation under s 17(1) to mark the boundaries of protected areas on the ground, this, Mr Howell argues, is an important part of the statutory context within which to construe s 14(1) and determine the degree of descriptive

h   certainty it requires. Again, if there is any failure by the Secretary of State to comply with his s 17(1) duty, or if the boundaries marked on the ground do not properly coincide with those of the area described in the byelaws themselves, then in those respects the byelaws will not be enforceable. That, indeed, is precisely what the Divisional Court held in *Bugg* with regard to the Alconbury byelaws (see [1993] 2 All ER 815 at 830, [1993] QB 473 at 504).

j   Those, then, are the rival contentions on the facts with regard to the question of certainty. What should be the legal approach?

Two competing approaches are canvassed, approaches which for convenience may be called respectively the *Kruse v Johnson* approach (see *Kruse v Johnson* [1898] 2 QB 91, [1895–9] All ER Rep 105) and the *Fawcett* approach (see *Fawcett Properties Ltd v Buckingham CC* [1960] 3 All ER 503, [1961] AC 636).

The *Kruse v Johnson* approach for which Mr Pleming contends is based on Mathew J's dictum in that case:

> '... a byelaw to be valid must, among other conditions, have two properties: it must be certain—that is, it must contain adequate information as to the duties of those who are to obey—and it must be reasonable.' (See [1898] 2 QB 91 at 108, [1895–9] All ER Rep 105 at 115.)

A more modern statement of essentially the same approach appears in Lord Lane CJ's judgment in *Staden v Tarjanyi* (1980) 78 LGR 614 at 623:

> '... to be valid, a byelaw, carrying as this one does penalties for infringement, must be certain and clear in the sense that anyone engaged upon the otherwise lawful pursuit of hang gliding must know with reasonable certainty when he is breaking the law and when he is not breaking the law. That proposition scarcely needs demonstration or authority.'

The rival approach urged by Mr Howell is to be found in Lord Denning's speech in *Fawcett* [1960] 3 All ER 503 at 517, [1961] AC 636 at 677–678:

> 'I can well understand that a bye-law will be held void for uncertainty if it can be given no meaning or no sensible or ascertainable meaning. But, if the uncertainty stems only from the fact that the words of the bye-law are ambiguous, it is well settled that it must, if possible, be given such a meaning as to make it reasonable and valid, rather than unreasonable and invalid ... I am of opinion that a planning condition is only void for uncertainty if it can be given no meaning or no sensible or ascertainable meaning, and not merely because it is ambiguous or leads to absurd results. It is the daily task of the courts to resolve ambiguities of language and to choose between them; and to construe words so as to avoid absurdities or to put up with them.'

A little later in the speech, in the course of indicating his preferred formulation as to the court's proper approach to reasonableness, Lord Denning said ([1960] 3 All ER 503 at 518, [1961] AC 636 at 679):

> '... it puts planning conditions on much the same footing as bye-laws made by a local authority, to which they are so closely akin. Indeed, I see no difference in principle between them. As with bye-laws, so with planning conditions.'

It appears from the beginning of the passage already cited from *Bugg* that the court there adopted the *Kruse v Johnson* approach; there had, indeed, been extensive citation of that line of authority whereas *Fawcett* and the subsequent planning condition cases had not apparently been before the court.

Mr Howell submits that whichever approach the court adopts, these particular byelaws ought not properly to be condemned for uncertainty. Least of all, he submits, should they be struck down on the *Fawcett* approach. Mr Pleming's submissions unsurprisingly lie at the opposite end of the spectrum. He argues that these byelaws would fail even the less stringent test set by *Fawcett*: there is simply no sufficient information provided by them from which to ascertain the areas protected.

Early in the judgment though this is, I have to say that I find Mr Howell's arguments compelling: even applying the *Kruse v Johnson* test I would uphold a these byelaws rather than condemn them for uncertainty. And this despite the considerable persuasive force inevitably attaching to the court's judgment in *Bugg*. Of course the plan here could have been better and clearer, as the 1996 plan now is. Of course too the boundaries could have been described, to include, for instance, just as in the original draft statutory instrument (but for whatever reason not in the byelaws as made) 'the outer perimeter walls and fences of HMS

b Forest Moor and Menwith Hill Station'. But Parliament plainly cannot have envisaged generally such a description of the boundaries—see s 2(5); and however narrow and precise the line on a map, there will always be, literally, a borderline of uncertainty. That should not, in my judgment, invalidate the byelaws and make them void and unenforceable even against those who deliberately and flagrantly trespass within the very centre of the protected areas.

c Mr Howell suggests that the Divisional Court's decision in *Bugg*, critical as it is of the byelaws' failure to describe the boundaries of the protected areas, may have been given per incuriam of s 2(5), and certainly no reference to that provision appears anywhere in the report, not even in the argument. We are told, however, that it was referred to in counsel's skeleton arguments and I am

d therefore inclined to regard the decision as based on rather wider grounds. Alas, I find myself in respectful disagreement with it.

It follows from this central conclusion that neither of the two important and difficult points of law argued before us strictly falls for decision. Since, however, we were treated to full and able argument on each, and since it is not impossible that it may be sought to carry this litigation further, I for my part think it right to

e address them.

When byelaws are challenged for uncertainty, should the court follow the *Kruse v Johnson* approach or the *Fawcett* approach?

In support of the *Kruse v Johnson* approach, Mr Pleming points to nearly 100 years of authority in which Mathew J's dictum has been cited with approval and

f apparently applied. It is, he acknowledges, a curiosity that so fundamental and entrenched a principle should find its origin in an obiter dictum in a dissenting judgment in a case concerned (like the three cases cited in support of the dictum) not with certainty but with reasonableness. Nevertheless, as early as 1901, in *Nash v Findlay* 18 TLR 92, Mathew J's test was expressly applied by Lord

g Alverstone CJ sitting with two of the judges who had been in the majority in *Kruse v Johnson*, and a byelaw there was held void for uncertainty. Amongst the subsequent cases in which Mathew J's dictum or an equivalent restatement of it are to be found are *Scott v Pilliner* [1904] 2 KB 855, *Leyton UDC v Chew* [1907] 2 KB 283, *A-G v Denby* [1925] 1 Ch 596, *United Bill Posting Co Ltd v Somerset CC* (1926) 42 TLR 537, *Staden v Tarjanyi* (1980) 78 LGR 614 and *R v Secretary of State for Trade*

h *and Industry, ex p Ford* (1984) 4 Tr L 150, all of which we examined.

As for *Fawcett*, Mr Pleming submits, first, that Lord Denning's dictum there, in so far as it equates byelaws with planning conditions, was itself obiter; and, second, that in any event *Fawcett* was concerned with uncertainty of language whereas here we are concerned with uncertainty of application. It is one thing,

j he submits, to require the courts to resolve the former; quite another for the courts to determine a byelaw's area of operation when the instrument itself lacks the necessary information. Lord Cohen's speech in *Fawcett*, he argues, supports only the former: explaining Viscount Simonds' dictum in *London and North Eastern Rly Co v Berriman* [1946] 1 All ER 255 at 270, [1946] AC 278 at 313–314 that 'A man is not to be put in peril upon an ambiguity', Lord Cohen said—

'This principle involves that, if a statutory provision is ambiguous, the
court should adopt any reasonable interpretation which would avoid the *a*
penalty, but the court should not, I think, strike a provision out of an Act on
the ground of uncertainty unless it is impossible to resolve the ambiguity
which it is said to contain.' (See [1960] 3 All ER 503 at 507, [1961] AC 636 at
662.)

Mr Howell submits to the contrary that whether or not Lord Denning's dictum *b*
in *Fawcett* is obiter with regard to byelaws (which he disputes), planning
conditions are closely analogous to them and no logical reasons exist for
distinguishing between them. The breach of either can be attended by criminal
consequences, admittedly, in the case of planning conditions, at one remove, but
that is immaterial. If anything, submits Mr Howell, one would expect a less *c*
stringent test of uncertainty for byelaws, which must cater to a wide range of
possibilities than for conditions, which are directed to more specific
circumstances.

As to Mr Pleming's contention that the *Fawcett* principle in any event applies
only to ambiguity of language rather than uncertainty of operation, Mr Howell
submits that this too would involve an illogical and unjustifiable distinction in *d*
approach. As Willmer LJ said in *Hall & Co Ltd v Shoreham-by-Sea UDC* [1964] 1 All
ER 1 at 5, [1964] 1 WLR 240 at 245 (another planning condition case in which
Fawcett was applied):

'It has been contended on behalf of the plaintiffs that conditions imposed *e*
by a local authority must be such that the developer can know exactly what
they involve before making up his mind whether to proceed with the
development contemplated ... I do not think, however, that this is the right
test to apply. The question is not whether the plaintiffs are left uncertain as
to how the conditions will operate. That may be very relevant in considering
whether the conditions are reasonable. Where uncertainty is alleged, the *f*
true question, as it seems to me, is whether the language of the conditions
makes sense, that is, is capable of a reasonable construction. This is in
accordance with the view expressed by LORD DENNING in *Fawcett* ...'

Similarly, as Woolf J observed in *Ex p Ford* (1984) 4 Trade LR 150 at 160, another
statutory instrument case: *g*

'As was made clear by a series of authorities, uncertainty of language rarely
creates the necessary degree of invalidity to cause the courts to intervene. It
seems to me that a similar approach has to be applied to uncertainty of
application, and especially in the area of consumer protection it is *h*
unfortunately inevitable that those who are responsible for supplying the
public will at times be put in the situation where they will have to make
difficult decisions as to whether or not they are infringing the law.'

If, clearly, the *Fawcett* principle applies equally to byelaws as to planning
conditions, and to uncertainty of application as well as to uncertainty of language, *j*
there can be no question as to which line of authority we must follow: the
planning condition cases are all in the House of Lords or Court of Appeal; the
byelaw cases all in the Divisional Court or before a single judge. *Fawcett* has been
followed in other planning condition cases in the Court of Appeal (see *Alderson v
Secretary of State for the Environment* (1984) 49 P & CR 307, a case where the Court
of Appeal overturned Webster J's ruling that 'locally' had no ascertainable

a meaning, as well as *Hall & Co Ltd v Shoreham-by-Sea UDC*). Since *Fawcett*, however, *Kruse v Johnson* appears still to have been followed in other byelaw (or similar) cases, notably, of those we were shown, *Staden v Tarjanyi*, *Ex p Ford* and, indeed, *Bugg* itself. Perhaps rather oddly, the interrelation between these two strains of authority seems scarcely to have been considered; the only specific reference to it appears in Diplock LJ's judgment in *Mixnam's Properties Ltd v Chertsey UDC* [1963] 2 All ER 787 at 798–799, [1964] 1 QB 214 at 235, 238, a case concerned with the conditions of a caravan site licence. Diplock LJ said:

> 'Failure to comply with a condition attached to a site licence is a criminal offence. The power to impose conditions is thus in effect a power to make subordinate legislation analogous to a power to make bye-laws. (See per LORD DENNING in *Fawcett Properties, Ltd.* v. *Buckingham County Council* ([1960] 3 All ER 503 at 517, [1961] AC 636).) The validity of such conditions is thus to be tested by the same principle as the validity of bye-laws ... Bye-laws have in the past been declared void for "uncertainty"; see *Nash* v. *Findlay* ((1901) 18 TLR 92) and *A.-G.* v. *Denby* ([1925] 1 Ch 596). Some doubt is cast on the correctness of "uncertainty" as a separate ground of invalidity by the speeches in the House of Lords in the recent case of *Fawcett Properties, Ltd.* v. *Buckingham County Council* ... but if the courts can declare subordinate legislation to be invalid for "uncertainty" as distinct from unenforceable, as in the case of a clause in a statute to which it is impossible to ascribe a meaning, this must be because Parliament is to be presumed not to have intended to authorise the subordinate legislative authority to make changes in the existing law which are uncertain.'

The only conditions in fact struck down in *Mixnam's Properties* as void for uncertainty were two which Danckwerts LJ found 'quite impossible to apply', one of which Diplock LJ described as 'so uncertain it is not possible to ascribe any intelligible meaning to the words'; the other he found ultra vires on a more general ground so that it was unnecessary to decide whether, because it was 'difficult to ascribe [to it] any intelligible meaning', it was also void for uncertainty (see [1963] 2 All ER 787 at 804–805, [1964] 1 QB 214 at 246–247). Although I do not think that *Mixnam's Properties* (which went on a different point to the House of Lords ([1964] 2 All ER 627, [1965] AC 735)) decides the present issue, it seems to me broadly to support Mr Howell's argument.

More importantly, however, Mr Howell makes, to my mind convincingly, these two further submissions. First, that the *Kruse v Johnson* test, whether formulated in terms of 'adequate information' (as by Mathew J), or of 'reasonable certainty' (as in *Staden v Tarjanyi*), itself is one of great uncertainty. It provides no criteria or principles by which to judge the adequacy of the information, or the degree of certainty, afforded by the byelaws. At what point does a byelaw become invalid for uncertainty? It seems to me insufficient to answer, as Mr Pleming does, that this can safely be left to the magistrates of the day or the judges on appeal. Better, surely, as with the *Fawcett* test, to treat the instrument as valid unless so uncertain in its language as to have no ascertainable meaning, or so unclear in its effect as to be incapable of certain application in any case (often on analysis essentially the same thing; see eg *Alderson*). Being a criminal provision, it will be wherever reasonably possible construed or, as the case may be, applied to avoid penalty.

Mr Howell's second and, as it seems to me, interrelated submission, is that, despite the language used and the approach ostensibly applied in all the byelaw

cases, these, almost without exception, can be seen on examination to have
produced a result entirely consistent with the *Fawcett* test. Some appear in the
end not to be uncertainty cases at all (see e g *Scott v Pilliner* [1904] 2 KB 855, where,
as Lord Denning pointed out in *Fawcett*, the byelaw was held void for
unreasonableness, not uncertainty). Pressed to indicate which of the byelaw
cases he contended would have been decided differently on a *Fawcett* approach,
Mr Pleming nominated *Nash v Findlay*, *Staden v Tarjanyi*, and *A-G v Denby*. In none
of these cases, however, does that seem to me at all clear. In *Nash v Findlay* the
court simply felt unable to ascribe any meaning whatever to a particular
provision, given the existence of other byelaws which appeared to include the
same area of misconduct. *Staden v Tarjanyi* was a case where the byelaw
impugned forbade any person, inter alia, to hang glide over a particular pleasure
ground. Given that *Lord Bernstein of Leigh v Skyviews and General Ltd* [1977] 2 All
ER 902, [1978] QB 479 had just held it permissible to fly at such a height that no
one can possibly be inconvenienced, Lord Lane CJ said ((1980) 78 LGR 614 at
623):

> 'It seems to me that to be valid the byelaw must set some lower level below
> which the glider must not fly. It is not for us to say whether that should be
> stipulated in feet or metres or whether it should be delineated by, if you like,
> the nuisance to those on the ground ... Some limitation must be put upon it
> ... There was no such limitation. Accordingly, it follows that the byelaw
> was invalid.'

The decision is explicable in terms of there having been no lawful touchstone of
liability whatever. Had a height been set, that would have cured the vice of
forbidding what was otherwise undoubtedly lawful flying. Had the criterion of
nuisance and annoyance been used, uncertain in its application though that no
doubt would have been, the court would still have found it acceptable.

A-G v Denby is a difficult case, which I do not propose to discuss at length.
Suffice it to say that the byelaw there in question was not in the event held
invalid; rather, it was held 'too uncertain for me to give effect to it *in this case*; that
on one construction there is no infringement, and on the other it is wholly
unreasonable' (see [1925] 1 Ch 596 at 616; my emphasis).

Certain other of the byelaw cases, moreover, strongly support the view that in
reality the court, however it chose to express itself, was upholding byelaws even
where they were undoubtedly of uncertain application. That seems to me
conspicuously to have been the case in *United Bill Posting Co Ltd v Somerset CC*
(1926) 42 TLR 537, and also in *Ex p Ford*. In *United Bill Posting* a byelaw was upheld
which forbade the exhibiting of advertisements 'so as to be visible from any
public highway ... and to disfigure the natural beauty of *the* landscape' (my
emphasis). The empowering statute had referred to 'the natural beauty of *a*
landscape'. The complaint that the byelaw did not specify the landscapes of
natural beauty to which it applied (as clearly it could have done) failed.

R v Secretary of State for Trade and Industry, ex p Ford (1984) 4 Tr L 150 was
concerned with an order banning the sale of scented erasers, 'scented' meaning
'smelling of food or flowers'. Woolf J noted that the application of the order gave
rise to difficulties (at 159):

> 'The question as to whether or not an eraser ... does in fact smell of food
> or flowers must be very much a matter of subjective judgment ... It is
> possible readily to envisage situations where different courts would come to

a different conclusions about the same eraser. That such a situation can be brought about by an order creating a criminal offence I have no hesitation in saying is highly undesirable.'

The order was nevertheless upheld.

b Why I describe this second submission of Mr Howell's as interrelated to his first is this: it is surely for the very reason that a literal application of the *Kruse v Johnson* test would of itself involve great uncertainty that the courts in fact give effect to byelaws even when it is often quite impossible to be sure at the margins whether or not a particular course of conduct would breach them. In my judgment, so long as in certain circumstances an offence will undoubtedly be committed, byelaws should (subject to any issues of severance such as arose in c *Hutchinson*) be upheld and to that extent enforced. If, of course, that test is failed, then indeed the byelaws should be struck down for uncertainty; Parliament could not have intended byelaws to be made which are incapable of any certain application. (There may, I recognise, be cases where byelaws are enacted which quite needlessly give rise to difficulties of application. Whether these should d properly be struck down for unreasonableness it is not presently necessary to decide.)

From all this it follows that the *Fawcett* test of uncertainty should in my judgment apply to byelaws just as to planning conditions. There is no sufficient reason to distinguish between the two classes of case. The *Fawcett* test, moreover, is the more satisfactory of the two tests because itself the more certain. e Even if not strictly bound to do so, therefore, I would adopt it as this court is free to do. On this approach, even assuming (which I respectfully doubt) that in reality it would generally make any practical difference to the result, there can be no doubt whatever that the present byelaws fall to be upheld.

I come finally to the issue of lawful justification. If, contrary to my own clear f conclusions, *Bugg* was right to hold these byelaws invalid for uncertainty, can they nevertheless provide a defence of lawful justification to the tortious claims now faced by these defendant constables for the arrests and detentions which they carried out in purported enforcement of them? Mr Pleming submits not, taking as his starting point Lord Lowry's speech in *DPP v Hutchinson* [1990] 2 All ER 836 at 850, [1990] 2 AC 783 at 819: 'The basic principle is that an ultra vires g enactment, such as a byelaw, is void ab initio and of no effect.'

That is, indeed, hardly a controversial proposition. Another authoritative statement to the same effect appears in Lord Diplock's speech in *F Hoffmann-La Roche & Co AG v Secretary of State for Trade and Industry* [1974] 2 All ER 1128 at 1154, [1975] AC 295 at 365 (a case, as we shall see, upon which Mr Howell h nevertheless places considerable reliance):

> 'It would ... be inconsistent with the doctrine of ultra vires as it has been developed in English law as a means of controlling abuse of power by the executive arm of government if the judgment of a court in proceedings j properly constituted that a statutory instrument was ultra vires were to have any lesser consequence in law than to render the instrument incapable of ever having had any legal effect on the rights or duties of the parties to the proceedings ...'

Invalidity is, in short, generally regarded as of retrospective, not prospective, effect.

Given that s 17(2) of the 1892 Act (and byelaw 4) permit arrest only if the
person arrested actually commits an offence, it would, submits Mr Pleming, be
fundamentally inconsistent with this basic principle now to regard the defendant
constables as having acted lawfully.

To that apparently formidable argument Mr Howell makes two main
responses, either, he submits, capable on its own of defeating it; taken together,
more compelling still.

The first centres on the decision of the House of Lords in *Wills v Bowley* [1982]
2 All ER 654, [1983] 1 AC 57. That case concerned a constable's power of arrest
under s 28 of the Town Police Clauses Act 1847, a section which *required* a
constable to 'take into custody, without warrant, and forthwith convey before a
justice, any person who within his view [meaning "in his sight"] commits any
such offence [a large spectrum of street offences, some serious, some trivial, then
being set out]'.

By a majority of three to two the House of Lords held that s 28 falls to be
construed so as to protect constables who arrest someone whom they honestly
(albeit mistakenly) believe on reasonable grounds they have seen committing a
stipulated offence. Lord Bridge said ([1982] 2 All ER 654 at 680–681, [1983] 1 AC
57 at 102):

'Parliament, in enacting any such provision, must have intended that any
person who *was* committing any of the specified offences, whether serious
or trivial, should be arrested and brought to justice, very often, no doubt,
because this might be the only way he could be brought to justice at all. But
the person making the arrest cannot determine guilt in advance; he cannot
know that guilt will in due course be established; his only protection, if he is
to have any, at the time of making the arrest must be found in his honest
belief on reasonable grounds that he has observed the commission of a
relevant offence by the person he arrests. If a power of arrest in flagrante
delicto is to be effective at all, the person who exercises it needs protection;
protection not only against liability to pay damages in tort, but, perhaps
more important, as the instant case shows, protection, so far as the law can
give it, against violent resistance to the reasonable force which a person
exercising a lawful power of arrest is entitled to use in order to effect and
maintain his arrest. If the protection the law affords is contingent and
unpredictable, how can Parliament reasonably have expected anyone to rely
on it? Yet, surely Parliament must have intended the protection to be relied
on in order that the power of arrest should be effective. Making an arrest can
never be an agreeable task and may often be very disagreeable; how much
more so if the law gives no assurance of protection.' (Lord Bridge's
emphasis.)

By the same token, submits Mr Howell, the constables here should be protected.

Not so, submits Mr Pleming, for what I understand to be two main reasons:
first, because of certain differences between the requirements respectively of s 28
there and of s 17(2) here; second, because *Wills v Bowley* is concerned only with
honest and reasonable mistakes of fact, not of law. Let me consider each in turn.

The main difference in the legislation on which Mr Pleming relies is that
whereas under s 28 of the 1847 Act the constable (who, incidentally, had no
option but to arrest the miscreant) was bound without more ado then to bring
him before a court, here, under s 17(2) of the 1892 Act, the constable has a
discretion not merely whether or not to arrest someone apparently in breach of

a the byelaws, but also, even if he does arrest him, whether then to bring him before a court or instead release him without charge; in practice, we are told, many are arrested and removed and not then prosecuted. True, Mr Pleming acknowledges, here as in *Wills v Bowley* the legislation encompasses a wide range of offences, the most serious of which no doubt involve considerations of public safety and security. At the other end of the spectrum, however, are offences as b venial as affixing leaflets to the outer side of the perimeter walls and fences. Where such a spectrum of seriousness exists, he submits, Lord Bridge's speech, properly understood, requires that before adopting the benevolent construction adopted there, the legislation must as there require that any offender will be automatically taken before a justice.

   I would reject this argument. There seems to me in this case, no less than in c *Wills v Bowley*, an obvious need for prompt action to secure public safety and security with regard to land appropriated for military use, and the mere fact that a constable is not bound to bring everyone arrested before the court ought not in principle to distinguish the two cases: s 17(2) involves essentially the same three sequential steps as s 28. In the result, had a constable arrested and ejected d someone whom he genuinely (although on the facts mistakenly) believed on reasonable grounds to be a trespasser, I see no good reason why a *Wills v Bowley* construction of s 17(2) should not be adopted.

   What then of the argument that such a construction cannot avail an arresting officer whose mistake was, as postulated here, one of law rather than fact?

e Clear it is that ordinarily a mistake of law, however understandable, cannot provide the lawful justification for an arrest where otherwise there is none (see e g *Bentley v Brudzinski* (1982) 75 Cr App R 217, *Collins v Wilcock* [1984] 3 All ER 374, [1984] 1 WLR 1172 and *Todd v DPP* [1996] Crim LR 344). Here, however, submits Mr Howell, looking at the matter as at the dates of these arrests, there was no mistake of law on the part of the arresting constables, certainly not in any f conventional sense. It was not as if the constables had, as in the usual case, misunderstood their legal powers; on the contrary, they were enforcing what at the time appeared to be perfectly valid byelaws; to have done otherwise would seemingly have involved them in a clear breach of their duties. This essentially is Mr Howell's second main argument and in support of it he relies heavily on *Hoffmann-La Roche*.

g The question arising there was whether the Crown should be required to give a cross-undertaking in damages when seeking an interlocutory injunction to enforce a statutory order which was under challenge on natural justice grounds. In holding not, it was emphasised by several of their Lordships that there is a duty to enforce the law and that the order had the full force of law unless and until it h could be shown to be ultra vires. As Lord Reid put it ([1974] 2 All ER 1128 at 1134, [1975] AC 295 at 341):

   'Dealing with alleged breaches of the law is a function of the Crown (or of a department of the executive) entirely different in character from its j function in protecting its proprietary right. It has more resemblance to the function of prosecuting those who are alleged to have committed an offence. A person who is prosecuted and found not guilty may have suffered serious loss by reason of the prosecution, but in general he has no legal claim against the prosecutor. In the absence of special circumstances I see no reason why the Crown, in seeking to enforce orders of this kind, should have to incur legal liability to the person alleged to be in breach of the order. It must be

borne in mind that an order made under statutory authority is as much the
law of the land as an Act of Parliament unless and until it has been found to *a*
be ultra vires.'

Lord Diplock said ([1974] 2 All ER 1128 at 1155, [1975] AC 295 at 367):

'The duty of the Crown to see that the law declared by the statutory
instrument is obeyed is not suspended by the commencement of *b*
proceedings in which the validity of the instrument is challenged. Prima
facie the Crown is entitled as of right to an interim injunction to enforce
obedience to it. To displace this right or to fetter it by the imposition of
conditions, it is for the defendant to show a strong prima facie case that the
statutory instrument is ultra vires.'
c

Mr Pleming's response to this argument is twofold. First, he reiterates the
basic principle as to the retrospective effect of any eventual finding of invalidity.
Second, he submits that in this particular case the byelaws were patently
defective, ie invalid on their face.

Mr Pleming seeks to illustrate the operation of the basic principle in this field *d*
by reference to such authorities as *R v Reading Justices, ex p South West Meat Ltd*
[1992] Crim LR 672 and *R v Central Criminal Court, ex p A J D Holdings Ltd* [1992]
Crim LR 669. In my judgment, however, neither avail him: critical to each was
the provision in s 15(1) of the Police and Criminal Evidence Act 1984 that 'an
entry on or search of premises under a warrant is unlawful unless it complies with
this section and section 16 below'. Once the court had found on the facts in each *e*
case that they did not so comply, the entry and search were necessarily held
unlawful. The cases simply did not concern the question whether there is legal
justification for those things done by a person discharging his duty to enforce the
apparent law if subsequently that law proves to be invalid. Nor to my mind does
Mr Pleming's argument derive any assistance from consideration of the statutory *f*
protection given to justices by the Justices of the Peace Act 1979 as amended, or
to constables by the Constables Protection Act 1750.

Mr Pleming's second argument, that the byelaws here were patently defective,
it is necessary to consider in a little more detail. Once again it takes as its starting
point the decision in *Bugg*. The Divisional Court there, Mr Pleming points out,
speaks of the present class of case (which it held susceptible of collateral *g*
challenge) as involving 'substantive invalidity' (as opposed to 'procedural
invalidity'), where the byelaw is 'on its face invalid' (ie where 'no evidence is
required', as for example, where it is 'patently unreasonable'). And the court
added ([1993] 2 All ER 815 at 827, [1993] QB 473 at 500):

'A member of the public is required to comply with byelaws even if he *h*
believes they have a procedural defect unless and until the law is held to be
invalid by a court of competent jurisdiction. If before this happens he
contravenes the byelaw, he commits an offence and can be punished. Where
the byelaw is substantively invalid, the position is different. No citizen is
required to comply with a law which is bad on its face. If the citizen is *j*
satisfied that that is the situation, he is entitled to ignore the law.'

This approach, moreover, was followed and applied in *R v Wicks* (1995) 93 LGR
377, an enforcement notice case, where, returning to the language of *Miller-Mead
v Minister of Housing and Local Government* [1963] 1 All ER 459, [1963] 2 QB 196, the
Court of Appeal, Criminal Division described Woolf LJ's 'substantive invalidity'

a   as akin to 'nullity', and his 'procedural invalidity' as relating to such matters (which 'would in almost all cases require ... evidence') as would render a notice invalid (see 93 LGR 377 at 382–383). The actual decision in R v Wicks was that the notice there, not being a nullity patently defective on its face, remained valid until quashed, something which only the High Court rather than the criminal court had jurisdiction to do.

b   This argument too, however, I would reject. By no stretch of the imagination can these byelaws be regarded as so patently defective on their face that the constables can properly be criticised for not having identified their deficiencies and declined to enforce them. The instrument, in Lord Radcliffe's celebrated phrase in *Smith v East Elloe RDC* [1956] 1 All ER 855 at 871, [1956] AC 736 at 769, 'bears no brand of invalidity upon its forehead'.

c   The same Divisional Court as eventually in *Bugg* held these byelaws invalid for uncertainty had, after all, the previous year in Miss Greaves' case regarded that very contention as unarguable.

        I can quite understand the concepts of 'substantive invalidity', 'procedural invalidity' and so forth in the context of determining whether or not collateral
d   challenges properly lie. In my judgment, however, they afford no help whatever in the present situation. There can be no question here of the constables lacking 'reasonable grounds' for believing these plaintiffs to have been breaching the law (the *Wills v Bowley* approach), nor of there being apparent to them 'a strong prima facie case that the statutory instrument [was] ultra vires' (Lord Diplock's phrase
e   in *Hoffmann-La Roche*). As it seems to me, the position can be no different whether byelaws are eventually condemned for substantive invalidity or for procedural invalidity: either way, as I repeat, the actions of the constables concerned (who might theoretically have heard the court dismiss Miss Greaves' judicial review application as unarguable) would be beyond criticism. (Having reached this conclusion I note but need not deal with Mr Howell's submission
f   that, even by *Bugg*'s own test of patent invalidity (ie where no evidence is required to establish it), absent the concession there made as to the width of the line on the plan representing 60 feet on the ground, evidence would in any event have been required so that the test is not satisfied here.)

        Although I do not pretend to have found this part of the case altogether easy,
g   I have come to the conclusion that Mr Howell's arguments are to be preferred here also.

        The central question raised here is whether these constables were acting tortiously in arresting the plaintiffs or whether instead they enjoy at common law a defence of lawful justification. This question, as it seems to me, falls to be
h   answered as at the time of the events complained of. At that time these byelaws were apparently valid; they were in law to be presumed valid; in the public interest, moreover, they needed to be enforced. It seems to me one thing to accept, as readily I do, that a subsequent declaration as to their invalidity operates retrospectively to entitle a person convicted of their breach to have that conviction set aside; quite another to hold that it transforms what, judged at the
j   time, was to be regarded as the lawful discharge of the constables' duty into what must later be found actionably tortious conduct.

        I do not understand this point ever to have been addressed before. In my judgment it is not covered by the general doctrine of retrospectivity with regard to the annulment of invalid instruments. I am not prepared to regard the many broad statements of principle as going this far.

On the face of it, any right of redress on the part of those arrested under what ultimately are found to be defective byelaws should be against the Secretary of *a* State as the maker of the invalid instrument. The Secretary of State is, indeed, here said to be liable on that ground. If, however, as Mr Pleming recognises may well be the case, no such claim succeeds, essentially because English law provides no cause of action for invalid administrative action as such, that is no basis for creating a cause of action instead against those, here the defendant constables, *b* who are not responsible for the invalidity. Nor is it a good ground for denying them the common law defence of lawful justification which should surely be available to them. Quite the contrary. I see no sound policy reasons for making innocent constables liable in law, even though such liability would be underwritten by public funds.

In my judgment, therefore, even if these byelaws are properly to be regarded *c* as void for uncertainty as the Divisional Court held in *Bugg*, that would not serve to deprive the constables here of a defence of lawful justification wherever they can show they were acting in the reasonable belief that the plaintiffs were committing a byelaw offence.

Rather than reformulate the preliminary issues yet again, I would suggest that *d* this be treated as a declaratory judgment.

PETER GIBSON LJ. The preliminary issues determined by the judge were essentially: (1) are the byelaws defective on their face on the ground that the area to which they relate is insufficiently identified, and, if so, are the byelaws invalid? and (2) if the byelaws are invalid, were they incapable of providing a lawful *e* justification for the arrest and detention of the plaintiffs? Both issues raised questions of general importance.

Byelaws are a widely used form of delegated legislation, a usual feature of which is that they prescribe what may or may not be done within a designated area and attach a penal sanction to any breach. They are to be found regulating, *f* for example, the parking in streets in a local authority's area and regulating commons, parks and communal gardens. If, therefore, the plaintiffs are right in their contention that the byelaws with which this case is concerned are uncertain and therefore invalid because they fail to provide adequate information as to the protected area, the principle thereby established would have wide application.

Mr Pleming QC in his powerful argument for the plaintiffs naturally placed *g* reliance on the judgment of the Divisional Court in *Bugg v DPP, Percy v DPP* [1993] 2 All ER 815, [1993] QB 473, to the effect that the byelaws were defective on their face because there was no description contained in the byelaws as to the boundary of the protected area. If the phrase 'lands belonging to the Secretary of State' in the specified parishes means *the* lands belonging to the Secretary of State, *h* as I believe, and the Divisional Court appears to have believed, it does, then in my judgment the protected area has been described with certainty. It is not suggested that the Secretary of State is unable to establish that the lands shown on the plan do belong to him. And if the area is certain, it follows that the boundary of the area is certain. Further, the reference to the plan for convenience *j* of identification means that the plan, whilst it cannot override the verbal description of the lands as belonging to the Secretary of State in the specified parishes, can be used as an aid to determining the protected area and hence its boundary. In my judgment, this not being an area to which s 2(5) of the Military Lands Act 1900 applied, it was not necessary to describe the boundary in the byelaws. I therefore respectfully disagree with the Divisional Court in so far as *a* their decision is based on the absence of a description of the boundary of the protected area in the byelaws.

Mr Pleming, in arguing for the invalidity of the byelaws, submitted that the description 'lands belonging to the Secretary of State' made it impossible for anyone walking in the area to know what land is referred to. I cannot accept that that is the right test. Mr Pleming was constrained to accept that the protected
b land might properly be described in the byelaws by reference to an Ordnance Survey plan or public register, but he submitted that the extrinsic evidence must be readily available to the public. I cannot see how this can properly be an ingredient of a test of certainty. So long as the description identifies the protected area by whatever means, the test of certainty is in my judgment satisfied. No doubt one of the reasons why Parliament required in s 17 of the Military Lands
c Act 1892 the marking of the boundaries of the areas to which byelaws apply was that members of the public in the neighbourhood of the protected area should know where the area began, but that marking, as the Divisional Court in *Bugg* rightly held, did not affect the question of certainty.

Another point taken by Mr Pleming is that uncertainty may be caused by the
d enlargement or reduction, after the byelaws are made, of the lands belonging to the Secretary of State. For my part, I do not accept that such enlargement or reduction creates any uncertainty. The meaning of the byelaws is that which they have when the byelaws are made. If the Secretary of State acquires more land, the byelaws will not apply to the further land; that would require a further decision by the Secretary of State to be taken in the light of the circumstances
e then obtaining to make byelaws apply to the further land. If the Secretary of State disposes of land subject to the byelaws, the land disposed of would no longer be subject to the byelaws, as they would cease to satisfy the condition of belonging to the Secretary of State. Further the plan would need amending, and no doubt in practice there would be new byelaws promulgated for the smaller area.

f In my judgment, if the correct test for the certainty of a byelaw is, as Mr Pleming submitted, that which was suggested by Mathew J in *Kruse v Johnson* [1898] 2 QB 91 at 108, [1895–9] All ER Rep 105 at 115, viz that it must contain adequate information as to the duties of those who are to obey, then in my judgment these byelaws passed that test. For these as well as the reasons given by Simon Brown LJ, I would allow this appeal.

g On the further point whether the correct test is that suggested by Mathew J or that suggested by Lord Denning in *Fawcett Properties Ltd v Buckingham CC* [1960] 3 All ER 503, [1961] AC 636 at 676–678 (the most material parts of which Simon Brown LJ has cited), I unhesitatingly prefer that of Lord Denning. The adequacy of information test is itself uncertain. Our attention has been drawn to Bennion
h *Statutory Interpretation* (2nd edn, 1992) p 326:

> '*Voidness for uncertainty* The interpreter is not permitted to declare an enactment containing a broad term or other ambiguous expression void for uncertainty. The uncertainty is intended to be resolved by the interpreter, whether an administrative official or the court. This can be looked on as a
> *j* delegation by Parliament of legislative power. A corresponding rule applies to uncertainty in statutory instruments and most other delegated legislation. The position is different with byelaws however. A byelaw may be declared void if uncertain in its terms.'

To my mind it is wrong in principle that the test of uncertainty should differ according to whether it applies to a byelaw on the one hand or to an enactment or delegated legislation other than a byelaw on the other. Further, it should be borne in mind that in *Kruse v Johnson* itself Lord Russell CJ (with whom Chitty LJ and Wright, Darling and Channell JJ agreed) urged that byelaws made by representative public bodies ought to be supported, if possible, and interpreted benevolently (see [1898] 2 QB 91 at 99, [1895–9] All ER Rep 105 at 110). There is no dispute but that if no meaning can be given to a byelaw, it must be invalid, and that if there is any reasonable doubt whether an unauthorised person has entered the protected area, that person will not be convicted of an offence under the byelaws. But where a sensible meaning can be given to the byelaws, and there is no reasonable doubt that the unauthorised person is within the protected area, I can see no sufficient reasons of policy or principle that should lead the court to conclude that the byelaws should be struck down on the ground of uncertainty.

For these reasons and the reasons explained by Simon Brown LJ in his judgment, I too would hold that the *Fawcett* test for uncertainty is to be preferred to that suggested by Mathew J in relation to byelaws.

On the second issue, I am in entire agreement with Simon Brown LJ

SCHIEMANN LJ. I agree with both judgments which have been delivered. The use of the phrase 'lands belonging to the Secretary of State' in the HMS Forest Moor and Menwith Hill Station Byelaws 1986, SI 1986/481, does not render them uncertain because whether or not lands do or do not belong to the Secretary of State can be ascertained with certainty, by resort to the courts if need be. The fact that it is conceivable that an individual walking in the area might well have difficulty in knowing, without making further inquiries, whether a particular square metre did or did not belong to the Secretary of State is, in my judgment, irrelevant to the question whether or not the byelaws are void for uncertainty.

I desire only to add a few words on what the position would have been had the court found the byelaws in question to be invalid.

Underlying this is a question which has intrigued administrative lawyers in different countries and to which they have given different answers. The question is this: once a court has declared an enactment to be invalid, from what point in time does the abrogation apply: retroactively from the time of the court's ruling (ex tunc) or only from the time of the enactment (ex nunc)? Historically, this has been a problem of far greater import in countries which have a court which can declare legislative acts void as being unconstitutional than it has been in this country, where traditionally it has only been the legality of byelaws and statutory instruments which has been the subject of legal challenge. Now that we are members of the European Union and the possibility arises that even provisions in Acts of Parliament can be declared illegal because of a conflict with Community law the question may well grow to be of greater importance in this country.

The ex tunc solution has an initial attractiveness. The law should never have been made and therefore one must proceed as though it never had been made. To do otherwise will in effect legalise the illegal and the courts are not in business to do that. Moreover, once the courts start to give some effect to illegal legislation, there will be less incentive for the legislator to refrain from such illegality.

The problem with the ex tunc solution is that it will often be the case that, between the making of the enactment in question and the declaration of its invalidity, many people will have regulated their lives on the assumption that the enactment was lawful. Society cannot function if all legislation has first to be tested in court for legality. In practice, money will have been spent, taxes *a* collected, businesses and property bought and sold and people arrested and perhaps imprisoned on the basis that what appears to be the law is the law.

It has been commonplace in our jurisprudence, as Simon Brown LJ points out, to speak of a basic principle that an ultra vires enactment is void ab initio and of no effect. This beguilingly simple formulation, as is widely acknowledged, conceals more than it reveals. Manifestly in daily life the enactment will have had
b an effect in the sense that people will have regulated their conduct in the light of it. Even in the law courts it will often be found to have had an effect because the courts will have given a remedy to a person disadvantaged by the application of the ultra vires enactment to him or because a decision, binding on the parties thereto, has been rendered on the basis of the apparent law or because some period of limitation has expired making it too late now to raise any point on
c illegality.

The policy questions which the law must address in this type of case are whether any and if so what remedy should be given to whom against whom in cases where persons have acted in reliance on what appears to be valid legislation. To approach these questions by rigidly applying to all circumstances a doctrine
d that the enactment which has been declared invalid was 'incapable of ever having had any legal effect upon the rights and duties to the parties' seems to me, with all respect to the strong stream of authority in our law to that effect, needlessly to restrict the possible answers which policy might require. For instance, in the context of the present case had we held the byelaws to be invalid, as it seems to me a sensible answer might be that no remedy should be given against the
e policeman who acted in good faith but that a remedy should be given against a Secretary of State who put into circulation invalid byelaws with the perfectly foreseeable consequence that policemen would act on the assumption that they were valid. We are not required in the present case to decide whether that is the answer given by our law as it stands. I merely give it as a possibility.

f It may be that, in the development of the law, future cases will draw on that part of our law which is applicable to cases containing a European Community element which shows a considerable amount of flexibility in dealing with this question. There are now many cases which examine the conflict which an ex tunc declaration produces with the principles of legal certainty, acquired rights and legitimate expectation. This is not the place to develop the point, there
g having understandably and sensibly been no reference to it at the bar and it being unnecessary to our decision. Relevant case law and discussions of the problems involved can be found, in the European context, in Wyatt and Dashwood *European Community Law* (3rd edn, 1993) pp 93–95, Schermers and Waelbroeck *Judicial Protection in the European Communities* (5th edn, 1991) pp 56–63, 441, 442,
h in the English context, in Craig *Administrative Law* (3rd edn, 1994) pp 472–475 and, in the French context, in Long *Les grands arrets de la jurisprudence administrative* (9th edn, 1990) pp 565–567.

So far as the present case is concerned, I would allow the appeal.

j *Appeal allowed. Leave to appeal to the House of Lords refused.*

Carolyn Toulmin   Barrister.

Kay Green and others v Twinsectra Ltd　　　　*a*

COURT OF APPEAL, CIVIL DIVISION
STAUGHTON, ALDOUS LJJ AND SIR JOHN MAY
22, 23 APRIL, 15 MAY 1996

b

*Landlord and tenant – Flats – Tenants' right to acquire landlord's reversion – Disposal
by landlord – Tenants' rights of first refusal – Landlord disposing of reversion without
giving tenants prior notice of disposal – Service of purchase notice by tenants on new
landlord – Whether new landlord under a duty to comply with purchase notice –
Whether purchase notice served by requisite majority of tenants – Whether purchase*　　*c*
notice valid – Landlord and Tenant Act 1987, ss 1, 12.

In February 1992 the landlord of six buildings, four of which contained flats and
two, houses and bungalows, sold the freeholds of the buildings, which were
registered under two separate titles, to T Ltd without giving the tenants of the
flats first refusal or notice of the proposed disposal as required by s 5 of the　*d*
Landlord and Tenant Act 1987. In July 1992 the tenants of flats in three of the
buildings served a purchase notice on T Ltd under s 12[a] of the 1987 Act requiring
T Ltd to convey the freehold of the buildings to them. T Ltd did not comply with
the notice and thereafter the tenants applied to the court for declarations that T
Ltd was in default in failing to do so and that they were entitled to acquire the　*e*
freehold of the buildings. The judge dismissed the application, holding that the
purchase notice had not been served by the requisite majority of tenants, since
the relevant 'premises' for the purposes of s 1[b] of the 1987 Act were all the
buildings containing flats, and those premises had to be comprised within one
title. He further held that the purchase notice was invalid in that it failed to
include one of the flats in the buildings and also required the transfer of buildings　*f*
containing houses and bungalows, in breach of s 12(3)(a)(i) of the 1987 Act. The
tenants appealed and on the appeal T Ltd contended that the 1987 Act did not
impose a duty on a new landlord to comply with a purchase notice.

Held – (1) Although the 1987 Act did not specifically state that a new landlord　*g*
who was served with a purchase notice had to give effect to it, the wording of s 12
was such as to require the new landlord to do so, since the section assumed that
the purchase notice operated so as to require disposal and provided a duty as to
the way the property had to be disposed. Moreover, since the purpose of the Act
was to confer on tenants of flats rights with respect to the acquisition by them of
their landlord's reversion, it was necessary that a new landlord should do so in　*h*
order to give effect to that purpose (see p 555 *g* to *j*, p 556 *b* and p 561 *g*, post);
Belvedere Court Management Ltd v Frogmore Developments Ltd [1996] 1 All ER 312 and
Denetower Ltd v Toop [1991] 3 All ER 661 explained.

(2) For the purposes of s 1 of the 1987 Act 'premises' consisted of the whole or
part of a building and the fact that the building was included within one or more　*j*
registered titles was irrelevant. Accordingly, in considering whether the purchase
notice had been served by the requisite majority of tenants, each building had to
be considered separately and it was not appropriate to take into account the

---

a　Section 12, so far as material, is set out at p 553 *c* to p 554 *a*, post
b　Section 1, so far as material, is set out at p 551 *f* to *j*, post

a fourth building containing flats. It followed, having regard to their number, that the purchase notice had been served by the requisite majority of tenants (see p 557 *c d g* and p 562 *b c*, post).

(3) To comply with s 12 of the 1987 Act a purchase notice had to be in writing and give adequate notice to the new landlord of the tenants' desire to have the new landlord's interest in the premises transferred to them. Those requirements *b* were imperative and therefore although one flat was not included in the purchase notice, as the notice required disposal of the freehold interest in the relevant building it would be absurd to understand the notice as only requiring part of the freehold to be transferred. The requirement in s 12(3)(a)(i), however, that a purchase notice should require the new landlord to dispose of the interest only so far as relating to the particular premises occupied by the tenants was directory *c* only. Accordingly, the fact that the purchase notice required the disposal also of buildings to which the 1987 Act did not apply, did not invalidate the notice. It followed that the purchase notice was valid and the appeal would therefore be allowed (see p 558 *e*, p 559 *h j* to p 560 *b d*, p 561 *b c* and p 562 *d* to *j*, post); *Denetower Ltd v Toop* [1991] 3 All ER 661 followed.

d
Notes

For enforcement of tenant's rights against new landlords, see 27(2) *Halsbury's Laws* (4th edn reissue) paras 1601–1609.

For the Landlord and Tenant Act 1987, ss 1, 12, see 23 *Halsbury's Statutes* (4th edn) (1989 reissue) 384, 399.
e

Cases referred to in judgments

Belvedere Court Management Ltd v Frogmore Developments Ltd [1996] 1 All ER 312, CA.
Denetower Ltd v Toop [1991] 3 All ER 661, [1991] 1 WLR 945, CA.
f *Howard v Bodington* (1877) 2 PD 203, Arches Ct.
Howard v Secretary of State for the Environment [1974] 1 All ER 644, [1975] QB 235, [1974] 2 WLR 459, CA.
IRC v Ayrshire Employers Mutual Insurance Association Ltd [1946] 1 All ER 637, HL.
Methuen-Campbell v Walters [1979] 1 All ER 606, [1979] QB 525, [1979] 2 WLR 113, *g*   CA.

Cases also cited or referred to in skeleton arguments

Cousins v Metropolitan Guarantee Ltd [1989] 2 EGLR 223.
Englefield Court Tenants v Skeels [1990] 2 EGLR 230.
h *Gardiner v Sevenoaks RDC* [1950] 2 All ER 84, DC.
Mabo v Queensland (1992) 107 ALR 1, Aust HC.
Mainwaring v Trustees of Henry Smith's Charity [1996] 2 All ER 220, CA.
Montagu (Samuel) & Co Ltd v Swiss Air Transport Co Ltd [1966] 1 All ER 814, [1966] 2 QB 306, CA.
j *Potts (or Riddell) v Reid* [1942] 2 All ER 161, [1943] AC 1, HL.
30 Upperton Gardens Management Ltd v Akano [1990] 2 EGLR 232.
Tropis Shipping Co Ltd v Ibex Property Corp Ltd (1967) 203 EG 133.
Williams v Secretary of State for Wales (1971) 23 P & CR 135.
Wrotham Park Estate Co v Parkside Homes Ltd [1974] 2 All ER 321, [1974] 1 WLR 798.

Appeal

By amended notice dated 27 January 1995 the applicants, Mr John Lewick Kay   *a*
Green and 17 other tenants of Tudor Court and Tudor House, Hanworth,
appealed from the decision of Judge Hull QC at Staines County Court on 23
August 1994 refusing their application for a declaration that the respondent,
Twinsectra Ltd, the new landlord of the properties, was in default in not
complying with a notice served by the applicants pursuant to s 12 of the Landlord   *b*
and Tenant Act 1987 requiring the disposal of the reversionary interest in the
property to them. The facts are set out in the judgment of Aldous LJ.

David Neuberger QC and *Edward Denehan* (instructed by *J E Kennedy & Co*, Harrow)
for the applicants.
Kim Lewison QC and *Simon Brilliant* (instructed by *Wallace & Partners*) for the   *c*
respondent.

Cur adv vult

15 May 1996. The following judgments were delivered.   *d*

ALDOUS LJ (giving the first judgment at the invitation of Staughton LJ). This is
an appeal from the decision of Judge Hull QC, which dismissed the applicants'
request for declarations that Twinsectra Ltd, the respondent, was in default in not
complying with a notice served pursuant to the Landlord and Tenant Act 1987
and therefore the applicants were entitled to require Twinsectra to transfer the   *e*
reversionary interest in certain property to them.

The appeal is concerned with the application and provisions of Pt I of the 1987
Act. That Act, as stated in the title, was passed inter alia 'to confer on tenants of
flats rights with respect to the acquisition by them of their landlord's reversion'.
In outline Pt I of the Act gives to certain tenants the right of first refusal to acquire   *f*
the landlord's reversion. Section 1 states that a landlord shall not make a 'relevant
disposal' affecting any premises to which Pt I of the Act applies without serving a
notice in accordance with s 5 of the Act. The premises are defined as those which
consist of the whole or part of a building and contain two or more flats held by
qualifying tenants and the number of the flats held by such tenants exceeds 50%
of the total number of flats contained in the premises. Sections 2 to 4 define who   *g*
are relevant landlords and qualifying tenants and what is a relevant disposal.
Section 5 requires a landlord who proposes to make a relevant disposal to serve a
notice in accordance with the section on the qualifying tenants, thereby giving
the tenants first refusal. Sections 6 to 10 are concerned with what happens after
the notice has been served.   *h*

Sections 11 to 17 come into effect when the original landlord has, in breach of
his obligations, disposed of his reversion to a new landlord. Section 11 requires
the new landlord to comply with a notice served by the requisite majority of
qualifying tenants requiring him to supply particulars of the terms on which the
original disposal was made. Section 12 gives the requisite majority of qualifying   *j*
tenants the right to serve a 'purchase notice' on the new landlord requiring him
to dispose of the estate or interest that was the subject of the original disposal on
terms on which it was made to a person or persons nominated by them for that
purpose. Section 13 gives to a rent assessment committee, called a leasehold
valuation tribunal, the jurisdiction to hear and determine questions arising in
relation to any matters specified in the purchase notice, the identity of the

a property or relating to other terms on which the disposal is to be made and any
question arising for determination in consequence of the provision in a purchase
notice such as is mentioned in s 12(3)(b). Sections 14 to 17 are concerned with
eventualities that may arise after service of a purchase notice pursuant to s 12.

Section 19 deals with enforcement of obligations under Pt I of the 1987 Act. It
provides that the court may, on the application of any person interested, make an
b order requiring any person who has made default in complying with any duty
imposed by any provision of Pt I of the Act to make good the default within an
appropriate time. That application cannot be made unless a notice has previously
been served on the person in question requiring him to make good the default
and more than 14 days have elapsed since the date of service of the notice.

c *The facts*
The named applicant is Mr John Lewick Kay Green, who is the nominated
representative of 17 tenants of Tudor Court and Tudor House, Castle Way,
Hanworth, in the London Borough of Hounslow. I will refer to them as 'the
applicants'.

d London and City Westcliffe Properties Ltd were the owners of Tudor Court,
Tudor House and Parr Court of Castle Way, Hanworth, in the London Borough
of Hounslow. Those properties consist of flats, bungalows and terrace houses
which are let. London and City decided to dispose of the freeholds, but failed to
serve a s 5 notice on the tenants of the properties. Instead, the freeholds, which
were registered at the London Registry under titles MX420465 and MX304042,
e were put up for auction as one lot with the particulars of sale drawing attention
to the fact that no s 5 notice had been served. They were purchased on 25
February 1992 by Twinsectra for £240,000 and it was registered as proprietor of
the freehold interest in the properties on 13 April 1992. On 1 May 1992 Mr Green,
as the nominated representative of the applicants, served on Twinsectra a s 11
f notice requiring it to supply particulars of the terms upon which the disposal was
made. Solicitors acting on behalf of Twinsectra replied to that notice giving the
information required by the 1987 Act, but stating that it was given without
prejudice to Twinsectra's contentions that the notice was not a valid notice under
s 11 and the premises were not premises to which Pt I of the Act applied. On 20
July 1992 a s 12 notice (the purchase notice) was served on Twinsectra by
g solicitors acting on behalf of Mr Green and on behalf of the 17 other long lease
tenants in Tudor Court and Tudor House whose names and addresses were
given in the notice. I shall have to come back to the terms of that notice, but in
effect it required Twinsectra to dispose of the freehold of a number of units
within Tudor House and Tudor Court to Mr Green, who was the nominated
h person as required by the section. An immaterial amendment was made nine
days later. Twinsectra failed to comply with the notice and these proceedings
were started on 12 November 1992.

Tudor Court consists of four buildings, which I will refer to as 'buildings 1, 2,
3 and 4'. Building 1 is the main building. It is an attractive sixteenth century
j domestic dwelling with the main part running north/south and attached to it,
two wings protruding in a westerly direction to form three sides of a courtyard,
now a garden. It has been converted so that it now contains seven flats and three
terrace houses, which are included in title MX304042.

Building 2 is situated to the west of the main part of building 1 and faces across
the courtyard. It is a later addition to the complex and consists of two
semi-detached bungalows. It is included in titles MX304042 and 420465.

Building 3 appears to have been built as servants' cottages. It is adjacent, but *a* not attached, to the northern wing of Tudor Court. As let, it contains two terrace houses and two bungalows. It is also included in both titles.

Building 4 is adjacent to the southern wing of Tudor Court. It is a modern purpose-built block of five flats, which is contained within title MX420465.

Around the buildings comprising Tudor Court is a garden and what was called the amenity land comprising ponds and trees. That garden abuts the garden of *b* Tudor House, which is situated to the west. It is a nineteenth century mansion, which has been divided into seven flats, with its own drive passing to the north of Tudor Court and terminating in Castle Way. It is within title MX420465.

Parr Court is a modern building consisting of about 44 flats, which is built around three sides of a court with lawns and ponds. It is situated to the *c* north-west of Tudor House and its grounds are separated from those of Tudor House by a wall. It is included within title MX420465.

With three exceptions, all the flats and houses in Tudor Court and all the flats in Tudor House are occupied under long leases at low rents on substantially the same terms. The leases gave access to the garden, but did not include the amenity land. Parr Court was let differently and some of the tenancies were *d* regulated tenancies.

The proceedings

Before the judge the applicants sought declarations that Twinsectra was in default in failing to comply with the provisions of the s 12 notice. It followed, *e* they alleged, that they were entitled to acquire the freehold of the seven flats in Tudor House and the buildings which comprised Tudor Court. On this appeal, they only challenged the judge's decision in respect of Tudor House and buildings 1 and 4 of Tudor Court. They were also concerned to ensure that this court decided the essential issues between the parties. They therefore applied to amend their pleading and notice of appeal so as to seek declarations: (i) that the *f* purchase notice, dated 27 July 1992, served on the respondent by the applicants is an effective notice under s 12 of the 1987 Act; (ii) that the respondent is in default in compliance with the purchase notice dated 27 July 1992 served on it by the applicants pursuant to s 12 of the 1987 Act; and (iii) that the applicants are therefore entitled to require the respondent to transfer the reversionary interest *g* in that part of building 1 Tudor Court, or in the alternative the reversionary interest in that part of building 1 Tudor Court, save for those parts of building 1 which do not comprise 'flats' within the meaning of s 60 of the 1987 Act, the reversionary interest in building 4 Tudor Court, and the reversionary interest in Tudor House with all appurtenances to such buildings.

As the respondents did not object, the court allowed the amendments leaving *h* to be decided the question of costs.

The judge dismissed the applicants' claim for declarations. He held that the notice had not been served by a nominee of the requisite majority of tenants because the applicants could not sever Parr Court from the application. He also held that the purchase notice was invalid for a number of reasons to which I have *j* to come. However, it is convenient at this stage of my judgment to set out the relevant parts of the purchase notice:

'FLATS 1, 1A, 1B, 2, 2A, 3, 3A, 4, 4A, 4B, 5, 5A, 6, 6A, 7, 8, 9, 10, 11, 12 Tudor Court and 1, 2, 3, 4, 5 & 6 Tudor House Castle Way, Hanworth, Middlesex. LANDLORD & TENANT ACT 1987. As solicitor for JOHN KAY GREEN of Flat 8 *a*   Tudor Court, the duly appointed nominee for the purposes of the above mentioned Act, on his own behalf and on behalf of the 19 other Long Lease Tenants whose names and addresses are specified at the foot of this notice. NOTICE IS HEREBY GIVEN pursuant to Section 12 of the above mentioned enactment that you are required to dispose of the estate or interest that you hold in the above mentioned premises (that estate or interest being part of

b   the subject matter of the original disposal thereof by instrument of transfer dated 25 February 1992 and made between London City & Westcliffe Properties Limited (1) and Twinsectra Limited (2)) to the above named JOHN KAY GREEN he being the person nominated for the purposes of the said Section 12 by the majority of the qualifying tenants of TUDOR COURT and TUDOR HOUSE flats whose names and addresses are specified at the foot of this

c   Notice AND FURTHER TAKE NOTICE that the terms on which the above mentioned majority of tenants require you to dispose of the said estate or interest to them are (1) the same terms on which the said estate or interest was disposed of to Twinsectra Limited; or (2) alternatively on such terms as may be determined by a rent assessment committee pursuant to Section

d   12(3)(b) of the above mentioned enactment.'

At the foot of the notice was listed the flats referred to at the start, together with the names and addresses of the tenants. They include all but one of the flats in Tudor House; all but two of the flats in building 1 and one house; one of the bungalows in building 2; two houses and one bungalow in building 3; and all but

e   one flat in building 4.

The 1987 Act

Although it will be necessary for me to refer to other sections of the 1987 Act, it is convenient to set out the most relevant parts of the sections at the heart of this case:

f

'**1.** *Qualifying tenants to have rights of first refusal on disposals by landlord.*—
(1) A landlord shall not make a relevant disposal affecting any premises to which at the time of the disposal this Part applies unless—(a) he has in accordance with section 5 previously served a notice under that section with respect to the disposal on the qualifying tenants of the flats contained in

g   those premises (being a notice by virtue of which rights of first refusal are conferred on those tenants); and (b) the disposal is made in accordance with the requirements of sections 6 to 10.

(2) Subject to subsections (3) and (4), this Part applies to premises if—(a) they consist of the whole or part of a building; and (b) they contain two or

h   more flats held by qualifying tenants; and (c) the number of flats held by such tenants exceeds 50 per cent of the total number of flats contained in the premises.

(3) This Part does not apply to premises falling within subsection (2) if— (a) any part or parts of the premises is or are occupied or intended to be

j   occupied otherwise than for residential purposes; and (b) the internal floor area of that part or those parts (taken together) exceeds 50 per cent of the internal floor area of the premises (taken as a whole); and for purposes of this subsection the internal floor area of any common parts shall be disregarded ...

5. *Requirement to serve notice conferring rights of first refusal.*—(1) Where, in the case of any premises to which this Part applies, the landlord proposes to make a relevant disposal affecting the premises, he shall serve a notice under this section on the qualifying tenants of the flats contained in the premises.

(2) A notice under this section must—(a) contain particulars of the principal terms of the disposal proposed by the landlord, including in particular—(i) the property to which it relates and the estate or interest in that property proposed to be disposed of, and (ii) the consideration required by the landlord for making the disposal; (b) state that the notice constitutes an offer by the landlord to dispose of the property on those terms which may be accepted by the requisite majority of qualifying tenants of the constituent flats; (c) specify a period within which that offer may be so accepted, being a period of not less than two months which is to begin with the date of service of the notice; and (d) specify a further period within which a person or persons may be nominated for the purposes of section 6, being a period of not less than two months which is to begin with the end of the period specified under paragraph (c).

(3) Where, as the result of a notice under this section being served on different tenants on different dates, the period specified in the notice under subsection (2)(c) would, apart from this subsection, end on different dates— (a) the notice shall have effect in relation to all the qualifying tenants on whom it is served as if it provided for that period to end with the latest of those dates, and for the period specified in the notice under subsection (2)(d) to begin with the end of that period; and (b) references in this Part to the period specified in the notice under subsection (2)(c) or (as the case may be) subsection (2)(d) shall be construed accordingly.

(4) Where a landlord has not served a notice under this section on all of the qualifying tenants on whom it was required to be served by virtue of subsection (1), he shall nevertheless be treated as having complied with that subsection if—(a) he has served such a notice on not less than 90 per cent of the qualifying tenants on whom it was so required to be served, or (b) where the qualifying tenants on whom it was so required to be served number less than ten, he has served such a notice on all but one of them.

(5) Where a landlord proposes to effect a transaction that would involve both—(a) a disposal of an estate or interest in the whole or part of a building constituting a relevant disposal affecting any premises to which this Part applies, and (b) a disposal of an estate or interest in the whole or part of another building (whether or not constituting a relevant disposal affecting any premises to which this Part applies) or more than one such disposal, the landlord shall, for the purpose of complying with this section in relation to any relevant disposal falling within paragraph (a) or (b) above, sever the transaction in such a way as to secure that, in the notice served by him under this section with respect to that disposal, the terms specified in pursuance of subsection (2)(a) are the terms on which he is willing to make that disposal ...

11. *Duty of new landlord to furnish particulars of disposal made in contravention of Part I.*—(1) Where—(a) a landlord has made a relevant disposal affecting any premises to which at the time of the disposal this Part applied ("the original disposal"), and (b) either no notice was served by the landlord under section 5 with respect to that disposal or it was made in contravention of any provision of sections 6 to 10, and (c) those premises are still premises to which this Part applies, the requisite majority of qualifying tenants of the constituent flats may, before the end of the period specified in subsection (2) below, serve a notice on the transferee under the original disposal requiring

a

him to furnish a person (whose name and address are specified for the purpose in the notice) with particulars of the terms on which the original disposal was made (including those relating to the consideration payable) and the date on which it was made; and in the following provisions of this Part the transferee under that disposal is referred to as "the new landlord".

(2) The period referred to in subsection (1) is the period of two months beginning with the date by which—(a) notices under section 3 of the Landlord and Tenant Act 1985 (in this Act referred to as "the 1985 Act") relating to the original disposal, or (b) documents of any other description indicating that the original disposal has taken place, have been served on the requisite majority of qualifying tenants of the constituent flats.

(3) Any person served with a notice in accordance with subsection (1) shall comply with the notice within the period of one month beginning with the date on which it is served on him.

12. *Right of qualifying tenants to compel sale etc. by new landlord.*—
(1) Where—(a) paragraphs (a) and (b) of section 11(1) apply to a relevant disposal affecting any premises to which at the time of the disposal this Part applied (other than a disposal consisting of such a surrender as is mentioned in section 15(1)(b)), and (b) those premises are still premises to which this Part applies, the requisite majority of qualifying tenants of the constituent flats may, before the end of the period specified in subsection (2), serve a notice ("a purchase notice") on the new landlord requiring him (except as provided by the following provisions of this Part) to dispose of the estate or interest that was the subject-matter of the original disposal, on terms on which it was made (including those relating to the consideration payable), to a person or persons nominated for the purposes of this section by any such majority of qualifying tenants of those flats.

(2) The period referred to in subsection (1) is—(a) in a case where a notice has been served on the new landlord under section 11(1), the period of three months beginning with the date on which a notice is served by him under section 11(3); and (b) in any other case, the period of three months beginning with the date mentioned in section 11(2).

(3) A purchase notice—(a) shall, where the estate or interest that was the subject-matter of the original disposal related to any property in addition to the premises to which this Part applied at the time of the disposal—(i) require the new landlord to dispose of that estate or interest only so far as relating to those premises, and (ii) require him to do so on the terms referred to in subsection (1) subject to such modifications as are necessary or expedient in the circumstances; (b) may, instead of specifying the estate or interest to be disposed of or any particular terms on which the disposal is to be made by the new landlord (whether doing so expressly or by reference to the original disposal), provide for that estate or interest, or (as the case may be) for any such terms, to be determined by a rent assessment committee in accordance with section 13.

(4) Where the property which the new landlord is required to dispose of in pursuance of the purchase notice has at any time since the original disposal become subject to any charge or other incumbrance, then, unless the court by order directs otherwise—(a) in the case of a charge to secure the payment of money or the performance of any other obligation by the new landlord or any other person, the instrument by virtue of which the property is disposed of by the new landlord to the person or persons nominated for the purposes

of this section shall (subject to the provisions of Part I of Schedule 1) operate
to discharge the property from that charge; and (b) in the case of any other
incumbrance, the property shall be so disposed of subject to the
incumbrance but with a reduction in the consideration payable to the new
landlord corresponding to the amount by which the existence of the
incumbrance reduces the value of the property ...'

The first issue

Twinsectra in its skeleton argument submitted that, even if it be assumed that
a landlord had a duty to comply with a purchase notice, the county court in this
case did not have jurisdiction to grant the declarations because the declarations
sought in the pleadings were said to be 'in aid of' an enforcement order and as no
default notice had been served, an enforcement notice could not be made so as
to trigger the court's powers under s 19 of the 1987 Act. That was a pleading
point and was one reason why the applicants requested the amendment to which
I have referred. It was not pressed at the hearing before us. However, the
amendment did not solve the question as to whether it would be right to grant
the declarations originally sought, even if the purchase notice was a valid notice.
Twinsectra submitted that even if it had been served with a valid notice, it was
not under an obligation to comply with it. If that is right there would be no
purpose in granting those declarations. Thus, the first question for decision is:
does a landlord, upon whom a valid purchase notice has been served, have to give
effect to it? Mr Lewison QC submitted that the 1987 Act did not contain any
requirement that a landlord, who was served with a s 12 purchase notice, need
comply with it. All that the section did was to provide for service of a notice in a
particular form. That, he submitted, was to be contrasted with the effect of
service of a s 5 notice. That constituted an offer which could be accepted by a
nominated person in accordance with the provisions of s 6. He also drew
attention to s 19, which empowers the court to 'make an order requiring any
person who has made default in complying with any duty imposed on him by any
provision of this Part to make good the default within such time as specified in
the order'. He submitted that the Act did impose duties as could be seen, for
example in s 1 ('a landlord shall not make'), s 5(1) ('he shall serve a notice'), s 5(5)
('the landlord shall, for the purpose ...'), and s 11(3) ('shall comply with the
notice'). In contrast s 12, he submitted, contained no such duty upon a landlord
to comply with the notice when served.

Mr Lewison referred us to the criticisms of the 1987 Act made by this court in
Belvedere Court Management Ltd v Frogmore Developments Ltd [1996] 1 All ER 312. In
that case landlords had sold flats to Frogmore without serving a s 5 notice. Prior
to receipt of a purchase notice, Frogmore granted certain leases in the block of
flats to another party. Bingham MR said (at 330–331):

'In *Denetower Ltd v Toop* [1991] 3 All ER 661 at 668, [1991] 1 WLR 945 at 952
Browne-Wilkinson V-C sitting in this court described the 1987 Act as
"ill-drafted, complicated and confused". The argument in this case has given
new force to this understated criticism. Some anomalies have already been
mentioned. There are others. Nothing in s 12 imposes on the new landlord
a duty not to dispose of his interest, such as is imposed on the original
landlord by s 6(1). It is unclear why not. There is nothing in s 12 which gives
the tenants a right to require a subsequent purchaser from the new landlord
to dispose of his interest to the tenants' nominee. A limited right is given by

a
s 16, but it is not equivalent to the right given by s 12(1) against the new landlord. It is again unclear why not. Counsel discounted the suggestion that an acceptance notice under s 6(1)(b) or a purchase notice under s 12(1) might create an equitable interest in the land capable of registration as a land charge or protection by a caution, and I am not inclined to disagree. But one could wish that the Act provided as many answers as it raised problems.'

b
Hobhouse LJ made a similar criticism. He said (at 331):

'The Act imposes certain obligations on landlords but does not match them with adequately expressed rights for the tenants. In some respects the drafting is extremely detailed, in others obvious situations have not been provided for. In places restrictive expressions are used—s 16 provides examples—but the reasons for the restrictions are not clear and the Act does not deal with the lacunae that result. Overall the drafting does not disclose a clear and consistent policy and it falls between the two stools of being both excessively and inadequately detailed.'

c

d
After referring to two cases he went on:

'The legislature does not seem to have appreciated what was involved in making the rights sought to be conferred on tenants effective. Whilst the drafting of fully effective provisions would not be unduly difficult (and has been achieved in other legislation covering similar matters), it is not the role of the court to construct such provisions if they are not to be found expressly or implicitly in the Act as drafted. The ease of the legislative task does not mean that the distinction between the roles of the courts and the legislature can be disregarded. The solutions to the problems posed have to be found, if at all, within the scope of the interpretative tools open to the courts to uncover and give effect to the statutory intention.'

e

f
Mr Lewison submitted that the words of Hobhouse LJ were applicable to the facts of this case and the court should not construct a duty which was not there. If there was a lacuna, as he submitted there was, it should be remedied by Parliament and not by the court.

Mr Neuberger QC, who appeared for the applicants, submitted that a landlord who was served with a purchase notice had to give effect to it. Although there was no section of the 1987 Act which so stated, the requirement was, in the words of Hobhouse LJ, 'found expressly or implicitly in the Act'. I believe he is right.

g

I have already set out part of the long title to the 1987 Act. It is an Act 'to confer on tenants of flats rights with respect to the acquisition by them of their landlord's reversion'.

h
To give effect to that, it is necessary that a landlord should, when served with a purchase notice, comply with it and to decide to the contrary would be failing to comply with the stated intention of the legislature. In any case, I believe that the words of s 12 are such as to require a landlord to give effect to the notice.

j
Section 12(1) enables qualifying tenants to serve a purchase notice on the new landlord, 'requiring him ... to dispose of the estate or interest that was the subject-matter of the original disposal'; and sub-s (4) refers to 'Where the property which the new landlord is required to dispose of in pursuance of the purchase notice ...' It goes on to state that 'the property shall be so disposed of ...' Thus the section assumes that the purchase notice operates so as to require disposal and provides a duty as to the way the property has to be disposed of.

Further, to accept the submission of Twinsectra would mean that ss 12 to 17 had no purpose as a landlord could refuse to comply with a purchase notice which *a* had been served. That is unreal.

I have not found it necessary, when concluding that there was a duty upon a landlord to give effect to a purchase notice, to rely upon the heading of s 12 which makes it clear that such a duty exists. Even so, I believe it clear that the section is concerned with the right of tenants to compel a sale by a new landlord. That *b* appears to have been the view of Bingham MR in *Belvedere* when he said in the passage that I have quoted: 'A limited right is given by s 16, but it is not equivalent to the right given by s 12(1) against the new landlord.'

The conclusion I have reached is consistent with the decision of the court in *Denetower* to grant the declarations which they did. If the judges had believed that the landlord did not have to give effect to the purchase notice, they would not *c* have granted the declarations which they did as to do so would not have resolved the essential issue between the parties.

The second issue

Was the purchase notice served by the requisite majority of qualifying tenants? *d*

Mr Lewison submitted that the notice was not served by the requisite majority of tenants of the relevant premises. He drew our attention to the way that the 1987 Act enables qualifying tenants to serve notices. Section 3 defines a qualifying tenant as a tenant of a flat under a tenancy other than certain tenancies such as protected shorthold tenancies. He accepted that those of the applicants who were tenants of flats were qualifying tenants within the definition, if they were *e* tenants of the relevant premises. He pointed out that a purchase notice could only be served by qualifying tenants where: 'paragraphs (a) and (b) of section 11(1) apply to a relevant disposal affecting any person to which … this Part applied.'

Section 11(1)(a) was concerned with relevant disposals affecting any premises to *f* which at the time of the disposal Pt I applied, and s 1(2) defined the premises to which Pt I applied in this way:

'… this Part applies to premises if—(a) they consist of the whole or part of a building; and (b) they contain two or more flats held by qualifying tenants; and (c) the number of flats held by such tenants exceeds 50 per cent of the *g* total number of flats contained in the premises.'

Mr Lewison submitted that the word 'premises' in s 1 meant, in this case, the complex as a whole meaning Tudor Court, Tudor House and Parr Court. If so, the applicants did not have the requisite majority defined in s 5(6). He also *h* submitted that 'premises' to which Pt I applied had to be comprised within one registered title. There were, he submitted, two estates in land capable of subsisting or of being conveyed, namely an estate in fee simple absolute in possession or a term of years absolute and that, by virtue of s 69 of the Land Registration Act 1925, each separate registered title was a separate estate in land. Therefore the 'premises' could not comprise more than one estate. Thus, he *j* submitted, the premises must be encompassed within one land registration title.

Those latter submissions found favour with the judge. He said:

'In addition, it appears to me that the word "premises" imports a requirement that the building or buildings or parts of buildings constituting the premises to which Part I applies must be held by the same title.

a "Premises" meant originally the commencement of a deed, setting out particulars of the property intended to be transferred thereby; hence it has come to mean the lands granted by a particular deed. If "premises" means something more than a building or part of a building, then I do not think it should be extended to include all the buildings held by a particular landlord, by whatever title they are held. The Act is expropriatory and the court
b should not be "too ready to give too liberal a construction"—see per Goff LJ in *Methuen-Campbell v Walters* [1979] 1 All ER 606 at 610, [1979] QB 525 at 529 dealing of course with the Leasehold Reform Act 1967.'

I cannot accept the conclusion of the judge that title is relevant. The premises must consist of the whole or part of a building which, as was made clear in
c *Belvedere*, could include a garden. The word 'premises' does not have a special meaning. It is a word which over the years has been applied to houses, land, shops, and the like with the result that it has come to mean real property of some kind. Thus the 1987 Act states that a landlord should not make a relevant disposal affecting any real property without serving a s 5 notice, if it consists of the whole or part of a building and it contains two or more flats held by qualifying tenants
d and the number of those flats exceeds 50% of the total. The fact that the building is included within one or more titles is irrelevant. It follows that the question of whether a relevant disposal of premises has been made has to be considered on a building by building basis. Thus when ascertaining whether the applicants were a requisite majority, it is not appropriate to take into account Parr Court. Each
e building must be considered separately.

In this case we are only concerned with Tudor House, and buildings 1 and 4 of Tudor Court and in each case the relevant applicants constituted the requisite majority of tenants in the building. Parr Court was a different building. If the tenants wished to purchase the freehold of that building, the question of whether they could do so would be for them to decide. Any decision they took could not
f affect the rights of the tenants of the other buildings. The contrary conclusion would be surprising. If the original landlord had complied with his duty under s 5, he would, under s 5(5), have had to sever each building from the others. Thus it would be surprising if the procedure laid down after transfer to a new landlord, placed the tenants of Tudor House in the position of being governed by the
g decisions of the tenants of Parr Court.

It follows that the purchase notice was served by the requisite majority of tenants of Tudor House and buildings 1 and 4 of Tudor Court.

The third issue

h A number of attacks were advanced against the content of the purchase notice which, it was submitted, rendered it invalid. Each needs consideration.

The purpose of Pt I of the 1987 Act was to give qualifying tenants a right of first refusal. To achieve that, s 1 placed a duty upon a landlord not to make a relevant disposal without serving a s 5 notice giving to the tenants a right to acquire the
j relevant estate or interest. Section 5 sets out in detail the form of the notice which the landlord has to serve. The offer made in the notice can be accepted by the tenants by serving an acceptance notice as provided for in s 6. In general, such difficulties in procedure which arise are borne by the landlord as he has to draft the relevant s 5 notice.

If the original landlord is in breach of his obligations under ss 1 and 5, the qualifying tenants have the right to acquire the estate from the new landlord by serving a s 12 notice. In this case, it is said that the content of that notice was not in accordance with s 12 and as a result it was invalid. If that be right, then the failure of the original landlord to serve a s 5 notice placed the tenants in a position in which they should not have been put.

I shall come to s 12, but it is important to bear in mind that the purpose of a purchase notice is to give to the new landlord adequate notice that the qualifying tenants of the building wish to acquire the freehold upon the terms of the original disposal or upon terms to be decided by the leasehold valuation tribunal. That was the view of Browne-Wilkinson VC in *Denetower* [1991] 3 All ER 661, [1991] 1 WLR 945, which was a case where it was alleged that the purchase notice was invalid as it failed to define the property adequately. He said:

'Given the complexity of the Act, a draftsman of a notice would be presented with an impossible task in seeking to specify in detail the exact property to be acquired. A notice in terms such as those contained in the present notice gives to the new landlord adequate notice of the claim. Details of the property to be acquired and the terms of the acquisition can in default of agreement be sorted out by the rent assessment committee on an application under s 13(1).' (See [1991] 3 All ER 661 at 669, [1991] 1 WLR 945 at 953.)

A purchase notice must give adequate notice to the new landlord of the qualifying tenants desire to purchase the estate or interest that they should have been offered by the original landlord. That is imperative, in the sense that it must be followed to the letter, but some of the other requirements of s 12 are only directory. That difference can arise as was made clear in *Howard v Secretary of State for the Environment* [1974] 1 All ER 644, [1975] QB 235. In that case, the Secretary of State contended that a notice of appeal was invalid as it failed to comply with the statutory obligation that it 'shall be made by notice in writing to the Minister, which shall indicate the Grounds of Appeal and state the facts upon which it is based'. The Secretary of State contended that the notice was invalid as it failed to provide details of the facts relied on. The court held that it was imperative to serve a notice of appeal in writing, but it was only directory that the notice of appeal had to contain the facts. Thus the notice of appeal was not invalid because it did not include all the facts which were going to be relied on. Lord Denning MR cited this passage from the speech of Lord Penzance in *Howard v Bodington* (1877) 2 PD 203 at 210:

'Now the distinction between matters that are directory and matters that are imperative is well known to us all in the common language of the courts at Westminster ... A thing has been ordered by the legislature to be done. What is the consequence if it is not done? In the case of statutes that are said to be imperative, the Courts have decided that if it is not done the whole thing fails, and the proceedings that follow upon it are all void. On the other hand, when the Courts hold a provision to be mandatory or directory, they say that, although such provision may not have been complied with, the subsequent proceedings do not fail.'

Later Lord Denning MR said ([1974] 1 All ER 644 at 648, [1975] QB 235 at 242):

'The section is no doubt imperative in that the notice of appeal must be in writing and must be made within the specified time. But I think it is only directory as to the contents. Take first the requirement as to the "grounds" a　of appeal. The section is either imperative in requiring "the grounds" to be indicated, or it is not. That must mean all or none. I cannot see any justification for the view that it is imperative as to *one* ground and not imperative as to the rest. If *one* was all that was necessary, an appellant would only have to put in one frivolous or hopeless ground and then amend later to add his real grounds. That would be a futile exercise. Then as to

b　"stating the facts". It cannot be supposed that the appellant must at all costs state all the facts on which he bases his appeal. He has to state the facts, not the evidence; and the facts may depend on evidence yet to be obtained; and may not be fully or sufficiently known at the time the notice of appeal is given. All things considered, it seems to me that the section, in so far as the "grounds" and "facts" are concerned, must be construed as directory only;

c　that is, as desiring information to be given about them. It is not to be supposed that an appeal should fail altogether simply because the grounds are not indicated, or the facts stated. Even if it is wanting in not giving them, it is not fatal. The defects can be remedied later, either before or at the hearing of the appeal, so long as an opportunity is afforded of dealing with

d　them.' (Lord Denning MR's emphasis.)

In *Belvedere*, Hobhouse LJ expressed his views as to the way that the 1987 Act should be construed using different language, but I believe arriving at the same result. He said ([1996] 1 All ER 312 at 335):

e　'By way of final comment I would add that I am strongly attracted to the view that legislation of the present kind should be evaluated and construed on an analytical basis. It should be considered which of the provisions are substantive and which are secondary, that is, simply part of the machinery of the legislation. Further, the provisions which fall into the latter category should be examined to assess whether they are essential parts of the

f　mechanics or merely supportive of the other provisions so that they need not be insisted on regardless of the circumstances. In other words, as in the construction of contractual and similar documents, the status and effect of the provision has to be assessed having regard to the scheme of the legislation as a whole and the role of that provision in that scheme—for example, whether some provision confers an option properly so called,

g　whether some provision is equivalent to a condition precedent, whether some requirement can be fulfilled in some other way or waived. Such an approach when applied to legislation such as the present would assist to enable the substantive rights to be given effect to and would help to avoid absurdities or unjustified lacunae.'

h　A s 12 notice must be in writing and served upon the new landlord in time. Further, it must give adequate notice of the requirement of the qualifying tenants to have the estate or interest in the premises, as defined in s 1, to be transferred to a nominated person. Those requirements are in my view imperative.

j　The first complaint as to the form of the notice made by Twinsectra was a failure to include Flat 7, Tudor House, in the notice. It was said that that failure was fatal to the validity of the purchase notice as a whole. That was accepted to be a valid complaint by the judge.

It is correct that Flat 7, Tudor House, is not included in the heading of the notice and therefore it is possible to read the notice as only relating to six flats in Tudor House. That, to my mind, would not give full effect to the notice that was

given. The notice required Twinsectra to dispose of the freehold interest that
Twinsectra held in 'the above mentioned premises'. Given that what was being *a*
referred to was a freehold interest in Tudor House, it would be absurd to
understand the notice as only requiring part of that freehold interest to be
transferred. Further, if there was doubt, the letter sent with the notice made it
clear that what was being referred to was the whole of the freehold interest in
Tudor House. I therefore conclude that the notice was not invalid on this *b*
ground.

Second, Twinsectra drew attention to s 12(3), which is concerned with an
acquisition where the original disposal included property in addition to premises
to which Pt I of the 1987 Act applied. In such a case, the subsection states that the
purchase notice should require the new landlord to dispose of the estate or
interest 'only' so far as relating to the particular premises and upon terms of the *c*
original disposal subject to such modifications as are necessary or expedient.

Twinsectra submitted that the purchase notice required transfer of all Tudor
Court, whether or not the buildings contained houses or bungalows and that the
inclusion of such units in the notice was a clear breach of s 12(3)(a)(i). That, the
judge held to be correct. *d*

The applicants accept that the purchase notice could advantageously have
been drafted in different terms. However, I believe that the requirements in
s 12(3)(a)(i) are only directory. In this case, the purchase notice included extra
property, but that did not invalidate the notice as a whole. It gave adequate
notice of the requirement of the qualifying tenants that the landlord should
transfer buildings 1 and 4 of Tudor Court and Tudor House. Further, it was clear *e*
that Parr Court was not included. The notice also stated that in the alternative to
disposal to them on the original terms, the terms were to be determined by a
leasehold valuation tribunal. Thus the landlord was given adequate notice that
the tenants of buildings 1 and 4 of Tudor Court and Tudor House wished to
acquire the freehold interest in them. That was in my view sufficient. *f*

Third, Twinsectra submitted that s 12(3)(a)(ii) stated that the purchase notice
should require the terms of the original disposal to be modified. That the notice
did not do. The notice required Twinsectra to—

> 'dispose of the said estate or interest to them [on] (1) the same terms on
> which the said estate or interest was disposed of to Twinsectra Ltd; or (2) *g*
> alternatively on such terms as may be determined by a rent assessment
> committee pursuant to Section 12(3)(b) of the above mentioned enactment.'

Although the notice could have been worded so as to refer to the words of
s 12(3)(a)(ii), there was, in my view, no need for it to do so. For practical
purposes, it was sufficient to make it clear to the landlord that the qualifying *h*
tenants wished to have the estate conveyed to them upon the same terms with
such appropriate modifications as would be agreed or settled by a leasehold
valuation tribunal. That, I believe, was the effect of the notice which was served.
It follows that for practical purposes Twinsectra could have been in no doubt,
after receipt of the notice, that the terms would have to be settled, in default of *j*
agreement, by a leasehold valuation tribunal.

It is an imperative requirement of s 12(3) that the qualifying tenants should
inform the new landlord of the property to be acquired, thereby informing him
that the qualifying tenants desire to acquire the estate or interest in that property
which was transferred to the new landlord in breach of the original landlord's
obligations under s 1. The provisions of s 12(3)(a) and (b) allowing the qualifying

a tenants to either acquire the whole of the property or sever, and to leave it to a leasehold valuation tribunal to sort out the estate or interest or terms, are in my view directory. I therefore conclude that this objection also fails.

I conclude that the notice served was a valid notice by the qualifying tenants of buildings 1 and 4 of Tudor Court and of Tudor House. In those circumstances, I would allow this appeal in so far as it relates to the tenants of those buildings and *b* grant declarations appropriate to the conclusion I have reached.

SIR JOHN MAY. I have had the opportunity of reading Aldous and Staughton LJJ's judgments in draft and I agree with them. Although we are differing from the decision of the learned judge below, I do not think it necessary to add anything on my own account. I too would allow this appeal and grant the *c* declarations to which Aldous and Staughton LJJ have referred.

STAUGHTON LJ. This is the most remarkable case of statutory interpretation that I have ever seen. It is as plain as can be what the purpose of Pt I of the Landlord and Tenant Act 1987 was—to enable tenants of flats to buy their *d* landlord's interest in the building if the landlord proposed to sell it to someone else, and to buy it from the purchaser if the landlord had actually done so. But nowhere does the statute say expressly that the tenants shall have that right against the new landlord. If that omission is fatal, Pt I of the 1987 Act is not worth the paper which it is written on. One can compare what Lord Simonds said in *IRC v Ayrshire Employers Mutual Insurance Association Ltd* [1946] 1 All ER 637 at 641:
e

> 'The case is an unusual one. The section under discussion, sect. 31 of the Finance Act, 1933, is clearly a remedial section, if that is a proper description of a section intended to bring further subject-matter within the ambit of taxation. It is at least clear what is the gap that is intended to be filled and hardly less clear how it is intended to fill that gap. Yet I can come to no other *f* conclusion than that the language of the section fails to achieve its apparent purpose and I must decline to insert words or phrases which might succeed where the draftsman failed.'

We are not left in such a state of impotence in this day and age, or with this *g* statute. As Aldous LJ has pointed out, the long title of the 1987 Act suggests that it confers on tenants rights with respect to the acquisition of their landlord's reversion. And s 12(1), which allows the tenants to serve a notice requiring the new landlord to dispose of his estate or interest to their nominee, by implication enacts that the landlord shall be obliged to comply with the requirement. If this *h* be constructive judicial legislation, then it is an example of what Bingham MR considered in *Belvedere Court Management Ltd v Frogmore Developments Ltd* [1996] 1 All ER 312 at 329 to be called for.

It seems to me that this conclusion is supported by the sidenote to s 12: 'Right of qualifying tenants to compel sale etc. by new landlord.' See also the sidenote *j* to s 17: 'Termination of rights against new landlord or subsequent purchaser.'

There is a strong argument for paying some attention to the marginal notes, while not allowing them to be decisive. After all, they are included in the copy of the bill that is before Parliament, although not susceptible to alteration by vote of the members but only by officials (see Bennion *Statutory Interpretation* (2nd edn, 1992) pp 486, 512–514). However, reliance on marginal notes in a statute for the present has to be regarded as controversial.

The other problems in this appeal relate to the content and extent of the purchase notice which the tenants gave. First, it is essential to decide what is *a* meant by the provision in s 1(2): '... this Part applies to premises if—(a) they consist of the whole or part of a building ...'

Although a different view seems to have been common ground before the judge, in my opinion more than one building cannot, in the ordinary way, be treated as comprised in premises for the purposes of the 1987 Act. There may be *b* an exception for outhouses and the like; but in general I consider that separate buildings must be treated separately. Otherwise there is very likely to be absurdity; the judge doubted whether the 1987 Act could then be made to work.

It follows that there could be no objection to the omission of Parr Court from the tenants' purchase notice, although (i) it was transferred to Twinsectra Ltd by a conveyance which included other buildings which featured in the purchase *c* notice, and (ii) it was registered in the same title as Tudor House and parts of Tudor Court. If Parr Court was properly omitted from the purchase notice, there was no lack of a qualifying majority of tenants for each of the buildings to which Pt I of the 1987 Act applied.

However, the inclusion of buildings 2 and 3 of Tudor Court in the purchase *d* notice was an infringement of s 12(3)(a)(i). That provides that where the original landlord's disposal included property in addition to the premises which the 1987 Act applied to, the notice must require the landlord to dispose of his estate or interest only so far as relating to those premises.

I cannot regard this defect in the tenants' purchase notice as so significant as to render it altogether invalid, for three reasons. In the first place, it was in all *e* probability caused by the original landlord's failure to serve a notice under s 5 and in doing so to sever the transaction as required by sub-s (5) of that section. Secondly, it must have been perfectly obvious to the new landlord which parts of Tudor Court could, and which could not, qualify under Pt I of the 1987 Act. And thirdly, the purchase notice allowed as an alternative that the terms might be *f* determined by a rent assessment committee, which would have jurisdiction under s 13(1)(a) to determine 'the identity of the property to be disposed of'. I would therefore conclude that the purchase notice did not fail to comply with s 12 in any respect that was imperative or mandatory, but at most where it was directory (see *Howard v Secretary of State for the Environment* [1974] 1 All ER 644, [1975] QB 235 and the judgment of Hobhouse LJ in the *Belvedere Court* case [1996] *g* 1 All ER 312 at 335).

It may be that there should strictly have been not one purchase notice served by the tenants but three, relating to the three buildings to which Pt I of the 1987 Act applied. However, I did not understand Mr Lewison to insist that there should have been three separate pieces of paper; and if he pressed the point, I *h* would not have held that any such requirement was imperative or mandatory.

Finally, there was a complaint that the purchase notice, by reason of the way it was drafted, referred only to flats 1 to 6 in Tudor House and not to flat 7. I would reject that argument for the reason given by Aldous LJ. All told, I would allow this appeal, and grant declarations as he proposes. *j*

Appeal allowed. Leave to appeal to the House of Lords refused.

L I Zysman Esq   Barrister.

Cargill International SA and another v Bangladesh Sugar and Food Industries Corp

QUEEN'S BENCH DIVISION (COMMERCIAL COURT)

MORISON J

13, 14, 15 MAY, 7 JUNE 1996

Contract – Bond – Performance bond – Plaintiffs providing performance bond in relation to contract for the supply and delivery of goods to the defendant – Bond liable to be forfeited for any breach of contract – Plaintiffs subsequently breaching contract and defendant making call on bond – Defendant not suffering loss to extent of value of bond – Whether plaintiff entitled to recover overpayment.

The plaintiff companies successfully tendered for the supply of sugar to the defendant governmental organisation. The tender offer was accepted subject to the receipt of a performance bond covering 10% of the total cost and freight value and was subsequently confirmed in writing by a contract dated 16 June 1994. The contract stipulated that the cargo would be transported in a vessel which was not more than 20 years old and would be delivered before 15 September 1994. Clause 13 provided that the plaintiffs' performance bond was liable to be forfeited if they failed to fulfil any of the terms and conditions of the contract and also if they were responsible for any loss or damage suffered by the defendant. In the event, the vessel used was over 20 years old and arrived some days late. The defendant therefore rejected the shipment and made a call on the bond under cl 13. The plaintiffs thereafter applied to the Commercial Court for, inter alia, an injunction restraining the defendants from drawing on the bond and a declaration that the defendant was not entitled to make any call on the bond or to retain any money so received on the ground that it had suffered no loss since the market for sugar had fallen, the defendants had replaced the rejected sugar at less than the contract price, and the plaintiffs themselves had paid the extra insurance required for the over-age vessel. The judge ordered the trial of certain preliminary issues, including whether the defendant was entitled to make a call for the full amount of the performance bond and, if so, whether it was entitled to retain all the moneys received by it.

Held – The defendant was entitled to make a call for the full amount of the performance bond, even if the breach of contract had caused it no loss, since the bond was not intended to represent an 'estimate' of the amount of damages to which it might be entitled for such breach but was a 'guarantee' of due performance. However, it was implicit in the nature of a bond that, in the absence of clear words to a different effect, when the bond was called there would at some stage in the future be an 'accounting' between the parties to determine their rights and obligations. Furthermore, in the instant case, there was an implied contractual term that the defendant would account to the plaintiffs for the proceeds received under the bond and would only retain the amount of any loss suffered as a result of the plaintiffs' breach. Accordingly, if the defendant had suffered no damage as a result of the plaintiffs' breach, any money received by it under the bond was recoverable the plaintiffs (see p 565 *b*, p 568 *h j*, p 573 *d e* and p 574 *a b*, post).

Australasian Conference Association Ltd v Mainline Constructions Pty Ltd (in liq) (1978) 141 CLR 335, *Wood Hall Ltd v Pipeline Authority* (1979) 141 CLR 443 and

State Trading Corp of India Ltd v E D & F Man (Sugar) Ltd (1981) Times, 22 July considered. *a*

Notes
For nature and effect of performance guarantees and bonds, see 41 *Halsbury's Laws* (4th edn) para 960.

Cases referred to in judgment
Australasian Conference Association Ltd v Mainline Constructions Pty Ltd (in liq) (1978) 141 CLR 335, Aust HC.
Comdel Commodities Ltd v Siporex Trade SA (No 2) [1990] 2 All ER 552, [1991] 1 AC 148, [1990] 3 WLR 1, HL.; *affg* [1990] 1 All ER 216, CA.
General Surety and Guarantee Co Ltd v Francis Parker Ltd (1977) 6 Build LR 16. *c*
Owen (Edward) Engineering Ltd v Barclays Bank International Ltd [1978] 1 All ER 976, [1978] QB 159, [1977] 3 WLR 764, CA.
Public Works Comr v Hills [1906] AC 368, [1904–7] All ER Rep 919, PC.
State Trading Corp of India Ltd v E D & F Man (Sugar) Ltd (1981) Times, 22 July, [1981] CA Transcript 307. *d*
Trafalgar House Construction (Regions) Ltd v General Surety and Guarantee Co Ltd [1995] 3 All ER 737, [1996] AC 199, [1995] 3 WLR 204, HL.
Wood Hall Ltd v Pipeline Authority (1979) 141 CLR 443, Aust HC.
Workers Trust and Merchant Bank Ltd v Dojap Investments Ltd [1993] 2 All ER 370, [1993] AC 573, [1993] 2 WLR 702, PC. *e*

Cases also cited or referred to in skeleton arguments
Comdel Commodities Ltd v Siporex Trade SA [1996] CA Transcript 196.
Congimex Cia Geral de Comercio Importadora e Exportadora SARL v Tradax Export SA [1983] 1 Lloyd's Rep 250, CA; *affg* [1981] 2 Lloyd's Rep 687.
Dunlop Pneumatic Tyre Co Ltd v New Garage and Motor Co Ltd [1915] AC 79, [1914– *f* 15] All ER Rep 739, HL.
Harbottle (R D) (Mercantile) Ltd v National Westminster Bank Ltd [1977] 2 All ER 862, [1978] QB 146.
I E Contractors Ltd v Lloyds Bank plc [1990] 2 Lloyd's Rep 496, CA; *affg* [1989] 2 Lloyd's Rep 205.
Potton Homes Ltd v Coleman Contractors Ltd (1984) 28 Build LR 19, CA. *g*
Siporex Trade SA v Banque Indosuez [1986] 2 Lloyd's Rep 146.
Stockloser v Johnson [1954] 1 All ER 630, [1954] 1 QB 476, CA.

Preliminary issues
By order made by Rix J on 2 May 1996 two preliminary issues were ordered to be *h* tried in an action brought by the plaintiffs, Cargill International SA, Geneva Branch and Cargill (HK) Ltd (the seller), for an injunction restraining the defendant, Bangladesh Sugar and Food Industries Corp (the buyer), from drawing on a performance bond provided by the seller as part of a contract for the sale and delivery of goods, and a declaration that the buyer was not entitled *j* to make any call on the bond or to retain any payment so received. The facts are set out in the judgment.

Stephen Males (instructed by *Middleton Potts*) for the seller.
Ajmalul Hossain (instructed by *Beale & Co*) for the buyer.

Cur adv vult

a
7 June 1996. The following judgment was delivered.

MORISON J. This is a trial of preliminary issues, in accordance with the order of Rix J dated 2 May 1996. The case raises, I think, an important question of law which is as yet undecided. The question is whether money paid under a performance bond to a party who has suffered no damage is recoverable by the
b other party. Lord Bridge in *Comdel Commodities Ltd v Siporex Trade SA (No 2)* [1990] 2 All ER 552 at 558, [1991] 1 AC 148 at 166 thought the point was 'certainly arguable'. The facts relevant to this trial may be shortly stated.

The facts
By a contract in writing and dated 16 June 1994 the plaintiffs (the seller) whom
c I shall also call Cargill, agreed to sell to the defendant (the buyer), the Bangladesh Sugar and Food Industries Corp, 12,500 metric tons (± 5% at seller's option) of sugar c & f(c) (cost, freight and commission) free out of Chittagong at a price of $US400·97 per metric ton. The defendant is a governmental organisation; it invited tenders for the supply of sugar. Cargill's tender offer of 28 May 1994 was
d accepted in principle, and a letter of intent was issued dated 30 May 1994. In that letter it was made clear that unless within seven days Cargill submitted a performance guarantee covering 10% of the total c & f value endorsed by an authorised bank of Bangladesh, the letter of intent would automatically be cancelled and Cargill's bid-bond (representing 1% of the value of the cargo) forfeited. Cargill arranged for the Dhaka branch of Banque Indosuez (the bank)
e to provide a letter of guarantee for $US526,273·15. The terms of the guarantee, the format of which had been stipulated in an annexure to the invitation to tender, were contained in a letter dated 4 June 1994, and are:

> '... we, Banque Indosuez, Dhaka hereby undertake and guarantee due
> signing and acceptance and performance of the contract by the supplier
f > [defined as Cargill] and we unconditionally and absolutely bind ourselves:
> I) To make payment of USD 526,273·15 ... to the corporation [the
> defendants] or as directed by [the defendants] in writing without any
> question whatsoever. II) To keep this guarantee valid and in force till 3
> (Three) months after arrival of the total quantity of contracted goods at the
g > Jetty of Chittagong Port and extendable for further period if so required by
> the [defendant]. The Guarantee is unconditional and it is expressly
> understood that the sole judge for deciding whether the suppliers have
> performed the contract and fulfilled the terms and conditions of the contract
> will be the [defendant] ... III) It is specifically stipulated and understood by
> us that any grant of time or indulgence to the suppliers without reference to
h > us shall not in any manner tend to absolve us from our liability to make
> payment as stipulated above under this guarantee.'

Thereafter, the parties negotiated the terms of a contract of sale which is contained in a written agreement dated 16 June 1994. Although this was a sale
j c & f(c) and, therefore, essentially an agreement for procurement and delivery of documents of title to goods, there was an express promise by the seller to ensure arrival of the cargo of sugar at Chittagong Port, Bangladesh before 15 September 1994 'positively'. There was a stipulation in the contract that the cargo would be transshipped in a vessel which was not more than 20 years old. There were, of course, many other stipulations governing the transportation, discharge and inspection of the goods. Clause 10 of the contract provided for payment by an irrevocable, confirmed and workable letter of credit payable at sight, such

document to be provided within seven days of the signing of the contract. Clauses 13 and 16(1) of the contract are of immediate relevance to the preliminary issues:

> '13. PERFORMANCE BOND: The SELLER has already submitted a performance Bond to the BUYER in the form of Bank Guarantee equivalent to 10% of the total offered C & F(C) value of ... Sugar. The Performance Bond is liable to be forfeited by the BUYER if the SELLER fails to fulfil any of the terms and conditions of this contract ... and also if any loss/damage occurs to the BUYER due to any fault of the SELLER ... 16. SPECIAL CLAUSE: i) The arrival period/ time is the essence of this contract. Therefore the SELLER shall strictly adhere to the arrival period/time stipulated in this contract. If the SELLER fails to do so, the BUYER shall be entitled to recover from the SELLER liquidated damage @ 2% of the contract value, as agreed, of the undelivered goods for each month or part of the month during which the delivery of the goods will be in arrear, or to terminate the contract and call back the LETTER OF CREDIT and also to forfeit the Performance Bond mentioned at clause 13.'

There is a dispute between the parties as to the performance of this contract. The buyer says that the vessel did not arrive at the Chittagong Port on time; and, furthermore, the vessel in which the goods were shipped was more than 20 years old. The buyer says it is entitled to forfeit the performance bond pursuant to cl 13. The seller contends that any late arrival was due to the buyer's default; and although the vessel was older than stipulated for, that was due to the buyer's failure in arranging, timeously, for a letter of credit which complied with the contract. That, in turn, delayed them in fixing a vessel for the voyage, and at that late stage only over-age vessels were available. The sellers say that the buyer has suffered no loss from any alleged breach. The market for sugar had fallen so that when the buyer rejected the goods he was able to replace them with sugar at a lower price than he had contracted to pay. As to the age of the vessel, the sellers had paid the extra insurance required for a vessel over 20 years old; the vessel had arrived and no loss has fallen on the buyer by reason of this alleged breach.

Both parties alleged that the other had repudiated the contract of sale. Their dispute involved a number of excursions into the courts, as the sellers tried to prevent the buyer from making a demand under the performance bond. Further, Cargill say that they have sold the cargo at a loss and have invoked the arbitration clause, under which all disputes arising out of the contract were to be referred to the Council of the Refined Sugar Association 'for settlement in accordance with the Rules relating to Arbitration'. Proceedings were extant in two jurisdictions. Sensibly, the parties have reached agreement for the orderly determination of their disputes by an agreement reached between them dated 12 April 1996. Under that agreement, Cargill have provided a bank guarantee for the same amount as the performance bond, which has been cancelled. The bank guarantee is to be treated in substitution for the performance bond in all respects and, therefore, the rights of the parties in relation thereto are governed by the terms of the bond and of the contract of sale. The parties agreed to discontinue all proceedings outside of the English courts.

The issues

The issues which the parties have agreed, and the court has decided, should be determined as preliminary issues are these.

a On the assumption that the plaintiffs were in breach of contract in one or both of two respects, namely the over-age of the vessel and its late arrival at the port of Chittagong: (1) whether the defendant was entitled to make a call for the full amount of the performance bond, if the breach or breaches of contract (a) caused no loss to the defendants, (b) caused some loss to the defendants which was less than the amount of the performance bond, or (c) caused some loss to the

b defendant which was equal to or greater than the amount of the performance bond; (2) whether, in the event of the defendant having obtained payment under the performance bond as a result of any such call as it was entitled to make, the defendant was entitled to retain (a) all of the moneys received by it, (b) only such amount as was equal to the amount of the loss suffered by it, or (c) some other, and if so what, amount.

c
The arguments

For the seller, Cargill, Mr Males submitted as follows. (1) Clause 13 of the sale contract specifies the circumstances in which the buyer is entitled to call on the bond and retain the proceeds. The fact that the bond is itself unconditional, as

d between the buyer and the bank, is immaterial. The bank is not concerned with the merits of any dispute under the sale contract; it is not in a position to judge whether the buyer is rightly asserting a breach and will, in the absence of any successful legal intervention by the seller, be entitled, and obliged, to pay on a buyer's demand, at least if that demand is made in good faith. (2) On a proper construction of cl 13, or, if necessary, as a matter of an implied term: A. The

e buyer was not entitled to make a call on the bond unless two conditions were satisfied, namely (a) a breach of contract by Cargill and (b) loss or damage suffered by the buyer as a result of that breach. B. Even if the buyer was to make a call on the bond, it would not be entitled to retain the proceeds thereof save to the extent that the same two conditions were satisfied. (3) Alternatively, the

f seller argues that if, on its true construction, cl 13 entitled the buyer to make a call on the bond and retain the proceeds regardless of the loss suffered, then the bond operates as a penalty, and the sellers are entitled to relief from that penalty in the form of an order for repayment of the amount of the bond, less any damage actually proved to have been suffered by the buyer as a result of the sellers' breach or breaches of contract.

g For the buyer, it was argued by Mr Hossain that: (1) on a proper construction of the contract of sale, this was not a contract for the delivery of sugar, rather a delivery of documents of title to sugar shipped on board a vessel chartered by the sellers. The date of arrival of the cargo stipulated in cl 5 ('The SELLER will ensure arrival of the vessel with the contracted quantity … at the Chittagong Port,

h Bangladesh before 15th September 1994 positively.') provided a date from which the date of shipment could be deduced. There was no date of shipment stipulated; subject to certain exclusions, the cargo could have been shipped from, say, Brazil or South Korea (as was in fact the case) and the duration of the voyage could vary substantially. The shipment date could, thus, vary. (2) Clause 13 of

j the contract specified the events which gave rise to the buyer's right to forfeit the performance bond. The first event was if the seller failed to fulfil any of the terms and conditions of the contract (whether or not damage was thereby caused). The second event, and it was a separate event as the words 'and also if' made clear, was if any loss or damage was suffered by the buyer ('occurs to the buyer') due to any fault of the seller. The second event provided for circumstances, such as negligent misstatement, which did not necessarily involve a breach of a term of

the contract. The right to forfeit arose if there was a breach of contract which
caused no loss or no recoverable loss. If the seller was at fault, in any respect, and   *a*
the buyer sustained a loss thereby, even if that loss would not have been
recoverable as a head of damage, the right to forfeit arose. (3) In any event, the
performance bond was unconditional and the buyer had an unfettered right to
call on the bank to honour its obligations thereunder. (4) The sellers were, in
effect, seeking relief from forfeiture. Such relief was only available where   *b*
proprietary or possessory rights are involved. This is a commercial contract
freely negotiated between parties at arm's length, not a contract or dispute
relating to land. (5) This was not in the nature of a penalty clause. The buyer
had a right to forfeit the bond whenever there was a breach, regardless of loss.
The buyer does not seek to make any claim under cl 13; it is content to forfeit the
bond.   *c*

I start with the commercial purpose of a performance bond. There is a wealth
of authority concerned with the question whether and in what circumstances an
interlocutory injunction may be granted (1) against the bank which issued the
bond to restrain it from paying in accordance with its terms, and (2) against the
beneficiary of the bond to prevent it from calling the bond.   *d*

The court will not grant an injunction in either case unless there has been a lack
of good faith. The justification for this lies in the commercial purpose of the
bond. Such a bond is, effectively, as valuable as a promissory note and is intended
to affect the 'tempo' of parties' obligations; in the sense that when an allegation
of breach of contract is made (in good faith), the beneficiary can call the bond and
receive its value pending the resolution of the contractual disputes. He does not   *e*
have to await the final determination of his rights before he receives some
moneys. On an application for an injunction, it is, therefore, not pertinent that
the beneficiary may be wrong to have called the bond because, after a trial or
arbitration, the breach of contract may not be established; otherwise, the court
would be frustrating the commercial purpose of the bond. The concept that   *f*
money must be paid without question, and the rights and wrongs argued about
later, is a familiar one in international trade, and substantial building contracts. A
performance bond may assume the characteristics of a guarantee, especially, if
not exclusively, in building contracts, where the beneficiary must show, as a
prerequisite for calling on the bond, that by reason of the contractor's
non-performance he has sustained damage (see *Trafalgar House Construction*   *g*
(Regions) Ltd v General Surety and Guarantee Co Ltd [1995] 3 All ER 737, [1996] AC
199).

However, it seems to me implicit in the nature of a bond, and in the approach
of the court to injunction applications, that, in the absence of some clear words
to a different effect, when the bond is called, there will, at some stage in the   *h*
future, be an 'accounting' between the parties in the sense that their rights and
obligations will be finally determined at some future date. The bond is not
intended to represent an 'estimate' of the amount of damages to which the
beneficiary may be entitled for the breach alleged to give rise to the right to call.
The bond is a 'guarantee' of due performance. If the amount of the bond is not   *j*
sufficient to satisfy the beneficiary's claim for damages, he can bring proceedings
for his loss. As far as I am aware, and no case was cited to me to suggest
otherwise, the performance bond is not intended to supplant the right to sue for
damages. Indeed, such a contention would conflict with what I believe to be the
commercial purpose of these instruments. Mr Hossain submitted that the
buyer's rights were exhausted when the bond was called, but he could give no

a support for the proposition; and he had, I think, no satisfactory explanation as to why his clients should have wished so to restrict their damages. The bond could be called in any number of circumstances, at least some of which could have caused his clients losses substantially in excess of the bond value. If he were right, then, presumably, the beneficiary would decline to call the bond; yet serious loss caused by a breach of contract was the very event for which the bond was

b required and given in the first place. I reject, entirely, his submission on this point, both as being without legal foundation and as lacking in commercial good sense.

Therefore, the question arises as to why, if the beneficiary can sue to recover what he has actually lost, the seller (in this case) should not be able to recover any overpayment. It would seem, in principle, correct that if a performance bond

c does not exhaust one party's rights, it should not exhaust the rights of the other party.

What I perceive to be correct in principle, is fortified by authority. In *State Trading Corp of India Ltd v E D & F Man (Sugar) Ltd* (1981) Times, 22 July Lord Denning MR said (in an injunction case):

d 'I may say that performance bonds fulfil a most useful role in international trade. If the seller defaults in making delivery, the buyer can operate the bond. He does not have to go to far away countries and sue for damages, or go through a long arbitration. He can get the damages at once which are due to him for breach of contract. The bond is given so that, on notice of default

e being given, the buyer can have his money in hand to meet his claim for damages for the seller's non-performance of contract. If he receives too much, that can be rectified later at an arbitration. The courts must see that these performance bonds are honoured.'

If the court had considered that an 'overpayment' could not be recovered, its

f approach to the grant of injunctive relief might have been different. Almost all cases where such relief has been sought are ones where the plaintiff is saying that there has been no breach, or that he has the benefit of some exclusion clause, or that the other contracting party has not suffered any loss. None of these contentions will suffice, partly because, I think, the court always recognised that the bonds affected the 'tempo' of the parties' obligations but not their substantive

g rights.

Support may also be found in two Australian cases. In the first, *Australasian Conference Association Ltd v Mainline Constructions Pty Ltd (in liq)* (1978) 141 CLR 335, the question before the court was whether the employer under a building contract made with a builder (Mainline) which subsequently went into

h liquidation was entitled to pay sub-contractors out of the performance bond moneys which it had called, and been paid by the builder's bank. It was the bank's position, inter alia, that the employer was obliged to account to it for any surplus after the sub-contractors had been paid off. The employer conceded that it was not entitled to retain any surplus, and the court clearly believed that to be correct,

j as did the other two parties. The court's conclusion was that the issue had to be determined by reference to the contract between the employer and Mainline; it concluded that the surplus should be released to Mainline and not to the bank. In a subsequent building case (an injunction case), *Wood Hall Ltd v Pipeline Authority* (1979) 141 CLR 443, the court held that the beneficiary was entitled to call the bond but that once paid, the 'money must be held as security for the contractor's due and faithful performance of the work' (see 141 CLR 443 at 454 per Gibbs J).

Both these cases lend (limited) support for the proposition that moneys paid
under a performance bond are designed to be used in accordance with the *a*
provisions of the contract and that any surplus is for the account of the party
which provided the bond.

In Hudson and Wallace *Hudson's Building and Engineering Contracts* (11th edn,
1994) vol 2, Ch 17 'Bonds and Guarantees', para 17·078 it is said:

> *b*
> 'It is generally assumed, and there is no real reason to doubt, that the
> Courts will provide a remedy by way of repayment to the other contracting
> party if a beneficiary who has been paid under an unconditional bond is
> ultimately shown to have called on it without justification: "I do not doubt
> that in such an event the money would be repayable, but it is not so certain
> it would be repayable with interest" [See *General Surety and Guarantee Co Ltd* *c*
> *v Francis Parker Ltd* [1977] 6 Build LR 16 at 21 per Donaldson J].'

The learned editor expresses the view that the claim for repayment can be put
in one of two ways:

> 'First, the payment by the bank ... being required in most cases under the *d*
> principal construction contract itself, or sometimes by a side-contract, must
> be regarded as being made by the bank as agent for the contractor and
> subject ... to an implied term for repayment if not in fact due. Secondly, it
> has been seen that in the case of a *conditional* bond, equity would not permit
> recovery of a sum in excess of the true debt or damages, as being a penalty, *e*
> so that by analogy in a case where the payment under the bond was
> obligatory and unavoidable, and indeed brought about by the owner's own
> act in making the call, it would be only logical to order repayment for the
> same reasons. Such a claim could also be based in quasi-contract on wider
> principles of unjust enrichment and unconscionability ... In cases where
> there has been no default at all on the part of the contractor, there would *f*
> additionally be a total failure of consideration for the payment. Questions of
> interest and costs pose considerable difficulties however.'   (Author's
> emphasis.)

In Keating *Building Contracts* (6th edn, 1995) p 275–276 under a paragraph
heading 'On demand bonds' the editor says: *g*

> 'Problems that they raise include whether an employer who calls an on
> demand bond has to account for the amount received, and if so, to whom
> and upon what legal principles ... It is submitted that, where in relation to a
> building contract a contractor has at the request of the employer procured *h*
> an unconditional bond, the court may depending on all the circumstances be
> able to imply into the building contract a term that the employer should
> account to the contractor for the proceeds of the bond. There may in some
> circumstances alternatively be a collateral contract to equivalent effect. If
> this were correct, where the employer's loss was either nil or less than the
> amount recovered under the bond, the contractor would be entitled to *j*
> recover in part or in whole.'

In a footnote, the editor indicates that—

> 'an implied term or collateral contract might more readily be found in
> building contracts than in contracts of sale. In building contracts, an on

a   demand bond is more likely to be seen as intended for security for performance than as a discount.'

No authority is cited for this note, although I would have thought it was based on some dicta of Lord Denning MR in *Edward Owen Engineering Ltd v Barclays Bank International Ltd* [1978] 1 All ER 976 at 982, [1978] QB 159 at 170 (an injunction case), where he said:

b

'It is obvious that that course of action can be followed, not only when there are substantial breaches of contract, but also when the breaches are insubstantial or trivial, in which case they bear the colour of a penalty or liquidated damages; or even when the breaches are merely allegations by the customer without any proof at all; or even when the breaches are
c   non-existent.   The performance guarantee then bears the colour of a discount on the price of 10 per cent or 5 per cent or as the case may be. The customer can always enforce payment by making a claim on the guarantee and it will then be passed down the line to the English supplier.   This possibility is so real that the English supplier if he is wise, will take it into
d   account when quoting his price for the contract.'

Whilst this case played an important part in the development of the court's practice not to interfere, at an interlocutory stage, with the workings of performance bonds I do not understand Lord Denning MR to be expressing a view as to the right of a supplier to recover any overpayment, and this is
e   reinforced to an extent, I think, by his reference to 'penalty'. Further, he referred to this case when he gave judgment in *State Trading Corp of India Ltd v ED & F Man (Sugar) Ltd*.   He gave no indication that what he was saying there was at odds with, or was intended to qualify, what he said in the earlier case.

In Benjamin *Sale of Goods* (4th edn, 1992) para 23-218, there is the following
f   passage:

'As the making of an excessive demand is, basically, a breach of the beneficiary's underlying contract, the amount ought to be regarded as repayable to the account party rather than to the bank.'

The learned editors assume that the overpayment may be recovered and infer
g   that the only question is whether the account party (the seller) or the bank is entitled to receive the repayment.   They rely upon the two Australian cases as supporting the conclusion that it is the account party and not the bank which is entitled to the moneys.

As a matter of general principle, therefore, in the light of the commercial
h   purpose of such bonds, the authorities to which I have referred and the textbook comments, I take the view that if there has been a call on a bond which turns out to exceed the true loss sustained, then the party who provided the bond is entitled to recover the overpayment.   It seems to me that the account party may hold the amount recovered in trust for the bank, (where, for example, the bank had not
j   been paid by him) but that does not affect his right to bring the claim in his own name.   In the normal course of events, the bank will have required its customer to provide it with appropriate security for the giving of the bond, which would be called upon as soon as the bank was required to pay.   On the facts of this case, no question of a trust or agency will arise.   In principle, I take the view that the account party is always entitled to receive the overpayment, since his entitlement is founded upon the contract between himself and the beneficiary.

I turn therefore to the contract between the parties. Under cl 13 the bond was 'liable to be forfeited ... if the SELLER fails to fulfil any of the terms and conditions of this contract ... and also if any loss/damage occurs to the BUYER due to any fault of the SELLER'. It seems to me that on a proper construction of this clause, there is no indication that it was the parties' intention that the bond would either satisfy the whole of the buyer's damages (see above), or prevent the seller from recovering any overpayment. The word 'forfeit' might be apt to suggest that once called, the bond moneys had 'gone' for good. But if it had been the intention of the parties to produce a result whereby the buyer could both call on the bond and sue for damages, whereas the seller forfeited his right to any overpayment, then much plainer words would have been required to take this case away from the general principles as I perceive them to be. That being so, it seems to me that treating the two parts of the clause disjunctively, and treating the right to forfeit as arising if either there was a breach or if any loss or damage occurred to the buyer due to any fault of the seller (which might not be a breach) would make commercial good sense. The buyer is stipulating clearly that, as between himself and the seller, all he needs to show to be entitled to call on the bond is a breach of contract; he need not show damage (although damage will almost always follow); if, on the other hand, say through a misrepresentation by the seller, damage was caused to the buyer then the right to call the bond was conferred by the second half of the clause. But in either event, there will be an 'accounting' at trial or arbitration to ensure that the buyer has not been underpaid or overpaid.

Further, it seems to me that the more natural reading of the clause is to treat the events giving rise to a right to 'forfeit' the bond as disjunctive. The words 'also if' would otherwise be unnecessary and the words 'due to any fault of the SELLER' would not lie easily with a construction which treated the only triggering event as a breach of contract ('fails to fulfil any of the terms and conditions of this contract').

In relation to cl 16, I cannot accept Mr Males' submission that the right to forfeit the bond is subject to the same conditions as to loss being suffered as provided for by cl 13. The words 'mentioned at' are, I think, no more than a reference back to cl 13, which is headed 'PERFORMANCE BOND'. I do not read these words as meaning 'the right to forfeit in the circumstances set out in clause 13'. It seems to me that cl 16 clearly provides that if the arrival period/time stipulated in the contract is not adhered to then the buyer will either be entitled to liquidated damages or to terminate the contract and call back the letter of credit and forfeit the bond. Again, the right, as between the parties, of the buyer to call on the bond is not conditional upon him showing any damage. On termination he is entitled to receive immediate payment of the bond moneys and sue for damages, and the seller, conversely, is entitled to recover any overpayment.

Although this point does not arise for decision, it seems to me unclear whether cll 16 and 13 are cumulative. If the goods arrive late and the buyer affirms the contract is he entitled to both liquidated damages and to forfeit the bond. It could be said that cl 16 was a self contained code for what happened on late arrival. I am asked to assume that the goods arrived late in breach of contract and that an over-age vessel was used to carry them, also in breach of contract. The latter breach would fall within the first part of cl 13; the former within cl 16. Even if cl 16 was self contained, and no argument to this effect was addressed to me, then the right to forfeit the bond existed by reason of the latter breach. If the two clauses operate cumulatively, so that where there is late arrival and the buyer affirms the contract, it will be seen that the buyer not only receives liquidated *a* damages (which would presumably be a genuine pre-estimate of the damages sustained) but also obtains a windfall payment of the moneys under the bond.

In my judgment, under no circumstances is the performance bond to provide to the buyer a windfall payment. That cannot have been the parties' intention: the bond could not be in stronger terms: the bank unconditionally and absolutely bound itself to make payment only to the buyer 'without any question

b whatsoever' and 'it is expressly understood that the sole judge for deciding whether the suppliers have performed the contract and fulfilled the terms and conditions of the contract will be' the buyers. As Lord Denning MR said, this type of bond can be called upon whenever there is a breach or perceived breach, however trivial. It surely cannot have been the parties' intention that the buyer who could so easily call on the bond should be able to retain for his own benefit

c a windfall profit. If that had been the parties' intention, then either no party would trade on those terms or the buyer would always pay 10% more than the market price.

The basis upon which recovery may be made in respect of an overpayment is, I think, contractual rather than quasi contractual. It seems to me that it is

d necessary to imply into the contract that moneys paid under the bond which exceeded the buyer's actual loss would be recoverable by the seller. I am content to adopt Mr Males' formulation of the term which is to be implied into the sale contract, as a matter of necessity or on the basis that the implication of such a term was so obvious that its incorporation in the contract went without saying: 'that the buyer will account to the seller for the proceeds of the bond, retaining

e only the amount of any loss suffered as a result of the seller's breach of contract.'

It is unnecessary to consider the interesting argument advanced on penalty. Had I been persuaded that there was a term of the contract between the parties which enabled the buyer to call on the bond when he had suffered no damage, and to retain the moneys, I would have held the provision to have been penal. In

f *Workers Trust and Merchant Bank Ltd v Dojap Investments Ltd* [1993] 2 All ER 370 at 376, [1993] AC 573 at 582 Lord Browne-Wilkinson said:

> 'There is clear authority that in a case of a sum paid by one party to another under the contract as security for the performance of that contract, a provision for its forfeiture in the event of non-performance is a penalty from
> *g* which the court will give relief by ordering repayment of the sum so paid, less any damage actually proved to have been suffered as a result of non-completion: *Public Works Comr v Hills* [1906] AC 368, [1904–7] All ER Rep 919.'

It seems to me that it is a fortiori where, as here, there has been a 'mere' breach

h not giving rise to non-completion of the contract. I do not, I hope without discourtesy to Mr Hossain's interesting argument, need to consider the line of cases on forfeiture of moneys already paid under a contract, or of analogous cases relating to the forfeiture of deposits. If provisions of a contract are penal, within principles which are well known, then the power to grant relief from their effect

j is undoubted. Relief from the effects of a penalty clause is akin to the right to relief from forfeiture in those cases where the court would grant specific performance of the contractual obligations, namely where the contract confers some proprietary or possessory interest.

In my view, the answer to the questions which I have been asked to determine are as follows. (1) Whether the defendant was entitled to make a call for the full amount of the performance bond, if the breach or breaches of contract (a) caused

no loss to the defendants, (b) caused some loss to the defendants which was less
than the amount of the performance bond, (c) caused some loss to the defendant
which was equal to or greater than the amount of the performance bond. Yes, in
all cases. (2) Whether, in the event of the defendant having obtained payment
under the performance bond as a result of any such call as it was entitled to make,
the defendant was entitled to retain: (a) all of the moneys received by it; (b) only
such amount as was equal to the amount of the loss suffered by it; or (c) some
other, and if so what, amount. The answer is (b).

I am grateful to both counsel for their interesting and helpful arguments to
which I have not done full justice in this judgment.

Order accordingly.

K Mydeen Esq   Barrister.

Practice Note

a

QUEEN'S BENCH DIVISION

LORD BINGHAM OF CORNHILL CJ, BLOFELD AND CRESSWELL JJ

15 OCTOBER 1996

b

Practice – Chambers proceedings – Queen's Bench Division – Chambers applications and appeals – Inter partes applications and appeals – Listing – General list – Chambers warned list – Estimate of length of hearing – Papers for perusal by judge – Skeleton argument or chronology.

c

LORD BINGHAM OF CORNHILL CJ gave the following direction at the sitting of the court. In order to expedite the hearing of summonses and appeals by the Queen's Bench judge in chambers, the procedure has been reorganised.

The existing practice direction ([1989] 1 All ER 1120, [1989] 1 WLR 359) is

d replaced by the following.

1. All inter partes applications and appeals to the Queen's Bench judge in chambers will initially be entered in a general list. They will be listed for hearing in Room E 101 or some other room at the Royal Courts of Justice on Tuesdays or Thursdays.

e Whenever it appears or is agreed that any application or appeal is likely to last more than 30 minutes, it will be transferred to the chambers warned list. If the parties agree that it is likely to last more than 30 minutes, the applicant/appellant must as soon as practicable, and in any event not later than 12 noon on the working day before the date given, transfer the case to the chambers warned list. If the parties do not so agree, or agree less than 24 hours before the date given,

f the parties must attend on the date given.

2. Causes in the chambers warned list will be listed in the Daily Cause List. This will be done by the clerk of the lists when he prepares the following day's list at 2.15 pm. The clerk of the lists will, where it is possible, accept 'offers' in the week in which the matter appears in the warned list. Fixtures will only be given

g in exceptional circumstances.

3. In order to ensure that a complete set of papers in proper order is available for the judge before hearing such applications and appeals, the parties must in advance of the hearing lodge in Room W 11/W 13 a bundle properly paged and indexed in date order containing copies of the following documents. (i) The

h notice of appeal or, as the case may be, the summons; (ii) the pleadings (if any); (iii) copies of all affidavits (together with copy exhibits thereto) upon which any party intends to rely; and (iv) any relevant order made in the action.

The bundle should be agreed. The originals of all affidavits intended to be relied on should be bespoken or produced at the hearing and all exhibits should

j be available. A skeleton argument and, where that would be helpful, a chronology should be lodged.

The bundle must be lodged not later than 48 hours after the parties have been notified that the case is to appear in the warned list. For cases to be heard in the general list, the bundle must be lodged at least 48 hours before the hearing. Skeleton arguments (with chronology) must be lodged not later than 24 hours before the hearing.

4. Except with leave of the judge, no document may be adduced in evidence
or relied on unless a copy of it has been lodged and the original produced.   a

Dilys Tausz   Barrister.

a   # Burrows v Brent London Borough Council

HOUSE OF LORDS

LORD BROWNE-WILKINSON, LORD KEITH OF KINKEL, LORD GRIFFITHS, LORD JAUNCEY
OF TULLICHETTLE AND LORD STEYN

b
22, 23 JULY, 31 OCTOBER 1996

Housing – Local authority houses – Possession – Security of tenure – Secure tenancy –
Possession order for non-payment of rent – Local authority and tenant entering into
agreement that authority would not evict if rent and instalments of arrears paid –
c   *Tenant failing to pay instalments – Whether agreement creating new secure tenancy –*
Whether local authority required to obtain new possession order before evicting tenant
for non-payment – Housing Act 1985, s 85(2)(3)(a).

The respondent was the tenant under a secure tenancy of a flat owned by the
d appellant council, and under Pt IV of the Housing Act 1985 her tenancy could not
be terminated by the landlord without a court order for possession. The
respondent fell into arrears with the rent and on 29 January 1992 the council
obtained a final order for possession in the county court under which the
respondent was ordered to pay arrears of £2,427·63 and to give up possession on
12 February. In accordance with a practice common among local authority
e landlords, the council entered into an agreement with the respondent on 5
February under which she agreed to pay the rent together with instalments of the
arrears. The agreement further stated that if payments ceased or were irregular
the council would seek to evict the respondent. The respondent failed to make
payments as required and the council issued a warrant for possession which was
f executed on 8 June 1994. Thereafter, the respondent brought an action against
the council seeking a declaration that she remained a tenant of the premises, a
mandatory injunction to be allowed back into them and damages for unlawful
eviction, contending that the effect of the February agreement was to create a
new secure tenancy or licence by operation of law which could only be
terminated by a further court order for possession. The county court judge
g granted the declaration and injunction sought. The council appealed to the
Court of Appeal, contending that the combined effect of the possession order and
the February agreement was that the respondent became a tolerated trespasser
who could continue in possession provided she fulfilled the conditions of the
agreement. The court dismissed the appeal on the grounds that since the
h respondent's original secure tenancy terminated on 12 February 1992 when she
was required to give up possession under the order made on 29 January 1992, the
February agreement could only take effect as an agreement to permit the
respondent to stay on after the original tenancy terminated on 12 February 1992
under a new right of occupation, either by way of a new tenancy or as a licensee,
j but in either case protected as a new secured tenancy under the 1985 Act. The
council appealed to the House of Lords, contending that since under s 85(2) and
(3)(a)[a] of the 1985 Act the court had power 'at any time before the execution of
the order' to postpone the date of possession and could make a suspended order
conditional on making 'payments in respect of occupation after the termination

_____

a   Section 85, so far as material, is set out at p 580 *j* to p 581 *a*, post

of the tenancy (mesne profits)', the original possession order remained in force
during the period of the agreement.

Held – An agreement between a local authority and a secure tenant who was in
arrears to the effect that a possession order (whether suspended on conditions or
immediate and unconditional) obtained by reason of the arrears would not be
executed provided the tenant observed the conditions of the agreement did not
operate to create a new secure tenancy requiring the local authority to obtain a
further possession order in the event of the tenant not observing the conditions.
Section 85(2) and (3)(a) of the 1985 Act demonstrated that the original tenancy
terminated by a possession order could be revived at any time until the original
order was executed. Since the possession order of 29 January 1992 had not been
executed at the time the agreement of 5 February was entered into the
respondent could have applied to the court at any time for an order varying the
date on which possession was to be given, thereby retrospectively reviving the
old secure tenancy together with its covenants. The parties to the agreement did
not have any intention of creating a new tenancy or licence; they only intended
that execution of the order should be deferred so long as the respondent complied
with the agreed conditions. It followed that while the respondent complied with
the agreed conditions the council was prevented from taking any steps which
would finally put an end to her right to apply to the court for an order reviving
the tenancy. By making the agreement of 5 February the appellant council did
not grant a new tenancy or licence to the respondent and the possession order
had therefore been properly enforced. The appeal would accordingly be allowed
(see p 581 j to p 582 d, p 583 e to p 584 d j to p 585 a b and p 588 c d, post).

Notes
For recovery of possession of a house let under a secure tenancy, see 27(2)
Halsbury's Laws (4th edn reissue) paras 1168–1190.

For the Housing Act 1985, s 85, see 21 *Halsbury's Statutes* (4th edn) (1990
reissue) 122.

Cases referred to in opinions
Greenwich London BC v Regan (1996) 28 HLR 469, CA.
Thompson v Elmbridge BC [1987] 1 WLR 1425, CA.

Appeal
Brent London Borough Council appealed from the decision of the Court of
Appeal (Butler Sloss, Otton and Auld LJJ) ((1995) 27 HLR 748) delivered on 12 July
1995 dismissing the council's appeal from the decision of Judge Finestein QC
sitting in the Willesden County Court on 19 August 1994 whereby he made a
declaration that the respondent, Diane Sarah Elizabeth Burrows, was a secure
tenant of the basement and ground floor flat at 28 Oxford Road, London, NW6,
and granted her an injunction ordering the council to re-admit her to the
premises. The facts are set out in the opinion of Lord Browne-Wilkinson.

Ashley Underwood and *Bryan McGuire* (instructed by *Paul Barber,* Wembley) for the
council.
David Neuberger QC and *William Geldart* (instructed by *Daniel & Harris*) for Miss
Burrows.

a   Their Lordships took time for consideration.

31 October 1996. The following opinions were delivered.

LORD BROWNE-WILKINSON. My Lords, this appeal raises a question as to the rights of a tenant of a dwelling house let by a local authority. Under Pt IV of
b   the Housing Act 1985 such tenancy is a 'secure tenancy'. A landlord cannot terminate a secure tenancy otherwise than by obtaining from the court an order for possession. Local authority landlords often obtain an order for possession against a secure tenant but then agree with the tenant that, whilst certain conditions are observed, the order will not be executed. The question is whether such an agreement operates so as to create a new secure tenancy which can only
c   be terminated if the landlord obtains a further order from the court.

On 6 August 1984 Brent London Borough Council (Brent) granted a tenancy of the basement and ground floor flat at 28 Oxford Road, London, NW6, jointly to the respondent, Miss Burrows, and her husband, Richard Allen. In January 1986 Mr Allen left the premises leaving Miss Burrows with her children. She fell
d   behind with her rent.

On 29 January 1992 Brent obtained a final order for possession against Miss Burrows and Mr Allen in the Willesden County Court. The order directed that the plaintiff should recover the sum of £2,427·63 being arrears of rent and costs. It further ordered 'that the defendant do give the plaintiff possession of the said land on' 12 February 1992. Thus, the order was not suspended: it was an
e   immediate order for possession on 12 February.

On 5 February 1992 Brent came to an arrangement with Miss Burrows, which was recorded in writing. It was made on a form which was designed for use by tenants prior to a possession hearing. The memorandum of the arrangements stated:

f
'I acknowledge that there are arrears of £2,313·41 on my rent account as at 27.1.92 … I understand that in these circumstances the London Borough of Brent will seek a possession order and judgment against me for the full amount of the arrears from the County Court. I agree to pay the rent charge of £2·67 due every week and, in addition, to reduce the arrears by regular
g   instalments of £3·00 per week. [There was then a section of the document which was only applicable when the document was to be signed before an order was made, which was crossed out.]   IF PAYMENTS CEASE OR ARE IRREGULAR THE COUNCIL WILL SEEK TO EVICT.'

Miss Burrows failed to make the payments in accordance with the agreement
h   of 5 February 1992. Brent issued a warrant for possession informing her that she would be evicted on 8 June 1994. Miss Burrows moved out on 7 June. The order was executed. She returned on 8 June 1994 to find herself locked out and the premises boarded up. She thereupon applied to the Willesden County Court seeking to have the bailiff's warrant and the possession order set aside but those
j   proceedings were dismissed.

On 4 July 1995 Miss Burrows commenced this action seeking a declaration that she remained a tenant and damages for unlawful eviction. She also sought a mandatory injunction to be allowed back into the premises. At the heart of her case was the contention that the effect of the arrangements made on 5 February 1992 was to create a new tenancy or licence by operation of law. By his judgment of 19 August 1994 Judge Finestein QC agreed with Miss Burrows' submissions

and ordered her reinstatement. He made the declaration and injunction asked
and referred the matter to the district judge for an assessment of damages.

In the course of his judgment, the judge found that: (1) Miss Burrows
understood, and this was part of the express agreement, that eviction would be a
penalty if she was in default; (2) it was not contemplated by her that when she
entered into the arrangement on 5 February she was entering into a tenancy; (3)
when she left the premises on 7 June 1994 it was not her state of mind that a new
tenancy had come into being as a result of the arrangement of 5 February 1992.

Brent appealed to the Court of Appeal (Butler Sloss, Otton and Auld LJJ)
((1995) 27 HLR 748), which dismissed the appeal. Brent appeal to your Lordships'
House.

Sections 79, 80 and 81 of the 1985 Act define the conditions which have to be
satisfied in order to constitute a 'secure tenancy'. Those conditions were satisfied
in the present case. It is important to note that under s 79(3) the provisions of
Pt IV of the Act apply to a 'licence to occupy a dwelling-house ... as they apply in
relation to a tenancy'. Therefore nothing in this case turns on the distinction
between a licence and a tenancy; if, by making the agreement not to enforce the
possession order, the local authority is to be taken to have granted a licence for
the tenant to continue in occupation the position will be just the same as if they
had granted a tenancy.

Section 82 provides as follows:

'(1) A secure tenancy which is either—(a) a weekly or other periodic
tenancy, or (b) a tenancy for a term certain but subject to termination by the
landlord, cannot be brought to an end by the landlord except by obtaining an
order of the court for the possession of the dwelling-house or an order under
subsection (3).

(2) Where the landlord obtains an order for the possession of the
dwelling-house, the tenancy ends on the date on which the tenant is to give
up possession in pursuance of the order ...'

It is important to note that the secure tenancy ends, not on the date on which
possession is in fact given up, but on the date on which the order requires the
defendant to give up possession.

Section 84 provides that the court shall not make an order for possession save
on one of the grounds mentioned in Sch 2 which include non-payment of rent.
In addition, in the case of non-payment of rent the court must also be satisfied
that it is reasonable to make the order. An order for possession cannot be made
unless the ground on which an order is to be sought has been specified in a prior
notice to be served on the tenant (see ss 83 and 84(3)).

Section 85 is central to the argument in this case. It provides:

'(1) Where proceedings are brought for possession of a dwelling-house let
under a secure tenancy [for the non-payment of rent] the court may adjourn
the proceedings for such period or periods as it thinks fit.

(2) On the making of an order for possession of such a dwelling-house on
any of those grounds, or at any time before the execution of the order, the
court may—(a) stay or suspend the execution of the order, or (b) postpone
the date of possession, for such period or periods as the court thinks fit.

(3) On such an adjournment, stay, suspension or postponement the
court—(a) shall impose conditions with respect to the payment by the tenant
of arrears of rent (if any) and rent or payments in respect of occupation after

a the termination of the tenancy (mesne profits), unless it considers that to do so would cause exceptional hardship to the tenant or would otherwise be unreasonable, and (b) may impose such other conditions as it thinks fit.

(4) If the conditions are complied with, the court may, if it thinks fit, discharge or rescind the order for possession ...'

b The argument for Miss Burrows, which the Court of Appeal accepted, is as follows. The order of 29 January 1992 directed that possession should be given on 12 February 1992. Therefore, by virtue of s 82(2), Miss Burrows' original secure tenancy terminated on that day. Yet, under the agreement of 5 February 1992 Miss Burrows remained in occupation of the house paying a 'rent charge' of £2·67 per week for such occupation. That agreement could not be effective to c alter or vary the order itself, but could only take effect as an agreement to permit Miss Burrows to stay on after her existing tenancy had terminated on 12 February 1992. This right of continued occupation can only be explained on the ground that the agreement conferred on Miss Burrows a new right of occupation, either by way of a new tenancy or as a licensee, it mattered not which. If it was a new d tenancy, it was a new secure tenancy; if it was only a licence, by virtue of s 79(3) Miss Burrows enjoyed the same protection as if it were a tenancy. In either event, the new secure tenancy or new licence could only be terminated by Brent applying to the court for a further court order terminating the new right (see s 82(1)).

The argument for Brent before the Court of Appeal was that the agreement of e 5 February was simply an agreement by Brent not to execute the possession order, provided that Miss Burrows complied with the agreed conditions. As the judge's findings demonstrated, Miss Burrows never intended that the agreement should create a tenancy and it was absurd to imagine that Brent, by granting Miss Burrows an indulgence in relation to a possession order which they had only just f obtained, should have intended to create a new right of occupation necessitating a further application to the court in order to obtain possession. In the period during which Brent agreed to forbear from enforcing the order, Miss Burrows was a mere 'tolerated trespasser'.

The Court of Appeal, whilst accepting that the crucial factor in determining Miss Burrows' rights was the intention of the parties, rejected Brent's contention g on the ground that it gave rise to manifest absurdities. At the rate for payment of arrears stipulated by the agreement of 5 February 1992 it would have taken Miss Burrows 14 years to pay them off during which time, if the argument of Brent was correct, she would be a mere trespasser. As a trespasser she would enjoy none of the rights of a tenant. Thus she could not require Brent to repair the house. She h would have no rights under the Defective Premises Act 1972. She would qualify as a homeless person under s 58 of the 1985 Act. Brent would have no right to evict her for any breach of the covenants in her tenancy, but only for breach of the conditions contained in the agreement of 5 February 1992. On the case as presented to the Court of Appeal their conclusion was inevitable. But the j significance of s 85 was not drawn to their attention. As a result of the recent decision of the Court of Appeal in *Greenwich London BC v Regan* (1996) 28 HLR 469 Brent advanced before your Lordships a far more compelling argument, viz: (1) although under s 82(2) the original tenancy came to an end on 12 February 1992 (being the date fixed by the order for giving possession) that was not necessarily the final position; (2) under s 85(2) the court has power to postpone the date of possession; (3) this power to postpone the date for possession is exercisable by the

court 'at any time before the execution of the order'. This shows that the power
can be exercised even after the date for possession specified in the order has
passed and the tenancy has thereby been terminated by virtue of s 82(2); (4) this
conclusion is re-enforced by s 85(3)(a), which postulates that the court can make
a suspended order conditional on making 'payments in respect of occupation
after the termination of the tenancy (mesne profits)'. This demonstrates that
there can come a time when, although the old tenancy has terminated and the
former tenant has remained in possession for which he is liable to pay mesne
profits as a trespasser, the court can until the original order is executed make an
order varying the date for the giving of possession thereby reviving the
previously defunct tenancy; (5) therefore, so far as the tenant is concerned, the
crucial event is the execution of the order for possession. Down to that date the
tenant can apply to the court for a variation of the original order substituting a
new date on which possession is to be given thereby reviving the old secure
tenancy. This revived tenancy will not be terminated under s 82 until the new
date for giving possession occurs; (6) that such revival of the old tenancy is
possible is demonstrated by s 85(4) which plainly assumes that on discharge or
rescission of the original order for possession, the old secure tenancy will revive.

I accept this analysis of the effect of s 85, which is largely derived from the
judgment of Millett LJ in *Greenwich London BC v Regan*. In that case, an order for
possession was made against a secure tenant, the order (as construed by the
Court of Appeal) providing for the giving of possession to be postponed so long
as arrears of rent were paid by instalments and the current rent was paid. The
tenant having failed to comply with the conditions in the order, the landlord and
the tenant agreed variations in the amount of the payments which were to be
made. The tenant having breached the terms of the order and the agreed terms,
the landlord applied for a warrant of execution. The tenant sought a stay of
execution. He submitted that the old tenancy had come to an end when he failed
to comply with the conditions imposed by the order (see *Thompson v Elmbridge BC*
[1987] 1 WLR 1425). He then submitted, in reliance on the decision of the Court
of Appeal in the instant case, that by agreeing to allow the former tenant to
remain in possession the landlord had created a new tenancy or licence and
therefore could not obtain possession under the old order.

The Court of Appeal in *Regan's* case, after analysing s 85 in much the same
terms as I have summarised above, posed the question whether the parties could,
by agreement, revive the expired tenancy without an order of the court. The
Court of Appeal held (in my view rightly) that the parties could not by agreement
vary the terms of the court order. But they held that by agreeing the new
conditions, the landlord waived the right to complain that failure to comply with
the conditions specified in the order constituted a breach of those latter
conditions. Consequently, there being no breach of the conditions imposed by
the order upon which the landlord could rely, the order remained in force, the
date for giving possession had not passed and therefore the old tenancy had not
been terminated. They distinguished the decision in the present case on the
ground that they were dealing with a suspended conditional order of the court
whereas in the instant case there is an immediate, unconditional order for
possession.

One factor which weighed heavily with the Court of Appeal in *Regan's* case (to
which I also attach importance) is the practical effect of the decision under appeal,
ie any consensual variation of an order for possession produces a new secure
tenancy or licence. Local authorities and other public housing authorities try to

a conduct their housing functions as humane and reasonable landlords. In so doing they frequently need to grant indulgences to their tenants to reflect changes in the tenants' circumstances. When applying for possession orders for non-payment of rent local authorities agree to the order being suspended upon the payment of arrears, the rate of payment being adjusted to meet the means of the tenant at the date of the order. If the tenant subsequently loses his job, the landlord will often

b be willing to reduce the rate of payment of arrears. Why should this not be done by agreement? Yet the effect of the local authority agreeing to such a reduction will be that the tenant, whilst keeping up his payments at the agreed reduced rate, will be in breach of the conditions specified by the order at the higher rate. If so his old tenancy will be terminated. On the view of the law adopted by the Court of Appeal in the present case, a new secure tenancy requiring a new order will

c come into existence. Similarly where, as with Miss Burrows, the court makes an immediate order for possession but the landlord grants an indulgence by agreeing not to execute the order immediately: if the Court of Appeal decision is correct, the effect of granting the indulgence is to create a new tenancy or licence and the local authority will have to obtain a new possession order. The practical result

d therefore will be either that the local authority will be reluctant to make reasonable and humane concessions by agreement or in every case will have to make an application to the court to vary the existing order so as to ensure that the old tenancy is not brought to an end. I find it impossible to believe that Parliament intended to produce such an unreasonable regime, penalising sensible agreements out of court and requiring repeated applications to an already

e overstretched court system.

What, then, is the correct legal analysis? I start from the proposition that where a former tenant is by agreement allowed to remain in possession of the demised property after the termination of the tenancy, the question in each case is quo animo the parties have so acted: depending upon the circumstances, their

f conduct may give rise to a new tenancy, a licence or some other arrangement. In the present case, on 5 February 1992 the parties plainly did not intend to create a new tenancy or licence, but only to defer the execution of the order so long as Miss Burrows complied with the agreed conditions. It cannot be right to impute to the parties an intention to create a legal relationship such as a secure tenancy or licence unless the legal structures within which they made their agreement

g force that conclusion.

A secure tenancy protected by Pt IV of the 1985 Act is not like an ordinary tenancy. It can only be terminated by an order of the court ordering possession to be given on a particular date or in a particular event. But even determination by order of the court is not final. Until the possession order is executed, the court

h can by variation of its order change the date on which possession is to be given and thereby revive a secure tenancy which has already been terminated. During the period between the date specified by the order for the giving of possession and the date on which the order is executed there is a period of limbo: the old tenancy has gone but may yet be revived by a further order of the court varying

j the date for possession. If the parties reach an agreement as to the continued occupation of the premises by the tenant during that limbo period, what intention is to be imputed to them?

In my judgment, little guidance is to be obtained from the cases where a tenant holds over after the termination of an ordinary tenancy where there is no possibility that the expired tenancy can revive. The position in relation to secure tenancies is sui generis. In my judgment, the agreement can and should take effect in the way the parties intend, ie it is an agreement by the landlords that, *a* upon the tenant complying with the agreed conditions, the landlords will forbear from executing the order, ie from taking the step which would finally put an end to the tenant's right to apply to the court for an order reviving the tenancy. There is no need to impute to the parties an intention to create a new tenancy or licence: the retention of possession and the payment of rent relate to occupation under the old tenancy which is in limbo but which may be revived. In these *b* circumstances I think it is fair to characterise the former tenant as a trespasser whom the landlord has agreed not to evict—a 'tolerated trespasser'—pending either the revival of the old tenancy or the breach of the agreed conditions.

Once the effect of s 85 is appreciated, the absurdities which led the Court of Appeal not to accept that Miss Burrows could be a tolerated trespasser disappear. Technically the old secure tenancy is, during the limbo period, no longer in *c* existence and therefore neither the repairing covenants in the tenancy nor the Defective Premises Act 1972 apply. But the tenant can at any time apply to the court for an order varying the date on which possession is to be given and thereby retrospectively revive the old secure tenancy, together with its covenants. If the tenant has complied with the agreed conditions, there can be little doubt that the *d* court would make the required order. Moreover, the tenant will not be a homeless person within s 58(2) of the 1985 Act because the tenant will be occupying the residence by virtue of any 'rule of law giving him the right to remain in occupation' (see s 58(2)(c)). If the tenant were in breach of any of the covenants in the old secure tenancy, Brent could apply to vary the order so as retrospectively to revive the old tenancy together with its covenants. *e*

Finally, there is a method (albeit a clumsy one) whereby the order for possession even if an immediate unconditional order, can be discharged or rescinded if so desired under s 85(4). The power in that subsection to discharge or rescind only arises 'if the conditions are complied with', a requirement which cannot be satisfied in the case of an unconditional order. But there is no reason *f* why the order cannot be discharged by consent or, if such consent is not forthcoming, by the court varying the original order so as to impose the agreed conditions and then discharging the varied order.

It was submitted that the fact that the tenancy was granted to Miss Burrows jointly with Mr Allen whereas the agreement of 5 February 1992 was made with *g* Miss Burrows alone, indicated that the agreement must have given rise to a new tenancy with Miss Burrows alone. Therefore there must be a new tenancy. However, since in my view on its proper analysis the arrangement contained in the agreement of 5 February 1992 gave rise to no new tenancy with anyone, that factor is irrelevant. *h*

I therefore reach the conclusion that, in the absence of special circumstances, an agreement by a landlord not to enforce strictly an order for possession, whether conditional or unconditional, does not create a new secure tenancy or licence under Pt IV of the 1985 Act. Brent, by making the agreement of 5 February 1992, did not grant a new tenancy or licence to Miss Burrows as from *j* 12 February 1992. It follows that the possession order of 29 January 1992 was properly enforced. I would therefore reverse the decisions of the Court of Appeal and the trial judge and dismiss Miss Burrows' action.

As Brent have succeeded on a point not taken in the courts below, I propose that there should be no order as to costs before your Lordships' House and the order for costs made in the courts below should remain undisturbed.

LORD KEITH OF KINKEL. My Lords, for the reasons given in the speech
a prepared by my noble and learned friend Lord Browne-Wilkinson, which I have
read in draft and with which I agree, I would allow this appeal.

LORD GRIFFITHS. My Lords, for the reasons given in the speeches prepared
by my noble and learned friends Lord Browne-Wilkinson and Lord Jauncey of
b Tullichettle, which I have read in draft and with which I agree, I would allow this
appeal.

LORD JAUNCEY OF TULLICHETTLE. My Lords, this appeal raises an
important question of principle in relation to the effect of forbearance by a
landlord to enforce an order for possession granted under s 82(2) of the Housing
c Act 1985. I have had the advantage of reading in draft the speech of my noble and
learned friend Lord Browne-Wilkinson and I gratefully adopt his account of the
factual background giving rise to this appeal.

Section 82(1) of the 1985 Act provides that a secure tenancy such as was
enjoyed by the respondent cannot be brought to an end by the landlord without
d an order of the court for possession. Section 82(2) provides:

'Where the landlord obtains an order for the possession of the
dwelling-house, the tenancy ends on the date on which the tenant is to give
up possession in pursuance of the order.'

This provision is mandatory with the result that occupation by the tenant after
e the date specified in the order ceases to be attributable to the original secure
tenancy. In view of the terms of that subsection the Court of Appeal ((1995) 27
HLR 748) concluded that the effect of the agreement of 5 February 1992 was to
grant to the respondent a new lease or licence to occupy which enjoyed the same
protection as the terminated tenancy. Before this House, Mr Underwood, for the
f appellants, advanced an argument which had not been deployed before the Court
of Appeal and which relied upon detailed consideration of s 85, which provides,
inter alia, as follows:

'(1) Where proceedings are brought for possession of a dwelling-house let
under a secure tenancy on any of the grounds set out in Part I or Part III of
g Schedule 2 (grounds 1 to 8 and 12 to 16: cases in which the court must be
satisfied that it is reasonable to make a possession order), the court may
adjourn the proceedings for such period or periods as it thinks fit.
(2) On the making of an order for possession of such a dwelling-house on
any of those grounds, or at any time before the execution of the order, the
h court may—(a) stay or suspend the execution of the order, or (b) postpone
the date of possession, for such period or periods as the court thinks fit.
(3) On such an adjournment, stay, suspension or postponement the
court—(a) shall impose conditions with respect to the payment by the tenant
of arrears of rent (if any) and rent or payments in respect of occupation after
the termination of the tenancy (mesne profits), unless it considers that to do
j so would cause exceptional hardship to the tenant or would otherwise be
unreasonable, and (b) may impose such other conditions as it thinks fit.
(4) If the conditions are complied with, the court may, if it thinks fit,
discharge or rescind the order for possession ...'

Subsections (1) and (2) cover three different situations which are in turn
reflected in sub-s (3). If the proceedings for a possession order are adjourned in

circumstances covered by sub-s (1) the secure tenancy will continue in force but the court is required by sub-s (3)(a) to impose conditions as to payment of any *a* arrears of rent and of future rent, subject always to questions of exceptional hardship and unreasonableness.   If the tenant fails to comply with these conditions the landlord will be entitled to go back to the court and seek an order for possession. If during the initial proceedings the court makes an order, but postpones the date of possession the tenancy will not be terminated under s 82(2) *b* until any condition imposed under sub-s (3) has been breached by the tenant (see *Thompson v Elmbridge BC* [1987] 1 WLR 1425). However, the court's power to make an order postponing the date of possession is not restricted to exercise on the first application for an order for possession but may be exercised on the application of either party at any time prior to execution of that order and even after the secure tenancy has ended by reason of s 82(2). This is made clear by the *c* words in s 85(2) 'or at any time before the execution of the order' (see also *Greenwich London BC v Regan* (1996) 28 HLR 469 at 476 per Millett LJ). In such an event the secure tenancy is reinstated or revived subject to any conditions imposed under sub-s (3).

However, whereas an order postponing the date of possession necessarily *d* affects the operation of s 82(2), an order staying or suspending the execution of an order for possession on a stated date has no effect on the operation of that subsection but merely postpones execution so long as the conditions of suspension are complied with. The reference to mesne profits in sub-s (3)(a) as contrasted with that to payment of rent is relevant to the period of occupation after such a suspension as well as to any period of occupation between the *e* termination of a tenancy under s 82 and the subsequent postponement of the date of possession under s 85(2)(a). The words are, in my view, particularly significant since they show that the 1985 Act contemplates the court requiring post-termination payments to be made by an occupier which are of a nature wholly inconsistent with the existence of any tenancy in his or her favour. *f* Subsection (4) is similarly inconsistent with the creation of a new tenancy because a discharge of an order for possession would only be effective if the tenancy to which the order related had not been superseded by a new tenancy. I therefore conclude that the court has power under s 85 not only to permit an individual to continue to occupy premises after a secure tenancy has determined without the creation of a new tenancy in his or her favour but also to revive the determined *g* secure tenancy on compliance by the individual with any stipulated conditions. During the period between the termination of the secure tenancy and either its revival or the execution of the order for possession the occupation of the former secure tenant derives not from any new lease but from the provisions of the 1985 Act which cast him in the role of what my noble and learned friend Lord *h* Browne-Wilkinson aptly describes as 'a tolerated trespasser'. Can the same result be achieved by agreement between the parties without the need to invoke the power of the court under s 85?

In *Greenwich London BC v Regan* the Court of Appeal considered an order for possession, which Millett LJ construed as one 'requiring the delivery of *j* possession to be postponed, in the first instance for 28 days and thereafter until there was a breach of the conditions of the order' (see (1996) 28 HLR 469 at 476). The tenant failed to comply with the terms of the order and the parties thereafter entered into a fresh agreement whereby the tenant agreed to make weekly payments of a lesser amount than those stipulated in the order. Some time later the tenant again defaulted on his payments and the landlords sought to execute a the order for possession. The tenant argued that the agreement between the parties varying the order had created a new tenancy and that therefore a new order for possession was required. This argument was rejected. Millett LJ, after pointing out the impracticability of a landlord applying to the court whenever he granted some indulgence to a tenant, went on to say (at 477):

b 'If, after a breach occurs and the tenancy is determined, and the Local Authority subsequently reaches agreement with the tenant the effect of which is to waive the breaches, then in my opinion in accordance with ordinary principle such breaches must be treated as if they had not occurred. It would follow from this that the tenancy must thereafter be treated as not having been determined. This appears to me to be the effect of an order c which leaves the determination of the tenancy to the occurrence of a breach of the conditions of the order, and which leaves the occurrence of a breach to be dependent upon whether the landlord treats it as such or agrees to waive the breach. If the landlord does more and agrees not only to waive a breach of the conditions on which the order has been suspended, but also to accept payment of the arrears by smaller instalments and over a longer d period than those provided for by the order, he thereby consents to such payments being treated as sufficient compliance with the order. This must either prevent the tenancy from being brought to an end or, if it has already been determined, prevent it from being so regarded.'

e He summarised the position in four paragraphs of which I repeat only two (at 478):

f '2. The Local Authority may waive the breach, in which case the tenancy continues as if there had been no breach. This is so whether the Local Authority agrees in advance not to treat the particular failure to comply with the terms of the order as bringing the tenancy to an end, or agrees to waive the breach after it has occurred. In either case the tenancy is treated as if it has not determined.

3. The local authority may agree a consensual variation in the terms of the order. It will be a question of fact in every case whether the agreement which the parties had entered into should be characterised as an agreement which creates a new tenancy, or merely as one which provides for a variation g in the terms on which the order has been suspended, waiving any past breaches and treating the tenancy as if it has not been terminated.'

Mr Neuberger QC, for the respondent, did not challenge, correctly in my view, the decision in *Greenwich London BC v Regan* but sought to distinguish it upon the h ground that whereas a landlord could waive a condition imposed on a tenant in a court order the parties could not by agreement alter the impact of s 82(2) on an unconditional order for possession. It followed that any agreement between the parties as to the respondent's continued occupation must constitute a new tenancy. Mr Underwood argued that such a result would be not only contrary to j the intention of the parties but to the whole scheme of the 1985 Act.

My Lords, I agree with Mr Neuberger that the impact of s 82(2) cannot be altered by agreement between the parties. However, for the reasons which I have already elaborated, that subsection cannot be looked at in isolation from the other sections, in particular s 85, of Pt IV of the 1985 Act. The whole scheme of that Part is to afford protection to the secure tenant and that is achieved in s 85 by conferring on the court flexible powers to continue an existing secure tenancy, to

revive a determined secure tenancy or to create a state of statutory limbo which
will afford to a defaulting tenant an opportunity to have restored to him all the   *a*
benefits of the secure tenancy when he has complied with stipulated conditions.
Parliament cannot have intended to penalise a landlord who acted within the
spirit of the 1985 Act by granting indulgences to defaulting tenants without going
through time-wasting and expensive court proceedings. Furthermore, a tenant
who has reached an agreement advantageous to himself is not thereby prevented   *b*
from making an application to the court under s 85(2) or (4). In this case the judge
found as a fact that neither party contemplated that the agreement of 5 February
1992 created a new tenancy and I can therefore see no reason why it should not
be given the same effect as an order of the court in similar terms suspending
execution of the order for possession of 29 January 1992. Such a result would
accord entirely with the spirit of the relevant statutory provisions, would be   *c*
consistent with the intention of the parties and would preserve all the
respondent's rights under sub-ss (2), (3) and (4) of s 85. For these reasons and for
those given by my noble and learned friend Lord Browne-Wilkinson I would
therefore allow the appeal.

LORD STEYN. My Lords, I have had the advantage of reading in draft the   *d*
speech prepared by my noble and learned friends Lord Browne-Wilkinson and
Lord Jauncey of Tullichettle. For the reasons they give I too would reverse the
decision of the Court of Appeal and dismiss the action.

Appeal allowed.   *e*

                                        Celia Fox   Barrister.

a

R v Crown Court at Liverpool and another, ex parte Cooke

QUEEN'S BENCH DIVISION

b LEGGATT LJ AND SIR IAIN GLIDEWELL

28 MARCH, 3 APRIL 1996

Nuisance – Statutory nuisance – Complaint to justices – Proceedings against local authority – Compensation for statutory nuisance – Extent of period of offence for which
c *compensation payable – Whether magistrates entitled to consider whole of period for which statutory nuisance existing – Powers of Criminal Courts Act 1973, s 35 – Environmental Protection Act 1990, s 82.*

The applicant council tenant contacted the respondent local authority alleging
d that the state of her accommodation, being subject to rodent infestation, damp and egress of foul water/sewage, gave rise to a statutory nuisance within the Environmental Protection Act 1990, and that the nuisance was the council's responsibility as landlord. On 24 October 1994 the applicant gave notice pursuant to s 82(6)[a] of the 1990 Act of intention to bring proceedings if the nuisance had not been remedied within 21 days of the date of that notice. She subsequently
e issued a complaint and, at the hearing before the magistrates, the council pleaded guilty. On 18 January 1995 the magistrates ordered the council to carry out specified works to abate the nuisance and to pay the applicant £3,000 in compensation pursuant to s 35[b] of the Powers of Criminal Courts Act 1973. The council appealed and the Crown Court reduced the compensation to be paid to
f £250, concluding that the period in respect of which compensation was payable was that between the issue of the complaint and the date of sentence. The applicant applied for judicial review of that decision, on the grounds that the judge had wrongly concluded that the award of compensation should not be such as to fully compensate the applicant on the basis used in awarding damages in the county court (ie the whole period for which the statutory nuisance was alleged
g to have existed).

Held – When assessing compensation under s 35 of the 1973 Act in respect of an offence of statutory nuisance by a landlord under s 82 of the 1990 Act, the court should take into account only the injury, loss or damage caused by the
h continuation of the nuisance from the date when the period stated in the complainant's s 82(6) notice expired to the date of the hearing. However, if the complainant should delay for more than six months after the expiry of the s 82(6) notice before making complaint to the magistrates, then the offence which could form the basis for compensation would not commence earlier than a date six
j months before the complaint was made. It followed that there was no warrant for considering the whole of the period for which the nuisance was alleged to have existed, and the application would be dismissed accordingly (see p 593 *e*, p 594 *h* to p 595 *fj* and p 598 *j* to p 599 *b*, post).

---

a   Section 82, so far as material, is se out at p 592 *a* to *g*, post
b   Section 35, so far as material, is set out at p 593 *c d*, post

Notes

For proceedings by a person aggrieved in respect of a statutory nuisance, see 38   *a*
Halsbury's Laws (4th edn) para 412.

For the Powers of Criminal Courts Act 1973, s 35, see 12 *Halsbury's Statutes* (4th edn) (1994 reissue) 601.

For the Environmental Protection Act 1990, s 82, see 35 *Halsbury's Statutes* (4th edn) (1993 reissue) 908.   *b*

Cases referred to in judgments

Botross v Fulham London Borough (1994) 16 Cr App R (S) 622, DC.
Davenport v Walsall Metropolitan BC (17 March 1995, unreported), DC.
Herbert v Lambeth London Borough (1991) 13 Cr App R (S) 489, DC.   *c*
Northern Ireland Trailers Ltd v Preston County Borough [1972] 1 All ER 260, [1972] 1 WLR 203, DC.
R v Inner London Crown Court, ex p Bentham [1989] 1 WLR 408, DC.
R v Newham Justices, ex p Hunt, R v Oxted Justices, ex p Franklin [1976] 1 All ER 839, [1976] 1 WLR 420, DC.
Sandwell Metropolitan BC v Bujok [1990] 3 All ER 385, [1990] 1 WLR 1350, HL; *affg*   *d*
(1989) 88 LGR 521, DC.

Cases also cited or referred to in skeleton arguments

Bond v Chief Constable of Kent [1983] 1 All ER 456, [1983] 1 WLR 40, DC.
Calabar Properties Ltd v Stitcher [1984] 3 All ER 759, [1984] 1 WLR 287, CA.   *e*
Chiodi's personal representative v De Marney (1988) 21 HLR 6, CA.
Coventry City Council v Doyle [1981] 2 All ER 184, [1981] 1 WLR 1325, DC.
Crutchley v Tonks (1993) 15 Cr App R (S) 627, CA.
Davies v Peterson (1988) 21 HLR 63, CA.
Hyde v Emery (1984) 6 Cr App R (S) 206, DC.   *f*
Joyce v Liverpool City Council, Wynne v Liverpool City Council [1995] 3 All ER 110, [1996] QB 252, CA.
R v Donovan (1982) 3 Cr App R (S) 192, CA.
R v Horsham Justices, ex p Richards [1985] 2 All ER 1114, [1985] 1 WLR 986, DC.
R v Kneeshaw [1974] 1 All ER 896, [1975] QB 57, CA.
R v Miller (1976) 68 Cr App R 56, CA.   *g*
R v Oddy [1974] 2 All ER 666, [1974] 1 WLR 1212, CA.
R v Thomson Holidays Ltd [1974] 1 All ER 823, [1974] QB 592, CA.
R v Vivian [1979] 1 All ER 48, [1979] 1 WLR 291, CA.
R v Warn [1937] 4 All ER 327, CCA.   *h*

Application for judicial review

The applicant, Jacqueline Anne Cooke, applied with leave of Tucker J given on 30 August 1995 for judicial review of the decision of the Crown Court at Liverpool (Judge Hamilton sitting with lay justices) made on 31 March 1995, whereby they allowed the appeal of the respondents, Liverpool City Council, to   *j*
the extent that the compensation order made by the stipendiary magistrate on 18 January 1995 in the sum of £3,000 in respect of statutory nuisance under s 82 of the Environmental Protection Act 1990 was to be replaced by an order for compensation payable by the council to the applicant in the sum of £250, by way of an order for certiorari to quash the said judgment, and an order remitting the

a decision for reconsideration, or an order for compensation in such amount as the High Court deemed just. The facts are set out in the judgment of Leggatt LJ.

Timothy King QC and *Ivan Wolfenden* (instructed by *Andrew H James*, Liverpool) for the applicant.

John Howell QC and *Ranjit Bhose* (instructed by *Peter Rhodes*, Liverpool) for the
b council.

Cur adv vult

3 April 1996. The following judgments were delivered.

c **LEGGATT LJ.** The applicant, Jacqueline Anne Cooke, applies by leave for judicial review of the judgment of Judge Hamilton sitting with lay justices in the Crown Court at Liverpool on 31 March 1995, by which the appeal of Liverpool City Council was allowed to the extent that a compensation order in the sum of £3,000 made in favour of the applicant on 18 January 1995 by Mr Tapp sitting as
d a stipendiary magistrate was replaced by an order for compensation in the sum of £250.

By letter dated 24 October 1994 notice was given of the applicant's intention to bring proceedings for an order under s 82(2) of the Environmental Protection Act 1990. The letter ended:

e
'We hereby give notice pursuant to section 82(7) of the Environmental Protection Act 1990 that our client proposes to bring proceedings in respect of statutory nuisance under section 79 of the Act after 21 days from the date of this letter if rodent infestation, damp and egress of foul water/sewage from the soil pipe [at] flat 33 referred to above have not been remedied to her
f satisfaction.'

A complaint was issued on 17 November 1994 alleging that—

'on this 17th day of November 1994 a statutory nuisance defined by section 79(a) and (e) of the Environmental Protection Act 1990 exists at 33a
g Hawkstone Street, Liverpool 8, Merseyside and continues to exist and the nuisance (particulars of which are given in the attached inspection report dated the 3rd day of November 1994) is the responsibility of the said Liverpool City Council and insofar as it results in defects in the structure and exterior of the said dwelling house is their responsibility as owners.'

h
On 21 December 1994 the city council pleaded guilty at the magistrates' court. On 18 January 1995 it was ordered that the city council should carry out specified works to abate the nuisance; that the city council should pay the applicant's costs of £2,171·50; and that the city council should pay £3,000 in compensation to the applicant. No evidence was heard on the amount of compensation to be
j awarded, which was not agreed. The award was based on the assumed continuance of a nuisance for the previous two and a half years. On appeal by the city council, the Crown Court reduced the compensation to be paid to £250 and imposed a fine of £500.

So far as material, s 82 of the 1990 Act provides:

'(1) A magistrates' court may act under this section on a complaint made
by any person on the ground that he is aggrieved by the existence of a
statutory nuisance.

(2) If the magistrates' court is satisfied that the alleged nuisance exists, or
that although abated it is likely to recur on the same premises, the court shall
make an order for either or both of the following purposes—(a) requiring the
defendant to abate the nuisance within a time specified in the order, and to
execute any works necessary for that purpose; (b) prohibiting a recurrence of
the nuisance, and requiring the defendant, within a time specified in the
order, to execute any works necessary to prevent the recurrence; and may
also impose on the defendant a fine not exceeding level 5 on the standard
scale.

(3) If the magistrates' court is satisfied that the alleged nuisance exists and
is such as, in the opinion of the court, to render the premises unfit for human
habitation, an order under subsection (2) above may prohibit the use of the
premises for human habitation until the premises are, to the satisfaction of
the court, rendered fit for that purpose.

(4) Proceedings for an order under subsection (2) above shall be
brought—(a) except in a case falling within paragraph (b) or (c) below,
against the person responsible for the nuisance; (b) where the nuisance arises
from any defect of a structural character, against the owner of the premises;
(c) where the person responsible for the nuisance cannot be found, against
the owner or occupier of the premises ...

(6) Before instituting proceedings for an order under subsection (2) above
against any person, the person aggrieved by the nuisance shall give to that
person such notice in writing of his intention to bring the proceedings as is
applicable to proceedings in respect of a nuisance of that description and the
notice shall specify the matter complained of.

(7) The notice of the bringing of proceedings in respect of a statutory
nuisance required by subsection (6) above which is applicable is—(a) in the
case of a nuisance falling within paragraph (g) of section 79(1) above, not less
than three days' notice; and (b) in the case of a nuisance of any other
description, not less than twenty-one days' notice ...

(12) Where on the hearing of proceedings for an order under subsection
(2) above it is proved that the alleged nuisance existed at the date of the
making of the complaint, then, whether or not at the date of the hearing it
still exists or is likely to recur, the court shall order the defendant (or
defendants in such proportions as appears fair and reasonable) to pay to the
person bringing the proceedings such amount as the court considers
reasonably sufficient to compensate him for any expenses properly incurred
by him in the proceedings ...'

The offence of which a person may be convicted under s 82(2) of the 1990 Act is
being the person responsible for the nuisance which the magistrates' court is
satisfied exists (or is likely to recur if it does not exist) on the hearing of the
proceedings for an order, or in certain circumstances being the owner or occupier
of the premises from which that nuisance arises (or is likely to recur). The offence
is committed on, and by reference to the state of affairs on, the day of the hearing.
There is no offence for which a person can be convicted in any proceedings for
an order under s 82(2) if a nuisance has existed, but has been abated before the
hearing and is not likely to recur. All that the court may do in such a case if a

a nuisance existed at the date of the making of the complaint is to order the defendants to pay the person bringing the proceedings compensation for any expenses properly incurred by him in the proceedings (see s 82(2), (4) and (12) of the 1990 Act).

For the purpose of this hearing it is accepted by the city council that a defendant who is fined, or to whom an order is directed, under s 82(2) of the 1990
b Act, is a person convicted of an offence for the purpose of s 35(1) of the Powers of Criminal Courts Act 1973 (as amended).

Section 35(1) of the 1973 Act provides, so far as material:

c 'Subject to the provisions of this Part of this Act and to section 40 of the Magistrates' Court Act 1980 (which imposes a monetary limit on the powers of a magistrates' court under this section), a court by or before which a person is convicted of an offence, instead of or in addition to dealing with him in any other way, may, on application or otherwise, make an order (in this Act referred to as "a compensation order") requiring him to pay compensation for any personal injury, loss or damage resulting from that
d offence or any other offence which is taken into consideration by the court in determining sentence ...'

The issue raised by this application is as to the extent of the magistrate's power under s 35 to make an order for compensation in respect of statutory nuisance.

Giving judgment, Judge Hamilton said:
e
'One of the most important arguments here is the "Day One" argument. The summons was issued on 17 November 1994, and only alleges that the statutory nuisance "exists" on that date. It was accepted by counsel on each side that a magistrates' court can only issue a summons relating to matters
f no more than six months earlier. In other words, the summons could have alleged that the nuisance existed from 17 May to 17 November 1994, "and still exists". But it did not. As the learned stipendiary magistrate reached his decision on penalty on 18 January 1995, the "Day One" argument means that he could only award compensation for that period of two months.'

g The judge then reviewed the facts, remarked that sufficient items remained in dispute to make it inappropriate to award 'full compensation', as the applicant was claiming it, held that her refusal of offers of alternative accommodation was unreasonable, and concluded:

h 'As a result of all this, because of the "Day One" argument and this question of alternative accommodation, we do not think it is safe to award Mrs Cooke compensation for any longer period than the two months between the date of the summons, and the learned stipendiary magistrate's decision. It would be quite wrong to take anything like the full amount of £2,000 for general compensation, and £800 for general damages. We
j accordingly assess such compensation in the total figure of £250. Of course, there is also the anomaly that the learned stipendiary magistrate imposed no fine at all for a serious case (as he found it to be), but concentrated entirely on compensation. This strikes us also as being wrong in principle. Bearing in mind that he apparently imposed no fine because of the amount to be awarded in compensation, we think it right to move some distance in the

opposite direction. While, therefore, the compensation is reduced to £250, we impose a fine of £500.'

The main submission of Mr King QC, for the applicant, which he reiterated in various forms, not always different, was that as a matter of common sense and public policy it would be absurd if magistrates dealing with a complaint of statutory nuisance were not entitled to consider, since it represents the existence of a state of affairs, the whole of the period for which it has existed. The city council having allowed the state of affairs to exist, the court is entitled to ask what the detrimental effect of its existence has been. Mr King submitted that, taking into account the evidence, the court is entitled in the exercise of its discretion to go back in time to see how long the state of affairs has existed. He relied on *Botross v Fulham London Borough* (1994) 16 Cr App R (S) 622 in which the principal question for this court was whether the proceedings were criminal in nature so as to give the court jurisdiction to make a compensation order. It was held that proof of the existence of a nuisance amounted to proof of a criminal offence. The court adopted the description of a statutory nuisance by Mann LJ in *R v Inner London Crown Court, ex p Bentham* [1989] 1 WLR 408 at 413: '... allowing premises to be in such a state as to be prejudicial to health.' Mr King pointed to the fact that there was no suggestion that the magistrates could not take account of the whole of the period for which the nuisance had endured.

Mr King also relied on *Sandwell Metropolitan BC v Bujok* [1990] 3 All ER 385, [1990] 1 WLR 1350 as showing that under the Public Health Act 1936 an offence was committed when a complaint was brought by the person aggrieved. The House of Lords held that a person was entitled to make a complaint against a local authority under s 94 of that Act without first serving an abatement notice. But s 82(6) and (7) of the 1990 Act, which remedies that deficiency, only requires the service of a notice, not an abatement notice. So it is not necessary to prove non-compliance as such, although it is of course necessary to prove the continued existence of the nuisance on the day of the hearing. Similarly, in *Herbert v Lambeth London Borough* (1991) 13 Cr App R (S) 489 this court held that a compensation order can be made on the basis of a finding of statutory nuisance. That finding, Mr King contended, was itself based on evidence of the continuing existence of a state of affairs. Once more there was no suggestion that the extent of the period which the court could consider was circumscribed. But in none of the cases cited was there any dispute about how much of a period of time for which a statutory nuisance has lasted may be taken into account by the court in assessing compensation.

The scheme of s 82 is to require a person aggrieved by a statutory nuisance to give to the person responsible for it 21 days' written notice of intention to bring proceedings and specifying the matter complained of. That is not an abatement notice, in the sense that proof of a failure to comply with it is necessary as a precondition of the bringing of proceedings. But its effect is comparable, since no proceedings can be instituted until after the expiry of the notice, and if the person responsible rectifies the matter complained of before the hearing, the nuisance is abated, and no offence is committed. If the statutory nuisance remains at the hearing date, an offence is committed. In addition, if the nuisance is proved to have existed when the proceedings were brought, whether or not it is abated before the hearing, the court may make a compensation order for any expenses properly incurred.

a
The power to make a compensation order under s 35 of the 1973 Act is, of course, not peculiar to statutory nuisance. So the power, and the monetary limit to which it is subject, were not themselves tailored to the requirements of statutory nuisance. It also seems unlikely that the legislature paid regard specifically to the period in respect of which compensation would be payable. By s 35 the court may make a compensation order 'for any personal injury, loss or

b
damage resulting from' the offence. The offence is of allowing a statutory nuisance to exist at the complainant's premises at the date of the hearing.

I see no warrant for construing s 82 (or s 35) so as to entitle the court to take account of the whole period for which the nuisance is alleged to have existed. That is not the subject of the complaint, which therefore gives no notice to the person responsible of the length of the period for which the nuisance is alleged to

c
have existed. The complaint in the present case, while incidentally relying on an inspection report of 3 November 1994, alleges the existence of a statutory nuisance only on 17 November 1994. The earliest means by which the court found that the appellants had had notice of the matter complained of was by letter of 24 October 1994.

d
In my judgment 'the offence', from which may have resulted personal injury, loss or damage capable of being the subject of a compensation order, is the statutory nuisance complained of, in so far as it exists at the date of the hearing and has existed since the date specified in the complaint, provided that that date is not before whichever is the later of: (a) the date when the statutory notice expired; and (b) a date not more than six months before the complaint was made.

e
Only by instituting proceedings can a complainant put the person responsible at risk of having a compensation order made against him. The statutory notice is not significant except in so far as the date of its expiry is the date before which no complaint may be made. So the court has no jurisdiction to make a compensation order in respect of any period before that date.

f
It seems to me obvious, and this court has often reiterated, that the magistrates' court is not a suitable court in which to entertain any but simple, straightforward claims for compensation. On the time scale I have indicated many, if not most, claims for statutory nuisance may be expected to fall within that description. Otherwise claimants must be left to bring proceedings in the

g
county court, which is more accustomed to assessing general damages. The mere fact that magistrates have power to award compensation up to a sum of £5,000 does not mean that it is always sensible for them to involve themselves in what are essentially civil claims.

Since the section provides for both alternatives, I see nothing contrary to

h
principle about ordering compensation 'instead of' rather than 'in addition to' a fine. If a compensation order is itself large enough to be punitive, as the magistrate's order was here, there is no occasion to impose a fine as well. If, on the other hand, the compensation order is relatively small, as the Crown Court decided it should be, it is necessary to add a fine for punitive effect.

j
In my judgment, the judge came to the right conclusion for substantially the right reasons, and I would dismiss the application.

SIR IAIN GLIDEWELL. Section 35 of the Powers of Criminal Courts Act 1973 empowers a court before which a person is convicted of an offence to order the offender to pay—

'compensation for any personal injury, loss or damage resulting from that *a* offence, or any other offence which is taken into consideration by the court in determining sentence ...'

Despite argument to the contrary by Mr Howell QC, for Liverpool City Council, the Crown Court did not take any offence into consideration in this case. The first question which arises before us is, what was the offence of which the city council was convicted at the Liverpool Magistrates' Court on 21 December 1994? *b* The offence is described in the information dated 17 November 1994 as follows:

'That on the 17th day of November 1994 a statutory nuisance defined by section 79(1)(a) and (e) of the Environmental Protection Act 1990 exists ... and continues to exist and that the nuisance is the responsibility of the said Liverpool City Council and in so far as it results in defects in the structure and *c* exterior of the said dwelling house is their responsibility as owners.'

The information does not specify the statutory provision which is said to have been contravened by the city council, but it does describe Mrs Cooke as being 'a person aggrieved for the purposes of section 82 of the said Act ...' It follows that the allegation must be that the council had committed an offence under s 82(2) of *d* the 1990 Act, which Leggatt LJ has set out in his judgment and which I therefore need not repeat.

Section 82(2) does not in terms create any offence. The operative part of the subsection empowers the magistrates' court, if satisfied on complaint that an alleged statutory nuisance exists or, if abated, is likely to recur, to make an order *e* requiring the defendant to abate the nuisance within a specified time, or prohibiting any recurrence as the case may be. Only if the defendant fails to comply with such an order within the specified time does the section provide expressly, in s 82(8), that he is guilty of an offence. However, s 82(2) also empowers the magistrates' court when making an order to impose on the defendant a fine. *f*

The concept of a fine for an unspecified offence fits somewhat uneasily into the wording of the remainder of the subsection, especially as the procedure for seeking an order is by way of complaint, which is appropriate for civil proceedings, not information, by which criminal proceedings are commenced. However, this court in *Botross v Fulham London Borough* (1994) 16 Cr App R (S) 622 *g* has decided that the power given by s 82(2) to impose a fine can only mean that the subsection does create an offence. That decision was followed by another decision of this court in *Davenport v Walsall Metropolitan BC* (17 March 1995, unreported). In that case the court decided that on a complaint under s 82(1) the magistrates are empowered to order the payment of compensation, but may in *h* their discretion decline to do so on the ground that the assessment of such compensation would be too complicated for the summary procedure. In neither of those cases was the court asked to define the limits of the offence from which the loss or damage for which compensation is claimed is said to result.

Both the Public Health Acts 1875 and 1936 contained, in similar terms, provisions which enabled local authorities to deal with statutory nuisances. The *j* scheme of these provisions, as set out in ss 93 and 94 of the 1936 Act, was as follows. (1) The service by the local authority of an abatement notice requiring the person responsible for a nuisance to abate it within a stated time. (2) A complaint to the magistrates by the local authority that the defendant had failed to comply with the abatement notice in the specified time. (3) 'If on the hearing

of a complaint it is proved that the alleged nuisance exists ... the court shall make
a an order (hereafter in this Act referred to as "a nuisance order") ... requiring the
defendant to comply with all or any of the requirements of the abatement notice,
or otherwise to abate the nuisance, within a time specified in the order ... and
may also impose on the defendant a fine ...' (See s 94.)

In *Northern Ireland Trailers Ltd v Preston County Borough* [1972] 1 All ER 260,
b [1972] 1 WLR 203 it was argued that proceedings under s 94 of the 1936 Act begun
by information, not by complaint, were a nullity. This court held that a failure to
comply with an abatement notice under s 94 was an offence, since the
magistrates might impose a fine on the defendant.

There were also provisions in the 1875 and 1936 Acts which enabled 'any
person aggrieved by' a statutory nuisance to make complaint about it to the
c magistrates. Section 99 of the 1936 Act provided:

> 'Complaint of the existence of statutory nuisance under this Act may be
> made to a justice of the peace by any person aggrieved by the nuisance, and
> thereupon the like proceeding shall be had, with the like incidents and
> consequences as to the making of orders, penalties for disobedience of orders
d > and otherwise, as in the case of a complaint by the local authority ...'

In *R v Newham Justices, ex p Hunt, R v Oxted Justices, ex p Franklin* [1976] 1 All ER
839 at 842, [1976] 1 WLR 420 at 424, in which the question was whether the
procedure under s 99 was a civil or criminal process, this court decided that 'the
proper interpretation of this section leads to the conclusion that the individual
e can by information invoke section 94'. Thus, the person responsible for a
statutory nuisance was guilty of an offence, but that offence was under s 94,
initiated by a complaint under s 99.

That decision was followed by this court in *R v Inner London Crown Court, ex p
Bentham* [1989] 1 WLR 408, in which Mann LJ, after reciting the history of the
f earlier decisions, said (at 413):

> 'On analysis, the position seems to be that proceedings are initiated by
> information under section 99, and that the information is then dealt with
> under section 94(2). It appears plain that the proceedings under section 94(2)
> are criminal in character. The offence is the wrongdoing which leads to
g > whatever order is in fact made; in this case, putting it generally, allowing
> premises to be in such a state as to be prejudicial to health.'

In *Sandwell Metropolitan BC v Bujok* [1990] 3 All ER 385, [1990] 1 WLR 1350 the
defendant council argued that a person aggrieved (in that case, as here, one of
their tenants) was required, before laying an information under s 99, to serve an
h abatement notice. That argument failed in this court ((1989) 88 LGR 521) and
before the House of Lords. In a speech with which all others agreed, Lord
Griffiths specifically approved the decision in *R v Newham Justices, ex p Hunt, R v
Oxted Justices, ex p Franklin*. However, he also said that he entirely agreed with
the following passage from the judgment of Watkins LJ in that case in this court
j ((1989) 88 LGR 521 at 534–535):

> '... it is surely repugnant to common sense that in the area of legal activity
> a local authority should be prosecuted by one of its tenants without first
> being given the opportunity by that tenant to remedy the consequences of a
> neglect to repair the dwelling that tenant occupies. In law there is no doubt
> that [the tenant] was entitled to commence proceedings without giving

notice of the state of the dwelling to the local authority. But in every other *a* conceivable way I regard that action as entirely wrong. Endless trouble to many people in courts and local authority offices and much money could be saved by the giving of notice of disrepair which it is to be supposed a local authority would appropriately react to. If they did not, then would be the time for a tenant to exercise the right to prosecute. I doubt whether there is anyone, a ratepayer especially, giving proper thought to such a situation as *b* we have been confronted with who would disagree with that approach to what surely is a commonplace problem.' (See ([1990] 3 All ER 385 at 389–390, [1990] 1 WLR 1350 at 1355–1356.)

In *Herbert v Lambeth London Borough* (1991) 13 Cr App R (S) 489 in which, apparently for the first time in this court, the question arose whether an *c* individual who had laid an information under s 99 of the 1936 Act was entitled to claim compensation, the court decided, following *R v Inner London Crown Court, ex p Bentham*, that in such a case the magistrates had the power to order compensation. Woolf LJ cited with approval the following passage from *Stone's Justices' Manual* para 3–85, p 843:
d

'"The machinery of a compensation order under this Act is intended for clear and simple cases. It must always be remembered that the civil rights of the victim remained, although the power to make a compensation order is not confined to the cases where there is a civil liability. A compensation order made by the court of trial can be extremely beneficial as long as it is *e* confined to simple, straightforward cases and generally cases where no great amount is at stake."' (See (1991) 13 Cr App R (S) 489 at 494.)

I turn at last to the provisions of the present Act. As compared with the 1936 Act, the 1990 Act made substantial changes in the procedure for dealing with statutory nuisances. Those important for present purposes are the following. (1) *f* As to proceedings by local authorities, s 80(1) and (2) of the 1990 Act provide for service by the authority of an abatement notice; s 80(3) gives, for the first time, a right to appeal to the magistrates court against an abatement notice; s 80(4) expressly makes it an offence to fail to comply with an abatement notice without reasonable excuse. (2) As to individual persons aggrieved, s 82 does not adopt *g* the wording of s 99 of the 1936 Act or its predecessors. Instead, s 82(2) describes in detail the magistrates' powers on the making of a complaint by a person aggrieved, including that of imposing a fine. Thus, the offence of which the person responsible for the nuisance is guilty, in accordance with the decision in *Botross v Fulham London Borough*, is an offence under s 82 itself. (3) However, no *h* doubt in order to meet the points made in the House of Lords in *Sandwell Metropolitan BC v Bujok* about the undesirability of making a defendant guilty of an offence of committing a statutory nuisance when he had had no notice from the complainant before the commencement of the proceedings in the magistrates court, by s 82(6) and (7) Parliament now requires the complainant to give such prior notice. *j*

It therefore follows that, if no such notice be given, or if within the period of the notice the matter complained of is rectified, there is no offence, and the court may make no order. Thus, it is in my view clear that an offence against s 82(2) is first committed when the s 82(6) notice expires without the complaint being rectified.

a   I therefore agree with Leggatt LJ that, in proceedings under s 82, compensation may be awarded only for such injury, loss or damage as is proved to have been caused by the continuance of the nuisance after the expiry of the period stated in the s 82(6) notice, until the date of the hearing. I also agree with him that if a complainant should delay for more than six months after the expiry of the s 82(6) notice before making complaint to the magistrates, then the offence which could

b   form the basis for compensation would not commence earlier than a date six months before the complaint was made. For these reasons, which do no more than supplement those of Leggatt LJ, I agree that this application for judicial review of the decision of the Crown Court at Liverpool of 31 March 1995 should be dismissed.

c   *Application dismissed. Leave to appeal refused.*

Dilys Tausz   Barrister.

Re H (a minor) (adoption: non-patrial)

COURT OF APPEAL, CIVIL DIVISION
STUART-SMITH, PETER GIBSON AND THORPE LJJ
26 APRIL, 3 MAY 1996

Adoption – Order – Discretion – Nationality – Immigration control – Application to adopt child with no right of abode in United Kingdom – Factors to be considered – Child granted leave to enter United Kingdom on family holiday – British relatives who were childless applying to adopt child – Whether welfare of child accurately balanced against public policy considerations of immigration control when determining whether to grant adoption order – Adoption Act 1976, s 6.

Mr and Mrs A, who were British citizens living in England, were unable to have children of their own. They had relatives of Pakistani nationality living in Pakistan who had a family of eight children. S was the sixth child. In July 1992 S, who was then aged 12, came to England with his father for a family wedding. While in England, S's father agreed that Mr and Mrs A should adopt S, who then lived with them as their son. The Home Office later refused an application for an extension of S's entry visa. Thereafter Mr and Mrs A lodged an appeal against the refusal and applied for an adoption order in respect of S, the consequence of which would be to grant him British citizenship and the right to live permanently in the United Kingdom. The Secretary of State opposed the application, and was joined as intervenor to the adoption proceedings. The judge allowed the application and granted an adoption order. The Secretary of State appealed, contending that it was a breach of the immigration rules to allow a child who had obtained entry to the country on one basis, but was subsequently the subject of an adoption application, leave to enter the United Kingdom where there had not been a genuine transfer of parental responsibility on the ground of the original parents' inability to care for the child. The Secretary of State further contended that a breach of immigration regulations or policy could only be outweighed by the promotion of the welfare of the child and not by any other consideration, and that since the application to adopt S was made for the personal benefit of Mr and Mrs A and not to promote or meet a welfare need of S, it should be refused.

Held – When determining an application by a British citizen to adopt a child from overseas, the court should have regard to the statutory considerations expressed in s 6[a] of the Adoption Act 1976 without the elaboration of stages or inflexible rules. The court should therefore carry out a balancing act between the welfare of the child throughout its childhood (which was the first, but not paramount, consideration) and the public policy considerations of immigration control, and while misuse of an adoption application as a device to circumvent immigration controls would always be refused, there was no justification in s 6 for the rejection of a genuine application merely on the ground that it was not primarily motivated by welfare considerations. In the instant case, although the applicants wished to adopt S because they could not have a child of their own and not to

---

a   Section 6, so far as material, provides: 'In reaching any decision relating to the adoption of a child a
     court … shall have regard to all the circumstances, first consideration being given to the need to
     safeguard and promote the welfare of the child throughout his childhood …'

a meet or satisfy a welfare need of S, the judge had correctly determined that the adoption application was genuine and not a device to obtain British citizenship; the welfare advantages to the child were real, significant and lasting and clearly outweighed the considerations of public policy in maintaining immigration regulations. It followed that the appeal would accordingly be dismissed (see p 604 *j* to p 605 *a c e*, p 606 *c* to *g j* and p 607 *a d* to *g*, post).

b Dictum of Hollings J in *Re H (a minor) (adoption: non-patrial)* [1982] 3 All ER 84 at 94 and of Balcombe LJ in *Re W (a minor)* [1985] 3 All ER 449 at 454 applied.

Re K (a minor) (adoption: nationality) [1994] 3 All ER 553 considered.

Notes

c For duty in adoption proceedings to promote a child's welfare, see 5(2) *Halsbury's Laws* (4th edn reissue) para 1068, and for a case on the subject, see 28(3) *Digest* (2nd reissue) 363, *3221*.

For the Adoption Act 1976, s 6, see 6 *Halsbury's Statutes* (4th edn) (1992 reissue) 227.

d **Cases referred to in judgments**

H (a minor) (adoption: non-patrial), Re [1982] 3 All ER 84, [1982] Fam 121, [1982] 3 WLR 501.

K (a minor) (adoption: nationality), Re [1994] 3 All ER 553, [1995] Fam 38, [1994] 3 WLR 572, CA; *rvsg* (5 September 1993, unreported), EAT.

e *W (a minor), Re* [1985] 3 All ER 449, [1986] Fam 54, [1985] 3 WLR 945, CA.

Case also cited or referred to in skeleton arguments

S (a minor), Re (16 November 1995, unreported), Fam D.

Appeal

f By notice dated 7 December 1995 the Secretary of State for the Home Department, as the intervenor in the proceedings, appealed from the order of Holman J ([1996] 1 FLR 717) made on 13 November 1995 whereby he made an adoption order in respect of a child, S, who was a foreign national with no independent right of abode in the United Kingdom, in favour of the applicants.

g The facts are set out in the judgment of Thorpe LJ.

Lisa Giovannetti (instructed by the *Treasury Solicitor*) for the Secretary of State.
Patricia Scotland QC and *Khadim Al'Hassan* (instructed by *John Delaney & Co*, Leeds) for the applicants.

h *Richard Bond* (instructed by the *Official Solicitor*) for the guardian ad litem.

Cur adv vult

3 May 1996. The following judgments were delivered.

j **THORPE LJ** (giving the first judgment at the invitation of Stuart-Smith LJ). This appeal concerns two related families and the arrangements that they made for one of the children, S, who was born on 22 May 1980 and who is therefore nearly 16 years of age. The appeal is brought by the Secretary of State for the Home Department, who challenges an adoption order made by Holman J ([1996] 1 FLR 717) on 13 November 1995 in respect of S and in favour of Mr A and Mrs A, the first and second respondents.

Mr and Mrs A are in their late thirties. They came to the United Kingdom in
the 1970s and married in 1978. They have both acquired UK citizenship and they   *a*
have a settled life in Halifax living above their shop. However, for 14 years after
their marriage they struggled in vain to conceive a child. Mr A was found to have
a low sperm count. IVF treatment proved ineffective. By 1992 they were
resigned to adoption.

MZ and ZB are a related couple. It seems that the two husbands are cousins,   *b*
as are the two wives. By contrast MZ and ZB have a quiverful of children. There
are eight in all ranging in age from 26 to 7 years. S is the sixth. The family lives
in Pakistan where MZ has secure employment and the whole family a very
comfortable standard of living. On 21 July 1992 MZ arrived in England with S and
two other of his children for a family wedding in Halifax. S's entry visa gave him
permission to remain in the United Kingdom for six months as a visitor. On 6   *c*
August 1992 S began to live with the first and second respondents as their son and
has so remained with them ever since. These circumstances and this chronology
inevitably give rise to many questions and some suspicions. However, the
circumstances were fully investigated by Holman J, who heard the first and
second respondents give oral evidence and accepted them as witnesses of truth.   *d*
The fundamental family arrangement was subsequently explained by S's mother
in these words:

> 'In Pakistan when a couple have no children and ask for one of yours you
> just give one as long as you know they are good people. God has given us so
> many children and they have none.'   *e*

Holman J found as follows ([1996] 1 FLR 717 at 721):

> 'I accept that it was only after S arrived in this country in July 1992 that the
> applicants proposed to the father that S might live with and be adopted by
> them, although the idea might have been forming in the minds of the
> applicants some time prior to that as they faced up to the impossibility of   *f*
> bearing a child of their own and the long delay, with no certainty at the end
> of it, before they might adopt one through their local social services. The
> purpose of the arrangement was not to give S the advantage of British
> citizenship or a right of abode here but to provide a child for these applicants
> who were desperate to have one. The arrangement was not entered into to   *g*
> meet or satisfy a welfare need of S. He was already being entirely
> appropriately and happily brought up by his natural family in Pakistan. But
> I am quite satisfied that all the adults nevertheless had his welfare in mind
> even if, objectively and again by Western cultural standards, what was done
> could not be regarded as in his best interests at the time. The applicants were   *h*
> convinced (as has proved to be the case) that they could offer a very good
> home and upbringing to S and bestow on him all their love as their only
> child. The natural parents were also satisfied that this was so. The natural
> father said to [the immigration officer] that "We thought they would love
> him more than us". S himself has said that at home in Pakistan he felt he had
> to vie with all his brothers and sisters for the love and attention of his parents,   *j*
> whereas with the applicants he alone would get all their attention and love.'

In March 1993 the Home Office refused an application for extension of H's
visa. In April an appeal was lodged against the refusal and an originating
application issued in the Halifax County Court seeking S's adoption. The
application was transferred to the High Court in August 1993 and in February

a 1994 the Secretary of State for the Home Department was joined as intervenor. After all the formal stages essential in an adoption application had been duly completed, the application came for trial before Holman J. The applicants were supported in their application by the Official Solicitor but opposed by the Secretary of State.

b Holman J recorded how well S had done in the applicants' care in the three years of their cohabitation. He said (at 722):

c 'During their oral evidence I was very struck by the strength and sincerity of each applicant's commitment to S, whom each undoubtedly now adores and is very proud of as if he was their own. Mrs A said with great sincerity "We feel that I bore him and he is our own child". She said "God gave this child to us".'

He had before him a letter that S had written to the Official Solicitor expressing his strong wish not only to remain with the applicants but to be adopted by them. He found (at 722):

d 'It is quite clear that the break between S and his natural parents is now real and permanent. He has very little written or telephone contact with them. He himself feels little tie with them now. Having parted with him in this way, they themselves have broken the link, and even if S had to return to Pakistan they would expect the applicants to continue to look after, and be responsible for, him.'

e The Secretary of State did not seek to reverse the family arrangement. He took the point of principle that an adoption order should be refused on the application of dicta from past cases as to how the balance should be held between immigration regulations and controls and welfare and other considerations urged f in support of adoption applications. Holman J, directing himself carefully from the three cited authorities, applied a two-stage approach. On the first stage, rejecting the submission of Miss Giovannetti, he held (at 724):

g 'But the desire of a childless couple to have a child whom they can call their own is a common and appropriate part of the motive of many adoption situations. The fact that this was the principal motive when S was first handed over does not mean that this application should fail at the first stage. The purpose of the first stage is to exclude applications which are not genuinely motivated to achieve the genuine benefits inherent in adoption itself rather than the incidental benefit of obtaining British citizenship and a h right of abode.'

Applying that direction to the facts he concluded (at 725):

'In my judgment this is a genuine adoption application motivated by the genuine advantages inherent in adoption itself and I can accordingly proceed j to the second stage.'

He defined the second stage in this sentence (at 724):

'It is only if the welfare considerations and any other legitimate considerations under section 6 clearly outweigh the immigration and public policy considerations that I may make an adoption order.'

He then reviewed all the relevant considerations at some length. He completed
the balance with these words (at 730):

> 'I have considered this balance with great care. I do bear in mind that
> Parliament itself, by s 1(5) of the British Nationality Act 1981 and by the
> [Immigration Act 1971], has contemplated that in certain circumstances
> nationality and right of abode may in effect be conferred by judicial decision
> rather than the discretion of the Secretary of State, and I bear in mind that
> under s 6 of the [Adoption Act 1976] I must give first consideration to the
> welfare of S. I have concluded that this case is genuine, that the welfare
> advantages to S are real, significant and lasting, and that they do clearly
> outweigh the substantial considerations of immigration policy. I should
> make an adoption order.'

Miss Giovannetti, by way of background to her submissions, draws attention
to rr 310 to 316 of the Statement of Changes in Immigration Rules (HC Paper
1994 No 395), which set the requirements for leave to enter for a child adopted
abroad. They amount to a relatively stringent code, including r 310(viii):

> '[A child who was] adopted due to the inability of the original parent(s) or
> current carer(s) to care for him and there has been a genuine transfer of
> parental responsibility to the adoptive parents ...'

S, had he been adopted abroad, would not have satisfied that condition. The
rules do not cover the case of a child where leave of entry is sought for the
purposes of a UK adoption. That situation is covered by Home Office circular
RON 117, which includes in para 3, 'We will also need to be satisfied that it is in
the child's best interests to be adopted' and in para 4: 'In particular we will wish
to be satisfied that the proposed adoption involves a genuine transfer of parental
responsibility on the ground of the original parents' inability to look after the
child.' Again, at date of entry S would not have satisfied those requirements.
Thus, Miss Giovannetti submits that to the further case of children who obtain
entry on one basis but who are subsequently the subject of an application to
adopt similar limitations should be applied.

Turning to authority Miss Giovannetti traces the development of the case law
from *Re H (a minor) (adoption: non-patrial)* [1982] 3 All ER 84, [1982] Fam 121,
through *Re W (a minor)* [1985] 3 All ER 449, [1986] Fam 54, to *Re K (a minor)
(adoption: nationality)* [1994] 3 All ER 553, [1995] Fam 38. In the first case she
concentrates upon the essential paragraph in the judgment of Hollings J, which I
must cite in full:

> 'What then should the approach of this court be in applications of this
> nature? Clearly, it must pay great regard to the "immigration decision" and
> in particular considerations of public policy and where relevant national
> security. It must be on its guard against the possibility of abuse; but the mere
> fact that nationality or patriality would result is not conclusive. It must treat
> welfare as the first consideration, outweighing any one other factor but not
> all factors. If the court considers on the evidence and information before it
> that the true motive of the application is based on the desire to achieve
> nationality and the right of abode rather than the general welfare of the
> minor then an adoption order should not be made. If on the other hand part
> of the motive, or it may be at least as much, is to achieve real emotional or
> psychological, social and legal benefit (s 19 apart) of adoption, then an

a adoption order may be proper, notwithstanding that this has the effect of overriding an immigration decision or even an immigration rule. In every case it is a matter of balancing welfare against public policy, and the wider the implications of the public policy aspect the less weight may be attached to the aspect of the welfare of the particular individual.' (See [1982] 3 All ER 84 at 94, [1982] Fam 121 at 133.)

b The second authority contains a passage which I regard as important. Balcombe LJ said ([1985] 3 All ER 449 at 454, [1986] Fam 54 at 62–63):

c 'In our judgment, when an application is made by a British citizen to adopt a foreign child, the following considerations apply. (1) The applicant should give notice of the application to the Home Office, to see whether the Secretary of State wishes to be added as a party to the application under r 15(3) of the Adoption Rules 1984. The court should ensure that this has been done. (2) When the court comes to consider the application on its merits it must, of course, give first consideration to the need to safeguard and promote the welfare of the child throughout its childhood. If only a short d period of that childhood remains, then clearly this factor carries less weight. (3) The court should also consider whether the welfare of the child would be better, or as well, promoted by another type of order which does not have the same effect on nationality and immigration as an adoption order, eg a custodianship order under Pt II of the Children Act 1975 when those e provisions are brought into force. (4) In any event the court should take into account those considerations of public policy in relation to the effect of an adoption order on nationality and the right of abode to which we have already referred, and should carry out the balancing act between welfare (being the first consideration) and public policy to which Hollings J referred [see [1982] 3 All ER 84 at 94, [1982] Fam 121 at 133], and which the courts are f having daily to carry out in all decisions relating to children.'

In the latest case Balcombe LJ said ([1994] 3 All ER 553 at 558, [1995] Fam 38 at 43):

g 'It was common ground that the judge adopted the correct two-stage approach: to consider first the motive for the application and only if satisfied that the true motive was not to achieve British nationality and the consequent right of abode for K, rather than to serve her general welfare, to proceed to the second stage, which is to carry out a balancing exercise between public policy and K's welfare, see generally Re H (a minor) (adoption: h non-patrial) [1982] 3 All ER 84, [1982] Fam 121, Re W (a minor) [1985] 3 All ER 449, [1986] Fam 54.'

Miss Giovannetti's essential submission is that in all these cases the court has balanced the motive to achieve nationality as against the motive to promote the j welfare of the child. A breach of immigration regulations or policy can only be outweighed by the promotion of the welfare of the child and not by any other consideration. Here she submits the applicants were not seeking to promote the welfare of the child but to resolve the personal tragedy of infertility. Therefore the application of the first-stage test properly formulated should have led to the dismissal of the application without any consideration of the second-stage test. In developing that submission she asks, in relation to the formulation of Hollings J, whose motive, the motive of the applicants or of the birth parents; and, at what date, the date of entry or the date of trial of the application?

Although these submissions are lucidly presented, I found them unconvincing. Of course in the ordinary adoption case a child the subject of adoption will have been abandoned by its parents or its parents will be disqualified by disability or conduct from providing adequate parenting themselves. In those circumstances it is natural that the court should pose the question in the form that it has been posed, namely is the aim of the application to achieve nationality or to promote welfare. But, as this exceptional case demonstrates, they are not the only aims that the court may have to consider. A pedantic commentary on the crucial sentence in the judgment of Hollings J might say that court applications do not have motives, still less desires. Clearly the court must be on guard against the possibility of abuse. In seeking to uphold immigration regulations and policy the court, in my judgment, should investigate whether the arrangement culminating in the adoption application is a device to circumvent immigration regulations and controls. I believe that that is only to restate in different words the direction formulated by Hollings J in the fifth sentence of the cited passage.

The paragraph cited from the judgment in *Re H* has subsequently been elevated into a two-stage test which does not seem to me to have been Hollings J's intention. It is not so stated in *Re W*. Mr Bond for the Official Solicitor says that it had that genesis in *Re K* at first instance (5 September 1993, unreported) and the development was adopted by Balcombe LJ in this court. I do not think that it is helpful. It seems to me that it risks complicating unnecessarily the essential judicial task. The Family Division judge must dispose of the adoption application by reference principally to s 6 of the Adoption Act 1976. By that section, he must have regard to all the circumstances, first, but not paramount, consideration being given to child welfare. He must also give due consideration to the ascertained wishes and feelings of the child in the light of the child's age and understanding. As the first consideration, welfare outweighs any one other but not all factors. Although not referred to in the section it is an important consideration that immigration regulations and policies should be upheld. A misuse of the right to apply for adoption as a device to circumvent immigration controls will always be fatal to an adoption application. Quite apart from immigration policy considerations, adults exposed in that way are likely to have forfeited the confidence in their maturity and responsibility which the judge must hold before committing to them a child on such an irrevocable basis. Nor can I conceive that in a case of blatant abuse the application might be rescued by the argument that subsequent delay has resulted in the development of circumstances justifying a submission that the refusal of the application would be contrary to the welfare consideration. In such circumstances even if the applicants have redeemed themselves to some extent as potential parents the public policy consideration is likely to outweigh the welfare consideration. But in the end each case must turn on its own particular facts and in determining the case the judge should have regard to the statutory considerations as expressed in s 6 without the elaboration of stages and with due regard to the considerations expressed by this court in the passage cited from in *Re W*.

Miss Scotland QC and Mr Bond in resisting the appeal both commended the judgment of Holman J as either impeccable or carefully crafted. The descriptions are well justified. The conclusions which he reached were clearly open to him within the discretion that he exercised and I would dismiss this appeal.

PETER GIBSON LJ. I entirely agree with the judgment of Thorpe LJ and I only
a add a few words of my own because it appears that the application of a two-stage
test has rapidly become the rigid practice in cases of the type now before us.

It is not in dispute that the court faced with an adoption application, which, if
successful, would nullify an adverse decision of the Secretary of State under the
Statement of Changes in Immigration Rules (HC Paper 1994 No 395),
b nevertheless has jurisdiction to consider that application and to make an adoption
order. It is plainly right that the court should have regard to the nationality and
immigration consequences of any order, and should be on its guard lest the
adoption proceedings are but a device to evade the immigration procedures and
policy. But whilst those matters are properly to be taken into account, it is in my
view wrong to elevate the guidance given by judges as to the approach to be
c adopted in such cases into a set of inflexible rules. Thus the contrast drawn
between a motive to achieve British nationality and a right of abode on the one
hand and a motive to serve the child's welfare, which was appropriate in the
circumstances of, for example, *Re K (a minor) (adoption: nationality)* [1994] 3 All ER
553, [1995] Fam 38 at 43, has been relied on by the Secretary of State in the
d different circumstances of the present case, where the judge has found that the
welfare of the child, whilst a consideration, was not the principal motive for the
application. Section 6 of the Adoption Act 1976, which governs the decision to
be taken by the court, does not refer to the motive for the application, though no
doubt it is one of the circumstances to which regard must be had. But the
relevance of welfare is, under the section, that it is that which needs to be
e safeguarded and promoted throughout the childhood of the child and to it first
consideration must be given by the court. In my judgment, the wording of the
section does not justify the rejection of a genuine adoption application simply on
the ground that it is not primarily motivated by welfare considerations.

In my opinion the judge, having satisfied himself that the adoption application
f was genuine and not a device to obtain British citizenship and a right of abode for
the child, impeccably balanced the public policy considerations and the welfare
considerations, when concluding that the welfare advantages to the child were
real, significant and lasting and clearly outweighed the substantial considerations
of immigration policy.

For these and the reasons given by Thorpe LJ, I too would dismiss this appeal.
g
STUART-SMITH LJ. I agree with both judgments.

Appeal dismissed. Leave to appeal to the House of Lords refused.

Paul Magrath Esq   Barrister.

Fuji Finance Inc v Aetna Life Insurance Co Ltd and another

COURT OF APPEAL, CIVIL DIVISION

HOBHOUSE, MORRITT LJJ AND SIR RALPH GIBSON

15, 16 MAY, 4 JULY 1996

Insurance – Contract of insurance – Nature of contract – Capital investment bond – Policy benefits on surrender or on death of life insured – Whether policy an 'insurance on the life of any person' – Whether contract a policy of life insurance – Life Assurance Act 1774, s 1.

In 1986 the plaintiff, a Panamanian investment company, took out a policy variously described as a life assurance policy or a capital investment bond, with the defendant insurance company and paid a single premium of £50,000. Under the policy, sums were payable on the death of the life assured, T (the prime mover behind the plaintiff's operations), or the early surrender of the policy and, either way, the sums payable were calculated by reference to the value of the units then allocated to the policy. If, however, the policyholder chose to surrender the policy within the first five years, the amount payable would be subject to a small discontinuance charge. A central feature of the policy was the 'switch' option, which entitled the policyholder to direct the insurer to convert units of an internal fund allocated to the policy to units of another fund. Within six years the policy had soared in value to over £1m due to T's astute use of the switch option. However, in 1991 the insurers altered the procedures of the switch option and thereafter T's return was negligible. The plaintiff claimed that the alteration of the policy terms constituted a repudiatory breach of contract and surrendered the policy. The insurers paid out surrender proceeds of £1,110,758·50, but the plaintiff, being dissatisfied, commenced proceedings for damages against them. On a trial of preliminary issues, the judge held that the policy was not an 'insurance on the life' of T within the meaning of s 1[a] of the Life Assurance Act 1774, but that it was not rendered unenforceable by virtue of s 16[b] of the Insurance Companies Act 1982, which restricted insurance companies to the business of insurance. The insurers appealed.

Held – The fact that the measure of the benefit payable on the surrender of a life assurance policy was the same as that payable on the death of the life assured did not prevent the contract from being recognised as 'insurance ... made ... on the life ... of any person' within s 1 of the 1774 Act, if the event on which the benefit was payable was sufficiently life or death related. Since the policy came to an end on the death of T, so that, subject to notification in the prescribed manner, the benefits then crystallised, the right to surrender was related to the continuance of life, for it could not be exercised by the plaintiff after T's death. It followed that the policy was a policy of life insurance within the 1774 Act and the appeal would accordingly be allowed on that ground (see p 618 *e g* to *j*, p 619 *f*, p 623 *j* and p 626 *j*, post).

---

a Section 1, so far as material, is set out at p 611 *h* to p 612 *a*, post
b Section 16, so far as material, is set out at p 612 *b c*, post

a   *Marac Life Assurance Ltd v IR Comr* [1986] 1 NZLR 694, *NM Superannuation Pty Ltd v Young* (1993) 113 ALR 39 and *Jones v AMP Perpetual Trustee Co NZ Ltd* [1994] 1 NZLR 690 considered.

Decision of Nicholls V-C [1994] 4 All ER 1025 reversed.

Notes

b   For principles common to all insurances, see 25 *Halsbury's Laws* (4th edn reissue) para 2.

For the basis of a contract for life insurance, see ibid, paras 525–528, and for cases on the subject, see 29(2) *Digest* (2nd reissue) 172–177, 4163–4171.

For the Life Assurance Act 1774, s 1, see 22 *Halsbury's Statutes* (4th edn) (1995 reissue) 8.

c   For the Insurance Companies Act 1982, s 16, see ibid 251.

Cases referred to in judgments

Archbolds (Freightage) Ltd v S Spanglett Ltd (Randall, third party) [1961] 1 All ER 417, [1961] 1 QB 374, [1961] 2 WLR 170, CA.

d   *Bedford Insurance Co Ltd v Instituto de Resseguros do Brasil* [1984] 3 All ER 766, [1985] QB 966, [1984] 3 WLR 726.

Cope v Rowlands (1836) 2 M & W 149, 150 ER 707.

Cornelius v Phillips [1918] AC 199, [1916–17] All ER Rep 685, HL.

Flood v Irish Provident Assurance Co Ltd [1912] 2 Ch 597n, Ir CA.

Gould v Curtis [1913] 3 KB 84, CA.

e   *Jones v AMP Perpetual Trustee Co NZ Ltd* [1994] 1 NZLR 690, NZ HC.

Joseph v Law Integrity Insurance Co Ltd [1912] 2 Ch 581, CA.

Mahmoud and Ispahani, Re an arbitration between [1921] 2 KB 716, [1921] All ER Rep 217, CA.

Marac Life Assurance Ltd v IR Comr [1986] 1 NZLR 694, NZ CA; *affg* (1985) 9 TRNZ

f   201, NZ HC.

National Standard Life Assurance Corp, Re [1918] 1 Ch 427.

NM Superannuation Pty Ltd v Young (1993) 113 ALR 39, Aust Fed Ct.

Phoenix General Insurance Co of Greece SA v Administratia Asigurarilor de Stat [1987] 2 All ER 152, [1988] QB 216, [1987] 2 WLR 512, CA.

Prudential Insurance Co v IRC [1904] 2 KB 658.

g

Appeal

The defendants, Aetna Life Insurance Co Ltd and Windsor Life Assurance Co Ltd (to which Aetna had transferred its long-term business), appealed with leave from the decision of Nicholls V-C ([1994] 4 All ER 1025, [1995] Ch 122) given on 7 July

h   1994 whereby he determined on a trial of two preliminary issues in an action brought by the plaintiff, Fuji Finance Inc (Fuji), against the defendants for damages for breach of contract, that a policy issued to Fuji on 24 October 1986 by Tyndall Assurance Ltd (which had subsequently transferred its undertakings and liabilities to Aetna) was not a policy of insurance within the meaning of s 1 of the

j   Life Assurance Act 1774 and was not rendered unenforceable by s 16 of the Insurance Companies Act 1982. By order of the Court of Appeal dated 12 March 1996 the Secretary of State for Trade and Industry was given leave to intervene in the proceedings. The facts are set out in the judgment of Morritt LJ.

Anthony Grabiner QC and *Daniel Toledano* (instructed by *White & Case*) for the defendants.

Nicholas Underhill QC and *Robert Powell-Jones* (instructed by *Peter Sewell & Co*) for
Fuji.

Ian Glick QC and *Jacob Grierson* (instructed by the *Treasury Solicitor*) for the
Secretary of State.

Cur adv vult

4 July 1996. The following judgments were delivered.

MORRITT LJ (giving the first judgment at the invitation of Hobhouse LJ). On
24 October 1986 Tyndall Assurance Ltd (Tyndall) issued to the plaintiff, Fuji
Finance Inc (Fuji), a company incorporated under the laws of Panama, what it
described variously as a life assurance policy or as a capital investment bond (the
policy), in consideration of a single premium of £50,000; the life assured was
stated to be Gary Robert Tait. The liabilities thereunder of Tyndall were
transferred to Aetna Life Insurance Co Ltd on 27 April 1987 and to Windsor Life
Assurance Co Ltd (Aetna) on 1 January 1994 pursuant to ss 49 and 50 of the
Insurance Companies Act 1982. On 7 July 1994 Nicholls V-C ([1994] 4 All ER
1025, [1995] Ch 122) declared in answer to two preliminary issues directed to be
tried by an order of Master Barratt made on 25 March 1994 that the policy was
not a policy of insurance within the meaning of s 1 of the Life Assurance Act 1774
and was not rendered unenforceable by s 16 of the 1982 Act. This is an appeal
brought with the leave of Nicholls V-C by the two life assurance companies from
those declarations. The Secretary of State for Trade and Industry was given leave
to intervene by an order of this court made on 12 March 1996. He supports the
life assurance companies on the first issue and Fuji on the second.

The policy required Tyndall to maintain certain funds as subdivisions of its
long-term business fund. Each of the nine funds represented a broad category of
investment as indicated by its name, such as the UK Equity Fund or the Property
Fund, and was divided into units of equal value. The policy, which was typical of
many such policies issued by Tyndall at the relevant time, linked the benefits
payable under it to the value at maturity of the units in the funds to which it was
linked. By the terms of the policy the policyholder might switch from one fund
to another by giving notice to Tyndall to that effect. Nevertheless, the allocation
of units was notional only for the purpose of determining benefits and the assets
of the funds remained the property of Tyndall.

The funds were valued periodically on prescribed valuation days so as to
determine bid and offer prices for the units therein; the former being the asset
value of the unit after certain specified deductions were treated as having been
made and the latter being 100/95ths of the bid price. If notice to switch was given
then the bid price of the units to be disposed of (less a small amount to cover the
administration expenses involved) was treated as invested at the bid price in the
units to be acquired on the next following valuation day at the bid prices then
ascertained. Such prices were published in the Financial Times on the day
following the valuation day.

Mr Tait established in correspondence with Tyndall before the policy was
taken out by Fuji a number of relevant matters which he contends became the
terms of the policy or of a contract collateral to it. Those claims have still to be
determined at the trial of the action, now fixed to commence in March 1997. So
far as material for present purposes, such matters relate to the timing of the
valuation of the investments in the fund and the time by which switching

a instructions had to be received. The procedure adopted by Tyndall was to fix the bid and offer prices of the units at between 9 am and 10 am on the valuation day on the basis of data taken from the Stock Exchange data stream at 4 pm the previous day. The prices so ascertained were published in the Financial Times for the following day but switch instructions would be accepted for that valuation day if they were given in writing or by fax before 2.30 pm on the valuation day.

b One consequence of this timing, which Mr Tait evidently appreciated, was that the well-informed investor could himself estimate on the morning of the valuation day the approximate bid price which Tyndall would have fixed though it would not be published until the following day. Armed with this information and with knowledge of how the market had moved on the morning of the valuation day the policyholder could give instructions by fax before 2.30 pm on *c* the valuation day for a switch in the certain knowledge that he would thereby make a profit or avoid a loss. Between 24 March 1986 and 24 April 1991 Mr Tait exercised the switch option on behalf of Fuji so as to increase the value of the benefits payable under the policy from £54,089·70 to £1,058,375, an annual average return of 90%.

d From and after 24 April 1991 Aetna, then entitled to the business and liable for the obligations of Tyndall, changed the time on each valuation date at which it fixed the prices for the units from 10 am to 4 pm. The later time meant that the publication deadline for the Financial Times to be published on the following day could not be met so that the prices so fixed were not publicised until the next day *e* but one. One result of the change was that thereafter it was necessary for Mr Tait to give instructions to switch by 2.30 pm before the time for fixing the unit prices. In this action, commenced by Fuji by a writ indorsed with a statement of claim issued on 21 April 1993, Fuji claims that such a change of procedure constituted a repudiation of the policy or the collateral contract. The reason, as claimed in para 13, is that the additional 24 hours' delay in the prices at which Aetna had *f* insisted on carrying out switches since 24 April 1991 removed the advantage previously enjoyed so that the average return achieved thereafter was a paltry 8%. Accordingly, on 26 May 1992 Fuji accepted such repudiation, surrendered the policy and received £1,110,758·50 from Aetna. However, in the action Fuji sues for damages for breach of contract, the suggested measure of which is put at *g* a sum equal to the average return of 90% per annum on the policy moneys compounded annually for the rest of the lifetime of Mr Tait. It has been calculated by Aetna that such a sum would be equivalent to the gross national product of the United Kingdom for 460,000 years; though in fact any damage claim established would be limited to the assets of the relevant funds.

h Sections 1 and 3 of the 1774 Act provide, so far as material:

> '[1] ... no insurance shall be made by any person or persons ... on the life or lives of any person or persons, or on any other event or events whatsoever, wherein the person or persons for whose use, benefit, or on *j* whose account such policy or policies shall be made, shall have no interest, or by way of gaming or wagering; and that every assurance made contrary to the true intent and meaning hereof shall be null and void to all intents and purposes whatsoever.
>
> **3.** And in all cases where the insured hath interest in such life or lives, event or events, no greater sum shall be recovered or received from the

insurer or insurers than the amount of value of the interest of the insured in such life or lives, or other event or events.'

Fuji accepts that it does not have an insurable interest on the life of Mr Tait in excess of the sum already paid on the surrender of the policy. Thus the policy is void under s 1 of the 1774 Act to the extent that Fuji does not have an insurable interest if it is an insurance on the life of any person; hence the first preliminary issue.

Section 16(1) of the 1982 Act provides:

'An insurance company to which this Part of this Act applies shall not carry on any activities, in the United Kingdom or elsewhere, otherwise than in connection with or for the purposes of its insurance business.'

If the policy was not an insurance on the life of any person then, Aetna claims, it was not insurance at all and, being prohibited by s 16(1), was and is illegal and void; hence the second preliminary issue.

Before turning to these issues it is necessary to set out in greater detail the material terms of the policy. As I have already indicated it is described as a life assurance policy and as a capital investment bond. The initial and only premium was £50,000. As no intermediary was involved Fuji was credited with having paid a premium of £52,770·44, being the sum which, less the usual commission of 5·25%, results in the sum of £50,000. As the premium paid was of an amount which entitled the policyholder to a bonus of 2·5% of the premium paid, the value of the units allocated to the policy was £54,089·70. Early surrender was discouraged by a discontinuance charge designed to recoup the bonus, starting at 2·5% in the first year and reducing by half a per cent a year so as to cease altogether at the end of the fourth year. By condition (10)(g) such charge also applied in the case of the life assured committing suicide within the first year of the policy. The date of birth of Mr Tait, which was not admitted, was given as 21 February 1945. Mr Tait was not required to undergo any medical examination. The conditions indorsed on the policy included the following:

'Definitions

Death Benefit Factor means at the Commencement Date the Death Benefit Factor shown in the Schedule and thereafter it shall be such amount as may be determined under the provisions of Condition (6), provided always that the Death Benefit Factor shall not any time exceed the Factor shown in the Appendix for the attained age of the Life Assured at that time.

Mortality Cost means the expected cost of mortality for a Policy Month calculated as the Death Benefit Factor multiplied by the Value of Units on the Next Valuation Day following the first day of the Policy Month less the Value of Units on such Valuation Day multiplied by one twelfth of such annual rate of mortality as the Actuary deems to be equitable having regard to the then age of the Life Assured, the sex of the Life Assured and the A1967–70 select tables for assured lives published by the Institute of Actuaries or such other tables as may be published subsequently by the said Institute ...

(5) BENEFIT ON DEATH On the death of the Life Assured the Company shall pay the Value of Units on the Next Valuation Day following receipt by the Company of written notification of death multiplied by the Death Benefit Factor at the date of death of the Life Assured ...

a
(7) BENEFIT ON SURRENDER   At any time after the Unit Allocation Date the Policyholder may by notice to the Company in writing surrender the Policy in exchange for a cash sum equal to the Value of Units on the Next Valuation Day following receipt of the notice reduced by the Discontinuance Charge calculated in accordance with the table endorsed on this Policy (if any) ...

b
(10) EXCEPTIONAL CIRCUMSTANCES   Where in the opinion of the Company it would, due to exceptional circumstances, be in the interest of other holders of policies linked to a particular Fund for the exercise of any of the options contained in Condition (4), (7) and (8) affecting such Fund to be delayed the Company may by notice in writing to the Policyholder require him to defer the exercise of such option for a period not exceeding six months.'

c
Though the definition of death benefit factor envisaged that the factor shown in the schedule might be altered under condition (6), that was not a possibility in this case as condition (6) was expressly excluded. In the schedule the death benefit factor was specified as 1.00, though in the brochure advertising such policies it was stated that 'on the death of a single premium account 101% of the bid value of units will become payable'. The former actuary of Aetna gave evidence by affidavit sworn on 17 June 1994 to the effect that the schedule was wrong and that Aetna would have regarded itself as bound to adopt a death benefit factor of 1.01. Nevertheless, the reamended defence served on 14 April 1994 avers that the death benefit factor was 1.00 and there has been no application for leave to amend. Nicholls V-C recorded that the matter had been argued before him on the basis that the preliminary issue should be determined on the assumption that the death benefit factor was indeed 1.00.

d

e

With those considerations in mind I turn to the first issue. In his judgment, Nicholls V-C considered the meaning of the words in s 1 of the 1774 Act 'insurance ... on the life ... of any person'. After referring to *Prudential Insurance Co v IRC* [1904] 2 KB 658, *Flood v Irish Provident Assurance Co Ltd* [1912] 2 Ch 597n, *Joseph v Law Integrity Insurance Co Ltd* [1912] 2 Ch 581 and *Gould v Curtis* [1913] 3 KB 84, he said ([1994] 4 All ER 1025 at 1031, [1995] Ch 122 at 130):

f

g
'To be within the scope of this prohibitory section, the contract must be, first, an insurance which, secondly, is on the life of a person. In the *Prudential* case, Channell J enunciated the essence of an insurance for this purpose: a contract under which a sum of money becomes payable on an event which is uncertain as to its timing or as to its happening at all. The second element ("on the life") requires that the uncertain event is one geared to the uncertainties of life.   This reading of s 1 accords with the now well-established understanding of what is meant by life insurance.   I appreciate that, as I have already observed, the decided cases were concerned with the application of particular statutory or other definitions concerned with life insurance. However, none of those cases turned on subtle nuances of language. Shining through the cases is a judicial appraisal of the essence of life insurance.   Moreover, if one were to seek to compare language, *Joseph's* case would be indistinguishable.   There the company's objects incorporated a reference to the business of life assurance within the meaning of the Life Assurance Companies Act 1870. That Act applied to companies which issued "policies of assurance upon human life". I can see no reason for interpreting the similar expression in the 1774 Act differently from the way

h

j

the Court of Appeal interpreted that expression in the 1870 Act. *a*
Accordingly, in my view, to be within s 1, a sum of money (or other benefit)
must be payable on an event uncertain, either as to its timing or as to its
happening at all, and that event must be dependent on the contingencies of
human life.'

Nicholls V-C then considered the terms of the policy in this case, apart from
that relating to the discontinuance charge. He observed that in accordance with *b*
conditions (5) and (7) the benefit payable on death or surrender was the same,
namely the value of the units on the next valuation day after the company
received notification of the death or request for payment. He rejected an
argument that because one of the events on which payment was due was death
the policy was necessarily one of life insurance on the ground that— *c*

'To be within s 1 the contract must not only be "on life", the contract must
also be a contract of "insurance". Accordingly it is necessary to identify the
uncertain event which triggers a payment by the insurer. I do not see how
an event can be regarded as triggering a payment if there is already in
existence, irrespective of the happening of that event, an obligation on the *d*
insurer to make that very same payment on request. When the event occurs,
the insured acquires nothing he did not already have. Nor, I add, does the
insured lose anything.' (See [1994] 4 All ER 1025 at 1032, [1995] Ch 122 at
131.)

Nicholls V-C considered that the absence of any mortality cost deduction *e*
confirmed that the formula for calculating the benefits was unaffected by any
consideration of the life expectancy of Mr Tait and was therefore consistent with
the policy not being an insurance on Mr Tait's life.

Nicholls V-C then turned to the significance of the discontinuance charge. He
concluded that an element of insurance on the life of Mr Tait was built in to that
provision. He decided nevertheless that this element did not render the policy *f*
one of insurance on a life. He took the relevant principle to be:

'If a contract has to be labelled either as a contract of insurance or as not a
contract of insurance, then it must be necessary to look at the overall
position in the case of a contract with elements of more than one nature. I
agree with the suggestion in *MacGillivray and Parkington on Insurance Law* (8th *g*
edn, 1988) para 7 that only where the principal object is to insure can a
contract as a whole be called a contract of insurance.' (See [1994] 4 All ER
1025 at 1034, [1995] Ch 122 at 133.)

Applying that principle, he thought that the capital investment bond was not a *h*
contract of insurance nor an insurance on the life of any person.

The insurance companies submit that he was wrong. They accept that
Nicholls V-C correctly stated the test for the existence of an insurance on the life
of any person to be the existence of an obligation to pay 'a sum of money (or
other benefit) ... payable on an event uncertain, either as to its timing or as to its
happening at all, and that event must be dependent of the contingencies of *j*
human life.' They contend that the capital investment bond satisfies that test.
First, they rely on condition (5) whereunder the benefit is payable on the death.
They submit that it is immaterial that the same sum of money is payable in other
circumstances; not least because the right to surrender is dependent on the
continuance of life. Second, they rely on the fact that on the death of Mr Tait the

a benefit is payable forthwith on notification to the insurance company without the insurance company having the right to postpone payment for six months as it has in the event of a surrender and exceptional circumstances within condition (10). Third, they rely on the fact that on death within the first five years (except by suicide in the first year) unlike surrender in the same period, the benefit payable is not reduced by the discontinuance charge. Fourth, they contend that the

b insurance element constituted by the discontinuance charge confirms the policy as one of insurance when construed as a whole. They submit that the principal object test applied by Nicholls V-C is wrong in law. Finally, they point to the fact that on the death of Mr Tait the policy comes to an end, thereby crystallising the benefits payable thereunder without the option to either party to continue it.

On this issue the Secretary of State supports the insurance companies. He

c submits that it is not an essential element of a policy of life insurance that the benefit on death or maturity should be more or different from that payable on surrender. He points out that in enacting the 1982 Act and the Financial Services Act 1986, Parliament regarded the activities of insurance and investment as complementary and not as mutually exclusive. Thus, s 1 of the 1982 Act defines

d long-term business by reference to Sch 1, which includes in para (3) the linked long-term business of effecting and carrying out contracts of insurance on human life where the benefits are wholly determined by reference to the value of property. The 1986 Act indicates a similar view in s 1 and Sch 10, where a contract which is long-term insurance business is also treated, with exceptions, as an investment.

e Both the insurance companies and the Secretary of State relied on cases to which Nicholls V-C had not been referred, namely *Marac Life Assurance Ltd v IR Comr* [1986] 1 NZLR 694, *NM Superannuation Pty Ltd v Young* (1993) 113 ALR 39 and *Jones v AMP Perpetual Trustee Co NZ Ltd* [1994] 1 NZLR 690. I think that these cases are of assistance. The authorities to which he was referred in this

f connection all predate by many years the considerable developments in the nature of the insurance obtainable in the last two decades. These three cases show how the courts of Australia and New Zealand have regarded the newer forms of policy.

In *Marac Life Assurance Ltd v IR Comr* the Court of Appeal in New Zealand was concerned with whether certain bonds were policies of life insurance for the

g purposes of the Life Insurance Act 1908, the Income Tax Act 1976 and the Securities Act 1978. The bonds provided for the payment of a single premium. The benefits were (a) the payment of a fixed sum on a particular date if the life assured survived that date, and (b) the payment of a sum equal to the single premium together with bonuses thereon at a percentage rate compounded

h annually up to the anniversary of the commencement of the policy occurring next after the death if the life assured died before the particular date. The policy conferred an option on the holder to extend it for further periods.

The argument for the Revenue, which sought to establish that the bonds were not policies of insurance, posed as the appropriate test whether the primary or dominant purpose of the bonds was life insurance or investment. The Court of

j Appeal was unanimous in its conclusion that the bonds were policies of insurance. Its approach is demonstrated by the passage in the judgment of Cooke J, where he said (at 697–698):

'With respect, I agree with Ongley J's conclusion on this part of the case, but not with all his reasoning. Some of his observations suggest that he saw the question as turning on a weighing of what he called the insurance element in the bonds as against what he called the investment element. In these bonds I do not see any such dichotomy or true contrast. In the general sense all life insurance is investment. What distinguishes it from other kinds of investment is that the gain or yield, if there is one, depends on the contingencies of human life. That is the case as regards all these bonds. Under each a fixed sum, being more than the premium, becomes payable to the policy holder or his personal representative (the 10 year bond carrying as well participation in surplus), but the date on which the fixed sum becomes payable depends on whether or not the life assured is continuing. It is true that the sum is calculated by adding to the premium a given percentage, and compounding the resulting figure if necessary; but only if death happens to occur on an exact anniversary of the commencement of the risk will the sum correspond to interest for the actual use of money. No reason is apparent for describing these contracts as anything other than life insurance. In essence they are very closely linked with the contingencies of human life. A contract of life insurance is not the less such because it is for a short term.'

The suggested test of primary or dominant purpose was also rejected. Thus Somers J said (at 715):

'Mr Jenkin accepted that the bonds contained an element of life insurance but submitted that it was necessary to posit a further test to see whether they were in substance life policies. That test he posed as being whether their primary or dominant purpose was life insurance such characteristic being itself determined by the emphasis the parties placed upon it. I am quite unable to accept that. One obvious answer is that there may be no correspondence of emphasis between the parties and that the holder of a bond may have a variety of purposes in acquiring it. Another rests on the ordinary rules about the construction of a contract. In the High Court Ongley J said ((1985) 9 TRNZ 201 at 209): "I have reached the conclusion, however, that the insurance content of the Marac Life Bonds of whatever term, is not properly to be regarded as negligible. It is sufficiently substantial to justify the arrangement entered into between the insurer and the bondholder being regarded as a contract of life insurance." While a case may arise in which that which is called life assurance by the parties proves upon analysis to be something different, I doubt whether an attempted weighing of "insurance content" in the way indicated by the Judge is possible or material. If the contract answers the common test of life insurance which necessarily embraces a risk by the insurer dependent on the length of human life it must I think be characterised as life insurance.'

Accordingly, this case recognised that the investment element of a policy, which has become such a feature of modern insurance, is consistent with its characterisation as a life policy.

In *NM Superannuation Pty Ltd v Young* (1993) 113 ALR 39 the Federal Court of Australia was concerned with whether the policy in question was a policy 'of life assurance or endowment assurance' within the meaning of the phrase as used in s 116 of the Bankruptcy Act 1966 so as to except it from the property of the bankrupt divisible amongst his creditors. The policy in question arose under an employees' superannuation scheme, which required the employer to fund policies to be issued to its employees by the trustees of the scheme. The events a on which benefits were payable included (a) retirement on or after his retirement date as defined, (b) death in employment before the age of 70 and (c) leaving the employment of the employer before the retirement date. In each of those events the benefits were the retirement accumulation as defined, namely the accumulated contributions made by the employer with interest accrued from payment of the contribution to the event in question.

b   The judge had held by reference to the judgment of Channell J in *Prudential Insurance Co v IRC* [1904] 2 KB 658 that the policy was not life insurance for there was no element of risk of loss to the insurer. This was rejected by the Federal Court. Hill J said (at 54):

c   'His Lordship then found the contract in question to be a contract of insurance, whether the benefits payable under it were looked at separately or together. Thus, a contract to pay a sum of money at a particular age was, in the relevant sense, "uncertain" for it was uncertain whether the assured would live to that age. Clearly enough the contract to pay an amount on death would be insurance because, although death was certain, the time of it happening was uncertain. The fact that a larger sum was payable in the
d   event of reaching the prescribed age rather than death, was a matter which his Lordship regarded as immaterial. The requirement of uncertainty, which was referred to by Channell J, was said by the learned trial judge to be uncertainty "as to both profit and loss to the insurer". This was said to be a distinguishing characteristic of a contract of insurance. There is nothing in
e   the comments of Channell J which leads to this conclusion. Indeed, in the present case, the element of uncertainty, in the sense that that word is used by Channell J, is clearly there. The retirement benefit, payable under cl 11, is uncertain because the member may die before reaching the retirement date and thus receive no benefit under that clause. The death benefit, payable under cl 13, is equally uncertain, not in the sense that death is
f   uncertain, but because the time of death is uncertain and that benefit will not be payable if the member retires before the event of death occurs. Equally, the benefit payable under cl 17 is uncertain because it will only be payable if death has not intervened. The fact that the quantum of the benefits is the same does not affect, in my view, the outcome.'

g
        Hill J equated the operation of the right of the policyholder under cl 17 (to payment in the event of leaving employment with that employer before his retirement date) with that of 'a provision that permits cancellation of the policy at any time, or in limited circumstances, with an amount becoming thereby payable to the person insured' (see (1993) 113 ALR 39 at 58). Thus Hill J did not
h   think that either the identity of benefit or the events of retirement or change of employment on which it was payable prevented its recognition as a life policy. His conclusion was that 'the policy is properly to be characterised as a policy of life insurance' (see 113 ALR 39 at 40).
        Finally, in *Jones v AMP Perpetual Trustee Co NZ Ltd* [1994] 1 NZLR 690 the High
j   Court of New Zealand was concerned with whether the policy effected by the trustee company was a policy of life or endowment insurance for the purpose of the investment power of the trustees under the trust deed establishing a superannuation fund. The provisions of the policy were very similar to those of the scheme in *NM Superannuation Pty Ltd v Young*. Thomas J did not consider that the fact that the same benefit, namely contributions paid plus interest, was

payable in the events of disability, retirement or death prevented the policy being recognised as a policy of life insurance.

For Fuji it was submitted that Nicholls V-C was right for substantially the reasons he gave. It was submitted that the payment of the benefit must be dependent on the happening of an event or contingency related to death or survival to a specified age or date. Counsel for Fuji accepted that a right to payment of premiums paid, or some other specified sum on earlier surrender, does not prevent the contract being one of life insurance provided that such right affords 'different and inherently inferior benefits to those payable on the specified event'. He subjected all the cases to which I have referred to a minute, but not over-lengthy, analysis to demonstrate that in each of them the benefits were payable on a life or death-related event and in none of them was the same benefit payable on a surrender at the volition of the policyholder. He contended that, leaving out the discontinuance charge which he submitted was not an element of insurance at all, the terms of conditions (5) and (7) provided for identical rights on both death and surrender. This contract was, in his submission, simply an investment contract dressed up as a life assurance. He also submitted that the provisions of the 1982 Act and the 1986 Act and the regulatory consequences on which the Secretary of State relied were not relevant considerations on the construction and application of the 1774 Act.

Though the argument ranged over a wide area, and I make no complaint on that score, in the end the point is a narrow one. Is the fact that, subject to certain exceptions, the measure of the benefit payable on surrender is the same as that payable on death sufficient to prevent this contract being recognised as 'insurance ... made ... on the life ... of any person'? For my part I do not think that it is.

The essence of life assurance, as emphasised in all the cases, is that the right to the benefits is related to life or death. The obvious case, like condition (5), is where the benefit is payable on death or its notification. But over the years other less obviously life or death-related events have been recognised as sufficient. Thus survival to a given date, as in *Joseph v Law Integrity Insurance Co Ltd* [1912] 2 Ch 581, or the exercise of an option to determine given only to the personal representatives of the policyholder, as in *Re National Standard Life Assurance Corp* [1918] 1 Ch 427, being alive and therefore able to retire or leave a specified employment, as in *NM Superannuation Pty Ltd v Young* (1993) 113 ALR 39, have all been recognised as being sufficiently related to life or death. In this case, as counsel for Fuji accepted, the policy came to an end on the death of Mr Tait so that, subject to notification in the prescribed manner, the benefits then crystallised. Thus the right to surrender was related to the continuance of life, for it could not be exercised by Fuji after the death of Mr Tait. I do not suggest that a policy which contained condition (7) without also including condition (5) would be a policy of life assurance. But I see no reason why a policy which contains both should be denied that character.

If the event on which a benefit is payable is sufficiently life or death-related, then I can see no reason in principle why it should matter if that benefit is the same as that payable on another life or death-related event. That is a matter for the insurer and it is well established that it is not necessary that the insurer should be exposed to any risk at all (see *Flood v Irish Provident Assurance Co Ltd* [1912] 2 Ch 597n and *NM Superannuation v Young*). This was evidently the view of Hill J in the last-mentioned case, as demonstrated in the passage I quoted earlier, and I agree with him.

But even if it is necessary that the benefits should differ between one event and another, I do not see any reason why the difference must arise from the description of, or formula for fixing, those benefits. There is no doubt, given the fluctuations in the market, that over the term of the life of Mr Tait the value of the benefits receivable will change from valuation day to valuation day. Except in the case of unusual stability in the market, it is almost inevitable that the value of the benefits payable on death will be different from the value payable on surrender, and the value payable on surrender will vary according to when the surrender occurs.

In my view there is nothing in condition (7) to nullify compliance by condition (5) with s 1 of the 1774 Act which, if it stood alone, is admitted. The various other matters relied on by Aetna confirm this conclusion. Thus Aetna has no right under condition (10) to defer payment on notification of the death of the life assured, on death within the first five years (except by suicide in the first year) the value of the units must be paid in full without the deduction of any discontinuance charge and, as Nicholls V-C observed, the whole policy is 'clothed in the vesture of life insurance', which is at least relevant, though by no means conclusive, to the characterisation of the policy (see [1994] 4 All ER 1025 at 1032, [1995] Ch 122 at 132).

For my part, I would accept the submissions of counsel for Fuji that the scope of and regulatory consequences which might arise under the 1982 Act and the 1986 Act are not relevant to this issue, but that question does not arise in the view that I have taken. Further, I do not accept that Nicholls V-C, by his reference to the principal object of the insurance, indicated that he was adopting some inappropriate test (see [1994] 4 All ER 1025 at 1034, [1995] Ch 122 at 133). Reading his judgment on this issue as a whole it is clear that he was correctly considering the characterisation of the policy as a whole and posing the question whether so read it was a policy of life insurance.

Accordingly, I would allow the appeal on the first issue. On that basis the second issue does not arise. But as concern has been expressed as to both the conclusion of Nicholls V-C and his reasoning, the issue was fully argued and as this case may go further I should express my views on it, albeit shortly. For this purpose it is necessary to assume that the policy was neither a contract of insurance nor an insurance on the life of any person.

Nicholls V-C started by considering the decision of this court in *Phoenix General Insurance Co of Greece SA v Administratia Asigurarilor de Stat* [1987] 2 All ER 152, [1988] QB 216 in relation to the effect of infringing what is now s 2 of the 1982 Act. He said ([1994] 4 All ER 1025 at 1036, [1995] Ch 122 at 135):

'In the present case the prohibition is against carrying on any "activities" other than those permitted. "Activities" is every bit as wide and comprehensive as the prohibition in the *Phoenix* case. "Activities", albeit loose and general, is a comprehensive expression in this context. It must be apt to embrace carrying out a non-insurance contract as well as effecting such a contract. For this reason I am unable to draw any sensible distinction between the language of the prohibition in the two sections.'

He then considered whether 'Parliament is to be taken to have intended to strike down all contracts entered into, perhaps unwittingly by the insurer and in good faith by the insured, in breach of s 16'. For the four reasons he then gave he considered that the section did not avoid the policy. The first was that the section implemented European directives (Council Directive (EEC) 73/239 on the co-ordination of laws etc relating to the taking up and pursuit of the business of *a* direct insurance other than life assurance and Council Directive (EEC) 79/267 on the co-ordination of laws, regulations and administrative provisions relating to the taking up and pursuit of the business of direct life assurance) designed only to limit the business activities of insurance companies. The second, and following from the first, was that if an equivalent limitation were incorporated into the *b* insurance companies' memoranda of association the policyholder would still enjoy a substantial measure of protection under ss 35, 35A and 35B of the Companies Act 1985 (as amended by s 108 of the Companies Act 1989). His third reason was that, in contrast to s 2, infringement of s 16 did not involve a criminal offence. He relied, fourthly, on the fact that after the decision of this court in the *Phoenix* case s 132 of the 1986 Act was enacted to enable the court, in its *c* discretion, to enforce contracts which infringed s 2. No such provision was made in respect of contracts which infringed s 16, which Nicholls V-C considered to be an a fortiori case (see [1994] 4 All ER 1025 at 1036–1037, [1995] Ch 122 at 136–137).

In conclusion Nicholls V-C said ([1994] 4 All ER 1025 at 1037, [1995] Ch 122 at 136–137): *d*

'In my view, these features taken together point to the conclusion that Parliament did not intend that a contract made by an insurance company in breach of the restriction in s 16 should be unlawful and unenforceable. Rather, s 16 is part of a regulatory framework, in respect of which the Secretary of State has wide-ranging powers and responsibilities. The *e* intended remedy for a default by an insurance company under s 16 lies in the powers of intervention conferred on the Secretary of State by the same part of the Act in which s 16 appears. Default under s 16 can trigger an exercise of those powers (see s 37(2)(b)(i)).'

The insurance companies submit that Nicholls V-C was wrong in this *f* conclusion. First, they submit, having rightly concluded that s 16 expressly prohibited the insurer from carrying on the activity in question, it was not open to Nicholls V-C, consistently with the judgment of Kerr LJ in the *Phoenix* case, to consider the issues of public policy to which he referred. Second, they submit that the considerations to which Nicholls V-C did refer do not lead to the *g* conclusion at which he arrived. They maintain that he misunderstood the purpose and effect of the European directives; that the provisions introduced into the 1985 Act by the 1989 Act cannot be used to construe the 1982 Act; that the existence or otherwise of a penalty for the infringement of s 16 is not material to whether that section prohibits the performance of the obligations undertaken by the insurance company, and that Parliament's treatment of invalidity under s 2 *h* shows that it requires legislation to enable the court to enforce a contract in contravention of s 16.

On this issue Fuji contended that Nicholls V-C was wrong in his initial conclusion that s 16 prohibited the issue of the policy to Fuji but supported his ultimate decision. The Secretary of State supported Fuji on this issue. By *j* agreement between them the argument on this issue was primarily presented by counsel for the Secretary of State.

In essence the argument for both sides commenced with the judgment of Kerr LJ in *Phoenix General Insurance Co of Greece SA v Administratia Asigurarilor de Stat*. That case concerned the effect of the prohibition then contained in s 2(1) of the

Insurance Companies Act 1974 (now s 2(1) of the 1982 Act) that, so far as relevant,
'No person shall carry on in Great Britain insurance business' without the
requisite authority. Insurance business was defined by s 83 (now s 95) as 'the
business of effecting and carrying out contracts of insurance'. The purpose of the
provision was described by Kerr LJ in these terms ([1987] 2 All ER 152 at 175,
[1988] QB 216 at 273):

'The statutory prohibitions are designed to protect the insured by seeking
to ensure that undesirable persons are not authorised to carry on insurance
business and that authorised insurers remain solvent. Good public policy
and common sense therefore require that contracts of insurance, even if
made by unauthorised insurers, should not be invalidated. To treat the
contracts as prohibited would of course prevent the insured from claiming
under the contract and would merely leave him with the doubtful remedy of
seeking to recover his premium as money had and received.'

Later he described the problem and the principle to be applied. He said ([1987] 2
All ER 152 at 176, [1988] QB 216 at 273–274):

'The problem is therefore to determine whether or not the 1974 Act
prohibits contracts of insurance by necessary implication, since it
undoubtedly does not do so expressly. In that context it seems to me that the
position can be summarised as follows. (i) Where a statute prohibits both
parties from concluding or performing a contract when both or either of
them have no authority to do so, the contract is impliedly prohibited: see [Re
an arbitration between Mahmoud and Ispahani] [1921] 2 KB 716, [1921] All ER
Rep 217 and its analysis by Pearce LJ in [Archbolds (Freightage) Ltd v S Spanglett
Ltd (Randall, third party)] [1961] 1 All ER 417, [1961] 1 QB 374 with which
Devlin LJ agreed. (ii) But where a statute merely prohibits one party from
entering into a contract without authority, and/or imposes a penalty on him
if he does so (ie a unilateral prohibition) it does not follow that the contract
itself is impliedly prohibited so as to render it illegal and void. Whether or
not the statute has this effect depends on considerations of public policy in
the light of the mischief which the statute is designed to prevent, its
language, scope and purpose, the consequences for the innocent party, and
any other relevant considerations. The statutes considered in Cope v
Rowlands ((1836) 2 M & W 149, 150 ER 707) and Cornelius v Phillips ([1918] A
C 199, [1916–17] All ER Rep 685) fell on one side of the line; the Food Act
1984 would clearly fall on the other. (iii) The Insurance Companies Act
1974 only imposes a unilateral prohibition on unauthorised insurers. If this
were merely to prohibit them from carrying on "the business of effecting
contracts of insurance" of a class for which they have no authority, then it
would clearly be open to the court to hold that considerations of public
policy preclude the implication that such contracts are prohibited and void.
But unfortunately the unilateral prohibition is not limited to the business of
"effecting contracts of insurance" but extends to the business of "carrying
out contracts of insurance". This is a form of statutory prohibition, albeit
only unilateral, which is not covered by any authority. However, in the
same way as Parker J in [Bedford Insurance Co Ltd v Instituto de Resseguros do
Brasil] [1984] 3 All ER 766, [1985] QB 966, I can see no convincing escape
from the conclusion that this extension of the prohibition has the
unfortunate effect that contracts made without authorisation are prohibited

by necessary implication and therefore void. Since the statute prohibits the
insurer from carrying out the contract (of which the most obvious example
is paying claims), how can the insured require the insurer to do an act which
is expressly forbidden by statute? And how can a court enforce a contract
against an unauthorised insurer when Parliament has expressly prohibited
him from carrying it out? In that situation there is simply no room for the
introduction of considerations of public policy. As Parker J said in the *Bedford*
case [1984] 3 All ER 766 at 775, [1985] QB 966 at 986: "... once it is concluded
that on its true construction the Act prohibited both contract and
performance, that is the public policy". (iv) It follows that, however
reluctantly, I feel bound to agree with the analysis of Parker J in the *Bedford*
case and his conclusion that contracts of insurance made by unauthorised
insurers are prohibited by the 1974 Act ...'

In reliance on this passage Aetna criticises Nicholls V-C in that, as they submit,
having rightly put the prohibition contained in s 16(1) into category (iii), he then
went on to consider the aspects of public policy which could only enter into the
debate if he had put the case into category (ii). For Fuji, it is contended that
Nicholls V-C should have put s 16 into category (ii), thereby entitling him to
consider the aspects of public policy to which he referred.

It is not clear to me that Nicholls V-C did put the case into category (iii). It
seems to me that when one reads his judgment on this issue as a whole it was
directed to the consideration of which of the two available categories, (ii) or (iii),
it should be put into and that the answer depended on the proper construction of
the section in the context of the Act as a whole. At all events it seems to me that
that is the first question to be determined.

I have already quoted s 16(1) of the 1982 Act. It was enacted to give effect to
the European directives which, in their original form, imposed an obligation on
member states to require an insurance undertaking to—

'limit its business activities [to the business of insurance] [to the business
referred to in this Directive] and operations directly arising therefrom, to the
exclusion of all other commercial business ...'

It is clear that s 16 imposes a unilateral prohibition on the insurance company
from carrying 'on any activities ... otherwise than in connection with or for the
purposes of its insurance business'. When the definition of insurance business is
imported from s 95 it includes the effecting and carrying out of insurance policies.
But, as pointed out by counsel for Fuji, it does so in relation to the insurance
business to which it is to be confined and not to the proscribed 'activities'. In this
respect the case is different from the *Phoenix* case, for the words of prohibition in
that case included the specific and unambiguous prohibition on effecting and
carrying out of contracts of insurance without authority. It was from those words
that the Court of Appeal derived the necessary implication that the contracts of
insurance themselves were prohibited.

The word 'activities' is, of course, very general and is capable of covering the
issue of the policy if it were not a policy of insurance. But I do not think that it
follows from its width that, as a matter of construction, the prohibition
necessarily goes that far. In the *Phoenix* case the court considered that a
prohibition on 'carrying on the business of effecting contracts of insurance'
would not have done so. The carrying out of the contract may be collateral to
the prohibition (cf *Archbolds (Freightage) Ltd v S Spanglett Ltd (Randall, third party)*

a [1961] 1 All ER 417, [1961] 1 QB 374). Accordingly, the first stage must be to ascertain as a matter of construction what is prohibited expressly or by necessary implication. This involves a consideration of the Act as a whole and the mischief it was designed to deal with, not as a consideration of public policy as such but as part of the normal processes of statutory construction.

b There are a number of matters which convince me that it is not necessary to imply into s 16(1) any prohibition on making or carrying out contracts outside the permitted limit. The first is the very width of the word used. It is so wide and general that I find it difficult to ascribe to Parliament the intention that anything which fell within the word was to be illegal and void. This is reinforced by the fact that there is no criminal sanction for its breach. Such an omission is, of course, by no means conclusive but the wider the prohibition the more surprising c the omission. If the prohibition is as all-embracing as Aetna submits then why are the directors and other individuals responsible for the chaos which must ensue from its infringement not made criminally responsible?

Not only is there no criminal sanction but there is an impressive array of regulatory remedies available to the Secretary of State in the event of an d infringement of s 16. He may withdraw authorisation altogether under s 11. Pursuant to s 37(1) he has wide powers of intervention, including the power to direct investments (s 38), to limit premium income (s 41), to require an actuary's investigation (s 42), to accelerate the time for the periodic returns required by other provisions of the Act (s 43), to appoint inspectors (s 43A, 44), to search e premises (s 44A) and to wind up the company (s 54). These powers are more than adequate to ensure compliance with s 16.

The purpose of the section, evident from the directives it was intended to implement, was to limit the scope of the undertakings' commercial activities. It is not a necessary implication from that purpose that every contract entered into in carrying on business in the forbidden sphere should be invalidated. Although f ss 35, 35A and 35B of the 1985 Act, to which Nicholls V-C referred, were not enacted until 1989, at the time of the enactment of the 1982 Act s 35 of the 1985 Act, which reproduced the provisions originally contained in s 9(1) of the European Communities Act 1972, did apply. That section would give some measure of protection to the person dealing in good faith with the company in g the unauthorised field without exonerating the management of the company.

I agree with Aetna that the provisions of s 132 of the 1986 Act cannot assist on the true construction of s 16 of the 1982 Act. First, the former Act is subsequent in time. Second, even if the assumption on which Parliament subsequently legislates may be prayed in aid, it is by no means clear what the assumption was. h To this extent I disagree with the judgment of Nicholls V-C.

In my view s 16 on its true construction does not invalidate activities undertaken otherwise that in connection with and for the purpose of its insurance business as defined. There is no express prohibition and in my view, given the purpose and context of the Act and having regard to its other provisions, no j necessary implication to that effect either. I agree with Nicholls V-C's overall conclusion. Accordingly, if the second issue arose for decision I would dismiss the appeal on that issue.

SIR RALPH GIBSON. I agree that the appeal should be allowed on the first issue for the reasons given by Morritt LJ

On that basis, as he has said, the second issue of illegality does not arise. Morritt LJ has noted the importance of the second issue and has expressed his view that, if the policy was neither a contract of insurance nor an insurance on the life of any person, s 16 of the Insurance Companies Act 1982 does not invalidate activities undertaken otherwise than in connection with and for the purposes of the insurance business as defined: and, accordingly, the contract upon which Fuji Finance Inc (Fuji) claims damages would not be avoided.

For my part I am not persuaded that, on the assumption stated, s 16 of the 1982 Act would leave the contract enforceable by Fuji.

The prohibition in s 16(1) is that 'the insurance company ... shall not carry on any activities ... otherwise than in connection with or for the purposes of its insurance business'; and, as Nicholls V-C observed ([1994] 4 All ER 1025 at 1035, [1995] Ch 122 at 134), on this assumption, Tyndall Assurance Ltd was prohibited from issuing Fuji's policy because the section restricts insurance companies to the business of insurance.

Since the Act does not spell out the consequences for a particular piece of prohibited business or of failure to comply with s 16, beyond stating that such a default is not a criminal offence (s 71(7)), the question for the court is whether it is clear, as a matter of necessary implication, that Parliament intended to render unenforceable the contract contained in the supposed policy. The relevant considerations for resolution of this question were stated by Devlin LJ in *Archbolds (Freightage) Ltd v S Spanglett Ltd (Randall, third party)* [1961] 1 All ER 417 at 425, [1961] 1 QB 374 at 390 to be 'the same as those that arise on the construction of every statute; one must have regard to the language used and to the scope and purpose of the statute': cited by Kerr LJ in *Phoenix General Insurance Co of Greece SA v Administratia Asigurarilor de Stat* [1987] 2 All ER 152 at 175, [1988] QB 216 at 272. Later in his judgment, Kerr LJ observed that the contrast between a contract of money lending and a contract of insurance made it clear why it is good public policy to refuse to enforce the former, but bad policy in the case of the latter because in both cases the legislation is designed to protect the customer but the protection which the customer requires is different in the two cases.

Kerr LJ continued ([1987] 2 All ER 152 at 175, [1988] QB 216 at 273):

> 'The statutory prohibitions are designed to protect the insured by seeking to ensure that undesirable persons are not authorised to carry on insurance business and that authorised insurers remain solvent. Good public policy and common sense therefore require that contracts of insurance, even if made by unauthorised insurers, should not be invalidated.'

He then observed that if the Insurance Companies Act 1974 permitted resort to considerations of public policy then there could only be one answer; but he concluded that the language of the express prohibition, namely the 'effecting and carrying out of contracts of insurance' rendered the contract unenforceable at the suit of the customer.

Nicholls V-C in this case accepted that the prohibition in s 16(1) of the 1982 Act is as wide and comprehensive as the prohibition in the *Phoenix* case. The word 'activities' is apt to embrace carrying out a non-insurance contract as well as effecting such a contract. Nevertheless, he held that Parliament is not to be taken 'to have intended to strike down all contracts entered into ... in breach of s 16', having regard to the genesis of s 16 in the European Directives (Council Directive (EEC) 73/239 on the co-ordination of laws etc relating to the taking up and

a pursuit of the business of direct insurance other than life assurance and Council
Directive (EEC) 79/267 on the co-ordination of laws, regulations and
administrative provisions relating to the taking up and pursuit of the business of
direct life assurance); to the provisions of ss 35, 35A and 35B of the Companies
Act 1985 as amended; to the express provision that default under s 16 is not a
criminal offence; and to s 132 of the Financial Services Act 1986, which gives to
b the court discretion with reference to a contract made in breach of s 2 of the 1982
Act but no discretion with reference to a contract made in breach of s 16. The
intended remedy for a default by an insurer under s 16 lay, in his view, in the
powers of intervention of the Secretary of State under the Act (see s 37(2)(b)(i)).

Morritt LJ has concluded that it is not necessary to imply into s 16(1) any
prohibition on making or carrying out contracts outside the permitted limit for
c reasons which he has set out, namely, in summary, the width and generality of
the wording of the prohibition coupled with the absence of criminal sanctions for
breach; and the array of regulatory remedies available to the Secretary of State in
the event of infringement of s 16. These powers are, in his view, more than
adequate to ensure compliance with s 16.

d I have found this point to be difficult. In the end, I prefer the view that, upon
the assumption made, the contract in this policy would be void.

The prohibition under s 2, of which the terms were considered in the *Phoenix*
case, is, with the definition imported, as follows: 'No person shall carry on any
insurance business of effecting and carrying out contacts of insurance ... unless
authorised to do so.'

e The prohibition under s 16(1), with the definition imported, is as follows:

> 'An insurance company ... shall not carry on any activities ... otherwise
> than in connection with or for the purposes of its business of effecting and
> carrying out contracts of insurance.'

f I respectfully agree with the obiter conclusion of this court in the *Phoenix* case
that the prohibition in s 2 had the effect of rendering void a contract which was
outside the authorised range of business. The prohibition in s 16(1) seems to me
to have been intended to have the same effect. The width of the provision does
not, in my judgment, suggest otherwise. The words 'in connection with or for
the purpose of' must be read as meaning 'in lawful connection with and for the
g lawful purposes of' the insurance business. A contract, which is not a permitted
contract of insurance, and which is not in such lawful connection or for such
lawful purposes, would therefore be void; but the mere fact that such a void
contract or contracts had been made would not affect the validity of other
activities which were in lawful connection with or for the lawful purposes of the
h insurance business.

Next, the availability of the regulatory remedies is not, in my judgment, of
decisive significance. It is common ground that the purposes of the legislation
include that of protecting the public and, in particular, the potential and the actual
customers of the insurance company. It does not assist or protect an individual
j customer, who has entered into a contract which the insurance company is
prohibited from making, for his contract to be rendered void; but later invocation
of the regulatory remedies will do nothing to protect other customers, who
already have valid contracts of insurance, against the possible effect upon the
solvency of the insurance company of the prohibited contract, and of other
similar contracts. I have no confident understanding of the degree of the risk of

the making of a sufficient number of prohibited contracts which may be of
sufficiently damaging effect to impair the solvency of an insurance company; but
I see no reason to disregard the risk as fanciful. I think it likely that Parliament
would have supposed that a casual breach of s 16 with reference to a particular
contract, which would gave rise to no threat to the solvency of the company,
would not cause a respectable insurance company to rely upon its own technical
breach of the prohibition so as to escape liability. Further, an individual
customer, whose contract might thus be rendered void, might in a significant
number of cases be protected by contractual rights against his broker or other
financial adviser.

If my view is right, it is obviously desirable for the discretion enacted by s 132
of the 1986 Act to be extended to enforcement of a contract made in breach of
s 16(1) of the 1982 Act.

HOBHOUSE LJ. Before Nicholls V-C ([1994] 4 All ER 1025, [1995] Ch 122) and
before this court two points of law were argued. They arose on the two issues
ordered to be tried as preliminary issues in the action. The first was whether the
contract contained in the document issued to the plaintiff was a contract of life
insurance. If it was, it was properly issued by the defendants to the plaintiff and
was enforceable but was subject to the provisions of the Life Assurance Act 1774.
The life assured was that of Gary Robert Tait. Accordingly, under s 3 of the 1774
Act: ' ... no greater sum shall be recovered or received from the insurer or
insurers than the amount of value of the interest of the insured in such life ...' It
is accepted that the sum already received by the plaintiff from the defendants fully
covers the maximum amount that it could recover under s 3. Therefore if the
relevant contract is a contract of life assurance, the plaintiff has no right to recover
substantial damages from the defendants in this action.

The second point only arises if the first issue is answered in the negative and
the contract is not a contract of insurance. It is accepted that, on this hypothesis,
s 16(1) of the Insurance Companies Act 1982 applies. That section provides:

'An insurance company to which this Part of this Act applies shall not carry
on any activities, in the United Kingdom or elsewhere, otherwise than in
connection with or for the purposes of its insurance business.'

The second point, therefore, is whether this provision renders the contract
unenforceable against the defendants. If it does, then it follows that the plaintiff's
claim in the action must fail.

Nicholls V-C decided both points in favour of the plaintiff. In his judgment,
therefore, the action was to proceed to a trial on the merits. The defendants have
appealed from his decision and have argued, in the alternative, that each of the
issues should be answered in the senses contended for by the defendants. If the
defendants succeed on either of the points which they have argued, it follows, as
I have already explained, that the plaintiff's claim in the action must fail. If the
defendants succeed on the first point, they not only do not need the second point
but the second point does not arise; in both senses it becomes academic.

Like Morritt LJ and Sir Ralph Gibson I consider that the defendants succeed on
the first point. It follows that the appeal must be allowed and that the judgment
of Nicholls V-C cannot stand. Under these circumstances, for reasons which I
will develop later in this judgment, I do not consider that it is desirable that this
court should determine the second issue. Any views expressed will be obiter.

The first issue
a
   In the relevant respect, the 1774 Act applies to any 'insurance' made 'on the life or lives of any person or persons'. What is an insurance on the life of a person has been before the courts on a number of occasions, particularly in the first two decades of this century when new types of life insurance contract were being developed and marketed as a means of investment or saving. The leading
b authorities are reviewed in the judgments of Nicholls V-C and Morritt LJ. Nicholls V-C summarised the law in these words ([1994] 4 All ER 1025 at 1031, [1995] Ch 122 at 130):

   'Accordingly, in my view, to be within s 1 a sum of money (or other benefit) must be payable on an event uncertain, either as to its timing or as
c   to its happening at all, and that event must be dependent on the contingencies of human life.'

These contingencies include the contingency of survival as well as of death (see *Gould v Curtis* [1913] 3 KB 84). By the terms of the contract, a sum is payable by
d the defendants to the plaintiff upon the death of Mr Tait. Further, if they be relevant, the sums payable upon partial or full surrender are dependent on the contingency of the survival of Mr Tait until the date when that right is exercised. What are the rights of the plaintiff at any moment in time under this contract are dependent upon the contingency of whether Mr Tait has died. The quantification of the defendants' liability under the contract at any given time is
e dependent upon other factors but this does not affect the character of the contract as a policy of life insurance. The terms of policies may take a wide variety of forms. There may be other rights given by the contract besides the right to be paid a sum dependent upon a contingency of human life. These other rights do not mean that there is not a contract of insurance. It is not necessary that the
f insurer should be exposed to a risk of loss (see *Joseph v Law Integrity Insurance Co Ltd* [1912] 2 Ch 581, following *Flood v Irish Provident Assurance Co Ltd* [1912] 2 Ch 597n). The sum recoverable on death may be greater than the sum recoverable on survival but this need not be the case and is not in many classes of life insurance. Indeed, the sum payable can be the same, the contingency affecting the time at which it becomes payable.
g
   Here the argument of the plaintiff is that the quantification of the sum at any given moment is the same whether Mr Tait is alive at that moment or has just died. But whether, at any given moment in time, any sum is payable depends upon whether Mr Tait had survived to that moment or has just died. This conclusion is confirmed by the additional cases cited to us from Australia and
h New Zealand, in particular *NM Superannuation Pty Ltd v Young* (1993) 113 ALR 39 and *Jones v AMP Perpetual Trustee Co NZ Ltd* [1994] 1 NZLR 690.
   Nicholls V-C's reason for accepting the plaintiff's argument was summed up in this passage ([1994] 4 All ER 1025 at 1032, [1995] Ch 122 at 131):

j   'To be within s 1 the contract must not only be "on life", the contract must also be a contract of "insurance". Accordingly it is necessary to identify the uncertain event which triggers a payment by the insurer. I do not see how an event can be regarded as triggering a payment if there is already in existence, irrespective of the happening of that event, an obligation of the insurer to make that very same payment on request. When the event occurs,

the insured acquires nothing he did not already have. Nor, I add, does the
insured lose anything.'

Here Nicholls V-C is applying a different criterion to that he adopted earlier and
which I have quoted. But he is, with respect, in any event confusing the valuation
of the right with its accrual. The death of Mr Tait crystallises and restricts the
rights of the plaintiff under the contract. The survival of Mr Tait enables the
plaintiff to exercise other rights at a later date, rights which because they are
exercisable at a different date or dates will have a different value to the value of
the right which would have accrued had Mr Tate died on the earlier date. All
these rights (and, if it be relevant, their value) remain contingent upon the death
or survival of Mr Tait which is an uncertain event.

Accordingly, the appeal succeeds on the first point. This contract was a policy
of life insurance. The plaintiff cannot make any further recovery in the action by
reason of s 3 of the 1774 Act.

The second issue

It has been a matter of judicial comment now for over 50 years that Parliament
causes unnecessary uncertainty by enacting provisions which prohibit or render
unlawful activities or actions without saying at the same time what is to be the
effect (if any) on the validity or enforceability of the transactions referred to. In
recent years parliamentary draftsmen seem to have heeded this advice but in the
case of s 16 of the 1982 Act they have not done so. That section leaves open to
argument whether its contravention renders transactions which are not related
to insurance business ineffective and unenforceable. As is evident from the
judgments of Morritt LJ and Sir Ralph Gibson, the arguments are nicely balanced.
The arguments which led to the conclusion of Nicholls V-C on this issue do not
seem to me to be at all persuasive (see [1994] 4 All ER 1025 at 1036, [1995] Ch 122
at 136). But it is clear both from the argument before us and from the judgment
of Morritt LJ that more persuasive arguments can be advanced. However, the
fact remains that this section forms part of a scheme which is intended to protect
the assets and solvency of insurance companies and to prevent those assets from
being diverted to liabilities which arise from business which is not insurance
business. If the arguments presented to us by Mr Glick QC, who appeared before
us on behalf of the Secretary of State and for whose assistance we are grateful,
were to be accepted, such an object might very well be frustrated. There are
forceful arguments consistent with previously decided cases to lead to the
conclusion expressed by Sir Ralph Gibson.

The only wholly satisfactory answer to this uncertainty would be for those
responsible for the legislation to make clear their intention by, for example,
making applicable to s 16 the discretion which already exists in s 132 of the 1986
Act or by some other express provision. As was pointed out by Mr Glick, the
overlap and interplay of the provisions regarding life insurance and other forms
of investment contract covered by this and other Acts and by European
legislation is of great practical and schematic importance. In my judgment it is
inappropriate for this court to express a view about a contentious question which
is hypothetical and does not arise on this appeal. Hopefully the uncertainty will
be remedied by legislation. If, however, that should not occur, an authoritative
judicial decision must await a case in which the need for such a decision arises.

Accordingly, beyond saying that I do not accept the reasons given by Nicholls
V-C for his conclusion, I express no view upon the second issue. The appeal will

a be allowed, the judgment of the court below will be set aside, and there will be substituted a single declaration in the terms of the first issue that the policy referred to in para 4 of the amended statement of claim was a policy of life assurance within the meaning of s 1 of the 1774 Act.

Appeal allowed. Leave to appeal to House of Lords refused.

b

Mary Rose Plummer   Barrister.

Lloyds Bank plc v Carrick and another

COURT OF APPEAL, CIVIL DIVISION
BELDAM, MORRITT LJJ AND SIR RALPH GIBSON
8, 9, 28 FEBRUARY 1996

Land charge – Failure to register – Estate contract – Contract void against purchaser of legal estate for money or money's worth – Mortgagee – Defendant agreeing to purchase property – Agreement not registered – Defendant paying purchase price but title not conveyed to defendant – Legal owner charging property to bank – Bank claiming possession on legal owner's default – Whether defendant entitled to assert bare trust, constructive trust or proprietary estoppel against bank – Land Charges Act 1972, s 4(6).

The second defendant was the sister-in-law of the first defendant, a building contractor who had a number of properties. When her husband (the first defendant's brother) died in 1982, the first defendant suggested that she sell the matrimonial home, pay the proceeds to him and move to a maisonette which he held on a long lease which would become hers. The second defendant accepted that offer, sold her house, paid the sum of £19,000 to her brother-in-law and moved into the maisonette. The title to the maisonette was unregistered and the lease remained in the first defendant's name. Thereafter, the second defendant was responsible for all outgoings on the property. In 1986 the first defendant charged the property to the plaintiff bank without informing the bank that his sister-in-law was living in the property or of the arrangements under which she did so. The bank did not itself make any inquiries as to who was in possession. In 1991 the bank sought repayment of the amount then owing by the first defendant, which amounted to some £89,000, and subsequently brought proceedings for possession of the property. The first defendant claimed that he held the property as bare trustee for the second defendant, who was joined as a party. The bank contended that her interest was registrable as a class C(iv) land charge (ie an unregistered estate contract), under the Land Charges Act 1972 and was void against the bank under s 4(6)[a] of that Act for want of registration. The county court judge dismissed the bank's claim on the grounds that because there was a bare trust there was no registrable interest and, further, that the bank's charge was subject to the second defendant's interest because, in failing to make inquiries of who was in possession of the property, it had constructive notice of her beneficial interest. The bank appealed. The second defendant accepted that the original agreement was a valid open contract for the purchase of the property which became enforceable by her when she partly performed it by entering into possession and paying the whole of the purchase price, that it remained uncompleted at the time the bank's legal charge was granted in 1986, and that if her only interest in the property was derived from the contract the bank was entitled to succeed because the contract was void as against the bank as an unregistered estate contract. However, she contended that her interest in the property was separate and distinct from that arising under the unregistered estate contract because it arose under either a bare trust, a constructive trust or a proprietary estoppel. The bank accepted that if it did so, it had constructive notice of that interest.

---

a   Section 4(6) is set out at p 636 j, post

Held – The appeal would be allowed for the following reasons—

a

(1) The arrangement between the defendants amounted to a specifically enforceable contract at the suit of the second defendant; the first defendant therefore became a trustee of the property for his sister-in-law and since she had paid the whole of the purchase price he was in fact a bare trustee and had no beneficial interest in the property. However, the second defendant's absolute

b beneficial interest originated in the contract and had no existence except as the equitable consequence of the contract and, as such, she was unable to assert the existence of a bare trust separate from the contract (see p 637 *g* to p 638 *c*, post).

(2) If there had been no contract between the parties, the second defendant might have been able to rely on a constructive trust similar to a wife's equitable interest where the title was registered in the sole name of the husband; but where

c there was a specifically enforceable contract the court was not entitled to superimpose a further constructive trust on the vendor in favour of the purchaser over that which already existed in consequence of the contractual relationship. Accordingly, the second defendant was not able to assert the existence of a constructive trust (see p 639 *b* to *f*, post); *Lloyds Bank plc v Rosset* [1990] 1 All ER

d 1111 distinguished.

(3) The second defendant's claim to assert a proprietary estoppel failed because the principles of proprietary estoppel could not be applied when, at the time of the relevant expenditure, there was already a bare trust arising in consequence of an enforceable contract to the same effect as the interest sought pursuant to the proprietary estoppel. Furthermore, any proprietary estoppel

e which the second defendant could enforce was against the first defendant, not the bank, in respect of those rights which his actions had encouraged her to have, i e that she was the beneficial owner of the property. Her expectations that she was entitled to have the property conveyed to her were defeated by the fact that the contract was not registered before the bank's charge was granted, and as against

f the first defendant she still retained her rights under a valid and enforceable contract but was prevented from enforcing them because he was unable to redeem the mortgage and obtain title to pass on to her. The beneficial owner under an unregistered contract could not defeat a mortgagee's interest and obtain indirectly by means of a proprietary estoppel that which s 4(6) of the 1972 Act, by specifically invalidating as against a mortgagee any unregistered contract by the

g estate owner for the conveyance of the legal estate, prevented him from obtaining directly under a contract declared to be void as against the mortgagee (see p 641 *d* to p 642 *d j*, post); *Western Fish Products Ltd v Penwith DC* [1981] 2 All ER 204 applied.

Per curiam. It is beyond doubt that s 14 of the Law of Property Act 1925 does

h not achieve for unregistered land that which s 70(1)(g) of the Land Registration Act 1925 achieves for registered land (see p 642 *f j*, post).

Notes

For equitable interests in land, see 16 *Halsbury's Laws* (4th edn reissue) paras 775–

j 781.

For estate contract and the effect of omission to register such a contract as a land charge, see 26 *Halsbury's Laws* (4th edn) paras 732–743.

For the Law of Property Act 1925, s 14, see 37 *Halsbury's Statutes* (4th edn) 94.

For the Land Registration Act 1925, s 70, see ibid 578.

For the Land Charges Act 1972, s 4, see ibid 412.

Cases referred to in judgments

Austin v Keele (1987) 61 ALJR 605, PC.

Bridges v Mees [1957] 2 All ER 577, [1957] Ch 475, [1957] 3 WLR 215.

Campbell Discount Co Ltd v Bridge [1961] 2 All ER 97, [1961] 1 QB 445, [1961] 2 WLR 596, CA; *rvsd* [1962] 1 All ER 385, [1962] AC 600, [1962] 2 WLR 439, HL.

Crabb v Arun DC [1975] 3 All ER 865, [1976] Ch 179, [1975] 3 WLR 847, CA.

Gissing v Gissing [1970] 2 All ER 780, [1971] AC 886, [1970] 3 WLR 255, HL.

Grant v Edwards [1986] 2 All ER 426, [1986] Ch 638, [1986] 3 WLR 114, CA.

Inwards v Baker [1965] 1 All ER 446, [1965] 2 QB 29, [1965] 2 WLR 212, CA.

Ives (E R) Investments Ltd v High [1967] 1 All ER 504, [1967] 2 QB 379, [1967] 2 WLR 789, CA.

Lloyds Bank plc v Rosset [1990] 1 All ER 1111, [1991] 1 AC 107, [1990] 2 WLR 867, HL.

Moorgate Mercantile Co Ltd v Twitchings [1975] 3 All ER 314, [1976] QB 225, [1975] 3 WLR 286, CA.

Ramsden v Dyson (1866) LR 1 HL 129.

Shiloh Spinners Ltd v Harding [1973] 1 All ER 90, [1973] AC 691, [1973] 2 WLR 28, HL.

Taylor Fashions Ltd v Liverpool Victoria Trustees Co Ltd [1981] 1 All ER 897, [1982] QB 133, [1981] 2 WLR 576.

Western Fish Products Ltd v Penwith DC [1981] 2 All ER 204, CA.

Willmott v Barber (1880) 15 Ch D 96.

Cases also cited or referred to in skeleton arguments

Abbey National Building Society v Cann [1990] 1 All ER 1085, [1991] 1 AC 56, HL.

Alderdale Estate Co v McGrory [1917] 1 Ch 414, CA; *rvsd* [1918] AC 503, [1918–19] All ER Rep 1184, HL.

Ashburn Anstalt v Arnold [1988] 2 All ER 147, [1989] Ch 1, CA.

Beesly v Hallwood Estates Ltd [1960] 2 All ER 314, [1960] 1 WLR 549; *affd* [1961] 1 All ER 90, [1961] Ch 105, CA.

Butcher v Stapeley (1685) 1 Vern 363, 23 ER 524.

Coventry Permanent Economic Building Society v Jones [1951] 1 All ER 901.

De Lusignan v Johnson (1973) 230 EG 499.

Gloag and Miller's Contract, Re (1883) 23 Ch D 320.

Hollington Bros Ltd v Rhodes [1951] 2 All ER 578.

Hyde v Pearce [1982] 1 All ER 1029, [1982] 1 WLR 560, CA.

Killner v France [1946] 2 All ER 83.

Lester v Foxcraft (1700) Colles 108, 1 ER 205.

Markfaith Investment Ltd v Chiap Hua Flashlights Ltd [1991] 2 AC 43, [1990] 2 WLR 1451, PC.

Midland Bank Trust Co Ltd v Green [1981] 1 All ER 153, [1981] AC 513, HL.

Milton v Procter [1989] NSW ConvR 56,959, NSW CA; *affd* 1988 NSW LEXIS 8800, NSW CA (Full Ct).

Monolithic Building Co, Re, Tacon v Monolithic Building Co [1915] 1 Ch 643, [1914–15] All ER Rep 249, Ch D & CA.

Phillips v Mobil Oil Co Ltd [1989] 3 All ER 97, [1989] 1 WLR 888, CA.

Pyke v Williams (1703) 2 Vern 455, 23 ER 891.

Ridley v De Geerts [1945] 2 All ER 654, CA.

Sharp v Milligan (1856) 22 Beav 606, 52 ER 1242; *affd* (1857) 23 Beav 419, 53 ER 165.

Timmins v Moreland Street Property Co Ltd [1957] 3 All ER 265, [1958] Ch 110, CA.

Tootal Clothing Ltd v Guinea Properties Ltd (1992) 64 P & CR 452.

a *Williams & Glyn's Bank Ltd v Boland* [1980] 2 All ER 408, [1980] 3 WLR 138, HL.
Wolverhampton and Walsall Rly Co v London and North Western Rly Co (1873) LR 16
   Eq 433.

Appeal
By notice dated 31 March 1995 the plaintiff, Lloyds Bank plc (the bank) appealed
b with leave of the Court of Appeal (Neill LJ and Cazalet J) granted on 31 March
1995 from the order of Mr Recorder Holmes given in the Cambridge County
Court on 5 July 1994 whereby he dismissed the bank's claim as mortgagee for
possession of the leasehold property known as 7 Derby Way, Newmarket,
Suffolk and made a declaration that the mortgagor, the first defendant, Michael
Robert Carrick, held the lease of that property in trust for his sister-in-law, the
c second defendant, Margaret Carrick, so that her interests in and rights over the
property were not subject to the bank's charge dated 25 November 1986. By
respondent's notice dated 6 June 1995 the second defendant contended that the
order should be affirmed on the additional ground that her expenditure on the
property prior to the legal charge was incurred in the belief encouraged by the
d first defendant that she was the beneficial owner of the property and thus gave
rise to an equity in her favour. The facts are set out in the judgment of Morritt LJ.

Josephine Hayes (instructed by *Taylor Vinters*, Cambridge) for the bank.
Neil Vickery (instructed by *Quirke & Co*, Croydon) for the defendants.

e   *Cur adv vult*

28 February 1996. The following judgments were delivered.

MORRITT LJ (giving the first judgment at the invitation of Beldam LJ). This is
an appeal of Lloyds Bank plc, to which I shall refer as 'the bank', from the order
f of Mr Recorder Holmes made in the Cambridge County Court on 5 July 1994. By
that order he dismissed the bank's claim as mortgagee for possession of leasehold
property known as 7 Derby Way, Newmarket, Suffolk and made a declaration
that the mortgagor, the first defendant Mr Carrick, held the lease of that property
in trust for the second defendant, Mrs Carrick, so that her interests in and rights
g over that property were not subject to the bank's charge dated 25 November
1986.
   The facts are simple and may be shortly stated. No 7 Derby Way, Newmarket
is a maisonette the title to which is unregistered. By a lease dated 4 August 1971
it was demised for a term of 99 years from 25 March 1971 in consideration of a
premium and a relatively nominal rent. There were no restrictions on the
h lessee's ability to assign the term, which, on 2 February 1982, was assigned to the
first defendant Mr Carrick who then lived in the maisonette.
   Mr Jeffrey Carrick was the brother of Mr Carrick and the husband of the second
defendant. Mr Jeffrey Carrick and Mrs Carrick, together with their two small
boys, lived in Edinburgh Road, Newmarket. Mr Jeffrey Carrick died in March
j 1982. After his death but before November 1982 there were discussions between
Mr Carrick and Mrs Carrick as to where she should live. Those discussions and
their aftermath were described by the recorder in the following terms:

   'The first defendant says that he told Mrs Carrick that, effectively, "If you
   like, you can come and live in this property [ie 7 Derby Way, Newmarket]".
   She was concerned whether she could afford to do so and whether she could

sell her house and what would happen. Suffice it to say that Mr Michael
Carrick, the first defendant, said to his sister-in-law "Put the property on the
market and what you get from the net proceeds of sale you can pay to this
property, which will become yours". Effectively, that is what happened.
Mrs Carrick, the second defendant, put her property on the market. She
realised a figure, which after deductions of repayment of mortgage (no doubt
estate agent's commission and legal expenses and the usual outgoings that
one incurs on a sale), amounted to around £19,000. As a result of completing
that, the £19,000 was paid over to the first defendant. The first defendant,
being a building contractor, had a number of other properties at the material
time and, in fact, went to live at another property, taking his then wife and
child with him, leaving Mrs Carrick to come and live in the property.'

Mrs Carrick and her two children moved into the maisonette in about November
1982.

In the course of his judgment the recorder referred to the existence of a charge
over the maisonette in favour of the bank existing at that time, but that seems to
be an error for the original document is dated 10 November 1983. At all events
Mrs Carrick became aware of it and raised the matter with Mr Carrick on a
number of occasions when he told her not to worry as he would sort it out. In
the event it was redeemed on 11 November 1986 some two weeks before the
execution of the charge with which this appeal is concerned. At some time before
it was redeemed works were carried out in the maisonette consisting of a kitchen
extension, central heating and damp proofing. They were effected by Mr Carrick
at a cost of about £5,000 but paid for by Mrs Carrick's father.

The legal charge on which the bank relies is dated 25 November 1986 and was
made between Mr Carrick and the bank to secure all monies due on any account
by the former to the latter. Mr Carrick, as beneficial owner, charged the lease of
the maisonette as security for those moneys. The charge was preceded by a
questionnaire signed by Mr Carrick to the effect that, to the best of his
knowledge, there were no persons other than the mortgagor who would then or
thereafter occupy the maisonette.

On 16 January 1991 and again on 9 August 1991 the bank demanded from Mr
Carrick the substantial sums then due from him to the bank. They were not paid
and the bank commenced these proceedings in the Cambridge County Court by
a summons issued on 27 February 1992 seeking against Mr Carrick a judgment
for £89,010·95 and interest thereon accruing at the rate of £53·18 per day and an
order for possession of the maisonette.

By his answer dated 8 March 1992 Mr Carrick admitted the money claim but,
in respect of the possession claim, he alleged that he was, and had been since a
time before the execution of the legal charge relied on by the bank, a bare trustee
of the maisonette for his sister-in-law. Accordingly Mrs Carrick was joined as the
second defendant and ordered to serve a defence. By her defence and
counterclaim served on 27 April 1992 Mrs Carrick claimed that Mr Carrick had
been a bare trustee for her of the long leasehold interest in the maisonette. The
material paragraphs are paras 5, 6, 9, 10 and 11, which are in the following terms:

'5. Pursuant to a suggestion made by the First Defendant to the Second
Defendant, the Second Defendant in or about October 1982 sold her former
matrimonial home and took up occupation at 7 Derby Way, Newmarket
which she has occupied at all material times since that date. 6. On the
directions of the Second Defendant the Solicitors who acted on the sale of

a the said matrimonial home paid the resulting proceeds of around £19,000 to
the order of the First Defendant. The said sum was for the acquisition of 7
Derby Way Newmarket by the Second Defendant ... 9. After the said
acquisition of 7 Derby Way Newmarket the Second Defendant was
responsible for and paid all outgoings relating to 7 Derby Way. 10. The
Second Defendant in or about 1983 had an extension built to 7 Derby Way
b at a cost of about £5,000 which the Second Defendant paid. 11. It was the
common intention of both the First and Second Defendants that 7 Derby
Way, Newmarket should become the property of the Second Defendant free
of all incumbrances.'

The bank replied to the effect that the interest of Mrs Carrick was registrable as a
c land charge of class C(iv), namely an estate contract, and was void against the
bank for want of registration. The bank sought particulars of the defence so as to
require Mrs Carrick to spell out the origin of the interest she claimed. The
particulars served by Mrs Carrick on 17 September 1993 contended:

'1. that no contract of sale was concluded between the First and Second
d Defendant in respect of the First Defendant's interest in 7 Derby Way;
2. that upon the Second Defendant entering into occupation of 7 Derby
Way and paying to the First Defendant the sum of about £19,000 as pleaded
in paragraph 6 of the Defence and Counterclaim, the First Defendant held his
interest in 7 Derby Way upon bare trust for the Second Defendant; 3. that
further and alternatively, the Second Defendant paid the said sum and
e entered into occupation of 7 Derby Way and acted as pleaded in paragraphs
9 and 10 of the Defence and Counterclaim, with the intention, which was a
common intention of the First and Second Defendants, that 7 Derby Way
was to be the Second Defendant's permanent home and that she was to be
absolutely entitled to the beneficial interest in it ...'

f Yet further particulars were sought from Mrs Carrick and given by her on 20
December 1993. These included the following passage:

'It was agreed that the Second Defendant would buy 7 Derby Way for
whatever she received upon the sale of 93 Edinburgh Road (in the event
about £19,000). The First Defendant told the Second Defendant not to
g worry about the matter further and that he would sort things out. The
Second Defendant thereafter left it up to the First Defendant to sort out the
legal formalities of the sale. The Second Defendant moved in to 7 Derby
Way on 19th November 1982. She paid the First Defendant the proceeds of
sale from 93 Edinburgh Road on about that date. Since then the Second
h Defendant has lived at 7 Derby Way and paid all the outgoings on it. The
agreement between the Defendants is not recorded in writing.'

The action was heard by the recorder on 4 July 1994. He heard evidence from
two bank officials and from Mr Carrick and Mrs Carrick. He gave judgment on
5 July 1994. The recorder set out the history of the case, the state of the pleadings
j and the documents of title relating to the maisonette. He expressed the view that
the case turned on the law so far as it relates to registrable interests and later,
whether there was a contract between Mr Carrick and Mrs Carrick. In respect of
these issues his conclusions were:

'In my view there was a contract that upon payment of the £19,000 by the
second defendant there arose, in my view, a bare trust. In other words, there

was nothing left vested in Mr Carrick (the first defendant) other than the
legal title. Mr Carrick had no rights to the property. He simply held the legal *a*
title upon trust. Mrs Carrick could have called for the legal title to be
conveyed to her by the first defendant as bare trustee. If, as I do, I follow that
through, the interest behind the bare trust is not registrable.'

On the basis that there was no registrable interest the recorder then went on
to consider whether the bank had notice of the interest of Mrs Carrick so that the *b*
legal charge took effect subject to it. He concluded on all the evidence that the
bank was not entitled to rely simply on the answer to the questionnaire, for one
or more of its officers knew that Mrs Carrick was resident in the maisonette and
had constructive notice of her beneficial interest for any enquiry of her would
have revealed it. The recorder declined to deal with a submission based on *c*
proprietary estoppel as, in his view, it had not been pleaded and did not arise.

The bank appeals with the leave of Neill LJ and Cazalet J granted on 31 March
1995. It contends that the recorder should have found that the only interest of
Mrs Carrick in the maisonette was an estate contract within the Land Charges Act
1972 and accordingly was void for want of registration as against the bank as the
purchaser of a legal estate for valuable consideration. *d*

By a respondent's notice served on 1 May 1995 Mrs Carrick contends that the
decision of the recorder should be upheld on the additional ground that her
expenditure on the improvements to the maisonette prior to the legal charge was
incurred in the belief encouraged by Mr Carrick that she was the owner of the
property and thus gave rise to an equity in her favour. She submits that the bank *e*
had notice of it and that such equity should be satisfied by the affirmation of the
recorder's order. It was accepted by counsel on her behalf that she could not go
outside the facts pleaded in her defence of which I have quoted the relevant
paragraphs. The other points referred to in the respondent's notice were
abandoned at the hearing.

It is convenient to consider first the relevant statutory provisions. The 1972 *f*
Act replaced the Land Charges Act 1925. So far as relevant it provides:

'... **2.** *The register of land charges.*—(1) If a charge on or obligation affecting
land falls into one of the classes described in this section, it may be registered
in the register of land charges as a land charge of that class ...
(4) A Class C land charge is any of the following (not being a local land *g*
charge), namely ... (iv) an estate contract; and for this purpose ... (iv) an
estate contract is a contract by an estate owner or by a person entitled at the
date of the contract to have a legal estate conveyed to him to convey or
create a legal estate, including a contract conferring either expressly or by *h*
statutory implication a valid option to purchase, a right of pre-emption or to
any other like right ...
4. ... (6) An estate contract and a land charge of Class D created or entered
into on or after 1st January 1926 shall be void as against a purchaser for
money or money's worth (or, in the case of an Inland Revenue charge, a
purchaser within the meaning of the Capital Transfer Tax Act 1984) of a legal *j*
estate in the land charged with it, unless the land charge is registered in the
appropriate register before the completion of the purchase ...'

Section 17 incorporates the definitions contained in the Law of Property Act 1925
of 'legal estate' and 'purchaser', which, it is common ground, include a charge by
way of legal mortgage and a mortgagee such as the bank.

a
So far as relevant, the Law of Property Act 1925 provides:

'199.   *Restrictions on constructive notice.*—(1) A purchaser shall not be
prejudicially affected by notice of—(i) any instrument or matter capable of
registration under the provisions of the Land Charges Act, 1925, or any
enactment which it replaces, which is void or not enforceable as against him
b
under that Act or enactment, by reason of the non-registration thereof ...'

In the light of these provisions and, no doubt, the consideration by each party
of the written argument of the other, the issues between them were narrowed
considerably.   First, it is accepted by Mrs Carrick that if her only interest in the
maisonette was derived from the contract which she accepts is void as against the
c bank as an unregistered estate contract then the appeal succeeds.   Second, Mrs
Carrick accepts that the original contract between her and Mr Carrick, as found
by the recorder, was a valid open contract for the purchase of the maisonette; that
it became enforceable by her when she partly performed it by entering into
possession and paying the whole of the purchase price but that it remained
executory, that is to say uncompleted, at the time of the legal charge to the bank
d
granted in November 1986.   Third, the bank accepts that if Mrs Carrick had an
interest in the maisonette not arising from but separate and distinct from the
unregistered contract, it was and is binding on the bank for, as found by the
recorder, the bank had notice of it.

Thus the issue argued on this appeal was whether Mrs Carrick had an interest
e in the maisonette separate and distinct from that which arose under the
unregistered estate contract which was capable of binding the bank as successor
in title to Mr Carrick.   For Mrs Carrick it was submitted that she did.   It was
contended that she was entitled to such an interest under a bare trust, a
constructive trust and by virtue of a proprietary estoppel.

f   I shall consider each of these points in due course.   But before doing so it is
necessary to consider the position of Mr Carrick and Mrs Carrick before the
charge to the bank was executed.   At the time it was made the contract was valid
but, as provided by s 40 of the Law of Property Act 1925, unenforceable for want
of a memorandum in writing or part performance.   It became enforceable when
in or about November 1982 Mrs Carrick paid the purchase price to Mr Carrick
g and went into possession.   One consequence of the contract becoming
enforceable was that it was specifically enforceable at the suit of Mrs Carrick.
Accordingly Mr Carrick became a trustee of the maisonette for Mrs Carrick.
Normally such trusteeship is of a peculiar kind because the vendor himself has a
beneficial interest in the property as explained in *Megarry and Wade on The Law of*
h *Real Property* (5th edn, 1984) p 602.   But in this case as Mrs Carrick had paid the
whole of the purchase price at the time the contract became enforceable Mr
Carrick as the vendor had no beneficial interest.   Thus he may properly be
described as a bare trustee (cf *Bridges v Mees* [1957] 2 All ER 577 at 581, [1957] Ch
475 at 485).   It follows that at all times after November 1982 Mrs Carrick was the
j absolute beneficial owner of the maisonette and Mr Carrick was a trustee of it
without any beneficial interest in it.

The argument for Mrs Carrick relied on the relative position at law and in
equity as I have described it to found the argument that such an absolute
equitable interest was not itself registrable but bound the bank as they had
constructive notice of it.   Counsel for Mrs Carrick accepted that such interest
came or started from the contract but, he contended, it matured into an interest

separate and distinct from the contract as soon as the purchase price was paid in
full.   *a*

For my part I am unable to accept this analysis. The payment of £19,000 by
Mrs Carrick to Mr Carrick did not as such and without more give her any interest
in the maisonette. Nor, prior to the conclusion of the contract, were the
circumstances such that Mrs Carrick could assert that her brother-in-law held the
maisonette on any trust for her benefit. The source and origin of the trust was *b*
the contract; the payment of the price by Mrs Carrick served only to make it a
bare trust by removing any beneficial interest of Mr Carrick. Section 4(6) of the
1972 Act avoids that contract as against the bank. The result, in my judgment,
must be that Mrs Carrick is unable to establish the bare trust as against the bank
for it has no existence except as the equitable consequence of the contract.
Accordingly I reject the contention founded on the bare trust.   *c*

The second contention for Mrs Carrick was to the effect that she was entitled
to the whole beneficial interest in the maisonette arising under a constructive
trust and that that interest was not registrable so that the bank, having had
constructive notice of it, took subject to it. For this proposition her Counsel
relied on the speech of Lord Bridge of Harwich in *Lloyds Bank plc v Rosset* [1990] 1 *d*
All ER 1111, [1991] 1 AC 107. That case was concerned with the question of what
must be established to entitle a wife to an equitable interest in registered land the
title to which is registered in the sole name of her husband. Lord Bridge of
Harwich said:

> 'The first and fundamental question which must always be resolved is *e*
> whether, independently of any inference to be drawn from the conduct of
> the parties in the course of sharing the house as their home and managing
> their joint affairs, there has at any time prior to acquisition, or exceptionally
> at some later date, been any agreement, arrangement or understanding
> reached between them that the property is to be shared beneficially. The
> finding of an agreement or arrangement to share in this sense can only, I *f*
> think, be based on evidence of express discussions between the partners,
> however imperfectly remembered and however imprecise their terms may
> have been. Once a finding to this effect is made it will only be necessary for
> the partner asserting a claim to a beneficial interest against the partner
> entitled to the legal estate to show that he or she has acted to his or her *g*
> detriment or significantly altered his or her position in reliance on the
> agreement in order to give rise to a constructive trust or a proprietary
> estoppel.' (See [1990] 1 All ER 1111 at 1118–1119, [1991] 1 AC 107 at 132.)

Counsel recognised that in this case the contract between Mr Carrick and Mrs *h*
Carrick was entered into after Mr Carrick had taken an assignment of the lease
into his own name. But he submitted that the same principle applied and for that
purpose relied on the statement of Lord Oliver of Aylmerton in giving the
opinion of the Privy Council in *Austin v Keele* (1987) 61 ALJR 605 at 609, where he
said
                                                                                j
> 'Although Lord Diplock [in *Gissing v Gissing* [1970] 2 All ER 780 at 790,
> [1971] AC 886 at 905] referred to the formation of a common intention "at
> the time of acquisition", the Court of Appeal expressed the view, with which
> their Lordships agree, that although it may be more difficult to prove the
> requisite intention in relation to property already held beneficially by the
> trustee, there is no reason in principle why the doctrine should be limited to

a
an intention formed at the time of the first acquisition of the property—an opinion echoed by Mustill L.J. in his judgment in *Grant v Edwards* ([1986] 2 All ER 426 at 435, [1986] Ch 638 at 651). In essence the doctrine is an application of proprietary estoppel and there is no reason in principle why it should be confined to the single event of acquisition of the property by the owner of the legal estate.'

b
Counsel for Mrs Carrick submitted that if there had been no contract then on the proper application of these principles there would have been a constructive trust in favour of Mrs Carrick. From this he argued that Mrs Carrick should not be in any worse position just because there was a contract.

In this case there was a trust of the maisonette for the benefit of Mrs Carrick c precisely because there had been an agreement between her and Mr Carrick which, for her part, she had substantially if not wholly performed. As between her and Mr Carrick such trust subsisted at all times after November 1982. I agree with counsel for the bank that there is no room in those circumstances for the implication or imposition of any further trust of the maisonette for the benefit of d Mrs Carrick. In *Lloyds Bank plc v Rosset* there was no contract which conferred any interest in the house on the wife. As with all such statements of principle the speech of Lord Bridge of Harwich must be read by reference to the facts of the case. So read there is nothing in it to suggest that where there is a specifically enforceable contract the court is entitled to superimpose a further constructive trust on the vendor in favour of the purchaser over that which already exists in e consequence of the contractual relationship.

It is true that on this footing the ultimate position of Mrs Carrick with the benefit of a specifically enforceable contract may be worse than it would have been if there had been no contract. But that is because she failed to do that which Parliament has ordained must be done if her interest is to prevail over that of the f bank, namely to register the estate contract. Her failure in that respect cannot, in my view, justify the implication or imposition of a trust after the execution of the charge when the dealings between Mr Carrick and Mrs Carrick before such execution did not. For these reasons I would reject the second point on which Mrs Carrick relied.

The third contention was that Mrs Carrick is entitled to the benefit of a g proprietary estoppel. Counsel on her behalf submitted by reference to the principles set out in *Snell's Equity* (29th edn, 1990) pp 574–576 that such an estoppel arose in her favour by virtue of the facts pleaded in her defence. He submitted that Mrs Carrick had paid the purchase price and carried out the improvements to the maisonette in the belief common to both her and Mr h Carrick and to that extent encouraged by him that she either did or would own it. Reliance was placed on the decisions of this court in *Inwards v Baker* [1965] 1 All ER 446, [1965] 2 QB 29 and *E R Ives Investments Ltd v High* [1967] 1 All ER 504, [1967] 2 QB 379 as establishing that such an estoppel gives rise to an interest in land capable of binding a successor in title with notice.

j
This was disputed by counsel for the bank. She submitted that such principles could not be applied to cases in which there was no belief or expectation of having or acquiring an interest in someone else's land. In this context she relied on *Western Fish Products Ltd v Penwith DC* [1981] 2 All ER 204. Further, she submitted that the facts did not warrant such an estoppel as they did not cover all the elements referred to as 'probanda' in *Wilmott v Barber* (1880) 15 Ch D 96 and were otherwise insufficient. In addition she submitted that such an estoppel

cannot give rise to an interest in land capable of binding successors in title with notice.   a

I would observe at the outset that it is a matter of some doubt whether the principles of proprietary estoppel differ from those of that species of constructive trust which was referred to by Lord Bridge of Harwich in *Lloyds Bank plc v Rosset*. In the passage from his speech which I have already quoted he treated the two labels as interchangeable. To the like effect is the passage in the advice of the   b
Privy Council in *Austin v Keele* (1987) 61 ALJR 605 given by Lord Oliver of Aylmerton, which I have also quoted. However that may be, the case under this head was put somewhat differently and should be considered on its own merits.

With regard to the second submission of counsel for the bank I think that it is now clear that to constitute the requisite estoppel it is not necessary to establish all of the five elements or 'probanda' referred to by Fry J in *Willmott v Barber*   c
(1880) 15 Ch D 96 at 105–106. In his judgment in *Taylor Fashions Ltd v Liverpool Victoria Trustees Co Ltd* [1981] 1 All ER 897, [1982] QB 133 Oliver J traced through the subsequent cases in which this question had been considered. I do not propose to repeat the process but would respectfully agree with the conclusion of Oliver J that proof of all those elements or 'probanda' is not necessary to found   d
an estoppel. For my part I agree with the proposition stated by Oliver J that—

> 'the more recent cases indicate, in my judgment, that the application of the
> *Ramsden v Dyson* (1866) LR 1 HL 129 principle (whether you call it
> proprietary estoppel, estoppel by acquiescence or estoppel by
> encouragement is really immaterial) requires a very much broader approach   e
> which is directed to ascertaining whether, in particular individual
> circumstances, it would be unconscionable for a party to be permitted to
> deny that which, knowingly or unknowingly, he has allowed or encouraged
> another to assume to his detriment rather than to inquiring whether the
> circumstances can be fitted within the confines of some preconceived
> formula serving as a universal yardstick for every form of unconscionable   f
> behaviour. So regarded, knowledge of the true position by the party alleged
> to be estopped becomes merely one of the relevant factors (it may even be a
> determining factor in certain cases) in the overall inquiry.' (See [1981] 1 All
> ER 897 at 915–916, [1982] QB 133 at 151–152.)

In *Western Fish Products Ltd v Penwith DC* the plaintiff carried out works on its   g
own land in reliance on statements made by an officer of the local planning authority that permission would be granted for its development. Planning permission was in due course refused and enforcement notices were served. The plaintiff then instituted proceedings for a declaration that it was entitled to the permissions the officer had represented that it would obtain, in reliance on which   h
the plaintiff had carried out the works on its own land. The claim failed on a number of grounds. In relation to the claim to a proprietary estoppel Megaw LJ giving the judgment of the court said ([1981] 2 All ER 204 at 218–219):

> 'We know of no case, and none has been cited to us, in which the principle   j
> set out in *Ramsden v Dyson* and *Crabb v Arun District Council* [1975] 3 All ER
> 865, [1976] Ch 179 has been applied otherwise than to rights and interests
> created in and over land. It may extend to other forms of property: see per
> Lord Denning MR in *Moorgate Mercantile Co Ltd v Twitchings* [1975] 3 All ER
> 314 at 323–324, [1976] QB 225 at 242. In our judgment there is no good
> reason for extending the principle further. As Harman LJ pointed out in
> *Campbell Discount Co Ltd v Bridge* [1961] 2 All ER 97 at 103, [1961] 1 QB 445 at

a   459, the system of equity has become a very precise one. The creation of new rights and remedies is a matter for Parliament, not the judges. In his reply counsel for the plaintiffs seemed to recognise that the reported cases did put limits to the application of the so-called concept of proprietary estoppel. He submitted that the plaintiffs' case was within that concept because what the defendant council, by their officers, had represented had,

b   to their knowledge, caused the plaintiffs to spend money on or in connection with their own land which they would not have otherwise spent. On their own case they have spent money in order to take advantage of existing rights over their own land which the defendant council by their officers had confirmed they possessed. There was no question of their acquiring any rights in relation to any other person's land, which is what proprietary

c   estoppel is concerned with.'

In my judgment the claim of Mrs Carrick fails on a number of grounds. First, as in the case of the constructive trust, I do not see how there is any room for the application of the principles of proprietary estoppel when at the time of the

d   relevant expenditure there was already a bare trust arising in consequence of an enforceable contract to the same effect as the interest sought pursuant to the proprietary estoppel. As the evidence showed Mrs Carrick knew of the need for a conveyance and was content that it should be deferred. Thus at the time that she paid the price and committed herself to the expenditure on the subsequent improvements she believed, rightly, that she was spending the money in respect

e   of her own property, albeit under an uncompleted contract. In this respect I see no relevant distinction between this case and that of *Western Fish Products Ltd v Penwith DC*.

Second, this is not a case in which the expectations of Mrs Carrick have been defeated by Mr Carrick seeking to resile from the position he had encouraged her

f   to expect. As far as he is concerned he has always accepted that she had contracted to buy the maisonette and had paid the price in full. As against him the contract is still binding and enforceable although, as he is unable to redeem the mortgage, he is in breach of contract for having charged the maisonette and in breach of trust for failing to account to Mrs Carrick for the money raised on the security of the maisonette. Mrs Carrick's expectations have been defeated

g   because the contract was not registered at any time before the charge was granted and Parliament has decreed that in those circumstances the contract is void against the bank.

Third, it was common ground that the right arising from a proprietary estoppel cannot exceed that which the party sought to be estopped encouraged the other

h   to believe that she had or would acquire. The party sought to be estopped is Mr Carrick. In so far as he encouraged Mrs Carrick to believe that she was or would become the beneficial owner of the maisonette there is no further right to be obtained for she was, and, subject to the charge, still is. But counsel for Mrs Carrick submits that Mr Carrick went further and encouraged her in the belief that she was or would become the legal owner of the maisonette. Apart from the

j   facts that this was never alleged in the defence of Mrs Carrick nor explored in evidence at the trial I do not think that it could avail Mrs Carrick. Section 4(6) of the 1972 Act invalidates, as against the bank, any unregistered contract by the estate owner for the conveyance of the legal estate. It cannot be unconscionable for the bank to rely on the non-registration of the contract. I do not see how it could be right to confer on Mrs Carrick indirectly, and by means of a proprietary estoppel binding on the bank, that which Parliament prevented her from

obtaining directly by the contract it has declared to be void. To avoid any future
misunderstanding I would emphasise that there was and is a valid and a
enforceable contract as against the vendor. Accordingly this case is quite unlike
those which may become more prevalent where there is no contract at all, not
because there was no agreement but because the agreement was not in writing
as now required by s 2 of the Law of Property (Miscellaneous Provisions) Act
1989.
b
   In my judgment, the claim based on proprietary estoppel fails. In the
circumstances it is unnecessary to consider further the submission of counsel for
the bank to the effect that a proprietary estoppel cannot give rise to an interest in
land capable of binding successors in title. This interesting argument will have to
await another day, though it is hard to see how in this court it can surmount the
hurdle constituted by the decision of this court in *E R Ives Investments Ltd v High* c
[1967] 1 All ER 504, [1967] 2 QB 379.
   For all these reasons I consider that the recorder was wrong to have held that
Mrs Carrick had any interest valid against the bank sufficient to constitute a
defence to the claim against her for possession of the maisonette. I would allow
this appeal.
d
   This result seems to me to be inevitable in the light of the provisions of the
1972 Act and of the Law of Property Act 1925 I quoted earlier. However, it
should be noted that the result would have been different if the title to the
maisonette had been registered. In such a case the interest of Mrs Carrick, who
was in possession of the maisonette and of whom no enquiry had been made,
would have been an overriding interest under s 70(1)(g) of the Land Registration e
Act 1925. As such it would have been binding on the bank.
   As the authors of *Megarry and Wade on The Law of Real Property* point out at pp
186–187 the same position would have been achieved under the Law of Property
Act 1922, for what is now s 14 of the Law of Property Act 1925 was then in a part
which also contained the legislation which subsequently became the Land f
Charges Act 1925.
   In my view it is beyond doubt that s 14 of the Law of Property Act 1925 does
not achieve for unregistered land that which s 70(1)(g) of the Land Registration
Act 1925 achieves for registered land, but whether that was originally intended or
is a quirk of the process of breaking up the Law of Property Act 1922 into,
amongst others, the Law of Property Act 1925 and the Land Charges Act 1925 is g
unclear. What is certain is that it must be for others to consider and for
Parliament to decide whether this distinction between registered and
unregistered land should continue, particularly as the system for the registration
of incumbrances in the case of unregistered land is by no means complete, as
shown by *Inwards v Baker* [1965] 1 All ER 446, [1965] 2 QB 29, *E R Ives Investments* h
Ltd v High [1967] 1 All ER 504, [1967] 2 QB 379 and *Shiloh Spinners Ltd v Harding*
[1973] 1 All ER 90, [1973] AC 691.

SIR RALPH GIBSON. I agree.

j
BELDAM LJ. For the reasons given by Morritt LJ, I agree that this appeal should
be allowed.

Appeal allowed.

L I Zysman Esq   Barrister

Cadogan and another v McGirk

COURT OF APPEAL, CIVIL DIVISION

WAITE, MILLETT AND THORPE LJJ

28 FEBRUARY, 25 APRIL 1996

Landlord and tenant – Leasehold enfranchisement – Premises – Flat – Appurtenance let with flat – Outhouse let with flat – Tenant having fixed term lease of second floor flat in block together with separate fixed term lease of storeroom on sixth floor – Tenant claiming new lease of flat on same terms as existing lease but including storeroom within demise – Whether tenant entitled to have storeroom included in new lease – Whether storeroom 'appurtenance' – Whether storeroom 'outhouse' – Whether storeroom part of flat – Leasehold Reform, Housing and Urban Development Act 1993, ss 62(2), 101(1).

The respondent was the tenant of a flat on the second floor of a mansion block owned by the applicants under a lease dated 12 December 1977 for a term of 26 years less 10 days from 24 June 1977. He was also the tenant for the same term of a storeroom on the sixth floor of the block under a separate lease which provided that the storeroom could be used for the 'storage of normal household goods and effects only' and could be assigned or sublet with the flat, but not separately. In 1994 the respondent served notice on the applicants under s 42[a] of the Leasehold Reform, Housing and Urban Development Act 1993 claiming to exercise his right to a new lease of the flat on the same terms as the existing lease, but including the storeroom within the demise, by virtue of s 62(2)[b] of the 1993 Act. The applicants accepted that the respondent was entitled to a new lease of the flat but contended that he was not entitled to have the storeroom included therein and they applied to the court for a declaration to that effect. The judge held that the respondent was entitled to have the storeroom included in the new lease on the ground that, while the storeroom was not an 'outhouse' within the meaning of s 62(2), it was an 'appurtenance' of the flat within the meaning of that subsection. The applicants appealed to the Court of Appeal, contending that the storeroom was not an 'appurtenance', since it was not within the curtilage of the flat and would not pass under an assignment of the flat without express mention. The respondent contended that the storeroom was an 'outhouse', or in the alternative, that the storeroom was part of the flat within the meaning of s 101(1)[c] of the 1993 Act.

Held – Although an 'appurtenance' within the meaning of s 62(2) of the 1993 Act had to be within the curtilage of the block, it did not have to be within the curtilage of the flat, since Parliament could not have intended that storerooms allocated to particular flats which would have been acquired from the landlord if the tenants had exercised their collective rights should be excluded from the new leases of the particular flats to which they had been allocated and be retained by the landlord even if all the tenants were to exercise their individual rights. Nor

---

a   Section 42, so far as material, provides: 'A claim by a qualifying tenant of a flat to exercise the right to acquire a new lease of a flat is made by the giving of notice of the claim under this section ...'

b   Section 62(2) is set out at p 647 *d*, post

c   Section 101(1), so far as material, is set out at p 647 *b c*, post

was it essential that the appurtenance should be capable of passing under an
assignment of the flat without express mention. Accordingly, since the *a*
storeroom belonged to, or was usually enjoyed with, the flat and was let to the
respondent with the flat, it was an 'appurtenance' of the flat within the meaning
of s 62(2). It was not, however, an 'outhouse' within the meaning of that
subsection since it was within the same building as the flat and not outside it or
in the grounds of the block. Neither was the storeroom part of the flat within the *b*
meaning of s 101(1) of the Act since there was no natural or physical relationship
between the storeroom and the flat. It followed that, on the basis that the
storeroom was an appurtenance, the respondent was entitled to have it included
in the new lease and the appeal would therefore be dismissed (see p 649 *d e g j*,
p 650 *a*, p 651 *f* to *j* and p 652 *b e f*, post).

Methuen-Campbell v Walters [1979] 1 All ER 606 distinguished. *c*

Notes
For the individual right of a tenant of a flat to acquire a new lease, see 27(2)
Halsbury's Laws (4th edn reissue) para 1523.

Cases referred to in judgments *d*
Barras v Aberdeen Steam Trawling and Fishing Co Ltd [1933] AC 402, [1933] All ER
Rep 52, HL.
Buszard v Capel (1828) 8 B & C 141, 108 ER 996; affd (1829) 6 Bing 150, 130 ER 1237,
Ex Ch.
Evans v Angell (1858) 26 Beav 202, 53 ER 874. *e*
Jones v Wrotham Park Settled Estates [1979] 1 All ER 286, sub nom Wentworth
Securities Ltd v Jones [1980] AC 74, [1979] 2 WLR 132, HL.
Manson v Duke of Westminster [1981] 2 All ER 40, [1981] QB 323, [1981] 2 WLR 428,
CA.
Methuen-Campbell v Walters [1979] 1 All ER 606, [1979] QB 525, [1979] 2 WLR 113, *f*
CA.
Trim v Sturminster RDC [1938] 2 All ER 168, [1938] 2 KB 508, CA.

Cases also cited or referred to in skeleton arguments
Annicola Investments Ltd v Minister of Housing and Local Government [1965] 3 All ER
850, [1968] 1 QB 631. *g*
A-G ex rel Yorkshire Derwent Trust Ltd v Brotherton [1992] 1 All ER 230, [1991] Ch
185, CA.
Bettisworth's Case, Hayward v Bettisworth (1580) 2 Co Rep 31b, 76 ER 482.
Camberwell (Wingfield Mews) No 2 Clearance Order, 1936, Re, Butler's Application
[1939] 1 All ER 590, [1939] 1 KB 570, CA. *h*
Dyer v Dorset CC [1989] QB 346, [1988] 3 WLR 213, CA.
London Corp v Cusack-Smith [1955] 1 All ER 302, [1955] AC 337, HL.
Pittalis v Grant [1989] 2 All ER 622, [1989] QB 605, CA.
Quillotex Co Ltd v Minister of Housing and Local Government [1965] 2 All ER 913,
[1966] 1 QB 704.
Sharpe v Duke Street Securities NV [1987] 2 EGLR 106, CA. *j*
Tandon v Trustees of Spurgeon's Homes [1982] 1 All ER 1086, [1982] AC 755, HL.

Appeal
By notice dated 17 November 1994 the applicants, the Hon Charles Gerald John
Cadogan, Viscount Chelsea, and Cadogan Estates Ltd, appealed from the order
of Judge Krikler on 26 October 1994, dismissing their originating motion for an

a order (i) declaring that the respondent, Donald Dea McGirk, was not entitled to acquire a new lease of Flat 3, Wyndham House, The Willett Building, Sloane Square, London SW1, which included the attic box room referred to in a notice under s 42 of the Leasehold Reform, Housing and Urban Development Act 1993 served by the respondent on 19 January 1994, and (ii) directing under para 9(2) of Sch 12 to the 1993 Act that the notice be amended to exclude the attic box room

b referred to therein. The facts are set out in the judgment of Millett LJ.

Anthony Radevsky (instructed by *Lee & Pembertons*) for the appellants.
John Male (instructed by *Bird & Bird*) for the respondent.

Cur adv vult

c
25 April 1996. The following judgments were delivered.

MILLETT LJ (giving the first judgment at the invitation of Waite LJ). The question in this appeal is whether an attic box storeroom on the sixth floor of a mansion block of flats forms part of the second floor flat to which it has been

d allocated. If it does, then the respondent is entitled to have the storeroom included in the new lease of his flat to be granted to him under the provisions of Ch II of Pt I of the Leasehold Reform, Housing and Urban Development Act 1993. If it does not, then the storeroom will be excluded from the new lease and the respondent's right to possession of the storeroom will come to an end in June

e 2003.
    The judge held that the storeroom was an 'appurtenance' of the flat within the meaning of s 62(2) of the 1993 Act. He rejected the respondent's alternative argument that it was an 'outhouse' within the subsection, from which decision the respondent appeals by his respondent's notice. We gave leave to the respondent to raise a yet further alternative before us, viz that the storeroom was

f part of the flat as defined by s 101(1) of the 1993 Act.

The facts
    The facts are straightforward and are not in dispute. The appellants, the Hon Charles Gerald John Cadogan, Viscount Chelsea, and Cadogan Estates Ltd, are

g the freehold owners of a building known as the Willett Building in Sloane Square. This comprises commercial premises in the basement and on the ground and part of the first floors. The upper floors are divided into two linked buildings known as Wyndham House and Wellesley House, which are purpose-built mansion blocks of residential flats.

h   The respondent, Donald Dea McGirk, is the tenant of flat 3, Wyndham House. Wyndham House contains ten flats and flat 3 is on the second floor. The respondent holds the flat under a lease dated 12 December 1977 for a term of 26 years less 10 days from 24 June 1977 at an annual rent of £100. The term expires on 13 June 2003.

j   The respondent is also the tenant of storeroom No 14 on the sixth or attic floor under an agreement also dated 12 December 1977 and for the same term as the flat at the annual rent of £1. Under the terms of the agreement; the storeroom may be used 'for the storage of normal household goods and effects only' and may be assigned or sublet with the flat but not separately.
    The respondent has lived in the flat since 1969. The flats in Wyndham House are spacious but are old-fashioned and short of storage space. There are no built-in cupboards or wardrobes. For this reason, storage spaces in the attic on

the sixth floor and in the basement were allotted to residents. The respondent
has had the use of storeroom 14 since 1969, though it was not included in a formal
lease to him until 1977. In that year, the respondent purchased his current
leasehold interest in the flat and on the same date entered into a separate
agreement for the storeroom. The respondent and his wife use it for storing
suitcases and seasonal clothing and bedding for which there is inadequate storage
space in the flat.

In January 1994 the respondent served a notice under s 42 of the 1993 Act
claiming to exercise his right to a new lease of his flat 'on the same terms as the
present lease ... but including the attic boxroom within the demise'. The
appellants accept that the respondent is entitled to a new lease of the flat but
dispute his entitlement to have the boxroom included therein. In May 1994 the
appellants issued proceedings in the West London County Court for a
declaration that the respondent was not entitled to have the storeroom included
in the new lease of his flat. On 26 October 1994, after the case had been
transferred to the Willesden County Court, Judge Krikler held that the
respondent was entitled to have the storeroom included in the new lease and
dismissed the application.

The legislation

Leasehold enfranchisement was introduced by the Leasehold Reform Act
1967. This gave residential tenants of houses held on long leases at low rents the
right to acquire either the freehold or an extended lease. The 1967 Act did not
apply to blocks of flats, and because of the definition of 'house' it excluded many
residential properties in single occupation, such as the mews house partly built
over a garage in different occupation, which would normally be regarded as
houses. The 1993 Act was passed in order to extend the benefits of leasehold
enfranchisement to tenants who were outside the protection of the 1967 Act. It
conferred rights of collective enfranchisement on the tenants of blocks of flats
who were collectively entitled to acquire the freehold of the premises in which
their flats were contained, and individual rights on each of the tenants to acquire
new 90-year leases of their own particular flats. The right to collective
enfranchisement is conferred by Ch I of Pt I of the 1993 Act, and the individual
right to acquire a new lease is conferred by Ch II of Pt I of the 1993 Act.

The individual right of a tenant to acquire a new lease of his particular flat is
conferred by s 39 of the 1993 Act. Section 39(2)(a) requires the tenant to be a
qualifying tenant of the flat. Section 39(3) incorporates ss 5, 7 and 8 of Ch I.
Section 5 defines 'qualifying tenant' as a tenant of the flat under a long lease at a
low rent. Section 7 defines 'long lease'. Section 7(6) provides:

> 'Where in the case of a flat there are at any time two or more separate
> leases, with the same landlord and the same tenant, and—(a) the property
> comprised in one of those leases consists of either the flat or a part of it (in
> either case with or without any appurtenant property), and (b) the property
> comprised in every other lease consists of either a part of the flat (with or
> without any appurtenant property) or appurtenant property only, then in
> relation to the property comprised in such of those leases as are long leases,
> this Chapter shall apply as it would if at that time—(i) there were a single
> lease of that property, and (ii) that lease were a long lease; but this subsection
> has effect subject to the operation of subsections (3) to (5) in relation to any
> of the separate leases.'

a 'Appurtenant property' is defined by s 1(7) (applied to s 7 by s 7(7)). This reads:

> 'In this section—"appurtenant property", in relation to a flat, means any garage, outhouse, garden, yard or appurtenances belonging to, or usually enjoyed with, the flat ...'

'Low rent' is defined by s 8.

b For the purposes of Pt I (that is to say, both Ch I and Ch II) 'flat' is defined by s 101(1). This reads:

> 'In this Part ... "flat" means a separate set of premises (whether or not on the same floor)—(a) which forms part of a building, and (b) which is constructed or adapted for use for the purposes of a dwelling, and (c) either
c the whole or a material part of which lies above or below some other part of the building ...'

For the purposes of Ch II only, 'flat' is given an extended meaning by s 62(2). This reads:

d
> 'Subject to subsection (3), references in this Chapter to a flat, in relation to a claim by a tenant under this Chapter, include any garage, outhouse, garden, yard and appurtenances belonging to, or usually enjoyed with, the flat and let to the tenant with the flat on the relevant date (or, in a case where an application is made under section 50(1), on the date of the making of the application).'

e Subsection (3) is not material.

It is clear that a tenant who obtains a new lease of his flat is entitled to exercise the rights of passage over the common parts and to use the lift and to enjoy the other easements and advantages to which he was formerly entitled. This is not dealt with expressly in Ch II of the 1993 Act, and there was some discussion
f before us whether such rights are 'appurtenances' of the flat and so within the extended definition of the flat in s 62(2), or come within s 57(1) which entitles the tenant to a new lease 'on the same terms as those of the existing lease'. In the absence of any indication to the contrary, I would have expected them to be treated as 'appurtenances'; the expression 'the terms of the lease' would ordinarily refer to the covenants and conditions of the lease rather than the extent
g of the demise. But s 57(1) provides for the terms of the existing lease to be modified (inter alia) to exclude from the new lease property included in the existing lease but not forming part of the flat. This is an indication that the expression 'terms of the existing lease' may need to be given a wider interpretation than would be usual. It is not, however, necessary to decide the
h point, and I prefer to leave it open for decision in a case where it is material to the result.

Principles of construction

There was some discussion before us of the proper approach which should be
j adopted to the construction of the 1993 Act. Two particular questions were canvassed. The first was whether the Act, being expropriatory in nature, must be strictly construed. A man, it was said, is not to have his property compulsorily acquired except by plain language. Support for this proposition may be found in the judgments of all three members of this court in *Methuen-Campbell v Walters* [1979] 1 All ER 606, [1979] QB 525, which was a decision on the 1967 Act. This is not, however, the approach which has been adopted since. In *Jones v Wrotham*

Park Settled Estates [1979] 1 All ER 286 at 295, [1980] AC 74 at 113 Lord Russell said
of this point: 'I attribute minimal if any force to this point, and regard only the   *a*
statutory provisions.' Similarly, in *Manson v Duke of Westminster* [1981] 2 All ER
40 at 48, [1981] QB 323 at 332 Stephenson LJ said: 'I would ... regard the
expropriatory nature of the 1967 Act as of little weight in construing its provisions
...' I respectfully agree. It would, in my opinion, be wrong to disregard the fact
that, while the 1993 Act may to some extent be regarded as expropriatory of the   *b*
landlord's interest, nevertheless it was passed for the benefit of tenants. It is the
duty of the court to construe the 1993 Act fairly and with a view, if possible, to
making it effective to confer on tenants those advantages which Parliament must
have intended them to enjoy.

The other question concerned the extent to which the court may obtain
guidance to the meaning of a word or phrase in a statute from judicial decisions   *c*
on the same word or phrase in earlier legislation. The correct approach was laid
down by Viscount Buckmaster in *Barras v Aberdeen Steam Trawling and Fishing Co
Ltd* [1933] AC 402 at 411, [1933] All ER Rep 52 at 55:

> 'It has long been a well established principle to be applied in the
> consideration of Acts of Parliament that where a word of doubtful meaning   *d*
> has received a clear judicial interpretation, the subsequent statute which
> incorporates the same word or the same phrase *in a similar context*, must be
> construed so that the word or phrase is interpreted according to the meaning
> that has previously been assigned to it.' (My emphasis.)

The rule has often been applied, but the qualification to which I have drawn   *e*
attention is of the first importance. The rule is invoked by the appellants in
relation to the meaning of the word 'appurtenances' in s 62(2), and I shall return
to the application of the rule when considering the meaning of the word in that
subsection.

There is, however, one further matter which, although not raised by either   *f*
party, is of general relevance when determining the effect of the statutory
provisions which are under consideration in the present case. The tenant of a flat
in a block of flats may have two distinct rights; an individual right under Ch II to
obtain a new lease of his particular flat, and a right to join with the other tenants
in exercising the collective right under Ch I to acquire the freehold interest in the
block. Even if all the tenants in a block exercise their individual rights to obtain   *g*
new leases of their own flats, the landlord will retain the ownership of the
common parts. If, on the other hand, the tenants exercise their collective right to
acquire the freehold interest in the entire block, they will acquire the common
parts. Given the close interrelation between Ch I and Ch II, I approach the
statutory definition of the premises to be included in the new lease of an   *h*
individual flat with a strong predisposition to assume that, if all the tenants were
to obtain new leases of their particular flats under Ch II, then with the sole
exception of the common parts the landlord would not retain any part of the
premises in which the flats are contained which he would not retain if they had
exercised their collective right to acquire the whole premises under Ch I.   *j*

Storage space and storage rooms which have been allocated to particular flats
are not, of course, comprised in the common parts (see s 4(2)). It is not clear
whether Wyndham House is within the definition of premises to which Ch I
applies, but the existence of the storerooms would not affect this question. If Ch I
does apply to Wyndham House and if sufficient of the tenants were to exercise
their collective rights of enfranchisement, they would be entitled to acquire the

a   freehold of Wyndham House and the storerooms in the attic and basement
     would be included in the property to be acquired.

Flat
       The first question is whether the storeroom on the sixth floor forms part of the
     flat on the second floor. This depends on whether it is part of the same 'separate
b   set of premises (whether or not on the same floor)' (see s 101(1) of the 1993 Act).
     The words in parenthesis make it clear that maisonettes are included, but they
     may have a wider effect than this. In my opinion, the word 'separate' suggests
     both 'physically separate' or 'set apart' and 'single' or 'regarded as a unit'. The
     definition is concerned with the physical configuration of the premises. It was
     conceded by the appellants that the rooms which form part of the flat do not have
c   to be contiguous. Many sets of chambers in the Inns of Court are physically
     divided by a common staircase and landing but they would, I think, be regarded
     as a single 'separate set of premises'. The question is one of fact and degree, and
     must largely be one of impression. The degree of proximity of any part of the
     premises which is not contiguous is likely to be decisive. I have come to the clear
d   conclusion that the storeroom on the sixth floor cannot be said to be part of the
     same separate set of premises as the rooms in the second floor flat. It was
     allocated to and let with the flat, but it does not form part of the flat.
       I do not reach this conclusion because the storeroom is held under a separate
     lease, for s 7(6) expressly contemplates the possibility of different parts of the
     same flat being let under separate leases. What is decisive to my mind is the
e   absence of any natural or physical relationship between the flat and the
     storeroom. The storeroom could equally well have been allocated to and let with
     any of the other flats; just as any of the other storerooms could equally well have
     been allocated to and let with the flat. Section 7(6) covers the case of a single
     physical unit comprised in two leases. In the present case there are two physical
f   units let together.

Outhouse
       The respondent submits that the storeroom is (i) outwith the flat, (ii) used in
     connection with the flat and ancillary to the flat, and (iii) belongs to the flat in the
     sense that it has been allocated to and let with the flat and may be assigned with
g   the flat.
       In my judgment, these facts are not sufficient to make the storeroom an
     'outhouse'. The essential characteristic of an outhouse is that it is outside. The
     Shorter Oxford English Dictionary defines 'outhouse' as—'a subsidiary building in
     the grounds of or adjoining a house, as a stable, barn, shed etc.'
h   The respondent argues that the question is whether the storeroom is an
     'outhouse' of the flat, not whether it is an 'outhouse' of Wyndham House; that
     the principal building is the flat, not Wyndham House; and that it is sufficient if
     the storeroom is outside the flat even if it is inside Wyndham House.
       I do not accept this. An 'outhouse' is an outbuilding or outside building in the
j   grounds of or adjoining a principal building. Neither s 1(7) nor s 62(2) requires
     the outhouse to be an 'outhouse of the flat'. It is sufficient if it is 'an outhouse ...
     belonging to, or usually enjoyed with, the flat'. In my opinion, it is sufficient if
     the outhouse is an outhouse in the grounds of or adjoining Wyndham House.
     Any such outhouse which was enjoyed with and let to the tenant of a particular
     flat with his flat would come within s 62(2) and so within the extended definition
     of the flat for the purposes of Ch II.

But it must be an 'outhouse', ie outside any other building. Like the judge, I cannot accept that a room within a building can properly be described as an 'outhouse' of another set of rooms within the same building. It is simply not an 'outhouse' at all.

Appurtenance

If the storeroom is an 'appurtenance' of the flat within the meaning of s 62(2) of the 1993 Act, then it is 'appurtenant property' within the meaning of s 1(7) which was 'let with' the flat within the meaning of s 7(6) and falls within the extended definition of 'the flat' in s 62(2).

The changing meaning of the word 'appurtenance' is traced in *Methuen-Campbell v Walters* [1979] 1 All ER 606 at 612–615, 620–621, [1979] QB 525 at 533–536, 542–543 in the judgments of Goff and Buckley LJJ respectively. It was formerly a term of art. Strictly it did not include land, but was restricted to incorporeal hereditaments. It was firmly established that land could not be appurtenant to other land (see *Co Litt* (18th edn, 1823) p 123b, section 184, *Buszard v Capel* (1828) 8 B & C 141, 108 ER 996 and other cases). This meaning, however, would yield to the context, and came in time to be replaced by another, viz anything which would pass under a conveyance of the principal subject matter without express mention (see *Evans v Angell* (1858) 26 Beav 202 at 205, 53 ER 874 at 875 per Romilly MR). The appurtenances of a house thus came to include the orchard, yard, curtilage and gardens of the house.

It was against that background that the Housing Act 1936 defined 'house' as including—'any yard, garden, outhouses, and appurtenances belonging thereto or usually enjoyed therewith.' In *Trim v Sturminster RDC* [1938] 2 All ER 168 at 170, [1938] 2 KB 508 at 516 Slesser LJ said:

> '... no case has been cited to us in which the word "appurtenances" has ever been extended to include land which does not fall within the curtilage of the yard of the house itself—that is, within the parcel of the demise of the house.'

As Goff LJ observed in *Methuen-Campbell v Walters* [1979] 1 All ER 606 at 614, [1979] QB 525 at 535 this confined the word 'appurtenances' to the curtilage of the house.

When in 1967 Parliament came to grant residential tenants under long leases at low rents the right to acquire the freehold or an extended lease of their houses, it adopted a similar but updated version of the same definition. Section 2(3) of the 1967 Act referred to—

> 'any garage, outhouse, garden, yard and appurtenances which at the relevant time are let to him with the house and are occupied with and used for the purposes of the house or any part of it by him or by another occupant.'

The main elements of the definition were unchanged except for the addition of the garage, but the qualifying words at the end of the definition were different. The words 'belonging thereto or usually enjoyed therewith' were replaced by the words 'let to him with the house and ... occupied with and used for the purposes of the house or any part of it'.

In *Methuen-Campbell v Walters* it was assumed that the word 'appurtenances' was apt to include land. Buckley LJ suggested that the reference to occupation and use was sufficient to admit such an interpretation (see [1979] 1 All ER 606 at

a 621, [1979] QB 525 at 543). But nothing could pass which was not within the
curtilage of the house and so capable of passing under a conveyance of the house
without express mention.

Section 62(2) of the 1993 Act reproduces the language of the definition of
'house' in s 2(3) of the 1967 Act, but the qualifying words at the end of the
definition return to the formula employed in the 1936 Act. It is not, however,
b suggested that this is sufficient to exclude land from the ambit of the word
'appurtenances'. In my judgment, it is too late now to suppose that Parliament
has returned to the older and stricter usage in this context.

The appellants, however, submit on the authority of *Methuen-Campbell v
Walters* that the storeroom is not an 'appurtenance' of the flat because (i) it is not
within the curtilage of the flat, and (ii) because it would not pass under an
c assignment of the flat without express mention. They invoke the principle of
statutory construction to which I have referred, and submit that the context is the
same, viz the right of a residential tenant to acquire a new lease of the demised
premises.

But the statutory context is not identical. There are two differences, one
d relatively minor and one more significant. The first is that the 1967 Act contained
no equivalent of s 7(6) of the 1993 Act. Given the presence of s 7(6), which
contemplates that appurtenant property may be contained in a separate demise
and that the separate demise may contain appurtenant property only, I find it
difficult to believe that Parliament can have intended to confine 'appurtenances'
to property which would pass under an assignment of the flat alone. I recognise
e that this is not a complete answer, for 'appurtenant property' includes a garage or
outhouse as well as 'appurtenances' properly so called; but the point is not
without significance. The essential qualification, it seems to me, is that the
appurtenant property should 'belong to, or [be] usually enjoyed with, the flat and
[be] let to the tenant with the flat on the relevant date', not that it should be
f capable of passing under an assignment of the flat without express mention.

But the main change in the context in which the statutory language falls to be
applied is that the 1967 Act applied to houses (as restrictively defined) and the
1993 Act applies to flats, including flats in mansion blocks of flats. The subject
matter of the 1967 Act was a house with its own curtilage. The subject matter of
Ch II of the 1993 Act, however, is a flat, which may or not have a curtilage (for a
g garden flat may have a garden and a basement flat may have an area) but which
also forms part of larger premises with their own curtilage. The 'appurtenance'
must be an appurtenance of the flat in the sense that it must belong to or be
usually enjoyed with the flat and must be let with the flat. The question is
whether it must also be within the curtilage (if any) of the flat or whether it is
h sufficient if it is contained within the premises of which the flat forms part or is
situate within the curtilage of those premises.

I am of opinion that the latter is sufficient. I am influenced by two
considerations. First, I find it difficult to believe that Parliament can have
intended that storerooms allocated to particular flats which would have been
j acquired from the landlord if the tenants had exercised their collective rights
should be excluded from the new leases of the particular flats to which they have
been allocated and be retained by the landlord even if all the tenants were to
exercise their individual rights. Secondly, Parliament cannot sensibly have
intended to distinguish between a right to make use of a storage or other space
and an actual demise of the space. If the appellants' construction of the 1993 Act
is right, a tenant of an upstairs flat who was granted the right to park his car in a

numbered parking space in the forecourt of his block of flats would be entitled to
have a similar right on the grant of a new lease of his flat; whereas a tenant who
had an actual demise of a parking space would not. The absurdity of this is all the
greater when it is remembered that if the tenant had a demise of a lock-up garage
and not merely a parking space he would be entitled to have it included in the
new lease.

The immediate context provides further support for the construction which I
have favoured. Just as the 'outhouse' must be in the grounds of the block of
which the flat forms part, so in my opinion the 'appurtenance', if consisting of
land or a building, must be within the curtilage of the block but need not be
within the curtilage (if any) of the flat. But whereas the 'outhouse' must be
outside the main building, the 'appurtenance' may be within it.

In my judgment, this approach gives proper weight to the meaning which has
been ascribed to the word 'appurtenance' in the 1967 Act but has proper regard
to the changed context in which the word is used in the 1993 Act. As I see it, it is
necessary first to identify the separate set of rooms within the building which
constitutes the flat; next to identify other areas within the building which, or the
right to enjoy which, may be appurtenant to the flat; and finally to consider the
grounds of the building in order to identify any garage, outhouse, garden, yard or
other erection or land within the curtilage of the building which, or the right to
enjoy which, is usually enjoyed and let to the tenant with the flat.

Conclusion

I conclude that the storeroom is not part of the flat as defined by s 101(1) of the
1993 Act and is not an 'outhouse' within the meaning of s 62(2); but that it is an
'appurtenance' of the flat within the meaning of the latter subsection, and that
accordingly the respondent is entitled to have it included in the new lease of his
flat. I would dismiss the appeal.

THORPE LJ. I agree.

WAITE LJ. I also agree.

Appeal dismissed. Leave to appeal to the House of Lords refused.

Paul Magrath Esq   Barrister.

a Knowles and another v Fire Brigades Union

COURT OF APPEAL, CIVIL DIVISION
NEILL, MILLETT AND PHILLIPS LJJ
1, 31 JULY 1996

b

Trade union – Expulsion of member – Power to expel member – Plaintiff members employed as full-time fire fighters – Union opposing full-time fire fighters undertaking additional retained duties – Members subsequently expelled for undertaking additional duties contrary to union policy – Whether members unjustifiably disciplined – Whether union policy constituting 'other industrial action' – Trade Union and Labour Relations c *(Consolidation) Act 1992, s 65(2)(a).*

The plaintiffs, two trade union members who were employed as full-time fire fighters, entered into contracts with their local authority employer to undertake additional duties at a former fire station on a retained basis. Retained fire fighters d were not in full-time employment with a fire brigade, but were paid an annual fee to be ready and on standby to be called out for fires and an extra fee for each fire to which they were summoned. The system of retained duties for full-time fire fighters was contrary to union policy and had been phased out, with the result that when the union learnt that the plaintiffs had been so enrolled it summoned them to a disciplinary hearing before its regional committee and subsequently e expelled them. The plaintiffs did not appeal against that decision, but they presented a complaint to an industrial tribunal pursuant to s 66[a] of the Trade Union and Labour Relations (Consolidation) Act 1992, contending that they had been 'unjustifiably disciplined' within the meaning of s 65(2)(a)[b] of the 1992 Act for 'failing to participate in or support a strike or other industrial action'. f Following a preliminary hearing, the tribunal ruled that the union's opposition to the additional contracts constituted 'other industrial action' and, in particular, that if pressure were put on an employer and, as a result, the employer was inhibited from acting in a way in which he would otherwise have acted, that amounted to 'other industrial action'. On the union's appeal, the appeal tribunal concluded that the industrial tribunal had applied the wrong test and, considering g that they were entitled to intervene, allowed the appeal on the ground that the union was not seeking by its ban to influence the way in which its members performed their tasks in their employment as full-time firemen. The plaintiffs appealed.

h **Held** – In the context of the 1992 Act, which plainly contemplated that industrial action was a serious step, the union's opposition to full-time fire fighters being employed in addition on retained fire fighting contracts did not constitute 'other industrial action' within the meaning of s 65(2)(a) of that Act. The union's policy did not require full-time workers to break or to depart from the terms of their existing contracts; it merely required employees not to undertake additional j work under new contracts. Further, there was no evidence to suggest that either the employer or the union contemplated that the 'pressure' exerted by the union required the support of a ballot, and the fact that other fire fighters had complied

---

a   Section 66, so far as material, provides: 'An individual who claims that he has been unjustifiably disciplined by a trade union may present a complaint against the union to an industrial tribunal ...'
b   Section 65, so far as material, is set out at p 657 *c d*, post

with the union's policy did not indicate that the union and its members had crossed the threshold into taking industrial action within the meaning of s 65. *a* The appeal tribunal had therefore been justified in concluding that the industrial tribunal had misdirected itself in treating pressure plus inhibition as a sufficient test of industrial action. The appeal would accordingly be dismissed (see p 662 *c* f to h, post).

Midlands Plastics v Till [1983] ICR 118 considered. *b*

Notes
For meaning of 'other industrial action', see 16 *Halsbury's Laws* (4th edn reissue) para 353, and for cases on the subject, see 20(2) *Digest* (2nd reissue) 89–92, *2160–2165.*

Cases referred to in judgments *c*
British Telecommunications plc v Ticehurst [1992] ICR 383, CA.
Coates v Modern Methods and Materials Ltd [1982] 3 All ER 946, [1983] QB 192, [1982] 3 WLR 764, CA.
Midlands Plastics v Till [1983] ICR 118, EAT.
Power Packing Casemakers Ltd v Faust [1983] 2 All ER 166, [1983] QB 471, [1983] 2 *d* WLR 439, CA; *affg* [1981] ICR 484, EAT.
Rasool v Hepworth Pipe Co Ltd [1980] ICR 494, EAT.

Cases also cited or referred to in skeleton arguments
Campion v Hamworthy Engineering Ltd [1987] ICR 966, CA.
Glenrose (Fish Merchants) Ltd v Chapman (11 December 1990, unreported), EAT. *e*
Lewis v E Mason & Sons [1994] IRLR 4, EAT.
Miles v Wakefield Metropolitan DC [1987] 1 All ER 1089, [1987] AC 539, HL.
Seaboard World Airlines Inc v Transport and General Workers' Union [1973] ICR 458, NIRC.

Appeal *f*
By notice dated 5 January 1996 Michael Knowles and David Johnson appealed with leave from the decision of the Employment Appeal Tribunal (Keene J, Mr Scott and Mr Tuffin) ([1996] IRLR 337) on 8 December 1995 overruling a decision of an industrial tribunal on 20 October 1993 that the policy of the respondent, the Fire Brigades Union (the union), opposing its members from taking on additional duties constituted 'other industrial action' within the meaning of s 65(2)(a) of the *g* Trade Union and Labour Relations (Consolidation) Act 1992. The facts are set out in the judgment of Neill LJ.

Jeremy McMullen QC and *Jonathan Gavaghan* (instructed by the *Free Representation Unit*) for the appellants. *h*
Laura Cox QC and *Nicholas Randall* (instructed by *Robin Thompson & Partners*) for the union.

Cur adv vult

31 July 1996. The following judgments were delivered.
j

NEILL LJ.

Introduction
The appellants in these consolidated appeals are Mr Michael Knowles and Mr David Johnson. The respondent is the Fire Brigades Union (the union).
The appeal is concerned with the circumstances in which the appellants were expelled from the union on 6 October 1992.

a   The appellants were employees of the Shropshire County Council, working at Telford at a fire station known as Tweedale Fire Station. They worked there as full-time fire fighters. It was a maintained station, which meant that it was manned by full-time fire fighters between 9 am and 6 pm. Between 6 pm and 9 am the next morning the station was manned by retained fire fighters. Retained fire fighters are not in full-time employment with a fire brigade, but are paid a fee *b* each year to be ready and on standby to be called out for fires. They receive an extra fee for each fire to which they are summoned.

   The conditions of service of persons employed in local fire brigades are set out in a scheme agreed by the National Joint Council for Local Authorities Fire Brigades (the national joint council). From time to time the national joint council publishes a booklet (known as 'the Grey Book') containing up-to-date details of *c* the scheme. The union and the National Association of Fire Officers are represented on the national joint council and send employees' representatives to meetings of the council.

   For many years there has been a difference of opinion between the union and the employers' representatives on the national joint council as to whether *d* full-time fire fighters should also be eligible to work part-time as retained fire fighters. For about 15 years, between 1961 and about 1976, a system was in force whereby full-time fire fighters were free to volunteer to undertake 'at stations wholly or partly manned by retained members obligations similar to those of retained members', provided that such arrangements did not prejudice standards of cover. A provision to this effect was included in section II of the Grey Book *e* (1974 edn). In 1974, however, it was decided at the annual conference of the union to seek the end of this system. It was felt that in the context of a modern highly skilled and technical fire service there was no place for such a system. At first the union's efforts to make a change met with resistance from the employers, but by 1977 the national joint council had decided that whole-time retained duties *f* should be phased out. In due course, the reference to whole-time retained duties was deleted from the Grey Book.

   In 1986, however, the employers approached the union again with a view to the reintroduction of retained duties for whole-time fire fighters. It was said that there were difficulties with the recruitment of retained fire fighters in a certain number of fire brigades and it was found that employers were often unwilling to *g* release their employees for fire calls during working time. As a result of this approach the national joint council set up a working party to examine the problems. The conclusions of the working party led to a proposal by the employers that whole-time retained duties should be reintroduced. This proposal, however, was unanimously rejected by the union at their annual *h* conference in 1989.

   On 13 December 1990 the general secretary of the union wrote to the members to explain the union's attitude to the employers' proposals. Towards the end of his letter the general secretary said:

j   'The Union has fought over many years for its members in a modern day Fire Service to have proper remuneration and proper working hours which reflect such a service. Employers and Governments have attempted during the same period to lead us back to the 1940s and 1950s. There are problems of recruiting retained personnel in a small number of Brigades mainly in the South of England. There are a number of reasons for this, not least of which is that the population living in extremely high cost housing in these areas are not the type of people interested in being Retained Firefighters. The

employment of Wholetime Firefighters on retained contracts would not
solve that problem as they cannot afford to live in these areas and, therefore,
cannot meet the laid down times [of] response ... The Employers have
stated that should we not reach agreement on this issue by the 11th February
1991 they will inform Fire Authorities that they will unilaterally withdraw
from the National Agreement which removed the wholetime/retained duty
system from the scheme of conditions of service as being an appropriate
system within the modern day Fire Service. The Executive Council firmly
believe that to concede to those threats would lead to our hard won pay,
conditions of service and most importantly jobs being decimated by these
proposals.'

The general secretary ended his letter by stating that the union's conference
would be recalled on 13 February 1991 and that the executive council would
recommend, inter alia: (a) the rejection of the reintroduction of the employment
of whole-time fire fighters on retained contracts; and (b) the commencement of
a campaign to eradicate from the fire service the whole-time/retained duty
system.

On 13 February 1991 the recalled annual conference of the union met in
Blackpool. At the conference, a resolution rejecting the reintroduction of the
employment of whole-time fire fighters on retained contracts was carried by a
majority of 40,983 votes to 742 votes. On the same day, the joint secretary wrote
to members of the union informing them of the result of the voting and asking
them to note the decisions of the conference.

Meanwhile at local level negotiations had taken place with the union about the
future of the Tweedale Fire Station. In July 1990 it was decided by the county
council that the Tweedale station should be reduced to a one-pump retained
station and that the appellants should be transferred to a fire station at Wellington
on a duty shift system.

Following the transfer of the appellants to the Wellington fire station they
applied, or perhaps were invited, to undertake retained duties at their former fire
station at Tweedale. They were both enrolled as retained fire fighters on 15 April
1992.

The fact that the appellants had so enrolled came to the attention of the union.
They were summoned to a disciplinary hearing before the regional committee of
the union. This committee recommended that the appellants should be expelled
and this recommendation was upheld by the union's main disciplinary
committee. On 6 October 1992 the general secretary wrote to the appellants to
inform them that the disciplinary committee had resolved that they should be
expelled. The second paragraph of the letter was in these terms:

'The decision of the Committee was that you had acted contrary to the
policies of the Union in that you undertook retained duties whilst still
employed as a Wholetime member of the Brigade in contravention of
Annual Conference policy.'

The appellants were informed that they had the right to appeal, but they did not
avail themselves of this opportunity.

The hearing before the industrial tribunal
On 27 October 1992 the appellants presented complaints against the union
pursuant to s 66 of the Trade Union and Labour Relations (Consolidation) Act

a 1992 claiming that they had been unjustifiably disciplined by the union. In the notices of appearance by the union it was contended that the appellants had been expelled for acting contrary to the policies of the union but it was denied that the expulsion was unlawful.

The right which the appellants sought to enforce by their complaints is that enshrined in s 64 of the 1992 Act. Section 64(1) is in these terms: 'An individual b who is or has been a member of a trade union has the right not to be unjustifiably disciplined by the union.' By s 64(2) it is provided that an individual is disciplined if a determination is made, inter alia, that he should be expelled from the union.

Section 65 of the 1992 Act contains a definition of the words 'unjustifiably disciplined'. So far as is material, s 65 provides:

c   '(1) An individual is unjustifiably disciplined by a trade union if the actual or supposed conduct which constitutes the reason, or one of the reasons, for disciplining him is—(a) conduct to which this section applies, or (b) something which is believed by the union to amount to such conduct ...

d   (2) This section applies to conduct which consists in—(a) failing to participate in or support a strike or other industrial action (whether by members of the union or by others), or indicating opposition to or a lack of support for such action ...

(7) In this section—"conduct" includes statements, acts and omissions ...'

e On 14 July 1993 a hearing took place at the industrial tribunal at which directions were given as to the future conduct of the proceedings. It was then agreed and directed that a preliminary point should be tried as to whether or not the union's 'policy of opposing a system of whole-time fire fighters being employed in addition on retained fire fighting contracts' constituted industrial action within the meaning of that phrase in s 65(2)(a) of the 1992 Act.

f The preliminary point was heard by the industrial tribunal on 20 October 1993. At the hearing evidence was given by Mr Cameron, the general secretary of the union, and by Mr Bryant, an executive council member of the union. Mr Bryant told the tribunal that he had had a number of meetings with the chief officer of the Shropshire fire brigade and that at these meetings he had insisted on union policy being maintained in relation to full-time fire fighters. We have seen the g minutes of a meeting held on 25 March 1991 which was attended by the deputy chief fire officer of the Shropshire fire brigade and by union officials including the branch chairman. It seems clear that at this meeting the deputy chief fire officer was informed that any full-time fire fighter who accepted a retained contract would be expelled from the union.

h In their full reasons, which were sent to the parties on 15 December 1993 the industrial tribunal, having referred to some authorities to which their attention had been drawn, stated their conclusions as follows:

'(9) We have not found these cases of much assistance. The only j   principles which seemed to emerge from them are, first, that the expression must be given a wide construction, secondly, the conduct need not involve a breach of contract and thirdly that the conduct must involve some pressure put on the employer by the employee, or of course by a union acting on behalf of employees in an attempt to force the employer to adopt a course of conduct which is different from that which the employer would adopt were such pressure not to be put upon him ...

(10) ... It does appear that the pressure has so far merely been an attempt
by the union to persuade local authorities not to engage in [offering retained
contracts].   There have not been even as yet any threats that if a local
authority does not fall into line and comply with the expressed joint
agreement, that there will be further action taken against it by its employees
on the instructions of the respondents. The respondents probably hope that
as it is a joint agreement they can achieve a result by pressure put on the
employers' side through the Joint Council. The fact remains, however, that
the policy of the Union, although we heard no evidence as to whether it
might financially inconvenience the local authorities, certainly prevents the
local authorities from carrying out the reorganisation of the fire service run
by them, in the manner in which they would wish to do it, namely, by the
full-time employed fire fighters being retained fire fighters when they are not
on duty as full-time fire fighters ... If the phrase is to be given a wide
meaning ... then this is industrial action, in that it is designed by the
respondents to bring pressure to bear on employers to adopt a certain course
of action and that this course of action inhibits the employer in the way in
which he might wish to carry out his duty to provide a fire service. There is
in this case we find something more than mere persuasion. The respondents
have indicated to their members their intention to enforce the Council
agreements by the adoption of those agreements as Union policy and this
brings pressure to bear on the employers who are met in the main with a
refusal by the respondents' members to accept these duties when offered
them.   This in our view amounts to industrial action, even though the
respondents might not have gone so far as to threaten industrial action in
support of their policy, but only attempted to deal with the matter by way of
persuasion. The point as we see it is that the employer when considering
how to organise the services which he provides, has to look over his shoulder
to see whether his proposals do not conflict with the settled policy of the
respondents. He is inhibited in what he wishes to do, by that settled policy
... The question is that the joint agreement has been reinforced by the
respondents making it a specific instruction to their members not to act in
this way. This in our view has the effect of making the conduct industrial
action.'

It followed, therefore, that the preliminary point was decided in favour of the
appellants.

The appeal to the Employment Appeal Tribunal

The union then appealed.

The judgment of the Employment Appeal Tribunal ([1996] IRLR 337) was
delivered by Keene J on 8 December 1995. In the judgment, reference was made
to what appeared to be the conclusion of the industrial tribunal that if pressure
were put on an employer and as a result the employer was inhibited from acting
in a way in which he otherwise would have acted, that amounted to 'other
industrial action'. The judgment continued (at 340–341):

'Pressure plus inhibition seemed to be sufficient in their judgment. We
take the view that that is the wrong approach. Not all things which seek to
put pressure on an employer will automatically and ipso facto amount to
industrial action, even though the employer may feel himself inhibited as a
result of the pressure. The lay members of this appeal tribunal emphasise

that if the industrial tribunal's approach were correct, it would lead to many

a negotiating sessions between employers and unions amounting to "other industrial action", because those negotiations regularly involve the application of pressure on employers by the union side threatening to take strike action or some other form of action and the employers' freedom of action is often constrained by the knowledge of such threats ... Not every

b action which involves pressure on an employer together with some effect on that employer's freedom of action will constitute "other industrial action". There must be some action directed against the employer with the object of obtaining some advantage for the employees ... Moreover, it is difficult to see how action which does not affect the performance of an employee's duties towards his employer in his existing job can constitute industrial

c action. The appellant union was, on the facts found, not seeking by its ban to affect or influence the way in which its members performed their tasks in their existing employment as full-time firemen.'

Accordingly, the Employment Appeal Tribunal, concluding that the industrial tribunal had applied the wrong test, considered that they were entitled to *d* intervene and allowed the appeal.

The appellants have now appealed to this court.

The appeal

In s 218 of the 1992 Act there is a definition of 'trade dispute' for the purposes *e* of Pt IV of the Act. Part IV is concerned with industrial relations. Trade dispute is defined as meaning a dispute between employers and workers, or between workers and workers, which is connected with one or more of certain specified matters including 'terms and conditions of employment, or the physical conditions in which any workers are required to work'.

Sections 64, 65 and 66 are in Pt I of the 1992 Act. This part is headed 'Trade *f* Unions'. The three sections are in Ch V of Pt I, which is headed 'Rights of Trade Union Members'. There is, however, no definition anywhere in the 1992 Act of the words 'other industrial action'.

It was argued on behalf of the appellants that in the absence of any statutory definition the question of whether there was or was not 'other industrial action' *g* was a question of fact which an industrial tribunal was particularly suited to determine.

Counsel for the appellants drew our attention to the decision of the Court of Appeal in *Power Packing Casemakers Ltd v Faust* [1983] 2 All ER 166, [1983] QB 471. In that case the Court of Appeal upheld the decision of the Employment Appeal Tribunal ([1981] ICR 484), who had decided that employees who had refused a *h* request by their employers to work overtime had taken part in 'other industrial action' within the meaning of s 62 of the Employment Protection (Consolidation) Act 1978. The question in issue in that case was whether the industrial tribunal had any jurisdiction to determine whether the dismissal was fair or unfair. In the course of his judgment, Stephenson LJ approved the refusal of the Employment *j* Appeal Tribunal to define the phrase 'other industrial action' in s 62 and their decision that the matter should be left to the good sense of industrial tribunals. Earlier in his judgment Stephenson LJ said ([1983] 2 All ER 166 at 170, [1983] QB 471 at 475):

'An industrial tribunal and the lay members of the appeal tribunal may be trusted to recognise industrial action when they see it, and that was how

both tribunals, as well as one appellant and one other witness, described the
employees' refusal to work overtime.'

Counsel also referred us to a passage in the judgment of Stephenson LJ in
Coates v Modern Methods and Materials Ltd [1982] 3 All ER 946 at 954, [1983] QB 192
at 205 (another case under s 62 of the 1978 Act), where the matter in issue was
whether the two employees concerned had been 'taking part in a strike'.
Stephenson LJ said:

> 'It ought to be easy to decide what "taking part in a strike" means and
> whether on proved or accepted facts a particular employee was or was not
> taking part in a strike. The industrial tribunal seem to have found it easy,
> because they unanimously decided that Mrs Leith was taking part ... I know
> that the construction of a statute is a question of law; but the meaning of
> ordinary words is not, and the meaning of "taking part in a strike" seems to
> me to be just the sort of question which an industrial jury is best fitted to
> decide.'

It was argued in the alternative on behalf of the appellants that, if the question
of what was meant by 'other industrial action' were to be more properly regarded
as a mixed question of fact and law rather than a question of pure fact, the
industrial tribunal did not misdirect themselves and there was no proper basis for
the intervention by the Employment Appeal Tribunal. It was to be noted that the
industrial tribunal made specific reference in para 8 of the reasons to the decision
in *Rasool v Hepworth Pipe Co Ltd* [1980] ICR 494, and that in para 10 they had
distinguished it on the basis that the steps taken by the union were not, as in
Rasool's case, merely acts preparatory to ascertaining the feelings of the
employees towards industrial action.

In *Rasool v Hepworth Pipe Co Ltd* the Employment Appeal Tribunal was
concerned with an argument that the attendance of employees at an
unauthorised mass meeting for the purpose of ascertaining the views of the
workforce with regard to impending wage negotiations constituted 'other
industrial action' within the meaning of the predecessor to s 62 of the 1978 Act.
Waterhouse J said (at 509):

> 'It is sufficient for us to say that it is probably incorrect to attempt to
> interpret the expression [other industrial action] narrowly in terms of specific
> intention and that the nature and effect of the concerted action are probably
> of greater importance. Nevertheless, in our judgment, attendance at an
> unauthorised meeting for the purpose indicated by the majority of the
> tribunal in the instant case falls short of "other industrial action." As the
> majority of the tribunal found, it is more properly regarded as trade union
> activity, even though a degree of disruption of the manufacturing process
> resulted.'

In addition counsel drew our attention to a phrase in the judgment of Ralph
Gibson LJ in *British Telecommunications plc v Ticehurst* [1992] ICR 383 at 398, where
he referred to the fact that Mrs Ticehurst had participated in 'the concerted
action' devised by the union. It was said that in the present case the appellants
had failed to participate in the concerted action which the union had devised,
namely that full-time fire fighters should refuse to enter into retained contracts.
A refusal to enter into retained contracts was analogous to a refusal to operate

a machines. Pressure was applied to the employers who suffered inconvenience and incurred the expense of employing new retained fire fighters.

On behalf of the union on the other hand it was argued that what constituted 'other industrial action' was plainly a mixed question of law and fact. In reaching their conclusions the industrial tribunal had failed to distinguish between: (a) acts preparatory to industrial action; (b) threats of industrial action; and (c) actual
b industrial action.

By failing to make this distinction they had reached a conclusion which was perverse on the facts found. It was important to note that the industrial tribunal stated in their reasons that they had heard no evidence as to whether the policy of the union 'might financially inconvenience the local authorities'. On the
c findings the effect of the policy went no further than to prevent the local authorities from carrying out the reorganisation of the fire service in the manner in which they might wish to do. The union had done no more than seek to persuade the county council not to offer retained contracts to whole-time fire fighters. No 'action' had been taken against the employers by the union nor had
d there been any threats of action.

It was accepted that a breach of contract was not a necessary prerequisite for a finding that there had been industrial action, though normally industrial action does amount to or involve a breach of contract. Counsel referred us to the decision of the Employment Appeal Tribunal in *Midland Plastics v Till* [1983] ICR
e 118. In that case, the employers had been informed by a member of the works committee that if the demands for a specified minimum wage were not met in full it was the workers' intention to take industrial action as from 11 am that day. In the interval between the receipt of the letter and 11 am four employees were asked by the management what action they were going to take if the demands were not met. They replied that they were going to abide by the wishes of the
f workforce. They were immediately dismissed. By a majority, the industrial tribunal concluded that the letter and the surrounding circumstances did not amount to 'other industrial action' within s 62 of the 1978 Act. The Employment Appeal Tribunal dismissed the employers' appeal. Browne-Wilkinson J said (at 123–124):

g

'The majority of the industrial tribunal have referred to the actions which, in normal contemplation, might be thought of as industrial action: walk-out, go-slow, working to rule, banning of overtime, picketing. We are far from saying that that is a comprehensive list. But if the employers are to succeed,
h as it seems to us, they must be able to show that the threat of taking industrial action can itself amount to taking industrial action. We reject that view ...   Unfortunately a substantial factor in industrial relations negotiations in this country is a display of power by one side in response to which the other side either does or does not yield to the wishes of the person
j displaying such power. The actual taking of industrial action is the last stage and is quite distinct from the stage at which the threat of it is being used as a negotiating weapon. Throughout the period of a strike notice what is bearing upon the employer is the risk to his business. We can see no distinction between what occurred in this case and the ordinary strike notice. In neither case has the matter matured into taking part in industrial action.'

Conclusion

a

I accept that the words 'other industrial action' are not to be narrowly construed. But they have to be looked at in a context where the transition from negotiations to action may have far-reaching consequences. We are not dealing in the present case with Pt V of the 1992 Act, which is concerned with industrial action, or with s 226 in Pt V, which provides that an act done by a trade union to induce a person to take part in industrial action is not protected unless the b industrial action has the support of a ballot. But it is to be noted that one of the rights conferred on trade union members by Ch V in Pt I is the right to a ballot before industrial action takes place (see s 62 of the 1992 Act).

Industrial action can take many forms, but, in the absence of any statutory definition, I do not think that any attempt at a paraphrase is likely to be useful. In my judgment, the question of what is industrial action for the purposes of s 65 of c the 1992 Act is a mixed question of fact and law. In large measure it is a question of fact, but the facts have to be judged in the context of the Act which plainly contemplates that industrial action is a serious step.

It is necessary to look at all the circumstances. These circumstances will include the contracts of employment of the employees and whether any breach d of or departure from the terms of the contract are involved, the effect on the employer of what is done or omitted, and the object which the union or the employees seek to achieve.

In the present case it seems to me that the following factors are relevant.

(a) At the date when the appellants were expelled from the union the policy e had been in force for over 18 months. The object to be achieved by the union's policy was to prevent a unilateral departure from the terms which had been agreed in 1977.

(b) The policy did not require full-time workers to break or to depart from the terms of their existing contracts. The policy merely required fire fighters not to f undertake additional work under new contracts.

(c) There is no evidence to suggest that either the county council or the union contemplated that the 'pressure' exerted by the union required the support of a ballot.

(d) There was some discussion at the hearing as to whether any of the other full-time fire fighters in Shropshire had actually refused offers of retained g contracts. Even in the absence of express evidence to this effect, however, it is reasonable to assume that some of the 45 other fire fighters did so refuse. But their compliance with the union's policy does not seem to me on the facts of this case to amount to a clear indication that the union and its members had crossed the threshold into taking industrial action within the meaning of s 65.   h

(e) The evidence of Mr Bryant, as recorded in para 6 of the reasons, shows that negotiations were being continued and that although the union were making clear that they intended to adhere to their policy, the breakdown which is almost implicit in the taking of industrial action had not occurred. As Browne-Wilkinson J said in *Midland Plastics v Till*, in the passage which I have already cited, 'the actual j taking of industrial action is the last stage and is quite distinct from the stage at which the threat of it is being used as a negotiating weapon'. One must also take account of the reaction of the lay members of the Employment Appeal Tribunal in the present case to the suggestion that the mere fact that an employer may feel himself inhibited as a result of pressure applied to him means that industrial action has been taken.

a   In my judgment, the Employment Appeal Tribunal were justified in concluding that the industrial tribunal had misdirected themselves in treating pressure plus inhibition as a sufficient test of industrial action. Furthermore, I think that counsel for the union was correct in her submission that the industrial tribunal failed sufficiently to distinguish between conduct which fell short even of a threat and actual 'industrial action' within the meaning of s 65 of the 1992

b   Act.
    Accordingly I would dismiss this appeal.

MILLETT LJ. I agree.

PHILLIPS LJ. I also agree.

c
Appeal dismissed.

Paul Magrath Esq   Barrister.

Warren v Warren

COURT OF APPEAL, CIVIL DIVISION
LORD WOOLF MR, BUTLER-SLOSS AND SAVILLE LJJ
22, 31 JULY 1996

Evidence – Witness – Judge – Compellability – Whether judge a compellable witness.

A judge (which for this purpose includes a master of the Supreme Court) cannot be compelled to give evidence of those matters of which he became aware relating to, and as a result of the performance of, his judicial functions. However, the judge will remain competent to give evidence, and if a situation arises where his evidence is vital, he should be able to be relied on not to allow the fact that he cannot be compelled to give evidence to stand in the way of his doing so (see p 670 *g* to *j*, p 671 *d* to *g j*, post).

Dictum of Cleasby B in *Duke of Buccleuch v Metropolitan Board of Works* [1861–73] All ER Rep 654 at 657 applied.

Notes

For compellability and privilege of witnesses, including judges, see 17 *Halsbury's Laws* (4th edn) paras 231–236, and for cases on the privilege of judges and arbitrators, see 22(2) *Digest* (2nd reissue) 155–157, 7481–7500.

Cases referred to in judgments

Buccleuch (Duke) v Metropolitan Board of Works (1872) LR 5 HL 418, [1861–73] All ER Rep 654.
McC v Mullan [1984] 3 All ER 908, [1985] AC 528, [1984] 3 WLR 1227, HL.
McKinley v McKinley [1960] 1 All ER 476, [1960] 1 WLR 120, Assizes.
R v Harvey (1858) 8 Cox CC 99, Assizes.
R v Morgan (1852) 6 Cox CC 107, Assizes.
Ridehalgh v Horsefield [1994] 3 All ER 848, [1994] Ch 205, [1994] 3 WLR 462, CA.
Sirros v Moore [1974] 3 All ER 776, [1975] QB 118, [1974] 3 WLR 459, CA.

Cases also cited or referred to in skeleton arguments

Barrister (wasted costs order), Re a (No 1 of 1991) [1992] 3 All ER 429, [1993] QB 293, CA.
Chelsea Man plc v Chelsea Girl Ltd [1988] FSR 217, DC.
Dawson v Dawson [1955] CA Transcript 190.
Florence v Lawson (1851) 17 LTOS 260, DC.
Hennie v Hennie [1972] CA Transcript 359.
Locke v Camberwell Health Authority [1991] 2 Med LR 249, CA.
Mileage Conference Group of the Tyre Manufacturers' Conference Ltd, Re agreement of [1966] 2 All ER 849, [1966] 1 WLR 1137, RPC.
R v Baines [1909] 1 KB 258, [1908–10] All ER Rep 328, DC.
R v Brighton County Court, ex p Westminster Press Ltd [1990] 2 All ER 732, [1990] 1 QB 628, DC.
R v Gazard (1838) 8 C & P 595, 173 ER 633, Assizes.
Ramlochan v R [1956] 2 All ER 577n, [1956] AC 475, PC.
Rudkin-Jones (CK) (a bankrupt), Re, ex p The Bankrupt v The Trustee of the Property of the Bankrupt [1964] 3 All ER 750, [1964] 1 WLR 1470, DC.

a
Senior v Holdsworth [1975] 2 All ER 1009, [1976] QB 23, CA.
Spectravest Inc v Aperknit Ltd [1988] FSR 161, DC.
W (an infant), Re [1971] 2 All ER 49, [1971] AC 682, HL.

Appeal

b
By notice dated 14 November 1994 Mr Gregory Francis Challenor appealed with leave from the order of Judge Davies in the Portsmouth County Court on 19 October 1994 that the appellant pay wasted costs relating to the transfer of proceedings in which he was the legal representative of Mr Stephen Paul Warren to the High Court on the basis that he had acted unreasonably in subpoenaing District Judge Cawood to give evidence in those proceedings. The facts are set c out in the judgment of Lord Woolf MR.

Paul McCormick (instructed by *Anderton & Co*, Portsmouth) for Mr Challenor.
Christopher Katkowski (instructed by the *Treasury Solicitor*) as amicus curiae.

Cur adv vult

d

31 July 1996. The following judgments were delivered.

LORD WOOLF MR. This appeal raises one point of considerable general importance. It is as to the immunity of judges from being compelled to give e evidence in proceedings in relation to functions which they have performed as judges. The point arose in the course of what should have been simple and straightforward proceedings ancillary to divorce proceedings between Mr and Mrs Warren. The ancillary proceedings related to the modest contents of the former matrimonial home. They have resulted in contempt proceedings and proceedings for a wasted costs order against the solicitor for Mr Warren, Mr f Gregory Challenor. This appeal is by Mr Challenor against a wasted costs order. The history of the proceedings vividly illustrates what can happen if the lawyers on both sides become excessively combative and lose any sense of proportion in relation to the issues involved.

g *The facts*

The parties were married on 28 September 1985. The decree absolute was pronounced on 27 May 1993. Mrs Warren was the petitioner. On 24 January 1994 Mr Warren made an ex parte application for an injunction to restrain his wife from disposing of the matrimonial property. He stated that he believed his h wife was imminently about to dispose of it in order to defeat his claim for ancillary financial relief. The schedule to the application referred to 47 different typical household items, which the husband said the wife had removed from the former matrimonial home without his consent while he was working in Germany. Mr Warren alleged he needed the property because in his absence he would be in difficulty in meeting his responsibilities under a joint residence order j for the children of the family.

This was the second ex parte application for an injunction by Mr Warren. The previous application had resulted in an application being made in the High Court to Singer J on 7 January 1994. That injunction had been discharged by District Judge Weintroub in the county court because there was no ancillary financial relief application pending.

In order to justify applying ex parte, Mr Warren said Mrs Warren would
dispose of the property if he gave notice. The application for the ex parte
injunction was successful and an ex parte injunction was granted on the 24
January 1994. This was followed by inter partes listing on 31 January but the case
was not reached and was heard on 1 February. By that time Mrs Warren had
sworn an affidavit which gave an account of events which was quite different
from that of Mr Warren. She concludes her affidavit by referring to further
proceedings and asking that an order which had been made in those proceedings
should be discharged. Both parties were represented by counsel. From a note
prepared by Mrs Warren's counsel, Paul Dugdale, it appears that long
negotiations took place on 31 January, and on 1 February 1994 the case was
'floating' but came before District Judge Cawood, who was able to offer 'a very
quick slot in his list just after lunch'. The district judge sensibly made a suggestion
that it seemed reasonable that fixtures from the previous matrimonial home
should be returned, and on that basis an undertaking was given by Mrs Warren,
the terms of which as amended before the order was drawn up are:

> 'LINDA ANNE WARREN was represented by counsel and gave an undertaking
> to the Court promising to return to the Respondent and until return not to
> cause any damage to the following chattels (1) All carpets pertaining to [the
> former matrimonial home] (2) All curtains save the bedroom curtains and
> curtain rails pertaining to the said property (3) Oven and Hob (4) The
> Rotary Washing Line and to arrange for all the said chattels to be ready for
> collection by [Mr Warren from Mrs Warren's then address at a specified time
> on 3 February 1994].'

The form which records the undertaking states that the meaning of an
undertaking and the consequences of failing to keep it were explained to Mrs
Warren. Mrs Warren signed the pro forma statement, indicating that she
understood the undertaking that she had given, and that if she broke any of the
promises to the court she might be sent to prison for contempt. The order which
was made by the court following the undertaking contained a similar list of the
four items to be returned.

Mr Warren attended to collect the items. He was accompanied by four people,
including a process server and certified court bailiff and a police constable. All the
listed items were not returned, the carpets did not include the underlay (which
had not been specifically mentioned in the undertaking) and the carpet was not
complete. Furthermore, certain of the curtains were missing, the cooker was
damaged, the kitchen carpet was slashed and a curtain rail was bent and broken.

The response to this situation was for Mr Warren's solicitors to take out an
application to commit Mrs Warren to prison. The application was issued on 28
February 1994. It was heard on 14 March 1994 when, for reasons I will explain, it
was adjourned. It was further adjourned on 15 March 1994. On 21 March there
was a directions hearing when the case was transferred to the High Court. On 13
May 1994 an offer was made by the husband to withdraw the committal
application. This was an unconditional offer but it was refused. On 13 June 1994
the committal application was listed before Thorpe J in the High Court at
Winchester where it was dismissed by consent.

Having recited that history of the committal proceedings, it is now necessary
to refer to an event which took place early in the committal proceedings which
explains at least in part why they were so prolonged. As a result of the committal
proceedings Mr Dugdale, Mrs Warren's counsel, swore an affidavit on 8 March

a 1994. In that affidavit he explained that he had been asked to make a note at the hearing on the day the undertaking was given and he was instructed by Mrs Warren that she did not believe the former matrimonial home had ever had any other curtains, beyond those in the bedroom and the lounge. Mr Dugdale states that he told this to Mr Warren's counsel, Mr McCormick. Mr Dugdale exhibited a note to the affidavit which he made contemporaneously and explains in the

b note how the curtains in the bedroom came to be omitted from the undertaking. He says that he had no doubt in his mind that the undertaking Mrs Warren gave to the court was to return the two sets of curtains for the lounge in the matrimonial home only. Unfortunately the undertaking certainly did not make this clear. Mr Dugdale, having prepared the affidavit, did not represent Mrs Warren on the day of the hearing on 14 March 1994. Another counsel did so, but

c Mr McCormick still represented Mr Warren.

The hearing on 14 March was before Judge Davies. At the outset of the proceedings, counsel then appearing on behalf of Mrs Warren objected to Mr McCormick (who had represented Mr Warren when the undertakings were given) still representing him notwithstanding that he might have to be a witness

d as to what Mr Dugdale stated had taken place if there was any dispute as to this. Having heard argument, the judge ruled that Mr Dugdale's evidence was relevant. The case then adjourned to the following day so that Mr McCormick could consider his position with the assistance of the Bar Council. During the course of the hearing, Mr McCormick indicated that his solicitors were considering calling District Judge Cawood to give evidence and arrangements

e would have to be made for the reception of his evidence. The judge however regarded that as a matter which was entirely for them, that is, the solicitors. The judge then adjourned the case until the following morning. The case was then adjourned as indicated. A summons for District Judge Cawood to give evidence was then issued and served on 16 March 1994. The district judge declined to be

f interviewed for the purpose of making a statement.

The application was then transferred to the High Court at Winchester on 21 March 1994. An ancillary relief hearing unconnected with the application to commit took place before District Judge Weintroub on 13 May 1994 during which it was suggested on behalf of Mr Warren that the committal proceedings could be withdrawn with no order for costs. This was followed up by a letter

g making the same offer on 24 May 1994. However the offer was not accepted and the matter was not dealt with by consent and instead, on 13 June 1994, with solicitors and counsel attending, the application was dismissed with consent.

There then followed the proceedings to show cause why a wasted costs order should not be made. The notice to show cause was dated 23 June 1994. The

h notice related both to Mr Warren's counsel, Mr McCormick, and to his solicitor, Mr Challenor. As far as Mr Challenor is concerned the matters relied on were as follows. (1) That he instructed Mr McCormick after he was aware Mrs Warren's solicitors were relying on the evidence of their former counsel, Mr Dugdale, in response to the application to commit. Here it is suggested that Mr Challenor

j caused the costs of the court hearings on 14 and 15 March 1994 to be wasted. (2) Secondly, it is suggested that Mr Challenor should have arranged for new representation for his client on 15 March. In relation to this allegation, it is said that the costs of that day were wasted. (3) Thirdly it is alleged, it having been confirmed on 14 and 15 March by counsel on behalf of Mrs Warren, that there was no issue as to the validity of the undertaking given by Mrs Warren, that Mr Challenor was unreasonable in subpoenaing District Judge Cawood and by so doing he caused the hearing fixed for 22 March 1994 to be vacated and costs to be wasted in respect of the hearing on 21 March 1994.

I am not concerned with the wasted costs application against Mr McCormick but it was said that, the matter having been brought to his attention, he failed to withdraw promptly or failed to communicate promptly his decision to withdraw and so caused the cost of the hearing of 15 March 1994 to be wasted. I have not any details about this, but to complete the history I should indicate that it is suggested by Mr Challenor that there was a further application for a wasted costs order which was dismissed at an initial stage without a hearing on the merits by District Judge Weintroub.

The application to show cause was adjourned on 30 June 1994 and then heard on three succeeding days, 15 and 18 August 1994 and 19 October 1994, on which date judgment was given. At the hearing, which was before Judge Davies, the second ground relied on as against Mr Challenor was abandoned.

The jurisdiction to make a wasted costs order is now contained in s 51 of the Supreme Court Act 1981 (as substituted by s 4 of the Courts and Legal Services Act 1990). That section, so far as relevant, is in the following terms:

'(1) Subject to the provisions of this or any other enactment and to the rules of court, the costs of and incidental to all proceedings in—(a) the civil division of the Court of Appeal; (b) the High Court; and (c) any county court, shall be in the discretion of the court ...

(6) In any proceedings mentioned in subsection (1), the court may disallow, or (as the case may be) order the legal or other representative concerned to meet, the whole of any wasted costs or such part of them as may be determined in accordance with rules of court.

(7) In subsection (6), "wasted costs" means any costs incurred by a party—(a) as a result of any improper, unreasonable or negligent act or omission on the part of any legal or other representative or any employee of such a representative; or (b) which, in the light of any such act or omission occurring after they were incurred, the court considers it is unreasonable to expect that party to pay ...

(13) In this section "legal or other representative," in relation to a party to proceedings, means any person exercising a right of audience or right to conduct litigation on his behalf.'

The section was considered by this court in *Ridehalgh v Horsefield* [1994] 3 All ER 848, [1994] Ch 205 and in his judgment Bingham MR gave guidance as to the proper approach to the requirement that, before a wasted costs order is made, there should be an 'improper, unreasonable or negligent act or omission on the part of any legal or other representative or any employee of such a representative'.

In dealing with the application, the judge drew attention to the passage in the judgment of Bingham MR, which reads:

'The procedure to be followed in determining applications for wasted costs must be laid down by courts so as to meet the requirements of the individual case before them. The overriding requirements are that any procedure must be fair and that it must be as simple and summary as fairness permits. Fairness requires that any respondent lawyer should be very clearly told what he is said to have done wrong and what is claimed. But the requirement of simplicity and summariness means that elaborate pleadings a should in general be avoided.' (See [1994] 3 All ER 848 at 867, [1994] Ch 205 at 238–239.)

The passage then goes on, and I quote further, because what is said is relevant here:

b 'No formal process of discovery will be appropriate. We cannot imagine circumstances in which the application should be permitted to interrogate the respondent lawyer, or vice versa. Hearings should be measured in hours and not in days or weeks. Judges must not reject a weapon which Parliament intended to be used for protection of those injured by the unjustifiable conduct of the other sides' lawyers, but they must be astute to control what threatens to become a new and costly form of satellite litigation.'

c I emphasise the concluding words of Bingham MR.

The judge, having directed herself in accordance with that authority, came to the conclusion that the time scale was so tight that Mr Challenor could not be criticised as alleged in the first ground. I wholly indorse her conclusion. She then
d turned to the third ground (ground two was no longer being pursued). As to this ground, she expressed the view that the summons was designed 'to harass the other side rather than advance the resolution of the case'. She then turned to the fact that District Judge Cawood had produced his notes of the hearing and she adds:

e 'In these circumstances it was inconceivable that the district judge could have had anything further to add which was relevant to the issues with which the court would have been concerned in dealing with the committal applications.'

Having come to that conclusion, she determined that Mr Challenor should pay
f the costs wasted by the need to transfer to the High Court, which were the costs of 21 March, and the additional costs in consequence of there being a transfer to the High Court.

I have set out above what Bingham MR said about satellite litigation in relation to wasted cost orders. What he had to say in relation to wasted costs orders can be applied to many other examples of satellite litigation, of which the application
g to commit in the circumstances of this case is a prime example. Mrs Warren was not represented before us, but even without that representation, it does appear to me that both sides have allowed the issues between this former husband and wife to be treated in a manner which is totally disproportionate to the nature of the issues involved. In my judgment, it would have been preferable if there had
h not been committal proceedings, and if there had not been the application for wasted costs. Both parties to the property proceedings were legally aided. The applications inevitably resulted in a very substantial expenditure in costs which in any event will fall on the legal aid fund. A less combative approach would have provided a much more satisfactory and expeditious results for the parties. Instead
j of the lawyers encouraging a reasonable approach to the resolution of the simple issues involved, they have smothered those issues in application after application and in so doing have achieved a great deal of wasted expenditure. The wasted cost application certainly did not accord with simple and summary procedure to which Bingham MR referred.

The wasted costs order having been made, we now have this appeal. Mr Challenor's case is very simple on the appeal. It was that Mrs Warren had given

the undertaking which was recorded and by calling the district judge he could
show this was the case. A district judge is in no different position to any other
witness when it comes to his being subpoenaed or summonsed and, as all
witnesses are required normally to give oral evidence, he behaved perfectly
reasonably in seeking to secure the judge's attendance. After all, the judge was in
the best position to give the evidence as to what happened at the time the
undertaking was given.

It was this approach to the calling of a judge that has given rise to the need to
consider the principle issue which I identified at the outset of this judgment.
Because of the general importance of this issue, the Attorney General was asked
to instruct an amicus. As a result, we have had the assistance of Mr Katkowski for
which we are grateful to the Attorney.

All the learning on this subject is consistent in indicating that judges of
whatever court are competent to give evidence. As to compellability, the
preponderance of authority indicates that while judges of the superior courts
cannot be compelled to give evidence, the judges of the inferior courts can be
compelled to do so (see *Phipson on Evidence* (14th edn, 1990) para 19–12, *Cross and
Taper on Evidence* (5th edn, 1979) p 530 and 17 *Halsbury's Laws* (4th edn) para 236).
The textbook writers comments are not however unqualified. Thus, *Phipson*
pp 475–476 says there—

> 'is no objection to the judge of an inferior court being called *in some
> circumstances, although it would seem highly undesirable to call such a witness
> unless there was absolutely no other means of proving some piece of evidence vital to
> the proceedings.*' (My emphasis.)

The earlier authorities on which the learning is based are far from impressive
being founded neither on principle or precedent and consist of little more than
off-the-cuff judicial reactions to particular situations (see as examples, *R v Harvey*
(1858) 8 Cox CC 99 and the comment of Byles J at Cornwall Assizes, which
contains the only clear statement of what is said to be the position, and *R v Morgan*
(1852) 6 Cox CC 107). In the more recent case of *McKinley v McKinley* [1960] 1 All
ER 476, [1960] 1 WLR 120 there is a detailed survey of what authority there is and
Wrangham J applies the general approach to a magistrate's clerk.

The precedents of any judge actually being called to give evidence are very thin
indeed. The most impressive authority is *Duke of Buccleuch v Metropolitan Board of
Works* (1872) LR 5 HL 418, [1861–73] All ER Rep 654. That case decided that
arbitrators are compellable but should not be questioned as to their reasons for
their award. In giving the answers of the judges to the questions posed, Cleasby
B made this general statement:

> 'With respect to those who fill the office of Judge it has been felt that there
> are grave objections to their conduct being made the subject of cross
> examination and comment (to which hardly any limit could be put) in
> relation to proceedings before them; and, as everything which they can
> properly prove can be proved by others, the Courts of law discountenance,
> and I think I may say prevent them being examined.' (See LR 5 HL 418 at
> 433, [1861–73] All ER Rep 654 at 657.)

It will be observed the statement makes no distinction between different classes
of judge.

A distinction does undoubtedly exist in the case of the magistrates' court and
is still part of the law relating to justices as Lord Bridge of Harwich made clear in

a   *McC v Mullan* [1984] 3 All ER 908 at 916, 922–924, [1985] AC 528 at 541, 550–551 when refusing to follow Lord Denning MR's attempt to sweep away the distinction in *Sirros v Moore* [1974] 3 All ER 776, [1975] QB 118. Although there is a clear constitutional distinction between High Court and other judges and the High Court and other courts, it does not follow that this provides a reason for distinguishing between judges so far as compellability to give evidence is

b concerned. If there was such a distinction in the past between judges of superior and other courts as to the compellability to give evidence (which is by no means clearly established) then it was difficult to understand the principle on which it was then based and even more difficult to justify it today. There has been a vast change in the extent of the jurisdiction of courts which are not generally regarded as superior courts since the nineteenth century, when the relevant judicial

c comments were made. District judges exercise both a High Court jurisdiction and a county court jurisdiction. The circuit judge's jurisdiction has been extended beyond recognition. In matrimonial matters in particular, there is a unified approach to jurisdiction.

    On examination, the authorities certainly do not stand in the way of the

d adoption of a more sensible approach which reflects the present position as to the relative jurisdiction of the judiciary as a whole. The justification for judges not being compellable identified by Cleasby B is, however, still valid. The amicus argued against extending the rule to all judges in case this could lead to injustice. However, I consider he overestimated the danger. The exception to the principle of compellability only applies to the judge being required to give evidence of

e those matters of which he became aware relating to and as a result of his performance of his judicial functions. If therefore, to take the example considered in argument, a murder is committed in the face of the court the judge could be compelled to give evidence as to the murder, since although he would have observed the murder when acting as a judge, the murder did not relate to his functions as a judge. The position is no different from that which would apply

f if the murder had taken place in the presence of the judge outside the court. It would be a collateral incident (see *Duke of Buccleuch v Metropolitan Board of Works* (1872) LR 5 HL 418 at 433, [1861–73] All ER Rep 654 at 657 and *Phipson* para 19–12).

    It is also important to remember that the judge will remain competent to give

g evidence, and if a situation arises where his evidence is vital, the judge should be able to be relied on not to allow the fact that he cannot be compelled to give evidence to stand in the way of his doing so.

    Mr Katkowski submitted that rather than putting the onus on the judge to avoid injustice, it would be preferable for the court to make the judge

h compellable but for this court to provide guidelines which made clear that the judge should only be called in exceptional circumstances and as a last resort. The difficulty I find with this approach is one of practicality. The guidelines could result in litigation as to whether it was appropriate to issue a summons or not and as this case vividly illustrates, litigation of this sort should not be encouraged.

j Nor do I consider it appropriate, as Mr Katkowski urged, to assume because there has not be a problem in the past there will not be a problem in the future. Accordingly it is my view that no judge in relation to his judicial functions is a compellable witness. For this purpose masters of the Supreme Court are of course judges.

    Returning therefore to consider the merits of this appeal, I accept that while the judge was not compellable, the appellant cannot be criticised for not

appreciating this.   Mr Challenor cannot therefore be said to have acted
unreasonably merely because he sought the attendance of the judge. It has to be   *a*
shown that he was acting unreasonably in the circumstances of this case in
seeking to summons the witness. Here, it has to be accepted, there was a dispute
as to what was the undertaking given by Mrs Warren and a ruling had been made
by Judge Davies that counsel's evidence was relevant. In normal circumstances,
bearing in mind the document that had been signed, this would be the only   *b*
evidence needed. However, the other side were relying on the evidence of their
counsel to qualify that evidence. So Mr Challenor says, in that position was it not
reasonable, putting on one side questions as to the dignity of the judge, for me to
obtain the best evidence in rebuttal, namely that of the judge? After all, the judge
could have agreed to be interviewed and this could have dispensed with the need
for his attendance. The judge's notes which were provided are not in themselves   *c*
conclusive that the evidence the judge could give would not further the evidence.
It was not, as Judge Davies said, inconceivable that the district judge could give
further evidence.

There is also another aspect; that is that in this case as a whole it would be
extremely unfair to single out one legal adviser for this treatment. The decision   *d*
to summons the judge was just one of the many examples of a totally
disproportionate approach being adopted. Mr Challenor's decision to summons
the judge has to be assessed against a background of inappropriate conduct on
both sides. The history of the case reflects no credit on the legal advisors on both
sides and I sympathise with the judge for wishing to demonstrate her disapproval.
However, I do not consider the order can stand and I would allow the appeal.   *e*

BUTLER-SLOSS LJ. I agree.

SAVILLE LJ. I agree.

Appeal allowed.   *f*

L I Zysman Esq   Barrister.

a # Lonrho Exports Ltd v Export Credits Guarantee Department

CHANCERY DIVISION

b LIGHTMAN J

8–12, 15–17, 19, 30 JULY 1996

Guarantee – Loss – Recovery – Guarantee relating to export contract between exporter and foreign buyer – Guarantors undertaking to pay 95 per cent of loss arising under contracts of sale by reason of political events or economic difficulties – Claim under
c *policy satisfied by insurer – Insurer recovering moneys from foreign government pursuant to international agreement for payment of outstanding debts – Character of receipt in hands of insurer as the Crown – Whether receipt a recovery by insurer governed by terms of policy – Whether exporter having proprietary interest in moneys recovered – Whether implied term in policy for payment of proportion of moneys to*
d *exporter on receipt and for payment of interest thereon.*

The plaintiff exported goods to Zambia and in 1975 entered into export credit guarantees with the Export Credits Guarantee Department (the ECGD). In return for the payment of a premium, the ECGD agreed to pay the plaintiff 95% of the amount of any loss arising under its contracts of sale with buyers in
e specified countries by reason of, inter alia, 'political events, or economic difficulties ... which prevent or delay the transfer of payments or deposits made in respect of the contract'. The ECGD was entitled to recover outstanding debts due from foreign debtors and was required under article 24 of the guarantee to pay the plaintiff a part of the debt recovered in proportion to its uninsured loss.
f By 1980 the plaintiff was owed substantial sums in US dollars by Zambian importers; but, as a result of foreign exchange restrictions introduced by the Zambian government, those sums could not be remitted to the plaintiff. Following a multilateral agreement for the rescheduling of its debts, Zambia entered into a bilateral agreement with the UK government (negotiated by the ECGD as representative of the Crown) for the payment of outstanding debts,
g including those which the ECGD sought to recover. In January 1984 the Bank of Zambia made a payment to the ECGD pursuant to the bilateral agreement (the 1984 payment), which was paid into the Consolidated Fund as required under s 14 of the Export Guarantees and Overseas Investment Act 1978. However, the Bank of Zambia failed to comply with the ECGD's requests to confirm the list of
h debts outstanding, with the result that in 1991 the ECGD paid three instalments of the dividend to the plaintiff. Thereafter, the plaintiff brought an action against the ECGD, claiming interest on its proportion of the 1984 payment for the period from its receipt in 1984 to the distribution of the dividend in 1991, on the basis that the ECGD had held the moneys on trust for the plaintiff during that period
j or, alternatively, that there was an implied term in the guarantees that a proportion of moneys recovered from foreign governments by the ECGD were to be paid to the plaintiff on receipt and that therefore interest was also due.

Held – The action would be dismissed for the following reasons—
    (1) Where an insurer exercised his subrogated right of recovery against a third party and recovered an amount in excess of the sum which he was entitled to

recoup, that surplus recovery was held by him on trust for the insured party. *a* Accordingly, if the plaintiff could establish that the 1984 payment included recoveries of the debts owed to it within the meaning of article 24 of the guarantees, the ECGD would hold the 1984 payment on trust: as to the sum referable to the plaintiff's debts, to pay a portion to itself in satisfaction of its right to a share, and as to the balance, to hold it on trust for the plaintiff absolutely (see p 690 *g* and p 691 *a b e*, post); *Lord Napier and Ettrick v Hunter, Lord Napier and* *b* *Ettrick v R F Kershaw Ltd* [1993] 1 All ER 385 considered.

(2) However, in concluding and performing obligations under a treaty such as the bilateral agreement with the government of Zambia, the Crown did not act as a trustee or agent for its own nationals; payments made to the United Kingdom under that agreement were therefore received by the Crown in a sovereign capacity and formed the absolute property of the state and, as such, they were not *c* recoveries for the purpose of article 24 of the guarantees. Indeed, if the 1984 payment had constituted a recovery, it would have been subject to the trust provisions in article 24 in favour of the various policyholders from the date of the payment, and the ECGD would have ceased to be able to comply with the international law obligations of the Crown under the bilateral agreement or *d* otherwise fulfil the responsibility of the Crown in conducting international relations. Moreover, the existence of an intention by the ECGD to make appropriations out of the 1984 payment as recoveries under the guarantees was not effective to appropriate any part of the 1984 payment to any specific debts; the intention was plainly to make appropriations only when the ECGD considered that the necessary agreement with the Bank of Zambia had been *e* reached and the necessary calculations made. It followed that the plaintiff was not entitled to any proprietary or other interest in the 1984 payment until the respective dates of the three payments made to it. In respect of the 1984 payment, the ECGD was at no time a trustee or subject to fiduciary duties owed to the plaintiff and therefore no question arose as to the grant of relief in respect of the *f* pleaded fiduciary duty to pay interest (see p 689 *d j*, p 693 *j* and p 694 *a* to *e j* to p 695 *d*, post); *Civilian War Claimants Association Ltd v R* [1931] All ER Rep 432 applied; *H Cousins & Co Ltd v D & C Carriers Ltd* [1971] 1 All ER 55 distinguished.

(3) Since the ECGD was absolutely entitled to the 1984 payment from the date of its receipt, it was never under any obligation under article 24 of the guarantees and only as a matter of bounty made the payments to the plaintiff, treating them *g* as the plaintiff's share of recoveries received, and since there was never any agreement between the ECGD and the Bank of Zambia to make those specific payments, it was clear that the plaintiff's contractual claim also failed (see p 696 *a*, post).

h

Notes

For export credit guarantee insurance, see 25 *Halsbury's Laws* (4th edn reissue) para 777.

Cases referred to in judgment *j*
Barcelona Traction Light and Power Co Ltd, Re 1970 ICJ Rep 3.
British Airways Board v Laker Airways Ltd [1984] 3 All ER 39, [1985] AC 58, [1984] 3 WLR 413, HL; *rvsg in part* [1983] 3 All ER 375, [1984] QB 142, CA.
Buck v A-G [1964] 2 All ER 663, [1965] Ch 745, [1964] 3 WLR 850; *affd* [1965] 1 All ER 882, [1965] Ch 745, [1965] 2 WLR 1053, CA.
Burnand v Rodocanachi Sons & Co (1882) 7 App Cas 333, HL.

a   *Civilian War Claimants Association Ltd v R* [1932] AC 14, [1931] All ER Rep 432, HL.
    Cousins (H) & Co Ltd v D & C Carriers Ltd [1971] 1 All ER 55, [1971] 2 QB 230,
        [1971] 2 WLR 85, CA
    German Property Administrator v Knoop [1933] Ch 439.
    Gschwind v Swiss Confederation (1932) 6 Annual Digest 242, Swiss Fed Ct.
    Littrell v USA (No 2) [1994] 4 All ER 203, [1995] 1 WLR 82, CA.
b   *Lonsdale (Earl) v A-G* [1982] 3 All ER 579, [1981] 1 WLR 887.
    Lucas (L) Ltd v Export Credits Guarantee Dept [1974] 2 All ER 889, [1974] 1 WLR 909,
        HL.
    *Maclaine Watson & Co Ltd v Dept of Trade and Industry, Maclaine Watson & Co Ltd
        v International Tin Council* [1989] 3 All ER 523, sub nom *J H Rayner (Mincing
        Lane) Ltd v Dept of Trade and Industry* [1990] 2 AC 418, [1989] 3 WLR 969, HL.
c   *Napier and Ettrick (Lord) v Hunter, Lord Napier and Ettrick v R F Kershaw Ltd* [1993]
        1 All ER 385, [1993] AC 713, [1993] 2 WLR 42, HL.
    Nissan v A-G [1969] 1 All ER 629, [1970] AC 179, [1969] 2 WLR 926, HL.
    Philipp Bros v Republic of Sierra Leone [1995] 1 Lloyd's Rep 289, CA.
    R v Secretary of State for Foreign and Commonwealth Affairs, ex p Pirbhai (1985) Times,
d   17 October, [1985] CA Transcript 582.
    Rustomjee v R (1876) 2 QBD 69, CA.
    Westdeutsche Landesbank Girozentrale v Islington London BC [1996] 2 All ER 961,
        [1996] 2 WLR 802, HL.
    Westland Helicopters Ltd v Arab Organisation for Industrialisation [1995] 2 All ER 387,
        [1995] QB 282, [1995] 2 WLR 126.

e

Action

By writ issued on 5 August 1992 the plaintiff, Lonrho Exports Ltd, commenced proceedings against the defendant, the Export Credits Guarantee Department, seeking interest on payments made to the plaintiff out of moneys received by the
f   defendant from the Bank of Zambia, as recoveries of debts which had been partially repaid to the plaintiff by the defendant pursuant to export credit guarantees. The facts are set out in the judgment.

Alan Boyle QC and *Alison Green* (instructed by *Cameron Markby Hewitt*) for the plaintiff.
g   *Roderick Cordara QC, Professor Christopher Greenwood* and *Philippa Hopkins* (instructed by the *Treasury Solicitor*) for the defendant.

Cur adv vult

h   30 July 1996. The following judgment was delivered.

LIGHTMAN J.

I. INTRODUCTION

The Export Credits Guarantee Department (the ECGD) guarantees the
j   payment of a percentage (normally 90% to 95%) of certain debts due from foreign debtors owed to United Kingdom exporters. These debts may be short term (payable in less than one year) or medium or long term (payable in a longer period). Sometimes before, and sometimes after, the ECGD has paid up under these guarantees, the ECGD makes recoveries from the foreign debtors and part of these recoveries (representing the uninsured part of the debts) is payable over by the ECGD to the exporters. This is a test case which raises three questions.

The first is what the ECGD describe in an internal memorandum as 'the hoary old chestnut' whether the exporters are entitled to interest on their share of the recoveries in respect of the period between receipt and disbursement of them by the ECGD. This depends on the as yet undecided question whether an insurer, who recovers a sum in excess of that which he is entitled to retain in recoupment of his payment to the insured, holds the balance as trustee for the insured. The ECGD have adopted what the memorandum describes as 'the party line' of denying such entitlement to interest. The second is whether a payment made by a foreign state to the Crown pursuant to a treaty in whole or in part in respect of such debts constitutes a recovery for this purpose. The third is whether, in a case where there is such a receipt from a foreign state, as an implied term of the guarantees the ECGD is obliged to pay interest from the date that the ECGD and the foreign state agree the policyholders to be paid and what they shall be paid out of such receipt.

The first stage in answering the third question must be to determine whether it is the Crown or the court which has to decide whether such an agreement has been reached between the ECGD and the foreign state. In this case, both parties by agreement have proceeded, and requested me to proceed, on the basis that as well as deciding this preliminary question, whether or not if I hold as a matter of law that the decision-maker is the Crown, none the less I should also decide on the evidence adduced whether (and if so when) such an agreement was reached. The reason for this is that this case may be taken on appeal (if leave is granted) as far as the House of Lords, and my finding may prove relevant on an appeal if my answer to the preliminary question is held to be wrong. With some misgiving I have decided to comply with the parties' request. I say more about this aspect of the case at the close of this judgment.

II. FACTS

(A) *The background*

Under ss 1 and 12 of the Export Guarantees and Overseas Investment Act 1978, since superseded by the Export and Investment Guarantees Act 1991, the Secretary of State acting by the ECGD (a department of the Secretary of State) for the purpose of encouraging trade with foreign countries (and accordingly of promoting the national interest) was given power to give guarantees on such terms and conditions as to consideration or otherwise as may be determined in connection with, inter alia, the export of goods and rendering of services. On 12 December 1975 the plaintiff, Lonrho Export Ltd (LEL), and the ECGD entered into two standard form contracts of insurance called an 'External Trade Guarantee' and a 'Comprehensive Short Term Guarantee' (the guarantees), which (so far as is material) were in the same terms. By the guarantees, in consideration of a premium paid by LEL, the ECGD undertook to cover certain risks of LEL in respect of short-term debts arising under contracts for the sale of goods to buyers in specified countries, including Zambia. In particular the ECGD agreed to pay to LEL 95% (being the guaranteed percentage) of the amount of any loss arising by reason of the occurrence of any of the specified causes of loss which LEL might sustain in connection with any contract to which the guarantees applied. One such event was 'political events, or economic difficulties ... which prevent or delay the transfer of payments or deposits made in respect of the contract'.

By 1979 or 1980, LEL was owed substantial sums (the LEL debts) in US dollars (dollars) and Deutschmarks (DMs) by Zambian buyers under contracts (the LEL a contracts) covered by the guarantees. The buyers deposited the equivalent in local currency with commercial banks in Zambia to purchase the necessary dollars and DMs, but the purchase could not proceed nor could these sums be remitted due to foreign exchange restrictions introduced by the Zambian government because of lack of the foreign currency to meet even these short term debts. This was a cause of loss covered by the guarantees. LEL (and a

b number of other exporters who likewise insured with the ECGD, in some cases for 90% and in others 95% of their losses) made claims against the ECGD for the guaranteed percentage of their debts and these claims were processed and paid. (It is agreed in principle between the parties for the purpose of these proceedings that the LEL contracts and losses fall within the guarantees, though the ECGD reserve the right to raise questions at a later stage in respect of any particular

c contract or loss.)

By 1983, Zambia's economy was in crisis. The lack of the hard currency urgently needed to pay its foreign debts, (long, medium and short) gave rise to an urgent need for some rescheduling of its debts, and in particular debts owed to foreign governments and debts guaranteed by state agencies. To this end Zambia

d participated in discussions of the so-called 'Paris Club'.

The Paris Club was established in 1956 as an informal grouping of western countries which meets monthly in Paris, and to which proposals may be brought by countries wishing to reschedule (normally long term) debts payable in hard currency as a result of government to government loans or the supply to nationals of goods, services or credit where the debts are insured by an official

e Export Credit Agency (such as the ECGD). (The London Club serves an equivalent function in the rescheduling of purely private debts.) Beyond the debtor and creditor nations, other interested international organisations take part, such as the World Bank, the International Monetary Fund and the Organisation for Economic Co-operation and Development. Once

f recommendations for debt restructuring on the part of the debtor country have been agreed, they are embodied in a multilateral agreed minute (which I shall call a 'multilateral agreement') signed by the debtor country and all the creditor countries. For the United Kingdom the multilateral agreement is signed by the head of the delegation, usually a Treasury official. Such a multilateral agreement has no legal force in international law. Each creditor country then negotiates a

g bilateral agreement (or treaty) with the debtor country, which sets out in detail the terms on which the debt is to be repaid and which is binding in international law. The bilateral agreement is necessary because creditor governments and their export credit agencies have different budgetary and legislative requirements to satisfy and it is not possible to cater for all of these in the multilateral

h agreement. For the United Kingdom the bilateral agreement in respect of export credit debt is negotiated by the International Debt Division of the ECGD, but, since it is a government treaty, it has to be formally signed by an ambassador or high commissioner or some other official of the Foreign and Commonwealth Office. Currently there are some 150 bilateral agreements either signed or in

j process of negotiation with 50 countries, and the total amount covered by these agreements is approximately £7·9bn. For the financial year ending 31 March 1992, recoveries totalled £400m, of which £330m represented payments of moratorium interest and £70m repayments of principal.

On 16 May 1983, after negotiations conducted on behalf of the United Kingdom by the Treasury, a multilateral agreement (the multilateral agreement) was made between the Zambian government and 12 other governments,

including that of the United Kingdom. The multilateral agreement, after reciting
in the preamble the serious economic and financial difficulties faced by Zambia   *a*
and the determination of the Zambian government to reduce the economic and
financial imbalances and reach targets agreed with the International Monetary
Fund, laid down general principles for the rescheduling of Zambia's international
long, medium and short term debt arising under obligations incurred before 1
January 1983. It was unusual (and the multilateral agreement with Zambia was   *b*
one of the first) to include short term debt in a rescheduling exercise, since debtor
countries normally have sufficient foreign currency reserves to pay short term
debts which often relate to the most basic supplies needed by a country. It is only
in cases of extreme economic failure that short term debts are rescheduled, and
compiling and verifying short term debt lists generally is more complicated than
compiling and verifying long term debt lists having regard to the larger number   *c*
of debts of a smaller value. As regards short term debts, the multilateral
agreement provided for repayment by ten half-yearly instalments and for
subsequent negotiation of bilateral agreements between the Zambian
government and each of the 12 other governments dealing with the nuts and
bolts of the rescheduling and in particular the interest rate payable in respect of   *d*
the moratorium period. It is clear in part from the terms of the bilateral
agreement subsequently negotiated (see article 3 and paragraph 4 of schedule 2)
and in part from the evidence of Mr Sapsted (to whom I must subsequently refer)
that debts were only eligible for payment where the debtor had deposited a sum
equal to the debt in local currency with a local commercial bank or the Bank of
Zambia (BOZ) and accordingly was only prevented from paying his debt in the   *e*
agreed currency by Zambian exchange control restrictions which disabled the
debtor from converting this sum into hard currency.

In order to progress the restructuring arrangements, it was necessary for the
ECGD to establish which United Kingdom nationals had claims which might fall
within the scope of the multilateral agreement, so that a list of creditors could be   *f*
agreed with Zambia and the amounts owed could be established. On 16 June
1983, therefore, ahead of execution of the anticipated bilateral agreement (but
with some knowledge of what its terms would be) the ECGD wrote to some 120
exporters whose debts it had guaranteed, and who had made a claim and received
payment from the ECGD (including LEL), in an attempt to establish which debts
were claimed by creditors to fall within the scope of the restructuring   *g*
arrangements. The standard letter informed them of the multilateral agreement,
and invited them by 7 July 1983 to complete an enclosed mandate and to list the
short term debts on which the ECGD had paid a claim. The letter stated: 'Please
note that this mandate only allows ECGD to act on your behalf in recovering
insured unpaid debt.' The mandate to be signed by policyholders stated: *h*

> 'We acknowledge receipt of your letter ... regarding the proposed
> agreement for the settlement of debts from the above country, and confirm
> that we agree to your negotiations of the terms set out therein, in respect of
> debts under our contracts guaranteed by ECGD.'
                                                                                           j
(It is to be noted that, whilst the letter referred to debts on which the ECGD had
paid a claim, the ECGD later included in lists of creditors of which it sought
agreement by BOZ creditors who had not been paid and indeed had not made a
claim.)

On 5 July 1983 LEL signed and returned the mandate to the ECGD, together
with a detailed schedule setting out the LEL debts totalling $US1,238,478 and

a   DM8,149,442. (LEL debts in DMs in respect of which a distribution by the ECGD was finally made totalled some DM7·6m of the total DM8 to 8·5m debt in DMs in respect of which a distribution was made; and LEL debts in dollars in respect of which the ECGD made a distribution was in the region of $US6–700,000. The LEL debts in total amounted to some 15% of the total short term debt.)

b   Most of the creditors responded, but only after 7 July 1983. The ECGD then set about preparing lists of the debts notified by its policyholders, with a view to obtaining their agreement by BOZ. For this purpose the ECGD first carefully checked the information obtained from the creditors against the records contained in the ECGD's files representing the information obtained when each policyholder made his claim on the ECGD under his policy, ie the information provided which satisfied the ECGD that the claim was covered by the policy.

c   The ECGD then prepared a list of the debts which appeared to it to be eligible for inclusion within the bilateral agreement. A first list was sent to the BOZ on 13 September 1983, and this was followed in time by a further four lists.

    On 30 December 1983 pursuant to the multilateral agreement the United Kingdom government entered into a bilateral agreement with the Zambian

d   government regarding the rescheduling of its debts (the bilateral agreement) (TS 23 (1984); Cmnd 9187). The negotiations were conducted by representatives of the ECGD in their capacity as representatives of the Crown and the bilateral agreement was signed by an official of the Foreign and Commonwealth Office on behalf of the United Kingdom. The bilateral agreement applied, inter alia, to

e   debts owed by a person resident or carrying on business in Zambia for the supply of goods from outside Zambia under a contract entered into before 1 January 1983 (article 2), ie it applied to all of the LEL debts. By article 4, the Zambian government undertook to pay its debts punctually and ensure that funds were transferred to the ECGD 'on behalf of creditors in the United Kingdom in the currency of the debt' sufficient to pay the short term debts in ten equal and

f   consecutive half-yearly instalments on 30 June and 31 December in each year commencing on 31 December 1983. Article 5 provided for interest to be paid to the ECGD on behalf of the creditors on any unsettled debt at 1% above LIBOR. Article 8 provided that the bilateral agreement and its implementation should not affect the rights and obligations of creditors and debtors under their credit contracts. Article 9 incorporated schedule 2, which (so far as is material) provided

g   as follows:

    'Rules   (1) The [ECGD] and [BOZ] shall agree a list of debts to which, by virtue of the provisions of Article 2 of this Agreement, this Agreement applies. (2) Such a list shall be completed as soon as possible. This list may

h   be reviewed from time to time at the request of the [ECGD] or [BOZ]. The agreement of both the [ECGD] and [BOZ] shall be necessary before the list may be altered or amended or added to. (3) Neither inability to complete the list referred to in paragraphs (1) and (2) of this Schedule nor delay in its completion shall prevent or delay the implementation of the other

j   provisions of this Agreement ... (5)(a) [BOZ] shall transfer the necessary amounts in the currency of the debt to the [ECGD] in the United Kingdom together with payment instructions in favour of the creditor to whom payment is due in accordance with this Agreement. (b) When making such transfer [BOZ] shall give the [ECGD] particulars of the debts and of the interest to which the transfers relate.'

(I shall refer to the above as 'the rules'.) (There were subsequent multilateral and bilateral agreements in particular in respect of obligations incurred after 1 January 1983, but they are not relevant to the issues in these proceedings.)

Zambia failed to comply with the schedule of payments set out in the bilateral agreement. The only payment ever made was a single payment made on account on 24 January 1984 of £5,881,221·20 (the 1984 payment). Section 14(1)(b) of the 1978 Act required that all sums received by the ECGD by virtue of the Act should be paid into the Consolidated Fund, which is a general fund. Receipts banked with the Consolidated Fund cannot be earmarked for specific purposes. (Section 1 of the Civil List Act 1952 placed on the ECGD a requirement to like effect in respect of 'hereditary revenues', a term which embraces such receipts). On receipt the ECGD paid the 1984 payment into a non-interest bearing account in the name of the ECGD at the Bank of England, and at the close of business the same day the balance was transferred to the Paymaster General's Account and thereby became part of the Consolidated Fund. Surplus moneys in the hands of the Paymaster General at the end of each day are put at the disposal of the National Loans Fund. The ECGD concede that the 1984 payment reduced by an equal amount the Crown's borrowing requirement and accordingly saved the Crown from incurring interest on such borrowing. The 1984 payment also constituted for the ECGD's accounting purposes and its 'balance sheet' a receipt, but provision was there made for payment of a portion of the 1984 payment (calculated on stylised assumptions) to policyholders, who were for this purpose referred to as 'sundry creditors'.

The 1984 payment, made following receipt of the first list of debt, was considerably less than the total sum claimed by United Kingdom creditors. It was described by BOZ in a letter dated 21 January 1984 (as to £3,276,380·33) as 'the total principal payments due on all outstanding Paris Club debits' and (as to £2,604,840·33) as 'a payment on account pending verification' of one quarter of the estimated amount of rescheduling interest of £10m due to 31 December 1983. No other instructions were given, still less those contemplated by paragraph 5(1) of the rules. The making of the 1984 payment before agreement of the list of creditors to be paid and of the character and amounts of the payments to be made in respect of individual debts was quite exceptional and not contemplated by the bilateral agreement. The bilateral agreement provided for payments of specific sums earmarked for specific debts. It is the fact that the 1984 payment was made ahead of the agreement of the debts in whose payment it should be applied that has given rise to the problems resulting in this litigation. It should however be said at once that (as Mr Sapsted said in his letter dated 5 June 1984 and confirmed in his evidence and as is reflected in the provision for sundry creditors in the ECGD accounts), the ECGD recognised immediately that part of the 1984 payment reflected the entitlement of policy holders and had to be paid over to those whose debts were agreed by BOZ. It was inconceivable that none would be paid to policyholders: a proportion would go to them, but there was a question as to which ones and how much. The issue in this case relates to the character of the entitlement of the policyholders, whether it was legal or moral only.

(B) *Overview of the exercise*

The ECGD then commenced the process of seeking the agreement of BOZ to the allocation of the 1984 payment between (1) different categories of debt ie short, medium and long term; (2) principal and interest; and (3) the individual debts. This was a requirement of the rules and a necessary prelude to the a allocation of any sum earmarked to an individual debt as between the ECGD and the policyholders. There were substantial delays in completing this process. The major stumbling block was the failure of BOZ to address the issue of the approval of individual debts with the attention and seriousness required.

The individuals principally concerned at the ECGD were between 1983 and September 1987 Mr Sapsted and thereafter his successor Mr Roderick, both of
b whom worked in Cardiff; and in Zambia Mr Brown and Mr Cordery who worked at the British High Commission in Lusaka and acted in a liaison capacity between the ECGD and BOZ. Mr Chipumbu was the deputy director National Debt Office at BOZ in Zambia until 1986, when he was replaced by Mr Gondwe, who in 1990 was in turn replaced by Mr Mwantza. Both Mr Sapsted and Mr Roderick gave evidence. They were both impressive witnesses, who clearly carried out
c their duties with a deep sense of responsibility and conscientiously. Entirely properly they conceived it to be their duty not to take advantage of any misunderstanding or error of approach on the part of BOZ in its first experience of this kind of exercise. To this end they adopted and remained faithful to the principle throughout the exercise that BOZ should not be treated as finally
d agreeing, or committing itself to payments of, any debts unless and until: (1) they were satisfied that BOZ thoroughly understood what it needed to do to protect the proper interests of BOZ in this regard (and in particular had verified with the commercial banks in Zambia each debt which BOZ agreed should be paid under the bilateral agreement) and accordingly that such consent was full and informed; and (2) (on the basis that the persons they were dealing with could not be
e expected to have authority to reach a binding agreement at a meeting without referring back to their superiors) such agreement or commitment was in writing.

There was one significant difference in approach between Mr Sapsted and Mr Roderick. Mr Sapsted took the view that the ECGD should expend the 1984 payment to the full extent of the moneys available in payment of each and every
f debt BOZ agreed should be paid as soon as such agreement was reached, and not awaiting agreement of other debts, even though the consequence would be that the balance available after such payment would prove insufficient to pay in full creditors whose debts were only agreed later and they might only receive a dividend. On this basis, when the debts in sterling and Swiss francs and their payment were finally agreed earlier than the other debts, they were paid in full.
g In Mr Sapsted's view there was no such agreement in respect of dollar or DM debts during the period that he was concerned.

Mr Roderick, however, took the view that the payment of the balance should not be paid to the other creditors until the total remaining indebtedness was agreed, so that all such creditors should share the balance pari passu. In Mr
h Roderick's view there was no such agreement during the period that he was concerned save that which the ECGD engineered and inferred after its final ultimatum in December 1990.

The task undertaken by the ECGD must not be underestimated. This was only one of a number of similar exercises on which it was involved over the period and
j the staff available was limited. Further it was aiming at a moving target, for over the period when agreement with BOZ was being sought some debts were paid direct and new (late) claims continued to come to light. But the real obstacle was the lack of the required co-operation from their partner in the exercise, BOZ. After the verification of debts by the ECGD, a similar exercise was called for on the part of BOZ, and this made serious demands on BOZ and, for whatever the reason, this exercise was not afforded by BOZ the required or (at times) any

degree of priority. There was little (if anything) in it for BOZ. In December 1986
the multilateral agreement expired and Zambia showed no interest in negotiating   *a*
a fresh agreement until 1990. Between 1986 and 1990, Zambia broke off relations
with the International Monetary Fund and the World Bank, fell into default in
respect of payments due to them as well as to the Export Credit Agencies of
various countries and indeed displayed a negative attitude to the Paris Club.
Only in 1990 when Zambia sought another Paris Club agreement did Zambia   *b*
seek to regularise its relations with international institutions and progress the
agreement of the debts. This no doubt aggravated and lengthened the whole
process. Mr Youd, head of the African section of the International Debt Division,
with evident justification, summarised the position in his evidence: 'In my
experience, the difficulties encountered in trying to achieve debt reconciliation
with Zambia were, along with Sudan, the most extreme that I have ever   *c*
encountered.'

(C) *Detailed history of agreement process*

On 28 March 1984 the ECGD sent a telex to the Head of Treasury in Kitwe
with a breakdown of the intended allocation of the 1984 payment on account to   *d*
the ECGD policyholders. On 5 June 1984 Mr Sapsted wrote to Mr Brown
expressing the view that part of this money was due to the policyholders and his
anxiety to avoid criticism for delay in making allocations to individual creditors,
and asking him to establish whether any of the debts were now approved and
seeking details. On 30 August 1984 Mr Brown telexed Mr Sapsted that Mr
Chipumbu had confirmed five lists of short term debts (which had previously   *e*
been sent by the ECGD to Mr Brown and supplied by him to Mr Chipumbu) and
also agreed the total figures in dollars and DMs. It is clear (if not common
ground) that the lists included the LEL debts. Mr Sapsted quite realistically (and
I think correctly) took the view that the confirmation was merely of the
arithmetic totalling up the figures in the lists, and there had been no verification   *f*
of the individual debts with the Zambian commercial banks (see, e g telex dated
16 May 1985).

On 18 February 1985 at a meeting in Cardiff Mr Sapsted provided Mr Brown
with a further composite debt list (the sixth list), which he passed on to Mr
Chipumbu. Mr Chipumbu however made no comments on the contents of this   *g*
list. On 26 April 1985 Mr Chipumbu telexed the ECGD requesting an urgent
indication by 3 May how the 1984 payment had been applied. The ECGD replied
that it was considering the details of the request.

On 8 May 1985 Mr Sapsted sent a telex to Mr Brown stating that the ECGD was
unable to allocate any of the 1984 payment to the ECGD policyholders until it   *h*
had received a response to the list of debts and confirmation of the individual
amounts and due dates; and requesting Mr Brown to visit Mr Chipumbu again
and establish 'how they are coping with our most recent version of the debt list'.
Mr Sapsted also said in the telex that he had telexed BOZ on 28 March 1984 with
the breakdowns of the ECGD's intended allocation to certain policyholders. In
his evidence Mr Sapsted acknowledged difficulty in reconciling these statements,   *j*
for there could be no allocation (intended or actual) until the debts had been
agreed. I am satisfied that at this time BOZ had not agreed the debts, and the
ECGD knew this, and that BOZ could not sensibly agree the debts until it had
verified them with the commercial banks with whom the debtors must have
deposited the necessary local currency.

a On 16 May 1985 Mr Cordery in Lusaka sent a telex to Mr Sapsted stating that the debt lists had been submitted to the commercial banks for verification but that only a few replies had been received and that Mr Cordery had now sent the sixth list for verification. By telex dated 10 June 1985 Mr Sapsted made it clear to Mr Cordery that the sixth list replaced all the earlier lists.

b On 24 June 1985 Mr Chipumbu met Mr Sapsted and a Mr Bannister at the ECGD's offices in Cardiff. Those present worked through the debt lists. Mr Chipumbu stated that he had passed the ECGD's lists to the commercial banks for verification and that on this basis BOZ had compiled a list of debts which it felt should be deleted or which required clarification. This list included four LEL debts. Mr Chipumbu stated that the remainder of the debts, which were the majority, would be agreed. The ECGD realised that the debts which BOZ was c asking to be deleted had already been deleted from the sixth list, a copy of which was given to Mr Chipumbu. Mr Chipumbu stated that he wanted the 1984 payment to be allocated to capital, but the ECGD insisted that in accordance with established practice it should be allocated to moratorium interest. Mr Chipumbu plainly accepted this, for BOZ thereafter proceeded on the basis that the 1984 d payment should be allocated to moratorium interest (see telex dated 14 March 1986). The meeting ended with a promise by Mr Chipumbu that he would revert in early July 'with the amounts which BOZ could agree as eligible for inclusion'.

On 5 July 1985 Mr Chipumbu sent a telex to the ECGD stating that BOZ 'confirm the 1983 agreement no.1 debt list' setting out the totals in the various e currencies. Mr Chipumbu added:

f 'The above total amounts are subject to final adjustments when the bills which we agreed should be followed up are attended to in due course. Having regard to the foregoing, please now proceed to make your proposed allocation of the Pds 5,831,221-20   As we agreed on Monday 24th June, 1985 Bank of Zambia has to approve your proposed allocation   Grateful therefore if your proposals can be made as soon as possible to enable you finalise the payments due to the British Exporters without further delay.'

g Accordingly subject to some queries which Mr Chipumbu had raised and of which he provided details at the June meeting and in respect of which he had received clarification at the meeting the debt lists were now ready to be agreed. On 30 July 1985 Mr Sapsted wrote to Mr Cordery that considerable progress had been made at the meeting and that both parties had agreed to follow up what was outstanding. On 4 September 1985 Mr Sapsted noted that Mr Chipumbu was told the ECGD's proposals for allocation.

h On 4 September 1985 in the course of a telephone conversation Mr Sapsted told Mr Chipumbu that 'our figures are now lower than those previously agreed due to further recoveries made direct'.

On 16 October 1985 the ECGD wrote to BOZ enclosing schedules setting out a breakdown of consolidated debt and moratorium interest due over the j remainder of the year (appendix A); details of how the ECGD had allocated (in the sense of appropriated to payment of moratorium interest) the January 1984 payment (appendix B); repayment programmes for the various categories of consolidated debt (schedules 1A and 2A); and the current payment position under each of the agreements (schedules 1B and 2B). In schedule 1A the relevant figure was $US5,371,904·86 and DM8,250,732·81

On 3 February 1986 Mr Sapsted sent a telex to Mr Chipumbu asking for a reply
on the question of the debt list and the ECGD's proposed method of allocation.   *a*
This was followed by a further meeting between Mr Sapsted and Mr Chipumbu
in London on 7 March 1986. On 14 March 1986 Mr Chipumbu sent a telex to Mr
Sapsted referring to the meeting on 7 March, confirming the amounts
rescheduled (stated in case of dollars as $US4,259,669·15 and in case of DMs
8,090,812·80) under the bilateral agreement and asked the ECGD to allocate the   *b*
1984 payment to exporters as to £4,905,265·56 in respect of moratorium interest
on short term debts as at 31 December 1982, as to £341,275·66 in respect of
moratorium interest in respect of long term debts at that date and as to
£634,679·98 in respect of moratorium interest in respect of long term maturities
due between 1 January 1983 and 31 December 1983. On 25 March 1986 Mr
Sapsted sent a telex to Mr Chipumbu acknowledging the telex of 14 March 1986   *c*
and stating 'I am now able to proceed with the initial stages of the allocation of
the amount paid in January 1984' and requesting comments on the debts not
approved by BOZ and the new debts of which details had been passed to Mr
Chipumbu at the meeting. Mr Chipumbu acknowledged on 25 April 1986. On
27 May 1986 Mr Sapsted wrote to Mr Chipumbu: *d*

'You have still to provide me with details of the debts which cannot be
agreed ie those debts contained in the computer listings for US Dollars,
D Marks and Sw Francs where your totals were less than mine ... the debts,
previously queried, where I gave you evidence of local currency deposit and
the new debts passed to you during our last meeting.'   *e*

On 17 July 1986 Mr Chipumbu telexed Mr Sapsted referring to the difficulty of
providing details of the disputed debts and invited the ECGD to proceed with the
payment of the sterling debt component whilst continuing to deal with the
outstanding difficulties in relation to other currency debts. By agreement, the   *f*
payment of the sterling and South African Rand debts did in fact later proceed.
Those creditors were paid in full.

On 25 July 1986 Mr Sapsted telexed Mr Chipumbu promising a list of new debts
plus a revised statement of account by mid-August. On 5 August 1986 Mr Sapsted
sent a list of new debts for agreement. On 23 October 1986 Mr Sapsted sent Mr   *g*
Chipumbu a telex chasing up a response. Between 23 October 1986 and 4
December 1987 no further effort was made by the ECGD to progress the
allocation of moneys due to LEL and other like policyholders. The reason was
the total absorption of the efforts of its staff on other far more substantial
recoveries from other countries (and in particular Tanzania and Nigeria) which
had a higher priority, in that they had far greater prospects of being productive in   *h*
terms of securing far greater recoveries for the ECGD and several thousand other
policyholders. (It is to be noted that whilst the ECGD secured payment for 91
exporters to Zambia, in 1987 the ECGD had responsibility for over 4,000
exporters in its rescheduling agreements with other debtor countries.) I am quite
satisfied that any further efforts would have yielded no better results than were   *j*
in fact achieved when the ECGD resumed its efforts, and indeed the contrary is
not even suggested.

On 4 December 1987 Mr Roderick, after apologising for the inactivity since
October 1986, requested an update regarding reconciliation of the debts. The
response from Mr Gondwe was that due to the lapse of time the documentation

a could not be located and to ask for copies of the agreements and schedules for reconciliation.

There followed protracted correspondence between the ECGD and BOZ during which little progress was made. The ECGD supplied further documentation to Mr Gondwe but he did not provide any substantive response over a long period. To secure progress, at a ministerial meeting on 1 March 1990,
b the problem was raised as a matter where a solution might be linked to the provision of aid to Zambia by the United Kingdom. This had some effect.

Mr Mwanza spent two weeks at the ECGD in Cardiff in March 1990 in order to reconcile Zambia's short and long term debt and this meeting resulted in some progress. On 17 April 1990 Mr Roderick wrote to Mr Mwanza confirming that he had taken back to Zambia a countersigned debt list of agreed debt. On 30 May
c 1990 Mr Mwanza promised a full report on the reconciled position including debts not agreed, and this was repeated on 7 August 1990, 17 October 1990 and 5 November 1990.

On 21 May 1990 Mr Roderick was driven to taking the most unusual step of giving an ultimatum to BOZ. He threatened to treat the debt lists as agreed
d unless some progress was made. This ultimatum prompted some, but only limited, further progress.

Ultimately, on 26 November 1990 the ECGD telexed BOZ that it would (unless BOZ objected within 24 hours) disburse the 1984 payment on the basis that the ECGD debt list was agreed; and on 14 December 1990 finally notified
e BOZ that allocation on this basis was now to proceed. The balance of the 1984 payment was not sufficient to pay the debts treated as agreed, and during the period between this date and 12 March 1991, the ECGD undertook the exercise of calculating the dividend payable in respect of each debt and the breakdown of that dividend between the part payable to the policyholder and the part to which the ECGD was entitled. No suggestion has been made that the period between
f 14 December 1990 and the dates of the various payments to LEL was more than was reasonably required for this purpose.

On 12 March 1991 the ECGD paid the first instalment of their share of the dividend to some 91 creditors. This included a payment to LEL of £524,033·66. This was followed on 11 April 1991 by payment of a second instalment of
g £7,028·77 and on 16 May 1991 of a third instalment of £106,812·64. The breakdown of the recoveries between the ECGD and policyholders (and in respect of the LEL debts between the ECGD and LEL) reflected the entitlement of the policyholder to (a) the entirety of the moratorium interest in respect of the period between the date that their debts became due and the date of payment of
h the policy moneys by the ECGD representing 90% or 95% of the loss; and to 5% or 10% of the moratorium interest in respect of the subsequent period. On 15 April 1991 LEL asked the ECGD whether the apportionments made to LEL included interest earned (or saved) by holding the moneys payable to LEL since 1984. There followed internal memoranda in which the response to this 'hoary old chestnut' was considered and the established policy (or 'party line') was
j adopted of rejecting such a request for interest. Accordingly, in the ECGD's reply dated 7 May 1991, the ECGD stated that moneys apportioned to LEL did not include any interest and that the ECGD 'has no authority to pay interest'. On 25 June 1991 LEL requested the ECGD to pay interest on the footing that the ECGD in recovering and holding these moneys was acting as LEL's agent or trustee. The ECGD in its reply dated 21 August denied that it had acted as either an agent

or a trustee. It nonetheless acknowledged that the ECGD would have been
obliged to pass on profits or interest arising from receipts in relation to LEL's   *a*
debts if it had received any, but there were no profits or interest earned on these
recoveries. On 20 November 1991 LEL's solicitors wrote to the ECGD claiming
interest. On 19 December 1991 the legal adviser to the ECGD denied that any
question of payment of interest arose. The letter accepted that in principle the
ECGD was under a duty to account for and pay over timeously moneys   *b*
recovered on behalf of its principal, but denied that there had been any breach of
such duty because LEL's debts could not be regarded as having been agreed until
November 1990, and as a consequence from January 1984 to November 1990
there were no moneys in the ECGD's hands that constituted a definable sum
owing to LEL.

LEL's solicitors wrote a formal letter before action on 22 May 1992. By letters   *c*
dated 5 June and 7 July 1992 the ECGD persuaded LEL not to issue proceedings
until the ECGD had taken advice from counsel. LEL gave a final deadline of the
end of July 1992 and this was accepted by the ECGD. This passed with no further
substantive response, and proceedings were issued on 5 August 1992. The ECGD
have agreed that by reason of this correspondence the period between 22 May   *d*
and 1 August 1992 shall not be taken into account for limitation purposes.

(D) *Findings*

For the reasons which I give when dealing with the international law aspects
of this case, I think that the question raised by LEL whether there ever was an   *e*
agreement of the debt lists and for payment to creditors out of the 1984 payment
before 14 December 1990 is one which is for the Executive and that the decision
of the ECGD that there was no such agreement before 14 December 1990 is
conclusive. I should accordingly accept and faithfully give effect to that
determination. None the less for the reason given at the commencement of this
judgment, I shall as requested independently make my own determination.   *f*

On the basis of the evidence before me I am satisfied that at no time did BOZ
finally agree with the ECGD the dollars or DMs debts, let alone that they should
be paid out of the 1984 payment. Accordingly I reject LEL's contention that there
was such a final agreement at some earlier date prior to 14 December 1990. On
this issue the correspondence only forms part (albeit an important part) of the   *g*
picture. There were no doubt further communications, oral and written,
between BOZ and the ECGD, of which no record remains and of which there is
no specific recollection. Three matters, as it seems to me, are of critical
importance. The first is the understanding that there was no such agreement on
the part of the experienced civil servants with the day to day responsibility for the   *h*
negotiations, namely Mr Sapsted and Mr Roderick, who are plainly men of total
integrity and whose evidence I fully accept. The second is the existence of every
incentive on their part and on the part of the ECGD to secure the agreement of
BOZ and distribution of the 1984 payment as soon as possible, and the absence of
any motive (let alone any suggested by LEL) for delay or failure to recognise such
an agreement if there was one. The third is the absence of any suggestion by   *j*
Zambia at any time of any such agreement. It is correct that at times there were
letters from and statements by BOZ which might be read as pointing to such an
agreement, but these were ambiguous, and on each occasion when the matter
was followed up, any suggestion of the conclusion of a final agreement
evaporated.

III. LAW

a   LEL's claim to interest is made on two alternative bases. The first is the existence of a proprietary interest in the 1984 payment giving rise to a liability on the part of the ECGD as trustee or fiduciary to pay interest; and the second is a contractual liability arising under implied terms of the guarantees. The ECGD denies the existence of such proprietary interest and the contractual claim. In the forefront of its defence, the ECGD places emphasis on what has been called the international law element in this case, which requires examination before proceeding further.

b

(A) *The international element*

The international law element in this case arises from the fact that the 1984
c   payment was made by BOZ to the ECGD in intended performance of the obligation of the government of Zambia under the bilateral agreement. The ECGD contend that by reason of these facts, in accordance with established principles of English law, under English law the ECGD held these moneys as beneficial owners free of any obligation to LEL and the other policyholders until it voluntarily decided to treat a substantial part of the 1984 payment as a recovery
d   under article 24 of the guarantees of the various policyholders (including LEL) by making payments to them. On this aspect of the case I should immediately express my appreciation for the invaluable assistance of Professor Greenwood, junior counsel on behalf of the ECGD.

The relevant established principles of English law relevant in this context may
e   be stated as follows.

(1) The conclusion of a treaty by the United Kingdom is a sovereign act carried out by the Crown in the exercise of the royal prerogative (see *Rustomjee v R* (1876) 2 QBD 69).

(2) Treaties do not form part of English domestic law unless given effect by statute. Unless given such effect by statute, they can neither create new, nor take
f   away existing, rights recognised by English law (see *Maclaine Watson & Co Ltd v Dept of Trade and Industry, Maclaine Watson & Co Ltd v International Tin Council* [1989] 3 All ER 523 at 529–530, 544–545, [1990] 2 AC 418 at 480–482, 500 per Lord Templeman and Lord Oliver).

(3) When the Crown espouses claims (eg of nationals who are creditors of
g   foreign states or nationals) and affords diplomatic protection (eg by the negotiation of a treaty providing for payment to the Crown for distribution to its nationals), under international law the Crown is maintaining its own right in its own name to such protection of its nationals (see *Re Barcelona Traction Light and Power Co Ltd* 1970 ICJ Rep 3 at 78–79).

(4) (Subject to (5) below) in concluding and performing the obligations under
h   such a treaty, the Crown does not act as agent or trustee for the nationals; and irrespective of the terms of the treaty and (as it seems to me) the characterisation of the payments by the treaty, payments made to the United Kingdom pursuant to such treaties are received by the Crown in a sovereign capacity and form the absolute property of the State (see *Civilian War Claimants Association Ltd v R* [1932]
j   AC 14, [1931] All ER Rep 432 and consider the decision to the like effect of the Swiss Federal Court in *Gschwind v Swiss Confederation* (1932) 6 Annual Digest 242 at 244–245 and the statement to like effect in the third American Law Institute's *Restatement of Foreign Relations Law* vol II p 348).

(5) There is nothing to prevent the Crown acting as agent or trustee if it chooses to do so (see *Nissan v A-G* [1969] 1 All ER 629 at 650–651, [1970] AC 179

at 223 per Lord Pearce). It may be that the Crown can, when it concludes or
performs a treaty, act as a trustee or agent for one or more nationals or *a*
corporations (see *Civilian War Claimants Association Ltd v R* [1932] AC 14 at 26–27,
[1931] All ER Rep 432 at 436 per Lord Atkin and *Buck v A-G* [1964] 2 All ER 663 at
669, [1965] Ch 745 at 759 per Wilberforce J, but see *Rustomjee v R* (1876) 2 QBD 69
at 74 per Lord Coleridge CJ). But, if this is so, there is a strong presumption
against the Crown fettering in this way its ability to conduct foreign relations in *b*
the interests of the United Kingdom as a whole and the Crown must expressly
declare its intention to act in this capacity before it will be held to have done so
(see *German Property Administrator v Knoop* [1933] Ch 439 at 455–456 per
Maugham J, citing Lord Atkin in the *Civilian War Claimants* case). For this
purpose it is quite insufficient that the Crown has espoused the individual's cause,
obtained from him his co-operation (including details of his claims to take up with *c*
the foreign government) and indeed has obtained acceptance of such claims by
the foreign government. The fact that under municipal law the Crown would
be held (if negotiating a private agreement rather than a treaty) to be negotiating
as agent or trustee is not sufficient if it is negotiating a treaty, where the Crown
must represent the national interest and take account of the widest range of *d*
considerations (see the cases cited above). There can be (as it seems to me) no
reason why the Crown cannot commit itself to hold any sum received under a
treaty as agent or trustee if the necessary intention is sufficiently clearly
established, though this would be quite exceptional.

(6) The entitlement of the Crown to retain the payments made to it is not, as *e*
a matter of English law, affected by the terms of the treaty or whatever the treaty
may provide regarding their distribution. Nor can the terms of the treaty affect
or qualify the sovereign character of the Crown's receipt of such payments or
imbue such receipt with the character eg of a recovery. The Crown has under
English law no legal or equitable, but at best a mere moral, obligation to fulfil
those terms. If the Crown fails to do so, the only remedies lie in Parliament or (at *f*
the instance of the foreign government) in international law proceedings (see
Philipp Bros v Republic of Sierra Leone [1995] 1 Lloyd's Rep 289).

(7) The Crown in distributing any payments received pursuant to a treaty may
determine the character to be borne by the payments it makes and earmark such
payments (eg as mere bounty or a payment in respect of the insured or uninsured *g*
element of a loss) and such determination and earmarking binds third parties (eg
insurers) (see *Burnand v Rodocanachi Sons & Co* (1882) 7 App Cas 333).

(8) Subject to (9), the interpretation of treaties not by statute incorporated into
municipal law and the decision whether or not they have been complied with are *h*
matters exclusively for the Crown in its conduct of foreign relations. The court
must speak with the same voice as the Executive and accordingly seek and follow
the interpretation adopted by the Crown, and not venture its own interpretation
(let alone its own interpretation if at variance with that of the Crown). Nor may
it seek to determine whether the parties have implemented its provisions in good
faith as required by international law (see *British Airways Board v Laker Airways Ltd* *j*
[1983] 3 All ER 375 at 402–403, [1984] QB 142 at 192–193 per Donaldson MR;
[1984] 3 All ER 39 at 49, [1985] AC 58 at 85–86 per Lord Diplock, *Littrell v USA (No
2)* [1994] 4 All ER 203 at 210–211, 216, [1995] 1 WLR 82 at 89, 94 and *Westland
Helicopters Ltd v Arab Organisation for Industrialisation* [1995] 2 All ER 387 at 399,
[1995] QB 282 at 294). For an example of the possible difficulties created where

a the court does construe a treaty, see Oppenheim *International Law*, (9th edn, 1992) vol 1 para 612, footnote 2.

(9) As exceptions (actual or apparent) to (8), (a) there are circumstances when the court may be called on to interpret a treaty (e g if its terms are incorporated into a domestic contract); and (b) reference may be made to the conclusion of a treaty and its terms for evidential purposes as part of the factual background

b against which a particular issue is to be determined (see *Maclaine Watson & Co Ltd v Dept of Trade and Industry, Maclaine Watson & Co Ltd v International Tin Council* [1989] 3 All ER 523 at 545, [1990] 2 AC 418 at 500–501 per Lord Oliver and *Littrell v USA (No 2)* [1994] 4 All ER 203 at 215, [1995] 1 WLR 82 at 93 per Hoffmann LJ).

(10) The courts will not adjudicate upon the transactions of or between

c sovereign states, and in all matters relating to foreign relations, judges should be circumspect and rarely should judges intervene where diplomats fear to tread (see *Maclaine Watson & Co Ltd* [1989] 3 All ER 523 at 544, [1990] 2 AC 418 at 499 per Lord Oliver and *R v Secretary of State for Foreign and Commonwealth Affairs, ex p Pirbhai* (1985) Times, 17 October.

d Applying these principles to the facts of this case:

(a) It is clear that the Crown in negotiating the terms and implementation of the multilateral and bilateral agreements did not negotiate as trustee or agent for the policyholders and owed no duties (under the guarantees or otherwise) to policyholders. The Crown espoused the cause of the ECGD and the

e policyholders and needed their co-operation, and the policyholders provided the wherewithal (e g execution of the mandates) for this purpose, but this was only one aspect of the national interest the Crown was concerned to secure. In particular the bilateral agreement was more than a mechanism to collect the policyholders' debts. It was part of a framework to deal with Zambia's economic crisis which had repercussions abroad (and in particular for the United Kingdom)

f and the implementation of the bilateral agreement involved more than a mechanical verification exercise; it involved the relations between two nation states.

(b) It was at all times for the Crown, and the Crown alone, to decide what the rules meant and required, the speed and intensity of its activity in agreeing the

g allocation between principal and interest and the lists of creditors with BOZ and whether BOZ had agreed the lists and the allocation. The conduct of the Crown in this respect (which with the consent of the ECGD has been thoroughly examined in these proceedings) is not open to question or evaluation by the court. In making these decisions and indeed in deciding (by way of ultimatum to

h Zambia) to require any objection on the part of BOZ to the final list and to the distribution to the creditors listed to be made within a period of time, the Crown had to exercise a delicate judgment in the foreign relations field. It is not for the court to say that the Crown in its dealings with BOZ should have behaved differently. The court must accept the Crown's position that the agreement of

j BOZ to the debts and their payment was concluded on 14 December 1990 and not before.

(c) The Crown received the 1984 payment in its sovereign capacity as the absolute property of the Crown. The provisions of the bilateral agreement could not and did not confer any rights on LEL or the other policyholders or characterise it otherwise.

(d) The Crown by the guarantees could bind itself to deal with the sums received from Zambia (including the 1984 payment) as there provided. Whether *a* it did so (as contended for by LEL) is a matter of construction of article 24.

(B) *Proprietary interest*

The proprietary claim made by LEL is to the effect that the ECGD at all times from the date of receipt held the 1984 payment on trust or subject to a fiduciary *b* obligation to pay over to LEL the due proportion representing LEL's share of the recovery made under the guarantees in respect of the LEL debts. LEL say that this share is reflected in and constituted by the total of the instalments paid in 1991 to LEL. This issue should, I think, be approached in three stages: (1) whether as a matter of law (without reference to the relevant terms of the guarantees) LEL had a proprietary interest in recoveries made by the ECGD. *c* (The relevance of this exercise is that the answer affords a guide, if there should emerge some real doubt or ambiguity in the construction of the guarantees (see *L Lucas Ltd v Export Credits Guarantee Dept* [1974] 2 All ER 889 at 897–898, [1974] 1 WLR 909 at 921); (2) whether under the terms of the guarantees LEL have such an interest; and (3) (which only arises if the answer to (2) is in the affirmative) *d* whether (in particular having regard to the source of the 1984 payment and the international law aspects of the case) the 1984 payment constitutes such a recovery.

(1) The general law

The general law on the rights of the insurer in respect of recoveries is *e* authoritatively stated in the decision of the House of Lords in *Lord Napier and Ettrick v Hunter, Lord Napier and Ettrick v R F Kershaw Ltd* [1993] 1 All ER 385, [1993] AC 713. The insured, who has been indemnified in whole or in part by an insurer, retains the right to enforce any cause of action against the party who occasioned the loss, but the insurer has the right in the name of the insured to enforce that *f* cause of action. If the insured obtains any recoveries, the insurer has an equitable lien on those recoveries to secure the amount due to the insurer from such recoveries, but subject to that lien the recoveries belong beneficially to the insured. The question raised in this case concerns the situation where the insurer obtains recoveries which exceed the sum which he is entitled to recoup himself *g* and whether he holds the balance on trust for the insured or is merely liable to pay over to the insured a sum equal to the balance either as debt or as moneys had and received. I have been told by counsel that there is no authority or textbook affording guidance on this question. If this is so, this is a remarkable lacuna, for the situation is one which must be met with in practice.

So far as there is absent any authoritative guidance, recourse must be had to *h* principle. The significant facts in such a situation are that: (a) the cause of action or right to recover belongs beneficially and (unless assigned) at law to the insured; (b) the insurer is entitled through the medium of the insured to enforce the cause of action to secure his recoupment; (c) whilst the House of Lords in *Lord Napier and Ettrick v Hunter* left open whether the insurer has an equitable charge on the *j* cause of action, he has an equitable lien on the recoveries. In short the insurer enforces a cause of action belonging beneficially to the insured for the joint benefit of the insured and the insurer and in the fruit of that endeavour the insurer has only a limited interest. The applicable principles in this situation lie in the law of mortgages which provides that a chargee who in exercise of his a rights as security holder obtains a payment or realisation exceeding his debt (e g by sale of the charged property) holds the surplus recoveries on trust for the mortgagor (see e g *Snell's Equity* (29th edn, 1990) p 416). As it seems to me, by parity of reasoning, the insurer holds the surplus recoveries on trust for the insured. The moneys in the hands of the insurer belong to the assured, subject only to the right of the insurer to retain the sum secured in his own favour. He

b is duty bound to divide up the moneys in his hands between the assured and himself in the shares reflecting their respective entitlement and to hold the insured's entitlement on trust for the insured. This conclusion does not involve the novel importation into commercial law of an equitable principle, let alone a principle inconsistent with the speed and certainty which are essential requirements for the orderly conduct of business affairs. It merely involves the

c application of traditional principles in an area where there is no reason why, and no suggestion in any authority that, those principles should not apply: consider *Westdeutsche Landesbank Girozentrale v Islington London BC* [1996] 2 All ER 961 at 973–974, 987, [1996] 2 WLR 802 at 814, 828. There is no reason why the insured's part of recoveries in the hands of the insurer should form part of the cash flow of

d the insurer available for the insurer's creditors. Equity has intervened to lend assistance to the insurer, not to deny the insured his equitable proprietary title to recoveries.

Accordingly in this case, ignoring the relevant terms of the guarantees, and putting to one side for the moment the fact that the ECGD (and therefore the Crown) is the insurer, so long as LEL could establish that the 1984 payment

e included recoveries in respect of the LEL debts, the ECGD would hold the 1984 payment on trust, as to the sum referable to the LEL debts, to pay a portion to itself in satisfaction of its right to a share and as to the balance on trust for LEL absolutely.

Mr Cordara has submitted that the facts that the insurer in this case is the

f Crown (and that there is accordingly no risk of its insolvency) and that the ECGD is under an obligation under s 14 of the 1978 Act to pay all receipts into the Consolidated Fund (and this includes the recoveries) make a difference. I totally disagree. The identity and qualities of the insurer are surely quite irrelevant. The fact that the ECGD, as the recipient of the recoveries, becomes subject to a statutory obligation under s 14 of the 1978 Act on receipt to deal with them in a

g manner which destroys their separate identity and the absence of any equitable charge on the part of LEL on the Consolidated Fund do not prevent the moneys on receipt being analysed or identified as trust moneys or the normal consequences flowing from such receipt in terms (in particular) of personal liability of the ECGD as trustee to the beneficiaries.

h Sections 1 and 12 of the 1978 Act confer upon the ECGD the power to enter into contracts on such terms as the ECGD think fit. If the normal consequences of receipt by the ECGD of recoveries were to be excluded, an express term to this effect in the guarantees would be expected.

j (2) The guarantees
It is appropriate to set out the two relevant articles of the guarantees:

'Article 23. ACTION AFTER PAYMENT OF CLAIM   a. Upon payment by the Insurer, the INSURED shall— i. take all steps which may be necessary or expedient, or which the Insurer may at any time require, to effect recoveries, whether from the buyer or from any guarantor or other person from whom

such recoveries may be made, including (if so required) the institution of
legal proceedings in any country; ii. upon request assign and transfer to the
Insurer the INSURED's rights in connection with any contract in respect of
which such payment has been made, including the right to receive any
moneys payable under such contract or the right to damages for any breach
thereof; iii. upon request deliver up to the Insurer any goods relating to any
contract in respect of which such payment has been made any documents
relating thereto and assign and transfer to the Insurer the INSURED's rights
and interest in any such goods and documents. iv. upon request assign,
deliver up or otherwise transfer to the Insurer any negotiable instruments,
guarantees or other securities relating to such goods or such contract ...

Article 24. RECOVERIES   a.i. All sums which are received by or on behalf
of the INSURED after the date of ascertainment of loss in relation to a
contract ... ii. all sums which are received by or on behalf of the INSURED in
respect of interest under a contract in relation to any period after the date of
payment of a claim under this Guarantee in respect of that contract; and
iii. all other sums whatsoever relating to a contract which are received by or
on behalf of the INSURED from any source after the date of ascertainment of
loss in relation to that contract, including (but not limited to) sums resulting
from the realisation of any security given for the amount owing under that
contract or from the resale of any goods or materials relating to that contract;
shall, immediately on receipt by the INSURED or a person acting on his
behalf ... be remitted to the Insurer. The INSURED hereby acknowledges and
declares that, until such sums are so remitted, the INSURED receives and holds
such sums in trust for the Insurer ... c. All sums referred to in paragraph a.
of this Article ... and all sums recovered by the Insurer relating to a contract
in respect of which a claim has been paid, shall after receipt by the Insurer be
divided between the Insurer and the INSURED in the proportion in which the
amount of loss ascertained in accordance with the Relevant Section is borne
by each of them respectively, whether or not such division results in the
retention by the Insurer of a greater or lesser sum than the amount paid by
the Insurer under this Guarantee in connection with that amount of loss:
Provided That, in respect of any claim paid by the Insurer in accordance with
the terms of the Pre-Credit Risk Section, the Insurer shall not be entitled by
virtue of this Article to any amount in excess of the amount which he has
paid to the INSURED under that Section in respect of that claim.'

I should first make two preliminary observations. (1) I reject Mr Cordara's
submission that there is any applicable rule of law to the effect that the guarantees
should be construed in a manner favourable to the Crown and against the other
party. The rule that grants by the Crown should be construed in favour of the
Crown has no application to ordinary commercial transactions, let alone those
where the contract is in a standard form: consider *Earl of Lonsdale v A-G* [1982] 3
All ER 579 at 615, [1982] 1 WLR 887 at 932. (2) The inclusion in article 24 of the
words 'whether or not such division results in the retention by the Insurer of a
greater or lesser sum than the amount paid by the Insurer under this Guarantee
in connection with that claim' is designed to negate the application of the decision
in *L Lucas Ltd v Export Credits Guarantee Dept* [1974] 2 All ER 889, [1974] 1 WLR
909, which held that, where such words are not included, the ECGD is not
entitled to share the benefit of any currency exchange profits.

a   Article 24(c) provides that all the recoveries shall be divided in defined shares between the ECGD and the policyholder. This language is apposite to the receipt by the ECGD of moneys which belong as to part to the ECGD and as to part to the policyholder, and constitutes, as it appears to me, an agreement by the ECGD to hold recoveries on trust for the policyholder and itself in such shares reflecting their respective entitlements. The language is not apposite to the creation of a
b   mere debtor-creditor relationship between the ECGD and the policyholder in respect of the policyholder's share. If difficulties arise in determining on receipt the respective entitlements of the ECGD and the policyholder, the appropriate course in any ordinary case as between a non-ECGD insurer and the insured is to pay the receipt into an interest bearing joint account in the names of both the insurer and the insured (see *Lord Napier and Ettrick v Hunter* [1993] 1 All ER 385 at
c   398, [1993] AC 713 at 739 per Lord Templeman). In the case of receipts of recoveries by the ECGD, s 14(1)(b) of the 1978 Act requires them to be paid into the Consolidated Fund. But this does not mean that the moneys cannot likewise be paid into an interest bearing joint account: (1) if the recoveries are received by the ECGD and paid into the Consolidated Fund, under s 14(2) of the 1978 Act the
d   ECGD may fulfil this obligation under the guarantees by withdrawing the sum from the Consolidated Fund and paying it into the appropriate joint account; and (2) in any case, before the recoveries are received by the ECGD, the ECGD may seek to arrange that, instead of their being paid to the ECGD alone, the recoveries are paid into such a joint account.

e   It is correct that the word 'trust' is not used in article 24(c), and the word 'trust' is used in article 24(a), but this has no significance as a guide to whether the ECGD is a trustee of recoveries under article 24(c). The explanation for the express use of the word 'trust' in article 24(a) is that article 24(a) imposes a trust on the policyholder holding recoveries where no trust would have otherwise existed, let alone a trust requiring the policyholder to remit the entirety of the
f   recoveries to the ECGD: the recoveries would belong beneficially to the policyholder subject only to an equitable lien in favour of the insurer. In the absence of such a provision the policyholder would be entitled to carry out the division of the recoveries between himself and the ECGD, and accordingly merely to remit to the ECGD the share to which the ECGD was entitled and which was secured by its lien. The imposition of the trust is the chosen
g   mechanism to entitle the ECGD in all cases to obtain immediately from the policyholder the full recoveries without any deduction and itself to carry out the division. This, of course, affords to the ECGD greater security: it is in no way dependent on the policyholder carrying out the division exercise properly, for it can carry it out itself. By contrast, the word 'trust' does not appear in article 24(c)
h   because under the established principles of law to which I have referred (leaving aside the language of article 24(c) providing for 'division') a trust exists anyway.

If I had found any ambiguity or had any doubt on the true construction of the guarantees, reference to these principles would have led me to the same result.

j   (3) Recovery

The critical issue is whether, and if so when, the 1984 payment constituted a recovery within the meaning of article 24. It was an inter-state payment made by the government of Zambia in satisfaction of a claim, not by the policyholders, but by the United Kingdom. The government of Zambia was not a debtor, and the Crown represented by the ECGD according to English law, (unless otherwise constrained by article 24), was free to deal with the 1984 payment (like any other payment made pursuant to a treaty) as it thought fit. There are, as it seems to me, two overwhelming reasons why the 1984 payment should be designated (like any other payment pursuant to a treaty) as a sovereign receipt available for distribution (according to international law) in accordance with the rules, but (according to English law) at the free discretion of the Crown, and not a recovery under any or all of the various ECGD policies unless and until distributed as such by the ECGD.

(a) If the 1984 payment is to be held to have any character beyond that of a sovereign receipt on the part of the Crown, it is necessary to analyse its character by reference to the terms of the bilateral agreement and most particularly the rules. But I do not think that this exercise is permissible, having regard to the principle to which I have referred, that the terms of the treaty should not be referred to for the purpose of qualifying the sovereign character of such a receipt or of imbuing such receipt with any other character. But if the exercise can be undertaken, a reference to the terms of the bilateral agreement reveals that the Crown is intended to be free to deal with the payment in a manner inconsistent with that which would be permissible if it were to be a recovery within the meaning of article 24. If and when the 1984 payment constituted a recovery, from that date the 1984 payment became subject to the trust provisions of article 24 in favour of the various policyholders, and (save in so far as the rules were consistent with such trust) the ECGD ceased to be able to comply with the international law obligations of the Crown under the bilateral agreement, or otherwise fulfil the responsibility of the Crown in conducting international relations in respect of the 1984 payment (e g to add or exclude debts as contemplated by the rules or repay to BOZ the whole or part if the national interests of the United Kingdom so required). This consideration must militate against analysing the 1984 payment as a recovery: such can scarcely have been the intent of BOZ or the Crown.

(b) There would be the most serious (indeed insuperable) difficulty in determining in respect of what insured debts and what part of such debts the 1984 payment was a recovery. At the date of the 1984 payment, it remained to be determined, in accordance with the rules or otherwise: (1) whether and in what proportions it should be applied in payment of long, medium or short term debts; (2) whether and in what proportion it should be applied in payment of principal and moratorium interest; and (3) what debts should be paid and whether all should be paid pari passu or whether the first debts to be agreed should be paid in full and the rest pro rata out of the balance. Only when these questions had been determined in a manner favourable to making a payment in respect of his debt could a policyholder have a prospect of a recovery in respect of his debt. These determinations were to be made (according to the bilateral agreement and so according to international law) by the ECGD jointly with BOZ. Neither LEL nor any other policyholder had any voice or right to invoke any jurisdiction of the court to make such a determination or challenge any determination by the ECGD. At best, part of the 1984 payment was a potential recovery under article 24 of the guarantees in respect of the LEL debts. Article 24 could not attach to any moneys until the potential became a reality.

There are many strong factors indicative from the very beginning of the intention of the ECGD to make appropriations out of future receipts from the government of Zambia and (from the date of the 1984 payment) out of the 1984 payment, as recoveries under the guarantees. These include (1) the letter dated a the 5 June 1984 from Mr Sapsted to Mr Brown in which he wrote that he considered part of the 1984 payment to be 'due to our policyholders' but that he was unable to begin allocation without the approval of individual debts by BOZ; (2) the 7 July letter and mandate; (3) the terms of the bilateral agreement; (4) the contents of the lists submitted for agreement (which included the various policyholders' including LEL's debts); (5) the correspondence between the

b ECGD and LEL acknowledging LEL's interest in the 1984 payment and the intention to make payments out of 'the recoveries' to LEL in respect of the LEL debts; and (6) the payments in fact later made to LEL and other policyholders. The intention I find established and unwavering, reflecting the international law and moral obligation on the part of the ECGD so to act. But the existence of such intention is not effective to appropriate any part of the 1984 payment to any

c specific debts (let alone the LEL debts), for the intention was plainly to make appropriations only when the ECGD considered that the necessary agreement with BOZ had been reached and the necessary calculations made.

Accordingly I hold that LEL at no time was entitled to any proprietary or other interest in the 1984 payment until the respective dates of the three payments

d made to them. In respect of the 1984 payment the ECGD was at no time a trustee or subject to fiduciary duties owed to LEL, (and not even under a duty to act in good faith towards LEL as submitted by Mr Boyle) and therefore no question arises of the grant of relief in respect of the pleaded fiduciary duty to pay interest. If I had found that the 1984 payment received by the ECGD as to the part paid over to LEL constituted a recovery within the meaning of article 24 in respect of

e the LEL debts from a date earlier than that on which it was paid over to LEL, I would have held that the ECGD received and held that part as trustee for LEL and itself and ordered the ECGD to pay interest. I would have considered it appropriate in this case, in order to effect full restitution and justice to LEL, to order the ECGD to pay compound interest, since the receipt and payment into the Consolidated Fund saved the Crown the cost of borrowing an equivalent sum

f and paying compound interest. I would have rejected any suggestion that there was any limitation defence, since it is common ground that the amount of the 1984 payment referable to the LEL debts and the amount payable to LEL could be and was only ascertained after 14 December 1990, less than two years before the issue of the writ in this action.

g
IV. CONTRACTUAL CLAIM

LEL has, very much as a secondary line of attack in the alternative to the fiduciary claim, argued that the ECGD and BOZ agreed at various dates prior to December 1990 the debts which the ECGD should pay out of the 1984 payment, that these included the LEL debts, and that in respect of the period between the

h date of such agreement and the dates of the three payments the ECGD should pay interest on the sums so agreed and paid. The pleaded legal basis was implied terms of the guarantees that the ECGD should (1) pay the sums due to LEL from the 1984 payment timeously or within a reasonable time from receipt; (2) place the 1984 payment in an interest bearing account earning the best possible rate of

j interest consistent with proper security; (3) account to LEL for any interest earned or that should have been earned on any moneys due to LEL from the 1984 payment; and (4) pay interest at a reasonable rate on the amount paid to LEL from the date of receipt by the ECGD to the date of payment to LEL. Alternatively, it was contended that the court had jurisdiction to grant interest in respect of the late payments.

In view of my finding that the ECGD was absolutely entitled to the 1984 payment from the date of its receipt, was never under any obligation under article 24 of the guarantees and only as a matter of bounty made the three payments to LEL treating such payments as LEL's share of recoveries received and that in any event there was never any such agreement between the ECGD and BOZ, the contractual claim must likewise fail.

I may add that, as a matter of law, the only one of the four suggested terms which can properly be implied in the guarantees is that requiring the ECGD to pay to LEL its share of any recoveries in respect of the LEL debts within a reasonable time of receipt. There was, however, no breach of this term, for there was no such recovery until the payment made to LEL. I can see no basis for implying any term regarding earning or payment of interest. The only case cited having even the semblance of a bearing on this question is *H Cousins & Co Ltd v D & C Carriers Ltd* [1971] 1 All ER 55, [1971] 2 QB 230, where it was held, applying the officious bystander's test, that a term might be implied as to the division between insurer and insured of interest awarded under the Law Reform (Miscellaneous Provisions) Act 1934. There was in that case a need to decide how moneys payable by the wrongdoer should be divided up between insurer and insured. The answer was that it was obvious that it should be shared in the manner that made good their respective losses. The decision in that case in no wise supports the implication of a term requiring the insured to assume the novel duties alleged. A fiduciary relationship between the parties alone could give rise to an obligation to pay interest; otherwise the relationship was simply that of debtor and creditor.

V. LIMITATION

The question of limitation accordingly does not arise. I should, however, briefly express my views on the one question of fact raised in case it may prove relevant on any appeal.

LEL from 18 July 1985 onwards sent a series of letters to the ECGD asking how the process of agreeing the debts with Zambia was proceeding. The ECGD replied that it hoped that the list would be agreed in the near future and that as soon as this was achieved an allocation would take place. LEL contend that the ECGD in its replies to these letters misrepresented and concealed the true position, which was that the lists had been agreed. There is in my view nothing in LEL's contention that the period of limitation should be extended by reason of this alleged misrepresentation and concealment, for there was no such agreement of lists and accordingly no misrepresentation or concealment. The ECGD conducted its correspondence with LEL with complete propriety and nothing relevant which should have been disclosed was withheld.

VI. CONCLUSION

I accordingly dismiss this action.

I should add that I consider it most undesirable (if it can be avoided) that (as has happened in the present case) the court should be called on at the same trial both to hear lengthy evidence and decide an issue of fact (in this case as to whether a final agreement of debt lists had been reached between the ECGD and BOZ), and to decide the issue of law whether that issue of fact is justiciable. It is plainly undesirable and embarrassing that the trial judge be placed in a position of having to decide questions of fact which, in the light of the answer to the issue of law, it may be in the public interest he should not enter upon. The examination of the

a
question is likely also to involve an unnecessary waste of the parties' costs and judicial time. This can and should be avoided by a determination of the issue of law as a preliminary issue or as the first stage of the trial. Unfortunately in this case there was no pre-trial review, which should have produced directions to this effect, and I was only made aware of this dilemma after the evidence was complete and I had heard Professor Greenwood's final submissions. Though I

b
have decided that the issue of fact is concluded by the determination of the Crown, I have with some hesitation decided the question of fact as though justiciable only because the parties (and most importantly the ECGD) have requested me to do so and accordingly (as I infer from the consent of the Crown to my following this course) there is no possible prejudice to the public interest in my doing so.

c

Action dismissed.

Celia Fox   Barrister.

Bristol and West Building Society v Mothew (t/a Stapley & Co)

a

COURT OF APPEAL, CIVIL DIVISION

STAUGHTON, MILLETT AND OTTON LJJ

b

21, 22 MAY, 24 JULY 1996

Solicitor – Negligence – Negligent misrepresentation – Mortgage transaction – Solicitor acting for both borrower and building society – Solicitor incorrectly reporting to society that borrower having no other indebtedness and that no second charge contemplated – c *Society relying on representations in report and making mortgage advance – Borrower subsequently defaulting on mortgage and society suffering loss when realising its security – Whether solicitor liable in negligence to society for net loss arising from borrower's subsequent default – Whether solicitor in breach of trust or fiduciary duty to society.*

d

In 1988 the defendant solicitor acted for the purchasers in the purchase of a property for £73,000 and also for the plaintiff building society to which they had applied for an advance of £59,000 towards the purchase price. The society offered to advance the loan on the security of a first mortgage of the property on condition that the purchasers personally provided the balance of the purchase price without resort to further borrowing and that no second mortgage or other loan was being arranged or contemplated in connection with the purchase. The society's standing instructions to solicitors acting for the society required the defendant to report prior to completion any proposal that the purchaser might arrange a second mortgage and shortly before the cheque was required to submit f a report confirming, inter alia, that to the best of his knowledge and belief the balance of the purchase price was being provided by the purchaser personally without resort to further borrowing. The purchasers owed money to a bank secured by a second charge on their existing property and the bank agreed to allow a small part of that debt (£3,350) to remain outstanding after the sale of the property and to be secured by a second charge on the new property. The g defendant was informed of these arrangements and gave an undertaking to the bank to hold the title deeds to its order pending registration. However, in breach of his instructions, the defendant inadvertently failed to inform the society of the arrangements and in his report confirmed that the balance of the purchase price was being provided by the purchasers personally. Following completion, the h purchasers executed a first charge in favour of the society and a second charge in favour of the bank. The purchasers later defaulted and the society realised less than £53,000 when it enforced its security. Thereafter, the society brought an action against the defendant to recover the whole of its net loss on the transaction, alleging breach of contract and negligence in failing to report the j purchasers' arrangements for a second mortgage (which were admitted) and breach of trust (which was denied). The district judge gave summary judgment for damages to be assessed in respect of the common law claims and summary judgment for the society for breach of trust for the sum claimed. On appeal, the judge affirmed the decision and the defendant appealed to the Court of Appeal. By a respondent's notice the society contended that it was entitled to judgment a for the sum claimed and not merely for damages to be assessed, in respect of its common law claims.

Held – (1) Where a lender sued his solicitor for having negligently given him incorrect advice or information it was sufficient for him to prove that he relied on the advice or information and he did not have to prove that he would not have
b acted as he did if he had been given the proper advice or the correct information. Accordingly, it was sufficient for the society to prove that it relied on the representations in the report and it did not have to prove that it would not have made the mortgage advance if it had known the true facts. However, it did not follow from the fact that the defendant's negligent statements caused the society to make the mortgage advance that the whole of the society's loss was
c attributable to his negligence, since in the case of a breach of duty to take care the measure of damages was not necessarily the full amount of the loss which the plaintiff had suffered by having entered into the transaction but only that part, if any, of such loss as was properly attributable to the inaccuracy of the information. The society would therefore be required to establish what loss, if any, was
d occasioned by the arrangements which the purchasers made with the bank and, therefore, damages remained to be assessed (see p 704 *d*, p 705 *j* to p 706 *a c* to *e*, p 707 *a b f*, p 718 *h* and p 720 *j*, post); *Downs v Chappell* [1996] 3 All ER 344 applied.
   (2) Since the defendant's conduct in providing incorrect information to the society was due to an oversight, it constituted a breach of duty of which he was unaware and, therefore, such conduct and his subsequent application of the
e mortgage money in accordance with his instructions did not constitute a breach of trust. Furthermore, the defendant was not guilty of breach of fiduciary duty since his failure to report the true state of affairs was due to an inadvertent failure and was not due to disloyalty or infidelity. Accordingly the appeal would be allowed and the cross-appeal dismissed (see p 709 *j* to p 710 *a*, p 712 *e*, p 715 *c d g*,
f p 717 *f* to *j*, p 718 *h*, p 719 *j* and p 720 *j*, post); *Permanent Building Society (in liq) v Wheeler* (1994) 14 ACSR 109 adopted.

Notes
For a solicitor's liability for negligence, see 44(1) *Halsbury's Laws* (4th edn reissue) paras 152–153, and for cases on the subject, see 44 *Digest* (Reissue) 132–133, *1306–*
g *1334*.

Cases referred to in judgments
Bolton Partners v Lambert (1889) 41 Ch D 295, CA.
Bristol and West Building Society v May May & Merrimans (a firm) [1996] 2 All ER
h   801.
Clark Boyce v Mouat [1993] 4 All ER 268, [1994] 1 AC 428, [1993] 3 WLR 1021, PC.
Commonwealth Bank of Australia v Smith (1991) 102 ALR 453, Aust Fed Ct.
Coomber, Re, Coomber v Coomber [1911] 1 Ch 723, CA.
Downs v Chappell [1996] 3 All ER 344, CA.
j *El Ajou v Dollar Land Holdings plc* [1993] 3 All ER 717.
Girardet v Crease & Co (1987) 11 BCLR (2d) 361, BC SC.
Henderson v Merrett Syndicates Ltd, Hallam-Eames v Merrett Syndicates Ltd, Hughes v Merrett Syndicates Ltd, Arbuthnott v Feltrim Underwriting Agencies Ltd, Deeny v Gooda Walker Ltd (in liq) [1994] 3 All ER 506, [1995] 2 AC 145, [1994] 3 WLR 761, HL.
Kelly v Cooper [1993] AC 205, [1993] 3 LRC 476, [1992] 3 WLR 936, PC.

Lac Minerals Ltd v International Corona Ltd [1989] 2 SCR 574, (1989) 61 DLR (4th)
        14, [1989] LRC (Comm) 932, Can SC.   *a*
Lewis v Hillman (1852) 3 HL Cas 607, 10 ER 239.
Lipkin Gorman (a firm) v Karpnale Ltd [1992] 4 All ER 512, [1991] 2 AC 548, [1991]
        3 WLR 10, HL.
Moody v Cox [1917] 2 Ch 71, [1916–17] All ER Rep 548, CA.
Mortgage Express Ltd v Bowerman & Partners (a firm) [1996] 2 All ER 836, CA.   *b*
Nocton v Lord Ashburton [1914] AC 932, [1914–15] All ER Rep 45, HL.
Permanent Building Society (in liq) v Wheeler (1994) 14 ACSR 109, W Aust SC.
South Australia Asset Management Corp v York Montague Ltd, United Bank of Kuwait
        plc v Prudential Property Services Ltd, Nykredit Mortgage Bank plc v Edward Erdman
        Group Ltd [1996] 3 All ER 365, [1996] 3 WLR 87, HL; *rvsg sub nom Banque*
        Bruxelles Lambert SA v Eagle Star Insurance Ltd [1995] 2 All ER 769, [1995] QB   *c*
        375, [1995] 2 WLR 607, CA.
Sykes v Midland Bank Executor and Trustee Co Ltd [1970] 2 All ER 471, [1971] 1 QB
        113, [1970] 3 WLR 273, CA.
Target Holdings Ltd v Redferns (a firm) [1995] 3 All ER 785, [1996] AC 421, [1995] 3
        WLR 352, HL.   *d*
Westdeutsche Landesbank Girozentrale v Islington London BC [1996] 2 All ER 961,
        [1996] 2 WLR 802, HL.

Cases also cited or referred to in skeleton arguments
A-G for Hong Kong v Reid [1994] 1 All ER 1, [1994] 1 AC 324, PC.
Alliance and Leicester Building Society v Edgestop Ltd (18 January 1991, unreported)   *e*
        Ch D.
Bishopsgate Investment Management Ltd v Maxwell (No 2) [1994] 1 All ER 261, CA.
Brickenden v London Loan and Savings Co [1934] 3 DLR 465, PC.
Canson Enterprises Ltd v Boughton & Co (1991) 85 DLR (4th) 129, Can SC.
Chase Manhattan Bank NA v Israel-British Bank (London) Ltd [1979] 3 All ER 1025,   *f*
        [1981] Ch 105.
Dawson (decd), Re, Union Fidelity Trustee Co Ltd v Perpetual Trustee Co Ltd [1966] 2
        NSWLR 211, NSW SC.
Farrington v Rowe McBride & Partners [1985] 1 NZLR 83, NZ CA.
Gemstone Corp of Australia Ltd v Grasso and Star Corp Ltd (1993) ACLC 653, S Aust
        SC.   *g*
Gray v New Augarita Porcupine Mines Ltd [1952] 3 DLR 1, PC.
McPherson v Watt (1877) 3 AC 254, HL.
Miller's Deed Trusts, Re (1978) 75 LS Gaz 454.
Nelson v Rye [1996] 2 All ER 186.
Nestle v National Westminster Bank plc [1994] 1 All ER 118, [1993] 1 WLR 1260, CA.   *h*
Sinclair v Brougham [1914] AC 398, [1914-15] All ER Rep 622, HL.
Wan v McDonald (1992) 105 ALR 473, Aust FedC.
Witten-Hannah v Davis [1995] 2 NZLR 141, NZ CA.

Interlocutory appeal   *j*
By notice dated 5 January 1996 the defendant, Anthony Paul Mothew, a solicitor
trading as Stapley & Co, appealed with leave of Nourse LJ from the order of
Chadwick J made on 27 July 1995 dismissing his appeal from the order of Deputy
District Judge Raskin made on 21 June 1995 giving summary judgment for the
plaintiff, Bristol and West Building Society (the society), for damages to be
assessed in respect of the society's common law claims for breach of contract and

a negligence and for the sum of £59,000 in respect of the society's claim for breach of trust. By a respondent's notice the society contended that it was entitled to judgment for the sum claimed and not merely for damages to be assessed in respect of its common law claims. The facts are set out in the judgment of Millett LJ.

b Jonathan Sumption QC and Glenn Campbell (instructed by Wansbroughs Willey Hargrave) for the defendant.
Nicholas Patten QC and Timothy Higginson (instructed by Osborne Clarke, Bristol) for the society.

Cur adv vult

c

24 July 1996. The following judgments were delivered.

MILLETT LJ (giving the first judgment at the invitation of Staughton LJ). This is an appeal brought by the defendant with the leave of the single Lord Justice
d from an order for summary judgment given initially by the district judge and affirmed (for different reasons) by Chadwick J. It raises important questions of principle in relation to a claim by a mortgagee to recover from the solicitor who was acting for both mortgagor and mortgagee the loss arising from the mortgagor's subsequent default.

The collapse in the property market which accompanied the recession at the
e beginning of the present decade caused mortgage lenders to suffer serious losses. Unable to recover their advances from the borrowers or by the enforcement of their security they have sought to recover them from the valuers or solicitors on whose valuations or advice they have relied. In some cases they have been the victims of a fraud to which the valuers and solicitors have been parties. In other
f cases, such as the present, they have been unable to accuse their solicitor of anything more serious than negligence. Believing that the common law rules of causation and remoteness of damage might not enable them to recover the whole amount of their loss they have turned to equity and alleged breach of trust or fiduciary duty. We have thus been concerned to decide just what is involved in these concepts.

g

THE FACTS
The facts are not in dispute. The defendant is a solicitor. In August 1988 he acted for a Mr and Mrs Towers in the purchase of 17 Thameshill Avenue, Romford (the property) for £73,000. In accordance with the usual practice he also
h acted for the Bristol and West Building Society (the society) to which the purchasers had applied for an advance of £59,000 in order to finance the purchase. (This was the Cheshunt Building Society, but its rights have since vested in the society.) In their application form the purchasers had stated that the balance of the purchase price of £14,000 was being provided by them personally and that
j they were not applying elsewhere for financial assistance towards the purchase price.

The society offered to advance to the purchasers £59,000 on the security of a first mortgage of the property on the express condition that unless otherwise agreed in writing the balance of the purchase price was to be provided by the purchasers personally without resort to further borrowing and that no second mortgage or other loan was being arranged or contemplated in connection with the purchase. The defendant was provided with the offer of advance (but not with the purchasers' application).   *a*

The society's standing instructions to solicitors acting for the society required them to report to the society prior to completion (inter alia):

> '(viii) Any proposal that the applicant may create a second mortgage or enter into a promissory note or otherwise borrow in order to finance part of the purchase price. (ix) Any incorrect information given in the solicitor's instructions. (x) Any other matters which ought to be brought to the notice of the Society as prospective mortgagee.'   *b*

The solicitor was required to submit a report on title and request for advance cheque to the society at least five clear working days before the cheque was required. This was done on a form by which the solicitor was asked to confirm   *c* (inter alia) that the title was good and marketable and might safely be accepted by the society; that to the best of his knowledge and belief the balance of the purchase money was being provided by the applicant personally without resort to further borrowing; and that the special conditions attached to the offer of advance had been, or would be, complied with.   *d*

Mr and Mrs Towers intended to provide the balance of the purchase price from the net proceeds of sale of their existing property after discharging a subsisting mortgage. As it happens, they owed money to Barclays Bank which was secured by a second charge on that property. They arranged with the bank to allow a small part of the debt (£3,350) to remain outstanding after the sale of the existing property and to be secured by a second charge on the new property. The   *e* defendant was informed of these arrangements and gave an undertaking to the bank to hold the title deeds to its order pending registration. Unfortunately, he either failed to appreciate that, although they related to old borrowing, these arrangements were a matter which he was required to report to the society, or he had forgotten or overlooked them when he made his report.   *f*

By his report dated 2 August 1988 the defendant confirmed that to the best of his knowledge and belief the balance of the purchase money was being provided by the applicants personally without resort to further borrowing and that the special conditions attached to the offer of advance had been or would be complied with. He failed to disclose the fact that Mr and Mrs Towers were making arrangements for a second mortgage in connection with the purchase.   *g*

It is conceded by the defendant that his statements were untrue and that his failure to report the purchasers' arrangements for a second mortgage was a breach of his instructions. The society alleges that the defendant acted negligently and in breach of contract, and this is admitted. There is no allegation of dishonesty or bad faith, and if any such allegation were made it would be   *h* strongly resisted. The society does not allege that the defendant made the statements in question knowing them to be untrue. It alleges only that he 'knew or ought to have known' that they were untrue, and this is consistent with oversight.

Following the receipt of the report the society forwarded a cheque for the   *j* amount of the advance to the defendant in readiness for completion on 30 August. Completion took place on that date when the mortgage advance was released to the vendor's solicitors as part of the purchase price for the property. Mr and Mrs Towers executed a first charge in favour of the society and a second charge in favour of the bank. On 25 November the defendant applied to the society for its consent to the registration of the second charge in favour of the *a* bank. The society granted its consent on 10 March 1989. It does not appear that the society was aware of the date of the bank's charge (and so was aware that it constituted a breach of the conditions of the advance) when it gave its consent, but it is alleged that the society must have learned of it shortly afterwards and nevertheless took no action.

b The purchasers defaulted after making only small repayments and the society enforced its security. The property was sold on 6 February 1991 and realised net proceeds of a little under £53,000. The society claimed to recover the whole of its net loss on the transaction from the defendant, alleging breach of contract, negligence and breach of trust. As I have already indicated, breach of contract and negligence are admitted; breach of trust is denied.

c It has always been the defendant's case that the society would not have been concerned by the purchasers' proposal to grant a second charge to the bank if this had been disclosed to it in August 1988; that it would still have proceeded with the transaction; and that it would have suffered precisely the same loss in that event. It is alleged that, in the heady days of 1988, when the property market was at its height and mortgage lenders were falling over themselves to advance *d* money to house purchasers, the society would not have been concerned by a proposal to grant a second charge to secure a relatively trivial indebtedness which did not even represent fresh borrowing; and it is contended that this is demonstrated by the lack of concern shown by the society when it was asked to give its consent to the registration of a second charge in March 1989. Despite the submissions of the society to the contrary, I am satisfied that, if legally relevant, *e* these allegations raise a triable issue.

The course of the proceedings below

It was common ground below that no damages would be recoverable at common law for breach of contract or tort unless the society could show that it *f* would not have proceeded with the transaction if it had been informed of the facts. The society, however, submitted that the position was different in equity. It alleged that the defendant had committed a breach of trust or fiduciary duty, and submitted that common law principles of causation and remoteness of damage have no application in such a case so that it was not necessary for the society to show that it would not have proceeded with the transaction if it had *g* been informed of the facts.

The district judge accepted these arguments. In respect of the common law claims for breach of contract and negligence she gave summary judgment for damages to be assessed. This was apparently on the basis that the judgment would leave it open to the defendant to contend that no loss was caused by the *h* breach.

The district judge also gave summary judgment for the society for breach of trust for the sum of £59,000 less the sums received by the society on the sale of the property, and this was affirmed by the judge, who was satisfied that there was no question or issue to be tried in the action and dismissed the appeal.

j *The course of the appeal*

In the course of the appeal the defendant submitted that, by consenting to the registration of the second charge, the society waived the breaches of which complaint is made; and that this raises a triable issue on liability which entitles him to unconditional leave to defend in relation to all the pleaded causes of action. In the absence of any evidence or reason to suppose that the society was aware of the date of the second charge when it gave its consent to its registration, I am not persuaded that there is a triable issue on waiver, and I would not disturb *a* the order below on this ground.

When the appeal was first argued before us it was still conceded by the society that it could not recover damages at common law for breach of contract or negligence unless it could show that it would not have proceeded with the mortgage advance if it had been informed of the facts. The society, however, *b* maintained that it could escape this principle because the defendant was also guilty of a breach of trust and that common law rules of causation and remoteness of damage have no application in such a case. The critical questions, therefore, appeared to be whether the defendant was guilty of a breach of trust or fiduciary duty and, if so, whether the society needed to prove that it would not still have proceeded with the transaction if it had been told of the facts. *c*

After we had reserved judgment on the appeal, however, the society informed us that it wished to resile from its concession. Relying on the recent decision of this court in *Downs v Chappell* [1996] 3 All ER 344, delivered on 3 April 1996, the society submitted that it was entitled to recover the whole of its net loss on the transaction by way of damages for negligence at common law without having to *d* establish that it would not have proceeded with the transaction if it had been informed of the facts. If correct, it submitted, this would be determinative of the case, and it would not be necessary for the society to rely on any breach of trust or fiduciary duty. Before the defendant's advisers could respond to this, speeches were delivered in the House of Lords in *South Australia Asset Management Corp v* *e* *York Montague Ltd, United Bank of Kuwait plc v Prudential Property Services Ltd, Nykredit Mortgage Bank plc v Edward Erdman Group Ltd* [1996] 3 All ER 365, [1996] 3 WLR 87. These were relevant to the common law position. For the reasons given by Staughton LJ, however, we decided that it was not necessary to restore the appeal for further argument. This was because the assessment of damages at common law is still pending. They will have to be assessed in conformity with *f* the decision of the House of Lords in the *South Australia* case and not with any gloss which, in the absence of argument, we may inadvertently have put upon that decision.

THE CLAIMS AT COMMON LAW *g*

The society has served a respondent's notice, in which it contends that it is entitled to judgment for the sum claimed, and not merely for damages to be assessed, in respect of its common law claims. If this is correct, then the society does not need to establish that the defendant was guilty of a breach of trust or fiduciary duty. *h*

This question depends upon an alleged difference between the tests of causation and remoteness of damage at common law and in equity. In a case of the present kind, however, two different questions of causation are involved and it is necessary to distinguish between them. Where a plaintiff claims that he has suffered loss by entering into a transaction as a result of negligent advice or *j* information provided by the defendant, the first question is whether the plaintiff can establish that the defendant's negligence caused him to enter into the transaction. If he cannot his claim must fail. But even if he can, it is not sufficient for him to establish that the transaction caused him loss. He must still show what (if any) part of his loss is attributable to the defendant's negligence. This is usually treated as a question of the measure of damages rather than causation, and for *a* convenience I shall so treat it in this judgment, but it must be acknowledged that it involves questions of causation.

In *Downs v Chappell* [1996] 3 All ER 344 the plaintiffs bought a small business in reliance on trading figures contained in a letter from the vendor's accountants which was forwarded to them by the vendor. The vendor knew that the figures contained in the letter were false. The plaintiffs sued the vendor for deceit and *b* the accountants for negligence. The judge accepted the plaintiffs' evidence that they would not have contracted to purchase the business without verification of the figures by the accountants. But he was not satisfied that they would not still have bought the business even if the correct figures had been supplied, and dismissed the action against both defendants.

This court allowed the plaintiffs' appeal against both defendants. Hobhouse LJ *c* gave the only reasoned judgment. In relation to the vendor, he pointed out that for a plaintiff to succeed in the tort of deceit it was necessary for him to prove (1) a fraudulent representation, (2) materiality and (3) inducement. All three elements had been proved. The judge had found that the representations did induce the plaintiffs to enter into the transaction: they would not have done so *d* without them. This was sufficient proof of causation. Whether the plaintiffs would have entered into the transaction if they had been told the truth was irrelevant.

We are not concerned with this part of the decision, since the present case is not one of fraud. But Hobhouse LJ held that the position was the same in relation to the accountants, who were charged with negligence only. Here the question *e* was not inducement but reliance. The relevant question was simply whether the plaintiffs had entered into the contract in reliance upon the figures contained in the accountants' letter. The judge had answered that question in the affirmative: the plaintiffs would not have entered into the contract if they had not been provided with the letter. The causal relationship between the accountants' *f* negligence and the plaintiffs' purchase was established. It was not necessary to consider whether the plaintiffs would have purchased the business if they had been supplied with the correct figures.

In the present case the society's claim is not for misrepresentation. Accordingly, questions of inducement and materiality are not relevant. Its claim lies in negligence, and the relevant concept is reliance. In considering the issue of *g* causation in an action for negligence brought by a client against his solicitor it appears from *Downs v Chappell* that it is necessary to distinguish between two different kinds of case.

Where a client sues his solicitor for having negligently failed to give him proper advice, he must show what advice should have been given and (on a balance of *h* probabilities) that if such advice had been given he would not entered into the relevant transaction or would not have entered into it on the terms he did. The same applies where the client's complaint is that the solicitor failed in his duty to give him material information. In *Sykes v Midland Bank Executor and Trustee Co Ltd* [1970] 2 All ER 471, [1971] 1 QB 113, which was concerned with a failure to give *j* proper advice, the plaintiff was unable to establish this and his claim to damages for negligence failed. In *Mortgage Express Ltd v Bowerman & Partners (a firm)* [1996] 2 All ER 836, which was concerned with a failure to convey information, the plaintiff was able to establish that if it had been given the information it would have withdrawn from the transaction and its claim succeeded.

Where, however, a client sues his solicitor for having negligently given him incorrect advice or for having negligently given him incorrect information, the position appears to be different. In such a case it is sufficient for the plaintiff to prove that he relied on the advice or information, that is to say that he would not have acted as he did if he had not been given such advice or information. It is not necessary for him to prove that he would not have acted as he did if he had been given the proper advice or the correct information. This was the position in *Downs v Chappell*.

In the present case the society makes complaints of both kinds. It alleges that the defendant negligently and in breach of his instructions failed to report the purchasers' proposed arrangements with the bank prior to completion. This is a claim of the first kind, and, if it were all, the society would have to establish that if it had been informed of those arrangements it would not have proceeded with the mortgage advance. But the defendant went further than this. He did not merely fail to report the arrangements to the society; he expressly represented to the society that no such arrangements existed. That brings the case within the second category. It follows from the decision of this court in *Downs v Chappell* that it is sufficient for the society to prove that it relied on the representations in the report. Although the judge spoke in terms of inducement, he plainly found reliance. The society's procedures were designed to ensure that no cheque would be issued in the absence of a satisfactory report from its solicitor.

In my judgment we are bound by the decision in *Downs v Chappell* to hold that the necessary causal link between the defendant's negligence and the mortgage advance was proved.

Measure of damages

It does not, however, follow from the fact that the defendant's negligent statements caused the society to make the mortgage advance that the whole of the society's loss is attributable to his negligence. Having regard to the date of the advance, some part at least of the society's loss may well be attributable to the fall in property values which had occurred by the time that it was able to sell the property.

In the *South Australia* case the House of Lords ruled definitively on the correct measure of damages for the negligent provision of information on which the plaintiff relied in entering into a transaction from which loss resulted. The only speech was delivered by Lord Hoffmann. He distinguished between the measure of damages for (1) breach of a contractual warranty and (2) breach of a duty (whether contractual or tortious) to take care (i) to give proper advice and (ii) to provide accurate information.

In the case of breach of warranty, the comparison is between the plaintiff's position as a result of entering into the transaction with what it would have been if the facts had been as warranted. The measure of damages is the extent to which the plaintiff would have been better off if the information had been right. In the case of a breach of duty to take care the measure of damages is the extent to which the plaintiff is worse off because the information was wrong. Since he entered into the transaction in reliance on the advice or information given to him by the defendant, the starting point is to compare his position as a result of entering into the transaction with what it would have been if he had not entered into the transaction at all.

But that is only the starting point. Lord Hoffmann distinguished between a duty to advise someone as to what course of action he should take and a duty to provide information for the purpose of enabling someone else to decide upon his course of action. In the former case, the defendant is liable for all the foreseeable a consequences of the action being taken. In the latter case, however, he is responsible only for the consequences of the information being wrong. The measure of damages is not necessarily the full amount of the loss which the plaintiff has suffered by having entered into the transaction but only that part, if any, of such loss as is properly attributable to the inaccuracy of the information. If the plaintiff would have suffered the same loss even if the facts had actually

b been as represented the defendant is not liable.

Accordingly, in this class of case the plaintiff must prove two things: first, that he has suffered loss; and second, that the loss fell within the scope of the duty he was owed. In the present case the society must prove what (if any) loss was occasioned by the arrangements which the purchasers had made with the bank.

c The society was told that Mr and Mrs Towers had no other indebtedness and that no second charge was contemplated. The existence of the second charge did not affect the society's security. The absence of any indebtedness to the bank would not have put money in the purchasers' pocket; it would merely have reduced their liabilities. Whether their liability to the bank affected their ability to make mortgage repayments to the society has yet to be established, but given

d the smallness of the liability its effect on the purchasers' ability to meet their obligations to the society may have been negligible. It may even be, for example, that the purchasers made no payments at all to the bank at the relevant time, and if so it is difficult to see how any part of the loss suffered by the society can be attributable to the inaccuracy of the information supplied to it by defendant. It would have occurred even if the information had been correct.

e

Conclusion

The society has proved the causal link between the defendant's negligence and the making of the mortgage advance but it has not yet established the amount of its loss (if any) which is properly attributable to the defendant's negligence.

f Damages remain to be assessed. We are bound by the decision of this court in *Downs v Chappell* to hold that the society will not have to prove that it would not have made the mortgage advance if it had known the true facts; but it will be required to establish what it has lost as a result of the existence of the second charge and the purchasers' indebtedness to the bank. It can maintain the money judgment which it has obtained below only if it can invoke equitable principles.

g

THE CLAIMS IN EQUITY

The judge's reasoning

The judge found that, in the events which happened, the defendant committed a breach of trust by applying the mortgage advance in the purchase of the property; that he was accordingly liable to restore the trust property, viz the £59,000 with interest less receipts; that no question of damages at common law or of compensation for loss arose; and that it was irrelevant whether, had it been told of the position, the society might still have chosen to make the advance notwithstanding the arrangements which had been made with the bank.

j Accordingly, the judge concluded that there was no question or issue to be tried in the action and gave summary judgment for the whole of the society's claim.

The judge's conclusion that the defendant had committed a breach of trust in applying the mortgage advance in the purchase of the property was based on the fact that he had obtained payment of the mortgage advance by misrepresentation. The judge said:

'It seems to me clear beyond argument that [the defendant] received the
cheque ... for £59,000 as a direct result of the misleading report which he had *a*
supplied to the society on 2 August 1988. The money was paid to the
defendant as a result of a misrepresentation made to the society by the
defendant ... *The effect, in my judgment, was that from the moment when [the]*
cheque for £59,000 was received by the [defendant] he held it upon a constructive
trust to return it forthwith to the society, unless authorised by the society to retain or *b*
dispose of it after full knowledge of the facts had been disclosed.' (My emphasis.)

In the judge's opinion it necessarily followed that the defendant's subsequent
application of the mortgage money in the purchase of the property constituted a
breach of trust. He said:

'In making that payment there is, in my view, no doubt that the defendant *c*
acted in breach of the trust which had been imposed upon him by the
circumstances in which he had received the society's cheque. That trust
required him to return the £59,000 to the society. Any payment of that
£59,000 to a third party, albeit to the vendors of the property, was a breach
of that trust.' *d*

The judge dismissed the submission that the society had to establish that it would
not have made the advance if it had known the facts. He said:

'But that point affords no defence to the [society]'s claim. It is nihil ad rem
that if the true position had been disclosed to the society, the society might *e*
or might not have issued an amended offer of advance. Liability to repay
arises in this case because the [defendant] received money from the society
as a result of his own misrepresentation. He cannot be heard to say that he
could retain that money against the society, or dispose of it to the vendors,
because, in other circumstances, the society might have chosen to make the
advance notwithstanding the borrowing from [the bank].' *f*

The judge did not explain why the consequence of the defendant's
misrepresentation was that he held the mortgage advance on a constructive trust
for the society, or why the defendant's authority to apply the money in
accordance with the society's instructions was determined, but he took the
opportunity to do so when he revisited these questions a few months later in *g*
Bristol and West Building Society v May May & Merrimans (a firm) [1996] 2 All ER
801 after two county court judges had declined to follow his decision in the
present case. The later case involved a number of transactions in which the same
society had made mortgage advances and suffered loss when the borrowers
defaulted which it sought to recover from the solicitors who had acted for both *h*
parties to the lending transactions. In some cases the solicitor knew nothing,
prior to the receipt of the cheque for the mortgage advance, which ought to have
led him to qualify his report, though he discovered the facts afterwards and
before he disbursed the money on completion. In other cases the solicitor's
breach of his instructions preceded his receipt of the mortgage advance, as it did *j*
in the present case.

The judge distinguished between the two groups of cases. In relation to the
first group he reluctantly felt compelled by the decision in *Target Holdings Ltd v*
Redferns (a firm) [1995] 3 All ER 785, [1996] AC 421 to conclude that, at least for
the purpose of an application for summary judgment, it was necessary for the
society to show that it would not have proceeded with the transaction if it had

a known the facts. In relation to the second group, however, where the society paid the cheque for the mortgage advance to the solicitor in response to a request based upon a warranty or representation which (as the judge put it) the solicitor 'knew or must be taken to have known' to be misleading, he confirmed his previous decision in the present case. He held that the society was entitled to succeed in such cases whether or not it would have still made the advance if it had known the facts.

b In the course of his judgment the judge explained how the constructive trust in question arose. It was, he said, because the solicitor had given misleading information to his client. This constituted a breach of fiduciary duty which enabled the court to impose a constructive trust on the property acquired as a result of the breach of duty. He said:

c
> '... where moneys have been received by the solicitor from the society following a request based upon a warranty or representation which he knew, or must be taken to have known, to be misleading in some material respect, equity will give a remedy in respect of any loss which the society may suffer as a result of its payment in reliance upon that request. That will be a remedy
d based upon breach of fiduciary duty and may, where necessary, take the form of the imposition of a constructive trust on those moneys to enforce the solicitor's obligation to return them to the society forthwith. The constructive trust imposed by equity to enforce the obligation to make immediate restitution overrides any express or implied trust which might
e otherwise arise out of any instructions given by [the society] when the money is paid to the solicitor. No reliance can be placed on those instructions, because they are vitiated by the breach of duty by which they were obtained ... In the absence of some fresh instructions, given by the society after full disclosure of the matters in respect of which it has been misled, the only course properly open to the solicitor is to repay the moneys
f to the society with interest.'

The judge evidently considered himself to be imposing a remedial constructive trust as the appropriate remedy for a prior breach of fiduciary duty.

The judge's references to the solicitor having made a representation which 'he knew, or must be taken as having known' to be misleading is not an accurate
g description of the facts of the present case. It is not alleged that the defendant 'knew or must be taken to have known' the facts, but only that he 'knew or ought to have known' them, which is a very different matter. In explaining his decision in the present case the judge said that the defendant's misrepresentation could not be described as innocent because he 'clearly had the knowledge which made
h the representation false'. That confuses knowledge with the means of knowledge. On the society's pleaded case the defendant must be taken to have known the facts at one time but to have forgotten or overlooked them so that they were not present to his mind when he came to complete his report to the society.

j It is not alleged that the defendant deliberately concealed the arrangements which the purchasers had made with their bank from the society or that he consciously intended to mislead it. Nothing in this judgment is intended to apply to such a case. My observations are confined to the case like the present where the provision of incorrect information by a solicitor to his client must be taken to have been due to an oversight. In such a case his breach of duty is unconscious; he will ex hypothesi be unaware of the fact that he has committed a breach of his

instructions; and if this means that his subsequent application of the mortgage
money constitutes a breach of trust then it will be a breach of a trust of which he   *a*
is unaware. I would not willingly treat such conduct as involving a breach of trust
or misapplication of trust money unless compelled by authority to do so, and in
my judgment neither principle nor authority compels such a conclusion.

Before us the defendant submits that, while he was guilty of negligence and
breach of contract, he was not guilty of a breach of trust or fiduciary duty. It is   *b*
convenient to take first the question of fiduciary duty, and then to consider the
question of breach of trust.

Breach of fiduciary duty

Despite the warning given by Fletcher Moulton LJ in *Re Coomber, Coomber v
Coomber* [1911] 1 Ch 723 at 728 this branch of the law has been bedevilled by   *c*
unthinking resort to verbal formulae. It is therefore necessary to begin by
defining one's terms. The expression 'fiduciary duty' is properly confined to
those duties which are peculiar to fiduciaries and the breach of which attracts
legal consequences differing from those consequent upon the breach of other
duties. Unless the expression is so limited it is lacking in practical utility. In this   *d*
sense it is obvious that not every breach of duty by a fiduciary is a breach of
fiduciary duty. I would indorse the observations of Southin J in *Girardet v Crease
& Co* (1987) 11 BCLR (2d) 361 where she said:

> 'The word "fiduciary" is flung around now as if it applied to all breaches of
> duty by solicitors, directors of companies and so forth ... That a lawyer can   *e*
> commit a breach of the special duty [of a fiduciary] ... by entering into a
> contract with the client without full disclosure ... and so forth is clear. But
> to say that simple carelessness in giving advice is such a breach is a perversion
> of words.'

These remarks were approved by La Forest J in *Lac Minerals Ltd v International*   *f*
Corona Ltd (1989) 61 DLR (4th) 14 at 28, where he said:

> '... not every legal claim arising out of a relationship with fiduciary
> incidents will give rise to a claim for a breach of fiduciary duty.'

It is similarly inappropriate to apply the expression to the obligation of a trustee   *g*
or other fiduciary to use proper skill and care in the discharge of his duties. If it is
confined to cases where the fiduciary nature of the duty has special legal
consequences, then the fact that the source of the duty is to be found in equity
rather than the common law does not make it a fiduciary duty. The common law
and equity each developed the duty of care, but they did so independently of each   *h*
other and the standard of care required is not always the same. But they
influenced each other, and today the substance of the resulting obligations is
more significant than their particular historic origin. In *Henderson v Merrett
Syndicates Ltd, Hallam-Eames v Merrett Syndicates Ltd, Hughes v Merrett Syndicates
Ltd, Arbuthnott v Feltrim Underwriting Agencies Ltd, Deeny v Gooda Walker Ltd (in liq)*
[1994] 3 All ER 506 at 543, [1995] 2 AC 145 at 205 Lord Browne-Wilkinson said: *j*

> 'The liability of a fiduciary for the negligent transaction of his duties is not
> a separate head of liability but the paradigm of the general duty to act with
> care imposed by law on those who take it upon themselves to act or advise
> others. Although the historical development of the rules of law and equity
> have, in the past, caused different labels to be stuck on different

a manifestations of the duty, in truth the duty of care on bailees carriers, trustees, directors, agents and others is the same duty: it arises from the circumstances in which the defendants were acting, not from their status or description. It is the fact that they have all assumed responsibility for the property or affairs of others which renders them liable for the careless performance of what they have undertaken to do, not the description of the b trade or position which they hold.'

I respectfully agree, and indorse the comment of Ipp J in *Permanent Building Society (in liq) v Wheeler* (1994) 14 ACSR 109 at 157 where he said:

'It is essential to bear in mind that the existence of a fiduciary relationship does not mean that every duty owed by a fiduciary to the beneficiary is a c fiduciary duty. In particular, a trustee's duty to exercise reasonable care, though equitable, is not specifically a fiduciary duty ...'

Ipp J explained this (at 158):

'The director's duty to exercise care and skill has nothing to do with any d position of disadvantage or vulnerability on the part of the company. It is not a duty that stems from the requirements of trust and confidence imposed on a fiduciary. In my opinion, that duty is not a fiduciary duty, although it is a duty actionable in the equitable jurisdiction of this court ... I consider that Hamilton owed PBS a duty, both in law and in equity, to exercise reasonable e care and skill, and PBS was able to mount a claim against him for breach of the legal duty, and, in the alternative, breach of the equitable duty. For the reasons I have expressed, in my view the equitable duty is not to be equated with or termed a "fiduciary" duty.'

I agree. Historical support for this analysis may be found in the passage in f Viscount Haldane LC's speech in *Nocton v Lord Ashburton* [1914] AC 932 at 956, [1914–15] All ER Rep 45 at 54. Discussing the old bill in Chancery for equitable compensation for breach of fiduciary duty, he said that he thought it probable that a demurrer for want of equity would always have lain to a bill which did no more than seek to enforce a claim for damages for negligence against a solicitor.

In my judgment this is not just a question of semantics. It goes to the very g heart of the concept of breach of fiduciary duty and the availability of equitable remedies.

Although the remedy which equity makes available for breach of the equitable duty of skill and care is equitable compensation rather than damages, this is merely the product of history and in this context is in my opinion a distinction h without a difference. Equitable compensation for breach of the duty of skill and care resembles common law damages in that it is awarded by way of compensation to the plaintiff for his loss. There is no reason in principle why the common law rules of causation, remoteness of damage and measure of damages should not be applied by analogy in such a case. It should not be confused with j equitable compensation for breach of fiduciary duty, which may be awarded in lieu of rescission or specific restitution.

This leaves those duties which are special to fiduciaries and which attract those remedies which are peculiar to the equitable jurisdiction and are primarily restitutionary or restorative rather than compensatory. A fiduciary is someone who has undertaken to act for or on behalf of another in a particular matter in circumstances which give rise to a relationship of trust and confidence. The

distinguishing obligation of a fiduciary is the obligation of loyalty. The principal
is entitled to the single-minded loyalty of his fiduciary. This core liability has *a*
several facets. A fiduciary must act in good faith; he must not make a profit out
of his trust; he must not place himself in a position where his duty and his interest
may conflict; he may not act for his own benefit or the benefit of a third person
without the informed consent of his principal. This is not intended to be an
exhaustive list, but it is sufficient to indicate the nature of fiduciary obligations. *b*
They are the defining characteristics of the fiduciary. As Dr Finn pointed out in
his classic work *Fiduciary Obligations* (1977) p 2, he is not subject to fiduciary
obligations because he is a fiduciary; it is because he is subject to them that he is
a fiduciary.

(In this survey I have left out of account the situation where the fiduciary deals
with his principal. In such a case he must prove affirmatively that the transaction *c*
is fair and that in the course of the negotiations he made full disclosure of all facts
material to the transaction. Even inadvertent failure to disclose will entitle the
principal to rescind the transaction. The rule is the same whether the fiduciary is
acting on his own behalf or on behalf of another. The principle need not be
further considered because it is does arise in the present case. The mortgage *d*
advance was negotiated directly between the society and the purchasers. The
defendant had nothing to do with the negotiations. He was instructed by the
society to carry out on its behalf a transaction which had already been agreed.)

The nature of the obligation determines the nature of the breach. The various
obligations of a fiduciary merely reflect different aspects of his core duties of
loyalty and fidelity. Breach of fiduciary obligation, therefore, connotes disloyalty *e*
or infidelity. Mere incompetence is not enough. A servant who loyally does his
incompetent best for his master is not unfaithful and is not guilty of a breach of
fiduciary duty.

In the present case it is clear that, if the defendant had been acting for the
society alone, his admitted negligence would not have exposed him to a charge *f*
of breach of fiduciary duty. Before us counsel for the society accepted as much,
but insisted that the fact that he also acted for the purchasers made all the
difference. So it is necessary to ask: why did the fact that the defendant was acting
for the purchasers as well as for the society convert the defendant's admitted
breach of his duty of skill and care into a breach of fiduciary duty? To answer this
question it is necessary to identify the fiduciary obligation of which he is alleged *g*
to have been in breach.

It is at this point, in my judgment, that the society's argument runs into
difficulty. A fiduciary who acts for two principals with potentially conflicting
interests without the informed consent of both is in breach of the obligation of
undivided loyalty; he puts himself in a position where his duty to one principal *h*
may conflict with his duty to the other: see *Clark Boyce v Mouat* [1993] 4 All ER 268,
[1994] 1 AC 428 and the cases there cited. This is sometimes described as 'the
double employment rule'. Breach of the rule automatically constitutes a breach
of fiduciary duty. But this is not something of which the society can complain. It
knew that the defendant was acting for the purchasers when it instructed him. *j*
Indeed, that was the very reason why it chose the defendant to act for it. The
potential conflict was of the society's own making (see *Finn* p 254 and *Kelly v
Cooper* [1993] AC 205, [1993] 3 LRC 476).

It was submitted on behalf of the society that this is irrelevant because the
defendant misled the society. It did not know of the arrangements which the
purchasers had made with their bank, and so could not be said to be 'fully

a informed' for the purpose of absolving the defendant from the operation of the double employment rule. The submission is misconceived. The society knew all the facts relevant to its choice of solicitor. Its decision to forward the cheque for the mortgage advance to the defendant and to instruct him to proceed was based on false information, but its earlier decision to employ the defendant despite the potentially conflicting interest of his other clients was a fully informed decision.

b   That, of course, is not the end of the matter. Even if a fiduciary is properly acting for two principals with potentially conflicting interests he must act in good faith in the interests of each and must not act with the intention of furthering the interests of one principal to the prejudice of those of the other (see *Finn* p 48). I shall call this 'the duty of good faith'. But it goes further than this. He must not allow the performance of his obligations to one principal to be influenced by his

c relationship with the other. He must serve each as faithfully and loyally as if he were his only principal. Conduct which is in breach of this duty need not be dishonest but it must be intentional. An unconscious omission which happens to benefit one principal at the expense of the other does not constitute a breach of fiduciary duty, though it may constitute a breach of the duty of skill and care.

d This is because the principle which is in play is that the fiduciary must not be inhibited by the existence of his other employment from serving the interests of his principal as faithfully and effectively as if he were the only employer. I shall call this 'the no inhibition principle'. Unless the fiduciary is inhibited or believes (whether rightly or wrongly) that he is inhibited in the performance of his duties to one principal by reason of his employment by the other, his failure to act is not

e attributable to the double employment.

    Finally, the fiduciary must take care not to find himself in a position where there is an *actual* conflict of duty so that he cannot fulfil his obligations to one principal without failing in his obligations to the other: see *Moody v Cox* [1917] 2 Ch 71, [1916–17] All ER Rep 548 and *Commonwealth Bank of Australia v Smith*

f (1991) 102 ALR 453. If he does, he may have no alternative but to cease to act for at least one and preferably both. The fact that he cannot fulfil his obligations to one principal without being in breach of his obligations to the other will not absolve him from liability. I shall call this 'the actual conflict rule'.

    In the present case the judge evidently thought that the defendant was in

g breach of both the duty of good faith and the actual conflict rule. In *Bristol and West Building Society v May May & Merrimans (a firm)* [1996] 2 All ER 801 at 817–818 he said:

        '... there can be no doubt that the requirement of unconscionable conduct

h   is present where a solicitor who is acting for both borrower and lender misrepresents to the lender some fact *which he knows, or must be taken to know,* will or may affect the lender's decision to proceed with the loan. In those circumstances the solicitor *is abusing his fiduciary relationship with one client, the lender, to obtain an advantage for his other client, the borrower.* It is as much "against the dictates of conscience" for a solicitor *knowingly to prefer the*

j   *interests of one client over those of another client* as it is for him to prefer his own interests over those of his client.' (My emphasis.)

    I respectfully agree; but no such allegation is made in the present case.

    As to the actual conflict rule, the judge said (at 832):

'First, in *Mothew*, the "agent" was a fiduciary who had put himself in a
position in which his duty to the lender *was* in conflict with the interests of *a*
his other client, the borrower.' (My emphasis.)

I do not accept this. By instructing him to act for them, the purchasers must be
taken to have authorised the defendant to complete the report without which the
mortgage advance would not have been forthcoming; and to complete it *b*
truthfully. The defendant was required by the society to report on the
purchasers' title as well as to confirm the absence of any further borrowing. The
two stood in exactly the same case. The defendant would not have been in
breach of his duty to the purchasers if he had disclosed the facts to the society any
more than if he had reported a defect in their title.

This proposition can be tested by considering what the defendant's position *c*
would have been if he had acted for the purchasers and another solicitor had been
instructed to act for the society. He would have been required to deduce the
purchasers' title to the satisfaction of the society's solicitor, and to confirm to him
that no further borrowing or second charge was in contemplation. His duty to
the purchasers would have required him to ascertain the facts from them and to *d*
report them to the society. Unless they told him the facts and instructed him to
lie to the society, instructions which he would be bound to refuse, his duty to the
purchasers would not inhibit him in providing full and truthful information to the
solicitor acting for the society.

In my judgment, the defendant was never in breach of the actual conflict rule.
It is not alleged that he acted in bad faith or that he deliberately withheld *e*
information because he wrongly believed that his duty to the purchasers required
him to do so. He was not guilty of a breach of fiduciary duty.

The judge relied on *Nocton v Lord Ashburton* [1914] AC 932, [1914–15] All ER
Rep 45 and *Commonwealth Bank of Australia v Smith* (1991) 102 ALR 453 to hold
that a party who pays money to his solicitor in reliance on a representation *known* *f*
by the solicitor to be false has a remedy in breach of fiduciary duty. Neither case
is authority for the proposition (though its correctness is not in issue); certainly
neither is authority for the proposition that a party who pays money to a solicitor
in reliance on a representation which the solicitor *ought to have known* to be false
has such a remedy.

In *Nocton v Lord Ashburton* a solicitor had an undisclosed personal interest in a *g*
transaction on which he gave his client advice which was to his own advantage
and the disadvantage of his client. The plaintiff pleaded breach of the duty of
good faith. In fact this was unnecessary; the existence of the defendant's
undisclosed interest was enough: see *Lewis v Hillman* (1852) 3 HL Cas 607, 10 ER
239. The plaintiff was entitled to receive, and thought that he was receiving, the *h*
disinterested advice of a solicitor with no other interest in the transaction.
Commonwealth Bank of Australia v Smith involved a breach of the actual conflict
rule. The defendant, who was acting for both parties to a proposed transaction,
placed himself in an impossible position by undertaking to advise one of them on
the merits of the transaction. *j*

In *Moody v Cox* [1917] 2 Ch 71, [1916–17] All ER Rep 548 a solicitor, who was
acting for both vendor and purchaser, was in possession of valuations which
showed that the property was not worth the price which the purchaser had
agreed to pay. He did not disclose them to the purchaser, and claimed that his
duty to the vendor precluded him from doing so. The purchaser was allowed to
rescind. The case bears a superficial resemblance to the present but there are two

a crucial differences: (i) the vendor was under no obligation to disclose the valuations to the purchaser and did not wish his solicitor do so; and (ii) the vendor and the solicitor tacitly agreed to conceal the valuations from the purchaser. The solicitor was in breach of both the duty of good faith and the actual conflict rule; his defence fell foul of the no inhibition principle.

b That was a case of deliberate concealment. Non-disclosure and concealment are two very different things. This has been a truism of the law from the time of Cicero, citing Diogenes of Babylon (see *De Officiis*, lib 3, c 12, 13). It is even enshrined, like other such truisms, in a Latin tag: aliud est celare, aliud tacere.

The society placed much reliance on a dictum by Lord Jauncey in *Clarke Boyce v Mouat* [1993] 4 All ER 268 at 275, [1994] 1 AC 428 at 437, where he said:

c   'Another case of breach [of fiduciary duty] is where a solicitor acts for both parties without disclosing this to one of them or where having disclosed it he fails, unbeknown to one party, to disclose to that party material facts relative to the other party of which he is aware.' (My emphasis.)

d But I do not think that Lord Jauncey meant to include an inadvertent failure which owes nothing to the double employment. Where such failure is to the advantage of the other party, the court will jealously scrutinise the facts to ensure that there has been nothing more than inadvertence, but there can be no justification for treating an unconscious failure as demonstrating a want of fidelity.

e In my judgment the distinction drawn by Ipp J in *Permanent Building Society (in liq) v Wheeler* (1994) 14 ACSR 109 is sound in principle and is decisive of the present case. On the society's pleaded case the fact that the defendant was acting for the purchasers played no part in his failure to report the true state of affairs to the society. It did not inhibit him from fulfilling his obligations to the society. It is consistent with its pleaded case that the defendant would have done so but for

f a negligent oversight. It would have been exactly the same if he had failed to notice and report the existence of a defect in the purchasers' title. To characterise either such failure as a breach of fiduciary duty because he was acting for both parties in a situation where that fact did not contribute to his failure is, in my opinion, to substitute a verbal formula for principle.

g In my judgment the judge's conclusion that the defendant was in breach of fiduciary duty cannot be supported. It follows that it cannot be sustained as a ground for holding the defendant to be in breach of a constructive trust of the mortgage money.

h *Breach of trust*
It is not disputed that from the time of its receipt by the defendant the mortgage money was trust money. It was client's money which belonged to the society and was properly paid into a client account. The defendant never claimed any beneficial interest in the money which remained throughout the property of

j the society in equity. The defendant held it in trust for the society but with the society's authority (and instructions) to apply it in the completion of the transaction of purchase and mortgage of the property. Those instructions were revocable but, unless previously revoked, the defendant was entitled and bound to act in accordance with them.

The society's instructions were not revoked before the defendant acted on them, and in my judgment there was no ground upon which the judge could properly conclude that his authority to apply the money in completing the transaction had determined.

If his judgment in the present case is considered without the benefit of his later explanation in *Bristol and West Building Society v May May & Merrimans (a firm)* [1996] 2 All ER 801, it would appear that the judge was of opinion that the defendant's authority to deal with the money was automatically vitiated by the fact that it (and the cheque itself) was obtained by misrepresentation. But that is contrary to principle. Misrepresentation makes a transaction voidable not void. It gives the representee the right to elect whether to rescind or affirm the transaction. The representor cannot anticipate his decision. Unless and until the representee elects to rescind the representor remains fully bound. The defendant's misrepresentations merely gave the society the right to elect to withdraw from the transaction on discovering the truth. Since its instructions to the defendant were revocable in any case, this did not materially alter the position so far as he was concerned, though it may have strengthened the society's position in relation to the purchasers.

The right to rescind for misrepresentation is an equity. Until it is exercised the beneficial interest in any property transferred in reliance on the representation remains vested in the transferee. In *El Ajou v Dollar Land Holdings plc* [1993] 3 All ER 717 at 734 I suggested that on rescission the equitable title might revest in the representee retrospectively at least to the extent necessary to support an equitable tracing claim. I was concerned to circumvent the supposed rule that there must be a fiduciary relationship or retained beneficial interest before resort may be had to the equitable tracing rules. The rule would have been productive of the most extraordinary anomalies in that case, and its existence continually threatens to frustrate attempts to develop a coherent law of restitution. Until the equitable tracing rules are made available in support of the ordinary common law claim for money had and received some problems will remain incapable of sensible resolution.

But all that is by the way. Whether or not there is a retrospective vesting for tracing purposes it is clear that on rescission the equitable title does not revest retrospectively *so as to cause an application of trust money which was properly authorised when made to be afterwards treated as a breach of trust*. In *Lipkin Gorman (a firm) v Karpnale Ltd* [1992] 4 All ER 512 at 528, [1991] 2 AC 548 at 573 Lord Goff said:

> 'Of course, "tracing" or "following" property into its product involves a decision by the owner of the original property to assert his title to the product in place of his original property. This is sometimes referred to as ratification. I myself would not so describe it; but it has, in my opinion, at least one feature in common with ratification, that it cannot be relied upon so as to render an innocent recipient a wrongdoer (cf *Bolton Partners v Lambert* (1889) 41 Ch D 295 at 307 per Cotton LJ: "... an act lawful at the time of its performance [cannot] be rendered unlawful, by the application of the doctrine of ratification.").'

In *Westdeutsche Landesbank Girozentrale v Islington London BC* [1996] 2 All ER 961 at 988, [1996] 2 WLR 802 at 828 Lord Browne-Wilkinson expressly rejected the possibility that a recipient of trust money could be personally liable, regardless of fault, for any subsequent payment away of the moneys to third parties even though, at the date of such payment, he was ignorant of the existence of any trust. He said:

a
'Since the equitable jurisdiction to enforce trusts depends upon the conscience of the holder of the legal interest being affected, he cannot be a trustee of the property if and so long as he is ignorant of the facts alleged to affect his conscience, ie until he is aware that he is intended to hold the property for the benefit of others in the case of an express or implied trust, or, in the case of a constructive trust, of the facts which are alleged to affect
b   his conscience.'

Mutatis mutandis that passage is directly applicable in the present case. The defendant knew that he was a trustee of the money for the society; but he did not realise that he had misled the society and could not know that his authority to complete had determined (if indeed it had). He could not be bound to repay the
c   money to the society so long as he was ignorant of the facts which had brought his authority to an end, for those are the facts which are alleged to affect his conscience and subject him to an obligation to return the money to the society.

Before us the society put forward a more sophisticated argument. The defendant's instructions, it pointed out, expressly required him to report the arrangements in question 'to the Society prior to completion'. This, it was
d   submitted, made it a condition of the defendant's authority to complete that he had complied with his obligation. Whether he knew it or not, he had no authority to complete. It was not necessary for the society to revoke his authority or withdraw from the transaction.

I do not accept this. The society's standing instructions did not clearly make
e   the defendant's authority to complete conditional on having complied with his instructions. Whether they did so or not is, of course, a question of construction, and it is possible that the society could adopt instructions which would have this effect. But it would in my judgment require very clear wording to produce so inconvenient and impractical a result. No solicitor could safely accept such
f   instructions, for he could never be certain that he was entitled to complete.

In my judgment the defendant's authority to apply the mortgage money in the completion of the purchase was not conditional on his having first complied with his contractual obligations to the society, was not vitiated by the misrepresentations for which he was responsible but of which he was unaware, and was effective to prevent his payment being a breach of trust. Given his state
g   of knowledge, he had no choice but to complete.

Conclusion

In my judgment the defendant was not guilty of breach of trust or fiduciary duty. This makes it unnecessary to consider what the consequences of such a
h   breach would have been. I would allow the appeal and set aside the money judgment. I would leave undisturbed the judgments for damages to be assessed for breach of contract and negligence, but make it clear that it does not follow that the society will establish any recoverable loss.

j   **OTTON LJ.** I have read with advantage the judgments of Millett and Staughton LJJ. I agree with the analysis and reasoning regarding breach of trust and of fiduciary duty. I wish only to add a few words on the extant common law claims.

I am satisfied that there was sufficient evidence before the judge to establish negligence on the part of the defendant. There was the requisite proximity between the parties, and there was foreseeability of damage. Thus a duty of care arose. This duty included answering correctly such questions as were posed by

the proposed lender and which it was reasonable for him to be required to
answer. The answer sought was one of fact and not opinion. The fact sought   *a*
could have been supplied accurately by information which was within his
knowledge. If it was not at his fingertips the information was either on file or
could easily have been obtained by direct inquiry of the intending purchaser. His
breach of duty occurred when he conveyed the inaccurate information to the
plaintiffs. The duty was not simply a duty not to act carelessly; it was a duty not   *b*
to inflict damage carelessly. Damage is the gist of the action.

The more complex issues are whether the inaccurate information given was
causative of damage, and if so what measure. To my mind it is not necessary to
adopt a particular procedural path to find the answer. I appreciate that Lord
Hoffmann suggests that it is first necessary to decide the kind of loss to which the
plaintiff is entitled (see *South Australia Management Corp v York Montague Ltd,*   *c*
United Bank of Kuwait plc v Prudential Property Services Ltd, Nykredit Mortgage Bank
plc v Edward Erdman Group Ltd [1996] 3 All ER 365, [1996] 3 WLR 87). This may
be appropriate in most cases where negligence/causation is involved. From a
practical point of view in some cases it may be more expedient to establish the
causal link between the negligent act or omission, and the reliance by the plaintiff   *d*
or the course of action which he was induced to take. The judge may find as a
fact that there was no reliance or that the plaintiff would have behaved in the
same or substantially the same manner if he had been given accurate information,
in either event the negligence had no causative potency. That is the end of the
matter. The chain is broken, there is no loss at all and there is no need to consider
or determine the kind of loss.   *e*

In other cases it may be appropriate to identify the type or particular head of
damage claimed. This may identify damage which is too remote and for which
no remedy lies (e g economic loss), and the claim in respect of it fails in limine. As
I concur that the damages award must now be set aside the issue of the measure
of damage, if any, is now at large.   *f*

I regard the evidence (in particular the hearsay evidence of Ms Samantha
Bennett at para 29 of Mr Prees' affidavit) as falling short of resolving the issues of
causation or damage. It does not (for example) address the possibility of a revised
offer if the accurate and full position had been explained to the plaintiffs.

I do not think it necessary to conclude whether there was a breach of contract.
This cause of action probably adds nothing to the case in negligence. It is unlikely   *g*
that there is any practical difference between a breach of the duty of care and a
breach of contract, or in the issues arising on causation, or the measure of
damages. If there is any issue it can be determined by the trial judge; I also
consider that there was no waiver.

For these reasons I consider that there are triable issues and they should be   *h*
determined by a judge at first instance.

I would therefore allow the appeal and remit the assessment of damages as
proposed by Staughton LJ and dismiss the respondent's notice.

STAUGHTON LJ. Mr Mothew made his report to the Cheshunt Building   *j*
Society on 2 August 1988. In it he answered one of the questions asked as follows:

> '[Q.] Please confirm that (to the best of your knowledge and belief) the
> balance of the purchase money is being provided by the applicant(s)
> personally without resort to further borrowing. If not please give details.
> [A.] Confirmed.'

a That was untrue. There were other aspects of the same error, but I need not go into them in detail. Although Mr Mothew had the means of knowledge in his possession, which could have brought the error to his attention, it is not said that he acted fraudulently or in bad faith.

The ordinary remedy of a client who has received wrong information or advice from his solicitor is to claim damages for negligence, whether as a breach of *b* contract or as a tort. For such a claim to give rise to substantial damages the building society would have to show that the breach of contract or negligence caused them loss. By their respondent's notice they seek to say that, if they had known the true facts, they would not have lent any money to Mr and Mrs Towers.

c The judge regarded that point as immaterial, since the building society succeeded on other grounds. If it is material, in my opinion it raises a triable issue. According to Samantha Bennett of the society's advances department, the offer of advance would have immediately been withdrawn if the society had known that even £3,350 was being borrowed elsewhere. In the nature of things Mr Mothew is unlikely to have evidence which directly controverts that statement. *d* But there are grounds for supposing that it may be open to question. I would not give judgment under RSC Ord 14 on the basis that it is true. If it is critical, the case must go to trial, perhaps with the aid of interrogatories and discovery of documents.

However, in this particular case the building society were not the sole clients *e* of Mr Mothew; he was also the solicitor acting for Mr and Mrs Towers. That is said to make all the difference, because Mr Mothew then became under a fiduciary duty to the building society. And the argument is that for breach of fiduciary duty the remedy does not depend on causation or remoteness; all that is necessary is that the loss would not have occurred *but for* the breach of duty.

f It seems to me wrong that a breach of contract or tort should become a breach of fiduciary duty in that way. I am glad to find that the authorities relied on by Millett LJ show that it is wrong. In my judgment Mr Mothew was in breach of a duty of care and nothing more. True he was in a situation where he owed duties to two clients, and those duties might conflict with each other. But he did not prefer the interest of one client to that of another; at most he was guilty of *g* negligence which had that unintended effect.

Alternatively it is said that Mr Mothew was in breach of trust because he paid away the trust fund contrary to his instructions. He did indeed hold the £59,000 in trust; it was not his own money. There was in my opinion an express or implied trust, and not (as the judge held) a constructive trust. But he did not pay *h* it away contrary to the society's instructions. The cheque reached Mr Mothew with a letter dated 23 August 1988, which in effect instructed him to use it for completion of the proposed purchase. That was what he did.

There being in my opinion no breach of fiduciary duty or breach of trust, it is unnecessary to consider what remedy such a breach might have afforded.

j Thus far the appeal succeeds, but there remains judgment on the cause of action at common law for damages to be assessed. Mr Sumption QC for the defendant says that even that must go, since there is a triable issue as to waiver by the building society. The problem that he faces is that, although the building society readily agreed when they were asked to consent to the registration of the second charge, they are not shown to have known that the second charge was contemplated and intended at the time of Mr Mothew's report. There has been

ample opportunity to produce evidence that they knew, if indeed they did. In my
judgment there was no waiver.

When the argument before us was concluded on 21 May that was all that we
had to decide. But we have since been asked to consider the judgment of
Hobhouse LJ in *Downs v Chappell* [1996] 3 All ER 344 and the speech of Lord
Hoffmann in *South Australia Asset Management Corp v York Montague Ltd, United
Bank of Kuwait plc v Prudential Property Services Ltd, Nykredit Mortgage Bank plc v
Edward Erdman Group Ltd* [1996] 3 All ER 365, [1996] 3 WLR 87. Such has been
the volume of litigation on the topic of loss to lenders following negligent
professional advice and the collapse of the property market that judges risk being
overtaken by new authority.

The Court of Appeal in the *South Australia* case (sub nom *Banque Bruxelles
Lambert SA v Eagle Star Insurance Co Ltd* [1995] 2 All ER 769, [1995] QB 375) began
with a reference to the well-known principle that damages should be as nearly as
possible the sum which would put the plaintiff in the position in which he would
have been if he had not been injured. That would lead to two possible answers
in the present case. (1) If there had been no report from Mr Mothew to the
building society, the money would not have been lent; the society would still
have its £59,000. There would have been no transaction, a phrase which I use not
as a label for anything but as a description of the fact. (2) If Mr Mothew had
provided an accurate report to the building society, then they might have been
content to proceed on the terms previously proposed, or they might have made
a revised offer, or they might have proceeded as in (1) above. There is a triable
issue as to that.

Left to myself, I would have ruled that (2) was the appropriate situation for the
judge to consider in assessing the damages. But I have to acknowledge that
Hobhouse LJ in *Downs v Chappell*, with the agreement of Butler-Sloss and Roch
LJJ, preferred method (1), both for fraudulent misrepresentation and for
negligence. Lord Hoffmann, as it seems to me, considered that either method
was the wrong place to begin: 'Before one can consider the principle on which
one should calculate the damages to which a plaintiff is entitled as compensation
for loss, it is necessary to decide for what kind of loss he is entitled...' (see [1996]
3 All ER 365 at 369, [1996] 3 WLR 87 at 92). There followed an exposition of the
problem and the answer to it, as set out in the judgment of Millett LJ.

For my part I feel that we should not at this stage purport to instruct the judge
who has to assess the damages by a paraphrase or interpretation of that decision,
for a number of reasons. First, we have not heard argument on it, and our
judgment is already long delayed by intervening material. I am told it would be
impractical for us to have a further hearing before October. Secondly, the judge
has yet to find the facts relating to the assessment of damages. Thirdly, the judge
must be guided by what Lord Hoffmann has said and not by any gloss of ours.

I would allow the appeal and remit the assessment of damages, either to
Chadwick J or to another judge of the Chancery Division as the exigencies of
business may require. The cross-appeal should be dismissed.

Appeal allowed. Cross-appeal dismissed.

Mary Rose Plummer   Barrister.

a

Trustee of the property of F C Jones & Sons (a firm) v Jones

COURT OF APPEAL, CIVIL DIVISION

b

NOURSE, BELDAM AND MILLETT LJJ

25 APRIL 1996

Restitution – Unjust enrichment – Investment profit – Entitlement to profit – Firm committing act of bankruptcy – Defendant obtaining funds from partners' joint account before firm adjudicated bankrupt – Defendant investing money and making
c *considerable profit – Trustee in bankruptcy claiming entitlement to original sum and profit – Whether trustee in bankruptcy entitled to trace investment profit.*

The partners of a firm committed an act of bankruptcy, but before they were adjudicated bankrupt, one of the partners drew three cheques totalling £11,700
d on a joint account held with another partner in favour of his wife, the defendant. The defendant paid the proceeds of the cheques into an account which she opened with a firm of commodity brokers in order to deal in potato futures. The defendant's investment proved to be highly profitable and she received two cheques totalling £50,760 from the commodity brokers which she paid into an account at R plc. She allowed her husband to withdraw £900 from the account
e leaving a balance of £49,860. Shortly thereafter the Official Receiver informed R plc of his claim to the money in the account. The defendant immediately demanded the release of the money and R plc interpleaded. An order was made on the interpleader summons that the money be paid into court. On the trial of the issues between the two claimants, the trustee in bankruptcy contended that
f the defendant never acquired any title to the money in the joint account since it had already vested in him under s 37 of the Bankruptcy Act 1914 when the act of bankruptcy was committed and that therefore the money in court represented the proceeds of her successful speculation with his money. The defendant conceded the trustee's entitlement to the original sum of £11,700, but contended that, in the absence of a constructive trust or fiduciary relationship justifying the
g intervention of equity, he could not recover the profits made by her use of the money. The deputy judge held that the defendant was a constructive trustee and that therefore, applying the equitable rules of tracing, the trustee was entitled to the money in court. The plaintiff appealed to the Court of Appeal.

h **Held** – Since the trustee was entitled to the money in the bankrupts' joint account from the date of the act of bankruptcy, the cheques which had been drawn in favour of the defendant were incapable of passing any legal or equitable title to her and, as such, she did not receive the money in a fiduciary capacity and was not a constructive trustee. However, the trustee could trace his money at
j common law into the money held in the defendant's account with the commodity brokers; and since the chose in action, which was vested in the defendant's name but which in reality belonged to the trustee, was not a right to payment from the brokers of the original amount deposited but a right to claim the balance, whether greater or less than the amount deposited, the trustee was entitled to the balance of the money in that account, including the profits made by the use of the money. It followed that the trustee was entitled to the money

in court and the appeal would accordingly be dismissed (see p 723 h j, p 724 f to h, p 726 h, p 727 g, p 728 f j, p 729 h, p 730 a d to f, p 731 c to h and p 732 b, post).
Lipkin Gorman (a firm) v Karpnale Ltd [1992] 4 All ER 512 applied.

Notes
For liability based on unjust enrichment, see 9 *Halsbury's Laws* (4th edn) para 640.

Cases referred to in judgments
A-G for Hong Kong v Reid [1994] 1 All ER 1, [1994] 1 AC 324, [1993] 3 WLR 1143, PC.

Agip (Africa) Ltd v Jackson [1992] 4 All ER 451, [1991] Ch 547, [1991] 3 WLR 116, CA; *affg* [1992] 4 All ER 385, [1990] Ch 265, [1989] 3 WLR 1367.

Banque Belge pour l'Etranger v Hambrouck [1921] 1 KB 321, CA.

Bishop, Re, ex p Claxton (1891) 8 Morr 221, DC.

Chase Manhattan Bank NA v Israel-British Bank (London) Ltd [1979] 3 All ER 1025, [1981] Ch 105, [1980] 2 WLR 202.

Clarke v Shee and Johnson (1774) 1 Cowp 197, 98 ER 1041.

Dennis (a bankrupt), Re [1995] 3 All ER 171, [1996] Ch 80, [1995] 3 WLR 367, CA.

Gunsbourg, Re [1920] 2 KB 426, sub nom *Re A Gunsbourg & Co Ltd, ex p Cook* [1920] All ER Rep 492, CA.

Hart, Re, ex p Green [1912] 3 KB 6, CA.

Hooson, Ex p, re Chapman & Shaw (1872) LR 8 Ch App 231.

Lipkin Gorman (a firm) v Karpnale Ltd [1992] 4 All ER 512, [1991] 2 AC 548, [1991] 3 WLR 10, HL.

Pollitt, Re, ex p Minor [1893] 1 QB 455, CA.

Taylor v Plumer (1815) 3 M & S 562, [1814–23] All ER Rep 167, 105 ER 721.

Cases also cited or referred to in skeleton arguments
Boscawen v Bajwa, Abbey National plc v Boscawen [1995] 4 All ER 769, [1996] 1 WLR 328, CA.

Clark (a bankrupt), Re, ex p trustee of the property of the bankrupt v Texaco Ltd [1975] 1 All ER 453, [1975] 1 WLR 559.

Dent (a bankrupt), Re, Trustee of the property of the bankrupt v Dent [1994] 2 All ER 904, [1994] 1 WLR 956, DC.

Diplock's Estate, Re, Diplock v White [1948] 2 All ER 318, [1948] Ch 465, CA; *affd* sub nom *Ministry of Health v Simpson* [1950] 2 All ER 1137, [1951] AC 251, HL.

Gray's Inn Construction Co Ltd, Re [1980] 1 All ER 814, [1980] 1 WLR 711, CA.

Hirth, Re, ex p the trustee [1899] 1 QB 612, CA.

James, Ex p, re Condon (1874) LR 9 Ch App 609, [1874–80] All ER Rep 388, CA.

Matthews (F B & C H) Ltd, Re [1982] 1 All ER 338, [1982] Ch 257, CA.

South Tyneside Metropolitan BC v Svenska International plc [1995] 1 All ER 545.

Westdeutsche Landesbank Girozentrale v Islington London BC [1994] 4 All ER 890, [1994] 1 WLR 938, CA; *rvsd* [1996] 2 All ER 961, [1996] 2 WLR 802, HL.

Appeal
By notice dated 7 April 1995 the defendant, Anne Jones, appealed from the decision of John Cherryman QC, sitting as a deputy judge of the High Court in the Cardiff District Registry, on 24 March 1995 whereby he ordered, inter alia, that certain moneys which had been paid into court be declared the property of

a the plaintiff, the trustee in bankruptcy of the property of F C Jones & Sons (a firm), and be paid out to him. The facts are set out in the judgment of Millett LJ.

James K Quirke (instructed by *Thursfields*, Kidderminster) for Mrs Jones.
Stephen Davies (instructed by *Eversheds*, Cardiff) for the trustee.

b **MILLETT LJ** (delivering the first judgment at the invitation of Nourse LJ). The firm of F C Jones & Sons carried on business as potato growers. There were three partners, Messrs F C Jones, F W J Jones and A C Jones. In 1984 the firm got into financial difficulties. A supplier obtained judgment against it. The judgment was not satisfied and a bankruptcy notice was issued. The partners failed to comply with the notice and thereby committed an act of bankruptcy. The judgment c creditor presented a bankruptcy petition, a receiving order was made and in due course the partners were adjudicated bankrupt.

In the meantime, that is to say after the act of bankruptcy and before the adjudication, Mrs Jones, the wife of Mr F W J Jones, opened an account with a firm of commodity brokers in order to deal on the London potato futures market. d Into this account she paid the proceeds of three cheques totalling £11,700. The cheques were all drawn by Mrs Jones' husband on the joint account of himself and Mr A C Jones at the local branch of Midland Bank.

Mrs Jones' dealings in potato futures proved to be highly profitable. She received two cheques totalling £50,760 from the commodity brokers and paid them into a call deposit account which she opened at R Raphael & Sons plc e (Raphaels). She allowed Mr F W J Jones to withdraw £900 from the account, leaving a balance of £49,860. Shortly afterwards the Official Receiver informed Raphaels of his claim to the money in the account. Mrs Jones immediately demanded the release of the money and Raphaels interpleaded.

Pursuant to an order made on the interpleader summons the money held by f Raphaels was paid into court and issues between the rival claimants were directed to be tried with the trustee in bankruptcy as plaintiff and Mrs Jones as defendant. In 1986 the proceedings were transferred to the Chancery Division where, after an unexplained lapse of nine years, they came on for hearing before Mr Cherryman QC, sitting as a deputy judge of the High Court in that division. g He found in favour of the trustee and ordered that the money in court be paid out to him. Mrs Jones now appeals from his decision.

The trustee's case, as presently formulated, is simplicity itself. The money in court represents the proceeds of Mrs Jones' successful speculation with the £11,700 which she received from her husband. The £11,700, in turn, was paid to her out of the joint account of two of the partners, who were afterwards h adjudicated bankrupt. The money was drawn from the joint account after the date of the act of bankruptcy on which the receiving order was made. All this is undisputed. But, says the trustee, the money in the joint account had already vested in him, for under s 37 of the Bankruptcy Act 1914 his title to the assets of the bankrupts related back to the date of the act of bankruptcy. Accordingly, Mrs j Jones never acquired any title to the money. The money which she received from her husband belonged to the trustee, and the money in court represents the proceeds of her successful speculation with his money.

The trustee submits that his title to the money in court is clear and unimpeachable unless Mrs Jones can take advantage of s 45 of the 1914 Act by proving (a) that she was paid the £11,700 as a creditor of the firm, and (b) that at

the time she received the money she had no notice of any available act of
bankruptcy. Counsel for Mrs Jones has disclaimed any contention that she was a
creditor of the firm, and he concedes that the trustee's claim is bound to succeed
in relation to the original sum of £11,700 with interest thereon. But, he submits,
the trustee cannot recover the profits which Mrs Jones made by the use of the
money because he cannot maintain a proprietary claim in equity, and he cannot
maintain a proprietary claim in equity because he cannot establish the existence
of a fiduciary relationship between Mrs Jones and the trustee.

Counsel for Mrs Jones submits that all claims by a trustee or liquidator to
recover payments to third parties, whether as fraudulent preferences (which are
voidable) or as dispositions by a company made after the commencement of the
winding up (which are void), must be made by way of an action for money had
and received; that this, being an action at law, is a personal claim; that it does not
matter whether the transaction which is impugned was void or merely voidable;
and that, in the absence of a constructive trust or fiduciary relationship which
would justify the intervention of equity, the trustee cannot recover the proceeds
of the profitable investment by the recipient of the money which he received.

The judge thought that Mrs Jones was a constructive trustee. He said:

'... the trustee really has no problem in establishing a fiduciary
relationship. In my view where, as here (due to the effect of the doctrine of
relation back), A pays B's money to C, B retains the beneficial title to the
money and C becomes a bare trustee (see *Chase Manhattan Bank NA v
Israel-British Bank (London) Ltd* [1979] 3 All ER 1025 at 1032, [1981] Ch 105 at
119).'

Founding himself on that reasoning, the deputy judge applied the equitable rules
of tracing.

It is, however, in my view plain that Mrs Jones did not receive the money in a
fiduciary capacity and that she did not become a constructive trustee. The deputy
judge's conclusion presupposes that A (who in this case is the bankrupts) had a
legal title to transfer. In the present case, however, the bankrupts had been
divested of all title by statute. Mr F W J Jones had no title at all in law or equity
to the money in the joint account at Midland Bank, and could confer no title on
Mrs Jones.

While, however, I accept the submissions of counsel for Mrs Jones that she did
not become a constructive trustee, I do not accept the proposition that the trustee
in bankruptcy is unable to recover the profits which Mrs Jones made by the use
of his money unless she can be shown to have received it in one or other of the
two capacities mentioned; nor do I consider it necessary for him to invoke the
assistance of equity in order to maintain his claim. In short, I do not accept the
main submission of counsel that the only action at law which was available to the
trustee was an action against Mrs Jones for money had and received.

It is, in my view, unhelpful to categorise the payment of the £11,700 to Mrs
Jones as either 'void' or 'voidable'. Neither term is strictly accurate. In order to
see why this is so it is necessary to consider the effect of the doctrine of relation
back under the old bankruptcy law. I recently had occasion to examine this in
detail in *Re Dennis (a bankrupt)* [1995] 3 All ER 171 at 190, [1996] Ch 80 at 104,
where I said:

'It is clear from the authorities that the relation back of the trustee's title
did not merely make the title of the debtor himself, or any person claiming

a   through the debtor, defeasible in the event of adjudication. If the debtor was
adjudicated bankrupt, then as from the date of the act of bankruptcy neither
the debtor nor any such person claiming under him who could not bring
himself within the protective provisions of the Bankruptcy Acts had any title
at all; as from that date title was vested in the trustee. The position of the
debtor and persons who claimed under him during the intermediate period
b   was extremely curious. They did not possess a defeasible title, but either an
indefeasible title if the act of bankruptcy was not followed by adjudication or
no title at all if it was. Outside the law of bankruptcy no similar ambulatory
title was known to the law.'

In saying this I was summarising the law expounded by this court in *Re Gunsbourg*
c   [1920] 2 KB 426, [1920] All ER Rep 492. In that case the debtor transferred his
assets to a company which he had formed. He afterwards committed an act of
bankruptcy on which he was adjudicated bankrupt. The company had sold some
of the assets which it had acquired from the debtor to a bona fide purchaser
without notice of the act of bankruptcy. The trustee impugned the transfer to the
company, which was held to be fraudulent and void and to constitute an act of
d   bankruptcy. The trustee then sought to recover from the purchaser the assets
which he had acquired from the company after the act of bankruptcy. The court
held that the title of the trustee related back to the earlier act of bankruptcy,
which consisted of the transfer to the company, and that neither the company nor
any subsequent purchaser could establish any title against the trustee. It was a
e   hard case, because the defendant was a bona fide purchaser without notice of the
act of bankruptcy; but he was unable to bring himself within the protective
provisions of s 45 of the 1914 Act, which were limited to persons who had dealt
directly with the bankrupt.

Lord Sterndale MR explained the way in which the doctrine of relation back
f   operated as follows ([1920] 2 KB 426 at 438, [1920] All ER Rep 492 at 495–496):

'If this be correct the position is exactly the same as if the bankrupt had
been in possession of goods belonging to another person, to which he had no
title, and had sold them to the original transferee who had then resold them.
In such a case neither the original nor any of the subsequent transferees
g   would take any title at all, and the true owner could recover the goods from
anyone in whose possession he found them. I know of no doctrine of law or
equity which would relieve any of the transferees in these circumstances. It
was however argued that this statement of Lord Esher cannot be taken to its
full extent and that it must be confined to avoiding dealings with his property
by the bankrupt himself after the date of relation back. This was founded on
h   the argument that the original transfer was not void but only voidable, and
that therefore any bona-fide purchase from the original transferee was
protected. I am not sure that void and voidable are quite apt expressions, but
clearly the transfer was not void at the moment it was made, for it might be
that no circumstances would ever arise in which a trustee's title would
j   accrue or the bankruptcy law apply. I will assume that voidable is a correct
expression to describe the nature of the transaction, and then it becomes
necessary to ascertain the effect of the avoidance caused by the making of the
receiving order. This seems to me to be quite different from the effect of
avoidance in the ordinary case of a voidable transfer where no principles of
bankruptcy law apply. In this latter case the title of the person avoiding the

transaction arises only from the time when he elects to avoid, and therefore
intervening bona-fide transactions are protected because the transferor up to
the date of avoidance had and could confer a good title. In the case under
consideration so soon as the receiving order is made the trustee at once gets
a title which relates back to the earliest act of bankruptcy within three
months of the receiving order, whether it be the one upon which the
receiving order is made or not, and therefore his position and rights are
entirely different from those of an ordinary person who elects to avoid a
voidable transaction.'

Warrington LJ cited the decision in *Re Hart, ex p Green* [1912] 3 KB 6 and
distinguished it on the ground that there the original disposal by the debtor was
prior to the act of bankruptcy, though the later transfer by the disponee to the
defendant was after it. In such a case the trustee could not succeed against a
transferee for value without notice. He continued ([1920] 2 KB 426 at 446, [1920]
All ER Rep 492 at 500):

> 'This seems to me to have no application to such a case as the present in
> which the effect of the subsequent bankruptcy is, without more, to vest the
> property in the trustee as from a date anterior to the dealing impeached …
> The statutory transfer passes the legal property in the goods to the trustee as
> from the commencement of the bankruptcy, and subsequent sales thereof by
> any person other than the trustee can confer no property on the purchaser
> …'

As I pointed out in *Re Dennis* [1995] 4 All ER 171 at 190, [1996] Ch 80 at 103:

> 'This could not be clearer. The transfer to the company constituted an act
> of bankruptcy. Had no adjudication followed, the transfer would have
> passed title to the company. It might still have been possible for the creditors
> to impugn it as a fraudulent conveyance, but then it could not have been
> avoided as against a bona fide purchaser for value without notice. The
> relation back of the trustee's title, however, did not strictly render the
> transaction either void or voidable; it operated automatically to divest the
> debtor at the date of the act of bankruptcy of any title to pass to the
> transferee, and this enabled the trustee to prevail against anyone who could
> not bring himself within the protective provisions of s 45.'

Accordingly, as from the date of the act of bankruptcy, the money in the
bankrupts' joint account at Midland Bank belonged to the trustee. The account
holders had no title to it at law or in equity. The cheques which they drew in
favour of Mrs Jones were not 'void' or 'voidable' but, in the events which
happened, they were incapable of passing any legal or equitable title. They were
not, however, without legal effect, for the bank honoured them. The result was
to affect the identity of the debtor but not the creditor and to put Mrs Jones in
possession of funds to which she had no title. A debt formally owed by Midland
Bank apparently to Messrs F W J Jones and A C Jones but in reality to their trustee
ultimately became a debt owed by Raphaels apparently to Mrs Jones but in reality
to the trustee.

What is the result? If the cheques had passed the legal title to Mrs Jones but not
the beneficial ownership, she would have received the money as constructive
trustee and be liable to a proprietary restitutionary claim in equity (sometimes,
though inaccurately, described as a tracing claim). Mrs Jones would have been

a obliged, not merely to account for the £11,700 which she had received, but to hand over the £11,700 in specie to the trustee. Her position would have been no different from that of an express trustee who held the money in trust for the trustee; or from that of Mr Reid in *A-G for Hong Kong v Reid* [1994] 1 All ER 1, [1994] 1 AC 324 whose liability to account for the profits which he made from investing a bribe was based on his obligation to pay it over to his principal as soon *b* as he received it. The existence of any such obligation has been disputed by commentators, but no one disputes that, if the obligation exists, it carries with it the duty to pay over or account for any profits made by the use of the money.

But Mrs Jones was not a constructive trustee. She had no legal title to the money. She had no title to it at all. She was merely in possession; that is to say, in a position to deal with it even though it did not belong to her. Counsel for Mrs *c* Jones says that it follows that she cannot be made liable to any kind of proprietary claim. He relies strongly for this purpose on *Ex p Hooson, re Chapman & Shaw* (1872) LR 8 Ch App 231, followed in *Re Bishop, ex p Claxton* (1891) 8 Morr 221, which are both cases concerned with fraudulent preference. In each case the debtor had paid a debt on the eve of his bankruptcy, the payment was found to *d* be a fraudulent preference and the creditor was ordered to repay the amount in question to the trustee in bankruptcy. The creditor failed to do so and was committed to prison under the Debtors Act 1869. That Act had abolished imprisonment for debt, but there were exceptions. One exception was 'default by a trustee or person acting in a fiduciary capacity'. The court held that there was no fiduciary relationship between the debtor and his creditors, still less *e* between the creditor whose debt was paid and the rest of the creditors. Given the fact that the payment was good when made and that it continued to bind the debtor himself, being voidable only at the instance of the trustee in bankruptcy, the conclusion was perhaps inevitable.

But those were cases in which the payment was valid when made and passed *f* a good though defeasible title to the recipient. He obtained legal title to the money and, since he was not a trustee, equitable title as well. He was free to deal with the money on his own account as he pleased. If he made a profit from the use of his own money, he was entitled to keep it. If he became bankrupt, the money would form part of his estate and the debtor's trustee would have to prove in his bankruptcy for the amount claimed. The present case is entirely *g* different. Mrs Jones had no title at all, at law or in equity. If she became bankrupt, the money would not vest in her trustee. But this would not be because it was trust property; it would be because it was not her property at all. If she made a profit, how could she have any claim to the profit made by the use of someone else's money?

h In my judgment she could not. If she were to retain the profit made by the use of the trustee's money, then, in the language of the modern law of restitution, she would be unjustly enriched at the expense of the trustee. If she were a constructive trustee of the money, a court of equity, as a court of conscience, would say that it was unconscionable for her to lay claim to the profit made by *j* the use of her beneficiary's money. It would, however, be a mistake to suppose that the common law courts disregarded considerations of conscience. Lord Mansfield CJ, who did much to develop the early law of restitution at common law, founded it firmly on the basis of good conscience and unjust enrichment.

It would, in my judgment, be absurd if a person with no title at all were in a stronger position to resist a proprietary claim by the true owner than one with a

bare legal title. In the present case equity has no role to play. The trustee must
bring his claim at common law. It follows that, if he has to trace his money, he *a*
must rely on common law tracing rules, and that he has no proprietary *remedy*.
But it does not follow that he has no proprietary *claim*. His claim is exclusively
proprietary. He claims the money because it belongs to him at law or represents
profits made by the use of money which belonged to him at law.

The trustee submits that he has no need to trace, since the facts are clear and *b*
undisputed. Mrs Jones did not mix the money with her own. The trustee's
money remained identifiable as such throughout. But, of course, he does have to
trace it in order to establish that the money which he claims represents his
money. Counsel for Mrs Jones acknowledges that the trustee can successfully
trace his money into her account at Raphaels, for his concession in respect of the
£11,700 acknowledges this. I do not understand how his concession that the *c*
trustee is entitled to £11,700 of the money in court is reconcilable with his
submission that the only cause of action available to the trustee is an action for
money had and received. I say this for two reasons. In the first place, the trustee
has never brought such an action, and any such action would now be long out of
time. In the second place, in an action for money had and received it would be *d*
irrelevant what Mrs Jones had done with the money after she received it. Her
liability would be based on her receipt of the money, and she would be personally
liable to a money judgment for £11,700. But while the trustee would be entitled
to a money judgment for that sum, he would not be entitled to any particular sum
of £11,700 such as the money in court in specie.
                                                                    e
But in my judgment the concession that the trustee can trace the money at
common law is rightly made. There are no factual difficulties of the kind which
proved fatal in this court to the common law claim in *Agip (Africa) Ltd v Jackson*
[1992] 4 All ER 451, [1991] Ch 547. It is not necessary to trace the passage of the
money through the clearing system or the London potato futures market. The
money which Mrs Jones paid into her account with the commodity brokers *f*
represented the proceeds of cheques which she received from her husband.
Those cheques represented money in the bankrupts' joint account at Midland
Bank which belonged to the trustee.

In *Lipkin Gorman (a firm) v Karpnale Ltd* [1992] 4 All ER 512 at 528, [1991] 2 AC
548 at 573, Lord Goff held that the plaintiffs could trace or follow their 'property *g*
into its product' for this 'involves a decision by the owner of the original property
to assert his title to the product in place of his original property'. In that case the
original property was the plaintiffs' chose in action, a debt owed by the bank to
the plaintiffs. Lord Goff held that the plaintiffs could—
                                                                    h
'trace their property at common law in that chose in action, or in any part
of it, into its product, ie cash drawn by Cass from their client account at the
bank.' (See [1992] 4 All ER 512 at 529, [1991] 2 AC 548 at 574.)

Accordingly, the trustee can follow the money in the joint account at Midland
Bank, which had been vested by statute in him, into the proceeds of the three *j*
cheques which Mrs Jones received from her husband. The trustee does not need
to follow the money from one recipient to another or follow it through the
clearing system; he can follow the cheques as they pass from hand to hand. It is
sufficient for him to be able to trace the money into the cheques and the cheques
into their proceeds.

a   In *Agip (Africa) Ltd v Jackson* [1992] 4 All ER 385 at 398, [1990] Ch 265 at 285 I said that the ability of the common law to trace an asset into a changed form in the same hands was established in *Taylor v Plumer* (1815) 3 M & S 562, [1814–23] All ER Rep 167. Lord Ellenborough CJ in that case had said:

b
> '... the product of or substitute for the original thing still follows the nature of the thing itself, as long as it can be ascertained to be such, and the right only ceases when the means of ascertainment fail, which is the case when the subject is turned into money, and mixed and confounded in a general mass of the same description.' (See 3 M & S 562 at 575, [1814–23] All ER Rep 167 at 171.)

c   In this it appears that I fell into a common error, for it has since been convincingly demonstrated that, although *Taylor v Plumer* was decided by a common law court, the court was in fact applying the rules of equity (see Lionel Smith, 'Tracing in *Taylor v Plumer*: Equity in the Court of King's Bench' (1995) LMCLQ 240).

   But this is no reason for concluding that the common law does not recognise claims to substitute assets or their products. Such claims were upheld by this *d* court in *Banque Belge pour l'Etranger v Hambrouck* [1921] 1 KB 321 and by the House of Lords in *Lipkin Gorman (a firm) v Karpnale Ltd* [1992] 4 All ER 512, [1991] 2 AC 548. It has been suggested by commentators that these cases are undermined by their misunderstanding of *Taylor v Plumer*, but that is not how the English doctrine of stare decisis operates. It would be more consistent with that doctrine *e* to say that, in recognising claims to substituted assets, equity must be taken to have followed the law, even though the law was not declared until later. Lord Ellenborough CJ gave no indication that, in following assets into their exchange products, equity had adopted a rule which was peculiar to itself or which went further than the common law.

   There is no merit in having distinct and differing tracing rules at law and in *f* equity, given that tracing is neither a right nor a remedy but merely the process by which the plaintiff establishes what has happened to his property and makes good his claim that the assets which he claims can properly be regarded as representing his property. The fact that there are different tracing rules at law and in equity is unfortunate though probably inevitable, but unnecessary *g* differences should not be created where they are not required by the different nature of legal and equitable doctrines and remedies. There is, in my view, even less merit in the present rule which precludes the invocation of the equitable tracing rules to support a common law claim; until that rule is swept away unnecessary obstacles to the development of a rational and coherent law of restitution will remain.

h
   Given that the trustee can trace his money at Midland Bank into the money in Mrs Jones' account with the commodity brokers, can he successfully assert a claim to that part of the money which represents the profit made by the use of his money? I have no doubt that, in the particular circumstances of this case, he can. There is no need to trace through the dealings on the London potato futures *j* market. If Mrs Jones, as the nominal account holder, had any entitlement to demand payment from the brokers, this was because of the terms of the contract which she made with them. Under the terms of that contract it is reasonable to infer that the brokers were authorised to deal in potato futures on her account, to debit her account with losses and to credit it with profits, and to pay her only the balance standing to her account. It is, in my opinion, impossible to separate

the chose in action constituted by the deposit of the trustee's money on those
terms from the terms upon which it was deposited. The chose in action, which   *a*
was vested in Mrs Jones' name but which in reality belonged to the trustee, was
not a right to payment from the brokers of the original amount deposited but a
right to claim the balance, whether greater or less than the amounted deposited;
and it is to that chose in action that the trustee now lays claim.

Given, then, that the trustee has established his legal claim to the £11,700 and   *b*
the profits earned by the use of his money, and has located the money, first, in
Mrs Jones' account with the commodity brokers and, later, in Mrs Jones' account
at Raphaels, I am satisfied that the common law has adequate remedies to enable
him to recover his property. He did not need to sue Mrs Jones; and he did not do
so. He was entitled to bring an action for debt against Raphaels and obtain an
order for payment. When he threatened to do so, Raphaels interpleaded, and the   *c*
issue between the trustee and Mrs Jones was which of them could give a good
receipt to Raphaels. That depended upon which of them had the legal title to the
chose in action. The money now being in court, the court can grant an
appropriate declaration and make an order for payment.

In my judgment, the trustee was entitled at law to the money in the joint   *d*
account of the bankrupts at Midland Bank, which had vested in him by statute.
He was similarly entitled to the balance of the money in Mrs Jones' account with
the commodity brokers, and the fact that it included profits made by the use of
that money is immaterial. He was similarly entitled to the money in Mrs Jones'
account at Raphaels and able to give them a good receipt for the money. Mrs
Jones never had any interest, legal or equitable, in any of those moneys. The   *e*
trustee is plainly entitled to the money in court and the judge was right to order
that it be paid out to him.

I would dismiss the appeal.

BELDAM LJ. I too would dismiss the appeal.   *f*

Millett LJ has set out the full facts of the case and has referred to the relevant
cases. The question for the court is whether Mrs Jones can retain profits from
dealing with £11,700 which in law belonged to the trustee in bankruptcy of F C
Jones & Sons. In *Re Dennis (a bankrupt)* [1995] 3 All ER 171, [1996] Ch 80 this court
held that where a debtor was adjudicated bankrupt the trustee's title to the
debtor's property related back to the first available act of bankruptcy and, further,   *g*
that it divested the debtor of title from that date. That decision, as Millett LJ has
indicated, was based on the judgment of this court in *Re Gunsbourg* [1920] 2 KB
426, [1920] All ER Rep 492. Lord Sterndale MR, after referring to Lord Esher
MR's judgment in *Re Pollitt, ex p Minor* [1893] 1 QB 455 at 457, said of the effect of
the relation back ([1920] 2 KB 426 at 438, [1920] All ER Rep 492 at 495):   *h*

> 'If this be correct the position is exactly the same as if the bankrupt had
> been in possession of goods belonging to another person, to which he had no
> title, and had sold them to the original transferee who had then resold them.
> In such a case neither the original nor any of the subsequent transferees
> would take any title at all, and the true owner could recover the goods from   *j*
> anyone in whose possession he found them. I know of no doctrine of law or
> equity which would relieve any of the transferees in these circumstances.'

At the date of the act of bankruptcy the partners apparently held an account with
Midland Bank which was sufficiently in credit to provide for the payment of three

a cheques totalling £11,700 to Mrs Jones, who deposited the cheques for collection with Drexel Burnham Lambert for the purpose of dealing in the London potato futures market. She subsequently gave instructions for investment of the money in various futures dealings, and was successful to the extent that the sum of £11,700 eventually increased to over £50,000. That amount having been paid to her, she deposited it in an account with Raphaels. The trustee in bankruptcy then

b claimed the asset represented by the balance standing to the credit of that account. It was argued that the trustee in bankruptcy could validly trace the original £11,700 through the account with Drexel Burnham Lambert and into the account with Raphaels, but to no greater extent could he claim the sum then standing to the credit of the account.

c There is now ample authority for the proposition that a person who can trace his property into its product, provided the product is identifiable as the product of his property, may lay legal claim to that property. As Lord Goff said in *Lipkin Gorman (a firm) v Karpnale Ltd* [1992] 4 All ER 512 at 528, [1991] 2 AC 548 at 573:

d 'Of course, "tracing" or "following" property into its product involves a decision by the owner of the original property to assert his title to the product in place of his original property.'

In my view, therefore, the trustee in this case could assert legal title to the debt which was due from Raphaels on the account represented by the original £11,700 and the proceeds of dealing with it.

e At no time did Mrs Jones have any legal or beneficial title to any of the sums paid into that account. It was argued by Mr Quirke that, because she had given the instructions for the futures dealings with the money, she was entitled to the profits which had accrued. He argued that, because Mrs Jones had no legal or equitable title, she could retain profits made by the use of the property which, had

f she had a legal title, she would have been bound to pay to the trustee. I cannot assent to this apparent absurdity. In my view she at no time had any legal title or equitable right to the property or to profits made by dealing with it. The trustee was legally entitled to the balance due from Raphaels on the account and not just to the sum of £11,700 originally deposited with Drexel Burnham Lambert.

I too would dismiss the appeal.

g

NOURSE LJ. I also agree that the appeal must be dismissed.

I recognise that our decision goes further than that of the House of Lords in *Lipkin Gorman (a firm) v Karpnale Ltd* [1992] 4 All ER 512, [1991] 2 AC 548, in that

h it holds that the action for money had and received entitles the legal owner to trace his property into its product, not only in the sense of property for which it is exchanged, but also in the sense of property representing the original and the profit made by the defendant's use of it.

Millett LJ has explained how that extension is justified on the particular facts of this case. But there is, I think, a broader justification to be found in the seminal

j judgment of Lord Mansfield CJ in *Clarke v Shee and Johnson* (1774) 1 Cowp 197 at 199–200, 98 ER 1041 at 1042, where he said of the action for money had and received:

'This is a liberal action in the nature of a bill in equity; and if, under the circumstances of the case, it appears that the defendant cannot in conscience retain what is the subject-matter of it, the plaintiff may well support this action.'

a

In my view, Mrs Jones cannot in conscience retain the profit any more than the original £11,700. She had no title to the original. She could not have made the profit without her use of it. She cannot, by making a profit through the use of money to which she had no title, acquire some better title to the profit.

b

Appeal dismissed. Leave to appeal to the House of Lords refused.

L I Zysman Esq   Barrister.

a
Kleinwort Benson Ltd v Birmingham City Council

b
COURT OF APPEAL, CIVIL DIVISION

EVANS, SAVILLE AND MORRITT LJJ

6, 7 MARCH, 9 MAY 1996

Contract – Failure of consideration – Recovery of money paid – Defence of passing on
c *or windfall gain – Local authority and bank entering into interest rate swap agreement*
– Bank hedging liabilities under other contracts and recouping part or whole of losses –
Agreement ultra vires local authority and void – Bank claiming in restitution for unjust
enrichment of local authority – Whether local authority unjustly enriched at expense of
bank – Whether local authority entitled to raise defence of passing on or windfall gain
d *in reliance on bank's hedging arrangements.*

In 1982 the defendant local authority entered into an interest rate swap contract
with the plaintiff bank. Such contracts were subsequently ruled by the House of
Lords to be ultra vires local authorities and void and the bank thereafter brought
an action against the local authority claiming restitution of £353,321·91, being the
e net amount it had paid to the local authority under the contract, on the basis of
unjust enrichment. The local authority applied for leave to amend its defence in
order to raise the defence of passing on (or windfall gain), ie that by reason of the
bank's own independent hedging arrangements, whereby it entered into various
parallel contracts with third parties designed to offset any risk arising from its
f contract with the local authority, the bank had not in fact suffered any or any
substantial loss as a result of the swaps transaction with the local authority. The
judge refused the application and entered final judgment for the bank. The local
authority appealed, contending principally that, in considering the bank's right to
restitution, the court had to take into account related transactions, which in the
instant case included any hedging arrangements entered into in order to protect
g the bank from suffering losses under the swaps contract.

Held – In order to establish a claim in restitution a plaintiff had to show that the
defendant had been unjustly enriched at the plaintiff's expense. That issue had to
h be determined by reference to the payer/payee relationship alone without any
regard to related transactions entered into by the payer with third parties; the
payee's obligation, which was correlative to the payer's right to restitution, was
to repay the amount he had received which it was unjust that he should keep, and
it would be inconsistent with the principle of repayment to give the concept of
loss a wider meaning equivalent to 'overall losses on the transaction'.
j Accordingly, no account was to be taken of the bank's hedging arrangements,
which were in any event too remote. It followed that the defence of passing on
(or windfall gain) was not available to the local authority and its appeal would
accordingly be dismissed (see p 741 *e f h*, p 742 *e f j* to p 743 *a c h* and p 750 *d*, post).

Kleinwort Benson Ltd v South Tyneside Metropolitan BC [1994] 4 All ER 972
approved.

Notes

For quasi-contract and restitution in the context of a failure of consideration, see   *a*
9 *Halsbury's Laws* (4th edn) paras 667–672.

Cases referred to in judgments

Air Canada v British Columbia (1989) 59 DLR (4th) 161, Can SC.

Amministrazione delle Finanze dello Stato v San Giorgio Case 199/82 [1983] ECR   *b*
3595.

Banque Belge pour l'Etranger v Hambrouck [1921] 1 KB 321, CA.

*British Westinghouse Electric and Manufacturing Co Ltd v Underground Electric
Railways Co of London Ltd* [1912] AC 673, [1911–13] All ER Rep 63, HL.

Chase Manhattan Bank NA v Israel-British Bank (London) Ltd [1979] 3 All ER 1025,   *c*
[1981] Ch 105, [1980] 2 WLR 202.

Comr of State Revenue v Royal Insurance Australia Ltd (1994) 126 ALR 1, Aust HC.

EC Commission v Italy Case 104/86 [1988] ECR 1799.

Fibrosa Spolka Akcyjna v Fairbairn Lawson Combe Barbour Ltd [1942] 2 All ER 122,
[1943] AC 32, HL.

Fils (Les) de Jules Bianco SA v Directeur Général des Douanes et des Droits Indirects Case   *d*
331/85 [1988] ECR 1099.

*Friends' Provident Life Office v Hillier Parker May & Rowden (a firm) (Estates and
General plc and ors, third parties)* [1995] 4 All ER 260, CA.

Hanover Shoe Inc v United Shoe Machinery Corp (1968) 392 US 481, US SC.

Hazell v Hammersmith and Fulham London BC [1991] 1 All ER 545, [1992] AC 1,   *e*
[1991] 2 WLR 372, HL; *rvsg* [1990] 3 All ER 33, [1990] 2 QB 697, [1990] 2 WLR
1038, CA.

Hussey v Eels [1990] 1 All ER 449, [1990] 2 QB 227, [1990] 2 WLR 234, CA.

Jones (R E) Ltd v Waring & Gillow Ltd [1926] AC 670, [1926] All ER Rep 36, HL.

Kelly v Solari (1841) 9 M & W 54, [1835–42] All ER Rep 320, 152 ER 24.   *f*

Kleinwort Benson Ltd v South Tyneside Metropolitan BC [1994] 4 All ER 972.

Lipkin Gorman (a firm) v Karpnale Ltd [1992] 4 All ER 512, [1991] 2 AC 548, [1991]
3 WLR 10, HL.

Mason v NSW (1959) 102 CLR 108, Aust HC.

Moses v Macferlan (1760) 2 Burr 1005, [1558–1774] All ER Rep 581, 97 ER 676.   *g*

123 East Fifty-Fourth Street Inc v US (1946) 157 F 2d 68, US Ct of Apps.

Pagnan (R) & Flli v Corbisa Industrial Agropacuaria Ltda [1971] 1 All ER 165, [1970]
1 WLR 1306, CA.

South Tyneside Metropolitan BC v Svenska International plc [1995] 1 All ER 545.

Westdeutsche Landesbank Girozentrale v Islington London BC, Kleinwort Benson Ltd v   *h*
Sandwell BC [1996] 2 All ER 961, HL; *rvsg* [1994] 4 All ER 890, [1994] 1 WLR 938,
CA; *affg in part* [1994] 4 All ER 890.

Woolwich Building Society v IRC (No 2) [1992] 3 All ER 737, [1993] AC 70, [1992] 3
WLR 366, HL.

Cases also cited or referred to in skeleton arguments   *j*

Allied Air Conditioning Inc v R (1994) 109 DLR (4th) 463, BC CA.

Cherubini Metal Works Ltd v Nova Scotia (1995) 137 NSR 2d 197, NS CA.

Customs and Excise Comrs v Fine Art Developments plc [1989] 1 All ER 502, [1989] AC
914, HL.

Sobeys Inc v Nova Scotia (1992) 112 NSR 2d 205, NS CA.

Appeal

a By notice dated 2 March 1995 Birmingham City Council (the local authority) appealed against the decision of Gatehouse J on 9 December 1994 whereby he refused leave for the local authority to amend its points of defence and counterclaim to the claim of Kleinwort Benson Ltd (the bank) for restitution to raise the defence of passing on or windfall gain and entered final judgment for the
b bank in the sum of £184,597·59. The facts are set out in the judgment of Evans LJ.

Nicholas Underhill QC and *Mark West* (instructed by *S A Dobson*, Birmingham) for the local authority.
Rhodri Davies (instructed by *Clifford Chance*) for the bank.

c   *Cur adv vult*

9 May 1996. The following judgments were delivered.

EVANS LJ. During the 1980s a number of local authorities entered the financial
d markets in order to trade in a new form of derivative, known as the interest rate swaps contract. Then the courts held that these contracts were ultra vires the local authorities and therefore void (see *Hazell v Hammersmith and Fulham London BC* [1991] 1 All ER 545, [1992] AC 1). That judgment launched what has been called a great raft of litigation (see Richard Nolan 'Change of position in anticipation of enrichment' (a commentary on *South Tyneside Metropolitan BC v*
e *Svenska International plc* [1995] 1 All ER 545) [1995] Lloyd's MCLQ 313 at 314). More than 100 writs were issued, mostly in the Commercial Court, claiming to recover the net amounts which had been paid out by one party or the other under the void contracts. In some cases the market rates of interest had moved against the local authorities, and they were the plaintiffs. In others, including the present,
f the banks had paid out more by way of differences than they had received, and they claimed to recover the net overpayment.

The right of recovery in both cases was established by a number of judgments, including that of Hobhouse J in *Kleinwort Benson Ltd v South Tyneside Metropolitan BC* [1994] 4 All ER 972 (*Swaps 2*). The claims fall within the principle of unjust enrichment, giving the plaintiffs a right to restitution which the courts have
g upheld.

The nature of an interest rate swaps contract was described in the judgment of Woolf LJ in the Divisional Court in *Hazell v Hammersmith and Fulham London BC* [1990] 3 All ER 33 at 63–66, [1990] 2 QB 697 at 739–743. The involvement of Kleinwort Benson, the present respondents (the bank), in this market was
h summarised in Hobhouse J's judgment in the *South Tyneside* (*Swaps 2*) case, based on the evidence given in that case. Although, as will appear below, no evidence was given in the present case, the bank accepts that Hobhouse J's summary is broadly accurate and relevant for present purposes.

j *These proceedings*
The bank claims to recover £353,321·91 as the net amount of payments made by it to the appellants, Birmingham City Council (the authority), under a swaps contract dated 23 September 1982 which ran until September 1987. The authority applied for leave to amend its points of defence so as to raise what has come to be known as the defence of 'passing on'. What this means for present purposes is that the authority seeks to assert that the bank has not in fact suffered

any, or any substantial loss as a result of these transactions. The reason given is
that the payments which the bank made to the authority and which it now claims   *a*
to recover were in fact matched by payments which it received from third parties
described as counter-parties under hedging arrangements which it made with
them. If those are the facts, says the authority, then the bank has suffered no, or
no substantial loss and its claim for restitution should fail.

This issue was raised in the *South Tyneside* proceedings and it was decided by   *b*
Hobhouse J in favour of the bank (see [1994] 4 All ER 972 at 987). In the present
case, Gatehouse J agreed with that judgment and refused the authority leave to
make the amendments which seek to raise this defence. The authority now
appeals, and so essentially this is an appeal against Hobhouse J's judgment on this
issue in the *South Tyneside* case.
                                                                                  c
Thus the form of 'passing on' alleged by the authority in the present case is the
bank's practice of hedging or otherwise covering itself against the risks inherent
in the swaps contract. Because there has been no discovery, the authority cannot
specify what arrangements of this sort were made in the present case, and so it
relies upon the general description of the bank's method of doing business to
which reference has already been made. There is no reason to suppose that the   *d*
method is atypical of other banks who were engaged in this market, and it would
be permissible to infer, even apart from Hobhouse J's judgment, that the bank did
hedge or cover the risks by one or more of the commercial means open to it.
Although it might take a position against the market to a limited extent or in
certain circumstances from time to time, the likelihood is that it conducted its   *e*
business so as to deal profitably by trade and counter-trade rather than expose
itself to market vagaries over the period in question.

Because the authority does not know what hedging or other arrangements the
bank did make, Mr Nicholas Underhill QC, for the authority, made his
submissions on two alternative bases; first, that the risks under this contract were
fully hedged by a further transaction with an identifiable counter-party, or   *f*
secondly, that the risks were covered to a greater or lesser extent and for part or
all of the period by some such arrangements made from time to time.

The law—general
                                                                                  g
The principle of unjust enrichment is recognised in English as in other systems
of law. It requires the recipient of money to repay it when the circumstances are
such that it is contrary to 'the ties of natural justice and equity' for him to retain
it (see Lord Mansfield CJ's celebrated dictum in *Moses v Macferlan* (1760) 2 Burr
1005 at 1012, [1558–1774] All ER Rep 581 at 585). How those circumstances may
be identified has been the subject of countless judicial decisions over the   *h*
centuries. A number of recognisable forms of action emerged from the mists of
legal history. These entitled the plaintiff to recover not damages, but a quantified
sum from a defendant who was not necessarily a wrongdoer and who was not
bound by any contract or express undertaking to pay the sum claimed by the
plaintiff. The circumstances in which such a non-contractual obligation can arise   *j*
are various; the recovery of money paid under a mistake of fact (though not,
historically and so far as English law is concerned, under a mistake of law), or
where the consideration in return for which the money was paid has failed, are
well established examples. Now, the mists have cleared still further. It is
recognised that these different forms spring from a single underlying principle,
which is described as the right to recover on grounds of unjust enrichment; that

a is to say, the defendant has been unjustly enriched by the payment made to him
and which the plaintiff seeks to recover.

The leading textbook authority defines the principle by reference, first, to Lord
Mansfield's dictum, and secondly, to the American Law Institute's *Restatement of
the Law, Restitution* (1937) (see Goff and Jones *The Law of Restitution* (4th edn,
1993) pp 12–13). Chapter 1 of the American *Restatement* reads simply as follows:

b   '§1. UNJUST ENRICHMENT   A person who has been unjustly enriched at the
      expense of another is required to make restitution to the other.'

That the principle forms part of English law has been authoritatively recognised
in two recent judgments of the House of Lords: *Lipkin Gorman (a firm) v Karpnale
c Ltd* [1992] 4 All ER 512, [1991] 2 AC 548 and *Woolwich Building Society v IRC (No 2)*
[1992] 3 All ER 737, [1993] AC 70.

Notwithstanding its roots in natural justice and equity, the principle does not
give the courts a discretionary power to order repayment whenever it seems in
the circumstance of the particular case just and equitable to do so:

d   'The recovery of money in restitution is not, as a general rule, a matter of
      discretion for the court. A claim to recover money at common law is made
      as a matter of right; and, even though the underlying principle of recovery is
      the principle of unjust enrichment, nevertheless, where recovery is denied,
      it is denied on the basis of legal principle.' (See *Lipkin Gorman* [1992] 4 All ER
      512 at 532, [1991] 2 AC 548 at 578 per Lord Goff.)

e
So the search for rules defining the circumstances in which the general principle
gives a remedy continues, and it is subject as always to the binding authority of
previous decisions. But the two House of Lords judgments recognise that this is
a developing area of the law and that the courts should be ready to apply the
f general principle when it is appropriate and consistent with authority to do so.
This applies to the scope of defences as well as to the extent of the plaintiff's right
of recovery. Later in his speech in *Lipkin Gorman* Lord Goff said, in relation to the
defendants' contention that they had 'changed their position' after or by reason
of receiving the payments in question and therefore should not be required to
refund them:

g
      'I am most anxious that, in recognising this defence to actions of
      restitution, nothing should be said at this stage to inhibit the development of
      the defence on a case by case basis, in the usual way.' (See [1992] 4 All ER
      512 at 534, [1991] 2 AC 548 at 580.)

h
Swaps cases
      The significance of *Westdeutsche Landesbank Girozentrale v Islington London BC,
Kleinwort Benson Ltd v Sandwell BC* [1994] 4 All ER 890, [1994] 1 WLR 938 (*Swaps
1*) (in which the judgment of Hobhouse J was upheld by the Court of Appeal), was
j that the plaintiff banks were held to have a right of recovery on the ground that
the swaps contracts being ultra vires the local authorities were void and of no
effect in law. This meant that in law no consideration was given for the payments
and the principle of unjust enrichment applied. The reasoning has been criticised
but there has been no appeal on this issue to the House of Lords, although an
appeal there on another issue is pending (see William Swadling 'Restitution for
No Consideration' (1994) 2 RLR 73).

It is also established that the right of recovery is limited to the net amount by which payments made under the void contracts have exceeded payments *a* received under them. This is because the payments received, although in respect of sums which became due from the opposing party at different dates from the payments made by the plaintiffs, nevertheless count as repayments of those amounts:

> 'Where payments both ways have been made the correct view is to treat *b* the later payment as, pro tanto, repayment of the earlier sum paid by the other party.' (See [1994] 4 All ER 890 at 929 per Hobhouse J.)

Either the bank or the local authority may be the plaintiff, depending on what payments have been made between them, and the same legal principles apply in both cases, although as the present appeal illustrates their application may be *c* different as between them.

The issue here is whether what is called the defence of passing on is available when the plaintiff is the bank. The hedging operations which it carries out in the normal course of its operations are not ones which would normally be undertaken by a local authority. But the same principle would apply if the local *d* authority was the plaintiff and the bank as defendant contended that because of a hedging operation or for any other reason the authority had not suffered the depletion of its assets which it is said is essential to found a claim. The essence of the defence is that the plaintiff ought not to recover the payment which has 'unjustly' enriched the defendant, if the result of restitution would be that the plaintiff, not being out of pocket, would himself receive a 'windfall gain' (see *e* *Comr of State Revenue v Royal Insurance Australia Ltd* (1994) 126 ALR 1 at 27 per Brennan J).

When the bank is plaintiff, as it is here, and its hedging activities have resulted in its making good part or all of the shortfall in payments by the local authority, then those activities become relevant if the authority raises this defence. The *f* converse situation arises if the bank is defendant, as it wrongly thought that it was (to the authority's counterclaim) in the *Westdeutsche Landesbank* case, and raises the 'change of position' defence. That defence was considered both in *Westdeutsche Landesbank* and in *South Tyneside Metropolitan BC v Svenska International plc* [1995] 1 All ER 545 at 558–568 per Clarke J and in both cases it failed. Whether those decisions are relevant to the present case is one of the *g* matters that has been raised in argument before us.

It is not disputed that the hedging arrangements, whatever form they take, are separate and independent contracts, not in any way conditional upon or related to the swaps contract itself. This is so, even if the hedge is a perfect match, ie the mirror image of the swaps contract, apart from the bank's profit or 'turn'. *h*

'Passing on' or 'windfall gain'

This defence has been considered by the Supreme Court of Canada in *Air Canada v British Columbia* (1989) 59 DLR (4th) 161 and twice by the High Court of Australia in *Mason v NSW* (1959) 102 CLR 108 and *Comr of State Revenue v Royal* *j* *Insurance Australia Ltd* (1994) 126 ALR 1. In these, as in numerous US authorities, the claim was for repayment of overpaid tax (in *Mason*'s case, statutory dues paid as fees). In such cases, the defence is raised when the plaintiff taxpayer has passed on the burden of the tax to his own customers and he will be under no obligation to reimburse them if he succeeds in recovering the tax which he has paid. Then it can be said that repayment will result in a windfall gain for him, or conversely,

a   that the benefit to the taxing authority even if it is properly regarded as 'unjust
enrichment' has not been at the taxpayer's expense.

Whether the defence is available in taxation cases under English law must be
regarded as uncertain. The taxpayer's right to recover tax paid under a void
statutory instrument was upheld in *Woolwich Building Society v IRC (No 2)* [1992]
3 All ER 737 at 764, [1993] AC 70 at 177, where Lord Goff said this with regard to
b   a passing on defence :

'It will be a matter for consideration whether the fact that the plaintiff has
passed on the tax or levy so that the burden has fallen on another should
provide a defence to his claim. Although this is contemplated by the Court
of Justice of the European Communities in [*Amministrazione delle Finanze
c   dello Stato v San Giorgio* Case 199/82 [1983] ECR 3595], it is evident from *Air
Canada v British Columbia* that the point is not without its difficulties; and the
availability of such a defence may depend upon the nature of the tax or other
levy.'

d   Lord Goff then referred to pending consultations by the Law Commission. Its
report, *Restitution: mistakes of law and ultra vires public authority receipts and
payments*   (Law Com No 227) (1994), has now been published and its
recommendations include '(20) it should be a defence to claims for the repayment
of taxes overpaid as a result of mistake that repayment will unjustly enrich the
claimant' (cf para 21 dealing with ultra vires claims). A statutory scheme has this
e   effect with regard to value added tax (VAT) (see the Value Added Tax Act 1994,
s 80(3)). But the Law Commission expressly excluded questions arising under
swaps contracts from its consideration and so there is nothing in its report of
direct relevance to the present case (see Law Com No 227, para 1·11).

Apparently there is no reported authority from Canada, Australia or the United
f   States where the defence has been raised, except to a claim for overpaid tax and
apart from an anti-trust suit in the United States where the defence was rejected
by the Supreme Court (see *Hanover Shoe Inc v United Shoe Machinery Corp* (1968)
392 US 481).

In my judgment, the taxation cases are of limited assistance in addressing the
question of general principle which is raised by the present appeal. There is a
g   public law element involved in them (see *Air Canada v British Columbia* (1989) 59
DLR (4th) 161 at 170 per Wilson J) and a further question, akin to agency, which
is whether the taxpayer should be regarded as having collected tax from his
customers on behalf of the taxing authority. Conversely, it may appear that any
tax recovered by him will be held by him as a fiduciary for his customers (see *123
h   East Fifty-Fourth Street Inc v US* (1946) 157 F 2d 68 per Judge L Hand). Statements
of principle in *Air Canada* are favourable to the appellants in the present case, but
the converse is true so far as the Australian cases are concerned. These judgments
are most relevant for present purposes, in my respectful view, for what they say
with regard to the private law of restitution, and in particular, the full survey of
j   the common law position by Mason CJ in *Comr of State Revenue v Royal Insurance
Australia Ltd* (1994) 126 ALR 1. His conclusion in that case was that 'the
Commissioner would have no defence to a restitutionary claim by Royal to
recover the mistaken payments of duty' and that even if it was established that
Royal charged the tax as a separate item on the policy holders it would be entitled
to recover the moneys which it would then hold as a constructive trustee (see
(1994) 126 ALR 1 at 18). In relation to restitutionary relief, which he distinguished

from the public law aspects, he quoted with approval what Windeyer J said in
Mason v NSW (1959) 102 CLR 108 at 146:   *a*

> 'If the defendant be improperly enriched on what legal principle can it
> claim to retain its ill-gotten gains merely because the plaintiffs have not, it is
> said, been correspondingly impoverished? The concept of impoverishment
> as a correlative of enrichment may have some place in some fields of
> continental law. It is foreign to our law. Even if there were any equity in   *b*
> favour of third parties attaching to the fruits of any judgment the plaintiffs
> might recover ... this circumstance would be quite irrelevant to the present
> proceedings. Certainly it would not enable the defendant to refuse to return
> moneys which it was not in law entitled to collect and which *ex hypothesi* it
> got by extortion.'   *c*

Mason CJ then said ((1994) 126 ALR 1 at 15):

> 'Restitutionary relief, as it has developed to this point in our law, does not
> seek to provide compensation for loss. Instead, it operates to restore to the
> plaintiff what has been transferred from the plaintiff to the defendant
> whereby the defendant has been unjustly enriched. As in the action for   *d*
> money had and received, the defendant comes under an obligation to
> account to the plaintiff for money which the defendant has received for the
> use of the plaintiff. The subtraction from the plaintiff's wealth enables one
> to say that the defendant's unjust enrichment has been "at the expense of the
> plaintiff", notwithstanding that the plaintiff may recoup the outgoing by   *e*
> means of transactions with third parties. On this approach, it would not
> matter that the plaintiff is or will be over-compensated because he or she has
> passed on the tax or charge to someone else. And it seems that there is no
> recorded instance of a court engaging in the daunting exercise of working
> out the actual loss sustained by the plaintiff and restricting the amount of an
> award to that measure.'   *f*

There are also judgments of the Court of Justice of the European
Communities, including *Amministrazione delle Finanze dello Stato v San Giorgio*
Case 199/82 [1983] ECR 3595 to which Lord Goff referred in *Woolwich Building
Society v IRC (No 2)* [1992] 3 All ER 737 at 764, [1993] AC 70 at 177. This too was
a claim to recover overpaid statutory charges. Italian law required the taxpayer   *g*
to prove that he had not passed them on to his customers and it imposed a burden
of proof upon him which it might be virtually impossible to discharge. The Court
of Justice held that this provision of Italian law was contrary to European law, but
the court's judgment and the opinion of Advocate General Mancini were in terms
which can be regarded as supporting the lawfulness of a passing on defence. This   *h*
approach was reaffirmed in *Les Fils de Jules Bianco SA v Directeur Général des
Douanes et des Droits Indirects* Case 331/85 [1988] ECR 1099, and in *EC Commission
v Italy* Case 104/86 [1988] ECR 1799 at 1815 (para 6) the court held:

> '... Community law does not require an order for the recovery of charges
> improperly made to be granted in conditions which would involve an unjust   *j*
> enrichment of those entitled. Thus it does not prevent the fact that the
> burden of such charges may have been passed on to other traders or to
> consumers from being taken into consideration.'

The opinion of Advocate General Sir Gordon Slynn in the former case shows the
difficulties that can arise when it becomes necessary to inquire whether the

a burden of the overpayment has been passed on to customers in the form of
increased charges for the taxpayer's goods or services. Economic factors come
into play: has the taxpayer by raising his prices reduced the demand for what he
supplies, so that he has not benefited overall? This prompts a further question:
why should it be assumed that a repayment of tax will not be passed on to future
customers in the form of reduced prices?

b   The present case is far removed from the taxation authorities. No element of
public law is involved. No question of a constructive trust or of any obligation to
account to customers can arise. This follows from the admitted fact that the
hedge contracts, even if they were perfect matches, were market transactions
independent of the swaps contract which were and remained binding on the bank
and third parties notwithstanding that the swaps contract was void. This also
c means that the bank paid its own money to the authority and for its own account:
no question of agency or any third party interest can arise.

Kleinwort Benson Ltd v South Tyneside Metropolitan BC
     The relevant part of the judgment of Hobhouse J is reported at [1994] 4 All ER
d 972 at 984–987. He held, first, that the defendants were seeking to invoke 'some
unspecific principle which derives not from the law of restitution but from some
concept of compensation'. He continued: 'Even in the simplest cases where
parties are dealing on a market, other individual contracts are in principle too
remote to be taken into account', and he held as a second ground of his decision
that the hedge contracts were too remote to be taken into account in any event.
e But the primary answer was that such considerations were not relevant to
restitution:

f   'What contracts or other transactions or engagements the plaintiffs may
     have entered into with third parties have nothing to do with the principle of
     restitution. Therefore it suffices in the present case for the plaintiffs to show
     that they were the payers of the relevant money, that the defendants were
     unjustly enriched by the payments and that there is no obstacle to
     restitution.'

     He held that in the law of taxation special considerations may apply and that there
g was no place in the law of restitution 'for some principle borrowed from the law
of compensation'.

Submissions
     Mr Underhill submits that, the law of compensation apart, there is a relevant
h restriction on the right to restitution, and that it is found in the express words of
the American *Restatement* definition: the plaintiff must show that the defendant is
unjustly enriched *at his (the plaintiff's) expense.* He relies upon the following
passage from P Birks *An Introduction to the Law of Restitution* (1985, revisd 1989)
p 132 under the heading 'At the Plaintiff's expense':

j   'The plaintiff must bring himself ... within these words. If he cannot he has
     not even a *prima facie* entitlement to sue. For the defendant may have been
     enriched, and unjustly, yet unless it happened at the plaintiff's expense it will
     seem to be no business of his. That is what Goulding, J., meant when he said
     that the words "unjust enrichment" fail on their own to identify any
     plaintiff.'

He submits further that there is no justification for interpreting this
requirement by reference to the relationship between the payer and the payee   *a*
alone. Regard should also be had to related transactions, including in the present
case any hedges which were entered into in order to protect the bank from
suffering losses under the swaps contract. The area of inquiry should be limited,
he concedes, by what he calls the normal rules of remoteness; but within those
limits the plaintiff cannot show that the defendant was enriched 'at his expense'   *b*
if after taking account of all the relevant transactions he suffered no or only a
smaller loss than the amount which he seeks to recover from the defendant.

Mr Rhodri Davies, for the bank, submits that the law of restitution as it is now
established does not recognise the claimed defence of passing on, except possibly
in the special case where the plaintiff seeks to recover overpaid tax. He carefully
analysed the authorities to show that there is no support, as he submits, for Mr   *c*
Underhill's contention, and he pointed to practical difficulties and certain
anomalies which might result if the defence was one of general application.
Among these anomalies was the possible conflict between a judgment in the
present case which recognised hedge contracts as providing a passing on defence,
though not as increasing the amount of the claim, and the judgments in the *South*   *d*
Tyneside and *Svenska* cases which have held, as he submits, that market
transactions with third parties do not enable the defendant to rely upon the
'change of position' defence, which logically he ought to be able to do if the
passing on defence was recognised.

Conclusion
I can accept Mr Underhill's submission that the phrase 'at the expense of' forms
part of the definition of a restitutionary claim and that the central issue is whether
that has to be interpreted by reference to the payer/payee relationship alone, as
distinct from other parts of what he calls the overall transaction. But I have no
doubt that the former interpretation is correct. This is because the payee's   *f*
obligation, which is correlative to the payer's right to restitution, is to refund or
repay the amount which he has received and which it is unjust that he should
keep. 'At his expense', in my judgment, serves to identify the person by or on
whose behalf the payment was made and to whom repayment is due (compare
Chase Manhattan Bank NA v Israel-British Bank (London) Ltd [1979] 3 All ER 1025 at
1037, [1981] Ch 105 at 125 per Goulding J and see Birks, p 132). That person,   *g*
having made the payment, is necessarily out of pocket to that extent, and the
defendant's obligation is to replenish his pocket when the circumstances are such
that the money should be returned.

If the payment was made for valuable consideration, then the payer did not
suffer 'loss' even though the payment was made by him. But if it appears, as it   *h*
did in the present case, that in law there was no consideration for it, then in that
sense the payer has suffered loss. His pocket is emptier than it would have been
if the money, or its value, was still there. But I would not give 'loss' any wider
meaning than that. In particular, it seems to me that it would be inconsistent
with the principle of repayment that 'loss' should be given some wider meaning   *j*
equivalent to 'overall losses on the transaction', even if 'the transaction' could be
sufficiently identified, or that the right to recover restitution should be limited to
the amount of 'loss' in that sense, though never increased above the amount of
the payment.

I therefore agree with the first of Hobhouse J's two reasons for holding that no
'passing on' defence arises in the present case. I agree with the second reason

a also. If the claim is treated as limited to compensation for loss in fact suffered, taking account of related transactions which are not too remote from it, then in my judgment such hedge contracts as were entered into by the bank in the normal course of its business were 'too remote' to be taken into account. Market rates are taken into account when assessing damages because the plaintiff comes under a duty to mitigate his loss and it is presumed that he has done so by

b entering the market for that purpose. It is only in special cases that actual transactions are taken into account (see *R Pagnan & Flli v Corbisa Industrial Agropacuaria Ltda* [1971] 1 All ER 165, [1970] 1 WLR 1306). But here, there was no duty on the bank to hedge the risks to which it was exposed under the swaps contract, and its claim for restitution is not based on any wrongdoing or breach of contract by the authority.

c   For these reasons, I would hold that the alleged passing on defence does not arise in the present case. Out of deference to the thorough and well-researched submissions which were so attractively presented to us, I would add just the following.

d   (1) This is not a proprietary claim, and Mr Underhill accepted that there could be no scope for a passing on defence if it was. It is a claim for restitution precisely because the plaintiff can only claim repayment of an equivalent amount of money to what he paid. That is a further reason, in my judgment, for defining the right to recovery in terms of that amount of money, and nothing else.

      (2) If it was necessary to have regard to the status of the 'change of position' defence, which in my judgment it is not, then I would agree with Mr Underhill's

e submission (in reply) that the existing authorities of *South Tyneside* and *Svenska* do not establish a clear rule that no such defence can be raised. The *Svenska* case in particular turned on special facts, and I prefer to express no view as to whether that defence, which was recognised in the *Lipkin Gorman* case, could ever be established by reference to market transactions.

f   (3) This is not a case where the payment which it is sought to recover was made to the defendant by a third party, not by the plaintiff. Again, it is unnecessary in my view to deal further with this different aspect of the problem.

      (4) Mr Davies astutely referred us to the judgments in *Banque Belge pour l'Etranger v Hambrouck* [1921] 1 KB 321 at 323, 325, 328–329, 331–332, 335, where the plaintiff bank was held to be entitled to recover a sum of money which it had

g paid out under its customer's cheque, regardless of whether or not it was liable to reimburse the amount debited to the customer's account. But there was some doubt as to the precise nature of the cause of action and in my judgment this authority gives some, but only limited support to the respondents' case (see [1921] 1 KB 321 at 332–333).

h   I would dismiss the appeal.

SAVILLE LJ. I agree. I also agree with the judgment of Morritt LJ, which I have had the advantage of reading in draft.

      The basis for this kind of unjust enrichment claim lies in the fact that the only

j right the payee can assert to the money he has received is that created by the contract under which it was paid. If that contract is void, then it inexorably follows that this right does not exist, and the payee has no right to that money. The payee is thus unjustly enriched, since there is no justification for the retention of money to which he has no right. Leaving aside defences such as change of position, that injustice can only be corrected by returning the money to the payer, whose performed obligation to pay only arose under the same

contract. That obligation to pay is correlative to the payee's right to receive and
retain the payment; and likewise does not in fact exist if the contract is void. In *a*
short, the payer was under no obligation to part with his money, nor the payee
any correlative right to receive or retain it. Justice is done by imposing an
obligation on the payee to repay the payer.

Looked at this way, which is the way Lord Wright analysed the matter in
Fibrosa Spolka Akcyjna v Fairbairn Lawson Combe Barbour Ltd [1942] 2 All ER 122 at *b*
137, [1943] AC 32 at 65, whether the payer is out of pocket or has recouped his
outlay from other sources is entirely irrelevant. The payee has been unjustly
enriched by receiving and retaining money he has received from the payer and to
which he has no right. He does not cease to be unjustly enriched because the
payer for one reason or another is not out of pocket. His obligation to return the
money is not based on any loss the payer may have sustained, but on the simple *c*
ground that it is unjust that he should keep something to which he has no right
and which he only received through the payer's performance of an obligation
which did not in fact exist.

The expression 'at the payer's expense' is a convenient way of describing the
need for the payer to show that his money was used to pay the payee. Thus, there *d*
may well be cases where this cannot be shown, but where in truth, for example,
the payer was only the conduit through which the funds of others passed to the
payee. What this expression does not justify is the importation of concepts of loss
or damage with their attendant concepts of mitigation, for these have nothing
whatever to do with the reason why our law imposes an obligation on the payee
to repay to the payer what he has no right to retain. I too would dismiss this *e*
appeal.

MORRITT LJ. In the circumstances described by Evans LJ, whose account I
gratefully adopt, the question for determination is whether the law of restitution
in England and Wales recognises the defence of passing on. If it does then it is not *f*
disputed that the appeal and the amendment to the defence for which leave is
sought should be allowed so that if the facts as disclosed at the trial warrant it
effect may be given to the defence.

Any consideration of the modern law of restitution is likely to start with the
speech of Lord Wright in *Fibrosa Spolka Akcyjna v Fairbairn Lawson Combe Barbour*
Ltd [1942] 2 All ER 122 at 135–136, [1943] AC 32 at 61: *g*

> 'It is clear that any civilised system of law is bound to provide remedies for
> cases of what has been called unjust enrichment or unjust benefit, that is, to
> prevent a man from retaining the money of, or some kind of benefit derived
> from, another which it is against conscience that he should keep. Such *h*
> remedies in English law are generically different from remedies in contract
> or in tort, and are now recognised to fall within a third category of the
> common law which has been called quasi-contract or restitution. The root
> idea was stated by three Lords of Appeal, LORD SHAW, LORD SUMNER and
> LORD CARSON, in *Jones* v. *Waring and Gillow* ([1926] AC 670, [1926] All ER Rep *j*
> 36), which dealt with a particular species of the category, namely, money
> paid under a mistake of fact. LORD SUMNER ([1926] AC 670 at 696, [1926] All
> ER Rep 36 at 47) referring to *Kelly* v. *Solari* ((1841) 9 M & W 54, [1835–42] All
> ER Rep 320), where money had been paid by an insurance company under
> the mistaken impression that it was due to an executrix under a policy which
> had in fact been cancelled, said: "There was no real intention on the

a company's part to enrich her." Payment under a mistake of fact is only one head of this category of the law. Another class is where, as in this case, there is prepayment on account of money to be paid as consideration for the performance of a contract which in the event becomes abortive and is not performed, so that the money never becomes due. There was in such circumstances no intention to enrich the payee.'

b It is noteworthy that the emphasis is on the provision of a remedy designed to prevent a defendant retaining that which, whether money or some other benefit, was derived from the plaintiff with no intention to enrich the defendant.

The researches of counsel did not reveal any reference to the benefit to the defendant being 'at the expense of the plaintiff' in any case originating in England *c* or Wales earlier than the decision of the House of Lords in *Lipkin Gorman (a firm) v Karpnale Ltd* [1992] 4 All ER 512, [1991] 2 AC 548. Lord Goff said:

'I accept that the solicitors' claim in the present case is founded upon the unjust enrichment of the club, and can only succeed if, in accordance with the principles of the law of restitution, the club was indeed unjustly enriched *d* at the expense of the solicitors. The claim for money had and received is not, as I have previously mentioned, founded upon any wrong committed by the club against the solicitors. But it does not, in my opinion, follow that the court has carte blanche to reject the solicitors, claim simply because it thinks it unfair or unjust in the circumstances to grant recovery. The recovery of money in restitution is not, as a general rule, a matter of discretion for the *e* court. A claim to recover money at common law is made as a matter of right; and, even though the underlying principle of recovery is the principle of unjust enrichment, nevertheless, where recovery is denied, it is denied on the basis of legal principle.' (See [1992] 4 All ER 512 at 532, [1991] 2 AC 548 at 578.)

f It is, I think, clear that the origin of the words 'at the expense of the plaintiff' is to be found in the American Law Institute's *Restatement of the law, Restitution* (1937), which states:

'§1. UNJUST ENRICHMENT. A person who has been unjustly enriched at the *g* expense of another is required to make restitution to the other.

Comment: a. A person is enriched if he has received a benefit (see Comment *b*). A person is unjustly enriched if the retention of the benefit would be unjust (see Comment *c*). A person obtains restitution when he is restored to the position he formerly occupied either by the return of something which he formerly had or by the receipt of its equivalent in money. Ordinarily, the *h* measure of restitution is the amount of enrichment received (see Comment *d*), but as stated in Comment *e*, if the loss suffered differs from the amount of benefit received, the measure of restitution may be more or less than the loss suffered or more or less than the enrichment.'

j [See judge's note, p 750, post, regarding further researches of counsel.]

The comment under *e* contains examples of cases where the benefit and loss do not coincide; but none of them suggests that if the enrichment of the defendant would be unjust he escapes liability because the plaintiff has not suffered a corresponding or any loss. With the exception of cases involving the repayment of tax to a trader who passed on the burden of the impost to his customers in the ordinary course of business, the researches of counsel have not

discovered any case in any country whose system of law is based on the common
law where the defence of passing on has been upheld. The weight of authority is *a*
to the opposite effect. Thus in *Mason v NSW* (1959) 102 CLR 108 at 146
Windeyer J said:

> 'It was argued that, even if they were otherwise entitled, the plaintiffs were
> in some way estopped from recovering because they had "passed on" to their *b*
> customers the amount paid for permits and are thus, it was said, not
> themselves at a loss. I can see no basis for this contention. Provided it be
> recognized that the action for money had and received is not only the origin
> of but, as developed, still determines the scope of the English law of
> quasi-contract, it seems to me not inapt to describe it as a law of "unjust
> enrichment". But accepting this, and I certainly see no need to-day to look *c*
> for the implication of a contract or to speak of the fiction of a contract when
> in reality there was no contract, still how does it avail the defendant? If the
> defendant be improperly enriched on what legal principle can it claim to
> retain its ill-gotten gains merely because the plaintiffs have not, it is said,
> been correspondingly impoverished? The concept of impoverishment as a
> correlative of enrichment may have some place in some fields of continental *d*
> law. It is foreign to our law. Even if there were any equity in favour of third
> parties attaching to the fruits of any judgment the plaintiffs might recover—
> and there is nothing proved at all remotely suggesting that there is—this
> circumstance would be quite irrelevant to the present proceedings.
> Certainly it would not enable the defendant to refuse to return moneys *e*
> which it was not in law entitled to collect and which *ex hypothesi* it got by
> extortion.'

In *Comr of State Revenue v Royal Insurance Australia Ltd* (1994) 126 ALR 1 at 14
Mason CJ approved that passage in the judgment of Windeyer J when he said:
f
> 'Historically, as I have already noted, the basis of restitutionary relief in
> English law was not compensation for loss or damage but restoration of
> what had been taken or received. The requirement that the defendant be
> unjustly enriched "at the expense of" the plaintiff can mean that the
> enrichment is "by doing wrong to" or "by subtraction from" the plaintiff.
> Hence a plaintiff can succeed by showing that he or she was the victim of a *g*
> wrong which enriched the defendant—that is not such a case—or that the
> defendant was enriched by receiving the plaintiff's money or property.
> When the plaintiff succeeds in a restitutionary claim, the court awards the
> plaintiff the monetary equivalent of what the defendant has taken or
> received, except in those cases in which the plaintiff is entitled to specific *h*
> proprietary relief. Because the object of restitutionary relief is to divest the
> defendant of what the defendant is not entitled to retain, the court does not
> assess the amount of its award by reference to the actual loss which the
> plaintiff has sustained. That is what Windeyer J was saying in *Mason v New
> South Wales* when he rejected the notion that impoverishment of the plaintiff *j*
> is a correlative of the defendant's unjust enrichment.'

The case for the appellants, Birmingham City Council (the authority), depends
on extending and applying to the facts of this case the propositions enunciated by
La Forest J in *Air Canada v British Columbia* (1989) 59 DLR (4th) 161 at 193–194,
where he said:

a
'The law of restitution is not intended to provide windfalls to plaintiffs who have suffered no loss. Its function is to ensure that where a plaintiff has been deprived of wealth that is either in his possession or would have accrued for his benefit, it is restored to him. The measure of restitutionary recovery is the gain the province made at the airlines' expense. If the airlines have not shown that they bore the burden of the tax, then they have not made out their claim. What the province received is relevant only in so far as it was received at the airlines' expense.'

b

The application in England of the principle referred to in that passage was considered and rejected by Hobhouse J in *Kleinwort Benson Ltd v South Tyneside Metropolitan BC* [1994] 4 All ER 972 at 984–985. He considered the principle and said:

c

'What is the legal principle which the defendants invoke? It can only be some unspecific principle which derives not from the law of restitution but from some concept of compensation. The essential features in what the defendants here are asking the court to do (and other defendants in similar actions) is to make an assessment of the loss suffered by the relevant plaintiff as if one were investigating a right to compensation. The argument involves problems of remoteness. Even in the simplest cases where parties are dealing on a market, other individual contracts are in principle too remote to be taken into account. Compensation is assessed by reference to the market, not by reference to individual contracts. Where the position is more complex and it is not a question of looking at individual contracts but at the overall position of the plaintiff which may change from time to time, the problems of remoteness become self-evident and the risk of entering into an infinite regress likewise become apparent. But the primary answer is that such considerations may be relevant to compensation but are not relevant to restitution. Here there is no problem about recognising a restitutionary remedy in personam against the defendants in favour of the plaintiffs. What contracts or other transactions or engagements the plaintiffs may have entered into with third parties have nothing to do with the principle of restitution. Therefore it suffices in the present case for the plaintiffs to show that they were the payers of the relevant money, that the defendants were unjustly enriched by the payments and that there is no obstacle to restitution. The problems which arise in different classes of case and are referred to in the textbooks, where the defendant has enjoyed some less tangible benefit and it does not derive from a payment made by the plaintiff to the defendant, do not arise for consideration in this case.'

d

e

f

g

h
Later he concluded ([1994] 4 All ER 972 at 987):

'In the present case I am concerned with payments made under void transactions where there is no question but that the relevant plaintiff made the payment on his own account and out of his own money. If the plaintiff is to be denied his remedy in respect of the sum which he has paid to the defendant and which it is unjust that the defendant should retain, it must be upon a basis that is relevant to the law of restitution and not some principle borrowed from the law of compensation. Further, the application of the principle, if it is to be adopted, must respect the principles of remoteness recognised in the law of compensation.'

j

Counsel for the authority contends that the propositions advanced by La Forest J *a* in *Air Canada v British Columbia* are consistent with the principles of the law of restitution in England, that Hobhouse J was wrong to have concluded otherwise and that such propositions should be applied in this case if the facts as established at trial warrant it. He submits that restitution does involve the concept of loss and hence compensation for they are inherent in the consideration of whether the enrichment of the defendant was 'at the expense of the plaintiff'. He accepts *b* that the recognition of the defence may give rise to considerable problems of knowing where to draw the line and suggests that suitable control mechanisms may be found in the application of two well established principles. The first is the burden of proof. It is suggested that once the plaintiff has shown that he had paid the sum claimed to the defendant then the burden would shift to the defendant to establish if he could that the loss had been passed on by the plaintiff. The *c* second is that in seeking to do so the court should apply principles well recognised in the assessment of damages for breach of contract or tort which require that the innocent party bring into account benefits derived from connected transactions. For my part, I do not accept any of these propositions.

I will consider first the suggested control mechanisms. The principle which *d* requires a plaintiff to bring into account in the assessment of damages benefits derived from connected transactions was established in *British Westinghouse Electric and Manufacturing Co Ltd v Underground Electric Railways Co of London Ltd* [1912] AC 673, [1911–13] All ER Rep 63 and has been considered in a number of cases since including *Hussey v Eels* [1990] 1 All ER 449, [1990] 2 QB 227. The principle is one aspect of the requirement that the plaintiff should mitigate his *e* loss. Thus, a benefit derived from a subsequent transaction arising out of the consequences of the original wrong and entered into by the plaintiff in the ordinary course of his business must be brought into account in assessing the loss sustained by virtue of the wrong.

But this principle can have no application to a claim to restitution such as is *f* made in this case. First, the claim is not founded on a wrong inflicted on the plaintiff but is for restitution of money paid by the plaintiff to the authority as money had and received to the use of the plaintiff. In such circumstances there is no duty to mitigate anything. But even if there were the principle on which the authority seeks to rely would not apply. Let it be assumed that there are two precisely matching equal but opposite interest rate swaps only one of which is *g* made with a local authority and therefore void. In such a case the valid transaction which the authority contends should be brought into account would have been concluded in reliance on the validity of the other, not on or as a consequence of its invalidity. Thus, even if the restitutionary claim were to depend on loss the usual rules as to mitigation would treat the matching swap *h* transaction as unconnected. In consequence any gain made as a result of it would not diminish the loss sustained as a result of the wrong. I can see no reason why the defendant to a claim for restitution based on the invalidity of a contract should be put in a better position than he would have been in if the claim had been for damages for the breach of a valid contract.

j

The idea that the evidential burden of proof of passing on might switch to the defendant when the plaintiff has produced evidence sufficient to establish his initial payment to the defendant is supported by the opinion of Advocate General Sir Gordon Slynn in *EC Commission v Italy* Case 104/86 [1988] ECR 1799 at 1810–1811. But Sir Gordon was not suggesting that such a principle somehow mitigated any perceived injustice in the suggested defence; he was concerned a   with whether the requirement of Italian law for documentary evidence was a material restriction. The switch of the onus of proof could do little to ameliorate the wide ranging practical consequences of a defence of passing on. It would be little consolation to a claimant required to disclose on discovery all its books and other records relevant to a defence of passing on to be told that the onus of proof rested on its adversary.

b   Accordingly I reject the suggestion that either of the control mechanisms relied on could have the effects for which the authority contends. It must follow that in the consideration of the suggested defence, to which I now return, it is necessary to face the practical consequences referred to by Hobhouse J down to and including the infinite regression. As I have already indicated I would reject the argument of the authority.

c   First, there is no doubt that in this case the respondent, Kleinwort Benson (the bank), was legally, and, if it is material, beneficially entitled to the money it paid to the authority. This is not a case in which the claimant held the money claimed as a bare trustee or tax collector such as, arguably, in *Air Canada v British Columbia* (1989) 59 DLR (4th) 161 or *123 East Fifty-Fourth Street Inc v US* (1946) 157 F 2d 68.

d   It is true, as shown in *Friends' Provident Life Office v Hillier Parker May & Rowden (a firm) (Estates and General plc and ors, third parties)* [1995] 4 All ER 260 at 272 on which the authority relied, that in certain statutory contexts compensation for damage may include restitution for unjust enrichment; but that cannot alter the fact that the claim of the bank is for restitution of the money it paid to the authority. The bank does not seek compensation for loss.

e   Second, the words 'at the expense of the plaintiff' on which the authority place such reliance do not appear in a statute and should not be construed or applied as if they did. In my view they do no more than point to the requirement that the immediate source of the unjust enrichment must be the plaintiff. Were it otherwise the decision of this court in *Banque Belge pour l'Etranger v Hambrouck*

f   [1921] 1 KB 321 would have been different. Some commentaries equate the phrase 'at the expense of' with a subtraction from the wealth of the plaintiff. No doubt this is a useful description. But the type of restitutionary claim with which this appeal is concerned relates to a subtraction from the plaintiff's gross wealth. The suggested defence of passing on would involve the different concept of a reduction in the net worth of the plaintiff.

g   Third, if the authority were permitted to retain that which the bank paid under the void swap it would have the result of giving effect to that which was ultra vires and void. Whilst the theory of restitution no longer involves the implication of any promise to repay, all those factors which go to establish the case for restitution would be nullified or undermined by a defence of passing on.

h   Fourth, I do not accept the proposition that if the loss has been passed on it is necessarily unjust for the claimant to recover what La Forest J in *Air Canada v British Columbia* (1989) 59 DLR (4th) 161 at 193–194 described as 'a windfall'. The concept of relative titles is not unfamiliar, for example in the case of trespass to land. If, in accordance with the relevant principles, the defendant has been

j   unjustly enriched by the payment by the plaintiff it seems to me that the plaintiff has a better title than the defendant to any 'windfall' available, not least so as to be in a position to satisfy any claim made against him by those from whom 'the windfall' was ultimately derived. I do not suggest that this is a proprietary claim, merely that proprietary principles are applicable by analogy to claims in personam (cf *Lipkin Gorman (a firm) v Karpnale Ltd* [1992] 4 All ER 512 at 527, [1991] 2 AC 548 at 572).

Fifth, if the defence is recognised it will place at the disposal of an unjustly *a* enriched defendant a powerful weapon with which to postpone the entry of judgment against him. I do not think that the fact that the recovery might in some cases represent a 'windfall' in the hands of the plaintiff is sufficient reason to enable an unjustly enriched defendant to delay recovery from him in the many cases where it would not.

Finally, there is the overwhelming weight of authority against the contentions *b* of the authority. Apart from the cases to which I have already referred the defence of passing on has been referred to in two other recent cases, namely *Amministrazione delle Finanze dello Stato v San Giorgio* Case 199/82 [1983] ECR 3595 and *Woolwich Building Society v IRC (No 2)* [1992] 3 All ER 737, [1993] AC 70. In the first, the Court of Justice of the European Communities concluded that Community law did not prevent a national legal system from disallowing the *c* repayment of charges which had been unduly levied on the ground that they had been passed on to the ultimate purchaser by incorporation in the price of goods. In the second, Lord Goff recognised that it would be a matter for consideration whether the fact that the plaintiff has passed on the tax or levy so that the burden has fallen on another should provide a defence to his claim. Neither of those *d* cases throws any light on the answer to the question posed by this appeal.

In my view, and in agreement with Evans and Saville LJJ, the relevant principles and precedents require the dismissal of this appeal.

Judge's note. I add this note to record the product of the further researches of counsel which they brought to our attention when our judgments were handed *e* down. The first use of the phrase 'at the expense of another' in the context of unjust enrichment published in the United States of America appears to be an article by J B Ames (then Bussey Professor of Law at the University of Harvard) 'The History of Assumpsit' (1888) 2 Harv LR 1, 52. He described the third class of quasi-contract as founded 'upon the fundamental principle of justice that no *f* one ought unjustly to enrich himself at the expense of another' (see (1888) 2 Harv LR 52 at 64). Later, he stated that 'the equitable principle which lies at the foundation of the great bulk of quasi-contracts, namely, that one person shall not unjustly enrich himself at the expense of another, has established itself very gradually in the Common Law' (at 66). The principle is stated in similar terms by William A Keener (then Kent Professor of Law in Columbia College) *Treatise on* *g* *the Law of Quasi-Contracts* (1893) p 19. Neither of those works refers to any authority or earlier work in which the phrase is to be found. Further, it is interesting to note that Professor Woodward, then Professor of Law in Leland Stanford Junior University, in his *The Law of Quasi-Contracts* published in Boston in 1913 does not use the phrase at all. Thus it would appear that Professor J B *h* Ames was the originator of the phrase which, though not initially commanding universal acceptance, was incorporated into the American *Restatement.*

Appeal dismissed. Leave to appeal to House of Lords refused.

Paul Magrath Esq Barrister. *j*

a   # R v Lord Chancellor, ex parte Maxwell

QUEEN'S BENCH DIVISION
HENRY LJ AND SACHS J
13, 14, 19 JUNE 1996

b

Judicial review – Lord Chancellor – Deployment of judges – High Court judge appointed to preside over fraud trial and ordering severance of counts in indictment at preparatory hearing – Trial proceeding in respect of two counts – Trial judge promoted to Court of Appeal during trial but continuing to sit as Crown Court judge until
c   *conclusion of trial at Lord Chancellor's request – Whether judge's refusal to deal with remaining counts in the absence of further request from Lord Chancellor unlawful – Whether trial of remaining counts 'ancillary matter relating to' first trial or 'proceedings arising out of' that trial – Whether Lord Chancellor's refusal to make request irrational – Supreme Court Act 1981, ss 8, 9(1)(4)(7) – Criminal Justice Act 1987, s 7.*

d

A High Court judge was appointed to preside over the trial of the applicant and his co-defendants who were charged with fraud in an indictment containing ten counts. The judge held a preparatory hearing under s 7 of the Criminal Justice Act 1987 and ordered that the counts in the indictment should be severed and that
e   two counts only should be tried initially. During the trial of those counts, the judge was promoted to the Court of Appeal but he continued to sit as a judge of the Crown Court at the Lord Chancellor's request under s 9(1) of the Supreme Court Act 1981 until the conclusion of the trial, when the applicant and his co-defendants were all acquitted. The prosecution then indicated that they intended to proceed with the trial of the remaining counts in the indictment;
f   however the judge refused to deal with them on the ground that in the absence of a further request from the Lord Chancellor he had no jurisdiction to do so. The Lord Chancellor refused to make such a request and the second trial was listed before another judge. The applicant applied for judicial review of the Lord Chancellor's decision, contending that it was unlawful for the judge not to deal with the remaining counts in the indictment since he was empowered to do so by
g   s 9(7)[a] of the 1981 Act and that the Lord Chancellor's decision was irrational.

Held – The application would be dismissed for the following reasons—

(1) Although a High Court judge had jurisdiction to sit in the Crown Court by virtue of s 8 of the 1981 Act, that section did not empower a lord justice of appeal
h   to do so. It followed that after his appointment as a lord justice the judge could only have conducted the trial of the remaining counts in the indictment if the Lord Chancellor had requested him to do so under s 9(1) or (4) of the 1981 Act. He was not empowered to do so by s 9(7) of the 1981 Act on the expiry of the original request since the trial of the remaining counts was not an 'ancillary
j   matter relating to' the first trial, nor did it constitute 'proceedings arising out of' that trial for the purposes of s 9(7). Furthermore, while in a serious and complex fraud case the judge who presided at the preparatory hearing should, save in exceptional circumstances, be the judge who conducted the trial, legal incapacity

---

a   Section 9(7) is set out at p 755 *b*, post

to continue to act as the trial judge constituted such exceptional circumstances (see p 754 *j* to p 755 *c*, p 757 *g* and p 758 *a*, post); *R v Southwark Crown Court, ex p Customs and Excise Comrs* [1993] 1 WLR 764 considered.

(2) In considering whether to request the judge to deal with the remaining counts in the indictment the Lord Chancellor had to decide on the best disposal of judicial manpower for the proper administration of justice and had to balance the contribution the judge could make in the trial of those counts against his broader contribution in the Court of Appeal and the wider interests of justice in having a Court of Appeal up to full strength at a critical time. That balance, and the weight to be given to various aspects of the process, were matters for the Lord Chancellor and not the court. Since the Lord Chancellor had approached the matter correctly and reached a decision within the discretion accorded to him, the contention that his decision was irrational was unsustainable (see p 758 *j* to p 759 *b*, post).

Per curiam. An administrative discretion relating to the deployment of judicial manpower is open to challenge by way of judicial review, but since realistically most such challenges were doomed to failure they should be discouraged and so critically examined at the leave stage (see p 759 *c d*, post).

Notes

For judicial composition of the Crown Court, see 10 *Halsbury's Laws* (4th edn) para 883.

For the nature of judicial review, see 1(1) *Halsbury's Laws* (4th edn reissue) para 60, and for cases on the subject, see 16 *Digest* (2nd reissue) 475–506, 3646–3723.

For the Supreme Court Act 1981, ss 8, 9, see 11 *Halsbury's Statutes* (4th edn) (1991 reissue) 975.

For the Criminal Justice Act 1987, s 7, see 12 *Halsbury's Statutes* (4th edn) (1994 reissue) 1115.

Cases referred to in judgment

R v Ministry of Defence, ex p Smith [1996] 1 All ER 257, [1996] QB 517, [1996] 2 WLR 305, CA.

R v Southwark Crown Court, ex p Customs and Excise Comrs [1993] 1 WLR 764, DC.

R v Tonner, R v Evans [1985] 1 All ER 807, [1985] 1 WLR 344, CA.

Cases also cited or referred to in skeleton arguments

Associated Provincial Picture Houses Ltd v Wednesbury Corp [1947] 2 All ER 680, [1948] 1 KB 223, CA.

Brind v Secretary of State for the Home Dept [1991] 1 All ER 720, [1991] 1 AC 696, HL.

Connelly v DPP [1964] 2 All ER 401, [1964] AC 1254, HL.

DPP v Humphrys [1976] 2 All ER 497, [1977] AC 1, HL.

R v Criminal Injuries Compensation Board, ex p P [1995] 1 All ER 870, [1995] 1 WLR 845, CA.

R v Kellard [1995] 2 Cr App R 134, CA.

Sambasivam v Public Prosecutor, Federation of Malaya [1950] AC 458, PC.

Application for judicial review

Kevin Francis Herbert Maxwell applied, with leave of Carnwath J granted on 27 March 1996, for an order of certiorari to quash the decision of the Lord Chancellor, communicated by letter on 9 February 1996 whereby he declined to request Phillips LJ under s 9(1) and (2) of the Supreme Court Act 1981 to act as a a judge of the Crown Court for the purpose of presiding over the remaining stages of a criminal case alleged against the applicant and his co-defendants in an indictment in January 1994 at the Central Criminal Court and for an order of mandamus that such a request be made. The facts are set out in the judgment of the court.

b *Alun Jones QC* and *Leah Saffian* (instructed by *Peters & Peters*) for Mr Maxwell.
Stephen Richards (instructed by the *Treasury Solicitor*) for the Lord Chancellor.
Nigel Pleming QC and *Mark Lucraft* (instructed by the *Solicitor for the Serious Fraud Office*) for the Serious Fraud Office.

Cur adv vult

c

19 June 1996. The following judgment of the court was delivered.

HENRY LJ. The applicant, Mr Kevin Maxwell, challenges the decision of the Lord Chancellor not to request (under s 9 of the Supreme Court Act 1981) Phillips
d LJ to act as a judge of the Crown Court for the purpose of presiding over the disposal of the remaining stages of the criminal case against Mr Maxwell and others. It seems to have come as some surprise to the profession that an administrative discretion relating to the deployment of judicial manpower could be the subject of such a challenge, and to that point we will return. But the first point to make clear is that no comparison or evaluation of the judicial qualities of
e the two judges is involved in this challenge and its resolution.

The matter arises in this way. In June 1992, the applicant, Mr Maxwell, was arrested and charged with fraud. In July 1993, the ten charges that had been preferred against him and his co-accused were transferred to the Central Criminal Court for trial under the serious fraud regime established by the Criminal Justice
f Act 1987. Phillips J was appointed the trial judge. On 19 January 1994 indictment no T930798 was preferred and signed, containing ten counts against Mr Maxwell and five co-defendants. The trial judge ordered a preparatory hearing in relation to those counts under s 7(1) of the 1987 Act. On 31 January 1994 the accused were arraigned, and all pleaded not guilty to all offences. The significance of arraignment under the serious fraud regime is that it marks the start of the trial
g (see s 8 of the 1987 Act).

The judge's first act in the preparatory hearing was to order severance of the counts in the indictment. To achieve manageability of the case before a jury, he restricted the first jury trial to counts 4 and 10 of the indictment. In so doing, he commented that even trial on those two counts alone went close to the limits of
h manageability. In the event, 61 days were spent on the preparatory hearing before the trial. That preparatory hearing was directed to the trial on counts 4 and 10. There were then 131 days of trial before the jury. That trial ended on 19 January 1996 with the acquittal of all defendants (including the applicant) on both counts.

j During the trial, an unusual event had occurred. On 2 October 1995 Her Majesty The Queen, pursuant to s 10(2) of the 1981 Act by letters patent appointed Phillips J to be a Lord Justice of Appeal. That appointment meant that he was no longer qualified under s 8 of the 1981 Act to sit as a judge of the Crown Court (as he had been doing to conduct this trial). He would only have such powers if the Lord Chancellor invited him to continue under s 9(1). As the balance of public interest clearly pointed to Phillips LJ concluding the trial of Mr

Maxwell and others on the counts 4 and 10, the Lord Chancellor requested him
to sit as a judge of the Crown Court to conclude that trial, and he accepted. But
for that request, he would not have had jurisdiction to continue.

That trial was concluded on 26 January 1996. On that date the prosecution
indicated that they intended to proceed with the trial of counts 1, 2 and 9 against
Mr Maxwell, Mr Trachtenberg and Mr Fuller, and a separate trial in relation to
counts 7 and 8 against Mr Stoney. At that hearing, Phillips LJ made it clear that
his jurisdiction to sit as a judge of the Crown Court did not extend to trying the
suggested second and third jury trials under the indictment. Counsel for Mr
Maxwell then invited the judge to proceed on the basis that —

> 'your Lordship is seised of this trial, which opened when the preparatory
> hearing began in January 1994, and there is no power in your Lordship to
> transfer any further disposal of any part of this trial to another judge.'

Phillips LJ made the point that he could hardly be required to deal with the
remaining counts as a matter of law if he had no jurisdiction to do so, and that
unless the Lord Chancellor requested him to do so he had no such jurisdiction.
Counsel for Mr Maxwell and Mr Trachtenberg made submissions to the court
both as to why he must conduct those trials, and second why he should. Mr
Maxwell's solicitors that evening wrote to the Lord Chancellor, asking him to
exercise his powers, stating:

> 'We contend that it is clearly in the interests of justice and in accordance
> with the law that Lord Justice Phillips should preside over the second trial.
> The reasons for this contention are summarised in the submission of Alun
> Jones QC which are contained in the attached transcript. In the
> circumstances we invite you to issue a further direction to Lord Justice
> Phillips to sit as a Crown Court Judge and to hear any further proceedings
> against Mr Kevin Maxwell.'

They followed that up with a letter of 29 January suggesting that it would be
arguably unlawful to appoint a new judge.

However, on 9 February, the Court Service wrote saying that the forthcoming
trial of Mr Maxwell and others would be listed before Buckley J.

That appointment prompted a judicial review challenge to the Lord
Chancellor's failure to request Phillips LJ to sit as a judge of the Crown Court for
the remaining stages of the trial, dealing with the remaining counts in the
indictment. That challenge asserted that the Lord Chancellor was bound in law
to issue such a request to Phillips LJ, submitting that the case was 'part heard'
under s 7(1) of the 1987 Act, and that having ordered a preparatory hearing in
relation to the trial of the indictment, the judge was thereafter bound to preside
over the trial or trials of all counts on that indictment in the absence of
exceptional circumstances such as ill-health. We would guess that that
submission was a determinative factor in the single judge granting the applicant
leave to bring the judicial review challenge now before us.

We examine the submission that it would be unlawful for Phillips LJ not to try
the remaining counts on the indictment. As a High Court judge, Phillips J had
jurisdiction to sit in the Crown Court by virtue of s 8 of the 1981 Act and High
Court judges routinely do so, whenever trying crime. But that section does not
empower Lords Justices of Appeal to sit in the Crown Court. In our judgment,
after his appointment, Phillips LJ would only be empowered to conduct the trial
of all the outstanding counts on the indictment if the Lord Chancellor requested

a him to do so under s 9(1) or (4), and no such request has been made. But it is
contended that s 9(7) empowers him so to sit. That subsection reads:

> 'Notwithstanding the expiry of any period for which a person is authorised
> by virtue of subsection (1) or (4) to act as a judge of a particular court—(a) he
> may attend at that court for the purpose of continuing to deal with, giving
> judgment in, or dealing with any ancillary matter relating to, any case begun
b > before him while acting as a judge of that court; and (b) for that purpose, and
> for the purpose of any proceedings arising out of any such case or matter, he
> shall be treated as being or, as the case may be, having been a judge of that
> court.'

c   The authority given to him as a result of his acceptances of the Lord
Chancellor's mid-trial request under sub-s (1) was to conclude the trial of counts
4 and 10. He has concluded that trial. The trial of the remaining counts are not
an ancillary matter relating to that trial, nor are they proceedings arising out of
that trial. It follows that in our judgment the Lord Chief Justice was quite right
to say in the letter of 1 February 1996 that the conclusion of the trial on counts 4
d and 10 terminated his powers pursuant to the request under s 9(1), which entitled
him to sit in the Crown Court despite his elevation. Therefore, unless the Lord
Chancellor specially requested Phillips LJ to try the remaining counts on the
indictment under s 9(1), the judge had no power to do so. The omission of Lords
Justices of Appeal from those whom Parliament has automatically empowered to
act as Crown Court judges in s 8 clearly shows that the Lord Chancellor (as the
e 'appropriate authority') has been entrusted with discretion as to whether or not
to issue such a request under s 9(1). There are no statutory limits placed on the
exercise of that discretion: it is a 'strong discretion'. The policy is clear: that in
matters of judicial deployment, Parliament does not seek to lay down how the
Lord Chancellor should exercise his discretion.

f   Recognising that the Lord Chancellor has such a discretion, Mr Jones QC for
Mr Maxwell mounts an irrationality challenge to the Lord Chancellor's decision
not to invite Phillips LJ to try the remaining counts on the indictment. In making
such a challenge, the applicant has a mountain to climb. In his decision not to
make this request, the Lord Chancellor was exercising a broad administrative
discretion. That discretion involved a balance between competing facets of the
g interests of justice. On the one hand, there was the best disposal of the remaining
counts in a single trial, albeit an important one. On the other, the broader
interests of justice in having at the present time a Court of Appeal up to strength
and manned as Her Majesty, on advice, had considered that it should be manned.
Parliament has entrusted that decision to the Lord Chancellor: he is answerable
h to Parliament for it.

These courts are not concerned with the merits of such decisions, but only
with the legality of them. The test in irrationality challenges of this kind was set
out by Bingham MR in *R v Ministry of Defence, ex p Smith* [1996] 1 All ER 257 at 263,
[1996] QB 517 at 554:

j
> 'The court may not interfere with the exercise of an administrative
> discretion on substantive grounds save where the court is satisfied that the
> decision is unreasonable in the sense that it is beyond the range of responses
> open to a reasonable decision-maker. But in judging whether the
> decision-maker has exceeded this margin of appreciation the human rights
> context is important. The more substantial the interference with human

rights, the more the court will require by way of justification before it is satisfied that the decision is reasonable in the sense outlined above.'

Decisions so unreasonable as to warrant interference jump off the page at you. For instance, when the Lord Chancellor requested Phillips LJ, on his appointment to the Court of Appeal, to conclude the trial of counts 4 and 10, that trial was at about the half-way stage. There had been 61 days of preparatory hearing, and the judge had been seised of the case for more than two years. If Phillips LJ had not been invited to sit to finish, all that time and expenditure would have been wasted, when (we cannot say 'only') another four months would complete the trial. The Lord Chancellor would never have contemplated not asking Phillips LJ to complete that trial, but had he so decided it seems to us that such a decision might be vulnerable to challenge as irrational. So the matter is justiciable, but the occasions when such a decision is struck down will, realistically, be rare indeed.

We start the irrationality inquiry by examining the power to order separate trials of counts in an indictment. Section 5(3) of the Indictments Act 1915 provides:

'Where, before trial, or at any stage of a trial, the court is of the opinion that a person accused may be prejudiced or embarrassed in his defence by reason of being charged with more than one offence in the same indictment, or that for any other reason it is desirable to direct that the person should be tried separately for any one or more offences charged in an indictment, the court may order a separate trial of any count or counts of such indictment.'

That is the source of the power of severance. The 'separate trial' normally begins when the jury is sworn and the defendant or defendants are put in charge of the jury (R v Tonner, R v Evans [1985] 1 All ER 807, [1985] 1 WLR 344); thus (absent the serious fraud complication) there is no difficulty in a fresh judge trying the severed count. But it is axiomatic that you cannot change the trial judge in mid-trial, that is, from the time that the jury has been empanelled, until the time that they return to the court room with their verdict.

The difficulty in relation to the serious fraud regime is that s 8 of the 1987 Act fixes an artificially early date for the commencement of the trial, namely at the commencement of the preparatory hearing, which will be before any questions of severance have been decided. That section reads:

'Commencement of trial and arraignment.—(1) If a judge orders a preparatory hearing, the trial shall begin with that hearing.
(2) Arraignment shall accordingly take place at the start of the preparatory hearing.'

The legislative source of that provision can be traced back to the Fraud Trials Committee Report (1986 HMSO), chaired by Lord Roskill. That committee found that pre-trial hearings were often ineffective and inefficient. They attached particular importance to them to achieve a just and efficient resolution of fraud trials, and therefore recommended (p 115, Recommendation 34): 'The judge presiding at the preparatory hearings must be the judge who, save in exceptional circumstances, is to conduct the trial.' The object of such hearings was to identify the issues, to expedite the proceedings, to assist the judge's management of the trial, and to deal with questions as to admissibility of evidence and other questions of law.

a   Though that report was published only ten years ago, experience since shows it have been written in what now seems an age of innocence. Internal evidence shows that the committee were envisaging preparatory hearings only lasting a day or two. The 61 days of preparatory hearing in Mr Maxwell's first trial is typical of experience since (and was a preparatory hearing limited to counts 4 and 10—though we are told there is a significant area of overlap with the Berlitz counts). Curiously too, the Roskill Report only refers to the question of

b   severance in a single sentence. Nor is the question of severance addressed either expressly or by necessary implication in the 1987 Act.

The commencement of the trial (and its consequences) in serious fraud cases was considered (albeit in a case uncomplicated by questions of severance) by the Divisional Court in *R v Southwark Crown Court, ex p Customs and Excise Comrs*

c   [1993] 1 WLR 764. That was a trial under the serious fraud regime. The court found that there was one preparatory hearing in existence, and that that had been conducted before Judge Anwyl-Davies QC. But the trial was listed for hearing before Judge Mota Singh QC, simply because of a direction by the presiding judge that Judge Anwyl-Davies should conduct the retrial of another case. The court

d   made the basic point that in a criminal trial there is no power to change the judge once the jury is sworn until the moment at which the jury returns to give its verdict (though another judge may take that verdict). They then applied that same principle by way of analogy to an unsevered trial of serious fraud ([1993] 1 WLR 764 at 772):

e   'Does the same principle apply to the trial of a serious and complex fraud? Must the same judge hear the preparatory hearing and the process before the jury? The advantages of having the same judge throughout the trial of a complex and serious fraud case are set out in paragraph 6.31 of the Fraud Trials Committee Report (1986 H.M.S.O.) chaired by Lord Roskill. It is there stated, at p. 88: "Almost all the witnesses who discussed this agreed in their

f   evidence that in principle the same judge should conduct the preparatory hearings and the trial itself." The 34th recommendation of that Committee reads at p. 182: "The judge presiding at the preparatory hearings must be the judge who, save in exceptional circumstances, is to conduct the trial." In our judgment, the correct principle is that stated in the 34th conclusion of the

g   Committee, namely, that the judge presiding at the preparatory hearings must be the judge who, save in exceptional circumstances, is to conduct the trial. Administrative convenience would not be a sufficient reason for changing the judge in a complex and serious fraud case between the preparatory hearings and the proceedings in front of the jury. What amounts to exceptional circumstances will have to be resolved on a case by

h   case basis. Clearly, the death or serious illness of the judge would qualify as an exceptional circumstance.'

That decision of another constitution of this court binds us unless we conclude that the earlier decision is clearly wrong. We do not think that it is. But what was

j   said, both by the Roskill Committee and also by the court, contemplated a whole (ie non-severed) trial of the indictment. We would not accept that 'exceptional circumstances' are necessarily the test where the trial has been severed. But if that is the test in such trials, then the level of the threshold required for exceptional circumstances must sensibly be lower in a severed trial where there has been no preparatory hearing specifically related to the severed counts (though there will usually be, as there is here, some degree of overlap) than in an unsevered trial where the preparatory hearing was focused on that trial. And in any event we have no hesitation in concluding that the legal incapacity to continue to act as the trial judge for the remaining counts which occurred when Phillips LJ's remit under s 9(1) expired with the conclusion of the trial of counts 4 and 10 must be capable of constituting exceptional circumstances. We reject entirely the suggestion that the reason for 'not requesting Phillips LJ was 'administrative convenience'. It quite plainly was not. The Lord Chancellor was deciding on the best deployment of judicial manpower in the proper administration of justice. That was the right criterion.

We come then to the critical question of judgment for the Lord Chancellor. The factual framework for that question is quite clear without going into detail. Phillips LJ undoubtedly is 'uniquely well placed' to try the remaining counts on this indictment. The Crown put the indictment forward as 'one fraud', and though there have been no preparatory hearings (nor orders other than severance) in relation to the remaining counts and though there will be a new jury or juries sworn in relation to them, the overlapping background knowledge he has of the case and the practical and legal problems thrown up by it, all justify the description 'uniquely well placed'. While the Serious Fraud Office do not support the application (because they do not see how the Lord Chancellor's decision can be called 'irrational'), they acknowledge that it would assist the future conduct of the case if it were conducted by Phillips LJ. Because of his familiarity with the subject-matter, he would have to do less reading or re-reading and would require less help from the parties. So the trials would start and so finish sooner, and be cheaper. As Mr Pleming QC put it: 'Life will be more difficult with a new judge. It will be harder work for everyone, but especially for the new judge.' All these disadvantages the Lord Chancellor recognised. While 'uniquely well placed', Phillips LJ is not irreplaceable. No judge in these circumstances ever would be, dealing as he will be with a new jury, and having to decide all rulings on the material before him. It will take longer for the new judge to master that material, but it is only a question of time before he does. This reflects the Lord Chief Justice's view expressed in opinion given to the Lord Chancellor that the remaining trials did not require to be tried by a Lord Justice.

The other side of the balance comprises the public interest in the Court of Appeal (effectively the final court in the country for all save the handful of cases which go to the House of Lords) being at full strength for a period of a year or more. That court is, in the words of Bingham MR, at the pivot of our legal system. Because it has been under-manned and under-resourced, it has not been able to keep up with the increased number of appeals. In his most recent report *The Court of Appeal Civil Division Review of the Legal Year* 1994–95 p 15, Bingham MR concluded:

'There is an urgent need for an increase in the judicial strength of the court. The alternative is delay of a length inconsistent with the due administration of justice.'

The Lord Chancellor accepts that there is a 'severe backlog'. Three additional appointments have recently been made, but the crisis continues. And it is not restricted to civil justice. There are similar pressures in crime, in the Court of Appeal Criminal Division, and the Divisional Court.

The Lord Chancellor had to decide on the best disposal of judicial manpower for the proper administration of justice. He had to balance the narrow, but more closely focused, contribution Phillips LJ could make in the trial of the remaining *a* counts, against his broader contribution in the Court of Appeal and the wider interests of justice in having a Court of Appeal up to full strength at a critical time. This balance, and the weight to be given to various aspects of the process, are all matters for the Lord Chancellor, and not for the reviewing court. The greater the element of policy in a decision, the greater the judicial reticence in reviewing it should be. Here there is a high degree of policy. The Lord Chancellor *b* approached the matter correctly, informed himself properly, consulted appropriately, and reached a decision well within the discretion accorded to him. This application accordingly must fail. In our judgment, irrationality on these facts is unsustainable.

A final word. We started by saying that there had been some surprise that a discretion relating to the deployment of judicial manpower could be the subject *c* of attack by judicial review. *R v Southwark Crown Court, ex p Customs and Excise Comrs* [1993] 1 WLR 764 and the illustration we have given of circumstances where such a question might well be reviewable show that there is no universal prohibition. But we wish to do all we can to discourage any comparable application relating to the deployment of judicial manpower. Experience shows *d* that an unusual application of this kind spawns imitations, even if the imitated application fails. We wish to discourage such applications. Given the ground rules of the review and the discretion entrusted to the decision-maker, the realistic assumption must be that the vast preponderance of such applications are doomed to failure and so should be critically examined at the leave stage. If the exceptional case comes along, it will be clearly just that, and that will be so clear *e* that these words will not deter either the applicant's advisors or the single judge.

Application dismissed.

Dilys Tausz   Barrister.

Providence Capitol Trustees Ltd v Ayres and another

CHANCERY DIVISION

CHADWICK J

13 JUNE 1996

Costs – Order for costs – Costs of appeal – Pensions Ombudsman – Liability of ombudsman for costs of successful appeal against his determination – Ombudsman properly named as party to appeal – Ombudsman not appearing at hearing of appeal or taking steps to defend his determination – Whether costs of appeal recoverable by successful appellant against ombudsman – RSC Ord 62, r 3(3).

On 7 June 1996 the court allowed an appeal under s 151(4)[a] of the Pension Schemes Act 1993 by the pensioneer trustee against a determination made by the Pensions Ombudsman following his investigation of a complaint and stood over the trustee's application that the Pensions Ombudsman should pay the costs of the appeal. The ombudsman resisted the application. The trustee relied on the direction in RSC Ord 62, r 3(3) that if the court thought fit to make any order as to costs, it should order the costs to follow the event unless it appeared to the court that in the circumstances of the case some other order should be made. The question arose whether the Pensions Ombudsman, who was properly named as a party to any appeal against his determination, should be at risk as to the costs of a successful appeal in circumstances where he did not appear at the hearing of the appeal or otherwise take any part in resisting a challenge to his determination.

Held – There was no inflexible rule that a successful litigant was entitled to expect to recover his costs from somebody. Where the tribunal whose decision was overturned on appeal appeared on the appeal and made itself party to the lis, it put itself at risk as to the costs of the appeal and it might expect to pay the costs of the appeal. However, it was only in exceptional circumstances that an order for costs would be made where the tribunal did not appear. Accordingly, it would be oppressive to make an order for costs against the Pensions Ombudsman in circumstances where his determination had been overturned on appeal but where he had not made himself a party to the lis by appearing at the appeal or taking steps to defend his determination. The application would therefore be dismissed (see p 763 b d j and p 765 g, post).

R v Kingston-upon-Hull Rent Tribunal, ex p Black [1949] 1 All ER 260 considered.

Notes

For jurisdiction and discretion to award costs, see 37 *Halsbury's Laws* (4th edn) paras 712–725, and for cases on the subject, see 37(3) *Digest* (Reissue) 230, 240, 4273–4275, 4350–4352.

---

a   Section 151(4), so far as material, provides: 'An appeal on a point of law shall lie to the High Court … from a determination or direction of the Pensions Ombudsman at the instance of any person falling within paragraphs (a) to (c) of subsection (3).'

Cases referred to in judgment

a

Dolphin Packaging Materials Ltd v Pensions Ombudsman (1993) Times, 2 December.
Miller v Stapleton [1996] 2 All ER 449.
R v Kingston-upon-Hull Rent Tribunal, ex p Black [1949] 1 All ER 260, DC.
R v Llanidloes Licensing Justices, ex p Davies [1957] 2 All ER 610, [1957] 1 WLR 809,
    DC.

b

R v Newcastle-under-Lyme Justices, ex p Massey [1995] 1 All ER 120, [1994] 1 WLR
    1684, DC.
Steele Ford & Newton (a firm) v CPS [1993] 2 All ER 769, sub nom *Holden & Co (a
    firm) v CPS (No 2)* [1994] 1 AC 22, [1993] 2 WLR 934, HL.

Cases also cited or referred to in skeleton arguments

c

Hamar v Pensions Ombudsman [1996] PLR 1.
R v Liverpool Justices, ex p Roberts [1960] 2 All ER 384, [1960] 1 WLR 585, DC.
R v Willesden Justices, ex p Utley [1947] 2 All ER 838, [1948] 1 KB 397, DC.
R v York City Justices, ex p Farmery (1988) 153 JP 257, DC.
Westminster City Council v Haywood [1996] 2 All ER 467, [1996] 3 WLR 563.

d

Application

By notice dated 2 March 1995 the appellant, Providence Capitol Trustees Ltd,
applied for an order that the second respondent, the Pensions Ombudsman, pay
the costs of its successful appeal under s 151(4) of the Pension Schemes Act 1993
from a determination made by the Pensions Ombudsman on 2 February 1995

e

following an investigation of a complaint made to him by the first respondent, Mr
Graham Ayres, in relation to a pension scheme known as the Axelstore Ltd Small
Self-Administered Scheme. The first respondent took no part in the application.
The facts are set out in the judgment.

f

Geoffrey Topham (instructed by *Hammond Suddards*) for the appellant trustee.
Christopher Nugee (instructed by *Paisner & Co*) for the Pensions Ombudsman.

CHADWICK J. On 7 June 1996 I allowed an appeal by the pensioneer trustee
against a determination made by the Pensions Ombudsman on 2 February 1995,
following his investigation of a complaint made to him by Mr Graham Ayres in

g

relation to a pension scheme known as the Axelstore Ltd Small Self-Administered
Scheme. The ombudsman had not appeared at the hearing of that appeal. At the
conclusion of my judgment I stood over the application of the appellant trustee
that the ombudsman should pay the costs of the appeal in order to give to the
ombudsman an opportunity to be heard. He has appeared by counsel to resist
the application for costs. It is on that application that I now rule.

h

The point is of some general importance. Should the Pensions Ombudsman,
who is properly named as a party to any appeal against his determination, be at
risk as to the costs of a successful appeal in circumstances where he does not
appear at the hearing of the appeal or otherwise take any part in resisting the
challenge to his determination?

j

The office of Pensions Ombudsman is established under Pt X of the Pension
Schemes Act 1993. His functions are prescribed by sub-ss (1) and (2) of s 146,
which are in these terms:

'(1) The Pensions Ombudsman may investigate and determine any
complaint made to him in writing by or on behalf of an authorised
complainant who alleges that he has sustained injustice in consequence of

maladministration in connection with any act or omission of the trustees or managers of an occupational pension scheme or personal pension scheme.   a

(2) The Pensions Ombudsman may also investigate and determine any dispute of fact or law which arises in relation to such a scheme between—(a) the trustees or managers of the scheme, and (b) an authorised complainant, and which is referred to him in writing by or on behalf of the authorised complainant ...'   b

Section 150(7) enables the ombudsman to refer any question of law to the High Court. Subject to that, he is to make his determination of the complaint or dispute, as the case may be, in the form of a written statement. That statement must contain the reasons for his determination (see s 151(1) of the 1993 Act). The determination is final and binding on the complainant and on the trustees, and on   c any persons claiming under them; subject to an appeal only on a point of law to the High Court (see s 151(3) and (4)).

An appeal against the determination of the Pensions Ombudsman is an appeal to which the provisions of RSC Ord 55 apply (see r 1 of that order). Order 55, r 4(1)(b) provides that notice of the originating motion by which such an appeal   d is commenced must be served on the person whose determination or decision is the subject of the appeal and on every party to the proceedings other than the appellant.

In the present case notice of the originating motion was served, correctly, on both the ombudsman and Mr Ayres. They are each named as a respondent and each is a party to the appeal for the purposes of s 151 of the Supreme Court Act   e 1981. In particular they are each a party for the purposes of RSC Ord 62. Order 62, r 3 provides:

'... (2) No party to any proceedings shall be entitled to recover any of the costs of those proceedings from any other party to those proceedings except   f under an order of the Court.

(3) If the Court in the exercise of its discretion sees fit to make any order as to the costs of any proceedings, the Court shall order the costs to follow the event, except where it appears to the Court that in the circumstances of the case some other order should be made as to the whole or any part of the   g costs ...'

In the present case the pensioneer trustee as successful appellant, for reasons which are understandable and to which I shall refer later in this judgment, does not seek costs against Mr Ayres. Further, although RSC Ord 62, r 6 enables a person who has been party to any proceedings in the capacity of trustee to   h recover the costs of those proceedings in so far as they are not recovered from any other party out of the fund held by him in that capacity, in the circumstances that are set out in my judgment of 7 June 1996 the trustee no longer holds any fund to which it could have recourse under that rule. Accordingly, unless the appellant can obtain an order for costs against the ombudsman, it will be left to bear the   j costs of its successful appeal out of its own funds.

It is in these circumstances that the trustee seeks an order that the ombudsman pay the costs of the appeal, relying upon the direction in RSC Ord 62, r 3(3) that, if the court thinks fit to make any order as to costs, it should order the costs to follow the event unless it appears to the court that in the circumstances of the case some other order should be made.

a   The question, therefore, is whether I should make any order for costs on this appeal; and if so whether there are any circumstances which make it appropriate to make some order other than that costs should follow the event, that is to say should be recoverable by the successful appellant against the Pensions Ombudsman as respondent. Questions of costs are of course to be decided by the court in the exercise of its discretion (see s 51(1) of the 1981 Act).

b   There is no inflexible rule that a successful litigant is entitled to expect to recover his costs from somebody (see the observations of Lord Bridge in *Steele Ford & Newton (a firm) v CPS* [1993] 2 All ER 769 at 779–780, [1994] 1 AC 22 at 39–40). Among the examples given by Lord Bridge is that of a party who has been the victim of a misjudgment by an inferior court or tribunal, and who obtains relief on an application for judicial review from the Divisional Court in

c   circumstances in which the court cannot hold either another party or the inferior tribunal itself liable in costs and there is no power to award costs from public funds.

         When the tribunal whose decision is overturned on appeal appears on the appeal and makes itself party to the lis, it puts itself at risk as to the costs of the

d   appeal; and if the appeal against its decision is successful it may expect to pay the costs of the appeal: see the observations of Lord Goddard CJ in *R v Kingston-upon-Hull Rent Tribunal, ex p Black* [1949] 1 All ER 260 and *R v Llanidloes Licensing Justices, ex p Davies* [1957] 2 All ER 610. But in circumstances where the tribunal does not appear and does not take part, it is only in exceptional cases that an order for costs will be made against it. For a recent summary of the principles

e   applicable to justices, see *R v Newcastle-under-Lyme Justices, ex p Massey* [1995] 1 All ER 120 at 126–127. Under para (iii) of that summary the court said:

f   'Justices who merely file affidavits and do not appear before the Divisional Court or the High Court will not, without more, normally be visited with a costs order … This is so despite the fact that, in judicial review proceedings, judges are served with notice of proceedings under Ord 53, r 5(3) and are therefore a party within s 151(1) of the 1981 Act. Albeit that they are a party, for over a century it has not generally been the practice to award costs against them in prerogative writ and judicial review proceedings and that practice, reiterated by successive Lords Chief Justice, must have been known

g   to Parliament at the time of the 1977 and subsequent amendments to Ord 3 and of the enactment of ss 31 and 52 of the 1981 Act and of the 1993 Act.'

         That that principle applies not only to justices but also to other tribunals appears from the decision of the Divisional Court in *R v Kingston-upon-Hull Rent Tribunal, ex p Black* [1949] 1 All ER 260; in particular in a trenchant observation of Lord

h   Goddard CJ, 'If there had been no appearance by the Tribunal of course we should not have given costs in this case'.

         In my view, those principles should guide me in the exercise of my discretion in the present case. It seems to me that it would be oppressive to make an order for costs against the Pensions Ombudsman in circumstances where his

j   determination has been overturned on appeal but where he has not made himself a party to the lis by appearing at the appeal or taking steps to defend his determination. It would be oppressive because the ombudsman has no choice whether or not to be named as a respondent and no power, once named as a respondent, to set aside his own order so as to avoid the need for the appeal proceeding. He is necessarily a party and, whether or not on further consideration he comes to the conclusion that his determination was wrong, there is nothing that he can do to prevent the appeal from proceeding. To visit a *a* party with an order for costs in circumstances in which he is unable to take any steps to avoid the costs incurred on the appeal seems to me to be oppressive and unfair.

Counsel for the appellant trustee urges me to take the view that what might at first sight appear oppressive and unfair is a necessary consequence of the scheme of the legislation. Parliament, having provided for a right of appeal against *b* determinations by the Pensions Ombudsman, must have anticipated that somebody would be required to bear the costs of such an appeal. Prima facie, so it is said, Parliament cannot have intended that the successful appellant should bear the costs. To attribute an intention that the costs of the appeal should be borne by the complainant who had succeeded before the ombudsman would be *c* to risk frustrating the purpose of the legislation. It would be likely to frustrate the purpose of the legislation if a relatively impoverished complainant, having obtained a determination in his favour through the summary procedure provided by Pt X of the 1993 Act, were then to be faced with the risk of bearing the costs of seeking to uphold that determination on an appeal brought by a trustee who might well have a much deeper pocket. If complainants fear that a determination *d* in their favour will not be effective unless they are prepared to risk the costs of upholding it on an appeal to the High Court, they may perhaps take the view that the summary procedure provided by Pt X of the 1993 Act is of little advantage to them.

It is considerations of that nature which, very properly, have led the trustee in *e* this case not to seek an order for costs against Mr Ayres. But the decision not to seek costs against Mr Ayres in this case does not lead to the conclusion that it is therefore correct to make an order for costs against the ombudsman. There will be many circumstances in which the complainant is able to bear the costs of resisting an appeal and in which there will be no reason for the appellant trustee not to seek, or for the court to refuse to make, an order for costs against him. *f* There will be other circumstances in which the trustee's costs of a successful appeal can be recovered by the trustee out of the trust fund pursuant to RSC Ord 62, r 6(2) and the general law.

Having those circumstances in mind it is, in my view, impossible to form the conclusion that Parliament intended to impose on the ombudsman the costs of *g* all successful appeals against his determination irrespective of whether he makes himself party to the lis. I find nothing in the 1993 Act which leads to the conclusion that, in exercising its discretion as to costs, the court should not follow the guidance that can be found in relation to appeals from other tribunals.

I have been referred to two decisions in relation to costs on appeals from the *h* Pensions Ombudsman. The first is a decision of Turner J in *Dolphin Packaging Materials Ltd v Pensions Ombudsman* (1993) Times, 2 December. The issue before the court was what direction should be given to the ombudsman in relation to his involvement in appeal proceedings to which he had been made party. He was seeking directions from the court on the question whether he should continue to *j* be a party to the appeal and, secondly, whether the personal representative of the former member of the relevant scheme was also a necessary party. In those circumstances, the ombudsman having sought directions from the court, the court made an order that he should pay the costs of obtaining those directions. That decision, of itself, gives no guidance as to the way the court should exercise its discretion in a case where the ombudsman has taken no part in the appeal.

a I was referred also to the decision of Carnwath J in *Miller v Stapleton* [1996] 2 All ER 449. In that case the ombudsman appeared and took part in the hearing of the appeal. The issue in which the ombudsman was interested was whether he had power to award compensation for distress and inconvenience. The court held that he did not have that power—a decision which has not been followed on this point in subsequent cases—and ordered that he should pay the costs of the *b* appeal. That, as it seems to me, is an example of a case in which the ombudsman, for good and understandable reasons, had made himself a party to the lis; and so, in accordance with the principles to which I have referred, had put himself at risk as to an order for costs.

I should, however, say a little as to the further argument based on observations of Turner J in the *Dolphin Packaging Materials* case. The judge took the view that *c* it was important that the Pensions Ombudsman had the opportunity to appear at an appeal, because without him it would be likely that points of law might not be addressed adequately by the complainant in person, with the result that the court might be asked to decide a difficult question of law without having heard full argument on both sides. The judge does not appear to have been referred to Ord *d* 55, r 4(1)(b), which plainly does entitle the ombudsman to be present at the hearing of the appeal. The judge decided the question on the basis that it was desirable that he should be present in order to assist the court.

I do not intend to cast any doubt on the proposition that in suitable cases it may be appropriate for the ombudsman to appear in order to argue questions of law for the assistance of the court. But, if he does so on his own initiative, he must *e* risk the possibility that an order for costs will be made against him if his arguments are unsuccessful. To avoid that risk he may think it appropriate either to refer the question of law to the court under s 150(7) of the 1993 Act before he makes his determination, or to apply to the court at an interlocutory stage of the appellate proceedings for a direction whether or not, in that particular case, the court would be assisted by his arguments. If such application is made, the court *f* will then be in a position to give such comfort as it thinks fit to the ombudsman in relation to the risk that an order for costs might be made against him.

For those reasons I dismiss the application for costs against the Pensions Ombudsman on the present appeal. The appellant having chosen not to seek costs against the other respondent, Mr Ayres, I make no order for costs on this *g* appeal.

Application dismissed.

Celia Fox   Barrister.

Practice Note

a

Medical treatment – Withdrawal of treatment – Insensate patient – Patient in persistent vegetative state – Practice – Sanction of High Court judge required before treatment terminated – Confirmation of diagnosis – Form of application – Parties to application – Evidence – Views of patient – Consultation with Official Solicitor.

b

The need for the prior sanction of a High Court judge

1. The termination of artificial feeding and hydration for patients in a vegetative state will in virtually all cases require the prior sanction of a High Court judge: *Airedale NHS Trust v Bland* [1993] 1 All ER 821 at 833, [1993] AC 789 at 805 per Sir Stephen Brown P and *Frenchay Healthcare NHS Trust v S* [1994] 2 All   c
ER 403, [1994] 1 WLR 601.

2. The diagnosis should be made in accordance with the most up-to-date generally accepted guidelines for the medical profession. A working group of the Royal College of Physicians issued guidance on the diagnosis and management of the permanent vegetative state (PVS) in March 1996. This has been indorsed by   d
the Conference of Medical Royal Colleges. The working group advises that the diagnosis of permanent vegetative state is not absolute but based on probabilities. Such a diagnosis may not reasonably be made until the patient has been in a continuing vegetative state following head injury for more than 12 months or following other causes of brain damage for more than six months. Before then, as soon as the patient's condition has stabilised, rehabilitative measures such as   e
coma arousal programmes, should be instituted (see *Airedale NHS Trust v Bland* [1993] 1 All ER 821 at 872, [1993] AC 789 at 870–871 per Lord Goff). It is not appropriate to apply to court for permission to terminate artificial feeding and hydration until the condition is judged to be permanent. In many cases it will be necessary to commission reports based on clinical and other observations of the   f
patient over a period of time

Applications to court

3. Applications to court should be by originating summons issued in the Family Division of the High Court seeking a declaration in the form set out in para 5 below. Subject to specific provisions below, the application should follow   g
the procedure laid down for sterilisation cases by the House of Lords in *F v West Berkshire Health Authority (Mental Health Act Commission intervening)* [1989] 2 All ER 545, [1990] 2 AC 1 and in the Official Solicitor's practice note ([1996] 2 FLR 111).

4. Applications to court in relation to minors should be made within wardship   h
proceedings. In such cases the applicant should seek the leave of the court for the termination of feeding and hydration, rather than a declaration. The form of relief set out in para 5 below should be amended accordingly.

5. The originating summons should seek relief in the following form:

'(1) It is declared that despite the inability of X to give a valid consent, the   j
plaintiffs and/or the responsible medical practitioners: (i) may lawfully discontinue all life-sustaining treatment and medical support measures (including ventilation, nutrition and hydration by artificial means) designed to keep X alive in his existing permanent vegetative state; and (ii) may lawfully furnish such treatment and nursing care whether at hospital or elsewhere under medical supervision as may be appropriate to ensure X

a
suffers the least distress and retains the greatest dignity until such time as his life comes to an end.

(2) It is ordered that in the event of a material change in the existing circumstances occurring before such withdrawal of treatment any party shall have liberty to apply for such further or other declaration or order as may be just.'

b
6. The case will normally be heard in open court. The court will, however, usually take steps to preserve the anonymity of the patient and the patient's family (and, where appropriate, the hospital) by making orders under s 11 of the Contempt of Court Act 1981: *Re G (adult patient: publicity)* [1995] 2 FLR 528. An order restricting publicity will continue to have effect notwithstanding the death

c
of the patient, unless and until an application is made to discharge it: *Re C (adult patient: restriction of publicity after death)* [1996] 1 FCR 605.

The parties

7. The applicant may be either the next of kin or other individual closely connected with the patient or the relevant district health authority/NHS Trust

d
(which in any event ought to be a party): *Re S (hospital patient: court's jurisdiction)* [1995] 3 All ER 290, [1996] Fam 1. The views of the next of kin or of others close to the patient cannot act as a veto to an application but they must be taken fully into account by the court: *Re G (persistent vegetative state)* [1995] 2 FCR 46.

8. The Official Solicitor should normally be invited to act as guardian ad litem

e
of the patient, who will inevitably be a patient within the meaning of RSC Ord 80. In any case in which the Official Solicitor does not represent the patient, he should be joined as a defendant or respondent.

The investigation

9. There should be at least two independent reports on the patient from

f
neurologists or other doctors experienced in assessing disturbances of consciousness. One of these reports will be commissioned by the Official Solicitor. The duties of doctors making the diagnosis are described in the report of the working group of the Royal College of Physicians as follows:

g
'They should undertake their own assessment separately and should write clearly the details of that assessment and their conclusion in the notes. They must ask medical and other clinical staff and relatives or carers about the reactions and responses of the patient and it is important that the assessors shall take into account the descriptions and comments given by relatives, carers and nursing staff who spend most time with the patient. The medical

h
practitioners shall separately perform a formal neurological examination and consider the results of those investigations which have been undertaken to identify the cause of the condition. It is helpful for nursing staff and relatives to be present during the examination; their role as responsible witnesses who spend a much longer time with the patient than can the medical practitioners must be recognised. It is to be emphasised that there is no urgency in making

j
the diagnosis of the permanent vegetative state. If there is any uncertainty in the mind of the assessor then the diagnosis shall not be made and a reassessment undertaken after further time has elapsed. The most important role of the medical practitioner in making the diagnosis is to ensure that the patient is not sentient and, in this respect, the views of the nursing staff, relatives and carers are of considerable importance and help.'

The views of the patient and others

10. The Official Solicitor's representative will normally require to interview the next of kin and others close to the patient as well as seeing the patient and those caring for him. The views of the patient may have been previously expressed, either in writing or otherwise. The High Court may determine the effect of a purported advance directive as to future medical treatment: *Re T (adult: refusal of medical treatment)* [1992] 4 All ER 649, [1993] Fam 95 and *Re C (adult: refusal of medical treatment)* [1994] 1 All ER 819, [1994] 1 WLR 290. In summary, the patient's previously expressed views, if any, will always be an important component in the decisions of the doctors and the court, particularly if they are clearly established and were intended to apply to the circumstances which have in fact arisen.

Consultation with the Official Solicitor

11. Members of the Official Solicitor's legal staff are prepared to discuss PVS cases before proceedings have been issued. Contact with the Official Solicitor may be made by telephoning 0171-911-7127 during office hours.

12. This practice note replaces the practice note dated March 1994 ([1994] 2 All ER 413).

PETER HARRIS
Official Solicitor.

26 July 1996

a # Smith New Court Securities Ltd v Scrimgeour Vickers (Asset Management) Ltd

HOUSE OF LORDS

b LORD BROWNE-WILKINSON, LORD KEITH OF KINKEL, LORD MUSTILL, LORD SLYNN OF HADLEY AND LORD STEYN

24–27 JUNE, 1–3, JULY, 21 NOVEMBER 1996

Damages – Measure of damages – Fraudulent misrepresentation – Plaintiff induced to purchase shares by fraudulent misrepresentation – Value of shares flawed by reason of
c *undiscovered fraud perpetrated on company issuing shares – Assessment of damages – Whether damages to be assessed on basis of difference between price paid and real value of shares at date of transaction taking into account undiscovered fraud – Whether damages to be assessed by reference to difference between price paid and open market price if market had known of fraud – Whether damages to be assessed at date of*
d *transaction.*

In July 1989 the plaintiff company, SNC, purchased a parcel of 28,141,424 shares in F Inc which had been pledged to a bank as security for a loan made by the bank to a client. When the client defaulted the bank forced a sale of the shares through the first defendants, stockbrokers owned by the bank. SNC was under the
e impression that it was in competition with two other bidders for the shares and bid a price of $82\frac{1}{4}$p per share, making a total consideration of £23,141,424 for the parcel. In September an announcement by F Inc that it had been the victim of a major fraud had a disastrous effect on its share price. Between November 1989 and April 1990 SNC sold the shares at prices between 30p and 40p, realising a total
f of £11,788,204 at a loss of £11,353,220 on the transaction as a whole. When the share price collapsed SNC investigated the circumstances of its purchase of the shares and discovered that there had not been two other bidders at the time of the sale. SNC brought proceedings against the first defendants and the bank claiming damages for fraudulent misrepresentation. SNC alleged that it had been induced to enter into the transaction by three false representations made by R, a senior
g executive of the bank and a director of the first defendants, to the effect that SNC would be in competition with two other bidders for the parcel of shares, second, that he would disclose the competing bids after SNC had made its bid thereby representing that he had in fact received other bids, and third, after SNC had bid 82p, that there had been other bids of 81p and 75 to 77p. The judge found that
h SNC had been induced to enter into the transaction by the second and third representations, both of which were false, but further found that the first representation had not been proved. He held that on the basis of the two false representations SNC was entitled to damages against the bank (as being vicariously liable for the misrepresentations made by R) assessed on the basis of the difference between the price paid and the real value of the shares at the date
j of the transaction, taking into account the then undiscovered fraud perpetrated on F Inc, that value being 44p, and not the market value if the representations had not been made, which was not less than 78p. The judge accordingly awarded damages of £10,764,005. The bank appealed to the Court of Appeal on the measure of damages, while SNC cross-appealed against the finding that the first representation had not been proved. The Court of Appeal upheld the cross-appeal on the grounds that the second and third representations, both of

which had been proved, were inexplicable unless the first representation had also been made. However, on the issue of damages, the court held that the correct measure of damages was the difference between the price paid by the buyer and the price which, without the misrepresentations, the shares would have fetched on the open market on the acquisition date and accordingly reduced the damages to £1,196,010. SNC and the bank appealed and cross-appealed to the House of Lords. On the damages issue, the bank contended that the loss attributable to the subsequent disclosure of the fraud by a third party was a misfortune risk and irrecoverable and that the cause of SNC's loss was its decision to retain the shares rather than sell them on immediately, while SNC contended that the law imposed liability in an action for deceit for consequences that were unforeseen and unforeseeable when the tortfeasor committed the wrong.

Held – (1) On the liability issue, the House of Lords would very rarely exercise its jurisdiction to disturb concurrent findings of fact by the trial judge and the Court of Appeal. Given that there was convincing evidence that SNC had fixed its bid on the basis that were other bids and that the issue of misrepresentation arose several months later, both the trial judge and the Court of Appeal were entitled to draw the conclusion that SNC had entered into the transaction as the result of actionable fraudulent misrepresentations. However, it was possible that there was a misunderstanding during the initial contact between R and SNC, at which the first representation was alleged to have been made, and therefore the judge was entitled to find that he was not satisfied that the first representation was made in sufficiently unequivocal terms for it to form the basis for an action in deceit. However, that finding did not affect the validity of the finding by both the trial judge and the Court of Appeal that the second and third representations were proved and that therefore the essentials of the tort of deceit had been established. The bank's cross-appeal on liability would accordingly be dismissed (see p 772 *j*, p 780 *h* to p 781 *a f*, p 782 *c*, p 786 *b* to *d*, p 787 *a b* and p 788 *b g* to *j*, post).

(2) On the damages issue, the primary rule was that a victim of fraud was entitled to compensation for all the actual loss, including consequential loss, directly flowing from the transaction induced by the deceit of the wrongdoer. The normal method of calculating the loss caused by the deceit was prima facie the price paid less the real value of the subject matter of the sale as at the date of the transaction or acquisition by the plaintiff. However, since the overriding principle was that the plaintiff should receive full compensation for the wrong suffered and the date of transaction rule was only a means of attempting to give effect to the overriding compensatory rule, that rule did not apply where either the misrepresentation continued to operate after the date of the acquisition of the asset so as to induce the plaintiff to retain the asset, or the circumstances of the case were such that the plaintiff was, by reason of the fraud, locked into the property. Any assessment of damages was limited by the normal rules relating to causation, remoteness and mitigation except that in the case of remoteness the victim of the fraud was entitled to compensation for all the actual loss directly flowing from the transaction induced by the wrongdoer, including heads of consequential loss, and not merely loss which was reasonably foreseeable. On the facts, SNC had been induced by the misrepresentations to purchase an asset that was already flawed by reason of the undiscovered fraud perpetrated on F Inc and were locked into the transaction by reason of the fraudulent misrepresentations, having bought the shares for a purpose and at a price which precluded them from sensibly disposing of them immediately. In those

a circumstances it could not be said that the loss flowed from SNC's decision to retain the shares. It followed that the amount of damages recoverable by SNC was the difference between the contract price and the amount actually realised by SNC on the resale of the shares. SNC's appeal would therefore be allowed (see p 775 *j*, p 777 *b* to *f*, p 778 *d f j* to p 779 *c g* to *j*, p 780 *b g h*, p 781 *a f*, p 790 *a b*, p 792 *a* to *h*, p 793 *a*, p 794 *a* to *f* and p 795 *c* to *j*, post); *Doyle v Olby (Ironmongers) Ltd*
b [1969] 2 All ER 119 applied; *Downs v Chappell* [1996] 3 All ER 344 overruled in part; *Twycross v Grant* (1877) 2 CPD 469, *Waddell v Blockey* (1879) 4 QBD 678, *Peek v Derry* (1887) 37 Ch D 541 and *McConnel v Wright* [1903] 1 Ch 546 doubted.

Decision of Court of Appeal [1994] 4 All ER 225 reversed.

Notes
c For fraudulent misrepresentation in general, see 31 *Halsbury's Laws* (4th edn) paras 1057–1062, and for cases on the subject, see 34 *Digest* (Reissue) 330–344, *2566–2726*.

For measure of damages for misrepresentation, see 31 *Halsbury's Laws* (4th edn) paras 1107–1109, and for cases on the subject, see 34 *Digest* (Reissue) 383–
d 387, *3126–3166*.

Cases referred to in opinions
A-G of Hong Kong v Wong Muk-ping [1987] 2 All ER 488, [1987] AC 501, [1987] 2 WLR 1033, PC.
Arkwright v Newbold (1881) 17 Ch D 301, Ch D and CA.
e *Cemp Properties (UK) Ltd v Dentsply Research and Development Corp (Denton Hall & Bergin, third party)* [1991] 2 EGLR 197, CA.
Clark v Urquhart, Stracey v Urquhart [1930] AC 28, HL.
County Personnel (Employment Agency) Ltd v Alan R Pulver & Co (a firm) [1987] 1 All ER 289, [1987] 1 WLR 916, CA.
f *Davidson v Tullock* (1860) 2 LT 97, HL.
Dodd Properties (Kent) Ltd v Canterbury City Council [1980] 1 All ER 928, [1980] 1 WLR 433, CA.
Doyle v Olby (Ironmongers) Ltd [1969] 2 All ER 119, [1969] 2 QB 158, [1969] 2 WLR 673, CA.
g *Downs v Chappell* [1996] 3 All ER 344, CA.
East v Maurer [1991] 2 All ER 733, [1991] 1 WLR 461, CA.
H and ors (minors) (sexual abuse: standard of proof) Re [1996] 1 All ER 1, [1996] AC 563, [1996] 2 WLR 8, HL.
IBL Ltd v Coussens [1991] 2 All ER 133, CA.
h *Johnson v Agnew* [1979] 1 All ER 883, [1980] AC 367, [1979] 2 WLR 487, HL.
Livingstone v Rawyards Coal Co (1880) 5 App Cas 25, HL.
McConnel v Wright [1903] 1 Ch 546, CA.
Overseas Tankship (UK) Ltd v Morts Dock and Engineering Co Ltd, The Wagon Mound [1961] 1 All ER 404, [1961] AC 388, [1961] 2 WLR 126, PC.
Pasley v Freeman (1789) 3 Durn & E 51, [1775–1802] All ER Rep 31, 100 ER 450.
j *Peek v Derry* (1887) 37 Ch D 541, CA; *rvsd* (1889) 14 App Cas 337, [1886–90] All ER Rep 1, HL.
Potts v Miller (1940) 64 CLR 282, Aust HC.
Royscot Trust Ltd v Rogerson [1991] 3 All ER 294, [1991] 2 QB 297, [1991] 3 WLR 57, CA.
Ruxley Electronics and Construction Ltd v Forsyth [1995] 3 All ER 268, [1996] AC 344, [1995] 3 WLR 118, HL.

Shepheard v Broome [1904] AC 342, HL; *affg* sub nom *Broome v Speak* [1903] 1 Ch
   586, CA.

Smith Kline & French Laboratories Ltd v Long [1988] 3 All ER 887, [1989] 1 WLR 1,
   CA.

*South Australia Asset Management Corp v York Montague Ltd, United Bank of Kuwait v
   Prudential Property Services Ltd, Nykredit Mortgage Bank plc v Edward Erdman
   Group Ltd* [1996] 3 All ER 365, [1996] 3 WLR 87, HL; *rvsg* sub nom *Banque
   Bruxelles Lambert SA v Eagle Star Insurance Co Ltd* [1995] 2 All ER 769, [1995] QB
   375, [1995] 2 WLR 607, CA.

Toteff v Antonas (1952) 87 CLR 647, Aust HC.

Twycross v Grant (1877) 2 CPD 469, CPD and CA.

Waddell v Blockey (1879) 4 QBD 678, CA.

Yorkshire Dale Steamship Co Ltd v Minister of War Transport [1942] AC 691, [1942] 2
   All ER 6, HL.

Appeal

The plaintiff, Smith New Court Securities Ltd (Smith), appealed from the
decision of the Court of Appeal (Nourse, Rose and Hoffmann LJJ) ([1994] 4 All ER
225, [1994] 1 WLR 1271) delivered on 17 February 1994 allowing the appeal of the
second defendant, Citibank NA (Citibank), from the judgment of Chadwick J
([1992] BCLC 1104) delivered on 25 March 1992 giving judgment for Smith
against Citibank in the sum of £10,764,005 and interest on Smith's claim for
damages for fraudulent misrepresentation brought against the first defendant,
Scrimgeour Vickers (Asset Management) Ltd, and Citibank arising out of the
purchase by Smith of a parcel of 28,141,424 shares in Ferranti International Signal
Inc on 21 July 1989 from Citibank acting through the first defendant as broker.
The Court of Appeal substituted an award of £1,196,010 damages payable by
Citibank to Smith. Citibank cross-appealed against that part of the Court of
Appeal's judgment reversing Chadwick J's finding that one of the
misrepresentations relied upon by Smith had not been proved. The facts are set
out in the opinion of Lord Browne-Wilkinson.

Anthony Grabiner QC, Ian Glick QC and *John McCaughran* (instructed by *Ashurst
   Morris Crisp*) for Smith.

Jonathan Sumption QC and *Anthony Mann QC* (instructed by *Wilde Sapte*) for
   Citibank.

Their Lordships took time for consideration.

21 November 1996. The following opinions were delivered.

LORD BROWNE-WILKINSON. My Lords, I have had the advantage of
reading in draft the speech to be delivered by my noble and learned friend Lord
Steyn. As to the issue of liability raised by the cross-appeal, I agree with his
reasoning and conclusions: I would restore the judge's finding that Smith New
Court Securities Ltd (Smith) had established that Citibank NA (through Mr
Roberts) fraudulently induced Smith to purchase the Ferranti shares by making
the second and third representations, but not the first representation.

The damages issue which is the subject matter of the appeal raises for decision
for the first time in your Lordships' House the question of the correct measure of
damages where a plaintiff has acquired property in reliance on a fraudulent

a misrepresentation made by the defendant. The position in the present case is complicated by the fact that there are two frauds involved. The first, 'Roberts fraud', is the fraudulent representation made by Mr Roberts on behalf of Citibank on 21 July 1989 which induced Smith to buy 28,141,424 Ferranti shares for £23,141,424. The second, 'Guerin fraud', is the fraud practised by Mr Guerin on Ferranti. Although the Guerin fraud was committed before 21 July 1989, its *b* existence was unknown to Citibank, Smith, Ferranti and the market until after that date. Shortly stated the question is who should bear the risk of the Guerin fraud: Smith, which still held the Ferranti shares when the Guerin fraud was discovered, or Citibank which by its servant had fraudulently induced Smith to buy the Ferranti shares.

The relevant facts lie within a comparatively narrow compass. The judge held *c* that Smith bought the Ferranti shares at $82\frac{1}{4}$p as a market making risk, i e with a view to holding them on its books over a comparatively long period to be sold on at a later date. He further held that Smith would not have bought at that price at all apart from the Roberts fraud. Such a purchase is to be contrasted with a 'bought deal' where the market maker buys the shares with a view to its agency *d* branch selling them on in smaller parcels to its clients, such sales usually taking place within a matter of hours. The judge held that, if Smith had been considering a bought deal, it could not have bid more than 78p, at which price Citibank would not have sold to Smith. From these facts, two points emerge: first, as a result of the Roberts fraud Smith bought the Ferranti shares with a view to holding them for a comparatively long period; second, if Smith had bid on the *e* basis of a bought deal, it would not have acquired the shares.

The history of the Ferranti shares subsequent to 21 July 1989 was as follows. On 11 August 1989 Ferranti published its annual reports and accounts for the year ending 31 March 1989 which confirmed the results stated in a preliminary announcement made on 14 July 1989. On 11 September 1989 the directors of *f* Ferranti announced that information had come to their attention which required a restatement of the 1989 accounts. At their request dealing in Ferranti shares was suspended. On 29 September the chairman of Ferranti wrote to the shareholders telling them that Ferranti had been the victim of a major fraud by Mr Guerin. Trading in Ferranti shares resumed on 3 October. On 17 November Ferranti published its revised audited accounts which showed that the effect of *g* the Guerin fraud was even worse than had been thought.

Smith had retained all the Ferranti shares which it had bought on 21 July. But from 20 November 1989 onwards Smith began to trickle these shares onto the market and obtained prices ranging from 49p down to 30p. By 30 April 1990 it had sold them all for a total of £11,788,204, i e at a loss of £11,353,220. It was not *h* suggested at the trial that Smith's retention of the shares until November 1989 or their subsequent sales were in any way unreasonable.

The judge found that Smith first learned of Mr Roberts' fraud on 5 December 1989 although there was evidence to suggest that by mid-November 1989 Smith was suspicious of the truth of Mr Roberts' representations. On 2 January 1990 *j* solicitors for Smith wrote to Citibank purporting to rescind the contract for the purchase of the 28m Ferranti shares. At the trial, the claim to rescind was persisted in until the closing speech for Smith when it was expressly abandoned for reasons not examined before your Lordships. Thereafter the only claim by Smith has been for damages for deceit. Both before the trial judge, Chadwick J ([1992] BCLC 1104) and the Court of Appeal, Nourse, Rose and Hoffmann LJJ ([1994] 4 All ER 225, [1994] 1 WLR 1271) the argument proceeded on the basis that, where a fraudulent misrepresentation has induced the plaintiff to enter into

a contract of purchase, the measure of damages is, in general, the difference
between the contract price and the true open market value of the property   *a*
purchased, *valued as at the date of the contract of purchase*. This was the law as laid
down in a series of cases decided at the end of the nineteenth century, usually in
relation to shares purchased in reliance on a fraudulent prospectus (see *Twycross
v Grant* (1877) 2 CPD 469, *Waddell v Blockey* (1879) 4 QBD 678 and *Peek v Derry*
(1887) 37 Ch D 541 and subsequently treated as settled law by the Court of Appeal   *b*
in *McConnel v Wright* [1903] 1 Ch 546). It was common ground that there was one
exception to this general rule: where the open market at the transaction date was
a false market, in the sense that the price was inflated because of a
misrepresentation made to the market generally *by the defendant*, the market
value is not decisive: in such circumstances the 'true' value as at the transaction
date has to be ascertained but with the benefit of hindsight (see *McConnel v*   *c*
Wright).

Now in the present case the market value of the Ferranti shares at the
transaction date (21 July 1989) was inflated, since the existence of the Guerin
fraud was then unknown: there was, in one sense, a false market. But that false
market was not attributable to the fraud of the defendant, Citibank: the Roberts   *d*
fraud had no impact on the open market price. The difference between
Chadwick J and the Court of Appeal lay in the fact that Chadwick J held that there
was a latent defect (ie the Guerin fraud) in the Ferranti shares and that, even
though the false market was not due to the fraud of Citibank, he had to find the
true value of the Ferranti shares, using hindsight. He accordingly valued the
Ferranti shares at what would have been their open market value had the market   *e*
known of the Guerin fraud on 21 July 1989. The judge fixed this value at 44p per
share giving a total true value of the shares on the transaction date of £12,382,226.
He accordingly awarded as damages the difference between the contract price
and that figure, ie £10,764,005.

The Court of Appeal on the other hand took the view that it was only   *f*
legitimate, in the case of quoted shares, to depart from the market price as at the
transaction date where that price was falsified *by the defendant's misrepresentation*.
In all other cases the market value has to be taken to be the quoted value. The
Court of Appeal therefore reduced the damages to £1,196,010, being the
difference between the contract price and the value of the shares at 78p a share,
being the value at which on 21 July 1989 Smith itself would have been prepared   *g*
to buy. The Court of Appeal was conscious that, in so holding, they were
throwing the whole risk of catastrophic events onto the innocent purchaser
rather than the fraudulent vendor. But they held that such injustice stemmed
from the rigidity of two rules (both of which had been common ground before
them): first, the denial of rescission where a plaintiff cannot return in specie the   *h*
very shares which were the subject matter of the fraudulent sale; second, the rule
which requires the damages to be calculated as at the date of sale.

As to the first rule referred to by the Court of Appeal, the reasons why Smith
abandoned their claim to rescind were not explored before your Lordships. I will
therefore say nothing about the point save that if the current law in fact provides
(as the Court of Appeal thought) that there is no right to rescind the contract for   *j*
the sale of quoted shares once the specific shares purchased have been sold, the
law will need to be closely looked at hereafter. Since in such a case other,
identical, shares can be purchased on the market, the defrauded purchaser can
offer substantial restitutio in integrum which is normally sufficient.

As to the second rule referred to by the Court of Appeal—the rule requiring
damages to be assessed as at the date of the transaction—Mr Grabiner, for Smith,

a submitted that the basis on which the nineteenth century cases were decided was erroneous and that later decisions show the right approach to the assessment of damages. I agree with those submissions and rather than consider the sterilities of the argument surrounding the nineteenth century cases proceed at once to consider the more modern law.

b As ever in considering damages in tort, the starting point must be to repeat, yet again, the well-known statement of Lord Blackburn in *Livingstone v Rawyards Coal Co* (1880) 5 App Cas 25 at 39:

> c 'I do not think there is any difference of opinion as to its being a general rule that, where any injury is to be compensated by damages, in settling the sum of money to be given for reparation of damages you should as nearly as possible get that sum of money which will put the party who has been injured, or who has suffered, in the same position as he would have been in if he had not sustained the wrong for which he is now getting his compensation or reparation.'

d To that statement he added these important words, which are less frequently quoted:

> 'That must be qualified by a great many things which may arise—such, for instance, as by the consideration whether the damage has been maliciously done, or whether it has been done with full knowledge that the person doing it was doing wrong. There could be no doubt that there you would say that everything would be taken into view that would go most against the wilful e wrongdoer—many things which you would properly allow in favour of an innocent mistaken trespasser would be disallowed as against a wilful and intentional trespasser on the ground that he must not qualify his own wrong, and various things of that sort.'

f In *Clark v Urquhart, Stracey v Urquhart* [1930] AC 28 at 67–68 Lord Atkin cast doubt on whether the measure of damages laid down in the nineteenth century cases as summarised in *McConnel v Wright* [1903] 1 Ch 546 was correct. He said:

> 'I find it difficult to suppose that there is any difference in the measure of damages in an action of deceit depending upon the nature of the transaction into which the plaintiff is fraudulently induced to enter. Whether he buys g shares or buys sugar, whether he subscribes for shares, or agrees to enter into a partnership, or in any other way alters his position to his detriment, in principle, the measure of damages should be the same, and whether estimated by a jury or a judge. I should have thought it would be based on the actual damage directly flowing from the fraudulent inducement. The h formula in *McConnel v. Wright* may be correct or it may be expressed in too rigid terms. I reserve the right to consider it if it should ever be in issue in this House.'

In the High Court of Australia, Dixon J in *Potts v Miller* (1940) 64 CLR 282 at 299–300, whilst loyally applying the old inflexible rule was plainly unhappy with j it (see also *Toteff v Antonas* (1952) 87 CLR 647).

The decision which restated the law correctly is *Doyle v Olby (Ironmongers) Ltd* [1969] 2 All ER 119, [1969] 2 QB 158. In that case the plaintiff had been induced by the fraudulent misrepresentation of the defendant to buy an ironmonger's business for £4,500 plus stock at a valuation of £5,000. Shortly after the purchase, he discovered the fraud and started the action. But despite this he had to remain in occupation: he had burned his boats and had to carry on with the business as

best he could. After three years, he managed to sell the business for £3,700, but
in the meantime he had incurred business debts. Lord Denning MR, after *a*
referring to Lord Atkin's dictum, stated the principle as follows ([1969] 2 All ER
119 at 122, [1969] 2 QB 158 at 167):

'On principle the distinction seems to be this: in contract, the defendant has
made a promise and broken it. The object of damages is to put the plaintiff *b*
in as good a position, as far as money can do it, as if the promise had been
performed. In fraud, the defendant has been guilty of a deliberate wrong by
inducing the plaintiff to act to his detriment. The object of damages is to
compensate the plaintiff for all the loss he has suffered, so far, again, as
money can do it. In contract, the damages are limited to what may
reasonably be supposed to have been in the contemplation of the parties. In *c*
fraud, they are not so limited. The defendant is bound to make reparation
for all the actual damages directly flowing from the fraudulent inducement.
The person who has been defrauded is entitled to say: "I would not have
entered into this bargain at all but for your representation. Owing to your
fraud, I have not only lost all the money I paid you, but, what is more, I have
been put to a large amount of extra expense as well and suffered this or that *d*
extra damages." All such damages can be recovered: and it does not lie in the
mouth of the fraudulent person to say that they could not reasonably have
been foreseen. For instance, in this very case the plaintiff has not only lost
the money which he paid for the business, which he would never have done
if there had been no fraud: he put all that money in and lost it; but also he has *e*
been put to expense and loss in trying to run a business which has turned out
to be a disaster for him. He is entitled to damages for all his loss, subject, of
course, to giving credit for any benefit that he has received. There is nothing
to be taken off in mitigation: for there is nothing more that he could have
done to reduce his loss. He did all that he could reasonably be expected to
do.' *f*

In the same case Winn LJ said ([1969] 2 All ER 119 at 123, [1969] 2 QB 158 at 168):

'It appears to me that in a case where there has been a breach of warranty
of authority, and still more clearly where there has been a tortious wrong
consisting of a fraudulent inducement, the proper starting point for any *g*
court called on to consider what damages are recoverable by the defrauded
person is to compare his position before the representation was made to him
with his position after it, brought about by that representation, always
bearing in mind that no element in the consequential position can be
regarded as attributable loss and damage if it be too remote a consequence: *h*
it would be too remote not necessarily because it was not contemplated by
the representor but in any case where the person deceived has not himself
behaved with reasonable prudence, reasonable common sense or can in any
true sense be said to have been the author of his own mis-fortune. The
damage that he seeks to recover must have flowed directly from the fraud *j*
perpetrated on him.'

The damages awarded by the Court of Appeal in that case were calculated
(admittedly on a rough and ready basis as to the figures) as follows: The plaintiff
was treated as having lost £9,500, the price paid for the business and stock.
Against this, he had to give credit for £3,500, ie not for the value of the business
at the transaction date but for the amount he actually received on the resale of

a the business three years later. To this £3,500 there were added other benefits which he had received so as to give a total of £7,000 benefits received to be set against the sum lost of £9,500, ie a balance of loss of £2,500. In addition, the plaintiff was awarded by way of consequential damages the sum of £3,000 in respect of liabilities incurred by him in running the business. Thus the total award for direct and consequential damages was £5,500 (see [1969] 2 All ER 119 at 124–125, [1969] 2 QB 158 at 169–170).

b   Doyle v Olby (Ironmongers) Ltd establishes four points. First, that the measure of damages where a contract has been induced by fraudulent misrepresentation is reparation for all the actual damage directly flowing from (ie caused by) entering into the transaction. Second, that in assessing such damages it is not an inflexible rule that the plaintiff must bring into account the value as at the transaction date

c of the asset acquired: although the point is not adverted to in the judgments, the basis on which the damages were computed shows that there can be circumstances in which it is proper to require a defendant only to bring into account the actual proceeds of the asset provided that he has acted reasonably in retaining it. Third, damages for deceit are not limited to those which were

d reasonably foreseeable.   Fourth, the damages recoverable can include consequential loss suffered by reason of having acquired the asset.

In my judgment Doyle v Olby (Ironmongers) Ltd was rightly decided on all these points. It is true, as to the second point, that there were not apparently cited to the Court of Appeal the nineteenth century cases which established the 'inflexible rule' that the asset acquired has to be valued as at the transaction date: the

e successful appellant was not legally represented.   But in my judgment the decision on this second point is correct. The old 'inflexible rule' is both wrong in principle and capable of producing manifest injustice. The defendant's fraud may have an effect continuing after the transaction is completed, eg if a sale of gold shares was induced by a misrepresentation that a new find had been made which

f was to be announced later it would plainly be wrong to assume that the plaintiff should have sold the shares before the announcement should have been made. Again, the acquisition of the asset may, as in Doyle v Olby (Ironmongers) Ltd itself, lock the purchaser into continuing to hold the asset until he can effect a resale. To say that in such a case the plaintiff has obtained the value of the asset as at the transaction date and must therefore bring it into account flies in the face of

g common sense: how can he be said to have received such a value if, despite his efforts, he has been unable to sell.

Doyle v Olby (Ironmongers) Ltd has subsequently been approved and followed by the Court of Appeal in East v Maurer [1991] 2 All ER 733, [1991] 1 WLR 461 and Downs v Chappell [1996] 3 All ER 344. In both cases the plaintiffs had purchased a

h business as a going concern in reliance on the defendant's fraudulent misrepresentation. In each case after discovery of the fraud they sold the business at a loss and recovered by way of damages the difference between the original purchase price and the price eventually realised on a resale, ie the old date of transaction rule was not applied. In South Australia Asset Management Corp v York Montague Ltd, United Bank of Kuwait v Prudential Property Services Ltd, Nykredit

j Mortgage Bank plc v Edward Erdman Group Ltd [1996] 3 All ER 365, [1996] 3 WLR 87 your Lordships treated the measure of damages for fraud as being in a special category regulated by the principles of Doyle v Olby (Ironmongers) Ltd.

Turning for a moment away from damages for deceit, the general rule in other areas of the law has been that damages are to be assessed as at the date the wrong was committed. But recent decisions have emphasised that this is only a general rule: where it is necessary in order adequately to compensate the plaintiff for the

damage suffered by reason of the defendant's wrong a different date of
assessment can be selected. Thus in the law of contract, the date of breach rule   a
'is not an absolute rule: if to follow it would give rise to injustice, the court has
power to fix such other date as may be appropriate in the circumstances' (see
Johnson v Agnew [1979] 1 All ER 883 at 896, [1980] AC 367 at 401 per Lord
Wilberforce). Similar flexibility applies in assessing damages for conversion (*IBL
Ltd v Coussens* [1991] 2 All ER 133) or for negligence (*Dodd Properties (Kent) Ltd v*   b
Canterbury City Council [1980] 1 All ER 928, [1980] 1 WLR 433). As Bingham LJ
said in *County Personnel (Employment Agency) Ltd v Alan R Pulver & Co (a firm)* [1987]
1 All ER 289 at 297, [1987] 1 WLR 916 at 925–926:

> 'While the general rule undoubtedly is that damages for tort or breach of
> contract are assessed at the date of the breach ... this rule also should not be   c
> mechanistically applied in circumstances where assessment at another date
> may more accurately reflect the overriding compensatory rule.'

In the light of these authorities the old nineteenth century cases can no longer
be treated as laying down a strict and inflexible rule. In many cases, even in
deceit, it will be appropriate to value the asset acquired as at the transaction date   d
if that truly reflects the value of what the plaintiff has obtained. Thus, if the asset
acquired is a readily marketable asset and there is no special feature (such as a
continuing misrepresentation or the purchaser being locked into a business that
he has acquired) the transaction date rule may well produce a fair result. The
plaintiff has acquired the asset and what he does with it thereafter is entirely up   e
to him, freed from any continuing adverse impact of the defendant's wrongful
act. The transaction date rule has one manifest advantage, namely that it avoids
any question of causation. One of the difficulties of either valuing the asset at a
later date or treating the actual receipt on realisation as being the value obtained
is that difficult questions of causation are bound to arise. In the period between
the transaction date and the date of valuation or resale other factors will have   f
influenced the value or resale price of the asset. It was the desire to avoid these
difficulties of causation which led to the adoption of the transaction date rule. But
in cases where property has been acquired in reliance on a fraudulent
misrepresentation there are likely to be many cases where the general rule has to
be departed from in order to give adequate compensation for the wrong done to   g
the plaintiff, in particular where the fraud continues to influence the conduct of
the plaintiff after the transaction is complete or where the result of the transaction
induced by fraud is to lock the plaintiff into continuing to hold the asset acquired.

Finally, it must be emphasised that the principle in *Doyle v Olby (Ironmongers)
Ltd* [1969] 2 All ER 119, [1969] 2 QB 158, strict though it is, still requires the   h
plaintiff to mitigate his loss once he is aware of the fraud. So long as he is not
aware of the fraud, no question of a duty to mitigate can arise. But once the fraud
has been discovered, if the plaintiff is not locked into the asset and the fraud has
ceased to operate on his mind, a failure to take reasonable steps to sell the
property may constitute a failure to mitigate his loss requiring him to bring the
value of the property into account as at the date when he discovered the fraud or   j
shortly thereafter.

In sum, in my judgment the following principles apply in assessing the
damages payable where the plaintiff has been induced by a fraudulent
misrepresentation to buy property.

(1) The defendant is bound to make reparation for all the damage directly
flowing from the transaction.

a (2) Although such damage need not have been foreseeable, it must have been directly caused by the transaction.

(3) In assessing such damage, the plaintiff is entitled to recover by way of damages the full price paid by him, but he must give credit for any benefits which he has received as a result of the transaction.

(4) As a general rule, the benefits received by him include the market value of b the property acquired as at the date of acquisition; but such general rule is not to be inflexibly applied where to do so would prevent him obtaining full compensation for the wrong suffered.

(5) Although the circumstances in which the general rule should not apply cannot be comprehensively stated, it will normally not apply where either (a) the misrepresentation has continued to operate after the date of the acquisition of the c asset so as to induce the plaintiff to retain the asset or (b) the circumstances of the case are such that the plaintiff is, by reason of the fraud, locked into the property.

(6) In addition, the plaintiff is entitled to recover consequential losses caused by the transaction.

(7) The plaintiff must take all reasonable steps to mitigate his loss once he has d discovered the fraud.

Before seeking to apply those principles to the present case, there are two points I must make. First, in *Downs v Chappell* [1996] 3 All ER 344 at 361 Hobhouse LJ, having quantified the recoverable damage very much along the lines that I have suggested, sought to cross-check his result by looking to see what the value of the business would have been if the misrepresentations had been true e and then comparing that value to the contract price. Whilst Hobhouse LJ accepted that this was not the correct measure of damages, he was seeking to check that the plaintiff was not being compensated for a general fall in market prices (for which the defendant was not accountable) rather than for the wrong done to him by the defendant. In my view, such a cross-check is not likely to be f helpful and is conducive to overelaboration both in the evidence and in argument. Second, in *Royscot Trust Ltd v Rogerson* [1991] 3 All ER 294, [1991] 2 QB 297 the *Doyle v Olby (Ironmongers) Ltd* measure of damages was adopted in assessing damages for innocent misrepresentation under the Misrepresentation Act 1967. I express no view on the correctness of that decision.

How then do those principles apply in the present case? First, there is no doubt g that the total loss incurred by Smith was caused by the Roberts fraud, unless it can be said that Smith's own decision to retain the shares until after the revelation of the Guerin fraud was a causative factor. The Guerin fraud had been committed before Smith acquired the shares on 21 July 1989. Unknown to everybody, on that date the shares were already pregnant with disaster. Accordingly when, h pursuant to the Roberts fraud, Smith acquired the Ferranti shares they were induced to purchase a flawed asset. This is not a case of the difficult kind that can arise where the depreciation in the asset acquired between the date of acquisition and the date of realisation may be due to factors affecting the market which have occurred after the date of the defendant's fraud. In the present case the loss was j incurred by reason of the purchasing of the shares which were pregnant with the loss and that purchase was caused by the Roberts fraud.

Can it then be said that the loss flowed not from Smith's acquisition but from Smith's decision to retain the shares? In my judgment it cannot. The judge found that the shares were acquired as a market making risk and at a price which Smith would only have paid for an acquisition as a market making risk. As such, Smith could not dispose of them on 21 July 1989 otherwise than at a loss. Smith were in a special sense locked into the shares having bought them for a purpose and at a price which precluded them from sensibly disposing of them. It was not alleged or found that Smith acted unreasonably in retaining the shares for as long as they *a* did or in realising them in the manner in which they did.

In the circumstances, it would not in my judgment compensate Smith for the actual loss they have suffered (ie the difference between the contract price and the resale price eventually realised) if Smith were required to give credit for the shares having a value of 78p on 21 July 1989. Having acquired the shares at 82¼p *b* for stock Smith could not commercially have sold on that date at 78p. It is not realistic to treat Smith as having received shares worth 78p each when in fact, in real life, they could not commercially have sold or realised the shares at that price on that date. In my judgment, this is one of those cases where to give full reparation to Smith, the benefit which Smith ought to bring into account to be set against its loss for the total purchase price paid should be the actual resale *c* price achieved by Smith when eventually the shares were sold.

Finally I must mention a point raised by Mr Sumption, namely that it is not open to Smith to argue before your Lordships that the damages should be assessed in the manner which I have proposed. On the pleadings, the damages claimed were the difference between the contract price and either the 'true value' *d* on 21 July 1989 or their value when the fraud was discovered. Mr Sumption urged, in addition to the point on the pleadings, that it would be unfair to Citibank to entertain the new argument since, if the point had been pleaded Citibank would itself have pleaded and led evidence of a failure by Smith to mitigate its loss and as to the reasonableness of Smith's conduct.

Although the pleading point is technically correct (and could be cured by *e* amendment) I am not satisfied that Citibank is prejudiced by allowing this point to be argued before your Lordships. In opening his case before the judge, Mr Grabiner conceded that, in any event, he could not recover more than Smith's actual realised loss. It could therefore have been an issue at the trial, if Citibank had chosen to make it one, whether Smith should have sold earlier or at a better *f* price. Indeed, as I understand it, those matters were investigated in that context at the trial and the judge found that Smith had acted reasonably. In the circumstances, I can see no injustice to Citibank in deciding this case on the new point raised before your Lordships.

For these reasons I would hold that the damages recoverable amount to £11,352,220 being the difference between the contract price and the amount *g* actually realised by Smith on the resale of the shares. However, as there was no appeal by Smith against the judge's assessment of the damages at £10,764,005, Smith's claim must be limited to that latter amount. I would therefore allow the appeal and restore the judge's order.

h

LORD KEITH OF KINKEL. My Lords, for the reasons given in the speeches to be delivered by my noble and learned friends Lord Browne-Wilkinson and Lord Steyn, which I have read in draft and with which I agree, I would allow the appeal, dismiss the cross-appeal and restore the order of the trial judge as to damages.

j

LORD MUSTILL. My Lords, the speech to be delivered by my noble and learned friend Lord Steyn deals with both liability and damages. On the issue of liability I gratefully adopt the analysis of law and fact, and agree that in respect of the second and third occasions it has, but in respect of the first it has not, been established that an actionable misrepresentation was made by Citibank NA (acting through Mr Roberts) to Smith New Court Securities Ltd (Smith). I also a agree that the conclusion regarding the first occasion, which differs from that of the Court of Appeal, does not affect the liability of Citibank for having induced Smith to enter into the purchase of Ferranti shares.

On the question of damages I further agree that they should be assessed on the basis of the difference between the contract price and the amount actually realised by Smith on the resale, and would therefore allow the appeal and restore

b the award of the trial judge on damages. On this aspect of the dispute I wish, however, to add a very few words. Notwithstanding the high authority of its source I cannot regard the judgment of Lord Denning MR in *Doyle v Olby (Ironmongers) Ltd* [1969] 2 All ER 119, [1969] 2 QB 158 as an invariable guide to the assessment of damages for fraudulent misrepresentation. The appeal in that case was not fully argued by counsel. The judgments were not reserved and do not

c sit very easily together. To my mind the propositions which on the argument of the present appeal were sought to be extracted from the decision were painted with too broad a brush to deal accurately with all the problems which may arise. True, the assessment of damages often involves so many unquantifiable contingencies and unverifiable assumptions that in many cases realism demands

d a rough and ready approach to the facts. True also that in a case of fraud there are good reasons for departing in some respect from the ordinary rules: and the irrelevance of foreseeability provides an example. Nevertheless, there are instances where more is required in the way of analysis than can be found in *Doyle v Olby (Ironmongers) Ltd* and this is one. For my part, I would suggest that in the future when faced with situations such as the present, courts would do well to be

e guided by the seven propositions set out by my noble and learned friend, Lord Browne-Wilkinson in the latter part of his speech. The fourth and fifth of these are, I believe, amply sufficient to show that the damages awarded by the judge ought to be upheld.

f **LORD SLYNN OF HADLEY.** My Lords, I have had the advantage of reading the text of the speech prepared by my noble and learned friends Lord Browne-Wilkinson and Lord Steyn. I agree that for the reasons they give the appeal of Smith New Court Securities Ltd should be allowed and that the order of Chadwick J as to damages be restored and that the cross-appeal on liability should be dismissed.

g **LORD STEYN.** My Lords, there is an appeal and cross-appeal against the judgment of the Court of Appeal dated 17 February 1994 to be considered. The Court of Appeal upheld a judgment dated 25 March 1992 by Chadwick J so far as he concluded that the plaintiffs in an action in the Chancery Division had established actionable fraudulent misrepresentations in respect of the sale of a

h parcel of shares. Despite the fact that Chadwick J had come to his conclusions in a witness action, the Court of Appeal held that he had misdirected himself on one aspect of the issues of fact on liability. Accordingly the Court of Appeal felt free to consider the case afresh without being rigidly bound by all the judge's findings of fact. In the result the Court of Appeal affirmed the judgment on liability of

j Chadwick J on additional grounds. The correctness of the Court of Appeal's decision on liability is the subject matter of the cross-appeal. The arguments on the cross-appeal were addressed to issues of pure fact. Moreover, in material respects the arguments of counsel for the cross-appellant challenged concurrent findings of fact of the trial judge and the Court of Appeal.

By contrast the appeal challenges the decision of the Court of Appeal on a question of principle, namely the correct measure of damages in an action for

deceit. The judge adopted a valuation method to assess damages and held that
the buyers were entitled to damages in a sum of the order of £10·7m. In arriving   *a*
at this conclusion the judge took into account a subsequent fall in the value of the
shares, which was caused by a pre-existing and unconnected fraud which had
been perpetrated on the company concerned. The Court of Appeal ruled that as
a matter of law the judge applied the wrong measure of damages, and that the
correct measure was the difference between the price paid by the buyer and the   *b*
price which, absent the misrepresentations, the shares would have fetched on the
open market on the acquisition date. It was common ground that on that date
the fraud perpetrated by the third party was not known to the market. On this
basis the Court of Appeal reduced the damages to which the buyers were entitled
to a sum of the order of £1·1m.

My Lords, a detailed review of the testimonial battleground at trial has left me   *c*
in no doubt that the cross-appeal ought to be dismissed. I will have to explain my
reasons for this firm conclusion in some detail. The helpful judgments of
Chadwick J and the Court of Appeal are now reported (see [1992] BCLC 1104
(Ch D); [1994] 4 All ER 225, [1994] 1 WLR 1271 (CA)). It is therefore possible to
deal with the cross-appeal on liability somewhat more economically than would   *d*
otherwise have been the case. I will then turn to the important question of law
as to the correct legal measure of damages. I will explain why I think that the
appeal should be allowed and that the award of damages made by Chadwick J
should be restored.

LIABILITY   *e*

The story of the Ferranti shares

In July 1988 Citibank NA, a company carrying on business as a bank in London,
made available a loan facility of £23m to Parent Industries Inc, a United States
company. As security for the loan Parent charged 28m shares in Ferranti
International Signal Inc to Citibank. A Mr Guerin, a former director of Ferranti,   *f*
was the beneficial owner of Parent. Mr Peck was Mr Guerin's man at Parent and
occupied the position of President. By mid-July 1989 Parent was in default under
the loan agreement. Citibank was urgently considering the realisation of the
security for its loan. In the phrase often used at the trial it was a 'forced sale'
situation.   *g*

On 21 July 1989 Citibank, acting through the brokers, Scrimgeour Vickers
(Asset Management) Ltd, sold the 28m Ferranti shares to Smith New Court
Securities Ltd (Smith) for about £23m, the price per share being 82¼p. Mr
Roberts, a senior employee of Citibank and director of Scrimgeour, arranged the
sale. In doing so he dealt with Mr Lewis and Mr Abrahams, two directors of   *h*
Smith and market makers by occupation.

At the trial the case of Smith was that Mr Roberts induced Smith by fraudulent
misrepresentations to buy the Ferranti shares. In order to understand the nature
of Smith's case it is necessary to explain the vicissitudes of the value of shares in
Ferranti. On 14 July 1989 Ferranti made a preliminary announcement of its   *j*
financial results for the year ended 31 March 1989. On the basis of that
information the market value of the parcel of Ferranti shares was probably of the
order of 78p to 82p per share, ie a few pence lower than the prices quoted on the
Stock Exchange. Ferranti, Citibank and Smith, as well as the individuals acting
for these companies, and the market generally, did not know that a massive fraud
had been perpetrated on Ferranti. In real terms the market price of the Ferranti
shares on 21 July 1989 was a fictitious price. There was a false market in Ferranti

a
shares. The fact of the fraud and its impact on the value of Ferranti shares only became known in September 1989. By a letter of 29 September 1989 together with unaudited group accounts the chairman of the board of Ferranti explained to shareholders that the fraud had caused a reduction in the net worth of the Ferranti Group as at 31 March 1989 of approximately £170m (from £370·8m to £198·5m) and a reduction in profit for the year of approximately £18m (from

b
£29·3m to £10·9m). In November 1989 Ferranti published the revised audited accounts for the year ended 31 March 1989. Those accounts confirmed the pessimistic predictions made in late September. In these changed circumstances, and between 20 November 1989 and 30 April 1990, Smith disposed of the Ferranti shares by selling them in the market in relatively small parcels at prices ranging from 49p per share to 30p per share. The difference between the total price paid

c
by Smith and the total of the prices received was £11·3m.

That brings me to the events of 21 July 1989 so far as they are relevant to the alleged fraudulent misrepresentations. In order to render the shape of the case intelligible it will be necessary to give a chronological account of the sequence of events, with the rival contentions of the parties as to the principal disputes

d
interspersed. Shortly before 9.30 am on 21 July 1989 Mr Roberts asked Mr Lewis whether Smith would be interested in buying the Ferranti shares. At 9.43 am Mr Lewis phoned Mr Roberts. Mr Abrahams was also a party to the conversation. The discussion lasted 13 minutes. Mr Lewis confirmed that Smith was interested in purchasing the Ferranti shares. Smith's case was that during the conversation Mr Roberts said that Smith would be in competition with two other bidders

e
interested in buying the Ferranti shares, namely a company in the Citicorp Group and another bidder not in the securities industry. Mr Roberts identified the first company as Citicorp Scrimgeour Vickers Ltd (CSV), a company carrying on business as stockbrokers and market makers in London. This was the first alleged representation. At trial Mr Roberts said that he went no further than to say that

f
there were at least two other parties interested. There was in fact no bidder for the Ferranti shares from outside the securities industry. The dispute as to what was said in the 9.43 am conversation was a major issue at the trial. What was not in issue was that Mr Lewis and Mr Abrahams came to believe that Smith would be in competition for the Ferranti shares with a bidder from outside the securities industry.

g
Following the 9.43 am conversation, Mr Abrahams and Mr Lewis attended a meeting with other employees of Smith to discuss whether Smith should bid for the Ferranti shares and, if so, at what price. Mr Lewis and Mr Abrahams told those present at the meeting that Smith would be bidding in competition against CSV and one other bidder from outside the securities industry. The decision

h
taken at the meeting was that Smith should bid 82p per share. The reasoning that led to this decision is of some relevance. The facts are common ground. Smith had a choice. It could have bought the shares as a 'bought deal' or as a market making risk. The first would have involved Smith buying the Ferranti shares and selling them through Smith's agency arm, at a profit, within a matter of hours to institutional clients. In a transaction of the magnitude of buying 28m shares in

j
Ferranti it would have been normal for Smith to do a bought deal. Instead Smith chose to do a transaction of the second type. This involved buying the shares with a view to holding them as a market making risk and only selling them as and when the opportunity or opportunities to do so might arise. Smith took the view that the Ferranti shares could not be sold to institutional clients at a price above 80p per share without a recommendation to clients, which Smith's agency arm was not prepared to give. In order to do a bought deal Smith would have had to

buy the Ferranti shares at below 80p. If Smith had not believed that it was in
competition with a bidder from outside the securities industry, it would have bid   *a*
for the shares at a price consistent with doing a bought deal at a profit. That price
would have been 78p per share. It was agreed that if Smith had bid 78p per share,
the bid would not have been accepted by Citibank.

In the presence of Mr Abrahams, Mr Lewis telephoned Mr Roberts at
10.42 am. This call lasted about two minutes. It was made some 20 minutes after   *b*
the conclusion of the pricing meeting. At the trial Mr Lewis and Mr Abrahams
testified that Mr Lewis told Mr Roberts that Smith had decided to bid for the
Ferranti shares; that Mr Lewis asked him to attend at Smith's offices so that Smith
could make the bid in person; and that Mr Lewis asked Mr Roberts to bring with
him the other two bids in sealed envelopes to Smith's offices. Mr Roberts agreed
that Mr Lewis asked him to come to Smith's offices to hear the bid. But Mr   *c*
Roberts denied that anything else was said about bringing the other bids in sealed
envelopes.

Mr Roberts arrived at the offices of Smith shortly after noon. A meeting then
took place between Mr Roberts and three employees of Smith, namely Mr Lewis,
Mr Abrahams and Mr Marks. Mr Marks had been present at the pricing meeting.   *d*
It is common ground that Mr Lewis said that Smith would bid 82p per share. Mr
Roberts did not have authority to accept the bid but he said that he would
recommend the bid. What is in dispute is the rest of the conversation. Mr Lewis
said that Mr Roberts said at the start of the meeting that he would disclose the
competing bids after Smith had made its bid. This was called the second
representation. Mr Lewis, Mr Abrahams and Mr Marks said that after Mr Lewis   *e*
made the bid at 82p Mr Roberts said that Aeritalia (an Italian company) had bid
81p for the shares and CSV had bid 75–77p. This was called the third
representation. Mr Roberts said that he made no mention of bids: he said that he
said that Aeritalia and CSV had given indications in the 81p and 75–77p regions.
Neither Aeritalia nor CSV had made any bid. It was conceded that if the second   *f*
and third representations had been made, they would have been fraudulently
made.

Mr Roberts returned to his office and told the decision makers at Citibank
about the bid. While the bid had formally lapsed because it was not immediately
accepted Smith remained a willing buyer of the Ferranti shares at 82p per share
throughout the afternoon. Shortly after 5.00 pm on the same day the bargain was   *g*
struck. It was done in a telephone conversation between Mr Lewis and Mr
Abrahams, on the Smith side, and Mr Fisher, a director and senior dealer at
Scrimgeour. The main reason for the additional ½p was to establish that the
contract was made after trading hours on Friday, 21 July, so that it would not
have to be reported under Stock Exchange rules until the following business day.   *h*

The rest of the story can be taken quite briefly. After the suspension of Ferranti
shares in September 1989, Smith started to investigate the circumstances in which
it had purchased the Ferranti shares. Smith discovered that Aeritalia had never
bid for the Ferranti shares. That discovery led to the institution of the
proceedings in January 1990.   *j*

The trial and the judgment of Chadwick J on liability

The trial took place between 25 November 1991 and 17 January 1992. The
judge gave judgment on 25 March 1992. He found that, in advance of earlier
criminal proceedings against Mr Roberts, Serious Fraud Office officials had asked
Mr Lewis and Mr Abrahams to pool their recollections; that they falsely denied
this at the criminal trial; and that in the civil trial they falsely pretended that they

a had forgotten how their statements came into existence. In the result the judge found that the first representation, which depended exclusively on the evidence of Mr Lewis and Mr Abrahams, had not been proved. But, in the light of the totality of the evidence before him, the judge found that Mr Roberts had made the second and third representations on behalf of Citibank; that those representations were false; and that Smith had been induced to enter into the

b contract by those fraudulent misrepresentations.

The appeal and the judgment of the Court of Appeal

Citibank appealed against the judge's findings on liability. Smith served a respondent's notice which invited the Court of Appeal to uphold the judge's

c conclusions on liability on additional grounds. And that is what the Court of Appeal did. The Court of Appeal held that the judge had misdirected himself in respect of the 9.43 am conversation by considering the credibility and reliability of Mr Lewis and Mr Abrahams in isolation. After a review of all the evidence the Court of Appeal found, as a matter of fact, that all three representations were made and made fraudulently and that they induced Smith to enter into the

d contract. In the result the Court of Appeal dismissed Citibank's appeal on liability.

The submissions for Citibank

Counsel for Citibank put in the forefront of his submissions the undisputed

e proposition that while as a matter of law fraud only has to be proved to the civil standard, proof to that standard must necessarily take into account the consideration that the more serious the allegation is, the greater the proof is needed to persuade a court that it can be satisfied that the allegation is established. In other words, the very gravity of an allegation of fraud is a circumstance which

f has to be weighed in the scale in deciding as to the balance of probabilities (see *Re H and ors (minors) (sexual abuse: standard of proof)* [1996] 1 All ER 1 at 16–18, [1996] AC 563 at 586–587 per Lord Nicholls of Birkenhead). But counsel accepted that both Chadwick J and the Court of Appeal correctly directed themselves in accordance with this standard.

g Counsel for Citibank reviewed the minutiae of the evidence. He highlighted undoubted inconsistencies between the accounts of Mr Lewis and Mr Abrahams. He argued that there were improbabilities inherent in their accounts. But throughout his speech there was the theme that since Chadwick J found on proper grounds that Mr Lewis and Mr Abrahams had lied it is impossible to sort

h out in their evidence truth from falsehood. That is an argument worthy of careful consideration. It has rightly been said that a cocktail of truth, falsity and evasion is a more powerful instrument of deception than undiluted falsehood. It is also difficult to detect. But counsel had to face the fact that on the third representation Mr Marks supported the accounts of Mr Lewis and Mr Abrahams. And at the trial counsel never challenged the credibility of Mr Marks. Counsel for Citibank put

j the matter quite simply: he said Mr Marks' evidence was too thin a thread to bear the weight of an elaborate case of fraud. Moreover, counsel argued that the Court of Appeal was not entitled to substitute their view for that of the judge on the first representation. Once it was accepted that the first representation had not been proved he said that it was simply impossible to be satisfied that the second and third representations were made. In the broadest outline these were the principal submissions of counsel for Citibank.

The approach to an attack on concurrent findings of fact

The principle is well settled that where there has been no misdirection on an issue of fact by the trial judge the presumption is that his conclusion on issues of fact is correct. The Court of Appeal will only reverse the trial judge on an issue of fact when it is convinced that his view is wrong. In such a case, if the Court of Appeal is left in doubt as to the correctness of the conclusion, it will not disturb it. That is the first difficulty in the way of upholding the arguments of counsel for Citibank. But there is an additional obstacle. The Court of Appeal upheld the findings of fact of the trial judge on the actionability of the second and third representations. While the jurisdiction of the House is not in doubt, it is most reluctant to disturb concurrent findings of fact. There are two reasons for this approach. First, the prime function of the House of Lords is to review questions of law of general public importance. That function it cannot properly discharge if it often has to hear appeals on pure fact. This point is underlined by the fact that, despite the economy of presentation of counsel, the hearing on liability lasted more than three days. Secondly, in the case of concurrent findings of fact, the House is confronted with the combined views of the first instance judge and the Court of Appeal. A suggestion that the House can be expected to take a different view on concurrent findings *of fact* generally gives rise to an initial sense of disbelief. Nevertheless, I must examine the merits of the argument of counsel for Citibank.

The reasons why the concurrent findings are unassailable

It seems to me that there are five principal reasons why the attack on the concurrent findings of fact must fail. First, having found that Mr Lewis and Mr Abrahams had lied on a collateral matter, the judge approached their evidence with great caution. Rightly, he rejected the notion that falsity in one thing involves falsity in all. Reviewing their accounts as to the second and third representations against the whole body of evidence he accepted, as he was entitled to do, their accounts. Secondly, the judge was plainly considerably influenced by the fact that on the third representation Mr Marks in all material respects supported Mr Lewis and Mr Abrahams. He accepted the evidence of Mr Marks. Thirdly, it is not in dispute that between 10.00 and 10.30 am on the morning of 21 July 1989, at the pricing meeting which was attended by Mr Lewis, Mr Abrahams and Mr Marks, Smith fixed their bid at 82p on the footing that they would be bidding in competition with two other bidders, one of whom was from outside the securities industry. This fact strongly supported Smith's case. Fourthly, while disputed by counsel for Citibank, it seems to me inescapable that on Citibank's theory of the case, Mr Lewis and Mr Abrahams fabricated the story that they had been told that there were other bidders and the price of the bids several months before the issue of misrepresentation arose. There is the undisputed evidence of Mr Smith, another employee of Smith, that the account of the rival bids surfaced on 21 July 1989, ie the day of the transaction. Given this fact, and Mr Marks' evidence, the theory of a fabrication is absurd. Fifthly, as against these factors, the judge had to weigh the evidence of Mr Roberts. The judge rejected Mr Roberts' evidence. That necessarily involved a finding that Mr Roberts gave untruthful evidence. The judge was entitled to take this course. Taking into account counsel's submissions I have reviewed the whole of the evidence of Mr Roberts, given over more than two days. He was a most unimpressive witness. He testified that at the midday meeting he had said that Aeritalia had given an indication (shorthand for saying they were interested parties) at 81p. It is perfectly clear, however, that Aeritalia was only interested in a an option to buy the Ferranti shares for two months. The sale of the shares was, however, a matter of urgency and both Citibank and Parent, acting through Mr Peck, wanted an outright sale. Mr Roberts said that he had been told by another Citibank employee that Mr Peck had said that Aeritalia might make an outright bid. In Mr Roberts' own words that was 'a zero possibility' by midday on 21 July 1989. Cumulatively, these five factors are sufficient in the particular b circumstances of this case to demonstrate convincingly that the attack on the concurrent findings of Chadwick J and the Court of Appeal must be rejected. In sustaining the second and third representations as actionable fraudulent misrepresentations Chadwick J in my judgment came to a correct conclusion. So far as the Court of Appeal affirmed the findings of Chadwick J, I am in respectful agreement with their concurrent views.

c

The Court of Appeal's views on the facts

It is now necessary to consider the exceptional course taken by the Court of Appeal regarding the first representation. It will be recollected that the judge did not find the first representation proved but he did find the second and third representations proved. The clue to this conclusion is to be found in the d following passage in the judgment at first instance ([1992] BCLC 1104 at 1116):

'... it would, in my view, be unsafe to make a finding of dishonesty against Mr Roberts on the unsupported evidence of Mr Lewis and Mr Abrahams. I approach the examination of the events of 21 July 1989 on the basis that little, if any, weight can be given to their evidence where it is in conflict with that e given by Mr Roberts.'

The Court of Appeal concluded that the judge erred by not subsequently reviewing this conclusion in the light of all the evidence. Counsel for Citibank vigorously challenged the conclusion of the Court of Appeal. It is necessary to f analyse the position on a step-by-step basis.

In making findings of credibility and reliability it is unsafe for a trial judge to compartmentalise the case. In *A-G of Hong Kong v Wong Muk-ping* [1987] 2 All ER 488 at 493, [1987] AC 501 at 510 Lord Bridge of Harwich explained:

'It is a commonplace of judicial experience that a witness who makes a g poor impression in the witness box may be found at the end of the day, when his evidence is considered in the light of all the other evidence bearing on the issue, to have been both truthful and accurate. Conversely, the evidence of a witness who at first seemed impressive and reliable may at the end of the day have to be rejected. Such experience suggests that it is dangerous to h assess the credibility of the evidence given by any witness in isolation from other evidence in the case which is capable of throwing light on its reliability ...'

In other words, an initial and provisional conclusion that a witness is not credible on a particular point may be falsified when considered against the possibilities, j probabilities and certainties emerging from the whole body of evidence before the court. That is the error into which the judge fell. He ought to have reconsidered his understandable unwillingness to act on the unsupported evidence of Mr Lewis and Mr Abrahams in respect of the first representation in the light of the evidence about the pricing meeting, Mr Marks' account and the inherent probabilities. There is no internal indication in his judgment that he ever did so.

It follows that the Court of Appeal was entitled to conclude that in respect of the first representation the trial judge misdirected himself. That meant that the *a* Court of Appeal was at large to disregard the judge's findings of fact, even though based on credibility. I understood counsel for Citibank at one stage to suggest that this vitiates all the judge's findings of fact and the whole case on fraud collapses. That is quite unrealistic. The impact of a misdirection is not governed by fixed rules. The appropriate course is dictated by considerations of common *b* sense and fairness as well as close attention to the nature of the misdirection and the circumstances of the particular case. Here the Court of Appeal was fully entitled to take the view that the misdirection only vitiated the judge's findings on the first representation. In all other respects the Court of Appeal was entitled to act on the judge's findings so far as they were unaffected by the misdirection.

On the first representation the Court of Appeal was entitled to come to its own *c* conclusion. The principal reasons for the conclusion of the Court of Appeal were spelt out as follows ([1994] 4 All ER 225 at 233, [1994] 1 WLR 1271 at 1279):

'Events at the pricing meeting and the making of the second and third representations as found by the judge are all inexplicable unless the first representation had also been made ... The judge failed to stand back and *d* consider his finding as to the first representation in the light of his findings as to the second and third. Had he done so, we have little doubt that he would have been driven to conclude, as we do, that the first representation was also made.'

In effect the Court of Appeal held that on the first representation the judge should *e* in all the circumstances also have accepted the evidence of Mr Lewis and Mr Abrahams, and rejected the evidence of Mr Roberts. To this extent I respectfully agree with the admittedly exceptional course taken by the Court of Appeal.

That is, however, not the end of the matter. On the first representation, counsel for Citibank was able to demonstrate that, even on an acceptance of the *f* evidence of Mr Lewis and Mr Abrahams, there was considerable scope for misunderstanding between the participants in the 9.43 am telephone conversation. In the discussions at 10.42 am and at midday Mr Lewis and Mr Abrahams on their evidence (and the evidence of Mr Marks) unambiguously spoke of actual bids. But Mr Lewis and Mr Abrahams were less clear about the *g* discussion at 9.43 am: they both said that Mr Roberts either spoke of bids or about bids to be made. Counsel for Smith argued that Mr Roberts impliedly represented that he had bona fide and reasonable grounds for saying that bids would be made that day and that he had no such grounds. There is force in this argument. But on any view that is a far less clear-cut position than existed in respect of the second and third representation. That brings me back to another *h* passage in the judgment at first instance. The judge said ([1992] BCLC 1104 at 1129):

'... I am not satisfied that the first representation was made in the earlier telephone conversations in the morning of 21 July 1989 in sufficiently *j* unequivocal terms for it to form the basis for an action in deceit ...'

Making due allowance for the judge's earlier misdirection, I attach weight to this passage. On balance I too am not persuaded that the evidence of Mr Lewis and Mr Abrahams established the first representation in clear enough terms sufficient to justify a finding of deceit. Differing from the Court of Appeal on the interpretation of the evidence of Mr Lewis and Mr Abrahams, I would hold that a in respect of the 9.43 am conversation an actionable fraudulent misrepresentation has not been established.

Conclusion on cross-appeal

In my view the conclusion that the actionability of the first representation has not been established does not affect the outcome of this appeal. The misrepresentations at the midday meeting on 21 July 1989 induced Smith to enter
b into the transaction shortly after 5 o'clock on that day. After all, the trial judge found on ample evidence (including that of Mr Marks) that Smith would have withdrawn from the transaction if these misrepresentations had not been made. The Court of Appeal agreed with this conclusion. So do I. The essentials of the tort of deceit were established. I would dismiss the cross-appeal on liability.

c
DAMAGES

The issue

Given the fact that the subsequent dramatic fall in the value of Ferranti shares was caused by the disclosure of an earlier fraud practised on Ferranti by a third
d party the question is whether Smith is entitled to recover against Citibank the entire loss arising from the fraudulently induced transaction. Smith submits that the Court of Appeal adopted the wrong measure. Smith seeks to recover damages calculated on the basis of the price paid less the aggregate of subsequent realisations. Citibank contends that the loss attributable to the subsequent disclosure of the fraud by a third party is a misfortune risk and is irrecoverable.
e Citibank argues that the Court of Appeal adopted the correct measure.

Horses and shares

The fraud perpetrated by Mr Roberts on Smith related to shares quoted on the Stock Exchange. Undoubtedly, the legal measure of damages in an action in deceit when applied to transactions in shares may throw up special problems. It
f is not simply a matter of the perception of the market as to the value of the shares. If loss is to be determined by way of the price paid less a valuation of the shares at a given date, the determination of the real or true value of the shares, absent the deceit forming the basis of the claim, may give rise to difficult hypothetical problems. Even more difficult problems arise if it is alleged that for extrinsic
g reasons there has been a false market, eg because investors have been misled by widespread false statements about the value of the stock of the company. None of these practical considerations justify the adoption of a special rule in respect of share transactions. The same legal principle must govern sales of shares, goods, a business or land. It is therefore possible to simplify the problem. The example given by Cockburn CJ in *Twycross v Grant* (1877) 2 CPD 469 is instructive. He said
h (at 544–545):

j 'If a man buys a horse, as a racehorse, on the false representation that it has won some great race, while in reality it is a horse of very inferior speed, and he pays ten or twenty times as much as the horse is worth, and after the buyer has got the animal home it dies of some latent disease inherent in its system at the time he bought it, he may claim the entire price he gave; the horse was by reason of the latent mischief worthless when he bought; but if it catches some disease and dies, the buyer cannot claim the entire value of the horse, which he is no longer in a condition to restore, but only the difference between the price he gave and the real value at the time he bought.'

Counsel for Citibank argued that Cockburn CJ erred in saying that if the horse *a* had some latent disease at the time of the transaction the buyer may claim the entire price he paid. He argued that in such a case there was no sufficient causal link between the latent disease and the eventual death of the horse. Counsel for Smith argued that the transaction, which was induced by deceit, directly led to the loss of the entire value of the horse. On any view it is clear that, if Cockburn CJ is right, the law imposes liability in an action for deceit for some *b* consequences that were unforeseen and unforeseeable when the tortfeasor committed the wrong. And if that is right it may tell us something about the correct disposal of the present case.

The justification for distinguishing between deceit and negligence
That brings me to the question of policy whether there is a justification for *c* differentiating between the extent of liability for civil wrongs depending on where in the sliding scale from strict liability to intentional wrongdoing the particular civil wrong fits in. It may be said that logical symmetry and a policy of not punishing intentional wrongdoers by civil remedies favour a uniform rule. On the other hand, it is a rational and defensible strategy to impose wider liability on an intentional wrongdoer. As Hart and Honoré *Causation in the Law* (2nd edn, *d* 1985) p 304 observed: 'an innocent plaintiff may, not without reason, call on a morally reprehensible defendant to pay the whole of the loss he has caused'. The exclusion of heads of loss in the law of negligence, which reflects considerations of legal policy, does not necessarily avail the intentional wrongdoer. Such a policy of imposing more stringent remedies on an intentional wrongdoer serves *e* two purposes. First it serves a deterrent purpose in discouraging fraud. Counsel for Citibank argued that the sole purpose of the law of tort generally, and the tort of deceit in particular, should be to compensate the victims of civil wrongs. That is far too narrow a view. Professor Glanville Williams identified four possible purposes of an action for damages in tort: appeasement, justice, deterrence and compensation (see 'The Aims of the Law of Tort' (1951) 4 CLP 137). He *f* concluded (p 172):

> 'Where possible the law seems to like to ride two or three horses at once; but occasionally a situation occurs where one must be selected. The tendency is then to choose the deterrent purpose for tort of intention, and the compensatory purpose for other torts.' *g*

And in the battle against fraud civil remedies can play a useful and beneficial role. Secondly, as between the fraudster and the innocent party, moral considerations militate in favour of requiring the fraudster to bear the risk of misfortunes directly caused by his fraud. I make no apology for referring to moral considerations. *h* The law and morality are inextricably interwoven. To a large extent the law is simply formulated and declared morality. And, as *Oliver Wendell Holmes, The Common Law* (1968) p 106 observed, the very notion of deceit with its overtones of wickedness is drawn from the moral world.

The old cases   *j*
For more than a hundred years at least English law has adopted a policy of imposing more extensive liability on intentional wrongdoers than on merely careless defendants. This policy was trenchantly spelt out by Lord Blackburn in *Livingstone v Rawyards Coal Co* (1880) 5 App Cas 25 at 39:

> 'There could be no doubt that there you would say that everything would be taken into view that would go most against the wilful wrongdoer—many

a
things which you would properly allow in favour of an innocent mistaken trespasser would be disallowed as against a wilful and intentional trespasser on the ground that he must not qualify his own wrong, and various things of that sort.'

Since Victorian times there have been great developments in our law of obligations. But there has been no retreat from the policy spelt out by Lord
b Blackburn. On the other hand, the way in which the law can distinguish between the intentional wrongdoer and a man who caused loss by a foolish but honest mistake was not worked out clearly in the old cases. *Pasley v Freeman* (1789) 3 Durn & E 51, [1775–1802] All ER Rep 31 decided more than 200 years ago, marks the emergence of the tort of deceit. In cases framed in deceit the measure of
c damages was held to involve ascertainment of the 'real' or 'face' value of the shares at the time of allotment or purchase: see *Davidson v Tullock* (1860) 2 LT 97, *Peek v Derry* (1887) 37 Ch D 541 (rvsd on liability (1889) 14 App Cas 337), *Arkwright v Newbold* (1881) 17 Ch D 301 (rvsd on liability) and *Broome v Speak* [1903] 1 Ch 586 (affd sub nom *Shepheard v Broome* [1904] AC 342). Except for some useful general observations on valuation as a method of measuring loss, and the explanation of
d the inquiry into a past hypothetical event in the sense of the valuation of shares absent the fraud, I do not think those cases help much. And, except for the obiter dictum of Cockburn CJ in *Twycross v Grant* (1877) 2 CPD 469 at 544, the earlier cases do not touch on the problems in the present case. Finally, even in the last century it was realised that there must be sensible and practical limits to the heads
e of loss for which even an intentional wrongdoer can be held liable. Thus in *Twycross v Grant* Cockburn CJ said that if the fraudulently misdescribed horse subsequently catches a disease and dies the buyer cannot claim the entire value of the horse. But it took a long time before the precise nature of those limitations were clearly understood and explained.

f *Doyle v Olby (Ironmongers) Ltd*
Eventually, the idea took root that an intentional wrongdoer is not entitled to the benefit of the reasonable foreseeability test of remoteness. He is to be held liable in respect of 'the actual damage directly flowing from the fraudulent inducement': see the obiter dictum of Lord Atkin in *Clark v Urquhart, Stracey v Urquhart* [1930] AC 28 at 68; and compare dicta of Dixon J in *Potts v Miller* (1940)
g 64 CLR 282 at 298–299 and in *Toteff v Antonas* (1952) 87 CLR 647 at 650. It was, however, not until the decision of the Court of Appeal in *Doyle v Olby (Ironmongers) Ltd* that the governing principles were clearly laid down. By fraudulent misrepresentation the defendant induced the plaintiff to buy a business. The trial judge awarded damages to the plaintiff on the basis of a
h contractual measure of damages, ie the cost of making good the representations. The Court of Appeal ruled that this was an error and substituted a higher figure assessed on the basis of the tort measure, ie restoration of the status quo ante. Lord Denning MR explained ([1969] 2 All ER 119 at 122, [1969] 2 QB at 167):

j
'In contract, the damages are limited to what may reasonably be supposed to have been in the contemplation of the parties. In fraud, they are not so limited. The defendant is bound to make reparation for all the actual damage directly flowing from the fraudulent inducement. The person who has been defrauded is entitled to say: "I would not have entered into this bargain at all but for your representation. Owing to your fraud, I have not only lost all the money I paid you, but, what is more, I have been put to a large amount of extra expense as well and suffered this or that extra

damages." All such damages can be recovered: and it does not lie in the
mouth of the fraudulent person to say that they could not reasonably have
been foreseen.'

Winn and Sachs LJJ expressed themselves in similar terms.

The logic of the decision in *Doyle v Olby (Ironmongers) Ltd* justifies the following
propositions.

(1) The plaintiff in an action for deceit is not entitled to be compensated in
accordance with the contractual measure of damage, ie the benefit of the bargain
measure. He is not entitled to be protected in respect of his positive interest in
the bargain.

(2) The plaintiff in an action for deceit is, however, entitled to be compensated
in respect of his negative interest. The aim is to put the plaintiff into the position
he would have been in if no false representation had been made.

(3) The practical difference between the two measures was lucidly explained
in a contemporary case note on *Doyle v Olby (Ironmongers) Ltd* (see Treitel
'Damages for Deceit' (1969) 32 MLR 558–559). The author said:

'If the plaintiff's bargain would have been a bad one, even on the
assumption that the representation was true, he will do best under the
tortious measure. If, on the assumption that the representation was true, his
bargain would have been a good one, he will do best under the first
contractual measure (under which he may recover something even if the
actual value of what he has recovered is greater than the price).'

(4) Concentrating on the tort measure, the remoteness test whether the loss
was reasonably foreseeable had been authoritatively laid down in *The Wagon
Mound* in respect of the tort of negligence a few years before *Doyle v Olby
(Ironmongers) Ltd* was decided: *Overseas Tankship (UK) Ltd v Morts Dock and
Engineering Co Ltd, The Wagon Mound* [1961] 1 All ER 404, [1961] AC 388. *Doyle v
Olby (Ironmongers) Ltd* settled that a wider test applies in an action for deceit.

(5) The dicta in all three judgments, as well as the actual calculation of
damages in *Doyle v Olby (Ironmongers) Ltd*, make it clear that the victim of the fraud
is entitled to compensation for all the actual loss directly flowing from the
transaction induced by the wrongdoer. That includes heads of consequential
loss.

(6) Significantly in the present context the rule in the previous paragraph is not
tied to any process of valuation at the date of the transaction. It is squarely based
on the overriding compensatory principle, widened in view of the fraud to cover
all direct consequences. The legal measure is to compare the position of the
plaintiff as it was before the fraudulent statement was made to him with his
position as it became as a result of his reliance on the fraudulent statement.

Doyle v Olby (Ironmongers) Ltd was subsequently applied by the Court of Appeal
in two Court of Appeal decisions: *East v Maurer* [1991] 2 All ER 733, [1991] 1 WLR
461 and *Smith Kline & French Laboratories Ltd v Long* [1988] 3 All ER 887, [1989] 1
WLR 1. *East v Maurer* is of some significance since it throws light on a point which
arose in argument. Counsel for Citibank argued that in the case of a fraudulently
induced sale of a business, loss of profits is only recoverable on the basis of the
contractual measure and never on the basis of the tort measure applicable to
fraud. This is an oversimplification. The plaintiff is not entitled to demand that
the defendant must pay to him the profits of the business as represented. On the
other hand, *East v Maurer* shows that an award based on the hypothetical
profitable business in which the plaintiff would have engaged but for deceit is

a permissible: it is classic consequential loss. Turning to the *Smith Kline* case it has been suggested that the *Doyle v Olby (Ironmongers) Ltd* rule was wrongly applied (see Burrows *Remedies for Torts and Breach of Contract* (2nd edn, 1994) pp 173–174). The correctness of that comment I need not examine. In my view it is sufficient to say that the principles emerging from *Doyle v Olby (Ironmongers) Ltd* are good law.

b *Side-tracking*
At the risk of being side-tracked I must now refer to two Court of Appeal decisions which were discussed in argument. In *Royscot Trust Ltd v Rogerson* [1991] 3 All ER 294, [1991] 2 QB 297 the Court of Appeal held that under s 2(1) of the Misrepresentation Act 1967 damages in respect of an honest but careless
c representation are to be calculated as if the representation had been made fraudulently. The question is whether the rather loose wording of the statute compels the court to treat a person who was morally innocent as if he was guilty of fraud when it comes to the measure of damages. There has been trenchant academic criticism of the *Royscot* case (see Richard Hooley 'Damages and the Misrepresentation Act 1967' (1991) 107 LQR 547–551). Since this point does not
d directly arise in the present case, I express no concluded view on the correctness of the decision in the *Royscot* case. The second case is the decision of the Court of Appeal in *Downs v Chappell* [1996] 3 All ER 344. The context is the rule that in an action for deceit the plaintiff is entitled to recover all his loss directly flowing from the fraudulently induced *transaction*. In the case of a negligent misrepresentation the rule is narrower: the recoverable loss does not extend
e beyond the consequences flowing from the negligent *misrepresentation* (see *Banque Bruxelles Lambert SA v Eagle Star Insurance Co Ltd* [1995] 2 All ER 769, [1995] QB 375). In *Downs v Chappell* Hobhouse LJ applied this narrower rule to an action for deceit. He enunciated the following 'qualification' of the conventional rule ([1996] 3 All ER 344 at 361):

f
'In my judgment, having determined what the plaintiffs have lost as a result of entering into the transaction—their contract with Mr Chappell—it is still appropriate to ask the question whether that loss can properly be treated as having been caused by the defendants' torts, notwithstanding that the torts caused the plaintiffs to enter into the transaction.'

g
That led Hobhouse LJ (at 362) 'to compare the loss consequent upon entering into the transaction with what would have been the position had the represented, or supposed, state of affairs actually existed'. The correctness of this proposition in a case of deceit was debated at the bar. Counsel for Citibank, in whose interest it was to adopt this proposition, felt some difficulty in doing so. In my view the
h orthodox and settled rule that the plaintiff is entitled to all losses directly flowing from the transaction caused by the deceit does not require a revision. In other words, it is not necessary in an action for deceit for the judge, after he had ascertained the loss directly flowing from the victim having entered into the transaction, to embark on a hypothetical reconstruction of what the parties
j would have agreed had the deceit not occurred. The rule in deceit is justified by the grounds already discussed. I would hold that on this point *Downs v Chappell* was wrongly decided.

The date if transaction rule
That brings me to the perceived difficulty caused by the date of transaction rule. The Court of Appeal ([1994] 4 All ER 225 at 237, [1994] 1 WLR 1271 at 1283) referred to the rigidity of 'the rule in *Waddell v Blockey* (1879) 4 QBD 678, which

requires the damages to be calculated as at the date of sale'. No doubt this view
was influenced by the shape of arguments before the Court of Appeal which
treated the central issue as being in reality a valuation exercise. It is right that the
normal method of calculating the loss caused by the deceit is the price paid less
the real value of the subject matter of the sale. To the extent that this method is
adopted, the selection of a date of valuation is necessary. And generally the date
of the transaction would be a practical and just date to adopt. But it is not always
so. It is only prima facie the right date. It may be appropriate to select a later date.
That follows from the fact that the valuation method is only a means of trying to
give effect to the overriding compensatory rule (see *Potts v Miller* (1940) 64 CLR
282 at 299 per Dixon J and *County Personnel (Employment Agency) Ltd v Alan R Pulver
& Co (a firm)* [1987] 1 All ER 289 at 297–298, [1987] 1 WLR 916 at 925–926 per
Bingham LJ). Moreover, and more importantly, the date of transaction rule is
simply a second order rule applicable only where the valuation method is
employed. If that method is inapposite, the court is entitled simply to assess the
loss flowing directly from the transaction without any reference to the date of
transaction or indeed any particular date. Such a course will be appropriate
whenever the overriding compensatory rule requires it. An example of such a
case is to be found in *Cemp Properties (UK) Ltd v Dentsply Research and Development
Corp (Denton Hall & Bergin, third party)* [1991] 2 EGLR 197 at 201 per Bingham LJ.
There is in truth only one legal measure of assessing damages in an action for
deceit: the plaintiff is entitled to recover as damages a sum representing the
financial loss flowing directly from his alteration of position under the
inducement of the fraudulent representations of the defendants. The analogy of
the assessment of damages in a contractual claim on the basis of cost of cure or
difference in value springs to mind. In *Ruxley Electronics and Construction Ltd v
Forsyth* [1995] 3 All ER 268 at 277, [1996] AC 344 at 360 Lord Mustill said: 'There
are not two alternative measures of damages, at opposite poles, but only one:
namely the loss truly suffered by the promisee.' In an action for deceit the price
paid less the valuation at the transaction date is simply a method of measuring
loss which will satisfactorily solve many cases. It is not a substitute for the single
legal measure: it is an application of it.

Causation

So far I have discussed in general terms the scope of a fraudster's liability in
accordance with the rule identified with *Doyle v Olby (Ironmongers) Ltd* [1969] 2 All
ER 119, [1969] 2 QB 158. It is now necessary to consider separately the three
limiting principles which, even in a case of deceit, serve to keep wrongdoers'
liability within practical and sensible limits. The three concepts are causation,
remoteness and mitigation. In practice the inquiries under these headings
overlap. But they are distinct legal concepts. For present purposes causation is
the most important. The major issue in the present case is whether there is a
causal link between the fraud and the loss arising by reason of the pre-existing
fraud perpetrated on Ferranti. How should this matter be approached? The
development of a single satisfactory theory of causation has taxed great academic
minds (see Hart and Honoré *Causation in the Law* (2nd edn, 1985) and Honoré
'Necessary and Sufficient Conditions in Tort Law' in Owen *Philosophical
Foundations of Tort Law* (1995) p 363). But, as yet, it seems to me that no
satisfactory theory capable of solving the infinite variety of practical problems has
been found. Our case law yields few secure footholds. But it is settled that at any
rate in the law of obligations causation is to be categorised as an issue of fact.
What has further been established is that the 'but for' test, although it often yields

a the right answer, does not always do so.   That has led judges to apply the pragmatic test whether the condition in question was a substantial factor in producing the result.   On other occasions judges assert that the guiding criterion is whether in common sense terms there is a sufficient causal connection (see *Yorkshire Dale Steamship Co Ltd v Minister of War Transport* [1942] 2 All ER 6 at 15, [1942] AC 691 at 706 per Lord Wright). There is no material difference between

b these two approaches.   While acknowledging that this hardly amounts to an intellectually satisfying theory of causation, that is how I must approach the question of causation.

Remoteness and mitigation

    The second limiting principle is remoteness. I have already discussed the special rule of remoteness developed by the courts in the context of deceit. This

c requirement is in issue in the present case: if there is a sufficient causal link it must still be shown that the entire loss suffered by Smith is a direct consequence of the fraudulently induced transaction.   The third limiting principle is the duty to mitigate. The plaintiff is not entitled to damages in respect of loss which he could reasonably have avoided. This limiting principle has no special features in the

d context of deceit. There is no issue under this heading and I need say no more about it.

Taking stock

    It is now necessary to take stock of the case. The distinctive features of the case are—(1) that the fraud of Mr Roberts induced Smith to buy the Ferranti shares,

e the value of which were already at the date of sale doomed to collapse due to the fraud practised on the company by a third party; and (2) that by reason of the fraud of Mr Roberts, Smith was induced to buy the shares as a market making risk, ie to hold on to the shares for sale at a later stage.

    In these circumstances Smith was truly locked into the transaction by reason of the fraud perpetrated on it.   And the causative influence of the fraud is not

f significantly   attenuated   or   diluted   by   other   causative   factors   acting simultaneously with or subsequent to the fraud. The position would have been different if the loss suffered by Smith arose from a subsequent fraud. That would be a case like the misrepresented horse in Cockburn CJ's example in *Twycross v Grant* (1877) 2 CPD 469 at 544–545, where the buyer plainly cannot recover the

g entire value of the horse if it subsequently catches a disease and dies. In the actual circumstances of this case I am satisfied that there was a sufficient causal link between the fraud and Smith's loss. Moreover, for substantially the same reasons, I would hold that Smith's losses, calculated on the basis of the difference between the price paid and the proceeds of subsequent realisations, flow directly

h from the fraud. In my view Smith would on this basis be entitled to recover the sum of about £11·3m. Smith merely seeks restoration of the order for payment of £10,764,005 which Chadwick J made on a different basis. In law Smith are entitled to succeed on this appeal to that extent.

Conclusion

j   I have not lost sight of counsel for Citibank's argument that, given the way the case was pleaded, Smith should not be allowed to succeed on this legal basis. In my view the argument that Citibank was prejudiced is quite unreal. I reject it.

    I would allow Smith's appeal on damages and restore the order of Chadwick J.

Appeal allowed. Cross-appeal dismissed.

                                        Celia Fox   Barrister.

Re Bank of Credit and Commerce International SA (No 10)

a

CHANCERY DIVISION (COMPANIES COURT)

SIR RICHARD SCOTT V-C

b

16–18, 22–25 JULY, 6 AUGUST 1996

Company – Winding up – Set-off – Mutual dealings – Company incorporated in Luxembourg – Principal liquidation in Luxembourg – English liquidation 'ancillary' to Luxembourg liquidation – Whether court having power to direct that particular parts of statutory winding-up scheme and particular winding-up rules should not apply – Jurisdiction – Discretion – Insolvency Rules 1986, r 4.90.

c

The bank, which was incorporated in Luxembourg and formed part of a group that carried on a banking business on an international scale, went into liquidation in Luxembourg on 3 January 1992. The Luxembourg winding-up order was *d* followed by a winding-up order made in England on 14 January 1992. In the course of the discussions between the liquidators which led to the pooling agreement, under which all the bank's assets would be pooled, the tracing and recovery of assets would be a joint enterprise and creditors in each liquidation would receive the same level of dividend from a central pool, it was recognised that the difference between the respective set-off laws of England and *e* Luxembourg presented a problem. It was accepted that Luxembourg was the country in which the principal liquidation would be taking place and that the liquidation in England was ancillary, but persons who were both creditors and debtors of the bank would, if obliged to prove in Luxembourg, be deprived of the advantage in an English winding up of the debts they owed being set off against *f* the debts owing to them. The English liquidators sought directions from the court on whether, before (i) releasing funds already held in the central pool to the Luxembourg liquidators of the bank for payment of dividends to creditors, and (ii) transmitting to the Luxembourg liquidators funds representing the proceeds of realisations made by the English liquidators, the English liquidators should make provision for various matters. The question arose whether or to what *g* extent the court could disapply r 4.90 of the Insolvency Rules 1986, which provided that an automatic self-executing offset took effect between debts owed by and debts owed to the insolvent company to and by a third party creditor/ debtor and that only the net balance would remain to be proved by the third party or sued for by the company, in order to allow the rules of Luxembourg *h* insolvency regarding set-off to apply.

Held – The court had no inherent or statutory power to disapply the statutory insolvency scheme. Where a foreign company was in liquidation in its country of incorporation, a winding up order made in England would normally be *j* regarded as giving rise to a winding up ancillary to that being conducted in the country of incorporation in that the English liquidators would have to get in and realise English assets and the liquidators in the principal liquidation would be best placed to declare the dividend and distribute the assets comprised in the pool. None the less, the ancillary character of an English winding up did not relieve an English court of the obligation to apply English law, including English insolvency a law, to the resolution of any issue arising in the winding up brought before the court. The court had power in an ancillary liquidation to direct liquidators to transmit funds to the principal liquidators in order to enable a pari passu distribution to worldwide creditors to be achieved but it had neither the power to disapply r 4.90 or any other substantive rule forming part of the statutory scheme under the Insolvency Act 1986 and the 1986 rules nor the power to relieve

b English liquidators in an ancillary winding up of the obligation to determine whether proofs of debt submitted to them should be admitted or that creditors whose claims they admitted received the pari passu dividend to which they were entitled. If, however, the court had jurisdiction to disapply r 4.90 it should not as a matter of discretion be exercised. Accordingly, r 4.90 applied to the English winding up and the question of what retentions should be made by the English

c liquidators to protect the positions of net creditors or net debtors had to be answered on that footing (see p 815 a b j, p 821 c to f, p 822 b f to j and p 824 c e, post).

Notes

d For mutual credit and set-off, see 3(2) Halsbury's Laws (4th edn reissue) paras 535–537, and for cases on the subject, see 5(1) Digest (2nd reissue) 359–361, 10751–10761.

For the Insolvency Rules 1986, r 4.90, see 3 Halsbury's Statutory Instruments (1995 reissue) 346.

e ## Cases referred to in judgment

Banco Ambrosiano Holding v Banco di Napoli International (No 1227/83) (23 December 1983), Luxembourg.

Bank of Credit and Commerce International SA, Re [1992] BCLC 570.

Bank of Credit and Commerce International SA, Re (No 2) [1992] BCLC 579.

f Bank of Credit and Commerce International SA, Re (No 3) [1993] BCLC 1490, CA; affg [1993] BCLC 106.

Bank of Credit and Commerce International SA, Re (No 10) [1995] 1 BCLC 362.

Commercial Bank of South Australia, Re (1886) 33 Ch D 174.

English Scottish and Australian Chartered Bank, Re [1893] 3 Ch 385; affd [1893] 3 Ch

g 385, [1891–4] All ER Rep 775, CA.

Federal Bank of Australia Ltd, Re (1893) 62 LJ Ch 561, Ch D and CA.

Felixstowe Dock and Rly Co v US Lines Inc [1988] 2 All ER 77, [1989] QB 360, [1989] 2 WLR 109.

Fitzgerald v Williams [1996] 2 All ER 171, [1996] 2 WLR 447, CA.

h Hibernian Merchants Ltd, Re [1957] 3 All ER 97, [1958] Ch 76, [1957] 3 WLR 486.

North Australian Territory Co Ltd v Goldsbrough Mort & Co Ltd (1889) 61 LT 716.

Queensland Mercantile Agency Co Ltd, Re (1888) 58 LT 878.

Sedgwick Collins & Co v Rossia Insurance Co of Petrograd (Employers' Liability Assurance Corp, garnishees) [1926] 1 KB 1, CA; affd sub nom Employers' Liability

j Assurance Corp v Sedgwick Collins & Co Ltd [1927] AC 95, [1926] All ER Rep 388, HL.

Shaw (Alfred) & Co Ltd, Re, ex p Mackenzie (1897) 8 QLJ 93, Qd SC.

Stein v Blake [1995] 2 All ER 961, [1996] AC 243, [1995] 2 WLR 710, HL.

Suidair International Airways Ltd (in liq), Re [1950] 2 All ER 920, [1951] Ch 165.

Vocalian (Foreign) Ltd, Re [1932] 2 Ch 196, [1932] All ER Rep 519.

Cases also cited or referred to in skeleton arguments

Abidin Daver, The [1984] 1 All ER 470, [1984] AC 398, HL.

Aectra Refining and Marketing Inc v Exmar NV [1995] 1 All ER 641, [1994] 1 WLR 1634, CA.

African Farms Ltd, Re (1906) TS 373, Transvaal SC.

Alabama New Orleans Texas and Pacific Junction Rly Co, Re [1891] 1 Ch 213, CA.

Amin Rasheed Shipping Corp v Kuwait Insurance Co, The Al Wahab [1983] 2 All ER 884, [1984] AC 50, HL.

Aratra Potato Co Ltd v Egyptian Navigation Co, The El Amria [1981] 2 Lloyd's Rep 119, CA.

Australian Federal Life and General Assurance Co Ltd [1931] VR 317, Vic SC.

Azoff-Don Commercial Bank, Re [1954] 1 All ER 947, [1954] Ch 315.

Baden v Société Générale pour Favoriser le Développement du Commerce et de l'Industrie en France SA (1982) [1992] 4 All ER 161, [1993] 1 WLR 509.

Banco de Portugal v Noddell (1880) 5 App Cas 161, HL.

Bank of Credit and Commerce International SA, Re (No 8) [1996] 2 All ER 121, [1996] Ch 245, CA.

Bank of Credit and Commerce International SA, Re (No 9) [1994] 3 All ER 764, [1994] 1 WLR 708, CA.

Bankers Trust International Ltd v Todd Shipyard Corp, The Halcyon Isle [1980] 3 All ER 197, [1981] AC 221, PC.

Banque des Marchands de Moscou (Koupetschesky) (in liq) v Kindersley [1950] 2 All ER 549, [1951] Ch 112, CA.

Banque Indosuez SA v Ferromet Resources Inc [1993] BCLC 112.

Blain, Ex p, re Sawers (1879) 12 Ch D 522, CA.

Cia Merabello San Nicholas SA, Re [1972] 3 All ER 448, [1973] Ch 75.

Clark (Inspector of Taxes) v Oceanic Contractors Inc [1983] 1 All ER 133, [1983] 2 AC 130, HL.

Commercial Bank of India, Re (1868) LR 6 Eq 517.

Continental Bank NA v Aeokos Cia Naviera SA [1994] 2 All ER 540, [1994] 1 WLR 588, CA.

Gibbs (Anthony) & Sons v La Société Industrielle et Commerciale des Métaux (1890) 25 QBD 399, [1886–90] All ER Rep 804, CA.

Halifax Building Society v Registry of Friendly Societies [1978] 3 All ER 403, [1978] 1 WLR 1544.

Hanak v Green [1958] 2 All ER 141, [1958] 2 QB 9, CA.

Harbour Assurance Co (UK) Ltd v Kansa General International Assurance Co Ltd [1993] 3 All ER 897, [1993] QB 701, CA.

Hiram Maxim Lamp Co, Re [1903] 1 Ch 70.

IIT, Re (1975) 58 DLR (3d) 55, Ont HC.

International Tin Council, Re [1987] 1 All ER 890, [1987] Ch 419; *affd* [1988] 3 All ER 257, [1989] Ch 309, CA.

International Westminster Bank plc v Okeanos Maritime Corp [1987] 3 All ER 137, sub nom *Re a Company (No 00359 of 1987)* [1988] Ch 210.

Jabbour (Fouad Bishara) v Custodian of Absentee's Property of State of Israel [1954] 1 All ER 145, [1954] 1 WLR 139.

Jarvis Conklin Mortgage Co, Re (1895) 11 TLR 373.

Joachimson v Swiss Bank Corp [1921] 3 KB 110, CA.

Kwok v Comr of Estate Duty [1988] 1 WLR 1035, PC.

Levasseur v Mason & Barry Ltd (1890) 63 LT 700.

Libyan Arab Foreign Bank v Bankers Trust Co [1989] 3 All ER 252, [1989] QB 728.

a   *MacFadyen & Co, Re, ex p Vizianagaram Co Ltd* [1908] 1 KB 675.

MacKinnon v Donaldson Lufkin & Jenrette Securities Corp [1986] 1 All ER 653, [1986] Ch 482.

Matheson Bros Ltd, Re (1884) 27 Ch D 225.

Melbourn, Ex p, re Melbourn (1870) LR 6 Ch App 64, LJJ.

Mersey Steel and Iron Co v Naylor Benzon & Co (1882) 9 QBD 648, CA; *affd* (1884) 9

b   App Cas 434, [1881–5] All ER Rep 365, HL.

MS Fashions Ltd v Bank of Credit and Commerce International SA (in liq) (No 2), High Street Services Ltd v Bank of Credit and Commerce International SA (in liq), Impexbond Ltd v Bank of Credit and Commerce International SA (in liq) [1993] 3 All ER 769, [1993] Ch 425, Ch D and CA.

National Bank of Greece and Athens SA v Metliss [1957] 3 All ER 608, [1958] AC 509,

c   HL.

National Benefit Assurance Co, Re [1927] 3 DLR 289, Man CA.

National Westminster Bank Ltd v Halesowen Presswork and Assemblies Ltd [1972] 1 All ER 641, [1972] AC 785, HL.

New York Life Insurance Co v Public Trustee [1924] 2 Ch 101, CA.

d   *New Zealand Loan and Mercantile Agency Co Ltd v Morrison* [1898] AC 349, PC.

NFU Development Trust Ltd, Re [1973] 1 All ER 135, [1972] 1 WLR 1548.

Oriental Inland Steam Co, Re (1874) LR 9 Ch App 557, LJJ.

Paramount Airways Ltd, Re [1992] 3 All ER 1, [1993] Ch 223, CA.

Real Estate Development Co, Re [1991] BCLC 210.

Rolls Razor Ltd v Cox [1967] 1 All ER 397, [1967] 1 QB 552, CA.

e   *Rossano v Manufacturers Life Insurance Co Ltd* [1962] 2 All ER 214, [1963] 2 QB 352.

Russian Bank for Foreign Trade, Re [1933] Ch 745.

Sefel Geophysical Ltd, Re (1988) 54 DLR (4th) 117, Alta QB.

Smith v Buchanan (1800) 1 East 6, 102 ER 3.

Sovereign Life Assurance Co v Dodd [1892] 2 QB 573, CA.

f   *Spiliada Maritime Corp v Cansulex Ltd, The Spiliada* [1986] 3 All ER 843, [1987] AC 460, HL.

Standard Insurance Co Ltd, Re [1968] Qd R 118, Qd SC.

Union Theatres Ltd, Re (1933) 35 WALR 89, W Aust SC.

Application

g   The English liquidators of Bank of Credit and Commerce International SA (BCCI SA) applied to the court, inter alia, for the following directions: That prior to (a) the English liquidators transmitting to the Luxembourg liquidators the proceeds of the realisations of SA Property (as defined in the pooling agreement) now or hereafter held by the English liquidators and/or (b) the English liquidators authorising funds available to them and now or hereafter held by or under the

h   control of the Luxembourg liquidators and the Cayman liquidators to be distributed by way of dividend, the English liquidators be authorised and directed to make a provision of \$US427m in respect of the potential rights of set-off available under English law to persons having material dealings with the English branches of BCCI SA outstanding at 3 January 1992, out of the provision referred

j   to above to pay first and subsequent dividends to persons having a deposit with or material claim arising out of a transaction with, the English branches of BCCI SA who would (applying English insolvency rules of set-off) be creditors of BCCI SA as at 3 January, at the same time and at the same rate as the Luxembourg liquidators pay first and subsequent dividends to creditors of BCCI SA, to retain the remainder of the provision referred to above and deal with the same in

accordance with the further directions of the court. The respondents to the
application were the Luxembourg liquidators of BCCI and representative
creditors and debtors of BCCI. The facts are set out in the judgment.

Michael Crystal QC, Martin Pascoe and *Fidelis Oditah* (instructed by *Lovell White Durrant*) for the English liquidators.

Nigel Davis QC (instructed by *Norton Rose*) for Arab Banking Corp BSC.

Hilary Heilbron QC (instructed by *Sheridans*) for Mr Ismael/The Rising Group (net debtor).

John Jarvis QC and *Sandy Shandro* (solicitor advocate) (instructed by *Clifford Chance*) for the Deposit Protection Board.

Ajmalul Hossain (instructed by *Specher Grier*) for employees (BCCI Campaign Committee).

Anthony Trace and *Michael Gibbon* (instructed by *Stephenson Harwood*) for BCC Gibraltar Ltd.

Robin Dicker (instructed by *Wilde Sapte*) for CM Fashions (Leeds) Ltd (net creditor).

Simon Mortimore QC (instructed by *Clifford Chance*) for Bank of China.

Susan Prevezer (instructed by *Lovell White Durrant*, agents for *Cains*, Isle of Man) for BCCI SA, Isle of Man.

Susan Prevezer (instructed by *Lovell White Durrant*, agents for *Sheppherd & Wedderburn* WS, Edinburgh) for BCCI SA, Scotland.

Ian Geering QC and *Richard Snowden* (instructed by *Hammond Suddards*) for BCCI SA, Luxembourg.

John Brisby QC (instructed by *Hammond Suddards*) for Peter Ackermann (creditor).

Barbara Dohmann QC and *Tom Beazley* (instructed by *Memery Crystal*) for the English liquidation committee.

Cur adv vult

6 August 1996. The following judgment was delivered.

SIR RICHARD SCOTT V-C.   This hearing has been occasioned by an
application made to the court by the English liquidators of Bank of Credit and
Commerce International SA (BCCI SA) for directions as to whether, before: (i)
releasing funds already held in the central pool (which I will later explain) to the
Luxembourg liquidators of BCCI SA for payment of dividends to creditors; and
(ii) transmitting to the Luxembourg liquidators funds representing the proceeds
of realisations made by the English liquidators, the English liquidators should
make provision for various matters. The English liquidators also seek directions
authorising them to pay out of the sums they retain certain limited dividends at
the same time and at the same rate as dividends are paid by the Luxembourg
liquidators. Although it is no more than an application for directions, the
application has raised some important and very difficult issues of principle. It is,
moreover, an application of very considerable practical importance to the many
thousands of BCCI depositors who have been waiting for over five years for some
dividend to be paid to them. The main issue for decision is whether or to what
extent this court can disapply r 4.90 of the Insolvency Rules 1986, SI 1986/1925,
in order to allow the rules of Luxembourg insolvency regarding set-off to apply.

I do not think I can adequately describe the issues that I must deal with without
first some rehearsal of the history of the BCCI liquidation. BCCI SA was
incorporated in Luxembourg and formed part of a group that carried on a
banking business on an international scale. BCCI SA was the wholly owned

a subsidiary of BCCI Holdings (Luxembourg) SA (BCCI Holdings). Some 77% of
the shares in BCCI Holdings were owned by the ruler of the emirate of Abu
Dhabi, the Crown Prince of the emirate and other Abu Dhabi government
entities. Another wholly owned subsidiary of BCCI Holdings was Bank of Credit
and Commerce International (Overseas) Ltd (BCCI Overseas). BCCI Overseas
was incorporated in the Cayman Islands. BCCI SA and BCCI Overseas carried on
b the group's banking business in many parts of the world. In most countries the
business was carried on through branches. In some countries, however, business
was carried on through the medium of subsidiary companies. For example, BCC
Gibraltar Ltd was incorporated in Gibraltar as a wholly-owned subsidiary of
BCCI SA for the purpose of carrying on the business in Gibraltar.

In 1972 the centre of operations of the BCCI Group was based in Abu Dhabi.
c Shortly thereafter it was moved to London. But in 1987 the group's central
treasury operations were moved from London back to Abu Dhabi and in the
summer of 1990 the central management of the group was also moved from
London to Abu Dhabi. By June 1991 the BCCI Group operated in some 69
countries. BCCI SA had some 47 branches, including 24 in the United Kingdom,
d covering 13 countries. BCCI Overseas had 63 branches covering 28 countries.
Other subsidiaries or affiliates of BCCI Holdings had some 260 branches covering
30 countries.

The group collapsed in the summer of 1991. Provisional liquidators of BCCI
SA were appointed in England on 5 July 1991 on the application of the Bank of
England.
e Similar action was taken by other regulators around the world with the
intention and effect of closing down the operations of the BCCI Group. In
Luxembourg a commissaire de surveillance was appointed on 8 July 1991. In the
Cayman Islands a receiver was appointed over BCCI Overseas and associated
companies on 5 July 1991, and on 22 July 1991 the Grand Court of the Cayman
Islands appointed provisional liquidators of BCCI Overseas and of International
f Credit and Investment Co (Overseas) Ltd (ICIC Overseas). Both the Court of
Session in Scotland and the High Court of the Isle of Man appointed provisional
liquidators of BCCI SA in their respective jurisdictions.

A petition to wind up BCCI SA founded on allegations contained in a draft
report that had been prepared by Price Waterhouse under s 41 of the Banking Act
g 1987 was presented by the Bank of England on 5 July 1991. When the petition
came before the court on 30 July 1991 it was adjourned for four months to enable
a possible restructuring support operation to be examined (see *Re Bank of Credit
and Commerce International SA* [1992] BCLC 570). In the course of his judgment
Browne-Wilkinson V-C referred to the nature of the problems that would have
h to be faced if a winding-up order were to be made. He said (at 577):

'This case raises, and will continue to raise, enormous problems. BCCI is
a Luxembourg bank; it is not an English bank. As I understand it, if a winding
up goes forward the assets of BCCI worldwide will be applicable for the
creditors of BCCI worldwide. The attempt to put a ring fence around the
j assets of the creditors to be found in any one jurisdiction is, at least under
English law as I understand it, not correct, and destined to failure. I believe
the position will prove to be the same in most other countries and
jurisdictions.'

In dealing with an application made on 27 August 1991 on behalf of a group of
creditors, Browne-Wilkinson V-C said:

'The second delicate aspect is the relationship between this court and the court of Luxembourg. BCCI is incorporated in Luxembourg which prima facie is the court where the prime winding-up proceedings, if it ever gets that far, will have to be conducted as being the law of the country of incorporation. Some suggestions have been made that in some way it is inappropriate that that should be the primary administration were a winding-up order to be made. That is not a view with which I can concur in any way. There is nothing to indicate that the court of Luxembourg would be in some way regarded as inappropriate, if otherwise under the general law that is the right court to administer the matter.' (See *Re Bank of Credit and Commerce International SA (No 2)* [1992] BCLC 579 at 581.)

On 2 December 1991, when the adjourned petition came back before the court, Nicholls V-C (who had replaced Sir Nicolas Browne-Wilkinson as Vice-Chancellor) referred to 'the truly gargantuan task of preserving and realising assets of BCCI worldwide', and went on:

'One has only to read the provisional liquidators' report to the court dated 29 November to see what a mammoth and difficult task this is. The BCCI group operated through branches or representative offices in 75 countries, each has its own legal system and some have exchange control restrictions. Further, the affairs of BCCI and Overseas are inextricably intermingled. Plainly, worldwide cooperation is essential if the assets in the different jurisdictions are to be realised to the best advantage of the creditors. Otherwise and all too obviously there is likely to be long drawn out litigation in many jurisdictions between the different parts of the BCCI group.'

He adjourned the petition to 14 January 1992.

On 3 January 1992 BCCI SA went into liquidation in Luxembourg, the country of its incorporation. Three liquidators were appointed. The winding-up order was made by Judge Welter. In a judgment submitted to the Law Courts in Luxembourg on 6 December 1991 and certified on 23 January 1992 she commented that 'the company ... transacted only some 10% of its worldwide business in Luxembourg, the preponderant volume being located in the United Kingdom', that 'the method of winding-up adopted by the court ... should ... take account of the non-conflicting provisions of English law' and that 'the court's main concern is to ensure that the rights of creditors are respected and an equal footing is maintained between them'. She went on as follows:

'Observance of the principle of equality of creditors means that it must be expressly stated that as from the date of the said judgment, no further payment (legal, judicial or contractual) can be made for the benefit of those who are both debtors and creditors of BCCI S.A. Consequently, these creditors must pay to the liquidators the sums originally due to the credit establishment and, with regard to their debts, accept the law of the dividend should the possibility of an offset provide them, where applicable, with payment in full. The only exception to the rule banning any offset, repeatedly confirmed in the case of bankruptcy, winding up or controlled management (Cf. in particular, Appeal Court, 2 March 1923, 11, 134; Luxembourg Court 30 July 1927, 11, 554; Commercial Court of Antwerp 2 March 1937, Pand. period. 1938, No. 226; Luxembourg Court 23 December 1983: *Banco Ambrosiano Holding -v- Banco di Napoli International* No. 1227/83 on the Roll) is where the sum owed and the debt have a common origin or a   relate to the same contract (cf. Luxembourg Court, 1 April 1977, 23, 556). The reference to articles 537 to 552 inclusive of the Commercial Code has the effect of regulating the rights of joint debtors, sureties, creditors under pledge and privileged creditors under movables and mortgage and privileged creditors under immoveables, by analogy with bankruptcy.'

b   It will be appreciated that the Luxembourg set-off rule, as stated by Judge Welter, produces a very different effect from that produced in English liquidations by r 4.90 of the 1986 rules. Under r 4.90 an automatic, self-executing offset between debts owed by and debts owed to the insolvent company to and by a third party creditor/debtor takes effect. Only the net balance will remain to be proved for by the third party or, as the case may be, sued for by the company.

c   One way of looking at the effect of r 4.90 is that the company's asset, namely the debt owed by the third party, becomes available to the third party as a security to set against the debt owed by the company. It follows from r 4.90 that a creditor of the company who also owes money to the company does not have to be content simply with an eventual dividend paid on the debt owed by the company.

d   Up to the extent of the debt that he or she owes to the company, the creditor will receive in respect of the debt owed by the company 100p in the pound. This state of affairs, an inevitable and intended consequence of r 4.90, does not treat the creditor who owes money to the company on an equal footing with creditors who do not owe money to the company. The latter recover only a dividend. The former are credited with 100p in the pound up to the extent of their debt to the

e   company.

Be that as it may, the order of the Luxembourg court of 3 January 1992: (i) confirmed the 'dissolution and winding-up' of BCCI SA; (ii) appointed Judge Welter as investigating judge; (iii) appointed three individuals as liquidators; and (iv) declared that 'as from [the date of the judgment] no further offset may be

f   made except in the case of linked debts arising under the same contract'. The order contained, of course, many other provisions as well.

The Luxembourg winding-up order on 3 January 1992 was followed by a winding-up order made in this jurisdiction on 14 January 1992. The order was that BCCI SA 'be wound up by this court under the provisions of the Insolvency Act 1986 ...'

g   One of the parties heard by the court when the English winding-up order was made was the Deposit Protection Board (the board). The board administers the Deposit Protection Scheme, a statutory scheme that was established by s 58 of the Banking Act 1987 to provide compensation to sterling depositors in the event of insolvency of an institution authorised to take deposits under the Act. BCCI SA

h   was such an institution. The level of compensation payable is an amount equal to 75% of a 'protected deposit' subject to a maximum payment to any one depositor of £15,000 (see s 60(1)). Section 58(1) requires the board to make the compensation payments 'as soon as practicable'. Under s 62 of the Act, where the board has made or is under a liability to make a compensation payment to a

j   depositor, the insolvent institution becomes liable to the board for an amount equal to the compensation payment made, or to be made, by the board. And the liquidator of the institution comes under a statutory duty to pay to the board, until the board has been fully repaid, dividends that would otherwise have been paid to the depositor.

The collapse of BCCI SA led to considerable pressure on the board, both from the government and the media, to make compensation payments to depositors

as soon as possible. Claim forms were sent to depositors as early as 22 July 1991
and by the time the winding-up order was made on 14 January 1992 it had   a
become clear that a sum of many millions would have to be paid by the board as
compensation under the scheme.

On the same day as the English winding-up order was made, a winding-up
order in respect of BCCI SA was made by the Court of Session in Scotland; and
on 15 January 1992 the High Court in the Isle of Man, too, made a winding-up   b
order. Both in Scotland and in the Isle of Man, BCCI SA had carried on its banking
business through branches.

And, also on 14 January 1992, the Grand Court of the Cayman Islands ordered
BCCI Overseas and associated BCCI companies to be wound up.

In the meantime, liquidation proceedings were in progress in the United States.
The United States, I understand, unlike England, Luxembourg and, I think, the   c
majority of European states, operates a 'ring fence' liquidation system under
which assets in its jurisdiction are applied first in or towards the discharge of debts
owing to domestic creditors. In addition, proceedings were instituted in the
United States against companies in the BCCI Group, including BCCI, for
infringements of federal regulatory requirements as well as for breaches of   d
anti-racketeering statutes. Discussions were in progress between the United
States authorities and the BCCI SA and BCCI Overseas liquidators outside the
United States regarding the resolution of the US proceedings. It was, naturally,
the wish of the Luxembourg, English and Cayman Islands liquidators to obtain
the release from the United States of as large a sum as possible in respect of
BCCI's US assets.   e

Also in progress were discussions between the Luxembourg, English and
Cayman Island liquidators regarding difficulties in deciding which BCCI assets
belonged to which BCCI company and which BCCI creditors and which BCCI
debtors were the creditors or debtors of which BCCI company. The manner in
which many of the BCCI books had been kept left the answers uncertain. The   f
possibility of lengthy and expensive litigation in order to reach some resolution
of these difficulties loomed. In addition, very important negotiations with the
Abu Dhabi majority shareholders had been commenced. The prospect that a
very substantial sum might be forthcoming from the majority shareholders was
a real possibility. But, of course, agreement between the respective BCCI
liquidators as to the basis on which any such sum would be paid and received, and   g
as to the manner in which the sum once received would be applied, was essential.

The discussions and negotiations to which I have referred led in due course to
a number of agreements being concluded. A so-called contribution agreement
was entered into with the Abu Dhabi majority shareholders. Under this
agreement, the majority shareholders agreed to provide a sum in excess of about   h
$US1·5bn upon terms which included their release from any further action being
brought or claim made against them by any of the BCCI liquidators. Claims
which had been made by the liquidators against Sheik Mahfouz were settled for
sums of $US245m and $US183m. And negotiations with the US authorities led to
an agreement for the release from the United States of $US240m. These funds   j
have been referred to collectively as 'global realisations'.

By an agreement dated 15 January 1993 (although not signed until May 1994)
made between the respective liquidators in Luxembourg, England and the
Cayman Islands, agreement was reached as to how the global realisations should
be allocated between them. The agreement (known as the 'Costs and Recoveries
Agreement') recited that arrangements had been agreed 'for dealing with certain

a projects which ... are agreed by the liquidators to be treated as Global Projects' and that the liquidators wished 'to set out their agreement for the sharing of the costs of and the recoveries from such projects'. Paragraph 3.2 of the agreement provided: 'All recoveries resulting from a Global Project shall be distributed to the liquidators in the Relevant Percentages forthwith after receipt thereof.'

Paragraph 5.1 of the agreement provided:

b
'This Agreement may only be terminated with respect to any Global Project upon the agreement of all the Liquidators and, in that event, on such terms as they mutually agree.'

The 'Relevant Percentages' as set out in the agreement, were 'English Liquidators—50%; Luxembourg Liquidators—10%; Overseas Liquidators— c 35%; Holdings Liquidators—5%'. Under a later agreement, whereby the ICIC companies brought assets into the global realisations pool, the relevant percentages were altered so as to enable a 2·5% share to be allocated to the ICIC companies. The English liquidators' percentage became 48·5%. The present position, therefore, is that the English liquidators are entitled to call for the d distribution to themselves for the purposes of the English liquidation of 48·5% of the global realisations.

The costs and recoveries agreement in its original form was approved by the Luxembourg court on 25 January 1994. The costs and recoveries agreement amended to take account of the ICIC companies 2·5% share was approved by the Luxembourg court on 31 January 1995.
e
The costs and recoveries agreement dealt with global realisations. In addition, however, the English liquidators have at their disposal the proceeds of realisations of English assets. These English realisations amount at present to some $US655m.

The most important agreement of all for present purposes is the pooling f agreement. It was, for reasons I have already indicated, well understood by each set of liquidators that co-operation between them was essential if the winding up was not to be lost in a morass of legal argument. Their objective was to create a structure under which all BCCI assets would be pooled, the tracing and recovery of assets would be a joint enterprise and creditors in each liquidation would g receive the same level of dividend from a central pool.

In the course of the discussions which led to the pooling agreement it was recognised that the difference between the respective set-off laws of England and Luxembourg presented a problem. On the one hand, Luxembourg, the country in which BCCI SA was incorporated, was the country in which the principal liquidation would be taking place. On the other hand, persons who were both h creditors and debtors of BCCI SA would, if obliged to prove in Luxembourg, be deprived of the advantage in an English winding-up of the debts they owed being set-off against the debts owing to them.

It is necessary for me to refer to a number of the provisions of the pooling agreement. The pooling agreement was dated 10 November 1994. The parties j were BCCI SA, BCCI SA's Luxembourg liquidators, BCCI SA's English liquidators, BCCI Overseas and BCCI Overseas' Cayman Islands liquidators. The recitals to the pooling agreement included the following:

'... (iv) one of the purposes of this Agreement is to provide for the property of SA and Overseas to be pooled and shared between them in the manner hereinafter set out; (v) it is expedient that so far as possible the affairs of all branches of SA and Overseas should be wound up or otherwise dealt with as part of a worldwide winding-up of each company.'

The agreement was expressed to be conditional on approval being obtained from the Luxembourg court, the English court and the Cayman Islands court.

Clause 3 of the pooling agreement, headed 'Distribution of Pool Property to Pool Creditors' included the following sub-clauses:

'3.1 Subject to Clause 3.11 below, the liabilities of SA in respect of which a creditor of SA is entitled to rank for a dividend in the liquidation of SA, and the amount for which he is entitled to rank for such dividend, shall be established by the Luxembourg Liquidators in the Luxembourg Liquidation in accordance with the laws of the Grand Duchy of Luxembourg (including its conflict of law rules) for the time being applicable ...

3.11 The individual entitlement of each Pool Creditor in respect of each distribution made in accordance with this Agreement shall be subject: (a) in the case of each creditor with an Admitted SA Claim to the laws of the Grand Duchy of Luxembourg, to the provisions of the Luxembourg Judgment and to such further orders and directions as may be made by the Luxembourg Court ...

3.18 Subject to Clause 3.21 below, no distribution to creditors of SA or of Overseas or of any Participating Subsidiary or of Holdings shall be made out of the Pool Realisation Accounts except a distribution made in accordance with this Part or with Part VII of this Agreement ...

3.21 The Luxembourg liquidators and the Cayman liquidators may make arrangements: (a) with the English Liquidators in relation to matters set out in clause 5.6 below ...'

No such arrangements as are referred to in cl 3.21(a) have, in the event, been made.

Part VII of the pooling agreement (referred to in cl 3.18) dealt with preferential payments.

It follows from the provisions of cl 3 that once realisations of BCCI assets reach the pool realisation accounts, the distribution of the money will, so far as unsecured creditors of BCCI SA are concerned, be the responsibility of the Luxembourg liquidators acting in accordance with Luxembourg law and under the supervision of the Luxembourg court.

I now come to cl 5 of the pooling agreement, headed 'The English Liquidation'. Clause 5 included the following relevant sub-clauses:

'5.1 Subject to Clause 5.3 below, SA, the Luxembourg Liquidators, Overseas and the Cayman Liquidators shall co-operate with the English Liquidators by the exchange of information, in the joint conduct of litigation, and by other means, as from time to time may seem expedient, with a view to the realisation by the English Liquidators of SA Property situated within the jurisdiction of the English Court.

5.2 Subject to Clause 5.3 below, the English Liquidators shall co-operate with SA, the Luxembourg Liquidators, Overseas and the Cayman Liquidators by the exchange of information, in the joint conduct of litigation, and by other means, as from time to time may seem expedient, with a view to the realisation by the Luxembourg Liquidators and/or the Cayman Liquidators of Overseas Property wherever situated and of SA Property situated outside the jurisdiction of the English Court.

5.3 Subject to any prohibitions or conditions imposed by the law of England and Wales and subject to Clause 5.4 below, the English Liquidators shall make the books and records of the branches of SA in England and Wales available for inspection and review by the Luxembourg Liquidators or by such person or persons as the Luxembourg Liquidators may appoint as their agent or agents for such purpose and shall respond to any queries raised by the Luxembourg Liquidators or by such person or persons as aforesaid (and upon request provide to the Luxembourg Liquidators or to such person or persons as aforesaid such information or copies of documents or other data as they may reasonably require) which relate to the affairs of such branches of SA.

5.4 Notwithstanding the provisions of Clauses 5.1, 5.2 and 5.3 above: (a) nothing in such Clauses shall require the Luxembourg Liquidators or the Cayman Liquidators to take any step which is contrary to an express direction of the Luxembourg Court or the Cayman Court respectively; and (b) nothing in such Clauses shall require the English Liquidators to take any step which is contrary to an express direction of the English Court.

5.5 It is the joint intention of the Luxembourg Liquidators, the Cayman Liquidators and the English Liquidators that, subject to such provision or arrangements being made in relation to the matters set out in Clause 5.6 below, and subject generally to such terms and conditions, as to the English Court may seem fit, the English Liquidators should transmit to the Luxembourg Liquidators to be dealt with by the Luxembourg Liquidators in accordance with the provisions of this Agreement all proceeds of the realisation of SA Property which are now or may hereafter be or come within the jurisdiction of the English Court.

5.6 The matters referred to in Clause 5.5 above are: (i) the payment of, or provision for, the English Costs; (ii) the payment in full of all English Preferential Claims; (iii) the recognition of all valid claims (whether based upon the existence of security or rules of law and equity or otherwise) having regard to which assets in the hands of the English Liquidators are not assets available for distribution to creditors in the English Liquidation but the property of the claimant; (iv) provision or arrangements for the benefit of debtors of SA liable to be sued in a Court in England and Wales which enables them to take advantage of any set-off or cross-claim which would have been available to them if they had been sued by the English Liquidators in the course of the English Liquidation; (v) provision or arrangements in relation to any claim (not being an English Preferential Claim) which would be admissible in the English Liquidation but would not be admissible (or would be admissible on different terms as to dividend) in the Luxembourg Liquidation; and (vi) provision or arrangements in relation to the claims and rights of persons who are entitled to compensation payments under Part II of the Banking Act 1987 (or who would be so entitled to such payments but for Section 61 of that Act), and in relation to the consequent claims and rights of the Deposit Protection Board thereunder, in order to protect such claims and rights.

5.7 With a view to achieving the objective described in Clause 5.5 above, the English Liquidators will use their best endeavours to obtain from the English Court such further or other orders and directions (whether by way of variation of or addition to the English Order or otherwise) as may be necessary or desirable to enable the said objective to be achieved.'

The 'English Order' referred to in cl 5.7 is the order of this court approving the pooling agreement; in the event, Nicholls V-C's order of 12 June 1992 was the *a* English order (see *Re Bank of Credit and Commerce International SA (No 3)* [1993] BCLC 106).

The reference in cl 5.5 to 'all proceeds of the realisation of SA Property which are now or may hereafter be or come within the jurisdiction of the English Court' is apt, in my opinion, in its ordinary meaning, to include the English liquidators' *b* 48·5% of the global realisations if and to the extent that the English liquidators should call for the share to be transmitted to them in England. Under the costs and recoveries agreement the English liquidators appear to me to have the right to so call.

The obligation of the English liquidators under cl 5.5 to transmit realisations of SA assets to the Luxembourg liquidators is expressed to be subject to *c* 'arrangements being made in relation to the matters set out in Clause 5.6'. These 'matters' include provision or arrangements which would enable BCCI SA debtors 'liable to be sued in a Court in England and Wales' to retain the benefit of r 4.90 set-off (see sub-para (iv)). Sub-paragraph (iv) appears to be authorising the English liquidators to make provision for a class of creditors/debtors limited *d* to those 'liable to be sued in a Court in England and Wales'.

If the sub-paragraph were to be applied so as to provide English creditors/debtors of BCCI SA with an advantage not available to BCCI SA's other creditors/debtors, a question might arise under art 6 of the EEC Treaty as to the legality of the provision. I will return to this point later.   *e*

No such difficulty arises in connection with sub-para (v) of cl 5.6. The claims to which sub-para (v) applies would include, in my opinion, claims of creditors proving for the net balance due to them after r 4.90 set-off had been applied. Claims thus calculated would not be admitted in the Luxembourg liquidation.

Clause 5.6(vi) contemplated in terms that provision for the claims of the *f* Deposit Protection Board might need to be made by the English liquidators.

Clause 6 of the pooling argument contained provision for liquidators of foreign branches or foreign subsidiaries of BCCI SA or BCCI Overseas to enter into branch participation agreements whereby they would, in effect, join the pooling agreement.

The terms of the pooling agreement and the contribution agreement having *g* been settled between the respective sets of liquidators, the process of obtaining the approval of the respective courts to these agreements was set in train.

The English liquidators' application for approval was dealt with by Nicholls V-C at a four-day hearing from 8 to 12 June 1992 (see *Re Bank of Credit and Commerce International SA (No 3)* [1993] BCLC 106). A number of creditors or *h* group of creditors appeared and objected. However, Nicholls V-C approved both agreements. The contents of his order dated 12 June 1992 approving the pooling agreement are of relevance. It was recited, inter alia—

'(iv) that it is expedient that the determination of the claims of the creditors *j* of BCCI SA (other than the claims of creditors whose claims are given preferential status on a liquidation of SA in a jurisdiction other than the Grand Duchy of Luxembourg and the distribution of assets of BCCI SA to such creditors (other than as aforesaid) should be carried out in accordance with one liquidation; and (v) that it is expedient that the liquidation in accordance with which such determination and distribution should be

a   carried out should be the liquidation of BCCI SA by the Luxembourg Court
     in Luxembourg.'

It was then ordered, so far as relevant:

     'Subject to: (i) the provisions of the Pooling Agreement ... being satisfied
     ... (ii) the terms and conditions set out in the Schedule to this Order and to
b   provisions being made for the matters referred to in the said Schedule in
     accordance with the said terms and conditions. The English Liquidators be
     at liberty to transmit to the Luxembourg Liquidators in Luxembourg for the
     purposes of the liquidation of BCCI SA by the Luxembourg Court all
     proceeds of the realisation of property of BCCI SA which are now or may
c   hereafter be or come within the jurisdiction of this Honourable Court (such
     proceeds being hereafter referred to as English Proceeds).'

The schedule to the order authorised the English liquidators to retain sufficient
funds out of the English proceeds to cover costs, charges and expenses of the
English liquidation, to cover any preferential claims and to cover any proprietary
d claims that ought to be made and, also, authorised them—

     'to make such arrangements with the Luxembourg Liquidators as they
     think fit to facilitate: (a) the ascertainment of the claims of the creditors
     (other than Preferential English Claims) which are capable of being admitted
     in the liquidation of BCCI SA in Luxembourg; (b) the qualification of such
e   claims; and (c) distributions to which creditors in respect of such claims may
     be entitled ...'

In his judgment, given on 12 June 1992, Nicholls V-C said about the pooling
agreement ([1993] BCLC 106 at 111):

f   '... I am in no doubt that the agreements are so plainly for the benefit of
     the creditors that I should approve them without further ado. I am satisfied
     that the affairs of BCCI SA and BCCI Overseas are so hopelessly intertwined
     that a pooling of their assets, with a distribution enabling the like dividend to
     be paid to both companies' creditors, is the only sensible way to proceed. It
     would make no sense to spend vast sums of money and much time in trying
g   to disentangle and unravel.'

One of the features of the contribution agreement, as it then stood, was that it
contained a provision barring from participation in the funds being provided by
the Abu Dhabi majority shareholders, any creditors who declined to release the
h majority shareholders from damages claims. To that extent, therefore, the
contribution agreement effected a variation in the pari passu scheme established
in this jurisdiction by the Insolvency Act 1986 and its statutory predecessors. It
was contended by a group of creditors who objected to the contribution
agreement that, inter alia, the court had no power, save by a formal scheme of
arrangement under s 425 of the Companies Act 1985, to authorise a distribution
j of assets in a winding up otherwise than in accordance with the statutory pari
passu scheme. Nicholls V-C said, simply (at 111):

     'I do not agree. The liquidators' powers under, paras 2 and 3 of Sch 4 to
     the Insolvency Act 1986, exercisable with the approval of the court, are wide
     and they are wide enough to cover this case.'

The objectors took this ultra vires point (with other points) to the Court of Appeal ([1993] BCLC 1490). The appeal was dismissed on 17 July 1992. As to the ultra vires point, Dillon LJ said (at 1510):

'As I see it, in a liquidation there can be a departure from the pari passu rule by a scheme of arrangement under s 425; but, equally, there can be a departure from the pari passu rule if it is merely ancillary to an exercise of any of the powers which are exercisable with the sanction of the court under Pt I of Sch 4 to the Insolvency Act 1986.'

The contribution agreement represented a compromise of claims and cross-claims between the BCCI companies and the majority shareholders. Since the liquidators had power to enter into a compromise agreement with the majority shareholders, they had power to agree, as a term of the compromise, to a variation of the strict pari passu rule.

The contribution agreement and the pooling agreement were approved also in the Grand Court of the Cayman Islands on 19 June 1992. On the same day the Cayman court adopted Insolvency Rules identical to those contained in the 1986 rules.

In Luxembourg, however, the application for approval of the two agreements, ran into difficulties. Both the agreements, as originally agreed, had contained a clause nominating English law as the proper law and England as the venue for the arbitration of any disputes. These provisions were objected to by Judge Welter in the Luxembourg hearings. She approved the agreements on 22 October 1992 subject to a requirement that the provisions regarding English law and regarding the venue of any arbitration should be deleted. The majority shareholders and the English and Cayman Island courts agreed to the deletions.

In Luxembourg, however, an appeal was lodged against the approval of the agreements, although the appeal against the pooling agreement approval was later withdrawn. On 27 October 1993 the Luxembourg appeal against the approval of the contribution agreement was allowed. It succeeded on the same point that had been argued unsuccessfully in this country, namely that the court had no power to permit a departure from a strict pari passu distribution among the unsecured creditors.

The refusal by the Luxembourg Appeal Court to accept the contribution agreement led to renewed negotiations between the majority shareholders and the respective sets of liquidators. In due course a revised contribution agreement with an increase to $1·8bn of the sum to be provided by the majority shareholders and the removal of the provision that might have led to a variation in the pari passu distribution rule was agreed. The revised contribution agreement (and the agreement under which the ICIC companies joined the pooling agreement and were allocated 2·5% of the global realisations), was approved by me on 19 December 1994 (see Re Bank of Credit and Commerce International SA (No 10) [1995] 1 BCLC 362), by the Grand Court in the Cayman Islands on 13 January 1995 and by the Luxembourg court on 31 January 1995. Again, however, the approval given by the Luxembourg court was appealed. But this time the appeal was withdrawn. The revised contribution agreement was formally completed on 14 May 1996.

The agreements to which I have referred all being in place and the BCCI realisations now totalling well over $2bn, the liquidators are anxious to declare and pay a first dividend as soon as possible. It is contemplated by the pooling a agreement that the BCCI SA dividend will be declared and paid by the Luxembourg liquidators.

The Luxembourg liquidators (and the Cayman Islands liquidators) have in mind a first dividend of 20%, to be followed later by another 20% dividend. For this to be possible funds must be released to the Luxembourg liquidators by the English liquidators. First, however, there must be a decision as to the amount of b the funds that need to be retained by the English liquidators under their control. That decision will determine what, if any, part of the English realisations can be transmitted to Luxembourg and what part of their 48·5% share of the global realisations they can release to the Luxembourg liquidators.

The English liquidators' report to the court dated 2 February 1996 raised eight separate matters in respect of which funds might need to be retained and in c respect of which directions from the court were thought to be needed. They were (1) set-off; (2) currency conversion; (3) claims admission procedures; (4) claims under examination; (5) claim valuation date; (6) the BCCI Scottish branch's letter of request; (7) the BCCI Isle of Man branch's letter of request; and (8) preferential claims. To these matters should now be added (9) the claims of d the Deposit Protection Board.

Some of these matters present no present problem. The Luxembourg liquidators have indicated that they propose to admit all claims in US dollars at 3 January 1992 exchange rates and to pay all dividends in US dollars. No provision need now be made in respect of currency conversion difficulties.

The 'claim valuation date' problem arises from the circumstance that the e Luxembourg liquidation commenced on 3 January 1992 but the English liquidation did not commence until 14 January 1992. Interest bearing claims would, therefore, accrue some ten days additional interest if proved in a English liquidation than would be able to be claimed in a Luxembourg liquidation. In their report of 20 February 1996, the English liquidators have expressed the view f that 'it would not be unfair for any creditor to receive a dividend based on claims calculated as at 3 January 1992' and that they 'do not consider it appropriate for any provision to be made for the different claim valuation date that would apply were the liquidation of BCCI SA a purely English liquidation'. I agree.

As to preferential claims, it is now common ground that the English liquidators should pay the preferential claims of all employees who were working for English g branches of BCCI SA. The provision to be made by the English liquidators will be calculated accordingly. No directions from the court are needed.

The other matters are all live. They raise a question as to the nature of a so-called 'ancillary' liquidation and as to the extent to which the court has power in a winding up to direct that particular parts of the statutory winding-up scheme h and particular winding-up rules shall not apply. It may be convenient if I describe briefly the problems that arise in respect of each of the still live matters.

(1) SET OFF

It was made clear by the terms of the 3 January 1992 order of the Luxembourg j court and the judgment given by Judge Welter that the Luxembourg liquidators would be required to restrict set-off to the very limited set-off recognised by Luxembourg law. Leaving aside that very limited set-off, the Luxembourg liquidators are required to collect all outstanding loans in full and to admit deposits in full for dividend purposes even where the loans and deposits were made to and made by the same person. A creditor/debtor will, therefore, be required to repay in full his or her liabilities to BCCI SA before receiving any dividend. If a loan is outstanding at the time a dividend is declared, the liquidators may apply the dividend in or towards discharge of the loan and sue for the balance, if any, of the loan. Alternatively, they may refuse to admit the proof submitted by the creditor/debtor and take action to recover the full amount of the loan. The Luxembourg liquidators have made clear that, as the rules on set-off in Luxembourg are regarded as a matter of public policy, they would not be able to sanction any arrangement which required them formally to recognise and apply rights of set-off wider than those which exist under local rules.

Under r 4.90 of the 1986 rules, by contrast, all mutual credits and debits are set-off so that only the net balance is provable in, or payable to, the liquidation. An account must be struck as at the commencement of the liquidation between the company and the creditor/debtor whereby all credits and debits are set-off regardless of the jurisdiction in which any credit or debit arose. In *Stein v Blake* [1995] 2 All ER 961 at 964, 967, [1996] AC 243 at 251, 255 Lord Hoffmann (with whose speech the other members of the House agreed) said:

> 'Bankruptcy set-off ... affects the substantive rights of the parties by enabling the bankrupt's creditor to use his indebtedness to the bankrupt as a form of security',

and that bankruptcy set-off 'is mandatory and self-executing and results, as of the bankruptcy date, in only a net balance being owing ...'

Every English winding up has a theoretical international application. The set-off brought about by r 4.90 applies, under English law, to every creditor and every debtor whether or not the proper law of the debt is English law.

The r 4.90 account, struck at the commencement of the winding up, will have the result that the creditor/debtor will be left either as a net creditor to prove for the balance or, as the case may be, as a net debtor to be sued for the balance, or, if the credits and debits were of exactly equal amounts, with no sum either owing or owed.

In their report to the court of 20 February 1996 the English liquidators gave details of the practical implication of the differences in set-off law between England and Luxembourg. Out of a total of some 36,000 proof of debt forms received by them, round about 6,000 were affected by r 4.90 set-off. These were broken down as follows. (1) Net creditors. Credit accounts with balances totalling in aggregate about $US300m, involving about 1,100 separate net creditors and where amounts outstanding on loan accounts totalling $US150m would be set-off under r 4.90, have been identified. (2) Net debtors. Loan accounts with a total of about $US765m outstanding, involving about 1,600 separate net debtors and where balances on credit accounts totalling $US121m would be set-off under r 4.90 have been identified.

There may be additional net creditors and net debtors who have not yet been identified.

If the net creditors were proving in England, they would, treating them as a block, receive dividends on the net balance of $150m. Assuming a dividend of 40%, the dividend paid would be $60m. In Luxembourg, by contrast, no dividend at all would be paid. The 40% dividend payable on the $300m would be $120m. But the $120m would be set against the $150m outstanding on loan accounts. So nothing would be paid to the net creditors and $30m would still be owed by them.

As to the net debtors, in England there is no credit balance in respect of which they can prove but they remain liable for the net debt of $644m (ie $765m minus

a
$121m). In Luxembourg they could prove for the $121m. The 40% dividend would be $48·4m. The $48·4m would be set against the $765m, leaving the debtors still liable to pay $716·6m.

The respective disadvantages to the net creditors and net debtors of depriving them of the benefit of r 4.90 and applying to them the Luxembourg winding-up rules is clear.

b

(2) CLAIMS ADMISSION PROCEDURES

The English liquidators have examined the 36,000 odd proofs that have been submitted to them by those creditors who had material dealings with the English branches of BCCI SA. Having done so, they have forwarded to the Luxembourg
c liquidators the proofs that have appeared to them (the English liquidators) to be in order. The Luxembourg liquidators have reviewed the claims but have indicated that for a variety of procedural reasons, they are at present unable to accept some 4,000 claims totalling $300m odd. The reasons relate to such matters as proof of identity, signature verification and minor discrepancies between bank records and proof forms. To the extent that these claims may eventually be
d rejected by the Luxembourg liquidators but would have been accepted by the English liquidators, the claimants will have been disadvantaged by the application of Luxembourg winding-up procedure rather than English winding-up procedure.

e (3) CLAIMS UNDER EXAMINATION

There are about 2,800 claims to an aggregate value of $694m that the English liquidators are currently examining. A significant number of these will turn out to be acceptable to the English liquidators and will be forwarded to Luxembourg. No doubt the Luxembourg liquidators' review will reveal the same sort of
f procedural problems in regard to some of those forwarded as arose in regard to the 4,000-odd claims mentioned in (2) above.

(4) THE SCOTTISH LIQUIDATION AND ISLE OF MAN LIQUIDATION

The Scottish liquidators of BCCI SA have been collecting the assets of the
g Scottish branch. They have been contemplating entering into a branch participation agreement in a form to be agreed with the Luxembourg liquidators (see cl 6 of the pooling agreement). They wish to be able to make similar provisions to those which the English liquidators are, under cl 5 of the pooling agreement, able to make. But it is not clear whether or not the Luxembourg
h liquidators will be willing to allow the same latitude to the Scottish liquidators under a branch participation agreement as has been allowed to the English liquidators under the pooling agreement.

In these circumstances, the Court of Session in Scotland has issued a letter of request dated 31 January 1996 to this court under s 426 of the 1986 Act. The letter
j of request asks this court to consider whether the English liquidators should be directed to make the same provision for persons who dealt with the Scottish branches of BCCI SA as are directed to be made for those who dealt with the English branches. The same point arises in connection with the Isle of Man liquidation. The High Court in the Isle of Man has issued a letter of request dated 2 February 1996 seeking the same assistance as is sought by the letter of request from the Court of Session.

(5) THE DEPOSIT PROTECTION BOARD

Under the Banking Act 1987 the English liquidators are placed under a *a* statutory duty to divert to the board dividends that would otherwise be payable to creditors to whom the board has made compensation payments. In calculating the amount of the compensation payments, the board sought and received the assistance of the English liquidators as to the amount of the indebtedness of BCCI SA to the respective creditors. In calculating the respective amounts, the English *b* liquidators applied r 4.90 where applicable. They had no choice but to do so. It may be, therefore, that the board must look to the English liquidators rather than to the Luxembourg liquidators for the diverted dividends that are due to them.

ANCILLARY LIQUIDATIONS

There is no doubt but that both Browne-Wilkinson V-C and Nicholls V-C, my *c* two distinguished predecessors, contemplated and intended that the winding up of BCCI SA in this country would be an 'ancillary' liquidation, with the Luxembourg liquidation constituting the principal liquidation.

I have already cited a number of passages from their respective judgments and need not, I think, add to that citation. The intention that the English liquidation *d* should be ancillary to that in Luxembourg is made manifest by the terms of the order of 12 July 1992 made by Nicholls V-C in approving the contribution agreement and the pooling agreement. The relevant terms of that order, too, I have already cited. It is equally clear from the terms of the Luxembourg winding-up order of 3 January 1992 and the several judgments of the *e* Luxembourg courts that the Luxembourg courts regard the Luxembourg winding up as the principal winding up.

This common ground leaves it, however, wholly unclear whether there are any, and if so what, limits to the extent to which English liquidators in a so-called 'ancillary' liquidation can decline to apply provisions of English insolvency law and procedure in deference to the insolvency law and procedure of the country *f* in which the principal winding up is taking place.

Mr Crystal QC, on behalf of the English liquidators, has placed before me all the relevant authorities in order to demonstrate the state of uncertainty in which the law appears to stand. Counsel for various net creditors have submitted that English liquidators have no power to disapply provisions of the statutory *g* insolvency scheme established under the Insolvency Act 1986 and its predecessors. If there is such power, it should not, they submit, as a matter of discretion be exercised so as to deprive creditors entitled to prove in England of benefits to which they would be entitled under the English insolvency scheme.

Counsel for the Luxembourg liquidators, Mr Geering QC, and counsel for *h* creditors who have no loans to offset have submitted that the English court does have a discretionary power to disapply in an English liquidation all or any parts of the statutory insolvency scheme and that, in the present case, all ordinary creditors, whether or not they have loans which under r 4.90 would be offset in England, should be required to prove in Luxembourg under Luxembourg rules *j* and procedure.

The first question, therefore, is whether this court does have the discretionary power contended for.

Just as companies are creatures of statute, so, too, the law and procedure governing the dissolution of companies is statutory. Many of the rules of winding up have been borrowed from bankruptcy law and practice (r 4.90 is an example) a but, none the less, the power of the courts to wind up companies is a statutory power.

Mr Brisby QC, counsel for a representative creditor with no loan to offset, ie a creditor in whose interest it would be that r 4.90 did not apply so as to allow creditor/debtors the benefit of r 4.90 set-off, submitted that the court had an inherent power to disapply r 4.90 or any other provisions of the statutory b insolvency scheme. I do not accept that there is any such inherent power. The courts have, in my judgment, no more inherent power to disapply the statutory insolvency scheme than to disapply the provisions of any other statute.

Alternatively, Mr Brisby suggested that s 125(1) of the 1986 Act could provide the requisite power. Section 125(1) provides:

c   'On hearing a winding-up petition the court may dismiss it, or adjourn the
      hearing conditionally or unconditionally, or make an interim order, or any
      other order that it thinks fit …'

The words invoked by Mr Brisby were 'any other order that it thinks fit'. These words cannot, in my opinion, bear the weight sought to be placed on d them. They must, surely, be read subject to the ejusdem generis rule and, so read, cannot authorise the coupling-up of a winding-up order with a direction disapplying some part of the statutory winding-up scheme.

Mr Geering referred me to a textbook, Smart *Cross-Border Insolvency* (1991) p 244. The author states:

e   '… if an ancillary winding up is ordered, the powers of the English
      liquidator may be restricted to collecting the English assets and settling a list
      of creditors. Finally, the assets so collected shall, after satisfying preferred
      creditors and other approved payments, be remitted to the foreign liquidator
      so that the claims of the creditors can be dealt with on an equal footing in one
      single liquidation.'
f

The good sense of the procedure outlined in this passage is evident, but the passage does not assist in the identification of the source of the court's power to give the recommended directions.

Mr Geering reminded me that Nicholls V-C, in approving the contribution agreement in its original form, and the Court of Appeal, in dismissing the appeal g against his order, had been prepared to approve the entry by the English liquidators into an agreement one effect of which might have been to vary the pari passu rule governing distributions to creditors. The contribution agreement represented, however, a compromise of claims and cross-claims between the liquidators and the Abu Dhabi majority shareholders. The variation of the pari h passu rule was a term of that compromise. The court has an undoubted power under s 167 of the 1986 Act to authorise liquidators to compromise claims and both Nicholls V-C and the Court of Appeal found the requisite power in that section. Section 167 is, however, of no relevance to the present issue.

Neither Mr Geering nor Mr Brisby, nor any other counsel who has addressed j me, has been able to point to any clear source of the alleged power of the court to authorise or direct liquidators in an English winding up to disapply parts of the statutory insolvency scheme.

There is, none the less, a long-standing line of authority describing an English liquidation as an 'ancillary' liquidation where the company concerned is a foreign company in liquidation in its country of incorporation and appearing to approve the placing of limits on the functions of the English liquidators.

In *Re Commercial Bank of South Australia* (1886) 33 Ch D 174 a petition had been presented in England to wind up an Australian bank. A petition to wind up the bank had been presented in Australia. North J held that notwithstanding the proceedings in Australia, the English creditors were entitled to have a winding-up order made in England. He then went on (at 178–179):

> 'But I will say this, that I think the winding-up here will be ancillary to a winding-up in *Australia*, and, if I have the control of the proceedings here, I will take care that there shall be no conflict between the two Courts, and I shall have regard to the interests of all the creditors and all the contributories, and shall endeavour to keep down the expenses of the winding-up so far as possible ... I do not think that I ought to insert any special directions in the order. But I think that the liquidator ought not to act without the special directions of the Judge in Chambers, except for the purpose of getting in the English assets and settling a list of the English creditors.'

It is not entirely clear what North J envisaged would be done with the English assets once the English liquidators had got them in. It is a fair inference, however, that he had in mind that the assets and the list of creditors would be transmitted to Australia so that the Australian liquidator could pay a dividend, pari passu, to all creditors. But, if that is a correct inference, the source of the court's power to authorise this to be done remains unrevealed.

Re Queensland Mercantile Agency Co Ltd (1888) 58 LT 878 was another case dealt with by North J. It involved a Queensland company which was the subject of winding-up orders made both in Queensland and in England. The winding-up order in England had, according to the report of the facts, directed that the winding up be ancillary to the winding up in Queensland. The issue in the case was whether an action brought against the company in Scotland should be stayed. North J said (at 879):

> 'The liquidation of the company is going on here. It is true that there is a liquidation of the company also going on in Queensland, where the head office of the company was situated. To a certain extent, I treat the winding-up here as ancillary to the winding-up there, but not to such an extent as to make this court an agent for the courts in Queensland ...'

This dictum is tantalisingly silent as to the effect of the English winding up being treated as ancillary to that in Queensland.

In *North Australian Territory Co Ltd v Goldsbrough Mort & Co Ltd* (1889) 61 LT 716 it was the English winding up which was the principal winding up. An English company entered into voluntary liquidation in England but a compulsory winding-up order was made against it in Australia. In describing the situation Kay J said (at 717):

> 'But they are not an Australian company; they are an English company. In Australia an order has been made for a compulsory winding-up. According to our law such an order might possibly be made, or something of that kind might be done, but in the case of an Australian company it would be confined to the property existing in this country, and would only be by way of assisting a winding-up which either was going on or was contemplated in Australia. It would only be to protect the property in this country, and the creditors in this country. That would be the only purpose of such an order ... The Australian courts have no jurisdiction to wind-up an English

a   company in this country. The winding-up in this country must go according
to the law of this country, and according to the law of the corporation, which
is a corporation in this country. Therefore any order made by the Australian
courts for winding-up in Australia would merely be ancillary, just as in the
converse case an order made in this country for winding-up an Australian
company could only be ancillary to any winding-up taking place in
b   Australia.'

This exposition seems to me to provide a valuable insight into what was meant
by an 'ancillary' winding up. The effective jurisdiction of the court is, for
winding-up purposes, necessarily territorial. English liquidators can get in assets
of the company that are within the jurisdiction of the court. But they can only
c   get in assets of the company that are outside the territorial jurisdiction of the
court if or to the extent that their title to control the company is recognised by
the courts of the country in which the assets are situated. The English statutory
insolvency scheme purports to have worldwide, not merely territorial, effect.
Every creditor of the company, wherever he may be resident and whatever may
d   be the proper law of his debt, can prove in an English liquidation. The liquidators
must get in and realise the company's assets as best they may whatever may be
the country in which the assets are situated. But if the company is incorporated
abroad, English liquidators' ability to get in and realise the company's foreign
assets will be very limited. It follows that if a foreign company has a winding-up
order made against it in its country of incorporation and a winding-up order
e   made against it in England, the English liquidators' role is likely, perforce, to be
limited to getting in, realising and distributing the English assets. It was in that
sense, I think, that Kay J was describing the English liquidation as 'merely ...
ancillary'. I would add, however, that Kay J's remark that the only purpose of the
'ancillary' winding up would be 'to protect the property in this country and the
f   creditors in this country' cannot, without qualification, be accepted as correct. It
is basic to an English winding up that English creditors cannot be ring-fenced and
treated more favourably than foreign creditors. The reference to 'creditors in this
country' must, therefore, be read as a reference to 'creditors who prove in this
country'.

g   *Re Federal Bank of Australia Ltd* (1893) 62 LJ Ch 561 was a decision of Vaughan
Williams J. The Federal Bank of Australia was a Victoria bank with a branch
office in London. A winding-up petition was presented in England. It was
discovered, however, that the bank was in voluntary liquidation under court
supervision in Victoria and, moreover, that a compulsory winding-up order had
been made in South Australia. Vaughan Williams J made a winding-up order. He
h   said (at 563):

'I assume that the principal liquidation will have to go on in Australia, and
I assume that the duties of the English liquidator will be ancillary only to the
action of those who have the conduct of the liquidation in Australia. But,
j   assuming that, the liquidator appointed under a compulsory order will be
able to act more efficiently as an assistant to the principal liquidators in the
colony. Under these circumstances I think the best thing I can do in the
interest of everybody concerned is to make a compulsory order, a
consequence of which will be that the official receiver will be the liquidator.
I shall limit his authority in the way which I have already stated ...'

It is clear from this passage that Vaughan Williams J was prepared to direct the liquidator not to carry out some of the functions that would, in any ordinary liquidation, have formed part of his duties. What is not clear from the report is what were the actual limits imposed on the liquidator's authority.

The case was appealed ((1893) 62 LJ Ch 561), but not on the ground that Vaughan Williams J had lacked the power to limit the liquidator's functions.

Vaughan Williams J was in action again in *Re English Scottish and Australian Chartered Bank* [1893] 3 Ch 385. The question for decision was whether a scheme of arrangement should be sanctioned in respect of an English bank whose business was principally in Australia. A winding-up order had been made against the bank. On the question whether the scheme should be sanctioned a point of construction of s 2 of the Joint Stock Companies Arrangement Act 1870 arose. Vaughan Williams J said (at 394):

'... in construing the statute, one must bear in mind the principles upon which liquidations are conducted, in different countries and in different Courts, of one concern. One knows that where there is a liquidation of one concern the general principle is—ascertain what is the domicil of the company in liquidation; let the Court of the country of domicil act as the principal Court to govern the liquidation; and let the other Courts act as ancillary, as far as they can, to the principal liquidation. But although that is so, it has always been held that the desire to assist in the main liquidation— the desire to act as ancillary to the Court where the main liquidation is going on—will not ever make the Court give up the forensic rules which govern the conduct of its own liquidation.'

This passage seems to me valuable for two reasons. First, it adds to the growing number of cases in which the propriety of an English winding up assuming an ancillary role is accepted. But, second, it expresses a potentially important limitation to the extent to which an English winding up can assume a subordinate role, namely the court will not ever give up 'the forensic rules which govern the conduct of its own liquidation'.

In *Sedgwick Collins & Co v Rossia Insurance Co of Petrograd (Employers' Liability Assurance Corp, garnishees)* [1926] 1 KB 1 at 13 Scrutton LJ remarked that 'winding-up orders here have hitherto been treated only as ancillary to the main liquidation and carefully limited in effect' and in *Re Vocalion (Foreign) Ltd* [1932] 2 Ch 196 at 207, [1932] All ER Rep 519 at 525 Maugham J said:

'The view of this Court is that the principal winding-up should be in the principal domicil of the Corporation, and that any other winding-up order should be ancillary to the principal winding-up ...'

He went on:

'The effect of one winding-up being ancillary to the principal winding-up has not, I think, been much considered in our Courts. This Court no doubt holds that in the winding-up here all creditors, whether British or foreign, who can prove their debts have equal rights; but it would seem that foreign courts do not always take the same view.'

In *Re Commercial Bank of South Australia* (1886) 33 Ch D 174 at 178–179 North J had said that the English liquidator in an ancillary winding up ought not to take any step other than to get in the English assets and settle a list of English creditors without obtaining the special directions of the court. In *Re Hibernian Merchants a* *Ltd* [1957] 3 All ER 97 at 98, [1958] Ch 76 at 78 Roxburgh J expressed the view that Vaughan Williams J had gone 'too far' in his remarks in *Re Federal Bank of Australia Ltd* about limiting the authority of the liquidator. He, Roxburgh J, went on to say ([1957] 3 All ER 97 at 99, [1958] Ch 76 at 79):

b 'I think that something in the nature of what NORTH, J., did in *Re Commercial Bank of South Australia* could be done, if desirable ... I do not think that the order [ie an order incorporating North J's direction referred to above] necessarily would be ultra vires, provided that it is construed as not in any way limiting the effect of the winding-up order but as reserving specially to the court certain matters in respect of which a liquidator is always at liberty to apply to the court under the general law if he desires to
c do so. If the order be so construed, it cannot, in my judgment, offend the statute ...'

The doubts expressed by Roxburgh J were implicit in remarks made by Wynn-Parry J in *Re Suidair International Airways Ltd (in liq)* [1950] 2 All ER 920,
d [1951] Ch 165. The case concerned a South African company against which a winding-up order was made in South Africa. A creditor of the company had obtained a judgment against the company in England and had commenced execution processes. A winding-up order was then made against the company in England. The question for decision was whether an order should be made under s 325 of the Companies Act 1948 allowing the creditor to retain the benefit of the
e execution processes. The execution would have been void under South African insolvency law. Wynn-Parry J cited the passage from the judgment of Vaughan Williams J in *Re English Scottish and Australian Chartered Bank* that I have cited above, and then continued ([1951] Ch 165 at 173–174; cf [1950] 2 All ER 920 at 924–925):

f 'It appears to me that that must be the common sense of the matter, and that that passage enunciates a principle which, so far as I know, has never been doubted. Then it is said that all that that passage refers to is questions of procedure; that s. 325 concerns a question of substantive law; and that therefore the passage, when properly regarded, is not any obstacle to the
g adoption by the court of the argument put forward on behalf of the liquidator. To that I would make two answers: first, I do not read Vaughan Williams, J., as confining himself to what, on a narrow view, may be said to be matters of procedure. I think that he intended his observations and the statement of the principle to apply to the decision of all questions arising in
h the ancillary liquidation. Secondly, even if that passage could be read otherwise, I should be prepared for myself to say that I can see no sound reason for distinguishing between matters of procedure viewed in that narrow sense and matters of substantive right. It appears to me that the simple principle is that this court sits to administer the assets of the South
j Africa company which are within its jurisdiction, and for that purpose administers, and administers only, the relevant English law; that is, primarily, the law as stated in the Companies Act, 1948, looked at in the light, where necessary, of the authorities. If that principle be adhered to, no confusion will result. If it is departed from, then for myself I cannot see how any other result would follow than the utmost possible confusion. Who could lay down as a clear and exhaustive proposition where the court was to

draw the line in any particular case between administering the English law and the law of the main liquidation?'

a

Felixstowe Dock and Rly Co v US Lines Inc [1988] 2 All ER 77, [1989] QB 360 concerned a company incorporated in the United States. A US court had made an order under ch 11 of the United States Federal Bankruptcy Code (11 USC §§ 1101–1174) staying all claims against the company within and outside the United States. Hirst J had to decide whether to give effect in England to this order so as to restrain the plaintiffs, trade creditors of the company, from continuing to prosecute proceedings in this country to recover payment for the services which they had provided. He referred, inter alia, to *Re English Scottish and Australian Chartered Bank, Re Vocalion (Foreign) Ltd* and *Re Suidair International Airways Ltd (in liq)* and accepted a submission that—

b

c

'the English practice is to regard the courts of the country of incorporation as the principal forum for controlling the winding up of a company but that, in so far as that company has assets here, the usual practice is to carry out an ancillary winding up in England in accordance with our own rules, while working in harmony with the foreign courts',

d

and that 'Applying this principle ... the English courts would not and should not favour an order which removed the English assets entirely outside their control' (see [1988] 2 All ER 77 at 93, [1989] QB 360 at 379).

Finally, I should refer to a Queensland case, *Re Alfred Shaw & Co Ltd, ex p Mackenzie* (1897) 8 QLJ 93. The case concerned a Victoria company in voluntary liquidation in Victoria and against which winding-up orders had been made in Queensland and in England. The company had carried on business in Queensland and in England but not, it seems, in Victoria. The Queensland liquidator applied to the court for leave to transmit assets to England in order to enable the English liquidator to pay a dividend to, inter alios, the creditors who had proved in Queensland. Griffiths CJ made the point that 'The proceedings upon a winding-up order in such a case ... can only operate as an administration of the local assets of the company, which cannot be dissolved except under the law of the country of its domicile' (see 8 QLJ 93 at 95). He said that 'the title of the liquidators of the domicile should be recognised, subject to local law', but that 'the formal title of the local liquidator is better than that of the foreign one'. After confirming that all creditors were entitled to share in the assets of the company pari passu, with no priority being given to local creditors, he said (at 96):

e

f

g

'I hold, further, in accordance with the dictum of North J. already cited, that in such a case the country of the domicile is to be treated as the locality of the principal administration, and that the administration by the courts of other countries in which the affairs of the company are administered, ought to be regarded as ancillary to that administration. It is indeed manifest that to a certain extent the administration is merely ancillary. For, as already pointed out, the court of a country which is not the country of the domicile of the company can only administer the assets which it finds within its jurisdiction ... Applying these principles, I hold that in the present case the principal, and, indeed, the only real winding-up must take place in Victoria, and that the proceedings in Queensland (as those in England) are merely ancillary. If then a winding-up order had been made by the Supreme Court of Victoria, and the liquidator appointed by that court had applied to this court, with the sanction of that court, for an order to transmit the proceeds

h

j

a   raised by the realisation of Queensland assets to him, I should have had no difficulty in dealing with the application.   No winding-up order has, however, been made in Victoria, and the Victorian liquidators are not parties to this application.   Moreover, the application is not for the transmission of funds realised from an ancillary administration in England to a principal administrator, but for their transmission to another ancillary administrator
b   in England.   Ought I, then under these circumstances, to accede to the application?'

In the event, Griffiths CJ adjourned the application to enable the Victoria liquidators to be joined.   This line of authority establishes, in my opinion, at least the following propositions.

c   (1) Where a foreign company is in liquidation in its country of incorporation, a winding-up order made in England will normally be regarded as giving rise to a winding up ancillary to that being conducted in the country of incorporation.

(2) The winding up in England will be ancillary in the sense that it will not be within the power of the English liquidators to get in and realise all the assets of
d   the company worldwide.   They will necessarily have to concentrate on getting in and realising the English assets.

(3) Since in order to achieve a pari passu distribution between all the company's creditors it will be necessary for there to be a pooling of the company's assets worldwide and for a dividend to be declared out of the assets comprised in that pool, the winding up in England will be ancillary in the sense,
e   also, that it will be the liquidators in the principal liquidation who will be best placed to declare the dividend and to distribute the assets in the pool accordingly.

(4) None the less, the ancillary character of an English winding up does not relieve an English court of the obligation to apply English law, including English insolvency law, to the resolution of any issue arising in the winding up which is
f   brought before the court.   It may be, of course, that English conflicts of law rules will lead to the application of some foreign law principle in order to resolve a particular issue.

Rule 4.90 of the 1986 rules is a substantive rule of English law.   *Stein v Blake* [1995] 2 All ER 961, [1996] AC 243 establishes that that is so.   Mr Geering, supported by Mr Brisby, submitted that the Insolvency Rules, as a whole, were
g   procedural and that it was only in that procedural context that r 4.90 created substantive rights.   The court had, they submitted, power to disapply these procedural rules, either in whole or in part, in deference to the rules of the principal liquidation.   They submitted that if that were not so, the court could not make any order varying any of the procedures prescribed by the 1986 Act and the
h   1986 rules.

They pointed, by way of example, to the transmission of assets to the principal liquidators in order for those liquidators to declare and pay dividends to creditors. Unless the court has power to direct English liquidators in an ancillary liquidation to transmit assets to the principal liquidators, an ancillary liquidation is
j   meaningless.   If the court does have power to give that direction, it follows that it does have power to disapply the part of the statutory insolvency scheme established by the 1986 Act and the 1986 rules that relates to payment of dividends.   The position, they submitted, is all or nothing.   Either the court has power to disapply any part of the statutory insolvency scheme that, in its discretion, it thinks fit to disapply, or it has no power to disapply any part of the statutory scheme.   The latter conclusion cannot stand in the face of the many

authorities that, over the past hundred years or more, have indorsed the
propriety of an English winding up being merely an ancillary winding up. Ergo,   *a*
the former conclusion must be the right one and the English liquidators do have
a discretionary power to disapply r 4.90.

I find the logic of these submissions compelling but I am not persuaded that
they are right.

I have already observed that the source of the discretionary power to disapply   *b*
at discretion parts of the statutory insolvency scheme can be found neither in
statute nor in any inherent common law power of the courts. There is, however,
another way in which powers can become vested in the courts, namely by
accretion of judicial decisions. In the early decisions in which the English
liquidations were described as 'ancillary', no attempt was made to spell out the
effect of placing that description on the winding up in question or to analyse the   *c*
source of the dispensing power that the court was exercising. Without,
apparently, any such analysis, the situation seems simply to have come to be
accepted that in an appropriate case, of which the paradigm would be a company
in liquidation in its country of incorporation, but against which a winding-up
order had been made in this country, the court could direct that the winding-up   *d*
in this country be treated as 'ancillary'. The implication of this direction was that
at some stage in the liquidation the court would authorise the English liquidators
to transmit the assets they had got in to the principal liquidators. Mr Geering and
Mr Brisby emphasised that, without that implication, the description of the
liquidation as ancillary becomes fairly meaningless. I agree and consequently
accept that the implication to which I have referred should be read into the   *e*
numerous judicial dicta in which the concept of an ancillary liquidator has been
indorsed. In Nicholls V-C's order of 12 June 1992 in this liquidation, the direction
to be implied in the earlier cases was spelled out in express terms. And his order
was approved by the Court of Appeal.

The accumulation of judicial indorsements of the concept of ancillary   *f*
liquidations have, in my judgment, produced a situation in which it has become
established that in an 'ancillary' liquidation the courts do have power to direct
liquidators to transmit funds to the principal liquidators in order to enable a pari
passu distribution to worldwide creditors to be achieved. The House of Lords
could declare such a direction to be ultra vires. But a first instance judge could
not do so and I doubt whether the Court of Appeal could now do so.   *g*

But the judicial authority which has established the power of the court to give,
in general terms, the direction to which I have referred has certainly not
established the power of the court to disapply r 4.90 or any other substantive rule
forming part of the statutory scheme under the 1986 Act and rules.

Nor, in my opinion, has this line of judicial authority established the power of   *h*
the court to relieve English liquidators in an ancillary winding up of the
obligation to determine whether proofs of debt submitted to them should be
admitted or to see to it, so far as they are able to do so, that creditors whose claims
they do admit receive the pari passu dividend to which, under the statutory
insolvency scheme, they are entitled.   *j*

My conclusion on this issue of jurisdiction is reinforced by a consideration of
the practical consequences that would follow in the present case if the court did
have power to disapply r 4.90 and purported to exercise that power. It may be
said, however, that this is a point that goes more to the question whether,
assuming the power exists, it should be exercised. To that issue of discretion I
now turn.

DISCRETION

a
(i) *Rule 4.90*

If r 4.90 is to be disapplied in the winding up of BCCI SA it must, in my opinion, be disapplied across the board. It could not be disapplied for one class of creditor/debtors but not for another class. Let me consider in turn the various classes of creditor/debtors.

b
(a) Creditor/debtors whose choses in action have English law as their proper law and who, on an application of r 4.90, would become net debtors

In relation to this class, the disapplication of r 4.90, even if it were jurisdictionally possible (which in my view it is not) would be wholly impracticable. This is a class of creditor/debtors who will not be submitting any
c proof in the bankruptcy. They are net debtors. If they are sued in England on the gross amount of their debt, they will be liable only for the net debt. If they are sued abroad and English law is applied to determine the quantum of the indebtedness, the same result will obtain. In respect of a number of these debtors their net debts, with or without court action, will by now already have been paid.
d The choses in action will have been extinguished. In relation to those whose net debts have not been paid, the only extant chose in action will be the net debt. *Stein v Blake* provides clear authority that that is so. To this class of creditor/debtors there can be no question of disapplying r 4.90.

e
(b) Creditor/debtors whose choses in action do not have English law as their proper law but who, on an application of r 4.90, would be net debtors

If these net debtors were to be sued in England they, too, would be liable only for the net debt. It may be that if they were sued abroad, and certainly if they were sued in Luxembourg, they would be liable for the gross amount of their debts. They would have a right to prove in the Luxembourg liquidation for the
f full amount of their deposits. So far as the English liquidation is concerned, however, a discriminatory disapplication of r 4.90, so as to disapply the rule to this class of net debtors but not to domestic net debtors would, in my opinion, be unthinkable. It would offend a fundamental principle of English winding-up procedure and, arguably, would constitute a breach of art 6 of the EEC Treaty (cf *Fitzgerald v Williams* [1996] 2 All ER 171, [1996] 2 WLR 447). If, as seems to me
g clear, r 4.90 cannot be disapplied in respect of domestic net debtors, it cannot, in my judgment, be disapplied in respect of any net debtors.

(c) Creditor/debtors whose choses in action have English law as their proper law but who, on an application of r 4.90, would be net creditors

h Members of this class could not be sued in England on the debts they owed BCCI SA. Those debts would have been extinguished by r 4.90. If sued in any foreign country which recognised the proper law of the debt as governing the extinguishing of the debt, the same result would be reached. Members of this class will, since the date of the winding-up order, 14 January 1992, have been
j proceeding on the footing that their debts have been extinguished and that they must prove for the net credit. Many members in this class have received sums from the Deposit Protection Board calculated on that footing.

It is, in my opinion, simply not practicable (even if it were jurisdictionally possible) to revive these extinguished debts. Moreover, if r 4.90 cannot be disapplied so as to revive the full amount of the debts of the net debtors, it cannot be disapplied so as to revive the debts of the net creditors. Otherwise persons with debts greater than the amount of their deposits might find themselves in a more favourable financial position than if they had owed debts less than the amount of their deposits. Rule 4.90 cannot be disapplied to this class of creditor/debtors.

(d) Creditor/debtors whose choses in action do not have English law as their proper law but who, on an application of r 4.90, would be net creditors

For the reasons given under (b) above, r 4.90 cannot be disapplied in respect of this class but allowed to apply to and benefit the domestic net creditors.

For the reasons given above, I have no hesitation, assuming I have jurisdiction to disapply r 4.90, in declining to do so. Mr Geering submitted that by Nicholls V-C's order of 12 June 1992 the decision that r 4.90 should be disapplied had already been taken. He so submitted on the footing that the order had approved the pooling agreement and that the pooling agreement contemplated that Luxembourg law and procedure on set-off would be applied. He accepted that it was implicit in his submission that the 12 June 1992 order had had retrospective effect, reviving the debts extinguished by r 4.90 and thereby altering rights that had previously accrued. This implication makes his submission one that it is impossible to accept. First, the pooling agreement in cl 5.6(iv) and (v) reserves the position as to set-off. Second, it is inconceivable that Nicholls V-C would have made an order intending it to have retrospective effect and to alter accrued rights or that the Court of Appeal would have regarded the order as having that effect without any express mention of such a thing in the judgments.

Accordingly, in my opinion, r 4.90 applies in the English winding up and must be given effect to. The question of what, if any, retentions should be made by the English liquidators to protect the positions of net creditors or net debtors must be answered on that footing.

(ii) *Claims and admissions*

If a proof is submitted to English liquidators, their duty under the statutory insolvency scheme is to consider it, to admit it or reject it and, if it is admitted, to pay a dividend on it accordingly (see rr 4.73–4.94 and rr 4.179–4.186 of the 1986 rules). If it is right (and I do not think it is) that in an English 'ancillary' liquidation, the court can direct the English liquidators to leave to the principal liquidators the decision as to whether or not a dividend should be paid to a creditor whose proof has been, or is fit to be, admitted by the English liquidators, the question is whether or to what extent that power should be exercised in the present case.

It is implicit in the concept of an ancillary liquidation that the English liquidators, having realised assets and settled a list of creditors, will transmit the assets and the list to the principal liquidators to enable a dividend to be declared and paid. The principal liquidators, following as they must the procedural rules required by the law and practice in their own country, are likely to subject the list of creditors to a process of review. In the present case there is no reason, in my opinion, why any point should be taken about the procedural requirements for verification of the claims or for identification of the claimants that are necessary under Luxembourg law and practice. If, however, it transpires (it has not yet so transpired) that the Luxembourg liquidators or the Luxembourg court reject for some substantive reason a proof that was originally submitted to the English liquidators and that either has been or would be admitted by the English a liquidators, a problem will arise. Assuming that the court has the requisite power to authorise the English liquidators to decline to pay a dividend to such a creditor, I do not see any sufficient reason why the court should exercise such power. Provision ought, in my opinion, to be made.

Provision

b #### The pooling agreement

Clause 5.6 of the pooling agreement enables the English liquidators, as a matter of contract between themselves and the Luxembourg liquidators, to make provision for debtors of BCCI SA liable to be sued in an English court and who could, if sued by the English liquidators, have relied on r 4.90 set-off.

c Rule 5.6(v) is of more general application. I have already expressed the view that it would be wrong to discriminate between those whose debts to or deposits with BCCI SA were subject to English law and those whose debts or deposits were subject to some foreign law. For the same reasons it would, in my opinion, be wrong to discriminate between debtors 'liable to be sued in a court in England and Wales' and debtors not so liable. In my judgment, provision made for the former (under sub-para (iv)) can and should equally be made for the latter (under sub-para (v)).

Mr Geering submitted also that any provision to be made should be made only out of the English realisations and should not extend to any part of the English liquidators' 48·5% in the global realisations. He told me that the Luxembourg e liquidators had been proceeding on the footing that English realisations alone would be used for such provision as this court might think it right to direct the English liquidators to make. He told me also that the Luxembourg liquidators would not be able to sign any authority for withdrawals to be made from the global realisations without the authority of the Luxembourg court. This point f applies to the Abu Dhabi funds which are, I understand, in a bank account requiring for withdrawals the signatures of all 13 liquidators. On the other hand the Sheik Mahfouz funds are in a bank account withdrawals from which could, I understand, be made by the English liquidators alone up to the amount of their 48·5% share. In any event, I cannot believe that Mr Geering's warning to me was necessary. The costs and recoveries agreement, dated 15 January 1993 but which g came into effect in May 1994, gives the English liquidators the right to call for the distribution to them of their 48·5% share in the Abu Dhabi funds for the purposes of the winding up. The agreement was approved by the Luxembourg court. Mr Geering told me that it was regarded as having been superseded by the pooling agreement. But I observe, first, that the costs and recoveries agreement h contained specific provision for its termination and according to its own terms is still on foot, and, second, that when the ICIC companies joined the pooling agreement, the costs and recoveries agreement, far from being treated as superseded, was amended so as to reflect the 2·5% share that was attributed to the ICIC companies and, on 31 January 1995, approved as amended by the Luxembourg court. The suggestion that the costs and recoveries agreement is no j longer effective does not impress me in the least. Nor do I see any reason to believe that the Luxembourg courts might take that view.

I propose, therefore, to consider what, if any, provisions should be made by the English liquidators on the footing, first, that the making of any such provisions is consistent with and authorised by the pooling agreement, and, secondly, that if in order to make such provisions the English liquidators need to draw on their share of the Abu Dhabi funds or the Sheik Mahfouz funds, they are entitled under *a* the costs and recoveries agreement to do so.

(1) NET CREDITORS AND NET DEBTORS

I have come to the clear conclusion that provision should be made by the English liquidators for the dividend that net creditors would receive in any English winding up but that no provision need be made for net debtors. As to net *b* debtors, the position is that, under English law, their debts are extinguished by r 4.90 save for the net debt. There is no credit for which they can prove. The English liquidators have no liability to any of them. It is possible that they may be sued in some foreign jurisdiction. What the result of that might be, I cannot tell. I imagine the result would depend on whether English law was the proper law of the debt and whether the foreign court recognised the effect of r 4.90 on *c* the debt. But even if the foreign court imposed a liability on the debtor in excess of the net debt that would have been produced by the application of r 4.90, the net debtor would have no recourse against the English liquidators. The result would be a matter between the Luxembourg liquidators (the assumed plaintiffs), the debtor and the foreign court. No provision need be made here. *d*

As to net creditors, no provision need be made for the debt to BCCI SA that, by the operation of r 4.90, would have been extinguished. In that respect, the net creditors' position would be no different from that of a net debtor. Provision should, however, be made for the dividend that the net creditor would be entitled to receive under English insolvency rules. The amount of the requisite provision has caused me some anxiety. It would be preferable if the provision could be *e* confined to the difference between the dividend payable in England and the dividend payable in Luxembourg. An example will explain what I have in mind. A creditor has a deposit of £1,000 and an outstanding loan of £200. He is a net creditor for £800 and, in England, would receive £320 if a 40% dividend were declared. In Luxembourg, the creditor would be entitled to a dividend of £400 *f* but the £400 would be applied in discharging the £200 loan. So the creditor would receive only £200. Prima facie, therefore, provision should be made in the sum of £120, the difference between £320 and £120. If that is done, however, it is possible that the Luxembourg liquidators will take the view that as to £120 the creditor will be receiving his dividend in England and that he should receive in Luxembourg only £80, ie £200 minus £120. I sought clarification from Mr *g* Geering as to whether or not the Luxembourg liquidators would seek to set off against any Luxembourg dividend the provision made for the creditor in England. He was not able to provide any clarification. It may be that the point would be one for the Luxembourg court.

In these circumstances, it seems to me that the English liquidators will have to *h* make provision for the full amount of the dividend payable to such a creditor ie £320. The creditor would, of course, as a condition of being paid the sum by the English liquidators, have to confirm that he had not received and would withdraw any claim to a dividend from the Luxembourg liquidators.

j

(2) CLAIMS AND ADMISSION PROCEDURES

Clause 5.6(v) of the pooling agreement contemplates that the English liquidators may make provision for claims 'which would be admissible in the English liquidation but would not be admissible ... in the Luxembourg liquidation'. If claims that have met the standard of proof requisite for admission in the English liquidation, a fortiori claims that have already been admitted in the a English liquidation, are rejected by the Luxembourg liquidators, dividends on those claims ought, in my view, to be paid by the English liquidators.

Mr Geering has submitted that a conclusion on those lines would, in effect, be reversing the decision already reached by Nicholls V-C that the English liquidation should be ancillary to the Luxembourg liquidation. I do not agree. First, there has never been any clarity as to what was contemplated by the

b direction that the English liquidation should be ancillary. Second, the pooling agreement expressly contemplates that the English liquidators may make provision for claims not admissible in the Luxembourg liquidation. Third, the English liquidators have, in my opinion, a statutory obligation which the court ought not to waive, even if it has power to do so, to pay or make provision for payment of claims that are admitted (or fit to be admitted). It is one thing to hold,

c as I do, that the court has power to authorise the English liquidators to transmit assets and a list of creditors to the foreign liquidators so that the foreign liquidators can declare and pay the dividend. It is quite another to hold that the court can authorise the transmission of assets to the foreign liquidators in circumstances which will lead to a creditor whose claim would be, or has been,

d admitted in England, receiving nothing either from the foreign liquidators (because they have rejected the proof) or from the English liquidators (because they have no assets left with which to pay the dividend).

In this respect, as generally, the English liquidators cannot, in my opinion, justify limiting the provisions they make to provisions in respect of claimants

e whose accounts were conducted at English branches of BCCI SA. All creditors should be treated alike. On the other hand, the English liquidators need not make provision for creditors of BCCI SA who have not submitted proofs to them. The provision to be made under this heading should be confined to creditors who have submitted proofs to the English liquidators.

f In deciding the quantum of provision that should be made, the English liquidators will have to endeavour to ascertain from the Luxembourg liquidators the extent to which the difficulties that the claimants, all of whose claims have, I understand, been accepted in England, are experiencing in having their claims accepted in Luxembourg are likely to lead to a final rejection of the claims. With the assistance of the Luxembourg liquidators I would expect that a reasonably

g accurate assessment of the provisions that are needed under this heading can be made. The principle on which provision should be made is, however, as I have stated it.

(3) THE DEPOSIT PROTECTION BOARD

h The English liquidators have a statutory obligation to make dividend payments to the board in respect of any compensation payments made by the board to BCCI SA depositors (see s 62 of the Banking Act 1987). In my judgment, this is not an obligation the performance of which can be delegated by the English liquidators to the Luxembourg liquidators. If, or to the extent that, the

j Luxembourg liquidators were to pay dividends to the board, those payments would, pro tanto, discharge the English liquidators' obligation. But neither the board nor the English liquidators should, in my view, be placed in a position in which the decision as to whether a dividend in respect of a particular compensation payment should be paid to the board or as to the amount to be paid to the board is taken by the Luxembourg liquidators or the Luxembourg court. In any event, the state of the evidence has left it unclear whether the status of the board as entitled to receive dividends that would otherwise have been paid to the compensated depositor is recognised by the Luxembourg courts.

There is, however, a further consideration. A number of the depositors who have been compensated by the board are depositors who had loans outstanding and owing to BCCI SA. In respect of all of these, r 4.90 applied so as to produce the net credit in respect of which the amount of compensation paid by the board was calculated. This net credit would not be recognised in Luxembourg as the sum in respect of which a proof could be submitted and on which a dividend would be paid. It is, accordingly, not clear that the amount of the compensation paid by the board to these net creditors would be regarded in Luxembourg as an amount on which a dividend to the board could properly be paid.

For all these reasons the board is entitled, in my opinion, to look to the English liquidators for payment of the dividend to which under s 62 of the Banking Act 1987 they will become entitled. The English liquidators must retain sufficient funds under their control for that purpose.

(4) THE SCOTTISH AND ISLE OF MAN BRANCHES OF BCCI SA

The insolvency regimes in Scotland and in the Isle of Man have similar set-off rules as in r 4.90. The net creditors who have proved in those jurisdictions would suffer the same disadvantages if they had to prove in Luxembourg as would be suffered by the English net creditors.

The position in these two jurisdictions is as follows. In Scotland, assets of about $5m have been collected; claims of about $127m have been submitted. In the Isle of Man assets of about $20m have been collected; claims of about $100m have been submitted. If these claims totalling $227m were transmitted to the English winding up, the English liquidators estimate that an additional set-off provision of $14m and an additional provision in respect of rejected claims of $6m may be necessary.

The court has been invited by each of the two letters of request to direct the English liquidators to make similar provision for the Scottish and Isle of Man claimants as is proposed to be made for claimants who have proved in the English liquidation. Section 426(4) of the 1986 Act requires me to assist the Manx and Scottish courts in response to their respective requests. I have a discretion as to the nature of the assistance to be provided.

In my view, it would in principle be right for net creditors in the two jurisdictions to be treated in the same way as net creditors who have proved in this jurisdiction. Similarly, I think creditors whose claims have been accepted by the Scottish or Isle of Man liquidators (as the case may be) should have the same provision made against the eventuality that their claims are rejected in Luxembourg as is to be made for creditors who have proved in England and whose claims have been accepted by the English liquidators. This is particularly appropriate in the case of the Isle of Man creditors having regard to the extent to which the Isle of Man branch was supervised by BCCI SA managers in London (see para 3 of the affidavit of Mr Vanderpump sworn on 15 July 1996).

I am of opinion, however, that if the English liquidators are to make provision for the Scottish and Isle of Man claimants, the assets collected in Scotland and the Isle of Man ought to be transmitted to the English liquidators.

It is not clear whether or to what extent the claims that have been made in Scotland and the Isle of Man have been transmitted to Luxembourg. I assume from the content of Mr Vanderpump's affidavit and that sworn by Mr Powdrill in Scotland that the claims have not yet been transmitted to Luxembourg. If that is *a* right, they should be so transmitted as soon as possible so that those that do not raise any difficulty can be accepted in Luxembourg and the provision to be made by the English liquidators can be limited accordingly.

GENERAL

b I have, I believe and hope, dealt with all the points of principle that need a decision in order for the necessary provisions to be quantified and, subject to those provisions, for the rest of the funds controlled by the English liquidators to be released or transferred, as the case may be, to the Luxembourg liquidators.

If, there are points that I have overlooked, they can be mentioned when I hand down this judgment.

c   *Order accordingly.*

Celia Fox   Barrister.

Hood Sailmakers Ltd v Axford and another

a

QUEEN'S BENCH DIVISION (CROWN OFFICE LIST)

CARNWATH J

14 MARCH, 2 APRIL 1996

b

Company – Director – Proceedings of directors – Written resolution – Resolution passed by one director while sole co-director absent from United Kingdom – Quorum for meeting of directors two – Director absent from United Kingdom not entitled to notice of meeting – Whether resolution valid – Companies Act 1948, Sch 1, Table A, Part 1, regs 98, 99, 106.

c

A and H were the directors of the UK subsidiary of a US-based company, although H lived in the United States and played no active part in the running of the company. The articles of the company incorporated regs 98[a], 99[b] and 106[c] of Table A. In May 1986 a major restructuring in the pension arrangements for the *d* benefit of employees and directors of the company took place and was effected by way of written resolutions of the board, produced and signed by A. H, who was in the United States, neither knew about, nor signed the resolutions. On H's retirement, W and B were appointed as directors. Following differences between the directors, A and B were removed from their directorships and dismissed from employment. The company subsequently refused to pay A and B their share of *e* the pension funds, claiming that the 1986 resolutions were invalid since they had only been signed by one director. A and B complained to the Pensions Ombudsman pursuant to the provisions of the Pension Schemes Act 1993. The ombudsman upheld the complaint, holding that the resolutions were valid on the ground that they complied with reg 106 of Table A, which was not subject to the *f* quorum provisions contained in reg 99, since under reg 98 H was not entitled to notice of a directors' meeting as he was absent from the United Kingdom. He further held that the company was in any event estopped from denying the validity of the resolutions. The company appealed to the High Court.

g

Held – A written resolution, passed in accordance with reg 106 of Table A signed by only one director of a company where the quorum fixed for transaction of any business of the directors was two, was invalid, notwithstanding that the sole co-director was outside the United Kingdom and thus not entitled to notice of a meeting of directors. Regulation 106 was not directed to making a fundamental change to the quorum requirements and a director could not evade the quorum *h* requirements simply by waiting for his fellow director or directors to leave the country. It followed that the resolutions of May 1986 were not valid resolutions. However, in the circumstances, there was sufficient evidence on which the ombudsman was entitled to be satisfied that W's involvement with and acquiescence in the new scheme made it unconscionable for the company now *j* to deny the validity of the resolutions. The appeal would accordingly be dismissed (see p 833 *c d*, p 834 *f* to *h* and p 836 *a* to *c*, post).

---

a   Regulation 98 is set out at p 832 *j* to p 833 *a* , post
b   Regulation 99 is set out at p 833 *a*, post
c   Regulation 106, so far as material, is set out at p 833 *b*, post

Notes

a For quorum requirements at meetings of directors, see 7(1) *Halsbury's Laws* (4th edn reissue) para 633, and for cases on the subject, see 9(2) *Digest* (2nd reissue) 246–250, 5016–5040.

For the current Table A, see the Companies (Tables A to F) Regulations 1985, SI 1985/805, as amended, 4 *Halsbury's Statutory Instruments* (1996 reissue) 501.

b
Cases referred to in judgment

A-G of Hong Kong v Humphreys Estate (Queen's Gardens) Ltd [1987] 2 All ER 387, [1987] AC 114, [1987] 2 WLR 343, PC.

Taylor Fashions Ltd v Liverpool Victoria Trustees Co Ltd, Old & Campbell Ltd v Liverpool Victoria Trustees Co Ltd [1981] 1 All ER 897, [1982] QB 133, [1981] 2

c WLR 576.

Cases also cited or referred to in skeleton arguments

Amalgamated Investment and Property Co Ltd (in liq) v Texas Commerce International Bank Ltd [1981] 1 All ER 923, [1982] QB 84; affd [1981] 3 All ER 577, [1982] QB 84, CA.

d
Courage Group's Pension Schemes, Re, Ryan v Imperial Brewing and Leisure Ltd [1987] 1 All ER 528, [1987] 1 WLR 495.

Mettoy Pension Trustees Ltd v Evans [1991] 2 All ER 513, [1990] 1 WLR 1587.

Appeal

e By notice dated 19 September 1995 the company, Hood Sailmakers Ltd, appealed from the decision of the Pensions Ombudsman given on 22 August 1995 whereby he held that written resolutions signed by one director of the company, effecting new pension arrangements for the benefit of the employees and directors, were valid, since the resolutions complied with reg 106 of Table A incorporated in the company's articles, and that the complainant directors, Mr Axford and Mr

f Bainbridge, were therefore entitled to the amounts attributable to their share in the pension fund. The facts are set out in the judgment.

Michael Norman (instructed by *Scott Bailey & Co*, Lymington) for the company.
James Clifford (instructed by *Blake Lapthorn*) for the complainants.

g
Cur adv vult

2 April 1996. The following judgment was delivered.

CARNWATH J.   This is an appeal against a decision of the Pensions
h Ombudsman given on 22 August 1995. It is brought under s 151(4) of the Pension Schemes Act 1993, by which an appeal lies to the High Court on a point of law only. The background is set out in the ombudsman's decision and a summary is sufficient for my purposes. The company was founded in the late 1960s as a subsidiary of a US-based company. It established a pension scheme in 1973 for
j the benefit of employees and directors, the company being sole trustee and administrator of the scheme. In May 1986 the first complainant, Mr Axford (Mr A), and a Mr Hood (Mr H), were the only directors of the company. Mr H was resident in the United States and had not played an active part in the company for some time.

On 9 May 1986 the company circulated an announcement to scheme members referring to a 'major restructuring in pension arrangements' to take place on 1

June. The intention was to set up a new scheme and to transfer into it the surplus
assets existing at the close of the old scheme. Two documents were completed   *a*
on 12 May 1986, each headed 'Board Resolution'. The first made amendments to
the scheme rules, including alterations to the winding-up rule. The second was
to wind up the scheme and secure the members' accrued rights to guaranteed
minimum pensions by the purchase of annuities; the balance of assets was then
to be transferred to the new scheme. On 20 May 1986 the company executed a   *b*
deed setting up a new scheme to commence as from 1 June. After 31 May 1986
no payments were made into the old scheme but payments were paid into the
new scheme. In September 1986 Mr H resigned as director and was replaced by
Mr Woodhouse (Mr W). At the same time the second complainant, Mr
Bainbridge (Mr B), was also made a director. On 23 September the manager of
the scheme, Anthony Gibbs Associates, wrote to the company to inform it that   *c*
the scheme had been wound up and the excess assets transferred into the new
scheme. On 14 October three further payments were made from the scheme
funds to secure guaranteed minimum pensions, to augment pensions and to
purchase annuity policies. On 23 October the funds left over were invested with
an insurance company, locked in for a five-year period expiring in 1991. Various   *d*
payments were made from moneys invested with the insurance company
between October 1986 and February 1990.

In April 1991 as a result of differences between the complainants and Mr W,
the complainants were summarily dismissed from employment and removed
from their directorships. In February 1992 an industrial tribunal found that the
dismissals were unfair. In October 1991, at the end of the lock-up period, the   *e*
company failed to pay the complainants' share of the funds. The company
claimed that the 1986 resolutions were invalid, since the second director, Mr H,
neither knew about, nor signed, the board resolutions.

The ombudsman upheld the complaint. He found that the resolutions were
valid since they complied with reg 106 of Table A (which had been incorporated   *f*
in the company's articles). Furthermore, he found that, even if that was
incorrect, the company was estopped from denying the validity of the
resolutions. He therefore directed the company to pay to the complainants'
pension providers the amounts attributable to each complainant's share of the
fund in accordance with a schedule which had been prepared by the manager.

                                                                                                       g

Issues

The principal issues which have been argued before me are. (1) Whether the
resolutions of 12 May 1986 were valid resolutions. (2) If not, whether the
company is estopped from denying their validity. (3) Whether, in any event, the
company was subject to a fiduciary duty, which in practice would achieve a   *h*
similar result to that achieved by the ombudsman's determination. (This issue
was not considered by the ombudsman himself.)

The first question raises a point of company law of general importance, which
appears not to have been the subject of previous judicial consideration. Table A
(of Sch 1 to the Companies Act 1948) deals with the proceedings of directors in   *j*
regs 98 to 106. So far as material they provide:

'98. The directors may meet together for the despatch of business, adjourn
and otherwise regulate their meetings, as they think fit … A director may,
and the secretary on the requisition of a director shall, at any time summon
a meeting of the directors. It shall not be necessary to give notice of a

a meeting of directors to any director for the time being absent from the United Kingdom.

99. The quorum necessary for the transaction of the business of the directors may be fixed by the directors, and unless so fixed shall be two ...

106. A resolution in writing, signed by all the directors for the time being entitled to receive notice of a meeting of the directors, shall be as valid and
b effectual as if it had been passed at a meeting of the directors duly convened and held.'

The complainants argued, and the ombudsman accepted, that, where one of two directors is absent from the United Kingdom, the other director may pass a valid resolution under reg 106, simply by signing a resolution to that effect, even
c though the quorum fixed by reg 99 for the transaction of any business is two. According to this submission, reg 106 is not expressly or impliedly subject to the quorum provisions; on the contrary it provides that so long as the resolution is signed by any directors entitled to receive notice, it is to be treated as passed at a meeting 'duly convened and held'. In this case, the only director apart from Mr A was absent from the United Kingdom and therefore was not entitled to receive
d notice.

Mr Norman, for the company, challenges this view on two grounds. First, he says that the documents of 12 May 1986, on which the ombudsman relies, are not in fact 'resolutions in writing' within the meaning of the article; they are expressed rather as 'certificates' of resolutions passed at a previous meeting.
e Secondly, he says that as a matter of law the ombudsman's construction of reg 106 is wrong, and that it is subject to the quorum requirement.

As to the first point, I accept that the documents could have been more happily worded. The basic form is the same in each case. Although it is headed 'Board Resolution', it is then referred to as 'Extract from the Minutes of a Meeting of the Directors held on 12th May 1986'. It concludes by the director, Mr A, and the
f secretary 'certifying' that the matters resolved upon are 'a true extract from the minutes of the said Board Meeting'. It seems to me, however, that these criticisms are ones of form rather than substance. The document is clearly intended to record a decision of the company and it is signed by Mr A as director. In my view, it is sufficient to comply with the formal requirements of reg 106.

g This leaves the question of law. I was referred to a number of extracts from the textbooks. None of these appear to suggest that reg 106 poses any difficulty, the implication being that it is simply there for convenience to avoid unnecessary meetings. Thus, in Gower's *Principles of Modern Company Law* (5th edn, 1992) p 160, the following appears:

h '... unless the regulations provide to the contrary, due notice must be given to all of [the directors] and a quorum must be present at a meeting which must be convened as such. Notice here merely means reasonable notice having regard to the practice of the company, and if all in fact meet without notice they may waive this requirement if they wish, but are not bound to do so. And although majority decision prevails, a meeting of the
j majority without notice to the minority is ineffective, for it could be that the persuasive oratory of the minority would have induced the majority to change their minds. But if all are agreed, a meeting may be a waste of time and hence it is usual to provide that a resolution in writing signed by all the directors shall be as valid and effectual as if it had been duly passed at a meeting.'

It is to be noted that the last sentence of this summary omits the point that the
resolution only has to be signed by those directors entitled to notice of the
meeting. Similarly in Pennington *Company Law* (7th edn, 1995) p 768, the
following appears:

> '... if all the directors agree informally on a certain matter without a board
> meeting being held, their unanimity is equivalent to a resolution passed at a
> board meeting, and is binding on the company. Table A provides expressly
> that this shall be so if the informal but unanimous resolution is reduced to
> writing and is signed by all the directors.'

Palmer's *Company Law* (1993) vol 2, para 8.301 similarly refers to the successor
of reg 106 (reg 93 of the Companies (Tables A to F) Regulations 1985, SI 1985/
805) as follows:

> 'It is, however, frequently impracticable for directors to meet to discuss a
> matter upon which a decision is needed, and, in order to enable the board to
> consider any such matter without being required to assemble together,
> articles usually provide that a resolution in writing signed by all the directors
> entitled to receive notice of a board meeting shall be as effective as if passed
> at a board meeting.'

It seems to me that reg 106 is ambiguous. The reference to the meeting being
'duly convened and held' could be taken as a reference, not only to the
establishment of the meeting, but also to the validity of the business conducted
at it. On the other hand, it might simply be indicating that the document is to be
treated as equivalent to a meeting, without prejudice to any other requirement
relating to the actual business transacted at it. I note that reg 99 refers specifically
to the quorum required 'for the transaction of business'. This tends to suggest
that, even if the meeting is validly convened and held, the requirement for a
quorum is to be treated as a separate matter relating to the particular items of
business on which reliance is placed. This view also accords with what I take to
be the purpose of the provisions. As suggested by the textbooks, the object of
reg 106 appears to be to avoid the need for a meeting where it would otherwise
be superfluous. It does not appear to be directed to making a fundamental
change to the quorum requirements. It would be odd if a director could evade
the quorum requirements simply by waiting for his fellow director or directors to
leave the country.

On this point therefore, I conclude that the ombudsman's view was wrong in
law and that, viewed on their own, the resolutions of May 1986 were not valid
resolutions.

This takes me to the second point, which is the issue of estoppel. As to this, the
ombudsman concluded as follows:

> '20. Moreover, given my finding that the company did no acts inconsistent
> with the existence of the resolutions between May 1986 and—at the
> earliest—the end of the lock-up period in October 1991, I find it is estopped
> from denying that it knew about the resolutions and agreed to treat them as
> valid. Clearly Mr A and Mr B cannot rely on the doctrine of estoppel when
> seeking to establish that the resolutions were valid in the first place, but the
> Company accepts that the resolutions were on the Company's pension file
> and I am not impressed by the argument that Mr W did not trouble himself
> with the file but left everything to Mr A and to Mr B. He can not be allowed

a
to wash his hands and then complain that they are clean. In any event, this would not explain why the Company did not dispute the validity of the resolutions between the months after Mr A and Mr B left the company, and the "discovery" of the "true position" after October 1991.'

b
In the notice of appeal, the company claimed that no estoppel could arise between the company and the complainants because during the relevant period the complainants were directors and/or company secretary. However, before me Mr Norman does not submit that the doctrine of estoppel is inapplicable in such a context. In practice of course, the company could only act or make representations through its directors or other human agencies. The complainants clearly cannot rely on any express or implied representations made
c
by themselves in that capacity. However, the reality of the matter was that Mr W had come on the scene as an independent voice. The effect of the ombudsman's decision is that it was incumbent upon him, if he was seeking to question the basis on which the new scheme was proceeding, to have done something about it. Had he done so, it would have been open to the complainants to take action while they still had a position within the company.
d
Mr Norman accepts that the doctrine of estoppel is a broad one. As it was put by Oliver J in *Taylor Fashions Ltd v Liverpool Victoria Trustees Co Ltd, Old & Campbell Ltd v Liverpool Victoria Trustees Co Ltd* [1981] 1 All ER 897 at 915, [1982] QB 133 at 151–152, the question is—

e
'directed to ascertaining whether, in particular individual circumstances, it would be unconscionable for a party to be permitted to deny that which, knowingly or unknowingly, he has allowed or encouraged another to assume to his detriment …'

f
Mr Norman refers me to *A-G of Hong Kong v Humphreys Estate (Queen's Gardens) Ltd* [1987] 2 All ER 387, [1987] AC 114, where the Privy Council reviewed the earlier authorities, including *Taylor Fashions*. That was a case where it was alleged that the government of Hong Kong had acted to their detriment on the basis of an understanding with the respondents that a particular agreement was to go ahead. Lord Templeman, giving the opinion of the Privy Council, said this ([1987] 2 All ER 387 at 392, [1987] AC 114 at 124):

g
'Their Lordships accept that the government acted to their detriment and to the knowledge of HKL in the hope that HKL would not withdraw from the agreement in principle. But in order to found an estoppel the government must go further. First the government must show that HKL created or encouraged a belief or expectation on the part of the government
h
that HKL would not withdraw from the agreement in principle. Second the government must show that the government relied on that belief or expectation. Their Lordships agree with the courts of Hong Kong that the government fell on both counts.'

j
By analogy, Mr Norman submits that the ombudsman has not shown in his decision any positive encouragement by Mr W or any reliance on such encouragement by the complainants. All that is said in para 20 is that the company did no acts inconsistent with the existence of the resolutions.
I do not read Lord Templeman as seeking to qualify Oliver J's formulation which speaks of 'allowing or encouraging'. In any event, it seems to me that the ombudsman's conclusion must be seen against the background of his earlier

findings as to the actions of the company pursuant to the May 1986 resolutions. He clearly took the view that the company proceeded on the basis of those resolutions; the new scheme was treated as effective, the old one revoked, and surplus assets paid into the new scheme. Mr W was as much involved in those actions as the complainants, and as a director he had as much responsibility as they did. In that context the ombudsman said that Mr W could not rely on his own failure to trouble himself with the details of the file. His acquiescence in that position is taken by the ombudsman as sufficient encouragement to make it unconscionable for him now to deny the validity of the resolution.

I have to bear in mind that the decision on matters of fact is not for me but for the ombudsman. It is only if he has applied some wrong principle of law that the court can intervene. This would only arise if there were no evidence upon which he could reasonably have concluded as he did. For the reasons I have given, if one takes the decision as a whole, it seems to me that he did have such evidence, and he was entitled to reach the conclusion he did.

Accordingly, the appeal must be dismissed. It is therefore unnecessary for me to consider the alternative ground raised by the complainants based on alleged fiduciary obligation.

Appeal dismissed.

Dilys Tausz   Barrister.

R v Bowen

a

COURT OF APPEAL, CRIMINAL DIVISION
STUART-SMITH LJ, BUCKLEY J AND JUDGE HYAM
23 FEBRUARY 1996, 5 MARCH 1996

b

Criminal law – Duress as a defence – Test of duress – Direction to jury – Relevant characteristics – Whether low intelligence a relevant characteristic.

The appellant, B, was charged with five specimen counts of obtaining services by deception relating to a course of conduct over some three years. At his trial B
c asserted that throughout the period he had acted under duress and gave evidence that two men had threatened to petrol-bomb him and his family if he did not obtain goods for them and told him that if he went to the police his family would be attacked. Two other witnesses gave evidence that B was a simple man who had difficulty reading and writing and who required assistance to cope with his
d work and a psychologist said that he was abnormally suggestible, vulnerable and had a low intelligence quotient of 68. The judge directed the jury to consider whether the words and conduct alleged by B in relation to the threats made against him would have driven a person of reasonable firmness of the same sex and age and in the same circumstances to have committed the offences. B was convicted and he appealed on the ground that his low intelligence was a relevant
e characteristic which should have been put to the jury.

Held – The fact that a defendant had or might have had a low intelligence quotient was not relevant to a defence of duress, since a low intelligence quotient, short of mental impairment or mental defectiveness, could not be said to be a
f characteristic which made those who had it less courageous and less able to withstand threats and pressure than an ordinary person. It followed on the facts that the judge's direction to the jury on the issue of duress was sufficient. The appeal would accordingly be dismissed (see p 845 *c* to *e*, post).

Notes
g For duress as a criminal defence, see 11(1) *Halsbury's Laws* (4th edn reissue) para 24, and for cases on the subject, see 14(1) *Digest* (2nd reissue) 73–78, 559–580.

Cases referred to in judgment
DPP v Camplin [1978] 2 All ER 168, [1978] AC 705, [1978] 2 WLR 679, HL.
h *R v Emery* (1992) 14 Cr App R (S) 394, CA.
R v Graham [1982] 1 All ER 801, [1982] 1 WLR 294, CA.
R v Hegarty [1994] Crim LR 353, CA.
R v Horne [1994] Crim LR 584, CA. ·
R v Howe [1987] 1 All ER 771, [1987] AC 417, [1987] 2 WLR 568, HL.
j *R v Hurst* [1995] 1 Cr App R 82, CA.
R v Morhall [1995] 3 All ER 659, [1996] AC 90, [1995] 3 WLR 330, HL.
R v Turner [1975] 1 All ER 70, [1975] QB 834, [1975] 2 WLR 56, CA.

Cases also cited or referred to in skeleton arguments
R v Hudson, R v Taylor [1971] 2 All ER 244, [1971] 2 QB 202, CA.
R v Pommell [1995] 2 Cr App R 607, CA.

Appeal against conviction

By notice dated 22 January 1996 Cecil Bowen appealed with leave against his
convictions in the Crown Court at Luton on five counts of obtaining services by
deception before Judge Marshall and a jury on 2 August 1995 on the ground that
the judge should have directed the jury to consider the characteristics of the
defendant when considering the defence of duress, including in particular the
possession of a low intelligence quotient. The facts are set out in the judgment
of the court.

Alison Levitt (assigned by the *Registrar of Criminal Appeals*) for the appellant.
Peter Gribble (instructed by *Crown Prosecution Service*, St Albans) for the Crown.

Cur adv vult

5 March 1996. The following judgment of the court was delivered.

STUART-SMITH LJ. On 2 August 1995 in the Crown Court at Luton the
appellant was convicted of five counts of obtaining services by deception. He was
subsequently sentenced to 18 months' imprisonment, concurrent on each count.
He now appeals against his convictions with leave of the single judge.

The five counts were specimen counts reflecting a large number of incidents
during the period January 1992 to June 1994. On some 40 occasions the appellant
had visited shops selling electrical goods and obtained a large number of them by
applying for 'instant credit'. On all occasions he had paid a proportion of the cost
by way of deposit. He had not completed payment of any of the goods
concerned. Payments were to be made in some cases by 'payment book' and in
others by 'direct debit'. There was evidence that some of the direct debits had
been cancelled by the appellant.

On all occasions he had given his correct name and bank details. On some
occasions he had given his correct address; on others not. The total amount of
credit obtained was about £20,000.

The appellant was arrested on 14 June 1994 as he attempted to buy a
'camcorder' using the same method. He was interviewed at some length without
a solicitor being present, though he had received some advice over the telephone.
After some initial prevarication he told the officers that he had obtained a large
number of goods that he subsequently sold and that, although he had made some
payments for them, he stopped paying the finance company.

He was interviewed again on 10 August 1994 when details of the various
agreements were put to him and he accepted that he had obtained the goods in
question. He said that he had stopped paying for the credit because he could see
little point in doing so when it was so easy and he had sold the goods as a way of
making a 'quick buck'. He said that he had not realised that what he was doing
was a criminal offence; he thought he was just getting himself into debt.

On 1 November 1994, after his appearance in the magistrates' court, he
attempted to obtain a repair on some equipment which he had previously
obtained by his deception. He was arrested and again interviewed, when he
acknowledged that the goods were the subject of the proceedings and had not
been paid for.

Apart from an oblique reference to threats in these last two interviews, there
was no mention of the events which were to form the basis of his defence of

a duress. The Crown's case was that the appellant had no intention of paying the amounts of the credit outstanding in respect of any of the goods in question.

The appellant gave evidence; he accepted that he had obtained the goods on credit and had made few payments. He asserted that throughout the period he had acted under duress. He had been approached first by an acquaintance when buying a television for himself, and asked what was needed to obtain credit.
b Thereafter two men had accosted him in a public house, and he had been threatened by them that he and his family would be petrol-bombed if he did not obtain goods for them. On each occasion he was told what goods the men required. He was told that if he went to the police his family would be attacked. He said that he had not told the police this in interview because he was worried about the possible repercussions.

c He called two witnesses to support this case, Mr Cowdry and Mr McKenna; both had convictions for dishonesty; both said the appellant was a simple man who had difficulty reading and writing and who required a great deal of assistance to cope with his job as a taxi driver. Mr McKenna said that he had seen two men apparently threatening the appellant, but had not gone to the police because the
d appellant asked him not to. In cross-examination Mr Cowdry said that he had become aware that the appellant had been threatened and had told him to go to the police, but had formed the impression that he was too frightened to do so.

Counsel for the defence had challenged the reliability of the interviews. Two psychologists were called, Ms Kingswood for the appellant and Dr Gudjonsson for the Crown. They gave evidence, both on a voire dire and before the jury. On
e the voire dire the judge rejected the defence submission that the interviews should be excluded. There is no appeal from that decision.

Before the jury Ms Kingswood said that the appellant had an intelligence quotient (IQ) of 68 and a reading age of a child of six years and eight months. His level of ability was in the lowest 2% of the population. She found him abnormally
f suggestible. She said he was unlikely to have appreciated the significance of the questions put to him. She felt he was a 'vulnerable' individual. Dr Gudjonsson did not accept these conclusions. He thought the appellant might be faking a poor result; he thought that the appellant's IQ was higher than 68.

The appeal is based on what Miss Levitt submits was a misdirection in law in relation to the defence of duress. The judge dealt with this matter in the
g summing up. He said:

'What is duress? It consists of words spoken or conduct on the part of another person which drives the defendant to commit the offence because at the time of it he has good cause to fear that either he or his immediate family
h will be severely injured if he does not do so. It also has to be the type of threat or conduct or words spoken that would have driven a person of reasonable firmness—that means really a normal person who is not of a particularly nervous disposition—in those circumstances of the sex and age of the defendant in the same circumstances to do the same thing. So, you have a number of steps to cover in that. The first is, were there any threats
j by words or conduct? If you come to the conclusion that there were not then of course duress does not even start to be considered, but if you come to the conclusion that there were or may have been then of course you have to consider whether they were of the type which would have driven a person of reasonable firmness of the [same] sex and age of the defendant and in the same circumstances as the defendant to have committed the offences.'

After summarising briefly the defence case on duress, he told the jury that if they believed the defendant, or thought he might be telling the truth, they should acquit. In other words, he told them to apply the first or subjective test.

He repeated the two-stage test; he did not use the expression 'sharing the characteristics' of the defendant, but again referred to his age and sex when dealing with the objective test. After rehearsing the defence evidence, he again posed the two-stage test in terms similar to those he had used previously. And finally, he told the jury that if they believed the defendant, or thought he might be telling the truth, they should acquit.

At the conclusion of the summing up Miss Levitt submitted that the judge should have included in his direction that the sober person of reasonable firmness was someone who shared the defendant's characteristics. The judge accepted that he had not used this expression; he considered that he did not have to do so. He said:

'This is a simple question. They either think they [the defence witnesses] are lying. If they do then he is guilty [and] duress does not come into it; or they think they are telling the truth or may be telling the truth in which case then it is duress.'

We should add that that was not in the presence of the jury.

Miss Levitt submits to this court that the judge was in error in omitting these words.

The classic statement of the law is to be found in the judgment of the Court of Appeal in *R v Graham* [1982] 1 All ER 801 at 806, [1982] 1 WLR 294 at 300. Lord Lane CJ, giving the judgment, quoted a passage from a Law Commission report, *Defences of General Application* (1977, Law Com No 83) para 2.28, which includes this passage:

'"Whether the words 'in his situation' comprehend more than the surrounding circumstances, and extend to the characteristics of the defendant himself, it is difficult to say, and for that reason we would not recommend without qualification the adoption of that solution. We think that there should be an objective element in the requirements of the defence so that in the final event it will be for the jury to determine whether the threat was one which the defendant in question could not reasonably have been expected to resist. This will allow the jury to take into account the nature of the offence committed, its relationship to the threats which the defendant believed to exist, the threats themselves and the circumstances in which they were made, and the personal characteristics of the defendant. The last consideration is, we feel, a most important one. Threats directed against a weak, immature or disabled person may well be much more compelling than the same threats directed against a normal healthy person." As a matter of public policy, it seems to us essential to limit the defence of duress by means of an objective criterion formulated in terms of reasonableness. Consistency of approach in defences to criminal liability is obviously desirable. Provocation and duress are analogous. In provocation the words or actions of one person break the self-control of another. In duress the words or actions of one person break the will of another. The law requires a defendant to have the self-control reasonably to be expected of the ordinary citizen in his situation. It should likewise require him to have the steadfastness reasonably to be expected of the ordinary citizen in his

a situation. So too with self-defence, in which the law permits the use of no more force than is reasonable in the circumstances. And, in general, if a mistake is to excuse what would otherwise be criminal, the mistake must be a reasonable one. It follows that we accept counsel for the Crown's submission that the direction in this case was too favourable to the appellant. The Crown having conceded that the issue of duress was open to the

b appellant and was raised on the evidence, the correct approach on the facts of this case would have been as follows: (1) was the defendant, or may he have been, impelled to act as he did because, as a result of what he reasonably believed King had said or done, he had good cause to fear that if he did not so act King would kill him or (if this is to be added) cause him serious physical injury? (2) if so, have the prosecution made the jury sure that a sober person

c of reasonable firmness, sharing the characteristics of the defendant, would not have responded to whatever he reasonably believed King said or did by taking part in the killing? The fact that a defendant's will to resist has been eroded by the voluntary consumption of drink or drugs or both is not relevant to this test.'

d This formulation was approved by the House of Lords in R v Howe [1987] 1 All ER 771 at 800, [1987] AC 417 at 458–459 per Lord Mackay of Clashfern.

But the question remains: what are the relevant characteristics of the accused to which the jury should have regard in considering the second objective test? This question has given rise to considerable difficulty in recent cases. It seems

e clear that age and sex are, and physical health or disability may be, relevant characteristics. But beyond that it is not altogether easy to determine from the authorities what others may be relevant.

In R v Emery (1992) 14 Cr App R (S) 394 the female defendant was convicted of cruelty which had resulted in the death of her child aged 11 months. On the same

f occasion the father of the child was convicted both of cruelty and assault causing actual bodily harm. At the trial, each of the accused maintained that the other was responsible for abusing the child. Emery was allowed to call expert evidence in support of the defence of duress. She claimed that because of her fear of the father she had totally lost her capacity to act independently of him. The effect of

g the expert's evidence was that medical science recognised a condition known as 'post-traumatic stress disorder' which can result from prolonged serious violence and abuse. The features of this disorder (also termed 'learned helplessness') includes an inability to resist or stand up to the abuser coupled with a dependence on the abuser which made the victim unable to seek help. The defence of duress was rejected by the jury; but the Court of Appeal, in deciding whether the

h sentence of four years was correct, had occasion to consider whether the medical evidence was rightly admitted. Lord Taylor CJ said (at 397):

'The nature of the condition for which Miss Emery's advisers contended was something with which juries would not necessarily be familiar. The

j medical expertise relating to this form of stress disorder is of comparatively recent development. It is complex and it is not known by the public at large. Accordingly we are quite satisfied that it was appropriate for the learned judge to decide that this evidence should be allowed. Of course there must be limits on the nature of the evidence which can be given by medical experts in this context.'

It appears, however, that the evidence of the doctors went further than elucidating the nature of post-traumatic stress disorder and sought to support the credibility of Miss Emery. Lord Taylor CJ said (at 398):

> 'The evidence should have gone no further than allowing for the doctors to give an expert account of the causes of the condition of dependent helplessness, the circumstances in which it might arise and what level of abuse would be required to produce it; what degree of isolation of the person in question one would expect to find before it appeared and what sort of personality factors might be involved. The issue the jury had to decide in regard to Miss Emery was, whether or not the prosecution had negatived duress, and therefore the question for the doctors was whether a woman of reasonable firmness with the characteristics of Miss Emery, if abused in the manner which she said, would have had her will crushed so that she could not have protected her child. It was not for the experts to go into the question whether what she had said by way of history as to what abuse had taken place was true or not.'

In *R v Hegarty* [1994] Crim LR 353 the appellant sought to call before the jury evidence of medical witnesses to testify to his mental instability; their reports described him as 'emotionally unstable' and in a 'grossly elevated neurotic state'. The judge refused to admit the evidence and his decision was upheld on appeal. In that case counsel for the appellant submitted that medical evidence might be admissible both for the purposes of the subjective test, namely whether the threats affect the accused in fact, and the objective test, namely how the person of reasonable firmness would react. Neill LJ, after referring to *R v Emery*, said:

> 'We accept that for the purpose of the subjective test medical evidence is admissible if the mental condition or abnormality of the defendant is relevant and the condition or abnormality and its effects lie outside the knowledge and experience of laymen.'

This is a reference to the well-known judgment of Lawton LJ in *R v Turner* [1975] 1 All ER 70, [1975] QB 834, on the purposes and limits of expert evidence. Neill LJ then went on to consider whether medical evidence was admissible in relation to the objective test. He said: 'As the medical evidence was not admissible to explain the reaction of the appellant himself, it was clearly not admissible in this case on the objective test.' He referred to *DPP v Camplin* [1978] 2 All ER 168, [1978] AC 705, a case on provocation, where the House of Lords rejected the submission that medical evidence was required to explain how a pregnant woman, a 15-year-old boy or a hunchback would react in the circumstances. This was a matter for the jury (see [1978] 2 All ER 168 esp at 178, [1978] AC 705 esp at 727 per Lord Simon).

Neill LJ said:

> 'We are quite satisfied that the medical evidence is not admissible as the law stands at present on the objective test in a case of duress. Furthermore, as the objective test predicates a "sober person of reasonable firmness", we see no scope for attributing to that hypothetical person as one of the characteristics of the defendant a pre-existing mental condition of being "emotionally unstable" or in a "grossly elevated neurotic state".'

In *R v Horne* [1994] Crim LR 584 the defence was duress. The appellant had sought to adduce psychiatric evidence to the effect that he was unusually pliable a and vulnerable to pressure. The judge refused to admit this evidence. He said that mental characteristics such as inherent weakness, vulnerability and susceptibility to threats were inconsistent with the requirements of an objective test. The Court of Appeal affirmed his view. The report concluded (at 585–586):

b 'The second limb of the test, which passed an objective test, required the jury to ask themselves whether a person of reasonable firmness, otherwise sharing the characteristics of the defendant, would or might have responded as he did to the threats to which he was subjected. If the standard for comparison was a person of reasonable firmness it must be irrelevant for the jury to consider any characteristics of the defendant which showed that he was not such a person, but was pliant or vulnerable to pressure. It would be
c a contradiction in terms to ask the jury this question, and then ask them to take into account, as one of his characteristics, that he was pliant or vulnerable.'

A similar approach was adopted by the Court of Appeal in R v Hurst [1995] 1 Cr App R 82. In that case the appellant at trial raised the defence of duress and
d sought to adduce the evidence of a psychiatrist, not of psychiatric disorder, but of the possible effects upon her of sexual abuse as a child. The judge refused to admit the evidence and his decision was upheld on appeal. The Court of Appeal held that the evidence of the psychiatrist amounted to no more than an impression he had formed on the basis of what he had been told of the effect of the appellant's history. However, Beldam LJ, who gave the judgment of the
e court, said (at 90):

'There is a further reason why, as it seems to us, even if Dr Mellett's evidence could have been interpreted as indicating that the appellant, due to her previous experiences, suffered from a personality defect which made her lack the firmness and resolution to be expected of someone of her age and
f sex, that it was, nevertheless, inadmissible.'

After referring to R v Graham, he said (at 91):

'So long as there is this objective element in the standard by which a person's reaction to duress by threats is to be judged, we find it hard to see
g how the person of reasonable firmness can be invested with the characteristic of a personality which lacks reasonable firmness, and although we appreciate the difficulty involved in trying to separate personal characteristics one from another, nevertheless we are bound by the formulation in the case of Graham, and on that basis Dr Mellett's evidence
h was irrelevant to any issue which the jury had to determine.'

Finally, Miss Levitt relied on the recent case of R v Morhall [1995] 3 All ER 659, [1996] AC 90. In that case the appellant's defence to the charge of murder was provocation. The House of Lords held that the fact that the appellant was addicted to glue sniffing was a relevant characteristic for the purpose of the
j objective test provided by s 3 of the Homicide Act 1957 where the taunt which provoked the loss of control related to the appellant's addiction to glue sniffing. Lord Goff of Chieveley said: 'The function of the [reasonable person] test is only to introduce, as a matter of policy, a standard of self-control which has to be complied with if provocation is to be established in law ...' He also considered that it was preferable to direct juries to consider—

'the power of self-control to be expected of an *ordinary* person of the age
and sex of the defendant, but in other respects sharing such of the
defendant's characteristics as they think would affect the gravity of the
provocation ...' (See [1995] 3 All ER 659 at 665–666, [1996] AC 90 at 98; Lord
Goff's emphasis.)

Questions of duress and provocation are similar, in that the two-fold test
applies in each case. So far as the objective test in provocation is concerned, the
question is that posed by Lord Goff to which we have referred. In the case of
duress, the question is: would an ordinary person sharing the characteristics of
the defendant be able to resist the threats made to him?

What principles are to be derived from these authorities? We think they are as
follows.

(1) The mere fact that the accused is more pliable, vulnerable, timid or
susceptible to threats than a normal person are not characteristics with which it
is legitimate to invest the reasonable/ordinary person for the purpose of
considering the objective test.

(2) The defendant may be in a category of persons who the jury may think less
able to resist pressure than people not within that category. Obvious examples
are age, where a young person may well not be so robust as a mature one;
possibly sex, though many women would doubtless consider they had as much
moral courage to resist pressure as men; pregnancy, where there is added fear for
the unborn child; serious physical disability, which may inhibit self protection;
recognised mental illness or psychiatric condition, such as post-traumatic stress
disorder leading to learned helplessness.

(3) Characteristics which may be relevant in considering provocation, because
they relate to the nature of the provocation itself, will not necessarily be relevant
in cases of duress. Thus homosexuality may be relevant to provocation if the
provocative words or conduct are related to this characteristic; it cannot be
relevant in duress, since there is no reason to think that homosexuals are less
robust in resisting threats of the kind that are relevant in duress cases.

(4) Characteristics due to self-induced abuse, such as alcohol, drugs or glue
sniffing, cannot be relevant.

(5) Psychiatric evidence may be admissible to show that the accused is
suffering from some mental illness, mental impairment or a recognised
psychiatric condition, provided persons generally suffering from such a condition
may be more susceptible to pressure and threats, and thus to assist the jury in
deciding whether a reasonable person suffering from such a condition might have
been impelled to act as the defendant did. It is not admissible simply to show that
in the doctor's opinion an accused, who is not suffering from such illness or
condition, is especially timid, suggestible or vulnerable to pressure and threats.
Nor is medical opinion admissible to bolster or support the credibility of the
accused.

(6) Where counsel wishes to submit that the accused has some characteristic
which falls within (2) above, this must be made plain to the judge. The question
may arise in relation to the admissibility of medical evidence of the nature set out
in (5). If so, the judge will have to rule at that stage. There may, however, be no
medical evidence, or, as in this case, medical evidence may have been introduced
for some other purpose, for example to challenge the admissibility or weight of a
confession. In such a case counsel must raise the question before speeches in the

a absence of the jury, so that the judge can rule whether the alleged characteristic is capable of being relevant. If he rules that it is, then he must leave it to the jury.

(7) In the absence of some direction from the judge as to what characteristics are capable of being regarded as relevant, we think that the direction approved in *R v Graham* without more will not be as helpful as it might be, since the jury may be tempted, especially if there is evidence, as there was in this case, relating to *b* suggestibility and vulnerability, to think that these are relevant. In most cases it is probably only the age and sex of the accused that is capable of being relevant. If so, the judge should, as he did in this case, confine the characteristics in question to these.

How are these principles to be applied in this case? Miss Levitt accepts, rightly in our opinion, that the evidence that the appellant was abnormally suggestible *c* and a vulnerable individual is irrelevant. But she submits that the fact that he had, or may have had, a low IQ of 68 is relevant, since it might inhibit his ability to seek the protection of the police. We do not agree. We do not see how low IQ, short of mental impairment or mental defectiveness, can be said to be a characteristic that makes those who have it less courageous and less able to withstand threats *d* and pressure. Moreover, we do not think that any such submission as is now made, based solely on the appellant's low IQ, was ever advanced at the trial. Furthermore, it is to be noted that in two places the judge told the jury that if they thought the appellant passed the subjective test they should acquit him. We are quite satisfied that in the circumstances of this case the judge's direction was sufficient. He directed the jury to consider the only two relevant characteristics, *e* namely age and sex. It would not have assisted them, and might well have confused them, if he had added, without qualification, that the person of reasonable firmness was one who shared the characteristics of the appellant. For these reasons, the appeal will be dismissed.

f *Appeal dismissed.*

N P Metcalfe Esq   Barrister.

R v Associated Octel Co Ltd

HOUSE OF LORDS

LORD MACKAY OF CLASHFERN LC, LORD GOFF OF CHIEVELEY, LORD JAUNCEY OF
TULLICHETTLE, LORD MUSTILL AND LORD HOFFMANN

8 JULY, 14 NOVEMBER 1996

*Health and safety at work – Employer's duties – Duty to other person's employees –
Duty to conduct undertaking in such a way as to ensure other person's employees not
exposed to risks to health and safety – 'Conduct his undertaking' – Independent
contractor's workman injured while working at employer's site – Whether employer
liable for injury to workman employed by independent contractor – Whether employer
liable if not in position to exercise control over work carried out by independent
contractor – Whether employer required to take reasonably practical steps to avoid risk
to independent contractors' employees arising from inadequacy of arrangements for
work carried out by independent contractor – Health and Safety at Work etc Act 1974,
s 3(1).*

The appellant operated a large chemical plant which was designated by the
Health and Safety Executive as a 'major hazard site' and, for a number of years,
it had used a small firm of specialist contractors for certain repairs.   The
contractors' eight employees were employed virtually full-time on the site and,
like all other contractors on the site, they operated under a 'permit to work'
system which required them to fill in a form for every job stating what was going
to be done and to obtain authorisation from the appellant's engineers, who
decided what safety precautions were needed and issued a 'safety certificate'
imposing conditions under which the work was to be done. The 'permit to work'
system was part of a statement of safety procedures which the appellant was
obliged to draw up and submit to the Health and Safety Executive.   While
undertaking repairs as part of the plant's annual maintenance, an employee of the
contractors was in a tank cleaning the lining by the light of an electric light bulb
attached to a lead when the light broke, causing a bucket of highly inflammable
acetone being used for the cleaning to ignite. The workman was badly burned in
the ensuing flash fire. The appellant was prosecuted for breach of s 3(1)[a] of the
Health and Safety at Work etc Act 1974, which imposed a duty on an employer
to 'conduct his undertaking' in such a way as to ensure, so far as reasonably
practicable, that persons not in his employment who might be affected thereby
were not exposed to risks to their health or safety.   At its trial the appellant
submitted that there was no case to answer because the injury to the workman
was not caused by the way in which it had conducted its undertaking within the
meaning of s 3(1), since he was an employee of independent contractors, the
cleaning of the tank was part of the conduct of their undertaking and the
appellant had no right to control the way in which its independent contractors
carried out their work. The judge rejected that submission; the appellant was
duly convicted and was fined £25,000. It appealed to the Court of Appeal, which
dismissed the appeal on the grounds that the phrase 'conduct his undertaking'
was wide enough to embrace the activities of independent contractors carrying

---

a   Section 3(1) is set out at p 849 *a*, post

a   out the cleaning, repair and maintenance which was necessary for the conduct of
    the employer's business or enterprise. The appellant appealed to the House of
    Lords.

    Held – An employer's vicarious liability for the tortious act of another was not to
    be confused with the duty imposed by s 3 of the 1974 Act upon the employer
b   himself, since vicarious liability depended on the nature of the contractual
    relationship between the employer and the tortfeasor and whether the tortfeasor
    was acting within the scope of his duties under a contract of employment,
    whereas the statutory duty was defined by reference to a certain kind of activity,
    namely the conduct by the employer of his undertaking irrespective of the nature
    of the contractual relationships by which he chose to conduct it.   Section 3
c   imposed a duty on an employer to conduct his undertaking in such a way that,
    subject to reasonable practicability, it did not create risks to people's health and
    safety. If the employer engaged an independent contractor to do work which
    formed part of the conduct of his undertaking, he was required by s 3(1) to
    stipulate for whatever conditions were reasonably practicable to avoid
d   employees of the independent contractor being exposed to such risks. In doing
    so he had to take reasonably practical steps to avoid risk to the contractor's
    employees which arose not merely from the physical state of the premises but
    also from the inadequacy of the arrangements made with the contractors for
    carrying out the work, and if he omitted to do so he could not claim that he was
    not in a position to exercise any control. The decisive question in determining
e   culpability under s 3, therefore, was not whether the employer was vicariously
    liable or in a position to exercise control over work carried out by an independent
    contractor but simply whether the activity in question could be described as part
    of the employer's undertaking, that being a question of fact in each case.
    Although the trial judge had been in error in not leaving to the jury the question
f   whether having the tank repaired was part of the conduct of the appellant's
    undertaking at its chemical plant, that question admitted of only a positive
    answer and a properly instructed jury would undoubtedly have convicted.
    Accordingly the appeal would be dismissed and the conviction affirmed (see p 848
    d to g, p 850 c to e j to p 851 c f g, p 852 b c and p 853 a b f g, post).
        RMC Roadstone Products Ltd v Jester [1994] 4 All ER 1037 doubted.
g   Decision of the Court of Appeal [1994] 4 All ER 1051 affirmed.

    Notes
    For duties of employers to persons other than their employees, see 20 *Halsbury's
    Laws* (4th edn reissue) para 555.
h   For the Health and Safety at Work etc Act 1974, s 3, see 19 *Halsbury's Statutes*
    (4th edn) (1994 reissue) 801.

    Cases referred to in opinions
    DPP v Stonehouse [1977] 2 All ER 909, [1978] AC 55, [1977] 3 All ER 143, HL.
j   *Mailer v Austin Rover Group Ltd* [1989] 2 All ER 1087, sub nom *Austin Rover Group
        Ltd v HM Inspector of Factories* [1990] 1 AC 619, [1989] 3 WLR 520, HL.
    R v Mara [1987] 1 All ER 478, [1987] 1 WLR 87, CA.
    R v Swan Hunter Shipbuilders Ltd [1982] 1 All ER 264, [1981] ICR 831, CA.
    RMC Roadstone Products Ltd v Jester [1994] 4 All ER 1037, [1994] ICR 456, DC.
    Stirland v DPP [1944] 2 All ER 13, [1944] AC 315, HL.

Appeal

Associated Octel Co Ltd (Octel) appealed with leave of the Appeal Committee
from the decision of the Court of Appeal, Criminal Division (Stuart-Smith LJ, Kay
and Dyson JJ) ([1994] 4 All ER 1051) delivered on 19 July 1994 dismissing Octel's
appeal against its conviction in the Crown Court at Chester before Judge Prosser
and a jury on 19 March 1993 of failing to discharge the duty imposed on it by s 3(1)
of the Health and Safety at Work etc Act 1974. The facts are set out in the opinion
of Lord Hoffmann.

Raymond Walker QC and Julian Waters (instructed by Hill Dickinson Davis Campbell,
   Liverpool) for Octel.
Hugh Carlisle QC and Ian Burnett (instructed by the Treasury Solicitor) for the
   Crown.

Their Lordships took time for consideration.

14 November 1996. The following opinions were delivered.

LORD MACKAY OF CLASHFERN LC. My Lords, I have had the advantage of
reading in draft the speech of my noble and learned friend Lord Hoffmann. For
the reasons he gives I would dismiss this appeal.

LORD GOFF OF CHIEVELEY. My Lords, I have had the advantage of reading
in draft the speech prepared by my noble and learned friend Lord Hoffmann. For
the reasons he gives I, too, would dismiss this appeal.

LORD JAUNCEY OF TULLICHETTLE. My Lords, I have had the advantage
of reading in draft the speech prepared by my noble and learned friend Lord
Hoffmann. For the reasons he gives I, too, would dismiss this appeal.

LORD MUSTILL. My Lords, I have had the advantage of reading in draft the
speech prepared by my noble and learned friend Lord Hoffmann. For the reasons
he gives I, too, would dismiss this appeal.

LORD HOFFMANN. My Lords, the appellant, Associated Octel Co Ltd (Octel),
operates a large chemical plant at Ellesmere Port. On 25 June 1990 there was an
accident at the chlorine works. The plant was shut down for its annual
maintenance and a small firm of specialist contractors called Resin Glass Products
Ltd (RGP) were engaged in repairing the lining of a tank. Mr Cuthbert, an
employee of RGP, was working in the tank by the light of an electric light bulb
attached to a lead. After grinding the damaged area of the lining, he had to clean
it down with acetone before applying a fibreglass matting patch with resin. He
had his supply of acetone in an old paint bucket which he had found in a refuse
bin. While he was applying the acetone with a brush, the light bulb broke. Some
of the liquid had probably dripped onto it. Acetone is volatile and gives off highly
inflammable vapour. As Mr Cuthbert was using an open bucket, there was a
good deal of vapour in the tank. The broken bulb caused a flash fire in which Mr
Cuthbert was badly burned.

Octel was prosecuted for breach of ss 3(1) and 33(1)(a) of the Health and Safety
at Work etc Act 1974. Section 3(1) reads as follows:

a 'It shall be the duty of every employer to conduct his undertaking in such a way as to ensure, so far as is reasonably practicable, that persons not in his employment who may be affected thereby are not thereby exposed to risks to their health or safety.'

Section 33(1) states that it is an offence for an employer not to discharge a duty to which he is subject by virtue of s 3.

b In voluntary particulars of the indictment, the Crown said that the conduct of Octel's undertaking upon which it relied was the manner and method by which works of maintenance and repair were carried out. The failure of duty was a failure to control the works so as to ensure that persons not in Octel's employment—Mr Cuthbert was, of course, employed by RGP and not by c Octel—were not exposed to risks to their health and safety.

At the trial the prosecution led evidence of the way in which the work had been arranged. Octel had been using RGP for a number of years. Its eight employees spent virtually all their time on the site. Like all other such contractors on Octel's site, they operated under what was called a 'permit to work' system. This meant d that for every job they had to fill in a form saying what they were going to do and obtain authorisation from Octel's engineers, who would consider what safety precautions were needed. Authorisation would be accompanied by a 'safety certificate' imposing conditions under which the work was to be done. The whole plant was designated by the Health and Safety Executive as a 'major hazard site' and the 'permit to work' system was part of a statement of safety e procedures which Octel was obliged to draw up and submit to the Executive. In addition, Octel needed to maintain control over the activities of contractors to discharge its statutory duty to its own employees under s 2(1) of the 1974 Act. This states: 'It shall be the duty of every employer to ensure, so far as is reasonably practicable, the health, safety and welfare at work of all his f employees.'

The duty includes an obligation to take such steps as are reasonably practicable to safeguard employees from being injured by the activities of contractors and their employees. For example, in *R v Swan Hunter Shipbuilders Ltd* [1982] 1 All ER 264, [1981] ICR 831 the defendants did not warn a contractor's workmen of the risk of fire from an oxygen-enriched atmosphere. As a result, one of them g accidentally started a fire in which eight employees died. The employers were convicted under s 2(1).

In the present case the Crown adduced evidence by way of advance rebuttal of a defence that prevention of the accident had not been reasonably practicable. It showed that the permit to work system had been operated in a perfunctory h manner. The RGP specification said that grinding would take place and so Octel supplied Mr Cuthbert with protective clothing and a face mask. But nothing was said about the use of acetone. Octel did not supply a special air lamp (which could have been specified on the standard form) or a closed container for the acetone or forced air extraction for the tank.

j At the close of the prosecution's case, Mr Walker QC submitted on behalf of Octel that there was no case to answer. He said that on the evidence the injury to Mr Cuthbert was not caused by the way in which Octel had conducted its undertaking within the meaning of s 3(1). RGP were independent contractors and the cleaning of the tank was part of the conduct of their undertaking. Control was essential to liability under s 3(1) and Octel had no right to control the way in which its independent contractors did their work.

Judge Prosser rejected the submission. He said that Octel's undertaking was the chemical business which it conducted on the site. The conduct of the undertaking included having the tank repaired, whether by employees or contractors. After this ruling, Octel closed its case without calling evidence. By s 40 the burden is upon the employer to prove that it was not reasonably practicable to take the precautions which would have avoided the risk. In summing up, the judge directed the jury that Octel conducted its undertaking by having the tank repaired by RGP. He drew attention to the fact that this had been done in a way which caused risk to Mr Cuthbert—a risk which had materialised— and that Octel had called no evidence in support of a defence that it had not been reasonably practicable to ask whether he would be using inflammable substances or to take appropriate precautions. Not surprisingly, the jury convicted. The judge fined Octel £25,000.

Octel's main ground of appeal to the Court of Appeal ([1994] 4 All ER1051) was that the judge had been wrong to reject its submission of no case to answer. The Court of Appeal rejected this argument and so would I. It is based on what seems to me a confusion between two quite different concepts: an employer's vicarious liability for the tortious act of another and a duty imposed upon the employer himself. Vicarious liability depends (with some exceptions) on the nature of the contractual relationship between the employer and the tortfeasor. There is liability if the tortfeasor was acting within the scope of his duties under a contract of employment. Otherwise, generally speaking, the employer is not vicariously liable. But s 3 is not concerned with vicarious liability. It imposes a duty upon the employer himself. That duty is defined by reference to a certain kind of activity, namely, the conduct by the employer of his undertaking. It is indifferent to the nature of the contractual relationships by which the employer chooses to conduct it.

What, then, amounts to the conduct by the employer of his undertaking? Mr Walker said that it meant carrying on activities over which the employer had control. In *Mailer v Austin Rover Group Ltd* [1989] 2 All ER 1087 at 1097, [1990] 1 AC 619 at 634 Lord Jauncey of Tullichettle said:

'Sections 2 and 3 impose duties in relation to safety on a single person, whether an individual or a corporation, who is in a position to exercise complete control over the matters to which the duties extend. An employer can control the conditions of work of his employees and the manner in which he conducts his undertaking.'

Mr Walker says that the absence of a right to control the way in which the work is done is traditionally the badge of an employer's relationship with an independent contractor. So, as RGP were independent contractors, it must follow that Octel was not in a position to exercise that complete control which is the basis of liability under s 3.

This again seems to me a confusion of thought. Lord Jauncey was stating what is, if I may respectfully say so, the self-evident proposition that a person conducting his own undertaking is free to decide how he will do so. Section 3 requires the employer to do so in a way which, subject to reasonable practicability, does not create risks to people's health and safety. If, therefore, the employer engages an independent contractor to do work which forms part of the conduct of the employer's undertaking, he must stipulate for whatever conditions are needed to avoid those risks and are reasonably practicable. He cannot, having omitted to do so, say that he was not in a position to exercise any a control. This is precisely why Octel insisted that its contractors adhere to the 'permit to work' system.

The concept of control as one of the tests for vicarious liability serves an altogether different purpose. An employer is free to engage either employees or independent contractors. If he engages employees, he will be vicariously liable for torts committed in the course of their employment. If he engages

b independent contractors, he will not. The law takes the contractual relationship as given and in some cases the control test helps to decide the category to which it belongs. But for the purposes of s 3, the category is not decisive.

The question, as it seems to me, is simply whether the activity in question can be described as part of the employer's undertaking. In most cases, the answer will be obvious. Octel's undertaking was running a chemical plant at Ellesmere Port.

c Anything which constituted running the plant was part of the conduct of its undertaking. But there will also be ancillary activities such as obtaining supplies, making deliveries, cleaning, maintenance and repairs which may give rise to more difficulty. In R v Mara [1987] 1 All ER 478 at 481, [1987] 1 WLR 87 at 90–91 Parker LJ said this about the cleaning of a factory:

d   'A factory, for example, may shut down on Saturdays and Sundays for manufacturing purposes, but the employer may have the premises cleaned by a contractor over the weekend. If the contractor's employees are exposed to risks to health or safety because machinery is left insecure, or vats containing noxious substances are left unfenced, it is, in our judgment, clear

e   that the factory owner is in breach of his duty under s 3(1). The way in which he conducts his undertaking is to close his factory for manufacturing purposes over the weekend and to have it cleaned during the shut down period. It would clearly be reasonably practicable to secure machinery and noxious vats, and on the plain wording of the section he would be in breach of his duty if he failed to do so.'

f
I entirely agree and I draw attention to the language used by the learned judge. It is part of the conduct of the undertaking, not merely to clean the factory, but also to have the factory cleaned by contractors. The employer must take reasonably practical steps to avoid risk to the contractors' servants which arise, not merely from the physical state of the premises (there are separate provisions

g for safety of premises in s 4) but also from the inadequacy of the arrangements which the employer makes with the contractors for how they will do the work.

Likewise, in the present case, I think that it was part of the conduct of Octel's undertaking at Ellesmere Port to have the chlorine tank repaired. But I would not accept the extreme position of Mr Carlisle QC for the Crown, who submitted

h that works of cleaning, repair and maintenance which are necessary for the conduct of the employer's business attract the duty under s 3(1). That would suggest that any repairs, cleaning or maintenance, wherever and by whomsoever they may be done, form part of the conduct by the employer of his undertaking. The cleaning of the office curtains at the dry cleaners, the repair of the sales

j manager's car in the garage, maintenance work on machinery returned to the manufacturer's factory: all would in principle impose upon the employer a duty under s 3(1) to ensure that they did not create risks to the health and safety of workers and others at the drycleaners, garage and factory respectively. Mr Carlisle said that the employer could always rely on the defence that it was not reasonably practicable to take steps to prevent risks arising from what other people did on their own premises. But I do not think that such a defence needs to be invoked. In the context of the Act, such activities cannot fairly be described as the conduct by the employer of his undertaking. If he has a repair shop as a part of his plant, that is an ancillary part of his undertaking. Likewise, as in this case, if he has independent contractors to do cleaning or repairs on his own premises, as an activity integrated with the general conduct of his business. But not in the case of activities carried on by another person entirely separately from his own.

It seems to me wrong to try to find some formula such as that of Mr Carlisle to take the place of the simple words of the statute. Whether the activity which has caused the risk amounts to part of the conduct by the employer of his undertaking must in each case be a question of fact. The place where the activity takes place will in the normal case be very important; possibly decisive. But one cannot lay down rigid rules. A difficult borderline case was *RMC Roadstone Products Ltd v Jester* [1994] 4 All ER 1037, [1994] ICR 456. The employers engaged contractors to repair a building. The employers were going to buy new asbestos sheets for the purpose but the contractors offered to remove some from an adjacent disused factory. The employers obtained the permission of the owner. Their projects manager inspected the site with the contractors and warned them to be careful. They offered to supply the contractors with equipment. One of the contractors fell through a skylight on the roof of the disused building and was killed. The employers were charged under s 3(1) and the justices convicted. They said that it was not necessary for the employers to control the site on which the work was done. They were in a position to give specific instructions to the contractors as to how it should be carried on. They therefore owed a duty under s 3(1).

The Divisional Court set aside the conviction. Smith J said ([1994] 4 All ER 1037 at 1047, [1994] ICR 456 at 470):

'I am unable to accept that the mere capacity or opportunity to exercise control over an activity is enough to bring that activity within the ambit of the employer's conduct of his undertaking. Before he can say that an activity is within his conduct of his undertaking, the employer must, in my judgment, either exercise some actual control over it or be under a duty to do so. If the principal chooses to leave the independent contractor to do the work in the way he thinks fit, I consider that the work is not within the ambit of the principal's conduct of his undertaking. It is wholly the contractor's undertaking.'

I am afraid that I cannot accept this reasoning, which seems to me to involve a circularity. The employer is under a duty under s 3(1) to exercise control over an activity if it forms part of the conduct of his undertaking. The existence of such a duty cannot therefore be the test for deciding whether the activity is part of the undertaking or not. Likewise, the question of whether an employer may leave an independent contractor to do the work as he thinks fit depends upon whether having the work done forms part of the employer's conduct of his undertaking. If it does, he owes a duty under s 3(1) to ensure that it is done without risk— subject, of course, to reasonable practicability, which may limit the extent to which the employer can supervise the activities of a specialist independent contractor. Although the case was very much on the borderline, I think that there was evidence upon which the justices were entitled to find in the particular circumstances of the case that having the asbestos sheets removed was part of the a employers' undertaking. The facts were a matter for them and their decision should not have been disturbed.

As the question of whether having the tank repaired was part of the conduct of Octel's undertaking was also one of fact, it should properly have been left to the jury. Even if, as I think, the only rational answer was Yes, it should still have been left to the jury (see *DPP v Stonehouse* [1977] 2 All ER 909, [1978] AC 55). The judge
b did not do so. The effect of the summing up was to direct the jury to find on this point for the prosecution. This was understandable because the case was conducted on the basis that the sole issue was whether the fact that RGP were independent contractors took the work outside the scope of Octel's undertaking. Having correctly ruled that it did not, the judge assumed that the matter was no longer in issue. But in my view there remained a question of fact which it was,
c strictly speaking, for the jury to decide.

The question then is whether this House should, as in *DPP v Stonehouse,* apply the proviso to s 2(1) of the Criminal Appeal Act 1968 and dismiss the appeal. The test for whether the proviso may be applied was laid down by this House in *Stirland v DPP* [1944] 2 All ER 13 at 15, [1944] AC 315 at 321. The House must be
d satisfied that 'a reasonable jury, after being properly directed, would, on the evidence properly admissible, without doubt convict'. In written submissions after the argument in the House, the appellants submitted that this test was not satisfied. They said that they elected to call no evidence after the judge had wrongly ruled in favour of the Crown's submission on the law. If the judge had construed the statute correctly, they would have been able to adduce evidence to
e show that they had no control over how the tank was repaired and that it was therefore not part of their undertaking.

If the appellants were right about the law, I think that there would be much force in this submission. But if, as I think, the question of fact which should have been left the jury is simply whether having the tank repaired was part of the
f conduct of Octel's chemical undertaking at Ellesmere Port, I cannot imagine what evidence could have been called by the appellants which would have led a properly instructed jury to return a negative answer. The tank was part of Octel's plant. The work formed part of a maintenance programme planned by Octel. The men who did the work, although employed by an independent contractor, were almost permanently integrated into Octel's larger operations. They worked
g under the permit to work system. Octel provided their safety equipment and lighting. None of these facts was disputed. In these circumstances, a properly instructed jury would undoubtedly have convicted. I would therefore apply the proviso, dismiss the appeal and affirm the conviction.

h *Appeal dismissed.*

Celia Fox   Barrister.

Secretary of State for Trade and Industry v   *a*
Rogers

COURT OF APPEAL, CIVIL DIVISION
SIR RICHARD SCOTT V-C, ROCH AND HENRY LJJ
2, 30 JULY 1996
b

Company – Director – Disqualification – Disqualification order – Procedure –
Summary procedure for making order – Director prepared to accept that conduct made
him unfit to be concerned in management of company if application dealt with
summarily – Agreed statement of facts – No allegation of dishonesty – Whether judge   *c*
entitled to make finding of dishonesty – Company Directors Disqualification Act 1986,
s 6.

The Secretary of State for Trade and Industry applied for a disqualification order
against the appellant pursuant to s 6ᵃ of the Company Directors Disqualification   *d*
Act 1986. The parties agreed that the proceedings should be dealt with by the
summary form of procedure. In accordance with that procedure an agreed
statement of facts was placed before the court, no oral evidence was given and it
was also informed that the parties had agreed that the appellant's conduct
brought him within the middle bracket of disqualification periods. There was no
allegation of dishonesty in the statement of facts. The appellant was   *e*
subsequently disqualified for a period of eight years. Thereafter, the judge
amended the transcript of his extempore judgment to include a finding of
dishonesty. The appellant appealed.

Held – There was no impropriety in directors disqualification cases in placing an   *f*
agreed statement of facts before the court and inviting it to deal with the
application on the basis of that statement. However, the court was not entitled
to consider the general scope of the disputed evidence and to speculate whether
the disputed facts might, if pursued, have been proved or to ask whether, if they
were proved, the seriousness of the unfitness would be affected. Accordingly,
where the summary form of procedure was used a judge could not, if dishonesty   *g*
formed no part of the agreed facts, properly conclude that the agreed facts
disclosed dishonesty. It followed that the judge had not been entitled to make the
finding of dishonesty; and, in the circumstances, the appropriate disqualification
period without any finding of dishonesty was eight years. The appeal would
therefore be allowed, the disqualification order set aside and a disqualification   *h*
period of eight years imposed afresh (see p 858 *g* to *j*, p 859 *b*, p 863 *d* to *f j* and
p 864 *b* to *d*, post).
   Re Carecraft Construction Co Ltd [1993] 4 All ER 499 considered.

Notes
   j
For powers and duties of the court to make disqualification orders, see 7(2)
Halsbury's Laws (4th edn reissue) paras 1417–1427.
   For the Company Directors Disqualification Act 1986, s 6, see 8 *Halsbury's*
Statutes (4th edn) (1991 reissue) 786.

a   Section 6, so far as material, is set out at p 857 *a* to *d*, post

Cases referred to in judgments

a

Carecraft Construction Co Ltd, Re [1993] 4 All ER 499, [1994] 1 WLR 172.

Sevenoaks Stationers (Retail) Ltd, Re [1991] 3 All ER 578, [1991] Ch 164, [1990] 3 WLR 1165, CA.

Cases also cited or referred to in skeleton arguments

b

Barry v Minturn [1913] AC 584, HL.

Bradfield Third Equitable Benefit Building Society v Borders [1941] 2 All ER 205, HL.

Bromley v Bromley [1964] 3 All ER 226, [1965] P 111, CA.

Cornhill Insurance plc v Cornhill Financial Services Ltd [1993] BCLC 914, CA.

Dellow's Will Trusts, Re, Lloyds Bank Ltd v Institute of Cancer Research [1964] 1 All ER

c

771, [1964] 1 WLR 451.

Derry v Peek (1889) 14 App Cas 337, [1886–90] All ER Rep 1, HL.

Harrison's Share under a Settlement, Re, Harrison v Harrison, Re Ropner's Settlement Trusts, Ropner v Ropner [1955] 1 All ER 185, [1955] Ch 260, CA.

Hazeltine Corp v International Computers Ltd [1980] FSR 521.

d

Hornal v Neuberger Products Ltd [1956] 3 All ER 970, [1957] 1 QB 247, CA.

Lake v Lake [1955] 2 All ER 538, [1955] P 336, CA.

Nocton v Lord Ashburton [1914] AC 932, [1914–15] All ER Rep 45, HL.

Patrick & Lyon Ltd, Re [1933] Ch 786, [1933] All ER Rep 590.

Polly Peck International plc, Re (No 2), Secretary of State for Trade and Industry v Ellis

e

[1994] 1 BCLC 574.

Probe Data Systems Ltd, Re (No 3), Secretary of State for Trade and Industry v Desai [1992] BCLC 405, CA.

R v Cripps, ex p Muldoon [1984] 2 All ER 705, [1984] QB 686, CA.

R v Cristini [1987] Crim LR 504, CA.

f

R v Ghosh [1982] 2 All ER 689, [1982] QB 1053, CA.

R v Lester (1975) 63 Cr App R 144, CA.

R v White [1987] Crim LR 505, CA.

Royal Brunei Airlines Sdn Bhd v Tan [1995] 3 All ER 97, [1995] 2 AC 378, PC.

Sheridan (Brian) Cars Ltd, Re, Official Receiver v Sheridan [1996] 1 BCLC 327.

Thynne (Marchioness of Bath) v Thynne (Marquis of Bath) [1955] 2 All ER 377, [1955]

g

P 272, CA.

Appeal

By notice dated 29 February 1996 the respondent, David Michael Rogers, appealed with leave of the Court of Appeal from the decision of Harman J made

h

on 14 December 1994 whereby it was ordered, pursuant to s 6 of the Company Directors Disqualification Act 1986, that Mr Rogers should not without the leave of the court be a director of a company or in any way, whether directly or indirectly, be concerned or take part in the promotion, formation or management of a company for a period of eight years beginning on 14 December

j

1994. The facts are set out in the judgment of Sir Richard Scott V-C.

David Chivers (instructed by *Bunkers*, Hove) for Mr Rogers.

A W H Charles and *Mark Cunningham* (instructed by the *Treasury Solicitor*) for the Secretary of State.

Cur adv vult

30 July 1996. The following judgments were delivered.

a

SIR RICHARD SCOTT V-C.   This appeal is brought in rather unusual circumstances.

By originating summons dated 30 June 1992 the Secretary of State for Trade and Industry applied to the court for a disqualification order under s 6 of the Company Directors Disqualification Act 1986 against the respondent, Mr Rogers   *b* (the appellant in these proceedings).

The application was based upon Mr Rogers' conduct as a director of three companies in the Brombard group of companies.   The companies in question were Brombard Securities Ltd (BSL), Brombard Financial Services Group plc (BFSG) and Brombard Financial Services Ltd (BFS).   Mr Rogers was the   *c* controlling director of the three companies and of the group as a whole.

The Secretary of State and Mr Rogers reached agreement for the proceedings to be dealt with by the summary form of procedure sanctioned by Ferris J in *Re Carecraft Construction Co Ltd* [1993] 4 All ER 499, [1994] 1 WLR 172.

The purpose of the *Carecraft* procedure (as I will call it) is to enable   *d* disqualification proceedings to be summarily dealt with in cases where: (a) facts regarding the director's conduct in managing the company or companies in question are either agreed or, at least, are not disputed; (b) the Secretary of State is willing for the case to be dealt with by the judge on the agreed (or not disputed) facts and does not consider it necessary to endeavour to prove the additional facts that have been alleged in the evidence filed in support of the summons; (c) the   *e* director is willing for the case to be dealt with by the judge on the agreed (or not disputed) facts and does not dispute that those facts require the court to make a disqualification order under s 6 of the 1986 Act; and (d) the Secretary of State and the director have reached agreement either as to the length of the disqualification period that would be appropriate or, at least, as to the bracket of years into which the disqualification period should fall.   *f*

Where the *Carecraft* procedure is employed, an agreed statement of facts is placed before the court, no oral evidence is given (so no cross-examination takes place), the court is informed of the bracket into which the parties agree the disqualification period should fall and the parties' counsel address the judge on that basis.   The procedure enables the case to be disposed of expeditiously and   *g* with a substantial saving of costs that would be incurred in a full blown trial.

Some concern was expressed at the time *Re Carecraft* was decided, and has been voiced in some quarters subsequently, as to the propriety of the Secretary of State and the respondent director presenting the judge with a virtual fait accompli. Since this is the first occasion on which this court has had to deal with an appeal   *h* against an order made in a case in which the *Carecraft* procedure has been employed (and in the nature of things such appeals should rarely, if ever, be necessary), we should, in my view, take the opportunity to express our view on the concerns that have been expressed.

Section 1(1) of the 1986 Act provides: *j*

'In the circumstances specified below in this Act a court may, and under section 6 shall, make against a person a disqualification order ... for a specified period beginning with the date of the order.'

Section 6 of the Act provides as follows:

'(1) The court shall make a disqualification order against a person in any
case where, on an application under this section, it is satisfied—(a) that he is
or has been a director of a company which has at any time become insolvent
(whether while he was a director or subsequently), and (b) that his conduct
as a director of that company (either taken alone or taken together with his
conduct as a director of any other company or companies) makes him unfit
to be concerned in the management of a company.

(2) For the purposes of this section and the next, a company becomes
insolvent if—(a) the company goes into liquidation at a time when its assets
are insufficient for the payment of its debts and other liabilities and the
expenses of the winding up, (b) an administration order is made in relation
to the company, or (c) an administrative receiver of the company is
appointed; and references to a person's conduct as a director of any company
or companies include, where that company or any of those companies has
become insolvent, that person's conduct in relation to any matter connected
with or arising out of the insolvency of that company ...

(4) Under this section the minimum period of disqualification is 2 years,
and the maximum period is 15 years.'

Section 7(1) provides:

'If it appears to the Secretary of State that it is expedient in the public
interest that a disqualification order under section 6 should be made against
any person, an application for the making of such an order against that
person may be made—(a) by the Secretary of State, or (b) if the Secretary of
State so directs in the case of a person who is or has been a director of a
company which is being wound up by the court in England and Wales, by
the official receiver.'

Section 8 enables the Secretary of State to apply for a disqualification order if it
appears to him from a report made on information obtained under the various
statutory provisions referred to in sub-s (1) that 'it is expedient in the public
interest that a disqualification order should be made'. Subsection (2) provides:

'The court may make a disqualification order against a person where, on
an application under this section, it is satisfied that his conduct in relation to
the company makes him unfit to be concerned in the management of a
company.'

Subsection (4) prescribes a maximum disqualification period of 15 years, but no
minimum period for orders made under s 8.

Section 9(1) provides as follows:

'Where it falls to a court to determine whether a person's conduct as a
director or shadow director of any particular company or companies makes
him unfit to be concerned in the management of a company, the court shall,
as respects his conduct as a director of that company or, as the case may be,
each of those companies, have regard in particular—(a) to the matters
mentioned in Part I of Schedule 1 to this Act, and (b) where the company has
become insolvent, to the matters mentioned in Part II of that Schedule; and
references in that Schedule to the director and the company are to be read
accordingly.'

The matters mentioned in Pt I of Sch 1 to the 1986 Act, to which the court is required by s 9 to have regard, include:

'1. Any misfeasance or breach of any fiduciary or other duty by the director in relation to the company.

2. Any misapplication or retention by the director of, or any conduct by the director giving rise to an obligation to account for, any money or other property of the company.

3. The extent of the director's responsibility for the company entering into any transaction liable to be set aside under Part XVI of the Insolvency Act (provisions against debt avoidance) ...'

They include, in addition, various failures to comply with bookkeeping requirements of the Companies Act. The matters mentioned in Pt II of Sch 1 include: 'The extent of the director's responsibility for the causes of the company becoming insolvent.'

It is for the Secretary of State (or the Official Receiver) and those advising him to decide what evidence to place before the court in support of an application under s 6 and in respect of the matters to which, under s 9, the court is required to have particular regard. If, having done so, the Secretary of State decides that certain allegations made in the affidavits filed in support of the application need not be pursued, it is not, in my opinion, the proper function of the court to insist that they be pursued. The function of the court, in directors' disqualification proceedings, as in civil litigation generally, is adversarial. It is for the applicant to decide what case to present to the court, what allegations to make, and what allegations, once made, should be persevered with. It is for the respondent director to decide what allegations to dispute and what allegations to accept. If the Secretary of State and the respondent director place before the court an agreed statement of the facts that are agreed and of the facts that the respondent does not propose to dispute and invite the court to deal with the case on the basis of that agreed statement, it is not for the court, in my judgment, to insist that other allegations be pursued (whether or not the allegations relate to s 9 matters) or that cross-examination of any deponent or of the director should take place. If the judge feels strongly enough that the course being taken by the Secretary of State is ill-advised, he or she can, I would think, adjourn the case for a short period and invite the Secretary of State to reconsider. But, thereapart, the function of the judge is to deal with the case that is put before the court by the parties. There is no impropriety in directors' disqualification cases or in any other civil proceedings in placing before the court an agreed statement of facts and inviting the court to deal with the case on the basis of that statement.

It follows from what I have said that the opinion expressed by Ferris J in *Re Carecraft Construction Co Ltd* [1993] 4 All ER 499 at 507, [1994] 1 WLR 172 at 181 that the Secretary of State 'cannot agree that matters to which regard must be had by s 9(1) shall be left out of account' needs some qualification. If the Secretary of State's evidence on these 'matters' is disputed, it is, in my opinion, open to the Secretary of State to agree with the respondent director that the relevant allegations will not be pursued. And I do not agree that 'in deciding whether or not to accept a proposal that an application shall be dealt with in a summary way, the court needs to consider not only the unchallenged or admitted evidence but also the general scope of the disputed evidence' (see [1993] 4 All ER 499 at 510, [1994] 1 WLR 172 at 183). A belief that the disputed evidence would, if it were accepted, 'substantially affect the seriousness of the unfitness' is not, in my opinion, something that can properly be taken into account. I repeat that, in my opinion, the Secretary of State is entitled to decide what allegations in support of the disqualification allegation he will put forward or, having put forward, will persist in. It is for the court to deal with the application on the admitted or proved facts. It is not for the court to speculate whether the disputed facts might, if pursued, be proved or to ask itself whether, if they were proved, the seriousness of the unfitness would be affected.

The parties cannot, however, by their agreement require a judge to find that the director's conduct as described in an agreed statement of facts warrants a disqualification order. I find it almost inconceivable that, in a case where the director agrees that his conduct warrants a disqualification order, the judge would not so find. But a judicial finding must remain a matter for the judge's judgment reached on the facts agreed or proved before him. Similarly, the parties cannot by their agreement require the judge to conclude that a disqualification order of a specified period or falling within a specified bracket should be made. That, too, must remain a matter of judicial judgment formed, of course, on the basis of the agreed statement of facts. It would, naturally, be unusual for a judge to disagree with a period of disqualification thought both by the Secretary of State and by the respondent director to be suitable. But the principle remains that the judge would not be bound by their agreement in that regard.

I have on previous occasions expressed the personal belief that it would be very sensible, in a case where the Secretary of State and the director agree that the director's conduct warrants and the public interest would be satisfied by a disqualification for a specified period, if the disqualification could be imposed by a formal undertaking entered into by the director without the necessity of a court order. A statutory amendment would, however, be necessary in order to give such an undertaking the same effect as a court order. For the time being, a disqualification period can only be imposed by order of a judge and the judge must be satisfied that the order is the right one to make on the agreed statement of facts.

In summary, the *Carecraft* procedure can effectively, and without the judge's consent, limit the facts on which the judge can base his judgment as to the order that should be made; but the *Carecraft* procedure cannot oblige the judge to make a disqualification order and cannot bind him as to the period of disqualification to be imposed. It is important, in my opinion, in cases where the *Carecraft* procedure is to be used, for the judge to have an opportunity to read the papers in advance. If the judge, on reading the papers, has any doubts as to whether a disqualification order should be made or as to whether the period should fall within the agreed bracket, the doubts should be voiced at the earliest possible moment so that parties can consider whether they, or either of them, would prefer a full trial. It would, I anticipate, be a very rare case in which any such doubts were entertained.

I must now return to the events of the present case. The parties having agreed that the *Carecraft* procedure should be adopted, a 'Statement of Agreed and Non-Agreed Facts was prepared'. The statement, under the heading 'Introduction', included the following paragraphs :

'1.3 The purpose of this Statement is to identify, in relation to the allegations of unfitness relied on by the Secretary of State, those facts which are either agreed or not agreed between the Secretary of State and the

Respondent. Save where specifically stated to be not agreed, all the facts set
out below are agreed between the Secretary of State and the Respondent.   *a*

1.4 The Secretary of State submits that, by reference to the undisputed
and agreed facts, the conduct of the Respondent as a director of the
companies referred to in Mr Baxendale's affidavit (sworn herein on 30th June
1992) has been such as to make him unfit to be concerned in the
management of a company and that, accordingly the Court is bound (by   *b*
Section 6(1) of the 1986 Act) to make a disqualification order against him.

1.5 It is submitted by the Secretary of State that, by reference to the
undisputed and agreed facts the conduct of the Respondent brings him
within the middle bracket of disqualification periods suggested by the Court
of Appeal in *Re Sevenoaks Stationers (Retailers) Ltd* ([1991] 3 All ER 578, [1991]
Ch 164). It is further submitted that the case falls towards the upper end of   *c*
the middle bracket.

1.6 The Respondent accepts that, by reference to the undisputed and
agreed facts the Court can be satisfied as to his unfitness to be concerned in
the management of a company, and that a disqualification order should be
made. He agrees that the case falls within the range mentioned above and   *d*
will make submissions to the Court as to the appropriate period.

1.7 Both the Secretary of State and the Respondent agree that the
admissions and concessions expressly and impliedly made in this Statement
are made only for the purpose of facilitating a "Carecraft" disposal of the
proceedings and are made entirely without prejudice to the Respondent's   *e*
rights in any other proceedings. They further agree that, if the Court is
unwilling to approve such a disposal, then no further reference may be made
by either party to this Statement during the course of these or any other
proceedings, nor any reliance placed on any of the admissions or concessions
contained herein. In any event this Statement shall remain confidential as
between the parties subject to any direction or order of the Court.'   *f*

The 'middle bracket of disqualification periods' suggested by the Court of Appeal
in *Re Sevenoaks Stationers (Retail) Ltd* was a period of six to ten years.

The statement then set out the 'Allegations of Unfitness' which had been made
in the affidavit evidence filed in support of the Secretary of State's application and
in relation to each allegation set out 'what parts of the Allegation are admitted by   *g*
the Respondent, and what not admitted by him, and those facts material to the
Allegation that are agreed and not agreed' (para 3.4 of the statement). It was not,
in my opinion, necessary for the statement to set out the facts that were not
agreed.

The parts of the allegations and the facts material to the allegations that were   *h*
agreed by Mr Rogers demonstrated a number of serious breaches by Mr Rogers
of the fiduciary duty that, as a director, he owed to each of the three Brombard
companies, that is to say, BSL, BFSG and BFS. It is important to emphasise,
however, that the statement of facts did not record any agreement by Mr Rogers
that he had acted dishonestly. Nor, in putting the statement of facts before the   *j*
judge, did the Secretary of State pursue any allegation that Mr Rogers had acted
dishonestly. It was important to Mr Rogers that there should not be any recorded
finding of dishonesty against him. He is a member of a professional chartered
association. Whatever view his association might take of a disqualification order
made against one of its members on the basis of the agreed facts contained in the
statement, the association would be bound to take a very serious view if an

a allegation of dishonesty were admitted by him or proved against him. Mr Rogers would, in that event, be likely to be facing expulsion or, at the least, suspension from membership. If the Secretary of State had thought it necessary to make and to pursue any allegation that Mr Rogers' conduct had been dishonest, Mr Rogers would not have agreed to the *Carecraft* procedure. He would have maintained the denials of dishonesty already contained in his affidavits sworn in response to

b the evidence filed in support of the application. He would have offered himself for cross-examination. He would, in the witness box, have continued to maintain his denials of dishonesty. But the Secretary of State did not think it necessary to pursue any allegation of dishonesty; so the *Carecraft* procedure was agreed upon and Mr Rogers did not need to defend in the witness box his innocence of dishonesty.

c   The case came before Harman J on 14 December 1994. The judge was taken through the agreed statement of facts and heard submissions from counsel for the Secretary of State and counsel for Mr Rogers as to where in the agreed six to ten years bracket the appropriate disqualification period fell. Counsel for Mr Rogers accepted in his submissions that a period in the top end of the bracket, that is to say, eight to ten years, would be appropriate.

d   Harman J gave an extempore judgment. He rehearsed the salient features of the parts of the allegations that were agreed to by Mr Rogers and the agreed facts material to them and summed up his conclusion with the following words:

e   'Upon that I am wholly satisfied that this is an appropriate case for the adoption of the *Carecraft* procedure. I am urged by both counsel to adopt that and I am satisfied of it. I have to be sure, as [Ferris J] pointed out, that Mr Rogers is unfit to be a director. I am so satisfied by a recital of the facts which I have briefly presented. The matters are made out in evidence and there is no doubt of the facts. I am therefore of the view that Mr Rogers must be disqualified.'

f Having expressed that conclusion on the facts, the judge turned his attention to the requisite period of disqualification. He expressed himself as 'satisfied that counsel are correct in suggesting that the middle bracket is the correct one and that the upper end of the middle bracket is the correct part of that' and, after an impeccable review of the mitigating factors that had been put forward on Mr

g Rogers' behalf, concluded that a period of eight years was the proper disqualification period that should be imposed on Mr Rogers.

      So far, so good; Mr Rogers left court without any imputation of dishonesty having been held proved against him; the Secretary of State was satisfied that a proper period of disqualification consistent with the public interest had been

h imposed. Both parties were content and justice had been seen to be done. Mr Rogers, obviously, had no thought of appealing against the judge's order.

      On 17 March 1995, some three months after the extempore judgment had been delivered, Mr Rogers and his legal advisers received the transcript of the judgment as amended and approved by Harman J. On reading the approved

j transcript they discovered that, after the passage in the judgment that I have cited, which ended with the sentence 'I am therefore of the view that Mr Rogers must be disqualified', Harman J had added the sentences: 'He clearly acted for his own benefit and to the harm of the companies of which he was a director. That was dishonest.' Mr Rogers was understandably aghast at the addition to the judgment of a finding of dishonesty. As he said, in an affidavit sworn on 16 February 1996, he had agreed to the *Carecraft* proceeding on an assurance that the

allegations of dishonesty which had been made against him and which he had
denied would not be pursued. His lawyers endeavoured, first, to confirm that   *a*
their and Mr Rogers' recollection that no reference to dishonesty had been made
in the extempore judgment was correct. They sought leave to listen to the tapes
of the extempore judgment. The Secretary of State consented to their doing so
but the mechanical recording department of the Royal Courts of Justice refused
access to the tapes in the absence of a court order. An application to Harman J   *b*
for the requisite leave was refused on 16 June 1995. After some difficulties
regarding the obtaining of legal aid had been dealt with, an application was made
to the Court of Appeal for leave to appeal against Harman J's substantive order
of 14 December 1994. The Secretary of State supported the application. Mr
Rogers had no quarrel with the order as such. What he objected to was the
finding of dishonesty contained in the approved judgment. On 26 February 1996   *c*
the Court of Appeal: (i) gave Mr Rogers leave to appeal against the substantive
order of 14 December 1994; (ii) gave both parties leave to listen to the mechanical
recording tape of the judgment as delivered extempore; and (iii) gave Mr Rogers
leave to appeal against Harman J's 'implied refusal to amend the terms of his
judgment'.
                                                                                   d
    In the skeleton submissions put before us by counsel there is some analysis of
the scope of the ability of a judge to alter under the so-called 'slip rule' an error in
an order made or a judgment given. In my opinion, what has happened in the
present case cannot lead to or be remedied by any use of the slip rule. Harman J's
addition to his judgment as delivered of the sentences, 'He clearly acted for his   *e*
own benefit and to the harm of the companies of which he was a director. That
was dishonest', was not done in error, or by oversight or inadvertence. It was a
deliberate and intended addition. A judge can be asked to correct under the slip
rule a particular sentence in a judgment or a particular part of an order. But if,
from the response to such a request or otherwise, it appears that the sentence was
deliberate and intended, that is the end of any use that can be made of the slip   *f*
rule. Nor, in my judgment, can the Court of Appeal apply the slip rule in a
manner contrary to the intentions of the first instance judge. It is for the judge to
decide what to say in his judgment and what order to make. The Court of Appeal
can say that he was wrong in law or that there was no evidence to justify a
particular finding, but it cannot apply the slip rule to correct a sentence in the
judgment that the judge intended to include. In so far as the notice of appeal in   *g*
the present case seeks an order that Harman J's judgment be amended by the
deletion of the sentences that he had added, the appeal cannot succeed. It is, as I
have said, for the judge to decide what to say in his judgment. Nor, in my
judgment, can it be said that a judge has acted improperly in adding to the
approved transcript a finding that he had not mentioned in the judgment as   *h*
delivered extempore. In giving any judgment, extempore or reserved, a judge
ought to mention the important features of the case that have led to the
conclusion he has reached and the decision he has made. If, in a director's
disqualification case, a judge concludes, whether rightly or wrongly is for this
purpose immaterial, that on the facts of the case the director has acted dishonestly   *j*
and that for that reason, perhaps among other reasons, a disqualification order for
a particular period ought to be made, it seems to me plain that the judge should
say so. To reach a conclusion that a director was unfit and that, say, a ten-year
disqualification period was appropriate on the basis of an unexpressed finding
that the director's conduct had been dishonest cannot be right. Both the director
and the Secretary of State would be entitled to know on what basis the judge had

a disqualified the director for a period of ten years. While a failure to mention some relatively trivial factor or factors that had been taken into account might be unexceptionable, a failure to mention that a conclusion of dishonesty had been reached would, in my opinion, be contrary to proper practice.

Harman J's amendment to the transcript of his extempore judgment made it clear that his conclusion that Mr Rogers was unfit and that a disqualification *b* period of eight years was appropriate was based in important part on a finding that Mr Rogers' conduct had been dishonest. That being so the judge was right to make the amendment to the transcript and cannot be criticised for having done so.

But that leaves the critical question whether the judge was entitled to make that finding of dishonesty. In my judgment, he was not. The case had come *c* before him on agreed facts. If the Secretary of State had thought it right to pursue allegations of dishonesty against Mr Rogers, either Mr Rogers would have had to agree that his conduct had been dishonest or the *Carecraft* procedure could not have been employed. If the case had gone to a full trial and Mr Rogers, having denied dishonesty in his affidavit evidence, had not had the allegation that he had *d* been dishonest put to him in cross-examination, counsel for the Secretary of State could not properly have invited the judge to conclude that Mr Rogers had been dishonest and the judge could not properly have so concluded. A fortiori, where the *Carecraft* procedure is being used a judge cannot, if dishonesty forms no part of the agreed (or not disputed) facts, properly conclude that the agreed facts disclose dishonesty.

e In my judgment, it was not open to Harman J to conclude that Mr Rogers' intention, in doing what it was agreed he had done, or in not doing what it was agreed he had not done, was a dishonest one. The agreed facts of the case put before the court by the Secretary of State with the agreement of Mr Rogers did not entitle the judge to attribute to Mr Rogers motives of dishonesty.

f It follows, therefore, that the judge's conclusion, first, that Mr Rogers was unfit to be a director and, second, that eight years was the appropriate disqualification period, was reached upon a basis not open to him. His order cannot stand.

It is not, however, necessary for us to remit the case to be reheard at first instance. Both parties remain content that the case should be dealt with on the basis of the agreed facts as set out in the 'Statement of Agreed and Non-Agreed *g* Facts'. Counsel for Mr Rogers accepts before us, as he accepted below, that the agreed facts justify a disqualification order and he accepts that the appropriate disqualification period falls somewhere in the top range of the six to ten years bracket. In the circumstances this court is in as good a position as a judge at first instance to deal with the case and, in my judgment, should do so.

h It is not necessary for me in this judgment to repeat the salient features of the case. They are set out with clarity in the judgment of Harman J. They establish, incontrovertibly, a case in which a disqualification order in the top range of the middle bracket is justified. An assessment of Mr Rogers' conduct must accept, and I do accept, that his conduct was not dishonest but it was, nonetheless, *j* conduct from which the public must be protected. Counsel for Mr Rogers, as I have said, has never contended otherwise than that an eight-year disqualification period is the minimum period that would be appropriate. I agree and, without any finding of dishonesty, would regard a disqualification for that period as being right in principle and merited by the circumstances.

In the result, therefore, there will be no alteration to the disqualification period imposed by the judge. But I would make clear that Mr Rogers leaves this court

without any finding of dishonesty against him and with the view of this court that
the finding of dishonesty made by Harman J and expressed in his approved
judgment was not justified.

I would add that the Secretary of State has throughout supported Mr Rogers in
his appeal to this court against the finding of dishonesty made below. In these
unusual circumstances, and although the disqualification period thought right by
this court is the same as that imposed by Harman J, I would be in favour of an
order allowing the appeal, setting aside the order made below, save as to costs,
and imposing afresh a disqualification period commencing from today and to
continue for eight years calculated from 14 December 1994. The disqualification
will comprehend the four statutory limbs and not simply the two that were
mentioned by the judge below.

ROCH LJ. I agree.

HENRY LJ. I also agree.

Appeal allowed.

Celia Fox   Barrister.

a # Goulding and another v James and another

CHANCERY DIVISION

LADDIE J
b

7 NOVEMBER 1996

Variation of trusts – Jurisdiction – Discretion – Proposed variation for benefit of persons unborn – Whether wishes of testatrix to be taken into account – Whether proposed
c *variation should be approved – Variation of Trusts Act 1958, s 1(1)(c).*

In 1992 the testatrix made a will under the terms of which her estate was to be divided into two equal parts to be given to her daughter, J, and the latter's husband. Their interest was to be given to the testatrix's grandson, M, contingent
d upon attaining the age of 40 years in the event of either of them predeceasing the testatrix. In 1994 the testatrix revoked the will and replaced it with a new will which provided for the creation of will trusts under which J had a life interest in possession of the residuary estate subject to which M was to take absolutely on surviving to age 40. However if M failed to attain the age of 40 or died before J, whether or not he had attained the age of 40, then the children of M living at the
e date of his death were to take absolutely by substitution. If J predeceased M then, whilst M was living and under 40, the will trustees had power to release the capital of the residuary estate to M, so defeating the interests of 'future borns'. The testatrix died in December 1994. J and M applied to the court for a variation of the will trusts under s 1(1)(c)[a] of the Variation of Trusts Act 1958. The new
f arrangement provided that from the date of the variation, the will would be varied and the residuary estate should devolve and be deemed to have devolved since the date of death of the testatrix as if the will had provided for the residuary estate to be held as to 45% for M absolutely and as to 45% for J absolutely. The remaining 10% of the residuary estate was to be put into a grandchildren's fund
g on trust. The will trustees accepted that the proposed variation was in the interests of the persons unborn but stated that there was evidence of the wishes of the testatrix of which the court ought to be aware, namely her desire to exclude her daughter from taking the capital of the residuary estate and her concern that her grandson should not receive capital until he reached the age of
h 40.

Held – The court had power under s 1 of the Variation of Trusts Act 1958 to decide whether in all the circumstances the variation should be allowed to proceed and the beneficiaries did not have an unqualified entitlement to alter or terminate the trust. In the instant case the court, in the exercise of its discretion,
j would not approve the variation sought since what the plaintiffs wished to do in major part was put in place an arrangement which was the complete opposite of what was provided for under the will and the settled intention of the testatrix. The application would therefore be dismissed (see p 869 *f* and p 870 *c d*, post).

---

a   Section 1(1), so far as material, is set out at p 866 *f g*, post

Notes
For jurisdiction of the court to vary trusts, see 48 *Halsbury's Laws* (4th edn reissue) *a*
paras 923–927, and for cases on the subject, see 48 *Digest* (Reissue) 458–471, *4235–4281*.

For the Variation of Trusts Act 1958, s 1, see 48 *Halsbury's Statutes* (4th edn)
(1995 reissue) 362.

b

Cases referred to in judgment
Burney's Settlement Trusts, Re [1961] 1 All ER 856, [1961] 1 WLR 545.
Remnant's Settlement Trusts, Re, Hooper v Wenhasten [1970] 2 All ER 554, [1970] Ch
560, [1970] 2 WLR 1103.
Saunders v Vautier (1841) 4 Beav 115, [1835–42] All ER Rep 58, 49 ER 282.
Steed's Will Trusts, Re, Sandford v Stevenson [1960] 1 All ER 487, [1960] Ch 407, *c*
[1960] 2 WLR 474, CA.

Summons
The plaintiffs, June Goulding and Marcus Geoffrey Goulding, the only living
beneficiaries under the trusts of the will dated 24 March 1994 of Violet Louise *d*
Froud deceased, applied for an order approving pursuant to the Variation of
Trusts Act 1958 an arrangement on behalf of all unborn persons who might be
interested under the trusts of the will. The defendants, John Michael James and
Peter James Daniel, were the executors and trustees of the will. The facts are set
out in the judgment.

e

Brian Green (instructed by *Wilsons*, Salisbury) for the plaintiffs.
David Halpern (instructed by *Boyes Turner & Burrows*, Reading) for the defendants.

LADDIE J. This is an application for the variation of a trust under the provisions
of s 1(1)(c) of the Variation of Trusts Act 1958. That provides: *f*

'Where property, whether real or personal, is held on trusts arising,
whether before or after the passing of this Act, under any will, settlement or
other disposition, the court may if it thinks fit by order approve on behalf of
... (c) any person unborn ... any arrangement (by whomsoever proposed,
and whether or not there is any other person beneficially interested who is *g*
capable of assenting thereto) varying or revoking all or any of the trusts, or
enlarging the powers of the trustees of managing or administering any of the
property subject to the trusts ...'

The manner in which this application comes before the court is as follows. In
1992 Mrs Violet Louise Froud made a will under the terms of which her estate *h*
was to be divided into two equal parts to be given to Mrs Froud's daughter, June
Goulding, and the latter's husband, Kenneth Goulding. Their interest was to be
given to Mrs Froud's grandson, Marcus Goulding, contingent upon attaining the
age of 40 years in the event of either June or Kenneth predeceasing Mrs Froud.
In circumstances to which I will return hereafter, in 1994 Mrs Froud revoked that *j*
will and replaced it with a new will, which provided, in so far as material, for the
creation of will trusts, under which the following provisions were put in place.
(i) June, the daughter, was given a life interest in possession of the residuary
estate subject to which Marcus was to take absolutely on surviving to age 40.
(ii) However if Marcus failed to attain the age of 40 or Marcus died before
June, whether or not he has attained the age of 40, the children of Marcus living

a at the date of his death were to take absolutely by substitution. [At the moment Marcus, although married, has no children. There are, in other words, no 'future borns'.]

(iii) If June predeceased Marcus then, whilst Marcus was living and under 40, the will trustees were to have power to release the capital of the residuary estate to Marcus. If that power were to be exercised it would, of course, defeat the b interests of the future born.

Mrs Froud died in December 1994 leaving a substantial estate. Now, June and Marcus have applied to the court for a variation of the will trusts. What they want to do is to put in place a new arrangement. The most important provisions of the new arrangement would be as follows. From the date of the variation, the will will be varied and the residuary estate shall devolve and be deemed to have c devolved since the date of death of Mrs Froud as if the will had provided for the residuary estate to be held as to 45% for Marcus absolutely and as to 45% for June absolutely. The remaining 10% of the residuary estate is to be put into a grandchildren's fund on trust. The purpose of that is to build up a fund for Marcus's children, if he should have any.

d Actuarial evidence has been put before me which shows that Marcus's putative children, for whom Mrs Froud's current will makes contingent provisions, would benefit from the arrangement being proposed in that their contingent interest can be calculated to have a value at the moment of 1·85%, or less, of the residuary estate. The arrangement will therefore make provision for a considerably larger sum than the current value of their interest to be put aside for them. That fund e is to be taken offshore and, according to the proposed variation, will be managed by professional trustees.

The defendants to this application are the trustees of Mrs Froud's will trusts. They are represented by Mr David Halpern. They do not challenge the assertion of the plaintiffs that the variation proposed by the plaintiffs may be viewed as f being in the interests of the persons unborn. However, although the defendants do not feel that it is within their remit to formally oppose the variation, they have taken the view that there are matters which they wish to put before the court which might have an impact on the court's exercise of its discretion under s 1(1)(c) of the Act.

g The materials which they have drawn to my attention may be summarised as follows. First, Mrs Froud made it clear to her solicitors and accountants that she did not want her daughter, June, to have any interest in her estate save in the income derived from it. There is a considerable body of material pointing to this. For example, her views were recorded in the following terms in the attendance note of one of her solicitors who attended on her to go through the new will:

h

'She was quite happy with [the will] and confirmed again that in no circumstances would she want her daughter touching any of the capital at any time.'

j It appears that the reason for this desire to exclude her daughter from the capital of the estate was because Mrs Froud had come to deeply mistrust her son-in-law, Kenneth. She also complained that her daughter and son-in-law had mistreated her physically. Whatever the underlying reasons, it was her desire to exclude her daughter from taking the capital of the residuary estate which was the reason for revoking her 1992 will and replacing it by the 1994 one. Secondly, the reason for the imposition of the restriction in her will that Marcus would not

take any part of the estate until he was 40 was because she thought that he was a   *a*
'free spirit' who had, at the time of her will, not settled down.

Mr Green, who appeared for the plaintiffs, did not dispute that Mrs Froud's
intentions and desires were as set out above although he asserted, and Mr
Halpern agreed, that there was no material upon which the court could decide
whether her mistrust of her son-in-law was well-founded or whether her
complaints of mistreatment were justified.   *b*

Mr Halpern drew my attention to three cases: *Re Steed's Will Trusts, Sandford v
Stevenson* [1960] 1 All ER 487, [1960] Ch 407, *Re Burney's Settlement Trusts* [1961] 1
All ER 856, [1961] 1 WLR 545 and *Re Remnant's Settlement Trusts, Hooper v
Wenhasten* [1970] 2 All ER 554, [1970] Ch 560. He said that in the first of these the
Court of Appeal established the principle that in exercising its powers under s 1
of the 1958 Act, the court had a discretion and that the settlor's clear intention   *c*
was a matter which it was appropriate to take into account. The other two cases
do not detract from the principle set out in *Re Steed's Will Trusts* but they are
examples of cases where, on the facts, the court saw fit to approve variations even
though those variations were inconsistent with, or as in *Re Remnant's Settlement
Trusts*, went totally against, the intentions of the settlor.   *d*

Mr Green conceded that the principles set out in *Re Steed's Will Trusts* bound
me. But he said that I should not lose sight of the fact that in that case the
variation being proposed was the lifting of a protective trust under the provisions
of s 1(1)(d) of the 1958 Act. The court had to look for someone whose interest
should be taken into account when deciding how to exercise its discretion and, by
the device of looking at the provisions of Rules of the Supreme Court requiring a   *e*
settlor, where alive, to be joined as a party, decided that the settlor's views should
be so taken into account. He pointed to the fact there is no statutory requirement
that the views or intentions of the settlor should be taken into account and that
Re Steed's Will Trusts must be approached on that basis. He also said that,
whatever the views expressed in *Re Steed's Will Trusts*, it is well known that   *f*
applications for variations of trusts are almost never refused by the court if the
variation could be shown to confer sufficient benefit on those on behalf of whom
the court's approval was sought. Indeed in his own experience of about 40 such
applications, he had never experienced such a refusal. I did not understand Mr
Halpern to disagree with this assessment of the practice in relation to these types
of cases.   *g*

Furthermore Mr Green reminded me of the rule in *Saunders v Vautier* (1841) 4
Beav 115, [1835–42] All ER Rep 58. The beneficiaries under a trust can, if sui juris
and together entitled to the whole beneficial interest, put an end to the trust and
direct the trustees to hand over the trust property as they direct. Therefore if
June and Marcus had, between them, an absolute entitlement to the residuary   *h*
estate, they could direct the trustees to hand that estate to them at any time and
in any manner they wished. In particular they could override, at their will, the
firmest and most deeply held contrary intention of the settlor. As Mr Halpern
agreed, even if the course to be adopted by the beneficiaries in such a case would
make the settlor turn in her grave, that would be beside the point. The fact that   *j*
the beneficiaries had an absolute entitlement to the residuary estate gave them an
unfettered right to do with it what they liked.

From this Mr Green argued that when a court is faced with an application for
a variation under s 1(1)(c), the prime concern to be borne in mind must be the
interests of the person or persons unborn. Although, in the light of *Re Steed's Will
Trusts*, he conceded, at least for the purpose of proceedings in the High Court,

a that the intentions of the settlor could not be ignored, they should be given only minor weight. They should not be allowed to become a veto. At times I got the distinct impression that what he really meant was that the intentions of the settlor should always be taken into account and then always dismissed as being insufficiently weighty.

b I am very conscious that I should not do something which upsets years of practice in this division. However I am not impressed by the fact that most if not all other applications for variations of trusts have been approved. It is clear, and Mr Green agreed, that in many applications the purpose behind the variation was fiscal. The variation could not be said to be contrary to the intention of the settlor but could be regarded as a more tax-efficient way of achieving more or less what c the settlor wanted. Furthermore Mr Green accepted that he had no personal experience of any other case in which the variation could be said to have gone completely contrary to the settlor's strongest wishes. He also said that, were this application to be rejected, it could be envisaged that in other cases extensive evidence relating to what the settlor did or did not intend and whether or not the intention was based on reasonable grounds would have to be put before the d court. I am not persuaded that there is really any likelihood of that happening. In any event, if such evidence is relevant to the proper exercise of the court's discretion under the Act, I do not see how I can pretend that the discretion does not exist simply to avoid the inconvenience which would be caused by parties putting in evidence which was relevant to its exercise.

e It appears to me that the distinction between a *Saunders v Vautier* type of case and an application under s 1 of the 1958 Act is important. As Mr Green pointed out, under the former, the settlor's intentions are irrelevant. The court has no power to intervene. But the position under s 1 is quite different. In the case of such applications the beneficiaries do not have an unqualified entitlement to alter or terminate the trust and the court does have the power and, indeed, the duty to f decide whether, in all the circumstances, the variation should be allowed to proceed. The difference between the two types of case is clear from *Re Steed's Will Trusts* itself. In that case Lord Evershed MR referred to the fact that under the Act, the discretion was framed in the widest possible language. No doubt with cases like *Saunders v Vautier* in mind he referred to the court's duty to g exercise 'this very wide and, indeed, revolutionary discretion'. The way in which the court should approach the exercise of the discretion was expressed as follows:

h '... the court must regard the proposal as a whole, and, so regarding it, then ask itself whether in the exercise of its jurisdiction it should approve that proposal on behalf of the person who cannot give a consent, because he is not in a position to do so. If that is a right premise, then it follows that the court is bound to look at the scheme as a whole, and when it does so, to consider, as surely it must, what really was the intention of the benefactor. That such is a proper approach is at least supported by the provisions of j R.S.C., Ord. 55, r. 14A(3A) ... which provides that in the case of an application under this Act, where there is a living settlor the living settlor is to be a party before the court. That rule seems to me to reinforce what I conceive to underly this provision, viz., that the court must, albeit that it is performing its duty on behalf of some person who cannot consent on his or her own part, regard the proposal in the light of the purpose of the trust as shown by the evidence of the will or settlement itself, and of any other relevant evidence available.' (See [1960] 1 All ER 487 at 493, [1960] Ch 407 at 420–421.)

I note, in passing, the reference to evidence relating to the purpose of the trust in the last sentence.

I think it was not disputed here that that part of the variation which sets aside 10% of the estate for putative grandchildren was seen as the price that June and Marcus were prepared to pay to override the restrictions in Mrs Froud's will designed to prevent the former having access to any capital and the latter from benefiting before he was 40. Had the variation only been concerned to overcome the restriction on Marcus, I probably would have had little trouble in giving approval. But that is not the case here.

It seems to me that what the plaintiffs wish to do in major part is put in place an arrangement which is the complete opposite of what was provided for under the will and the settled intention of Mrs Froud. Since I have a discretion to exercise, I shall exercise it. I have come to the conclusion that this is a case in which it would not be appropriate to give approval to the variation sought and I will dismiss the application.

Application dismissed. Leave to appeal granted.

This case went on appeal on 5 December 1996 and judgment was delivered on 10 December.

Celia Fox   Barrister.

Re C (a minor) (interim care order: residential assessment)

HOUSE OF LORDS

LORD BROWNE-WILKINSON, LORD GRIFFITHS, LORD LLOYD OF BERWICK, LORD NICHOLLS OF BIRKENHEAD AND LORD HOPE OF CRAIGHEAD

30, 31 OCTOBER, 28 NOVEMBER 1996

Family proceedings – Care order – Conditions to be satisfied before making care order – Assessment of parents and child – Jurisdiction of court to order assessment before deciding to make care order – Residential assessment – Court having jurisdiction to give appropriate directions with regard to medical or psychiatric examination 'or other assessment' of child – Other assessment of child – Whether court having jurisdiction to order residential assessment of parents and child – Children Act 1989, s 38(6).

A four-month-old child was admitted to hospital where he was found to have sustained non-accidental injuries. The child's parents, both of whom were young and immature, were not able to give a satisfactory explanation of the injuries. The local authority obtained an emergency protection order and an interim care order was made under s 38 of the Children Act 1989. Social workers employed by the local authority concluded after a prolonged investigation of the child and his parents that the best course of action was an in-depth assessment of the child and the parents together at a residential unit to be undertaken as soon as possible. That conclusion was supported by an independent report by a clinical psychologist. However, the local authority refused to agree to, or pay for, the residential assessment which was proposed and decided to apply for a care order so that the child could be placed in a permanent alternative placement with a view to adoption. An application was made to the Family Division prior to the final hearing of care proceedings for directions under s 38(6)[a] of the 1989 Act, which provided that where the court made an interim care order or interim supervision order it could give such directions as it considered appropriate 'with regard to the medical or psychiatric examination or other assessment of the child'. The judge held that she had jurisdiction under s 38(6) to order a residential assessment and, having weighed the cost (estimated at £18,000 to £24,000) against the recommendations from the social workers, the psychologist and the guardian ad litem that residential assessment would be of value and was essential if the parents were to have any hope of keeping the child, decided to exercise her discretion by ordering the local authority to carry out the residential assessment. The local authority appealed to the Court of Appeal, which allowed the appeal on the grounds that it was bound by previous Court of Appeal authority to hold that the court had no jurisdiction under s 38(6) to order such residential assessment because 'other assessment of the child' in s 38(6) was to be construed as ejusdem generis with the words 'medical or psychiatric examination' and did not embrace examination or assessment of any other person in relation to the child. The parents appealed to the House of Lords.

---

a   Section 38(6) is set out at p 874 g, post

Held – The 1989 Act was to be construed purposively so as to give effect to the underlying intentions of Parliament. The court could only make a final care order under s 31 if the court was satisfied that the child was suffering or likely to suffer significant harm which was attributable either to the care being given to the child not being what it was reasonable to expect a parent to give to him or to the fact that the child was beyond parental control. The purpose of s 38(6) was to enable the court to obtain the information necessary for its own decision whether to make a final care order or merely an interim care order, notwithstanding that in all other respects control over the child rested with the local authority. The court had to have such powers to override the views of the local authority as were necessary to enable the court to discharge properly its function of deciding whether or not to accede to the local authority's application to take the child away from its parents by obtaining a care order. To allow the local authority to decide what evidence is to go before the court at the final hearing would allow the local authority by administrative decision to pre-empt the court's judicial decision. Accordingly, s 38(6) and (7), broadly construed, conferred jurisdiction on the court to order or prohibit any assessment which involved the participation of the child and was directed to providing the court with the material which, in the court's view, was required to enable it to reach a proper decision at the final hearing of the application for a full care order. However, in exercising its discretion whether to order any particular examination or assessment, the court was required to take into account the cost of the proposed assessment and the fact that local authorities' resources were notoriously limited. The parents' appeal would therefore be allowed (see p 875 h, p 876 a e to g, p 877 e to g, p 878 c, p 879 g h and p 880 b to e, post).

Notes

For care orders, see 5(2) *Halsbury's Laws* (4th edn reissue) 788

For the Children Act 1989, s 38, see 6 *Halsbury's Statutes* (4th edn) (1992 reissue) 441.

Cases referred to in opinions

A v Liverpool City Council [1981] 2 All ER 385, [1982] AC 363, [1981] 2 WLR 948, HL.

KP (a minor), Re (11 October 1995, unreported), Fam D.

L (a minor) (interim care order), Re [1996] 2 FCR 706, CA.

L (a minor) (police investigation: privilege), Re [1996] 2 All ER 78, [1996] 2 WLR 395, HL.

M (minors) (interim care order: directions), Re [1996] 3 FCR 137, CA.

Appeal

The parents of a child, T, appealed from the decision of the Court of Appeal (Butler-Sloss, Waite and Roch LJJ) given on 30 September 1996 allowing the appeal of Oldham Borough Council from the decision of Hogg J given on 16 July 1996 directing that the local authority carry out a residential assessment of T and the parents prior to the final hearing of care proceedings in respect of T. The facts are set out in the opinion of Lord Browne-Wilkinson.

Anthony Rumbelow QC and *Gillian Irving* (instructed by *Sharpe Pritchard*, agents for *Booth & Middleton*, Oldham) for the mother.

a *Anthony Rumbelow QC* and *Anthony Hayden* (instructed by *Sharpe Pritchard*, agents for *Norcross Lees & Riches*, Oldham) for the father.
   David Harris QC and *Maureen Roody* (instructed by *G F Smith*, Oldham) for the local authority.
   Lesley Newton and *Ceri Warnock* (instructed by *Temperley Taylor*, Manchester) for the guardian ad litem.

b
   Their Lordships took time for consideration.

   28 November 1996. The following opinions were delivered.

c **LORD BROWNE-WILKINSON.** My Lords, this appeal concerns a child, T, who was born on 11 June 1995. At the end of October 1995 he was taken to hospital where he was found to be suffering from serious injuries which, in the view of an experienced consultant paediatrician, were non-accidental. His parents, in whose care he had been, were young and inexperienced, the mother being 17 at the time of his birth and the father 16. They are immature and have
d a difficult relationship with each other. They lack family backing. They are unable to give any satisfactory explanation of how T came to suffer his injuries.
   On 1 November 1995 the local authority obtained an emergency protection order. On 9 November 1995 Oldham justices made an interim care order under s 38 of the Children Act 1989, which order has since been periodically extended from time to time. They have appointed a guardian ad litem for T. After T's
e discharge from hospital, he was placed by the authority with foster parents with whom he is still living. It is not yet known whether he has suffered permanent brain damage.
   Social workers employed by the local authority conducted a prolonged investigation of T and his parents over a period of some seven months. They
f reported to the court in what has been called the 'Orange Book assessment' that, although the parents were deficient in parenting skills and their relationship was difficult, they had made progress in their caring for T, with whom they had had contact for some four to five hours daily from Monday to Friday in each week. They expressed the following conclusion:

g   'At this stage in the assessment we feel that a more in-depth assessment at a residential unit is essential and should be undertaken as soon as possible. This placement would need to be fully supervised in an attempt to test out for longer and more realistic periods of time the parents' ability to cope whilst affording T protection. The gap in the assessment so far has clearly been the lack of opportunity to assess the parents' ability to cope over long
h   periods of time and in particular stressful situations. This would enable the parents' care to be observed at night times where there are regular occasions when T has little sleep, and is difficult to settle. These situations can be demanding and stressful for carers, especially if this continues for consecutive nights as is the situation with T.'

j
   There has also been an assessment of the parents by a clinical psychologist who supported the proposal for a residential assessment of T and the parents together.
   The guardian ad litem, having seen the reports of the social workers and the psychologist, reported her views to the court. She recognised that this was a very high risk case. She pointed to the severe injuries suffered by T as a baby of which there was no adequate explanation and to the youth, immaturity and

unsatisfactory relationship of the parents. On the other side, she drew attention
to the commitment shown by the parents in attending five days a week for four *a*
to five hours for supervised contact with T and the improvement in their
parenting skills. She expressed her conclusion as follows:

> 'It is my view that it is inappropriate to make a final decision on T's future
> placement without the information which could be obtained from a
> residential assessment. Even if there is only a slight possibility that T could *b*
> be rehabilitated with his parents I feel this possibility should, in fairness to T,
> be fully explored.'

Despite the recommendation made by their own social workers that
residential assessment would be desirable, the local authority did not agree. It
was initially indicated that the refusal of the local authority to countenance a *c*
residential assessment was based on financial grounds: the proposed residential
assessment would cost some £18,000 to £24,000. However, the reasons put
forward by the assistant director of social services to the court were not linked to
money. She considered in detail what she called the crucial areas: the lack of
explanation of the injuries, the lack of frankness by the parents as to the cause of *d*
the injuries, the unstable relationship between the parents, the lack of the
parenting skills necessary to deal with T's special needs and the fact that the
demands of those special needs would produce the stress on the parents which
may have led to them injuring T. In the light of those factors, she expressed the
view that any consideration of rehabilitation with his parents would expose T to
an unacceptable level of risk. She further said that, at the final hearing for a care *e*
order, the local authority would press for a care order with a view to T being
placed in a permanent alternative placement, presumably with a view to
adoption. In short, the local authority was not prepared to agree to, or pay for,
the residential assessment which was proposed.

It was in those circumstances that the case came before Hogg J on the hearing *f*
of an application that she should make a direction under s 38(6) of the 1989 Act
that T and his parents should be the subject of a residential assessment at a
specified place. Section 38(6) provides:

> 'Where the court makes an interim care order, or interim supervision
> order, it may give such directions (if any) as it considers appropriate with *g*
> regard to the medical or psychiatric examination or other assessment of the
> child; but if the child is of sufficient understanding to make an informed
> decision he may refuse to submit to the examination or other assessment.'

Before the judge, the local authority submitted that the court had no power
under the subsection to direct the local authority to carry out the residential *h*
assessment proposed. The judge rejected this submission. She founded her
decision on a decision of Singer J in *Re KP (a minor)* (11 October 1995, unreported).
Unfortunately, but not surprisingly, the judge's attention was not drawn to a then
unreported decision, *Re M (minors) (interim care order: directions)* [1996] 3 FCR 137,
delivered by the Court of Appeal the week before, holding that there was no *j*
jurisdiction under s 38(6) to order such residential assessment. Having held that
she had jurisdiction, Hogg J then considered the exercise of her supposed
discretionary power. She weighed the factors put forward by the local authority,
including the estimated cost of £24,000 and the consequent use of its resources.
She also took into account the delay involved in such assessment. She weighed
these factors against the recommendations from the social workers, the

a psychologist and the guardian ad litem that residential assessment would be of value and, indeed, essential if the parents were to have any hope of keeping T. She decided in the exercise of her discretion that the proposed residential assessment should take place, broadly on the grounds that, in view of the unexplained injuries to T, there was no possibility that the court would allow T to live with his parents unless the residential assessment demonstrated that there was no unacceptable risk in so doing: the decision by the local authority not to
b have such an assessment effectively pre-empted the court's decision at the final hearing of the local authority's application for a care order.

The local authority appealed to the Court of Appeal (Butler-Sloss, Waite and Roch LJJ). The primary ground of appeal was that the judge had no jurisdiction to make the order. Butler-Sloss LJ (with whom the other Lords Justices agreed)
c held that the Court of Appeal was bound by its earlier decision in *Re M (minors) (interim care order: directions)* and allowed the appeal. But she was plainly unhappy at the result. Having expressed a hope in *Re M (minors) (interim care order: directions)* that a local authority would normally pay attention to a judge's decision that an assessment was necessary because of the spirit of co-operation between the local authority and the court inherent in the machinery of the 1989
d Act, such co-operation had not taken place in the present case. She expressed the view that at some stage your Lordships' House might have to reconsider the true construction of this section.

T's parents appeal against that decision. Your Lordships are therefore faced with a short, but important, point on the construction of s 38(6).
e

Before considering the exact point at issue, it is important to put s 38(6) in context. Before the passing of the 1989 Act, the court, in the exercise of its wardship jurisdiction, retained a degree of control over its wards, even if the child was in the care of the local authority. Due to the decision of your Lordships'
f House in *A v Liverpool City Council* [1981] 2 All ER 385, [1982] AC 363, those powers were, as a matter of practice, limited so as to be exercised only when there were gaps in the statutory regime or in support of the powers of the local authority. Apart from such cases, it was the local authority who had the power and the duty to make decisions as to the welfare of the child in its care. This approach was strengthened by the 1989 Act, which by s 100 expressly excludes
g the wardship jurisdiction in certain cases.

Part IV of the Act contains a code regulating care and supervision orders (public law cases). Section 31 provides that the court may make a care or supervision order on the application of a local authority or of a very limited class of other applicants. The order, if made, places the child in the care of the local
h authority. But a final order can only be made if the threshold laid down by s 31(2) is crossed, ie the court is satisfied that the child is suffering or is likely to suffer significant harm and that such harm is attributable either to the care being given to the child not being what it would be reasonable to expect a parent to give to him or to the fact that the child is beyond parental control.

j There are three points to note about a final care order under s 31. First, it is the court which has to decide whether or not to make a care order. Second, before the court can make an order it has to be satisfied that the harm being suffered or anticipated is attributable to the actual or anticipated care being received by the child, an issue likely to be dominated by the evidence as to the abilities and conduct of the parents and the relationship between the child and those parents. Third, the threshold can be crossed where the harm is due to the child being

beyond parental control, an issue on which the relationship between the child
and his parents is central.

In many cases, including the present, the determination of the question
whether the court should make a final care order under s 31 requires information
to be gathered as to the child's circumstances and for that information to be
placed before the court to enable it to make its decision. But there are many cases
where the child will be at risk in the period pending final determination of the
application for a care order. To meet this need, s 38 provides for the making of
an interim care order where proceedings for a care order under s 31 are
adjourned. The threshold applicable to interim care orders is lower than that laid
down by s 31(2) for final orders: the court only has to be satisfied that 'there are
reasonable grounds for believing' that the requirements of s 31(2) are satisfied. If
so satisfied, the court may make an interim care order of limited duration,
initially for not more than eight weeks and on any renewal for not more than a
further four weeks.

The effect of a care order is laid down by s 33. In general, this section applies
as much to interim care orders as to final orders since the words 'a care order' are
defined to include both: s 31(11). When a care order is made, s 33 requires the
local authority to receive and keep the child in its care: sub-s (1). The local
authority is given parental responsibility for the child and (with certain
exceptions) the power to determine the extent to which parents and others
having parental responsibility for the child are allowed to meet such
responsibilities: sub-s (3).

Therefore the context in which s 38(6) has to be considered is this. The child
is in the care of the local authority under an interim care order pending the
decision by the court whether or not to make a final care order. Under the
interim care order the decision-making power as to the care, residence and
general welfare of the child is vested in the local authority, not in the court.
However, for the purpose of making its ultimate decision whether to grant a full
care order, the court will need the help of social workers, doctors and others as
to the child and his circumstances. Information and assessments from these
sources are necessary not only to determine whether the s 31 threshold has been
crossed (including the cause of the existing or anticipated harm to the child from
its existing circumstances) but also in exercising its discretion whether or not to
make a final care order. It is the practice of the courts to require the local
authority seeking a final care order to put forward a care plan for the court to
consider in exercising such discretion. Section 38(6) deals with the interaction
between the powers of the local authority entitled to make decisions as to the
child's welfare in the interim and the needs of the court to have access to the
relevant information and assessments so as to be able to make the ultimate
decision. It must always be borne in mind that in exercising its jurisdiction under
the Act, the court's function is investigative and non-adversarial: *Re L (a minor)*
(police investigation: privilege) [1996] 2 All ER 78 at 84–85, [1996] 2 WLR 395 at 401–
402.

Against that background, I turn to consider the construction of s 38(6), which
I have already quoted. It is important also to refer to s 38(7), which provides:

'A direction under subsection (6) may be to the effect that there is to be—
(a) no such examination or assessment; or (b) no such examination or
assessment unless the court directs otherwise.'

a There are two possible constructions of sub-ss (6) and (7), one narrow, the other purposive and broader. The Court of Appeal in *Re M (minors) (interim care order: directions)* [1996] 3 FCR 137 adopted the narrow view. They held that the words 'other assessment of the child' had to be construed as ejusdem generis with the words 'medical or psychiatric examination'. They attached decisive importance to the fact that the subsection only refers to the examination or assessment 'of the
b child' and makes no reference to the examination or assessment of any other person in relation to the child. They further held that for the court to order a residential assessment of the parents and child together at a specified place would involve the court in an unwarranted usurpation by the court of the local authority's power (as the authority having parental responsibility under the interim care order) to regulate where the child is to reside. In addition to
c supporting the arguments of the Court of Appeal in *Re M (minors) (interim care order: directions)*, Mr Harris QC for the local authority in the present appeal submitted that Parliament cannot have intended the court to have power to require the local authority against its own judgment to expend scarce resources: he submitted that the local authority is the only body which can properly assess
d how such resources are to be allocated as between the social services and the other services it has to provide and as between the various calls on its social services budget.

My Lords, I cannot accept this narrow construction of the subsection. The Act should be construed purposively so as to give effect to the underlying intentions of Parliament. As I have sought to demonstrate, the dividing line between the
e functions of the court on the one hand and the local authority on the other is that a child in interim care is subject to control of the local authority, the court having no power to interfere with the local authority's decisions save in specified cases. The cases where, despite that overall control, the court is to have power to intervene are set out, inter alia, in sub-ss (6) and (7). The purpose of sub-s (6) is
f to enable the court to obtain the information necessary for its own decision, notwithstanding the control over the child which in all other respects rests with the local authority. I therefore approach the subsection on the basis that the court is to have such powers to override the views of the local authority as are necessary to enable the court to discharge properly its function of deciding
g whether or not to accede to the local authority's application to take the child away from its parents by obtaining a care order. To allow the local authority to decide what evidence is to go before the court at the final hearing would be in many cases, including the present, to allow the local authority by administrative decision to pre-empt the court's judicial decision.

h This broad approach is supported by consideration of sub-s (7) which does not appear to have been drawn to the attention of the Court of Appeal either in *Re M (minors) (interim care order: directions)* or in the present case. Subsection (7) confers on the court the power to prohibit an examination or assessment which the local authority is proposing to make. It is manifestly directed to the type of conduct by
j social services revealed by the Cleveland Inquiry (Report of the inquiry into Child Abuse in Cleveland 1987 (1988) (Cm 412)), ie repeated interviews and assessments of the child and his parents which are detrimental to the child. This negative control by the court cannot have been intended to be limited to cases where the child, and only the child, is to be assessed. If it is to be fully effective to prevent damage to the child, the power under sub-s (7) must also extend to cases where it is proposed to assess the relationship between the parents and the child.

I am not convinced by the reasons which persuaded the Court of Appeal in
Re M (minors) (interim care order: directions) to adopt the narrow construction
limiting the ambit of the section to assessments of the child alone, such
assessments to be of the same type as medical or psychiatric examinations. First,
I can see no reason for the application of the ejusdem generis principle. What is
the genus?   Subsection (6) refer not to the 'medical psychiatric or other
examination' of the child but to 'other *assessment*' of the child. Some assessments,
even if confined to the child itself, may not involve any examination of that child,
yet plainly such an assessment is authorised by the subsection. I can find no genus
to which the principle can apply.

Next, it is true that sub-ss (6) and (7) only refer to the assessment 'of the child'
and not, as is proposed in the present case, a joint assessment of the child and the
parents, including the parents' attitude and behaviour towards the child. But it is
impossible to assess a young child divorced from his environment.   The
interaction between the child and his parents or other persons looking after him
is an essential element in making any assessment of the child. This is shown
particularly clearly by cases in which the courts have to decide whether the
threshold requirements of s 31 are satisfied because of the harm to the child that
is likely to be suffered because the child is beyond parental control. How can the
court determine that issue without considering the relationship between the
child and the parents? The court has no power to order the parents to take part
in any assessment against their wishes, any more than, as the final words of sub-s
(6) show, the court can order the child to do so if the child is capable of making
an informed decision. But what the interests of justice require is not a power to
compel the parent to take part in such assessment but a power in the court to
override the powers over the child which the local authority would otherwise
enjoy under the interim care order. If the narrower construction were to be
adopted the local authority could simply refuse to allow the child to take part in
any assessment with his parents.

The Court of Appeal in *Re M (minors) (interim care order: directions)* were much
influenced by the consideration that by making an order for residential
assessment at a defined place the court would be interfering with the local
authority's power under s 23 to fix the child's place of residence. It has been
decided by the Court of Appeal in *Re L (a minor) (interim care order)* [1996] 2 FCR
706 that the court, in making an interim care order, has no power to impose
conditions on the care order as to where the child should reside. *Re L (a minor)*
(interim care order) raised no question on the powers of the court to order
residential assessments under s 38(6) but Ward LJ ([1996] 2 FCR 706 at 711–712)
expressed concluded views on this question which the Court of Appeal in *Re M*
(minors) (interim care order: directions) followed. Ward LJ said that the court had
no power to order a residential assessment at a specified place. Millett LJ, whilst
agreeing with Ward LJ on the only issue before the court, expressed the view that
a judge could impose 'a condition which is consequential upon the giving of
directions for a residential assessment under section 38(6) ...' I can attach no
weight, one way or the other, to these obiter dicta. Ward LJ does not seem to
have appreciated that the whole purpose of s 38(6) is to override the powers
which, apart from it, the local authority would have under an interim care order
to refuse to permit any examination or assessment. He makes no reference to
s 38(7).

Mr Harris sought to develop the argument by saying that, if the court could
order residential assessment at a specified place, that would override the duties of

a the local authority as to the placement of children within their care imposed under s 23(2). The conditions under which such placement can be made are further regulated by regulations made by the Secretary of State (Arrangements for Placement of Children (General) Regulations 1991, SI 1991/890, and Placement of Children with Parents etc Regulations 1991, SI 1991/893). I do not accept this submission. Section 23 and the regulations made thereunder are

b concerned with placements made by the local authority with foster parents and others: s 38 is not dealing with that issue at all. It is providing for the assessment of the child for the purpose of assisting the court in its assessment of the child's best interests. An order specifying where and with whom that assessment is to take place is not 'a placement' within s 23 at all.

c Much the most powerful of Mr Harris's submissions is that based on the expenditure of scarce resources by the local authority in the carrying out of an expensive assessment. In the overwhelming majority of care cases, the parties are in straitened circumstances and there is no one to pay for any examination or assessment under s 38(6) other than the local authority. In the present case, the proposed residential assessment is going to cost some £24,000 and the local

d authority, taking as it does a gloomy view of the result of the assessment, considers that expenditure on that scale is not a sensible allocation of its limited resources, a decision which it is far better qualified to take than the court. I accept the force of this submission but it proves too much. Mr Harris was not able to argue that if the court directed a medical examination of the child himself, which examination would be very expensive, the local authority could refuse to carry it

e out simply on the grounds of the expense involved and the unwise allocation of limited resources. In such a case, it will be for the court to take into account in deciding whether or not to make an order for the medical examination the expense that it involves. If that is so, the issue of resources cannot affect the proper construction of sub-s (6). The consideration of the resource consequences

f of making the order must be the same whether the court is making an order for medical examination of the child or an order for the other assessment of the child. Therefore it is impossible to construe s 38(6) in the narrow sense simply because the court is less suitable than the local authority to assess the financial considerations.

g In my judgment, therefore, sub-ss (6) and (7) of s 38 of the Act are to be broadly construed. They confer jurisdiction on the court to order or prohibit any assessment which involves the participation of the child and is directed to providing the court with the material which, in the view of the court, is required to enable it to reach a proper decision at the final hearing of the application for a full care order. In exercising its discretion whether to order any particular

h examination or assessment, the court will take into account the cost of the proposed assessment and the fact that local authorities' resources are notoriously limited.

Since the point does not directly arise for decision in the present case, I express no final view on whether, on an application under s 38(6), it is appropriate for the

j court to enter into a detailed consideration of the resources of the local authority and the allocation of such resources. As at present advised the course adopted by Hogg J in the present case seems to me entirely satisfactory. In exercising her discretion she took into account the substantial cost of the proposed residential assessment and the fact that the local authority had limited resources to allocate. Having weighed that factor in the balance, she exercised her discretion to make the order sought. Mr Harris argued that this exercise of her discretion was

erroneous in that the judge ought to have insisted on having fuller evidence as to
the resources available to the local authority to meet the cost of the residential
assessment.   This submission is plainly ill-founded.   Whether or not it is
appropriate for the judge to consider in such cases the allocation of resources by
the local authority, it was for the local authority to put before the judge any
evidence they wished her to consider. They cannot be heard to complain if she
exercised her discretion on the basis of the only evidence put before her.

For these reasons I would allow the appeal and restore the order of Hogg J.

LORD GRIFFITHS. My Lords, I have had the advantage of reading in draft the
speech prepared by my noble and learned friend Lord Browne-Wilkinson. For
the reasons he has given, I, too, would allow this appeal.

LORD LLOYD OF BERWICK. My Lords, I have had the advantage of reading
in draft the speech prepared by my noble and learned friend Lord
Browne-Wilkinson. For the reasons he has given, I, too, would allow this appeal.

LORD NICHOLLS OF BIRKENHEAD. My Lords, I have had the advantage of
reading a draft of the speech of my noble and learned friend Lord
Browne-Wilkinson. For the reasons he has given, I, too, would allow this appeal.

LORD HOPE OF CRAIGHEAD. My Lords, for the reasons given in the speech
to be delivered by my noble and learned friend Lord Browne-Wilkinson, which I
have read in draft and with which I agree, I, too, would allow this appeal.

Appeal allowed.

Celia Fox   Barrister.

a   # Forbes v Wandsworth Health Authority

COURT OF APPEAL, CIVIL DIVISION

STUART-SMITH, EVANS AND ROCH LJJ

b
22, 23 JANUARY, 14 MARCH 1996

Limitation of action – Personal injury claim – Plaintiff's knowledge – Date of
plaintiff's knowledge that injury was significant – Date on which plaintiff first had
knowledge that injury attributable to defendant's act or omission – Whether action
c   *statute-barred – Exercise of discretion by court – Limitation Act 1980, ss 11, 14, 33.*

In October 1982 the plaintiff, who had a long history of circulatory problems, was
admitted to hospital for a by-pass operation on his left leg. The operation was not
a success, nor was a second operation carried out at 11.45 am the following day,
d   and in order to prevent gangrene and save the plaintiff's life, the leg was
amputated. In June 1991 the plaintiff consulted a solicitor, through whom, in
October 1992, the advice of a vascular surgeon was obtained that the delay in
initiating action to restore the blood supply to the plaintiff's leg following
occlusion of the graft had caused irreversible muscle ischaemia resulting in the
e   amputation. On 10 December 1992 the plaintiff issued proceedings against the
defendant health authority, claiming damages in respect of the negligent failure
to perform the second operation sooner. The health authority contended that
the plaintiff's claim had arisen more than three years before the issue of
proceedings and that his cause of action was accordingly time-barred under
ss 11(4)(b)[a] and 14(1)[b] of the Limitation Act 1980, which provided that the time
f   limit for actions for personal injuries was three years from the date of knowledge
of the person injured, which was defined as the date on which the plaintiff first
had knowledge (a) that the injury was significant, and (b) that it was attributable
in whole or in part to the act or omission which was alleged to constitute
negligence. The judge determined the limitation question as a preliminary issue
g   in favour of the plaintiff, holding that until he received the advice of the surgeon
in October 1992 the plaintiff had no actual knowledge because he had no reason
to suspect that the removal of his leg was due to the failure to carry out the
second operation sooner; and that he had no constructive knowledge within the
meaning of s 14(3)[c] of the 1980 Act because it would not have been reasonable to
expect him (taking account of his position, circumstances, character and
h   intelligence) to seek suitable medical advice and thereby acquire the relevant
knowledge before he in fact did. The judge further held that, if he had come to a
contrary conclusion, he would have exercised his discretion in the plaintiff's
favour to disapply the three-year limitation period under s 33[d] of the 1980 Act.
Following the trial of the preliminary issue, the plaintiff died and his wife was
j   substituted as plaintiff. The defendant health authority appealed to the Court of
Appeal.

---

a   Section 11(4)(b) is set out at p 885 *a*, post
b   Section 14(1) is set out at p 885 *b*, post
c   Section 14(3) is set out at p 885 *d*, post
d   Section 33, so far as material, is set out at p 892 *f* to *j*, post

Held – (1) For the purposes of s 14(1) of the 1980 Act the plaintiff knew that his
injury, namely the amputation of his leg, was significant within a very short time
of the operation, since that was not the inevitable consequence of the operations
performed on him. He did not, though, know that that injury was attributable to
the omission to carry out the second operation sooner until he received the
surgeon's advice in 1992. It followed that the judge had been correct in holding
that the plaintiff had no actual knowledge until that date. However, where a
plaintiff expected that an operation would be successful and it was not, with the
result that he sustained a major injury, a reasonable man would take advice
reasonably promptly if he was minded to make a claim and if he did not, he would
be fixed with constructive knowledge of the matters set out in s 14(1). It followed
that (Roch LJ dissenting), the plaintiff should have sought expert medical advice
12 to 18 months after he came out of hospital, by which time he would have had
time to overcome his shock and take stock of his disability and its consequences.
Accordingly, the plaintiff did have constructive knowledge of the relevant facts
and therefore the action was not commenced within the limitation period (see
p 885 *f j* to p 886 *a d e*, p 889 *b* to *d j* to p 890 *b j*, p 891 *j*, p 896 *d e*, p 897 *e* to *h*, p 899 *j*
and p 900 *c*, post).

(2) (Per Stuart-Smith and Evans LJJ) The court would not, however, exercise
its discretion under s 33 of the 1980 Act to disapply the limitation period, having
regard to the potentially serious prejudice to the defendant if the action was
permitted to proceed after such long delay, by reason of the inability to now
locate relevant medical records and witnesses, the fading of memories, the
difficulty for expert witnesses of placing themselves into the standard of medical
practice of 14 years before and the fact that the plaintiff's case was supported by
scanty evidence and had only modest prospects of success. The appeal would
accordingly be allowed (see p 892 *a*, p 893 *d e h j*, p 894 *b j*, p 895 *g* and p 900 *a b*,
post); *Dale v British Coal Corp* [1992] PIQR P373 applied.

Per curiam. It is difficult to see how the individual character and intelligence
of the plaintiff in a personal injury case can be relevant when the court is
considering whether the plaintiff had constructive knowledge within the
meaning of s 14(3)(b) of the 1980 Act that the injury was significant and
attributable to the act or omission alleged to constitute negligence (see p 891 *f*,
p 899 *c* to *f* and p 901 *c* to *f*, post); dictum of Purchas LJ in *Nash v Eli Lilly & Co*,
Berger v Eli Lilly & Co [1993] 4 All ER 383 at 399 doubted.

Notes

For limitation period in personal injury actions and date of plaintiff's knowledge
for purposes of the application of the limitation period, see 28 *Halsbury's Laws* (4th
edn) paras 691–692.

For court's powers to override the limitation period in personal injury actions,
see ibid para 684, and for cases on the subject, see 32(2) *Digest* (2nd reissue) 449–
461, 3408–3441.

For the Limitation Act 1980, ss 11, 14, 33, see 24 *Halsbury's Statutes* (4th edn)
(1989 reissue) 657, 661, 686.

Cases referred to in judgments

Bolam v Friern Hospital Management Committee [1957] 2 All ER 118, [1957] 1 WLR
582.
Broadley v Guy Clapham & Co [1994] 4 All ER 439, CA.
Dale v British Coal Corp [1992] PIQR P373, CA.
Davis v Ministry of Defence (1985) Times, 7 August, [1985] CA Transcript 413.

a *Dobbie v Medway Health Authority* [1994] 4 All ER 450, [1994] 1 WLR 1234, CA.
Hallam-Eames v Merrett (1995) Times, 25 January, [1995] CA Transcript 11.
Jones v Liverpool Health Authority (1995) 30 BMLR 1, CA.
Lye v Marks & Spencer plc (1988) Times, 15 February, [1988] CA Transcript 97.
Nash v Eli Lilly & Co, Berger v Eli Lilly & Co [1993] 4 All ER 383, [1993] 1 WLR 782, CA.
b *R v Bowen* [1996] 4 All ER 837, CA.
R v Hurst [1995] 1 Cr App R 82, CA.
Smith v West Lancashire Health Authority [1995] PIQR P514, CA.
Wilkinson v Ancliff (BLT) Ltd [1986] 3 All ER 427, [1986] 1 WLR 1352, CA.

c **Interlocutory appeal**

By notice dated 23 January 1995 the defendant, Wandsworth Health Authority, appealed from the decision of Judge Peter Baker QC, sitting as a deputy judge of the High Court, made on 11 August 1994, that the claim by the plaintiff, Mr Nelson Vernon Dugald Forbes, for damages for medical negligence was not *d* statute-barred on the grounds that it was commenced outside the three-year limitation period specified by s 11 of the Limitation Act 1980. The plaintiff died on 5 February 1995 and his wife, Mrs Jean Mavis Cecilia Forbes, was substituted as plaintiff pursuant to RSC Ord 15, r 7 on 2 August 1995. The facts are set out in the judgment of Stuart-Smith LJ.

e *Christopher Limb* (instructed by *Heptonstalls*, Goole) for the plaintiff.
Martin Spencer (instructed by *Capsticks*) for the defendant.

Cur adv vult

f 14 March 1996. The following judgments were delivered.

STUART-SMITH LJ. This is an appeal from a ruling on a preliminary issue of Judge Baker QC, sitting as a deputy judge of the High Court on 11 August 1994, that the plaintiff's claim is not statute-barred under the Limitation Act 1980. The action concerns an allegation of medical negligence in relation to the treatment *g* of Nelson Forbes (the deceased) who died pending this appeal on 5 February 1995. It relates to the treatment received by the deceased during his admission to the defendant's hospital in October 1982. Mrs Forbes, his widow and personal representative, was substituted as plaintiff under RSC Ord 15, r 7 on 2 August 1995.

h   The writ was issued on 10 December 1992, more than seven years after expiry of the primary limitation period. The question whether the action is statute-barred depends upon whether the date of knowledge of the deceased as defined in s 14 of the 1980 Act was within three years of the issue of the writ. If it was not, then the question arises whether s 11 of the 1980 Act should be disapplied, having regard to the provisions of s 33.
j   The judge, who in addition to the affidavit evidence, heard oral evidence from the deceased and Mrs Forbes, held that the deceased had no actual or constructive knowledge within the meaning of s 14 until he had, through his solicitors, received the advice of a vascular surgeon in October 1992. He therefore decided the issue in the plaintiff's favour. He expressed the view that had he reached a contrary conclusion he would have exercised his discretion under s 33 in favour of the plaintiff.

The deceased was 56 when he was admitted to the defendant's hospital on 16
October 1982. He had a long history of circulatory problems, including two
previous by-pass operations, one in each leg. These operations were carried out
in 1975 and 1978; they were successfully carried out by Mr Gillespie. It was
because of these previous successful operations that the deceased, who then lived
in Yorkshire, wished to be treated again by Mr Gillespie, and he was therefore
transferred to the defendant's hospital.

There is uncertainty as to the precise date, whether it was 24 or 25 October,
that a further by-pass operation was attempted by Mr Gillespie. Nothing turns
on the precise date, and I shall take the date of the first operation as 24 October.
It was not successful and a second operation was carried out at 11.45 am the next
day, 25 October. Unfortunately that, too, was not successful. The deceased was
told that in order to prevent gangrene, and save his life, it was necessary to
amputate the leg. He eventually agreed to this step and the operation was carried
out on 5 November 1982. It is clear that if he had not had the operation the leg
would probably have had to be amputated in due course in any event.

It is not alleged that the decision to operate or the decision to amputate was
wrong. The sole allegation is that it was negligent not to perform the second
operation sooner, specifically as soon as possible after 5 pm on 24 October when
no pulses could be felt in the deceased's left foot and the foot was cool. It is
alleged that if Mr Gillespie had operated sooner, the amputation could have been
avoided. The statement of claim does not explain why this should be so and the
information provided by the plaintiff's solicitor as to the basis of the case is sparse
in the extreme. He merely states in his affidavit that he obtained a report in
October 1992 from an unnamed vascular surgeon and—

> 'the report concluded that the medical staff employed by the defendant
> delayed, following the occlusion of the graft (on 24 October) in initiating
> action to restore the blood supply such that irreversible muscle ischaemia
> resulted in amputation'.

It must, I think, be the plaintiff's case that if the second operation had been
performed sooner, it would have had a good chance of success. But if it too failed,
despite more prompt action, it would seem that the leg would have required
amputation.

It was not until 1991 that the deceased took any steps to obtain professional
advice. By that time, Mrs Forbes was finding the strain of looking after the
deceased to be increasingly arduous. She went to stay with her daughter, who
suggested that it might be possible to obtain some money to help with his care.
She suggested consulting a solicitor. Somewhat reluctantly it seems, the
deceased agreed to this and Mr Burman, the plaintiff's solicitor, was consulted on
26 June 1991. He took steps to obtain the medical records which were available
and instructed a vascular surgeon to advise on the basis of those records. His
report was provided in October 1992.

Section 11 of the 1980 Act provides, so far as is relevant, as follows:

> '(1) This section applies to any action for damages for negligence ... where
> the damages claimed by the plaintiff for the negligence ... consist of or
> include damages in respect of personal injuries ...
> (3) An action to which this section applies shall not be brought after the
> expiration of the period applicable in accordance with subsections (4) or (5)
> below.

a
'(4) Except where subsection (5) below applies, the period applicable is three years from—(a) the date on which the cause of action accrued; or (b) the date of knowledge (if later) of the person injured ...'

Section 14 provides, so far as is relevant:

b
'(1) In sections 11 and 12 of this Act references to a person's date of knowledge are references to the date on which he first had knowledge of the following facts—(a) that the injury in question was significant; and (b) that the injury was attributable in whole or in part to the act or omission which is alleged to constitute negligence, nuisance or breach of duty ... and knowledge that any acts or omissions did or did not, as a matter of law, involve negligence, nuisance or breach of duty is irrelevant.
c
(2) For the purposes of this section an injury is significant if the person whose date of knowledge is in question would reasonably have considered it sufficiently serious to justify his instituting proceedings for damages against a defendant who did not dispute liability and was able to satisfy a judgment.
d
(3) For the purposes of this section a person's knowledge includes knowledge which he might reasonably have been expected to acquire—(a) from facts observable or ascertainable by him; or (b) from facts ascertainable by him with the help of medical or other appropriate expert advice which it is reasonable for him to seek; but a person shall not be fixed under this subsection with knowledge of a fact ascertainable only with the help of
e
expert advice so long as he has taken all reasonable steps to obtain (and, where appropriate, to act on) that advice.'

The judge held that the plaintiff had no actual knowledge because he had no reason to suspect or think that the removal of his leg was due to the act or omission of the defendant that was alleged to constitute negligence. In this case
f
the negligence is said to consist of an omission, namely to operate sooner than in fact was done. It is said that this delay, from about 5 pm (or such later time as is appropriate) until 11.45 am the next day, was the cause of the injury and that delay was negligent. It is not sufficient that the plaintiff knew that he had lost his leg and that there was in fact a period of time between the first and second operation.
g
Mr Limb, on behalf of the plaintiff, argued before the judge and in this court that the plaintiff did not even know that he was injured (within s 11(4)) or that the injury was significant (within s 14(1)(a)) until he obtained the medical advice in 1991. He submits that there is a problem in medical negligence cases where the plaintiff is diseased or injured prior to treatment and does not necessarily expect
h
to be free from disease or injury after treatment. The disease or pre-existing injury may continue or worsen after treatment and such deterioration may be no more than a natural continuation of the problem. The difficulty in determining what amounts to a significant injury is illustrated in *Nash v Eli Lilly & Co, Berger v Eli Lilly & Co* [1993] 4 All ER 383, [1993] 1 WLR 782. In that case, which was
j
concerned with the drug Opren, it was said by the Court of Appeal that 'until the degree of photosensitivy, for example, was sufficient to indicate that the drug was causing a significant injury, namely, an effect completely outside that of an acceptable side effect, it could not reasonably be said that the patient was aware of a "significant injury"' (see [1993] 4 All ER 383 at 391, [1993] 1 WLR 782 at 791). Whatever may be the position with unwanted side effects of drugs, which may be expected to a greater or lesser extent, I have no doubt that Mr Spencer, on

behalf of the defendant, is right in submitting that the injury in this case was the
amputation—as pleaded in the statement of claim—and that it was a significant
one.

This point was considered by the Court of Appeal in *Dobbie v Medway Health
Authority* [1994] 4 All ER 450 at 463, [1994] 1 WLR 1234 at 1248, where a similar
argument was advanced. Steyn LJ said:

> 'The simple answer to this construction is to be found in the ordinary
> meaning of the words of s 14(1). The contextual meaning of "injury" in
> s 14(1) is a personal injury without any further gloss other than the express
> definition of "significant" in s 14(2).'

In *Broadley v Guy Clapham* [1994] 4 All ER 439 at 443 Turner J, stating the test
for what amounted to an injury, said '[the plaintiff] did know, that what she was
suffering from was something other than the direct and inevitable consequence
of the operation that was performed'. That may well be a sufficient test in this
type of case, for it was certainly not an inevitable consequence of the operations
on 24 and 25 October that the plaintiff would lose his leg. But it does not cover
the case where the plaintiff is advised to have his leg removed, but it is said that
the advice was negligent. It seems to me that the injury is still the loss of the leg,
the cause of the injury was the surgeon's advice. In my opinion, therefore, the
plaintiff knew of the injury and knew that it was significant within a very short
time of the operation.

Did the plaintiff know prior to receipt of the opinion by the vascular surgeon
in 1992 that the loss of his leg was attributable in whole or in part to the omission
to operate sooner than 11.45 am on the second day?

The judge's approach is supported by two decisions of this court. The first is
Smith v West Lancashire Health Authority [1995] PIQR P514. On 12 November 1981
the plaintiff sustained injury to his right hand. A doctor employed by the
defendant health authority diagnosed an uncomplicated fracture to the ring
finger, but failed to diagnose a fracture of the little finger or dislocation of the ring
finger. Conservative treatment was prescribed. On 5 January 1982 the plaintiff
had to undergo an urgent operation for the open reduction of the fracture
dislocation. Delay was the problem, as in this case. Russell LJ, with whose
judgment Wall J agreed, said (at P517):

> 'As earlier indicated, the omission alleged in this case was essentially the
> omission to operate promptly. It was that omission which allegedly
> constituted negligence, together with the failure properly to diagnose.
> When did the patient first have knowledge of that omission? The reality is
> that he did not know that there had been an omission to operate at all until
> he was so advised by Mr Downie to that effect. True, he knew that he had
> not had an operation on or about November 12, 1981, but that knowledge
> cannot, in my judgment, be knowledge of an omission "which is alleged to
> constitute negligence". One cannot know of an omission without knowing
> what it is that is omitted. In this case, that was an operation to reduce the
> fracture dislocations, as opposed to conservative treatment. Simply to tell
> the plaintiff that the first course of treatment had not worked, is not the same
> as imbuing the plaintiff with a knowledge of an omission to operate.'

The second case is *Hallam-Eames v Merrett* (1995) Times, 25 January.
Hoffmann LJ gave the judgment of the court, consisting of Bingham MR and

a Saville LJ. After reciting the trial judge's construction of the similar provision contained in s 14A(8)(a), he said:

> 'In our judgment this is an over-simplification of the reasoning in *Broadley* and *Dobbie*. If all that was necessary was that a plaintiff should have known that the damage was attributable to an act or omission of the defendant, the statute would have said so. Instead, it speaks of the damage being
> *b* attributable to the act or omission which is alleged to constitute negligence. In other words, the act or omission of which the plaintiff must have knowledge must be that which is causally relevant for the purposes of an allegation of negligence.'

c And he said:

> 'The plaintiff does not have to know that he has a cause of action or that the defendant's acts can be characterised in law as negligent or as falling short of some standard of professional or other behaviour. But, as Hoffmann LJ said in *Broadley*, the words "which is alleged to constitute negligence" serve
> *d* to *identify* the facts of which the plaintiff must have knowledge. He must have known the facts which can fairly be described as constituting the negligence of which he complains. It may be that knowledge of such facts will also serve to bring home to him the fact that the defendant has been negligent or at fault. But that is not in itself a reason for saying that he need not have known them.' (My emphasis.)

e

Mr Spencer submitted that was too narrow a construction. First, he referred to a dictum of May LJ in *Davis v Ministry of Defence* (1985) Times, 7 August, where he rejected the construction that 'attributable' was the same as 'caused by'. He said it means 'capable of being attributed to', in that case the working conditions
f to which he was exposed by the respondents. This approach was approved and adopted by the Court of Appeal in *Wilkinson v Ancliff (BLT) Ltd* [1986] 3 All ER 427, [1986] 1 WLR 1352 (Slade and Croom-Johnson LJJ).

So far so good; but it does not answer the question here. Second, he relied on certain dicta in the judgments of the Court of Appeal in *Dobbie*'s case. In that case the plaintiff had her breast removed; shortly afterwards she learned that the lump
g in it was not cancerous. So it is clear that she had actual knowledge that a mistake had been made. Bingham MR said ([1994] 4 All ER 450 at 456, [1994] 1 WLR 1234 at 1240):

> 'It cannot plausibly be suggested that the words "act or omission" import
> *h* any requirement that such act or omission should be actionable or tortious, since that would stultify the closing words of s 14(1) and would moreover flout the recommendation on which the legislation was admittedly founded. In *Wilkinson v Ancliff (BLT) Ltd* [1986] 3 All ER 427 at 436, [1986] 1 WLR 1352 at 1362 reference was made to a submission of counsel based on the use of the words "act or omission" rather than "conduct" in s 14(1)(b). I do not
> *j* understand the court to have accepted that submission. But it is customary in discussing tortious liability to refer to acts and omissions, and I do not think the meaning of s 14(1)(b) would be any different had the reference been to conduct. Time starts to run against the claimant when he knows that the personal injury on which he founds his claim is capable of being attributed to something done or not done by the defendant whom he wishes to sue.'

With all respect to Bingham MR, it may well be that acts or omissions of the
defendant can be said to be his conduct; and in that case the defendant's act,
which was subsequently alleged to be negligent, was the removal of the breast;
but it is not easy to see how in the case of an omission this statement gives effect
to the words 'which is alleged to constitute negligence'.

After the passage I have already cited from *Dobbie's* case, Steyn LJ continued
([1994] 4 All ER 450 at 463, [1994] 1 WLR 1234 at 1248):

> 'The word "act" does not by itself describe something which ought not to
> have been done. And it would be impossible to attach a qualitative element
> to "omission" but not to "act".'

Those passages taken at face value do tend to support Mr Spencer's submission
that all that the plaintiff needs to know is that there was a period of time between
the first and second operations, that the second operation was not successful, and
that in consequence of the second operation not being successful, his leg was
amputated.

Next, Mr Spencer submits that on a proper analysis, the facts of this case are
indistinguishable from those in *Jones v Liverpool Health Authority* (1995) 30
BMLR 1. That was a case where the ultimate complaint was delayed treatment
complicated by lack of anticoagulant treatment. The original cause of the
problem arose when an arteriogram was performed on 5 September 1974 and
infection was set up in the plaintiff's leg as the catheter was inserted into his
femoral artery. That was a risk of the operation and was not negligent, although
at first the plaintiff did not realise that. It was not until the plaintiff was advised
by a vascular surgeon in October 1991 (after issue of a writ in 1987) that it was the
delay in taking corrective treatment until an operation on 23 October 1974 and
lack of anticoagulant treatment was eventually established as the basis of the
claim in negligence.

Mr Spencer submits that the non-negligent injury caused by the catheter is
equivalent to the underlying pathology in the present case. That is what required
treatment; Mr Jones knew it was not treated until 23 October 1974, and he knew
it was then unsuccessfully treated in the following year. Those facts, contends Mr
Spencer, are equivalent to the knowledge the deceased had here. He knew the
first operation was unsuccessful, he knew when the second operation was
performed, he knew it had been unsuccessful. But the facts of that case are
complicated by the fact that in 1977 the plaintiff was advised by a surgeon, Mr
Bloor. He said that the insertion of the catheter was not due to negligence, which
was the only issue considered at that stage. He did not deal with the question of
delay at all.

Although it is possible to equate the facts in that case with the present case, it
seems to me that in the judgment of the court, the part played by Mr Bloor was
crucial. Glidewell LJ, with whose judgment Morritt LJ and Sir John May agreed,
said (at 18):

> 'To use Hoffmann LJ's phrase in [*Broadley v Guy Clapham & Co* [1994] 4 All
> ER 439], when the plaintiff received Mr Bloor's report, he knew the facts
> which constitute the essence of his present complaint. What he did not
> know at that stage was that, to use Steyn LJ's phrase in *Dobbie v Medway
> Health Authority* ([1994] 4 All ER 450, [1994] 1 WLR 1234), he had a possible
> cause of action. In my judgment, on the authorities to which I have referred,
> it is clear that knowledge of the latter kind is not necessary to affect the

plaintiff with knowledge for the purposes of s 14(1) and (3). Put another way, if a person has been advised by one consultant, who considers on the information put before him that the plaintiff probably does not have a cause of action, and years later the plaintiff is advised by another consultant that, upon precisely the same facts he has a possible cause of action, he cannot thereafter claim that he did not gain knowledge for the purposes of ss 11 and 14 of the 1980 Act until he received the later opinion.'

In many medical negligence cases the plaintiff will not know that his injury is attributable to the omission of the defendant alleged to constitute negligence, in the sense that it is capable of being attributable to that omission, until he is also told that the defendant has been negligent. But that does not alter the fact that there is a distinction between causation and negligence; the first is relevant to s 14(1); the second is not. The fact that in such cases it may be necessary for the plaintiff also to know of the negligence before he can identify the omission alleged to have been negligent is nothing to the point. It does not mean that he falls foul of the closing words of s 14(1). For these reasons, I consider that the judge was correct in holding that there was no actual knowledge.

The judge dealt with the question of constructive knowledge. He said:

'As to constructive knowledge, the approach, it is submitted, and I agree, is to determine what the plaintiff should have realised or obtained, asking no more of him than is reasonable. That is a standard of reasonableness objective, but must take into account his position, circumstances, character and intelligence. That follows from *Nash v Eli Lilly & Co* [1993] 4 All ER 383, [1993] 1 WLR 782. And so would it have been reasonable to expect the plaintiff to make inquiries before in fact he did? On that issue, the burden is on the defendants to show that he should have done. In my judgment, nothing occurred in the intervening period between his treatment and the approach to solicitors—which may initially, from what I made of the evidence, not even have been, of itself, particularly to launch a negligence action, the approach to solicitors when it was made. It may well be that if the plaintiff had been a dissatisfied or a complaining man he might have started a train of inquiry somewhat earlier, but as I have said, he was a man who had every confidence in those treating him.'

Turning to the words of s 14(3), it is clear that the deceased could reasonably have been expected to acquire the relevant knowledge with the help of suitable medical advice. The real question is, whether it was reasonable for him to seek that advice. If it was, he took no steps at all to do so. One of the problems with the language of s 14(3)(b) is that two alternative courses of action may be perfectly reasonable. Thus it may be perfectly reasonable for a person who is not cured when he hoped to be to say 'Oh well, it is just one of those things. I expect the doctors did their best'; alternatively the explanation for the lack of success may be due to want of care on the part of those in whose charge he was, in which case it would be perfectly reasonable to take a second opinion. And I do not think that the person who adopts the first alternative can necessarily be said to be acting unreasonably. But he is in effect making a choice, either consciously by deciding to do nothing, or unconsciously by in fact doing nothing. Can a person who has effectively made this choice many years later, and without any alteration of circumstances, change his mind and then seek advice which reveals that all along he had a claim? I think not. It seems to me that where, as here, the plaintiff

expected or at least hoped that the operation would be successful and it
manifestly was not, with the result that he sustained a major injury, a reasonable
man of moderate intelligence, such as the deceased, if he thought about the
matter, would say that the lack of success was 'either just one of those things, a
risk of the operation or something may have gone wrong and there may have
been a want of care; I do not know which, but if I am ever to make a claim, I must
find out'.

In my judgment, any other construction would make the 1980 Act unworkable
since a plaintiff could delay indefinitely before seeking expert advice and say, as
the deceased did in this case, I had no occasion to seek it earlier. He would
therefore be able, as of right, to bring the action, no matter how many years had
elapsed. This is contrary to the whole purpose of the 1980 Act which is to prevent
defendants being vexed by stale claims which it is no longer possible to contest.
The primary limitation period in personal injury actions is therefore three years
from the date when the cause of action occurred. This is modified when the
plaintiff does not know, and could not reasonably discover with the assistance of
expert advice, matters essential to his cause of action. If he can bring himself
within the provisions of ss 11(4) and 14 he has an absolute right to bring the action
and no question of discretion arises. Section 33, in my opinion, is designed to give
the court an ultimate discretion in cases such as this, so that it can allow the
plaintiff to sue if it is equitable to do so.

I referred earlier to a subsequent alteration of circumstances. An example of
this would be if the initial injury, though significant, appeared to be not so serious
as to affect the plaintiff's enjoyment of life, but subsequently proved to be much
more serious, the fact that the plaintiff initially did nothing to find out the cause
of the injury should not preclude him; the time to take advice may well have been
when the gravity of the injury became apparent.

Something may turn on the advice or information that the plaintiff is given by
the defendant's employees in whose care he was. If he was deceived or misled
into thinking that nothing had gone wrong, when it was known or suspected that
an error was made, then the plaintiff's inaction in reliance on that advice should
not be held against him. But there is nothing of that sort here. In his evidence
Mr Forbes said that he had confidence in Mr Gillespie and that at no time was it
suggested to him that a mistake had been made or that delay had led to the
amputation. That is hardly surprising because it is clear that Mr Gillespie is still
confident that no mistake was made. And I decline to infer that any of the
defendant's personnel involved thought or suspected that there had been a
mistake. The deceased does not suggest that any explanation for the lack of
success was given to him, other than, as is alleged in para 5 of the defence, Mr
Gillespie had told him prior to the operation that because of the poor state of his
arteries the operation might not be a success.

In my judgment, a reasonable man in the position of the deceased, who knew
that the operation had been unsuccessful, that he had suffered a major injury
which would seriously affect his enjoyment of life in the future, would affect his
employability on the labour market, if he had any, and would impose substantial
burdens on his wife and family in looking after him, if he is minded to make a
claim at any time, should and would take advice reasonably promptly.

I do not think this will result in patients becoming 'action-happy' or in
ambulance chasing solicitors touting for work. Where the injury or disability is
not serious, most patients do not dream of suing unless it is obvious that
something has gone wrong which suggests want of care.

a The judge seems to have thought in the passage I have cited that the fact that nothing occurred between the deceased's return from hospital and his consulting a solicitor in 1991 in some way excused him. I do not think this can be so. Otherwise, a plaintiff could delay indefinitely in seeking advice. Nor do I consider that the fact that the deceased had confidence in Mr Gillespie absolves him. Most patients have confidence in their doctors until they find they have made a b mistake. And, as Mr Spencer pointed out, if the question is raised, has Mr Gillespie made a mistake, one cannot answer that question in the negative by saying that you have confidence in him.

The judge directed himself that the standard of reasonableness was objective, but must take into account his position, circumstances, character and intelligence and cited the judgment of this court in *Nash v Eli Lilly & Co* [1993] 4 All ER 383 at c 399, [1993] 1 WLR 782 at 799, where Purchas LJ said:

'The standard of reasonableness in connection with the observations and/ or the effort to ascertain are therefore finally objective but must be qualified to take into consideration the position, and circumstances and character of the plaintiff. Turning to [s 14(3)(b) of the 1980 Act], this subsection deals
d with facts ascertainable with the help of advice from outside expert sources, which, in the circumstances of the case, it is reasonable for the plaintiff to seek. As the whole of this section is dealing with claims for personal injury the specific reference to medical advice is understandable; but it clearly extends to other experts whom it would be reasonable to expect the plaintiff
e to consult. In considering whether or not the inquiry is, or is not, reasonable, the situation, character and intelligence of the plaintiff must be relevant.'

Like Roch LJ I have difficulty in seeing how the individual character and intelligence of the plaintiff can be relevant in an objective test. Similar problems have arisen in the criminal law in relation to the defence of provocation and f duress. In both these cases there is a dual test: the subjective one, was the accused in fact provoked or overborne by threats to act as he did; and the objective one, would an ordinary person sharing the characteristics of the accused be provoked to act as he did, or in the case of duress, would an ordinary person of reasonable firmness, sharing the accused's characteristics, have given way to the threats. This objective test has given rise to considerable difficulty in recent cases, g especially in the case of duress as to what characteristics are relevant and what are not. The mere fact that an accused is more suggestible, vulnerable or timid than a normal person of his age and sex is not relevant because it undermines the objective test which requires him to be of reasonable firmness of mind (see *R v Hurst* [1995] 1 Cr App R 82); the jury have to consider how a person sharing a h characteristic of the accused, in the sense, for example, that a young person, a pregnant woman or a person suffering a severe personal or mental disability would react. Since the jury may think that such people in general may be more vulnerable to pressure (see also *R v Bowen* [1996] 4 All ER 837).

It does not seem to me that the fact that a plaintiff is more trusting, incurious, j indolent, resigned or uncomplaining by nature can be a relevant characteristic, since this, too, undermines any objective approach.

I have come to the conclusion, therefore, that in the circumstances of this case the deceased did have constructive knowledge. That knowledge could not be attributed to him immediately he came out of hospital; clearly he would have to have time to overcome the shock, take stock of his grave disability and its consequences and seek advice. That would take about 12 to 18 months.

It is not necessary in this case to consider the closing words of s 14(3), since the deceased took no steps to obtain advice.

That being so, it is necessary to consider the effect of s 33 of the 1980 Act. The judge expressed the opinion that had he not found in the plaintiff's favour under s 14, he would have exercised his discretion under s 33 in his favour. This gives rise to the question whether in the circumstances this court must now exercise its discretion afresh, if we differ from the judge on his primary finding, or whether the defendant is appealing against an exercise of discretion, with the result that the restrictive approach that this court adopts to such appeals should apply. But for one feature, this might prove to be a difficult and important question. That feature is the death of Mr Forbes between the trial of the preliminary point and the appeal. That is a new situation which to my mind undoubtedly affects the exercise of discretion under s 33, if for no other reason than that the potential damages recoverable for the benefit of the estate of the deceased are significantly less than they would have been if the deceased were still alive. No damages for pain, suffering and loss of amenity can be recovered for any period after the death, and the claim for future cost of care, aids and appliances, said by Mr Burman in his affidavit to amount to an annual cost of £13,000, will not be recoverable. I adhere to the view I expressed in *Dale v British Coal Corp* [1992] PIQR P373 at P385, with which I understand Steyn LJ to have agreed, though Dillon LJ (at P386) reserved his opinion on the point.

Accordingly, in my opinion, this court must exercise its own discretion in the light of the relevant facts, paying due regard to any findings of fact made by the trial judge. Section 33 of the 1980 Act, so far as is relevant, is in these terms:

'(1) If it appears to the court that it would be equitable to allow an action to proceed having regard to the degree to which—(a) the provisions of section 11 or 12 of this Act prejudice the plaintiff or any person whom he represents; and (b) any decision of the court under this subsection would prejudice the defendant or any person whom he represents; the court may direct that those provisions shall not apply to the action, or shall not apply to any specified cause of action to which the action relates ...

(3) In acting under this section the court shall have regard to all the circumstances of the case and in particular to—(a) the length of, and the reasons for, the delay on the part of the plaintiff; (b) the extent to which, having regard to the delay, the evidence adduced or likely to be adduced by the plaintiff or the defendant is or is likely to be less cogent than if the action had been brought within the time allowed by section 11 or (as the case may be) by section 12 ... (f) the steps, if any, taken by the plaintiff to obtain medical, legal or other expert advice and the nature of any such advice he may have received.

(4) In a case where the person injured died when, because of section 11, he could no longer maintain an action and recover damages in respect of the injury, the court shall have regard in particular to the length of, and the reasons for, the delay on the part of the deceased ...'

The first point that Mr Spencer makes is that s 33 is not relevant at all in the present circumstances and the court has no jurisdiction to exercise its discretion. The plaintiff is now Mrs Forbes, who is suing on behalf of the estate. As such, Mr Spencer submits, that she is not representing persons within sub-s (1)(a). That expression is only apt to deal with a claim under the Fatal Accidents Acts, where *a* the claim is brought for the benefit of identified beneficiaries. Furthermore, he says that an estate is not a person or persons.

Subsection (4), however, clearly contemplates that an action may be brought in respect of personal injuries sustained by a person who is deceased before the claim is brought. I see no reason why it should not equally apply if he dies after an action is brought. Such an action is brought for the benefit of the estate, and *b* ultimately for the benefit of the beneficiaries. Something may turn on the identity of these; if they are not the deceased's dependants, but some charity or other institution like a cats' home, I should be inclined to think that the prejudice was small. But I am prepared to assume in this case that the plaintiff herself as widow is the main beneficiary, and that she has a need for any sums that might be awarded.

c So far as the defendant is concerned, in addition to the inevitable prejudice in losing a limitation defence, a number of specific matters are put forward. First, as a result of certain insurance arrangements which have recently occurred, the health authority will have to bear a greater share of the damages and costs than it would have done previously, when more favourable arrangements existed with *d* the medical defence institutions.

Secondly, medical records, including the operating theatre register, cannot be found. And, although the charts are available, it is no longer possible to identify the nurses on duty during the critical period of 5 pm on 24 October to 11 am on 25 October. The judge said he bore this in mind. But it is difficult to know what weight he attached to it. Since the allegations in the statement of claim relate to *e* this period, and include failure to act by the nursing staff, it seems to me that this is a potentially serious prejudice to the defendant not to be able to call these witnesses. Moreover, it is clear from his statement exhibited to an affidavit of the plaintiff's solicitor that Mr Gillespie now has no recollection of the matter, other than what appears in the records. Mr Gillespie undoubtedly took a very keen *f* interest in this patient, and it seems reasonable to suppose that much nearer the time he would have had a recollection which went further than the records now extant, which do not include the operating theatre register. Although in the defence the defendant justifies its actions in the light of the information recorded in the extant records, particularly where the alleged sin is one of omission and not commission, the defendant is gravely prejudiced by the delay, whereas the *g* plaintiff, who even when the deceased was alive, could have little or no factual input into the case, is not. Her case really depends on the acceptance of the view of the unknown vascular surgeon.

Mr Limb sought to counter this argument by submitting that most medical negligence cases are conducted on the basis that the defendant's witnesses can *h* remember nothing that is not in the contemporary records, and therefore there is no handicap to the defendant in this case since the records, save for the operating register, are extant. I do not agree; that may well be so when there is a very long delay. But, if the claim is made reasonably promptly, the defendant has an opportunity of taking statements from all relevant witnesses who are still *j* available. Their memories can frequently be stimulated by reference to the contemporary records; something which many years later is quite impossible, even if the witnesses can be identified. There is, I think, a striking example of that in this case. Paragraph 11(d) of the defence states that the nursing staff overnight were not able to feel a pulse in the leg, and this is relied upon as a contra-indication to immediate operation. This is based on the hospital notes. Mr Limb said that it would be the evidence of the vascular surgeon that nurses

often made mistakes and think that they can feel pulses when they cannot. Much *a*
may therefore depend on the skill and experience of the nurses involved; but the
defendant cannot identify them. There is a further problem caused by excessive
delay in medical negligence cases. The court is concerned with acceptable
standards of medical practice in 1982. With the best will in the world it is not
always easy, where medical science and practice has progressed over the years,
for experts to put themselves back into the standard of the day, now 14 years ago. *b*
Although in theory this may be a difficulty that affects both sides, in practice it
often presents more difficulty for the defence since recent advances which affect
current opinion have to be ignored. To my mind, the judge, who understandably
did not deal at any length with this aspect of the case because of his view that the
limitation period had not expired, seriously underestimated the evidential
prejudice to the defendant and in this respect I think, if no other, his exercise of *c*
discretion was plainly wrong.

There is a further aspect which is relevant to consideration of the exercise of
discretion under s 33. That is the strength of the plaintiff's case. The judge was
not invited to consider this. But if, as I consider we must, this court must exercise
its discretion afresh, it is a relevant consideration. In *Dale*'s case [1992] PIQR P373 *d*
at P380–P381 I said:

'The first concerns the relevance of the plaintiff's prospects of success in
the action and the evidence necessary to be adduced to establish those
prospects. Although not one of the matters specifically dealt with in
paragraphs (a) to (f) of section 33(3), it is one of the circumstances of the case *e*
which the court should take into account in considering the balance of
hardship. Plainly it is more prejudicial to a plaintiff to be deprived of a cause
of action when it is almost bound to succeed, as for example an injured
passenger in a motor vehicle, than one that looks highly speculative.
Equally, although it is always prejudicial to a defendant to be deprived of a
defence under the Limitation Act, it may be less inequitable or unfair where *f*
the plaintiff has a strong case and more unfair where he has a weak one. But
where as here the limitation issue is tried and determined before the merits
of the claim, the court cannot and should not attempt to determine the
merits on affidavit evidence. All that can be done and should be done is for
the judge to take an overall view of the prospects of success; a judge who is *g*
experienced in this type of litigation should have no difficulty in doing so.'

And in *Nash v Eli Lilly & Co* [1993] 4 All ER 383 at 403, [1993] 1 WLR 782 at 804
Purchas LJ said:

'For the reasons given below we accept that in these cases, if it is shown *h*
that the claim is a poor case lacking in merit, there may be significant and
relevant prejudice to the defendants if the limitation provisions are
disapplied.'

This is especially so where the plaintiff is impecunious, as for example if she is
legally aided, since the defendant cannot recover the costs of a successful defence *j*
(see *Lye v Marks & Spencer plc* (1988) Times, 15 February).

The court can, of course, only take a broad view of the matter at this stage. But
in this case the evidence adduced to support the plaintiff's case is scanty in the
extreme and consists of the plaintiff's solicitor's statement that the report from
the unnamed vascular surgeon 'criticised the delay and stated that if it had not
occurred, on balance of probabilities, the amputation would have been avoided'.

a   In *Dale's* case [1992] PIQR P373 at P382 I said:

'The onus is on the plaintiff to satisfy the court that the primary limitation
period should not apply. He must show that there is evidence which, if
accepted, will establish the necessary ingredients of his cause of action. In
many cases his own evidence on affidavit may suffice. If it is accepted, then
b   he should succeed. It is not normally appropriate for the defendants to try
and counter the evidence at that stage. The matter cannot be tried on
affidavit, and as I have said the best the judge can do is to take a view of the
prospects. But where it is necessary to show that prudent employers
customarily adopt specific precautions not taken by the defendants, or that
the defendants knew or ought to have known of some special risk peculiar to
c   the plaintiff, this may well have to be established by expert evidence, which
should either be exhibited, or at the very least the plaintiff's solicitor should
depose that he is so advised and the source of his information.'

In this case the defendant sought disclosure of the plaintiff's expert's report.
This was refused. The district judge ordered disclosure; but his decision was
d   reversed on appeal, apparently on the basis that the plaintiff should not be
ordered to produce an expert's report without it being in exchange for the
defendant's experts'. The plaintiff is no doubt entitled to take this stand. But if
he does so, he runs the risk that a bald statement culled from it may not carry very
much weight.

e   At most here there was some 17 hours' delay; in practice it was almost certainly
less than that. In a very fully pleaded defence drafted, we are told, from the
records still available, the defendant has set out the factual considerations which
determined their course of conduct. We also have a statement from Mr Gillespie
obtained on behalf of and exhibited as part of the plaintiff's case. Although not
surprisingly he does not deal in terms with the allegation now made, he gives
f   reasons why he is now particularly distressed at the allegation of incompetence
and negligence and by implication refutes them. It must be borne in mind that in
a medical negligence case the plaintiff has to overcome the difficult hurdle of the
Bolam test (see *Bolam v Friern Hospital Management Committee* [1957] 2 All ER 118,
[1957] 1 WLR 582). Taking a broad view of the plaintiff's chances of success on
g   the material available, I have to say that I can only regard them as modest.

For all these reasons, I have come to the conclusion that the court should not
exercise discretion in favour of the plaintiff. I would allow the appeal and
determine the preliminary issue in the defendant's favour.

h   **EVANS LJ.** In an action claiming damages for personal injury caused by
negligence of the defendant, the limitation period is three years from the date on
which the cause of action accrued or, if later, 'the date of knowledge ... of the
person injured' (s 11(4) of the Limitation Act 1980).

The injured person's 'date of knowledge' is defined in s 14(1) of the 1980 Act.
The facts which must be known are (a) that the injury was significant (further
j   defined in sub-s (2)) and—

'(b) that the injury was attributable in whole or in part to the act or
omission which is alleged to constitute negligence ... and knowledge that
any acts or omissions did or did not, as a matter of law, involve negligence
... is irrelevant.'

The plaintiff in any action of this kind has to prove that he suffered injury which was caused by the negligent act or omission of the defendant. Proof of negligence may require evidence of the practices of 'reasonable men' and, where negligence is alleged against a professional man, of the standard reasonably to be expected of a qualified practitioner placed as the defendant was.

The clear wording of sub-s (1) is sufficient to show that the relevant facts are more limited than those which together constitute the cause of action which the plaintiff alleges against the defendant. They are that the injury was 'significant' and that it was attributed to an act or omission of the defendant. The defendant must show that the plaintiff knew these facts in order to establish the limitation defence. To assert that the limitation period does not begin to run until the plaintiff also knows that the alleged act or omission was also actionable or tortious would be to 'stultify the closing words' of the subsection (see *Dobbie v Medway Health Authority* [1994] 4 All ER 450 at 456, [1994] 1 WLR 1234 at 1240 per Bingham MR).

In most personal injury cases the statutory tests are unlikely to be difficult to apply, but it has already become apparent from a number of decided cases that problems do arise where medical negligence is alleged. The present case is an example of this. First, what is meant by 'injury'? Where the plaintiff has undergone surgery with his or her informed consent, the wound is not an 'injury' in a legal sense at all. But amputation is the most explicit form of 'injury' in any other sense, and I agree with Stuart-Smith LJ for the reasons he gives that Mr Forbes suffered significant injury within s 14 when his leg was amputated in the further operation carried out on 5 November 1982.

When he brought this action in December 1992 (he has since died), Mr Forbes alleged that the cause of this injury was the negligence of those who treated him on 24 to 25 October 1982. They operated in the afternoon in order to relieve circulatory problems in his leg, but the operation was unsuccessful. They operated again at 11.45 the following morning, but circulation was not restored. The amputation became necessary in order to prevent gangrene and to save Mr Forbes' life.

He knew therefore that Mr Gillespie, the surgeon, and his team had caused the injury which he suffered. It is not suggested that the operations, though the first two were unsuccessful, were not properly and competently carried out. The allegation, so far as can be ascertained from the statement of claim and the plaintiff's solicitor's affidavit, which refers to an unnamed consultant vascular surgeon, is that the second operation should have been performed more promptly, on the evening of 24 October or during the night, and not left until the following day.

So Mr Spencer contends on behalf of the defendants that all the statutory ingredients of knowledge were present to Mr Forbes when or soon after the amputation took place. Putting aside all question of negligence or fault, as s 14(1) requires one to do, he submits that Mr Forbes knew then that Mr Gillespie or his team were responsible for the delay which in fact occurred. He knew about his injury and who had caused it. The Court of Appeal rejected in *Dobbie v Medway Health Authority* [1994] 4 All ER 450 at 457, [1994] 1 WLR 1234 at 1240 the contention that the limitation period did not commence until he also knew that 'something had gone wrong'.

There is, however, in my judgment a vital difference between the facts of *Dobbie* and the present case. There, the cause of the injury was the alleged negligence of the defendant surgeon in removing the plaintiff's breast when it

a   was not cancerous as he supposed. Negligent or not, that was the defendant's
     positive act. The present case on the other hand is one of omission. It is alleged
     that the surgeon or his team were negligent in failing to perform the second
     operation before they did. That omission was the cause of the plaintiff's injury,
     if negligence is proved.

         The defendant says that because Mr Forbes knew that he was not operated on
b   until the following morning, therefore he knew, putting all questions of fault or
     negligence on one side, that there was this omission and that delay had occurred.
     Mr Spencer relies among other authorities on the following passage in Steyn LJ's
     judgment in *Dobbie v Medway Health Authority* [1994] 4 All ER 450 at 463, [1994] 1
     WLR 1234 at 1248:

c   'The word "act" does not by itself describe something which ought not to
         have been done. And it would be impossible to attach a qualitative element
         to "omission" but not to "act".'

         I respectfully agree that the statute excludes any qualitative element from
     either acts or omissions, but in my judgment it is impossible to identify an
d   omission except by reference to an act which could have been done. It would be
     wrong and contrary to the section to say 'should have been done' or 'ought to
     have been done'; but the fact that nothing was done does not constitute an
     'omission', in my view, unless something could have been done—regardless of
     whether it ought to have been done or not. Certainly, the plaintiff's injury
e   cannot be said to be attributable to any omission by the defendant unless the
     defendant could have acted to prevent it.

         Of what fact, therefore, was Mr Forbes ignorant until he received the medical
     advice which led to him bringing these proceedings for negligence in 1992? I
     would say that he did not know until then that there was, as is now alleged, a lost
     opportunity to prevent the injury which he later suffered. That is a question of
f   medical *science* of which he was unaware. It is a different question depending on
     medical *practice* whether the operation should have been carried out sooner than
     it was. That is the question whether the omission was negligent, which is not
     relevant under s 14(1).

         I believe that this conclusion is consistent with other authorities to which
g   Stuart-Smith LJ has referred, including *Smith v West Lancashire Health Authority*
     [1995] PIQR P514 (Russell LJ) and *Hallam-Eames v Merrett* (1995) Times, 25
     January. The decision in *Jones v Liverpool Health Authority* (1995) 30 BMLR 1, I
     would agree, depends upon the part played in that case by the first consultant, Mr
     Bloor, as described in the passage from the judgment quoted by him.

h   I agree, therefore, both with Stuart-Smith LJ and with the judge that actual
     knowledge within s 14(1) has not been proved against the plaintiff here.

Constructive knowledge

         Section 14(3) adds to the plaintiff's actual knowledge, such knowledge as 'he
     might reasonably have been expected to acquire ... (b) from facts ascertainable by
j   him with the help of medical or other appropriate expert advice which it is
     reasonable for him to seek', followed by:

         '... but a person shall not be fixed under this subsection with knowledge of
         a fact ascertainable only with the help of expert advice so long as he has taken
         all reasonable steps to obtain (and, where appropriate, to act on) that advice.'

My first observation on this subsection is that it is concerned, like sub-s (1), with the facts of which the plaintiff had knowledge, or is deemed to have had knowledge, for the purposes of s 11. The relevant fact in the present case, for the reasons given above, is that there was, as is alleged, an opportunity for Mr Forbes' leg to be saved if a second operation was performed earlier than it was, an opportunity which was lost. This fact must be taken to have been within his knowledge if it was ascertainable with the help of medical advice which it was reasonable for him to seek (sub-s (3)(b)). I agree that the qualification 'but a person shall not be fixed' does not raise any separate issue in the present case. The question is, should it be held that it was reasonable for Mr Forbes to seek medical advice, after the amputation (in 1982) and more than three years before the writ was issued (before 1989)? If he had done so, then it must be assumed that he would have been told the alleged fact that his leg could have been saved by a prompt second operation on 24 October 1982.

I have found this the most difficult issue in this case. Part of the difficulty arises because the evidence is incomplete, as it must necessarily be when the limitation defence is decided as a preliminary issue. What advice was given to Mr Forbes before the first operation? Was he told that there was a substantial risk, if the operation failed, that his leg would have to be amputated? If so, within what sort of period? What was he told were the chances of success, or of failure?

We may infer that the reason for the operation was to prevent the risk that circulation in the leg would become blocked, leading to gangrene and the very precaution that became necessary—amputation of the leg. But Mr Gillespie must have held out some chances of success, and so it can be said that the failure of both operations and the consequent need to amputate must have been some indication, not that 'something had gone wrong', but that there had been a chance to save the leg, which had not materialised in the result.

Whilst this does not establish actual knowledge of the (alleged) lost opportunity to save his leg, nevertheless it may have been sufficient to make it reasonable for Mr Forbes to take medical advice (ie to consult another doctor) when the outcome was as significant an 'injury' as it was.

Against this, a striking feature of the case is the implicit trust, no doubt well justified, which he had in Mr Gillespie's professional skills. To say that he ought reasonably to have taken a second opinion is to encourage, it is suggested, all post-operation patients to do just that, merely on the off chance that they may find that they can recover damages for negligence. This in its turn could encourage 'ambulance chasers' among lawyers and diminish the trust which builds up between patients and the overwhelming majority of doctors who treat them.

The answer to this submission, I am sure, is that each case must depend upon its own facts. The statute applies a test of reasonableness, and it would be wrong to introduce categories or general rules as to what is reasonable, or not.

Another feature of the present case is that Mr Forbes consulted a second doctor when he did, seven or eight years after the amputation, not because he believed, even then, that the amputation was unnecessary or could have been avoided, but because his wife, the present plaintiff, found that the problems of looking after him were becoming insurmountable for her, and they wondered about financial help. Put another way, if it was appropriate for him to question Mr Gillespie's treatment then, was it not equally reasonable to do so as soon as he took stock after the amputation in 1982?

a   I agree with Stuart-Smith LJ that it is relevant to consider the scheme of the
     1980 Act, taking account both of the postponed start of the limitation period
     under s 11 and the discretionary power to extend it under s 33. Since there is a
     wide discretionary power to extend the period in circumstances which
     Parliament has defined in s 33, there is no clear requirement to construe the
     knowledge provisions in s 14 narrowly or in favour of individual plaintiffs. I
b   therefore consider that they should be interpreted neutrally so that in respect of
     constructive knowledge under s 14(3) an objective standard applies.

     By this standard, it seems to me that it was reasonable for Mr Forbes to obtain
     a second medical opinion in the circumstances of this case. This is primarily
     because of the seriousness of the injury and the history of treatment which he had
c   undergone. I doubt, however, whether it is appropriate to regard this issue in
     terms of a decision made consciously or unconsciously by Mr Forbes, whether to
     accept his lot or to consider making a claim. If the question is whether,
     objectively and reasonably, he could be expected to have obtained further advice,
     then I do not see that his actual mental processes are relevant at all.

d   This leads to the disquiet expressed by Stuart-Smith and Roch LJJ as to the
     statement in the judgment of this court in *Nash v Eli Lilly & Co, Berger v Eli Lilly &
     Co* [1993] 4 All ER 383 at 399, [1993] 1 WLR 782 at 799: 'In considering whether
     or not the inquiry is, or is not, reasonable, the situation, character and intelligence
     of the plaintiff must be relevant.' As to situation, there is no difficulty. The
     reasonable man must be placed in the situation that the plaintiff was. The
e   references to character and intelligence, however, suggest that regard should be
     had to personal characteristics of the plaintiff, and this I find difficult to square
     with the application of an objective and therefore equal standard. Moreover, as
     Stuart-Smith LJ points out, the kind of inquiry would become necessary which
     has to be undertaken in criminal cases where provocation is a possible defence to
f   a charge of murder, and as many authorities indicate this has not proved an easy
     task.

     If this qualified-objective approach was held in *Nash v Eli Lilly & Co* to be the
     correct interpretation of the subsection then of course the decision is binding on
     us; but I do not read the judgment as going that far. There is only the one-line
     statement, already quoted, and no indication in the report that this particular
g   nuance of meaning was argued in that appeal. It may also be possible to give the
     references to character and intelligence a limited meaning, for there could be
     circumstances where the nature of the alleged negligence was such that those
     attributes of the 'reasonable man' might be relevant in applying the objective test.
     No such considerations arise in the present case.

h   The court's statement was repeated and acted upon by the judge in the present
     case, and he may well have regarded it as qualifying the objective test, thus
     causing him to take account of the personal characteristics of Mr Forbes, whom
     he heard and saw in the witness box. It was natural and understandable that he
     should adopt that approach, but for the reasons given above I would hold that the
j   objective test alone must be applied and that it is necessary for this court to
     reassess this issue.

     Not without considerable hesitation, therefore, I concur with Stuart-Smith LJ's
     conclusion that Mr Forbes ought reasonably to have taken further medical advice
     soon after the amputation, if he ever intended to do so, and that in the
     circumstances he had constructive knowledge of the relevant facts within s 14(3).

Discretion: s 33

Here, I agree that the court's discretion should be exercised afresh and that the *a* plaintiff should not be granted an extension of time under s 33. The principal factor in my judgment is that on the evidence before us the plaintiff's claim seems to have only a very limited, almost negligible chance of success, and this factor does not appear to have been taken into account by the judge. I prefer to express no view on the question whether the judge's exercise of his discretion should be *b* disregarded where it is given as a second reason, and therefore obiter, for the decision he reached.

ROCH LJ. I agree with and respectfully adopt Stuart-Smith LJ's conclusion and reasoning on the first issue raised by this appeal, namely: did the deceased himself have knowledge of the facts identified in s 14(1) of the Limitation Act 1980 more *c* than three years before the commencement of proceedings on 10 December 1992?

I have the misfortune to part company with Stuart-Smith LJ's judgment on the second issue, namely whether the deceased's knowledge prior to 10 December 1989 included knowledge that there had been an omission to which the *d* amputation of his leg was attributable because that was knowledge which he might reasonably have been expected to acquire from facts ascertainable by him with the help of medical expert advice which it was reasonable for him to seek.

Clearly the knowledge needed to complete knowledge of the kind to start the three-year period running could have been provided to the deceased by expert medical advice, because there is no suggestion that there has been a sudden *e* advance in medical knowledge in this field between October 1982 and December 1989. Further, I agree with Stuart-Smith LJ that if it was reasonable for the deceased to seek expert medical advice, then the proviso to s 14(3)(b) cannot help the deceased because he took no step to obtain that advice, and therefore could not have been heard to say that he had taken all reasonable steps to obtain and *f* act on expert medical advice.

The question that the judge had to answer was: 'Was it reasonable for him to seek advice from a medical expert prior to 10 December 1989?' In my opinion the judge asked himself the correct question and the issues in this part of the appeal are: Did the judge misdirect himself on the law and, if he did not, did he reach a decision that was clearly wrong? With regard to the second issue it has to be *g* recalled that the judge saw and heard the deceased.

The judge's directions to himself on the law are to be found as follows:

'As to constructive knowledge, the approach, it is submitted and I agree, is to determine what the plaintiff should have realised or obtained, asking no *h* more of him than is reasonable. That is a standard of reasonableness [which is] objective, but must take into account his position, circumstances, character and intelligence. That follows from *Nash v Eli Lilly & Co, Berger v Eli Lilly & Co* [1993] 4 All ER 383, [1993] 1 WLR 782. And so would it have been reasonable to expect the plaintiff to make inquiries before in fact he did? *j* On that issue, the burden is on the defendants to show that he should have done.'

The judge's directions to himself were based on the decision of this court in *Nash v Eli Lilly & Co* [1993] 4 All ER 383 at 399, [1993] 1 WLR 782 at 801, where this court dealt with the question of constructive knowledge, saying:

a   'On this basis, in our judgment, the proper approach is to determine what this plaintiff should have observed or ascertained, while asking no more of him than is reasonable. The standard of reasonableness in connection with the observations and/or the effort to ascertain are therefore finally objective but must be qualified to take into consideration the position, and circumstances and character of the plaintiff.'

b   This court concluded this part of its judgment by saying: 'But this is an area [the area of constructive knowledge under s 14(3)] in which the onus of proving constructive knowledge is on the defendants.' (See [1993] 4 All ER 383 at 400, [1993] 1 WLR 782 at 801.)

     I must confess that I have difficulty with the first of the above passages from the judgment in *Nash*'s case. If the standard of reasonableness is objective, then the position, circumstances and character of a would-be plaintiff cannot be relevant although the circumstances in which the would-be plaintiff found himself at the time it is said he should have sought expert advice would be relevant. Nevertheless *Nash*'s case is a decision of this court and the judge and we are bound by it. An application of those principles means that the judge who saw and heard the deceased is in a much better position to answer the question which the section poses, namely: 'Was it reasonable for the deceased to seek the advice of a medical expert prior to the 10 December 1989?'

     Were the test to be a wholly objective test, then the conclusion that I would have reached in the present case would have been that it had been reasonable for the deceased to seek advice of a medical expert prior to 10 December 1989, for the reasons given by Stuart-Smith LJ. Because the judge had to take account of the deceased's position, circumstances and character and because the judge saw and heard the deceased, I am not prepared to hold that the judge was clearly wrong in the conclusion that he came to on this issue.

f   In this case, the operations performed by Mr Gillespie were carried out to try to save the deceased's leg, which, if the operations were unsuccessful, would inevitably be lost. The deceased had a high opinion of and great trust in Mr Gillespie. We do not have evidence of what the deceased was told by Mr Gillespie and other doctors before, between and after the two operations, but it is reasonable to suppose that he was told that the attempt to restore circulation to the leg might not succeed; that if it did not succeed the leg would have to be amputated if the deceased himself was to survive; and that following the two operations he was told all that could have been done to restore circulation to the leg had been done; that he believed that to be so and there was nothing of which he knew to cast doubt on the proposition that Mr Gillespie and his team had done all that could humanly have been done.

h   The fact that in 1991 the deceased went to solicitors at the insistence of his wife and daughter to inquire whether financial assistance was available to cope with his increasing needs for care does not, in my judgment, provide evidence that it would have been reasonable for the deceased to seek expert medical advice earlier. No doubt expert medical advice was sought at the solicitor's suggestion and one must be careful not to convert the question posed by s 14(3)(b) of the Act into a different question: 'Should the would-be plaintiff have consulted a solicitor earlier?' In this case as far as the deceased was concerned it was not a matter of things going wrong so much as a matter of things not going right.

     In my view, it would be unfortunate if the question asked in s 14(3)(b) were to be resolved by imputing to a would-be plaintiff an unconscious decision to do

nothing and then requiring him to stand by that 'decision'. Such an approach
would encourage those undergoing medical treatment which did not achieve the *a*
desired result to go automatically to another specialist for an opinion as to
whether the treatment given could have been made more effective.

On present authority, in my judgment, the judge was correct in asking himself
the question: 'Have the defendants proved that in this case Mr Forbes should
reasonably have sought expert medical advice prior to 10 December 1989?' This *b*
is not a case, in my judgment, where this court can say that the answer given by
the judge to that question was clearly wrong. I would dismiss this appeal.

Appeal allowed.

Paul Magrath Esq　　Barrister.　*c*

R v Secretary of State for Transport, ex parte Richmond upon Thames London Borough Council and others (No 4)

COURT OF APPEAL, CIVIL DIVISION
LEGGATT, MORRITT AND BROOKE LJJ
18, 19, 26 JULY 1996

Air traffic – Noise nuisance – Landing and take-off – Restrictions on landing and taking off to avoid, limit or mitigate noise – Secretary of State proposing new night flying restrictions at airport – Restrictions specifying aggregated seasonal limits – Restrictions for summer period allowing more noise than actually experienced under earlier restrictions – Whether restrictions invalid owing to doctrine of legitimate expectation, inadequacy of reasons or irrationality.

In August 1995 the Secretary of State, acting under powers conferred on him by s 78(3)[a] of the Civil Aviation Act 1982, made an order imposing new night flight restrictions at Heathrow, Gatwick and Stansted airports for various periods from October 1995 to 1998. The decision followed consultation papers issued in January 1993, March 1995 and June 1995 and imposed aggregated seasonal limits on the maximum number of aircraft movements permitted at the airport. The restrictions in respect of the summer periods allowed more noise than that which had actually been experienced in the summer of 1988, but less noise than that which had been permitted under the restrictions in force at that time. The applicant local authorities, whose inhabitants were affected by aircraft noise, applied for judicial review of the Secretary of State's decision. The judge dismissed their application and the applicants appealed to the Court of Appeal, contending that the Secretary of State's decision (i) infringed the legitimate expectation of local residents that the benefit of the previous policy would not be withdrawn without rational grounds being given on which they could comment, (ii) failed to give adequate reasons, and (iii) was irrational.

Held – (1) In the context of the exercise by the Secretary of State of his powers under s 78(3) of the 1982 Act, what was important was that people should be able to understand the policy objectives he had identified when he began the decision-making process and that they had a chance of making informed submissions to him about the way in which he should exercise his powers against that policy background. That was the situation in the instant case, since the 1993 and subsequent consultation papers had set out the proposals fairly and rationally in an intelligible policy context. It followed that the Secretary of State had not infringed the legitimate expectation of local residents (see p 914 *e*, p 916 *j* and p 923 *h*, post).

(2) In the procedural circumstances of the present case, it was appropriate to read the brief reasons given by the Secretary of State for his decision alongside the

---

a   Section 78(3), so far as material, provides: 'If the Secretary of State considers it appropriate, for the purpose of avoiding, limiting or mitigating the effect of noise and vibration connected with taking-off or landing of aircraft ... he may ... specify the maximum number of occasions on which aircraft ... may be permitted to take off or land ... during periods so specified ...'

consultation paper which defined the main issues likely to inform his choice. Having regard to the fact that the Secretary of State was under no legal duty to spell out why he preferred one set of arguments to another, it followed that those reasons were adequate since they enabled the reader to know what conclusions he had reached on the 'principal important controversial issues' (see p 919 *h j*, p 921 *h*, p 922 *j* and p 923 *h*, post); *Bolton Metropolitan DC v Secretary of State for the Environment* (1995) 71 P & CR 309 applied.

(3) There were no grounds on the facts for holding that the Secretary of State's decision was irrational and, accordingly, the appeal would be dismissed (see p 923 *d g h*, post).

Decision of Jowitt J [1996] 4 All ER 93 affirmed.

Notes

For noise and vibration on aerodromes, see 2 *Halsbury's Laws* (4th edn reissue) para 1185.

For the Civil Aviation Act 1982, s 78, see 4 *Halsbury's Statutes* (4th edn) (1987 reissue) 201.

Cases referred to in judgments

Associated Provincial Picture Houses Ltd v Wednesbury Corp [1947] 2 All ER 680, [1948] 1 KB 223, CA.

Bolton Metropolitan DC v Secretary of State for the Environment (1995) 71 P & CR 309, HL.

Brind v Secretary of State for the Home Dept [1991] 1 All ER 720, [1991] 1 AC 696, [1991] 2 WLR 588, HL.

Bugdaycay v Secretary of State for the Home Dept [1987] 1 All ER 940, [1987] AC 514, [1987] 2 WLR 606, HL.

Council of Civil Service Unions v Minister for the Civil Service [1984] 3 All ER 935, [1985] AC 374, [1984] 3 WLR 1174, HL.

Doody v Secretary of State for the Home Dept [1993] 3 All ER 92, [1994] 1 AC 531, [1993] 3 WLR 154, HL.

Gransden (E C) & Co Ltd v Secretary of State for the Environment (1985) 54 P & CR 86; *affd* (1985) 54 P & CR 361, CA.

Hope v Secretary of State for the Environment (1975) 31 P & CR 120.

Lloyd v McMahon [1987] 1 All ER 1118, [1987] AC 625, [1987] 2 WLR 821, HL.

Powell and Rayner v UK (21 February 1990, Series A No 172 4), ECt HR.

R v City of London Corp, ex p Matson (1995) 8 Admin LR 49, CA.

R v Civil Service Appeal Board, ex p Cunningham [1991] 4 All ER 310, CA.

R v Devon CC, ex p Baker, R v Durham CC, ex p Curtis [1995] 1 All ER 73, CA.

R v Higher Education Funding Council, ex p Institute of Dental Surgery [1994] 1 All ER 651, [1994] 1 WLR 242, DC.

R v Kensington and Chelsea Royal London BC, ex p Grillo [1996] 2 FCR 56, CA.

R v Ministry of Defence, ex p Smith [1996] 1 All ER 257, [1996] QB 517, [1996] 2 WLR 305, CA.

R v Rochdale Metropolitan BC, ex p Schemet (1992) 91 LGR 425.

R v Secretary of State for Transport, ex p Richmond upon Thames London BC [1994] 1 All ER 577, [1994] 1 WLR 74.

R v Secretary of State for Transport, ex p Richmond upon Thames London BC (No 2) [1995] Env LR 390.

R v Secretary of State for Transport, ex p Richmond upon Thames London BC (No 3) (1995) Times, 11 May.

a   *Save Britain's Heritage v Secretary of State for the Environment* [1991] 2 All ER 10, sub
     nom *Save Britain's Heritage v Number 1 Poultry Ltd* [1991] 1 WLR 153, HL.

Cases also cited or referred to in skeleton arguments
Ali v Secretary of State for the Home Dept [1984] 1 All ER 1009, [1984] 1 WLR 663,
     CA.
b   *Findlay v Secretary of State for the Home Dept* [1984] 3 All ER 801, [1985] AC 318, HL.
     Great Portland Estates plc v Westminster City Council [1984] 3 All ER 744, [1985] AC
     661, HL.
     Ladd v Marshall [1954] 3 All ER 745, [1954] 1 WLR 1489, CA.
     Lonrho plc v Secretary of State for Trade and Industry [1989] 2 All ER 609, [1989] 1
c   WLR 525, HL.
     Piggott Bros & Co Ltd v Jackson [1992] ICR 85, CA.
     R v Brent London BC, ex p Gunning (1985) 84 LGR 168.
     R v Immigration Appeal Tribunal, ex p Dhunna [1992] Imm AR 457.
     R v Immigration Appeal Tribunal, ex p Khan (Mahmud) [1983] 2 All ER 420, [1983] QB
d   790, CA.
     R v Jockey Club, ex p RAM Racecourses Ltd [1993] 2 All ER 225, DC.

Appeal
Hillingdon London Borough Council and Slough Borough Council appealed
with leave granted by Schiemann LJ from the judgment of Jowitt J ([1996] 4 All
e   ER 93, [1996] 1 WLR 1005) delivered on 8 March 1996 dismissing an application
for judicial review of the decision of the Secretary of State for Transport,
announced in a press notice on 16 August 1995, to introduce new night flying
restrictions at major London airports. At the hearing of the appeal the court
granted leave for the other four original applicants to be joined in the appeal,
f   namely Richmond upon Thames London Borough Council, Hounslow London
Borough Council, Surrey County Council and Windsor and Maidenhead Royal
Borough Council. The facts are set out in the judgment of Brooke LJ.

     Charles George QC and *Helen Mountfield* (instructed by *Richard Buxton*, Cambridge)
          for the appellants.
g   *Ian Burnett* and *Mark Shaw* (instructed by the *Treasury Solicitor*) for the
          respondent.

                                                                    Cur adv vult

h   26 July 1996. The following judgments were delivered.

BROOKE LJ (giving the first judgment at the invitation of Leggatt LJ). This case
is all about aircraft noise at Heathrow at night. Parliament has given the
Secretary of State power to exercise control in this matter if he thinks fit, and
j   controls of this kind have been exercised in one way or another since 1962. In
1988 when he came to exercise this power, which is to be found in s 78(3) of the
Civil Aviation Act 1982, he decided to limit aircraft movements at night to 2,750
during what he called the summer period and 3,000 during the winter period. For
this purpose the night was generally defined as lasting between 11.30 pm and 6
am, being extended to 6.30 am on winter weekdays and 8 am for winter Sundays
and for summer Sunday departures. A complete ban was imposed on scheduled

movements of certain noisier aircraft between 12.30 am and 5 am. This decision controlled the position between 1988 and 1993.

In fact only about 1,830 aircraft movements (as opposed to the 2,750 permitted) took place in the summer period of 1988, and it is this difference between the permitted level and the actual level of movements which has fuelled much of the litigation on this topic in the last 18 months.

Ever since 1993 the minister has been concerned to set a new level for the next five-year period, which ends in 1998. The first decision he made, in July 1993, was set aside two months later by Laws J on the basis that the way in which he purported to exercise his powers did not comply with the requirements of the statute (see *R v Secretary of State for Transport, ex p Richmond upon Thames London BC* [1994] 1 All ER 577, [1994] 1 WLR 74). He then made two short-term decisions (covering the periods between October 1993 and March 1994, and between March 1994 and October 1994 respectively) before making a long-term decision in May 1994 which was to embrace the period between October 1994 and the end of the summer season in 1998. These decisions, too, were declared to be unlawful, on this occasion by Latham J in December 1994 (see *R v Secretary of State for Transport, ex p Richmond upon Thames London BC (No 2)* [1995] Env LR 390).

In 1995 the minister tried again. He issued a short consultation paper in March 1995, in which he endeavoured to correct the deficiencies identified by Latham J. This led to a further challenge, on this occasion to the legal validity of the new consultation process, which the Court of Appeal, differing from Sedley J (see *R v Secretary of State for Transport, ex p Richmond upon Thames London BC (No 3)* (1995) Times, 11 May) considered to be properly arguable. Rather than wait for the outcome of a further substantive hearing, the minister published a short supplemental consultation paper in June, and came to a further decision, in relation to the next three years, on 16 August 1995. It is this decision which is the subject of the present challenge. Six local authorities whose inhabitants are to a greater or lesser extent affected by aircraft noise at Heathrow were parties to the new application, and when this was dismissed by Jowitt J ([1996] 4 All ER 93, [1996] 1 WLR 1005) in March 1996, two of them, Hillingdon London Borough Council and Slough Borough Council, appealed to this court, and at the hearing of the appeal the court granted leave for the other four original applicants to be joined in the appeal. The appeal was expedited by order of Schiemann LJ, given at the same time as he granted leave to appeal.

It is an important feature of this case that since 1993 new arrangements have been used as the basis for deciding how many night-time aircraft movements the minister should permit.

Under this new scheme there is a weighting system which differentiates between different aircraft depending on the noise they emit. For all practical purposes the lowest weighting is 0.5 (a level associated with so-called Whisper Jets like the BAe 146), and subsequent categories are weighted at 1, 2 and 4—and then at 8 and 16 for the two noisiest types. The large aircraft used for night flights to and from the Pacific Rim are said to be mostly in the 2–4 band: Concorde has a weighting of 16. The Department of Transport has calculated that if this banding system had been in operation in 1988, the permitted number of 'quota count points of noise' at Heathrow in the summer period of that year would have been about 8,000, and the number actually experienced was just over 5,200: the comparative figure for the summer of 1992, when the movements quota was almost fully taken up, but by quieter aircraft, was 5,430. In the intervening *a* summers the number would have been higher. At Gatwick, on the other hand, the permitted number of movements was for all practical purposes taken up, so that these differences between actual and permitted numbers did not exist.

The minister's decision in August 1995, like all its immediate predecessors, introduced a new permitted level of 7,000 'quota count points of noise' at Heathrow in the summer and 5,000 in the winter. A new 'night quota period'

b between 11.30 pm and 6 am was introduced and the new limits were to be applied to this period only. There was also to be a maximum limit on the number of permitted movements, on which nothing turns. In what have been called 'night shoulder periods', between 11 pm and 11.30 pm, and between 6 am and 7 am, there were now to be no limits on movements of aircraft categorised as Quota Count (QC) 4 or lower, but controls were still to be in place for the noisier

c aircraft categorised as QC8 or 16: no scheduled landing or take-off was to be permitted for any aircraft in these categories between 11 pm and 6 am, or for QC16 aircraft between 6 am and 7 am. In addition, a long-standing rule that aircraft must be flown between 11 pm and 7 am in such a way that they did not exceed a noise level known as 102 PNdB (which is said to cover QC16 aircraft and most QC8 aircraft) remained firmly in place.

d For all except the noisiest aircraft, therefore, the new regime removed the controls that had previously existed between 6 am and 6.30 am (on winter weekdays) and between 6 am and 8 am (for winter Sundays and summer Sunday departures): among other things, there was now to be no control on QC8 aircraft which could comply with the noise limit requirement from 6 am onwards. It also

e changed the position between 11.30 pm and 6 am. For this period it had the effect of reducing the maximum number of permitted movements as compared with what had been allowed in 1988, but it permitted significantly more 'quota count points of noise' than had actually been experienced in the summer of that year. As I have said, no scheduled movements of the two noisier categories of

f aircraft were to be permitted for a longer period than had existed under the previous regime.

Of the five points of challenge originally presented to Jowitt J, three survive for our consideration. These arise from arguments founded on the doctrine of legitimate expectation, on alleged inadequacy of reasons, and on alleged irrationality. Arguments based on the interpretation of the minister's statutory

g powers have been abandoned. In order to understand the points that are now being put, it is necessary to say something first about the historical context in which this application is set.

Aircraft noise at night is a topic which rouses considerable passions among those who live close to major airports. The English common law does not give

h them a right to sleep as such, but in the ordinary way their comfort and health is protected by the law of tort, which regulates conduct as between neighbours by such mechanisms as the law of nuisance (which is based on the concept of a reasonable amount of give and take) or the law of negligence (which creates duties of care to avoid unreasonable amounts of noise which may cause

j foreseeable injury to health). If, however, the noise-creator's activities are sanctioned by statute (for example by ministers acting under statutory powers) the common law right to damages, or the equitable right to seek injunctive relief, are removed (see, in the present context, s 76(1) of the 1982 Act).

In a more overtly rights-based system of law, such as that created by the European Convention on Human Rights (the Convention for the Protection of Human Rights and Fundamental Freedoms (Rome, 4 November 1950; TS 71

(1953); Cmd 8969)), the balance between the rights of the individual and the rights of the State (which represents more extensive public interests) is achieved through different mechanisms. This was illustrated in *Powell and Rayner v UK* (European Court of Human Rights, judgment of 21 February 1990, Series A No 172 4 at 18). The court then accepted, in the context of an application made under art 8(1) of the convention, that noise generated by aircraft in the vicinity of airports can affect 'the quality of [a person's] private life and the scope for enjoying the amenities of his home'. However, although art 8(1) recognises 'the right to respect for [everyone's] private and family life, his home ...', this is qualified by art 8(2) which permits such 'interference by a public authority with the exercise of this right ... as is ... necessary ... in the interests of ... the economic well-being of the country'. The final effect, therefore, is the same, although the route is different. The United Kingdom is bound by treaty to observe the convention and, although it is not part of our national law, ministers must be presumed to have intended to comply with its requirements when exercising powers conferred on them by Parliament unless there is evidence of a clear Parliamentary intention to contrary effect (see *Brind v Secretary of State for the Home Dept* [1991] 1 All ER 720, [1991] 1 AC 696).

In its 1985 White Paper on Airports Policy (1985, Cmnd 9542) the government had refused to contemplate a complete ban on all aircraft movement at night, although this had been recommended in the recent report on development proposals relating to Stansted and Heathrow airports. Although it sympathised with the intention which lay behind the inspector's recommendation, it considered that such a major step should not be taken without the fullest consideration of its effects on the aviation industry, and in particular on charter airlines and their passengers.

The government said in the White Paper that it was committed to mitigating as far as practicable the effects of aircraft noise and other disturbance and that its objective continued to be to bring about progressive reductions in aircraft noise at night at these airports, allowing only movements by quieter aircraft. It said that its policy on night noise was firmly based on research into the relationship between aircraft and sleep disturbance, and that in order to preserve a balance between environmental and aviation interests this should continue to be the basis for decisions. It added that it was committed to doing everything practicable to ensure that the noise climate improved, and that it would continue to support the operational measures that were necessary; in particular the continued use of quiet take-off and landing procedures and runway alternation.

Government policy in this matter between 1988 and 1993 was founded on the objectives set out in a consultation paper published in November 1987. This revealed a four-point strategy. (1) To continue to improve the night noise climate so that disturbance of people's sleep was further reduced; (2) to allow airlines to continue to provide some scheduled movements during the night period; (3) to enable the two airports to continue to offer a 24-hour service; and (4) to encourage airlines to continue to invest in quieter modern aircraft.

This paper set out the history of night flight restrictions at Heathrow since 1962. When quotas were last set, for a seven-year period, in 1981, these had had the purpose of phasing out night flights by the older noisier aircraft and, as had been promised at that time, the government had undertaken a further review of night restrictions, which was now complete. It considered that it was important that Heathrow's facilities should be available during the night to meet essential minimum needs and, although the demand for night flights was not great, a especially in the small hours, it believed that it was necessary that the airport should continue to be able to offer night movements to airlines who needed to accommodate particular schedules, and to cope with emergencies.

The airlines had wanted the night period to finish at 6 am every day, winter and summer. They had also wanted modern quieter aeroplanes to be allowed to fly at night without restrictions. The government rejected both these requests.

b The existing summer and winter quotas at Heathrow were not then being fully used and the government was not convinced that the benefits to the airlines of the extra flights would justify the disturbance they would cause. Although in this paper the expression 'the night noise climate' referred to the period between 11 pm and 7 am, the language of para 41 of that paper shows that the government was then using the expression 'the night period' as meaning the

c concept that was later to be described as 'the night quota period', whereas in the January 1993 paper a different meaning was adopted for this expression. This was another matter which gave rise to later difficulties.

At that time aircraft were banded into three categories, depending on the amount of noise they emitted. I will call these bands A, B and C. Band A were to

d be banned at night completely, take-offs by band B aircraft (identified as aeroplanes previously categorised as 'quieter', such as the B747) were to be banned between 12.30 am and 5 am, and the night noise limit of 102 PNdB was to continue. This apart, a simple quota of 2,750 (summer) and 3,000 (winter) was proposed for bands B and C night movements at Heathrow. These quotas were described as being set at about the present level of usage (and therefore smaller

e than the present quota of 3,650/3,250) to provide the flexibility to schedule a modest number of flights at night.

Following consultation, these proposals formed the basis of the minister's decision on 10 February 1988 which covered the period between 1988 and 1993. From the terms in which he announced his decision to Parliament can be gleaned

f what was later described as his undertaking 'not to allow a worsening of noise at night and ideally to improve it'. There is no reason to suppose that when he referred to the 'night noise climate' he was not referring to the period between 11 pm and 7 am.

In January 1993 the government published a new consultation paper in which it published its proposals for restricting night flights at Heathrow, Gatwick and

g Stansted for the five-year period beginning in October 1993. It pointed out that the first two of these airports had enormous importance not only for the local economies but the national economy as well, and it mentioned at the outset the arrangements being made in a European context to phase out completely the older, noisier aircraft by the year 2002. The competing pressures are clearly

h identified in the last two of the five objectives set out at the start of the paper:

'... (d) continue to protect local communities from excessive noise levels at night; (e) ensure that the competitive influences affecting UK airports and airlines and the wider employment and economic implications are taken into account.'

j

In paras 5 to 23 of the paper were set out, in summary form, the different considerations the government believed it would need to take into account. It repeated that the underlying principle behind the night flying restrictions had remained unchanged since 1962; to strike a balance between airlines wishing to operate services at night and people living round the airport who did not want

their sleep disturbed by aircraft noise. It mentioned the technological
developments which had led to aircraft becoming progressively quieter and the
extensive research project that had been commissioned in 1990 to provide
information on sleep disturbance. Paragraphs 8 and 9 reflected awareness of local
people's concerns that night flights at these airports should be further restricted,
if not banned altogether. Paragraphs 10 to 15, on the other hand, described the
demands being made for night flights.

The paper set out the argument that if UK restrictions meant that some flights
were not as convenient or that their costs were higher than competitors abroad
could offer, passengers would prefer alternatives that better suited their
requirements. In this context mention was made of three major European
airports at Paris, Amsterdam and Frankfurt, which either had no restrictions or
less onerous ones than Heathrow and Gatwick. Quite apart from the immediate
loss of business, concern was expressed about the consequential diminution in
status of UK airports and airlines, which in turn would diminish the attractions of
London and the United Kingdom generally for investment and international
commerce.

Three types of service were singled out for particular mention. The first were
flights from the Asia-Pacific region, a major growth area, which used to land early
in the daytime after stopping en route and were now able to complete their
journeys non-stop and therefore sought to land during the night period. The
second related to the special needs of charter companies who were operating in
a highly competitive, price sensitive market and whose commercial viability
depended on the high utilisation of their aircraft. The third was the continuing
demand for some all-cargo flights at night carrying mail and other time-sensitive
cargoes such as newspapers and perishable goods.

After mentioning certain anomalies in the present A, B and C system of
classification, and the way in which airlines' scheduling difficulties were
exacerbated by the changes in the definition of 'night' between the winter and
summer seasons and between weekdays and Sundays in winter, the paper
described the results of the recent research into sleep disturbance. This was said
to have been the most comprehensive of its kind ever conducted. It found that
external noise levels below 80 dB(A) (if measured outside the home, about the
same noise as would be heard at nearly 500 feet from an Intercity train travelling
at 95 mph) were very unlikely to cause any increase in the normal rate of
disturbance in someone's sleep, and with noise levels in the range of 80–95 dB(A)
the likelihood of the average person being awakened was about 1 in 75. The
research was said to have established that the number of disturbances caused by
aircraft noise was so small that it had a negligible effect on overall normal
disturbance rates.

In para 24 of the paper the government said that it was in the light of these
considerations that it had developed its new night quota proposals which I have
set out earlier in this judgment. EPNdB is a specialised noise unit used for aircraft
noise certification testing, and at the consultation stage the government was
proposing to give a nil weighting to aircraft whose noise level was below 90
EPNdB (which equated to a peak noise level of about 75 dB(A)): it was later
persuaded that these aircraft should each count 0.5 towards the new quotas. The
government's proposals were set out very clearly, but unhappily the paper
contained in para 34, immediately under the heading, 'Size of New Quota', the
following passage:

a   'Since 1988, more of the quieter types of aircraft have been acquired by
airlines, improving the night noise climate. In keeping with the undertaking
given in 1988 not to allow a worsening of noise at night, and ideally to
improve it, it is proposed that the quota for the next 5 years based on the new
quota system should be set at a level so as to keep overall noise levels below
those in 1988. For Heathrow the proposed summer noise quota is 7,000 …
b   The 1988 summer quota for Heathrow would have been about 8,000 if
calculated on the new basis …'

No mention was made in this paragraph of the fact that the actual number of
night movements at Heathrow that summer would have represented a noise
quota of only just over 5,200, so that if all the new permitted movements were
c   taken up, overall noise levels at Heathrow during the summer would increase
significantly.
    I need not dwell very long on the history of the matter between January 1993
and June 1995. As I have said, Laws J set aside the minister's original decision
because the new restrictions did not 'specify the maximum number of occasions
d   on which aircraft of descriptions so specified may be permitted to … land' (as
required by s 78(3)(b) of the 1982 Act), but only sought to impose control by
reference to levels of exposure to noise. Latham J, for his part, declared the next
three decisions unlawful because the minister had failed to provide a full and fair
consultation process (because of the misleading effect of para 34 of the
consultation paper) and had failed to take into account the fact that his decisions
e   would permit movements at Heathrow which would produce greater noise than
that experienced there in 1988, contrary to his expressed policy. The Court of
Appeal considered that the challenge to the March 1995 consultation paper was
properly arguable because the Secretary of State had failed to acknowledge in it
that he had in any way departed from the policy announced by his predecessor in
f   1988.
    The March 1995 consultation paper had been a brief, six-page document in
which the numbers were again set out and it was said that the proposal 'was to
impose noise quotas so that the maximum level of noise generated would be less
than the level which could have been generated by aircraft operating to the full
extent permitted in summer 1988, assuming the same mix of aircraft types as
g   actually operated at night at those airports in summer 1988'.
    In the June 1995 paper, which was issued as a supplement to the March paper,
the Secretary of State accepted the court's view that para 34 of the January 1993
paper had been misleading in relation to Heathrow. He now set out in very clear
terms the comparison he was using. He said that he believed that it was right to
h   compare what was allowed in summer 1988 with what it was proposed to allow
for summers under the new system. And he made it clear that his policies and the
proposals based on them did in fact allow more noise than was experienced from
aircraft movements that counted against the quotas in summer 1988, and
acknowledged that this was contrary to the policy as expressed in para 34 of the
j   1993 paper.
    On 16 August 1995 the minister announced his decision that all the details of
the new night flying restrictions regime would remain as previously announced.
He said that the government was committed to achieving and sustaining the
objectives identified in January 1993 and that the responses received to the two
recent consultation papers continued to show the polarisation to which his
predecessor had referred the previous year. He also described measures other

than the night restrictions regime which were being pursued as means of reducing disturbance for people affected by aircraft noise.   *a*

The first ground of challenge to this decision is based on the doctrine of legitimate expectation. This case has been put before us in a rather different way to the way it was put before the judge. The appellants rely on the second of the four broad categories of case identified by Simon Brown LJ in *R v Devon CC, ex p Baker, R v Durham CC, ex p Curtis* [1995] 1 All ER 73 at 88. In this class of case the   *b* claimant has an interest in some benefit which he or she hopes to retain and the expectation arises because his or her interest in it is one that the law holds protected by the requirements of procedural fairness. The law recognises that the interest cannot properly be withdrawn without the claimant being given an opportunity to comment and without the authority communicating rational grounds for any adverse decision.   *c*

An example of this type of case is to be found in the judgment of Roch J in *R v Rochdale Metropolitan BC, ex p Schemet* (1992) 91 LGR 425. A local education authority had announced the abandonment of its policy of paying travelling expenses to the parents of children who attended schools maintained by a neighbouring authority and, although the council had never made any promise   *d* to such parents and the applicant had received no assurance from the council, Roch J held that the parents of children at 'extra district schools' already receiving travel passes—

> 'had a legitimate expectation that that benefit would continue until there had been communicated to them some rational grounds for withdrawing it   *e* on which they had been given an opportunity to comment.' (See 91 LGR 425 at 445–446.)

In *Ex p Baker* [1995] 1 All ER 73 at 90 Simon Brown LJ sought to identify the interests which the law recognises to be of a character which require the protection of procedural fairness. He found the answer in Lord Diplock's speech   *f* in *Council of Civil Service Unions v Minister for the Civil Service* [1984] 3 All ER 935 at 949, [1985] AC 374 at 408, namely cases where a claimant had in the past been permitted to enjoy some benefit or advantage. Simon Brown LJ added (at 90–91):

> 'Whether or not he can then legitimately expect procedural fairness, and if so to what extent, will depend upon the court's view of what fairness   *g* demands in all the circumstances of the case ... In short, the concept of legitimate expectation when used ... in the category 2 sense seems to me no more than a recognition and embodiment of the unsurprising principle that the demands of fairness are likely to be somewhat higher when an authority contemplates depriving someone of an existing benefit or advantage than   *h* when the claimant is a bare applicant for a future benefit.'

The way that the appellants put their case under this head of their argument is to say that the effect of the 1985 policy as reinforced by the 1988 undertaking has been that the inhabitants of their areas suffered fewer aircraft movements at night (legalised trespass) and less noise at night (legalised nuisance) than would   *j* otherwise have been the case. Even though the 1988 decision was expressed to cover only the next five years, the 1995 decision, involving as it did an increase in aircraft movements and noise, constituted the withdrawal of a benefit or advantage (ie the benefit of the previous policy) which they could legitimately expect to be permitted to continue to enjoy. They do not claim any right to its continuance, but merely that it should not be withdrawn 'until there has been a communicated to them some rational grounds for withdrawing it on which they had been given the opportunity to comment' (see [1984] 3 All ER 935 at 949, [1985] AC 374 at 408 per Lord Diplock).

They maintain that the consultation documents do not set out rational grounds sufficient to satisfy this test. They base this contention on five main grounds. First, those documents do not explain the reasons for the change of b policy which permits more noise than was previously experienced, nor how the new proposals were still consistent with the Secretary of State's previous policy. Secondly, they do not explain what the new policy is. Thirdly, they do not explain how the proposals would 'maintain the essential balance between the interests of the airline industry and local people': the appellants quote extracts from the 1987 consultation paper to advance their point that arguments which c were at that time being rejected were now being accepted without explanation of the change of attitude. Fourthly, they do not explain how the noise climate in the night period (11 pm to 7 am), as opposed to the night quota period (11.30 pm to 6 am), was likely to change, especially since the Secretary of State had reduced the length of the latter by his decontrols. Fifthly, they did not explain why a d different conclusion in respect of decontrolling the 'early morning shoulder period' (6 to 7 am) was proposed, compared with that reached in 1987 when such a change had been ruled out 'because of increased disturbance during the early morning period'.

In the context of these complaints, the chief executive of the London Borough e of Richmond upon Thames had written to the department in May 1995 asking how the noise climate for the whole of the night period was likely to change and on 5 July he reiterated this request. He included in that letter the results of local research which suggested that noise levels in 1993–94 had increased by 30% during the night period and by 15% during the night quota period, as compared with the base year of 1988–89. He did not receive a substantive reply to these f letters.

The judge rejected the appellants' complaints quite briefly. He said that consultees knew what the Secretary of State's policy was for the 1993–98 period and that what had been called the 1988 undertaking was not part of that policy. They also knew what the Secretary of State's proposals were and they knew the g matters to which they should direct their representations. The appellants retort that the status of the 1988 undertaking (and of the 1985 White Paper policy) and the nature of the Secretary of State's policy in regard to the night period were wholly unclear and that they were and are still entitled to further reasoning, and a further opportunity to make representations in the light of that reasoning, h before the Secretary of State reaches his final decision.

When considering the appellants' arguments, it is reasonable to observe that the documents placed before the court reveal a fairly continuous thread of broad government policy ever since 1985, viz:

1985—To continue to bring about progressive reductions in aircraft noise at j night, allowing only movements by quieter aircraft; research into the relationship between aircraft and sleep disturbance would continue to be the basis for decisions on night noise. 1987—To continue to improve the night noise climate so that disturbance of people's sleep was further reduced; to allow airlines to continue to provide some scheduled movements during the night period. 1988— Not to allow a worsening of noise at night and ideally to improve it. 1993—To continue to protect local communities from excessive noise at night; to ensure that the competitive influences affecting UK airports and airlines and the wider employment and economic implications are taken into account.

In the context of planning law, which has a very complex statutory framework, it is well established that the appropriate authority must have regard to any relevant policy and that if it is going to depart from such a policy it must give clear reasons for doing so in order that the recipient of a decision may know why it is being made as an exception to the policy and the grounds upon which it was made. If the authority fails to understand the policy, then the decision will be as defective as it would be if no regard had been paid to the policy in the first place (see *E C Gransden & Co Ltd v Secretary of State for the Environment* (1985) 54 P & CR 86 at 94 per Woolf J). Mr George observed to us that people are likely to take 'locational' decisions about where to live and where to develop their businesses after studying published development plans and the official circulars that contain planning policy guidance, and that they are entitled to expect, as a general rule, that published policies will be followed.

It is always unwise to transfer principles established in one branch of administrative law too slavishly into another. In the present context there is no comparable statutory framework and it is clear from the evidence that the Secretary of State, as the decision-maker, was in the practice of taking decisions covering predetermined periods (since 1981, of seven years in the first instance, and then of five years at a time). It follows that what was important, in the context of the way he exercised his s 78(3) powers, was that people should be able to understand the policy objectives he identified when he began the decision-making process covering the next predetermined period and that they would have a chance of making informed submissions to him about the way in which he should exercise his powers against that policy background. It would, of course, be important for a planning inspector to be able to identify the broad aims of government policy on aircraft noise at night (as currently in the case of the inspector at the inquiry into the proposed fifth terminal at Heathrow, who has set aside a discrete period of his inquiry next year to consider noise issues), but in my judgment in the present context it is sufficient for the minister to have identified with adequate clarity the policy objectives which are to guide him when making his decision for the next finite period: it is Parliament, not the courts, which should hold him accountable if it wishes to query or challenge the policies he has chosen.

The main thrust of the appellants' criticism is that the 1993 consultation paper failed adequately to spell out how the proposal to change the regime in the night shoulder periods, and particularly the introduction of a broad measure of decontrol between 6 am and 6.30 am on winter weekdays, was consistent with government policy. In my judgment, however, the policy considerations which have impelled this change are reasonably clear from a careful reading of that consultation paper, and the representations we have seen make it equally clear that two, at least, of the appellant councils knew exactly what was being proposed and took the opportunity to comment very fully on the proposals.

Nobody reading that paper, for instance, could have been in any doubt that in certain respects things had moved on since 1987. For example, certain types of aircraft were now quieter (because of technological advances), certain types of aircraft could now fly direct to England non-stop from South Asia and the Pacific Rim countries (for the same reason), air movements to and from those destinations were likely to be a growth area over the next 20 years, and recent research had revealed quite favourable findings in relation to the extent that a external noise caused sleep disturbance. The consultation paper also showed that the government was now inclined to put more emphasis on economic factors than had perhaps been evident in its 1987 White Paper.

All these matters would have been evident to anyone reading that paper, and the later consultation papers published in March and June 1995 successfully, in my judgment, cancelled out any misleading impression that might have been
b obtained from reading para 34 of the original paper. It was now clear that the minister was intending to proceed by comparing the permitted noise climate in the basic 1988 summer 'night quota period' with the noise climate he was willing to permit in the summer night quota period under the future arrangements. In other words, the expression 'not to allow a worsening of noise at night' should be taken to refer to the level of noise which had previously been permitted, as
c opposed to that which had actually been experienced.

Ms Duthie, who is the head of the division of the Department of Transport which has responsibility for night flying, has also explained on affirmation that one of the minister's objectives in 1993 was to achieve identical night flying restrictions at all the three airports: under the 1988–93 regime there was the
d special rule banning departures at Heathrow between 6 am and 8 am on Sunday mornings in the summer which was now being abrogated. This consideration apart, she added that para 19 of the January 1993 consultation paper furnished an explanation for the reduction of the length of the night quota period. This reads:

e 'Airlines' scheduling difficulties are also exacerbated by the changes in the definition of "night" between the seasons and between weekdays and Sundays in winter. With scheduled services increasingly following a common pattern week by week throughout the year, it would be appropriate to standardise the hours covered by the quota.'

Although Latham J recorded in his judgment the minister's view that the extra
f restrictions on the noisiest two categories of aircraft during the night period were seen as offsetting the reduction in the time covered by the quota periods, particularly in the early morning, Ms Duthie said that this counter-balancing was not subject to any arithmetical calculation and that it was not being suggested that there was an exact correlation between these two features.

In my judgment, these passages in the consultation paper sufficiently identified
g the matters the government would be likely to consider, when balancing the fourth and fifth objectives it had identified at the start of that paper and the policy context in which they would be considered, and I do not consider that the appellants' criticisms in this regard are well founded. Although they complain that the desirability of standardising the schedules was only adverted to by one
h airline and by the British Airports Authority in their responses to the consultation, it is for the minister, not the court, to determine what weight to give to the advantages of making this change.

As to the appellants' complaint that the government ought to have explained how the noise climate in the whole of the night period was likely to change, there
j is, in my judgment, a limit to the amount that it is reasonable to require a statutory authority to spell out in a consultation document. The fact that changes were being proposed to the length of what are now being called 'the night shoulder periods', and the restrictions they would contain, was completely clear in the 1993 paper, and the way was open to objectors to do their own calculations to try to persuade the minister that the increased noise level he would be permitting was such that the balance he was seeking to strike should be struck in

some different way. Similarly, both the 1987 and the 1993 consultation papers were public documents, and the way was open to objectors to argue that the same reasons that had held good for restricting decontrol should still hold sway, albeit in different circumstances, in 1993–98.

Because the appellants complained that they were taken by surprise by the judge's finding that the 1988 undertaking was now a dead letter, we permitted them to put before us the 1985 White Paper and some of the evidence recently given by the department's principal witness on noise policy at the ongoing public inquiry into a fifth terminal at Heathrow. The effect of this evidence was that the government's approach to tackling aircraft noise which was set out in section 8 of the 1985 White Paper had not changed in essence since then. The inspector was told that the government was concerned to strike a balance between various interests in the various measures it adopted to reduce noise and to encourage noise mitigation and the use of quieter aircraft. He was also told that although there was always an element of 'balance' in policy, the emphasis now being given to the need to balance consideration of environmental impacts alongside economic benefits was an area in which policy had developed rather than changed substantially.

I can see nothing in this evidence to deflect me from the view that the Secretary of State understood what government policy was and that he had made clear the extent to which he was consciously departing from previous policy in the proposals he was making in the 1993 consultation paper. No doubt, if he had had wind of the complaint now being made (which did not surface in all the voluminous complaints made in the course of the earlier applications to which I have referred) he would have made clear in the 1995 papers the extent to which he was well aware that by ending the night quota period at 6 am throughout the year, there might have been a smaller difference between the permitted winter 'quota count points of noise' in 1988 and those permitted in 1993. I do not, however, consider that he was under any legal duty to point out the obvious. He has now made it clear that he appreciated that para 34 of the 1993 paper was misleading and that he is aware that his proposals involve, at Heathrow, a worsening of the noise climate to some extent.

I do not consider it useful, in this context, to enter into a semantic argument as to whether respondents to the consultation paper should have appreciated that the 1988 undertaking was dead, as the judge held, or whether it was still alive in principle, but subject to the interpretation that the noise climate meant the permitted climate, not the actual climate, which is what the evidence suggests. Nor do I consider it useful to analyse the explanations being given by the department's lawyers in the spring and summer of 1995: the text of what is complained of is set out in the judge's judgment and I need not repeat it here (see [1996] 4 All ER 93 at 105, [1996] 1 WLR 1005 at 1018). I agree with the judge's interpretation of this explanation and the matter does not justify any further exposition.

For all these reasons I consider that the consultation papers set out the proposals fairly and rationally in an intelligible policy context and, although as I have said the matter was not put in the same way before the judge, I agree with his view that this part of the appellants' challenge should be dismissed.

The appellants' second head of challenge is based on inadequacy of reasons. Section 78(3) of the 1982 Act does not require the Secretary of State to give reasons and the appellants accept that the law does not at present recognise a general duty to give reasons for an administrative decision (see *Doody v Secretary* a *of State for the Home Dept* [1993] 3 All ER 92 at 110, [1994] 1 AC 531 at 564 per Lord Mustill). They derive, however, from the decision of this court in *R v Kensington and Chelsea Royal London BC, ex p Grillo* [1996] 2 FCR 56 the principle that a duty to give reasons may be implied in appropriate circumstances. In that case the court approved a dictum of the Divisional Court in *R v Higher Education Funding Council, ex p Institute of Dental Surgery* [1994] 1 All ER 651 at 671, [1994] 1 WLR 242

b at 263, to the effect that 'where the subject-matter is an interest so highly regarded by the law—for example, personal liberty', fairness required that reasons, at least for particular decisions, should be given as of right: where, on the other hand, a decision appears aberrant, fairness may require reasons so that the recipient may know whether the aberration is in the legal sense real (and so challengeable) or apparent.

c   The appellants put their case on adequacy of reasons in two main ways. First, they say that a fundamental right was being interfered with, and since there was no remedy for their inhabitants at common law or under the convention, and their only protection was by way of judicial review proceedings, they contend that the need for adequate reasons was manifest. Quite apart from the

d significance of the fact that the proposals involve their inhabitants being subjected to an increased nuisance by noise of which they have no legal right to complain, they argue that the Court of Appeal now recognises that 'the human rights dimension' is part of the relevant background to the formulation and exercise of administrative policy and that proper justification should be given for a decision which involves an infringement of such rights (see *R v Ministry of*

e *Defence, ex p Smith* [1996] 1 All ER 257 at 266, 272–273; [1996] QB 517 at 558, 564–565).

    Alternatively, the appellants give three reasons for contending that this is a case in which a decision should be regarded as aberrant. First, because although the Secretary of State has acknowledged that his new proposals were contrary to the

f previous policy, he has never explained why, when and to what extent the 1988 undertaking was altered. Secondly, because the new proposals are contrary to the still extant noise policy set out in the 1985 White Paper. Thirdly, because the statements made by the department's legal representatives in the course of 1995 were so incomprehensible as to introduce aberrancy to the minister's eventual decision: I have already averted to this last point, which does not call for any

g further treatment.

    The appellants developed their arguments on the inadequacy of reasons under the same five heads they had used to support their contentions on legitimate expectation. First, although the minister admitted a change of policy in the June 1995 consultation paper, no reference to this change was made in the August

h decision letter (which said that in certain respects the 1987 policies were being continued), and no explanation was given for the admitted change of policy. Secondly, the minister did not explain what his new policy was.

    Their third contention is that although the decision letter contained the concept that the proposals 'represent[ed] a sharing of the benefits so far achieved

j by quicker aircraft, between local people and the airlines and their customers' it did not explain how this had been achieved. Although it had been said that there was a balancing between decontrol of previously controlled periods and additional controls on noisier aircraft, the appellants maintained that this had not taken place, and the minister now admitted that there was no exact correlation.

    Fourthly, the appellants complain that no explanation has been given of how the noise climate in the night period (as opposed to the night quota period) was

likely to change, even though the Secretary of State maintained that one of his
policy objectives was to continue to protect local communities from excessive
aircraft noise at night.   Finally, no explanation at all had been given for the
different decision on de-controlling the night shoulder period, or for the altered
balance now being struck between 'the economic well-being of the country' and
the right of the appellants' inhabitants to respect for their home, private and
family life.

In support of their arguments based on inadequacy of reasons the appellants
rely on the well-known passages in the speech of Lord Bridge in *Save Britain's
Heritage v Secretary of State for the Environment* [1991] 2 All ER 10 at 22, 23, [1991] 1
WLR 153 at 165, 166.   In the first of these passages Lord Bridge described as
'particularly well expressed' a passage in the judgment of Phillips J in *Hope v
Secretary of State for the Environment* (1975) 31 P & CR 120 at 123:

> '... the decision must be such that it enables the appellant to understand on
> what grounds the appeal has been decided and be in sufficient detail to
> enable him to know what conclusions the inspector has reached on the
> principal important controversial issues.'

In the second passage Lord Bridge said that he—

> 'certainly accept[ed] that the reasons should enable a person who is
> entitled to contest the decision to make a proper assessment as to whether
> the decision should be challenged.'

The judge dealt with this challenge by saying that any duty to give reasons in this
case must be based on the doctrine of legitimate expectation and that he did not
see that that doctrine could be applied differently to the giving of reasons so as to
require a breadth of detail of reasons beyond the ambit of previous practice and
utterances.

In analysing the appellants' arguments I begin by observing that they accepted
that where reasons for an administrative decision are required they do not have
to be detailed or elaborate and that it is sufficient if they explain why the decision
was reached.   They also do not quarrel with the judge's view that a passage from
a consultation paper, when read with a passage from the decision, may throw
light on the reasons lying behind the decision.   Even in a case where the relevant
statutory scheme expressly required the minister to have regard to every material
consideration and to give reasons for his ultimate decision, the House of Lords
defined the scope of the duty to give reasons in these terms:

> 'What the Secretary of State must do is to state his reasons in sufficient
> detail to enable the reader to know what conclusion he has reached on the
> "principal important controversial issues".   To require him to refer to every
> material consideration, however insignificant, and to deal with every
> argument, however peripheral, would be to impose an unjustifiable burden.'
> (See *Bolton Metropolitan DC v Secretary of State for the Environment* (1995) 71 P
> & CR 309 at 314 per Lord Lloyd of Berwick (with whose speech the other
> four Law Lords agreed).)

A little earlier, Lord Lloyd had said (71 P & CR 309 at 313):

> 'There is nothing in the statutory language which requires him, in stating
> his reasons, to deal specifically with every material consideration.   Otherwise
> his task would never be done.   The decision letter would be as long as the

a   inspector's report. He has to have *regard* to every material consideration; but he need not mention them all.' (Lord Lloyd's emphasis.)

Here the statute has prescribed no particular procedures for the decision-making process, no express duty to have regard to every material consideration, and no specific duty to give reasons. In so far as duties may be introduced by rules of natural justice, the governing principles are to be found in the speech of Lord

b   Bridge in *Lloyd v McMahon* [1987] 1 All ER 1118 at 1161, [1987] AC 625 at 702:

'... rules of natural justice are not engraved on tablets of stone. To use the phrase which better expresses the underlying concept, what the requirements of fairness demand when any body, domestic, administrative

c   or judicial, has to make a decision which will affect the rights of individuals depends on the character of the decision-making body, the kind of decision it has to make and the statutory or other framework in which it operates. In particular it is well established that when a statute has conferred on any body the power to make decisions affecting individuals, the courts will not only require the procedure prescribed by the statute to be followed, but will

d   readily imply so much and no more to be introduced by way of additional procedural safeguards as will ensure the attainment of fairness.'

The present case is concerned, among other things, with the right of people living near Heathrow Airport to enjoy reasonably quiet nights (a right linked, as I have said, to the rights recognised by art 8(1) of the convention). The procedure

e   the Secretary of State decided to adopt, both to ensure the attainment of fairness and also to accommodate such people's legitimate expectation that they would be entitled to make representations to him before he made any changes to the regime for restricting night flying at Heathrow, was to issue a consultation paper (with later supplements to accommodate decisions of the courts or the

f   complaints of the appellants and others), and later, when he had had a chance to consider all the representations he had received, to publish a short press notice announcing his decision and giving brief reasons for it. No doubt if Parliament had not been in recess in mid-August, his decision would have been furnished to Parliament, whether in the form of a written answer or otherwise, and he would always be liable to be called to Parliament to account for his decision and to give

g   reasons to explain it further.

This is not, therefore, a case in which a decision-maker has given no reasons (contrast *R v Civil Service Appeal Board, ex p Cunningham* [1991] 4 All ER 310 and *R v City of London Corp, ex p Matson* (1995) 8 Admin LR 49). The minister has given reasons, albeit brief ones.

h   The question the court has to decide, therefore, is whether the reasons in fact given by the minister enable the reader to know what conclusions he has reached on the principal important controversial issues.

A procedure in which a minister starts a decision-making process by publishing a full consultation paper which contains his own provisional proposals is different

j   from a procedure in which he passively awaits the report of an inspector on the merits of a proposal made by a third party, and in any scrutiny of the adequacy of the minister's reasons for his decision in such circumstances it is, in my judgment, appropriate to read his reasons alongside the consultation paper which defined the main issues which were likely to inform his choice. The 'principal important controversial issues' he had to decide were: (1) whether to go ahead with his new scheme based on noise quotas and, if so, how large should the new quotas be and

what period of the night should they embrace; (2) whether to continue with
extended restrictions for all aircraft movements from 6 am onwards on winter   *a*
weekdays (till 6.30 am), winter Sundays (till 8 am) and for summer Sunday
departures (till 8 am) or to introduce new arrangements (and if so what) banning
noisier aircraft during some or all of those periods; and (3) what restrictions he
should impose on scheduled movements of noisier aircraft and whether he
should extend them to a time (and if so what) earlier than 11.30 pm.   *b*

In his announcement on 16 August 1995 the minister gave his answers on all
these points. He also restated the five policy objectives which had informed the
pre-1993 review and said that the government was committed to achieving and
sustaining those objectives. He restated the government's aim to maintain a fair
balance between the interests of local people and the airline industry including its
customers. He said that differences between the new regime and the 1988–93   *c*
regime represented a sharing of the benefits so far achieved by quieter aircraft,
between local people and the airlines and their customers. He said in terms that
he had given careful consideration to all the responses he had received to the two
recent consultation papers, which were being made available for public scrutiny
for a six-month period. He also made it clear that he had ensured that the   *d*
maximum possible level of noise which could be generated against the new
movements limits would be less than the level which could have been generated
by aircraft operating to the full extent permitted in the summer of 1988.

Mr Burnett, who appears for the minister, contends that the minister has by
these means fulfilled his legal obligations. I now turn to consider the appellants'
grounds for maintaining that he has not.   *e*

I consider first the complaints that he has changed his policy without giving
reasons or explaining what his new policy is. In my judgment, these complaints
are not well-founded in law. On the face of it, Parliament has given the Secretary
of State an unfettered discretion as to how he will exercise his powers under
s 78(3) of the 1982 Act. He has chosen to go about the decision-making process   *f*
in the way I have described, and in advance of making a relevant decision he has
published the policy objectives which will inform his choice and has invited
interested parties to make representations to him, in particular on the issues he
has identified. Once the problems created by para 34 of the first paper were
resolved, everyone would know that his policy objectives were those set out at
the start of the 1993 paper, subject to the caveat that the permitted noise levels   *g*
for the periods when noise quotas were in operation would not be allowed to
increase. He does not have to repeat this all over again when he gives reasons for
his eventual decision.

The appellants' complaint about the lack of reasons being given to show how
the proposals would maintain the essential balance between the interests of the   *h*
airline industry and local people is, in my judgment, equally ill-founded. As I
have said, the 1993 consultation paper showed how things had changed on a
number of fronts since 1987 and I know of no principle of law which would
require a minister to go back to an earlier consultation paper and explain, item by
item, why he is now taking a different approach to that taken by his predecessor.   *j*
He has set out the competing considerations. He has set out his policy objectives.
He has allowed time for representations to be made and he has carefully
considered them, and he has announced his decision, which involved balancing
competing and often irreconcilable interests, with express reference to all these
matters. In argument before Latham J, for instance, counsel for the Secretary of
State had accepted that standardising the periods of restriction was bound to

a increase the number of early morning aircraft movements, but he pointed out that in return the Secretary of State had effectively prohibited the movement of the two noisiest categories of aircraft during the night period (at least until 6 am). In my judgment, the law does not require the Secretary of State to go further than he in fact went when giving reasons for his decision in this regard.

b The next complaint relates to his failure to explain the likely effect of the relaxation of restrictions from 6 am onwards compared with the previous regime. It would no doubt have been courteous for the minister to have furnished Richmond's chief executive with the information he sought, but he was not in my judgment obliged to do so as a matter of law. He had explained quite clearly what his proposals and his policy objectives were, and the contemporary arguments for relaxing the regime to some extent from 6 am onwards, to c accommodate no doubt the three types of special case identified in the consultation paper and the request for standardised schedules, were all quite evident. He had also, eventually, made it clear how he intended to make comparisons between the night noise climate at different times. The way had been open to the appellants to persuade him, by force of argument and no doubt d by other means available to them in the political forum, to reach a different conclusion from that which he proposed from 6 am onwards, but I do not consider that he went wrong in law in failing to give this matter specific attention in his decision-letter. The appellants' real complaint is that he did not give their side of the case the favourable attention they believed it deserved. That is not a matter for the courts.

e The appellants' next specific complaint is that the minister has reached a different decision as to de-controlling the shoulder period, as compared with that reached in the 1987 White Paper, without explaining why. To a great extent this is a specific rehash of earlier more generalised complaints. Nobody reading the 1993 consultation paper alongside the 1987 Paper could fail to notice that greater f weight was now being given to economic factors and that in this respect, as I have already said, there were a number of important new considerations which could well attract more weight than had been given to similar considerations in 1987. Moreover the government had always made it clear that its decisions in this area would be informed by the results of research into the relationship between aircraft noise and sleep disturbance, and the new research evidence mentioned in g the 1993 paper was a new factor which could influence a decision-maker in taking a slightly different decision, even if it is correct that this evidence did not specifically embrace the issue of 'sleep prevention' between 6 and 6.30 am in the wintertime. For reasons similar to those I have given already, I do not consider that the minister was under any legal duty to spell out the reasons why he h eventually confirmed his earlier proposal to prefer one set of arguments to another.

I turn now to the argument that insufficient justification has been given of the infringement of the 'right to sleep' that this decision entailed. In *R v Ministry of Defence, ex p Smith* [1996] 1 All ER 257 at 263, [1996] QB 517 at 554 Bingham MR j accepted, as an accurate distillation of the principles laid down by the House of Lords in *Bugdaycay v Secretary of State for the Home Dept* [1987] 1 All ER 940, [1987] AC 514 and *Brind v Secretary of State for the Home Dept* [1991] 1 All ER 720, [1991] 1 AC 696, the following submission by counsel:

'The court may not interfere with the exercise of an administrative discretion on substantive grounds save where the court is satisfied that the decision is unreasonable in the sense that it is beyond the range of responses open to a reasonable decision-maker.   But in judging whether the *a* decision-maker has exceeded this margin of appreciation the human rights context is important. The more substantial the interference with human rights, the more the court will require by way of justification before it is satisfied that the decision is reasonable in the sense outlined above.'

b

Well-known passages in the speech of Lord Bridge in the first of these cases (see [1987] 1 All ER 940 at 952, [1987] AC 514 at 531) and in the speeches of Lord Bridge and Lord Templeman in the second (see [1991] 1 All ER 720 at 723, 725–726, [1991] 1 AC 696 at 748–749, 751) are the source of this clear exposition of the current state of the law. It is instructive in the present context to note that in *Ex p* *Smith* Bingham MR rejected a submission by the Ministry of Defence that a test *c* more exacting than the *Wednesbury* test of irrationality was appropriate in the context of a policy decision by ministers (see *Associated Provincial Picture Houses Ltd v Wednesbury Corp* [1947] 2 All ER 680, [1948] 1 KB 223). He said ([1996] 1 All ER 257 at 264, [1996] QB 517 at 556):

d

'The greater the policy content of a decision, and the more remote the subject matter of a decision from ordinary judicial experience, the more hesitant the courts must necessarily be in holding a decision to be irrational. That is good law and, like most good law, common sense. Where decisions of a policy-laden ... nature are in issue, even greater caution than normal must be shown in applying the test, but the test itself is sufficiently flexible to *e* cover all situations.'

The right to respect for one's home and family life (carrying with it in this context the connotation of the right, acknowledged by the common law, to the enjoyment of nights at home undisturbed by unreasonable nuisance from noise) *f* is of course quite different from the rights to life and liberty or the rights of homosexuals which Bingham MR went on to consider in the next passage of his judgment. But it is a right of a type which the courts are increasingly willing to recognise as worthy of specific attention within the framework of the approach now helpfully identified in *Ex p Smith*.

Using this approach, I am satisfied that the minister furnished sufficient *g* justification for his decision, albeit that it impinges on the rights of people to enjoy nights undisturbed by unreasonable nuisance from noise, particularly from 6 a m onwards, and that his decision cannot be impugned on this ground.

I am also satisfied that the decision cannot properly be described as aberrant, and in that sense calling for further reasons by way of justification than the *h* minister has been willing to supply. Once the arguments based on an alleged confusion of policy have been set on one side, the minister's reasons are in my judgment sufficiently clear and the decision does not warrant that pejorative epithet. I accept the cogency of the appellants' criticism of the way in which the minister, through his lawyers and otherwise, sought to maintain for a long time *j* his stance that his policy was completely consistent with earlier policy statements, but so far as the present decision is concerned, in my judgment the minister has given adequate reasons and sufficient justification for his conclusion that it is reasonable, on balance, to run the risk of diminishing to some degree local people's ability to sleep at nights because of the other countervailing considerations to which he has now been willing to give greater weight.

a I turn finally to the third ground of challenge. If rational reasons are set out for a proposal to change a scheme for restricting aircraft movements, and adequate reasons are given for the eventual decision, a challenge based on irrationality faces formidably high hurdles (see *Brind v Secretary of State for the Home Dept* [1991] 1 All ER 720 at 731, 737–738, [1991] 1 AC 696 at 757–758, 764–765). I accept Mr George QC's submission that these three heads of challenge may be mutually b independent of one another and that an attack may succeed on any one of these grounds when it has failed on one or more of the others (see e g *R v City of London Corp, ex p Matson* (1995) 8 Admin LR 49, where the challenge failed on irrationality but succeeded on the absence of reasons). In the present case, however, there is such a large overlap between the appellants' arguments based on irrationality and their arguments on the other heads of challenge that I can deal with this part of c the case quite briefly.

In so far as Mr George attacks the decision for what he calls 'policy-related irrationality' I have set out my reasons for rejecting this ground of attack. Although to a great extent the Secretary of State was the author of his own misfortunes by including para 34 in the original consultation paper and by d accompanying that paper with a press notice in somewhat tendentious terms, these errors had, in my judgment, been successfully eradicated by June 1995 at the latest, and I agree with the judge that there is no basis now for arguing that the new policy is *Wednesbury* irrational.

I have also set out already my reasons for my conclusion that it was not irrational to give greater weight in 1993 than in 1987 to the arguments in support e of an earlier end to the night quota period in winter, or to consider that that part of government policy which consisted of phasing out or restricting the noisier aircraft could properly be put in the balance when considering whether the benefits so far achieved by quieter aircraft were indeed being shared between local people and the airlines and their customers. As to the absence of evidence f from research on the effect of noise on 'sleep prevention' (ie when someone wakes up in the early morning and cannot get to sleep again), I accept Mr Burnett's submission that the minister could not reasonably be criticised for not relying on evidence that did not at present exist and that the present state of the research evidence on sleep disturbance was a factor he could reasonably take into account.

g For all these reasons, although the appellants' case was put rather differently in certain respects, and we had the benefit of the additional policy evidence to which I have referred, I am satisfied that their challenge fails on all the three surviving grounds and that the judge was right to dismiss it. I would accordingly dismiss the appeal.

h
MORRITT LJ. I agree.

LEGGATT LJ. I agree.

j *Appeal dismissed.*

12 November 1996. The Appeal Committee of the House of Lords (Lord Mustill, Lord Steyn and Lord Hoffmann) refused leave to appeal.

L I Zysman Esq   Barrister.

R v Bristol Magistrates' Court, ex parte Hodge   *a*

QUEEN'S BENCH DIVISION (CROWN OFFICE LIST)
CAZALET J
8, 29 JULY, 30 AUGUST 1996

b

Husband and wife – Maintenance – Arrears – Wife signing enforcement permission – Husband seeking remission – Magistrates remitting arrears – Whether magistrates notifying wife of intention to remit arrears – Magistrates' Courts Rules 1981, r 44.

Husband and wife – Maintenance – Arrears – Remission – Magistrates failing to notify   *c*
wife of intention to remit arrears – Magistrates remitting arrears – No provision for appeal against remission of arrears – Whether wife to proceed by way of case stated or judicial review – Magistrates' Courts Act 1980, s 95 – Magistrates' Courts Rules 1981, r 44.

The mother and father were divorced and, in subsequent ancillary relief   *d*
proceedings, the county court ordered the father to make periodical payments in respect of the children of the family. The orders were registered in the magistrates' court. Arrears accrued and the mother applied for enforcement permission; she signed the relevant form, which included the words 'the whole or part of the arrears accruing under the order may be remitted by the justices',   *e*
and returned it as requested to the clerk to the justices. The father disputed the amount of arrears outstanding. There followed a number of hearings, which the mother did not attend, and she received various letters from the clerk in which no reference was made to remitting the arrears. On 8 February 1995 the clerk wrote again informing the mother that the father had disputed the amount of the arrears and requesting that she submit her observations by 15 February, but again   *f*
no reference was made to remission of arrears. The mother personally answered the clerk's letter, stating what she maintained were the arrears owing and contending that there was a balance left to pay. That letter reached the court before the hearing of 15 February, which the father attended in person. Thereafter, the clerk wrote to the mother saying that the court had remitted part   *g*
of the arrears and had ordered the father to pay the remainder at a weekly rate. The mother accepted that the justices had been entitled to remit a part of the sum remitted; but, although there was some compliance, there was a continuing default and in June 1995 a further complaint was issued for arrears. At a hearing on 21 June 1995 the justices, by letter written to the mother on the same day, remitted in full the arrears owing. The mother applied for judicial review of the   *h*
orders made by the justices on 15 February and 21 June 1995, contending that she had been given no opportunity to make representations nor had she been notified of any intention to remit arrears. The question also arose whether the correct appeal or reviewing procedure was by way of case stated or by judicial review pursuant to RSC Ord 53.   *j*

Held – (1) The justices were in breach of r 44(1)[a] of the Magistrates' Courts Rules 1981 in making an order remitting the whole or any part of arrears due under an

---

a   Rule 44(1) is set out at p 928 *j* to 929 *b*, post

a order enforceable under s 95[b] of the Magistrates' Courts Act 1980 without first notifying the applicant that it was their intention so to do. The notice of enforcement permission which the applicant had signed was merely a statement of the power of the justices to remit arrears, not of an intention so to do. The applicant had not therefore been given the opportunity to make representations to the court within the provisions of r 44(1). Further, the father had raised

b matters of conduct at the hearing which might have had a bearing upon the justices' decision, and it would have been appropriate that the applicant's account as to those matters should also have been put before the court. Accordingly, the orders were flawed and the justices were not entitled to remit the arrears as they had purported to do (see p 929 c to f j, post).

(2) It would have been open to the applicant to seek to have stated a case of

c construction as to whether, by their enforcement permission notice, the justices had given adequate notice to the applicant within the requirements of r 44(1) of their intention to remit arrears. However, the time to proceed by way of case stated had passed and the court had no power to extend the time for such an application. It followed that the only route open to the applicant to challenge the

d orders was by an application for judicial review. Although the court would not exercise its jurisdiction to grant judicial review where other remedies were available and had not been used, in the instant case the applicant had followed the course stated in the textbooks, and the issue of the application for leave was in time for the second of the two orders. It would therefore be appropriate for the court to exercise its discretion and make an order of certiorari quashing the

e justices' orders (see p 931 c to p 932 b, post); R v Dover Magistrates' Court, ex p Kidner [1983] 1 All ER 475 distinguished; Berry v Berry [1986] 2 All ER 948 followed.

Notes

For remission of arrears due under orders enforceable as affiliation orders, see 29

f Halsbury's Laws (4th edn) para 427.

For the Magistrates' Courts Act 1980, s 95, see 27 Halsbury's Statutes (4th edn) (1992 reissue) 251.

For the Magistrates' Courts Rules, r 44, see 11 Halsbury's Statutory Instruments (1995 reissue) 488.

g

Cases referred to in judgment

Berry v Berry [1986] 2 All ER 948, [1987] Fam 1, [1986] 3 WLR 257, CA.
Fletcher v Fletcher [1985] 2 All ER 260, [1985] Fam 92, [1985] 2 WLR 985, DC.
Michael v Gowland [1977] 2 All ER 328, [1977] 1 WLR 296, DC.

h R v Dover Magistrates' Court, ex p Kidner [1983] 1 All ER 475.
R v Epping and Harlow General Comrs, ex p Goldstraw [1983] 3 All ER 257, CA.
R v York City Justices, ex p Farmery (1988) 153 JP 257, DC.

Cases also cited or referred to in skeleton arguments

j R v Hastings Licensing Justices, ex p John Lovibond & Sons Ltd [1968] 2 All ER 270, [1968] 1 WLR 735, DC.
R v Liverpool Justices, ex p Roberts [1960] 2 All ER 384, [1960] 1 WLR 585, DC.

---

b   Section 95, so far as material, provides: '... a magistrates' court may remit the whole or any part of the sum due under the [maintenance] order ...'

Application for judicial review

Linda Mary Hodge applied with leave granted by Sir Stephen Brown P on 17 January 1996 for judicial review by way of orders of certiorari to quash the decisions made by the Bristol justices sitting in the Bristol Magistrates' Court on 15 February 1995 and 21 June 1995 whereby arrears of maintenance due to the applicant under a periodical payments order were remitted. The respondents took no part in the proceedings. The facts are set out in the judgment.

Tim Lawson-Cruttenden (instructed by *David Burrows*, Bristol) for the applicant.

Cur adv vult

30 August 1996. The following judgment was delivered.

CAZALET J. This is an application for judicial review in respect of orders made by the Bristol justices on 15 February 1995 and 21 June 1995 whereby arrears of maintenance were remitted which were due under a periodical payments order.

The only party who appears before me is the applicant, Linda Mary Hodge. She is represented by a solicitor advocate. The respondents, the Bristol magistrates, do not appear and are not represented, although they have submitted a short skeleton argument as to costs in the event of this application succeeding.

I start by summarising the background. The applicant was formerly married to Michael John Rees. There were two children of their family, Kelly Anne Rees, who was born on 15 December 1976 and who is now 19 years, and Nicholas John Rees, who was born on 17 June 1978, but who died on 11 May 1995, shortly before his eighteenth birthday.

The applicant and Mr Rees were divorced in 1982. On 12 August 1983 the Bristol County Court, in ancillary relief proceedings between the parties, made an order by consent settling their financial and property claims. In particular, Mr Rees was ordered to pay periodical payments to the children at the rate of £12 each per week until each child attained the age of 17 or ceased full-time education if later, or further order.

After various further applications, the court, on 15 September 1987, varied the original periodical payments orders to the sum of £17·50 each for the two children. Accordingly, Mr Rees had to pay the sum of £35 per week in total for the two children. There were no further variations of these orders; they were subsequently registered in the Bristol Magistrates' Court.

Arrears accrued, and on 5 October 1994 the applicant applied for enforcement permission. To this end she signed a form headed 'Bristol Magistrates' Court— Enforcement Permission'. The material part of the form reads as follows:

'I hereby give the clerk to the justices permission to take such enforcement action as he deems necessary for the recovery of payments due under the above order. I understand that as a result of the proceedings taken on my behalf against the Defendant namely Michael J. Rees, he may be committed to prison and/or the whole or part of the arrears accruing under the order may be remitted by the justices. Current Arrears: £962·50.'

That document was signed by the applicant and dated 5 October 1994. It was returned, as was requested on the face of the document, to the clerk to the a justices, accounts department, Bristol Magistrates' Court. It is not in dispute that this was the only form that the applicant signed.

The events which then followed are set out in affidavits or exhibits to affidavits which have been filed. The initial hearing of the complaint in respect of the arrears took place on 3 January 1995. At that hearing Mr Rees disputed that the amount of arrears outstanding was as much as the £962·50 specified by the b applicant in the document entitled enforcement permission. The applicant did not attend that hearing. Accordingly, the hearing of the complaint was adjourned until 31 January 1995 and Mr Rees was instructed to produce to the court, by 17 January 1995, a list of the payments which he said that he had made so that this list could be sent to the applicant for her comments. This list was duly produced by Mr Rees but, for reasons with which I need not concern myself, it was not sent c to the applicant in time for her to answer by 31 January 1995. Consequently, the complaint was further adjourned until 15 February 1995 to enable the applicant to do so.

By letter dated 30 January 1995 the clerk to the Bristol justices wrote to the applicant enclosing Mr Rees' alleged list of payments. This latter document was d detailed and went back to 1992. The clerk asked that the applicant's observations on that list should be sent to the court prior to 15 February 1995. Nothing was stated in that letter in regard to remission of arrears.

By letter of 8 February 1995 the clerk to the justices also sent copies of the list of payments produced by Mr Rees and his letter, to the applicant's solicitors. On the same day the clerk to the justices wrote again to the applicant telling the e applicant that, on 3 January 1995 at the first hearing, Mr Rees had in fact disputed the amount of the arrears, saying in particular that he had accepted that £210 arrears had accrued in respect of Kelly since she had left school in August 1993 but that she had started work during the same month, that is prior to her seventeenth birthday. Once again, the clerk to the justices asked for the applicant's f observations to be available by 15 February. Again there was no reference to a remission of arrears.

By letter dated February 1995 the applicant personally answered the clerk's letters. Her letter reached the court before the hearing of 15 February 1995. In that letter the applicant stated what she maintained were the arrears owing under the two orders. It was her contention that, after giving due credit for payments g made, some of which in particular had been received more recently, there was a balance left to pay as of 12 February 1995 amounting to £952·50.

Mr Rees attended the hearing on 15 February 1995 in person. The applicant did not attend. Evidence on oath was given by Mr Rees. He made various statements in regard to a misunderstanding about his having thought that the h order in Kelly's favour had ceased when she left school. However by a letter dated 15 February 1995 the clerk, following that hearing, wrote to the applicant saying that the court had remitted the sum of £648·50 (in fact the letter stated £684·50 but this was corrected in a subsequent letter to the lower figure) and had ordered Mr Rees to pay at the rate of £30·00 per week (that is £17·50 under the j order plus £12·50 a week off the arrears of £664).

In a further letter dated 6 March 1995 the clerk wrote to the applicant's solicitors indicating how the justices had arrived at these figures. It is not necessary for me to go into the detail of them, save to say that the applicant accepts that of the sum remitted of £648·50, the justices were entitled to remit £297·50. This she acknowledged and, indeed, acknowledged in her calculations up to 12 February 1995 (as per her letter to the justices) was a sum which had been

paid to her by Mr Rees by a cheque which had been postdated to 31 January 1995
and which had been sent direct to her and had been met on or about that day.

The court sheets show that there was a further arrears hearing on 12 April 1995
when Mr Rees was ordered to pay arrears of £804·00 by way of a lump sum
payment of £240, followed by weekly instalments of £12·50. Although there was
some compliance with the orders there was a continuing default in meeting the
full order and on 1 June 1995 a further complaint was issued for arrears.

The affidavit of Mr Antoine Mark John Rendell, court clerk to the Bristol
magistrates, sworn on 12 March 1996 deals with the hearing of that complaint
before the justices on 21 June 1995. Mr Rees attended in person and was not
represented. The applicant did not appear. Mr Rees disputed his liability for the
arrears put to him and gave evidence indicating why he considered that he was
justified in refusing to pay the arrears. Again I need not concern myself with the
detail of this. The essential point is that at that hearing of 21 June 1995 the
justices, confirmed by letter dated 21 June 1995 and written to the applicant,
remitted in full the arrears then owing which they held to amount to £584.

As to that amount of arrears, I make this point. If one takes the figure of £865
arrears set out in the applicant's affidavit, sworn on 18 September 1995 in support
of this application, and excludes the figure of £351, which she maintains was the
subject of erroneous findings by the magistrates at the hearing of 15 February
1995 when they held that this sum was either not owing or had been paid by Mr
Rees, then her figure alleged to be owing as at 21 June 1995 is reduced to £514. In
fact, the justices held that the sum then owing by way of arrears amounted to
£584. It may be that the justices took into account an additional four weeks
maintenance; namely the sum of £70, since this amount is the difference between
the two figures. I take the matter no further since, if it is appropriate, these figures
can be calculated at some later hearing. Suffice it to say that if one bears in mind
that issue was joined on the £351 remitted on the first hearing on 15 February
1995, then there is a small difference between what the applicant contended as
being, and the justices held to have been the arrears due on 21 June 1995.

Mr Lawson-Cruttenden, who appears on behalf of the applicant, contends that
the application raises two issues.

First, he maintains that the Bristol justices were not entitled to remit arrears
due from Mr Rees to the applicant in respect of child maintenance without giving
her an opportunity to make representations concerning such remission either
orally or in writing, and that no such opportunity was given to the applicant.

The documents before me indicate that the only reference made by the justices
or their clerk to the court's powers to remit arrears in whole or in part was as set
out on the notice of enforcement permission dated 5 October 1994 and signed by
the applicant to which I have already referred. However, the correspondence
which then followed, both to the applicant in person and to her solicitors, whilst
referring specifically to the issue as to the amount of arrears made no reference
either to the applicant or to her solicitors that the justices intended to remit, or
might form the intention of remitting, arrears at either the hearing of 15 February
1995 or that of 21 June 1995.

The power of the magistrates' court to remit arrears is contained in s 95 of the
Magistrates' Courts Act 1980. Rule 44(1) of the Magistrates' Courts Rules 1981,
SI 1981/552, provides:

> 'Before remitting the whole or any part of a sum due under a magistrates'
> court maintenance order or order enforceable as a magistrates' court

a   maintenance order under section 95 of the Act of 1980, the court shall, except
      save where it appears to it to be unnecessary or impracticable to do so, cause
      the person in whose favour the order is made or, if that person is a child, the
      child or the person with whom the child has his home to be notified of its
      intention and shall afford to such person a reasonable opportunity to make
      representations to the court, either orally at an adjourned hearing of the
b   complaint for enforcement or in writing and such representation shall be
      considered by the court.'

Mr Lawson-Cruttenden submits that there was a clear failure by the justices in
this case to notify the applicant of their intention to remit arrears at each of the
two hearings in question. He maintains that by failing to give such notice the
c justices were in breach of the mandatory provisions of r 44(1).

      I consider that submission to be properly made. The notice of enforcement
permission, in my view, was no more than a statement of the power of the
justices. It did not state that they had the intention of remitting arrears either in
whole or in part. I consider that the applicant should have been given notice by
d the justices through their clerk before they remitted any arrears at either of the
two hearings that it was their intention so to do. The applicant would then have
been given an opportunity to make representations to the court within the
provisions of r 44(1). She was not given this opportunity. I also note that such
communications as there were between the court and her, following her signing
the enforcement procedure notice, raised expressly the amount of the arrears and
e did not assert any intention to remit. The letter which the applicant received
after the court hearing of 15 February 1995 was retrospective, in that she was then
told that at the hearing of 15 February 1995 there had been a remission of certain
arrears (see letter from the justices' clerk of 15 February 1995). It is also to be
noted that the justices heard evidence from Mr Rees which went as to matters of
f conduct. His evidence as to this may have played some part on the minds of the
justices in the exercise of their discretion; but in any event, it would appear on the
face of it to have been appropriate that the applicant's account as to any such
matters should also have been put before the court if these were in fact relevant
and material to the exercise of the court's discretion.

      Under r 44(1) it is open to the court to waive the giving of such notice if it
g appears to be unnecessary or impracticable so to do. I do not think that it could
be argued that such a situation arose in this case even though a matter of two or
three days after the hearing of 15 February 1995, the applicant was put on notice
by letter that certain arrears had been remitted at that hearing. Should she then
have been put on notice by implication of an intention to remit at a later hearing?
h I do not think so. Furthermore, there is no evidence on the papers before me that
the applicant was given any notice of the later hearing of 21 June 1995. Indeed,
even if she was, there was no notice given by the justices that they intended to
consider a further remission of arrears at that hearing.

      For the reasons which I have given the justices, in my view, failed to comply at
j each of the hearings of 15 February and 21 June 1995 with the provisions of
r 44(1), in that they omitted to give notice of their intention to remit arrears either
in whole or in part in circumstances whereby they could not bring themselves
within the exempting proviso of the rule. In those circumstances their orders
remitting arrears at the two hearings were flawed and accordingly, in my view,
the answer to the first question raised on behalf of the applicant is that the Bristol
justices were not entitled to remit the arrears as they purported to do.

The second question which follows concerns the correct appeal/reviewing
procedure. Should this be by way of case stated or by judicial review pursuant to
RSC Ord 53?

This case has proceeded by judicial review pursuant to *R v Dover Magistrates'*
Court, ex p Kidner [1983] 1 All ER 475. In *Stone's Justices' Manual* (128th edn, 1996)
vol 1, para 1-5973, in the notes to r 44(1), it is stated:

> '(a) If there is a failure to give notice, as required, the High Court will
> entertain an application for judicial review to quash the order remitting
> arrears; see *R v Dover Magistrates' Court, ex p Kidner* ([1983] 1 All ER 475) ...'

A like note to r 44(1) appears in *The Family Court Practice* (1996) p 1675. Mr
Lawson-Cruttenden submits that, in the light of this authority, the applicant has
followed the correct procedure.

In *R v Dover Magistrates' Court, ex p Kidner* [1983] 1 All ER 475 the court was
concerned with an application by a wife for remission of certain arrears due under
a child order. The justices had failed to notify the wife of the husband's
application for remission of arrears but, not withstanding that, they remitted
arrears which had risen. In allowing the husband's motion for a judicial review
of the justices' order, the court held as follows (at 476):

> 'By failing to give the wife notice under r 44 of the 1981 rules before
> remitting the arrears of maintenance, the magistrates had denied the wife an
> opportunity to make representation to the court in a matter in respect of
> which she had a real interest, for a remission of arrears would result in her
> receiving less money under the maintenance order. Since there was no
> power to appeal against a remission of arrears under an order made under
> the [Guardianship of Infants Act] 1971, it was appropriate to make an order
> of certiorari quashing the magistrates' order and remitting the matter to the
> magistrates so that they could reconsider the husband's application after
> giving the wife notice of it. The wife's application would accordingly be
> granted ...'

The question of whether there is an appeal from a decision relating to the
remission of arrears was considered in two later cases, *Fletcher v Fletcher* [1985] 2
All ER 260, [1985] Fam 92 and *Berry v Berry* [1986] 2 All ER 948, [1987] Fam 1. Both
those decisions make clear that there is no appeal to the High Court against an
order granting or refusing remission. In *Berry v Berry* [1986] 2 All ER 948 at 956,
[1987] Fam 1 at 22, a case in which the husband appealed by notice of motion
against variation and remission orders, the Court of Appeal held as follows:

> 'There is no provision for a right of appeal to the High Court against the
> granting or refusal of an enforcement order. The only way in which such an
> order can be questioned is by case stated under s 111 of the 1980 Act'.

Section 111(1) of the 1980 Act provides as follows:

> 'Any person who was a party to any proceedings before a magistrates'
> court or is aggrieved by the conviction, order, determination or other
> proceeding of the court may question the proceeding on the ground that it
> is wrong in law or is in excess of jurisdiction by applying to the justices
> composing the court to state a case for the opinion of the High Court on the
> question of law or jurisdiction involved; but a person shall not make an
> application under this section in respect of a decision against which he has a

a right of appeal to the High Court or which by virtue of any enactment passed after 31st December 1979 is final.'

Mr Lawson-Cruttenden accepts that there is no power of appeal available to him, but has argued that it was not open to the applicant here to proceed by way of case stated. He maintains that the justices' failure to give notice of intention to remit arrears pursuant to the requirements of r 44(1) was a procedural error

b which could not give rise to redress by way of case stated. Mr Lawson-Cruttenden maintains that the proper route by which to challenge such a procedural irregularity is by way of judicial review; indeed he submits that this was the very course followed in *R v Dover Magistrates' Court, ex p Kidner* [1983] 1 All ER 475 in like circumstances. He submits that the justices here neither erred

c in law nor acted in excess of jurisdiction.

I do not consider that this submission is correctly made. It seems to me that it would clearly have been open to the applicant to seek to have stated a case on the particular point. She would, in her case, have set out the facts upon which she relied and asserted that the justices had misconstrued the provisions of r 44(1).

d The essence of the case would have been one of construction as to whether by their enforcement permission notice the justices had given adequate notice to the applicant within the requirements of r 44(1) of their intention to remit arrears or whether in the present case in any event it was unnecessary or impracticable so to do.

However, it is not now open to the applicant to proceed by way of case stated.

e Section 111(2) of the 1980 Act provides that any application under sub-s (1) must be made within 21 days after the day on which the decision of the magistrates' court was given. Accordingly, the applicant is well out of time; but in any event there is no power in the court to extend the time for an application to state a case (see *Michael v Gowland* [1977] 2 All ER 328, [1977] 1 WLR 296). It therefore

f follows that, because the applicant is out of time in applying for a case to be stated, the only way in which she can now seek to challenge the two orders remitting arrears is by an application for judicial review.

In cases where there is an application for a judicial review, I bear in mind that, save in exceptional circumstances, the jurisdiction to grant judicial review will not be exercised where other remedies have been available and have not been

g used (see in particular *R v Epping and Harlow General Comrs, ex p Goldstraw* [1983] 3 All ER 257).

In my view, the applicant should have proceeded by way of case stated. Whilst I bear in mind the procedure which was followed in *R v Dover Magistrates' Court, ex p Kidner* it does not appear that the question of reopening the irregularity by

h way of case stated was put to the court. Furthermore, the later Court of Appeal decision in *Berry v Berry* [1986] 2 All ER 948, [1987] Fam 1 makes it clear that a decision in regard to remission of arrears can only be challenged by way of case stated pursuant to s 111 of the 1980 Act.

However, although in my view, this applicant has not exhausted the remedies

j available to her, she was, as Mr Lawson-Cruttenden pointed out, following the course stated in the textbooks which followed *R v Dover Magistrates' Court, ex p Kidner* [1983] 1 All ER 475, as the appropriate one to take in the circumstances. Further, the issue of the application for leave on 20 September 1995 was in time in regard to the later of the two orders. In the circumstances of this particular case I consider that it is appropriate for the court to exercise its residual discretion here and grant judicial review of the two orders in question. Nevertheless, I

should point out that it seems to me that a party in a comparable position in
future should pursue his remedy by way of case stated and the indulgence
granted on the particular facts of this case may well have to be reconsidered.

I accordingly quash the two orders of 15 February 1995 and 21 June 1995 made
by the Bristol justices and direct that the enforcement permission notices be
reheard by a fresh panel of justices. I should also point out that express notice of
any intention by the justices to remit arrears, if that should be the case, must be
given to the applicant pursuant to the provisions of r 44(1) of the 1981 rules.

As to the question of costs Mr Lawson-Cruttenden indicated that in the light of
R v York City Justices, ex p Farmery (1988) 153 JP 257 he would not pursue an order
for costs against the justices here. In that decision the Divisional Court held—

> '(i) that costs would only be awarded against justices in the rarest of
> circumstances when they have done something which calls for strong
> disapproval; and (ii) that it was the practice not to grant costs against justices
> merely because they have made a mistake in law, but only if they have acted
> perversely or with some disregard for the elementary principles which every
> court ought to obey, and even then only if it was a flagrant instance.' (See
> 153 JP 257 at 258.)

Mr Lawson-Cruttenden accepted that, in the circumstances of this case, and
applying that test, he could not establish that this was a proper case for an award
of costs to be made against the justices. Accordingly, I make no order as to costs
save that, if appropriate, there be legal aid taxation of the applicant's costs.

Order accordingly.

Carolyn Toulmin   Barrister.

a
Re Senator Hanseatische
Verwaltungsgesellschaft mbH and another

COURT OF APPEAL, CIVIL DIVISION

b
LORD WOOLF MR, SAVILLE AND MILLETT LJJ

15, 16, 17, 24 JULY 1996

Gaming – Lottery – Receipt of money by chance – Money circulation scheme resembling chain letter – Scheme consisting of payment for memberships – Members having right to recruit further members, thereby obtaining commission – Commission payable by all
c new members joining further down family tree – Whether participants receiving money by exercise of skill in recruitment of new members, or by chance – Whether scheme an unlawful lottery.

Two companies, SHV and TMG, operated a scheme consisting entirely of the
d recruitment of participants, which was held out to members as an investment scheme with the possibility of significant rewards. Participants originally paid £2,500 (later increased to £3,000) to become members and, once recruited, had the right, but no obligation, to recruit further members and obtain commission from the recruitment. They were then entitled to commissions on the sale of participations by their recruits and by those whom their recruits recruited in their
e turn. The Secretary of State for Trade and Industry intervened on the basis that the sole or main business of SHV and TMG in the United Kingdom was the operation of the scheme and, since the scheme was either an unlawful lottery or had (in itself or through its underlying administrative structure) undesirable characteristics, it was just and equitable for the companies running it to be wound
f up; and that meanwhile the promoters of the scheme should be prevented from operating it. The Secretary of State accordingly issued winding-up petitions against the two companies pursuant to his powers under s 124A of the Insolvency Act 1986 and applied to the court for the appointment of a provisional liquidator. The judge declined to appoint a provisional liquidator, but enjoined SHV and TMG from continuing to operate the scheme pending the hearing of the
g winding-up petitions. SHV and TMG appealed, contending that it was an essential feature of a lottery that money or other prizes should be distributed entirely by chance, but that, in the instant case, the receipt of commission by the participants depended upon the exercise of skill in persuading others to pay to join the scheme, so that the scheme could not be a lottery.
h

Held – A scheme could be a lottery even if some of the rewards were gained by the application of an element of skill on the part of the participant, provided the scheme to a substantial extent offered other rewards dependent entirely on chance. In the absence of any statutory definition, the determination of whether
j a particular scheme was a lottery was a matter for interpretation by the court, which should adopt a commonsense rather than an over-analytical approach. In the case of a multi-lateral snowball or money circulation scheme, such as that at issue, it was clear that while a given member might be able, by the exercise of his own skill, to select and persuade others to join the scheme, whether additional members joined further down the line was, so far as the original participant was concerned, entirely a matter of chance. It followed that the scheme, which

closely resembled a chain letter, was an unlawful lottery and, accordingly, the
appeal would be dismissed (see p 937 *a c h* to p 938 *c*, p 940 *b c j*, p 941 *f g j* to p 942   *a*
a d to *j* and p 943 *j* to p 944 *e*, post).

DPP v Phillips [1934] All ER Rep 414 and *Seay v Eastwood* [1976] 3 All ER 153
approved.

Notes

b

For the elements of a lottery, and offences in connection with unlawful lotteries,
see 4(1) *Halsbury's Laws* (4th edn reissue) paras 148–153, and for cases on the
subject, see 7(1) *Digest* (2nd reissue) 73–81, *398–443*.

For the Insolvency Act 1986, s 124A, see 8 *Halsbury's Statutes* (4th edn) (1991
reissue) 849.

c

Cases referred to in judgments

Atkinson v Murrell [1972] 2 All ER 31, [1972] 2 QB 274, [1972] 2 WLR 509, DC; *affd*
    [1972] 2 All ER 1131, [1973] AC 289, [1972] 3 WLR 465, HL.
Barnes v Strathern 1929 JC 41, HC of Just.
Boucher v Rowsell [1947] 1 All ER 870, DC.   *d*
DPP v Phillips [1935] 1 KB 391, [1934] All ER Rep 414, DC.
Hall v Cox [1899] 1 QB 198, CA.
Imperial Tobacco Ltd v A-G [1980] 1 All ER 866, [1981] AC 718, [1980] 2 WLR 466,
    HL.
Jacob (Walter L) & Co Ltd, Re [1989] BCLC 345, CA.   *e*
Koscot Interplanetary (UK) Ltd, Re, re Koscot AG (31 July 1972, unreported), Ch D.
Moore v Elphick [1945] 2 All ER 155, DC.
Reader's Digest Association Ltd v Williams [1976] 3 All ER 737, [1976] 1 WLR 1109,
    DC.
Scott v DPP [1914] 2 KB 868, [1914–15] All ER Rep 825, DC.
Seay v Eastwood [1976] 3 All ER 153, [1976] 1 WLR 1117, HL.   *f*
Taylor v Smetten (1883) 11 QBD 207, DC.
Whitbread & Co Ltd v Bell, Bell v Whitbread & Co Ltd [1970] 2 All ER 64, [1970] 2 QB
    547, [1970] 2 WLR 1025, DC.

Cases also cited or referred to in skeleton arguments

g

Alchemy Marketing, Re (4 July 1994, unreported), Ch D.
Associated Newspapers, Ex p (1959) 57 SR (NSW) 550, NSW CA.
Bamford Publishers Ltd, Re (1977) Times, 4 June.
Barker v Mumby [1939] 1 All ER 611.
Company, Re a (No 001951 of 1987) [1988] BCLC 182.   *h*
Company, Re a (No 003102 of 1991), ex p Nyckeln Finance Co Ltd [1991] BCLC 350.
DPP v Bradfute & Associates Ltd [1967] 1 All ER 112, [1967] 2 QB 291, DC.
Global Pioneers Ltd, Re (2 November 1994, unreported), Ch D.
Hasta International Ltd, Re (29 February 1996, unreported), Ct of Sess.
Hibernian Merchants Ltd, Re [1957] 3 All ER 97, [1958] Ch 76.   *j*
Highfield Commodities Ltd, Re [1984] 3 All ER 884, [1985] 1 WLR 149.
International Tin Council, Re [1987] 1 All ER 890, [1987] Ch 419; *affd sub nom*
    Maclaine Watson & Co Ltd v Dept of Trade and Industry, Re International Tin
    Council, Maclaine Watson & Co Ltd v International Tin Council, Maclaine Watson
    & Co Ltd v International Tin Council (No 2) [1988] 3 All ER 257, [1989] Ch 309,
    CA.

a International Westminster Bank plc v Okeanos Maritime Corp [1987] 3 All ER 137, sub
nom Re a Company (No 00359 of 1987) [1988] Ch 210.
McLean v Murch [1934] NZLR s 7, NZ SC.
One Life Ltd v Roy (2 July 1996, unreported), Ch D.
Singette Ltd v Martin [1970] 3 All ER 938, [1971] AC 407, HL.

b **Appeal**

By notice dated 21 June 1996 Senator Hanseatische Verwaltungsgesellschaft
mbH and Titan Marketing Gesellschaft appealed with leave from the order of Sir
Richard Scott V-C dated 14 June 1996, whereby he granted an injunction
preventing the appellants from operating a money circulation scheme known as
c the Titan scheme in the United Kingdom, pending the hearing of a winding-up
petition brought by the Secretary of State for Trade and Industry in the exercise
of his powers under s 124A of the Insolvency Act 1986. The facts are set out in
the judgment of Saville LJ.

d Edward Bannister QC, Clive H Jones and Paul Kennedy (instructed by Charles Buckley)
for the appellants.
Roger Kaye QC and Guy Newey (instructed by the Treasury Solicitor) for the
Secretary of State.

Cur adv vult

e
24 July 1996. The following judgments were delivered.

SAVILLE LJ (giving the first judgment at the invitation of Lord Woolf MR). On
9 May 1996 the Secretary of State for Trade and Industry issued winding-up
f petitions against Senator Hanseatische Verwaltungsgesellschaft mbH (SHV),
Titan Marketing Gesellschaft (TMG) and Titan Business Club and shortly
afterwards applied to the court for the appointment of a provisional liquidator.
The matter came before Sir Richard Scott V-C, who on 14 June refused to appoint
a provisional liquidator, but instead enjoined SHV and TMG pending the hearing
of the winding-up petition from (in effect) continuing to operate in this country
g what is known as the Titan scheme. From this decision SHV and TMG appeal
with the leave of Sir Richard Scott V-C. Since the Titan Business Club appears to
be no more than a name used by SHV and TMG for the purposes of the Titan
scheme, it has played no separate part in the proceedings.

The petitions are issued under the powers given to the Secretary of State under
h s 124A of the Insolvency Act 1986. This section provides, among other things,
that where it appears to the Secretary of State from any report made or
information obtained under Pt XIV of the Companies Act 1985 (company
investigations etc) that it is expedient in the public interest that a company should
be wound up, he may present a petition for it to be wound up if the court thinks
j it just and equitable for it to be so.

The case made by the Secretary of State is in effect that the sole or main
business of the appellants in this country is the operation of the Titan scheme; and
that since this scheme is either an unlawful lottery or has (in itself or through its
underlying administrative structure) undesirable characteristics, it is just and
equitable for those running it to be wound up; and that meanwhile the promoters
of the scheme should be stopped from operating it.

Section 1 of the Lotteries and Amusements Act 1976 provides that lotteries which do not constitute gaming are unlawful, except as provided in that Act. It is not suggested that the scheme is gaming or a lottery permitted by this Act. Sir Richard Scott V-C held that the scheme was an unlawful lottery. He also considered that the Secretary of State had established a fairly arguable case that the administrative structure underlying the scheme, while not illegal, was highly unsatisfactory, highly suspicious and thoroughly undesirable.

Mr Bannister QC on behalf of the appellants accepted, in my view wholly correctly, that if the Titan scheme was a lottery, then it would be difficult (to say the least) to challenge the interim orders made by the judge. However, his argument was, in short, that the scheme was not a lottery and that since s 124A of the 1986 Act only applied to unlawful activities, there was no proper basis for the orders made by Sir Richard Scott V-C. In these circumstances the first question is whether or not the scheme is an unlawful lottery. To answer that question it is necessary only to look at the scheme operated by the appellants and not at the full background to the case, which Sir Richard Scott V-C has set out in his judgment.

The Titan scheme, at least as it operates in this country, is based upon invitations to become members of the Titan Business Club. In order to take up the invitation, the person concerned attends a recruitment meeting organised by persons described as self-employed consultants of SHV, is interviewed by one of these consultants, signs an application form and pays what was originally £2,500, but which was recently increased to £3,000. The new recruit then becomes what is called a junior partner with the right (but no obligation) to seek to introduce, by the same means, new members to the Titan Business Club. The junior partner receives £450 for each of the first two new members he successfully introduces, which comes from the money paid by those new members. He receives no more from those first two new members, but if and when he successfully introduces a third new member he becomes what is called a senior partner and receives £1,220 from the money paid by that new member. In addition, for each of the first two new members which that new member in turn successfully introduces, the senior partner will receive £770 from the money paid by them; and so on down the line, since each new member becomes a junior and then (if and when he successfully introduces a third new member) a senior partner, and is treated in the way I have described. If a senior partner successfully introduces more than three members they are treated in the same way as the third introduction, so that the senior partner gets £1,220 from each of them, £770 from each of the first two introduced by them, £770 from the first two in turn introduced down the line and so on.

Under this scheme, therefore, £1,220 of the £2,500 or £3,000 paid by each new member is received by the junior or senior partner concerned. The balance is distributed among the consultants and the appellants. As will be appreciated from the foregoing, a new member will make £450 from each of the first two members he introduces, £1,220 from each of the subsequent members he introduces, and further amounts of £770, the number of which (if any) depend entirely on the success of the latter members in introducing two new members and so on down the chain of the particular family tree in question. At least in theory, very large amounts indeed could be generated by this means, given each new layer of membership is successful in introducing new members. The scheme therefore provides the organisers and their self-employed consultants with half the amounts paid by members, and the latter with the chance of recouping their a outlay and making money when and if other members join. The scheme has no other purpose.

There is no statutory definition of a lottery. Mr Bannister submitted that an essential feature of a lottery is the distribution of money or other prizes entirely by chance or, in other words, by the equivalent of drawing lots. He cited *Taylor v Smetten* (1883) 11 QBD 207, *Hall v Cox* [1899] 1 QB 198 and *Scott v DPP* [1914] 2

b KB 868, [1914–15] All ER Rep 825, which do indeed support this general proposition. Building on this, Mr Bannister submitted that since the receipt by participants, whether junior or senior partners, depended upon the exercise of skill in persuading others to join the scheme, this essential feature was lacking and the scheme could not be a lottery.

In my judgment the correct starting point in any given case of this kind is to

c adopt the approach suggested by Lord Wilberforce in *Seay v Eastwood* [1976] 3 All ER 153, [1976] 1 WLR 1117. This case was concerned with the question whether the playing on fruit machines installed in a betting shop could be said to be part of the licensed business of bookmaking carried on at those premises, but the following passage from the speech of Lord Wilberforce is of general application:

d   'Legislation against, or controlling, gaming, wagering and betting is many centuries old in the United Kingdom. With only moderate success Parliament has endeavoured to keep up with the enormous variety of these activities which has arisen from the ingenuity of gamblers and of people who exploit them. It is impossible to frame accurate definitions which can cover

e   every such variety; attempts to do so may indeed be counter-productive, since each added precision merely provides an incentive to devise a variant which eludes it. So the legislation contains a number of expressions which are not, or not precisely defined: bet, wager, lottery, gaming, are examples of this. As to these, while sections appear in various Acts saying that a particular activity is, or is deemed to be, within the word, the general

f   meaning is left to be decided by the courts as cases arise under the common law. The process, and I think it is a very sound one, is then for magistrates, using their local knowledge, experience of the world and common sense, to give a sensible interpretation of the expressions used, subject to control of their decision by a court itself experienced in deciding this type of question.

g   When, as should rarely occur, higher appellate courts are required to review these cases, they should, in my opinion, endorse decisions which they can see have been reached and confirmed in this way. Refined analytical tools are not suitable instruments in this context.' (See [1976] 3 All ER 153 at 155, [1976] 1 WLR 1117 at 1121.)

h As can be seen from this passage, an over-analytical approach should not be adopted, but rather one of common sense. In the present case, the reality of the matter is undoubtedly that those persuaded to join the scheme did so and paid their money in the hope of the rewards that would result from those afterwards joining their particular family tree. True, it may be said that a given member

j might be able, by the exercise of his own skill, to select and persuade others to attend a recruitment meeting and (if they were acceptable) to induce them to become a member. By doing so that person would recover £450 or (after the second success) £1,220 from each, but the scheme does not stop there, for once a member becomes a senior partner there is a chance that other and potentially much greater glittering prizes will come (if at all) from further down the family tree. Whether or not they do depends on the success or failure of others down the line. The fact that those down the line might themselves exercise skill in persuading others to join is to my mind irrelevant, since whether they can and do, *a* and indeed whether further members join for whatever reason is, so far as any particular senior partner participant is concerned, entirely a matter of chance. It seems to me that a scheme can be a lottery even if some of the rewards can be said to be gained by the application of an element of skill on the part of the participant, provided the scheme to a substantial extent offers other rewards *b* dependent entirely on chance (see e g *Boucher v Rowsell* [1947] 1 All ER 870). Mr Bannister submitted that a senior partner might in fact exercise skill in helping to persuade others down the line to join the scheme, but there is no evidence that this happens and indeed on the face of it would be most unlikely to happen, since it would be in the interests of the senior partner to recruit a possible new member himself (thereby getting £1,220 instead of £770) and thus to deprive members *c* further down the line of the reward from making a successful introduction themselves.

Mr Bannister also submitted that the self-employed consultants or others who run the recruitment meetings exercise skill in persuading people to sign up to the scheme and pay their money. This is undoubtedly true. As more fully described *d* by Sir Richard Scott V-C, the meetings are conducted in what can perhaps be described as a revivalist style, with music and chanting and the oft-repeated promise of the chance of great rewards for those wise and clever enough to join Titan. Mr Bannister also submitted that since this skill was being exercised on behalf of the existing members, this was again sufficient to prevent the scheme from being a lottery. In this connection Mr Bannister relied on *Moore v Elphick* *e* [1945] 2 All ER 155, which is authority for the proposition that if participants in what would otherwise amount to a lottery rely upon the application of skill by their agent to generate prizes, the skill will be treated as their own and the scheme will not be a lottery for that reason. The difficulty with this argument is that there is no evidence to suggest that those running the recruitment meetings do so as *f* agents for the members. Mr Bannister relied on the application form which describes SHV as managing the scheme, but this comes nowhere near demonstrating that SHV or the consultants run the recruitment meetings as agents, especially when it is remembered that they stand to make money themselves from the introduction of new members. In truth it seems to me that the skill deployed at the meetings is deployed by and for the promoters of the *g* scheme, and not the participants.

Sir Richard Scott V-C, after reviewing all the relevant authorities, concluded that there was no real point of distinction to be drawn between the present scheme and that held to be an unlawful lottery by the Divisional Court in *DPP v Phillips* [1935] 1 KB 391, [1934] All ER Rep 414. As I understood him, Mr Bannister *h* in the end did not seriously suggest that this case was distinguishable; his main submission being simply that it was wrongly decided.

In my judgment *DPP v Phillips* is good law and is indeed indistinguishable from the present case in all material respects. It has in fact been cited and relied upon in subsequent cases with no hint of disapproval. The facts of that case and the *j* holding are conveniently set out in the headnote in the following terms:

'A company, having bought a quantity of note cases at a price of less than 1s. 6d. each, devised a scheme for selling them at a profit, and issued to the public a leaflet in accordance with the terms of which the scheme was conducted. The leaflet informed a person desirous of participating in the a scheme that on filling up and sending in an attached order form together with 1*l*. there would be sent to him a note case and a supply of the leaflets the order forms of which would be marked with a number allotted to him; that he should get other persons to give orders for note cases, using these forms; that he would be entitled to no benefit from the first three of these orders, but would be paid a commission of 10*s*. on every other order received

b on his forms and on sales made as a result of these orders; that whenever an order was received on one of his forms, after the first three, a supply of forms also marked with his number would be sent to the buyer, and that the participant would be paid a commission of 10*s*. on each of the first three sales made by every one to whom one of the forms so numbered was sent; and that there was no time limit to the scheme, but that the maximum

c commission payable to a participant was 20,000*l*.:—*Held*, that, inasmuch as, with the exception of commissions resulting from orders directly obtained by the participant himself, all the commissions which he received would result from orders given by persons over whom he had no control and would depend so far as he was concerned not upon his skill or work but upon pure

d chance, the scheme was a "lottery" within the meaning of the Lotteries Act, 1823, s. 41.' (See [1935] 1 KB 391.)

In the course of his judgment Lord Hewart CJ said ([1935] 1 KB 391 at 401, [1934] All ER Rep 414 at 416):

e 'What is it that is being done? There is here the publication of a scheme. What is the nature of that scheme? Is it not a scheme in the words, cited from Webster's Dictionary and approved by Hawkins J. in the well known case of *Taylor* v. *Smetten* ((1883) 11 QBD 207), for the "distribution of prizes by lot or chance"? There is no magic in the word "distribution." The word "payment" will do just as well. There is no magic in the word "prizes."

f "Commission" or "reward" will do just as well. Here, as it seems to me, it is quite obvious that the person who accepts the invitation contained in this leaflet is paying the sum of 1*l*. in order that he may have the opportunity of setting a ball rolling, over whose revolutions, after the first four at any rate, he will have no control, and it is a pure matter of chance whether the return

g upon his money will prove to be a few shillings or a great many pounds. I need not elaborate the matter. I think that this leaflet speaks for itself, and has the word "lottery" written all over it.'

To my mind this passage exemplifies (some 40 years in advance) the approach suggested by Lord Wilberforce, and I would respectfully approve it together with

h the reasoning in the rest of that judgment and that to be found in the judgments of Branson and du Parcq JJ in the same case. Mr Bannister submitted that the error into which this court fell was to confuse want of control with lot or pure chance, since in that case and the present, the element of skill of the member in selecting and inducing others to join can itself be said to some extent to be

j instrumental in leading others to join down the line. To my mind, however, such an argument is a good example of the over-analysis deprecated by Lord Wilberforce. Mr Bannister also instanced cases where leases were granted for a rent dependent on profits over which the lessor had no control, or where managers of an insurance company obtain 'override' commissions from the activities of subordinates over whom they also have no control, as demonstrating that there is a difference between lack of control and the necessarily random chance of a prize or reward created by a lottery properly so-called. In my view, however, Mr Bannister is again seeking to over-analyse the matter, since as a matter of ordinary language no one would describe such commercial arrangements as entailing that the lessor or the manager was participating in a lottery. In the present case, however, it seems to me that this is precisely what those who join the Titan scheme are doing. They pay their money for one reason only, namely to gain the chance, and it is only a chance, of reaping rewards from those who in turn pay and join for the same reason. One source at least of the potential rewards comes from those over whom the participant has no control, and to my mind it follows as a matter of ordinary language and common sense that in this respect at least the participant is taking part in a scheme properly described as the distribution of prizes or rewards entirely by chance. In other words, looked at as a whole, this scheme too has the word 'lottery' written all over it.

In these circumstances I would dismiss this appeal and it is unnecessary to consider the submission of the Secretary of State to the effect that even if the scheme was not an unlawful lottery, nevertheless there was a proper basis for the winding-up petition and thus for interim relief. It is thus also unnecessary to go into further details of the case, all of which, as I have said, are comprehensively set out in the judgment of Sir Richard Scott V-C. I should, however, add that I was entirely unpersuaded by Mr Bannister's submission that (leaving aside such cases as may arise, for example, under the regulatory provisions of the Financial Services Act 1986), s 124A of the Insolvency Act 1986 only applies where it can be shown that a company is acting unlawfully, because its business or its business methods are illegal. To my mind there is nothing in the section that suggests that it is so limited. On the contrary the phrases used (namely 'expedient in the public interest' and 'just and equitable') to my mind indicate that Parliament did not intend to impose such a restriction, but instead simply decided to leave the Secretary of State to form a view as to what was expedient in the public interest and the court then to decide on the material before it whether the justice and equity of the case dictated that the company concerned should be wound up (see e g *Re Walter L Jacob & Co Ltd* [1989] BCLC 345 at 352–353 per Nicholls LJ).

There are two further points that I should mention. First, the Secretary of State sought and obtained leave (as did the appellants) to adduce further evidence before this court. I have looked at this material, but to my mind it took the matter on which I have reached my decision no further. Second, it seemed at one stage that Mr Kaye QC on behalf of the Secretary of State was advancing a submission that we should interfere with the decision of Sir Richard Scott V-C by substituting the appointment of a provisional liquidator in place of the injunctive relief ordered. Suffice to say that on this interlocutory matter I was quite unpersuaded that there were any good grounds for taking such a course.

MILLETT LJ. I have had the advantage of reading in draft the judgment of Saville LJ. I am in full agreement with him, and with his reasons, that the Titan scheme is a lottery. I add a few words of my own in deference to the careful and lucid submissions which were advanced by Mr Bannister QC on behalf of the appellants and because of the general importance of the subject.

Although lotteries have been unlawful for more than two hundred years, Parliament has never attempted a definition. The reason for this is not far to seek. It may be found in the words of Lord Justice General (Clyde) in *Barnes v Strathern* 1929 JC 41 at 46:

a   'There is no limit to the ingenuity of the devisers of projects such as this,
       and there is, accordingly, no end to the variety of schemes which may
       constitute a lottery.'

In *Seay v Eastwood* [1976] 3 All ER 153 at 155, [1976] 1 WLR 1117 at 1121 Lord
Wilberforce commented:

b   'It is impossible to frame accurate definitions which can cover every such
       variety; attempts to do so may indeed be counter-productive, since each
       added precision merely provides an incentive to devise a variant which
       eludes it.'

       So Parliament has left it to the courts to decide what constitutes a lottery by
c references to the general underlying idea. They have consistently held that what
   lies at the heart of the concept is 'the distribution of prizes by lot or chance' (see
   Taylor v Smetten (1883) 11 QBD 207, *Atkinson v Murrell* [1972] 2 All ER 31, [1972] 2
   QB 274, *Whitbread & Co Ltd v Bell, Bell v Whitbread & Co Ltd* [1970] 2 All ER 64,
   [1970] 2 QB 547, *Reader's Digest Association Ltd v Williams* [1976] 3 All ER 737,
d [1976] 1 WLR 1109 and *Imperial Tobacco Ltd v A-G* [1980] 1 All ER 866, [1981] AC
   718). This is a description, not a definition. There is no magic in the word
   'prizes': any form of reward or commission is sufficient (see *DPP v Phillips* [1935]
   1 KB 391, [1934] All ER Rep 414). The distribution must depend entirely on
   chance: the presence of any element of skill means that the scheme is not a lottery
   (see *Hall v Cox* [1899] 1 QB 198 and *Scott v DPP* [1914] 2 KB 868, [1914–15] All ER
e Rep 825). But this refers to the skill of the competitor in achieving a winning
   result; not to the skill of the promoter in selling tickets.
       The Titan scheme is a multi-level snowball or money circulation scheme. As
   such, it most closely resembles the chain letter, versions of which have
   consistently been held to be lotteries. It has little in common with the traditional
f form of lottery in which participants pay nominal sums to buy tickets entitling
   them to take part in a draw for prizes. In the Titan scheme they pay substantial
   sums to take part, and thus may be said to buy tickets. But there is no draw and
   there are no prizes, at least in the traditional sense. Participants pay for the right
   to sell tickets to further participants and obtain commission from the sales. There
   is nothing beyond the sale of tickets and the distribution of the proceeds of sale.
g The scheme consists entirely of the sale of participations in itself.
       These features led Mr Bannister to submit that there is no lottery.
   Commissions on the sale of participations, he said, are not distributed at random
   but strictly in accordance with pre-set rules, and depend on the skill and effort of
   those who introduce the new participants. This is correct as far as it goes.
h Participants do not join in order to take part in any kind of competition, for there
   is none. Each new participant pays his money in order in his turn to become
   effectively a promoter of the scheme and earn commission from the sale of
   further participations. Such skill and effort as are expended by participants are
   expended in promoting the scheme, not in winning a competition.
j   But people do not join such schemes without the hope of rewards out of all
   proportion to the effort required of them, and the Titan scheme is no exception.
   Recruits are induced to part with substantial sums by the prospect of easy money
   and very large gains. This is due to the multi-level character of the scheme.
   Participants can recover their initial outlay by themselves directly recruiting new
   members, though they have to recruit at least four new members to achieve this.
   In order to achieve the spectacular rewards which are held out to them, they

depend on commissions from the sale of participations by their recruits and by
those whom their recruits have recruited in their turn, and so on down the line   *a*
apparently ad infinitum. Whether any commission on such indirect sales will
ever be earned, and if so how much, is due to factors which are completely
beyond the control of the original participant and are wholly unpredictable.

It was the presence of this feature which was held in *DPP v Phillips* [1935] 1 KB
391, [1934] All ER Rep 414 to make the scheme there under consideration an   *b*
unlawful lottery. Mr Bannister rightly conceded that the Titan scheme is not
distinguishable in any material respect from the scheme in that case. He
submitted that the case was wrongly decided and invited us to overrule it. But
both schemes are well within the mischief which the Lottery Acts have been
enacted to prevent. I think, not only that the case was rightly decided, but that a
decision to the contrary would emasculate the Lottery Acts and lead to the   *c*
introduction of a great many schemes whose legitimacy would depend upon the
kind of overelaborate analysis against which Lord Wilberforce warned in *Seay v
Eastwood* [1976] 3 All ER 153, [1976] 1 WLR 1117.

It is, however, another feature of the scheme which is far more pernicious and
which gives much greater cause for concern. This is the certainty that the scheme   *d*
will cause loss to a large number of people, and that the longer the scheme is
allowed to continue the greater the number who will inevitably suffer loss. This
is the necessary consequence of the fact that, in order to recover his money (let
alone make a profit), each new participant must recruit several further
participants, who then find themselves in the same situation. Those who have
only just joined can have had no opportunity to enlist further members. Until   *e*
they do so they have lost their money. Yet at every stage of the life of the scheme
from start to finish such members not only greatly outnumber those who
recruited them, but outnumber all other members of the scheme put together.

The number of persons who are sufficiently gullible to be persuaded to join
may be very large but it is obviously finite; so is the amount of money which can   *f*
be raised by a scheme of this kind. The scheme is bound to come to an end
sooner or later. When it does most of its members will have lost their money.
This is not merely likely; it is a mathematical certainty. It is as certain as the fact
that the organisers, who take almost two thirds of the money paid by each new
participant, will have made a substantial profit. The scheme is merely a device
for enabling the organisers and a relatively small number of early recruits to make   *g*
potentially very large profits at the expense of the much larger number of those
who are recruited later. Every new participant is in truth gambling on the
scheme continuing long enough for him to recover his money and, he hopes,
make a profit. But the scheme is not, of course, held out to him on this basis.

Schemes of this kind are inherently objectionable and the court has   *h*
consistently held that it is just and equitable to wind up the companies which
operate them. They tend to be sold on a false and deceptive basis, sometimes
explicit but usually implicit, that they are a certain source of profit for those who
join and are capable of lasting indefinitely. A particular vice of such schemes is
that they encourage similar dishonesty on the part of their members, who can   *j*
recover their money only at the expense of new members whom they induce to
enter the scheme. In *Re Koscot Interplanetary (UK) Ltd, Re Koscot AG* (31 July 1972,
unreported) Megarry J said:

'Once they had paid their money, the only real prospect that they had of
recovering it or of making a profit was to induce others to part with their

a money in a similar way. I cannot imagine that any resolutely honest man, once he had discovered the true nature of the scheme, would attempt to get his money back by inducing others to purchase franchises; and for such a man there is little save a prospect of a loss. But some honest men are less than resolutely so; and for them there is the temptation, to which some may yield, of recouping themselves at the expense of those of their friends and

b acquaintances who can be beguiled into buying a franchise. There are others who are simply gullible or deluded, and for them there may come the temptation to find others of their kind. For all these, and others, there is the choice between bearing the loss themselves and spreading the fraud. The scheme was one which had the quality of both effecting a swindle and tending to corrupt those swindled by making them confederates with the

c company in a dishonest scheme.'

That is strong language, but in my opinion such language is amply warranted by any scheme which must be sold to the public on an implicitly false basis or which cannot be sold at all. Like any lottery, it holds out the promise of spectacular rewards for the few at the expense of the many. Unlike the ordinary lottery,

d however, it does not charge nominal sums to enter to people who knowingly and for their own amusement risk a small sum in the remote hope of a great prize. If the Secretary of State's allegations are to be believed, the Titan scheme pretends to be a commercial operation in which the public are encouraged to 'invest' substantial moneys, often borrowed, in what, from the point of view of the

e 'investors' as a whole, is cynically set up as a loss-making venture.

If the Secretary of State makes good his allegations, he is plainly entitled to the view that it is expedient in the public interest that the company be wound up in order to protect the public by bringing the scheme to an end. I reject Mr Bannister's submission that the Secretary of State has no business to intervene in

f a case where no illegal activity is being carried on. The expression 'expedient in the public interest' is of the widest import; it means what it says. The Secretary of State has a right, and some would say a duty, to apply to the court to protect members of the public who deal with the company from suffering inevitable loss, whether this derives from illegal activity or not. A common case in which he intervenes is where an insolvent company continues to trade by paying its debts

g as they fall due out of money obtained from new creditors. The insolvency is the cause of the eventual loss, but it is the need to protect the public, not the insolvency, which grounds the Secretary of State's application for a winding-up order in such cases. The analogy with his allegations in the present case, while not exact, is close.

h The safeguard for the individual is that the decision to wind up the company is not left to the Secretary of State but to the court, which must consider whether it is just and equitable to do so. In reaching its decision the court will take into account the interests of all parties, present members and creditors of the company and present participants in the scheme, as well as the interests of the

j public who may hereafter have dealings with the company.

Sir Richard Scott V-C was plainly right to impose a temporary cessation of business pending the hearing of the winding-up petition. Given the nature of the scheme and the serious possibility that the Secretary of State will make good his allegations, a temporary cessation of the company's activities must be desirable. We were told that there are at present nearly 10,000 members of the scheme in the United Kingdom. At least 7,000 of them must have lost all or some of their

money and be seeking to recruit at least four further members in order to recover
their money. It cannot be right to allow the scheme to continue in operation a
pending the hearing of the petition, by which time, if they have been successful,
there could be 50,000 members, of whom at least 35,000 would be out of pocket.

Sir Richard Scott V-C declined to appoint a provisional liquidator and granted
temporary injunctions against the company instead. Neither remedy is likely to
be completely effective to prevent the organisers from setting up a similar b
scheme in the name of another entity and making use of the membership of the
existing scheme to continue their activities. In the absence of suitable
undertakings from the individuals behind the scheme to refrain from doing this,
I would for my part have thought it much the better course to appoint a
provisional liquidator. This would have a number of advantages. It would put
in place an independent officer of the court to take charge of the company's c
activities pending the hearing of the petition and to be a focal point for the present
members to turn to for advice as to their position. He would also be entitled to
obtain possession of the current membership lists and ensure that they could not
be used, without the approval of the court, to operate similar schemes pending
the hearing of the petition. But the Secretary of State did not press us to vary Sir d
Richard Scott V-C's order, and I am not prepared to go so far as to say that he
erred in principle in the way in which he exercised his discretion.

I agree that the appeal must be dismissed.

LORD WOOLF MR. I agree with the reasons given by Saville and Millett LJJ for
saying this appeal should be dismissed. I note what Millett LJ says about the e
advantages of appointing a provisional liquidator and agree with this. However,
these advantages would not justify interfering with the decision of Sir Richard
Scott V-C as to the relief which should be granted, which I do not regard as being
in any way inappropriate.

The judgments on this appeal make it clear that schemes of this sort are illegal. f
They involve those who set up, promote, purvey and administer the scheme in
criminal offences. This I hope will deter those who may be tempted to create
clones of Titan.

Appeal dismissed.

g

L I Zysman Esq   Barrister.

R v Secretary of State for the Home Department, ex parte Rahman

QUEEN'S BENCH DIVISION (CROWN OFFICE LIST)
COLLINS J
26 JUNE 1996

Immigration – Illegal entrant – Detention pending deportation – Habeas corpus – Evidence – Hearsay – Whether court entitled to take into account hearsay evidence relied on by Secretary of State on application for habeas corpus.

The applicant came to the United Kingdom from Bangladesh, having obtained a certificate of entitlement to the right of abode in order to join his father, S, who was a British citizen by registration. Thereafter, two denunciatory letters asserting that he was not S's son led entry clearance officers in Bangladesh to make inquiries, through interpreters, of the inhabitants of two local villages as to the applicant's true name and paternity. The villagers' responses were translated and, together with an interview of the applicant, they satisfied the Secretary of State that the applicant was not S's son and that he had obtained the certificate of entitlement by deception. The applicant was served with notice that he was an illegal entrant and detained under para 16 of Sch 2 to the Immigration Act 1971 pending his deportation. The applicant applied for a writ of habeas corpus, contending that as the villagers' evidence was hearsay and so inadmissible, the court could not take it into account in determining whether the Secretary of State had proved that he was an illegal entrant.

Held – Although habeas corpus remained an important weapon against attempts to restrict the liberty of the individual in an unauthorised fashion, the distinction between habeas corpus and judicial review in immigration cases was merely one of form and not substance. Accordingly, when hearing an application for habeas corpus by a person detained pending deportation after a decision by the Secretary of State that he was an illegal entrant, the court could take account of all the material which the Secretary of State had relied on in reaching his decision, even if that material was hearsay, since such material could be taken into account on an application for judicial review. It was however for the court to decide what weight to attach to the material which formed the basis of the Secretary of State's decision. Having regard to that material, the fact that the applicant was not S's son and so had obtained the certificate of entitlement by deception had been proved to the requisite standard. The application would therefore be dismissed (see p 950 c f to h, p 952 d to j, p 954 f and p 960 c d, post).

Khawaja v Secretary of State for the Home Dept [1983] 1 All ER 765 applied.

Notes
For entitlement to apply for writ of habeas corpus ad subjiciendum, see 1(1) *Halsbury's Laws* (4th edn reissue) para 245, and for nature of judicial review, see ibid para 60.

For meaning of hearsay, circumstances in which admissible and weight to be attached to it, see 17 *Halsbury's Laws* (4th edn) paras 11, 53 and 55.

For the Immigration Act 1971, Sch 2, para 16, see 31 *Halsbury's Statutes* (4th edn) (1994 reissue) 109.

Cases referred to in judgment

Bushel's Case (1670) T Jo 13, 84 ER 1123.

Ejaz v Secretary of State for Home Affairs [1978] CA Transcript 777.

Guerin, Re (1888) 60 LT 538, DC.

Khawaja v Secretary of State for the Home Dept [1983] 1 All ER 765, [1984] AC 74, [1983] 2 WLR 321, HL.

R v Brixton Prison Governor, ex p Ahson [1969] 2 All ER 347, [1969] 2 QB 222, [1969] 2 WLR 618, DC.

R v Oldham Justices, ex p Cawley [1996] 1 All ER 464, [1996] 2 WLR 681, DC.

R v Secretary of State for the Home Dept, ex p Hussain [1978] 2 All ER 423, [1978] 1 WLR 700, DC and CA.

R v Secretary of State for the Home Dept, ex p Muboyayi [1991] 4 All ER 72, [1992] QB 244, [1991] 3 WLR 442, CA.

R v Secretary of State for the Home Office, ex p Muse [1992] Imm AR 282.

Zamir v Secretary of State for the Home Dept [1980] 2 All ER 768, [1980] AC 930, [1980] 3 WLR 249, HL.

Application for habeas corpus

The applicant, Saidur Rahman, who had been detained as an illegal entrant under para 16 of Sch 2 to the Immigration Act 1971 pending deportation, applied for a writ of habeas corpus ad subjiciendum seeking his release from Bedford Prison. The facts are set out in the judgment.

Michael Shrimpton (instructed by *Saf Awan*, Luton) for the applicant.
Mark Shaw (instructed by the *Treasury Solicitor*) for the Secretary of State.

COLLINS J. This is an application for a writ of habeas corpus on behalf of Mr Saidur Rahman. The reason for the proceedings is that Mr Rahman obtained in 1989 a certificate of entitlement to the right of abode in the United Kingdom in order to join his father, Abdus Somed (who was a British citizen by registration) who was living here at the time.

Having arrived in this country, he was the subject of two denunciatory letters which asserted that he was not the son of Abdus Somed. The first of those letters also asserted that the son whom he brought back with him, together with his wife, in 1991 was not his. So far as that allegation is concerned, which relates to one of the two sons called Rone, it is admittedly true because DNA tests were carried out which established that Rone was not the son of the applicant and his wife. The Secretary of State made inquiries through entry clearance officers in Bangladesh. The result of those inquiries satisfied him, together with an interview of the applicant, that he was not the son of Abdus Somed and, therefore, had obtained the certificate of entitlement by deception.

Accordingly, on 3 August 1993 he was served with a notice that he was an illegal entrant and was detained under para 16 of Sch 2 to the Immigration Act 1971 pending his removal from this country.

On 11 August 1993 he applied to the vacation judge, Clarke J, for judicial review in the form of certiorari and for a writ of habeas corpus. On 16 August Clarke J refused bail and adjourned the case. At that stage it seems to have been accepted that judicial review was not an appropriate remedy and that the matter should proceed as an application for habeas corpus. Clarke J gave various directions as to the service of evidence. Those directions were not complied with. For some reason neither side progressed the matter. This was, no doubt, a partly because by then the applicant had been released on bail. I am not sure whether he has been granted a form of temporary admission or whether he is still on bail, but the net result is that he is at liberty and has been able to remain in this country pending the outcome of these proceedings. That, as I say, may explain to some extent the rather lengthy delay that has occurred before this matter has come before me.

b   In the meantime there has been the gathering of some further evidence on the part of the Secretary of State and a body of evidence on behalf of the applicant, the applicant seeking to put forward material in support of his contention that he is, indeed, the son of Abdus Somed and is properly entitled, and was at all times properly entitled, to the certificate of entitlement.

    Before I go into the facts in greater detail, I should deal with a preliminary
c point, a very important point, which has been raised by Mr Shrimpton on behalf of the applicant. The point relates to the nature of the evidence that the Secretary of State can put before the court.

    As I have said, the Secretary of State, through entry clearance officers, made inquiries in Bangladesh. Those inquiries included, and much of the Secretary of
d State's conclusions were based on, two visits that were made to the villages where the applicant lived, where his wife lived and where his alleged father lived.

    The first such visit took place on 15 February 1993. That was by two entry clearance officers to the village of Holdarpur, which is the village in which the applicant said he and his wife and two sons lived in the house of his father, Abdus Somed. In fact his wife, Rina, if the relationship is correct, is his first cousin.

e   The second village visit took place on 1 December 1993 and that was to the village of Nittarchok. It is a village, I believe, some ten miles or so away from Holdarpur. It was the village alleged to be his true home village where his true father had lived. I said 'had' because his true father, if the Home Office is right, had died some time before. Abdus Somed himself had died in April 1994 but was
f still alive when the visit was made in 1993. He was one of those seen by the entry clearance officers and there is an issue about what he is alleged to have said to them.

    In the course of the visits the entry clearance officers interviewed, through interpreters, a number of villagers. They were interviewed in the sense that they showed them photographs of the applicant, his wife, his children and his alleged
g father, and they sought the reaction of various villagers to those photographs. According to them, the reaction was that he was not, in the case of the villagers at Holdarpur, the son of Abdus and, in the case of the villagers at Nittarchok, that he was indeed an inhabitant of that village, that his father was a man called Suraj Ali and that he was really called Surab Ali.

h   The evidence of all this is contained in affidavits from two of the entry clearance officers who made the visits in question and who reported what they discovered in the course of those visits. That evidence, Mr Shrimpton submits (clearly correctly) is hearsay. Indeed, it is not only single hearsay but double hearsay because it is evidence that was given through interpreters. It is not
j suggested that the entry clearance officers themselves understood the relevant dialect that was being used and would have been able to understand what was being said unless the matter was interpreted. Accordingly, says Mr Shrimpton, that would have been clearly inadmissible in any legal proceedings in this country and the same principle must apply to the factual decision that I have to reach in this case, the factual decision being whether the Secretary of State has proved that the deceptions were made so that the applicant is an illegal entrant.

That, of course, results from *Khawaja v Secretary of State for the Home Dept* [1983] 1 All ER 765, [1984] AC 74. That case established that on an application to the court (in that case for judicial review) of an immigration officer's order detaining any person as an illegal entrant it was the court's duty to inquire whether there had been sufficient evidence to justify the immigration officer's belief that the entry had been illegal, and that the court was not limited merely to inquiring whether the decision of the immigration officer was a reasonable one. The court, therefore, has a fact-finding role and, says Mr Shrimpton, whatever may be the position theoretically in judicial review, it is quite plain in habeas corpus, hence the importance of going by way of habeas corpus in this case, that the court's role is one which must be carried out on proper, by which I mean admissible, evidence.

He obtained some support for that submission from *R v Governor of Brixton Prison, ex p Ahson* [1969] 2 All ER 347, [1969] 2 QB 222. That was a case involving the detention of a number of Pakistanis who were found wandering the countryside with wet clothing and it was alleged (with some plausibility) that they had come illegally into the country within the previous 24 hours. The significance of 'within 24 hours' was that under the law, as it then stood, applicants could only be removed or refused admission if they were apprehended within 24 hours of having entered the country. It is perhaps to be noted that counsel then appearing for the Home Office put the facts in this way:

> These 11 men were found wandering on a sunny morning, with their shoes and trousers wet, stained and, in some cases, sandy, hopelessly lost and facing in the opposite direction to which they insisted they were going. Duly authorised immigration officers were satisfied that the men had come in clandestinely, and that they had arrived in the preceding 24 hours.' (See [1969] 2 QB 222 at 226.)

He went on to submit that that was the only realistic inference which could be drawn from the facts. The court, by majority, were not prepared to accept that. They applied the criminal standard and indicated that they did not find it proved that the men had come in within the previous 24 hours. The matter that is of importance for our purposes relates to a statement that had been obtained from one of the men who, apparently, was not before the court and was not one of the applicants, no doubt because in that statement he had admitted that he, and indeed all of them, had come in within the previous 24 hours. Mr Quintin Hogg QC for the applicants submitted (at 224):

> 'The statements attributed to [this particular individual] are hearsay and should not be admitted into consideration for he has not sworn an affidavit nor has he given evidence.'

Unfortunately the basis upon which that material was treated is not entirely clear from the judgments that were given, there being three judgments in the case, because Ashworth J dissented. He said, in relation to this particular point:

> 'In giving this answer [ie the answer to the question whether he could be sure they had been in the country for less than 24 hours] I have disregarded entirely the statements attributed to [the individual that I have referred to] which were placed before the court de bene esse but which in my judgment are inadmissible.' (See [1969] 2 All ER 347 at 358, [1969] 2 QB 222 at 238.)

That is clear support, on the face of it, for Mr Shrimpton's contention.

a   Blain J dealt with the matter as follows ([1969] 2 All ER 347 at 361, [1969] 2 QB 222 at 241):

> '... in particular the evidence of what the [relevant gentleman] said, either as a go-between or as interpreter or otherwise I find no more convincing than that of the immigration officers, particularly as there is no affidavit from that person before the court, and for that matter it is by no means clear how much of what he said would be understood by the applicants in the examples in which they were present to hear it.'

It seems from that (and Mr Shrimpton, I think, accepts) that Blain J appears to be approving the matter on the basis of weight rather than on the basis of
c   admissibility of the statement of the gentleman concerned. That leaves Lord Parker CJ, who dealt with the matter as follows ([1969] 2 All ER 347 at 350–351, [1969] 2 QB 222 at 230):

> 'Further, according to the police, the Indian to whom I referred admitted that he had been with the other 11 Pakistanis, and that they all landed that
d   morning ... However, it is only right to say that the evidence in regard to that is pure hearsay, because the Indian concerned has not sworn an affidavit and has not given evidence before this court, and accordingly I disregard anything which it is said that he, the Indian, said.'

e   It is not, I confess, clear to me whether Lord Parker CJ in that passage was saying that he disregarded it because it was hearsay and therefore carried no weight or he disregarded it because it was hearsay and was inadmissible. He certainly does not say, in terms, that it was inadmissible and he does not appear to have refused to consider it.

Accordingly, as it seems to me, the likely approach that he was taking was
f   weight. However, I do not think that this case will turn on whether I am correct in my construction of what Lord Parker CJ, or indeed Blain J, said in 1968 because it seems to me that the matter is covered, at least inferentially, by what their Lordships said in *Khawaja*'s case. Before we reach *Khawaja*, Mr Shaw, on behalf of the Home Office, has relied particularly on *Ejaz v Secretary of State for the Home Affairs* [1978] CA Transcript 777.
g   In that case, in which the leading judgment was given by Roskill LJ, the court was approaching the matter on the basis of the review jurisdiction which prevailed between the decision in *R v Secretary of State for the Home Dept, ex p Hussain* [1978] 2 All ER 423, [1978] 1 WLR 700 and the decision of *Khawaja* which swept it away. In those circumstances the indications by the court that material
h   was admissible, or could be considered by the court, which could have been considered by the Secretary of State, albeit not strictly admissible, is entirely understandable. Indeed, it would have been extraordinary if the decision had gone any other way. The approach is made clear by what Roskill LJ said:

j   'I accept Mr Woolf's argument that the part which the evidence of the informers played was probably no more than to "trigger off" the inquiries, and that the real basis of the Secretary of State's decision that this applicant was an illegal entrant was that which is set out in those two passages in the affidavits to which I have referred—after a carefully reasoned and considered assessment and appraisal of the evidence before the Secretary of State. The appraisal of such evidence, whatever its source, whether it be direct evidence or hearsay, is a matter for the Secretary of State, as has often been said before in these cases.'

As I said, that clearly reflects the then approach of the courts to illegal entrants, an approach which culminated in the decision of the House of Lords in *Zamir v Secretary of State for the Home Dept* [1980] 2 All ER 768, [1980] AC 930. It is a decision which, as we all know, was held to be wrong in *Khawaja*, *Khawaja* indicating that the correct approach was the precedent fact approach.

It seems to me that there is great force, when one looks at the matter overall, in the submissions made by Mr Shaw. Albeit the court in this particular sort of case has a fact-finding role, it is in reality still reviewing the decision of the Secretary of State. Mr Shrimpton accepts that if this were judicial review, then the court could take account of the material which was properly taken into account by the Secretary of State, albeit not strictly admissible. Indeed, that is one of the reasons he advances for the need to preserve the remedy of habeas corpus in these cases because, he says, the role of the court in habeas corpus is truly fact-finding and is not truly a review jurisdiction.

It would be strange, it may be thought, if the Secretary of State were entitled to reach a decision whether a person was an illegal entrant based upon material which was not admissible in a court of law, and were to decide properly on that material that a person was an illegal entrant. If that were challenged and the court then itself independently carried out the fact-finding exercise, if Mr Shrimpton is correct, the court would be precluded from relying upon some of the material that the Secretary of State relied upon, simply because it was not admissible in a court of law.

In the context of an administrative decision and, more particularly, in the context of a decision which has to be taken where material is obtained from far-flung places and in forms which might not easily be translated into admissible evidence in an English court, it is somewhat strange that the Secretary of State could reach a decision which may be overturned simply because material he can properly rely upon cannot be put before the English court. That would, effectively, create something of a lottery and it would be a matter of chance whether someone chose to challenge the finding by the Secretary of State. If he did choose to challenge it, he might well persuade a court, if limited to admissible evidence, that there was insufficient evidence to establish that he was an illegal entrant.

That suggests to me that the material that can be put before the court ought to include all material which can properly be taken into account by the Secretary of State whether it be hearsay or not. Of course, both the Secretary of State, and the court will give such weight as they consider proper to that evidence. If that were not so, then there would be a distinction, and an artificial distinction, between the remedies available on judicial review and habeas corpus. One of the things that *Khawaja* makes clear is that the distinction is not one of substance and merely one of form.

I have said that there are indications in *Khawaja* that the approach I have suggested is the correct one. It is to be noted that the facts of the other case which was considered with *Khawaja*, which was called *Khera*, included material in an affidavit by the immigration officer that Mr Khera had said something or had not said something of materiality to a medical officer who had examined him in India. There was no evidence before the court from the medical examiner or indeed from anyone who had been present at the medical examination. Nonetheless, it a does not seem to have occurred to any of their Lordships to question the admissibility of that material. They certainly questioned the weight of it, deciding that it did not amount to sufficient proof together with such other evidence as there was, and on that ground they allowed Khera's appeal.

Lord Templeman said ([1983] 1 All ER 765 at 795, [1984] AC 74 at 128):

b   'In habeas corpus and judicial review proceedings evidence will be by affidavit, subject to cross-examination at the discretion of the court. It may be necessary for the court to reach a conclusion on the available information and without the benefit of oral evidence or of a prolonged investigation in the country of origin of the entrant. If fraud has been concealed for a number of years, witnesses of recorded statements may not be available to provide
c   affidavits as to the circumstances in which those statements were prepared, composed and signed. Those statements may appear before the court as exhibits to affidavits from persons in whose custody the statements have been preserved. It will be for the court to determine what weight to attach to any of the information provided. It will be for the court to consider any
d   explanations furnished by the entrant and his witnesses and to judge the reliability of the entrant under cross-examination. In Khera's case, for example, it is said that there was available a record of Khera's medical examination bearing the thumb-print or signature of Khera himself and the signature of the medical officer. The record is said to have contained the statement that Khera was unmarried. The medical officer might or might
e   not have been available, and might or might not have recollected the interview. Faced with any such record Khera himself could have given evidence and been cross-examined as to the recorded statement that he was unmarried. It would have been open to the court on consideration of the record and other circumstances, and on consideration of the
f   cross-examination of Khera, to have decided that fraud was not made out.'

It is perfectly plain, in my judgment, from those passages that Lord Templeman was not suggesting (indeed quite the contrary) that the material was not admissible. What he was indicating was that it was for the court to decide its weight. Lord Bridge referred to this matter briefly, saying ([1983] 1 All ER 765 at
g 792, [1984] AC 74 at 124):

      'I would add that the inherent difficulties of discovering and proving the true facts in many immigration cases can afford no valid ground for lowering or relaxing the standard of proof required. If unlimited leave to enter was granted perhaps years before and the essential facts relied on to establish the
h   fraud alleged can only be proved by documentary and affidavit evidence of past events which occurred in some remote part of the Indian subcontinent, the courts should be less, rather than more, ready to accept anything short of convincing proof.'

j That merely reflects that the court should be very careful not to attach great weight to material which has been untested and which cannot be put into a form which would render it admissible in a court of law. I do not think it is necessary to refer to any other passages of the speeches, save to note that Lord Scarman, in dealing with the relationship between habeas corpus and judicial review, said ([1983] 1 All ER 765 at 782, [1984] AC 74 at 111):

'There are, of course, procedural differences between habeas corpus and the modern statutory judicial review ... *Zamir* ... was a case of habeas corpus; in the instant cases the effective relief sought is certiorari to quash the immigration officer's decision. But the nature of the remedy sought cannot affect the principle of the law. In both cases liberty is in issue. "Judicial review" under RSC Ord 53 ... is available only by leave of the court. The writ of habeas corpus issues as of right. But the difference arises not in the law's substance but from the nature of the remedy appropriate to the case. The writ issues as of right summoning into court the person in whose custody the subject is. It gets the custodian into court; but discharge from custody is not possible unless "the party hath a probable cause to be delivered", as Vaughan CJ put it (see *Bushel's Case* (1670) T Jo 13, 84 ER 1123) in words quoted by Blackstone (3 Bl Com (12th edn, 1794) 132). This remains the law today and effectually puts habeas corpus in like case with the other form of judicial review.'

Mr Shrimpton is singularly unhappy with that passage, indeed with the whole approach in *Khawaja*, which seeks, as it were, to amalgamate the remedies of habeas corpus and judicial review. He is anxious that nothing that I say should do anything to diminish the importance of habeas corpus as an independent remedy. It is certainly the case that historically, and indeed still today, habeas corpus is a very important weapon in the hands of the court against any attempts to restrict the liberty of the individual in an unauthorised fashion.

However in reality, in my judgment, as Lord Scarman indicated, one has to look at the context in which the remedy has been sought. Here the context is a decision of the Secretary of State that the individual in question was an illegal entrant. That is an administrative decision which he has to form by virtue of the responsibilities placed upon him by the Immigration Act 1971. If that decision is challenged, the court has to decide for itself on looking at the material which was available to the Secretary of State or which is available to the court if there is further material before the court (because it is perfectly clear from the authorities, which I do not need to go into in any detail, which include *R v Secretary of State for the Home Office, ex p Muse* [1992] Imm AR 282) that the court is entitled to look at any fresh material that exists.

It seems to me that it is wholly right, sensible and proper that the court should be able to look at any such material. Of course, it is a matter for the Secretary of State to decide how he chooses to present that material. If he chooses to present it in such a way as is hearsay or hearsay upon hearsay then he runs the risk that the court will attach that much less weight to it. In certain circumstances it may obviously be impossible for him to produce the material in any other way. This case provides an example because it was clearly impractical for him to produce the villagers as witnesses and impractical, too, to go further than the entry clearance officers who made the visits. It is, therefore, for me to decide what weight should be attached to that material.

It seems to me that any other approach would perpetuate the distinction between judicial review and habeas corpus which *Khawaja* expressly indicated should not exist. Furthermore, it seems to me that what I have suggested should be the correct approach is supported, at least inferentially, by the recent decision of the Divisional Court in *R v Oldham Justices, ex p Cawley* [1996] 1 All ER 464, [1996] 2 WLR 681. That was a case involving the alleged unlawful committal to prison of fine defaulters. The court in that case was concerned to decide whether

a   judicial review or habeas corpus was the appropriate remedy. Simon Brown LJ
     said ([1996] 1 All ER 464 at 476, [1996] 2 WLR 681 at 694):

> 'This approach recognises the applicants' need to establish an error of law
> in the underlying decisions committing them to custody, but contends that
> this can properly be done by habeas corpus application, particularly where,
> as here, the applicants start by producing a defective warrant. I have to say
b> that although the jurisdictional difficulties confronting the applicants in this
> regard may well be fewer than those which in my judgment defeat their first
> argument, so too are the attractions fewer. The reality is that as judicial
> review has developed into an ever more flexible and responsive jurisdiction,
> the need for a parallel, blunter remedy by way of habeas corpus has
c> diminished. That said, this ancient writ plainly remains part of our
> constitutional heritage and it is certainly not for this court to deny a
> jurisdiction which in law it enjoys. The question is: in what circumstances is
> it available? The interrelation between habeas corpus and judicial review
> was recently considered by the Law Commission in their October 1994
> Report (Law Com No 226) ... Although the Commission noted that "the
d> case law is riddled with contradictions", it nevertheless concluded against
> subsuming habeas corpus into the judicial review procedure, albeit at the
> same time suggesting that the scope of review in both should be essentially
> the same.'

     He then goes on to refer to the immigration cases recognising, as indeed do I, that
e   the habeas corpus is clearly available as an alternative remedy and there is no
     suggestion that these proceedings are in improper form. They clearly are proper,
     although judicial review would equally clearly have been an alternative remedy.
         He cites a passage of Taylor LJ's judgment in *R v Secretary of State for the Home
     Dept, ex p Muboyayi* [1991] 4 All ER 72 at 91, [1992] QB 244 at 269:

f> 'The great writ of habeas corpus has over the centuries been a flexible
> remedy adaptable to changing circumstances. Time was when it was used
> in conjunction with certiorari in a manner characterised as certiorari in aid of
> habeas corpus. I see no reason why, in the changed circumstances of the
> 1990s and especially in immigration cases involving applicants entering and
g> being removed from the jurisdiction, the roles of these two remedies should
> not be reversed so as to provide habeas corpus in aid of certiorari.'

     That was an observation made in the context of the then law when bail could not
     be granted to applicants unless they applied for habeas corpus. That anomaly has
     now disappeared. It seems to me that the whole tenor of the cases following on
h   from *Khawaja* established that there should be no difference in the approach of
     the court to judicial review and to habeas corpus. Of course, the safeguards that
     are applicable to habeas corpus must be reflected in judicial review. In my
     judgment they are, but it is not a necessary safeguard in the context of
     immigration cases and in the context of the issues which have to be determined
j   that the court should be limited to evidence which is admissible in a court of law.
     It seems to me, as I have said, that the court is indeed entitled to have regard to
     all the material to which the Secretary of State could properly have had regard.
         I should mention one argument raised by Mr Shrimpton in support of his
     contention, which was that historically it was clear that it was open to an
     applicant for habeas corpus to seek and to receive a trial by jury of any factual
     issue which was raised. He refers me in that regard to an authority where that

precisely happened (see *Re Guerin* (1888) 60 LT 538). Guerin was an unfortunate
gentleman, who was accused of theft in France. They said that he was a
Frenchman and required his extradition. He said that he was an Englishman and
could not be extradited. The issue whether he was an Englishman was ordered
to be tried by a jury. He unfortunately received a judge who gave a misdirection,
namely that the onus was on him to establish that he was an Englishman,
whereas it ought to have been the other way round. As a result of that, the jury
found that he was not an Englishman and he was duly extradited and found
himself on Devil's Island. Twenty years later or so he escaped. He came back to
this country and there was a further attempt to extradite him. He raised the same
point. On this occasion, in 1907, the matter was tried in the more usual fashion
that one recognises with habeas corpus and the court, perhaps feeling that
enough was enough, decided on the correct application of the burden of proof
that it had not been established that he was not an Englishman. Accordingly, he
was not further extradited.

He has referred also to a Privy Council case in 1901, which I need not specify,
in which the Privy Council recognised in New Zealand the right to trial by jury.
Mr Shrimpton is not aware of any case since *Re Guerin* or the New Zealand case
where there ever has been a trial by jury in a habeas corpus matter. In my
judgment any application, if made now, would fall on singularly stony ground.
However, he makes the point in the context of his submission that if there was a
right to trial by jury then it is improbable, in those circumstances, that the court
would have countenanced the admission of any evidence other than evidence
that was strictly admissible. That may or may not be so, but the position in the
1890s and the early 1900s really cannot dictate the present day position, as was
made clear by Simon Brown LJ in *Ex p Cawley*. Indeed, following the dictum of
Taylor LJ the application of these remedies has developed over the years and
what may have been right for 1900 is not necessarily right for 1996.

Accordingly, in my judgment, the material which the Secretary of State wishes
to rely upon, in particular the village visits, is admissible before me. I too am
entitled to take it into account in deciding whether I am satisfied that the
Secretary of State has proved that the applicant is an illegal entrant. The standard
of proof, again, is quite clearly established by *Khawaja* as being the civil standard,
but the gravity of the matter will dictate the standard which must be applied. In
this case what is being alleged is that the applicant was guilty of fraud, told lies in
order to obtain the certificate, and that accordingly the certificate should be
removed, he himself should be removed from the country and is liable to be put
into custody pending such removal. It seems to me, in those circumstances, that
I ought to approach the matter (and I do) on the basis that if I have any reasonable
doubt as to whether the matter is proved, I should resolve that in favour of the
applicant. That is the standard which I propose to apply.

Mr Shaw was concerned that I should not, as a matter of language, apply the
criminal standard of proof because that is what *Khawaja* says does not apply. That
is, of course, technically right but in reality where one is dealing with a case such
as this, nothing less than that sort of an approach seems to me to be appropriate.
Therefore, it is necessary to look at the circumstances in slightly more detail.

I have already referred to the denunciatory letters. The first such letter came
in October 1991. It asserted that the applicant's true name was not Saidur
Rahman but was Mohammed Surab Ali Talukder and, secondly, that the child
Rone, in respect of whom the applicant was seeking entry clearance as his son,
was not his son nor his wife's son but the son of his sister-in-law. As a result of

a that allegation being made, the applicant's wife was interviewed. In the course of that interview she asserted still that both children were hers and her husband's. She was asked whether her husband had any enemies in the village and she said no. That was an interview that took place on 14 January 1992.

There was then a DNA examination and the result of that, which was sent to the Home Office in April 1992, indicated that Rone could not be the true son of b the parents. That has since, inevitably, been admitted by the applicant and his wife.

Accordingly, it is perfectly clear that he was a person who was prepared to tell lies in order to obtain an immigration advantage, on this occasion for Rone, whom he pretended was his son. Furthermore there was produced a birth certificate which purported to show that Rone was the true son of the applicant c and his wife. The significance of that is the applicant has himself produced a birth certificate purporting to show that he was the son of Abdus Somed. The point is also made that the applicant is someone who has been prepared to produce a false birth certificate and thus one does not apply to the birth certificate that he has produced the weight that one would otherwise apply to it.

d Mr Shrimpton, on the other hand, says, rightly, that the mere fact that there is one false document does not mean that the other document must be false. He says that the birth certificate is important evidence and that, on the face of it, the Home Office has had the opportunity of making inquiries, of inspecting the original register and of undertaking scientific tests to see whether the certificate is bogus. I do not think the scientific tests would necessarily have achieved much, e but the investigations of the original register in Bangladesh perhaps might. One knows not.

The fact is, again, that the applicant has clearly not helped himself (to put it no higher) by producing the false birth certificate in relation to his alleged son and in telling the lies to the authorities in order to try to get him into the country. He f seeks to explain that in an affidavit sworn by him in May 1996 (very recently) saying:

> 'My wife's eldest sister ... and her husband ... (who are very poor) begged me and my wife to take their son Rone ... with us to England by falsely claiming that he was my son. I did not want to do this. I was emotionally g pressurised by all my family to go through it. Due to constant mental pressure from everyone, and their persistent crying, followed by threats by the [parents] to take their own lives, I eventually relented, with great reluctance, and agreed to take Rone as my own son. At that time my wife and I did not have any children of our own.'

h

That, in my judgment, is not a satisfactory answer, particularly since, as far as I am aware, it has been put forward for the first time in an affidavit sworn as recently as last month.

The second denunciatory letter came in April 1992. That also referred to Rone j and went on to say that Rina's husband's name was Mr Surab Ali Talukder, the son of Sonai Ali Talukder, and that the village he lived in was a village called Nittarchok, therefore, effectively, giving the same information as had been given in the previous letter. That led to the village visit, in the course of which, on the material before me, the entry clearance officers established (they thought) that the applicant was not the son of an Abdus Somed of that village but came from a village some distance away.

Mr Shrimpton advises caution and points out that the interviews were carried *a* on through interpreters and warns of the dangers of misunderstandings. As I have said, what in fact the entry clearance officers did was to go with photographs and put the photographs to the individuals. They received answers from those that they saw which identified, or not, the people in question.

One recognises the dangers of misunderstandings through interpreters but, equally, when people have been shown photographs and asked about names, it *b* is usually fairly easy to tell whether they are saying yes or no when asked to recognise someone, even without an interpreter being present, and also experienced entry clearance officers would, one expects, be able to recognise names when names were stated, even if they could not understand the language otherwise. Accordingly, as it seems to me, the scope for misunderstandings in the sort of exercise that the entry clearance officers were carrying out is perhaps *c* somewhat less than it might be in certain other situations. It is not an overwhelming point but it is a factor which one is entitled to take into account.

In the course of that visit they not only saw various villagers but they also saw the alleged father, Abdus Somed and Rina, the wife. The record of questions and answers is this. I say the 'record'. It was the practice of the entry clearance *d* officers to take a tape recorder and to record the conversations. They would then get, through the interpreters' translation, the questions and answers and would then note those down. The tapes, unfortunately were not retained (understandably, because otherwise there would no doubt be shelves and shelves of these tapes) but were used again for the same purpose. Hence it has not been possible to obtain the originals of that first visit, although the originals of the *e* second visit have been obtained. Sadly they do not help because they are, apparently, too indistinct to give any possibility of understanding the original questions and answers.

In any event, the relevant questions are these. First of all, she was asked about Rone and she was asked about her children: *f*

'Q. That's your only child, isn't it? A. No, I've got one called Rone.

Q. But, the blood test has shown that Rone's not your child. A. Yes, that's right. I've only got one son.

Q. Why did you try to take your sister's child to UK? A. Well, it's a poor *g* country. Everybody wants to help one another.

Q. Now, can you tell me what your husband's real name is because I know it's not Saidur Rahman. A. It's Saidur Rahman.'

The entry clearance officer then said that he had turned to the alleged father, *h* Abdus Somed, and asked him:

'You've not been truthful with us, Mr Somed. You have taken a boy to UK who's not your son. Your niece's husband is not your son, is he? A. I brought him up.

Q. The whole village has told us that he's not your son, he's not even from *j* this village. Now please tell me the truth. A. He's a poor child. I brought him up, so I took him to UK.

Q. Who is he really? A. Well, I'm a sick man, I can't really remember everything.

Q. I'm sure you can remember who that boy really is.'

a The old man made no reply, so the question was repeated to Rina and she then said:

> 'His name is Surab, and his real name is Saidur.
> Q. Which village is Surab from? A. He's from Nittarchok. It's near Hobiganj:
> Q. And who is his real father? A. Suruz Ali.
b
> Q. And why did your uncle take that boy to the UK? A. He brought him up and took him to UK. We are only three sisters, we've got no brothers so later on my uncle arranged the marriage.'

If that is an accurate record of what the two were then saying, clearly each is accepting (the wife explicitly, the father less so) that there was no father/son
c relationship between the two.

Rina has subsequently sworn an affidavit, dated 28 December 1995, in which she rejects that account. She states that the questions were:

> 'Are you Mrs Rina Akthar? A. Yes, I am Rina Akthar.
> Q. How many children have you got? A. I have one child and his name is
d Jone Ahmed.
> Q. What is your husband's name? A. Saidur Rahman.
> At which the people from the High Commission said that is not my husband's name. His name is Surab Ali, His father is Suruj Ali of village Nittarchok. At which I said that is not true, but the people from the High
e Commission said that they have received information that my husband is not who he claims to be.
> Q. Is Saidur Rahman related to you? A. He is my first cousin. I have known him all my life and I am married to him.
> After that, the people from the High Commission said that they are leaving and will see what the Home Office has to do about my husband and then
f notify me of what decision the Home Office makes. They also told me that they received a letter from someone who told them that my husband is living under a different identity.'

If that be right the account given by the entry clearance officer is simply wrong. Either he is making it up or the interpreter has the matter hopelessly wrong.
g It is interesting to note that in his affidavit the applicant says this about it:

> 'I deny that this version of events is even remotely true [ie the version I read out before the version of the entry clearance officer]. My wife telephoned me that very same evening from Bangladesh and informed me of
h the visit by the immigration officers. She told me that pressure had been placed on her to admit that I was not Saidur Rahman. She informed me that she did not make these admissions despite the pressure exerted on her.'

Then he referred to the affidavit. The affidavit does not, on the face of it, refer to any pressure. It is a straightforward question and answer session and she gives
j the account which supports the applicant and does not suggest that the entry clearance officers put any pressure on her.

Mr Shaw submits that if she did say what was alleged against her in February 1993 that is of great significance, because it was contrary to her interest to make those admissions at that time, since she was applying to join her husband in the United Kingdom. He says that the affidavit which was prepared much later for the purpose of these proceedings is clearly self-serving, as indeed it clearly is.

As far as the father is concerned, he too has sworn an affidavit subsequently. That is dated 16 August 1993. He says:

'I, Md Abdus Samad S/O Late Abdul Hashim of Vill Haldarpur ... age about 70 years, by faith Muslim, by profession cultivation and by nationality Bangladeshi, do hereby solemnly affirm and declare as follows. That Md Saidur Rahman is my son. He was born at the aforesaid address on 29th July, 1967. The name of his mother is Momjan Bibi. The statement made above is explained to me in full and having understood that it is written according to my dictation I put my thumb impression below. Further to mention I cannot write anything on paper due to my physical condition.'

There then is a thumbprint and an insertion of Mr Ahmed describing himself as an advocate, confirms the identity.

Also produced is a medical report, or what purports to be a medical report, dated 4 October 1993. It certifies that Abdus Somed was seen by the doctor on 4 October 1993 for physical examination. It goes on: 'He is suffering from senile dementia. He is ill health and taking supportive medication.' What is said is, if he did say what the entry clearance officers alleged he said in February 1993, he was suffering from senile dementia and it is not possible to rely on anything that is there recorded.

That argument is all very well but, as it seems to me, the applicant cannot have it all ways because he puts forward the affidavit of August 1993, sworn, I suppose, when the senile dementia still existed. I do not think it is suggested that senile dementia is a condition that comes and goes depending on the seasons. What weight does one attach to the affidavit? Either it is all weightless or none of it, as it seems to me. In reality, too, I have the evidence of the entry clearance officer that the old man did not appear to misunderstand or to be unable to comprehend or to be suffering in any way from any condition which meant that what he said appeared unreliable. Certainly no one said that and one would expect Rina, perhaps, to have said: 'You cannot rely on everything he says. I am afraid he is not with us.'

Accordingly, in my judgment, the gravest possible doubt is cast upon both the alleged medical report and the affidavit of August 1993.

There then followed, as I have indicated, a visit to Nittarchok in December 1993. Similar confirmatory information is obtained according to the entry clearance officers. Mr Simpson was the officer in question. I have before me an affidavit from him, together with his report that he made immediately following the visit. He describes showing photographs and getting immediate recognition of the photograph of Surab Ali. Again, I make the same point about interpretation. Recognition of that sort of photograph and the giving of a name is not something that one would have thought is easy to misunderstand. He then refers to two people who were apparently trying to stop the villagers talking to the entry clearance officers. They, according to what he was later told, were the applicant's brothers who were trying, the inference is, to stop the truth being told.

Again, if that evidence is to be relied upon, there is further confirmation that the position is as the denunciatory letters indicated.

Mr Shrimpton says that it is all very well, but all that really does is to raise suspicions. We do not know because we are not able to test the reliability of the village visits. Furthermore, he says that a number of those villagers have been traced, that their identities had been provided by the Home Office, and that most a   of them have been seen since and have produced affidavits in which they state, effectively, that the evidence put forward by the entry clearance officers is wrong, and that they never identified the applicant as anyone other than Saidur Rahman, the son of Abdus Somed.

So far as the first visit is concerned, that is to say the villagers from Holdarpur, there are a number of affidavits which are in identical terms. They say (this is
b   standard), having set out their names:

'In February 1993 in Holderpur village, I was approached by some people who showed me some photographs of Saidur Rahman and Rina Akhter. They asked me my name. I was asked if I knew them and I said yes. I do not remember saying anything else. Saidur Rahman, S/O Late Abdus Somed is
c   married to his cousin, Rina Akhter D/O Abdul Johur. They married in 1988. They have one child Jone Ahmed. Abdus Somed passed away in April 1994. Saidur Rahman lives in UK. The statements made above are true to the best of my knowledge and belief. I put my signature below.'

Then there is a thumbprint, which again is certified by someone describing
d   himself as an advocate.

The slightly curious thing about these standard form affidavits is that they say, each of them: 'I do not remember saying anything else.' One might have expected them to say in slightly different forms that 'I confirmed' that they were who they alleged they were. But no. It seems to me that the weight to be attached to those affidavits is very small indeed. I am afraid the same must be said
e   of all the other virtually standard form affidavits which have been collected from Holdarpur and from the other villagers seeking to assert that the entry clearance officers' accounts are incorrect.

Similarly, there has been produced an extract from the voting register which is said to show that the applicant was on the register in the village as the son of
f   Abdus Somed.

The entry clearance officer, Mr Simpson, in his affidavit, says:

'I have one final and general comment on the material relied upon by the Applicant. I understand that the Applicant has admitted that he is not the father of Rone Ahmed. This inevitably means that the birth certificate ... put
g   forward ... is false. In my experience in Bangladesh (based upon real cases I have worked on and upon information given to me by local people) it is not difficult to obtain forged official documents such as birth certificates. False official and non-official documents are easily available on the payment of a small bribe. In paragraph 10 of his affidavit the Applicant exhibits a copy of
h   the 1990 voting list for Holderpur which contains his name. No proof of identity was required in 1990 in order to appear on this voting list. It was compiled for the 1991 elections but the accuracy of the lists was criticised and discredited by all the opposition parties. For the May 1996 elections the opposition parties campaigned for fresh voting lists, claiming that the ruling
j   party had rigged those previous in circulation. In addition, I am aware that it is a common practice to take a voting list to a private printer and have it renumbered and reprinted to include extra names. The normal price is about ... (2·50) [the equivalent]. There are also standard prices for falsifying other documents from birth certificates to full British passports (5,000). It is impossible for me to tell from photocopies whether any of the documents relied upon by the Applicant are false. Often false documents are very

difficult to detect because they are constructed from 'official' rubber stamps easily available from the bazaars.' a

It seems to me that I am perfectly entitled to have regard to that evidence from an experienced entry clearance officer who has worked in Bangladesh. I fully recognise that lies may be told and false documents put forward in order to bolster a case which is, in fact, a true case which the individual believes he may b have difficulty in establishing. I fully recognise that lies in themselves do not necessarily prove the deception in the material particular that is alleged in any individual case. However, notwithstanding that and notwithstanding the fact I recognise that the material has not been tested and there are always the possibilities for error when one is dealing through interpreters, I am quite satisfied on the material before me that it has been proved to the requisite c standard that this applicant was not the son of Abdus Somed and did obtain the certificate of entitlement by deception.

The matters that I have gone through persuade me that that is the only decision which I can reasonably come to on the material that is before me. In those circumstances this application for habeas corpus must be rejected. d

I would only add this, as I said in the introduction to this in dealing with the preliminary point, it seems to me that now there is no practical difference between the approach the court has to adopt to a judicial review and to a habeas corpus. True it is that habeas issues as of right, in a sense that the matter is investigated by the court without the need for any leave to be obtained. However, in a case where there is a factual issue as to whether a person is e properly to be regarded as an illegal entrant it would be a very rare case in which a court would refuse leave. Effectively, it could only say that it was unarguable if the evidence produced was so overwhelming that there was no chance that the applicant could, effectively, get around it. But where any factual issue is raised and, particularly having regard to the burden and standard of proof required as a f result of *Khawaja*, it seems to me, as I say, that leave is bound to be granted. Mr Shrimpton recognises in this case that Clarke J would almost certainly have granted leave if judicial review were being pursued.

It seems to me that the remedies available in judicial review are much more appropriate in cases such as this and, for my part, I would consider that prima facie challenges such as this ought to be brought by way of judicial review. g However, having said that I cannot of course prevent, nor would I wish anything that I say to tend to prevent, anyone who wishes to do so to bring proceedings by habeas corpus, because quite clearly there is jurisdiction so to do. It seems to me that there should be an encouragement (to put it no higher) to proceed by way of judicial review in these cases rather than by way of habeas corpus. Further than h that I do not think it would be proper for me to go.

Application dismissed. Leave to appeal granted.

Dilys Tausz Barrister. j

a # R v Crown Court at Guildford, ex parte Director of Public Prosecutions

R v Crown Court at Southwark, ex parte Bowles

b QUEEN'S BENCH DIVISION

SIMON BROWN LJ AND GAGE J

9, 17 OCTOBER 1996

Criminal evidence – Special procedure material – Access to special procedure material
c *– Application for production of special procedure material – Test to be applied in determining application – Dominant purpose of application – Police and Criminal Evidence Act 1984, s 9 – Criminal Justice Act 1988, s 93H.*

In two applications for judicial review the issue arose, having regard to the court's
d similar powers under s 9[a] of and Sch 1 to the Police and Criminal Evidence Act 1984, as to the circumstances in which an application would be appropriate under s 93H[b] of the Criminal Justice Act 1988, which provided that a constable might apply to a circuit judge for an order for the production of special procedure material implicated in a criminal offence where there were 'reasonable grounds for suspecting' that someone had benefited from criminal conduct.

e   In the first case, the Director of Public Prosecutions challenged the Crown Court judge's refusal to grant an order under s 93H for the production of details of bank accounts in which funds earned through prostitution were held. In the second case, a certified accountant sought judicial review of the judge's order under s 93H requiring her to produce business records relating to the false
f income and expenditure of two clients accused of dishonesty offences. The Director of Public Prosecutions contended in each case that, where a person was reasonably suspected of a crime of gain, s 93H had effectively superseded s 9 as the relevant power for investigating not merely the extent or whereabouts of the proceeds of criminal conduct but also whether any person had benefited from such conduct. The accountant contended that s 93H was directed solely towards
g assisting in the recovery of the actual proceeds of crime and that it had no application to the investigation of crime as such.

Held – (1) Where an order for the production of material was sought, an application under s 93H of the 1988 Act would be appropriate if the dominant
h purpose of the application was to determine, in respect of criminal offending, whether and, if so, to what extent someone had benefited from it or the whereabouts of the proceeds. However, where the production of the material was sought for criminal investigation purposes to determine whether an offence had been committed and, if so, to provide evidence of that offence, the
j application should be made under s 9 of the 1984 Act (see p 966 *a j*, p 967 *d* to *f* and p 969 *j*, post).

    (2) In the first case, it was clear that the police were seeking production of the bank's documents predominantly to determine the extent to which the accused

---

a   Section 9, so far as material, is set out at p 964 *d*, post
b   Section 93H, so far as material, is set out at p 963 *b* to *h*, post

had benefited from their offending and the whereabouts of their gains; it was therefore appropriate that an order for production should be made under s 93H *a* and the refusal to grant the order would be quashed accordingly. In the second case, it was less clear that the predominant reason the police sought the documents was essentially with a view to obtaining a restraint order, rather than investigating further the alleged criminality of the accountant's clients; it was doubtful whether the correct question had been asked either by the court or the *b* police and, in those circumstances, the production order would be quashed until a final decision had been made as to the appropriate statutory power to be used (see p 968 *d* and p 969 *e* to *g j*, post).

Notes

For special procedure generally, see 11(1) *Halsbury's Laws* (4th edn reissue) paras *c* 673–678.

For the Police and Criminal Evidence Act 1984, s 9, see 12 *Halsbury's Statutes* (4th edn) (1994 reissue) 858.

Cases referred to in judgments *d*

R v Crown Court at Lewes, ex p Hill (1990) 93 Cr App R 60, DC.
R v Maidstone Crown Court, ex p Waitt [1988] Crim LR 384, DC.

Cases also cited or referred to in skeleton arguments

Barclays Bank plc v Taylor [1989] 3 All ER 563, [1989] 1 WLR 1066, CA.
Pepper (Inspector of Taxes) v Hart [1993] 1 All ER 42, [1993] AC 593, HL. *e*

Applications for judicial review

R v Crown Court at Guildford, ex p DPP

The Director of Public Prosecutions applied, with leave of Buxton J granted on *f* 22 July 1996, for an order of certiorari to quash the decision of Judge Bull QC in the Crown Court at Guildford on 11 April 1996 whereby he refused to make an order under s 93H of the Criminal Justice Act 1988 for the production of bank records held by the London Branch of the Philippine National Bank relating to two accounts in which the proceeds of prostitution were held. The facts are set *g* out in the judgment of Simon Brown LJ.

R v Crown Court at Southwark, ex p Bowles

Karen Bowles, a certified accountant, applied, with leave of Buxton J granted on 6 August 1996, for an order of certiorari to quash the decision of Judge Peter *h* Jackson in the Crown Court at Southwark on 29 March 1996 whereby he granted an order under s 93H of the Criminal Justice Act 1988 for the production of records held by her relating to the business operations of her clients, who were facing charges of dishonesty connected with the running of their company, Associate Business Management Ltd. The facts are set out in the judgment of Simon Brown LJ. *j*

Andrew Mitchell (instructed by the *Crown Prosecution Service,* Guildford) for the DPP.
Robin Johnson (instructed by *Wainwright & Cummins*) for Mrs Bowles.

Cur adv vult

a 17 October 1996. The following judgments were delivered.

SIMON BROWN LJ. These two judicial review applications are both concerned with the proper construction and application of s 93H of the Criminal Justice Act 1988, a provision inserted into that Act by s 11 of the Proceeds of Crime Act 1995 with effect from 1 November 1995. Let me at once set out its material parts:

b

'(1) A constable may, for the purposes of an investigation into whether any person has benefited from any criminal conduct or into the extent or whereabouts of the proceeds of any criminal conduct, apply to a Circuit judge for an order under subsection (2) below in relation to particular material or material of a particular description.

c

(2) If, on such an application, the judge is satisfied that the conditions in subsection (4) below are fulfilled, he may make an order that the person who appears to him to be in possession of the material to which the application relates shall—(a) produce it to a constable for him to take away, or (b) give a constable access to it, within such period as the order may specify. This subsection has effect subject to section 93J(11) below [High Court orders in respect of government departments].

d

(3) The period to be specified in an order under subsection (2) above shall be seven days unless it appears to the judge that a longer or shorter period would be appropriate in the particular circumstances of the application.

(4) The conditions referred to in subsection (2) above are—(a) that there are reasonable grounds for suspecting that a specified person has benefited from any criminal conduct; (b) that there are reasonable grounds for suspecting that the material to which the application relates—(i) is likely to be of substantial value (whether by itself or together with other material) to the investigation for the purposes of which the application is made; and (ii) does not consist of or include items subject to legal privilege or excluded material; and (c) that there are reasonable grounds for believing that it is in the public interest, having regard—(i) to the benefit likely to accrue to the investigation if the material is obtained, and (ii) to the circumstances under which the person in possession of the material holds it, that the material should be produced or that access to it should be given.

e

f

(5) Where the judge makes an order under subsection (2)(b) above in relation to material on any premises he may, on the application of a constable, order any person who appears to him to be entitled to grant entry to the premises to allow a constable to enter the premises to obtain access to the material.

g

(6) An application under subsection (1) or (5) above may be made ex parte to a judge in chambers ...'

h

On the first listed motion, which I shall call 'the Guildford case', the applicant is the Director of Public Prosecutions (the DPP), who challenges the Crown Court judge's refusal on 11 April 1996 to grant a s 93H production order, and who complains that the judge construed this new power too restrictively.

j On the second motion, the Southwark case, the applicant is Mrs Karen Bowles, a certified accountant, who challenges that court's decision on 29 March 1996 to make a s 93H production order in respect of certain clients' documents in her keeping, and who complains that the judge construed the power too widely.

At the heart of the argument in both cases lies a comparison between the s 93H power and the power to make similar orders under s 9 of and Sch 1 to the Police and Criminal Evidence Act 1984 (PACE), the difficulty in the case consisting of determining the precise interrelationship between them.

The documents involved in both cases fall within the definition of 'special procedure material' in s 14 of PACE:

'(1) In this Act "special procedure material" means—(a) material to which subsection (2) below applies ...

(2) Subject to the following provisions of this section, this subsection applies to material, other than items subject to legal privilege and excluded material [personal records such as doctor's notes (see s 11 of PACE)], in the possession of a person who—(a) acquired or created it in the course of any trade, business, profession or other occupation or for the purpose of any paid or unpaid office; and (b) holds it subject—(i) to an express or implied undertaking to hold it in confidence ...'

This definition of 'special procedure material' is imported into s 93H by sub-s (12)(a).

Prior to 1 November 1995 the only way in which special procedure material had been available to the prosecution (save in certain limited circumstances under s 7 of the Bankers' Books Evidence Act 1879) was under s 9(1) of PACE:

'A constable may obtain access to excluded material or special procedure material for the purposes of a criminal investigation by making an application under Schedule 1 below and in accordance with that Schedule.'

Schedule 1 to PACE, under the heading 'Special procedure', provides, so far as relevant:

'1. If on an application made by a constable a circuit judge is satisfied that one or other of the sets of access conditions is fulfilled, he may make an order under paragraph 4 below.

2. The first set of access conditions is fulfilled if—(a) there are reasonable grounds for believing—(i) that a serious arrestable offence has been committed; (ii) that there is material which consists of special procedure material or includes special procedure material and does not also include excluded material on premises specified in the application; (iii) that the material is likely to be of substantial value (whether by itself or together with other material) to the investigation in connection with which the application is made; and (iv) that the material is likely to be relevant evidence; (b) other methods of obtaining the material—(i) have been tried without success; or (ii) have not been tried because it appeared that they were bound to fail; and (c) it is in the public interest, having regard—(i) to the benefit likely to accrue to the investigation if the material is obtained; and (ii) to the circumstances under which the person in possession of the material holds it, that the material should be produced or that access to it should be given ...

4. An order under this paragraph is an order that the person who appears to the circuit judge to be in possession of the material to which the application relates shall—(a) produce it to a constable for him to take away; or (b) give a constable access to it, not later than the end of the period of seven days from the date of the order or the end of such longer period as the order may specify ...'

It is worth noting at this point certain clear differences between the s 93H power and that provided by s 9 of PACE: (a) applications under s 93H can be a   made ex parte; those under s 9 must be inter partes; (b) s 9 applications must relate to a 'serious arrestable offence'; no such requirement arises under s 93H; (c) under s 9, information cannot be obtained either from government departments or to assist in foreign investigations; s 93H is not similarly restricted; (d) the s 9 power arises only when there exist 'reasonable grounds for *believing*' (para 2(a) of Sch 1) that an offence has been committed. The s 93H power

b   involves a lower threshold test: that there are 'reasonable grounds for *suspecting*' (s 93H(4)(a)) that someone has benefited from criminal conduct.

    In short, the s 9 power where it applies is in various respects the more limited of the two but by definition—by virtue of para 2(b)(ii) of Sch 1 to PACE—the requirement that other methods of obtaining the material have not been tried because it appeared that they were bound to fail—it does not apply in

c   circumstances where on its true construction s 93H does.

    It is convenient next to indicate in broad terms the rival contentions before us: those of Mr Mitchell who appears for the DPP in both cases, and those of Mr Johnson who represents Mrs Bowles alone.

    Mr Mitchell's essential submission is that wherever anyone is reasonably

d   suspected of an acquisition offence (a crime of gain), s 93H has effectively superseded s 9: s 93H now provides the relevant power for investigating whether a crime of gain has been committed. It expressly permits applications for the purpose of investigating, not merely 'the extent or whereabouts of the proceeds of any criminal conduct', but also 'whether any person has benefited from any criminal conduct'. An investigation into whether someone has benefited from

e   crime cannot sensibly be distinguished from an investigation into whether that person committed a crime in the first place. Take the average fraud: to ask whether or not X in a given transaction acted fraudulently is to ask equally whether X benefited from criminal conduct. If a complainant alleges loss, that is also an allegation of benefit by another.

f   Mr Johnson's contrary argument is that s 93H is directed solely towards assisting in the recovery of the proceeds of criminal conduct: it has no application to the investigation of crime as such. There are, he submits, within the legislation, a number of clear indications that the power was introduced with a view to depriving the criminal of his ill-gotten gains rather than actually investigating crime. The main pointers are these.

g
    (1) The long title to the 1995 Act:

        'An Act to make further provision for and in relation to the recovery of the proceeds of criminal conduct; to make further provision for facilitating the enforcement of overseas forfeiture and restraint orders; and for connected

h   purposes.'

    (2) Section 93H, as added by amendment to the 1988 Act, appears in Pt VI of that Act, which is itself headed: 'Confiscation of the proceeds of an offence'.

    (3) Section 93H itself is headed: 'Investigations into the proceeds of criminal

j   conduct.'

    (4) Section 15(2) of the 1995 Act provides:

        'For the purposes of sections 21 and 22 of [PACE—with regard to access to, and copying and retention of, seized material] an investigation into whether any person has benefited from any criminal conduct or into the extent or whereabouts of the proceeds of any criminal conduct shall be treated (so far as that would not otherwise be the case) as if it were an investigation of, or in connection with, an offence.'

Implicit in this is Parliament's recognition of a difference between an investigation into whether someone has benefited from crime and an investigation into an offence—'a criminal investigation' as s 9 puts it.

(5) Perhaps most tellingly of all, the contrast falls to be made between s 93H(4)(a) of the 1988 Act and s 55(4)(a) of the Drug Trafficking Act 1994 (originally s 27 of the Drug Trafficking Offences Act 1986). I have already set out sub-s (4) of s 93H. What is to be noted is that it is in every respect identical to s 55(4) of the 1994 Act save only (immaterially) that the word 'purposes' in s 93H(4)(b)(i) appears in the singular in s 55(4)(b)(i) and, this being the material distinction, instead of the condition in s 93H(4)(a) that 'there are reasonable grounds for suspecting that a specified person has benefited from any criminal conduct', the equivalent condition in s 55(4)(a) is that 'there are reasonable grounds for suspecting that a specified person *has carried on or* has benefited from drug trafficking'. It is, he submits, perfectly obvious that the omission from s 93H of the words 'has carried on' is deliberate and that Parliament thereby intended to focus this later provision more specifically upon investigating the benefits of crime than is the case under the drug trafficking legislation.

Mr Mitchell submits that the words 'as carried on' within the drug trafficking legislation are there to enable investigations into drug trafficking whether or not benefit has resulted but that these words would be otiose in s 93H. I find myself in some difficulty in understanding why.

Mr Johnson's arguments seem to me powerful ones indeed. Parliament can hardly have been intending in this way to bring about what to all intents and purposes would be the substantial repeal of s 9. I say substantial repeal because, if Mr Mitchell's submissions are sound, then the only remaining scope for the s 9 power would be (a) in the unlikely event that special procedure material is required for the investigation of non-acquisition offences, (b) if the crime of gain has failed, for example, mortgage fraud in a falling market, or (c) if the offence was at such an early stage that no possibility of benefit had arisen, for example, an embryonic fraudulent conspiracy.

Nor should s 93H readily be construed in such a way that Parliament is found unwittingly to have achieved this result. After all, even s 9 is recognised as 'a serious inroad upon the liberty of the subject' (see *R v Maidstone Crown Court, ex p Waitt* [1988] Crim LR 384 per Lloyd LJ, cited by Bingham LJ in *R v Crown Court at Lewes, ex p Hill* (1990) 93 Cr App Rep 60 at 66). As already explained, s 93H makes more serious inroads still. Were these powers to overlap it would be a remarkable thing to find Parliament precluding—by virtue of para 2(b)(ii) of Sch 1 to PACE—the use of the less rather than the more draconian of these two powers.

In my judgment, therefore, it would be wrong to construe the words in s 93H(1): 'an investigation into whether any person has benefited from any criminal conduct', for all the world as if they were synonymous with 'an investigation into whether any conduct from which a person has benefited was criminal'—effectively the construction for which Mr Mitchell contends.

It is at this point, however, that the real difficulties in the case arise: how to determine what properly is an investigation into the proceeds of criminal conduct within the scope of s 93H, and what can still only be investigated, if at all, under the more stringent controls applying to s 9. Wherein lies the true difference *a* between, on the one hand, a s 93H financial investigation and, on the other, a s 9 criminal investigation?

At one stage of his argument Mr Johnson sought to contend that a s 93H application can only properly be made prior to conviction where the trial is imminently contemplated and the Crown is ready to proceed on the evidence that they already have. If at this stage further incriminating evidence were to

b come to light following a s 93H production order, the judge might well rule it inadmissible under s 78 of PACE as evidence which it would at that late stage be unfair to admit. (Implicit in this submission is Mr Johnson's (correct) acknowledgment that evidence produced by or consequent on a production order is in the ordinary way admissible at trial and not confined in its use to restraint or confiscation proceedings.)

c That contention, however, seems to me plainly unsustainable. As Mr Mitchell pointed out, investigations into benefit may well be required at a very early stage, perhaps even before anyone is charged, particularly for restraint orders which may be sought not only against potential defendants but also, for example, against donees. There can be no temporal bar as such to the seeking of s 93H

d orders.

What then is the touchstone by which to decide whether a s 93H application should be made by the prosecuting authority and, other conditions being satisfied, granted by the court? I can find no better way of expressing it than to say that the question to be asked is this: what is the dominant purpose of the

e application: is it for criminal investigation purposes, to determine whether an offence has been committed and, if so, to provide evidence of that offence, or is it to determine, in respect of criminal offending—although not necessarily a specific offence which the prosecution already has reasonable grounds for believing (rather than merely suspecting) has been committed—whether (and, if so, to what extent) someone has benefited from it, or the whereabouts of the

f proceeds.

With these considerations in mind let me now turn finally to the facts of these two cases.

The Guildford case

g The basic facts here, appearing from the information sworn by a detective sergeant in support of the s 93H application, was that in early March 1996 a Mr and Mrs Imms were arrested and charged with numerous offences involving children and prostitution. Mr Imms was charged with living off the immoral earnings of his wife and others, Mrs Imms with exercising control and direction

h over a prostitute. A search warrant had been executed at their home address in January and it was known from the documentation then found and from interviews with the defendants that certain moneys earned from prostitution had been credited to two accounts held with the Philippine National Bank in the Philippines through their London branch. The information deposed that this

j branch holds records of these credits which it has refused to disclose and it was against the bank that the production order was sought.

The essence of Judge Bull QC's reasoning for refusing a s 93H order—and let it be noted that he was provided with wholly inadequate assistance in the construction of the statute—appears to have been, first that there were other avenues open to the prosecution before they needed to resort to s 93H, notably an application under s 7 of the Bankers' Books Evidence Act 1879, and second that

he had not been shown all the factual material necessary to found a satisfactory
application, in particular the transcripts of interviews with the defendants.

As to the first of those reasons, Mr Mitchell concedes that the material could
indeed have been obtained under the 1879 Act. He points out, however, that
there is no equivalent in the 1988 Act to para 2(b)(ii) of Sch 1 to PACE and that
accordingly *Ex p Hill*, where a s 9 order was refused because of the availability of
the 1879 Act, had no application. Judge Bull was not declining to make the s 93H
order as a matter of discretion but rather on the basis that 'I do not have the
power ... unless other matters have been tried first'. In that he was wrong. He
would in my judgment have been entitled to reject the application as a matter of
discretion on the basis that it was not in the public interest to use the s 93H power
because the 1879 Act was also available and was the more appropriate, but that
docs not appcar to havc bccn his rcasoning.

As to the judge's second reason, frankly there was no possible need for him to
have seen the interviews. The detective sergeant had already given oral evidence
that the defendants had admitted at interview that the money had come from
prostitution and other such activities.

If in those circumstances one asks the question I earlier posed, it seems to me
plain that the police here were indeed seeking production of the bank's
documents predominantly, if not exclusively, to determine the extent to which
the accused had benefited from their offending and the whereabouts of their
gains.

The Southwark case

The factual basis upon which Mrs Bowles brought her challenge was as
follows. Amongst her clients are a Mr and Mrs Peaty, trading as Associate
Business Management Ltd (ABM). This couple, as she knows, face charges of
dishonesty connected with the running of ABM. She is, however, unaware of the
details. On 29 March 1996 a production order was made against her requiring
that she—

> 'should give a constable access to and supply such originals and copies as
> may be necessary of the material to which the application relates, namely all
> files, documents and accounts and other records used in the ordinary course
> of business (howsoever recorded) ... paid cheques, inter-account transfers,
> telegraphic transfers and correspondence ... in relation to her dealings with
> ABM and any other material relating to [Mr or Mrs] Peaty [within seven
> days].'

Mrs Bowles has at all times behaved with the utmost propriety. She contacted
her professional body for advice and was told that she would be open to
professional disciplinary proceedings if she complied with the order and it was
later held to be unlawful. She is anxious to co-operate with the authorities but is
advised by her lawyers that, although the Crown is certainly entitled to the
material she holds, that entitlement arises under s 9 of PACE (it being undisputed
that these frauds are 'serious arrestable offences'), and not under s 93H.

Until this court hearing, Mrs Bowles had not seen the information sworn in
support of the production order. That is now before us and, so far as material,
can be summarised as follows. ABM purported to be a management consultancy
business which prior to going into voluntary liquidation at the end of 1994 was
run by Mr and Mrs Peaty. Its business operation, carried on since 1987, was the
placing of adverts in the broadsheet press (primarily the Daily Telegraph) aimed

a at recruiting redundant executives. Applicants would visit the Peatys' business premises, and enter an interviewing and selection process. An applicant would be assured of an income from existing ABM clientele between £25,000 and £40,000 per annum. The recruit would be required to pay a joining fee generally of £7,500 plus value added tax. A police investigation commenced in 1994 following receipt of a complaint from a consultant that despite his payment, and

b ABM's assurances, no work nor promised income had been forthcoming. Inquiries showed that over 100 people 'joined' ABM during the period 1991 to 1994 (records prior to this being very limited), and that ABM obtained an income exceeding £750,000. Further, inquiries into the disposal of this income have shown that the bulk had been used to the personal and private benefit of Mr and Mrs Peaty, including the total financing of their house purchase and of a second

c home in Scotland. Since 1991 ABM's accounts have been prepared by Mrs Bowles. It is said that those accounts failed to account properly for either the income or expenditure of the company and that the police believe that the information supplied by the company to Mrs Bowles has been either bogus or misleading. The information deposed that Mrs Bowles had declined to assist by producing the relevant documentation, claiming client confidentiality. It

d concluded thus: 'The production order requested, given the refusal by Mrs Bowles to co-operate, is the only way in which this matter can be resolved.'

That, of course, begs the very question to be decided here. True, if s 93H applies, then it displaces s 9. But it only applies if in reality the predominant reason the police seek these documents from Mrs Bowles is essentially with a

e view to their obtaining present restraint orders (and ultimately no doubt confiscation orders) rather than further investigating Mr and Mrs Peaty's alleged criminality. It seems to me altogether less than clear that this is so and, given the way the prosecuting authorities appear hitherto to have been directing themselves in law—doubtless consistently with Mr Mitchell's submissions to this

f court—I doubt whether they or, no less importantly, the judge who made the order, asked themselves the correct question.

In these circumstances it seems to me necessary to quash the production order in the Southwark case, although clearly Mrs Bowles must retain all the relevant papers and ultimately surrender them up when a final decision is made as to which is the appropriate statutory power to be used.

g In the result, I would allow both these judicial review applications, quashing respectively the refusal of a production order in the Guildford case and the grant of a production order in the Southwark case.

Finally, I note the agreement of both counsel at the conclusion of the argument, to which we gave our blessing, that whatever the outcome of these

h challenges there should be no order for costs save for payment of Mrs Bowles' costs in the Southwark case out of central funds. We so order.

GAGE J. I agree.

j *Order accordingly.*

Dilys Tausz   Barrister.

Boss Group Ltd v Boss France SA

a

COURT OF APPEAL, CIVIL DIVISION
RUSSELL, SAVILLE AND OTTON LJJ
19 MARCH, 2 APRIL 1996

b

Conflict of laws – Jurisdiction – Challenge to jurisdiction – Whether English courts having special jurisdiction – Contract – Matters relating to a contract – Existence of contract denied – Whether disputed existence of contract constituting a 'matter relating to a contract' – Civil Jurisdiction and Judgments Act 1982, Sch 1, art 5(1).

In September 1994 the plaintiff commenced proceedings by writ in England
seeking, inter alia, a declaration that no contract of distributorship of its products
in France existed between it and the defendant, who had previously sought to
establish the existence of such a contract and to claim damages for its breach in
French proceedings against the plaintiff. In November 1994 the defendant
applied by summons under RSC Ord 12, r 8 to set aside or stay the proceedings
on the grounds that the court did not have jurisdiction to hear the matter under
art 5(1)[a] of the Convention on Jurisdiction and the Enforcement of Judgments in
Civil and Commercial Matters 1968 (as set out in Sch 1 to the Civil Jurisdiction
and Judgments Act 1982), which provided that persons domiciled in a contracting
state could be sued in the courts of another contracting state in matters relating
to a contract if that was the place of performance of the obligation in question,
and that declaratory relief should not be granted since the claim for a negative
declaration represented forum shopping. The master set aside the writ and
dismissed the action, and his decision was affirmed by the judge, who held that
art 5(1) of the 1968 convention could not be invoked by a plaintiff who denied the
existence of any contractual relationship with the defendant, and that since the
defendant had made no threat to commence litigation in England and the matters
in issue had already been ventilated in the French courts and could and should be
resolved there, he would in the exercise of his discretion decline to allow the
proceedings to continue. The plaintiff appealed to the Court of Appeal.

c

d

e

f

Held – (1) It was no answer to a claim for jurisdiction under art 5(1) of the 1968
convention that the plaintiff was asserting that no contract ever came into
existence, since the word 'contract' in art 5(1) could not be read as only including
cases where the existence of a contract was unchallengeable or unchallenged, and
the article was not confined to actions to enforce a contract or to obtain
recompense for its breach, but referred generally to matters relating to a contract.
It was however incumbent on the plaintiff to satisfy the court that there was a
good arguable case that there was a matter relating to a contract in issue between
the parties, and in the instant case the plaintiff could do so by relying on the fact
that the defendant was seeking to enforce a contract against it. Furthermore, on
the facts there was also a good arguable case that the disputed obligation was to
be performed in England (see p 974 *j* to p 975 *g j* and p 977 *f*, post); *Effer SpA v
Kantner* Case 38/81 [1982] ECR 825 applied.

g

h

j

(2) Jurisdiction under the 1968 convention was not a matter of discretion.
Accordingly, if art 5(1) was applicable, it was the duty of the court to apply it and

---

a   Article 5(1), so far as material, is set out at p 974 *e*, post *a* ·the judge was therefore wrong in holding that he had a discretion in the matter. Furthermore, the application of the convention did not depend on considerations of forum conveniens and while the court looked very carefully at proceedings for negative declarations, caution in that regard could not be used as a substantive ground for declining jurisdiction under the convention since that would derogate from it. The court would, however, be astute to prevent art 5(1) from being used

b in frivolous or vexatious cases. Since the proceedings brought by the plaintiff could not be categorised as objectionable on those grounds and the charge of forum shopping could not be made good as art 5(1) was an exception to the general jurisdictional rule of domicile, it followed that the court did have jurisdiction under art 5(1) to entertain the plaintiff's claim and the appeal would accordingly be allowed (see p 976 *g* to p 977 *d f*, post); *Tesam Distribution Ltd v*

c *Schuh Mode Team GmbH* [1990] I L Pr 149 applied.

Notes

For jurisdiction of the courts under the Convention on Jurisdiction and Enforcement of Judgments in Civil and Commercial Matters 1968, see 8(1)

d *Halsbury's Laws* (4th edn reissue) paras 618–623, 641 and for cases on the subject, see 11(2) *Digest* (2nd reissue) 235–237, 1417–1421.

For the Civil Jurisdiction and Judgments Act 1982, Sch 1, art 5, see 11 *Halsbury's Statutes* (4th edn) (1991 reissue) 1136.

Cases referred to in judgments

e *Camilla Cotton Oil Co v Granadex SA, Shawnee Processors Inc v Granadex SA* [1976] 2 Lloyd's Rep 10, HL.

Clay, Re, Clay v Booth, re deed of indemnity [1919] 1 Ch 66, [1918–19] All ER Rep 94, CA.

Custom Made Commercial Ltd v Stawa Metallbau GmbH Case C-288/92 [1994] ECR

f I-2913.

Effer SpA v Kantner Case 38/81 [1982] ECR 825.

Guaranty Trust Co of New York v Hannay & Co [1915] 2 KB 536, [1914–15] All ER Rep 24, CA.

Maciej Rataj, The, Tatry (cargo owners) v Maciej Rataj (owners) C-Case 406/92 [1995]

g All ER (EC) 229, ECJ.

Medway Packaging Ltd v Meurer Maschinen GmbH & Co [1990] 2 Lloyd's Rep 112, CA.

Midland Bank plc v Laker Airways Ltd [1986] 1 All ER 526, [1986] QB 689, [1986] 2 WLR 707, CA.

h *New England Reinsurance Corp v Messoghios Insurance Co SA* [1992] 2 Lloyd's Rep 251, CA.

Shenavai v Kreischer Case 266/85 [1987] ECR 239.

Tesam Distribution Ltd v Schuh Mode Team GmbH [1990] I L Pr 149, CA.

Union Transport Group plc v Continental Lines SA [1992] 1 All ER 161, [1992] 1 WLR

j 15, HL.

Cases also cited or referred to in skeleton arguments

Arcado SPRL v Havilland SA Case 9/87 [1988] ECR 1539.

Barnato, Re, Joel v Sanges [1949] 1 All ER 515, [1949] Ch 258, CA.

Booker v Bell [1989] 1 Lloyd's Rep 516.

BP Exploration Co (Libya) Ltd v Hunt [1976] 3 All ER 879, [1976] 1 WLR 788.

Cia Naviera Micro SA v Shipley International Inc, The Parouth [1982] 2 Lloyd's Rep 351.

Desert Sun Loan Corp v Hill [1996] 2 All ER 847, CA.

DR Insurance Co v Central National Insurance Co [1996] 1 Lloyd's Rep 74.

DSV Silo- und Verwaltungsgesellschaft mbH v Sennar (owners), The Sennar [1985] 2 All ER 104, [1985] 1 WLR 490, HL.

Ealing London Borough v Race Relations Board [1971] 1 All ER 424, [1971] 1 QB 309; rvsd [1972] 1 All ER 105, [1972] AC 342, HL.

Ets A de Bloos SPRL v Société en commandite par actions Bouyer Case 14/76 [1976] ECR 1497.

Finnish Marine Insurance Co Ltd v Protective National Insurance Co [1989] 2 All ER 929, [1990] QB 1078.

Gulf Bank KSC v Mitsubishi Heavy Industries Ltd [1994] 1 Lloyd's Rep 323.

Gulf Bank KSC v Mitsubishi Heavy Industries Ltd (No 2) [1994] 2 Lloyd's Rep 145, CA.

Hoffmann v Krieg Case 145/86 [1988] ECR 645.

Hutton (E F) & Co (London) Ltd v Mofarrij [1989] 2 All ER 633, [1989] 1 WLR 488, CA.

Jakob Handte GmbH v Traitements mécano-chimiques des surfaces (TMCS) Case C-26/92 [1992] ECR I-3967.

Kalfelis v Bankhaus Schröder, Münchmeyer, Hengst & Co Case 189/87 [1988] ECR 5565.

Kleinwort Benson Ltd v Glasgow City Council [1996] 2 All ER 257, [1996] 2 WLR 655, CA; rvsg [1994] 4 All ER 865, [1993] QB 429.

London Passenger Transport Board v Moscrop [1942] 1 All ER 97, [1942] AC 344, HL.

Marc Rich & Co AG v Societa Italiana Impianti PA Case C-190/89 [1991] ECR I-3855.

Martin Peters Bauunternehmung GmbH v Zuid Nederlandse AannemersVereniging Case 34/82 [1983] ECR 987.

Maxwell Communications Corp plc, Re (No 2) [1992] BCC 757.

Molnlycke AB v Procter & Gamble Ltd [1992] 4 All ER 47, [1992] 1 WLR 1112, CA.

North Eastern Marine Engineering Co v Leeds Forge Co [1906] 1 Ch 324; affd [1906] 2 Ch 498, CA.

R v Governor of Brixton Prison, ex p Osman (No 1) [1992] 1 All ER 108, [1991] 1 WLR 281, DC.

Saipem SpA v Dredging VO2 BV, The Volvox Hollandia [1988] 2 Lloyd's Rep 361, CA.

Seaconsar Far East Ltd v Bank Markazi Jomhouri Islami Iran [1993] 4 All ER 456, [1994] 1 AC 438, HL.

Somafer SA v Saar-Ferngas AG Case 33/78 [1978] ECR 2183.

Trade Indemnity plc v Försäkringsaktiebolaget Njord (in liq) [1995] 1 All ER 796.

Appeal

By notice dated 21 September 1995 the plaintiff, Boss Group Ltd, appealed with leave granted on 15 September 1995 from the decision of Garland J on 12 April 1995 whereby he dismissed the plaintiff's appeal against the order of Master Eyre on 21 March 1995 dismissing the plaintiff's action for declaratory relief against the defendant, Boss France SA. The facts are set out in the judgment of Saville LJ.

David Donaldson QC and *Adrian Briggs* (instructed by *Wilmer Cutler & Pickering*) for the plaintiff.

Thomas Lowe (instructed by *D J Freeman*) for the defendant.

Cur adv vult

a

2 April 1996. The following judgments were delivered.

SAVILLE LJ (giving the first judgment at the invitation of Russell LJ). Until April 1994 the English company, Lancer Boss Group Ltd, was (as part of a group of companies) engaged in the business of manufacturing and selling fork-lift trucks as well as associated equipment and spare parts. In 1967 Boss France SA was incorporated as a French subsidiary of this English company for the purpose of importing and distributing its products in France and thereafter became the sole distributor of those products in France.

b

In April 1994 Lancer Boss Group Ltd went into administrative receivership. In the following month, the receivers and others sold the shares in Boss France SA to a M Dupuy for one franc, and other assets of Lancer Boss Group Ltd to another English company, which is now called Boss Group Ltd, and which is owned by a German corporation with its own French distributor.

c

For a short time after these changes, Boss France SA placed orders with Boss Group Ltd, which this company accepted. However, on 22 June 1994 Boss Group Ltd informed Boss France SA that it was terminating any arrangement between these two companies. Soon after, it became apparent not only that Boss Group Ltd was refusing to make any further deliveries to Boss France SA, but also that it had instead, started using its owner's French distributor in France.

d

Boss France SA took the view that this amounted to a breach of an exclusive distributorship agreement for France which bound Boss Group Ltd, and on 8 July 1994 commenced proceedings against Boss Group Ltd and the new distributor in the Tribunal de Commerce de Corbeil Essonnes. Boss France SA succeeded in obtaining orders from this court restraining the new distributor from holding itself out as a distributor of Boss equipment, and requiring Boss Group Ltd to continue to supply Boss France SA, as well as ancillary orders penalising any delay in deliveries and setting up an inquiry into the damages sustained by Boss France SA.

e

f

Boss Group Ltd appealed to the Court of Appeal in Paris, who, in effect, reversed this decision except in relation to products ordered by Boss France SA before 22 June 1994.

g

On 28 September 1994 (which was before the matter came before the Court of Appeal in Paris) Boss Group Ltd served an English writ on Boss Group SA in France. In these proceedings, Boss Group Ltd claimed the following relief:

'1. A declaration that the Plaintiff is not, and has at no material time been, under an obligation to the Defendant to supply and deliver the Plaintiff's equipment, or any equipment of any third party, upon the terms previously supplied by Old Boss or at all. [The reference in this paragraph to 'Old Boss' is a reference to Lancer Boss Group Ltd and its English subsidiaries.]

h

2. A declaration that there is and has been no contract of distributorship, or any other contract, between the Plaintiff and the Defendant herein pursuant to which the Defendant is entitled to act as distributor, whether exclusive or otherwise, of the Plaintiff's machinery in France.

j

3. Alternatively, a declaration that any contract of distributorship between the Plaintiff and the Defendant has been lawfully terminated by the Plaintiff and that the Plaintiff has no liability to the Defendant in respect of it.

4. A declaration that all and any contracts between the Plaintiff and the Defendant which have not been lawfully terminated have been fully performed by the Plaintiff.

5. A declaration that the Plaintiff is entitled to appoint a distributor of its machinery in France, other than the Defendant herein.'

On 29 November 1994 (and before the Court of Appeal in Paris had given its judgment) Boss France SA issued a summons under RSC Ord 12, r 8 to set aside or stay these proceedings. By a later amendment to this summons, Boss France SA set out the basis for this application in the following terms:

'1) The Defendant disputes special jurisdiction under Article 5(1) of the 1968 Brussels Convention on Jurisdiction and the Enforcement of Judgments in Civil and Commercial Matters.

2) The claim for a negative declaration represents forum shopping and declaratory relief should not be granted in such circumstances or in any event.'

On 21 March 1995 Master Eyre set aside the writ and dismissed the action. The plaintiff appealed but on 12 April 1995 Garland J dismissed the appeal. With leave of this court (granted in September 1995) the matter now comes before us.

The Civil Jurisdiction and Judgments Act 1982 incorporates the amended Brussels Convention on Jurisdiction and the Enforcement of Judgments in Civil and Commercial Matters into our law. The convention is set out in Sch 1. Article 5 of the convention provides as follows:

'A person domiciled in a Contracting State may, in another Contracting State, be sued: (1) in matters relating to a contract, in the courts for the place of performance of the obligation in question ...'

France and this country are, of course, contracting states.

Garland J held that this article could not be invoked by a plaintiff who was denying the existence of any contractual relationship with the defendant. He also appeared to decide that, since Boss France SA had made no threat to commence litigation here, since the matters in issue had already been ventilated in the French courts, and since 'these matters can and should be resolved in the French courts', he would in the exercise of his discretion decline to allow proceedings for 'negative declarations' to continue here. I start by considering the first of these reasons.

Articles 21 to 23 of the convention deal with what is to happen when proceedings are brought in more than one contracting state. In general terms, the rule is that the court first seized is to have jurisdiction and that courts in other contracting states should decline jurisdiction or stay proceedings brought before them. In the present case, it is important to note that it is not suggested that the French court was the court first seized of the matters in issue. It appears from the material put before us that the proceedings in France were of a provisional kind where the court did not seek to adjudicate finally upon the substantive merits of the case, which would, if heard in France, be considered by another court altogether. Thus, in the present case the question is whether this court has jurisdiction under art 5(1) and not whether another court was first seized.

Article 5(1) refers 'to matters relating to a contract', and gives the courts 'for the place of performance of the obligation in question' jurisdiction over such matters. It is well settled that it is no answer to a claim for jurisdiction under this article that the respondent is asserting that no contract ever came into existence (see *Effer SpA v Kantner* Case 38/81 [1982] ECR 825). In other words, the fact that at the end of the day the court seized of the matter may conclude that there was a indeed no contract is neither here nor there, provided that at the time when the court has to decide whether or not it has jurisdiction it is satisfied that the requirements of the article are met. It follows that the word 'contract' cannot be read as only including cases where the existence of a contract is unchallengeable or unchallenged.

b To my mind there are 'matters relating to a contract' in the present case. There is a lively dispute between the parties as to whether there is a contract between them under which the defendant is the exclusive distributor for the plaintiff in France. It is true that the plaintiff, who seeks to sue here, is asserting that no such contract exists, but equally the defendant is asserting the contrary. In my judgment, the fact that it is this way round does not make the article inapplicable. Article 5(1) is not confined to actions to enforce a contract or to c obtain recompense for its breach, but refers generally to 'matters relating to a contract'.

The defendant submits that assertions are not enough, since the court must be satisfied that the essential prerequisites for jurisdiction exist. Building on this, it submits that it is incumbent on a plaintiff to satisfy the court at least that there is d a good arguable case that such prerequisites do exist, and relies on authorities such as *New England Reinsurance Corp v Messoghios Insurance Co SA* [1992] 2 Lloyd's Rep 251 for that proposition. Since the plaintiff is claiming that there was no contract, the defendant submits that it inevitably follows that the plaintiff cannot fulfil this requirement.

I agree with the premises on which this argument is based, but to my mind the e conclusion does not follow. The article allows a party to be sued in matters relating to a contract in the courts for the place of performance of the obligation in question. That party in the present case is the defendant company. It seems to me that it is entirely illogical and wrong for that party to assert that there is a contract and that the plaintiff has broken it (which is what the defendant has done f in France, where it has itself relied on art 5(1) whilst simultaneously contending the contrary here in order to avoid the application of art 5(1)). To my mind, in a case such as the present, the plaintiff establishes a good arguable case that there is a matter relating to a contract by relying on the fact that this is what the defendant is contending against it. Unless the defendant withdraws its contentions (which it has not done), it seems to me that it cannot challenge the g jurisdiction on the basis that it should not be sued here because there is (contrary to those contentions) no contract. Once one has removed the self-contradictory stance taken up by the defendant, it seems to me that it is self-evident that there are matters relating to a contract between the parties.

The next matter is the place of performance of the obligation in question. h Where there are a number of obligations, the one in question is the principal obligation in dispute between the parties (see *Shenavai v Kreischer* Case 266/85 [1987] ECR 239 and *Union Transport Group plc v Continental Lines SA* [1992] 1 All ER 161, [1992] 1 WLR 15).

The obligation in dispute in the present case is that the plaintiff is bound to j supply only the defendant with its products for distribution in France. There could, perhaps, be said to be two obligations, one to supply the defendant, and the other not to supply anyone else. However, whichever way it is put, it seems to me that there is a good arguable case that these obligations (if they existed at all) fell to be performed in this country. So far as supply is concerned, it is now common ground that the products were in the past delivered to the defendant exworks Leighton Buzzard, and it is not suggested that the alleged continuing

exclusive distributorship contract contained any different term. Indeed, it would
be odd if such a suggestion were to be made, since it is the defendant's case that
the contract upon which it relies arose through the past course of dealing. As to
what could be described as the negative obligation not to supply others, I take the
view that this is probably performable everywhere, including both here and
France (see *Medway Packaging Ltd v Meurer Maschinen GmbH & Co* [1990] 2 Lloyd's
Rep 112). At this point I should note that both parties were content to proceed
on the basis that the Contracts (Applicable Law) Act 1990 did not apply to this
case, so that I have sought to categorise the place of performance on the basis of
common law conflict of law principles. Applying those principles, I take the view
(for the purpose of the question of jurisdiction) that the putative proper law of the
disputed contract is probably English law. However, even if it is French law,
there is nothing to suggest that the obligations are only performable in France
and not here, or that French law differs from English law in this regard. Indeed,
as I have noted, it is common ground that the alleged obligation to deliver was to
do so in England.

The defendant also sought to challenge the jurisdiction of the court on the
grounds that it had never contended that it had made an English law contract
with the plaintiff, but that its rights arose from contractual rights and obligations
existing under French law. Thus, it was submitted for the defendant, the court
should decline jurisdiction on the ground that the plaintiff was seeking
declarations in respect of a matter which was not in dispute between the parties,
relying on such cases as *Re Clay, Clay v Booth, re deed of indemnity* [1919] 1 Ch 66,
[1918–19] All ER Rep 94 and *Midland Bank plc v Laker Airways Ltd* [1986] 1 All ER
526, [1986] QB 689.

In my view this argument begs the question, which is whether the proper law
of the alleged contract is English or French law. The plaintiff contends that it is
English, the defendant, that it is French. There is a dispute between them about
this. As I have said, it seems to me that it is well arguable that the applicable law
is English. This does not mean that the plaintiff is seeking relief in respect of
something which the defendant is not disputing; indeed it means the precise
opposite.

I now turn to the second reason given by Garland J for declining jurisdiction.
In my judgment, this contains two errors.

In the first place, the judge appeared to consider that the application of art 5(1)
was a matter for his discretion. This is not the law. If the article is applicable it is
the duty of the court to apply it. Jurisdiction under the convention is not a matter
of discretion, as Nicholls LJ pointed out in *Tesam Distribution Ltd v Schuh Mode
Team GmbH* [1990] I L Pr 149 at 158.

In the second place, the judge seems to have decided as he did on the grounds
that France was the more convenient forum for the resolution of the dispute.
This again is not the law. The application of the convention does not depend on
considerations of forum conveniens (see *Custom Made Commercial Ltd v Stawa
Metallbau GmbH* Case C-288/92 [1994] ECR I-2913 and *The Maciej Rataj, Tatry
(cargo owners) v Maciej Rataj (owners)* C-Case 406/92 [1995] All ER (EC) 229).

It is of course the case that the English courts look very carefully at proceedings
for negative declarations (see *Guaranty Trust Co of New York v Hannay & Co* [1915]
2 KB 536, [1914–15] All ER Rep 24 and *Camilla Cotton Oil Co v Granadex SA,
Shawnee Processors Inc v Granadex SA* [1976] 2 Lloyd's Rep 10 at 14 per Lord
Wilberforce). This does not, however, mean that caution in this regard can be
used as a substantive ground for declining jurisdiction under the convention, for

a this would derogate from the convention. What it does mean is that the court will be astute to prevent the article from being used in frivolous or vexatious cases, just as it is astute to stop summarily cases where the plaintiff seeking to establish a contract cannot show that there is a serious issue which calls for a trial for its proper determination (see *Tesam Distribution Ltd v Schuh Mode Team GmbH* [1990] I L Pr 149 at 158). In such cases, the court is simply preventing the party

b concerned from abusing its process.

In my judgment the proceedings brought by the plaintiff cannot be categorised as objectionable on these grounds. The defendant contended that the plaintiff was indulging in forum shopping and that since art 5(1) was an exception to the general jurisdictional rule of domicile under art 2, they should be discouraged from doing so. In my view, this argument lies ill in the mouth of the defendant

c and in any event also begs the question. The defendant itself has attempted to bring substantive proceedings in France against the plaintiff, relying on art 5(1), notwithstanding that the domicile of the plaintiff is in this country. In any event, the charge of forum shopping can only be made good by assuming that a party which takes advantage of the convention exceptions to the general rule of

d domicile is somehow doing something illegitimate; but that assumption cannot be sustained if in truth one of the exceptions is applicable.

Finally, the defendant submitted that the plaintiff was estopped from contending that the place of performance was other than in France by the decision of the Court of Appeal in Paris. In my view, this argument is quite unsustainable. It is clear from the material before us that the views of that court

e were expressed in the context of the provisional proceedings and are in no way binding in France on any court that might deal there with the matter on a substantive basis. To my mind it follows that the requirement of finality is absent, so that no question of estoppel can arise.

For these reasons I would allow this appeal.

f **OTTON LJ.** I agree.

RUSSELL LJ. I also agree.

Appeal allowed. Leave to appeal to the House of Lords refused.

g
Paul Magrath Esq   Barrister.

Agnew and others v
Lansförsäkringsbølagens AB

a

QUEEN'S BENCH DIVISION (COMMERCIAL COURT)

MANCE J

17 JUNE, 30 JULY 1996

b

Conflict of laws – Jurisdiction – Challenge to jurisdiction – Contracts between parties domiciled in convention countries – Plaintiffs claiming jurisdiction of English court over defendant domiciled in Sweden – Plaintiffs seeking to avoid contracts for breach of duty of disclosure before contracts entered into – Plaintiffs claiming entitlement to sue *c* *in matters relating to contract in courts for place of performance of obligation in question – Whether duty of disclosure 'obligation in question' – Civil Jurisdiction and Judgments Act 1982, Sch 3C, art 5(1).*

The plaintiffs, Lloyd's underwriters and English and Scottish companies carrying *d* on reinsurance business in the London market, entered into reinsurance contracts with the defendant, a Swedish insurance company operating in Stockholm. Pursuant to the contracts, the plaintiffs underwrote various participations on primary and excess layer reinsurances in respect of the defendant's exposure as insurer under a contract for the supply of underwater valves for use in off-shore oil fields. Thereafter, the plaintiffs alleged that the *e* defendant had falsely represented that the valves were 'tried and tested', so that the reinsurances had been induced by material misrepresentations entitling them · to avoid their participations. The plaintiffs accordingly issued proceedings against the defendant in England, relying on art 5(1)[a] of the Lugano Convention on Jurisdiction and the Enforcement of Judgments in Civil and Commercial *f* Matters 1988 (as set out in Sch 3C to the Civil Jurisdiction and Judgments Act 1982), which gave jurisdiction to the courts of the place of performance of the obligation in question in claims arising from matters relating to a contract. The defendant applied to set aside the writ, contending that art 5 did not apply to the claim and that the English courts had no jurisdiction, since the duty to make a fair presentation of the risk when making reinsurance contracts could not constitute *g* a relevant 'obligation' for the purposes of art 5(1).

Held – Whether an action related to a contract and to the performance of an obligation for the purposes of art 5(1) of the 1988 convention had to be answered by reference to the system and objectives of the convention. Accordingly, *h* although the duty to make a fair presentation of the risk, by giving full disclosure and avoiding misrepresentation, arose in the negotiation of the contract and extra-contractually as a matter of national law, it was nevertheless an 'obligation' within the meaning of art 5(1), since art 5(1) drew no express distinction between obligations arising in the context of negotiation of a contract and obligations *j* arising under or after the contract. It followed that as the plaintiffs' claims concerned the performance of obligations in England within the meaning of art 5(1), and also constituted a matter 'relating to a contract' within the meaning of that article, the English courts had jurisdiction under the 1988 convention, and

---

a   Article 5(1), so far as material, is set out at p 981 *c*, post

a the application would therefore be dismissed (see p 989 *c f*, p 992 *g* and p 994 *g*, post).

Martin Peters Bauunternehmung GmbH v Zuid Nederlandse Aannemers Vereniging Case 34/82 [1983] ECR 987 applied.

Trade Indemnity plc v Försäkringsaktiebølaget Njord (in liq) [1995] 1 All ER 796 not followed.

b
Notes
For insurer's duties of disclosure and good faith, see 25 *Halsbury's Laws* (4th edn reissue) paras 349–362, and for cases on the subject, see 29(2) *Digest* (2nd reissue) 9–21, *2967–3034.*

c For jurisdiction of the courts under the Brussels Convention on Jurisdiction and the Enforcement of Judgments in Civil and Commercial Matters 1968 (and parallel provisions under the Lugano Convention), see 8(1) *Halsbury's Laws* (4th edn reissue) paras 618–623, 631, and for cases on the subject, see 11(2) *Digest* (2nd reissue) 235–237, *1417–1421.*

For the Civil Jurisdiction and Judgments Act 1982, Sch 3C, art 5, see 11
d Halsbury's Statutes (4th edn) (1991 reissue) 1168.

Cases referred to in judgment
Bank of Nova Scotia v Hellenic Mutual War Risks Association (Bermuda) Ltd, The Good Luck [1989] 3 All ER 628, [1990] 1 QB 818, [1990] 2 WLR 547, CA; *rvsd* [1991] 3 All ER 1, [1992] 1 AC 233, [1991] 2 WLR 1279, HL.
e
Banque Financière de la Cité SA v Westgate Insurance Co Ltd [1990] 2 All ER 947, [1991] 2 AC 249, [1990] 3 WLR 364, HL; *affg* [1989] 2 All ER 952, sub nom *Banque Keyser Ullmann SA v Skandia (UK) Insurance Co Ltd* [1990] 1 QB 665, [1989] 3 WLR 364, CA.
Black King Shipping Corp v Massie, The Litsion Pride [1985] 1 Lloyd's Rep 437.
f Boss Group Ltd v Boss France SA [1996] 4 All ER 970, CA.
Carter v Boehm (1766) 3 Burr 1905, [1558–1774] All ER Rep 183, 97 ER 1162.
Custom Made Commercial Ltd v Stawa Metallbau GmbH Case C-288/92 [1994] ECR I-2913.
Effer SpA v Kantner Case 38/81 [1982] ECR 825.
g Ets A de Bloos SPRL v Société en commandite par actions Bouyer Case 14/76 [1976] ECR 1497.
Hedley Byrne & Co Ltd v Heller & Partners Ltd [1963] 2 All ER 575, [1964] AC 465, [1963] 3 WLR 101, HL.
Industrie Tessili Italiana Como v Dunlop AG Case 12/76 [1976] ECR 1473.
h Ivenel v Schwab Case 133/81 [1982] ECR 1891.
Kalfelis v Bankhaus Schröder, Münchmeyer, Hengst & Co Case 189/87 [1988] ECR 5565.
Kleinwort Benson Ltd v Glasgow City Council [1996] 2 All ER 257, [1996] 2 WLR 655, CA.
j Merchants' and Manufacturers' Insurance Co Ltd v Hunt [1941] 1 All ER 123, [1941] 1 KB 295, CA.
Pan Atlantic Insurance Co Ltd v Pine Top Insurance Co Ltd [1994] 3 All ER 581, [1995] 1 AC 501, [1994] 3 WLR 677, HL.
Peters (Martin) Bauunternehmung GmbH v Zuid Nederlandse Aannemers Vereniging Case 34/82 [1983] ECR 987.
Shenavai v Kreischer Case 266/85 [1987] ECR 239.

Shevill v Presse Alliance SA Case C-68/93 [1995] All ER (EC) 289, [1995] 2 AC 18, [1995] 2 WLR 499, ECJ.

Soc ISI v Soc CPAV (1983, Cour de Cassation), *Rev Crit* 516.

Trade Indemnity plc v Försäkringsaktiebølaget Njord (in liq) [1995] 1 All ER 796.

Union Transport Group plc v Continental Lines SA [1992] 1 All ER 161, [1992] 1 WLR 15, HL.

Cases also cited or referred to in skeleton arguments

New England Reinsurance Corp v Messoghios Insurance Co SA [1992] 2 Lloyd's Rep 251, CA.

SPRL Arcado v SA Haviland Case 9/87 [1988] ECR 1539.

Tesam Distribution Ltd v Schuh Mode Team GmbH [1990] I L Pr 149, CA.

Application

By summons dated 6 November 1995 the defendants, Lansförsäkringsbølagens AB, a Swedish insurance company, applied under RSC Ord 12, r 8, for an order setting aside the writ in an action brought against them by ten plaintiffs, being Ian Charles Agnew, suing on his own behalf and in a representative capacity on behalf of all the members of several Lloyd's syndicates, and nine others, in which they sought to avoid contracts of reinsurance. The defendants challenged the jurisdiction of the English court on the ground that art 5(1) of the Lugano Convention on Jurisdiction and the Enforcement of Judgments in Civil and Commercial Matters did not apply to the plaintiffs' claim. The facts are set out in the judgment.

Andrew Lydiard (instructed by *Clyde & Co*) for the plaintiffs.
Michael Ashe QC (instructed by *Rosling King*) for the defendants.

Cur adv vult

30 July 1996. The following judgment was delivered.

MANCE J.

Introduction

The plaintiffs are Lloyd's underwriters and English or (in the case of the second plaintiffs) Scottish companies, carrying on reinsurance business in the London market. The defendants are a Swedish insurance company carrying on business in Stockholm. The defendants issued guarantee insurance to ABB Vetco Gray UK Ltd (ABB) in respect of obligations arising under a contract to supply Norsk Hydro with underwater valves (Christmas trees) for use in the Troll oil field in the Norwegian sector of the North Sea. The plaintiffs as reinsurers underwrote various participations on primary and excess layer reinsurances in respect of the defendants' exposure to ABB.

The plaintiffs claim in this action that the reinsurances were induced by material misrepresentations entitling them to avoid their participations. They seek declarations accordingly. Representations are said to have been made to the effect that the valves were 'bog standard' and/or 'tried and tested'. They are said to have been incorrect. The plaintiffs make the alternative claim that the defendants were in breach of an express warranty in the reinsurances to the effect that the valves were not and would not be prototypes. Neither party suggested a that this was other than a very secondary claim and Mr Lydiard did not rely on it for any purpose relevant before me.

Sweden is party to the Lugano Convention on Jurisdiction and the Enforcement of Judgments in Civil and Commercial Matters of 16 September 1988 (the convention), and the writ was indorsed with a certificate that this court had power to hear the claim under the Civil Jurisdiction and Judgments Act 1982.

b Whether this is so depends upon the scope and construction of art 5(1) of the convention, set out by virtue of s 1(3) of and Sch 1 to the Civil Jurisdiction and Judgments Act 1991 as Sch 3C to the 1982 Act. The defendants apply by summons dated 6 November 1995 under RSC Ord 12, r 8 to set aside the writ on the ground that art 5(1) does not apply to the present claim.

Article 5 provides:

c
'A person domiciled in a Contracting State may, in another Contracting State, be sued: (1) in matters relating to a contract, in the courts for the place of performance of the obligation in question ... (3) in matters relating to tort, delict or quasi-delict, in the courts for the place where the harmful event occurred ...'

d
When the present summons was issued, the defendants had in their favour the benefit of a decision of Rix J in *Trade Indemnity plc v Försäkringsaktiebølaget Njord (in liq)* [1995] 1 All ER 796. The plaintiffs ask me to reconsider aspects of that decision. On 25 January 1996 the Court of Appeal reached a majority decision in *Kleinwort Benson Ltd v Glasgow City Council* [1996] 2 All ER 257, [1996] 2 WLR 655

e which, the plaintiffs submit, offers them encouragement in that invitation. Subsequently, there has been a still more recent decision of the Court of Appeal on art 5(1) in *Boss Group Ltd v Boss France SA* [1996] 4 All ER 970.

For the plaintiffs to bring themselves within art 5(1) in this case, three criteria must be satisfied. (1) The matter must be one 'relating to a contract'; (2) there

f must be an 'obligation' in question in the action in the sense of the article; and (3) England must be the place for performance of any such obligation.

Mr Ashe QC for the defendants accepted that the present matter is one 'relating to a contract'. Rix J's decision is to like effect. Mr Ashe added, however, that he reserved the right to contend the contrary in a higher court. In these circumstances, and since the point is one of law and in some degree inter-related

g with the second criterion, I shall express some views on it myself, though necessarily without the benefit of contrary argument.

Before me the submissions have focused on the second criterion. It has been common ground that the claim concerns the defendants' duty to make a fair presentation of (and so not to misrepresent) the risk to the plaintiffs as reinsurers

h when making the reinsurance contracts. The issue has been whether that duty constitutes an 'obligation' in the sense of art 5(1).

If the first two criteria are satisfied, it was common ground that the third is also satisfied. The duty to make a fair presentation fell due for performance in London and any misrepresentation took place in the course of the brokers'

j presentation of the risk to the reinsurers in their offices or underwriting boxes in London.

Legal principles under the convention

The basic principle of jurisdiction under the convention is that persons domiciled in a contracting state should be sued in that state whatever their nationality (art 2). Article 3 introduces a number of special heads of jurisdiction, set out in section 2 (arts 5–6A). The basic sphere of operation of art 5(1) is defined *a* by the first criterion identified above, which is to be given an independent convention interpretation. As the European Court decided in *Martin Peters Bauunternehmung GmbH v Zuid Nederlandse Aannemers Vereniging* Case 34/82 [1983] ECR 987 at 1002 (paras 9–10):

b

'9 Thus the concept of matters relating to a contract serves as a criterion to define the scope of one of the rules of special jurisdiction available to the plaintiff ... [and] should not be interpreted simply as referring to the national law of one or other of the States concerned.

10 Therefore ... the concept of matters relating to a contract should be . regarded as an independent concept which, for the purpose of the *c* application of the Convention, must be interpreted by reference chiefly to the system and objectives of the Convention, in order to ensure that it is fully effective.'

The European Court in *Kalfelis v Bankhaus Schröder, Münchmeyer, Hengst & Co* *d* Case 189/87 [1988] ECR 5565 at 5585 (para 19) reiterated this point and applied it in the context of art 5(3). It also said that—

'the "special jurisdictions" enumerated in Articles 5 and 6 of the Convention constitute derogations from the principle that jurisdiction is vested in the courts of the State where the defendant is domiciled and as such *e* must be interpreted restrictively. It must therefore be recognized that a court which has jurisdiction under Article 5(3) over an action in so far as it is based on tort or delict does not have jurisdiction over that action in so far as it is not so based.'

Peters contains some guidance as to 'the system and objectives' which were in *f* mind when art 5(1) was introduced. The issue was whether claims to enforce obligations to pay money alleged to have been based in the relationship existing between an association in the building industry and its members by virtue of their membership were 'matters relating to a contract' within art 5(1). Holding that they were, the court said ([1983] ECR 987 at 1002 (paras 11–13)):

g

'11 In this regard it should be pointed out that although Article 5 makes provision in a number of cases for a special jurisdiction which the plaintiff may choose, this is because of the existence, in certain clearly-defined situations, of a particularly close connecting factor between a dispute and the court which may be called upon to hear it, with a view to the efficacious *h* conduct of the proceedings.

12 In that context, the designation by Article 5(1) of the Convention of the courts for the place of performance of the obligation in question expresses the concern that, because of the close links created by a contract between the parties thereto, it should be possible for all the difficulties which may arise *j* on the occasion of the performance of a contractual obligation to be brought before the same court: that for the place of performance of the obligation.

13 In that regard it appears that membership of an association creates between the members close links of the same kind as those which are created between the parties to a contract and that consequently the obligations to

a   which the national court refers may be regarded as contractual for the
       purpose of the application of Article 5(1) of the Convention.'

In considering a second question put by the Hoge Raad der Nederlanden
(whether a distinction should be drawn according to whether the obligation in
question arose simply from the act of becoming a member or resulted from that
act in conjunction with a decision made by an organ of the association), the
b European Court said ([1983] ECR 987 at 1003 (para 17)):

       'It should be noted that multiplication of the bases of jurisdiction in one
       and the same type of case is not likely to encourage legal certainty and
       effective legal protection throughout the territory of the Community. The
       provisions of the Convention should therefore be interpreted in such a way
c   that the court seised is not required to declare that it has jurisdiction to
       adjudicate upon certain applications but has no jurisdiction to hear certain
       other applications, even though they are closely related. Moreover, respect
       for the purposes and spirit of the Convention requires an interpretation of
       Article 5 which enables the national court to rule on its own jurisdiction
d   without being compelled to consider the substance of the case.'

In its further decision in *Shenavai v Kreischer* Case 266/85 [1987] ECR 239, the
European Court determined as the general rule under art 5(1), that the relevant
obligation is that on which the plaintiff's action is based. It adopted in this respect
its own previous approach in *Ets A de Bloos SPRL v Société en commandite par actions
e Bouyer* Case 14/76 [1976] ECR 1497, and limited another of its decisions, *Ivenel v
Schwab* Case 133/81 [1982] ECR 1891. It explained and relied on the underlying
rationale of art 5(1) as follows:

       '... no such uncertainty exists for most contracts if regard is had solely to
       the contractual obligation whose performance is sought in the judicial
f   proceedings. The place in which that obligation is to be performed usually
       constitutes the closest connecting factor between the dispute and the court
       having jurisdiction over it, and it is this connecting factor which explains
       why, in contractual matters, it is the court of the place of performance of the
       obligation which has jurisdiction.' (See [1987] ECR 239 at 256 (para 18).)

g The contractual obligation whose performance is sought refers to the primary
contractual obligation broken, rather than to any secondary obligation to pay
damages or any other remedy which may arise at law consequential on the
breach (see *de Bloos* [1976] ECR 1497 at 1509 (paras 16–17)). Otherwise, the
plaintiffs' own domicile could have become an automatic forum without any real
h connection with the underlying dispute.
       There is no doubt about the application of art 5(1) to claims to dissolve (or, in
English terminology, determine) a contract for breach of an obligation arising
under its terms (see *de Bloos* [1976] ECR 1497 at 1509 (para 16) and 1511 (answer
1)).
       The court in *Shenavai* dealt with the situation where several contractual
j obligations are in issue as follows ([1987] ECR 239 at 256 (para 19)):

       'Admittedly, the above rule does not afford a solution in the particular case
       of a dispute concerned with a number of obligations arising under the same
       contract and forming the basis of the proceedings commenced by the
       plaintiff. However, in such a case the court before which the matter is

brought will, when determining whether it has jurisdiction, be guided by the
maxim *accessorium sequitur principale*; in other words, where various
obligations are at issue, it will be the principal obligation which will
determine its jurisdiction ...'

Subsequent English authorities have noted the underlying rationale of art 5(1)
(viz the existence in a matter relating to contract of the particularly close
relationship likely to exist between any dispute and the courts of the place of
performance of the obligation in question) in decisions on its scope (see *Union
Transport Group plc v Continental Lines SA* [1992] 1 All ER 161 at 168, [1992] 1 WLR
15 at 23 per Lord Goff and *Kleinwort Benson Ltd v Glasgow City Council* [1996] 2 All
ER 257 at 271, 273–275, [1996] 2 WLR 655 at 669, 671–673 per Roch and Millett
LJJ; [1996] 2 All ER 257 at 265, [1996] 2 WLR 655 at 663 per Leggatt LJ (dissenting
in the result)).

The underlying rationale of art 5(1) has some limits as a guide to
interpretation. I mention two points. The first derives from *Kalfelis*, which raised
for consideration the relationship of arts 5(1) and 5(3). The claims were for
contractual liability (breach of an obligation to provide information, tort and
unjust enrichment). The plaintiffs' case was that all these claims could be
brought within art 5(3). Advocate General Darmon in contrast would have
applied the approach adopted in *Peters* so widely as to bring all of them within
art 5(1) (see [1988] ECR 5565 at 5577–5578). The European Court's actual
conclusion was more circumspect and did not indorse either approach. It ruled
that—

'the term "matters relating to tort, delict or quasi-delict" within the
meaning of Article 5(3) of the Convention must be regarded as an
independent concept covering all actions which seek to establish the liability
of a defendant and which are not related to a "contract" within Article 5(1)'
(See [1988] ECR 5565 at 5585 (paras 17–18) and 5587 (para 2(a).)

Secondly, although the underlying rationale of art 5(1) is that explained in *Peters*
([1983] ECR 987), 'the criterion employed in that provision is not the connection
with the court seised but, rather, only the place of performance of the obligation
which forms the basis of the legal proceedings'.[b] This is a quotation from *Custom
Made Commercial Ltd v Stawa Metallbau GmbH* Case C-288/92 [1994] ECR I-2913 at
2956 (para 14), where the court upheld the jurisdiction of the place of
performance in a case of jurisdiction based upon the buyer's obligation under the
law governing the contract to pay the price to the seller at the seller's place of
business. The court did so in the interests of certainty and simplicity, although
the effect could be to confer jurisdiction on a court which had no connection with
the dispute and which was also that of the seller's domicile. In the former respect,
it differed from the advice of Advocate General Lenz (although even he had
resisted any suggestion that art 5(1) should be turned into 'a vague *forum*

---

b   The actual decision in *Kalfelis* was that art 5(3) could not serve to 'channel' before a single forum all
     aspects of a dispute involving claims of a variety of different legal natures. There may still be some
     scope for regarding art 5(1) as serving to 'channel' and 'centralise' before a single forum all aspects
     in dispute, where a matter relating principally to contract raises claims of different legal natures,
     non-contractual as well as contractual. This is a theme addressed by Advocate General Darmon,
     but not decided by the court, in several subsequent cases (see e g *Shevill v Presse Alliance SA* [1995] All
     ER (EC) 289 at 302, [1995] 2 AC 18 at 45 (paras 76–78)). It is unnecessary to go into it in the present
     case.

conveniens rule' (see [1994] ECR I–2913 at 2929 (para 63)). In the latter respect, I note that even Advocate General Lenz would have regarded it as of no real weight, as an objection to a particular interpretation of art 5(1), that it would lead to jurisdiction in the place of a plaintiff's domicile. He put the matter as follows ([1994] ECR I-2913 at 2922 (para 32)):

> '... Neither can it be contested that, in view of the aforementioned articles, "apart from the cases expressly provided for, the Convention appears clearly hostile towards the attribution of jurisdiction to the courts of the plaintiff's domicile". Yet such "exceptions" to the conditions laid down by Article 5 et seq. are by no means rare. Articles 13 and 14 on jurisdiction over consumer contracts show this clearly. The court having jurisdiction under Article 5(3) (place where the harmful event occurred) may turn out, in the event, to be the court of the plaintiff's domicile. There is therefore no justification for inferring conclusions favouring a particular interpretation from the Convention's more or less marked "antipathy" to the plaintiff's court.'

'Matter relating to a contract'

I turn to the present circumstances. The defendants accept that the matter is one 'relating to a contract'. In my judgment this concession is well-founded. The matter is on any objective appreciation intimately concerned with and closely related to the contracts which (it is not in dispute) were here actually made between the defendants as insurers and the plaintiffs as reinsurers. The whole gist of the plaintiffs' complaint is that such contracts were made, but (confining attention to the plaintiffs' primary case) that their making was induced by the defendants' misrepresentations through their brokers. Based on that complaint the plaintiffs claim declarations establishing their entitlement to avoid the contracts.

In any textbook or comparative legal scheme, the issues which arise would fall under the general classification of contract. English arbitration authority, cited by Rix J, also indicates that as a matter of language there is no difficulty in recognising them as arising 'in relation to or in connection with' a contract.

The defendants emphasise authorities stating that the right to avoid an insurance contract, whether for non-disclosure or positive misrepresentation of material fact, arises not under any term of the contract, but independently under the general law. In the case of misrepresentation, its source in the general law was said, in *Merchants' and Manufacturers' Insurance Co Ltd v Hunt* [1941] 1 All ER 123 at 128, 137, [1941] 1 KB 295 at 312, 318 per Scott and Luxmoore LJJ, to be 'the jurisdiction originally exercised by the Courts of Equity to prevent imposition'. In *Banque Financière de la Cité SA v Westgate Insurance Co Ltd* [1989] 2 All ER 952 at 996, [1990] 1 QB 665 at 779 the Court of Appeal considered (albeit obiter in view of the later House of Lords decision) that the right to avoid a contract uberrimae fidei in case of non-disclosure must be founded on the same jurisdiction. In *Bank of Nova Scotia v Hellenic Mutual War Risks Association (Bermuda) Ltd, The Good Luck* [1989] 3 All ER 628, [1990] 1 QB 818, the Court of Appeal considered (again, obiter for like reason) that the same must apply as regards any obligation of utmost good faith continuing during the course of such a contract once made. I can leave aside whether it can be right to assign to equity sole credit for a principle of avoidance for failure to make a fair presentation of the risk, identified authoritatively in Lord Mansfield CJ's court (see *Carter v Boehm* (1766) 3 Burr

1905, [1558–1774] All ER Rep 183). The principle which Lord Mansfield CJ stated did not survive as the general contractual principle which he advocated, but it did survive in an insurance context—particularly in marine insurance law—while the non-marine context of *Carter v Boehm* itself would suggest some wider insurance application at least. Lord Mustill's speech in *Pan Atlantic Insurance Co Ltd v Pine Top Insurance Co Ltd* [1994] 3 All ER 581 at 612–613, [1995] 1 AC 501 at 543–544 contains discussion of the roles of common law and equity in this area, and of various theories upon which the doctrine of good faith has been explained as operating. In considering whether the matter is one 'relating to a contract' within art 5(1), it seems to me that such questions can largely be ignored, as being of no more than historical and domestic interest. I will, however, proceed on the basis that the duty of good faith exists, as Mr Ashe submitted, as a matter of general law outside the contract. Further, the remedy for its breach is now established to be avoidance, not damages. In the House of Lords in *Banque Financière de la Cité SA v Westgate Insurance Co Ltd* [1990] 2 All ER 947, [1991] 2 AC 249 Lord Templeman, with whose speech all other members of the House concurred, took the opportunity to agree expressly with the Court of Appeal on this point. The possibility of another remedy in some cases of positive misrepresentation under s 2 of the Misrepresentation Act 1967 can, it appears to me, be disregarded for present purposes. Any claims for positive misstatement which might exist under the principle of *Hedley Byrne & Co Ltd v Heller & Partners Ltd* [1963] 2 All ER 575, [1964] AC 465 depend upon proof of additional ingredients such as duty and negligence or deceit.

These points do nothing to undermine the conclusion that a claim for a declaration establishing a plaintiff's right to avoid a contract for breach of such a duty is a claim 'relating to a contract' within the meaning of art 5(1). The fact that the remedy is avoidance emphasises the reality that, without the making of the contract, the matter would never come before a court at all. Jurisprudentially and in some legal contexts (eg in the context of contracts requiring to be supported in writing or of limitation), it may no doubt make sense to identify 'sanctionless obligations'. In the present context, the duty to present the risk fairly or without misrepresentation is only ever likely to be significant when and if a contract has actually been made as a result. The duty is often referred to as a 'pre-contract' obligation. It can, however, also be described as an obligation to make full disclosure and to avoid misrepresentation *when* entering into an insurance contract. Sections 17 to 20 of the Marine Insurance Act 1906 prefer the former approach, expressing the relevant duties as arising 'before the contract is concluded' or 'during the negotiations', but in each case the premise is that a contract has been made.

Counsel for the defendants was therefore, in my judgment, right to concede that the present matter is one 'relating to a contract' or, here, contracts.

Obligation in question in the sense of art 5(1)

I turn to the question, whether the duty to make a fair presentation, by giving full disclosure and avoiding misrepresentation, is an obligation in the sense of art 5(1), carrying with it a place for performance which would in this case (and indeed commonly) be the place where the reinsurance contract was negotiated. The European Court, in the decisions to which I have referred, has on a number of occasions made reference to 'the contractual obligation [or right]' forming the basis of the legal proceedings and to the obligation referred to in art 5(1) as being a one which 'arises under the contract' (see for example *de Bloos* [1976] ECR 1497 at 1508 (paras 11, 14), *Peters* [1983] ECR 987 at 1002 (para 12) and *Shenavai v Kreischer* [1987] ECR 239 at 258 (para 18)). In none of these cases was the nature of the obligations embraced by art 5(1) directly in issue. I read the European Court's use of such phrases as being in context no more than a convenient shorthand to identify the general area (represented by the first criterion) in which

b any obligation embraced by art 5(1) must arise. The Court of Appeal's reasoning in *Kleinwort Benson Ltd v Glasgow City Council* [1996] 2 All ER 257, [1996] 2 WLR 655 is in the same sense.

Peters, as Rix J pointed out, does, however, address the meaning of the concept of 'contract' in art 5(1). In giving that concept an autonomous convention

c meaning, *Peters* likewise extended the nature of the obligations falling within the article. It was common ground in *Peters* that, under Dutch law (in contrast to what was described by the Advocate General as 'the prevailing tendency of the legal system of the Community States'), membership of an association did not create contractual relationships. The liabilities to which it gave rise were 'institutional' or, in other words, based on status and the general law rather than

d contract. Nonetheless, the court held that they were 'close links of the same kind as those which are created between the parties to a contract' (or, as Rix J summarised it, 'closely akin to contract'). The obligations imposed by Dutch law were thus to be 'regarded as contractual for the purpose of the application of Article 5(1)' (see [1983] ECR 987 at 1002 (para 13)).

e *Peters* does not provide a direct answer to the present situation, where (a) there are actual contracts both under the governing national law and, on any autonomous view, (b) there are claims to avoid these contracts, (c) the matter is thus one clearly 'relating to' the contracts, but (d) the 'obligation', non-performance of which gives rise to the claims, arises in the context of the

f contractual negotiations and does so (in terms of national law) extra-contractually under the general law. The observations of the European Court in *Peters* [1983] ECR 987 at 1002, 1003 (paras 12 and 17) do, however, make it legitimate to consider the consequences of any conclusion that the duty to make a fair presentation falls inside or outside the scope of art 5(1), an aspect to

g which I return at the end of this judgment.

Peters holds that the non-contractual classification of an obligation under national law is not conclusive when determining whether there is a 'matter relating to a contract' within art 5(1). Whether there is any obligation at all for the purpose of the second criterion is a different question. Whether this question

h is to be answered solely or primarily by reference to national law, or is subject to a parallel requirement that it satisfy some autonomous legal conception, as Rix J may have had in mind (see [1995] 1 All ER 896 at 815), was not addressed before me and does not appear to have been directly addressed in any of the European Court authorities on art 5(1). The fact that national law determines the law

j applicable to the legal relationship and the place for performance under the third criterion (see *Industrie Tessili Italiana Como v Dunlop AG* Case 12/76 [1976] ECR 1473) suggests that there must be an obligation under national law for performance. The requirement that the obligation to be performed in the state whose jurisdiction is invoked should be 'in question', and the test stated in *Shenavai* for cases where there is more than one such obligation, are convention

matters. Beyond that, it might be thought that the basic parameters for the
application of art 5(1) are sufficiently set at convention level by the first criterion[c]. *a*

So far as national law is concerned, both parties' submissions before me
accepted the existence of the extra-contractual duties of good faith and fair
presentation (including obligations to avoid misrepresentation) on which the
plaintiffs' case is founded. It is true that in *Pine Top Pan Atlantic Insurance Co Ltd v
Pine Top Insurance Co Ltd* [1994] 3 All ER 581 at 612–613, [1995] 1 AC 501 at 544 *b*
Lord Mustill left open all questions of analysis bearing on the nature of the duty
of good faith. But the weight of authority and usage certainly points towards the
analysis in terms of extra-contractual obligation which the parties adopted before
me.

In concluding that such obligations fall outside a boundary to be placed under
the convention on the conception of 'obligation' in art 5(1), the main factor that *c*
Rix J relied on was not that they are extra-contractual, but that they arise before,
and in the circumstances of formation of, the contract. Posing the question
whether the claims were 'apposite to be the subject matter of an article which
provides an exceptional jurisdiction based upon the connecting link of the place
of performance in matters relating to contract', he gave a negative answer (see *d*
[1995] 1 All ER 796 at 819ff). Article 5(1) was, he said, concerned with the place
where contracts are to be performed, not with the place where contracts are to
be made.

Rix J drew in support on a passage in the Jenard Report on the Brussels
Convention (OJ 1979 C59 p1 at pp 23–24), explaining why 'only the jurisdiction
of the forum solutionis has been retained' as a special or exceptional head of *e*
jurisdiction in the contractual field. Three reasons were given by Mr Jenard:
firstly, that it would be unwise to introduce too many different heads of
jurisdiction; secondly, that, although the previous Benelux Treaty of 24
November 1961 recognised as a head of jurisdiction the place where the
obligation arose, this would involve considerable changes for some other *f*
countries; and, thirdly, that:

> 'There was also concern that acceptance of the jurisdiction of the courts for
> the place where the obligation arose might sanction, by indirect means, the
> jurisdiction of the forum of the plaintiff. To have accepted this forum would
> have created tremendous problems of classification, in particular in the case *g*
> of contracts concluded by parties who are absent.'

Rix J considered that—

> 'it would infringe this distinction to hold that an obligation to avoid
> misrepresentations or non-disclosures in the making of a contract is an *h*
> obligation which founds jurisdiction at the place of performance. After all,
> such an obligation gives no right to contractual performance at all or to
> damages in lieu. The only remedy for its breach is the right to avoid the

---

c   In an exceptional case, if recognition of a national law duty as an obligation under art 5(1) would *j*
'impair the effectiveness of the Convention', there could still be scope for looking beyond national
law. But national law would on this approach normally be the sole test. Support for such an
analysis may derive from the European Court's reasoning and decision with respect to 'the place
where the harmful event occurred', the criterion for jurisdiction in a matter relating to tort within
art 5(3) (see *Shevill v Presse Alliance SA* [1995] All ER (EC) 289 at 318–319, [1995] 2 AC 18 at 63–64
(paras 34–41)), which came to my attention after writing the text to which this footnote is
appended.

a
contract, or, in the case of negligence or deceit, a right to damages in tort and not in contract.' (See [1995] 1 All ER 796 at 820.)

I differ from Rix J on the significance and weight of these points. The fact that art 5(1) is a special or exceptional jurisdiction in relation to the general jurisdiction based on domicile under art 2, does not by itself carry matters very

b
far. Although art 5(1) is a special jurisdiction, it was introduced for what were perceived as good reasons, and the primary inquiry must be whether the present circumstances fall within its proper scope, correctly interpreted. The statement in *Kalfelis* [1988] ECR 5565 at 5585 (para 19) that the special jurisdictions should be construed restrictively was deployed there to exclude from the scope of art 5(3) actions not based on tort or delict at all. Questions as to what actions are

c
based on tort or delict within art 5(3), or (here) what actions relate to a contract and (to the extent that it is appropriate to look beyond national law) to the performance of an obligation within art 5(1), are ones which must be answered 'by reference chiefly to the system and objectives of the convention' (see *Peters*). *Kleinwort Benson* and *Boss Group* both show the Court of Appeal seeking to

d
ascertain and apply the proper scope of art 5(1) in relation to the particular circumstances of those cases.

The fact that a particular construction of art 5(1) may happen to lead to the same jurisdiction as would follow if the convention had adopted a scheme conferring jurisdiction on the state of the place where the contract was made or the obligation arose or the plaintiff has its domicile also presents no necessary

e
objection to such construction. That is shown by the decision in *Custom Made Commercial Ltd v Stawa Metallbau GmbH* Case C-288/92 [1994] ECR I-2913, to which I have already referred. *Custom Made* was decided in the European Court in the fortnight between submissions and judgment in *Trade Indemnity* and it seems clear that it was not before Rix J.

f
Article 5(1) draws no express distinction between obligations arising in the context of negotiation of a contract and obligations arising under or after the contract. Once it is concluded (as here) that the matter relates to a contract, the only inquiries expressly required under art 5(1) are whether the matter involves an obligation, (or, if it involves more than one obligation, what is the principal obligation) and then, where that obligation was or would be due for

g
performance. If (as here) the matter turns on the issue of whether the defendants through their brokers properly performed their unquestioned duty of fair presentation in London, that would seem on its face to satisfy the requirements of art 5(1). The defendants submit that this is to put the cart before the horse. The fact that there is a place for performance cannot, they submit, determine the proper meaning of 'obligation'. As I have indicated, it seems to me open to doubt

h
how far the draughtsmen of the convention ever contemplated the possibility that there would be matters 'relating to a contract' and turning on the defendants' performance of duties recognised under national law in that regard, where the duties in question might yet be said not to constitute 'obligations' in the sense of

j
art 5(1).

Assuming a dual test whereby an 'obligation' in a matter relating to a contract must both exist under national law and satisfy some further conception to be derived from the general scheme and objectives of the convention, it is relevant to consider the rationale of art 5(1) and its applicability in the present context. The rationale, stressed in *Peters*, *Shenavai v Kreischer* and the English authorities mentioned above, is that there will normally be a close relationship between the place of performance and the court which is most convenient to determine the matter. That rationale will not always be satisfied and is not itself the criterion of jurisdiction (see *Custom Made*). But it can be said with assurance of the duty of fair presentation, that the place for its performance is very likely to be the place which is also convenient for the determination of disputes arising out of its asserted breach. One has only to think of the disputes which often arise as to what was said or shown in the course of placing between the brokers and underwriters. Of course there can also be disputes about other matters, such as whether a particular representation was or was not true, which may involve investigation elsewhere in the world. Article 5(1) is on any view designed as a simple and sometimes, perhaps, blunt test. Compared with other matters, such as claims for payment of the price or other moneys under commercial contracts, the place of performance of the duty of fair presentation appears to me, as much as if not more than most, to offer a sensible and convenient jurisdiction. In the light of the European and English authorities cited above, this is a factor of relevance in deciding whether to recognise pre-contract duties of disclosure as sufficient 'obligations' in the sense of art 5(1)^d.

In my view, any general distinction between pre-contract and post-contract duties looks at matters too broadly and from the wrong angle in the context of the convention. When and if a case involving questions relating to the formation of a contract falls outside art 5(1), it appears to me that it does so, not or not necessarily because it relates to the formation of the contract, but because there is no duty in question at all, and therefore no performance or place of performance of any obligation. The necessary connecting factors prescribed by art 5(1) are simply not there.

It is significant that the Court of Appeal decision in *Kleinwort Benson* points not to a simple distinction between issues relating to formation and subsequent performance, but to a different distinction. Matters relating to the formation of a contract would include issues about the correspondence of offer and acceptance, form, consideration (under English law), capacity, authority, illegality, mistake, misrepresentation and duress. But Millett LJ said ([1996] 2 All ER 257 at 274, [1996] 2 WLR 655 at 672):

> 'There is a real difference between the case where negotiations have not led to a concluded contract, where there is no contract at all, and the case where they have led to a contract, so that there is an agreement in fact, but one of the parties lacks contractual capacity, so that there is no contract in law.'

The parties in *Kleinwort Benson* had purported to enter into what were to all outward appearances interest swap contracts which were in law, as later held, outside the local authority's power and void. The bank sued to recover the sums paid to the local authority under the void contracts on grounds of unjust enrichment. The issue before the Court of Appeal was whether the matter was one 'relating to a contract'. Roch and Millett LJJ gave a broad European meaning to the concept of contract, which, as Millett LJ concluded, embraced 'at its irreducible minimum ... a consensual arrangement intended to create legal

---

d   It also demonstrates that to recognise the place of performance of the duty of fair presentation as relevant under art 5(1) would not 'impair the effectiveness of the Convention', if that is the only proviso to the applicability of national law to determine the existence of an obligation under art 5(1): see footnote c above.

a relations and to be legally enforceable' (see [1996] 2 All ER 257 at 273, [1996] 2
   WLR 655 at 671). On the 'central question' whether the word in art 5(1) included
   a void contract, Millett LJ said:

> 'The respondents say No. A void contract is a nullity. It is not a contract.
> It has no legal effect. It gives rise to no legal obligations. There is no place
> of performance. If one party claims to recover money paid pursuant to it, his
b > claim is not a contractual claim. The action lies in restitution, not contract.
> The recipient's obligation to repay is not a contractual obligation. It does not
> arise from the void contract, which is incapable of generating any legal rights
> and obligations. It arises solely by reason of the original payment and
> because the recipient would be unjustly enriched if he were allowed to retain
c > it. These are powerful arguments, but I am not persuaded by them. They
> appear to me to depend upon the kind of analysis which is employed by a
> national law in the classification of causes of action for domestic purposes,
> rather than the very broad and unanalytical approach which the convention
> requires. Even if every member state treats a contract as a nullity if one of
> the parties lacks capacity, this should not be treated as if it were a rule of
d > natural law and of universal application.' (See [1996] 2 All ER 257 at 273–274,
> [1996] 2 WLR 655 at 671.)

It was not in issue in *Kleinwort Benson* that, if the matter related to a contract, it
also involved an obligation, performance of which was due in England. The
obligation in question was, at least for Millett LJ, not the obligation to repay, but
e the defendant council's obligation under the swap 'contract', which it was
incapable of performing (see [1996] 2 All ER 257 at 275, [1996] 2 WLR 655 at 673).

Millett LJ's analysis demonstrates why, on the basis of the broad approach to
the concept of contract adopted in *Kleinwort Benson*, some disputes going to
formation may nonetheless involve contractual obligations within the meaning
f of art 5(1). A similar approach to the Court of Appeal's in *Kleinwort Benson*
appears to have been adopted by the French Cour de Cassation in a decision
noted in *Dicey and Morris on The Conflict of Laws* (12th edn, 1993) vol 1, p 357, n 93.
The case is *Soc ISI v Soc CPAV* (1983, Cour de Cassation), *Rev Crit* 516, where the
claim was to have a contract annulled (and recover compensation) on grounds of
the impossibility or illicitness of its performance, and the court applied art 5(1) by
g reference to the obligations of the defendants which were, according to the
plaintiffs' case, incapable of being performed.

There is another reason why it is easy to envisage issues relating to matters
concerning the formation of a valid contract coming before a court with
jurisdiction under art 5(1). A claim for performance (or for damages for
h non-performance) of a contract may be met by a denial of any contract, or of
authority or capacity to make any contract or by a defence that any contract was
illegal or made under mistake or duress. In such a case, a court may have
jurisdiction under art 5(1) 'even when the existence of the contract on which the
claim is based is in dispute between the parties' (see *Effer SpA v Kantner* Case 38/
j 81 [1982] ECR 825, a case where the only answer to the plaintiff's claim for fees
was that his contract had been with a third party, not the defendant). The English
courts have held in this context that a plaintiff needs to show no more than a good
arguable case in favour of the alleged contract in order to establish jurisdiction
under art 5(1).

If there are problems about the potential application of art 5(1) to issues
concerning the formation of contracts, they are thus most likely to arise in

practice in a situation where a plaintiff is himself seeking a declaration that no contractual consensus was ever reached. Even in this context, however, the most recent Court of Appeal decision in *Boss Group* [1996] 4 All ER 970 indicates that jurisdiction may exist under art 5(1). Boss France SA was contending that Boss Group Ltd was bound by an exclusive distributorship agreement for France. Boss Group Ltd brought the English action to establish that it was not party to any contract with Boss France SA or that, if it had ever been, the agreement had been determined and that it was under no liability to make supplies pursuant to any further orders received from Boss France SA. The Court of Appeal held that (1) the existence of the dispute meant that there was a 'matter relating to a contract', even for the purposes of Boss Group Ltd's claim, and (2) there was an obligation in question consisting of Boss Group Ltd's (disputed) obligation to honour further orders from Boss France SA which (there was a good arguable case for saying) would, if it existed, have fallen due for performance by Boss Group Ltd in England.

The present plaintiffs face a different and, it may I think be said, in some respects easier task under art 5(1) than the plaintiffs in *Kleinwort Benson* or, a fortiori, *Boss Group*. Here, a contract was admittedly and indubitably made, the matter relates to that contract and the primary relief available at law involves a claim to avoid the contract. The basis for the plaintiffs' claim to avoid is alleged misrepresentation, involving non-performance by the defendants of a duty of fair presentation. The defendants' submission is simply that this type of duty cannot constitute a relevant obligation for the purpose of art 5(1). I note that in *Kleinwort Benson* [1996] 2 All ER 257 at 276, [1996] 2 WLR 655 at 674 Millett LJ left for future consideration the question whether the word 'contract' in art 5(1) might be capable of including 'anticipated contract', adding:

'... I would not exclude it as a possibility. Many civilian systems require good faith in the negotiation of a proposed contract. Is a breach of such an obligation not "a matter relating to a contract"? I pose the question, not to suggest an answer, but to indicate that the answer is by no means obvious.'

In the present case, contracts have actually been made and it is, as I have said, both common ground and clear that the matter relates to those contracts. The further question whether the obligation of good faith or fair presentation is of a nature capable of falling within art 5(1) can and should be in my judgment answered affirmatively. Neither the fact that the obligation arises extra-contractually as a matter of law, nor the fact that it arises in the negotiation of the contract appears to me to represent any valid reason for disregarding it in the context of the present 'matter relating to a contract'.

Although not directly concerned with the present issues, two additional passages in *Kleinwort Benson* are, at lowest, consistent with the conclusion which I have reached. The first appears in Roch LJ's judgment ([1996] 2 All ER 257 at 270, [1996] 2 WLR 655 at 667):

'The word "obligation" in article 5(1) is not confined to contractual obligations ... In my opinion, the absence of any qualification of the word "obligation" throws light on the meaning to be given to the words "a contract".'

The second is from Millett LJ ([1996] 2 All ER 257 at 273, [1996] 2 WLR 655 at 671):

a
'The expression "matters relating to a contract" is not, in my opinion, to be equated with "contractual causes of action" or "the enforcement of contractual obligations" or even "claims based on contract".'

Both these passages embrace a concept of obligation under art 5(1) which is wide enough to cover duties, such as the duty of fair presentation, which are closely associated with, though not part of the relevant contract.

b

Other considerations

A number of other considerations also appear to me to militate in favour of recognising the present duty as an obligation in the sense of art 5(1).

Firstly, it is not uncommon for parties to agree an express warranty covering matters which would otherwise fall within the general duty of fair presentation. It is quite possible for this to occur in a reinsurance context (which is the only insurance context to which art 5(1) is relevant). To take an example, an insurer or reinsurer could require a warranty that there were 'no known [or reported] losses' when accepting a participation in respect of risks already incepted. Such a warranty gives rise to a right to avoid if untrue, although it is also promissory and so carries, potentially, a remedy in damages, however rarely material. The presence of an express warranty covering matters which would otherwise fall within the general duty of fair presentation would preclude the distinctions presently suggested between obligations arising under the contract and pre-contractual obligations arising at general law. The contract would be broken from its outset. Further, in the example just postulated (although not, of course, in the case of every such warranty) the breach would occur as and where the contract was made. If the defendants' submissions were upheld, they would mean that plaintiffs could rely upon art 5(1) where matters of fair presentation had been elevated to the status of a warranty, but could not do so to pursue a claim for misrepresentation or non-disclosure affecting the contract.

c

d

e

f
That breach of warranty, where alleged, will commonly be the dominant claim, and will as such carry jurisdiction under the principle in *Shenavai v Kreischer* Case 266/85 [1987] ECR 239 at 256 (para 19), if the case otherwise falls within art 5(1), is clear not only because breach of an express warranty justifies avoidance under English law without proof of materiality or inducement, but also because an express warranty will commonly supersede or render otiose disclosure (see s 18(3)(d) of the 1906 Act, which reflects for marine insurance, a principle general to all insurance). In the present case, however, the misrepresentations alleged are different, more expansive and more explicit than the alleged warranty and it is common ground that the warranty claim is secondary. The warranty claim will therefore on its face be within the court's jurisdiction, if the court has jurisdiction over the misrepresentation claims under art 5(1). The place of performance of the alleged warranty was, in these circumstances, not discussed before me.

g

h

The relationship of the pre-contractual duty of fair presentation with other aspects of the general duty of good faith, in my view, also merits consideration. The pre-contractual duty is probably best regarded as an aspect of an overriding duty of good faith, which itself operates, if and as the context requires, on a continuing basis (see *Black King Shipping Corp v Massie, The Litsion Pride* [1985] 1 Lloyd's Rep 437 at 508, 511–512 per Hirst J and ss 17ff of the 1906 Act). To take one instance, there may be a duty of disclosure, where the contract gives the insured an option to seek extended cover or (on a limited basis) in a claims

j

context; the remedy for breach is usually avoidance—here, of the extension or, in the claims context (without going into matters not yet perhaps finally resolved by authority), of either the claim or the whole cover. Mr Gee QC, counsel for the defendants before Rix J, was inclined to accept in *Trade Indemnity* that, had the case involved the *post*-contractual aspect of the continuing duty of good faith, a claim based on breach of that duty could properly have been said to involve an 'obligation' in the sense of art 5(1) (see [1995] 1 All ER 796 at 818). Rix J did not himself decide this, saying merely that it might well be so (see at 820). Such a duty can be very closely connected with particular contract terms. In this very case, the contracts appear to have been for periods of three and a half years, but one of them (the Fenchurch excess contract) is expressed to have been subject to full review after 18 and 30 months. That in turn is said to have connoted an obligation to make full disclosure for the purposes of such reviews. The obligation is pleaded as arising as a matter of construction. An alternative analysis (depending on the particular contract wording) may however be, either in this case or in some other case which can readily be envisaged, that the obligation of disclosure in such a situation is simply an aspect of the continuing duty of good faith, which is capable of arising during the course of an insurance context where there is an appropriate contractual context for such a duty (cf *Black King Shipping Corp v Massie, The Litsion Pride* [1985] 1 Lloyd's Rep 437 at 511–512 per Hirst J). It would be odd if the application of art 5(1) in this situation were to depend on a determination whether the duty of disclosure arose as a matter of construction or general law. If, as I think, both would fall within art 5(1), it would also be odd that the application of art 5(1) should vary according to whether the claim was to set aside the contract as originally made ab initio, or the contract as from the date of an intermediate review called for under its terms. Similar observations apply to the duty of disclosure on a party seeking, under an insurance facility, to invoke a 'held covered' or other extension clause to obtain cover in respect of a subject matter or period which would otherwise not be insured. Any distinction between pre-contract and post-contract duties appears to me to break down in such situations.

Conclusion

For these reasons, I have come to a conclusion different from that to which Rix J came in *Trade Indemnity*. In my judgment, the present claims to avoid not only constitute a matter 'relating to a contract', but also concern the performance of obligations in England within the meaning of art 5(1). I therefore dismiss the defendants' application to set aside the proceedings under Ord 12, r 8.

Application dismissed.

K Mydeen Esq   Barrister.

McCausland and another v Duncan Lawrie Ltd and another

COURT OF APPEAL, CIVIL DIVISION
NEILL, MORRITT LJJ AND TUCKER J
1 MAY, 6 JUNE 1996

Sale of land – Contract – Form of contract – Variation – Formalities required – Whether variation of contract for sale of land requiring same formalities applying to formation of contract – Whether alteration of completion date required to be incorporated in one document signed by or on behalf of both parties – Law of Property (Miscellaneous Provisions) Act 1989, s 2.

By a written agreement dated 26 January 1995 the vendors agreed to sell and the purchasers agreed to buy a property for £210,000. Under the terms of the contract the purchasers agreed to pay a holding deposit of £1,000 and the balance of £209,000 on completion, the date of which was stated to be 26 March 1995, which was in fact a Sunday. The contract further provided that if the purchasers did not complete on the completion date the full 10% deposit became payable. When the vendors' solicitor realised that the completion date was a Sunday he wrote to the purchasers' solicitor suggesting that completion be rearranged for Friday, 24 March. The purchasers' solicitor replied that he had been instructed that completion could take place on the new date suggested. However, the purchasers failed to complete on that date and the vendors forthwith issued a completion notice demanding the balance on the full 10% deposit, amounting to £20,000. The purchasers asked for an extension of time in which to complete. The vendors refused, rescinded the contract and issued proceedings to recover the balance of the deposit. The purchasers paid the amount claimed but without prejudice to their right to recover that sum if it was found that the vendors had not been entitled to serve the notice to complete. In proceedings brought by the purchasers claiming specific performance of the original contract and damages, the judge ordered that their statement of claim be struck out on the ground that s 2[a] of the Law of Property (Miscellaneous Provisions) Act 1989 did not apply to the variation of a contract and therefore the completion date was 24 March. The purchasers appealed.

Held – Where a contract for the sale of land was varied, the formalities prescribed by s 2 of the 1989 Act for the creation of a valid contract for the sale or other disposition of an interest in land applied also to the variation of the contract, and accordingly the contract as varied had to be in writing and incorporated in one document, or each document if contracts were exchanged, and signed by or on behalf of each party to the contract. Since the alteration of the completion date had not been incorporated in one document signed by or on behalf of both parties that variation of the contract did not comply with s 2. The statement of claim had therefore been wrongly struck out. The appeal would therefore be allowed and the statement of claim reinstated (see p 1000 *g* to *j*, p 1001 *e*, p 1002 *a c*, p 1003 *b* and p 1006 *f* to p 1007 *a e*, post).

Dictum of Shearman J in *Williams v Moss' Empires Ltd* [1915] 3 KB 242 at 246 applied.

---

a   Section 2, so far as material, is set out at p 997 h j, post

Notes

For requirements for a contract for the sale of land, see 42 *Halsbury's Laws* (4th edn) paras 27–46.

Cases referred to in judgments

Berry v Berry [1929] 2 KB 316, [1929] All ER Rep 281, DC.
Beswick v Beswick [1967] 2 All ER 1197, [1968] AC 58, [1967] 3 WLR 932, HL.
Commission for the New Towns v Cooper (GB) Ltd [1995] 2 All ER 929, [1995] Ch 259, [1995] 2 WLR 677, CA.
Firstpost Homes Ltd v Johnson [1995] 4 All ER 355, [1995] 1 WLR 1567, CA.
Giraud v Richmond (1846) 2 CB 835, 135 ER 1172.
Goss v Lord Nugent (1833) 5 B & Ad 58, [1824–34] All ER Rep 305, 110 ER 713.
Hunt v South Eastern Rly Co (1875) 45 LJQB 87.
Marshall v Lynn (1840) 6 M & W 109, 151 ER 342.
Morris v Baron & Co [1918] AC 1, HL.
Noble v Ward (1867) LR 2 Ex 135.
Ogle v Earl Vane (1868) LR 3 QB 272, Ex Ch.
Sanderson v Graves (1875) LR 10 Ex 234.
Stead v Dawber (1839) 10 Ad & El 57, 113 ER 22.
Stowell v Robinson (1837) 3 Bing NC 928, 132 ER 668.
Thornhill v Neats (1860) 8 CBNS 831, 141 ER 1392.
Williams v Moss' Empires Ltd [1915] 3 KB 242, DC.

Cases also cited or referred to in skeleton arguments

Besseler Waechter Glover & Co v South Derwent Coal Co Ltd [1937] 4 All ER 552, [1938] 1 KB 408.
Harvey v Grabham (1836) 5 Ad & El 61, 111 ER 1089.
Marshall v Lynn (1840) 6 M & W 109, 151 ER 342.
Mitas v Hyams [1951] 2 TLR 1215, CA.
Notcutt v Universal Equipment Co (London) Ltd [1986] 3 All ER 582, [1986] 1 WLR 641, CA.
Payne v Zafiropoyloy [1994] CLY 3513.
Plymouth Corp v Harvey [1971] 1 All ER 623, [1971] 1 WLR 549.
Robinson v Page (1826) 3 Russ 114, 38 ER 519.
Spiro v Glencrown Properties Ltd [1991] 1 All ER 600, [1991] Ch 537.
Tootal Clothing Ltd v Guinea Properties Management Ltd [1992] 2 EGLR 80, CA.

Appeal

By notice dated 14 November 1995 Piers Conolly McCausland and Elisabeth Maria Rionagh McCausland appealed with leave granted by Millett LJ on 9 November 1995 from the decision of Knox J delivered on 7 July 1995 striking out their statement of claim against the respondents, Duncan Lawrie Ltd and SIS Securities Ltd, for specific performance of the contract of sale dated 26 January 1995 made between the parties for the sale and purchase of the property at No 1 Beechmore Road, London SW11, and damages. The judge also ordered that a caution registered against the property in the Land Registry by the appellants be cancelled. The facts are set out in the judgment of Neill LJ.

David Neuberger QC and *William Geldart* (instructed by *H C L Hanne & Co*) for the appellants.
Philip Shepherd (instructed by *Swepstone Walsh*) for the respondents.

Cur adv vult

a 6 June 1996. The following judgments were delivered.

NEILL LJ. This appeal raises a question of some importance as to the meaning and effect of s 2 of the Law of Property (Miscellaneous Provisions) Act 1989.

Contracts for the sale of an interest in land have for centuries been attended by certain legal formalities. For about 250 years the proof of such contracts was *b* governed by s 4 of the Statute of Frauds (1677), though from an early date the effects of the statutory rule were mitigated by the equitable doctrine of part performance. In 1925 s 4 of the 1677 Act was replaced by s 40 of the Law of Property Act 1925, which provided:

c '(1) No action may be brought upon any contract for the sale or other disposition of land or any interest in land, unless the agreement upon which such action is brought, or some memorandum or note thereof, is in writing, and signed by the party to be charged or by some other person thereunto by him lawfully authorised.

(2) This section applies to contracts whether made before or after the commencement of this Act and does not affect the law relating to part *d* performance, or sales by the court.'

It may be noted that the sidenote to the section stated 'Contracts for sale, etc, of land to be in writing'. But in fact a contract not complying with the section was not illegal or void. It was merely unenforceable.

e In practice, both s 4 of the 1677 Act and s 40 of the 1925 Act gave rise to difficulties. In particular the doctrine of part performance led to uncertainty in its application to the facts of individual cases. There were calls for reform and in 1985 the Law Commission produced a working paper (No 92). The working paper was followed in 1987 by a Law Commission report, *Transfer of Land: Formalities for Contracts for Sale etc of Land* (Law Com No 164), which *f* recommended that, with certain specified exceptions, all contracts for the sale or other dispositions of interests in land should have to be in writing signed by all parties in order to be valid. A draft Bill incorporating the commission's recommendations was attached to the report.

The 1989 Act gave legislative effect to a number of the reforms relating to land *g* law which had been proposed by the Law Commission in the previous few years. Section 2 introduced the recommendations in report No 164, though there were some differences between s 2 and the corresponding clause in the draft Bill attached to the report.

So far as is material, s 2 was in these terms:

h '(1) A contract for the sale or other disposition of an interest in land can only be made in writing and only by incorporating all the terms which the parties have expressly agreed in one document or, where contracts are exchanged, in each.

(2) The terms may be incorporated in a document either by being set out in it or by reference to some other document.

j (3) The document incorporating the terms or, where contracts are exchanged, one of the documents incorporating them (but not necessarily the same one) must be signed by or on behalf of each party to the contract ...'

By s 2(6) 'interest in land' was defined as 'any estate, interest or charge in or over land or in or over the proceeds of sale of land'. By s 2(8) it was provided that s 40 of the 1925 Act should cease to have effect but by s 2(7) it was further

provided that nothing in the section should apply in relation to contracts made
before the section came into force.

I propose to turn next to the facts.

THE FACTS

I can state the relevant facts quite shortly. Duncan Lawrie Ltd, the first
respondent, is a bank. SIS Securities Ltd (SIS), the second respondent, is a
property company. The two companies have a common parent.

In 1991 Mr and Mrs McCausland, the appellants, brought proceedings against
Duncan Lawrie seeking specific performance of an alleged agreement for the sale
to them of the property known as 1 Beechmore Road, London SW11 (the
property). At about the time when these proceedings were issued the appellants
registered a caution in the Land Registry against the property. It is unnecessary
for the purposes of this judgment to investigate the circumstances which gave
rise to these earlier proceedings. The 1991 proceedings were settled on 26
January 1995. It was a term of the settlement that the property would be sold to
the appellants for £210,000. The 1991 proceedings were formally compromised
by a Tomlin order dated 7 February 1995.

By a written agreement dated 26 January 1995 SIS, as seller, agreed to sell the
property to the appellants for the sum of £210,000. The written agreement
incorporated the Standard Conditions of Sale (2nd edn) and also contained a
number of special conditions. The agreement provided for the payment of a
deposit of £1,000 and for a balance of £209,000. The completion date was stated
to be 26 March 1995.

By the combined effect of standard condition 6.1.2 and special condition 5(b)
the balance of the purchase price of £209,000 was due to be paid by 2.30 pm on
the completion date. By standard condition 6.8.1 it was provided that at any time
on or after the completion date a party who was ready able and willing to
complete might give the other a notice to complete. By special condition 6 it was
provided that if the buyers did not complete on the completion date the balance
of the full 10% deposit would become payable.

A few days after the contract was signed the solicitor acting for Duncan Lawrie
and SIS realised that 26 March 1995 was a Sunday. I shall call the two companies
'the bank'. He therefore wrote the following letter to the appellants' solicitors
dated 3 February 1995:

'... I note that the completion date in the Contract is 26th March which is
a Sunday, and I therefore suggest that completion be re-arranged for Friday
the 24th March. I await your confirmation.'

A few days later the appellants' solicitors replied:

'Thank you for your letter dated 13 February 1995 [I understand that this
letter was a reminder of the letter of 3 February] and I have now received
instructions that completion can take place on 24 March 1995.'

On Friday, 24 March 1995 the bank's solicitors sent a fax to Mr Grimes, a
partner with the appellants' solicitors, asking him to confirm that the completion
moneys had been transmitted to the bank's account that morning. The balance
of the purchase price was not so transmitted, however, and accordingly later that
day the bank's solicitors sent a completion notice to the appellants and to their
solicitors. The accompanying letter was in these terms:

'As completion did not take place today, and in accordance with the
Agreement dated 26th January 1995 made between SIS Securities Limited (1)
and Piers Conolly McCausland and Elizabeth Maria Rionagh
McCausland (2), I enclose a Completion Notice pursuant to the above
Agreement and look forward to receiving £20,000 in accordance with Special
Condition 6 of the Agreement. If the above sum is not payable forthwith my
clients will be applying for summary judgement and your clients should also
be aware that interest is payable at the Contract rate from exchange of the
Agreement until actual payment is received by my clients. I look forward to
hearing from you by return.'

I should also refer to the first part of the notice to complete which was addressed
to the appellants and headed by the name of the property. The notice continued:

'We the undersigned as Solicitors for and on behalf of SIS Securities
Limited ... ("the Seller"): 1. Refer to the contract dated the 26th January
1995 ("the Contract") by which you agreed to buy from the Seller the
Property known as 1 Beechmore Road, Battersea, London SW11; 2. State
that the sale of the Property has not been completed on the date fixed in the
Contract for completion and that the Seller is ready, able and willing to
complete; 3. Give you notice under condition 6.8 of the Standard
Conditions of Sale (2nd Edition) ... to complete the transaction in
accordance with that condition ...'

On 3 April 1995 the appellants' solicitors wrote to the bank's solicitors:

'We write further to our telephone conversation with your Mr Eliades this
afternoon concerning the request for additional time in which to complete
this transaction. We appreciate that the notice to complete expires this
Friday. The request is for an additional four working days to expire on
Thursday 13 April before Good Friday, to enable our client to raise the
finance to complete.'

The bank, however, was unwilling to grant an extension and on 5 April the bank's
solicitors wrote to say that completion had to take place on or before 7 April in
accordance with the notice to complete.

Mr Grimes made a further attempt on Friday, 7 April to obtain an extension to
Monday, 10 April but this attempt failed. On 7 April the bank's solicitors sent a
notice to rescind the contract of sale.

On 18 April 1995 the bank issued proceedings claiming the balance of the
deposit together with interest. Those proceedings were later compromised by
the payment by the appellants of the balance of the deposit. But this payment was
made without prejudice to the appellants' right to recover this sum if it were
found that the bank had not been entitled to serve the notice to complete on 24
March.

On 14 June 1995 the appellants brought the present proceedings against both
Duncan Lawrie Ltd and SIS Securities Ltd. I propose, however, to continue to
refer to these two companies collectively as the bank.

The claim by the appellants as set out in the statement of claim was to the effect
that there had been no valid variation of the contractual completion date and that
accordingly there had been no valid rescission of the contract of sale. The
appellants claimed specific performance of the contract of sale dated 26 January

1995 and damages. On 21 June the first appellant registered a caution against the property in the Land Registry.

On 30 June 1995 the bank issued a notice of motion seeking an order for the cancellation of the caution and for the striking out of the statement of claim. The motion was heard by Knox J on 7 July 1995.

THE JUDGE'S JUDGMENT

In the course of his judgment the judge set out the material parts of s 2 of the 1989 Act. Later he continued:

'It does seem to me that the limitation that is in terms created is one on the making of a contract for the sale or other disposition of an interest in land, and I do not discern within the four corners of the section a requirement that variations of an existing and, ex hypothesi, enforceable provision for the sale or disposition of an interest in land have themselves to be made in one document or where contracts are exchanged in each ... The conclusion that I have come to is that where there is initially a duly signed contract which complies with s 2(1) of the 1989 Act in incorporating all its terms, the requirement is satisfied and it is open to the parties, if they so agree of course, to vary one or more of those terms and that so far as that variation is concerned what matters is that it should be proved in the ordinary way. The alternative produces a result which seems to me to go beyond what Parliament can reasonably be expected to have intended, and this is a very good example because nothing could be much more simple and straightforward than the actual agreement for the alteration of the completion date from the Sunday for perfectly sensible commercial reasons to the preceding Friday.'

In these circumstances the judge made an order that the caution be cancelled and that the statement of claim be struck out. The action was thereupon dismissed.

The judge refused leave to appeal but leave was subsequently granted by Millett LJ on 9 November 1995.

THE APPEAL

It was argued on behalf of the appellants that if the contract dated 26 January 1995 had been varied by the exchange of correspondence the contract which the bank was relying on was the contract as varied by the correspondence. It was not a case of two collateral contracts. Furthermore, even if it were possible to treat this case as one where there had been an exchange of contracts for the purposes of s 2(1), it was necessary, by virtue of s 2(2), for the terms to be incorporated 'in a document either by being set out in it or by reference to some other document'.

It was accepted on behalf of the bank that s 2 of the 1989 Act contains strict provisions relating to the formation of a contract for the sale or other disposition of an interest in land. But it was submitted that s 2 has not altered the law on oral variations of a contract. It has always been the law that oral variations of written contracts are capable of proof. The manner of proof is a rule of evidence. There was nothing in s 2 to show that the variation of a contract had to comply with the formalities prescribed in the statute.

Our attention was drawn to s 82 of the Consumer Credit Act 1974, which contains provisions relating to the variation of 'regulated agreements' as defined in s 189(1) of the Act. In the case of consumer credit Parliament had provided that *a* the regulated agreement, as modified by any variation, should comply with the prescribed formalities. There was no similar provision in the 1989 Act.

Furthermore, it was submitted, it was a general principle of the law that in construing a statute the courts will not attribute to Parliament an intention to bring about a fundamental change in the law 'by a sidewind'. Counsel referred us to passages in the speeches of Lord Hodson and Lord Guest in *Beswick v*
b *Beswick* [1967] 2 All ER 1197 at 1206, 1210, [1968] AC 58 at 79, 85.

It was further argued on behalf of the bank that the appellants were estopped from recovering damages or being granted specific performance. By the letter of 14 February 1995 it was represented on behalf of the appellants that the completion date would be 24 March 1995. By their subsequent conduct the appellants and their solicitors had accepted that completion was due to take place
c and should have taken place on Friday 24 March. It was not until the issue of these proceedings that any objection was raised to the variation of the completion date. Had the bank had notice that the variation of the completion date was being challenged another notice to complete could have been sent. We were referred to para 11 of the affidavit of Ms Rhory Robertson sworn on 3 July
d 1995 from which it appeared that the appellants would not have been able to complete before 21 April 1995.

I propose to deal with these arguments under two headings: (1) the variation and (2) estoppel.

e *The variation*

I feel bound to reject the arguments on this issue advanced on behalf of the bank. The principle of construction that Parliament is not to be intended to have amended the law 'by a sidewind' is of importance when one is construing a consolidation Act. But, as Peter Gibson LJ explained in *Firstpost Homes Ltd v Johnson* [1995] 4 All ER 355 at 358, [1995] 1 WLR 1567 at 1571, s 2 of the 1989 Act
f was intended to effect a major change in the law:

> 'Section 2 brought about a markedly different regime from that which obtained hitherto. Whereas under s 40 of the 1925 Act contracts which did not comply with its requirements were not void but were merely
g unenforceable by action, contracts which do not comply with s 2 of the 1989 Act are ineffective: a contract for the sale of an interest in land can only be made in writing and in conformity with the other provisions of s 2. Whereas an oral contract was allowed and enforceable provided that it was evidenced in writing and the memorandum or note thereof was signed by or on behalf of the party against whom it was sought to be enforced, oral contracts are
h now of no effect and all contracts must be signed by or on behalf of all the parties. Whereas the contract or the memorandum or note evidencing the contract previously could be contained in more than one document, only one document is now allowed (save where contracts are exchanged) although reference to another document may be permitted in the
j circumstances laid down in s 2(2) and (3). Whereas the memorandum or note needed for s 40 of the 1925 Act did not have to contain every term of the contract, all the terms must now be contained in the document in question. Whereas the doctrine of part performance allowed certain contracts otherwise unenforceable to be enforced, that doctrine now has no application.'

It seems to me to be clear that Parliament intended to introduce new and strict requirements as to the formalities to be observed for the creation of a valid disposition of an interest in land. As Stuart-Smith LJ noted in *Commission for the New Towns v Cooper (GB) Ltd* [1995] 2 All ER 929 at 952, [1995] Ch 259 at 287, the section enacted by Parliament was materially different from that drafted by the Law Commission. Under s 2 all the terms of the contract have to be incorporated in the signed document.

What then is the contract on which the bank seeks to rely? It was said by counsel for the bank that the bank relied on the contract dated 26 January which was created in a form which complied with s 2 and that this contract was later varied in a manner which would have been recognised by the common law and by the courts of equity.

In my judgment, however, counsel for the appellants was correct when he submitted that the formalities prescribed by s 2 have to be applied to the contract as varied. This was not a case where the agreement between the parties was concluded by an exchange of contracts. The only document signed by both parties was the contract dated 26 January 1995.

The law in this regard is made plain in the speech of Lord Parmoor in *Morris v Baron & Co* [1918] AC 1 at 39, where he referred with approval to the following passage in the judgment of Shearman J in *Williams v Moss' Empires Ltd* [1915] 3 KB 242 at 246:

> 'The principle ... is where there is alleged to have been a variation of a written contract by a new parol contract, which incorporates some of the terms of the old contract, the new contract must be looked at in its entirety, and if the terms of the new contract when thus considered are such that by reason of the Statute of Frauds it cannot be given in evidence unless in writing, then being an unenforceable contract it cannot operate to effect a variation of the original contract ... whenever the parties vary a material term of an existing contract they are in effect entering into a new contract, the terms of which must be looked at in their entirety, and if the new contract is one which is required to be in writing but is not in writing, then it must be wholly disregarded and the parties are relegated to their rights under the original contract.'

In *Morris v Baron* the House of Lords was concerned with a contract for the sale of goods which was required by s 4 of the Sale of Goods Act 1893 to be evidenced in writing. It seems to me, however, that the principle approved by Lord Parmoor is directly applicable in this case. Furthermore, there are other passages in the speeches in *Morris v Baron* which show that if a contract is required to be in writing, variations which are not in writing cannot be relied upon (see [1918] AC 1 at 12, 16 per Lord Finlay LC and Viscount Haldane). Lord Atkinson explained the matter as follows (at 31):

> 'The foundation, I think, on which that rule rests is that after the agreed variation the contract of the parties is not the original contract which had been reduced into writing, but that contract as varied, that of this latter in its entirety there is no written evidence, and it therefore cannot in its entirety be enforced.'

We have had the advantage of a fuller argument than the judge had. With the benefit of that fuller argument I am satisfied that on this issue the judge reached the wrong conclusion and that the appeal must be allowed.

Estoppel

a
I have indicated earlier in this judgment the nature of the estoppel on which the bank would seek to rely. I am satisfied, however, that this issue cannot be resolved without evidence. I propose to say nothing further about it save that I consider that the point is plainly arguable.

b   CONCLUSION
In these circumstances I would allow the appeal and reinstate the statement of claim. The matter should proceed to trial if the parties cannot reach some agreement. If the action does proceed the bank will be able to raise the defence of estoppel if so advised.

c   **MORRITT LJ.** In 1987 the Law Commission recommended that contracts for the sale or other disposition of an interest in land should only be capable of being made in writing (see *Transfer of Land: Formalities for Contracts for Sale etc of Land* (Law Com No 164)). This was to be contrasted with the requirement, which had prevailed for several centuries and was then contained in s 40 of the Law of
d   Property Act 1925, that such a contract might be made orally but would only be enforceable if there was a written note or memorandum thereof signed by the party against whom it was sought to enforce the contract or his agent or if it had been partly performed by the person seeking to enforce the contract. The reasons for the recommendation were to avoid the uncertainties arising from the doctrine of part performance, to ensure mutuality between both parties to the
e   contract and to avoid the continuing uncertainty surrounding the operation of s 40 of the 1925 Act notwithstanding its long history (see paras 1.7 and 1.8).

This recommendation was accepted and in 1989 Parliament enacted the Law of Property (Miscellaneous Provisions) Act 1989, which provides, so far as material to this appeal:

f
'... **2.**—(1) A contract for the sale or other disposition of an interest in land can only be made in writing and only by incorporating all the terms which the parties have expressly agreed in one document or, where contracts are exchanged, in each.

(2) The terms may be incorporated in a document either by being set out
g   in it or by reference to some other document.

(3) The document incorporating the terms or, where contracts are exchanged, one of the documents incorporating them (but not necessarily the same one) must be signed by or on behalf of each party to the contract ... and nothing in this section affects the creation or operation of resulting,
h   implied or constructive trusts ...

(6) In this section—"disposition" has the same meaning as in the Law of Property Act 1925; "interest in land" means any estate, interest or charge in or over land or in or over the proceeds of sale of land ...

(8) Section 40 of the Law of Property Act 1925 (which is superseded by this
j   section) shall cease to have effect ...'

As Stuart-Smith LJ pointed out in *Commission for the New Towns v Cooper (GB) Ltd* [1995] 2 All ER 929 at 952, [1995] Ch 259 at 287, that section is not in the same terms as the draft Bill submitted by the Law Commission with their report so that it should not be assumed that the Act implements the recommendations of the Law Commission in all respects. It is material to this appeal to note one respect

in which the form proposed by the Law Commission differs from that which
Parliament enacted. In the draft Bill sub-cl (1) provided:

> 'No contract for the sale or other disposition of an interest in land shall
> come into being unless the contract is in writing and—(a) all the express
> terms of the contract are incorporated (whether expressly or by reference) in
> one document or each of two or more documents; and (b) that document or,
> as the case may be, one of those documents (though not necessarily the same
> one) is signed by or on behalf of each party to the contract.'

The former, but not the latter, requires all the terms of the contract to be
contained in one document or in each document involved in an exchange of
contracts. The latter would have permitted a contract contained in one or each
of two or more documents, whether or not exchanged as a contract. This
suggests that Parliament intended to require greater formality in the creation of
a contract for the sale of land than that suggested by the Law Commission.

The question on this appeal, namely whether the formalities required for the
creation of a contract for the sale or other disposition of an interest in land are also
required for its variation, was not considered by the Law Commission in its
report. Accordingly, the answer to it must be ascertained by a consideration of
the words used in the Act and the objects which the Act was intended to achieve
without any preconceptions stemming from the provisions of s 40 of the 1925
Act.

As the judge observed, the section, read literally, applies to the making of the
contract only. From this he deduced that where, as in this case, the contract was
undoubtedly made as required by the section and therefore valid there was no
requirement that the subsequent variation should likewise comply so long as the
agreement to vary it was proved in the ordinary way. If it were relevant to
consider whether there was an agreement to vary a contract to which the section
applies without also considering whether the original contract had been varied it
might well be that the section would not apply to the contract to vary; by itself it
might not be a contract for the sale or other disposition of an interest in land.

But that is not the question which arises in this case. The question here is
whether the contract for the sale of the land was varied so as to justify the notice
to complete served by the vendor. Thus the vendor has to establish that the
contract with the purchaser provided that the sale of the property was to be
completed on Friday, 24 March. For that purpose he has to demonstrate that
there is a document or two documents which were exchanged containing all the
terms of that contract and signed by both parties. Obviously he cannot do that
for the completion date he relies on is different from that specified in the contract
and there is no other document which is signed by both parties.

A similar problem arose in relation to the provision which was formerly
contained in s 4 of the Sale of Goods Act 1893 requiring a contract for the sale of
goods of more than £10 in value to be evidenced in writing. The question arose
in *Morris v Baron & Co* [1918] AC 1, where such a contract duly made was
subsequently varied without the same formality. Lord Atkinson stated the
relevant principle to be applied in these terms (at 31):

> 'There is nothing in all this inconsistent with the well established rule that
> a contract which the law requires to be evidenced by writing cannot be
> varied by parol: *Goss* v. *Lord Nugent* ((1833) 5 B & Ad 58, [1824–34] All ER Rep
> 305); *Stead* v. *Dawber* ((1839) 10 Ad & El 57, 113 ER 22); *Noble* v. *Ward* ((1867)

a LR 2 Ex 135); *Sanderson* v. *Graves* ((1875) LR 10 Ex 234). The foundation, I think, on which that rule rests is that after the agreed variation the contract of the parties is not the original contract which had been reduced into writing, but that contract as varied, that of this latter in its entirety there is no written evidence, and it therefore cannot in its entirety be enforced. There is a clear distinction, however, between cases such as these and cases

b like *Ogle* v. *Earl Vane* ((1868) LR 3 QB 272) where one party at the request of and for the convenience of the other forebears to perform the contract in some particular respect strictly according to its letter. As, for instance, where one party, bound to deliver goods sold upon a certain day, at the request of and for the convenience of the other postpones delivery to a later day. In such a case the contract is not varied at all, but the mode and manner of its

c performance is, for the reasons mentioned, altered. Moreover, rescission of a contract, whether written or parol, need not be express. It may be implied, and it will be implied legitimately, where the parties have entered into a new contract entirely or to an extent going to the very root of the first inconsistent with it: *Hunt* v. *South Eastern Ry. Co.* ((1875) 45 LJQB 87);

d *Thornhill* v. *Neats* ((1860) 8 CBNS 831, 141 ER 1392).'

To similar effect is the passage from the speech of Lord Parmoor, where he said (at 39):

e 'There is no reason to dissent from the opinion expressed by Shearman J. in *Williams* v. *Moss' Empires, Ld.* ([1915] 3 KB 242) and approved by Swinfen Eady L.J., although for the reasons given above, it is not, in my opinion, applicable to the present case. "The principle as laid down by Willes J., who delivered the judgment of the Court, in *Noble* v. *Ward* ((1867) LR 2 Ex 135) is where there is alleged to have been a variation of a written contract by a new

f parol contract, which incorporates some of the terms of the old contract, the new contract must be looked at in its entirety, and if the terms of the new contract when thus considered are such that by reason of the Statute of Frauds it cannot be given in evidence unless in writing, then being an unenforceable contract it cannot operate to effect a variation of the original

g contract. That principle is to be found in a number of cases, which I need not to refer to in detail." After referring to the cases of *Goss* v. *Lord Nugent* ((1833) 5 B & Ad 58, [1824–34] All ER Rep 305), *Stead* v. *Dawber* ((1839) 10 Ad & El 57, 113 ER 22), *Giraud* v. *Richmond* ((1846) 2 CB 835, 135 ER 1172), *Marshall* v. *Lynn* ((1840) 6 M & W 109, 151 ER 342) and *Stowell* v. *Robinson* ((1837) 3 Bing NC 928, 132 ER 668) the learned judge continues: "Those cases show

h that whenever the parties vary a material term of an existing contract they are in effect entering into a new contract, the terms of which must be looked at in their entirety, and if the new contract is one which is required to be in writing but is not in writing, then it must be wholly disregarded and the parties are relegated to their rights under the original contract." Unless the

j principle is maintained that it is not admissible to vary the terms of a contract in writing by a subsequent parol contract, which in itself would be required to be in writing to be enforceable, the safeguards provided either by the Statute of Frauds or the Sale of Goods Act, 1893, might be practically evaded and rendered of little value as a protection against fraud or to ensure certainty.'

In this case there is no suggestion of voluntary forbearance of the type referred to by Lord Atkinson nor of rescission of the contract altogether which may well be capable of being done otherwise than in writing. Nor in my view can there be any doubt but that the contractual date for completion is a material term if only because it specifies the time from which one or other party is entitled to serve a notice to complete and make time of the essence.

For the vendors it was submitted that to require the variation of the contract to comply with the same formalities as required for its original formation would be unnecessary, liable to give rise to serious inconvenience and therefore not what Parliament intended. It was suggested that such formality was unnecessary as the parol evidence rule excluding oral evidence tending to add to, subtract from, or vary or qualify a written contract would apply. In that event the variation would have to be in writing anyway, though not necessarily in the form required by s 2.

As counsel for the purchasers pointed out, the parol evidence rule only applies to the ascertainment of the original intention of the parties when the contract was made. That rule does not apply to the subsequent variation of the written contract; cf *Berry v Berry* [1929] 2 KB 316, [1929] All ER Rep 281 and *Chitty on Contracts* (27th edn, 1994) para 20-29. Accordingly, a subsequent variation of a contract for the sale of land would not have to be in writing independently of s 2 of the 1989 Act. It is not to be presumed that Parliament intended that although the original contract could only be formed in compliance with the formalities required by that section it might be varied orally given the substantial effect that such variations may have.

It was suggested by counsel for the purchasers that the formality required for a variation was not very great. He submitted that it would be sufficient for the solicitors for vendor and purchaser to sign the same memorandum expressly incorporating the terms of the original contract and setting out the agreed variation. He suggested that this was hardly more onerous than agreeing a variation in correspondence in so far as that had been the previous practice.

The choice lies between permitting a variation, however fundamental, to be made without any formality at all and requiring it to satisfy s 2. In my view it is evident that Parliament intended the latter. There would be little point in requiring that the original contract comply with s 2 if it might be varied wholly informally. Further, the respect in which the Act differs from the Bill proposed by the Law Commission indicates that Parliament intended more, rather than less, formality than that recommended by the Law Commission.

In his speech in *Morris v Baron* [1918] AC 1 at 39 Lord Parmoor recognised, in approving the judgment of Willes J, that equivalent formality is only required for the variation of 'a material term'. Thus the formalities prescribed by s 2 must be observed in order to effect a variation of a term material to the contract for the sale or other disposition of an interest in land but are not required for a variation which is immaterial in that respect. There is no doubt that in this case the term was material in that respect as it advanced the contractual date for completion and therefore the time when either party might make time of the essence by the service of a notice to complete. But it does not follow that s 2 must be observed in order to secure the variation of a term which is immaterial.

Thus, whilst understanding the reasons which the judge considered justified his conclusion and having had more time than he did to consider the point, I do not agree with him. In my judgment, the variation of a term material to a contract for the sale or other disposition of an interest in land must comply with a the formalities prescribed by s 2 of the 1989 Act if either party is to be able to enforce such contract as varied. Accordingly, I think that the judge was wrong to have struck out the statement of claim on the footing that s 2 did not apply in this case.

The vendors sought to support the order striking out the statement of claim and dismissing the action on the alternative ground that the agreement to vary
b the original contract gave rise to an estoppel precluding the purchasers from denying that the completion date was 24 March rather than 26 March. For the purchasers it was submitted that this ground might be sufficient to justify leave to defend if an application were made for summary judgment but was not so clearly right as to warrant the order made. It was submitted for the purchasers that one of the points the judge at trial would have to consider would be whether
c the court should give effect to an estoppel so as thereby to produce indirectly a result which Parliament had deliberately prevented being achieved directly by contract.

In my judgment, the claim for an estoppel is not so plain as to warrant striking out the action at this stage. Rather it is a defence available to the vendor if the
d action proceeds to trial. Section 2 does not give rise to any illegality if its terms are not observed and the need for an estoppel arises in just those circumstances where there is no enforceable contract. For my part I would not place weight on the contention that an estoppel such as the vendor would advance is impossible as a matter of law but it still has to be made out as a matter of fact.

For these reasons and the reasons given by Neill LJ I would allow this appeal.

e
TUCKER J. I agree with both judgments and have nothing to add.

Appeal allowed.

Paul Magrath Esq   Barrister.

Berkoff v Burchill and another

a

COURT OF APPEAL, CIVIL DIVISION

NEILL, MILLETT AND PHILLIPS LJJ

2, 31 JULY 1996

b

Libel and slander – Defamatory words – Words capable of defamatory meaning – Publication of words regarding physical appearance of plaintiff – Plaintiff claiming that words meant that he was 'hideously ugly' and were therefore defamatory – Whether meaning pleaded capable of being defamatory.

c

The first defendant was a journalist and writer who at the material time was retained to write articles about the cinema for a newspaper published by the second defendant. The plaintiff, a well-known actor, director and writer, brought an action for damages for libel against the defendants on the ground that in two articles they had made statements which meant and were understood to mean that he was 'hideously ugly' and therefore were defamatory, since they would tend to expose him to ridicule and/or would tend to cause other people to shun or avoid him. Following the issue by the defendants of a summons under RSC Ord 14A, the judge held that the meaning of the words pleaded by the plaintiff was capable of being defamatory and he dismissed the defendants' application for the action to be dismissed. The defendants appealed, contending that the characteristic of the tort of defamation was injury to reputation and the fact that a statement might injure feelings or cause annoyance was irrelevant to the question whether it was defamatory.

d

e

Held (Millett LJ dissenting) – While insults which did not diminish a person's standing among other people did not found an action for libel or slander, words were capable of being defamatory of a plaintiff if they held him up to contempt, scorn or ridicule or tended to exclude him from society, notwithstanding that they neither imputed disgraceful conduct to him nor any lack of skill or efficiency in the conduct of his trade or business or professional activity. Whether they were so capable in a particular case had to be answered in relation to the plaintiff's claim, taking into account the context in which they were published. In the instant case, the words might have been understood to mean that the plaintiff was not merely physically unattractive in appearance, but actually repulsive. To say that of someone in the public eye who made his living, in part at least, as an actor could be defamatory, since it was capable of lowering his standing in the estimation of the public and of making him an object of ridicule. It followed that it would be inappropriate to withdraw the matter from the consideration of a jury and the appeal would accordingly be dismissed (see p 1013 *h j*, p 1018 *d* to *h* and p 1021 *f* to *h*, post).

f

g

h

Notes

j

For defamatory statements, see 28 *Halsbury's Laws* (4th edn) paras 39–57, and for cases on the subject, see 32(1) *Digest* (2nd reissue) 145–190, *1150–1545*.

Cases referred to in judgments

Boyd v Mirror Newspapers Ltd [1980] 2 NSWLR 449, NSW SC.

a   *Capital and Counties Bank Ltd v George Henty & Sons* (1882) 7 App Cas 741, [1881–
      5] All ER Rep 86, HL; *affg* (1880) 5 CPD 514, CA.
    Cropp v Tilney (1693) 3 Salk 225, 90 ER 1132.
    De Libellis Famosis (1605) 5 Co Rep 125a, 77 ER 250.
    Drummond-Jackson v British Medical Association [1970] 1 All ER 1094, [1970] 1 WLR
      688, CA.
b   *Dunlop Rubber Co Ltd v Dunlop* [1921] 1 AC 367, [1920] All ER Rep 745, HL.
    Manning v Hill (A-G for Ontario and ors, interveners) (1995) 126 DLR (4th) 129, Can
      SC.
    Mason v Jennings (1680) T Raym 401, 83 ER 209.
    Morgan v Lingen (1863) 8 LT 800, NP.
    Parmiter v Coupland (1840) 6 M & W 105, 151 ER 340.
c   *Rosenblatt v Baer* (1966) 383 US 75, US SC.
    Scott v Sampson (1882) 8 QBD 491, [1881–5] All ER Rep 628, DC.
    Sim v Stretch [1936] 2 All ER 1237, HL.
    Tournier v National Provincial Union Bank of England Ltd [1924] 1 KB 461, [1923] All
      ER Rep 550, CA.
d   *Villers v Monsley* (1769) 2 Wils 403, 95 ER 886.
    Winyard v Tatler Publishing Co Ltd (1991) Independent, 16 August, [1991] CA
      Transcript 707.
    Youssoupoff v Metro-Goldwyn-Mayer Pictures Ltd (1934) 50 TLR 581, CA.
    Zbyszko v New York American Inc (1930) 228 App Div 277, NY SC.

e
Case also cited or referred to in skeleton arguments
Dolby v Newnes (1887) 3 TLR 393, NP.

Appeal

f   By notice dated 23 October 1995 the defendants, Julie Burchill and Times
    Newspapers Ltd, appealed with leave from the decision of Sir Maurice Drake
    sitting as a judge of the High Court on 20 September 1995 whereby he answered
    the question in the defendants' summons under RSC Ord 14A, in an action
    brought against them by the plaintiff, Steven Berkoff, for damages for libel, by
    deciding that to call a person 'hideously ugly' was capable of being defamatory.
g   The facts are set out in the judgment of Neill LJ.

James Price QC (instructed by *Theodore Goddard*) for the defendants.
Manuel Barca (instructed by *Mishcon de Reya*) for the plaintiff.

Cur adv vult

h
31 July 1996. The following judgments were delivered.

NEILL LJ.

j   INTRODUCTION
    This appeal raises questions as to the meaning of the word 'defamatory' and as
    to the nature of an action for defamation.
        The facts can be stated quite shortly. The plaintiff, Mr Steven Berkoff, is an
    actor, director and writer who is well known for his work on stage, screen and
    television. The first defendant, Miss Julie Burchill, is a journalist and writer who
    at the material times was retained to write articles about the cinema for the

Sunday Times. The second defendants, Times Newspapers Ltd, are the
publishers of the Sunday Times.   a

In the issue of the Sunday Times dated 30 January 1994 Miss Burchill wrote a
review of the film 'The Age of Innocence'. In the course of the review, in a
general reference to film directors, Miss Burchill wrote: '... film directors, from
Hitchcock to Berkoff, are notoriously hideous-looking people ...' Nine months
later Miss Burchill returned to the same theme in a review of the film   b
'Frankenstein'. In this review, which was published in the issue of the Sunday
Times dated 6 November 1994, Miss Burchill described a character in the film
called 'the Creature'. She wrote:

> 'The Creature is made as a vessel for Waldman's brain, and rejected in
> disgust when it comes out scarred and primeval. It's a very new look for the   c
> Creature—no bolts in the neck or flat-top hairdo—and I think it works; it's a
> lot like Stephen Berkoff, only marginally better-looking.'

Following the publication of the second article Mr Berkoff made an immediate
complaint. The complaint was rejected, however, and on 1 March 1995 Mr
Berkoff issued a writ. In para 6 of the statement of claim, which was served on   d
the same day as the writ was issued, it was alleged that the passages in the two
articles which I have set out meant and were understood to mean that Mr Berkoff
was hideously ugly. It is to be noted that in para 5 of the statement of claim, after
the words in the second article of which complaint was made had been set out, it
was pleaded that the plaintiff would rely on the full text of the article for context.

The defendants then issued a summons pursuant to RSC Ord 14A seeking an   e
order that the following question of law might be determined: '... whether the
meaning pleaded in paragraph 6 of the Statement of Claim ... is capable of being
defamatory ...' The summons also included an application for an order that if it
were determined that the meaning was not defamatory the action should be
dismissed.   f

The summons was heard by Sir Maurice Drake sitting as a judge of the High
Court. After hearing argument the judge dismissed the defendants' application,
but he gave the defendants leave to appeal.

The primary submission on behalf of Mr Berkoff before the judge was that the
meaning was defamatory because to call a person 'hideously ugly' would tend to
expose him to ridicule. As a subsidiary submission it was contended that such a   g
description would tend to cause other people to shun or avoid Mr Berkoff. The
judge stated his conclusion as follows:

> 'I must say I am doubtful whether to call a person "hideously ugly" exposes
> that person to ridicule, but I have come to the conclusion that it is likely to   h
> lead ordinary reasonable people to shun the plaintiff, despite the fact that
> being hideously ugly is no reflection on a person's character or good
> reputation. For that reason, albeit with hesitation, I hold that to call a person
> "hideously ugly" is defamatory. If justification is pleaded, that will involve
> the jury deciding whether the plea is made out.'   j

THE LAW

Before stating my conclusion I propose to examine the relevant question of law
under three headings. (1) The scope of the present application. (2) Definitions
of 'defamatory'. (3) Additional guidance from decided cases. I turn to the first
heading.

The scope of the present application

a   No order has been made as to the mode of trial in this case. One must therefore proceed on the basis that the action is likely to be tried, if at all, with a jury. The question of fact: libel or no libel, is a matter for the jury. But the court has jurisdiction to rule that as a matter of law words are incapable of being defamatory.

b   A striking example of the exercise of this jurisdiction is provided by the decision of the House of Lords in *Capital and Counties Bank Ltd v George Henty & Sons* (1882) 7 App Cas 741, [1881–5] All ER Rep 86. In that case the defendants sent a circular to a large number of their customers stating: 'Henty & Sons hereby give notice that they will not receive in payment cheques drawn on any of the branches of the Capital and Counties Bank.' The contents of the circular became known and

c   there was a run on the bank. Nevertheless it was held by the House of Lords, affirming the majority decision of the Court of Appeal ((1880) 5 CPD 514), that in their natural meaning the words were not capable in law of being defamatory. It may be noted that the issue had been left to the jury at the trial but they had been unable to agree.

d   It is clear, however, that the court should exercise great caution before concluding that words are incapable of a defamatory meaning. In the present case the position is somewhat different because a specified meaning has been isolated and the preliminary issue requires the determination of the single question, whether that meaning is capable of being defamatory. The practice of pleading inferential meanings is of course to be encouraged where it is

e   appropriate and it may often enable the court to dispose of extravagant inferential meanings under the new procedure enshrined in Ord 82, r 3A(1). But there may be cases, of which this perhaps is one, where the inferential meaning may not provide a wholly adequate paraphrase for the words complained of. Thus it was suggested in the review that the appearance of the 'marginally better-looking'

f   creature was such that it was 'rejected in disgust' when it came out 'scarred and primeval'.

I turn next to consider some of the definitions of the word 'defamatory'.

Definitions of 'defamatory'

g   I am not aware of any entirely satisfactory definition of the word 'defamatory'. It may be convenient, however, to collect together some of the definitions which have been used and approved in the past.

(1) The classic definition is that given by Lord Wensleydale (then Parke B) in *Parmiter v Coupland* (1840) 6 M & W 105 at 108, 151 ER 340 at 341–342. He said that in cases of libel it was for the judge to give a legal definition of the offence

h   which he defined as being:

> 'A publication, without justification or lawful excuse, which is calculated to injure the reputation of another, by exposing him to hatred, contempt, or ridicule ...'

j   It is to be noted that in *Tournier v National Provincial Union Bank of England Ltd* [1924] 1 KB 461 at 477, [1923] All ER Rep 550 at 557 Scrutton LJ said that he did not think that this 'ancient formula' was sufficient in all cases, because words might damage the reputation of a man as a business man which no one would connect with hatred, ridicule or contempt. Atkin LJ expressed a similar opinion ([1924] 1 KB 461 at 486–487, [1923] All ER Rep 550 at 561):

'I do not think that it is a sufficient direction to a jury on what is meant by "defamatory" to say, without more, that it means: Were the words calculated to expose the plaintiff to hatred, ridicule or contempt, in the mind of a reasonable man? The formula is well known to lawyers, but it is obvious that suggestions might be made very injurious to a man's character in business which would not, in the ordinary sense, excite either hate, ridicule, or contempt—for example, an imputation of a clever fraud which, however much to be condemned morally and legally, might yet not excite what a member of a jury might understand as hatred, or contempt.'

(2) In *Scott v Sampson* (1882) 8 QBD 491, [1881–5] All ER Rep 628 the Divisional Court was concerned with the question as to the evidence which might be called by a defendant relating to the character of the plaintiff. Cave J explained the nature of the right which is concerned in an action for defamation (8 QBD 491 at 503, [1881–5] All ER Rep 628 at 634):

'Speaking generally the law recognizes in every man a right to have the estimation in which he stands in the opinion of others unaffected by false statements to his discredit; and if such false statements are made without lawful excuse, and damage results to the person of whom they are made, he has a right of action.'

But, as was pointed out in the Faulks Committee *Report of the Committee on Defamation* (Cmnd 5909) para 62, the word 'discredit' is itself incapable of precise explication. Nevertheless, in *Youssoupoff v Metro-Goldwyn-Mayer Pictures Ltd* (1934) 50 TLR 581 Scrutton LJ said that he thought that it was difficult to improve upon the language of this definition.

(3) In *Sim v Stretch* [1936] 2 All ER 1237 at 1240 Lord Atkin expressed the view that the definition in *Parmiter v Coupland* was probably too narrow and that the question was complicated by having to consider the person or class of persons whose reaction to the publication provided the relevant test. He concluded this passage in his speech:

'... after collating the opinions of many authorities I propose in the present case the test: would the words tend to lower the plaintiff in the estimation of right-thinking members of society generally?'

(4) As I have already observed, both Scrutton and Atkin LJJ in *Tournier's* case drew attention to words which damage the reputation of a man as a business man. In *Drummond-Jackson v British Medical Association* [1970] 1 All ER 1094, [1970] 1 WLR 688 the Court of Appeal was concerned with an article in a medical journal which, it was suggested, impugned the plaintiff's reputation as a dentist. Lord Pearson said:

'... words may be defamatory of a trader or business man or professional man, although they do not impute any moral fault or defect of personal character. They [can] be defamatory of him if they impute lack of qualification, knowledge, skill, capacity, judgment or efficiency in the conduct of his trade or business or professional activity ...' (See [1970] 1 All ER 1094 at 1104, [1970] 1 WLR 688 at 698–699.)

It is therefore necessary in some cases to consider the occupation of the plaintiff.

(5) In *Youssoupoff v Metro-Goldwyn-Mayer Pictures Ltd* (1934) 50 TLR 581 at 587
a Slesser LJ expanded the *Parmiter v Coupland* definition to include words which
cause a person to be shunned or avoided. He said:

> '... not only is the matter defamatory if it brings the plaintiff into hatred,
> ridicule, or contempt by reason of some moral discredit on [the plaintiff's]
> part, but also if it tends to make the plaintiff be shunned and avoided and that
b > without any moral discredit on [the plaintiff's] part. It is for that reason that
> persons who have been alleged to have been insane, or to be suffering from
> certain diseases, and other cases where no direct moral responsibility could
> be placed upon them, have been held to be entitled to bring an action to
> protect their reputation and their honour.'

c Slesser LJ added, in relation to the facts in that case:

> 'One may, I think, take judicial notice of the fact that a lady of whom it has
> been said that she has been ravished, albeit against her will, has suffered in
> social reputation and in opportunities of receiving respectable consideration
> from the world.'
d
(6) The Faulks Committee in their report recommended that for the purpose
of civil cases the following definition of defamation should be adopted (para 65):

> 'Defamation shall consist of the publication to a third party of matter
> which in all the circumstances would be likely to affect a person adversely in
e > the estimation of reasonable people generally.'

(7) In the American Law Institute's Restatement of the Law of Torts (2nd edn,
1977) § 559 the following definition is given:

> 'A communication is defamatory if it tends so to harm the reputation of
> another as to lower him in the estimation of the community or to deter third
f > persons from associating or dealing with him.'

(8) In some of the Australian states a definition of 'defamatory matter' is
contained in the Code. In the Queensland Criminal Code § 366, the following
definition is given:

g > 'Any imputation concerning any person, or any member of his family,
> whether living or dead, by which the reputation of that person is likely to be
> injured, or by which he is likely to be injured in his profession or trade, or by
> which other persons are likely to be induced to shun or avoid or ridicule or
> despise him ...'

h   It will be seen from this collection of definitions that words may be
defamatory, even though they neither impute disgraceful conduct to the plaintiff
nor any lack of skill or efficiency in the conduct of his trade or business or
professional activity, if they hold him up to contempt, scorn or ridicule or tend to
exclude him from society. On the other hand, insults which do not diminish a
j man's standing among other people do not found an action for libel or slander.
The exact borderline may often be difficult to define.
    The case for Mr Berkoff is that the charge that he is 'hideously ugly' exposes
him to ridicule, and/or alternatively, will cause him to be shunned or avoided. I
turn therefore to such guidance as can be found in any of the decided cases to
which we were either referred by counsel or to which my own limited researches
have led me.

Guidance from decided cases

It will be convenient to consider the cases chronologically.

(1) In *Cropp v Tilney* (1693) 3 Salk 225, 90 ER 1132 the plaintiff complained of a publication which he said had resulted in his failing to be elected as a member of Parliament. The words of which he complained are irrelevant for present purposes, but it is to be noted that Holt CJ said (3 Salk 225 at 226, 90 ER 1132):

> 'Scandalous matter is not necessary to make a libel, it is enough if the defendant induces an ill opinion to be had of the plaintiff, or to make him contemptible and ridiculous; as for instance, an action was brought by the husband for riding Skimmington, and adjudged that it lay, because it made him ridiculous, and exposed him.'

It seems that the reference by Holt CJ was to the decision in *Mason v Jennings* (1680) T Raym 401, 83 ER 209, where the phrase 'riding Skimmington' was taken to imply that the plaintiff's wife beat him.

(2) In *Villers v Monsley* (1769) 2 Wils 403, 95 ER 886 the plaintiff complained of some verses written by the defendant which suggested that the plaintiff smelt of brimstone and which included the line: 'You old stinking, old nasty, old itchy old toad ...' The court upheld the plaintiff's award of sixpence damages which he had received at Warwickshire Assizes. Lord Wilmot CJ said (2 Wils 403 at 403–404, 95 ER 886 at 886–887):

> '... if any man deliberately or maliciously publishes any thing in writing concerning another which renders him ridiculous, or tends to hinder mankind from associating or having intercourse with him, an action well lies against such publisher. I see no difference between this and the cases of leprosy and plague; and it is admitted that an action lies in those cases ... Nobody will eat, drink, or have any intercourse with a person who has the itch and stinks of brimstone; therefore I think this libel actionable, and that judgment must be for the plaintiff.'

The other members of the court agreed. Gould J said (2 Wils 403 at 404, 95 ER 886 at 887):

> 'What is the reason why saying a man has the leprosy or plague is actionable? [It] is because the having of either cuts a man off from society; so the writing and publishing maliciously that a man has the itch and stinks of brimstone, cuts him off from society. I think the publishing any thing of a man that renders him ridiculous is a libel and actionable ...'

(3) In *Dunlop Rubber Co Ltd v Dunlop* [1921] 1 AC 367, [1920] All ER Rep 745 the plaintiff, who was the inventor of a pneumatic tyre, had assigned his interest in the invention to the defendant company. The plaintiff lived in Ireland. In 1891 the plaintiff had presented the defendants' predecessors in title with a portrait bust of himself and his signature to be used as a trade mark. Later, however, the defendants, without his permission, exhibited advertisements containing pictures intended to represent him, but the features, which were adapted from the portrait bust, were placed upon the body of a very tall man dressed in an exaggeratedly foppish manner, wearing a tall white hat, a white waistcoat, and carrying a cane and eyeglass. The plaintiff had obtained an injunction against the defendant company in the Chancery Division in Ireland and the injunction was upheld by the Court of Appeal in Ireland. On appeal to the House of Lords it was argued that leave should not have been given in Ireland to serve a writ in London.

But in the course of his speech dismissing the appeal Lord Birkenhead LC said
([1921] 1 AC 367 at 372, [1920] All ER Rep 745 at 747):

'... it was said in the Court below, and it has been said in other cases which
were cited to us as authorities, that such an injunction would not be granted,
and ought not to be granted, unless the Court was satisfied of the existence
of a serious libel, unless indeed it was prepared confidently and completely
to anticipate what the view of a jury would be when it tried the case. I am
not sure that in some of the passages cited the case was not in this particular
put rather too high. It is sufficient for me to say that the judges who tried this
case have reached the conclusion (and I agree with them) that the exhibition
of these pictures constituted a circumstance in which that which was done
was at least capable of a defamatory meaning.'

It is to be noted that the claim in the writ for an injunction was to restrain the
defendant from publishing any advertisements etc which contained pictures
representing the plaintiff 'in absurd or unsuitable costumes or attitudes, or
caricatures of him, or otherwise calculated to expose him to public ridicule or
contempt by misrepresenting his appearance or costume'.

(4) In *Zbyszko v New York American Inc* (1930) 228 App Div 277 the plaintiff, who
was a wrestler, complained of references to him in an article published by the
defendant on the theory of evolution. The article called attention to the
structural resemblance between man and the gorilla. Near the top of the page
appeared a photograph of the plaintiff in a wrestling pose and under it the words:
'Stanislaus Zbyszko, the Wrestler, not Fundamentally Different from the Gorilla
in Physique.' In close proximity to the photograph of the plaintiff was a
photograph of a gorilla (described in the law report as 'hideous looking') which
was stated to be a mounted specimen of the Great Kivu gorilla in Lord
Rothschild's museum in England.

The plaintiff's action, in which it was pleaded that 'the plaintiff enjoyed an
international reputation for dignity ... kindliness, intelligence and culture', was
struck out by the Supreme Court for New York County but the case was
reinstated by the Appellate Division. It was held that the tendency of the article
was to disgrace him and bring him into ridicule and contempt. Judge McAvoy
said (at 413):

'Any written article is actionable ... if it tends to expose the plaintiff to
public contempt, ridicule, aversion, or disgrace, or induce an evil opinion of
him in the minds of others and deprives him of their society. It is not
necessary that words impute disgraceful conduct to the plaintiff. If they
render him contemptible or ridiculous, he is equally entitled to redress.'

The court therefore held that the case could not be struck out before trial.

(5) In *Youssoupoff v Metro-Goldwyn-Mayer Pictures Ltd* (1934) 50 TLR 581 the
plaintiff complained that she could be identified with the character Princess
Natasha in the film 'Rasputin, the Mad Monk'. The princess claimed damages on
the basis that the film suggested that, by reason of her identification with
'Princess Natasha', she had been seduced by Rasputin. The princess was awarded
£25,000 damages. In the Court of Appeal it was contended that if the film
indicated any relations between Rasputin and 'Natasha' it indicated a rape of
Natasha and not a seduction. Slesser LJ considered the defamatory nature of the
film (at 587):

'I, for myself, cannot see that from the plaintiff's point of view it matters in the least whether this libel suggests that she has been seduced or ravished. The question whether she is or is not the more or the less moral seems to me immaterial in considering this question whether she has been defamed, and for this reason, that, as has been frequently pointed out in libel, not only is the matter defamatory if it brings the plaintiff into hatred, ridicule, or contempt by reason of some moral discredit on her part, but also if tends to make the plaintiff be shunned and avoided and that without any moral discredit on her part. It is for that reason that persons who have been alleged to have been insane, or to be suffering from certain diseases, and other cases where no direct moral responsibility could be placed upon them, have been held to be entitled to bring an action to protect their reputation and their honour.'

Later he added (at 588):

'When this woman is defamed in her sexual purity I do not think that the precise manner in which she has been despoiled of her innocence and virginity is a matter which a jury can properly be asked to consider.'

(6) In *Winyard v Tatler Publishing Co Ltd* (1991) Independent, 16 August the Tatler magazine published an article which contained a reference to a residential health spa of which Mr Stephen Winyard and Mrs Winyard, his mother, were directors. Mrs Winyard complained of a sentence which was in these terms:

'His mother, Gaynor Winyard, is an internationally renowned beauty therapist (known more familiarly on the beautician circuit as "the international boot").'

One of the meanings of 'boot' relied on by Mrs Winyard was that it meant 'an ugly harridan'. At the trial the judge considered a submission that in this meaning the word 'boot' was not capable of being defamatory. He said:

'In their context, applied to a lady who is in the alleged libel itself described as "a beauty therapist" and "someone on the beautician circuit" to call such a person "an ugly harridan" is in my view something beyond mere ridicule. It is ridicule, no doubt. But it is ridicule which the jury, if it thought right, would be entitled, within the well-known definition (which I am not going to repeat here but I shall state to the jury) of finding to be defamatory.'

It seems that the 'well-known definition' was that of Lord Atkin in *Sim v Stretch* [1936] 2 All ER 1237 at 1240: '... would the words tend to lower the plaintiff in the estimation of right-thinking members of society generally?'

In his judgment in the Court of Appeal, Staughton LJ referred to the judge's ruling:

'It may well be that in some cases to say that a woman is old and ugly, or haggard, would do no more than cause injury to her feelings, and would not affect her character or reputation. But the judge evidently felt that a different view might be taken if she was a beauty therapist. It is not, apparently, that she would have failed to exercise her skills in preserving her own appearance, but that others might not wish her to be in charge of their treatment. I entirely agree with the judge's ruling on this point; it was open for the jury, if they thought fit, to find that this meaning of the word "boot" lowered Mrs Winyard's character or reputation. Whether they did reach that conclusion a   we do not know. It may be that their verdict was entirely based on the innuendo meaning of a promiscuous slut, which (if established) was far more serious.'

(7) In *Manning v Hill* (*A-G for Ontario and ors, interveners*) (1995) 126 DLR (4th) 129 the Supreme Court of Canada was concerned with the relationship between the common law action for defamation and the Canadian Charter of Rights and
b   Freedoms. In the course of his judgment, with which the majority of the court agreed, Cory J considered the nature of actions for defamation and the values which require to be balanced. He traced the history of proceedings designed to protect the reputation of an individual (see 126 DLR (4th) 129 at 160). Starting with the provisions of the Mosaic Code, he came to the origins of the modern law
c   of libel arising out of *De Libellis Famosis* (1605) 5 Co Rep 125a, 77 ER 250. He continued (at 162–163):

       'Though the law of defamation no longer serves as a bulwark against the duel and blood feud, the protection of reputation remains of vital importance ... reputation is the "fundamental foundation on which people
d   are able to interact with each other in social environments". At the same time, it serves the equally or perhaps more fundamentally important purpose of fostering our self-image and sense of self-worth. This sentiment was eloquently expressed by Stewart J in *Rosenblatt v. Baer* ((1966) 383 US 75 at 92) who stated: "The right of a man to the protection of his own reputation from unjustified invasion and wrongful hurt reflects no more than our basic
e   concept of the essential dignity and worth of every human being—a concept at the root of any decent system of ordered liberty."'

THE APPEAL
       It was argued by counsel on behalf of the defendants that the defining
f   characteristic of the tort of defamation is injury to reputation. The fact that a statement may injure feelings or cause annoyance is irrelevant to the question whether it is defamatory. He reminded us of Lord Atkin's words in *Sim v Stretch* [1936] 2 All ER 1237 at 1242 that though the freedom of juries to award damages for injury to reputation was one of the safeguards of liberty, the protection was undermined 'when exhibitions of bad manners or discourtesy are placed on the
g   same level as attacks on character, and are treated as actionable wrongs'.

       Counsel accepted that it was also defamatory to say of a man that he was suffering from certain diseases. But he submitted that a distinction had to be drawn between an allegation that someone was physically unwholesome and an allegation that someone was physically aesthetically unpleasing. It could not be
h   defamatory to say that an individual had a streaming cold or influenza, so the test of being 'shunned or avoided' cannot be applied without qualification. It was also to be noted that it was not suggested in *Youssoupoff*'s case that there was no evidence on which it could be found that the passages complained of were defamatory of the princess (see (1934) 50 TLR 581 at 586 per Greer LJ).

j   Counsel for Mr Berkoff on the other hand, contended that the present case fell into the residual class where words may be defamatory even though they do not involve an attack on a plaintiff's reputation in the conventional sense. Mr Berkoff, it was said, is an actor and a person in the public eye. It was submitted that it was necessary to look at all the circumstances. If this were done it was a matter for the jury to decide whether the words complained of had passed beyond mere abuse and had become defamatory by exposing Mr Berkoff to ridicule or by causing him to be shunned or avoided. It was suggested that these two passages would reduce the respect with which he was regarded. The words complained of might affect Mr Berkoff's standing among the public, particularly theatre-goers, and among casting directors.

In his helpful submissions on behalf of the defendants, Mr Price QC rightly underlined the central characteristic of an action for defamation as being a remedy for publications which damage a person's reputation. But the word 'reputation', by its association with phrases such as 'business reputation', 'professional reputation' or 'reputation for honesty', may obscure the fact that in this context the word is to be interpreted in a broad sense as comprehending all aspects of a person's standing in the community. A man who is held up as a figure of fun may be defeated in his claim for damages by, for example, a plea of fair comment, or, if he succeeds on liability, the compensation which he receives from a jury may be very small. But nevertheless, the publication of which he complains may be defamatory of him because it affects in an adverse manner the attitude of other people towards him.

It was argued on behalf of Mr Berkoff that in considering whether words were capable of a defamatory meaning it was necessary to take into account every possible group of persons to whom the words might apply. Could the words be defamatory of anyone? In my opinion this is not the right test. Mr Price was, I think, correct when he submitted that the question has to be answered in relation to the claim by the plaintiff. But if this is done, one has to look at the words and judge them in the context in which they were published. Indeed, as I pointed out earlier, it is pleaded in the statement of claim that reliance will be placed on the context. It may be that in some contexts the words 'hideously ugly' could not be understood in a defamatory sense, but one has to consider the words in the surroundings in which they appear. This task is particularly important in relation to the second article.

It is trite law that the meaning of words in a libel action is determined by the reaction of the ordinary reader and not by the intention of the publisher, but the perceived intention of the publisher may colour the meaning. In the present case it would, in my view, be open to a jury to conclude that in the context the remarks about Mr Berkoff gave the impression that he was not merely physically unattractive in appearance but actually repulsive. It seems to me that to say this of someone in the public eye who makes his living, in part at least, as an actor, is capable of lowering his standing in the estimation of the public and of making him an object of ridicule

I confess that I have found this to be a far from easy case, but in the end I am satisfied that it would be wrong to decide this preliminary issue in a way which would withdraw the matter completely from the consideration of a jury.

I would dismiss the appeal.

MILLETT LJ. Many a true word is spoken in jest. Many a false one too. But chaff and banter are not defamatory, and even serious imputations are not actionable if no one would take them to be meant seriously. The question, however, is how the words would be understood, not how they were meant, and that issue is pre-eminently one for the jury. So, however difficult it may be, we must assume that Miss Julie Burchill might be taken seriously. The question then is: is it defamatory to say of a man that he is 'hideously ugly'?

Mr Berkoff is a director, actor and writer. Physical beauty is not a qualification for a director or writer. Mr Berkoff does not plead that he plays romantic leads a or that the words complained of impugn his professional ability. In any case, I do not think that it can be defamatory to say of an actor that he is unsuitable to play particular roles.

How then can the words complained of injure Mr Berkoff's reputation? They are an attack on his appearance, not on his reputation. It is submitted on his behalf that they would cause people 'to shun and avoid him' and would 'bring
b him into ridicule'. Ridicule, it will be recalled, is the second member of a well-known trinity.

The submission illustrates the danger of trusting to verbal formulae. Defamation has never been satisfactorily defined. All attempted definitions are illustrative. None of them is exhaustive. All can be misleading if they cause one to forget that defamation is an attack on reputation, that is on a man's standing
c in the world.

The cases in which words have been held to be defamatory because they would cause the plaintiff to be shunned or avoided, or 'cut off from society', have hitherto been confined to allegations that he suffers from leprosy or the plague or the itch or is noisome and smelly (see *Villers v Monsley* (1769) 2 Wils 403, 95 ER
d 886). I agree with Phillips LJ and for the reasons which he gives that an allegation of ugliness is not of that character. It is a common experience that ugly people have satisfactory social lives—Boris Karloff is not known to have been a recluse— and it is a popular belief for the truth of which I am unable to vouch that ugly men are particularly attractive to women.

I have no doubt that the words complained of were intended to ridicule Mr
e Berkoff, but I do not think that they made him look ridiculous or lowered his reputation in the eyes of ordinary people. There are only two cases which have been cited to us which are at all comparable. In *Winyard v Tatler Publishing Co Ltd* (1991) Independent, 16 August it was held to be defamatory to call a professional beautician 'an ugly harridan', not because it reflected on her professional ability,
f but because some of her customers might not wish to be attended by an ugly beautician. I find the decision difficult to understand, since the reasoning suggests that the cause of action would more properly be classified as malicious falsehood rather than defamation, so that actual loss of custom would have to be proved.

The other case is *Zbyszko v New York American Inc* (1930) 228 App Div 277. A
g newspaper published a photograph of a particularly repulsive gorilla. Next to it appeared a photograph of the plaintiff above the caption: 'Stanislaus Zbyszko, the Wrestler, Not Fundamentally Different from the Gorilla in Physique.' The statement of claim alleged that this had caused the plaintiff to be shunned and avoided by his wife (who presumably had not noticed her husband's physique
h until it was pointed out to her by the newspaper), his relatives, neighbours, friends and business associates, and had injured him in his professional calling. The Appellate Division of the New York Supreme Court held that the caption was capable of being defamatory. The case was presumably cited to us as persuasive authority. I find it singularly unpersuasive except as a demonstration
j of the lengths of absurdity to which an enthusiastic New York lawyer will go in pleading his case.

The line between mockery and defamation may sometimes be difficult to draw. When it is, it should be left to the jury to draw it. Despite the respect which is due to the opinion of Neill LJ, whose experience in this field is unrivalled, I am not persuaded that the present case could properly be put on the wrong side of the line. A decision that it is an actionable wrong to describe a man as

'hideously ugly' would be an unwarranted restriction on free speech. And if a
bald statement to this effect would not be capable of being defamatory, I do not
see how a humorously exaggerated observation to the like effect could be.
People must be allowed to poke fun at one another without fear of litigation. It
is one thing to ridicule a man; it is another to expose him to ridicule. Miss Burchill
made a cheap joke at Mr Berkoff's expense; she may thereby have demeaned
herself, but I do not believe that she defamed Mr Berkoff.

If I have appeared to treat Mr Berkoff's claim with unjudicial levity it is because
I find it impossible to take it seriously. Despite the views of my brethren, who are
both far more experienced than I am, I remain of the opinion that the proceedings
are as frivolous as Miss Burchill's article. The time of the court ought not to be
taken up with either of them. I would allow the appeal and dismiss the action.

PHILLIPS LJ. In almost every case in the books, words which have been held to
be defamatory have been words which have denigrated the character or
personality of the plaintiff, not the corporeal envelope housing that personality.
The law of defamation protects reputation, and reputation is not generally
dependent upon physical appearance. Exceptionally there has been a handful of
cases where words have been held defamatory, notwithstanding that they do not
attack character or personality.

In *Boyd v Mirror Newspapers Ltd* [1980] 2 NSWLR 449 at 453 as Hunt J observed:

> 'At common law, in general, an imputation, to be defamatory of the
> plaintiff, must be disparaging of him ... I say that this is "in general" the
> position, as the common law also recognizes as defamatory an imputation
> which, although not disparaging, tends to make other persons "shun or
> avoid" the plaintiff, for example, by attributing to him that he is insane:
> *Morgan v Lingen* ((1863) 8 LT 800); or by attributing to her that she has been
> raped ... as well as an imputation that displays the plaintiff in a ridiculous
> light, notwithstanding the absence of any moral blame on his part ...'

'Shun or avoid'

It is not easy to find the touchstone by which to judge whether words are
defamatory which tend to make other persons shun or avoid the plaintiff, but it
is axiomatic that the words must relate to an attribute of the plaintiff in respect of
which hearsay alone is enough to provoke this reaction. That was once true of a
statement that a woman had been raped and would still be true of a statement
that a person has a serious infectious or contagious disease, or is physically
unwholesome or is mentally deranged. There is precedent for holding all such
statements defamatory. There is, however, with one possible exception, no
precedent for holding it defamatory to describe a person as ugly. In my
judgment, such a statement differs in principle from those statements about a
person's physical condition which have been held to be defamatory. Those
statements have, in every case, been allegations of fact—illness, madness,
filthiness or defilement. Hearsay factual statements about a person's physical
condition can clearly be capable of causing those who hear or read them to avoid
the subject of them. In contrast, a statement that a person is ugly, or hideously
ugly, is a statement of subjective appreciation of that individual's features. To a
degree both beauty and ugliness are in the eye of the beholder. It is, perhaps, just
possible to think of a right minded person shunning one of his fellow men
because of a subjective distaste for his features. What I find impossible to accept

a is that a right minded person would shun another merely because a third party had expressed distaste for that other person's features.

It is perhaps for this reason that statements disparaging, however strongly, a person's features—and many such statements must have been published—have never been the subject of a successful claim for defamation.

My conclusion is that a statement that a person is hideously ugly does not fall
b into that category of statements that are defamatory because they tend to make people shun or avoid the plaintiff.

Ridicule

The class of cases where it has been held defamatory, or potentially defamatory, to damage a plaintiff's reputation by exposing him to ridicule is too
c elusive to encapsulate in any definition. No case demonstrates this better than *Dunlop Rubber Co Ltd v Dunlop* [1921] 1 AC 367, [1920] All ER Rep 745, the facts of which have been outlined by Neill LJ. The preliminary point which is the subject of this appeal does not require us to decide whether the publications complained of are capable of constituting defamation of the plaintiff. The question which we
d are asked to answer is whether 'the meaning pleaded in para 6 of the statement of claim is capable of being defamatory'. The defendants' skeleton argument opened with the following proposition:

'The question of law for decision is whether a statement that an individual is ugly is capable of being defamatory. If this statement is defamatory in one
e case, it must be in all cases (in the absence of any distinguishing features of a particular case), so that there is no distinction to be drawn between the technical issue of law, whether it is capable of being defamatory, and the technical issue of fact, whether it is defamatory.'

I cannot accept this proposition. Where the issue is whether words have
f damaged a plaintiff's reputation by exposing him to ridicule, that question cannot be answered simply by considering whether the natural and ordinary meaning of the words used is defamatory per se. The question has to be considered in the light of the actual words used and the circumstance in which they are used. There are many ways of indicating that a person is hideously ugly, ranging from
g a simple statement of opinion to that effect, which I feel could never be defamatory, to words plainly intended to convey that message by way of ridicule. The words used in this case fall into the latter category. Whether they have exposed the plaintiff to ridicule to the extent that his reputation has been damaged must be answered by the jury. The preliminary point raised by the
h defendants cannot be answered in the affirmative and this appeal should be dismissed.

Appeal dismissed.

Paul Magrath Esq   Barrister.

Practice Note

a

CHANCERY DIVISION (COMPANIES COURT)
SIR RICHARD SCOTT V-C
27 NOVEMBER 1996

b

Practice – Chancery Division – Companies Court – Schemes of arrangement and reductions of capital – Arrangements for hearing.

SIR RICHARD SCOTT V-C gave the following direction at the sitting of the court.

c

1. Chancery Practice Direction (6) Companies (other than insolvency) is amended by deleting para E (as amended) and substituting the following:

'E. Schemes of arrangement and reductions of capital: hearing.

1. This para E applies to (a) schemes of arrangement under ss 425 to 427A of the Companies Act 1985, whether made with creditors or members; (b) schemes for the transfer of the whole or part of the long-term business of an insurance company to which Sch 2C to the Insurance Companies Act 1982 (as amended) applies, and (c) reductions of capital, share premium account and capital redemption reserve. References in this para E to "schemes" are to schemes falling within (a) or (b) above, and references in this para E to reductions are to reductions falling within (c) above.

d

e

2. Petitions to sanction schemes of arrangement will be heard by the Companies Court judge.

3. Petitions to confirm reductions will be heard by the Companies Court registrar unless otherwise ordered. The registrar will hear petitions to confirm reductions in open court on a Wednesday each week after completion of the list of winding-up petitions.

f

4. Schemes and reductions in the long vacation.

The following requirements must be satisfied for a hearing to be fixed to sanction a scheme and/or confirm a reduction in the long vacation. (a) The application is one in which for financial, commercial or economic reasons a hearing before the end of the long vacation is desirable. This category will include cases of mergers and takeovers which arise in the summer and are likely to be affected by market fluctuations. (b) The application is one which could not with reasonable diligence have been made and prosecuted in time to be heard before the long vacation begins.

g

An informal application in chambers, to the court manager, accompanied by an advocate's certificate that requirements (a) and (b) are satisfied, must be made as soon as possible so that a suitable timetable may be settled, including a date for hearing.

h

In the case of reductions to be heard by the registrar, certain applications which do not fall within the above categories will be heard provided (i) that there is an urgent need for a hearing or (ii) that there is sufficient time available after the registrar has disposed of the urgent applications.

j

Applications to the registrar in chambers for orders convening meetings to consider schemes and for directions on reduction applications will continue to be heard during the long vacation. Provided notice is given to the court before the long vacation begins, a timetable will be fixed which will enable

a any necessary documents to be settled in chambers and enable the registrar
to hear the application.

The vacation judge will be available to hear petitions to sanction schemes
and any petitions to confirm reductions which require to be heard by a judge
on one Wednesday in August and two Wednesdays in September on dates
to be arranged and subsequently notified in the Long Vacation Notice which
b is printed in the Daily Cause List.

The vacation judge may also hear petitions to sanction schemes or confirm
reductions on other days if he thinks fit.'

2. Chancery Practice Direction (10) Insolvency, B Companies is amended by
deleting para (vi)(iii)(aa).

c

Celia Fox   Barrister.

Practice Note

CHANCERY DIVISION (COMPANIES COURT)
SIR RICHARD SCOTT V-C
27 NOVEMBER 1996

Practice – Chancery Division – Companies Court – Insolvency proceedings – Applications for appointment of provisional liquidator – Procedure.

SIR RICHARD SCOTT V-C gave the following direction at the sitting of the court.

1. Applications for an order appointing a provisional liquidator can at present be made either to the Companies Court judge or to the Companies Court registrar.

2. These applications may have far-reaching implications for the company involved and in future they should, like applications for the appointment of an administrator or the grant of an interlocutory injunction, be made to the Companies Court judge.

3. The judge may, if he thinks fit, direct that the application be heard in camera.

4. The following sub-paragraph shall be inserted into para (vi)(i) of the Chancery Practice Direction (10) Insolvency, B Companies, immediately after the existing sub-para (c):

'(cc) Applications for the appointment of a provisional liquidator.'

Celia Fox Barrister.

End of Volume 4